John A. Farrell

RICHARD NIXON

John A. Farrell is the author of *Clarence Darrow: Attorney for the Damned*, which won the Los Angeles Times Book Prize for Biography, and *Tip O'Neill and the Democratic Century*, which won the D. B. Hardeman Prize for the best book on Congress. He is a contributing editor to *Politico* magazine, following a prizewinning career as a newspaperman, most notably at *The Denver Post* and *The Boston Globe*, where he worked as a White House correspondent and served on the Spotlight investigative team.

www.jafarrell.com

Also by John A. Farrell

Clarence Darrow: Attorney for the Damned

Tip O'Neill and the Democratic Century

RICHARD
NIXON

RICHARD
NIXON

The Life

John A. Farrell

VINTAGE BOOKS
A Division of Penguin Random House LLC
New York

FIRST VINTAGE BOOKS EDITION, FEBRUARY 2018

Copyright © 2017 by John A. Farrell

The Library of Congress has cataloged the Doubleday edition as follows:
Names: Farrell, John A. (John Aloysius), author.
Title: Richard Nixon : the life / John A. Farrell.
Description: New York : Doubleday, 2017.
Identifiers: LCCN 2016049856 (print) | LCCN 2016052160 (ebook)
Subjects: LCSH: Nixon, Richard M. (Richard Milhous), 1913–1994. | Presidents—
United States—Biography. | United States—Politics and government—1969–1974. |
BISAC: BIOGRAPHY & AUTOBIOGRAPHY / Presidents & Heads of State. |
BIOGRAPHY & AUTOBIOGRAPHY / Political. | HISTORY /
United States / 20th Century.
Classification: LCC E856.F37 2017 (print) | LCC E856 (ebook) |
DDC 973.924092 [B]—dc23
LC record available at https://lccn.loc.gov/2016049856

Vintage Books Trade Paperback ISBN: 978-0-345-80496-9
eBook ISBN: 978-0-385-53736-0

Author photograph © Kathy Kupka
Book design by Michael Collica

www.vintagebooks.com

Printed in the United States of America
10 9 8 7 6 5 4 3 2 1

To Marjorie Farrell and J. Craig Baker,
with whom I shared these times

Contents

1. The Dragon Slayer 1

2. "I Had to Win" 18

3. As American as Thanksgiving 42

4. Death, God, Love, and War 65

5. A Kind of Man the Country Needs 80

6. HUAC 93

7. A Tragedy of History 104

8. The Pink Lady 129

9. The Great Train Robbery 158

10. Checkers 177

11. A Candidate for the Little Man 198

12. McCarthy 210

13. The New Nixon 235

14. The Desolate Night of Man's Inhumanity 247

15. The Field of Pending Battle 260

16. Nixon vs. Kennedy 276

17. Wilderness 294

18. The Greatest Comeback 312

19. Nixon's War 347

20. Not Fish nor Fowl 371

21. Drawing the Sword 397

22. The Road to Watergate 416

23. The Week That Changed the World 435

24. A Third-Rate Burglary 465

25. A Fairly Reasonable Interval 485

26. Cancer on the Presidency 503

27. The Final Days 517

28. Exile 534

Acknowledgments 559

Notes 565

Bibliography 689

Illustration Credits 701

Index 703

RICHARD
NIXON

1

The Dragon Slayer

THE UNITED STATES had throttled its foes with steel. Now it was time to stand down and go home. Navy lieutenant John Renneburg was stationed at the Glenn L. Martin Company aeronautics complex near Baltimore in the summer of 1945. It was a sprawling plant where the firm's big flying boats were built, then tested on the Chesapeake's tranquil waters. In a single year at the conflict's peak, American factories churned out ninety-six thousand warplanes—almost as many as those manufactured by Nazi Germany in seven years of war. The Martin plant was emblematic: one of the largest aviation works in the world, with fifty thousand employees building seaplanes, bombers, and other aircraft.

With victory, the nation faced a vast demobilization. The press brimmed with foreboding about the pain of "reconversion" to a peacetime economy. The army sent out thirty thousand telegrams canceling 95 percent of its orders for artillery, tanks, and other instruments of war. The navy stopped construction on a hundred ships. What the government needed now were regiments of lawyers to settle its contracts. That was Lieutenant Renneburg's job until new orders arrived. He was going home, just as soon as he could train a replacement.

The man the navy sent was a dark-haired, dark-eyed veteran of the fighting in the Pacific, Lieutenant Richard Nixon. After returning from the Solomon Islands, Nixon had been given a course on federal contracting. He and his wife, Pat, bounced from Washington to Philadelphia to New York and ultimately to Stansbury Manor, a complex of two-story apartment buildings on a cove near the Martin airfield. In this pleasant backwater, he and Renneburg spent their days haggling with the firm's accountants on behalf of the navy's Bureau of Aeronautics.

Renneburg found Nixon smart and serious, yet amiable. The work was demanding, "and about the only chance we would have to relax would be when we would walk down to the officers' mess," a bit more than a quarter mile away. They spoke about music, for which they were both enthusiasts, and swapped stories about their wartime experiences. Inevitably, the conversation turned to civilian life, Renneburg remembered, and one day "I asked him what he was planning to do."

It was a warm day, Indian summer. Nixon didn't really know, he told his colleague as they ambled. The navy had offered him a promotion to commander. The world of business beckoned, and he and Pat were entranced by Manhattan. If nothing else turned up, his law partners had kept his old job open in his little hometown of Whittier, California. And then—out of the blue, Nixon said—he had gotten a letter from some folks back home who wanted him to run for Congress. It was a long shot: he would be challenging a five-term incumbent. Nevertheless, intrigued, he had waited for the cheaper nightly long-distance rates and discussed it over the telephone.

"I'm not a politician," Nixon told Renneburg. "I probably would be defeated."

"I hope they didn't reverse the charges," his colleague said.

"No, they didn't." Nixon smiled. "They seemed to be serious."

Renneburg urged him to accept the offer. He admired Nixon's qualities and thought he'd make a good congressman—a voice for a new generation in uniform coming home from war and seeking to build a better world.

"Even if you get defeated, you might get some clients," Renneburg told him. "Somebody might remember the name of Nixon."

FOR THE VERY few who knew him well, the notion of "Congressman Nixon" was not exceptionally odd. All his life, he'd displayed an interest in history and politics. He was disciplined, hardworking, bright, and earnest, and had shown a rudimentary knack at winning school and club elections in Whittier. But those whipstitch contests were years ago. The congressman who represented the Twelfth Congressional District—Representative Jerry Voorhis—was a sturdy veteran of the House Democratic majority propelled to office by Franklin D. Roosevelt's mighty New Deal coalition. In polls of the capital's press corps, and of his fellow congressmen, the handsome, pipe-smoking Voorhis won top-ten rankings for diligence and integrity. He was the son of a retired automobile executive whose wealth could finance his campaigns. His constituent service earned him the loyalty of the district's farmers and citrus ranchers, for whom he ably labored on the House Agriculture Committee, a coveted perch. In the three most recent elections, the Republicans had tried to supplant him with a popular coach, a celebrity preacher, and a respected businessman. He had whipped them all.

Richard Nixon—Dick, to his friends and family; Nick in the navy; Nixie in college and Gus during law school—was thirty-two years old in 1945; not a bad-looking guy in his dress blues. "He looked so different: younger, real tanned, thinner, and of course very handsome in his blue uniform with all the braid and the white cap," Pat wrote his parents.

Age would accentuate the flaws in his features—jowls, the spatulate nose and receding hairline—but not for decades. His hair was thick and black and wavy. His deep-set eyes were the darkest brown, and his face pleasantly symmetrical, especially if he'd just relax and grin. Glee clubs and choirs prized his voice, and he was a more than capable pianist. He liked Chopin and Brahms. "He is a romanticist at heart, but he doesn't like to let this show," a music teacher would recall.

Nixon had played on the football team in college, but only because they needed bodies to fill out the squad, for he was no athlete. His feet were big, his chest narrow, and his shoulders sloped. The navy had taught him to stand up straight, but his natural posture was to slouch, hands dangling.

His mind was his defining feature. It was sharp and analytical; his memory remarkable. He enjoyed little more than sprawling in an armchair with a yellow legal pad, chin on his chest, legs on a footrest, thoughts marching through his head. He liked it there, in that restless mind. It was where, in the unhappy times of his boyhood, he had fled. He was a daydreamer, a cloud counter, a bookworm as a youth, and at night he would lie in bed listening to the train whistles, conjuring the marvelous places he would go. He could be there with you without being there, seem like he was listening while his thoughts were far away. He passed folks on the street and didn't see them; walked into them in hallways, offered a distracted nod and half a wave, and kept going. Some thought he was stuck-up, rude, or dour.

He wasn't easy to like. He knew it, and it hurt. "All over town people talk about what a good natured fellow Don is and wonder how he could have such a sour puss brother," he had written from the South Pacific in 1943, describing himself in a wartime "V mail" to his niece Laurene, the newborn baby daughter of his brother Donald. He welcomed her to the world, gave her "the scuttlebutt about your new relations," and touched, as a Quaker, on war's iniquity: "My hope for you is that when you are 17 your boyfriend won't have to use V mail to write."

It was a sweet letter, and some who saw that side of him found his awkwardness, that ungainly shyness, endearing. A friend liked to tell a story about Dick helping out with the dishes after dinner, leaving the kitchen and drifting through the house with a single glass, wiping it over and over, well past dry, transfixed by a speech he was crafting in his mind for an upcoming high school debate. It was a distinctive personality, peculiar even. Some accepted his preoccupation, but others saw calculation and gave him no credit for his dreaming.

He was given to small kindnesses, to bringing red roses to shut-ins, or sending little gifts of money to those who had fallen on hard times. At law school he befriended a disabled young man, put him on his ticket in a student election, and carried him up granite steps to class. He was a striver, a self-improver, and so—given the faults in his personality—an actor. If in small talk he was achingly inept, during high school and college he had thrust himself onstage—in school plays, collegiate debate, and public speaking competitions. He became a fine performer, his teachers recalled. His self-discipline was legendary, his preparation thorough. Others might come to rehearsal without knowing their lines; not Dick Nixon. He could lose himself in craft, ingest emotions, and affect and excite an audience. He yearned, above all, to be a great man. He had that sense of drama.

Nixon was looking to jump-start his life in those weeks after the war for, truth be told, he was a bit of a flop. He had excelled in high school and been offered an opportunity to study at Harvard or Yale, but his family's tottering finances prohibited it, and so he had attended little Whittier College, enrollment four hundred, where the faculty was well intentioned but undistinguished. There he could live at home and continue to work at his father's grocery store. It galled him. The crowning moment in his schooling was the day he was accepted, with a scholarship, to study law at Duke University. He showed not just happiness, but bliss at the prospect of escape. He was "not only fun, he was joyous, abandoned—the only time I remember him that way," his college girlfriend said. But though he graduated from Duke with honors, he could not find work with a Wall Street firm. He applied, without success, to the Federal Bureau of Investigation. Finally, his mother prevailed upon a family friend to give Dick a desk in a local law office, and back he slunk, Mr. Nobody from Nowhere. Nixon's first notable case was a disaster: he and the firm were sued for negligence and penalized thousands of dollars. He went bust at business, too. A scheme to market frozen orange juice failed, leaving him fending off irate creditors.

He was luckier in love. Pat was a spirited beauty—a gypsy, a vagabond, he fancied her—with looks that had earned her bit roles in Hollywood and a job modeling clothes in a swank Los Angeles department store as she worked her way through the University of Southern California. He was drawn to her pilgrim soul. Thelma Catherine Ryan (like Dick, she collected nicknames: Buddy in her youth and Pat as she grew older) was a fellow striver. She had been born in a Nevada mining camp, orphaned in her teens, and compelled to assume the household chores—cooking, laundry, cleaning—for herself and two brothers. Free of that drudgery, college degree in hand, she had no wish to be tied down and had resisted Dick's advances. His intensity was off-putting. But he persevered—for resilience was another of his defining traits—and in time she came to see him as a man of destiny. As a gift, she gave him a figurine, a mounted knight on a charger. She was "willing to submerge her entire life to him," said a friend. Her faith was his great asset.

For their honeymoon they filled a car's trunk with canned goods and set off on a road trip through the Southwest and Mexico. As a wedding prank, their friends had stripped the labels from the cans, and they'd end up eating stew for breakfast. For their first anniversary, they drove to New Orleans, split an order of Oysters Rockefeller at Antoine's, and rode a steamer around the Caribbean. In 1941, they had leapt at the opportunity to move to Washington, where big things were happening. But Nixon's work as a bureaucrat in the Office of Price Administration, writing rationing rules, was stifling, and he felt out of place among the East Coast whiz kids—the Ivy League liberals and bright, left-leaning Jewish attorneys who served the New Deal as men-at-arms. Six months after Pearl Harbor, recognizing his duty and yearning for excitement, he enlisted.

They sent him to a navy air training station—carved, incongruously, from the landlocked cornfields of Ottumwa, Iowa. He was newly married and a Quaker, and it was safe there in the Midwest, pushing paper. But displaying his sense of obligation, he lobbied for a transfer to combat. "Sir, I have a letter from Lt. (jg) Richard Nixon . . . now in Ottumwa, Iowa— legal officer & crying his heart out" to get into Air Combat Intelligence, a superior noted. "He is a good one . . . young, no children & *wants* A.C.I." A man could get himself killed, friends told him. Dick should leave the fighting to the single men, Pat's brother advised. But Nixon was insistent, and ultimately, the navy shrugged and dispatched the young lieutenant to the war zone.

In the South Pacific, Nixon served on a series of island outposts where he supervised the work of a combat air transport team, moving ammunition, reinforcements, and food and medicine to the front, and the wounded to the rear. He wrote to Pat, telling her not to worry about the recurrent Japanese shelling and bombing, for only the morons who refused to take shelter got killed, and his bunker on Bougainville was roomy and protective—with a roof of logs and sandbags. There was plenty of downtime, much of which he whiled away in the discordant style of a fighting

Quaker—reading his Bible or playing poker. He sent aching letters to her and read voraciously, copying down odd lines of speech and poetry, tearing out articles from magazines and newspapers and jotting his thoughts in the margins, or in journals he kept, about such disparate subjects as the female enigma, the ability of civilian populations to endure strategic bombing, the role of China in world affairs, and the dark sides of human nature.

In a moment of self-recognition, perhaps, he jotted down a line, attributed to Tennyson, from a pulpy short story in *Collier's* magazine: *The most virtuous hearts have a touch of hell's own fire in them.*

"He was struck by what he was learning about men," said Albert Upton, a favorite college instructor with whom Dick corresponded. "It was the first opportunity that he had ever had, I think, to see how much evil there is in the world around you, not just how much evil there is in Shanghai or Timbuktu, but how much evil there may even be in Whittier, California, where supposedly everybody goes to church." Nixon came to loathe the disorder and waste of war. Writing to Upton, he spoke of the need for moral rearmament, a Christian movement that taught brotherhood, peace, and spiritual purity. His heroes were Abraham Lincoln and Theodore Roosevelt, and Woodrow Wilson, who had tried to build a structure for peace and convey America's democratic values to the world. "Men's hearts wait upon us," Wilson had said in his first inaugural—words that Nixon would one day cite in speeches. "Who dares fail to try?"

There is cool and there is square, and Richard Milhous Nixon was nothing if not square. Duty called. Work got done. Yet he was no martinet, and something of a happy finagler, treating his enlisted men to a ham dinner after helping to "liberate" the meat from a passing plane and finding beer for the Seabees, who in turn built a comfortable hut—complete with shower—for Nick and his fellow officers. He was generous with the loot. Pilots relished the offerings at "Nick's Snack Shop," the hut at the airfield where they could wind down over hamburgers, coffee, or cold pineapple juice between missions. He learned how to cuss. And for a good Quaker boy, raised in a pious community, he proved a shark at cards. The amount of his winnings would be exaggerated over the years, but by the time the war was over, lumped in with what he and Pat saved from their paychecks, they had put aside some $10,000.

After fourteen months his tour was over. He flew out, with a refueling stop at a Pacific island. "It was one of those rare nights . . . a soft full moon, not as warm as usual, just the whisper of a breeze in the air," he would remember, and he strolled to stretch his legs. He came upon the "lonesome beauty" of a military cemetery—"no lawn, no monuments, the simplicity of white crosses in the white sand"—and pondered the loss. He yearned "for the building of a new world, which would not know the horror of war." And then he was home and caressing Pat at an airport gate.

They were in New York when, on August 14, the Japanese surrender was announced. With two million other revelers, Pat and Dick headed to Times Square. They walked around the city, through downtown's ethnic neighborhoods and up Fifth Avenue. "It was the largest, happiest mob I ever saw. Service men were kissing all the unescorted girls and the girls didn't mind a bit. . . . Chinatown looked like Christmas Eve with Fourth of July thrown in. . . . Flags, banners and decorations of all description covered the buildings," he wrote his parents. He and Pat stopped in at St. Patrick's Cathedral, crowded with the faithful offering prayers of thanks. "I only hope we can keep this peace," he wrote.

Years later, remembering, Nixon saw the war as "the catalyst" that had transformed his interest in politics into a sense of mission. He was a realist about human behavior, but his generation had an obligation, he believed, to find a better way. "He seemed to be dreaming about some new order which would make wars impossible," said Gretchen King, who had befriended Pat while her husband was at war and spent time with the couple after he returned. "He impressed us in those days as an idealistic dreamer."

The war "turned a great many of them with a very high idealistic feeling into politics," said Adela Rogers St. Johns, a California journalist and Whittier neighbor who came to know Dick well. "He came back with that very strong feeling, that we fought a war, a good many men had died to save this country, and now, let us make it what those boys had died for."

AND YET . . . Congress. No matter how he'd grown, he was still Dick from Whittier, that "eddy on the stream of life," as a college classmate called it. People there were isolated and parochial: by choice they kept the highways outside town. Sure, the Quakers saw him as a fair-haired boy—he had been elected to student office in college, chosen to lead the junior Kiwanis club, and appointed to serve as an assistant city attorney. But he had never campaigned for public office and was thoroughly unknown in the rest of the vast Twelfth District. The lives of American presidents are often cast as Horatio Alger tales, and the stories of their rise barnacled with myths. Yet few came so far, so fast, so alone, as Nixon. Not the governor of California or his aides, nor any member of the state's delegation to Congress knew Richard Nixon's name. He was, he would remember, "somebody who was nothing."

And charm, for Nixon, was an act of will. He had endured a dismal childhood, awash in gloom and grief. Two of his brothers died of gruesome illnesses. His father, Frank Nixon, was a cranky blowhard—a grade-school dropout who had come west from Ohio, married into local Quaker gentility, been staked by his in-laws to a farm in nearby Yorba Linda, and managed to fail at growing lemons in one of the planet's most bountiful citrus belts. Frank moved from farming to pumping gas and then opened a grocery store. They lived not in the tree-lined neighborhoods of town, but out on the highway, where Frank peddled groceries from an abandoned church. He conferred resentment to his son.

In the South Pacific, Dick had joined in camaraderie and learned how to lead. But the notion that he could return to California after four years away, engage the voters of the sprawling Twelfth District, and defeat a veteran congressman seemed inconceivable. He had no name, no fortune, no political machine.

WHAT HE HAD was Herman Perry.

It was Perry, the vice president and branch manager of the Bank of America in Whittier, who had sent the letter inviting Nixon to challenge Voorhis. It arrived by airmail. "Dear Dick," Perry wrote on September 29, 1945. "I am writing you this short note to ask you if you would like to be a candidate for Congress on the Republican ticket." The banker didn't offer much information. The incumbent was a Democrat, he noted, and the voters in the district were split almost evenly between Democrats and Republicans. In a postscript he remembered to ask Nixon: "Are you a registered voter in California?"

Perry, a native Indianan, was a man of stature in Whittier. He had arrived in Southern California in 1906, when the town had but a few hundred families, at the height of one of the Southland's booms. Ads hailing a West Coast paradise had dotted newspapers across the Midwest, luring people to Los Angeles and its sensuous climate. Two railway companies ran a thousand miles of streetcar line, like radials in a spider's web, west toward the beaches and out into the empty desert. The city fathers, with infamous duplicity, swiped a precious water supply from the far-off Owens Valley. Thickets of oil derricks dotted the coastal plain. Hollywood was incorporated, and daft developers launched projects like Venice-by-the-

Sea, complete with canals and gondolas. The population of Los Angeles County soared from 33,000 in 1880 to 504,000 in 1910. Most of "the Folks," as they were called, were transplants from the heartland: shopkeepers like Perry or farm folk like the Milhous clan—who dismantled their Indiana home and shipped the timbers, doors, and windows by train for reassembly in Whittier.

The town had been founded at century's turn by prosperous, cliquish Quakers, who gave it its insular character. They were of a western strain of the faith: less plain and pacifist, more smug and businesslike. "I was never asked inside a Friend's house, in the more than forty years I lived in Whittier," recalled the writer M. F. K. Fisher, the daughter of the local newspaper editor, an Anglican. Many of the townsfolk were gentle and fine, but others in "that land of thees and thous and daily snubs" were "sanctimonious bastards," she remembered. Drinking was outlawed, smoking, card playing, dancing, and flirtation discouraged.

Perry shifted to finance, rising to the role of local consul for California's own Bank of America, whose monopolistic practices fueled its transformation from a San Francisco storefront to the world's largest bank. Stout and stouthearted, he was the town's Mr. Republican: representing his neighbors on the county committee and making sure that their sober sentiments were reflected at the polls on Election Day. People called him "Uncle Herman," but his style was as stern as it was avuncular. In that part of Los Angeles County, "he *was* Bank of America," Donald Fantz, an appliance store owner, recalled, and "it was a privilege to be able to go and pull up your chair alongside his desk if you had some problems or something, and talk them over with him." Yet Perry was "ruled by his head, certainly, and not by his heart. I mean, he was a banker, first and foremost. Herman Perry would react on cold facts."

Among those who had turned to Perry for loans was Frank Nixon, who arrived in Whittier from Ohio in 1907. Perry had been a guest at Frank's wedding to Hannah, a classmate of Herman's and the daughter of fellow Hoosiers. The bank's credit helped the Nixon store survive the Depression, and Perry's son Hubert attended high school and college with Dick. When Dick returned to Whittier from law school at Duke, his office was in the Bank of America building, the Beaux Arts landmark on Philadelphia Steet that towered above the groves of citrus like a Crusader castle on the Levantine plain.

Herman Perry had two great unmet goals in life: to be a lawyer and to serve in Congress. And he found in Dick "a kind of fulfillment of his own ambitions," said Hubert, who had tried and failed at law school himself.

"I . . . might even say that I thought my dad was disappointed in me and looked upon Nixon as his favorite son. . . . He saw in Dick Nixon his own dreams that he couldn't make happen."

IN 1944, DON LYCAN, a vice president for Signal Oil & Gas, the largest independent oil company on the West Coast, had called on his friend Herman. Lycan was leading a drive to dump Voorhis, but since the oil industry was a scandalous font of corruption at the time, he had come in need of a front man. Perry was willing to play the role, but it was a fool's errand, he told the oilman: the congressman was too popular. Not so, Lycan argued. "If we really get serious we could beat him." The country was heading hell-bent to socialism and Voorhis had to be stopped. Lycan promised Perry that California's oil and business interests would supply the necessary funds.

Voorhis, a graduate of Hotchkiss and Yale, held views that decidedly tilted left. In his youth, during the Depression, he had been a member of the Socialist Party, and in Congress he had angered more than oil executives. His proposals to increase the authority of the Federal Reserve Board vexed banks. He infuriated manufacturers and big agricultural interests with his support of labor unions. He sought to subject insurance companies to tougher antitrust rules. And when voting for the New Deal's expansive structure of price controls, rationing, and commercial regulations, Voorhis irked many of the conservative small-town businessmen who, with the farmers and citrus ranchers, were core voters in his district. They had kept an aggrieved silence during the crises of war and depression but now were finding their voice. Roosevelt's programs sapped individual initiative, these self-made men believed; made people soft, serf-like, and dependent on government.

As Perry predicted, the 1944 campaign was a failure. The Republican candidate, oilman Roy McLaughlin, was "a very presentable elderly man," as one of his fund-raisers put it, but he lacked the vim to unseat Voorhis. The Republicans tried to make an issue of the congressman's support from left-leaning labor unions, but McLaughlin was not the kind of gut fighter to call Voorhis a Communist and make it stick. Nor was the moment ripe: it was still wartime, and Uncle Joe Stalin was America's ally.

Knowing that McLaughlin was headed for defeat, Perry retained $500 from the $2,000 that Lycan had given him. A seed had taken root. When they met again in 1945 to assess the situation, the convert was preaching to the prophet. Perry knew a young man—a navy lieutenant named

Nixon—who could beat Voorhis. He would write him, Perry told Lycan, and use the $500 to buy him an airplane ticket to California. And one more thing, Perry said: they would need much more than $2,000 this time. The oilman heard him out, grunted, and said, "All right, go ahead. My friends and I will supply you with the additional funds."

THERE WAS LITTLE chance that Dick and Pat would not leap at the opportunity—they pictured each other, after all, as a bold chevalier and his gypsy love. "I was a bit naïve . . . a dragon slayer I suppose," said Dick. But in their Maryland apartment, reading and rereading Perry's letter, they suppressed their excitement, forced themselves to act responsibly, and weighed the prospects. Money was the chief consideration: the election was a year away, and Dick would have no paycheck once he left the navy. They had their $10,000 to fall back on, but no home or car. Moreover, Pat was pregnant, and the baby due in February. Yet the war had given them, like many in that generation, a taste for the dance with fate. They saw this was their shot—the moment they had been chasing since the mean days of their youth, their ticket out of dullsville. Pat "liked adventure," Dick remembered. "She knew my interests. . . . She thought that it was very important to live an exciting life."

"I married a crusader," Pat would say, in turn. "I suppose there never was much question about it."

The odds, a year out, looked "relatively hopeless," but Nixon had a hunch that times were changing. Roosevelt had died in April 1945. Folks were tired of the regimentations of the New Deal and the war; sick of sacrifice, hungry for latitude and liberty. They wanted to fill their cars with gas, "use a second chunk of butter, watch the long lazy curl of a fishing line flicker in the sunlight, or get royally tight, without feeling that they were cheating some GI in the flak over Berlin or on the bloody ash of Iwo Jima," wrote the Cold War chronicler Eric Goldman. While stationed in the South Pacific, Dick had met Harold Stassen, the Republican "boy governor" of Minnesota, who had resigned his office to serve in the navy. They talked about postwar politics, and Stassen predicted a "radical change in the political weather" when the fighting was over. A young veteran, running as a fresh new voice, could "cash in," Nixon concluded.

So this was risk, but not folly. Perry's letter "sparked something" in his friend Dick, Hubert Perry remembered, "like a minister getting a call from Jesus." Dick and Pat didn't have much, so they didn't have much to lose. And as his friend Renneburg said: if Nixon was defeated, he could use the publicity and the connections he would make to land at a big Los Angeles law firm. Dick told Pat: "Let's do it."

It wasn't quite that simple, Herman Perry warned him when they spoke on the telephone in the first week of October. Nixon would have to audition before a group of Republican activists and survive a primary. There were names floating in the press—men like General George Patton, the war hero, and Walter Dexter, the state superintendent of education—who could have the nomination if they wanted it. But Pat and Dick were all in. "After having been away for such a long time . . . it was certainly a wonderful surprise to learn that I was even being considered," he wrote Perry in a follow-up letter on October 6. "I feel very strongly that Jerry Voorhis can be beaten and I'd welcome the opportunity to take a crack at him." He promised to wage "an aggressive, vigorous campaign of practical liberalism" to replace "Voorhis's particular brand of New Deal." The congressman's "lack of a military record won't help him, particularly since most of the boys will be home and voting," Nixon noted. He had just been promoted to Lieutenant Commander and with his savings would be able "to stand the financial expense" of a yearlong campaign. He promised "to tear Voorhis to pieces."

THE REPUBLICAN ESTABLISHMENT was not as ardent. The party machinery in the Twelfth District was dominated by a handful of aged men and women who had concluded that it was hopeless "to get a substantial person to run against Mr. Voorhis, because he was defeating his opponents by such huge majorities," recalled Earl Adams, a young, politically minded lawyer from San Marino. "Very few people wanted to be crucified." Nor would there be help from Washington or Sacramento. Governor Earl Warren was Republican, but almost in name only. Like the popular former governor and U.S. senator Hiram Johnson, who died that year after thirty-four years in office, Warren ran as an independent progressive Republican, appealing to all persuasions in California's unpartisan political tradition, and staying out of local races. The Twelfth District had undergone redistricting after the 1940 census, and Republican lawmakers had stripped Voorhis of some of his stronger wards in East Los Angeles, yet he had prevailed in 1942 and 1944. Voorhis couldn't be beat, the Republican elders decided, certainly not by some navy lieutenant.

"My first impression of Nixon was that here was a serious, determined, somewhat gawky young fellow who was out on a sort of a giant-killer operation," recalled Kyle Palmer, the chief political writer for the *Los*

Angeles Times, the region's biggest newspaper. Palmer, a likable tough guy with piratical instincts, acted with the blessing of the paper's conservative owners as the state's premier political power broker. "The Republicans—including myself—generally felt that it was a forlorn effort."

And so, if it were to succeed, the crusade would have to be launched outside the normal party channels. It emerged in the form of the ad hoc "Twelfth Congressional District Republican Candidate and Fact Finding Committee," which came to be known as the "Committee of 100" (for the approximate number of its members) or, to themselves, as "the Amateurs."

Roy Day, a gruff forty-four-year-old advertising salesman from Pomona, was the organizer. He ran the commercial printing business of a local newspaper and was one of those indispensable men who answered a community's call when its service groups—the Lions Club, the Chamber of Commerce, the Campfire Girls—needed an indefatigable wheel horse. He was an adman, a booster. Bullheaded, he had been drawn into politics in 1944 when a Republican state legislator died in mid-election, and Day organized a friend's victorious write-in campaign. The experience had exposed him to his party's complacency. "I got disgusted," he recalled. "We were blowing our own ball game."

Day volunteered to serve and, with the blessings of the Los Angeles county chairman, recruited the rump "fact-finding" team. He picked the number—one hundred—out of the air and roamed the district, talking to Republican club women, local committeemen, and business leaders like Perry; Roy Crocker, fifty-two, a savings and loan executive from tony San Marino; and J. Arthur Kruse, forty-seven, the chairman of a thrift from the district's biggest community, Alhambra.

"We younger men didn't realize that it was impossible. We were ignorant," recalled insurance man Frank Jorgensen, forty-three, a self-described "irascible son of a bitch" from San Marino. "We young bucks came in and got busy. . . . We didn't know top from bottom how to run a campaign. Except we were businessmen and we knew how to sell. We took the position that a political campaign was nothing more than selling a product." The initial gathering was at Eaton's, a sprawling hotel and restaurant on Route 66, near the Santa Anita racetrack. Over coffee or lunch, in hotel meeting rooms and at neighborhood cocktail parties, they refined their vision of a winning candidate: Young. Educated. Married. A veteran. Most of all, an aggressive campaigner.

The Twelfth District was the largest and most rural in Los Angeles County, a polyhedron with clusters of towns at its vertices and several hundred square miles of citrus, walnut, and avocado groves and dust-brown hills and ridges in between. At the base were Nixon's old haunts of Whittier and La Habra, where Perry and his associate at the Bank of America, Harold Lutz, were raising money and organizing the Friends. To the east were Claremont, San Dimas, and Pomona, an eclectic mix of college and farm towns, home to Voorhis and Day. And to the west, closest to downtown Los Angeles, were heavily populated suburbs, with Democratic precincts in El Monte and Monterey Park, fast-growing Alhambra and San Gabriel, and the lushly gardened lanes of San Marino and South Pasadena. There were "powerful" economic interests that would back Republican candidates in the 1946 campaign, Day promised Dexter, who was thinking it over. But the Amateurs themselves were small businessmen: Babbitts, not Vanderbilts. It went without saying that they were anti-union, anti-Roosevelt, and anti-Communist. "A lot of us felt that Roosevelt had been very soft on Communism," Jorgensen recalled. "I think he was befuddled a good deal of the time and fooled by Stalin."

The Amateurs issued a press release, announcing their search for a Cinderella: it was a novel approach, far from the smoke-filled rooms, and it drew some interest from the local press. They were dismayed at the first crop of pretenders, which included a right-wing bigot and a self-declared Republican who, upon investigation, turned out to be a Socialist. "My God . . . let's don't waste our time," Jorgensen thought. Then Perry spread the word. "Some of the people in the Whittier area are interested in suggesting the name of Lt. Richard Nixon. . . . He has had over three years of war service," Perry wrote the Amateurs. Nixon was a skilled orator and "comes from good Quaker stock. . . . He is a very aggressive individual."

Inquiries were made. "I found out Dick didn't have money, that he . . . worked his way through college. This made an impression on me," Day recalled. Jorgensen and his San Marino buddies rode over to Whittier, dropped in at Nixon's former law firm, and assessed his parents at the family store. "Everything I have been able to learn regarding this man is all to the good," Day wrote to Perry on October 12. "I believe it would be very much worth his while to arrange to be at our next meeting."

Patton was never a serious option, and by Christmas he was dead, killed in a car crash in Europe. Herman Perry's arm-twisting removed Dexter, a former president of Whittier College, whose career the banker had long promoted.

On October 16 Perry informed Nixon that Dexter was out of the race, and that Dick should make plans to come west to make a presentation to the Committee of 100 and have lunch with the area's top Republicans so that they could "look you over."

They needed to pull some strings—commercial air travel was difficult to schedule in those weeks after the war—but Nixon secured a ticket to Los Angeles. On the evening of Thursday, November 1, he spoke to forty friends and family members gathered at a testimonial dinner in his honor at the Dinner Bell Ranch in Whittier. The young veterans coming home wanted opportunity, Nixon said: "They don't want . . . government employment or bread lines. They want a fair chance at the American way of life." Roy Day was in the audience, studying Nixon carefully. By the end of the evening, he was exultant. "That's saleable merchandise," Day told his friends.

Nixon cleared the next hurdle at the University Club in downtown Los Angeles that Friday, at a lunch with Republican leaders in an upstairs private dining room. Perry was out of town so Dick, still in his navy uniform, was escorted by Tom Bewley, his old law partner, and Gerald Kepple, a former assemblyman from Whittier. Day and Jorgensen and some others from the San Marino group were there, and representatives of various Republican factions, including McIntyre Faries, the GOP national committeeman, and John Garland, a real estate developer who had married into the Chandler family, which owned and ran the *Los Angeles Times.*

Garland was skeptical about this "mysterious" navy officer that the Amateurs were touting. But "I immediately liked him because he was totally frank, completely open," he recalled. Nixon wanted a commitment that the money would be there if he ran. Jorgensen assured him that fundraising would not be a problem. They discussed the district, its voting patterns, and other matters. At the end Dick stood and told them, "I'm in your hands."

At the William Penn Hotel in Whittier that night, Nixon made his formal pitch to the Committee of 100. He spoke on the virtues of free enterprise and again of the need for "practical" liberalism. He was not a hard-line conservative, for he had witnessed, in war and depression, how Americans could employ an active, muscular government and achieve great things. Dick's father, who had shaped his son's political leanings, was a latitudinarian populist, while Hannah and her family were progressive Republicans. A New Deal program had helped Dick pay for law school. But Nixon shared his audience's decided belief that now—the crises abated—a continuing drift toward a planned economy was perilous. "I made a ten-minute speech," he would recall. "I did rather well, apparently." Indeed. In all three appearances, he dazzled. "He was excellent. He was just an unbelievable choice. It was like finding a diamond," Lutz marveled. "It was like saying goodbye at the gate to the race horse."

Dick took a red-eye back to Maryland. His hopes were lifted a few days later, when he received the reviews of his visit from Bewley. "The entire district is thrilled," the lawyer wrote. "I think you will get the nomination by a landslide. . . . The thing took hold and is going over big." In his own letter to Nixon, Day promised "off the record" that the Amateurs would fix the vote to make sure Nixon was selected. "Frankly Dick, we feel we have SOMETHING AND SOMEBODY to sell to this district now, and are going to do our very best to close the deal," he wrote.

Not everyone in Whittier cheered. To his friend Osmyn Stout, who had served on their college debating team with Nixon, the Amateurs represented "the most conservative, reactionary people" in the district. Stout, a pacifist, had thought of Dick as a forward-thinking, kind, and "exemplary" idealist. But now Nixon was aligned with the narrow-minded forces of conformity, Stout concluded: "He had sold his soul."

As Day promised, the first ballot was sixty-three for Nixon and fourteen for two also-rans. Pat and Dick had stayed up late in Maryland, awaiting word. It came two hours after midnight. "Dick, the nomination is yours!" Day shouted. When Perry called a few moments later, Nixon recalled a lesson that his mother had taught him—a gentleman has never heard the punch line—and acted as if he was just getting the news. The navy wanted him in New York in the morning, but he and Pat, chattering, never got to bed.

Nixon was exhilarated. He was soon on the train to Washington to confer with Republican Party officials, GOP congressional leaders, and members of the California delegation. "The main emphasis should be on the constructive program we have to offer," he wrote Perry. He suggested that they seek the backing of the local college faculties and told of a speech he was writing, to be given in the churches, urging racial tolerance. "I'm sure we can win," Nixon said. "And that we can retain our integrity as well because we shall only say what we believe and do."

THERE WAS THIS, too. While visiting Washington, Nixon had hit upon a line of attack. The capital's left-wingers—the "fellow travelers"—were "wild about" Voorhis, Nixon reported. The Republican Party researchers had quite a file on the congressman and his voting record. It would be guilt by association, for everyone knew that Voorhis was no Communist, but if they could portray him as a Red dupe, "I believe we can make Mr. Voorhis sweat."

Dick pulled out his yellow pads, filling line after line with notes and reminders, intent on leaving nothing to chance: *Set up budget . . . office furniture . . . need for paid workers . . . call on newspapers, former candidates, leaders . . . arrange church and lodge and veterans meetings . . . set up lists for mailings . . . billboards . . . bumper stickers . . . Nixon clubs each town (now) . . . study V. voting record.*

This was his hour; his chance to *be* someone. To excise the hurt. To stake his claim. He needed to win, and his plans revealed his hunger, and an incipient susceptibility to intrigue.

Set up . . . spies in V. camp, he wrote.

"I Had to Win"

S O THEY WENT west, Pat and Dick, back to the nowhere they had sought to escape. It was hard on Pat; she was in her third trimester, and discovering the lot of a candidate's wife. The Quaker ladies never had thought she was good enough for Dick, and the matrons of San Marino sneered at her sense of fashion. "We were the rawest of amateurs," Pat remembered. "Our friends were sympathetic but dubious, and the real politicians were scornful." At first the couple stayed with Dick's parents, Frank and Hannah. They were given his brother Eddie's bedroom, in the back of the house. "Richard is studying. Don't bother him," Hannah told her youngest. "He's . . . reading up a storm and making notes."

It wasn't quiet enough, and soon Dick was fleeing the house for the home of his legal secretary, where he could pull out his foolscap and make his lists (*set up community chairmen . . . arrange day meetings and calls . . . set up political rallies . . .*), dictate letters, and leave Pat to his parents. When the time came to write his kickoff speech, he escaped to a cottage loaned by friends, on Balboa Island off nearby Newport Beach. "He wanted to be where there was no telephone and people didn't know where he was," Florence Sucksdorf recalled. In return, the Sucksdorfs got a leg of lamb from brother Don's meat counter at the Nixon store—no small gift amid the postwar shortages. Indeed, the lingering scarcities were a recurring problem. Pat had given Dick's outdated suits away during the war, and he couldn't keep campaigning in uniform. Roy Day prevailed upon a Pomona haberdasher, who dug out a suit from the store's basement. Nixon wore it for months. Finding a pair of wide-enough shoes was an issue; so was Nixon's taste in ties. His audiences would never hear what he had to say, Day told him, if his garish neckwear continued to distract them.

An unexpected hurdle was Nixon's uneasiness with women. Coffees, teas, and house parties were an essential element of campaigning, and he could not bring himself to look female voters in the eye. It was an acute problem in a state where Republican ladies' groups were among the party's prized assets and California girls working the assembly lines in the aerospace and other defense plants had made a mighty contribution toward winning the war. Like Pat, many were returning to their homes with an expanded sense of independence. A candidate needed to court their votes. Yet Nixon "was very timid around women," Day recalled. "He's anything but a coward . . . he just felt that women kind of bugged him. . . . He wasn't that way around men at all."

Day had to coach him, warning the candidate that unless he looked *all* the voters squarely in the eye, women would see him as shifty. Nixon worked at it, drawing on his acting skills. To test him, Day invited students from all-female Scripps College to a coffee. They sat in a circle on the floor, interrogating Nixon, who responded, to Day's great relief, by taking each pointed question, complimenting the questioner, and tugging the women toward his position without being confrontational. The glad-handing never came easy, but once Nixon was persuaded that it was necessary, he buckled down and got it done.

Happily, for Nixon, most of his audiences were male. American men, in these years before television and its diversions, were joiners. Organizations like the Elks, the Masons, and the Lions were sources of fellowship, networking, and community service. Dick had hardly returned to Whittier before he was out talking to the Optimist Club on January 14, to the Rotary luncheon three days later, to a Kiwanis event in nearby Norwalk on January 28, and to the Lions Club "den" on January 31. On he roamed, to the Pomona Valley realtors, Rotary Club, and Lions. To the South Pasadena Rotarians, Masons, and Chamber of Commerce. To the St. James Episcopal men's club, the San Marino and Alhambra Kiwanians, and the El Monte Lions. By the end of March he had notched thirty-six speaking engagements, addressing some 3,700 people.

The service clubs were purportedly nonpartisan, so Nixon titled his talks "A Serviceman Looks to the Future" or "The Veteran in Peacetime." He would tell about the day on Bougainville when the order came down to unload thirty airplanes packed with rockets and reload them with wounded soldiers for the return trip to the hospital on Guadalcanal. His crew was a microcosm of America, he'd say, with a Texan and a New Yorker, a Mexican American and an American Indian, a boy with wealthy parents and the son of a railroad engineer. In the best American spirit they came together to fulfill their mission. Now they were home and hoping to chase their dreams. Their country owed them that, said Nixon, but government wage and price controls and other regimentations were stifling.

Dick was drawing on personal experience, as he and Pat were increasingly desperate to find a home and an automobile amid the country's economic turbulence. Detroit had manufactured 100,000 tanks during the war, but retooling to make cars took time, and the demand for housing for millions of returning veterans far exceeded the supply. The Truman administration had retained the wartime controls, hoping to cap inflation. Suppliers responded by hoarding crops, livestock, consumer goods, and raw materials, forcing housewives to haggle with black market traffickers of meat, furniture, nylon stockings, blue jeans, and other essentials. "My most pressing problems now are finding a place to live and buying a car," Nixon wrote Perry. "I have an order in for a Ford. . . . chances aren't too good." And for a father-to-be, he said, "the housing problem is a terrible one."

He and Pat were still living with his folks on February 21 when she interrupted Dick's breakfast with the news that she had gone into labor. He bundled her up, carried her down the stairs, and took her to the hospital. They expected a boy, whom they planned to name Richard. The doctors assured Dick they had hours yet, and he left to attend a political gathering in Los Angeles. The baby was born while he was gone. It was a difficult breech delivery, and Patricia "Tricia" Nixon came into the world with a broken shoulder. The candidate gave reporters a statement that managed to be both corny and sententious. "She is the only boss I recognize," Nixon said, and then, "Patricia is a lucky girl. She will grow up in the finest state of the Union in the greatest country on earth. She will grow up, go to school and when the time comes she will register and vote Republican."

Driving through Whittier, Dick stopped and rolled down the window to ask Waymeth Garrett, a boyhood friend, if he knew of any places for rent. Sure, Garrett said, he had a house to lease on Walnut Street. It came with a Servel refrigerator and a Wedgewood stove, and Dick made a quick U-turn to seal the deal, at $35 a month. The Nixons soon discovered the reason for the vacancy: there were hundreds of minks, kept in cages by Garrett on the lot next door, that squealed and stank. "They're kind of noisy, aren't they?" Nixon asked his landlord, after several sleepless nights.*

The times tried even Pat's vagabond soul. "The odor is something terrible," she told her friend Edith Holt, but "we couldn't find anything else." Dick's mom would babysit Tricia while Pat worked on the campaign during the day, but Hannah let the baby sleep, forcing Pat to stay up at night with a radio for company. The minks would shriek when she stepped out-

---

* "It used to bother Richard quite a bit," Garrett remembered. The market for minks never took off and ultimately, "we killed all the mink and made my wife a fur coat."

side to hang the diapers to dry. As a candidate's wife she couldn't relax, as she liked, with a cigarette in public. She worried about the family's finances. They had "saved every dime we could to have a home," Pat told Holt. "Now we're going to spend it all on this politics thing."

There were few furnishings in the duplex—the living room held a crib and a sofa, stacks of newspapers, and issues of the *Congressional Record*. Day and the others had to squat on the floor during strategy sessions. Their campaign headquarters was no palace, either. They moved an old leather couch to an office in downtown Whittier and borrowed a typewriter for Pat to use in answering correspondence. A proud Eddie, who had just earned his driver's license, drove the Nixon delivery truck, plastered with campaign billboards, around town and in local parades. Frank was his typical self—"overly enthusiastic" and bending ears, his youngest son recalled.

In his first partisan disquisition, Nixon opened with a dig at Truman and the Democrats over the postwar shortages of fashion and consumer goods. "No more encouraging sight could greet a candidate for office than to see a group of women take time on a busy Monday afternoon to hear him make his maiden political talk—particularly when we hadn't promised that a pair of nylons would be given as a door prize," he told the members of the San Gabriel and Alhambra Women's Club. He couldn't offer them stockings, Nixon said, because there were none to be had. "We'll leave the Democrats the job of making promises they can't keep. They are experienced at this sort of thing."

For some groups, Nixon dug deeper. The news, as winter turned to spring, was about the evil Communists. On March 5, Winston Churchill appeared at a small Missouri college in the company of Harry Truman. "A shadow has fallen upon the scenes so lately lighted by the Allied victory," Churchill declared. "From Stettin in the Baltic to Trieste in the Adriatic, an iron curtain has descended across the Continent." Roosevelt had believed that, with charm and patience, he could handle Stalin. Churchill was as sure that the Soviet dictator was immune to all persuasions, save military strength.

Nixon had his own iron curtain speech that spring. He titled it "The Challenge to Democracy" and reworked it as the campaign progressed. It began with a tour of Russian history—"a tragic story of war, starvation, torture, rape, murder and slavery"—of which the Soviet dictatorship was but the latest chapter. Isolationist sentiment was strong in the Republican Party; other, more belligerent factions were demanding a preemptive attack on the Soviet Union, or a war to liberate the nations of Eastern Europe. Nixon struck a middle way. He had been briefed on the Red peril in his visits with party leaders in Washington, but his speech just as certainly reflected the long hours of study and thought he gave to world affairs. It was enlightened for a rustic candidate, calling not for war but for the active containment of Soviet adventurism—for American deployment of economic, political, and military might to "hold the line for the growth of democratic ideals" that would one day topple the totalitarian state. He recognized, as well, the seductive danger of resorting to the enemy's tactics. "We must use means that conform to the highest moral standards," he said.

It was a smart speech, and whether he was talking about foreign or domestic affairs, Nixon impressed his audiences. Most times, he went on without a script. "Richard Nixon presented his platform with the agile perfection of an accomplished public speaker, attorney and debater," a Voorhis supporter reported to the congressman. "He had memorized it almost in entirety, word for word, and his speech lasted 40 minutes." Another Voorhis supporter, a local postmaster, sent a warning to the congressman after seeing Nixon work a Lions Club gathering. "He carried the group by storm," the man wrote. "He is dangerous. . . . I'm getting nervous about the situation, Jerry."

Veterans were treasured targets—especially those of Nixon's generation, now home after years away. Thousands were moving to California, whose splendors they had sampled while serving in, or passing through, the state during the war. The American Legion posts and VFW halls were supposed to be free of partisan politics, but Nixon found a way to make his pitch. "Nixon is setting a pretty fast pace," Voorhis adviser Jack Long warned the congressman on April 1. "He has joined the Legion and also the VFW and . . . he just drops into the Post meetings very informally and quite often and . . . has quite a bit to say about veteran needs and what he . . . will do when he gets in Congress. These young World War II veterans know very little about your work."

FOR SOUTHERN CALIFORNIA's conservatives, Nixon's promise of economic liberty was a tonic. Many had read Friedrich Hayek's alarum, *The Road to Serfdom* (if not the book then at least the condensed version in the *Reader's Digest*), a surprise bestseller that equated modern liberalism with totalitarianism. A tide was stirring, there and elsewhere, among people who felt that they were not being heard in Washington, for whom the East was a distant place where Ivy Leaguers leaned on formulas, not faith; where right and wrong were relative, and modernists and Manhattanites made sport of their plain ways. Not Richard Nixon. He knew them, knew their hopes and worries, shared their values and resentments.

"That boy worked his way. It wasn't handed to him. His father wasn't a millionaire—he had a little store," said Hannah Weegar, one of the first believers. "There was never anything flashy about Dick Nixon."

Folks came by the little office on Philadelphia Street to stuff envelopes or to chip in a dollar for printing and advertising costs. Pat long remembered an aged woman, nearly blind, who came to lick stamps. Their supporters made phone calls, distributed leaflets, organized coffee klatches, and filled the seats at rallies. The local seamstresses donated their time and made clothes for Pat. "It was really a grassroots movement if there ever was one," said Kathryn Bewley, the daughter of Nixon's law partner, remembering that first election. "I have never known of a campaign in which there was so much friendship and love as there was in this; enthusiasm . . . real affection, real concern about the whole situation, a feeling of respect for Dick, confidence in what he could do and . . . a willingness to help him in any way."

His first brochure proclaimed it: "Richard Nixon is one of us."

THE TWELFTH DISTRICT, a quilt of small communities, had dozens of daily and weekly newspapers. The publishers and editors were conservative— Rex Kennedy, the editor of the Whittier paper, was a local Republican Party official—generally members of the Lions or Rotary clubs, and often on hand to hear Nixon speak. If not, Dick made a point of stopping by on his way through town, delivering a publicity kit and a promise to buy ads. In many of those papers, the warmth of the news coverage would be in direct proportion to the advertising space a candidate purchased. "These newspapers are often financed, practically, by the back page [ad] which would be taken by some big market. And if someone got hold of the market owner . . . or we bought an ad for $300 or something like that, we could often get an editorial," one Amateur recalled. "People would read the editorial and then they'd say, 'Well, this little newspaper has no axe to grind. . . . It is our paper.'" Roy Day's employer, the Pomona newspaper, was for Nixon; the Whittier paper was behind him, and in Alhambra a young journalist named Herb Klein was smitten; his newspaper would blister Voorhis throughout the campaign, and he would promote Nixon, on and off, for years.

But building a grassroots movement took time. There were nights when two dozen people showed up in a hall with hundreds of empty seats. And cash was scarce. Day and Jorgensen had the same experience in their very different communities: seeing friends cross the street to avoid their solicitation of $20 for the campaign. Garland dug into his pocket for the initial batch of promotional material—the NIXON FOR CONGRESS bumper stickers that were distributed to the Committee of 100. "All of them were very pleased to have something tangible for the first time," Nixon wrote him. It was the end of March; he had been campaigning for three months.

The bookkeeping, by necessity, was creative. "I can remember time and time again of Frank Jorgensen calling . . . asking me to come down to his place . . . [as] it was a Friday, and we had these bills to meet," Adams recalled. "We . . . issued checks and then beat the rushes over the weekend to get the money." Jorgensen and others sat down with their Christmas card lists, typed out letters asking for donations, and held $25 dinners at their homes. The resources they raised went to mailings. There was no money to rent billboard space, and the newspaper ads were small and few. "The money is not coming in," Day moaned. At times, "I have had to dig down in my pocket for $200."

As the primary approached, Day sent out "newsgrams" to the Amateur network, making it clear there would be no infusion of funds from head-quarters: Nixon supporters would need to raise their own money for ads, signs, and mailings. There were moments that brought Pat to tears—like the day when the campaign literature came back from the printer but she didn't have the cash to pay for postage. She was devastated, as well, after handing out bundles of pamphlets to young "volunteers" who stole off and trashed them. She told a friend that it "was the most heart-breaking thing she ever experienced, because she had worked so hard, and she thought these kids were honest, you know, and were going to go out and pass them out from door to door."

Even the staunch had doubts. A friend of Roy Day's proposed a wa-ger: he would pay his pal a dollar for every vote by which Nixon beat Voorhis—if Day would do likewise if the congressman beat Nixon. Day turned it down. He couldn't afford, he told himself, to lose several thou-sand dollars. Nixon conferred with Adams about a job in his law firm should Voorhis prevail.

The opposition remained confident, bordering on complacent. "It will be a very interesting campaign and perhaps the cleanest one that you have had to face so far as your opponent personally is concerned," the congress-man's father, Charles Voorhis, told his son. "I feel very sanguine about the result."

Nixon had no consequential Republican contenders to worry him in the primary election, which took place on June 4. The results bore troubling news, nonetheless. In California's cross-filing system—where Republican candidates could also file to run in the Democratic primary, and vice versa—Voorhis had won a total of seven thousand more votes than Nixon. If it had been the actual election, Dick would have been on the downside of a landslide.*

"Many people were disappointed," Nixon admitted in a letter to Day. To stop the "sniping" and "keep the wolves away," he acknowledged the need to make changes, and to buck up the troops. "I think you could point out that here I was, a candidate unknown in the district in January, against a man 10 years in Congress; that we used none of our big guns, purposely (suggesting we really are holding back some stuff—as we are); that Voorhis polled 60 percent of the total on both tickets cast in the primary in 1944 and only 53.5 percent in 1946, which is really something," Dick wrote. "I really believe that."

But it was a solemn Nixon who, after the primary, joined Pat and another couple on a road trip to British Columbia. The vacation was supposed to refresh the candidate, but for most of the drive north he was silent and withdrawn, ruminating on the race. When they arrived in Port Angeles near Olympic National Park in Washington, Dick stayed in the hotel room, brooding, as Pat and their friends took in the sights.

IN ANALYZING HIS campaign's performance, Nixon saw two missing requisites. The first great need was money. For that, Dick would turn to Herman Perry. And Perry would tap Oil. Many factors make a winning crusade, and Nixon would later dismiss suggestions that the energy companies played a dominant role in his 1946 campaign; but the evidence buried in Perry's files shows how the oilmen interceded, breathing life into Nixon's candidacy.

The California oil industry had emerged at century's turn as a colossus—topping all states and nations in production. But Americans learned how its growth was greased when the Teapot Dome scandal blew in during the 1920s. One of California's pioneering drillers—Edward Doheny, a prodi-

* Voorhis received 25,048 votes in his Democratic primary victory. He also got 12,125 votes in the Republican balloting. Nixon won the Republican contest with 24,397 votes, but scored only 5,077 votes in the Democratic primary. A local judge, extrapolating the results for the usual bigger turnout of a general election, predicted that Voorhis would be reelected in November by precisely 11,723 votes.

gious contributor to political candidates and causes—had been granted one of the sweetheart deals unearthed in the affair to develop the U.S. Navy oil reserves at Elk Hills, California. After the bruising the industry took in Teapot Dome, it was thought that the oilmen might behave with more propriety. Not so. On May 21, 1943, Voorhis had taken to the House floor and exposed a federal contract that gave Standard Oil propitious and exclusive rights to the oil at Elk Hills, then the most important wartime reserve. The contract was subsequently ruled illegal, and the terms of the deal were rewritten. Voorhis had riled Oil, as well, with a contrary stance on the "tidelands" controversy. When states like Texas and California came into the Union, the issue of who owned the coastal seabed was a trivial matter and left unsettled. It became a mighty point of contention, however, as America shifted to a carbon economy and huge oil and gas deposits were discovered offshore. California was one of several states that leased its tidelands, as they were known, to oil companies in the years before the war. But on September 28, 1945, Truman proclaimed that the federal government owned the rights to the submerged lands and minerals.

It was probably a coincidence that, the very next day, Perry sat down and wrote Dick to suggest he run for Congress. But Voorhis was one of just three California representatives—and the only one from a contestable district—who backed Truman and the federal control of offshore oil. For the oilmen of the big producing states, returning the tidelands to state control—where officials were more easily suborned—was a holy cause.

Clearly, it was in Oil's interest to replace Voorhis. And Don Lycan, who had enlisted Perry in the cause back in 1944, was just one of the banker's friends in the industry. Major oil discoveries in neighboring Santa Fe Springs had brought the energy companies to Whittier. Perry did business with them at the Bank of America. Nixon's law firm—Wingert & Bewley—was built, to a significant degree, upon its oil clientele. Among Lycan's associates were his fellow directors at Signal Oil, Harry March and Samuel Mosher, yet another Perry pal. And Signal, in turn, had an intimate relationship with Standard Oil, which marketed its products.

The oilmen had wasted no time approaching Nixon. In February 1946 he received a letter from J. Paull Marshall, a Republican lawyer who had worked with Nixon at OPA and now counseled him on his run for Congress. "I have had a good talk with Harry March about you," wrote Marshall, who was about to leave the navy to start work as a lobbyist for the industry. Signal was "vitally interested in the tidelands oil question" and would like to meet Nixon and explore the candidate's thoughts on the issue.

"I certainly appreciate your speaking to [March] about me because from what you say, he can be of a great deal of assistance in the campaign," Nixon told Marshall. "I am interested in the Tidelands Oil question and I believe that my attitude on that question is somewhat similar to his."

Now, with the results of the primary election in hand, Nixon outlined his money woes to Perry. The banker asked him for a detailed budget showing what it would cost to defeat Voorhis. Dick gave him a thorough accounting in a letter on August 16.

They had no money for radio, Nixon told Perry. The campaign hoped to use "a considerable amount of outdoor advertising" but that was "depending upon the amount of our budget," he wrote. "During the primaries we had no billboards whatever." The number and quality of the mailings would depend on the size of the campaign treasury. There were plans to run advertisements in the district's thirty newspapers, but they could not afford to do so until October. He wanted to deluge the local papers with photographs and press releases, but "here, again" the PR campaign was "limited by the fact that our budget will not allow any considerable expenditures." Republican volunteers could canvass the friendly precincts, but he needed cash to pay workers in the Democratic wards and to hire young veterans to work the VFW halls.

On August 22, after a meeting in Los Angeles, Perry forwarded Nixon's list to Standard Oil executives Stanley Natcher and Floyd Bryant at their offices in San Francisco. "For the reasons we have already discussed," said Perry, the money should be funneled through a back channel, not the official Nixon campaign. He asked for $6,945 for mailings, canvassers, advertisements, and clerical help.* Within weeks, Nixon had a professional ad agency under contract, and eighteen large billboards bearing his name and face were being erected around the district. In all, Perry estimated that he raised $7,300 for Nixon that year.

Herman Perry "could get money from Standard on a personal basis," his son Hubert would recall. "This was all kept very quiet by my dad so that no one, including Nixon, knew where the funds came from." The secrecy was essential, as the corrupting effects of Oil's campaign practices were again dominating the nation's front pages. California oilman Edwin Pauley, a well-known Democratic fund-raiser (and the future employer of Nixon's friend, lawyer Paull Marshall), had been grilled by Congress—and his nomination as undersecretary of the navy scuttled—over charges that he had offered $300,000 to the Democratic Party if Truman dropped the

* The equivalent of about $85,000 in 2015.

federal claim to the tidelands. When the president asked Interior Secretary
Harold Ickes to vouch for Pauley, Ickes resigned, held a press conference,
and told three hundred reporters, "I don't care to stay in an administration
where I am expected to commit perjury."

THE OTHER MISSING requisite was in Nixon's campaign pitch; his message
needed punch. His talks about the veteran in peacetime were stale. In April,
Nixon received a note from an up-and-coming political consultant whom
Day had hired on a part-time basis. "I hope you will pardon the frankness
of this letter," the fellow wrote. But urgency required it. The campaign
needed "meat," he said. "Sending out laudatory statements about you from
people in the district will not do the trick."

His name was Murray Chotiner, and he was a thirty-six-year-old attorney from Los Angeles. He was a slick operator with a clientele that ran
to gamblers and bookies, and a passion for politics—a moon-faced man
given to flashy suits, loud ties, and lovely women. (He and his pal Kyle
Palmer went through wives like other men replaced their lawn mowers.)
Chotiner was a political prodigy. He had attended UCLA, graduated from
law school at twenty, opened an eponymous consulting firm, and directed
Earl Warren's campaign in Southern California in 1942. He alienated the
governor by asking him to intervene on behalf of an unsavory client—
"Chotiner was nothing but a two-bit crook," Warren aide Warren Olney
would insist—but in the fall of 1945, when the Amateurs launched their
drive, the Republican hierarchy assigned Chotiner to babysit. Day put him
on the payroll for a flat retainer of $500.

If Nixon wanted meat, Murray was his butcher. Above all, Chotiner
valued aggressiveness.

There was never much mystery about what Nixon would fling at
Voorhis in the fall. From his first trips to Washington in 1945 Nixon had
been told by GOP officials how Voorhis was beloved by the "pinko" crowd
and voted with "the most radical element" in Congress. But sculpting the
argument was another matter. Together, Nixon and Chotiner combed
Voorhis's record, looking for votes they could cite as proof that the congressman was a wild-eyed radical. "I forwarded to you the voting record
of Jerry Voorhis on significant measures for the 76th, 77th and 78th Congresses. . . . Enclosed is a voting record of Voorhis for the 75th Congress,"
Chotiner wrote Nixon on August 14. "For your purposes . . . rely on the
complete record for the 79th Congress, which we have compiled, as well as
the record of important measures for the previous sessions as supplied by

the Republican National Committee." Nixon later hailed the "tremendous value" of Chotiner's help.

By selectively dicing the public record, Dick made Jerry seem what he was not. The incumbent's signature accomplishment was the Voorhis Act of 1940, which singled out Communists and other subversives and required that they register with the U.S. government. It sprang from his service on the House Committee on Un-American Activities (HUAC), a panel created to investigate extremists in the years before and during World War II. The act's passage, during Voorhis's second term in Congress, gave the lie to Nixon's plans to portray the congressman as both an unsavory radical and an ineffective legislator. So Nixon erased history, omitting all mention in his campaign propaganda of the congressman's first three terms. The standard by which Voorhis was judged became "the last four years." Nixon zeroed in, for instance, on a vote cast by the congressman in 1945 against a resolution making HUAC a permanent committee. Who was Voorhis protecting? Didn't he recognize the Communist threat? Thus was Voorhis—reviled by actual Communists as a "Red-baiter"—transformed into a fellow traveler.

Nixon would attribute his 1946 success to his moderation. Throughout the campaign, he stressed lunch-bucket issues and the Truman administration's mishandling of the economy. He took several opportunities to speak up for civil rights. He denounced Southern racists like the right-wing demagogue Gerald L. K. Smith and Mississippi senator Theodore Bilbo and declared them "just as dangerous on the right as the Communists . . . on the left." And he accepted an honorary membership in a local NAACP chapter—no small gesture in an election where an incendiary fair employment measure was on the ballot and the Ku Klux Klan was burning crosses in Los Angeles.

That said, Nixon spent the fall relentlessly on the attack. "Whatever people said . . . I was not dull," he would remember. As the campaign manager for Senator Bill Knowland, Chotiner had been smearing the Democratic challenger—decorated war veteran Will Rogers Jr.—as a Communist dupe. Now he taught the Amateurs how to hone the Nixon campaign's assaults. "I don't completely respect a lot of the ways he operated," Day said. But "I learned a lot about politics from Murray." Chotiner was "a shrewd little man," recalled Merrell Small, another Warren adviser. "Very persuasive, and kind of oily and flattering—but watch him. Watch him."

Among those who objected was Pat. She and Dick had entered the race as a team; now he was brushing her aside. Politics was a man's world, Pat discovered, and when she criticized Chotiner's preference for "a harsh, even hurtful" campaign, Dick dismissed her. "The subject of Murray" and his "hard-line, street smart" tactics became "a non-subject" for the couple, her daughter Julie would write. Gypsy Pat was squeezed into the mold of candidate's wife, attending teas and coffees, relegated to background scenery as "her fiercely won independence was chipped away."

VOORHIS WAS NO great shakes as a politician, but neither was he clueless. He recognized the damning effect that Democratic fumbling on the economy and the truculent tactics of organized labor would have on the party's candidates. Freed from their wartime obligation to keep peace with management, America's unions had reverted to prewar militancy, and millions of striking steel, coal, railway, auto, manufacturing, and meat workers walked off the job in one of the most contentious years in labor relations the country would ever know. As Truman and the Democrats in Congress dithered over wage and price controls, veterans and their families slept in tents or cars, meat and other staples vanished from the shelves, and the cost of living soared.

Truman's grasp of foreign policy was also looking shaky. He had squired the bellicose Churchill to Missouri, then baffled his countrymen—and split the Democrats—by approving the more conciliatory approach to the Soviet Union proposed by Commerce Secretary Henry Wallace. Then, under pressure from the press and public, Truman had reversed himself again, castigating and firing Wallace. "What with the coal strike, the OPA [Office of Price Administration], the putting out of business of our livestock people, the confusion in foreign policy . . . and a hundred other things, I think Mr. Nixon on the whole has a pretty easy task ahead of him," Voorhis wrote his dad. "The main point in his favor will be that he was not a Congressman and does not have responsibility for all the things that make the people mad."

Indeed, a Boston-based advertising agency had coined a slogan that Republicans employed with great effect across the land that year: "Had enough?"

Voorhis would have been wise to change the subject: to concoct an issue or—as Chotiner would have told him—to savage the opposition. At the very least, the congressman could have spent more time in California. But from his college days, as an outsider among the eastern elites at Hotchkiss and Yale, Voorhis had chosen sanctimony as a form of self-identity. When others in his class moved on to Wall Street, he worked as a laborer to mix with the masses. With his family's fortune, he helped found a school for orphaned boys. His first foray into politics was with the quixotic End Poverty in California (EPIC) movement—the 1934 gubernatorial campaign of socialist-turned-Democrat Upton Sinclair. Voorhis was a loose-money man with a convoluted theory, which he wove into a book, about debt and economics and the Federal Reserve. His talks were long, often humorless, and dense. "I can think of no speech that I ever heard him give in which he did not, at some point, mention his monetary theories," said Leisa Bronson, a union organizer and Voorhis devotee. "I don't believe that one person in ten understood them."

The congressman disdained political combat, weighed every vote as if it were the most important of the age, and believed it was essential that he run a "dignified" campaign. He chose to stay in Washington through the first eight months of 1946 to debate the vital issues on the House floor. He was there when a bill to overturn Truman's claim to the tidelands reached the chamber. "From a purely political standpoint I may be foolish to take the position that I do," Voorhis told the House, "but I cannot conscientiously vote for this bill. . . . I can point to case after case after case in various states where the oil has been allowed to be wasted and exploited without anything like adequate returns to the people." He voted to support the president, infuriating California chauvinists and oil interests.

"He was a very devout representative of the people. Now: a politician? Jerry was not a good politician. I don't mean that unkindly, he just wasn't," said a campaign adviser, Stanley Long.

The hard men in Washington didn't hide their opinion of this erstwhile Mr. Smith. "Voorhis is an earnest, if ineffectual little man, a do-gooder who stumbles and bumbles . . . getting nowhere with all his puny might," was Secretary Ickes's private evaluation.

"I was very often extremely frustrated and downhearted," Voorhis would admit, "when I felt that you couldn't do what was really right." He worked hectically, alarming his family and friends. "If it were not for the fact that I feel you are needed badly in Washington I could almost hope that you would not have to go back again," Charles Voorhis wrote his son. There were signs that the congressman shared his father's ambivalence. In a congratulatory note to Nixon after Tricia was born, Voorhis had groused: "This job is truly a man-killer." Nixon scented weakness.

It was August before Voorhis left Washington for California. He chose to drive cross-country with his family, and the long hours behind the wheel brought on a siege of hemorrhoids. He stopped in Utah for emergency surgery and suffered a reaction to the spinal anesthesia. Homecoming events were canceled, and for weeks he battled nausea, headaches, and sleeplessness. And when Voorhis at last returned to the district, he was welcomed by a thunderous Nixon salvo that accused him of siding with the Communists against the interests of his constituents.

A GROWING FEAR of Communism was a factor in that year after the war. Running for Congress in Massachusetts, a young John F. Kennedy was telling the voters: "The freedom-loving countries of the world must stop Soviet Russia now, or be destroyed." J. Edgar Hoover, the director of the FBI, appeared before the American Legion convention in San Francisco and warned that there were 100,000 active Communists working to subvert democracy in America. The U.S. Chamber of Commerce, the lobbying voice of American business, hired Father John Cronin, a Roman Catholic priest, to prepare a pamphlet titled "Communist Infiltration of the United States" and distributed 400,000 copies. "We will have to set up some firing squads in every good-sized city and town in the country," one Chamber official wrote a colleague, in order to "liquidate the Reds and Pink Benedict Arnolds."

In California, the voters had been pounded for months by screaming headlines about HUAC's investigations of actors, writers, and film producers—and the often violent struggle over Red influence in the electrical workers', longshoremen's, and Hollywood studio unions, where film star Ronald Reagan was capturing attention with his battle against the Communists, and sluggers clashed at the gates of MGM. The Republican Party chairman, Carroll Reece, styled the election as a choice between "Communism and Republicanism."

"There was a lot of fear," Frank Jorgensen, the Amateur, recalled. Their campaign never made an outright accusation that Voorhis was a Communist, Jorgensen said. They did not have to. The "connotation" was enough.

The thread on which Nixon hung the charge was a provisional endorsement that Voorhis had gotten, back in March, from the Los Angeles chapter of the National Citizens' Political Action Committee, a harmless group of left-wing activists. The NC-PAC, however, was a spinoff of the Congress of Industrial Organizations, the militant labor group that had its own political action committee—the powerful CIO-PAC, regularly called "the PAC." And several of the CIO's member unions had been infiltrated and dominated by Communists. "The CIO is drunk with power. They have had a good taste of it. They like it. And I suspect that they feel strong enough to get it," Charles Voorhis warned his son. There was no question "but that CIO is saturated with the more radical elements of our society . . . including the real Communists."

The congressman thus ordered his campaign workers to steer clear of the CIO and its PAC. To a California leader of the United Auto Workers, a CIO affiliate, Voorhis wrote: "I am frankly deeply concerned over the degree to which the Communists have succeeded in getting hold of some of the organizations, and I definitely do not want their support, nor would they be justified in giving it to me, from their point of view."

The problem Voorhis faced was that he generally depended on labor and progressive groups for votes, funds, and campaign workers. Now he was making distinctions, wooing some and rejecting others. It left him conflicted: "I do not want to be discourteous" to liberal supporters "who are really quite all right," he told his dad. So Voorhis wavered. His admirers had battled Hollywood's actual Communists "every inch of the way" to get Voorhis that local NC-PAC blessing. But in June, Voorhis wrote the NC-PAC director, repudiating the organization unless it publicly renounced Communism. Then he changed his mind and didn't mail the letter. Later he wrote in the margin, "Not sent. Should have been."

Nixon had no taste for such fine distinctions and reckoned the voters would not either. "Nixon moved in and took the anti-Communist line. It was, I'm sure, in accordance with his beliefs and . . . it was the biggest, hottest issue . . . a gut issue," Amateur Mac Faries recalled. The argument was syllogistic: Voorhis was endorsed by NC-PAC . . . the NC-PAC was aligned with the CIO . . . ergo, Voorhis was a stooge for Communists. Faries and a few others balked. But when he "objected to the strength Nixon was putting into his efforts on the Red issue," Faries said, "my objections were overruled."

Nice guys and sissies don't win elections, Roy Day liked to say. In April, the Nixon campaign conflated the dreamy NC-PAC liberals and the CIO-PAC hard-liners into "the PAC." By the end of the summer, it was "the communist-dominated PAC," and the Nixon campaign was warning that Voorhis "consistently voted the PAC line." The canard soon appeared in the district's newspapers—where the Nixon campaign was now buying ads—and began to catch on among the public.

"How did Jerry get away with his support of the Communist Party line, representing a district made up of folks who believe in the American way of life and free enterprise?" Klein's Alhambra paper asked. "About the only possible explanation is that a majority of the voters in the 12th District were deceived." Young Dick Nixon was to be credited for exposing such duplicity. "He will not be found lined up with those members of Congress who toe the CIO-PAC Communist Party line as Jerry did."

The Democrats sensed the danger. "Many people not acquainted with your real views have the remarkable impression either that you are a wild-eyed radical or that you are a 'stooge' of the CIO-PAC," warned Paul Bullock, a Voorhis supporter, in a letter to the congressman.

In the last week of August, the Whittier and Alhambra newspapers shared a blistering editorial, layered with Hayek's philosophy and frosted with Nixon's opposition research, urging the farmers and small business-men who had been helped by Voorhis to stop trading their "political soul" for the constituent services his office so effectively rendered. "If this country ever falls into the grasp of a totalitarian dictator it is not likely to come through a Communist revolution," the editorial said. "It will come because those who profess to believe in freedom are willing to sell their fellow citizens into serfdom for a mess of pottage in the form of political favors from the very radicals who change our form of government. This is exactly what happened in Germany. It is the most dangerous threat to the American way of life in our own country today."

Nixon pressed the point in a Labor Day address in Whittier. "It is a satisfaction and a privilege to accept the challenge of the PAC," he said. "I will not, in the course of this campaign, remain silent concerning the radical doctrines fostered by this and other extreme left-wing elements that are seeking to eliminate representation of all the people from the American form of government." The campaign started handing out thimbles imprinted with the slogan NIXON FOR CONGRESS—PUT THE NEEDLE IN THE P.A.C. The gimmick proved to be a hit.

Finally, on September 11, Voorhis responded, with large, signed ads in the district's bigger newspapers accusing Nixon of making "an untrue claim" and demanding that the Republicans produce the evidence. Day had returned to his job at the printing plant, and Harrison McCall, a veteran organizer, was managing Nixon's campaign. He promised the press: "We will offer the proof at the proper time."

THE PROPER TIME arrived two days later, on a soft, warm California evening, as an overflow crowd jammed the auditorium at the South Pasadena junior high school for a meet-the-candidates forum. In their exchange of notes after Tricia was born, Voorhis had casually offered to join Nixon onstage in the fall to discuss the issues. Both campaigns were divided on the matter and spent the summer chewing it over. There were those in the Voorhis camp who saw no payoff in giving a challenger that kind of exposure, and there were Nixon advisers who were wary of taking on a congressman who, in a decade on the House floor, had no doubt mastered the art of debate. But once the question was out there, neither candidate could back away gracefully. Each agreed to attend the Pasadena event—on Republican turf, but staged by local progressives.

Stand-ins for the Senate hopefuls (Chotiner was there on Senator Knowland's behalf) warmed up a festive, even rowdy, crowd. Then Voorhis gave his opening remarks and Nixon—by prearrangement—arrived late, to whoops from his supporters. The thunderbolts struck in the question-and-answer session that capped the evening. Both sides had salted the crowd with partisans, armed with accusations. When the issue of the PAC was raised, Voorhis challenged Nixon, demanding that he produce "proof" of an endorsement. Striding across the stage with studied magniloquence (honed in amateur theater), Nixon shoved a piece of paper into his rival's hands. It was the preliminary list of favored candidacies from the local NC-PAC chapter, and it took Voorhis by surprise. He had forgotten, missed, or dismissed its import.

Why . . . this was not the PAC . . . this was a different group, Voorhis sputtered, clinging to the distinction. But Nixon was in his face, reading aloud the names of the many individuals who served as leaders for both organizations. It was clear, Nixon magisterially concluded, that the two groups were one and the same. Like a triumphant prosecutor, he turned and strode back to his podium. Nixon's supporters went wild.

"At this critical moment," Voorhis had "fumbled and was flustered," said Bullock, who was serving as the timekeeper. Tired and rusty, the congressman doddered through the rest of the evening, his windiness no match for Nixon's practiced, punishing jabs.

To Voorhis loyalists, Nixon's performance seemed "transparently political, self-serving, superficial, and, sometimes, downright corny," Bullock said. "The magnitude of Nixon's triumph did not immediately dawn on us." But as he left the auditorium, Voorhis fell in with Congressman Chet Holifield, a savvy Los Angeles Democrat.

"Jerry, he murdered you," Holifield said.

THE VOORHIS CAMPAIGN never recovered. "It was such a demoralizing kind of an evening," Long recalled. As the news of Nixon's march across the stage swept the district, it was clear that the trajectory of the campaign had been transformed.

"It begins to look like there is a real possibility" that Nixon could win, McCall wrote his sister. The debate "has started the voters talking . . . and that is just what Nixon needed." Dick seized the moment. "It made me known," he would recall. Voorhis "should never have accepted the challenge." On September 16, Nixon spoke to an audience in Pomona, with a growing group of journalists on hand. "There are those walking in high, official places in our country who would destroy our constitutional principles through socialization of American free institutions," Nixon warned. "These are the people who front for un-American elements, wittingly or otherwise." The "radical PAC and its adherents would deprive the people of liberty."

McCall sent telegrams to Kyle Palmer and Ray Haight, the Republican national committeeman, announcing that Nixon had fought himself into a photo finish, "through no help on your part." Their eyes opened, the Republican leaders agreed to fuel an eleventh-hour push. Haight later claimed that 70 percent of the Nixon expenditures in 1946 came from opportunistic, election-eve donors. Palmer put aside his skepticism, and the *Times* joined the local scribes, touting the remarkable GOP tyro of the Twelfth Congressional District, who was giving Voorhis "the fight of his life." The newspaper's owners were favorably impressed: the Chandlers now thought Nixon was a comer.

Dick's campaign treasury, saved from its midsummer drought by the emergency injection of oil money, spilled over with donations from commercial interests eager to be in on the kill. "It has been very discouraging to us to bet on losing horses during the past ten or twelve years," stockbroker R. N. Gregory wrote to his associates, soliciting money for the cause. "However, it is a long lane that has no turning and I am more confident than ever that Nixon has a good chance to win." Executives told employees to donate and to mask the contribution on their expense accounts. The Republican Party—recognizing that Truman's troubles had given them an unparalleled opportunity to take control of Congress in this midterm election—splashed a bull's-eye on Voorhis. Reports reached Voorhis that business interests from as far away as Wall Street were pulling out their checkbooks to defeat him.

"Money came in very slowly until the debates started," Crocker recalled, "and then money came in, all we needed."

Voorhis, dismayed, tried to make an issue of Nixon's spending. "Who is paying for the big Nixon signs?" the congressman's ads demanded. But it was virtually impossible to get an answer. The election laws were riddled with loopholes.

Nixon's inclination was to take advantage of such openings—even as he stretched the law beyond breaking.

"Under the law a candidate is required to report all contributions to his campaign, either financial or otherwise and if he does not do so he can be subjected to some pretty serious penalties," Nixon told Perry, who had asked him to write and thank one donor of billboard space. "For that reason, I do not believe it would be wise to write a letter . . . thanking him expressly for the use of the billboard because [it would be evidence that] such a contribution is known by the candidate and comes within the requirements of the law.

"I shall, however, write him a general letter thanking him for his support and then I will personally mention the matter to him when I see him," Nixon wrote.

The Nixon campaign, in its official report, said it spent $17,774. Years later, Day and Nixon admitted that the number was more like $40,000—about $500,000 after adjusting for inflation. But that was an estimate. No one actually knew, since thousands of dollars were raised and spent by individual operators like Perry, came as in-kind donations, or got channeled, at the end, via the Republican Party.

SEEKING TO RECOUP after the Pasadena massacre, Voorhis accepted Nixon's challenge to hold four more debates. In the sleepy Twelfth District, the political blood sport seized the fancy of the voters. More than a thousand people showed up for each of the final three contests, in Pomona, Monrovia, and San Gabriel. "The crowd got bigger and bigger," Holifield remembers, and Voorhis "got slaughtered every time."*

"It was deplorable. . . . [Nixon] would give these half-truths, innuendos," Dick's old debate teammate Osmyn Stout recalled. He registered his objection with Nixon. "You have to do this to become a candidate," Dick replied.

As Voorhis struggled to explain the NC-PAC endorsement, Nixon upped the ante. "ON ALL ISSUES INVOLVING RUSSIA, the CIO Political Action Committee looks after the interests of Russia against the interest of America," the Nixon ads charged. And of forty-six selected votes, Voorhis had strayed from the PAC's side only three times. "REMEMBER,

---

* Nixon had balked at first. Unlike Voorhis, he devoted days of study to each confrontation, and feared the time it would take from campaigning. But Chotiner sealed it. "Dick," he said, "when you're behind you don't play it safe. You must run a high risk campaign." After Nixon acceded Chotiner told him: "Good. I've already arranged for an announcement."

Voorhis is a former registered Socialist and his voting record in Congress is more Socialistic and Communistic than Democratic."

Voorhis stayed up all night dissecting the fine print, discovering that many of the forty-six votes Nixon cited were for routine New Deal legislation. "We got out a little pamphlet about it which we tried to distribute without too much success," he recalled. "The newspapers . . . wouldn't put my stuff in." His meager response was eclipsed by Nixon's next blast—that Voorhis had failed to get any of his bills from the last four years enacted into law, except for a measure shifting federal jurisdiction over rabbits (the district had many rabbit farms) from the Department of the Interior to the Department of Agriculture.

"I assume you have to be a rabbit to have representation in the Twelfth Congressional District," Nixon told a crowd.

"Oh, I made an awful mess" of the moment in the San Gabriel debate when Nixon brought up the rabbit bill, Voorhis recalled. "I just stood up in consternation and amazement—and got booed by his claque."

As Voorhis tried to describe the tortuous ways of Congress to his constituents, and how lawmakers shape bills that don't always bear their names, the PAC issue reared up again—with news that Radio Moscow had endorsed the CIO's slate of candidates. And on it went. Why didn't Voorhis vote to make HUAC a permanent body? Why didn't he serve in World War II? Why did he vote to give United Nations relief funds to Soviet bloc nations? Why did he vote, so many times, with Congressman Vito Marcantonio of Harlem, that well-known fellow traveler?

And "every time that I would say that something wasn't true . . . the response was always, 'Voorhis is using unfair tactics by accusing Dick Nixon of lying.' This was used over and over," Voorhis recalled. One pro-Nixon group called the "War Veterans Non-Partisan Voters League" slammed Voorhis for launching "slanderous attacks" against the challenger. Despite the rumors that were sweeping the district about oil company bagmen, there was "not a nickel of oil company money" in the Nixon campaign, the group insisted, and demanded: "What kind of a man is this Congressman Voorhis? Who is he to make scurrilous statements about an honest, clean, forthright young American who fought in defense of his country in the stinking mud and jungle of the Solomons? Coming from a man like Voorhis who stayed safely behind the front in Washington, smear statements are most inappropriate."

In the thrum of one Nixon ad, as Election Day approached, the drumbeats came together, and all the melodies merged.

Are you satisfied with present conditions? Can you buy meat? A new car? A refrigerator? The clothes you need? A vote for Nixon is a vote for change. Where are all those new houses you were promised? A vote for Nixon is a vote for change. Do you want a congressman who voted only three times out of 46 against the Communist-dominated PAC? A vote for Nixon is a vote for change. Do you know that your present congressman introduced 132 public bills in the last four years and only one of them was passed? That the one bill adopted transferred activities concerning rabbits from one federal department to another? A vote for Nixon is a vote for new, progressive and practical leadership. Vote for change.

Voorhis was a sensitive man—proud and vain about his record. He yearned for a genteel discussion. Nixon was anything but genteel. And many of the district's Democrats were starting to regard Dick—who they once considered an honorable challenger—as a sneak, a trickster, a hatchet man. An image was aborning. "He was wonderful," said Faries, yet also "much more personal . . . than some of us would have wished."

A Quaker elder from Whittier—Herschel Folger of the First Friends Church—was alarmed. "I feel much concerned . . . pertaining to various incidents in your campaign," Folger wrote Nixon. The extreme partisanship, the win-at-any-cost attitude, the "petty politics" of the race against Voorhis "made me sick at heart."

Yet the truth was that the Voorhis campaign was a shambles: underfunded, uncertain, and unable to capitalize on what doubts the voters might have had about Nixon's tactics. "My campaigns were never well organized," the congressman would admit. And the demographic tide then swamping California was running against him. The postwar migration added "a lot of new residents that didn't know even what district they were in. They had no idea at all [that] . . . Jerry Voorhis has been working with the old line people on agricultural assistance and . . . on numerous problems," said Stephen Zetterberg, another of the congressman's advisers. "Nixon was speaking to the newer groups of people that . . . hadn't even heard of Jerry Voorhis." And Voorhis had no strategy to reach them.

Across the land, the New Deal coalition was crumbling. It was a historic Election Day, as Republicans took control of both houses of Congress for the first time since 1930.

In California, a Nixon campaign gimmick persuaded voters to answer their telephones in the final days with a cheery, "Vote Nixon for Congress."

If they answered that way and it was the Nixon campaign calling, they were told, they could win a toaster. It was said that there were ugly phone calls as well—short, from unknown sources—in which an anonymous caller asked: "Did you know that Jerry Voorhis is a communist?"

The Election Day verdict was unmistakable. Zita Remley was with Voorhis that afternoon, and phoned a friend at Alhambra city hall to obtain the early returns. "Nixon was . . . far ahead," she recalled. Moments later, Voorhis saw his doom in the numbers from San Gabriel. "He was very white and sort of quiet. . . . He just sort of put his head in his hands," Remley said.

The Nixons read a different set of early returns. Sobbing, Pat fled home. "What's the matter?" asked their landlord. "He's losing," she cried. Then a fuller set of results came in, and it was clear that Dick was on his way to a smashing victory. He swept every corner of the district—even the congressman's hometown—and won with 56 percent of the votes.

Dick packed Pat into the car, and they made the rounds of victory parties—including one rowdy celebration where Jorgensen was stripped of his trousers, which were flung onto a chandelier. "Pat and I were happier," Nixon recalled, "than we were ever to be again in my political career."

VOORHIS WAS DESTROYED. He fled elective politics, infuriating Democrats who thought he should have waged a rematch in 1948—if only to keep the district competitive. Instead, it became a Republican stronghold. Many blamed him for an atrocious performance. "People always expect a candidate to hit hard. It's a spectacle that they enjoy . . . and when a candidate disappoints them in this regard and doesn't hit hard, it's a letdown," said Leisa Bronson. "Jerry was temperamentally ill-equipped to follow this line of strategy. . . . Not equipped to go in with the hard slugging."

Voorhis did not argue. "I had been the congressman for ten years. I'd done the best I could. And I really felt if the voters wanted to throw me out, by golly, okay," he recalled. "I'm afraid this was on my mind the whole time. . . . I hated a fight." But if Voorhis was candid about his flaws—and for decades declined to publicly complain about Nixon's tactics—in private there was fury in his circles.

"Entrenched interests have . . . conducted the most vicious and powerful campaign against you that money could buy," Charles Voorhis wrote his son. "Experts from the outside, highly trained in the art of lying and misrepresentation," had sown "misstatements over and over again."

The congressman's own message to Nixon was, at best, correct. Voorhis wished Dick well but ended by writing, "I have refrained for reasons which I am sure you will understand from making any references . . . to the circumstances of the campaign recently conducted in our district. It would only have spoiled the letter."

IN HIS MARCH toward Congress, Richard Nixon had displayed many of the formidable qualities that would carry him to power and renown. On exhibit, there at the start, were qualities he would demonstrate time and again. Audacity. Resourcefulness. Resilience. Toil. He showed political prescience, and an almost visceral identification with the longings of his constituency.

Yet in that campaign, as well, are inklings of tragedy—portents of a slide into "the deepest valley" of disgrace. Some were idiosyncracies—the awkwardness and detachment, surmounted by will. Others were more troubling: the erosion of worthy purpose, and its supplanting by expediency. The great, haunting need, and chronic insecurity. The use of smears. In the crucible of the presidency such cracks could give way, and such a man could shatter.

Some months later, after Nixon was established in Washington, lobbyist Stanley Long, the Voorhis adviser, joined him for lunch. They revisited the campaign.

"Of course I knew Jerry Voorhis wasn't a Communist," Nixon told him. And of course he understood how a congressman could contribute to the legislative process without passing bills that bore his name. But "you're just being naïve," Nixon said when Long objected. "I had to win. That's something you don't understand. The important thing was to win."

Win he must. Win he had. Richard Nixon was going to Congress. In four years he would be a U.S. senator; in six the vice president of the United States of America.

As American as Thanksgiving

T HE YOUNG CALIFORNIA congressman who arrived on Capitol Hill after the 1946 election rode rave reviews from the press. Dick Nixon was marked as a man to watch and his victory as an emblem of the year's historic turns. "Serious and energetic, he is indicative of the change in political trends, the increasing emphasis on youth and a genuine desire to serve the country," a *Washington Times Herald* reporter wrote. "If he bears out his promise he will go far."

Nixon turned thirty-four in January 1947. He was of above-average height for his time, an inch shy of six feet. He and his colleagues may have looked like vaudeville comics in their double-breasted suits with baggy pants and aileron lapels, but his clothes cloaked a trim frame. He joined a Congress comprised almost exclusively of white Christian men, confident in American supremacy and secure in their own unchallengeable place atop the social order. With his pretty wife and golden-haired daughter, the freshman Republican was popular with news photographers. They posed the family on bicycles with the Jefferson Memorial in the background and the cherry blossoms about their heads.

Nixon "looks like the boy who lived down the block from all of us," the *Times Herald* reporter wrote. "He's as typically American as Thanksgiving."

HE WAS BORN on January 9, 1913, in the front bedroom of the little gabled bungalow that his father had built on the outskirts of Yorba Linda. The doctor came by horse and buggy. It was a tiny town of some two hundred people, out amid the sage and the cactus. His father was exultant at the coming of a second son.

The Nixons were Scotch-Irish Protestants who had arrived in the colonies in the early eighteenth century, settling near Wilmington, Delaware. The patriarch, James Nixon, fared well, leaving his descendants two large farms, "my Negro man named Ned," and "a Negro woman named Nance."

His son George was an American patriot who served with George Washington at Trenton and Princeton, and later at the battle of Brandywine. After the war, he rambled west. A grandson, George Nixon III, enlisted in the Ohio volunteers at the age of forty and was killed on the slopes of Cemetery Ridge fighting for the Union at Gettysburg. His son Samuel, one of nine children left fatherless, was Richard Nixon's grandfather.

Samuel farmed, taught school, and delivered mail. He married a teacher, Sarah Wadsworth, who bore five children. Their third child was Frank, who was seven years old when Sarah's death from tuberculosis rocked the family. Samuel had sold his Ohio farm, packed his children in a wagon, and roamed the South in search of a warmer climate that might save his beloved from consumption. Now he was indigent, and heartbroken.

"Thus began a struggle of hardship and poverty as great in degree as any . . . in displaced families," Frank's brother Ernest recalled. Frank was dispatched to live with relatives. He was taunted at school and pummeled by bullies. "People thought they were almost white trash, they were so terribly poor," Alice Nixon Linton, his niece, recalled. "Day after day, Uncle Frank would march to school and know that after school he was going to take a terrible beating."

Samuel remarried, but his children found their stepmother cruel. Frank fled home without finishing grade school and rambled, across the Great Plains to the Rocky Mountains and back, an industrious nomad—shepherd, lineman, farmhand, carpenter, potter—who would never forget the pinch of poverty. He paused for a time in Columbus, where he helped lead fellow streetcar motormen in a protest for better working conditions and a cab sheltered from winter's cold. In 1907, frostbite inspired him to seek the warmth and promise of Southern California. He found work driving for the Red Cars, a regional Los Angeles trolley system, until he was dismissed after colliding with an automobile. He was laboring as a farmhand near Whittier, sampling a bevy of the local girls, when at a Valentine's Day party at the East Whittier meetinghouse, he met Hannah Milhous.

"I loved at first sight," Frank recalled, "among all the fair maidens I had met and love affairs which was many. . . . God bless her and it saved my life." He offered to take Hannah home, and she consented. They chose a long and wandering route through the orange groves. "And was it not a thrill to help her out of the buggy and hold her hand?" he remembered. "How I would have liked to steal a kiss which I dared not do."

He was back the next day, with a bouquet of violets. Frank noted, approvingly—for his father had warned him that fast girls snuggled close on the buggy seat—how Hannah kept a respectful distance. In March, he was invited to her birthday party and kissed her in the vestibule of the Milhous home. "That first kiss, oh that first kiss," he wrote. "The kiss of my life."

THE MILHOUS CLAN was from a rare sort of immigrant stock: Irish Quakers. The Society of Friends, as they called themselves, were individualistic and anticlerical. They believed that each person could forge a private relationship with the Divine, without the yoke of priests or popes. The early Friends were pacifists and abolitionists and laborers for social justice. They wore plain clothes, abhorred music and dance and other frivolities, and kept their own plain manner of speaking, using "thee" and "thy" instead of "you" and "your." William Penn's colony served as the faith's American foothold, and it was to southeast Pennsylvania that Thomas and Sarah Milhous, of Timahoe, Ireland, migrated in 1729.

Over the years, the Milhouses trekked the same trails as the Nixons, making their way across the Allegheny Mountains to the rich fields of the Midwest. They too were quietly industrious. The first noteworthy shoots were Joshua and Elizabeth Milhous, an Indiana nurseryman and his wife, notable because their lives served as the inspiration for *The Friendly Persuasion*, a fictional account of rural Quaker life written by a great-granddaughter, Jessamyn West. It tells the story of a Quaker family struggling with the modern versus the traditional and the challenge of pacifism during the Civil War.

Time, and westward migration, transformed the Quakers. Though some kept to the old ways, others embraced the trappings—preachers, choirs, and steeples—and doctrines of American Protestantism. They abandoned their social ministry and became more materialistic and self-satisfied. "It was rather a pity," West would write, skewering her family's smugness, "that there had to be for biological reasons an admission of non-Milhous blood into our life-stream."

Franklin Milhous, the oldest son of Joshua and Elizabeth, grew prosperous in the family nursery business in Indiana. His first wife bore two children before dying. He remarried, to the sturdier Almira Burdg. In 1897 they completed the clan's transcontinental passage, arriving in the new Quaker colony of Whittier, some twenty miles east of Los Angeles. They were midlife adventurers, looking for sunshine and hoping to cash in on the latest California boom. "It was abroad in those days: the notion to move out," Jessamyn recalled. "To go West."

—

FRANKLIN AND ALMIRA had a son and six daughters, bringing the number of Milhous children to nine. Hannah was a middle child—bright but plain, quiet, and overlooked in that big, busy household. It was an act of escape, with maybe a hint of desperation, when she took up with Frank, the randy farmhand. He was almost thirty, a man with little schooling but much worldly experience; she was a cloistered twenty-three-year-old—no old maid but fretful still—drawn to his vigor. Hannah abandoned her studies and they married quickly, after a four-month courtship, in June 1908. "The groom is a successful young business man of high ideals," the *Whittier News* reported.

But the Milhous family was dismayed. They "looked down on Uncle Frank. I could feel that keenly, because he wasn't well educated and he had a gruff manner," his niece Alice recalled. Almira liked to write poetry, and saw Hannah off with a foreboding bit of verse: *You'll get your reward for such service given / If not here on earth, you'll get it in heaven.* Hannah's younger sister Olive climbed a pepper tree in the yard and carved her displeasure into the wood: "Hannah is a bad girl."

Frank felt the scorn. He converted to his wife's faith, but could never claim the elect rank of "birthright" Quaker. He was a curt, disgruntled son-in-law, meeting obligations but breezing in and out of family gatherings or remaining behind, at home or in the car, when Hannah took their children to visit her parents and sisters.

Franklin Milhous augmented his nursery business by speculating in land, and he sold Frank and Hannah a property to farm in far-off Lindsay, an isolated outpost in the Central Valley. Hannah could not abide the loneliness, and after a year the couple moved to another Milhous parcel, the ten-acre plot in Yorba Linda, on which Frank planted lemon trees from his father-in-law's nursery stock.

Despite the fact it was so much closer—only fifteen miles from Whittier—Yorba Linda in 1912 was much like Lindsay: if not a frontier, it was still the California outback, a place for pioneers. There was a block-long street of stores called Main, a blacksmith who shared his shop with the barber, a druggist, and grocer and, eventually, a church built by the townsfolk. When one entrepreneur thought to make money selling liquor, he was foiled by a boycott. The townfolk bought him out and interred his license.

A panoramic photograph taken from a nearby hill shows the Nixon farm on the outskirts of town, on a naked plain amid ranks of skeletal saplings. Coyotes, buzzards, and rattlesnakes kept them company. When the Santa Ana winds roared down the mountain passes, the dirt and tumbleweed flew, and the little houses shook. Like Kansans searching the skies for signs of a funnel-shaped cloud, the farmers of Yorba Linda scanned the eastern horizon for the telltale pillars of dust that signaled the Santa Ana, braced their homes with planks, and shooed their children to shelter.

"It was just a little cottage," said Helen Neushutz, a friend of Hannah, recalling the Nixon home. "Dust. Dust everywhere. Starting little trees, you know. It was poor, I tell you, and it wasn't too good citrus land." The soil on Frank's spread was dry and thin, with hard adobe beneath. The trees grew but didn't yield much fruit. Looking back, Yorba Linda's old-timers would offer varied explanations for his failure at husbandry. He chose to farm a hilltop instead of the richer bottomland. His citrus stock was poor. He couldn't afford or didn't believe in fertilizer. He was stubborn and inflexible and refused advice. He didn't have the gift. Whatever the cause the outcome was plain: as other men made fortunes around him, Frank Nixon couldn't grow lemons.

HANNAH HAD A little sewing room, but there were few comforts and no indoor toilet in their home, and no electricity until 1916. The babies had bureau drawers for cribs; then, as boys, they bunked together, two to a bed, in the attic. A table, piano, and a stone fireplace dominated the living area. The distillate stove was cranky and dangerous, and Frank was burned badly on his face and arms when it tipped and fell, and he lifted the flaming mess to carry it outside, saving the family from greater tragedy. These were wretched years for Hannah. "Isn't it a whole lot nicer . . . to be on a big general ranch like yours than waiting and waiting for a few little lemon trees to grow and be so *miserably poor* all the while?" Hannah wrote her sister. They had a horse, a cow, chickens, a beehive for honey, and a garden. But forty years later, she remembered nights when there was nothing to serve for dinner but cornmeal.

Children kept arriving. Dick's father was a lusty type—a fanny pincher and a "horny old devil," in the words of a friend. Frank had to guard himself when dancing with women at church suppers, lest his tumescence show. Harold was the eldest boy, born in 1909. Richard arrived in 1913. Donald was born in 1914 and Arthur in 1918. A late surprise, Edward, came along in 1930, when Hannah was forty-five and Frank was fifty-three. The growing brood increased their financial pressures, and both showed signs of strain. Frank was loud and crotchety, plagued by stomach trouble and "nervous headaches." In the years to come, he would suffer a bleeding ulcer. The "overworked" Hannah was given to "nervous breakdowns," her family and friends recalled. At times she retreated to her parents' home, leaving the boys with hired girls.

The Nixon boys looked up to Frank and honored his struggle. Young Harold expressed their feelings in a schoolboy poem.

Only a dad neither rich or proud / Toiling, starving from day to day / Merely one of the surging crowd / Facing what ever may come his way . . .

Only a dad coming home at the end of day / Home to his wife and boys united / Sitting before the fire he begins to pray / For a light to shine on paths unlighted.

The household was noted, however, for its physical and emotional severity. Frank and Hannah loved their sons, but theirs was a time when children got whippings, at times with belts, sticks, or switches. With four unruly boys, a hair-trigger temper, and his mounting frustrations, Frank smacked and manhandled Dick and his brothers. "I just got through giving him a spanking for being in the ditch and I'll give him one now if he don't stay off that roof," Frank growled to a neighbor, after catching Dick in an irrigation canal and then bellowing at him to get down from a rafter. "If you like water, have some water," Frank raged on another occasion, yanking his boys from the canal and then slinging them back in. "Frank! You'll kill them!" said one of Hannah's sisters, aghast at his behavior. "He swatted them but good," said Dick's cousin Merle West. Hannah had to stand "as a buffer between Frank and the children," recalled Mary Rez, one of the hired girls.

"There are parents that can persuade kids to do things without physical punishment," but Frank was "a different kind," said Austin Marshburn, a Yorba Linda neighbor. "Frank had a temper and didn't always control it like he should."

The boys watched and learned from their father's behavior. Eldo West was flabbergasted when he visited the Nixons, years later, and heard Frank's sons cruelly pillorying their father. They had taken his vilification for years, and now relished the opportunity to dish it back.

Hannah was quite the opposite. "Two more temperamentally different people can hardly be imagined," Richard remembered. She kept it all in: her frustrations, her anger, her love. "In her whole life, I never heard her say to me, or to anyone else, 'I love you,'" he recalled. Her sister Jane said of Hannah's self-possession, "It was really not natural."

To some degree, this was the Quaker way: the relationship with God and the world was something to be worked out privately, and in silence. When praying, Hannah would close herself off in a closet. "I tried not to yell at my children," she recalled. "It does something to a child." Instead, she employed distance as a tool to discipline the boys. Frank and Hannah "were both explosive persons, one outwardly so, one inwardly," their granddaughter Lawrene recalled. Hannah "exploded inside" and "gave everybody the silent treatment, which just killed them, because she was so sweet. . . . She kept at it for days."

"I just can't stand it," Arthur would say. "Tell her to give me a spanking."

THROUGHOUT HIS YEARS as a public figure, Richard Nixon scorned psychoanalysis, dismissing suggestions that his diverse array of strengths and flaws was a consequential legacy of his childhood. There were many who agreed with him. They attributed the dark strains of his personality not to some early misery, but to the scarring effect of decades of intense political combat or the challenges common to his generation, of hard times and war.

"It is entirely usual that he would have determined from youth to try to make a mark," said a friend and colleague, Maurice Stans, casting Nixon as Ragged Dick, the Alger hero. "That picture of a young man struggling up from poverty all the way to the presidency is an un-complex one and does not require the psychological analyses to which he has been subjected. . . . He was an ambitious, capable American living the great dream, working hard all the way."

But other Nixon confidants were inclined to search for a formative trauma to explain his difficult personality. "Richard Nixon went up the walls of life with his claws," his friend and aide Bryce Harlow would venture. "I suspect that my gifted friend somewhere in his youth, maybe when he was very young or in his teens, got badly hurt by someone he cared for very deeply or trusted totally—a parent, a dear friend, a lover, a confidante. Somewhere I figure someone hurt him badly."

The drive to fill emotional voids, win parental approval, and bask in public acclaim has motivated many a corporate and political chieftain. Some go further along the continuum, meeting the description of a narcissistic personality offered by the twentieth-century psychoanalyst Heinz Kohut. Their lives are marked by a "hyperidealistic" drive and adulthoods in which grandiose goals and rich romantic visions are substitutes for meaningful relationships.

"Behind it lie low self-esteem and depression—a deep sense of uncared-for worthlessness and rejection, and incessant hunger for response, a yearning for reassurance," Kohut wrote. "All in all, the excited hypervitality for the patient must be understood as an attempt to counteract through self-stimulation a feeling of inner deadness and depression. As children these patients had felt emotionally unresponded to and had tried to overcome their loneliness and depression through . . . grandiose fantasies."

Dick was born at one of those moments when Hannah, already weakened by Harold's birth, was recoiling from the demands of motherhood and retreating to her childhood home. A sickly child, he competed for emotional nourishment with a cousin whom Hannah was breast-feeding for her sister. When they returned to Yorba Linda, Dick had to share his mother's attentions with Harold, a clamorous toddler. Then Hannah was hospitalized for a mastoidectomy, and Dick was sent to live with relatives. He was little more than a year old when Hannah became pregnant again: Donald was her third baby in five years. Not long after, Frank's widowed sister and her two boys moved in with the Nixons, crowding the house and staying for months.

Harold was a classic eldest child: charming, outgoing, and daring, full of laughter. He delighted his father as "the brightest and strongest, handsomest and best" of his sons. Don was a chubby, likable chuckler. Richard, the awkward middle son, struggled for his place in the family. He craved closeness, warmth, and affection; would seek it all his life. He was a "mama's baby," making more demands on Hannah than the others, his aunt Olive recalled. When rebuffed, he would conclude that he—the sourpuss child—was no easy thing to love. That hurt. So even as he reached out, he pulled back—fearful and suspecting that failure and rejection were his lot. "He had a fastidiousness about him," his cousin, and occasional babysitter, Jessamyn West remembered. "He was not . . . one you wanted to cuddle, though he may have longed for it."

In his first six months of life, Richard suffered through bouts of measles and cholera and, later, a serious case of pneumonia. At the age of three, he was thrown from a horse-drawn wagon and struck by its metal wheel. The gash in his scalp ran across his head, and the flow of blood left Hannah aghast, fearing at first that the accident had killed him. For the rest of his life he combed his hair back to cover the scar.

HAROLD WAS DISTINCTLY Nixon, but Dick was a jumble of Milhous and Nixon traits. Like Hannah, Dick was shy and cerebral. "Intense . . . and not outgoing," said Rez, the hired girl, who was sent to the Nixons by a local preacher to help the family cope. "He lived more within himself." And, like Hannah, Dick shied from confrontation. Watching her, he learned: Let his brothers take on their volatile father; Dick would evade and maneuver. "Don't argue with him," Dick told his siblings. "You'll have a better chance of getting what you want." Frank "had a hot temper, and I learned very early that the only way to deal with him was to abide by the rules he laid down," Dick would recall. "Otherwise, I would probably have felt the touch of the ruler or the strap."

Searching for footing in the unsettled land between glacier and volcano, Nixon found that scholastic achievement won both parents' esteem. He was a bookworm by nature; now he worked diligently: studying by Hannah's side, reading, and practicing the piano and the violin. He learned one of her favorite musical pieces—"Rustle of Spring"—and played it all his life.

"My father was not so controlled. He was explosive, dynamic. My mother was very controlled and I became that way," Nixon would remember. "I'm a disciplined person. . . . I cry inside. . . . My emotions are controlled."

But when frustrated, he raged. His infant wails could be heard at the neighbors'. An aunt remembered Frank climbing down from his tractor and telling Hannah to "keep that boy quiet" or "I'll do it for you." Dick bashed a playmate with the blunt end of a hatchet in an argument over a jar of tadpoles. When he joined other children in games, he insisted on setting the rules, and if he lost he would give way to a tantrum and throw himself on the floor, wailing and kicking his legs. "He was a terrible loser. He'd get so angry when he lost . . . angry for himself for not having lived up to his idea of perfection," a cousin, Edith Nunes, recalled.

"Far from being the cold or prim or restrained fellow that people have [Richard] pegged as being . . . he is a man full of passion, a man full of feeling," said Jessamyn West. But "he has the example of his father, and he is determined to keep a close rein on himself. . . . It is not coldness . . . it is control."

So the two sides clashed and swirled: the good Quaker son, trying to win Hannah's love, against Frank's battling, angry boy.

"There was plenty of character and steadiness and intelligence on the Milhous side, but this is kind of like having a warhead without anything to propel it," said his cousin Jessamyn. "The power and the motion . . . to carry that—and to take the chance—came from Frank."

Throughout his life, Richard had the habit of acknowledging a fear or a feeling and then, wary that he had disclosed too much, instantly amending the thought. So he described his childhood.

"There were times when I suppose we were tempted to run away and all that sort of thing," he would recall. "But on the other hand it was a happy home."

As a schoolboy Richard posed with his violin for a commercial photographer. Two photos survive the session; in one he looks cheerful, in the other bordering on sinister. "People react to fear, not love," he told an aide as president. "They don't teach that in Sunday school, but it's true."

YORBA LINDA HAD its glories, for this was California before freeways, smog, and subdivisions. There were hillsides to hike, and hollows for hiding. Frank would pack the boys up and take them and their friends to Laguna Beach, where they ate hot dogs, camped on the sand, and drifted asleep to the sound of the surf. There were square dances and potluck suppers and Sunday school picnics. Families escaped the summer heat amid the towering sycamore trees and crystalline waters of Santa Ana Canyon, or climbed Mount Baldy to play in snow. There were stands of blue-green barley, "the lordliest of crops," West recalled, and hills covered with baby blue eyes, lupine, and Indian paintbrush. Dick never forgot the sweet scent of the orange blossoms.

The Anaheim Union Water Company's steep-banked irrigation ditch snaked through the town, right by the Nixon property, offering endless opportunities for mischief. It was guarded by a roving zanjero, but its lure as playground and swimming hole was irresistible. It was where Dick, like most of the local urchins, learned to swim, "taught" by bigger boys, who threw him in to see him thrash and splash.

The town's little school had two grades in each classroom, and a cast-iron stove to ward off the morning chill. The daily curriculum was simple: Arithmetic. Reading. Recess. Spelling. Lunch. Penmanship. Reading. Arithmetic. Language. Geography. The schoolteachers were young women, imported and saddled with oppressive rules—no dating, no dancing, and no talking to men on the street—in that insular community. They were told where to live, and with whom, and compelled to cook dinner on hot plates in their rented rooms. It was "a very, very strict place . . . the most strange experience there, that I never want to go through again. It was terrible," Dick's first-grade teacher, Mary Skidmore, recalled.

Even while barefoot, Hannah's boys wore clean, white, ironed shirts. "Please call my son Richard, and never Dick," she told the teacher. "I named him Richard." He was a prodigious reader of newspapers, books—*Lad: A Dog, Treasure Island, The Swiss Family Robinson*—and borrowed copies of *The National Geographic Magazine.* He skipped second grade. His instructors remembered him as a solemn and businesslike student. "He absorbed knowledge of any kind like a blotter," a teacher remembered.

Dick lost himself in fantasies, in "the land of make believe," he called it. His family would find him hiding beneath a bed, or out under a tree, reading tales of great men and high adventure and "the far off places I wanted to go." Or in a field, staring up at the clouds or the stars, lost in a trancelike reverie. For generations of American boys, born in the lonesome heartland, the wail of a train whistle spoke of a world outside their farms and fields. So it did with Dick.

To augment his income, Frank cut and sold firewood, hired out as a carpenter, and started a land-clearing business with a neighbor, pooling their funds to buy the town's first tractor. When oil fields opened nearby, he worked as a roustabout. Hannah labored in a packinghouse, and the boys worked as field hands during harvest time. It kept the family going. But in 1922 Frank finally surrendered his dreams of a flourishing citrus ranch. Since oranges and lemons would not make him rich, maybe that booming phenomenon—the automobile—would. He studied the road-ways, counted the cars, and chose a corner on Whittier Boulevard—El Camino Real—where he bought land and opened a gas station.

"He had failed. So he had to come back . . . with his tail between his legs and start again," said Merle West.

WHITTIER HAD WIDE streets, a thriving business district, a college, and social strata. The wealthier lived on a shaded hillside, amid flowers, tower-ing palms, and eucalyptus trees. The Nixons lived on the highway in less-fashionable East Whittier, at a crossroads surrounded by orange, lemon, and walnut groves. Frank paid $5,000 for the property, on which he built a gas station, a two-car garage with second-story living quarters, and, later, a house. Two sprawling citrus operations—the Leffingwell Ranch across the street and the Murphy Ranch to the north—provided a clientele, includ-ing a number of Mexican laborers.

"There was quite a bit of money in town. Dick didn't have any of it," his friend Hubert Perry recalled. "But between the oil men and the people in the ranching business it was a very successful little isolated community."

Yorba Linda had no wrong side of the tracks, but the same could not be said for Whittier. The Quakers were gentle people, but they could be "hypocritical, smug, self-satisfied," writer M. F. K. Fisher recalled. The wealthy huddled with their own kind in a select group of pews on Sun-days. A part of the church "was theirs. If you got over there, you might be snubbed," a Whittier College professor remembered.

Dick was "outside the immediate group in which my family moved," said Robert Blake, an acquaintance from Whittier. "The people that lived in East Whittier in those days physically were somewhat removed from us. The Nixons went to different schools and lived a different kind of life. . . . We were aware of the problems their parents had in making the store go. . . . It was not a close social relationship our families had, in any way."

So Dick felt slights. The Nixons were not pariahs, however, as the move did put Frank and his family back in the orbit of his respectable Milhous in-laws. Sundays and holidays were notable affairs, with adults sitting around a twenty-foot-long table and children perched with plates of food on the stairs that wound upward from the front hall. The yard was filled with games at family picnics, and with fireworks on Independence Day. Christmas was happily Dickensian with the music-loving Franklin Milhous, in his ill-fitting hairpiece, playing the role of joyous old Fezziwig. The doors to the parlor were kept shut for days, as the grown-ups wrapped presents and decorated the tree, and then thrown open on Christmas morning.

After Franklin's death, in 1919, Almira ruled as the family matriarch. Her son Ezra was not a learned man, and he moved his large family around Southern California as he cleared and leveled land with a team of horses. The Nixon boys visited them in the summertime and joined in horseback rides and rabbit hunts, skinny-dipping in rural reservoirs, and plain hearty meals of mashed potatoes, beans, and gravy. "I don't think we ever owned a bathing suit when we were growing up. We would leave the house on a run, each one trying to see who would be the first one in the reservoir," Dick's cousin Franklin recalled. "The first pair of britches would come off as we went out the door."

Frank sold gasoline and tires and, to meet the demand of his rural clientele, added a small store to the gas station, stocked with produce and basic groceries. He saw opportunity when the Quakers built a new meetinghouse. He bought the old church building, hired workmen, and, with trucks and rollers, had it toted down Whittier Boulevard to his property. The layout was reversed, with the belfry in the rear, where Frank kept an office, and an eye on the shoppers below.

The market grew with boom times in the Roaring Twenties. Soon Frank was leasing the gas station to others and focusing on the grocery. There were racks of produce and a hanging scale, a meat counter, and shelves of canned and packaged goods. The family extended credit, boxed orders, and made deliveries. Frank stocked tobacco, but not liquor, and kept a revolver handy to discourage robbery. Hannah's homemade pies were a huge draw, and when she was away, Frank took his turn rising early and doing the baking himself.

As Don grew older he played a bigger role, managing the meat counter, buying refrigerators, adding a small café. Soon it was a place where the country-club crowd would stop on the way home from golf to buy meat. Over time, the Nixons hired help—nephews and nieces and neighbors—to assist them. But cantankerous Frank ruled the roost through Richard's boyhood, and wrung every cent out of his family's hide. "What did the boys do?" said Harry Schuyler, a neighbor. "They worked. From the time they were able to work, they worked. What did they do when they got home from school? They worked."

Frank often quoted God's imprecation to Adam and Eve as they were driven from paradise for their sinfulness: "In the sweat of thy face shalt thou eat bread." After all his hardscrabble years, he had found success— but at a cost. He "was a highly acquisitive person and a slave driver. He worked all his children and he worked his wife," said his nephew by marriage, Leonidas Dodson. "Richard had a very tough time of it, but that didn't stem . . . from economic necessity. It stemmed rather from a strong-willed, rather grasping" father.

Frank was known to perform charitable acts—carrying groceries through floodwaters to the homes of Mexican farmworkers; bringing medicine, on foot in the rain, for an ailing nephew; and taking care of his widowed sister and her children. When a massive earthquake shattered Long Beach, Frank instinctively, and immediately, drove there to help. In Yorba Linda, he had been known for his spirited evocation of Christian charity in a popular Sunday school class. During the Great Depression, the Nixon store allowed the jobless to purchase food on credit, and Frank carried their debts on his books through the hardest of times.

But mostly Frank was remembered for his loud, crotchety self. He held grudges against neighbors over property line disputes and other long-gone transactions—refusing to carry bags of groceries for one woman, even when she was eight months pregnant. He argued with anyone: customers, sons, neighbors, and salesmen. A guileless niece who helped Hannah clean the house remembered finding nickels and dimes on the windowsills and, years later, learning that the coins had been planted by Frank, to test her honesty. "People . . . wouldn't give two cents for Frank," said Merle West.

Many of Frank's rants dealt with politics. There was no fixed star in his beliefs: he moved around the populist heavens. His legacy to Richard was a distinct brand of Republicanism, built upon resentment of the big forces—

crooked Business or profligate Government—that exploited hard-pressed common folk. Among his fancied banes were big chain stores, owned by Jews, out to crush small operators like the Nixons.

As ALWAYS, DICK did well in his studies. He completed the fifth and sixth grades in East Whittier and then, midway through the seventh grade, went to live with an aunt in far-off Lindsay for six months, ostensibly to profit from her music lessons. His high school years were similarly divided, between schools in Fullerton (where he bivouacked with another aunt) and Whittier.

As an elementary school assignment when he was ten, Dick wrote a piteous letter, which Hannah kept as a remembrance.

> My Dear Master:
>   The two boys that you left me with are very bad to me. Their dog, Jim, is very old and he will never talk or play with me.
>   One Saturday the boys went hunting. Jim and myself went with them. While going through the woods one of the boys triped and fell on me. I lost my temper and bit him. He kiked me in the side and we started on. While we were walking I saw a black round thing in a tree. I hit it with my paw. A swarm of black thing came out of it. I felt pain all over. I started to run and as both of my eys were swelled shut I fell into a pond. When I got home I was very sore, I wish you would come home right now.
>   Your good dog
>   Richard

Dick never forgot the spring day in 1925 when his family arrived in Lindsay to take him home. Young Arthur, the little brother whom he adored, asked their parents for permission to give Dick a kiss. A few weeks later, Arthur was dead, taken by an illness that the doctors guessed was tubercular meningitis—a strain of tuberculosis that attacked the nervous system. One day Arthur had complained of sleepiness, the next his parents were coming downstairs sobbing, and Frank was telling Dick, "They say the little darling is going to die." Dick and his brothers were sent to stay with an aunt, who woke them one night with the awful news.

At home, the twelve-year-old Richard "slipped into a big chair and sat staring into space, silent and dry-eyed in the undemonstrative way in which, because of his choked deep feeling, he was always to face tragedy," his mother remembered. In a heartfelt college essay, Dick recalled Arthur's "unusually beautiful eyes; black eyes which seem to sparkle with hidden fire and to beckon us to come on some secret journey which will carry us to the land of make believe."

Arthur's death spurred the first stirrings of fatalism in Dick, but not the last. He was fourteen when Harold returned from a boarding school in New England coughing up blood.

In Yorba Linda, the Nixon boys had been raised on raw milk from the family cow, in part because Frank was fussy and didn't put stock in newfangled notions like pasteurization. "He refused to pay any attention to the doctor's warning that the cow ought to be tested for tuberculosis," Richard remembered. "Our family paid a heavy price." The survivors came to believe that the milk bore the tuberculosis bacilli, and so the seeds of tragedy.

Arthur's death was mercifully quick. Harold took six years to die. He was a gallant, if uncooperative patient, determined to wring what thrills he could from his time left on the planet. He raced a Ford hot rod through the fields, chased girls, gambled, and stayed out late. Behind the bravado, he wrestled with dread.

AND SO DICK's teenage years—all that time twixt twelve and twenty, of new stirrings, excitement, and exploration—were steeped in horror. The Nixon home was draped in grief after Arthur's death, and with the fear that Harold—and maybe Dick and Don, for tuberculosis can smolder in those exposed to the disease—would follow their little brother to the grave. The boiled plates and cutlery, the sweat-soaked sheets, the smell of the alcohol rubs—every wheeze and cough and show of bloody phlegm from Harold—served as dark forebodings.

For a time, Frank put Harold in a sanitarium. Then, fleeing its fogs and clammy dawns, Hannah and her eldest boy left Whittier for the dry mountain air of Prescott, Arizona, home to a colony of tuberculosis patients. She cooked and kept house for Harold and three other doomed young men who boarded with them. In the summers of his high school years, Richard would visit, taking odd jobs—chicken plucking, pool boy, carnival barker—to earn money. Back home, he shared lonely meals— fried food or warmed-up canned fare—with Frank and Don, all suffering from grief and missing Hannah. Dick never learned to savor food—it was mostly just a fuel.

Dick lost himself in work. No one toted as many books or spent more time in the library. His mother came to believe that, with Arthur dead and Harold dying, Dick's "need to succeed" was driven by a survivor's remorse. "Unconsciously . . . I think that Richard may have felt a kind of guilt that . . . he was alive," Hannah concluded. "It seemed that Richard was trying to be three sons in one, striving even harder than before to make up . . . for our loss."

Thus Dick, the transfer student who missed half the seventh grade at East Whittier elementary school, became president of the eighth-grade class. Asked to list his goals, he spoke of traveling overseas, and attending Columbia University. "I would like to study law and enter politics for an occupation," he wrote, "so that I might be of some good to the people." His family kept their gifted child supplied with books about American heroes, and inspirational verse by Edgar Guest and Rudyard Kipling. Dick hung verses by Longfellow, given him by his grandmother, over his bed:

Lives of great men oft' remind us,
We can make our lives sublime,
And departing, leave behind us,
Footprints on the sands of time.

Footprints that perhaps another
Sailing o'er life's stormy main
A forlorn and shipwrecked brother
Seeing may take heart again.

He was an A student in high school, and the town's prizewinning young orator. In 1929, speaking on "Our Privileges Under the Constitution," he pled for order and security, taking a cramped view of constitutional protections like the First Amendment and warning of those "who use them as a cloak for covering libelous, indecent and injurious statements."

"Should the morals of the nation be offended and polluted in the name of freedom of speech or freedom of the press?" he asked. "In the words of Lincoln, the individual can have no rights against the best interests of society."

Dick was on the high school debate team, earned a spot on the junior varsity football squad, performed in the drama club plays, and played the violin in the school orchestra. He lost an election for student body president, but took on the duties of "general manager," organizing sports and events and activities. He was a type of young man known to generations of American teenagers who looked with a mix of admiration and disdain upon the preternaturally smart. "He was, pretty much, a brain," said his cousin Merle.

At Fullerton High School, Dick was so resolute and square that his actions bordered on prissy. He liked his shirts ironed just so. He gargled and checked his breath before leaving the house each morning. "He didn't partake in rough play. . . . I never remember him as being a roughhouser," a pal recalled. "He always had a big smile when he smiled . . . but he didn't smile too often."

The other boys at Fullerton embraced a fad: wearing corduroy pants every day and refusing to wash them until they were downright filthy. Dick declined, and announced his disdain for riding the bus: his school-mates were loud and they smelled, he said. He was "not much of a mixer," Hannah recalled. "Not much for social chatter—or any other kind of talk. He was so tight-lipped . . . that he could always be trusted with a secret."

"Richard was always so serious that we always thought he never had any fun," said Anne Gillmore, a neighbor. "I think he was more or less of a loner. You'd see him sitting on the steps either staring into space or reading a book," said Albert Haendiges, a high school classmate. Dick could be lured to a game of tennis with his brothers, or touch football on the road outside the store. But schoolwork and reading or chores would beckon, and he would drift away. The reminiscences of Whittier youths are peppered with stories of driving by the Nixon home and seeing Richard studying at the dining room table in the hours after midnight. There were more than a few classmates, Merle West recalled, who thought Dick was sanctimonious, priggish, and a teacher's pet. They "hated Richard . . . couldn't stand the guy," West said.

DICK WAS GIFTED, but he lacked Harold's manly charm or Arthur's gentle beauty, and he knew it. He was devoted to Hannah, but her emotional remove increased with the care his brothers needed, her grief at their deaths, and the endless hours she consigned to work and church. Dick was shuffled around, dispatched to live with relatives, never, until college, finishing at a school where he began. He lived every day by the virtues with which the Nixons survived: toil, self-reliance, and endurance. "You shared the adversity and you grew stronger and took care of yourself," he would recall, "not having your mother to lean on."

The hard times left their mark. They bred in him a deep resentment of those who had it easy—who with good looks, illustrious ancestry, wealth, or personality seemed to glide through life. Like Frank, he gnawed at grievances, was prone to fits of temper. Straining to take the place of his lost brothers—to be brilliant for his mother and manly for his dad—he could be tense, solemn. A cousin, prized like Dick as a musician by their family, remembered her first visit to the Nixon home. As she entered the house he purposefully ignored her, sat down, and banged out the jarring "Flight of the Bumblebee" on the piano.

When Dick became ill with fever in his senior year in high school, his family fretted that he had worked himself sick. "I suppose you have studied too hard and read too much and overtaxed your nerves," his grandmother wrote. She told him of her own bout with "nervous frustration" and suggested that with enough willpower he could overcome his weaknesses.

"I found out that one can control their nerves to a great extent," she wrote. "I . . . said to myself—Now there is no use of this it must be stopped. Then be determined to make it so."

GIRLS WERE A new frontier; they would remember him, riding the bus to Fullerton, making faces at them. "He made quite an issue of girls—that he was a woman-hater . . . he was going to be a bachelor all his life," a classmate recalled. Puberty had brought new, unsettling feelings to Dick—and "this was his self-defense."

Frank may have had "amorous propensities," as Jessamyn West recalled, but the Milhous family's view of sexuality left "maiming inhibitions" among its young. The sexual instruction for Jessamyn and her cousins was "don't talk about it. . . . don't play with it. . . . keep it covered up." Years later, Dick would confide to a wartime buddy that he remained a virgin until his late twenties, throughout high school, college, and law school.

Richard did worry about manliness. He began to watch his weight, went out for football, refused to wear an apron in the store, and closed the blinds when it came his turn to wash the dishes. His mother later mocked her boy's first explorations with the female sex. "What dates he had . . . he talked not of romance, but about such things as what might have happened if the Persians had conquered the Greeks," she said.

And yet, from the start, there were girls—distant cousins and classmates—who were drawn to this boy they found mysterious, attractive, and kind. "I used to think he was very handsome. I thought his eyes were just beautiful. He has dark eyes. He has so much expression in them," said cousin Jo Marcelle. Another, Alice Nixon, thought he was "such a quiet, remote boy, studying so hard" that "he didn't seem to be of this world." But "there was a warmth underneath, and if you get through this shell, there is a wonderful person, an understanding person."

In the summer of 1929, Hannah became pregnant with Edward. Dick was sixteen and entering his senior year at Whittier High School. If he expressed any anger or embarrassment to his mother or father for their procreative recklessness, the record has not survived. Hannah, home from Arizona, found him changed: less dependent, more involved with life outside their home, including his female classmates. One girl, in particular, had a claim on his affections. Her name was Ola Florence Welch, and they had come together as the leads in a Latin Club production of the *Aeneid,* dressed in ill-fitting costumes, awkwardly performing a love scene that spurred their teenage audience to erupt in catcalls and laughter. Dick and Ola were mortified. His first mushy note to Ola was contrite. He had stalked out of rehearsal. "I have to apologize for the caddish way I acted Saturday evening. I certainly wish now I could have kept my temper in my pocket," he wrote. "Please don't think I'm that way all the time."

In fact, he was smitten. "I've tried to figure out why I'm so cracked about you," he said, and listed the reasons. "You are not a boy chaser. You use your brains to good purposes. You never show your anger to anyone. You are talented in other lines besides studying (dramatist, music etc.) and most of all 'You are just you.' That's the only way I can put it."

He signed it, "Love from Dick Nixon."

They survived that inauspicious beginning and started dating. She was cute and bubbly, popular, and fascinated by this dark and serious boy who talked to her of politics, history, and international affairs. She was his first love, and he hers.

THE WORLD OUTSIDE was sliding toward bedlam. Mussolini had seized power in Italy, the Nazis were marshaling their strength in Germany, and the Japanese were preparing to invade Manchuria. In Dick's senior year in high school, the stock market crashed, a trigger to the Great Depression. Harvard and Yale alumni came calling, offering him the opportunity to apply for an academic scholarship. But with the economic chaos, a new baby, and the costs of caring for Harold, the Nixon family could not afford to send its brightest son away, or to cover room and board in far-off Cambridge or New Haven. In the fall of 1930, Dick entered Whittier College—his tuition covered by a small bequest left by his grandfather Franklin. The freshmen, remembering his performance as the student manager in high school, immediately elected him class president.

The Depression shadowed his college years, but there was time for romance and horseplay, there in snuggly Whittier, and Dick learned to enjoy himself. He bought his first car—a Model A Ford. He competed in several sports at Whittier, added current hits to his repertoire on the piano, led the glee club on a statewide tour, and in San Francisco visited his first speakeasy (where he was more impressed by the saucy barmaid than the Tom Collins she served him) with teammates from the far-roaming debate squad. He grew in self-assurance, became a less awkward and more personable individual. A to-do list he made at the time, tracking his furious pace, included classwork, debate, student government, glee club, the athletic board, football, and the school plays.

His classmates—sobered by the era's financial and political turmoil, some skipping meals and selling blood to get by—were moving in his direction. These were serious times, and they came to appreciate his diligence and resilience. There were those who sneered at the grocer's boy who rose at 3:30 a.m. to drive to Los Angeles in the family truck and buy fruit and vegetables for the Nixon market. Ola's girlfriends thought him odd. And there were more than a few who laughed when he joined the varsity football squad, warmed the bench, and never won his letter. But many saw, and admired, Nixon's guts. And brains. Besides, Whittier College was tiny. With but some hundred students in the class of 1934, Dick had no host of competitors for student leadership.

The Whittier athletic teams were "never blessed with a lot of great material," said John Arrambide, one of the better football players. "I can remember [Dick] on the ground most of the time, but we'd pick him up and he'd be ready for the next play. That's what we admired about him. He never got into a ball game, but he was there and took it every week."

An exception, in the gloom of the Depression, was the Franklins—a select society whose members fancied themselves the campus elite, and proffered no invitation to the kid from East Whittier. "They were the haves and we were the have-nots, see?" Dick would recall. So he helped organize a rival club, dominated by the school's athletes, who called themselves the Orthogonians. They made virtue of their rank as plebs and proles and displayed a laudable blindness to class, ethnicity, and race. Let the Franklins wear tuxedos for the yearbook photograph: the Orthogonians would pose in open-collared shirts. The Franklins had fancy balls and dinners; the Orthogonians reveled at bean suppers. They accepted African Americans. Their mascot was the wild boar, and their motto was "Beans, Brains, Brawn and Bowels."

"Dick was taken into this organization to give the group some dignity, scholastically speaking," Keith Wood, an early Orthogonian, recalled. "Our founders did not want us to be known as an unintelligent bunch of athletes."

Nixon was an enthusiast, helping to devise the club's constitution, the lyrics of the club song, and its sadistic initiation rites. His ardor flagged only at the club's "knock and boost" meetings, in which the young men assessed their own, and each other's, strengths and weaknesses. As with any self-analysis, Nixon found the sessions excruciating. "It was such an invasion of privacy," he recalled. "To have this laying on a couch or discussing all these things and so forth and so on: no way for me. I could never do it."

"There is something that restrains from within," Thomas Bewley would recall. "He feels deeply. He is emotional. He wants to be a good fellow. He wants you to love him, but there is a feeling of caution there."

THE ORTHOGONIANS HAD an additional virtue: they provided a base for Dick's ventures in campus politics. Having the jocks on one's side never hurt. He also earned support by promoting his classmates' interests before the college administration—defending those who got into trouble or, as in his senior year, leading a movement for dancing on campus. It was the signature issue of his victorious campaign for student government president, in which he made the pragmatic argument (after testing it out on his pious Milhous relatives) that it was better to be sock-hopping in Whittier than jitterbugging in a roadhouse.

Not that he was a great dancer. Having skipped a grade in elementary school, Dick was one of the youngest in his class at Whittier—only seventeen when he started college—and lagging in the social graces. He "was not a ladies' man," said classmate Janet Triggs. "He didn't have the glamour about him that attracts the opposite sex. He wasn't sexy." But the social scene was important on campus, especially for a prospective student leader. So he would "ask a girl to go to something for the sake of being able to go," she said.

"He was always apart," his cousin Edith Nunes remembered. "He didn't go helling around with the rest of us. He didn't approve of it. He used to scold me for wearing too much lipstick." Edith, and a few others, glimpsed the private Dick—the nervous, anxious Dick—pacing before going onstage, where he then astounded them by performing with aplomb.

Ola helped. They were a college couple, at times inseparable, who roller-skated, danced, kissed, quarreled, broke apart, dated others, made up, and got back together. It was "stormy," she recalled. "He'd be harsh and I'd cry." Unlike Janet Triggs, Ola found him sexy, she confessed, but there was no "hanky-panky." One summer night, at the end of their junior year, Dick "became soft and tender and told me how much he loved me," she remembered. They decided to marry and began to save money for a ring. "I thought Dick was wonderful . . . so strong, so clever, so articulate," she recalled. "He wrote me notes which I just couldn't believe, they had such beautiful words and thoughts."

But his inscription in Ola's yearbook was rife with doubt and a pitiable self-loathing.

He had enjoyed portraying lovers in a college play with her, he wrote, "even though I have always detested making love in public—or anywhere else for that matter."

They had "some pretty good times together in spite of my intense bashfulness and inherent dumbness," he added.

Whenever Ola "threw me over for bigger and better men," he wrote, "it was good for me and a godsend for her."

Dick focused on French, history, and English, with just two math classes and no science courses, in his four years at Whittier. His finer qualities—his intellect, drive, and tenacity—brought him high regard from several members of the faculty, who took a personal interest. The football coach, "Chief" Wallace Newman, fueled Nixon's ache for winning at almost any cost. Paul Smith, his history professor, laded him with broadening, supplementary readings—like the ten-volume biography of Abraham Lincoln written by John Hay and John Nicolay. And Albert Upton, the drama coach, taught Dick how to step out of his introverted self onstage. It was Upton who introduced Dick to the pacifistic philosophy of Leo Tolstoy, whose works Nixon inhaled and whose lessons he embraced.

Nixon was going to college during the Depression. In itself, that was an accomplishment. But there is no pretending that Dick got an excellent education. "It was a poverty-stricken little local-yokel college," Upton remembered.

—

In Arthur's dying, Dick had seen God devour an innocent. Eight years later, in his junior year at Whittier, he witnessed the dying of the wide-grinned, valiant Harold.

When Hannah returned home to give birth to Edward, Harold had remained in Arizona. Dick, with his rich life of the mind, might have endured such a separation. But the high-spirited Harold found the life of a consumptive terrifyingly lonely.

"I'm so awful discouraged. . . . If I could only sleep better at night and not think about home and the past," Harold wrote Hannah. "Last night, mother . . . I began thinking of Arthur, and wished I could be lying out there with him. . . . I cried for a long time."

Harold's parents relented and told him to come home. Frank built a homemade camper, and they planned a monthlong trip. They were back after three days. Harold was too weak. "It was really worth doing," he told Dick, "to see the blossoms . . . to see the snow on the mountains." On a day in March 1933, Dick and Harold went into town to buy their mother an electric mixer for her birthday. A day later, while Dick was at school, studying in the library, Harold died. Why was it, Frank asked friends, that "the best of the fold are taken?"

Once again, Dick sat stoically, unresponsive, lost in grief and locked in agony. "He didn't let it out," Ola Florence recalled. Arthur's death had arrived like a bolt of lightning; Harold's dying had been one long, ghastly trip through hell.

4

Death, God, Love, and War

I N THE MONTHS after Harold's death, with the aid of a provocative senior-year philosophy course, Dick field-stripped his faith. It would rest now on reason, not revelation. He needed to rectify the cruelty and indifference of the universe with the myths he had learned as a child in Sunday school. Where was that gentle Jesus, that mighty and beneficent God, when Arthur and Harold and those who loved them had pleaded for alleviation?

"My parents . . . had ground into me, with the aid of the church, all the fundamental ideas in their strictest interpretation. The infallibility of the Bible, the miracles, even the whale story, all these I accepted as facts when I entered college four years ago," Dick wrote in a journal he kept for the class. Now "many of those childhood ideas have been destroyed."

He was searching, as well, for moral purpose—for a way to balance the lessons of the gospel with the epochal new discoveries in behavioral science, relativity, and evolution. "We are never satisfied with just living. We must know why we live," he wrote. "Where my study will lead I do not know, but certainly any system of ideas would be better than this absurd collection of science, religion and philosophy that I now have."

His conclusions were vaguely deist, in a way that Thomas Jefferson, Benjamin Franklin, and other sons of the Enlightenment might approve. Man acted in a fathomless Creation, he decided, where agonies and joys were random results, not the constructs of an intervening God. Yet at the same time, Dick retained a reverence for the teachings of Christ, which offered an answer to the chaos of modernism, and modern life. It might even be possible, he theorized, by living a life of Christlike virtue, to reach a kind of transcendence. "It is not necessary to show that Jesus rose from the dead on the third day and then lived on earth for forty days with his disciples before ascending into heaven. The important fact is that Jesus lived and taught a life so perfect that he continued to live and grow after his death in the hearts of men," Nixon wrote. "It may be true that the Resurrection story is a myth, but symbolically it teaches the great lesson that men who achieve the highest values in their lives may gain immortality."

Slowly, he came to terms. Not hopeless or despairing but wary—a realist, a fatalist, a bit messianic. Though the world was a callous place, men could still play a thrilling role. Woodrow Wilson, the "inspired idealist," had "made a nation believe that they were fighting for peace, for world democracy, for international friendship. Always holding himself above the level of cheap propaganda, he led his country into war, he fired his soldiers with patriotic zeal; he revitalized the Allied troops; all because he had an ideal, the ideal of World Peace. . . .

"Illogical? Insane? Yes, but the fact we must acknowledge is that man can be inspired to fight for the cause of peace. . . .

"My beliefs are shattered, but in their place a new philosophy has been built," Dick concluded. "A process of enlightenment and purification has taken place."

RICHARD NIXON ENTERED law school in the fall of 1934, at the age of twenty-one. His days at Duke were much like his time at Whittier College. He studied furiously, haunted the stacks, and graduated near the top of his class. He left a generally favorable impression and prevailed in a few extracurricular contests, like the contest for the presidency of the law school bar association. He had coveted this opportunity for postgraduate study and made the most of it.

It was no easy jog. Dick took money from relatives and menial jobs to get by. He wrote to tell his parents that, in addition to his classes and part-time work, he was studying six hours a day. He was "scared to death that he was going to flunk out," a classmate recalled. Nixon's classmates were favorite sons themselves, and from bigger, better stages than Whittier. There were moments when, despondent, he thought about leaving. "I've almost decided that I don't like this law business. No fooling. I'm getting almost disgusted," Dick told Ola.

"He wrote these sad letters," she would remember. "He sounded like he was close to quitting two or three times." An aunt wrote to Dick, urging him to relax, and included her remedy for hemorrhoids.

Nixon got by on grit. As at Whittier, he left a somewhat divided body of opinion among his classmates, many of who came from moneyed families. They joked about his "iron butt," and his well-worn wardrobe. They lauded his commitment, his drive, the hours he was in the library—but a contingent found him unpleasant, and even his pals called him Gloomy

Gus. "He never expected anything good to happen to him or to anyone close to him which wasn't earned," said classmate Lyman Brownfield. "Any time someone started blowing rosy bubbles, you could count on Nixon to burst them with a little sharp prick."

Dick lived in rented rooms in Durham, most memorably in a cabin in the woods during his senior year, where he, Brownfield, and two other aspiring barristers shared two brass double beds. They named it Whippoorwill Manor. It had no electricity, or indoor plumbing. They stashed their towels and shaving kits on campus and showered in the gym. He would dress in the morning chill, then trot through the forest to the fairy-tale campus, with its arches, stained glass, and spires. "Let me tell you about the nuttiest of the nutty Nixons," he wrote Ola. "He remains a stolid bachelor and I think his hair is beginning to thin out. He doesn't smoke, he drinks very little, he swears less and he is as crazy as ever. He still thinks an awful lot of his mother."

WHO KNOWS WHY couples drift apart? But many do as lives take different courses. So it was with Dick and Ola.

They were assertive individuals, proud, and new to the traps of love. And Dick had a hard time dealing with success. He knew how to handle toil, adversity, loss, and grief. You bled, bound your wounds, and soldiered on. But acclaim, well, that was intoxicating. He had ended his Whittier College years on a roll, tasting popularity. They wrote nice things about him in the yearbook. He didn't know how to govern his response.

"Deep down he had this insecure side to him," Ola recalled. "When he ran . . . for student body president he was really down, absolutely sure that he wasn't going to win.

"Then when he won, he went up and changed for a time, and became so different," she remembered. "He suddenly started dating other girls and I was left thinking, maybe now he's president he's changed."

Harold's death may have played a role: grief may have provoked an emotional deadness, or recklessness. Or perhaps he resented what he needed so much—or feared that which held such power to hurt him. Ola was still the person Dick called to share in his joy when he learned he was going to Duke. He wrote to her, often, from North Carolina—as if marriage was inevitable. But when he returned to California, after his first year of studies, he learned she was seeing another man.

"If I never see you again it will be too soon," he shouted, and slammed down the phone. He refused to accept it. For weeks he sent her letters.

Some were terribly self-denigrating: he likened himself to "a bad penny" that was "impossible to get rid of"; he wrote, "and when a person is worth even less than that the impossibility becomes complete."

In early 1936, just a few months before her wedding, she at last convinced him. It was over. "Finally I have become wise!" he wrote. "I regret having embarrassed you."

"In the year and a half I've been at Duke, I've realized more than ever the perfection, the splendor, the grandeur of my mother's character," he told her. "Incapable of selfishness she is to me a supreme ideal. And you have taken your place with her in my heart—as an example for which all men should strive.

"Old memories are slowly fading away. New ones are taking their place," he said. "But I shall always remember the kindness, the beauty, the loveliness that was, that is, and shall for ever be Ola Florence Welch."

A few months later she was married, and their relationship ended. She had been an important part of his life for six years. Now she was gone.

"Sometimes I think I never really knew him," Ola would recall, "and I was as close to him as anyone."

LIFE AT DUKE went on. Dick ate Milky Ways for breakfast and lived out of a single trunk, wearing the same red sweater, day after day, and alternating his few pairs of underwear until they were torn and dingy. He played handball for exercise, cheered himself hoarse for Duke's football team, and composed an arid article on automobile liability for the law journal. On breaks, he toured Washington, Baltimore, and New York. He was struck by the East's deciduous greenery, and its teeming cities chock with ethnic enclaves and tough-talking workmen. In the capital, he attended his first major-league ball games, watching Joe DiMaggio's Yankees take a double-header from the Senators.

In North Carolina, Richard witnessed how the South enforced segregation. He was moved by the plight of southern blacks; he found their treatment horrid, and unfair. He showed empathy, as well, to Fred Cady, the polio victim he befriended and helped bear up the stairs to class, to Charles Rhyne, a hospitalized classmate, and to Oren Mollenkopf, who never forgot how Dick found time to counsel him, offering "a kind word for a confused, homesick and frightened young man when he needed it the most."

"Nixon disclosed himself from the beginning as what I call a true liberal," his housemate Brownfield recalled. "He was strongly sympathetic to the rights of the individual, particularly when the individual found himself opposed by the unequal and artificially created force of big government, big society or big business." It was in his skepticism about New Deal solutions that Dick displayed his conservatism. He "never felt that an individual could transfer his responsibilities to the government and at the same time keep his freedom."

Nixon's one known law school escapade took place at the end of his second year at Duke, when he and two other students—all of whose scholarships depended on continued academic excellence—could not wait for grades to be posted. One climbed through a transom to unlock the dean's office, where they pawed through the files to see how they ranked, and were relieved to discover they had all survived.

After Ola, Dick didn't date at Duke. He was "rather a plodder," a female classmate, Farley Hunter, recalled. "Solemn . . . not an easy conversationalist." She and the other women in his class found him "worthy, admirable, hard-working but rather dull . . . [with] a lack of vivacity and gaiety and savoir-faire." Years later, after reading in *Time* magazine that Dick had been elected to the House, Hunter remembers thinking, "Good old Dick. Imagine him being in Congress. I can't think of anybody less likely."

DUKE WAS AN aspiring university built on tobacco money—not yet a citadel of the meritocracy. Its law school graduates tended to return home after graduation, to hang out their shingle or join a local practice, or take a job in government. The Ivy League packed the Wall Street firms with graduates; Duke did not.

And while Nixon was obviously bright and hardworking he was "not terribly imaginative or profound," said Professor Lon Fuller. "There was the suggestion of an intellectual inferiority complex." The last thing Dick's proud but fragile ego needed, after escaping Whittier, was rejection. Yet that is what he got.

Nixon had glowing letters of recommendation from the Duke faculty and scored interviews with New York law firms, but received no offers. Having dabbled in criminal justice during an internship with the Durham district attorney, he applied to the Federal Bureau of Investigation. The FBI took a long look at Nixon, and what it found it liked. But his application fell through the cracks.

Nixon graduated, third in his class, in the spring of 1937. His family, including the redoubtable Almira, drove across the country to see him get his diploma. The great escape was over. He had tried to leap and failed.

Squeezed in the car with Frank and Hannah, Don and Ed and Almira, he headed back to Whittier.

NIXON NEVER TOOK failure well. He would brood and sulk, find foes to blame and hate. But then—he'd rebound. He would rein in his resentment, pull out a yellow pad, start his lists, summon the will to carry on. No one could mistake him for Pollyanna, but there existed, within the angry man, a resolute optimist.

The first signs of that legendary resilience came in the years after Duke. He slunk back to Whittier at the age of twenty-four, morose, with no prospects in hand. Hannah had prevailed upon Tom Bewley to offer her son a position in his law firm. It was a fine little legal partnership, woven in the town's life, handling all the mundane tasks of the local citizenry—oil leases, matrimonial disputes, tax issues, probate. But life with Wingert & Bewley was a far cry and a continent from Wall Street or Capitol Hill. For three years of law school, he had been jousting with brilliant classmates and professors, debating the wisdom of Brandeis and Cardozo, dissecting Roosevelt's flaws. Now he would be helping farmers draft their wills.

Dick took the California bar exam in September. With no other options, he joined the firm, at $50 a month. He worked diligently, stayed late, took lunch at his desk, and thoroughly bungled his first big case.

Nixon thought about resigning, but Bewley accepted the responsibility. He had given Dick a simple matter to handle, just days after Nixon passed the bar. Dick had naively asked the opposing attorney for advice and been snookered. The outraged client sued Wingert & Bewley for malpractice, accusing them of negligence, carelessness, and incompetence. The firm settled, paying the client $4,800.*

NIXON WAS GREEN, and still quite square. When the Wingert family took him on his first trip to a racetrack, he declined to bet on a horse; when they brought him to a lively Mexican restaurant in old town Los Angeles, he refused to have a drink. "I never once remember Dick relaxing . . . not for a minute," Bewley would recall. "I saw him laugh only once. And in all that time I never went to lunch with Dick just for fun." He was terrible at divorce cases: he blushed a deep red when hearing his female clients describing their sexual incompatibility with their husbands. "Any kind

---

* About $60,000 today.

of personal confession" was "embarrassing to me personally," he would recall. He was absolutely appalled when, in front of his secretary, he had to interview a couple who had been caught having sex in a public park. "Women who were complainers, naggers, who had small petty grievances but wanted to inflict punishment on the husband annoyed him," Bewley recalled. Dick called them "bitches on wheels." He did better with the cold logic of tax cases, and in a part-time position as city attorney, during which he helped preserve Whittier's virtue by stopping a local café from selling liquor.

In 1939, Wingert & Bewley invited Dick to become a partner, and he opened a branch (a homemade desk in an empty space in a local real estate office) in La Habra. By then he had embarked upon a second track—as an entrepreneur, a vendor of frozen orange juice. For a get-rich scheme it had promise—future generations would embrace frozen fruit juice as a nigh-miraculous concoction—but when the twenty-five-year-old Nixon corralled a group of local investors and accepted the title of president of "Citra-Frost," the science of draining the water from the juice and freezing the concentrate was a decade away. Try as they might, the Citra-Frost lads could not find a way to package the juice without spoiling or spillage. The company lacked capital, as well. Dick worked with his usual fury, and even Frank showed up at night to squeeze the oranges. But Citra-Frost went bankrupt, wounding Nixon, his law firm, and the individuals who invested money. "You'll find people here," Bewley recalled, decades later, that still "hate his guts because of that."

To boost Dick's social standing, Frank and Hannah purchased a fancy home on a hillside above Whittier College, with a turret and gracious gardens. But as the decade drew toward its conclusion, the promise of Whittier College's golden boy had soured. Dick thought about moving to Cuba and starting over. Aside from his family's love, and his own indomitable dreams, he had just one thing going for him. Her name was Patricia Ryan.

THEY MET AT a local theater group, at auditions for a comic mystery called *The Dark Tower*, in early 1938. Both landed bit parts—he as a young playwright, and she as a vamp—that called for onstage flirtation. Dick was smitten. He asked her out, and she turned him down. A few nights later, he asked again. Once more, she laughed him off. "Don't laugh," he told her, "someday I'm going to marry you."

In March, he surprised her with roses on her birthday. "Gee Dick— guess I am a pretty lucky Irishman!" she wrote. "*Best of all* was knowing you remembered." But it was a one-sided romance, there at the start. Pat had fled the family truck farm in dusty Artesia, and a job swabbing floors and clerking at a bank, and moved to New York City after high school, where she helped tend the dying in a Catholic hospital for tuberculosis patients in the Bronx. There she found poise, and sophistication, promotions, and admirers. She had lost just enough of her teenage chubbiness, was now a sleek strawberry blond with standout cheekbones and, Dick thought, "a strangely sad but lovely smile."

Pat had returned to California, where she worked her way through the University of Southern California, stood around a few Hollywood sets, and was hired as a business teacher at Whittier High School. She saw through the movieland taradiddles. Acting was such low-paying work that "girls are tempted to accept presents and attentions," she told her brother.

She epitomized "the American working girl," said her friend and fellow teacher, Helene Drown. Pat had her independence, dance cards filled with men, wanted to have fun—and hoped to leave hard times behind her. "She had gaiety and a love for life and a sparkle in her eye," said Drown.

Moreover, Pat found Dick's courting bizarre. Within days of meeting her, he had introduced her to his parents. Soon he was showing up at night, begging her to take walks around town with him. When she closed her apartment door on him, he slipped notes beneath it. "Yes, I know I'm crazy," he wrote, "and that . . . I don't take hints, but you see, Miss Pat, I like you!"

She would marvel, years later, at his servile willingness to drive her to Los Angeles on weekends, where he knew she had dates with other men. "Please forgive me for acting like a sorehead when you gently ushered me out the other night," he wrote, after one of her attempts to dump him. "You must have thought I was trying to put on the attitude that I didn't really give a darn. . . .

"May I say now what I should have said then: I appreciated immeasurably those little rides and chats with you. . . .

"You see I too live in a world of make believe—especially in this love business. And sometimes I fear I don't know when I'm serious and when not! But I can honestly say that Patricia is one fine girl, that I like her immensely, and that though she isn't going to give me a chance to propose to her for fear of hurting me! and though she insulted my ego just a bit . . . I still remember her."

At times, he was grandiloquent. In one letter Dick likened her to an "Irish gypsy who radiates all that is happy and beautiful" and thanked her for leaving "a note addressed to a struggling barrister who looks from a window and dreams." For "though he is a prosaic person, his heart was filled with that grand poetic music, which makes us wish for those we love the realization of great dreams," he wrote.

In September, after losing track of Pat that summer (she had moved without giving him her new address), he wrote, pleadingly, to her at school. He needed "so very much to see you again—after class, before breakfast, Sunday or any time you might be able to stand me!" She relented and sent him her address. "Social note—romantic?" she wrote, in her sardonic way. "In case I don't see you before why don't you come early Wednesday . . . and I'll see if I can burn a hamburger for you."

For though she resisted, they had much in common. She too had spent childhood on ten acres in the boondocks, working the farm, yearning to fly. She, too, had grown up with a volatile father and a mollifying mother—an experience that led them each, despite other strengths, to shirk personal confrontations. "I detest temper. I detest scenes. I just can't be that way. I saw it with my father," Pat would tell her daughter Julie. Dick had lost two brothers to tuberculosis; Pat saw it claim her dad. She and Dick both skipped second grade, loved their books, joined in debate and school politics, took to the stage. They never belonged to the very elite at school but were too smart and disciplined to be ignored.

And they both had chips on their shoulders. "The moneyed class come in and ask us to do their shopping," Pat wrote an aunt, after finding work as a "collegienne"—a model and salesgirl—at Bullock's, a swank department store on Wilshire Boulevard, during her USC years. "They sit in luxurious chairs while we go all over the store and gather things for them to choose from. . . . I drape the lovely velvet robes etc. around me, grin at the fat, rich customers and . . . they buy."

Years later, she would tell journalist Gloria Steinem: "I never had time to think about things like . . . who I wanted to be, or who I admired, or to have ideas. I never had time to dream about being anyone else. I had to work. . . . I've never had it easy. I'm not like all you . . . all those people who had it easy." Had she asked, Pat would have discovered that Steinem's childhood was, if anything, even tougher than her own.

A professor at USC recalls the long days that Pat kept—working at the student cafeteria, the library, and on faculty research projects. "It always used to disturb me how tired her face was in repose," he said. "She stood out from the empty-headed, overdressed little sorority girls of that era like a good piece of literature on a shelf of paperbacks."

She and Dick were prodigious strivers, with that almost freakish discipline. It was this—their shared affinity for dreams, and unwavering resolve—that finally brought them together. It surely wasn't Dick's prospects. Their courtship straddled his time of trials, when Wingert & Bewley was defending itself against the charges of legal malpractice and Citra-Frost was failing. But Pat recognized the "drive" in Dick. "He was going places, and he always saw the possibilities."

In February 1940, on the second anniversary of their meeting, he vowed: "When the winds blow and the rains fall and the sun shines through the clouds, as it is now, he still resolves as he did then, that nothing so fine ever happened to him or anyone else as falling in love with Thee—my dearest heart." On a night in March they drove to Dana Point, near San Clemente. And, finally, she accepted his proposal of marriage. He sent her a ring in a basket of flowers.

"Living together will make us both grow—and by reason of it we shall realize our dreams," he told her. "It is our job to go forth together and accomplish great ends."

The wedding was a modest affair (times were tough, and the bride had been orphaned) on a Friday in June 1940, at the Mission Inn in Riverside. It was only when they applied for the marriage license that Dick learned Pat's name was Thelma. Nor had she told him of the sad, harsh circumstances of her childhood. Nor had he really explained the Citra-Frost debacle. "Pat still knows little about it and I prefer to handle it that way," he told Bewley.

Dick "thought often about his brothers' deaths," his daughter Julie would write. "It may have helped him to talk about that pain, and yet he was joining his life with a woman for whom death was a taboo subject, a hurt so deep it was sacredly, privately her own. She pushed grief out of her consciousness, unwilling to open scars. . . . Both would find it difficult in the years ahead to break through their reserve and discuss their deepest feelings."

But what was that, to a cavalier and his gypsy love? And so they went forth together.

THEIR COURTSHIP TOOK place in troubled times. Japan continued its conquests in Asia, invading China, razing much of Shanghai and Nanjing, and threatening Southeast Asia, Indonesia, and the Philippines. From 1936 to 1939, fascists and Communists took opposing sides, using locals as proxies, in the civil war in Spain. In March 1938, with fanfare and panoply about the reunification of Germanic peoples, Adolf Hitler sent his armies into Austria, claiming it for the Nazi Reich. All that summer, the Führer stormed and raged, threatening war with Czechoslovakia if it did not cede its German-speaking regions to the Nazis. The horrors of the Great War were fresh in many minds, and Dick and Pat were among the millions worldwide who lauded British prime minister Neville Chamberlain for appeasing the dictator and agreeing to the dismemberment of Czechoslovakia at a summit meeting in Munich. "My good friends," Chamberlain told his countrymen and the world, "a British Prime Minister has returned from Germany bringing peace with honor. I believe it is peace for our time. Go home and get a nice quiet sleep."

Peace with honor and a nice quiet sleep sounded good to Dick and Pat. They were just starting out, and the prospect of American involvement in a war of European quarrels was abhorrent. "I came from a Quaker background. I was as close to being a pacifist as anybody could be," Dick remembered. "I thought at that time that Chamberlain was the greatest man alive, and when I read Churchill's all-out criticism of Chamberlain I thought Churchill was a madman."

So the West slumbered as the emboldened Nazis stepped up the persecution of German Jews. Six months later, Hitler seized the rest of Czechoslovakia. In August 1939, the Germans signed a nonaggression pact with the Soviets, and in September the two mighty bullies carved up Poland. Chamberlain left office in disgrace, cursed in history with the title "appeaser." The war that resulted would claim 60 million lives, and the lesson of Munich would guide a generation: totalitarian hoodlums must be met by strength, early, before they gathered power and momentum and it took a cataclysm to strip them of their fangs.

PAT KNEW THAT Dick's intent to "accomplish great ends" was likely to lead to politics. They had but a year to do the things young married couples do in peacetime—dancing and ice skating, cocktails, spaghetti dinners and charades—before taking up the life of public service. Great things were happening. The country was bracing for war. In the spring of 1940, Dick gave some talks at the local service clubs after hearing that Whittier's state assemblyman might step down. In the end, the incumbent ran for reelection, but Dick returned to the circuit in the fall, speaking on behalf of the Republican presidential candidate, Wendell Willkie.

And then, after one of Dick's old law professors recommended him to the newly formed Office of Price Administration, Nixon was offered a job as a staff attorney in the nation's capital. With Pat's encouragement, he accepted. Whittier had not welcomed the new Mrs. Nixon, and it did not break her heart to leave. Though Dick was clearly the pleader, the good ladies of the town "thought Pat was ambitious" and had ensnared him, Dick's aunt Edith recalled. "I heard that . . . accusation of her character." His law partner's daughter heard it too. "It was a gossipy town—terribly so," said Judith Wingert Loubet. "Some people felt that he should have been going with a girl from, you know, a better family . . . [a woman] that didn't work. . . . They were very unfair to her."

Pat and Dick were still in California, preparing to move east when, as they left a cinema one Sunday evening, they heard the news from Pearl Harbor.

The couple arrived in Washington a month later, on Dick's birthday, after driving across the country through snow and ice. The OPA's mission had changed—from fighting inflation to designing and administering a vast system of rationing during wartime. Dick worked on the rubber and tire regulations. He lasted three months. He was fine at the work— earning quick promotions and better pay—and his duties were expanded to encompass gasoline and other critical materials. But he came to detest the bureaucratic backbiting and resisted the New Deal's left-wing orientation. He had various protections from the draft—his job, his wife, and his Quaker faith—but he felt an obligation to do his part fighting fascism. It was a perilous gambit, but enlisting and attending an officer candidate school offered a promise of a good war. Combat was a great leveler: from Alexander Hamilton to Ulysses S. Grant, military service had given otherwise precluded opportunities to men of no means or social standing. And no one with Dick's ambition could fail to recognize that time in uniform would be an almost indispensable prerequisite for leadership after the war.

After an idyllic final vacation in New England with Pat, Dick reported to naval officer training school at Quonset Point, Rhode Island, in August 1942. He marked time in Iowa (where the Californians got a taste of a Midwest winter, with weeks of subzero weather, and savored the boxes of citrus fruit his parents mailed them) before the navy agreed to send him to the front.

Nixon had requested carrier duty—perilous work for, as he noted in his correspondence, there were two fewer flattops after the *Lexington* and the *Yorktown* got sunk in the battles of the Coral Sea and Midway. On the air base in Ottumwa he hosted a radio show, helped incorporate the officers' club, aided his fellow officers with their tax returns, and served as an aide to the executive officer. All the while, he lobbied for a transfer.

The navy's need for bodies gave him his opportunity. He received his orders to report to the South Pacific in May 1943. He arrived in the Solomon Islands, a string of isles off the northeast shoulder of Australia, in June. He had sailed from San Francisco after bidding good-bye to a stoic Hannah and blubbering Frank at Union Station in Los Angeles. As they waited for his ship to depart, Dick and Pat toured San Francisco, sampling its famous delicacies, but neither was in the mood for merriment. "We've been to all the eating places," he told Bewley, but "are really too much on edge to enjoy it very much."

Dick's stint in Ottumwa saved him from the fiercest battle of the Solomons campaign: the fight for Guadalcanal, which had ended with an American victory in February 1943. Nixon arrived as the Allied forces went on the offensive, island-hopping toward Rabaul, the Japanese fortress on New Britain. The war in the South Pacific was iconic, fought at Henderson Field and Iron Bottom Sound and the Slot, and inspiring Broadway characters like Nellie Forbush and Mister Roberts. Among the other navy officers who served there were John Kennedy, Ben Bradlee, Harold Stassen, and John Mitchell—and a Marine lieutenant named Joe McCarthy—whose paths would cross Nixon's after the war.

Nixon was an officer in the South Pacific Air Transport Command, known as SCAT, under Admiral William "Bull" Halsey. His tour began in rear-echelon safety, but by the autumn and winter of 1943 Dick had persuaded the navy to send him "up the line," and he saw duty on Guadalcanal and Vella Lavella and, finally, at the front on Bougainville, where the counterattacking Japanese were still bombing and shelling the American invasion forces. "He wanted to get into something where the smell of combat was closer," one of his superiors, Carl Fleps, recalled.

On Bougainville, Dick's hut was destroyed by Japanese artillery fire as he huddled in a nearby foxhole. After the barrage, said tent mate Hollis Dole, he and Dick counted thirty-five shell holes within a hundred-foot radius. On another night, he felt an eight-inch poisonous centipede crawl upon him in his sleep. He bolted up and threw it off. It landed on the sleeping Dole and stung him—sending him to the hospital in awful pain.

Halsey's next hop was to Green Island, where Nixon took part in the invasion, only to find that the Japanese had largely abandoned the island.

The landing was a cakewalk, and he had no trouble setting up the SCAT command at an airstrip the Seabees carved from the jungle. It was there, vainly trying to save the dying men in a crashed, burning bomber, that he had his most searing glimpse of twentieth-century warfare. "I can still see the wedding ring on the charred hand of one of the crewmen," he would recall, of the bodies they pulled from the wreckage.

By all accounts, he served ably and was popular with his men. Yet some saw signs of the tension in his personality. There were glimpses of Gloomy Gus. "Nixon always seemed to be two people: one, very quiet, very much in the background, and actually somewhat morose," Dole recalled. "But when the chips were down it was just as if he were electrified. He knew what to say, how to say it, and he became quite animated and smiled."

On the beach during the Green Island landings, Nixon met a fellow navy lieutenant, James Stewart, who became his friend and second in command, shared his quarters, and taught him poker. Amid the boredom of war, with a weekly beer ration and no place to spend their money, there were plenty of pigeons who played, rashly, for thrills. Dick played coolly, patiently, to win. "When I knew that I didn't have the cards," he would remember, "I got the hell out."

PAT HAD STAYED on after Dick's troop ship left San Francisco. She found work, ending up as an analyst for the OPA. Their correspondence in the war years shows a loving couple weathering the storm. "All of me loves all of you all the time," he wrote, reassuring her when they were first separated. "I certainly am not the Romeo type and you are so beautiful."

Before shipping out to the South Pacific, Dick had prepared a handwritten will, leaving all to Pat and requesting a "simple and inexpensive" funeral. "The remarriage of my wife after my decease shall have no effect whatsoever on her right under my will," he wrote. "I believe that such action by her would be for the best."

Dick asked her to have her photograph taken and sent to him, and was thrilled by the result. The other guys on Green Island could not believe, he told her, that he had such a lovely girl. "Everybody raved—wondered how I happened to rate! (I do too.)," he wrote. He sent her stuffed koala bears for her birthday, wrote her a letter from a cargo plane, ten thousand feet above the Pacific ("I love you just the same up here as down below"), and listed the sunsets he watched without her.

"I just can't think of a thing to write about except our good times together—from the day we met—in February 1938. Remember how you treated me then?! Laguna, Mexico City, Havana, Panama, Washington D.C., Maine, Boston, Charlotte, Chicago—yes, even Ottumwa—what a wonderful five years. I love you always," he wrote.

But it wasn't all sighs and laughter. The months apart put pressure on the relationship. Pat rediscovered her taste for freedom. "I have to admit that I am pretty self-reliant and if I didn't love you I would feel very differently," she warned him, as he prepared to head home. "These many months you have been away have been full of interest, and had I not missed you so much and had I been footloose, could have been extremely happy.

"So, Sweet, you'll always have to love me lots and never let me change my feelings for you."

Having evaded the Japanese shrapnel, Dick's only injury was a nasty case of jungle fungus, which he carried home to the States. He was happy to get back to loving arms, while still proud of the great crusade in which he had played a role.

"I really haven't done more than I should—but have had the good luck to be assigned to jobs where there was work to be done," he told Pat. "At least my overseas experience has satisfied my yen *to do* something and I feel so much better than if I had stayed in Ottumwa."

The navy sent Nixon to Alameda Air Station on the San Francisco Bay, then summoned him to the East to study and apply the federal contracting laws. Dick and Pat were eating dinner at Bookbinder's restaurant in Philadelphia when they heard that Franklin Roosevelt had died and Harry Truman was now president. Nixon was in New York when he caught his first glimpse of General Dwight Eisenhower, being honored in a ticker-tape parade. Then it was on to Baltimore, and the letter from Herman Perry.

5

A Kind of Man the Country Needs

A FRAUGHT AND CHILLY capital welcomed Dick and Pat in January 1947. On their previous stint in Washington they had been lucky, renting an apartment in Alexandria on their first day in town. Fortune wasn't smiling this time, and they were mired with baby Tricia in a hotel for weeks before finding a duplex in the Park Fairfax neighborhood in nearby Virginia. His office turf was no grander: seniority ruled in the allotment of work space, and Representative Nixon was relegated to the fifth floor of the older House (now Cannon) office building.

They confessed to feeling lost at first, awash in reminders of their greenhorn status. Invited to an "informal" dinner party at the home of a veteran congressman, the Nixons showed up in their best cocktail party attire— and learned that "informal" was a code for tuxedos and floor-length frocks.* Their lives had changed. Be careful, Perry warned his protégé. Every ideologue, self-promoter, and special interest lobbyist would be looking to sink his hooks in a freshman representative. "You are a marked man. . . . Smile at them and listen but don't promise anything," Perry advised. "Be careful where you go and who you counsel with."

Dick and Pat found a city teetering between the joys of victory and the fears of the atomic age. Americans had cheered, hugged, danced at the news of Germany's surrender. They did again when Japan capitulated, but the accounts of atomic ruin brought dusk to the celebration. The new age was "a strange place," *Time* magazine reported, "full of weird symbols and the smell of death." The war itself sank to "minor significance," said the editors. Harry Truman, and most of his countrymen, believed that the incinerations of Hiroshima and Nagasaki were merciful acts, saving a million or more Japanese and Americans who would have died had the war dragged on. If so, it was "mercy born of a ruthless force," *Time* said. "The

---

* "Formal" meant white tie and tails.

weapon had been used by those on whom civilization could best hope to depend, but the demonstration of power against living creatures . . . created a bottomless wound."

Essayists scrambled for metaphors and found Faust, who sold his soul, or Prometheus, who stole fire from heaven and was condemned by the gods not to death, but to perpetual anguish. For it was only a matter of time—five years the prediction—before the Soviet Union built an A-bomb: that same totalitarian state that had aligned itself with Adolf Hitler in 1939, helped him crush Poland, built the Gulag, and sacrificed 27 million inhabitants in the war, the worst such immolation ever. The Soviets ruled Eastern Europe, threatened Iran, Greece, and Turkey. Three days after the Japanese surrendered, a clerk from the Soviet embassy in Ottawa had defected and given the disbelieving West the first news of the Red spy rings that had bored into the nucleus of the Manhattan Project at Los Alamos and stolen the bomb makers' secrets.

The war had begun with the fall of Poland. Now the war was over, yet the Poles were not free. Nor were the Czechs, the Hungarians, or the subjugated peoples of the Baltic and the Balkans. By October 1945 the U.S. military was drafting contingency plans for an American surprise attack on the Soviet Union employing twenty to thirty atomic weapons. The greatest of wars did not end; it only cooled.

In early 1946, George Kennan, a U.S. expert on Soviet behavior, had sent a famous dispatch—his "long telegram"—to Washington from the American embassy in Moscow. The Soviet Union was an aggressive, totalitarian, imperialistic state, he wrote. Its leaders would invariably portray others as enemies to justify "the dictatorship without which they did not know how to rule, for cruelties they did not dare not to inflict." They were "committed fanatically to the belief" that there could be no coexistence, Kennan said, and determined that "our society be disrupted, our traditional way of life be destroyed, the international authority of our state be broken."

And so, as Nixon settled into life in Congress, the specter of Communism, at home and abroad, commanded center stage. Eisenhower, the liberator of Europe, had urged his superiors to seek an accommodation with the Russians—until their behavior transformed his outlook. "Russia is definitely out to communize the world," Ike wrote in his diary. "It promotes starvation, unrest, anarchy. . . . We face a battle to extinction between the two systems."

At home, "the Reds, phonies and 'parlor pinks' seem to be banded together and are becoming a national danger," Truman confided to his own private journal. "I am afraid they are a sabotage front for Uncle Joe Stalin."

THE COLD WAR would reach monstrous scope, with forty thousand nuclear warheads poised for use around the world, far more than were needed for a cataclysm that could wipe out civilization. Americans craved peace; they got horror. They had traded one enemy for another, and even more perilous times. There was cause to suspect betrayal. There was an allure to hate. And in that a country could destroy itself.

For that was the other hazard—identified by Kennan, right there at the beginning. Americans must not overreact, he warned; not sacrifice their liberties or submit to fear. They must demonstrate to other peoples that a nation can be strong without political witch hunts, secret police, or imperial cruelties. "We must have courage and self-confidence to cling to our own methods and conceptions of human society," Kennan wrote. "The greatest danger that can befall us in coping with this problem of Soviet Communism, is that we shall allow ourselves to become like those with whom we are coping."

It had happened during the war. In a ghastly progression, the fascist bombings of Rotterdam and Coventry begat a ruthless Allied airborne campaign upon the populations of Japan and Germany. It took many more airplanes, but the firebombings of Dresden and Tokyo were just slightly less efficient at incinerating children than the atomic assault on Hiroshima.

The Cold War—that struggle to resist those conjoined perils of enmity abroad and terror at home—would define American life for almost five decades. It was in that climate that Richard Nixon entered politics; in that era he pursued his great ambitions.

As PERRY PREDICTED, the new congressman was tested quickly—on an issue judged urgent by home-state real estate interests. During the 1946 campaign, maneuvering to corral votes, Nixon had joined Voorhis in full-throated opposition to the Whittier Narrows Dam, a flood-control project near his hometown. The resultant reservoir would flood parts of neighboring El Monte, uniting the people there against it. "I shall oppose construction of the Whittier Narrows Dam to the limit of my ability," Nixon had promised. Once elected, he did not renege. "I honestly believe the dam should not be built," he wrote Perry. Moreover, Nixon had the means to stop it: the competition for federal funds was fierce, and the appropriators had plenty of other projects to fund—where the local congressmen were supplicants, not foes.

But after the election, almost immediately, Perry's reputation as Nixon's mentor drew a horde of local landowners, business boosters, and municipal officials to the banker's office, where they browbeat, begged, and bullied to try to get the congressman to change his stand. Road building and home-building were stalled, they claimed. The Los Angeles Chamber of Commerce, the U.S. Army Corps of Engineers, Senator Bill Knowland, and the politically connected oilman Ed Pauley were among those pressuring Nixon to relent. He learned that a syndicate of investors had bought land downstream, which would soar in value once the dam was built.

"The heat is on," Perry told his protégé. Pauley later bragged of how he bullied Nixon to take a broader view of the controversy, which would help in future statewide elections. He met with Nixon at a dinner party at oil lobbyist J. Paull Marshall's home in Washington and informed the freshman congressman that "we in southern California" viewed his parochialism "as a mistake" that "might prevent him later from becoming Senator."

Nixon tried to oblige, but his attempts to broker a compromise ran into resistance from Whittier's town fathers, who opposed the leading alternative site for the dam—Plan B. So Nixon stuck it out. For more than a year he testified against the dam and blocked the appropriation of funds, buying time and leverage for his old law partner, Tom Bewley, to negotiate an agreement that both Whittier and El Monte found palatable.

Nixon was learning. The Plan B settlement, which was similar to a compromise proposed by Voorhis, still displaced some two thousand people. But it was "probably the best job I've done since coming to Washington," he wrote his old Amateur friend Roy Day in the spring of 1948. "This type of behind the scenes work is far more effective than going out and making a speech on the floor of the House before half a dozen listeners."

NIXON WAS PLEASED with his committee assignments as well. Speaker Joe Martin had seen the merit of promoting a young star from the West. Nixon received a seat he requested on the House Education and Labor Committee, whose members were crafting the Republican majority's top legislative priority—a measure to curb the influence of organized labor that would become law as the Taft-Hartley Act. He also got a seat on the House Committee on Un-American Activities. Both offered fine platforms to extend themes he had deployed in the 1946 campaign: the need to take labor down a notch, and to battle Red subversion. "He was one of the few who got an extra committee also—Unamerican Activities—so he is pleased about that as they will have the duty of cleaning up the Communistic forces," Pat wrote his folks.

With Republicans in control of Congress, the labor bill moved swiftly. It was their signature domestic achievement—a rollback of privileges granted to unions by the New Deal's landmark Wagner Act. The Taft-Hartley legislation gave the president the authority to declare a cooling-off period and delay strikes that affected the national interest; outlawed sympathy strikes and boycotts; authorized right-to-work laws; put limits on union political activity; and, in a section later ruled unconstitutional, required that union officers submit signed affidavits to the government declaring they were not Communists.

Nixon sat across from another notable freshman on the committee, a twenty-nine-year-old Democrat from Massachusetts who joined him that spring in McKeesport, in the southwest Pennsylvania steel country, to debate the legislation before union and corporate leaders. "Young Kennedy . . . went with me and we discussed the Labor bill on opposite sides in a spirited but rather clean 'debate.' The reception to my end was good, considering the locale and audience," Nixon wrote a friend in California. Given the reigning public mood about unions and Communism, John F. Kennedy had offered a delicate critique of Taft-Hartley in McKeesport. Nixon was more vigorous in his support. "He won that one," Kennedy would joke when, as president, he revisited the town. "And we went on to other things."

On the midnight train to Washington, they shared a sleeping car and sat around—the ambassador's son and the shopkeeper's boy—discussing their passion for foreign affairs. Kennedy respected the man who took down Jerry Voorhis, and Nixon was intrigued with the gallant from Choate, Harvard, and Palm Beach. "Neither of us was a backslapper, and we both were uncomfortable with boisterous displays of superficial camaraderie," Nixon would remember. "He was shy . . . but it was shyness born of an instinct that guarded privacy and concealed emotions. I understood these qualities because I shared them." Soon Dick and Pat were attending parties at Kennedy's town house in Georgetown. When John Kennedy married Jacqueline Bouvier, the Nixons were invited to the wedding.

Friendships aside, Nixon voted like a Southern California Republican. Judith Wingert Loubet, the daughter of his senior law partner, was disillusioned. Where was the "practical liberal" she had worked to elect? "I had hoped that Dick was going to be a champion of the underdog and the poor man," she recalled. "I felt that once he got to Congress he was a little dazzled. . . . Too often he sided with the companies rather than what would have been for the general good."

Nixon's staff was tiny—administrative aide Bill Arnold and a couple of secretaries—and Pat was often drafted to help with the office mail. Frank and Hannah had bought a farm in Pennsylvania to fulfill a long-nurtured dream and be close to their son. They made frequent visits to Washington, where they and "a very satisfactory colored woman . . . just as clean as can be" were employed to help out with Tricia, the congressman reported. The family's finances were stretched, so Dick used campaign donations for political obligations like secretarial help, Christmas cards, and telephone bills. It was an accepted practice but would prove toweringly troublesome a few years down the road.

For expertise, Nixon reached out around the city, tapping veteran hands like HUAC counsel Robert Stripling, newsman Bert Andrews of the *New York Herald Tribune,* and Father John Cronin, a lobbyist for the Roman Catholic hierarchy who seasoned his fierce anti-Communism with a sense of social justice. In the months to come, they would play important roles in making Nixon a national figure. In the meantime, he was just another face. Bryce Harlow, a savvy young congressional aide, first met him at a stag dinner and found the congressman quiet and polite and "not then anything to react to." In time, Nixon would demonstrate that "he was smarter than the pack," Harlow said. "He was more committed and energetic and he worked harder." But "that was not discernable" at first sight.

THE UNITED STATES had emerged from World War II as a military and economic titan, with dominance in world affairs to rival ancient Rome. Though home to just 7 percent of the planet's inhabitants, it pumped 62 percent of its oil, made 57 percent of its steel, and built 80 percent of its automobiles. The homeland was unscathed, the factories and farmlands intact, and the number of casualties was blessedly small—there would be no shortage of skilled, battle-tested leaders in the postwar era. The rest of the world offered a study in contrast. Germany and Japan were in ashes. Even victors—the British, French, and Soviets—had suffered terrible ruin in the war, a killing winter, and a freakish drought that followed. Europe was "a rubble-heap, a charnel house, a breeding ground of pestilence and hate," Winston Churchill warned. In February 1947 the British sent word to Truman: they could no longer guard the eastern Mediterranean. If Greece and Turkey were to be saved from Communism, America would have to do it.

Truman decided to act. "Mr. President, if that is what you want there is only one way to get it. That is to make a personal appearance before Congress and scare hell out of the country," Senator Arthur Vandenberg, a Republican from Michigan, advised him. Nixon was in the chamber on March 12, when the president addressed a joint session of Congress and declared America's determination to defend weaker nations from Communist aggression. It became known as the Truman Doctrine. A few weeks later, Truman launched a federal Red hunt—a loyalty probe of government employees. Congress joined the president in enacting the National Security Act of 1947, establishing the Central Intelligence Agency, the National Security Council, the Department of Defense, and other pillars of the national security state.

Nixon backed Truman's request for $400 million for Greece and Turkey, despite the misgivings of some of the Amateurs in California. They were members of a Republican wing—"the Old Guard"—led by Senator Robert Taft of Ohio, who favored a noninterventionist foreign policy and a reduction in the reach and powers of government. Their isolationist sentiments flared after Secretary of State George Marshall proposed, in a June 5 speech at Harvard, that the United States would have to rescue the rest of Europe as well. The ungrateful socialists of Europe should be left to their "suffering," not bailed out by the "so called Marshall Plan," a half dozen of Nixon's early supporters wrote him. Truman's strategy was "right down Stalin's alley."

"The socialized states of western Europe and England have already . . . gone far toward embracing Communism. By nationalizing their means of production they are accomplishing the greater part of the Communist program," the Amateurs said. "It is very doubtful if we can buy these people off . . . by giving them further funds to promote the very form of economic Communism against which we seek to protect them." They warned Nixon not to be taken in by State Department and European "propaganda."

In another letter, Herman Perry was succinct. "We will just be pouring the money down a rat hole to help the undeserving in Europe and tax the people in the United States to death," Perry wrote. "Frankly, I trust that in the future you will be extremely careful in getting too far involved in this bungling thinking."

The Marshall Plan was a defining issue, which Nixon could not dodge.

In early July he was invited to the Oval Office and massaged by Truman. And on July 29, Nixon picked up his morning paper to discover that the Speaker had named him to a select bipartisan committee that would travel to Europe under the leadership of Representative Christian Herter, a Massachusetts Republican, to investigate conditions and report back to the House. Nixon was now at the hub of a national debate on the use of American power. A slip, and his career might end right there.

The nineteen House members in the Herter mission represented a cross-section of regional interests and blocs. Nixon and his colleagues were to fan out across the continent, consult with European leaders, and advise Congress on the need for—and the soundness of—the $13 billion European Recovery Program that Marshall had proposed. Leading commentators—columnists Joseph and Stewart Alsop and *New York Times* Washington bureau chief Arthur Krock among them—described the mission as a historic test of Congress's ability to rise beyond its habitual myopia.

Nixon, in his first review from the *Times,* was defined as a "very serious and industrious student of government and the world situation." This was no junket, the Alsops wrote, for the committee had "none of the House good-time Charlies or professional baby-kissers or incorrigible victims of the terrible oratory habit." Instead, the Speaker had chosen "men who would work, and were ready to take a hard trip." Nixon was proud of the appointment, but he had no illusions about the challenge. He knew what his Amateurs thought of Marshall's plan, and he pretty well knew what he would discover overseas. Congressional Republicans had been hearing from former president Herbert Hoover, an expert on international relief, who was convinced that America must act if Europe was to be saved.

Nixon confronted the classic question raised by Edmund Burke in his speech to the electors of Bristol. Did he owe his constituency his obedience or his judgment? Six months into his first term in political office, Nixon was facing another question of conscience, and this time more than a California water project was at stake. The future of freedom might be riding on his performance.

THE HERTER MISSION departed from New York on the liner *Queen Mary* at the end of August. Pat and his parents bid farewell to Dick from the dock, after they'd all attended a performance of the hit Broadway musical *Oklahoma!* From mid-ocean the congressman wrote his wife, raving about the shipboard luxuries, while insisting he was working hard. It was a refrain he'd employ throughout the six-week trip, as he chronicled the wonders of London, Paris, Berlin, Athens, Rome, Naples, Pompeii, Venice, and other sites, described the sumptuous meals and wines, and otherwise carried on about the fascinating time he was having.

For the vagabond gypsy who was left behind in the noxious Washington summer, laboring on the office mail, dealing with her aged in-laws, and tending to an infant in those days before central air-conditioning, it wasn't easy reading:

> Dearest—The hectic pace continues but tonight at least we are in a beautiful place, the Excelsior Hotel on Lido isle at Venice. Venice is just like the books & pictures described it. The Army had a motor boat & took us up the Grand Canal & for a quick look at the cathedral, the famous palaces & bridges. . . .
>
> Yesterday we took a car from Milan to Turin—about three hours. Visited rice farmers, factories & the famous Martini Rossi winery where we had lunch. You should have seen the lunch—cold sliced ham to start—ravioli—chicken—fruit & cheese with all kinds of wine & champagne & brandy to top it off. . . .
>
> We left Turin at 6 & arrived home by 9, just in time to go to the famous La Scala opera house to see "Manon." We were guests of honor & they played the Star Spangled Banner at the end of the 1st act with the spot on our box! . . .
>
> After we arrived here we went for a swim before supper, & the surf was wonderful.
>
> This may sound like a junket! But it has been a hard, tough trip & we are really learning things. The pleasure will have to wait until we can come together.
>
> All my love, I miss you . . . Dick

In fairness to Nixon, it *was* a tough trip. His letters to Pat cloaked the dangers and omitted the more grisly episodes. He toured Germany's sepulchral cities, ventured to the front lines of the Greek civil war, and witnessed bloody violence as Italians fought Yugoslavian Communists in the streets of Trieste. He was part of a subcommittee, assigned to southern Europe, that called itself "Jenkins Raiders" after its leader, Representative Thomas Jenkins, a Republican from Ohio. Their motto—"Don't stay too long in one place"—reflected the pace. The American correspondents who encountered Nixon on the trip admired him. "Nixon came up where the action was while the others . . . stayed down in the fleshpots of Athens," said the *Baltimore Sun*'s veteran war correspondent Phil Potter. "There was a curiosity and an energy to him."

The kid from Whittier was thrilled by the formal sessions—tea with the prime minister at 10 Downing Street in London, a duel of wits with Communist labor leaders in Italy, consultations in Paris—but he made a point of breaking free from his handlers and roaming among the people. In the Ruhr, Nixon and a colleague had German-speaking guides take them through the shattered streets of Essen. They found families living in cellars, without sunlight or proper ventilation, many stricken by disease. There was "a children's hospital in which 200 children were suffering from advanced stages of tuberculosis," Nixon confided in a diary of the trip.

> They called it a hospital, but it was a great long barn with very little heat and light. We thought we had seen destruction in Britain but until we saw the cities of Germany we had seen nothing at all. Hamburg, Berlin and the other German cities looked up at us just like great gaunt skeletons. . . . As we passed through the city of Berlin we went through block after block, mile after mile of complete utter desolation and destruction. . . . We could not understand how it was possible that three million people could be living in the city, but they are living there like a bunch of starved rats in the ruins.
>
> We stood in the great hall of what was once Hitler's Reich Chancellery, and as we looked at the ruins and realized what destruction a dictator had brought upon himself and his people by reason of his totalitarian aggression, small thin-faced German boys attempted to sell us the medals which their fathers had won during the war.

Economic activity was indeed lagging—but from malnutrition, not socialist coddling. Workers were given supplementary servings of food to increase their production at the mines and factories, but smuggled it home to keep their families from starving. It was the same at the special soup kitchens that the Allies ran to keep children fed.

Nixon, of course, was moved by the plight of the maltreated tuberculosis patients. Representative Eugene Cox of Georgia, a flinty conservative, gave all his candy, soap, and spare clothing to a group of German children after watching the eldest, a ten-year-old, hand her precious piece of chocolate to a baby sister. And in Greece, Representative James Richards of South Carolina emptied his wallet to a young woman who told the delegation how, during torture, the Communists had cut off one of her breasts.

The port of Trieste was a contested city—a "free territory" on the Adriatic divided like Berlin between Communist and Western forces. In their mid-September visit, Nixon witnessed the Red tactics firsthand. He left his hotel for a closer look as a column of Communists paraded, roaring in song, arms raised and fists clenched, sowing riot and disorder in which two bystanders were killed as he watched—a woman who was thrown to the ground and hit her head on a curb, and a man decapitated by a grenade. Nixon roamed through the city, chronicling the violence. His colleagues called it "Nixon's Charge."

At the Yugoslav border, Nixon took a lesson from the heroics of Lieutenant William Ochs and the twelve U.S. infantrymen under his command, who refused to yield ground to a column of two thousand Yugoslavian soldiers armed with artillery. No shots were fired, and eventually the Yugoslavs stood down. The Communists would probe for weakness, Nixon concluded, but back off if met by resolve.

It was the lesson of Munich. "We learned to our sorrow in the events leading up to World War II that appeasement of a totalitarian aggressor eventually leads to war," Nixon informed his diary. "We must not fall into the same error in our dealings with another totalitarian aggressor at this time, because if we do a third World War will sweep over the world with destruction even more terrible."

The Communist bullying left an impression, but it did not override Nixon's conviction that the Europeans would stand fast for freedom if they got the aid Marshall promised. Empty bellies, not bayonets, were the threat. That was also the analysis that Nixon received from the top-shelf advisers Herter had recruited to brief the mission—the State Department's Charles "Chip" Bohlen, future CIA chief Allen Dulles, and General Lucius Clay, the Allied commander in Berlin—on down to Rosetta Rubsamen, a Foreign Service officer at the U.S. embassy in Italy who served as Nixon's guide in Rome.

The liberal Rubsamen was captivated by the heart and discernment with which Nixon salted his instinctive conservatism in their long, intense discussions. Their instant friendship belied Nixon's image as a sourpuss. "I am afraid that I teased you too much when you were here, and made myself out for a wild revolutionary and unconventional woman," she wrote him, fondly. "So just take everything I said with a grain of salt, though I still hold the opinion that certain things like the danger of Communism in Italy are very much exaggerated."

"I am sorry that you were in Rome for so short a time," she concluded. "There are more things you might have enjoyed seeing, and we could have mapped a little strategy. But I am ever so glad that I did meet you and know you." They corresponded in the months ahead, and she kept him informed on conditions in Italy as the Marshall Plan was debated in Washington.

NIXON GOT HOME in mid-October. His reunion with Pat was a happy one; their daughter Julie was born nine months later. His service on the Herter committee left him with no doubts about the need for urgent action, and an unshakable conviction that, as a matter of both politics and policy, he needed to sell George Marshall's plan to the skeptics back home. Out came the yellow legal pads. He outlined his thoughts for a speech he would deliver over and over in the weeks to come.

"Communism is spreading like a cancer thru the life blood of Eu. feeding upon the fears, the hunger & misery of the people," he wrote. France and Italy could "go Commie," and then England would have to kneel to Russia. The Europeans "are willing to work, they want freedom, hate totalitarianism, above all else they want peace & where they have a minimum of food & shelter & security and a chance for freedom & peace they will resist the totalitarian pressure."

Nixon gave a nod to his Amateur friends about the danger of giving "blank checks to inefficient, weak & corrupt govts," but there was no doubt where he stood in the faceoff between isolationists and internationalists. "We must remember that we are a part of the world, that we cannot bury our heads in the sand in isolation, because if we do the cause of freedom and democracy will be lost not only in Eu. It will be lost here."

Nixon crisscrossed his district, making that speech. His constituents listened, asked questions, and many were persuaded. So it happened, across the land. Endorsed by the Herter committee, the Marshall Plan was approved by the House and Senate. It helped save Western Europe and went down in postwar history as an American strategic, diplomatic, and humanitarian triumph.

And, in the process, Nixon won his wager. Seven months after he returned from Europe, the voters brought back a verdict on their new congressman's performance. In the state's cross-filing primary in June, he clinched both the Republican and Democratic nominations for Congress, assuring his reelection. The people had concluded that Edmund Burke was right. Nixon had given them his best judgment, and they thanked him for it.

At a Georgetown dinner party that spring, John Kennedy regaled a guest with talk about the keen mind and admirable realism of this young congressman from California. Dick Nixon, said Kennedy, was the kind of man the country needed.

6

HUAC

THE MARSHALL PLAN and the Truman Doctrine were noble responses to the threat posed by Soviet predation. But there was a home front in the Cold War, too. Here, the issues were not addressed with bipartisan equanimity. At home things got ugly. From 1946 through 1954, the United States tore at its innards as scoundrels discovered the political payoff from maligning foes as disloyal, as treasonous, as traitors. For the unscrupulous, it made little difference if the charges were true, or somewhat so, or not. It would become known as the McCarthy Era, after its worst fomenter, Senator Joseph McCarthy, a bully from Wisconsin. But Richard Nixon, in his time on the House Committee on Un-American Activities, was a precursor, a John the Baptist, a kind of prophet who showed others the way. And for breaking the trail that led to McCarthyism, he too was tainted—at times with cause, at other times unfairly.

Dick Nixon, idealist, arrived in Washington at the beginning of an era in which the presentiments of Communist aggression became real—with armed face-offs in Berlin, Cuba, and the Middle East and proxy wars in Korea and Southeast Asia in which 240,000 Americans would be killed or wounded in the next three decades. He learned, almost immediately, how the U.S. government was suffused with Soviet agents during World War II. As a patriot and a partisan, he challenged the Truman administration to investigate the security lapses. When the White House moved with insufficient vigor, he saw the political opportunity and took it as his duty to expose the Communist agents himself.

In all this, Nixon made enemies. He entered the arena willingly, eagerly—fully cognizant that there would be both rewards and risks. He strove to be responsible. But this was Frank Nixon's son, Coach Newman's tiger: his instinct was to push, and push, and push. He was raw and unschooled in this competition, and his instincts sometimes failed him.

He could project as unctuous or nasty as, too frequently, he marred victory with excess. The journals of the left, like the *New Republic* and the *Nation,* soon made up their minds. They found Nixon demonic. Even centrist Democrats like Harry Truman and Sam Rayburn, the House leader from Texas, became his enemies. Sensitive as he was, and as insecure and easily bruised as he was, and brooding and self-centered and self-contained as he was, Nixon could not shrug off their criticism. It wounded him, and he lashed back. The vicious cycle persisted all his life.

THERE IS NO doubt that what Nixon suspected was true: the governments of the United States and Great Britain had been penetrated by Soviet spies during World War II, some of whom stole valuable military secrets, most famously the specifications for the atomic bomb. The alarming reversals of the postwar years—the loss of Eastern Europe, the fall of China to the Communists, the Soviet acquisition of atomic weapons—fed fears of treachery. "The Soviet Union was now a superpower, unabashedly hostile to us, operating all over the world through fifth columns of national communist parties," Secretary of State Dean Acheson would recall. "Russian agents were doubtless numerous and active."

But it is equally true that the United States was never in danger of a Communist insurrection led by its flaky homespun Reds. There were Communists in the theater and film industries, in labor unions, civil rights groups, and college faculties. A few were men and women of quality. But many were losers: a motley collection of self-aggrandizing utopians and mushy-headed sentimentalists, adrift in the drama of their lives. They posed a threat, as a fifth column, only in the feverish minds of equally crazed counterparts on the right. Red-baiters like Nixon, McCarthy, and FBI director J. Edgar Hoover were "tilting at windmills," the longtime Soviet ambassador to the United States, Anatoly Dobrynin, would recall. The "mammoth and unprecedented hunt for communists failed to uncover anything but the most minuscule number."

"The American Communist Party was never taken seriously in Moscow," Dobrynin said. "No one in the Soviet leadership, including the most zealous supporters of communism, ever talked seriously about any concrete prospects for communism in the United States."

Yet, at the time, Americans just *didn't know.* The tragedy is that their government *did* know, and that the witch hunts were unwarranted. In 1946, army cryptographers working for the Venona Project had cracked a Soviet diplomatic code, giving them a view of Communist espionage in the United States. They identified dozens of Soviet intelligence officers and the agents they ran, from the atomic labs in Los Alamos to the State Department in Washington.

No one was told. To protect its code-breaking breakthrough, the government kept its triumph secret. And "because the deciphered Venona messages were classified and unknown to the public, demagogues such as McCarthy had the opportunity to mix together accurate information . . . with falsehoods," wrote Cold War historians John Earl Haynes and Harvey Klehr. Honorable men, like George Marshall, were smeared by the right, and actual traitors, like Julius Rosenberg, the atom spy, became left-wing martyrs. As a CIA study would later conclude, the price for keeping Venona concealed was "a 40-year debate that contributed to the corrosion of the public's trust in government and faith in the honesty of its intelligence and law enforcement agencies."

It all seemed worse than it was, and better to err on the side of safety. And there were plenty of Commie stalkers in harness—had been since the Red Scare of the 1920s. The FBI had bulging files, and so did the U.S. Chamber of Commerce and the Roman Catholic bishops. As did HUAC, eager to get into the game under its new Republican leadership.

The Republicans had scored with their Red-baiting tactics in the 1946 election, and Nixon was one of many who advised that the party should exploit the issue in the 1948 congressional and presidential contests. HUAC gave him a platform to test the theory, and make a name. He began immediately. In his first speech in Congress, on February 18, 1947, he assailed the "foreign-directed conspiracy" whose "aim and purpose was to undermine and destroy the government of the United States."

"The principal character of this conspiracy," Nixon charged, was Gerhart Eisler, "alias Berger, alias Brown, alias Gerhart, alias Edwards, alias Liptzin, alias Eisman, a seasoned agent of the Communist International, who had been shuttling back and forth between Moscow and the United States from as early as 1933, to direct and master mind the political and espionage activities of the Communist Party in the United States."

Reporters found Eisler, a small, bald, bespectacled man, living in a $35-a-month apartment in Queens. He was charged with contempt of Congress after insisting on reading a defiant statement before he would answer the committee's questions. He then stowed away on a ship bound for Europe and made his way to East Germany, where he took a position in the Communist government.

—

FROM THE FIRST, Nixon recognized that his service to the cause held both danger and promise. Among the more educated Americans of the campuses and cities, and in the establishment press, HUAC was seen as a claque of clowns.

"The Committee," as it became known, was set up in 1938 as a special body to investigate individuals and organizations with fascist or Communist sympathies. It was chaired by Representative Martin Dies, a Democrat from Beaumont, Texas, and soon shifted its focus from the German American Bund and Japanese American "fifth columns" to scrutinize Communist influence in American labor unions, theater, and motion pictures. Its tactics were nigh as underhanded as those it was charged to investigate. Its subpoenas were accompanied by press releases that all but declared the witness guilty. Those who refused to answer were judged in contempt, and faced a term in prison. Those who exercised their Fifth Amendment guarantee against self-incrimination risked the blacklist.

"The Committee's members were the least intelligent in Congress because no decent man wanted to serve on it," wrote a *Time* magazine editor—a reformed Communist by the name of Whittaker Chambers. "They were uncouth, undignified and ungrammatical. They were rude and ruthless. They smeared innocent people on insufficient evidence or no evidence at all. They bullied witnesses and made sensational statements unfounded in fact. When, occasionally, they did seem to strike a fresh scent, they promptly lost it by all shouting at once or by making some ridiculous fumble."

HUAC seemed to specialize in silliness—at one point entertaining a witness who testified that America's dimpled sweetheart, the child actress Shirley Temple, was a Communist dupe. In closed-door hearings, actors James Cagney and Humphrey Bogart were named as threats to the Republic. "I don't think that committee could have located a Communist in Red Square in Moscow on May Day in front of Lenin's Tomb," said George Reedy, a newsman who covered the panel. The committee was flecked with members of Congress who loathed blacks and Jews. Some of the congressmen would happily say so. Democratic representative John Rankin, a particularly nasty bigot from Itawamba County, Mississippi, railed about "kikes" and "niggers" in his speeches.

"Not all Jews are Communists, but my information is that 75 percent of the members of the Communist Party in this country are Yiddish," Rankin told the House. "They have for their purpose the undermining and destroying [of] this country."

Meanwhile, HUAC declined to investigate the Ku Klux Klan because it was, Rankin insisted, "an old American institution."

"Mr. Rankin: he was a very prejudiced man," Robert Stripling would recall. If Stripling had his prejudices, he kept them in rein, and he seemed as happy chasing Nazis as he was pursuing Reds. A savvy lad from East Texas, he had wangled a patronage job as a doorkeeper in the House from his hometown congressman and risen to chief investigator. When Dies departed, the hound-faced Stripling stayed on—clipping the *Daily Worker,* compiling files from the mastheads of the left, making enemies at the White House, and surviving by feeding the press.

J. Parnell Thomas, a Republican from New Jersey, took over as HUAC's new chairman with the change of party control in January 1947. His reign was marred by a federal corruption probe, which would one day land him in prison with the very men he persecuted. On his good days he looked like an "apoplectic tomato," a *Time* reporter noted. The stress didn't help his ulcers, and he chaired some hearings in his government hospital room, clad in bathrobe and pajamas. He was "small, narrow-minded, petty, emotional, vindictive, and blindly partisan," wrote Robert Carr, a Dartmouth College law professor, in a contemporary analysis. "That he should have ended his career branded as a criminal was . . . a perverse, almost incredible turn of fate by which he had been made to suffer the same torture he had inflicted upon some of his own victims."

Given the committee's standing, Nixon's work on HUAC was perilous, recalled Father John Cronin, the veteran anti-Communist: "When he took membership upon the House committee, he did this knowing that it had proved the road to oblivion for many of its members." The congressman was initially defensive. "I should also like to say a word concerning my work on the Un-American Activities Committee," Nixon wrote to his supporters. "I realize that considerable criticism has been made of this committee in the past because it has sometimes made charges which could not be backed up by facts."

Nixon's discomfort increased when Thomas and his staff opened hearings on the Communist threat in the early months of 1947 and almost instantly trained their sights on Hollywood. Their chosen witnesses complained that films like *The Best Years of Our Lives,* an award-winning portrayal of the ordeal that GIs suffered coming home from World War II, were "degrading American institutions." Hollywood had extolled the bravery of the country's Russian allies during the war and had a tradition dating back to the Depression of portraying bankers as greedy and capitalists as oafs. It was an outrage, Thomas said. He enlisted Hoover's cooperation and held closed-door sessions in Los Angeles, harvesting names of film industry Communists.

Nixon did not participate in the Los Angeles hearings or volunteer for the HUAC subcommittee that was investigating Hollywood. He was wary: the film industry was a major employer in California, and many of its actors and executives were active in politics as partisans, celebrity fund-raisers, or donors. Besides, the committee's hearing schedule clashed with his duties on the Herter mission and his need to get back to his district and explain his support for the Marshall Plan.

Yet the young congressman was appreciative of HUAC's efforts. That spring he had a long conversation with the actor Ronald Reagan, a repentant New Dealer who was making a name for himself resisting Communist influence in the Screen Actors Guild. "I believe that he can be extremely helpful in the committee's investigation," Nixon told Herman Perry. "I am going to make every effort to see that he is called as a witness." The actor was a perfect fit for Nixon's favored strategy: to make HUAC more respectable. "Reagan would make a particularly good witness in view of the fact that he is classified as a liberal and as such could not be accused of simply being a red-baiting reactionary."

The committee was delighted to hear from Reagan, who joined Gary Cooper and other movie stars before standing-room-only crowds and an army of reporters and cameramen at public hearings in October. "I am a witch-hunter if the witches are Communists," the actor Adolphe Menjou proudly declared. But Reagan, though joining in the condemnation of Communism, defended Hollywood and free speech with homey eloquence. "In opposing these people, the best thing to do is make democracy work," Reagan said. "I believe that, as Thomas Jefferson put it, if all the American people know all of the facts they will never make a mistake."

The hearings were a spectacle, with the right's Ayn Rand and the left's Bertolt Brecht taking their turns at the microphone and an airplane full of Hollywood stars, led by Bogart and Lauren Bacall, barnstorming the heartland on their way to Washington in a cavalcade for artistic freedom. Nixon sat in on the first week's sessions, where he nudged Jack Warner of Warner Brothers to make more anti-Communist movies, but ducked the ugly climax. He wasn't there when a band of contemptuous screenwriters defied the dictatorial chairman and refused to answer questions about their membership in the Communist Party.

"I could answer it, but if I did, I would hate myself in the morning," writer Ring Lardner Jr. told the committee. He and the others were charged with contempt of Congress, put on trial, imprisoned, and blacklisted—and revered forever in liberal martyrology as the Hollywood Ten.

Nixon was wise to miss that showdown. It was far more dignified and productive to express his opposition to Communism in the measured cadences of a young statesman, with his firsthand accounts from Berlin and Greece and Trieste, than to get into a brawl with the movie industry.

He paid a price regardless. "I surely appreciated your letter . . . regarding my work on the Un-American Activities Committee," Nixon wrote campaign aide Harrison McCall. "If you could see some of the letters I have received vilifying the committee . . . you would realize why a word of encouragement is appreciated."

THE CONTEMPT CITATIONS for the Hollywood Ten came to the floor of the House for its approval in late November, and Nixon stood with his fellow committee members.

Representative Emanuel Celler, a liberal Democrat from Brooklyn, accused the committee of practicing "a little totalitarianism to preserve our democracy."

"How . . . do we combat Communism?" asked Representative Helen Gahagan Douglas, a California Democrat. "Certainly not by setting in motion a wave of hysteria."

This prompted Rankin to accuse his liberal colleagues of "giving aid and comfort to these Communists."

With relish, Rankin read aloud the actual, foreign-sounding names of Jewish movie stars, including those known to the public as Danny Kaye (David Daniel Kamirsky), Edward G. Robinson (Emanuel Goldenberg), and Melvyn Douglas (Melvyn Hesselberg), as proof of their disloyalty. Rankin knew, of course, that Douglas was married to the congresswoman from California.

Nixon had the task of following the malodorous Rankin and closing the debate on the contempt charge filed against screenwriter Dalton Trumbo, who would spend almost a year in prison, and a decade on the Hollywood blacklist—and win two Academy Awards for screenplays written under other names.*

"It is unfortunate that in the various proceedings which are brought

---

* The films were *Roman Holiday* (1953) and *The Brave One* (1956). He was freed from the blacklist and credited for his screenplays after writing the scripts for the 1960 sagas *Exodus* and *Spartacus*.

before this House by the Committee on Un-American Activities there are times that we have a tendency to indulge in emotionalism," Nixon said, trying to disassociate himself from Rankin. "We must recognize that in legislating on matters which involve freedom of expression and freedom of speech and political affiliations we are operating in a very tender area of the law in which the greatest care and discretion should be exercised."

That said, Nixon argued, the matter was not complicated. House committees had a historic, recognized power to investigate. And what Thomas liked to call "the $64 question"—"Are you now or have you ever been a member of the Communist Party?"—was a valid inquiry. For refusing to answer, Trumbo and his comrades were guilty of contempt, Nixon said. The House agreed—in Trumbo's case by a vote of 240 to 16.

The committee went on for years, chasing Reds in Hollywood, summoning actors and writers and directors for a grilling before the cameras, and clapping them with contempt citations if they refused, as many in conscience did refuse, to "name names" of their associates. Those who cooperated—like the choreographer Jerome Robbins (*West Side Story*) or director Elia Kazan (*A Streetcar Named Desire, On the Waterfront*)—were vilified as informers.

"The blacklist was a time of evil and . . . no one on either side who survived it came through untouched by evil. Caught in a situation that had passed beyond the control of mere individuals, each person reacted as his nature, his needs, his convictions and his particular circumstances compelled him to," Trumbo said generously, years later. "It will do no good to search for villains or heroes or saints or devils because there were none; there were only victims."

Nixon had steered clear of the committee's most abusive practices—and he did so again in the spring of 1948, when he chaired a HUAC subcommittee charged with writing legislation to ensure domestic security. From his efforts—in which he was joined by Representative Karl Mundt, a Republican from South Dakota—came the Subversive Activities Control Act, better known as the Mundt-Nixon bill.

There was scant need for the measure, which tightened controls already in place. Federal prosecutors were well armed with the Foreign Agents Registration Act of 1938 and the Voorhis and Smith Acts of 1940. Together, these measures saddled subversives with the burden of declaring themselves as tools of a foreign power and facing prosecution if advocating the violent overthrow of the U.S. government. Indeed, under the existing laws, the leaders of the Communist Party in the United States were indicted that summer. The chief virtue of Nixon's proposal was that it vented steam and preempted calls to outlaw the Communist Party—an action, said Hoover, that would drive the Reds underground and make his job harder.

The other virtue of Mundt-Nixon was the publicity it generated for its sponsors. Mundt was running for the Senate and Nixon for reelection, with an eye on a statewide race someday. His timing, and his luck, had paid off once again. After his work on Taft-Hartley and the Marshall Plan, he was now in the thick of the big debate on Communist subversion.

Nixon worked hard to seem earnest and fair. He consulted Wall Street lawyer (and future secretary of state) John Foster Dulles, Arthur Garfield Hays of the American Civil Liberties Union, and other legal experts about the legislation. When chairing a hearing, he asked questions thoughtfully, ruled fairly, and gave witnesses the freedom to elaborate and explain. He did so even as he suffered from two fractured arms, broken in a tumble on icy steps when, carrying Tricia, he could not catch himself or break the fall. The pain was excruciating, and three or four attendants had to hold him down when his injuries were x-rayed.*

Nixon "is at pains to try and keep the committee on a legally sound path and has a considerable reputation for fairness to witnesses," the *New York Times* reported. When Hays appeared before Nixon's subcommittee, Nixon joined in some learned jousting with the famous First Amendment lawyer and did not try to silence him. Nixon's fairness "confirms my faith in the American system of government," said Hays when it was over, marveling that a member of HUAC could be so evenhanded.

"It was kind of you," Hays wrote, in a follow-up note to Nixon a few weeks later. "I realize my views on these subjects are not popular these days, but I appreciate an opportunity to express them without earning personal ill will."

NOT ALL OF Nixon's actions were so faith confirming. He was dwelling in a scoundrels' den, and it was difficult to escape the stain. He joined in the practice of leaking HUAC's confidential files to conservative supporters: Murray Chotiner got access to the committee files on a political opponent, and Herman Perry was sent HUAC files to tar left-wing speakers at

---

* For the rest of his life, his tailors would be challenged: one arm was shorter than the other.

Whittier College. "I was glad to be able to furnish you some dope. . . . The information which comes from our committee files has been checked and double-checked and is quite reliable for the most part," Nixon wrote Perry. "I certainly regret that some of our Quaker Friends tie into the Communist groups as they often do."

There were times when Nixon's ear deserted him. So it was when HUAC turned its attention to Edward Condon, a physicist directing the National Bureau of Standards. In early 1948, without allowing Condon to respond, HUAC issued a report that libeled the scientist as a security risk and suggested he had ties to Soviet espionage. The committee "disgusted many observers because it had smeared witnesses on insufficient grounds or without giving them a chance to get their stories on the record," the *Herald Tribune*'s Bert Andrews would recall, and the Condon case was one such "shameful" incident. The HUAC report cited a letter from Hoover that noted the physicist's acquaintance with Nathan Silvermaster, a suspected spy. But the committee purposefully omitted the exculpatory conclusion to Hoover's letter, in which the FBI director absolved Condon of any treasonous intent. HUAC had "touched its nadir of bad judgment," wrote the British journalist Alistair Cooke, a keen observer of the era. "The . . . source of this very serious charge was an FBI letter that actually cleared Dr. Condon."

Rather than apologizing, HUAC doubled down—demanding to see Condon's personnel file. Truman, with a broad claim of presidential privilege, refused to hand it over. Whipped on by Nixon and others, the House of Representatives then voted to assert its prerogatives. The scientific and academic community and the nation's press responded in full throat, condemning the latest HUAC "smear." The controversy snowballed, and in the cloakrooms and corridors, other Republicans expressed anger for being placed, once again, in a difficult position. "We are getting some panning from our colleagues . . . as a consequence . . . of the Condon situation," Mundt warned Thomas.

In letters to friends, Nixon now acknowledged the committee's blunder and tried to distance himself. "The Condon case is one in which Thomas, without question, followed a bad procedure," he wrote. "I was not a member of the subcommittee which issued the original report. I intend to press for a full and open hearing" that would "either clear Condon of all charges, or clear the committee of the charges that have been made against it."

But the damage was done. That spring, for the first time, Nixon picked up the morning newspaper and found he was a target of the *Washington Post* cartoonist Herbert Block, who signed his work "Herblock." The drawing showed Lady Liberty tied to a stake as three plump figures dressed in Puritan garb, labeled "Nixon" and "Mundt" and "Thomas," piled wood around her feet and "Thomas" declared, "We got to burn the evil spirits out of her."

THE MUNDT-NIXON BILL came before the House in May, with Nixon as the floor manager. Rankin was his usual distasteful self, muttering about Jews and foreigners. Liberal Democrats railed against this latest affront to the Bill of Rights. Noting how previous statutes had failed to stem the anti-Communist hysteria, Celler predicted that "this bill will fail of its purpose and next year a still more drastic and still more Draconian bill will be the spawn of proscriptive minds."

The legislation became a shuttlecock, as well, in the race for the Republican presidential nomination with Harold Stassen (mistakenly) supporting it and New York governor Thomas Dewey (mistakenly) opposing it in a national radio forum because they both (mistakenly) believed that it outlawed the Communist Party. There were members of the House who seemed similarly confused, but the legislation won overwhelming approval and passed by a 319–58 vote. Mundt-Nixon was destined to die in the Senate, but not before Nixon won further acclaim as a young man of substance, a congressman to be reckoned with.

"As you know, I felt compelled to vote against the bill you so ably presented to the House," wrote John Heselton, a liberal Republican from Massachusetts, in a note to Nixon. "But I would be most unhappy if anyone were to construe that vote as the slightest reflection upon what I honestly believed to be a tremendously effective, conscientious and able effort on your part."

Nixon had this consoling thought: Dewey would undoubtedly beat Truman in November, and the Republicans would control both Congress and the White House in 1949. They would pass a bill in the next Congress, he thought, and a Republican president would sign it. All the conventional wisdom said so.

A Tragedy of History

O N INDEPENDENCE DAY in 1948, Dick drove Pat to Columbia Hospital in Washington, where, in the early morning hours of the following day, she gave birth to a nine-pound, six-ounce girl. They named the baby Julie. It was a welcome, happy event for a couple who had endured the rigors of hard times, war, and campaigning. With a five-month congressional recess ahead, and no real opposition to Dick's reelection, he and Pat looked forward to spending more time together, and the revitalizing effects of a long vacation. They needed it to refresh their marriage.

Pat had built a life for herself in New York and Los Angeles before they were married, and again in San Francisco while Dick served in the navy. She had given it up to return to Whittier and the role of a candidate's spouse. She was never a complete enthusiast of "this politics thing." A few days after the 1946 victory she had told one of Dick's law school classmates, with wistful regret, how she'd failed to sell her husband on a life as a lawyer in Palm Springs, a desert resort that, she was certain, would boom after the war. Washington had its majesty, but not for congressional wives, who took hat-making classes or rolled bandages for the Red Cross, or went visiting, or to teas with white gloves and calling cards. She'd been sentenced to chores in Dick's office, and to stay at home with Tricia as he toured Europe. She felt taken for granted and mourned the loss of "the camaraderie and carefree times" of their early years. Pat voiced her discontent when Dick returned from the Herter mission. Surprised, he responded with customary reticence, pledging his renewed devotion—in a letter. He promised to spend more time at home.

Time, for comers, is a scant commodity. The Mundt-Nixon bill, the Marshall Plan, and his reelection commanded Dick's attention in the winter and spring, and the Republican national convention in Philadelphia, which crowned Dewey as the presidential candidate, commandeered the early summer. Dick, a Stassen man, was consigned to the galleries, but he enjoyed squiring his dad around; together, they looked at an exhibit of that new wonder, television. Hannah arrived in Washington to help with the new baby but fell ill, and Pat now had three needing her care: her mother-in-law, two-year-old Tricia, and Julie.

Harry Truman then ruined Pat's hopes for a restorative August break. Evoking a seldom-used prerogative, the president called the Republican Congress back into session, challenging the "do-nothing" lawmakers to take action on a range of issues. Dick had to vow, swear, pledge to Pat: After Election Day, they would reenact the Caribbean cruise they took in 1941. They would leave the girls with Frank and Hannah and spend December on a slow boat to Panama. He guaranteed it.

THE COMMUNISTS DECLINED to cooperate. In early 1948, the Russians had completed their takeover of Czechoslovakia, an event marked by the death of Czech foreign minister Jan Masaryk, who jumped or fell or was thrown from an upper-story window after failing to secure his country's freedom. Talk of war with Russia filled America's coffee shops and living rooms, and the newspapers carried tidings of the U.S. atomic weapons tests at Eniwetok atoll. In June, Stalin ordered his forces to seal off West Berlin, touching off the first explosive Cold War crisis and evoking a heroic response: the storied Berlin airlift of fuel and food. (The Yanks called it "Operation Vittles.") The Soviet superiority in troops and tanks was overwhelming, and the Allied war chiefs made plans to abandon the German plain, drop back, and hold the Red Army at the Rhine. Truman dispatched a fleet of B-29 bombers to Europe; it was not lost on anyone that these were the planes that hauled the A-bombs. The Berlin crisis lasted almost a year before Stalin relented. There was no time for celebration, as a pair of equally alarming events left Americans unnerved: the Soviets tested their first atomic weapon, and the Communists under Mao Zedong completed the conquest of China. Against this backdrop, Richard Nixon would conduct two relentless campaigns: a hunt for Soviet spies and a race for the U.S. Senate. The first would make the second, and the second would fuel the first. A crisis, Nixon believed, was also an opportunity.

AS THE MEMBERS of Congress trudged back to the glory of August in Washington, HUAC's leaders were still hobbling from the beating they'd taken in the Condon fiasco. An unlikely source—the Truman administration—bailed them out. In midsummer, a federal grand jury probing subversion indicted twelve leaders of the Communist Party of the United States. The Justice Department's success in the case underscored the argument made by civil libertarians that the Mundt-Nixon bill was gratuitous, but it was a boon to HUAC, freeing up the federal witnesses, whose testimony turned the committee in a profitable direction.

The prosecutors' star witness captured the public's fancy. Elizabeth Bentley, a Vassar graduate, had fallen in love with a Communist spymaster named Jacob Golos and served him as a courier, carrying messages, funds, and stolen documents between party officials and the Red spies in the nation's capital. When her Bolshevik lover suffered a fatal heart attack, Bentley's life crumbled. She left the Communists in 1944, approached the FBI, and threw open the windows on Soviet espionage.

Though Bentley was a plain, plump, dark-haired woman, the newspapers portrayed her as a blond sexpot—the "Red Spy Queen"—a Mata Hari of the atomic age. For Republicans, furious at the White House and with zero desire to take up the president's agenda, her accounts of Communist penetration were a wondrous gift. Bentley's story let the GOP switch the subject from the banners Truman was raising on the economy, farm prices, and civil rights. They could knock the administration for a shocking lapse of security—indicative, no doubt, of a lax and forgiving attitude toward Communism. A Red hunt was in order. "If the White House refuses . . . to turn over personnel files, we will crucify the administration," Mundt wrote a colleague. "If they do, we are going to be able to dig out more stuff to plague them in the fall campaign." With Truman's proposals dead on arrival and Republicans wielding the gavels, the special session morphed into a circus of intrigues.

Bentley told her story to Senate investigators, and then to HUAC, in a public hearing on July 31. She named a high-ranking Treasury official, Harry Dexter White, and a score of other New Deal officials as Soviet agents. When White and others denied the allegations, HUAC was vilified, again, for inculpating people without allowing them the opportunity to respond. Needing to shore up Bentley's testimony, staffer Robert Stripling took "a forlorn shot in the dark," and subpoenaed Whittaker Chambers.

CHAMBERS WAS A graying editor at *Time* magazine, a cardiac patient drifting toward retirement, who spent much of his time at a farm in Westminster, Maryland. It wasn't likely he knew much about Bentley. He had fled the Communist Party in 1938 after six years as a drone in the underground. His tale was known to the FBI, which had interviewed him several times, and to a thriving camp of anti-Communist gumshoes, politicos, and reporters. "The story . . . had been floating around Washington for many years," Stripling would recall. "It was nothing new." But on August 3 Chambers appeared before HUAC, seconded Bentley's testimony about Soviet espionage, and produced his own roster of Communists in government. And on his list was Alger Hiss.

The reporters at the press table looked up. This was news. Bentley had not mentioned Hiss. He was then president of the Carnegie Endowment for International Peace, a prestigious institution. He had served as a top State Department official before and during the war, and been a Sherpa for Franklin Roosevelt at the Yalta summit, where Churchill, Stalin, and Roosevelt made their postwar plans and promises. He was a midwife to the birth of the United Nations. And all that time, according to the mumbling Chambers, Hiss was a Communist.

IT WAS TRUE. For as much as they were different, Hiss and Chambers were alike. They were misfits craving ballast: two boys who had fled the wreck of families razed by drink, madness, and suicide. They sought "a moral solution" in "a world of moral confusion," Chambers would say. And "at that crossroads the evil thing, Communism, lies in waiting."

Hiss had a carapace of cool. Thin and dapper, he was a graduate of Johns Hopkins University and Harvard Law School, a golden laddie of the New Deal and the protégé of Supreme Court justices. He possessed a "strong romantic streak," his friend and lawyer William Marbury would recall. He was "perfectly capable of any amount of self-sacrifice for a cause." But behind the charm, Hiss nurtured secrets. His father, despairing over financial reversals, had slashed his own throat with a razor, leaving Alger and four siblings to their mother, an adamant woman who strove to preserve a sheen of gentility. A dissolute brother died a young man. A mentally troubled sister killed herself. His mother greeted Alger's marriage to Priscilla Hobson, a divorcée, with a telegram that said: DO NOT TAKE THIS FATAL STEP.

Chambers was a visage of shamble and ruin, a self-loathing homosexual dismissed as a student from Columbia University for blasphemous writings. His father left the family when Chambers was seven years old to live with a male lover. His mother would gather her two sons, lock the bedroom door at night, and sleep with an ax by her side to protect them from imagined terrors. His grandmother, who lived with the family, had psychotic episodes, and his younger brother, after several failed attempts,

finally succeeded at suicide. Chambers showed his solidarity with the pro-
letariat, and sent a sign to the world of his soul's decay by refusing to
care for his teeth. For years they were "a devastation of empty sockets and
blackened stumps," a friend recalled, a memorable physical feature that
would play a role in what followed. He "was made of the stuff of which
the founders of religious cults and sects are built," his friend, the journalist
Isaac Levine, would remember. "He craved the adulation of disciples and
fancied himself as a prophet of history. . . . His ego cried for a mythologi-
cal halo."

Chambers and Hiss seized on Marx's vision of equality and Lenin's cult
of discipline to bring meaning and order to their lives. "One cannot escape
the conclusion that the tragedy of his family, rather than the crisis of history, shaped Whittaker Chambers' decision," wrote Arthur Schlesinger Jr.,
noting how Chambers joined the Communist movement amid the prosperity of the Roaring Twenties, not the gloom of the Depression. Communism had offered "the appeal of large-scale historic process, in which
to surrender the self," said William F. Buckley Jr., who was to become
Chambers's friend.

The cause that led Hiss and Chambers to treason was not without
appeal in the United States. The inequities of the industrial age and the
desperate conditions in the factories, mines, and tenements had drawn
millions of left-leaning Americans, over the years, to a movement that
Samuel Gompers called Labor, Eugene Debs and Sidney Hillman knew as
Socialism, and John Reed found in Communism. "I have seen the future;
and it works," wrote the muckraker Lincoln Steffens after returning from
Russia in 1919. When others faltered, America's Communists had rescued
the Scottsboro boys from the hangmen in Alabama and taken up arms
against fascism in the Spanish Civil War. In intellectual and artistic circles,
it could be something of a rite of passage. "Practically every young man has
been through a phase when he has been interested in Communist activities
of some kind," said Adolf Berle, the State Department official who supervised U.S. intelligence during World War II. In 1939, more than three
hundred American intellectuals, including men like Ernest Hemingway,
James Thurber, and Dashiell Hammett, signed an open letter heralding
the Soviet Union's progress and urging Americans to reject the "fantastic
falsehood that the USSR and the totalitarian states are basically alike."

The liberal infatuation with Communism abated when the news of
Stalin's purges reached America and the Soviet leader struck a nonaggression pact with Hitler to dismember Poland. But the alliance of the two
gangster statesmen did not last long. By the time America entered the war,

at the end of 1941, the Nazis and Soviets were locked in combat on the Eastern Front. For Americans, Stalin became "Uncle Joe," an irreplaceable ally in the great crusade against Germany, Italy, and Japan. "To cross this bridge I would hold hands with the Devil," Roosevelt told a friend.

In 1933, at the age of twenty-eight, Hiss had come to Washington, joining a team of brilliant leftist lawyers in the Agricultural Adjustment Administration, the New Deal agency coping with the crisis in rural America. While at the AAA, Hiss and others were enrolled in the Communist Party by Harold Ware, a farming expert who organized an underground cell. Hiss moved to Capitol Hill, where he worked as the counsel for a Senate investigation of the arms industry, and then to the Department of State. When Ware was killed in an automobile accident, control of the cell moved to a Soviet spymaster who enjoined Hiss and Chambers to steal secrets for Soviet military intelligence. Chambers abandoned the Communist faith in 1938, but Hiss kept spying through the war years as he climbed through the ranks and became a top adviser to Secretary of State Edward Stettinius Jr.

The full cost of Hiss's treason is not known. By the end of World War II he had access to military and atomic secrets. Yet when Hiss and Chambers were betraying their country in 1937 and 1938, they did not endanger America's men in arms: most of what the pair stole for Stalin were confidential U.S. government assessments of Japanese and Nazi actions and intentions. Thus could the two men justify their treachery. After all, Roosevelt's FBI pursued German saboteurs and Japanese Americans, not ragtag Communists, during the war. It was only toward the conflict's end, as the Soviet Union's ravenous appetites became clear, that men were judged in a transformed now for what they had done in a very different then. "Transport yourself back," a prosecutor in the Hiss case would urge the jury. "There were people who felt that the advance of Nazism and fascism . . . was being stemmed or stopped by nobody but the Russians. . . . You can see how a person of Chambers's intellect or Hiss's intellect could become . . . involved with that type of thinking."

It was difficult for Nixon, sizing up the "unkempt, disorderly" Chambers that August morning, to ascertain the intellect at all. He found the witness "short, fat, so soft-spoken that it was often necessary to ask him to repeat what he said, his clothes un-pressed, his manner almost diffident."

Nixon had raised no objection when others suggested that Chambers's testimony should be public. He had joined his fellow lawmakers, the committee's staff, a parade of reporters and spectators, and the skittish witness (for Chambers, not unreasonably, feared he was a target for assassination) as they trouped across the street from the committee's offices to the spacious Ways and Means room in the new House (now Longworth) office building.

Aside from the name of Alger Hiss, Nixon thought that the Chambers testimony was "pretty tame stuff." Chambers had buttressed Bentley's account, but without her knack for lively details—like how she stashed military secrets, on microfilm, in her knitting bag. And—a crucial point—Chambers had lied under oath, denying that the agents he handled were spies. The primary purpose of the Communist cells, he told the committee, was not to steal secrets but to infiltrate the government and help mold policy.

Chambers testified about how, as he prepared to flee the underground, he had gone to Hiss and begged his friend to accompany him. Hiss was wrenched by their parting and wept, but declined. "I was very fond of Mr. Hiss," said Chambers.

Tame stuff or not, Nixon was instantly aware of the political potential of the testimony. "Mr. Chambers," he said, as the hearing neared its end. "You indicated that nine years ago you came to Washington and reported to the government authorities concerning the Communists who were in the government."

Yes, said Chambers. He told the panel how he had gone to Berle and told all he knew: "I named specific names, Mr. Hiss among them."

"Mr. Chambers," asked Nixon. "Were you informed of any action that was taken as a result of your report to the government?"

"No; I was not," said Chambers. "I assumed that action would be taken right away which was, of course, rather naïve of me, and it wasn't until a great deal later that I discovered apparently nothing had been done."

"No action was taken," Nixon repeated. The New Dealers had covered it up. It was the theme, he later recalled, "that I was to develop throughout the balance of the case."

HISS NOW FACED a choice. He could seek the shelter of the Fifth Amendment, claiming its protection from self-incrimination. Or, like Chambers, he could hide among half-truths. Yes, Hiss might have said, he had a youthful flirtation with Communism. Yes, he'd paid his party dues. And yes, he had deceived his New Deal colleagues. But he was a patriot who hated Hitler. Secretaries of state and Supreme Court justices would vouch for him. His diplomatic record was flawless. It was all so long ago. Hiss may have gotten away with it. Chambers played that hand, stayed out of prison, and was posthumously awarded a Presidential Medal of Freedom.

But Hiss, as Stripling put it, was a "big fish." He had more at stake than Chambers. He would no doubt lose his job, maybe his career, and surely his reputation. And HUAC would make him play the rat, compel him to name names or, like the Hollywood Ten, face a prison cell for contempt. It was better to deny it all, Hiss decided. He would not betray the cause. He would brazen it out. He sent a telegram to the committee, demanding an opportunity to clear his name, saying: I DO NOT KNOW MR. CHAMBERS AND INSOFAR AS I AM AWARE HAVE NEVER LAID EYES ON HIM.

HISS GOT HIS invitation to testify and converted his appearance before the committee into a triumph. The August 5 hearing was conducted in the cavernous Caucus Room of the old House office building, where the seats were filled with spectators, fanning themselves as the ventilation system struggled with the summer heat. The table for the press was jammed with newspaper reporters; the congressmen on the dais appeared and vanished in a veil of cigarette smoke. Alone at the microphone, Hiss faced the inquisition.

"Hiss was . . . good looking . . . sophisticated, Ivy League dressed, Ivy League manner. He was everything that an elegant Washington executive should be in the New Deal era," Nixon would recall. "And with his clipped words and his very professional way of answering questions, a very careful way, he was a very effective witness."

"His performance . . . was as brilliant as Chambers had been lackluster," Nixon noted. "As suave and well-groomed as Chambers was unkempt and ill at ease."

Hiss started by dispensing with the Question. "I am not and have never been a member of the Communist Party," he said. None of his friends were Communists. He didn't know anybody named Whittaker Chambers. When shown a photograph of his accuser, Hiss evoked a fond response from the crowd. The photo rather looked, he said, like Karl Mundt.

"A titter of laughter swept through the press and through the front rows of the seats reserved for . . . Hiss's friends from the Georgetown, diplomatic set," Nixon recalled. "When they laughed, Hiss rather turned and smiled to everybody concerned in a very satisfied cat-that-swallowed-the-canary manner."

Hiss capped his day with a farewell salvo. "I am not happy that I didn't have a chance to meet with the committee privately before there was such a great public press display of what I consider completely unfounded charges against me," he scolded. "Denials do not always catch up with charges."

When Hiss had finished, a congressman or two led the line of well-wishers who came to shake his hand. "He left the hearing room . . . as if he were being carried off the football field as the halfback that had scored the winning touchdown," Nixon recalled. At home that evening Mundt told his wife, "The committee has certainly gotten hold of the wrong man."

Stripling's pals in the press corps shook their heads. The day was a catastrophe, perhaps fatal, for the committee, they said. A reporter from Chicago accosted Nixon at lunch. "This committee, in putting Chambers on the stand without checking his testimony first, has been guilty of calumny," he said. The Washington *Evening Star* had a front-page cartoon portraying HUAC as an overflowing sewer with the caption "Be Careful— You Might Get Splattered." And at his usual Thursday press conference, "Give 'em Hell Harry" was true to form. Was the hunt for Commies a "red herring?" he was asked. You bet, Truman said. HUAC was doing "irreparable harm."

Hiss's testimony seemed to have carried the day. "As a spectacle it had been superb," Chambers recalled. "It might have succeeded, too, but for one fact—the fact that is never foreseen. One of the Committee members was a man with one of those direct minds which has an inner ear for the ring of truth."

After lunch, when the gloomy HUAC members convened to consider their options, "everyone was convinced that a great injustice had been done," Nixon recalled. Bury it, some said; send the whole mess over to the Department of Justice, and let them decide who was lying.

"The committee was in, virtually, panic. . . . I must say I was tempted to do what most of the committee wanted to do, drop the case and get on with something else," Nixon recalled. And yet, alone, he maintained that they should stay the course.

"One man. Richard Nixon argued quietly but firmly against a switch from the Hiss investigation," Chambers would remember. "He pled the necessity of reaching truth."

IT IS DIFFICULT to find an adjective that sufficiently describes Nixon's audacity. He was a first-term congressman from a faraway district lacking great institutions of learning or influence. His few potent allies—Southern California's oilmen and the *Los Angeles Times*—were parochial powers. Mentors like Christian Herter urged him to cut his losses. Berle and others feared that Chambers was "a screwball."

"They were all against me," Nixon would recall. He was already being caricatured as an opportunist, trampling on civil liberties—this would further taint his reputation as a serious young man and a levelheaded student of world affairs. The newspapers, professors, the Democratic Party—the liberal establishment—were mobilizing. They took the attack on Alger Hiss as a Republican assault upon the New Deal.

Only the wily Stripling stood with Nixon. They both thought Hiss was evasive.

"You say you have never seen Mr. Chambers?" Stripling had asked the witness.

"The name means absolutely nothing to me," Hiss had replied. It sounded like a denial, but didn't address the question.

Hiss was "too smooth," said Nixon. They might not be able to prove he was a Communist, he told his colleagues, but their quarry had done more than just deny it: Hiss had sworn that he never knew Chambers at all. It was the bold, categorical sweep of that denial that made Hiss so believable. Yet if the two men had conspired for years, shared a great cause, and embraced in a tearful good-bye, then surely Chambers had something—some document, recollection, or trail—that would prove their relationship was real, and that Alger Hiss was lying. Nixon proposed to question Chambers further. He persuaded his grumpy colleagues to let him try. All right, they said. See what you can find.

NIXON DID NOT hazard all on a whim. He had reason to believe that Hiss was a Communist, for Father John Cronin had told him so.

Cronin was a Catholic intellectual, a warrior "in the defense of human dignity," he liked to say. He backed civil rights for black Americans and the rights of the working class to organize and became a fervent anti-Communist after watching the Reds infiltrate the labor movement. He took up arms: investigating, sounding the alarm in reports to his bishops, and serving as a conduit to the press and public for frustrated FBI and State Department agents who "were so distressed by the misinformation and naiveté of the American public that they were desperately seeking outlets," he would recall.

Representative Charles Kersten of Wisconsin, a fellow watchman, had introduced Cronin to Nixon in early 1947. The priest found the new congressman an eager pupil. "A twenty minute appointment was made," said Cronin. "The actual meeting took two hours."

"The story told in Mr. Nixon's office was dramatic and possibly lurid," Cronin remembered. They discussed "Communist espionage, especially atomic espionage; Communist penetration into government, including influential areas in the State and Treasury Departments; and the agonizingly slow reaction of the Executive Department to authentic reports on this situation. Names were given in the interview: Alger Hiss, Harry Dexter White . . . and many others."

Nixon reckoned that if he went after Hiss, he could count on the help of Cronin and his cohorts. The priest would serve as a go-between, collecting information from the FBI and passing it to Nixon via the congressman's private phone line.

Nixon knew, too, that if he brought down Hiss, the political dividends could be substantial. California had a vulnerable U.S. senator—Democrat Sheridan Downey—who was up for reelection in 1950. By the summer of 1948 Nixon was scheduling speeches around the state, and had Roy Day and others making discreet inquiries about "the Senator deal."

AND NIXON HAD a personal reason to pursue Alger Hiss: he just didn't like the man. The feeling had grown throughout the hearing, as Hiss failed to conceal his scorn for his inquisitors.

"He looked down his nose at the committee," Nixon recalled. "We were obviously, in his mind, the rather bumbling know-nothings who, in the minds of intellectuals and particularly the diplomatic set, generally inhabit the Congress."

Hiss's elitism would cost him dearly. Nothing more effectually raised Nixon's hackles.

At one point in the hearing, Nixon had compelled Hiss to admit that one of his mentors was Justice Felix Frankfurter, a Roosevelt appointee to the Supreme Court. Hiss had resisted, citing the committee's recklessness.

"Is it necessary?" Hiss asked Nixon. "There are so many witnesses who use names rather loosely before your committee."

Nixon flushed red. "He was rather insolent to me," he remembered. "From that time my suspicion concerning him continued to grow."

And though the stenographer missed the exchange (or it was edited out, as was sometimes the case at a member's request), Stripling always maintained that Hiss sealed his doom when asked by Nixon to name his alma mater.

"Johns Hopkins and Harvard," Hiss is said to have replied. "And I believe your college is Whittier?"

From that point on, Stripling said, it was personal: "Nixon had his hat set for Hiss."

On August 7, Nixon led a HUAC delegation to New York, where they summoned Chambers from his desk at *Time* to quiz him in a closed-door courtroom in the federal courthouse at Foley Square.

"I grilled him for two and a half hours on everything a man should know about another man if he knew him," Nixon would remember. He pressed Chambers for details about Hiss and his wife, his house, his hobbies, his mannerisms and habits. And as the day played out, it seemed more and more likely that Chambers was telling the truth. The witness knew a fair amount about the Hiss family, their home, their cocker spaniel, their terms of endearment. Chambers spoke about an old Ford that Alger had loaned him with windshield wipers that were worked by hand; a childhood job that Hiss had, delivering water from Druid Hill Park in Baltimore; and a prothonotary warbler that Hiss and his wife had spotted while bird-watching.

"I never saw one," said Chambers, sounding envious. "I am also fond of birds."

Nixon and the others trouped back to Washington, where the committee investigators confirmed much of what Chambers had told them. "It was obvious that either Chambers knew Hiss and Hiss was lying," said Nixon. "Or that Chambers had a very, very deep-seated motive which caused him to want to destroy Hiss, and he concocted a story after having studied Hiss's life." He decided he needed to know Chambers better. There were rumors about the witness, true and false, about his mental stability, drinking, and sexual proclivities. "There was a gnawing doubt in the back of my mind," Nixon would recall. "This was a bizarre tale." If Chambers had a grudge against Hiss, it was possible he had spied on the family, recording the mundane particulars of their lives. And so the congressman drove to Westminster and sat for hours talking with Chambers on the porch overlooking the fields. He met Esther Chambers, the witness's wife, and was struck by her dark features and prim Quaker manner. By the end of the day, "I was not convinced that everything" Chambers said about Hiss "was true. I still thought there could be a possibility that he had some motive for destroying Hiss . . . but that he knew him, I was convinced."

NIXON WAS REMINDED of the risk that he was taking when Harry Dexter White was summoned to testify, and gave a spirited performance before the committee. The distinguished-looking Treasury official denied he was a Communist, or a spy, and won rousing applause for his defense of American liberties. With his usual ham-handedness, Chairman Thomas taunted the witness when White, citing a heart condition, asked for breaks in the hearing. Three days later, White died of a heart attack. To many, it looked like he'd been hounded to death.

The Hiss case now dominated Nixon's life, his "absorption . . . almost frightening," his daughter would record. He hammered at the piano or paced the yard at his parents' farm, too tense to eat, ignoring Hannah's calls to dinner. He spent nights in his office, dozing on the couch or catching a few winks of sleep and a shower in a Capitol Hill hotel. His staff would take his suits to a one-hour dry cleaner. Pat and the girls didn't see him, and when he did come home he was mean and snappish. Nixon was "a troubled man," said the journalist Isaac Levine. "There was the Quaker in him, the pacifist, betraying occasional indecisiveness, perhaps a facet of insecurity. On the other hand, there was the able lawyer of all-absorbing ambition." Nixon knew that "a single mistake would be fatal," Cronin recalled.

Nixon looked for allies—taking transcripts of the Chambers testimony to William Rogers, the counsel to the Senate committee that had grilled Elizabeth Bentley, and to Bert Andrews, the *New York Herald Tribune* bureau chief who had won a Pulitzer Prize for exposing excesses in Truman's loyalty program. And with Congressman Charles Kersten at his side, Nixon traveled to New York to meet with John Foster Dulles, a leading adviser to Dewey.

Nixon was collecting more than moral support. He was soliciting the Dewey campaign's permission to proceed. Dulles was in an awkward position; the august Wall Street lawyer was in line to serve as the next Republican secretary of state but had been one of those who recommended Hiss for the job at the Carnegie Endowment. If Nixon exposed Hiss as a Communist, the blowback could hurt Dulles. Under such circumstances, Nixon had no trouble obtaining an audience at Dewey's headquarters at the Roosevelt Hotel. Joining Dulles was his brother, Allen, and Christian Herter. The young man from Whittier was conferring with the party elders, impressing them with his judgment, and earning their gratitude.

After reading the testimony, the Dulles brothers shook their heads at the compelling evidence of their friend Alger's treason and told Nixon to forge ahead.

Nixon then took Stripling, and Andrews, to visit Chambers at the farm in Westminster. They, too, became believers—though Stripling nursed a hunch that Chambers was holding something back.

NIXON NOW STARRED in three HUAC hearings that transformed the case. The first took place behind closed doors in Washington on the afternoon of Monday, August 16, when Hiss was confronted with the details of his life that Chambers had related to the committee. He sensed the danger and tried, too late, to recast the controversy. "The issue is not whether this man knew me," Hiss contended. "The issue is whether . . . I am a member of the Communist Party." Badgered by Nixon and the others, Hiss now said that he recalled a tenant—a writer named George Crosley—who had sublet his apartment, given him a rug, and taken the Ford with the hand-cranked windshield wipers off his hands. Crosley had very bad teeth, and his wife was dark-featured, Hiss said. He confirmed other details that Chambers had supplied about the Hiss family: their addresses, nicknames, and the breed, name, and kennel of their dog. And, yes, he and his wife were bird-watchers, Hiss said.

"Did you ever see a prothonotary warbler?" asked Representative John McDowell, a Pennsylvania newspaper publisher.

"I have right here on the Potomac," Hiss gushed. "Beautiful yellow head, a gorgeous bird."

It was clear that Hiss knew Chambers, if, perhaps, by another name. As far as that went, Chambers had been telling the truth.

IT WAS TIME to put Hiss and Chambers in a room together. Early the next morning, Nixon and McDowell trekked again to New York. They summoned Hiss to a closed-door hearing in a Commodore Hotel suite and brought in Chambers to confront him.

Hiss stalled, insisting that he could not identify Chambers as Crosley until he heard the witness talk. Then he wanted to examine his teeth. It was, Nixon later wrote Dulles, "one of the most unconvincing acts that I have ever seen put on by a supposedly intelligent man."

"Are you George Crosley?" Hiss asked.

"Not to my knowledge," said Chambers. "You are Alger Hiss, I believe."

"I certainly am."

"That was my recollection."

At one point, Nixon suggested that Chambers take an oath to testify truthfully, and Hiss sneered, "That is a good idea."

"I want no interruptions from you," Nixon barked.

Hiss objected to Nixon's tone of voice and—accurately—accused him of leaking defaming information to the press. Their hate for each other was out in the open.

"I don't need to ask Mr. Whittaker Chambers any more questions," Hiss declared. "I am now perfectly prepared to identify this man as George Crosley."

Fists clenched, Hiss accosted his old friend and dared him to repeat his accusations in public, where he was subject to the laws of libel. "I challenge you to do it, and I hope you will do it damned quickly," he said.

A HUAC staffer took Hiss by the elbow and tugged him away. He stormed out. The room was silent. Then Stripling said to Chambers: "Hi-ya, Mistah Crawzli."

THE FINAL SHOWDOWN took place in Washington, in the Caucus Room, on August 25, before banks of television and newsreel cameras that would sear the imagery of the Hiss case into American memory. Spectators filled the chairs and lined the walls, and hundreds of disappointed latecomers waited in the corridors outside. Washington "society" had discovered the controversy, the *Evening Star* reported, and attended "in the greatest of air-conditioned comfort." Among the celebrated onlookers was Representative Nixon's "blonde, good-looking wife, seated in the third row . . . hanging on his every word." Radio announcers kept up a steady whisper into their microphones, and reporters thrust bulletins into the hands of copy boys who rushed them to the newsrooms. "The air was heavy with the ominous and ultimate charges of modern history: treason, espionage and insanity," the *Nation* magazine reported.

It was the first House hearing carried by television. Each side knew what the other would say: Nixon and Hiss had leaked their versions of the face-off at the Commodore to the press. And so it was a contest of performance. Could Hiss win back the audience with his pose of wronged innocence? Could Chambers, with his plodding certainty, overcome a dashing adversary?

Hiss and Chambers restaged their face-to-face encounter for the cameras, and then Hiss took the witness chair. He was "a tall, well-groomed, handsome young man, adroit in manner, diplomatic in his speech," the *New York Times*'s James Reston reported. Nixon's questions of the witness "were detailed and often acid."

Hiss cited the long list of eminent men who had worked with him in government and would attest to his character.

"They saw my every gesture, my every movement, my every facial expression. They heard the tones in which I spoke, the words I uttered, the words spoken by others in my presence. They knew my every act relating to official business," he told the committee. "All are persons of unimpeachable character, in a position to know my work from day to day and hour to hour through many years. Ask them if they ever found in me anything except the highest adherence to duty and honor."

Americans should compare their affirmations with the word of Chambers, a confessed "liar, spy and traitor . . . unbalanced or worse," Hiss said.

After many hours, Chambers had his turn. "He is a short, round, jowly little man," Reston wrote. "He talked well with just a trace of hoarseness and lisp." Morning had turned into afternoon, and afternoon to evening. The cameras were still rolling. Again, Chambers offered his array of telling details.

Then Nixon asked him: "Is there any grudge you have against Mr. Hiss?"

As an informer, Chambers was an object of contempt. He had to persuade the public that he wasn't crazy, or addled with hate. He needed to cast his actions as a holy mission, a noble duty. The words that followed would echo through the years.

"The story has spread that in testifying against Mr. Hiss I am working out some old grudge, or motives of revenge or hatred," Chambers said slowly, ever painfully so. "I do not hate Mr. Hiss. We were close friends, but we were caught in a tragedy of history.

"Mr. Hiss represents the concealed enemy against which we are all fighting, and I am fighting. I have testified against him in remorse and pity, but in a moment of historic jeopardy in which this nation now stands, so help me God, I could not do otherwise."

THE HEARING HAD convened at 10:30 a.m. It ended at 8 that night. It had been a "vicious battle," packed with "spine tingling moments," Andrews reported, "one of the most tensely dramatic congressional hearings in America's history."

Hiss had impressed, with his list of celebrated mentors and associates. His point seemed well taken. How could he have acted as an advocate of

Communism? How could he have pushed damaging policies without all those great men noticing, and objecting? There were two possibilities. The first was that Chambers was lying—an increasingly unlikely scenario, as more and more details of his testimony checked out. The alternate was that Hiss was more than a Communist sympathizer—he was, in fact, a spy. The very soul of espionage is to infiltrate without stirring alarm. If Hiss had overtly promoted the Soviet Union's interests he would never have been trusted with the secrets that he stole. The attestations of his distinguished colleagues didn't clear Hiss—they demonstrated how very fine a spy he was.

Why hadn't Chambers told Congress the full extent of Hiss's activities? He claimed, then and later, that compassion stayed his hand. He was battling Communism, he said, and not his old comrades, whom he hoped to shield from the pain of prosecution. Perhaps, but to expose Hiss's espionage he would have to expose his own. Chambers was shrewd, and served the story in digestible morsels. "He sits and lights his pipe, he is cold and calculating, and he knows exactly what he will do three weeks hence," Stripling said. By the time he revealed his own treason, Chambers was a right-wing hero and had allies like Nixon to protect him.

HISS NOW MADE a god-awful error. He filed suit against Chambers for slander, presuming that if his old friend had proof of their iniquities, he would have produced it. In the course of the pretrial wrangling, Chambers was ordered by the court to disclose any evidence in his possession. He called at the home of his wife's nephew, who had hidden a lumpy envelope of microfilm and documents in a dusty dumbwaiter for him more than a decade ago. Chambers retained the microfilm but surrendered the documents to Hiss's stupefied lawyers, who turned them over to the government. They were typed copies of top-secret papers and handwritten notes—proof that Hiss was a Soviet agent.

The case was at another crossroads. Truman had completed his storied, victorious comeback against Dewey, and the Democrats had wrested control of the House and Senate from the Republicans. It seemed likely that the Democrats would abolish HUAC and broom the Hiss case. Nixon was in Washington after an exhausting autumn in which his party's leaders, eager to promote their new star, had sent him around the country to speak about the perils of "Cold War Treason." He was beginning to assemble the pieces for a Senate campaign in 1950—but first he had to take Pat on the

Caribbean cruise he had promised. He was in his office in early December, tying up loose ends, when Stripling brought him a visitor.

The man was Nicholas Vazzana, a member of the Chambers legal team who knew that his client had surrendered the stack of purloined documents. Vazzana was worried that the Justice Department would indict Chambers for perjury and let Hiss skate free. With enough nods and winks (for he feared the court's wrath if he were caught leaking), Vazzana gave Stripling and Nixon a tantalizing account of big doings in the slander case. "Alger Hiss," he said, had "better go shoot himself."

Nixon and Stripling adjourned to a Capitol Hill restaurant for lunch, where Stripling urged that they go see Chambers. Nixon was scheduled to leave for New York the next morning, where he and Pat had a ship to catch. The one thing he could not do was cancel the cruise on the eve of their departure. Pat would never forgive him.

"I'm so goddamned sick and tired of this case. I don't want to hear any more about it and I'm going to Panama! The hell with it, and you, and the whole damn business," he told Stripling.

So went their lunch: Nixon in a rage, torn by his conflicting obligations, and Stripling bristling from the scolding. Neither enjoyed his food. The standoff continued as they walked back to the office, and only after Stripling, heading out the door, car keys in hand, made one last entreaty did the congressman capitulate. "Goddamn it," he said, "if it will shut your mouth, I'll go."

They drove in strained silence the now-familiar route to Westminster. They arrived at milking time and had to cool their heels while Chambers finished with his cows.

"I have heard by rumor that you dropped a bombshell," Stripling told Chambers.

There had indeed been a bombshell in the slander case, Chambers acknowledged, and there were more to come. But that was all he'd say. Like Vazzana, he feared a contempt citation and would only communicate with cues and hints.

"What do you think he's got?" Nixon asked Stripling as they drove back to Washington.

"I don't know," said Stripling, but it could "blow the dome" right off the Capitol.

"I don't think he's got a thing," said Nixon.

—

NIXON WAS TOO bright to fool himself that way. On his way out of town the next morning, he stopped at the HUAC offices, leaving Stripling a directive to subpoena any evidence that Chambers still possessed. Then Dick and Pat got on a boat and sailed away.

Stripling served Chambers with the subpoena and dispatched two HUAC investigators to collect what was hidden in Westminster. At the Chambers farm they stumbled about with flashlights in the dark until the witness located a carved-out pumpkin in his garden, reached inside, and produced the cans of microfilm.

"I think this is what you are looking for," he said.

The investigators brought Stripling the film the next morning. He commandeered a men's room for use as a darkroom and called for an enlarger. Soon he was phoning around the country to HUAC members with news that the committee had evidence of espionage. There were secret government documents on the microfilm. Chambers and Hiss had been more than just Communists, they were spies.

Despite their harsh exchanges, Stripling remained loyal to Nixon. He recognized that when others had balked, the California congressman kept the case alive and deserved to be there for the laurels. "This was Mr. Nixon's case . . . and he had gotten on a boat," Stripling said. He alerted Nixon aide Bill Arnold and the *Trib*'s Bert Andrews, and they showered the steamship *Panama* with telegrams.

SECOND BOMBSHELL OBTAINED BY SUBPOENA I A.M. FRIDAY, Stripling's wire said. CASE CLINCHED. INFORMATION AMAZING. HEAT IS ON. . . . IMMEDIATE ACTION APPEARS NECESSARY. CAN YOU POSSIBLY GET BACK.

Stripling could only stall for so long. Mundt alerted the press, and the Saturday morning newspapers carried the saga of the "Pumpkin Papers" to the captivated public. And still there was no sign of Nixon.

GRAVE MISTAKE FOR YOU PERSONALLY TO LET ANYBODY ELSE GRAB THE BALL AFTER YOU HAVE CARRIED IT SO LONG, Arnold advised his boss.

YOU SHOULD BE HERE TO GET LIONS SHARE CREDIT YOU DESERVE, Andrews wired him. THESE FACTS ARE DYNAMITE. He sent his love to Pat, signing the telegram VACATION WRECKER ANDREWS.

Dick had received the first telegram while having dinner at the captain's table Friday night. "Here we go again," said Pat. After a night of intense consultations with his spouse, Dick accepted Stripling's offer to have the Coast Guard pick him up by seaplane in the Bahamas.

ESSENTIAL I ATTEND HEARING TUESDAY ARRANGE NAVY PICKUP BY ALL MEANS, he wired Arnold. Nixon's dramatic return added to the story, as newspaper and newsreel photographers caught him stepping off the seaplane and then posing in the office with Stripling, examining the microfilm with a magnifying glass.

Pat's return was not so newsworthy. She sailed on to Jamaica, left the cruise ship, and flew home alone.

Nixon's hour of victory was marred by one miscalculation that almost cost Chambers his life. As they prepared to reveal their findings to the press, Nixon and Stripling were asked by a photographer if they had checked the standard numbering of the film to determine its manufacturing date. Stripling called upon an Eastman Kodak lobbyist, who relayed the question to his company headquarters and returned with awful news: the film had been produced after 1945, not in the years when Hiss and Chambers were collaborating. The provenance of the photographs was in question, and Chambers's tale about the dusty dumbwaiter seemed a lie. They thought "we had been taken," Nixon would recall.

Chambers wasn't there to blame, but Vazzana was. "This is the end of my political career! This is all your fault!" Nixon howled. And when Chambers was reached by telephone in New York, Nixon turned his fury at him.

"It cannot be true, but I cannot explain it," said Chambers. "God must be against me."

"You better have a better answer than that," Nixon said.

Kodak rescued them. After further investigation, the company reported, it had concluded that the microfilm did indeed date to the 1930s. Stripling let out a yell, grabbed Nixon, and whirled him around the room. They had been spared a supper of crow before hundreds of waiting newsmen. They tried but failed to get Chambers on the phone. He had gone off and bought poison with which, a few days later, he unsuccessfully tried to end his life.

"Poor Chambers," Nixon said. "No one ever believes him at first."

The Hiss case had been "broken." The Red-hunting federal prosecutors who unearthed Elizabeth Bentley and indicted the Communist Party leadership now summoned Chambers and Hiss to testify.

Chambers recanted his previous lies. They had indeed been Soviet spies and not, as he had maintained, merely Communist sympathizers. He described for the grand jury how Hiss smuggled secret records home at night, where his wife, Priscilla, typed up copies that Chambers turned over to their Soviet spymasters.

The statute of limitations had run out for espionage, but Hiss and Chambers faced prison for perjury. The case against Chambers was open-and-shut, but Nixon came to his defense, accusing the Truman adminis-tration of persecuting a courageous witness in order to cover up its failures. And if Chambers were charged with perjury, Nixon argued, the case against Hiss would be fatally corroded. "You can't indict your main witness for perjury and expect the other case to stand up," he said.

Nixon was loyal, and protective. When Chambers confessed his homo-sexuality to the FBI, Nixon met with Esther Chambers, gently coun-seled her, and offered no judgment about her husband's past behavior or sexual orientation. "She said imaginative creative people wanted to explore all things & defended C that way—but was obviously disturbed," Nixon recorded in a diary entry. "Said nevertheless she was behind him 100%."

"I told her I wanted her to tell C I wished him well . . . and that a lot of people were behind him," Nixon wrote. "She seemed immensely pleased."

The Justice Department summoned Nixon before the grand jury, where the prosecutors challenged him to supply proof of his accusations of a White House cover-up. He quickly yielded. If that was how people had interpreted what he said, Nixon said, then he was sorry. He had meant no harm. "I certainly have no evidence to back that up," he admitted. But under mounting public pressure, the Truman administration came to see things Nixon's way. On December 15, Hiss was indicted for perjury. Chambers, the witness, was not. Years later, Nixon would recall his role in the trials of Alger Hiss with relish. He had "won the Hiss case in the papers," he would tell his White House aides. "I had to leak stuff all over the place.

"A committee of Congress is a double weapon. It destroys a man's repu-tation in public. And if it turns its files over to the Department of Justice for prosecution, they will prosecute the poor bastards," Nixon would recall. "I did it to Hiss."

IN HIS FIRST two years in Washington, Richard Nixon had amazed the capital time and again. The "handsome, strong-jawed Republican fresh-man," as one newsmagazine called him, had helped to push the Taft-Hartley and Mundt-Nixon bills through the House, provided crucial support for the Marshall Plan, and worked to temper HUAC's excesses. And then, when others hung back, Nixon had exposed a high-ranking

Soviet spy. It was, said commentator Fulton Lewis, "undoubtedly the most brilliant record . . . by any young congressman in a great many years."

Many expressed their admiration. "I was immediately struck by his probing intelligence, his obvious distinction among a committee of mediocre witch hunters," the British writer Alistair Cooke recalled. "He opened his eyes and ears impartially to Hiss's story, noted an early discrepancy, and correctly diagnosed Hiss's legal pedantries. . . . Once he felt for sure that Hiss was a consummate liar, he went after him with merciless skill."

But there were others, friend and foe, who were forming more pejorative impressions of Nixon. Lone wolf, they said. Glory hound. Opportunist. "Mr. Nixon never saw fit to share," Stripling recalled. He "played it solo all the way."

At one point, Stripling had rebuked his young ally. Nixon had gone "limber tail" during the Hollywood Ten investigation, Stripling chided him. He had disassociated himself from Thomas and the others when the going was tough, but now he was hogging the spotlight. "I don't think you realize you're not in the bush league," Stripling said. "You're in the majors now. You can't undermine the committee."

Karl Mundt's administrative assistant complained as well. "It was understandable that you should seek honor for yourself . . . and perhaps play down and ignore the contributions of others," W. E. O'Brien wrote Nixon. "But when you joined in a slur on the committee methods . . . that was going . . . too far."

J. Edgar Hoover was also wary. "To get a headline," Nixon had "played both sides against the middle," an FBI confidant told his boss after Nixon criticized the bureau for a lack of investigatory fervor. "I agree," the director wrote back. Former FBI agents on the HUAC staff spied on Nixon and reported to Hoover when the congressman, suspecting that the G-men were dragging their feet, sought to haul the director before the committee. They told him how Nixon had bragged that HUAC did more to stop Communist spying in three days than the FBI had done in eight years. Word reached Nixon of Hoover's displeasure, and he sought to patch things up, assuring Assistant Director Lou Nichols and others how much he admired the FBI director. But Hoover was no stranger to ambition. "This fellow Nixon blows hot and cold," the director told Nichols.

AND THOSE WERE Nixon's allies. The Hiss case put his name on the nation's front pages for weeks. He had tangled with President Truman, challenged the liberal order, matched wits with a New Deal darling, and come away triumphant. If he expected universal acclaim, he was to be disappointed. As in the campaign against Voorhis, where Nixon had taken the theme of anti-Communism past what many considered fair play, his zeal got the better of him, exposing him to retaliation.

On December 20, after undergoing questioning by the FBI, Laurence Duggan, a friend and former State Department colleague of Alger Hiss, jumped or fell from the sixteenth-floor window of his office in midtown Manhattan. Mundt and Nixon called a midnight press conference to claim credit for HUAC's role in exposing Duggan as a Red agent. He was one of six State Department officials who had worked for the Soviets, they said. When the press asked for the names of the other alleged spies, Mundt joked: "We'll release the others as they jump out of windows."

It was Christmastime. Communist or not, Duggan was a gentle soul who left a wife and four children behind, and his death evoked memories of how Harry Dexter White had died after being taunted by HUAC the previous summer.

Nixon and Mundt were pilloried. "At a stroke [the committee] has undone months of genuine effort . . . to correct past excesses and bring its procedures within the limits of reason and fairness," the *Herald Tribune* announced. A "dead man's character is being destroyed," said Edward R. Murrow, the CBS reporter, in his evening broadcast.

The poet Archibald MacLeish wrote "The Black Day: To the Memory of Laurence Duggan." It was published in the *Herald Tribune* and elsewhere:

> *. . . God help that country where the informer's shame*
> *Outshouts the decent silence to defame*
> *The dead man's honor and defile his name.*

And so the Hiss case left Nixon and Chambers marked men.

"The educated, progressive middle class, especially in its upper reaches, rallied to the cause and person of Alger Hiss, confident in his perfect innocence, deeply stirred by the pathos of what they never doubted was the injustice," wrote the literary critic Lionel Trilling, who had known Chambers in college. "Whittaker Chambers was regarded with loathing."

"The anti-Chambers whispering campaign was one of the most repellent of modern history," the liberal historian Arthur Schlesinger Jr. would recall.

The witness could retreat to his Maryland farm, write a book, and fade from view. Not so Nixon. Over time, Trilling observed, the loathing that intellectuals had for Chambers was transferred to Richard Nixon. So were the slurs. For if Alger Hiss was Jean Valjean, then Nixon must be Javert.

"I was to be subjected to the most unprincipled and vicious smear campaign of any public official in that period," Nixon remembered. "Bigamy, forgery, drunkenness, insanity, thievery, anti-Semitism, perjury, and the whole gamut of misconduct in public office . . . were among the charges that were hurled against me, some publicly and others through whispering campaigns, which were even more difficult to counteract."

Any politician would wince at such treatment. Nixon, congenitally insecure and too new to have grown a thick skin, was tormented. He had done his duty, served his country, and foiled America's enemies. And for this he was defamed by the liberal press and the left-leaning intelligentsia? What kind of awful, selfish people were they?

The Hiss case—that story of Whit and Alger, of the papers in the pumpkin, the broken-down Ford, and the yellow-chested warbler— reached beyond the usual political dispute. It was polarizing and personal. Andrews had warned Nixon in that telegram, summoning him back from sea. DOCUMENTS INCREDIBLY HOT. LINK TO HISS SEEMS CERTAIN . . . MY LIBERAL FRIENDS DON'T LOVE ME NO MORE. NOR YOU.

JUST AS IT molded Nixon, the Hiss case shaped the political climate in the formative days of the Cold War.

It was an "epitomizing drama," Chambers said. "The two irreconcilable faiths of our time—Communism and Freedom—came to grips in the persons of two . . . resolute men," he wrote. "With dark certitude, both knew . . . that the Great Case could end only in the destruction of one or both . . . just as the history of our times . . . can end only in the destruction of one or both of the contending forces."

Chambers was never less than dramatic, but plainspoken Democrats recognized the stakes. There was "political dynamite" in the Communism issue, Speaker Sam Rayburn told a congressional correspondent. "Don't doubt that."

For those on the left who had dabbled in radical doctrines in their youth, the Hiss case induced guilt, or at least defensiveness. Throughout the liberal community, it raised the alarm at how "the primitives," as Dean Acheson called the right's rabble-rousers, could employ calamitous witch hunts to undercut Roosevelt's legacy.

For Republicans, the Hiss case was a rallying point, bringing together

Bob Taft's Old Guard, young literati like William F. Buckley Jr., the blue-collar admirers of Senator McCarthy, and an inchoate crop of Sunbelt activists whose conservative passion, once harnessed, would lead to Republican disaster, rebirth, and triumph before century's end. The case inspired them all, inflamed their hostility toward the Ivy League elite, and confirmed their suspicions that the postwar reversals in Eastern Europe and China could be traced to treason and treachery.

And it would send Richard Nixon to the U.S. Senate.

8
_____

The Pink Lady

T HE CENTRAL VALLEY runs for five hundred miles through the
core of California, from the snow-topped volcanic cones of Mount
Shasta in the north to the Tehachapi crests that mark the notional
border between Northern and Southern California, just south of Bakersfield. It's about as big as West Virginia and, when irrigated, its soils are
marvelously rich. Two rivers pass through the valley, though not, for the
early Anglo settlers, conveniently: the San Joaquin River watershed contained two-thirds of the arable land, but only a third of the water. In Gold
Rush days, more than a few forty-niners were drawn to the valley's old
Spanish ranchos, and they soon concocted schemes to irrigate the semiarid
plain. The most ambitious—to divert the excess waters of the Sacramento
River to the thirstier San Joaquin valley—was deemed too expensive until
1935, when the federal Bureau of Reclamation signed on to build the
Central Valley Project, a multibillion-dollar lattice of hundred-mile-long
canals, towering dams, and reservoirs.

The government's goal, as with most of its reclamation projects, was
to dot the land with family farms. And so there were limits: no individual
could have federal water for more than 160 acres.* Progressive Republicans
and Democrats in Washington wished to steer the water to farmers, not
to the railroads and other big landowners. "The object of the Reclamation
Act is not so much to irrigate the land as it is to make homes," said Frederick Newell, the first chief of the bureau. "It is to bring about a condition
whereby that land shall be put into the hands of the small owner, whereby
a man with a family can get enough." Franklin Roosevelt embraced the
ideal. He saw the Central Valley as a vast canvas with 100,000 families,
mostly refugees from the Dust Bowl, finding a future on small farms fed

_____

* In California, a community property state, married couples could obtain federal water
for 320 acres.

by federal water and power. It was part of the New Deal's redistributive catechism.

The flat and open valley, however, was ideal for big, mechanized agricultural operations that profit from economies of scale. Huge family and corporate spreads came to dominate towns and counties, using migrant laborers displaced from the Great Plains by depression, drought, and dust storms. The big landowners coveted the cheap federal water and took aim at the 160-acre limit. They found allies in ideologues opposed to federal planning (one congressman accused Roosevelt of "trying to . . . force Communism upon the people") and, in the next of the chain of serendipitous developments that transformed Richard Nixon's life, in the state's senior U.S. senator, Sheridan Downey.

DOWNEY, SIXTY-FIVE, WAS a quirky kind of Democrat: "A genial, unobtrusive, generally shrewd, occasionally naïve and somewhat contradictive individual," as the *Los Angeles Times* put it in 1949. He had started out in politics as a liberal, run for lieutenant governor on a Democratic ticket with the gubernatorial hopeful, socialist Upton Sinclair, in 1934, and made his name peddling crackpot public pension plans. After unhorsing a conservative Democratic incumbent in the 1938 election, Downey drifted right himself. In the Senate he supported state control of the tidelands oil and saw the 160-acre limit as an element in a plot "to institute totalitarian rule." He feuded with reclamation officials, authored a protest book called *They Would Rule the Valley,* and introduced a measure in Congress to exempt the Central Valley Project from the acreage limit.

The dream of the valley as a Jeffersonian sanctum was fading. But not yet in every heart. Representative Helen Gahagan Douglas, of Los Angeles, a votary of Roosevelt, nurtured his vision. She saw things as a choice between "a land where people live, where there are homes, schools, a community" or a desolate landscape "where no one lives, where you just raise food and then you truck people in, a migrant people . . . where the children don't go to school, they live under impossible conditions, they don't have health treatment, they work at low wages." She concluded that Downey must be punished for his apostasy and she resolved to challenge him in the Democratic primary.

"La Gahagan," as her staff and others called her, was a marvelous piece of work. Tall and lovely, with a seraphic voice and a million-bucks grin, she had defied her wealthy parents, dropped out of Barnard College, and starred on Broadway in the Roaring Twenties. Columnist Heywood Broun famously called her "ten of the twelve most beautiful women in the world," and she married a dashing actor, Melvyn Douglas. The couple moved to Hollywood and joined the phalanx of movie stars in left-wing politics, an enthusiasm amplified by her 1937 singing tour of Europe, which took Douglas to Germany. When she got home she "joined everything anti-Nazi I could join," she recalled.

Douglas was particularly moved by the plight of the California farmworkers. She was drawn to action: visiting the migrants in their squalid camps, organizing Christmas parties for their children, testifying before Congress, and stoking the already formidable impact of John Steinbeck's book *The Grapes of Wrath*. She and her husband were invited to the White House and befriended by Franklin and Eleanor. By 1940 Helen was a Democratic national committeewoman, and in 1944 she won a downtown Los Angeles congressional seat.

In Congress, Helen was—like her friend Jerry Voorhis—more show horse than workhorse. "She had an artistic mind rather than an orderly mind," as one follower put it. But Douglas was an earnest diva, putting in the necessary hours of study to master the issues, facing down mossbacks like John Rankin, and winning the regard of Democratic leaders Sam Rayburn and John McCormack. She used the House as a platform to speak out for civil liberties, for women, for civil rights, and the African American veterans of World War II. She conveyed her enthusiasms for Henry Wallace, for the United Nations, and for international control of atomic energy. And she opposed the Truman Doctrine, HUAC, and bills policing Communists.

"The well-to-do regard her as a traitor to her class. . . . The conservatives regard her as a confidential agent of Stalin," wrote her chief strategist, Ed Lybeck, candidly assessing her weaknesses in a memo. "The Communists regard her as a Social Fascist (whatever the hell that is). . . . The Daughters of the Confederacy (there are a lot of them) refer to her as a 'nigger-lover.' . . . The Catholics (heavy in the South West section) will always regard her as an agent of the Anti-Christ because she supported the Spanish Loyalists. . . . She talks and votes against the Tidelands oil steal. . . . Money is almost impossible to get." Furthermore, "hers is the wrong sex politically," Lybeck said. She met resentment and envy "on the part of men who figure they should have the job and on the part of women who think that she's got what they haven't."

With the surety conveyed by lifelong celebrity, Douglas, forty-nine, waved off critics. When Melvyn was serving in the military overseas, she barely hid her romantic fling with Lyndon Johnson. She refused to gauge or alter course in response to more conservative breezes. She was well cast—La Pasionaria of the American left—and the Eastern press had many kind things to say about this glamorous oddity: a confident, swell-looking star giving a fine performance in a man's role. For her fellow liberals, her passion could be mesmerizing. "We regarded her as a lady, as an angel, as someone . . . we admired and loved," said labor organizer Tilford Dudley.

India Edwards, a more levelheaded Democrat, spoke of how the Douglas "idolaters" persuaded themselves that the congresswoman's "aura" would carry the day. "They just allowed their admiration and worship—it amounted to that—of Helen to do away with whatever common sense they might have had."

The state's Democratic chieftains implored Douglas to drop her schismatic challenge. They promised to clear the field if she would run against Republican senator William Knowland in 1952. When she declined, the party's moneymen urged her, at the least, to reverse her stand on the tidelands issue and tap the coffers of the oil industry. She refused. "As for money, I don't know where it's coming from," Douglas admitted to her top adviser. But she knew who would line up on the other side. "Oil money, utility money, Associated Farmers [agribusiness] money, plus real estate and NAM [National Association of Manufacturers] money poured in against me," she told a supporter, adding with bravado: "This doesn't frighten me one bit." She would rely on New Deal liberals, the state's labor unions, minorities, and her celebrity. And so she rode out to save the 160-acre limit and fulfill Roosevelt's dream, as she saw it, of "cheap power and land for the people."

"Downey is done for," she vowed. "A great liberal party cannot be built with such men." In October 1949 she declared herself a candidate.

NIXON, MEANWHILE, HAD been weighing the risks of "the Senator deal" since the summer of 1948. It had beckoned throughout his grueling march in the Hiss case, and as his status as a rising star in the House of Representatives diminished when the Democrats reclaimed the chamber. He may not have grasped the full extent of his party's dismal prospects—even Nixon's formidable analytic powers could not have detected that Republicans would control the House for just two of the next forty years—but he viewed with disdain the life of an ineffectual back-bencher. He had coasted to reelection in 1948, but several of his friends in Congress—two HUAC colleagues and his friend Charles Kersten among them—had lost their seats as Truman and the Democrats rallied to beat Dewey, a lesson on the flukiness of politics. The Senate race, on the other hand, had allure. With Republican governor Earl Warren and Republican lieutenant governor Goodwin "Goodie" Knight, the road through Sacramento was congested. Bill Knowland, the scion of a Northern California newspaper family, appeared to have a lock on the state's other Senate seat. In the foreseeable future, challenging Downey was Nixon's best opportunity for advancement.

And advancing was on his mind. The Senate campaign is the first instance in which young Dick Nixon, a second-term congressman not yet forty, let slip that the reach of his own ambition extended to the White House. In the spring of 1950, in several speeches, he defended his lack of experience by comparing himself to Abraham Lincoln, the unknown ex-congressman who used the fame of his debates with U.S. senator Stephen Douglas to propel himself to the presidency in 1860. "I must very strongly urge" that Nixon drop the analogy, wrote Bernard Brennan, a new adviser. "I know that you do not mean it in the way that it sounds as it hits the audience, but the reaction is that . . . your course of conduct will lead you to the presidency.

"I firmly believe that it ultimately will, and I have so expressed myself in a few intimate groups," Brennan wrote, urging Nixon to burn the letter once read. "But it could be very damaging to have this impression get out."*

BRENNAN WAS ON hand because, as Nixon contemplated his latest quest, he had shuffled his advisers. In January 1949, the irascible Frank Jorgensen had hosted Herman Perry and Roy Day and a few others for dinner at his San Marino home, where he found his fellow Amateurs conflicted. "Herman stated that he was of the opinion that you would be wise to continue your service in the House," Jorgensen reported to Nixon. "Day felt that you could whip Abraham Lincoln, if necessary, in the senator fight." Perry was fretting about his pals in the oil industry, who would not want to risk their investment on so speculative a venture.

Quietly, Nixon dispatched Jorgensen to woo Brennan, a Los Angeles attorney who led the Glendale Kiwanis, served as a director of the metropolitan water authority, and had helped run the Warren and Dewey campaigns in Southern California. Like Jorgensen, Brennan was in his late

---

* On several occasions in his career, Nixon was counseled by his advisers to burn potentially injurious evidence and declined to do so.

forties, old enough to see the chance and young enough to chase it. He was "crafty and clever and devious," one of California's pioneering political PR men, Herbert Baus, would recall. Brennan signed on immediately and, in the course of an intense, three-hour dinner, gave Jorgy the lowdown on the state's political landscape. Before a month was out, Brennan and Nixon were confidants, and Perry's influence was fading.

"I have never been insistent on 'sure-fire' deals," Nixon told Brennan in a March 14 letter. All he wanted was "a good fighting chance" and "I would be inclined to take it."

DICK HAD PAT to consider, as well. A Senate race was a big leap, which Nixon could not make without her. Like millions of postwar couples coping with the outcome of the baby boom, they were seeking a measure of permanency and shopping for a house in the suburbs. He found a local developer, William Hughes, who offered them a sweet deal on a home he was building on Honeysuckle Lane, on the southern flanks of Whittier. Their first stake in the American Dream was a flat-roofed one-story dwelling with a single bathroom and a party line for the telephone, on a tract beside a golf club.

The local gossips feasted on the news. "There is some concern *around here about your house deal.* What is the score?" Herman Perry wrote Nixon. It was "perfectly legitimate," Dick replied, employing a phrase that, when deployed to assure legitimacy, should always stir the skeptic. Years later, Hughes acknowledged that "I gave him an extra good price." But when Hughes tried to throw in the appliances as well, Nixon had insisted on buying his own, just as he purchased his Oldsmobiles, from friendly dealers in town. He reasoned that the $13,000 price tag for the house (and whatever break he got on his car and refrigerator) was justified by the promotional value the businessmen reaped by having a congressman as a customer.

Pat found reasons to sign on for the yearlong Senate campaign. Despite her frustrations with politics, she still saw her husband as a paladin—not a time-biding hack like so many of his colleagues, ploddingly compiling seniority in the House. And a Senate term was six years long—offering time to catch one's breath, and spend time with the family. California was a huge state, with a growing role in national politics, and Dick would need to spend time on the road—but he'd no longer face the biennial roulette of a member of the House. They thought that in the Senate they might find "a little more peace," Nixon recalled.

WITH PAT ON board, Dick drew up a checklist of hurdles. He needed funds—$100,000 to $125,000 to start, Perry told him—to demonstrate the dream was viable. He had to obtain the blessings of Bill Knowland and Earl Warren—and Lieutenant Governor Goodie Knight would need to stay out of the Senate race. For all this, and more, it was essential that Nixon secure the support of Kyle Palmer, the political editor of the *Los Angeles Times*. Palmer, Nixon recognized, was the "decisive factor."

The *Times* had emerged from the din of frontier days as the Southland's journalistic, and political, behemoth. Its owners were descendants of General Harrison Gray Otis, a fierce, walrus-like reactionary whose rapacity was matched only by his hatred of labor unions—who bombed his newspaper in retaliation, killing twenty, in 1910. Otis and his son-in-law, Harry Chandler, were instrumental in the scheme to steal water for Los Angeles from the far-off Owens Valley, securing both the city's growth and the soaring value of the land they owned via secret real estate syndicates. Otis "sits there in senile dementia with gangrene heart and rotting brain, grimacing at every reform, chattering impotently at all things that are decent, frothing, fuming, violently gibbering, going down to his grave in snarling infamy," said the Progressive candidate Hiram Johnson when running for governor in 1910.

Norman Chandler was the general's handsome grandson. He was not as truculent as his buccaneering forebears, and so did not inspire such florid vilification. But Norman was as determined to keep California booming, business friendly, and safe from profligate liberals. The *Times* allied itself with two conservative newspapers from Northern California— the *Oakland Tribune* and the *San Francisco Chronicle*—and could usually rely on the right-wing populists in the Hearst chain to join them in countering liberal influence. In 1949 the *Times* was rich, domineering, and everywhere. Its core readership was "a tightly-knit cohesive group, piously voting the behests of the *Los Angeles Times* and absolutely impervious to propaganda, threat, cajolery or thought," wrote a Democratic strategist. Norman's happy duty was to perpetuate its success. And since he didn't care for the grime of politics, he let Kyle be "the kingmaker," Californian H. R. Haldeman, Nixon's future White House chief of staff, would recall. "Nixon was one of the kings he decided to make, and did."

Palmer, jolly cynic and voluptuary, was, as might be expected in a native Tennessean, a marvelous little raconteur. He would host Republican hopefuls at his table at Perrino's restaurant or have them to his home on the beach at Malibu, where they shared highballs and fine wines with local elites, then moved to the dining room, perched above the ocean, for a splendid meal, drinks, and cigars—pausing in unspoken, common reverence at the moment when the sun dipped into the sea. "Kyle was always living over his head, and there was always a new wife," Norman's wife Dorothy grumbled. But the columnist was an indispensable Thomas Cromwell—scheming, twisting arms, and bringing ruin to candidates who did not kowtow. "Kyle came into Warren's office as a publisher, not a reporter," recalled Verne Scoggins, the governor's press aide. "They knew that he was speaking as the voice of Norman Chandler."

There were a few Democrats, like then attorney general Edmund "Pat" Brown, who could sweet-talk Palmer. But what Kyle really liked were Republicans who *won:* the popular Warren, despite his liberal lapses, was a favorite. The anointed received loving treatment, and their foes simply vanished from the pages of the *Times.* "Forget it," Palmer told Turner Catledge, who showed up to cover a California election for the *New York Times* and marveled at the blackout treatment given left-leaning candidates. "We don't go for that kind of crap that you have back in New York—of being obliged to print both sides."

When Nixon made his trek to the *Times's* downtown fortress back in 1946, Palmer had introduced him to Norman Chandler and commended his starry-eyed campaign against Jerry Voorhis in a patronizing column. The *Times* had not clambered aboard the bandwagon until the last days of Nixon's race, and Palmer was too good at what he did not to recognize his error. He kept watch on Nixon in Washington, through the Herter mission and the Hiss affair, and became a Nixon enthusiast.

TRADITION WAS ON Nixon's side, for Northern and Southern California generally split the state's two Senate seats. When then senator Hiram Johnson died in 1945, the Chandlers had supported the Knowland family—publishers of the *Oakland Tribune* and Governor Warren's longtime sponsors—when the governor named young Bill Knowland to fill the vacancy. The Warren-Knowland forces were thus obliged to back the *Times* in the selection of the 1950 nominee. "Whoever the *Times* lays its hands on for the race in 1950 . . . all three newspapers will support," Jorgensen told Nixon, in a three-page, single-spaced report on his discussions with Brennan. They urged Nixon to keep wooing Palmer. He did so, with success. "Through Kyle Palmer we have been in touch with Nixon," Norman Chandler informed a friend in mid-July. "He will receive *Times* support should he decide to enter the race."

Nixon was thrilled. Palmer "was always looking for talent, always looking for bench strength," said Robert Finch, a young Republican operative who knew both men well. Nixon became Palmer's "protégé." He represented youth, for one thing—that new generation, home from war, free of musty thinking. The bold young man who brought down Alger Hiss was ideally suited for a state whose rootless electorate was wont to reward image over experience. On the far side of the country, John Kennedy had won his House seat with the slogan "A New Generation Offers a Leader." Like Kennedy, Nixon seemed fresh, modern, and in tune with the coming age of expressways, jet airplanes, ad men, television, and teeming suburbs.

In California, new was almost always good. And Palmer was seeing his state transmogrify. The 1950 census would reveal that California had doubled in size in the two decades since 1930, with a population of more than 10 million people. It would double again by 1970. With all those new residents came new seats in Congress, and more clout in the Electoral College. Palmer had a vision of a California president, beholden to the *Times.* Warren had sought the White House and settled for a spot as Dewey's running mate in 1948. The governor would no doubt try again in 1952. But if Warren could not cinch the crown, then maybe one day Nixon could. "Kyle was influential in creating the image of Nixon the white knight . . . the clean young war veteran . . . good family . . . straight . . . modern guy," the state's longtime Democratic leader, Paul Ziffren, recalled.

Nixon was "a remarkable figure," Palmer told his readers. "Young enough to be bold and wise enough to be prudent. . . . If ever you saw a young man eager for the fray, full of vitality and strong of purpose, that man is Richard Nixon."

PALMER'S IMPRIMATUR WAS a signal for Southern California fund-raisers to start collecting money, and for Warren and Knowland to come aboard. Meanwhile, the newsman passed the word to Knight and other potential Senate candidates: if you want the paper's friendship, find another contest. Other shoots were thriving. Since the day they had met in the South Pacific during the war, Nixon had courted and supported the quixotic Republican presidential hopeful Harold Stassen of Minnesota. Now Stassen's California followers returned the favor, giving Nixon an all-important base in Northern California. "Being somewhat of a gambler, it would seem to me that the gamble on the state-wide race is not as great as the one we took in going against Voorhis," Nixon wrote Day. "Some people will say that there was not so much to lose then as there is now, but I am not inclined to agree."

"Although it is admittedly a long shot," Nixon wrote Jorgensen, "it presents such an unusual opportunity that the risk is worth taking." The GOP would retake the House only if there was a Republican wave in 1950, Nixon reasoned, and if that was the case why not ride it to the Senate? "I do not see any great gain in remaining a member of the House," he confided, "if it means that we would simply be a vocal but ineffective minority."

When Congress adjourned at the end of August, Dick packed Pat and the girls into the car and drove to California. He hoped to spend time on the beach, meet with his closest advisers, make a speaking tour of Northern California, and reach a final decision. It was time to "either get in or get out," he told Day. "When a man's star is up, he has to go," Day told the others.

Brennan agreed to act as a campaign chairman, and he and Jorgensen met with Murray Chotiner, who was hired as the day-to-day manager. Nixon was in Washington, that fall, when word came that Helen Douglas was going to challenge Downey. Her emergence as a picador in a gory Democratic corrida clinched the deal. Perry's allies in the oil business made one last attempt to rein in the congressman, but Nixon brushed them off. In early November, at the same Pomona clubhouse where he launched his race for the House in 1946, he announced his candidacy for the U.S. Senate.

The choice, he told his audience, was nothing less than liberty or bondage. They could dress it up, but Truman's stewardship of FDR's legacy was "the same old socialist baloney any way you slice it," Nixon said. "We must put on a fighting, rocking, socking campaign," he said. "We will raise a banner of freedom."

CAMPAIGNS CAN BE memorable when candidates and strategists mesh seamlessly with each other and the times. For Richard Nixon and Murray Chotiner, 1950 was such a year. They were hungry and driven, willing to spend a year of eighteen-hour workdays. They were drill sergeants: insistent that all factors were considered, all details attended, and every order met. They were ruthless. And they were righteous. They believed that Downey was weak and sick, needing to be culled from the herd, and that Helen Douglas, given the opportunity, would cuddle up to Stalin and destroy the American way.

Attack was Chotiner's metier. "There are many people who say we don't want that kind of campaign in our state. They say we want to conduct a constructive campaign," he would tell attendees at a GOP campaign school. "I say to you in all sincerity that if you do not deflate the opposition candidate before your own campaign gets started, the odds are that you are going to be doomed." He was a student of Machiavelli, and had a Hobbesian view of democracy. He urged his students to develop a strong back—the better to thwart backstabbers—and a thick neck, to "withstand those who are going to try to slice your throat." Chotiner liked to quote Teddy Roosevelt: "The law of life is the fundamental law of strife." He appealed to Nixon's truculent side—to a dark streak inherited from his father. "Sometimes I loathed Murray Chotiner—we all did," wrote journalist Adela Rogers St. Johns in a letter to Nixon a few years later. "He was a brute in many ways. But never, never, never was he cold or indifferent and NEVER once in my whole time in the early campaigns did I hear him say 'I'—or Chotiner—never. He was violent, hot and NIXON, NIXON, NIXON."

Chotiner asked for an exorbitant sum—$60,000, Jorgensen recalled—to run the campaign, and settled for $937.50 a month to start. He immediately went to work on the pending details. The campaign lacked a worthy photograph of the candidate for its advertising and press releases . . . 20th Century Fox would donate the services of a photographer . . . the session would take place at the movie studio, "around nine o'clock in the morning when one's facial characteristics are best," he told Nixon. They would then travel to the office, where "the letters to the State and County Committee members will be ready for your signature. . . . We can put them in the mail that same day." The campaign's starting budget, of around $3,500 per month, doubled in November to tout Nixon's candidacy with ads in 117 newspapers and a live statewide radio broadcast. By the June primary, Chotiner had organized three thousand volunteers. His rules were specific, and all were accountable. As each county chairman declared himself for Nixon, Chotiner sent him a list of what the campaign pledged to provide: leased billboards, four statewide radio broadcasts, forty inches of advertising for the local newspaper, prepared radio spots, and press releases. Each county, Chotiner instructed, would be expected to raise its own funds for local newspaper, radio, and television ads, and to tailor and run direct mail, door-to-door, and phone bank operations.

Nixon's immediate challenge was to become known by millions of people outside his district who had barely heard of him—in cities like San Diego and San Francisco, in the new suburban subdivisions, and in far-flung rural counties. In late 1949, Chotiner and an aide embarked on a listening tour of California—calling on dozens of local publishers and editors, asking their opinions, and inquiring about campaign advertising rates. "As soon as a man announces his candidacy . . . the newspapers feel that if he wants publicity he can come around and start . . . advertising," Chotiner recalled. Chotiner wrote summaries of his visits so Nixon could replay the newsmen's opinions back to them, flattering the journalists when they met. It helped, as well, that Murray followed up by sending cases of liquor to the newsrooms at Christmas.

Recognizing that North and South had different political cultures—the San Francisco Bay Republicans being more cosmopolitan—Nixon's team set up separate campaign committees for the two halves of the state. John Dinkelspiel, an attorney and World War II veteran, led the Northern California campaign with a core of enthusiasts who had been drawn together in support of Stassen's presidential ambitions and found the same forward-thinking qualities in Nixon. "Like all young warriors, you have dreams of a better country when you return," Dinkelspiel recalled.

In a conversation with Representative Hugh Scott of Pennsylvania, Chotiner heard of a Republican candidate who had traveled through Philadelphia in a sound truck playing music and then parked on a corner to offer a few remarks. "Now there is nothing new in using a sound truck in a campaign," Chotiner told Nixon. "But the candidate doesn't very often go along with it. . . . If you will do this there is no question in my mind that within one week the word will spread throughout the entire state that Dick Nixon is on the march, and that he is putting on the kind of campaign that will make old Sheridan Downey tremble."

In the margin of the memo, Nixon wrote, "Yes" and underlined it twice. They refined the idea, and Dick and Pat hit the road in a wood-paneled Mercury, on loan from a friendly car dealer. "He and his party will be traveling in a station wagon, which will be equipped with record playing equipment and public address system," Chotiner instructed the local chairmen. "The car will stop at some suitable place in a particular community. The driver of the car will play a couple of records to attract a crowd, and Dick will then make a five or ten minute informal talk to those who gather." To each local leader went detailed instructions on greeting the candidate as he entered town, staging a fifteen-minute walk through the central business district ("to meet the people on 'Main Street' such as barbers, druggists, clerks etc."), arranging for interviews with the local newspaper or radio station, and drumming up a crowd to hear Nixon speak from his perch on the hood or tailgate.

CHOTINER WAS MORE than a mechanic. As a researcher, and strategist, he helped cast Nixon's message. California, with its aspiring families and their middle-class values, was primed to go Republican—but what kind of Republican? Chotiner had learned from watching Earl Warren, who wooed voters with government services. After witnessing Dewey's 1948 collapse, Chotiner warned that the Republican Party must not be just the party of "No." He used health care as an example, and a mythical "Tom Jones" family to illustrate the point. "Tom Jones wants his own family doctor; he wants a doctor who knows all about him, his wife, and children. He likes to think of his doctor as his family counselor," Chotiner wrote. "But Tom Jones knows that if a serious illness should strike one of his family, he couldn't pay the doctor or hospital bills; or if he has been able to save up something over a period of years his life savings will be wiped out.

"So what happens? The [Truman] plan of health insurance sounds good to him because it tells him it will take care of his doctor and hospital bills. What does the Republican Party do? It shouts from the housetops and cries to the world that this is socialized medicine."

Well, "maybe it is," Chotiner wrote, "but the Republican Party must do something more than point out the evils of the administration's plan—it must show that it is ready to meet the needs of Tom Jones when illness strikes."

And so Congressman Nixon joined with other Republican moderates to introduce a national health insurance plan in which the states and federal governments would subsidize the purchase of insurance from private companies. "Our bill involves neither socialized medicine nor medicine for indigents only," the announcement said. "It recognizes that the problem of medical care for the people is urgent and that government should participate in its solution." In a state where the Democratic Party had a three-to-two advantage in registered voters, Nixon would have to corral hundreds of thousands of Democrats to win. The campaign needed "to present your sensible, firm side of the story in a simple, down-to-earth, personalized manner," Chotiner told him. Nixon had chosen a strategist who, like the candidate, was unapologetically pragmatic.

Chotiner had a final virtue: Kyle Palmer liked him and respected his judgment. When Republicans "down in the yacht club" sneered at Murray's streetwise manner and Jewish ancestry, Democratic leader Paul Ziffren recalled, it was Palmer who defended him. "When you are dying," Palmer told them, "you don't argue whether the doctor is Jewish." Merrell Small, an adviser of Governor Warren, was one of many who deplored Chotiner as a "shrewd little Jew." But Nixon didn't care—nor did he hesitate to back an Irish Catholic candidate named Patrick Hillings as his successor in the House, despite rampant anti-Catholicism in his district.

The Palmer connection clicked again when Nixon's last respectable Republican opponent—Judge Fred Houser—was endorsed by a subcommittee of the California Republican Assembly, a group of party activists meeting at Pebble Beach. On the Sunday that the full selection committee was to meet and ratify the choice, the *Los Angeles Times* took the remarkable step of endorsing "Nixon for U.S. Senator" in a stirring editorial, nine months before the election. The signal from the Chandlers did the trick. The Nixon forces reversed the subcommittee results, and he won the nod by a single vote.

Nixon was getting "the breaks," wrote Palmer. There was but one unhappy note: Perry and Day felt discarded—as did Nixon's 1946 campaign director Harrison McCall—watching Nixon ride off with Brennan and Chotiner. Day and Perry bickered, and Day quit the campaign for several months. "People who are going to choose up sides with Nixon should remember the poem about the chambered Nautilus—the little creature that always outgrows its shell," Ziffren would say. "Otherwise, they may be shocked when he sheds them."

IN THE CAMPAIGN press releases, Nixon was described as a "virile" and "fearless" and "red-blooded" defender of America. But his claim to these honorifics lay in his pursuit of Alger Hiss, and as 1949 turned toward 1950, the judicial system was not cooperating. Judge Samuel Kaufman had declared a mistrial after the jurors in the first Hiss trial announced that they were deadlocked. History has attributed the deadlock to a bravura performance by Lloyd Stryker, the defense attorney, but a petulant Nixon blamed the judge—and publicly called for an investigation of Kaufman and the jury foreman. He wrote long memos and funneled information and advice to the prosecutors. "As you probably realize Dick has a heck of a lot at stake in the outcome," journalist Victor Lasky wrote prosecutor Thomas Murphy. "I got a couple of things which he thought you should like to know, based on his many dealings with our boy, Alger."

Hiss cooperated in his own demise by switching lawyers. In the retrial it was Murphy who impressed, before a more sympathetic judge and jury, and on January 21, 1950, the spy was found guilty of perjury.

When pinned down by reporters and asked for his reaction to the Hiss verdict, Secretary of State Acheson directed them to the Gospel of Matthew, in which Jesus instructed his followers to show compassion to the sick, the destitute, and the imprisoned. Nixon stayed on the attack: Acheson's reference to the gospel was "disgusting," he said. There was no room for craven sentiments in the hunt to unclothe "traitors in the high councils of our own government."

Five days after the verdict, the thematic unveiling for Nixon's candidacy took place on the House floor. The title of his four-hour speech was "The Hiss Case—A Lesson for the American People." It was told like a detective story, tracking the spy hunt from start to finish, with Nixon as heroic sleuth. In the months ahead he had it reprinted and mailed across the land. The first salvo went to fifty thousand Democrats in Southern California, thirty thousand voters in the northern part of the state, and seven thousand newspapers around the country. It told the whole twisting tale of the Ford, the prothonotary warbler, and the papers in the pumpkin.

"We are not just dealing with espionage agents who get thirty pieces of silver to obtain the blueprints of a new weapon," Nixon said, but with "a far more sinister type of activity because it permits the enemy to guide and shape our policy."

A few days later, using that exact phrase and other sentiments that he cribbed from Nixon's speech, Senator Joseph McCarthy, the Republican from Wisconsin, launched the era that would bear his name.

"Tail Gunner Joe" was a roguish lout who had cast about for something to say in a series of Lincoln Day speeches in the hinterlands, and seized on the issue of Communist subversion. "I have here in my hand a list of 205—a list of names that were made known to the Secretary of State as being members of the Communist Party and who nevertheless are still working and shaping policy in the State Department," McCarthy told a gathering of Wheeling, West Virginia, Republicans on February 9. The Associated Press picked up the story and McCarthy was soon basking in national attention. When reporters demanded that the senator supply the names, McCarthy brushed them aside, often with a cynical wink. In truth, he had no such list, and the number was always changing, from 205 to 57 to 81. It did not matter. The witch hunt was on. He had his Hiss case. "I have found a pumpkin," McCarthy crowed.

McCarthy was a farm boy from an Irish Catholic family that had set-tled on the shores of Lake Winnebago. He had plowed his way through Marquette University, emerging with a law degree, and got himself elected a local judge. What credit he deserves for enlisting in the Marines at the age of thirty-three is tarnished by his brazen exaggeration of his war record upon returning home from the South Pacific.

Newspapers published searing editorials branding the senator as a demagogue. The Truman administration sneered at his tactics. Senate Democrats joined the fight, accosting McCarthy in a wild nighttime session on February 20—and discrediting the senator's allegations in weeks of special hearings. It made no difference. The Democrats only spurred the Republicans to defend one of their own. When Senator Margaret Chase Smith of Maine made an eloquent appeal to the conscience of her fellow Republican senators—"The nation sorely needs a Republican victory. But I don't want to see the Republican Party ride to political victory on the Four Horsemen of Calumny: fear, ignorance, bigotry and smear"—only a handful stood by her. The Red Scare, they were discovering, meant votes.

THE PESTILENCE OF "McCarthyism," as cartoonist Herblock dubbed it, flourished amid a cascade of events that marked 1950 as an especially fearful moment in the Cold War. Hiss was convicted on January 21. Ten days later, Truman announced that, in response to the Soviet Union's deto-nation of an atomic device, the United States would develop the hydro-gen bomb. A few days passed, and the government revealed how Klaus Fuchs and other Soviet spies had stolen America's atomic secrets. And as the weeks went by—as the Hollywood Ten were marched off to prison, and David Greenglass and Julius and Ethel Rosenberg were arrested and charged as spies—fear of Communism reached epic proportions. The Truman administration launched a review of U.S. national security policy, which led to proposals for a military buildup, and when Robert Oppen-heimer was asked for his advice, he told his interlocutors: "If one is hon-est the most probable view of the future is that of war, exploding atomic bombs, death, and the end of most freedom." It was that spring, with little note, and near-universal acquiescence, that Truman dismissed Franklin Roosevelt's qualms about aligning the United States on the wrong side of an anticolonial war of independence and approved the first multimillion-dollar aid package for French Indochina.

—

NIXON THOUGHT McCARTHY was a valuable ally, but reckless. He worried about a backlash. "Even when you are right, they will give you a rough time," Nixon advised the senator. "When you happen to be wrong, they will kill you." Nixon urged him to take pains to be accurate; to describe his prey as "fellow travelers" and security threats and not—as could not be proven—as "card-carrying Communists." McCarthy beefed up his staff with veterans of the Bentley and Hiss affairs and studied the files that Nixon gave him. "There was a certain identity of purpose which they had," McCarthy aide Roy Cohn recalled about Nixon and his boss, "which made them friendly."

In Northern California, John Dinkelspiel had qualms: he advised Brennan to "soft pedal" the issue. Nixon initially agreed. On more than one occasion in the spring of 1950, he spoke out on behalf of civil liberties, and he urged Truman to appoint a bipartisan commission to investigate McCarthy's charges. Not for the last time, Nixon defended Oppenheimer, whose left-wing dalliances in the 1930s had made him a quarry of the Red hunt. NIXON CHAMPIONS DR. OPPENHEIMER, read the headline in the *New York Times,* and Oppenheimer wrote to thank him. "Dick Nixon fired with a rifle, not with a shotgun," said Malcolm Champlin, a Northern California supporter, describing the difference between Nixon and McCarthy.

But as Nixon saw the mail pour in, read the editorials from the heartland, and heard the roar of the crowds, he and Chotiner were persuaded that it was time to dust off the tactics they had used against Voorhis. Commie bashing was always on Nixon's dance card; now it became his constant companion.

"I do not question the advisability of placing more emphasis upon other issues than un-American activities as the campaign develops. However, I do know that outside of so-called intellectual circles, the Hiss case has been tremendously effective in getting us the support we need," Nixon advised Brennan on March 3. "As Murray will tell you, literally hundreds of letters have come in from all over the country . . . most people have pledged their support as a result of the case . . . editorials have been written."

In April, Nixon learned that a condensed version of *Seeds of Treason,* a book on the Hiss case written with Nixon's cooperation by journalists Victor Lasky and Ralph de Toledano, would be published in *Reader's Digest,* the nation's biggest-selling magazine. The campaign prepared to mail out 500,000 reprints. In May, a nasty Red-baiting campaign waged by Congressman George Smathers unseated the leftist senator Claude Pepper in the Florida Democratic primary. Nixon met with Smathers and obtained a copy of *The Red Record of Senator Claude Pepper,* the pamphlet the Florida congressman had distributed. "If Helen is your opponent," Karl Mundt advised Nixon, "something of a similar nature might well be prepared."

And it was in May that the Republican senatorial committee in Washington mailed out a fact sheet to GOP Senate hopefuls: an analysis of the congressional voting records of Democratic candidates, showing their similarities to that of the very left-wing representative Vito Marcantonio of East Harlem. It was a hoary ploy, which Republican tacticians had been using for years. But it seemed to have fresh resonance in that spring of 1950, and Chotiner passed the Douglas-Marcantonio comparison to friends in the press.

"There's no use trying to talk about anything else," Nixon told Dinkelspiel. "It's all the people want to talk about."

THE DEMOCRATIC PRIMARY was as tumultuous as the times. Downey rattled the contest in early March by leaking word that he would not seek reelection. Then he reconsidered and announced he would run. But by month's end he was out of the race for good, pleading ill health. Replacing Downey as the candidate of the establishment Democrats was Manchester Boddy, the publisher of the Los Angeles *Daily News*.

As a candidate, Boddy was more than a crank—but just. He had started life as a poor farm boy, lifted himself by selling flatirons, pots and pans, and encyclopedias door-to-door, and arrived in California to nurse his lungs after being gassed on the Western Front during World War I. He purchased the liberal *News* after its owners ran it into bankruptcy, bet on the popularity of the New Deal, and rode Roosevelt's coattails to wealth and respectability. But the *News* returned to its natural state of insolvency after the war, and only huge loans from local business interests kept the paper afloat. Boddy wasn't only a hit man for the oilmen and others in the anybody-but-Douglas camp, but that was one role he played. Starting late, little known, he never had a chance.

Boddy's contribution to the contest was his hammering of Douglas, as he sought to capitalize on the public's anxiety over the Communist threat. He linked her to Marcantonio and christened her "the Pink Lady." On the eve of the primary, Downey joined in. Smarting from his treatment by the congresswoman, he told a statewide radio audience that Douglas was fine at "reading the lines provided by her publicity agents" but "failed utterly" to possess "the fundamental ability and qualifications" to serve in the Senate. She had voted against the Truman Doctrine, and against more funding for HUAC. In doing so, Downey said, she "gave comfort to the Soviet tyranny."

HARD WORK MAKES Fortune friendly. In early April, Dick and Pat set off in their station wagon on a pilgrimage that would take them fifteen thousand miles over the next two months. A wall map at campaign headquarters tracked their progress through the boondocks. Their days were long, unforgivingly so. They started on April 3 in Maricopa and Bakersfield, at the bottom of the Central Valley, where Nixon blasted the "socialistic planners" and "political demagogues" who supported the 160-acre limit on water. The most grinding stretch began on Monday morning, April 10, after a brief break for Easter. They left Fresno at 7:30 a.m. and at 8 they were in Clovis, twelve miles away, for a breakfast meeting. By 9:30 they had driven another fifteen miles, to Sanger. Then seventeen miles to Orange Cove. Seven miles to Orosi. Six miles to Dinuba. They had lunch at Reedley and progressed that afternoon through Kingsburg, Selma, Riverdale, Carruthers, and Fowler before heading back to Fresno for an early-evening reception and a nighttime public meeting that returned them to their hotel room just before midnight.

The next day, and the day after, and the days after that were more of the same: the woody arriving at a town; the music drawing a crowd; Dick shaking hands on Main Street, standing on the tailgate to speak and take questions, and then packing up, waving good-bye; and on up the highway, through the fields, to the next crossroads, a dozen or so miles away. As Dick spoke, Pat distributed thimbles emblazed with the motto SAFEGUARD THE AMERICAN HOME.

When they passed through Lindsay, Nixon noted some familiar faces in the audience. His footloose uncle Ezra had finally settled there with his nine children, who seemed similarly fertile. "Will my relatives please stand up?" the candidate asked. A third of the crowd rose, to general applause and laughter. Lying awake in the middle of the night, Dick would review the next day's schedule in his mind, analyzing his upcoming audiences. On the road between stops, he would scrawl four or five ideas on the back of his itinerary. Nixon liked to walk around a town or city before he spoke, to get a feel for the community. He tried to arrive early at his events and listened with one ear to the chatter in the background as he met and greeted folks. "You get the feel and you get the way the wind is blowing," he told a friend.

The reviews were good. In Berkeley, Nixon spoke at Sather Gate at the

University of California. "To the great surprise of most of us," a Douglas supporter warned her, "he gave a magnificent speech." Nixon had defused critics and silenced the hecklers. "If he is only a fraction as effective as he was here you have a formidable opponent on your hands." Her opponent was "impressive," Douglas would concede. "He had the appearance of a worried, decent man courageously doing his best for his country." Seeming to be "perplexed and concerned," Nixon would ask the crowds: "Why has she followed the Communist line so many times?"

With Boddy and Douglas clawing at each other, Nixon saw a chance to repeat his 1948 coup and claim the nomination of both parties. Perry was dispatched to raise funds from the Bank of America and the oil industry, and a mailing was sent out to Democratic voters, detailing Nixon's wartime experience, lovely family, and congressional record—and somehow failing to mention that he was, in fact, a Republican. Boddy howled, and charged Nixon with duplicity. A full-page ad in the *News* warned the voters to beware of "Tricky Dick."

DOUGLAS AND NIXON prevailed in their party primaries and squared off for a battle in the fall. Nixon marked victory by hosting a weekend get-together of his top advisers at the San Ysidro Ranch outside Santa Barbara, where they discussed the novel challenge that he would face by running against a woman. Chotiner had been wrestling with the matter for a while. In a long memo, he made the case for abolishing the luxury tax, a wartime holdover that covered, among other things, cosmetics and handbags. "It is an established fact that women can best be appealed to emotionally," Chotiner wrote. They could be counted on to "wax enthusiastic about a man who lets them know—in a dignified way, of course—that he likes his women pretty and he likes them feminine and understands that women have found that cosmetics are a necessity if they are to keep their jobs and men."

As for handbags, "men have pockets in their pants. Women do not have pockets. There is no place for them to carry their wallets, grocery lists, fountain pens, compacts, cigarettes and the thousand and one other items that a woman carries," Chotiner said. "Of course, they *could* have pockets large enough, but it would not do much for their pretty figures to be weighed down and bulged out by such a variety of lumps and bumps."

Many of these adorable, dizzy dames, scheming to keep their men, would doubtless resent Helen Douglas, Chotiner said. Her decision to leave the home and venture into the manly world of politics would be seen as a quiet rebuke to women who chose, in keeping with culture, church, and state, the prescribed roles of wife and mom, secretary, nurse, or teacher.

But for all Chotiner's musing about lipstick and curvy figures, he and Nixon concluded that, with the headlines screaming about Joe McCarthy, the Pink Lady route was surest. It had to be handled delicately—Nixon could not be seen as a bully. Best to counterpunch: to wait for Douglas to launch the first attack, portray her as a harridan, and return fire. The campaign was still making plans when Nixon returned to Congress for a short summer session. On June 24, like most of official Washington, he left the sultry capital for cooler climes. He was on his way to California when the news broke that the North Korean Communists, supported by Stalin and Mao, had invaded South Korea.

The United States was again at war. Communism was no theoretical danger: the soldiers killing American boys were driving Soviet tanks and wearing red stars. The reeling U.S. and South Korean forces were trapped in the "Pusan Perimeter," in the southeast corner of the Korean peninsula. There would be no Dunkirk. "We will die fighting together," the American commander told his troops. The news from the front was grim until September, when General Douglas MacArthur outflanked the North Koreans with a daring amphibious landing at Inchon. Now it was the Reds who fled, and MacArthur chased them north toward the border with China, unfazed by reports that Chinese "volunteers" had begun to join the fighting.

Nixon and Douglas supported President Truman in this moment of crisis. Nixon remained a believer in the lesson of Munich—that aggression must be met with strength. That summer, he shared the company of former president Hoover at "Cave Man Camp" in the annual Bohemian Grove encampment near Sonoma, where Dwight Eisenhower was a featured speaker. If Ike gave a perceptive critique of Truman's or MacArthur's handling of the war, Nixon chose not to record it. He was most impressed by the effect of the Eisenhower "mystique" on the conservative Old Guard campers.

DOUGLAS AND HER advisers were not fools. They had seen what happened to Voorhis in 1946, and watched Downey and Boddy twist and distort her record in the spring. She concluded that a preemptive attack on Nixon was her best hope. He had voted against a $60 million aid bill for South Korea the previous January. With that vote, she now charged, Nixon had helped cause the Korean War. The bill's failure had thrown the Korean economy "into panic," she declared, and "may have convinced Moscow" that "America was so divided and so little interested in Korea . . . that aggressive action could be taken there without fear of effective resistance."

Nixon fumed. He had voted against the measure, he contended, because the bill had not included funds for Chiang Kai-shek's regime on the island of Formosa. It was a typical play on the Hill—to hold out for something better by opposing the original proposal—just the kind of legislative quirk that Nixon had exploited when distorting Jerry Voorhis's record. But Douglas (unlike Nixon in 1946) didn't have the press on her side, to make the charge stick. Quite the opposite: in a Sunday column, Palmer mocked her "ridiculous linking of Nixon with her old legislative pal and collaborator, Marcantonio."

By striking first, Douglas opened herself to Nixon's onslaught. It would have come regardless, but she gave Nixon an opportunity to retaliate from the advantageous pose of affronted innocent. To supplement the Marcantonio material, Nixon had hired right-wing researcher and polemicist Edna Lonigan, a conspiracist who believed that Douglas was a Soviet agent and that the labor movement and the Democratic Party—even the New York state Republican Party, led then by Governor Thomas Dewey—had been "taken over" by Communists. Lonigan spent the summer poring over old copies of the *Daily Worker* and aggregating names from the letterheads of left-wing organizations. She decided that while there was no clear evidence of Douglas's treason, "every word and action . . . conforms to a precise pattern, as if one of the ablest [Communist] strategists wrote the words, and she delivered them." The "pattern" was a blueprint for a Communist takeover of America, drafted in Moscow itself, she concluded. "The Communist plan for 1950 is to secure as many places in Congress for active agents or stooges as possible, so that their Fifth Column can control our war preparations and confuse us to defeat."

Nixon brushed aside the ravings, but he studied Lonigan's reports, made suggestions, and otherwise encouraged her to keep digging. Chotiner thought they had all the ammo they needed. "You can take any vote and you can find that a man as conservative as Bob Taft voted the same way as Marcantonio for different reasons," he believed. That summer, he had one-page comparisons of the Douglas-Marcantonio voting records drawn up. In July, he printed a batch on pink paper and had them distributed throughout California. They caught on, and soon "the pink sheet" was a staple at Nixon events, with its warning about "the Douglas–Marcantonio

Axis." Some half a million copies were handed out. Chotiner would insist, over the years, that the color of the paper was an inadvertent choice. Nixon's files made no such claim. "The choice of the color pink was reasonable in that the word 'pinko' generally connoted one soft on Communism which was, indeed, Nixon's conclusion as to Mrs. Douglas," a memo from one of his other advisers noted.

"The comparison of Mrs. Douglas to Marcantonio was unfair," Nixon's friend and sometime aide Herb Klein would recall. It "left the wrong impression that the two had voted in alliance. Douglas was in no way closely associated with the New York congressman and voted independently. The pink sheet was a smearing distortion."

But Klein was not calling the shots. Brennan kicked off the fall campaign with an August 30 press release:

> During five years in Congress Helen Douglas has voted 353 times exactly as has Vito Marcantonio, the notorious Communist party-line congressman from New York. The import of the votes is more significant than their number.
>
> Both Helen Douglas and Marcantonio voted against establishing the Committee on Un-American Activities and on four separate times they have fought appropriations for investigations by the committee, which, among many other meritorious services, disclosed "the seeds of treason" sown by Alger Hiss.
>
> Helen Douglas and Marcantonio voted against military and economic aid to Greece and Turkey. Had they prevailed and had aid been denied, these countries would now be behind Communist Russia's Iron Curtain. They both opposed aid to anti-Communist China and to Formosa. They both sought to give Korea economic aid only, not the military assistance so desperately needed.
>
> Three times Helen Douglas and Marcantonio have voted in opposition to contempt proceedings against persons and organizations refusing to reveal records or answer whether they were Communists. Twice Helen Douglas and Marcantonio voted against loyalty checks for federal employees. They also voted against the Subversive Activities Control Act of 1948, requiring Communists and Communist-controlled organizations to register with the Attorney General. And even since Communist armies began their march into Korea, Helen Douglas and Marcantonio voted against the Security Bill. . . .
>
> How can Helen Douglas, capable actress that she is, take up so

strange a role as a foe of Communism? And why does she, when she has so deservedly earned the title of "the pink lady"? Perhaps she has just heard of the chameleon that changes color to suit conditions. Or perhaps Helen Douglas has decided pink isn't becoming anymore, or at least while we are in a bloody war with Communists.

Brennan's broadside set the tone. Chotiner's goal was to set all of California talking about Douglas and her treachery. He sent out a fat "Manual of Information" with an array of "Sample Statements" to Nixon supporters, showing them how to turn word of mouth in their communities against her. "Let's not forget that she favored giving away our atomic secrets, that she voted against aid to Greece and Turkey and that she opposed Communist-control legislation," a sample statement said. "All these votes gave comfort to the Communists." The words were carefully chosen. Giving "aid and comfort" to the enemy is a constitutional definition of treason. Accompanying the script were precise instructions on casting and timing: "To be used, if possible, by a woman coming to Nixon's defense right after Mrs. Douglas has been in your community."

AT THE END of August, Douglas faced a test of character when the old Mundt-Nixon bill, which had been reintroduced as the "Subversive Activities Control Act," came to the floor of the House. She could have cited the wartime emergency and, with 354 of her Democratic and Republican colleagues, voted for the legislation. Instead, she was one of just twenty to oppose it.

"I will not sacrifice the liberty of the American people on an altar of hysteria erected by those without vision, without faith, without courage, who cringe in fear before a handful of crackpots," she declared.

Just before the vote, she had called her campaign team in Los Angeles.

"You know what I am going to do . . ." she told them.

"Yes, Helen, we know," said an adviser, speaking for them all at headquarters.

"Okay," she said. "Just wanted to tell you, because you know what this might mean."

It was why they loved her. And why others believed she was a fool.

John Kennedy dropped by Nixon's office with a check for $1,000. His father, Kennedy told the startled Nixon staff, wanted their boss to win. Like the independent oilmen Edwin Pauley and John B. Elliott, and other royalist Democrats, the wealthy Joseph Kennedy voted with his checkbook.

"Isn't this something," Nixon marveled when he heard. "Isn't this something."

KYLE PALMER, MEANWHILE, was warming to the task of keelhauling Douglas. He began during the primary, calling her a "scolding woman" and urging Boddy to stop "pussyfooting" and "in a political sense, of course—to slap her around a little bit."

In early September, Palmer used some variation of the adjective *emotional* nine times in a column on Douglas. "The lady appears as a veritable political butterfly, flitting from flower to flower and bower to bower," he wrote. Bowers are garden structures, but the word is also used for bedrooms. She was "superficial" and "dramatic," wrote Palmer, and "emotionally attracted to the left wing doctrinaires of her day—the boys and girls whose views and objectives range all the way from the lighter shades of political pink to the deeper shades of red."

As for Nixon, he had "that something extra . . . a combination of rare humility, cold steel competence, an exceptionally keen mind and a comprehensive integrity that embraces not only his convictions but his willingness to fight for them."

FEW DAYS PASSED without a volley from Nixon that autumn. "The contest centers on . . . Communism," his campaign announced. In the pink sheets and bulletins, stump speeches and radio talks, he and his men drummed it over and over and over again. In early October, Nixon likened Douglas to Asian scholar Owen Lattimore—a favorite target of Joe McCarthy—and blamed her for the Korean War. "Mrs. Douglas aligned herself with the Lattimore clique in the State Department which adopted the appeasement policy in Asia that led to Korea," Nixon said, espousing Edna Lonigan's right-wing conspiracy theories. "This action by Mrs. Douglas has been established to have come just two weeks after [the American Communist leader] William Z. Foster transmitted his instructions from the Kremlin to the Communist national committee."

A few days later, on a statewide radio broadcast from Sacramento, Nixon once more raised the specter of treason: "If this had been the only act of my opponent which has given comfort to the Communists, we could ignore it. But it is not." He proclaimed that it was "time to take the gloves off."

"If there is a smear involved, let it be remembered that the record itself is doing the smearing," Nixon told a radio audience on October 24. "Mrs. Douglas made that record. I didn't."

On October 29, the Nixon campaign offered more of Lonigan's work: a list of the "Communist or subversive" organizations—like the Civil Rights Congress, a left-wing variant of the NAACP—with which Douglas had "associated." Her sin: she had spoken at one of its dinners, along with novelist Dashiell Hammett and the singer Paul Robeson.

"We do not say that Mrs. Douglas is a Communist," said the campaign press release. "We do say that both in and out of Congress she has been active for measures and causes that have been either inspired or approved by the Communist Party." This was "proof without a doubt that Helen Gahagan Douglas has given aid and comfort to the Communists."

In a scene out of the Salem witch trials, the Nixon campaign urged Douglas to "confess" and renounce her transgressions. It lamented, through crocodile tears, that "Mrs. Douglas remains deaf and blind to the redemptive possibilities of recantation."

WELL ORGANIZED, AND competently funded, the Nixon campaign chugged away. California was "a garden of Richard Nixon billboards," Douglas would recall. He kicked off the fall campaign with a jet-age version of a whistle-stop tour: flying from San Diego to Los Angeles to Fresno and San Francisco on September 18. Douglas coped as she could. She borrowed a tactic from Lyndon Johnson, who had used a helicopter to win a Senate seat in Texas in 1948, and hopped about the state in a copter, visiting town squares and farm wives in their kitchens. She engaged in her own bit of smearing when lumping Nixon with McCarthy in a "backwash of young men in dark shirts." To a labor audience she called Nixon a "demagogue" with a taste for "nice unadulterated fascism."

The Douglas campaign ran ads that scolded Nixon: "Thou Shalt Not Bear False Witness!" And when the *Independent Review,* a liberal publication, warned Californians to beware of "Nixon's Big Lie," she had the editorial distributed as a leaflet.

"Fairminded and thoughtful citizens of California are now beginning to realize that there is an organized and paid-for political conspiracy to defame Congresswoman Helen Gahagan Douglas by falsely accusing her through infamous insinuation and whispered innuendo of being a Communist," the editorial said. "Little Tricky Dick Nixon" and the "Nixon gang of political hatchetmen" were engaged in "a political lynching" that was "based on Hitler's theory that a lie, if repeated constantly, will finally be believed."

Yet Douglas was hamstrung by her shortage of money and the blackout by the press. Her campaign reported raising some $156,000, while Nixon later estimated that his campaign spent $750,000—a significant amount in those days before television was the preferred medium, and campaign costs soared.

Nixon was outperforming Douglas on the campaign trail as well. He gave his advisers the reins to criticize his performance. "Your speeches are too long," Brennan told him. He was using the phrase "in conclusion" three or four times per talk. It made people "restless, and increases their feeling that you do not have terminal facilities." Douglas had the same problem but, unlike Nixon, she failed to correct it. "She would stand there in the sun by the hour talking about the water," her aide Evelyn Chavoor recalled. "You can't go talk about 160-acre limitations, and reclamation and water when somebody is talking about your Communist leanings, and here we were in the midst of the war in Korea."

"For God's sake Helen, that's enough," Chavoor would plead.

"We had a tailgate rally at Douglas Aircraft with thousands of guys that belonged to the . . . unions gathered around. And what did Helen talk about? A hundred and sixty acres! They couldn't care less," campaign adviser Alvin Meyers remembered. "She was at the wrong place too often at the wrong time. . . . She often spoke about issues . . . with no relation to her audience."

Neither the White House nor the Democratic National Committee made a significant political investment in California. Truman made one nonpolitical speech in San Francisco. Other party headliners, like Vice President Alben Barkley, Averell Harriman, and Eleanor Roosevelt, failed to pierce the Red-baiting din. Nixon had broken the Democrats' spirit, Chavoor recalled: "With all this calumny poured down upon you day in and day out, day in and day out, you finally get an attitude of crawling into a shell." The Democratic drive in California was "a fantastically inept campaign," the liberal correspondent Carey McWilliams wrote in the *Nation*.

"The campaign management was horrible," Democratic strategist Don Bradley recalled. "We didn't know what ads were going to run, and hadn't met the payroll for quite a while . . . all kinds of communication problems. . . . It was a mess."

The tidings of a Democratic defeat were there in California's well-regarded Field Poll. In mid-October, Nixon was beating Douglas 39 to 27. By the end of the month, as the undecided voters took sides, Nixon's lead was solid, at 49–39. At that point, his cause was reinforced by the roar of newspaper headlines reporting the attacks by Chinese troops in Korea. As late as October 30, Americans had been assured that the allied drive through North Korea was proceeding with few hitches. On Wednesday, October 31, and for every day in that final week of the 1950 campaign, they were stunned by front-page reports that MacArthur's forces were being "chewed up" by the combined Red Chinese and North Korean armies, and retreating south in disarray.

Nixon leapt into a 13-point lead. Across the country, Senate candidates were riding Red-baiting into office. The events in Korea helped McCarthy and his allies bring down two Democratic antagonists he had targeted that fall: Senator Millard Tydings of Maryland—who had conducted the Senate investigation of McCarthy and his charges—and the Democratic Senate leader, Scott Lucas of Illinois.

Nixon capitalized on the setbacks in Korea with a final salvo, seizing on his opponent's reluctance to ban China from the United Nations. It was rough stuff.

"In the last few days and hours, the armed forces of an unfriendly government, Red China, have been thrown into the Korean War with the result that American forces are being forced to retreat, and are suffering heavy casualties," Nixon told the voters on the weekend before the election. "At this moment, a candidate seeking to represent the people of California in the highest legislative body in the land, the US Senate, which ratifies treaties and confirms presidential appointments, flatly refuses to answer the direct question as to whether she supports the government of Red China or whether she opposes it."

"Doesn't she read the newspapers?" Nixon asked. "Or doesn't she care whether American lives are being snuffed out by a ruthless aggressor?"

NIXON WAS ANXIOUS on Election Day. After voting in Whittier, he did some live TV spots and took Pat to the beach—then fled the chilly weather for a warm movie theater. They received the returns at his downtown headquarters that night. He had crushed Helen Douglas, with 59 percent of the vote. As the night progressed, Nixon went over to the *Times* to be interviewed on the Chandler-owned radio station. "His Senate victory was our victory," one of the paper's political reporters, Robert Hartmann, would recall.

Frank and Hannah, Don and his wife, and Pat accompanied Dick, and all were invited to celebrate his triumph, and have a bite to eat, in the publisher's upstairs apartment. The elder Nixons asked for milk to drink. But Dick took the Chandlers aside and asked if they could slip some bourbon in his milk: he didn't want Frank and Hannah to see him drinking. Dorothy found it distasteful, and peculiar, for a man to hide that from his parents. He was a United States senator, even if he was just thirty-seven years old.

The Great Train Robbery

RICHARD NIXON'S DEFEAT of Helen Douglas had not come without a cost. In his tilts with Voorhis, Hiss, and Douglas, Nixon had vanquished three bannerets of New Deal nobility. The left now identified him "as a menace to liberalism," Bryce Harlow, Republican strategist, recalled. "He was tough. He liked rolling in the dust."

"Voorhis was . . . the darling of Washington, D.C. The media, the liberals and the leftists of the day all loved Jerry," said Harlow. "So when Nixon came he was already marked. The Washington press disliked him before they met him."

Nixon then claimed fame by "unfrocking Alger Hiss—a most unsettling business, once again, for the liberal establishment," said Harlow. "He runs against a lady leftist from California and beats her too. . . . Now the Washington jackals had a hard fix on him."

It wasn't just Washington. The Senate race had smudged Nixon's name in California too. Douglas and her allies spent the last six weeks of her campaign trying to make Nixon's character the overriding issue. She failed, but her argument left its mark, along with the nickname Tricky Dick.

"We were not proud of Dick. . . . We felt that he was making a wrong persecution," said Nixon's old Orthogonian clubmate, Dean Triggs. "It wasn't ethical," his wife Jewel added.

"I was disgusted," said Richard Harris, still another Whittier classmate. "It was a smear campaign."

Nixon's family heard the grumbling. It was Dick's debate training, his uncle Oscar Marshburn suggested, that spurred him to be so aggressive. "Maybe his statements were misunderstood or maybe he got a little overambitious. I don't know," said Marshburn. He "may have made insinuations that he couldn't prove . . . and from the large group that was backing Helen Gahagan Douglas, these things could be interpreted as maybe being dirty."

Nixon's own analysis of the Senate election was accurate, as far as it went: Douglas had "waged a campaign that would not be equaled for stridency, ineptness and self-righteousness." And as a woman, Douglas lost the votes of traditionalists. But there had been moments during the election when even Nixon shook his head at his campaign's tactics. It was "a helluva shoddy way to win," he told one supporter. Then he would brace himself and say, "I knew all this about politics before I got in it, so there's no point in bitching about it now."

Douglas blamed her loss on the Korean War, which had a disproportionate impact on Californians, there on the Pacific Rim. Once North Korea marched on Seoul, "Nixon might well have won . . . even without the campaign of character assassination," she said. But the liberal enmity spilled into print. Carey McWilliams, a left-wing writer-activist who would soon become the editor of the *Nation,* took his fellow Californian to task in a magazine article late in the campaign. He accused Nixon of "brazen demagoguery" and "an astonishing capacity for petty malice." Herblock continued to feature Nixon in his cartoons, as a symbol of dirty campaigning and a threat to civil liberties. Tricky Dick was becoming a caricature.

NIXON WAS SWORN in a month early, on December 4, 1950, when Sheridan Downey—moving on to a job as a lobbyist—resigned to give his replacement a few weeks' extra seniority in the Senate. Across the Hill, in the House of Representatives, Nixon was succeeded by his protégé, Pat Hillings. As a senator from a huge and distant state, Nixon's payroll and expenses and office allowances grew. He stocked his third-floor quarters in the Senate office building with new aides, most notably a thirty-three-year-old secretary named Rose Mary Woods, whom he had met when they both worked on the Herter mission. The men on Nixon's staff would come and go with the years, but the women often served for decades. Woods, and other secretaries, came to worship "the Boss," as they called him, and became known as his "vestal virgins." They were, said advance man Aylett Cotton, "dedicated . . . to the same degree that a nun is dedicated to God." The war had opened new opportunities for women, and though many bowed out when the boys returned home, others stayed on in the workplace. More than a few became executive secretaries, administrative assistants, and alter egos to powerful men. Woods was one such woman. She had come to Washington from her native Ohio to work for the wartime government, hung around, and became Nixon's personal secretary. More than just a typist, though there was plenty of that, Woods was a gatekeeper, a detail person, and a trusted keeper of secrets.

Dick and Pat sold the house on Honeysuckle Lane in Whittier for a $4,000 gain on their $13,000 investment and bought a $41,000 white brick home on Tilden Street in northwest Washington. His $12,500 salary was augmented by the $7,000 in honoraria he earned giving speeches.

The poses Nixon struck for news and publicity photographs over the years—Dick raking the yard, Dick on the bike with Pat and baby Tricia, Dick at Christmas with his girls—cloaked a less than typical, and sometimes less than happy, family life, as did the comments dished to feature writers, which portrayed Dick as mostly perfect and Pat as a kind of supermom. In fact, the marriage was as storm-tossed as most. There was gossip on the Hill about Nixon's fondness for the nightlife, and reports of marital tensions. Pat sent a steady stream of sardonic wisecracks to her friend Helene Drown about his evasion of domestic duties.

"I have moved so many times and the actual process has always been gruesome," she told Helene. "Dick is always too busy, at least *his* story, so I do all the lugging, worrying and cussing."

"Our lawn is 2 ft. tall—Dick mowed it once and boasted blisters," Pat wrote. "However, our colored man hasn't shown up so Dick said he'd take another try at it. I'll telegraph you when it happens." The Nixons had a gardener and a housekeeper—unmentioned in the feature stories about the family—and a television, to keep the girls amused. Their backyard had a swing set and a wading pool from Sears.

Their relationship was tested continually. "This grind and the responsibility . . . is wearing," Pat told Helene. "We are so busy that we don't find the time for any close friends and just fun." At one point, when Pat was angry and refusing to speak to him, Dick begged Hannah to come and plead his case. "Not speaking?" Woods told one of Nixon's cousins, remembering the couple's spats, why, there were days when Pat locked him out of the house.

When the Senate was not in session, Nixon was in motion, darting about the country, giving speeches in twenty-one states. His schedule fattened his checkbook and introduced him to grateful Republican audiences in Akron, Wichita, Des Moines, and other exotic ports of call. Temptation accompanied success. Aides recalled Nixon and his friend Bill Rogers out around town in the company of young ladies.

—

"BALZAC ONCE WROTE that politicians are 'monsters of self-possession.' Yet while we may show this veneer on the outside, inside the turmoil becomes almost unbearable," Nixon would write a decade later. His rapid ascent through unknown territory was taking its toll on this intense young man. He had experienced periods of melancholy and exhaustion during the crises of the Hiss case; now the stress in his life presented as painful tension in his back and neck, a facial tic, sleeplessness, and, on at least one occasion, an "oppressive feeling" of pain in his chest. At the podium during one speech, Nixon felt like he was blacking out. In time, he developed chronic stomach troubles.

"I only recall a couple occasions when I was with him when he seemed completely lighthearted," said Cotton, who worked with Nixon throughout the 1950s. "He has a great many cares and worries to think about most of the time and he spends most of the time thinking of them."

A magazine profile noted his unique intensity. "If his geniality ever led him into a huddle more convivial than a cloakroom parley, no one on Capitol Hill knows about it," the author wrote. "Nixon is almost hermit-like in his association with others. . . . Nor does Nixon spend any time at those . . . time killing pastimes most public men pursue to relax. He has no hobbies."

Representative Gerald Ford of Michigan and his wife, Betty, arrived in the capital two years after the Nixons and, finding they had many things in common, befriended the couple. Nixon was a moody fellow, Ford discovered—joyously banging out a song on the piano for the House Chowder and Marching Club, then slipping into silence. "One minute he was outgoing, extrovert, the next reflective, even sullen," Ford recalled. "His moodiness drained a lot out of him."

Ford recalled Pat as "very reserved, very unemotional, shy . . . in the background . . . always under total self-control."

"Very seldom did she offer an opinion on anything; but she was interested, observing and listening, never missing anything you said," Ford said. "She seemed to be getting it in her mind and cataloging it. What she did with it, I don't know."

SHERIDAN DOWNEY, ULCER sufferer, sent Nixon a book, *The Will to Live*, written by Dr. Arnold Hutschnecker, who specialized in treating the physical manifestations of modern disorders like stress and anxiety. The New York doctor took Nixon as a patient and would advise, comfort, and minister to him, on and off, for the rest of Nixon's life. He told him to moderate his consumption of alcohol, avoid hard-to-digest foods, and get regular exercise. Over time, Hutschnecker would prescribe an array of tranquilizers to make Nixon relax, stimulants to rev him up, and barbiturates and other pills to help him sleep.

The doctor also listened sympathetically when Nixon spoke about his upbringing and his home life. Hutschnecker was not a practicing psychiatrist, but over time he developed his own theories about his patient's psyche. Sometimes, indiscreetly, he alluded to them in interviews or in writings.

Nixon threw himself so furiously into his work to mask deep insecurities, the doctor believed. Frank had been demanding; Hannah remote, and frequently absent. Nixon wrestled with conflicting feelings from his childhood—the craving for his mother's love and attention, and the hurt he felt when Hannah withheld it. "He did have this tension," Hutschnecker told Nixon biographer Jonathan Aitken. "The root cause of it was his drive, his ambition, his insecurities." Hutschnecker concluded that Dick "felt he owed everything to his mother—his superior intellect, his success and his ideals. The driving force of his life was that he wanted to prove to his mother that he was a good boy. He could not be a loser because that would mean he was letting his mother down."

In the fall of 1951, a crisis had occurred—perhaps the chest pain and near blackout that Hutschnecker later described in his notes. "Dick is more tired mentally than I have ever seen him," Pat told Helene. "The doctor told him he would have to get away and also take it easier." Hutschnecker prescribed regular doses of the restorative sunshine of Nixon's boyhood. Pat pried Dick away for a Sea Island, Georgia, vacation. "It was a real rest for Dick, but not long enough," she told Helene. After Christmas, Nixon went alone to Florida. On an earlier trip, Senator George Smathers had put him in touch with a high school classmate, a Cuban American businessman named Charles "Bebe" Rebozo, who could take Nixon out on his boat. Rebozo and Smathers were known in the Capitol for the recreational services they provided senators in Florida. John Kennedy and Lyndon Johnson were among Smathers's close friends. Nixon wasn't like the other partying pols. "Don't ever send another dull fellow like that down here again," Rebozo had reportedly told Smathers. "He doesn't drink whiskey, he doesn't chase women, he doesn't even play golf."

But in time, Nixon and Rebozo developed an abiding friendship. "He had a depth and a genuineness about him which didn't come through because of his shyness, but I saw it," Rebozo said, recalling their early acquaintance. "I knew that he would return and that we would become friends. I can't explain why, except to say that it was perhaps the attraction of opposites. He's a kind of genius. I just muddle through."

"Bebe knew that I was somewhat of a loner, that if I wanted his opinion I'd ask for it," Nixon remembered. "He's never one that wanted to sit down at the throne and have me confide in him."

In the spring of 1952, the Nixons and the Drowns went to Hawaii. Counting Christmas break, it was Dick's fourth therapeutic vacation in six months.

DICK AND PAT had taken a step upward in the capital's social strata, but McCarthy's debut and the bitterly fought 1950 elections left irremediable wounds in Washington. Joseph Alsop was an influential columnist, with a specialty in U.S. foreign policy, whose regard Nixon coveted. The young senator was pleased to be invited to dinner at the newsman's Georgetown home, but the evening was ruined when Averell Harriman, a friend of Helen Douglas, arrived and, seeing Nixon, loudly declared, "I will not break bread with that man!" Alsop's sister-in-law, another guest, was happy to see Nixon go. She found Dick and Pat uptight, like "two little dolls"—or the monitors at a high school dance.

Nixon was involved in another famous clash that, like the Harriman story, became a metaphor for the times. A little more than a week after being sworn in, the new senator and his wife had been invited by a Washington hostess to a dinner dance at the Sulgrave Club, a Beaux Arts mansion on Dupont Circle. Among the guests were columnist Drew Pearson and Senator McCarthy, who fell into a spirited argument. As Pearson went to leave that night, McCarthy caught up to him in the cloakroom, kneed him in the groin, and knocked him to the floor. Nixon arrived in time to save Pearson from a beating. He stepped between the two men, said, "Let a Quaker stop this fight," and led McCarthy away.

"As usual, he hit below the belt," Pearson said of his attacker.

IF NIXON HAD reservations about McCarthy they didn't keep him from joining his committee—in a seat the chairman opened by dumping the insufficiently militant Senator Margaret Chase Smith. In his maiden speech in the Senate, Nixon indulged in a little Red-baiting of his own, as he criticized Harry Truman for firing General Douglas MacArthur. "The Communists and the stooges for the Communists are happy, because the president has given them exactly what they have been after: General

MacArthur's scalp," he said. Nixon urged the United States to expand the war in Korea and bomb the supply lines in China.

But Nixon was no loutish partisan. In an exchange of letters, he upheld the right of the Berkeley school board to host Paul Robeson, an accused Communist, at the local high school. "I do not believe that we should follow the example of the totalitarian nations through the suppression of a free expression of ideas," Nixon told one critic. He won regard in the press when, while employing the committee's investigative powers to expose some of the Truman administration's corruption—officials had accepted fees, freezers, and mink coats from businessmen seeking favors—he declared that the Republican and Democratic national chairmen, each of whom was tied to various seamy acts, should both resign. The evenhandedness would cost him—Republican chairman Guy Gabrielson survived, and blocked Nixon from a keynote role in the upcoming national convention in Chicago—but it helped Nixon skate by his own faint brush with scandal when it was disclosed that the Republican campaign committee had laundered a $5,000 donation for him with the help of a shady influence peddler.

The intrigue of politics absorbed Nixon. He had scarcely moved into his new office before exchanging letters with Kyle Palmer about the national political landscape and the 1952 presidential race. The Republicans recognized the importance of California, Texas, and the other fast-growing Sunbelt states. Starting with Warren's selection as the vice-presidential candidate in 1948, the GOP would put a Californian, Texan, or Arizonan on the national ticket in fourteen of the next sixteen presidential elections. It seemed likely that whoever won the presidential nomination in 1952— the leading contenders were Senator Robert Taft and General Dwight Eisenhower—would look westward for a running mate.

Nixon liked Eisenhower's chances, and the general's stands on the issues. He was an internationalist, like Nixon. Having wielded its power during World War II, Ike was comfortable with the role of muscular government and felt no burning compulsion to dismantle popular domestic programs, like Social Security. Best of all, Eisenhower was a genuine hero who could clinch the votes of millions of Democrats and independent voters, and chip away at the Democratic hold on the South. For all of Taft's talents, Eisenhower would be the better bet to claim the White House. "If we are to win, we had better get together on our strongest electable man and start building him up now," Nixon wrote Palmer in January 1951. "Otherwise, Taft will win the nomination virtually by default."

And so Nixon set out to help Eisenhower, and perhaps to become his running mate. It was a relatively straightforward courtship. Ike did the reaching out, and the two met in Paris in May 1951. Nixon was attending a world health conference in Geneva, and the general, after a stint as the president of Columbia University, had returned to uniform to organize the forces of the newly established North Atlantic Treaty Organization (NATO). Nixon presented himself as a qualified young subaltern. Eisenhower came out from behind his desk and joined him on a couch; they spoke for forty-five minutes, and discussed world affairs and the Hiss case. Nixon was impressed by Ike's presence, but also his solicitous manner. He had an "incomparable ability" of "showing just as much interest when he listened as when he spoke."

Nixon was strong on the three issues the Republicans would employ in 1952—the fiasco of Korea, Democratic corruption, and the threat of Communism. He shared Eisenhower's views of America's place in the world and had supported NATO when Taft and others opposed it. Nixon was conservative, but he "knew the world was round," Thomas Dewey, Ike's political docent, would remember. Eisenhower had read *Seeds of Treason* and approved of the decorous tactics that Nixon had employed to expose Alger Hiss. He did not lump Nixon with McCarthy or the Old Guard conservatives, whom he sneered at, in private, as "disciples of hate." Nixon and Eisenhower had been on the same side—for academic freedom—when opposing a HUAC inquiry into "subversive" textbooks in 1949.

Three weeks later, back in the States, Nixon attended a confidential strategy meeting organized by the Stassen forces on a private estate in Clarksboro, New Jersey. The Minnesotan pledged to enter the Republican presidential primaries as a stopgap candidate—to hold a place for Ike and stand down if Eisenhower decided to run. It would keep Taft from seizing the nomination, Stassen said. That summer a liquor executive named Ellis Slater, one of Ike's golf and bridge buddies, represented the general at the Bohemian Club festivities. Slater suggested, and his campmates all agreed, that Ike and Dick would be an excellent ticket.

THE BUG IN Nixon's bowl was Earl Warren, who wanted to be president, but disdained the grubby process of claiming the prize. In this he was like Eisenhower, and, indeed, both were more complex than they seemed. They each had escaped impoverished boyhoods—Warren in Bakersfield and Eisenhower in Abilene—and succeeded via ruthless purpose, concealed behind masks of rectitude. Neither was an ideologue. Each liked to see himself, for political advantage and personal gratification, as a statesman soaring above the fray.

The governor "was a man who wanted everyone to support him when he was running for office, but never wanted to give anyone else any help when the other fellow was running. . . . It was all for Warren," said Nixon's pal Earl Adams. "If he saw anyone coming on up from the ranks and developing power, he would devise ways to cut the fellow down."

Ike was playing it coy, remaining in Europe, waiting to be drafted by an adoring public. Warren chose a similarly indirect strategy: instead of challenging Taft outright, he declared himself a favorite-son candidate— hoping that the convention would turn to him once the others had fought to a standstill. It put Nixon and Warren on colliding courses.

They were never close. There was bad blood, dating back to the 1946 campaign, when the lone-wolf Warren, keeping his usual distance from Republican candidates, had given Nixon no assistance. Indeed, he had said nice things about Jerry Voorhis and blocked Stassen's plans to come to California and campaign on Nixon's behalf. "Right then, a slow burn was kindled in Richard Nixon," his campaign aide Bill Arnold recalled.

Four years later, Warren had acceded to Nixon's Senate bid, but then made national news by announcing that he would stay neutral in the general election. He disapproved of Nixon's Red-baiting, and of Murray Chotiner. "Earl wants to get in the big league, and the professionals in that league don't understand this refusal to help the rest of the ticket," a commiserative Representative John Phillips, a fellow California Republican, wrote Nixon. There was "a furor on the floor" of the House of Representatives "when Earl said he didn't intend to come out for you!"

Nixon and his friends were outraged. Warren had been typically "selfish," Herman Perry wrote Nixon. "Unless a man is a crook he is entitled to the united support of the party he represents. Warren's eleventh hour confession will not go with me and 80 percent of the real Republicans."

When Warren fared poorly in the Republican Party presidential primaries in early 1952, Pat gloated in a letter to her friend Helene Drown: "Warren's showing in Oregon was sad," she wrote. "I'm not crying."

WARREN'S STRATEGY WAS to keep the California delegation aligned behind him, hoping that neither Eisenhower nor Taft would be nominated on the first ballot in Chicago. But Nixon wanted Ike to clinch the nomination, preferably with his help. Throughout the spring of 1952, Nixon was in regular contact with the general's political commanders—Dewey, Senator Henry Cabot Lodge Jr. of Massachusetts, who was Ike's campaign manager, and delegate hunter Herbert Brownell Jr., the most gifted Republican strategist of his day.* It was all necessarily conditional, but they let Nixon know that if he served as a "fifth column" in California, he had a fine chance of becoming the general's running mate.

In early May, Nixon gave a bravura performance before New York Republicans at the Waldorf Astoria in Manhattan, speaking concisely and eloquently, without a text, to meet the complicated requirements of a party dinner and a simultaneous radio broadcast. Dewey stubbed out his cigarette and shook Nixon's hand. "That was a hell of a speech," he said. "Make me a promise; don't get fat, don't get spoiled, you will be President someday." Afterwards, Nixon was invited to the governor's hotel suite, where Dewey dangled the vice-presidential nomination. In the coming days, Nixon met with Brownell, Ike's friend Lucius Clay, and an array of other Eisenhower associates so they could size him up. At a Gridiron dinner, Dewey and Brownell again raised the issue of the vice presidency. So did Lodge, in a conversation on the Senate floor. "I couldn't think of anybody else who could keep the California delegation in line," said Lodge. "I approached him on the Senate floor, well before the convention, and asked him if he would be interested in the vice presidency. 'Who wouldn't?' he said. Not very elegant, but that's what he said." It was all very secret.

CALIFORNIA'S SEVENTY DELEGATES were to be chosen in the state's Republican primary election in June. Only New York's delegation was bigger. Nixon could not oppose Warren with an Eisenhower slate; the governor was too strong, had too many favors owed, and chits to trade. Moreover, Nixon's base was divided. Some of his supporters, like Dana Smith, Roy Day, and Chotiner, sided with Ike. Others, like Bernard Brennan, respected Governor Warren's role as leader of the party. And a vocal segment from Nixon's camp, like Herman Perry and Tom Bewley, wanted Taft: many of them threw in with Representative Thomas Werdel of Bakersfield, who was rallying the state's conservatives to embarrass Warren, with whom they had been feuding for years. "There were a number of us that had some real principles which we stuck to, realizing that we

* Brownell was a former national chairman, the manager of Dewey's 1944 and 1948 presidential campaigns, and a future attorney general.

couldn't accomplish anything with Nixon or Warren because neither of them had any real principles. They were both open field runners," said Keith McCormac, one of the Werdel organizers.

Given the turmoil, the best Nixon could do was to join Warren and Bill Knowland—another vice-presidential prospect—in a Solomonic alliance. They agreed to work together to defeat the Werdel slate, with each man getting to name a third of the state's delegates to the convention. Warren went along because—by custom, law, and honor—all the delegates on the slate would be bound to him, as a favorite son, unless he should release them. Nixon was content with the arrangement, which allowed him to pursue his own agenda, securing what he could for Eisenhower. In a statement just before the June 3 primary, Nixon belittled Warren's hopes of winning the nomination and promised California Republicans that "once Governor Warren releases the delegation, we shall be free to look over the field and select the man best qualified."

The Warren-Nixon-Knowland slate prevailed, by a two-to-one margin. But Nixon soon poked the governor with another banderilla: informing his constituents that Warren's chances were hopeless and asking, via a poll he mailed out, if the voters preferred Eisenhower or Taft as an alternative. When a few last-minute substitutions were made in the delegation, Brennan made sure the replacements were Nixon loyalists. Despite a warning from Kyle Palmer ("Honorable men don't stab their friends—or enemies—in the back!"), Nixon was doing all he could to spoil Warren's hopes.

"I don't believe that any of us should have any illusions on the possibilities of Warren being selected for the top spot," Nixon wrote in a "personal and confidential" letter to Brennan. "I am laying these facts right on the line."

NOMINATING CONVENTIONS ARE creatures of the party: run by the faithful to reward the loyal. But Eisenhower had only just declared himself Republican. His strength lay in his widespread appeal, and his ability to lure new voters into the ranks. By the time Ike entered the race, Taft had locked up the Midwest and assembled a tidy lead among the delegates.

Dewey and Lodge corralled the Northeast for Eisenhower. Warren had California. That left the South as the pivotal region—and so it played out, in a series of confrontations between the Taft and Eisenhower forces in Georgia, Texas, and Louisiana. The Republican party machinery, controlled by Taft's Old Guard, was overwhelmed by a surge of new voters who showed up for Ike at local meetings and state conventions. Taft's loyalists contended that the newcomers were not true Republicans and moved to disqualify them. Ike's followers squawked and filed appeals. The convention would make the final decision, and the fate of the contested southern delegates would determine the nomination. And California, with its seventy votes, would have a determining impact.

Ike's advisers were crafty and cloaked themselves in principle. The country was sick of Truman-era bosses, corruption, and cronyism, they argued—Republican candidates would not be able to tap the public outrage if Taft's backroom tactics foiled the will of the people. The GOP governors, organized by Dewey, declared their support for "fair play." Earl Warren went along, believing that he needed to blunt Taft's momentum.

Nixon had arrived in Chicago a few days before the convention convened to serve on the platform committee. There he watched his friend Bill Rogers, Brownell, and others mount Ike's counterattack. Nixon did what he could to help. The political press was trumpeting the inexorable Old Guard "steamroller" when, as a rising young Republican star—and supposedly neutral—Nixon embraced the fair-play movement and branded Taft a loser.

"If the Republican Party approves the Texas grab we will be announcing to the country that we believe ruthless machine politics is wrong only when the Democrats use it," he said, in comments that made the front page of the *New York Times* and other newspapers. The Republicans needed a hero, like Ike, to tug Democrats and independents to their side. The party "can't hope to win this November if it limits its membership to the minority which has not been large enough to win four national elections."

NIXON THEN LEFT Chicago on Friday, July 4, and flew to Denver to join Warren and the California delegation on the chartered train that was taking them to the convention. ("The convention train . . . that's when most of the politicking is done," Pat told Helene Drown.) As they left California, and wound their way through the mountains and canyons, the mood had been festive. Jack Drown chatted about the University of California's football prospects with Warren, who was relaxing in the lead car with his family. The governor's daughters danced to the music from a radio. The delegates munched on Greek butter cakes, baked by the mother of George Christopher, a future mayor of San Francisco. And they sang, to the tune of "California, Here I Come," the Warren campaign song:

Old Chicago, here we come
Right straight through to Washington
We're in it
To win it
It can be done
Earl Warren, has boosters
From Old Maine to Oregon
We'll take every gol'darn state
Ike and Taft you're just too late
We're all for the Warren slate
California's Native Son!

But as the train sped through the prairie night, Nixon and his lieutenants were singing a different tune. Warren's hope for a deadlocked convention was a fantasy, they told their fellow delegates. Taft's "Texas grab" was unfair and could lead the party to ruin. But if the Californians sided with Eisenhower, they could support fair play, help put the general over the top, and keep from being left out in the cold. Nixon showed the delegates copies of the glowing responses about Eisenhower he had received in his poll—concealing the fact that Taft had actually "won" the survey. Since most of the delegates preferred Ike over Taft, Nixon found a receptive audience—except in the governor's private car, where Warren got word of the backstabbing. The good times vanished. Warren was "furious," said aide Merrell Small. "He was convinced they were soliciting first-ballot votes for Eisenhower."

"I have felt the tension in the train mounting . . . since Dick got on board," Nixon's friend Aylett Cotton, a delegate from the Bay Area, confided in a letter to his wife. "The Warren people want to stick with Warren. . . . The others fear that such a policy would lead to the nomination of Taft. . . . They want California to swing to Ike. . . . There will be a showdown."

NIXON ACCOMPLISHED WHAT he set out to do. The "great train robbery," as it came to be known, bled Warren and nudged the delegates toward Eisenhower. Nixon left the train on Saturday afternoon, before it reached Chicago, and so was not cornered by newsmen or photographers when the California delegates, blowing whistles and waving Warren signs and chanting their choruses of "California, Here I Come," climbed on buses for the ride to their hotel. (The Taft troops in the streets were singing "Onward Christian Soldiers.") Chotiner was in charge of various logistical details for the delegation in Chicago, and some of the Warren delegates would insist, for years, that he bedecked their buses with Eisenhower banners, not with the blue and gold Warren signs.

There would be three showdown votes. The initial confrontation was on the agenda for Monday. It would decide whether contested delegates could vote on credential challenges to other delegations before their own status was resolved. This abstruse parliamentary question shaped up as the initial test of strength that would show whether Taft's "steamroller" could be stopped. Nixon and Warren appeared to share a common interest: halting Taft. In reality, Warren had misread the situation. As events would show, the Eisenhower and Nixon alliance was the lethal danger, not Taft.

There was plenty of talk about fairness, but "it seems improbable that Nixon was motivated by . . . lofty principles," Small recalled. "Although he was very new in the business, he had an instinctive political craftiness."

"During a caucus of the California delegation [Nixon] vigorously supported Warren's request for a vote in favor of seating the Eisenhower delegates," Small remembered. "He could seem to be giving assistance to Warren while actually helping to foreclose the governor's one hope for the nomination."

The Californians supported the fair-play argument despite Knowland's energetic efforts (the Taft forces had been dangling the vice-presidential nomination before him) to broker a deal that would divide the delegation's votes, and thus help Taft. The Old Guard steamroller stalled.

TOO LATE, WARREN recognized Ike's momentum, and the extent of Nixon's scheming. On Monday, when making a courtesy call on Eisenhower, the governor had been flabbergasted to find Chotiner in Ike's suite, working with Ike's captains. "Nixon was selling out Warren," said political reporter Dick Bergholz. "Both Warren and Knowland were bitter as hell."

Warren seethed, and took action. On Tuesday he sent a mutual friend—Paul Davis—to visit Eisenhower. "The problem is this," Warren instructed Davis. "We have a traitor in our delegation. It's Nixon. He, like all the rest, took the oath that he would vote for me . . . but he has not paid attention to his oath and immediately upon being elected, started working for Eisenhower and has been doing so ever since. . . . He is actively in touch with the Eisenhower people. I wish you would tell General Eisenhower that we resent his people infiltrating, through Nixon into our delegation, and ask him to have it stopped."

Eisenhower brushed Davis off. "We are definitely leaving California alone," he said. And that was, more or less, true. Brownell and his floor manager, Governor Sherman Adams of New Hampshire, had done the math. The other states with favorite sons had cut their deals, and Ike's lieutenants didn't need the California delegates for the presidential roll call, so long as Nixon kept the state in line during the "fair play" procedural showdowns. Warren could have his moment in the spotlight. They would not humiliate him by stealing his delegates. But there would be no dead-lock. The convention would not be turning to a dark horse.

Eisenhower sent a message back to Warren. "I think it is highly desirable that for the vice president we have a young man such as Richard Nixon," he told Davis. Nixon was young, aggressive, and able. "He looks like the right type." Eisenhower may have been vetting Nixon with Warren—giving the governor an opportunity to show cause and object—or he might have been warning Warren to stop tossing words like *traitor* around. The "traitor" was going to be on the ticket.

Now that the convention had determined who would vote, the pen-ultimate showdown—the last before the roll call of the states—was on whether to seat the Eisenhower delegates from the South. It was "*the test*," Brownell recalled. The California delegates caucused on Wednes-day, July 9, shortly after 8 a.m. in a conference room at the Knickerbocker Hotel, sitting at rows of tables covered in green cloth. The dynamics had changed—Warren's hopes were still being flattened, but now Eisenhower was driving the steamroller. The debate was heated. A noisy tide of report-ers and photographers swept in, signaling that Ike was on the way. Nixon escorted Eisenhower to the rostrum, where the general charmed and fired up the delegates (drawing laughs when he compared the Democrats to the Abilene town drunk) and left amid another mob scene. Nixon then closed the debate. "It was marvelous," Cotton told his diary that night. "It was about a two-minute talk and it could be the two minute talk that will result in Ike's nomination. . . . I felt weak afterward. I doubt if the convention will again provide the drama and excitement."

Eisenhower's charisma and Nixon's remarks gave Ike the second vic-tory he *had* to have. California's seventy votes were still legally bound to Warren in the balloting for the nomination, but in the crucial creden-tials challenge that night—the win Ike needed to secure those southern ballots—the Californians voted sixty-two to eight to seat the Eisenhower delegates. It was a ripsnorting battle, played out on national television, with an unforgettable scene of Taft's spokesman, Senator Everett Dirksen of Illinois, shaking a finger at Dewey and, amid thunderous booing, saying: "We followed you before, and you took us down the path to defeat."

Eisenhower would not forget what Nixon had done. Aylett Cotton got his first hint of the general's gratitude when he went to Nixon's suite to congratulate him on his caucus speech. He found him on the phone with the press, issuing pro forma denials of that day's screaming headline, in the Chicago *Daily News,* announcing that Ike had the convention in hand and would choose Nixon as a running mate. His friend Dick "was very pleased" at the results of the caucus, Cotton recorded. "He was also pleased at the headline."

WARREN SAW, AND rued, his folly. In stopping Taft, he had only helped Ike. At the California caucus on Thursday, he thanked his supporters but went out of the way to snub Nixon. "The slight was perfectly obvious, as it was intended to be," Cotton recorded. The governor believed "Dick was trying to sabotage him." From that day on, "Warren hated Nixon," Republican fund-raiser Asa Call remembered. Over the years, Warren would tell mutual acquaintances how "Nixon cut my throat from here to here" and gesture with his finger across his neck.

The final roll call began just before noon on Friday and ended soon after. The Californians might have done themselves some good by switching their votes to Ike at the end of the first ballot, as he needed nine additional votes to win. But Ike's captains were honorable men and let Warren have his moment. An able Stassen lieutenant—a lawyer with a bright future named Warren Burger—switched the Minnesota delegation's votes to Eisenhower, giving Ike the prize. After the customary celebration, the convention recessed until evening, at which time it would hear from the general and approve his choice of a running mate.

GIVEN THE IMPORTANCE of the vice presidency—so recently demonstrated by Roosevelt's death and Truman's ascension—it is remarkable that the sixty-one-year-old Eisenhower did not give more time and thought to selection of a running mate. Yet that is the way the vice presidency had been handled for most of American history: as a ticket-balancing plum for a man not destined for greater things. Seven vice presidents had become president when a chief executive died, including the relatively recent examples of Theodore Roosevelt (1901), Calvin Coolidge (1923), and Harry Truman (1945), but since the modern system was put in place in 1804, only Martin Van Buren, in 1836, had finished out his term and gone on to win the presidency himself. The vice presidency was a political Boot Hill, home to the remains of such illustrious Americans as Garret Hobart and Hannibal Hamlin.

Brownell, who had brought decisiveness, order, and the fair-play strategy to Ike's campaign, had a serious talk about the topic with the general at dinner on Thursday. The candidate responded with a list of names, which included Nixon. Brownell and Dewey and Lodge all approved of the choice: Nixon was a war veteran with a photogenic family, demonstrated talents and energy, and a California address. His work as an anti-Communist was a bridge to the Old Guard, and (though he had markedly refrained from applauding when Joe McCarthy addressed the convention) he would serve as a happy spear-carrier, eviscerating Democrats over Korea, Communism, and corruption. Meanwhile, the heroic liberator of Europe could take the high road. "I wanted him as a running mate because he is dynamic, direct and square," Ike later told a Nixon admirer.

As the delegates broke for lunch on Friday, Ike's men led a council of several dozen party leaders in a parlor at Eisenhower headquarters in the Conrad Hilton Hotel. Some doffed their coats, and many lit up cigarettes or cigars. The smoke-filled consultations reminded New Hampshire's Sherman Adams of "a ward committee in Philadelphia discussing the selection of a candidate for alderman." Brownell and Dewey worked deftly, as if naming the running mate was an open question, and allowed various cheerleaders to extoll the virtues of fine fellows like Taft and Dirksen. Only when the field had been thinned did Dewey, who was chairing the meeting, ask, "What about Nixon?" and proceed to answer his own question. They talked a bit, and held a vote; no one objected, and after cheering themselves for their afternoon's work, Brownell picked up the phone.

IN THE YEARS to come, Dick and Pat and their friends would tell stories of how surprised they were, and how Nixon was caught napping—literally—by the phone call informing him that he had been selected. "Wake up Dick! It's you," Hillings was said to have shouted after answering Brownell's call in Nixon's hotel suite. Pat was at lunch at the downstairs coffee shop with Helene Drown and Phyllis Chotiner. She was so startled when the news came over the restaurant's television that a bite of sandwich tumbled from her mouth. Indeed, the final word must have rocked them—the gypsy and her knight. They had ridden from obscurity to a spot on a national ticket in six years.

Yet they were not totally unprepared. Earlier that year they had spent an evening discussing the vice presidency with the indomitable Alice Roosevelt Longworth, who told them all about her father, who found the job a bore but was rewarded with the presidency when William McKinley was assassinated. And Nixon needed his nap because he had been up all the night before, in earnest discussion, trying to persuade his hesitant wife that they should accept Ike's offer.

The issue was straightforward: Pat loathed politics. It took Dick away from her and the girls, relegated her to a subsidiary role, and tied him up in knots of tension, endangering his health and their marriage—when he could find the time to come home. They had just won a yearlong Senate campaign: wasn't that enough? And on both their minds was what being a vice president at the age of thirty-nine would mean: the pressure-packed decision on whether to seek the presidency when Ike stepped down, and the unrelenting demand to act flawlessly in the glare of national attention so that, in 1956 or 1960, Nixon would appear seasoned and ready to lead the nation.

Just before dawn, Nixon summoned Chotiner, who gave them his lay of the land. "The junior senator from California doesn't amount to anything. There comes a time when you have to go up or out," Chotiner told them. "Suppose you are a candidate [for vice president] and we lose? You're still the junior senator and haven't lost anything." The vice presidency didn't commit them to a presidential run—and if not, well, no vice president, leaving office in his mid-forties, with his contacts and prestige, would ever have to worry about making a living.

The Nixons were still debating it when Chotiner returned to bed. Dawn arrived. Hoping, perhaps, that the cup might still pass, Pat went along.

AND THEN IT *had* happened. Nixon hurriedly dressed—skipping a shower and a shave—and went to see Ike for a somewhat awkward fifteen-minute discussion. Would he join the crusade? Ike asked. You bet, said Nixon. He then made the long trip back to the convention hall, to find the breathless Pat. "I'm amazed, flabbergasted, weak and speechless," she told reporters. The band played "Anchors Aweigh" as Nixon entered the hall. He scrawled lines for a brief, forgettable acceptance speech while sitting amid his Californians, who shielded him from intruding reporters and well-wishing delegates. He was named by acclamation. The Californians cheered. Pat kissed him, and kissed him again.

Eisenhower had met with Taft to heal the rifts in the party, and Nixon saw it as his task to further the reconciliation process. His acceptance speech lauded Taft and the Old Guard—lavishly—so that some of Ike's supporters thought Nixon showed too much independence, and too little gratitude. In prime time they were on the podium, with Nixon holding Eisenhower's hand aloft, and Pat smiling, in a distinctive print dress with coin-like dots. After a midnight reception to honor the Nixons (in which Warren, with a frozen smile, served on the receiving line), Pat left the next morning for Washington, leaving Dick with the thousand political details that needed his attention.

"Eisenhower comes along. He needs California. For that reason he takes Nixon. Lightning has struck," Bryce Harlow recalled. "That's the way of politics—surging success or plunging defeat—a tempestuous way of life."

Aylett Cotton grabbed a bottle of scotch and found Dick in the Nixons' suite. "He said that he had had three hours sleep in the last 48," Cotton said. "And he looked it."

Checkers

HOME FROM CHICAGO, Pat was stunned. She had to retire the polka-dot dress she had worn at the convention: so many people had seen her wearing it, on their new TV sets, that it was instantly overexposed. People would think she had no other wardrobe. She consigned it to a closet. Television had demonstrated its phenomenal power in the spring of 1951, when a series of broadcast hearings on organized crime chaired by Senator Estes Kefauver gripped America's attention. It seemed like the whole nation broke from its daily routine to watch the mob bosses stammer, perspire, and prevaricate. TV stars like Roy Rogers and Milton Berle were now mainstays of American culture. The Chicago convention was another landmark. For the first time, the machinations of national politics—the drama of the "fair play" fight and Ike's come-from-behind victory—had been played out in millions of living rooms, like a sports event, with commentary offered by a flock of soon-to-be-celebrity newsmen, including Walter Cronkite.

The television cameras were there when Dick and Pat, per superstition and tradition, kicked off the fall campaign in Pomona, in his old congressional district, on September 17. Some fifteen thousand people jammed the rail yard to see the Nixons off on a whistle-stop tour. The couple's excitement was laced with nostalgia: they had made a sentimental visit to Pat's birthplace in Ely, Nevada, the day before and spent the night at the Mission Inn in Riverside, where they had been married in 1940. A sizable contingent from Whittier, with Frank Nixon, costumed as a railroad engineer, led the cheers as the *Dick Nixon Special* pulled away, with Dick on the train's rear platform, imploring all to "come along on this great crusade!"

"The tracks stood out under angled floodlights, creating a vision of the path to glory," journalist and author Earl Mazo wrote. "Hundreds of magnetized listeners found themselves following behind the crawling train with Nixon's outstretched arms seemingly their goal. If it were possible, thousands of television viewers would have joined the trek." The idolators were not part of the plan, and Nixon chewed out his friend and advance man Jack Drown for the mistake. His aides calmed him down and convinced him that the scene, in fact, had been quite memorable.

NIXON HAD SPENT the two months since the convention preparing for the fall contest, alternating strategy sessions at Eisenhower headquarters in the Brown Palace hotel in Denver with the kinds of abasing stunts—Dick in waders, learning to fly-fish with Ike; Dick in Maine wrestling with a giant lobster—that vice-presidential candidates are subjected to. To help heal the rift between the Taft and Eisenhower wings of the party, he had stationed himself at the door of the Ohio state convention to shake hands with three thousand Republicans. He made the cover of *Time,* and Pat offered a sketch of the Nixons' family life in the *Saturday Evening Post.* The article, crafted with the help of a professional writer, was headlined I SAY HE'S A WONDERFUL GUY. She promised its readers, "we come from typical, everyday American families that have had to work for what they got."

The hoopla "was wearing, but intensely exciting," Nixon would recall. "Our hopes for the future could not have been higher." Dick slipped away to the Atlantic beaches for a short vacation with his girls. Their friends were happy, thrilled, and ambitious. "Will see you at the White House in 1960!" the exultant Herman Perry wrote to Nixon's secretary, Dorothy Cox.

When scuttling Earl Warren's dreams, Nixon had hung a fourth trophy on his wall of liberal scalps, joining those of Voorhis, Hiss, and Douglas. Now he drew his sights on a fifth. In late July, the Democrats chose Adlai Stevenson as their presidential nominee. The Illinois governor was the scion of a famous family, a graduate of Choate and Princeton, and a favorite of the press. His arch wit and literacy appealed to a generation of journalists who, soured by the century's savagery, brought irony and cynicism to their coverage. Nixon was a prim Galahad, self-righteous and irony-free; the journalists were darker knights.

Nixon savored the opportunity to take on Stevenson. Among his other sins, the Illinois governor had served as a character witness for Alger Hiss. Nixon put his new research director—former congressman George MacKinnon—to work, and solicited advice from Eisenhower campaign aide Bill Rogers, Father John Cronin (both of whom had advised him in the Hiss case), and others. His staff gathered reports of "Stevenson's Communist Affiliations." A reporter from St. Louis passed on a tip that the governor was homosexual. Nixon insisted he would never use it. "Even if I thought there was anything to that story about Stevenson's being a queer (which I don't) I wouldn't dream of allowing it to be used in the campaign," Nixon wrote back. "This personal stuff (true or false) is below the belt." But in early September, on a shakedown cruise of New England, Nixon made sport of Stevenson's masculinity, labeling him "Sidesaddle Adlai" and snorting, "Let the other side serve up the clever quips which send the State Department cocktail set into gales of giggles."*

In the coming years, Nixon grew a fine hate for Stevenson. "To me he was the so-called 'liberal-intellectual' at his worst—plagued with Hamlet-like indecision, tittering at his own quips, assuming a superior, mincing attitude toward the so-called run-of-the-mill politician which character-izes the Georgetown, Ivy League social set to whom he is the second com-ing of Christ," Nixon confided to a diary in 1961. "He was a man who was all veneer and no substance, a perfect pigeon to be taken in by Hiss' veneer and to fail to see Chambers' substance." Dick was especially agitated when the press compared Stevenson to Woodrow Wilson, "one of my Quaker mother's heroes." It was "sacrilege," he wrote.

To the crowds in New England, Nixon previewed his role in the upcom-ing campaign. "If the record itself smears, let it smear," he said. "If the dry rot of corruption and Communism, which has eaten deep into our body politic during the past seven years, can only be chopped out with a hatchet, then let's call for a hatchet."

HATCHETS CAN CUT both ways. Nixon was all but daring his foes to strike. Liberal journals like the *New Republic* and the *Reporter* had writers comb-ing California for dirt. Ernest Brashear, a left-leaning labor reporter for the Los Angeles *Daily News,* asked, "Who is Richard Nixon?" in the Septem-ber 1 and 8 editions of the *New Republic,* informing his readers how Nixon had "garroted Mrs. Douglas politically with the strands of unreasoning, hatred and fear." The Warren faction of his home-state Republicans still seethed. "I have to nominate that dirty son of a bitch?" Bill Knowland had reportedly asked when urged to give the nominating address for Nixon at the convention.

"All is not well," Perry warned a friend. "Some of the Warrenites would

---

* The allegation was abroad. The FBI had been told by a New York City police detective in April that Stevenson was a homosexual, based on an uncorroborated report from Bradley University athletes arrested for fixing games, who sought to trade information for leniency. FBI director J. Edgar Hoover ordered the preparation of a "blind memorandum" for the files, and for distribution to unknown recipients.

be tickled to death to see Dick lose California in the coming election." Nixon had not left Chicago before newsmen began to hear rumors about the vice-presidential nominee—that he was anti-Semitic, and the benefi_ciary of a slush fund maintained by a group of wealthy businessmen.

The charge of anti-Semitism was not new. It had surfaced in the Senate campaign but was given short shrift by reporters who witnessed Nixon's relationship with Murray Chotiner and John Dinkelspiel. Whatever provincial bigotry Nixon took from Whittier did not prevent him from interacting comfortably with minorities—as long as they were on his side. In 1950, and now, again, in the summer of 1952, Chotiner enlisted California's Jewish leaders to vouch for Nixon's fair-mindedness.

The "slush fund" was another matter. Over the years Nixon had been paid $100 here, $1,000 there—passed on by Perry, Frank Jorgensen, or others—to help him meet the cost of political obligations, like mailings and travel, that exceeded his congressional allowance. "I personally feel we cannot expect a young man of Mr. Nixon's ability to carry these expenses out of his own salary," Perry wrote in a fund-raising letter to oilman Stan Natcher in 1948, thanking him for his role in raising $1,000. It was a scattershot process until the fall of 1950, when, as the senator-elect for a huge state three thousand miles from Washington, Nixon and his supporters recognized the need for a more structured system. Thus was born the "Nixon Sustaining Fund." Administered by Dana Smith, the Pasadena banker, it reached the tidy sum of $18,235.*

In letters to potential contributors, Smith laid out the ground rules. The maximum yearly contribution would be $500—"so that it can never be charged that anyone is contributing so much as to think he is entitled to special favors"—and only donors who had "supported Dick from the start" could participate. They aimed to maintain a balance of from $20,000 to $25,000, and to use it for airfare, postage, long-distance telephone calls, advertising, and the senator's twenty thousand Christmas cards. Brennan and Chotiner and Smith did most of the fund-raising, but Nixon was intimately involved, scheduling meetings with the donors "so that they could feel they were in on the know" and to "inform them of the services which are available in our office that I am sure many of them are not using and which we would be only too glad to furnish."

After Nixon was chosen as Ike's running mate, his friends arranged for a "surprise." Money was pouring in, and they could now allot $500 a month in "household expenses," paid directly to the Nixons, that would

* About $160,000 in 2015, after adjusting for inflation.

His deep-set eyes were the darkest brown, and his face pleasantly symmetrical. The young Dick Nixon in football gear (center), for the Whittier College team.

For the folks of California farm country, a family portrait was an important, solemn event. Here are Frank and Hannah Nixon, with Harold standing by his father, Donald on his mother's lap, and young Richard at her side.

Had he not become a politician, Richard Nixon said, he might have been a musician. He was an accomplished pianist, and here he poses with his violin. He was, his music teacher decided, "a romanticist at heart, but he doesn't like to let this show."

The Nixon brothers in Yorba Linda. The two on the right—Harold and Arthur—would die young, leaving Dick (standing beside Harold) "staring into space," his mother recalled, "in the undemonstrative way in which, because of his choked deep feeling, he was always to face tragedy."

Yorba Linda was a whistle-stop in the California outback. The Nixon farm is the small building just to the left of the cluster of larger homes and barns in the upper-right of the top photograph. The house that Frank Nixon built (center) was "just a little cottage," and there was "Dust. Dust everywhere," a family friend recalled. The children went to school barefooted, but his mother made sure that Richard (seated on the ground at far right in the bottom row) always had a clean white shirt.

The adolescent Nixon. In the left-hand photo, he is on the left, standing alongside his father, his brother Don, and the characteristically high-spirited Harold, who is mugging for the camera. On the right is his first love, Ola Florence Welch. Ola found him mysterious and sexy—but in austere Whittier, there was no "hanky-panky," she recalled. He, in turn, compared her with his mother—"incapable of selfishness"—and spoke with her of marriage. He was shattered when she dropped him for another man. "I shall always remember the kindness, the beauty, the loveliness that was, that is, and shall for ever be Ola Florence Welch," he wrote her.

The Nixon store, with a grocery clerk, and the produce bins that were Dick's responsibility. He would rise at three in the morning to drive to Los Angeles to buy vegetables at the farmers' market and then head to class.

Thelma "Buddy" Ryan would become Pat Nixon. Orphaned in her youth, she spent much of her time cooking, cleaning, and helping her brothers run the family farm. But she found time for academic accomplishment and popularity in high school—here posing beside a roadster of the era.

After meeting Pat at a community theater production, Dick launched an intense courtship, determined to wear down her initial coolness. Just to see her, he would offer to drive her to Los Angeles, where she dated other men. Slowly, she came to see him as a man of destiny. This is the photograph she sent him when he was stationed in the South Pacific.

Nixon, shirtless and with pith helmet in the tropical heat, on the job as a combat air traffic controller in the Pacific. He is standing in front of "Nick's Snack Shop"—a counter he set up to offer hamburgers and cold juice to the pilots at the airfield.

Richard Nixon in 1946, home from the war
and back in California to run for Congress.

Dick and Pat pose with baby Tricia in the first of many publicity shots depicting them as the
quintessential postwar middle-class family. Nixon struck a chord with those he called "the forgotten Americans." His campaign literature boasted that he was "one of us."

The political elite dismissed Nixon's candidacy, but he won the enthusiastic support of a hundred or so Republican "Amateurs," who recruited him to challenge Jerry Voorhis. The fourth man from the right is Herman Perry, the local banker who served as Nixon's political mentor and secret fund-raiser. Nixon's law partner, Thomas Bewley, is second from the left. And third from the left is Nixon's college football coach, "Chief" Wallace Newman.

Representative Jerry Voorhis was an entrenched liberal Democrat, unprepared for the aggressive Red-baiting tactics that his opponent, Richard Nixon, employed.

Nixon was soon identified as a bright and energetic comer in the House of Representatives, and named by Republican leaders to an important overseas mission to Europe led by Representative Christian Herter of Massachusetts to weigh the necessity of what became known as the Marshall Plan.

Among the other notable freshmen in the House of Representatives Class of 1946 was the boyish John F. Kennedy, seen here in the back row, standing next to Nixon, at a press conference.

The Republicans had captured Congress for the first time since the onslaught of the Great Depression, and Nixon was seen as emblematic of the changes in Washington. Here, he and Pat and Tricia pose in the spring of his first term among the cherry blossoms near the Jefferson Memorial.

The Hiss case gave Nixon his first taste of national acclaim. Here, he poses with Robert Stripling, an aide for the House Committee on Un-American Activities, examining microfilm recovered from a pumpkin patch at the Maryland farm of Whittaker Chambers.

Relentless drive and ambition propelled Nixon into the Senate in 1950. Here he can be seen standing on the tailgate of the station wagon that carried the congressman and his wife through the farmland, small towns, and cities of California.

DOUGLAS-MARCANTONIO VOTING RECORD

Many persons have requested a comparison of the voting records of Congresswoman Helen Douglas and the notorious Communist party-liner, Congressman Vito Marcantonio of New York.

Mrs. Douglas and Marcantonio have been members of Congress together since January 1, 1945. During that period, Mrs. Douglas voted the same as Marcantonio 354 times. While it should not be expected that a member of the House of Representatives should always vote in opposition to Marcantonio, it is significant to note, not only the great number of times which Mrs. Douglas voted in agreement with him, but also the issues on which almost without exception they always saw eye to eye, to-wit: Un-American Activities and Internal Security.

Here is the Record!

VOTES AGAINST COMMITTEE ON UN-AMERICAN ACTIVITIES

Both Douglas and Marcantonio voted against establishing the Committee on Un-American Activities. 1/3/45. Bill passed.

Both voted on three separate occasions against contempt proceedings against persons and organizations which refused to reveal records or answer whether they were Communists. 4/16/46, 6/26/46, 11/24/47. Bills passed.

Both voted on four separate occasions against allowing funds for investigation by the Un-American Activities Committee. 5/17/46, 5/9/48, 2/9/49, 3/23/50. (The last vote was 348 to 12.) All bills passed.

COMMUNIST-LINE FOREIGN POLICY VOTES

Both voted against Greek-Turkish Aid Bill. 5/9/47. (It has been established that without this aid Greece and Turkey would long since have gone behind the Iron Curtain.) Bill passed.

Both voted on two occasions against free press amendment to UNRRA appropriation bill, providing that no funds should be furnished any country which refused to allow free access to the news of activities of the UNRRA by press and radio representatives of the United States. 11/1/45, 6/28/46. Bills passed. (This would in effect have denied American relief funds to Communist dominated countries.)

Both voted against refusing Foreign Relief to Soviet-dominated countries UNLESS supervised by Americans. 4/30/47. Bill passed 324 to 75.

VOTE AGAINST NATIONAL DEFENSE

Both voted against the Selective Service Act of 1948. 6/18/48. Bill passed.

VOTES AGAINST LOYALTY AND SECURITY LEGISLATION

Both voted on two separate occasions against bills requiring loyalty checks for Federal employees. 7/15/47, 6/29/49. Bills passed.

Both voted against the Subversive Activities Control Act of 1948, requiring registration with the Attorney General of Communist party members and communist controlled organizations. Bill passed, $19 to 58. 5/19/48. AND AFTER KOREA both again voted against it. Bill passed 8/29/50. 354 to 20.

AFTER KOREA, on July 12, 1950, Marcantonio and Douglas and 12 others voted against the Security Bill, to permit the heads of key National Defense departments, such as the Atomic Energy Commission, to discharge government workers found to be poor security risks! Bill passed, 327 to 14.

VOTE AGAINST CALIFORNIA

Both recorded against confirming title to Tidelands in California and the other states affected. 4/30/48. Bill passed 257-29.

VOTES AGAINST CONGRESSIONAL INVESTIGATION OF COMMUNIST AND OTHER ILLEGAL ACTIVITIES

Both voted against investigating the "whitewash" of the AMERASIA case. 4/18/46. Bill passed.

Both voted against investigating why the Soviet Union was buying as many as 60,000 United States patents at one time. 5/4/47. Bill passed.

Both voted against continuing investigation of numerous instances of illegal actions by OPA and the War Labor Board. 1/18/45. Bill passed.

Both voted on two occasions against allowing Congress to have access to government records necessary to the conduct of investigations by Senate and House Committees. 4/22/48, 5/13/48. Bills passed.

ON ALL OF THE ABOVE VOTES which have occurred since Congressman Nixon took office on January 1, 1947, HE has voted exactly opposite to the Douglas-Marcantonio Axis!

After studying the voting comparison between Mrs. Douglas and Marcantonio, is it any wonder that the Communist line newspaper, the Daily People's World, in its lead editorial on January 31, 1950, labeled Congressman Nixon as "The Man To Beat" in this Senate race and that the Communist newspaper, the New York Daily Worker, in the issue of July 28, 1947, selected Mrs. Douglas along with Marcantonio as "One of the Heroes of the 80th Congress."

REMEMBER! The United States Senate votes on ratifying international treaties and confirming presidential appointments. Would California send Marcantonio to the United States Senate?

NIXON FOR U. S. SENATOR CAMPAIGN COMMITTEE

NORTHERN CALIFORNIA	CENTRAL CALIFORNIA	SOUTHERN CALIFORNIA
John Walton Dinkelspiel, Chairman	B. M. Hoblick, Chairman	Bernard Brennan, Chairman
1151 Market Street	820 Van Ness Avenue	117 W. 9th St., Los Angeles
San Francisco—Underhill 3-1416	Fresno—Phone 44116	TRinity 0661

Nixon's successful strategy portrayed his Democratic opponent, the liberal Representative Helen Gahagan Douglas of Los Angeles, as a Red dupe.

In the pictured "pink sheet," Nixon charged that Douglas was soft on Communism.

The Nixons—Pat, Tricia, Julie, and Dick—on the beach with a very famous cocker spaniel, Checkers. When Dwight D. Eisenhower chose Nixon as his running mate in 1952, critics claimed that Dick had profited from a political slush fund. Nixon went on national television (below) to plead his case, and mockingly noted that his family had accepted the gift of a puppy from a supporter. "The kids love the dog," Nixon said. "We're gonna keep it." The Checkers speech "was an astonishing act of self-resuscitation," an Eisenhower speechwriter would recall.

Ike and Dick had an awkward relationship, and Eisenhower thought seriously about dropping Nixon from the ticket in 1952 and in 1956. The generational gulf was great, and the two men had quite different personalities. Ike was a war hero, a man's man, with a coterie of pals with whom he played golf and cards. Nixon was an introvert, and insecure, always struggling to win the president's approval. On the left, Dick tees off. On the right, he steps out with Pat; the president; Ike's wife, Mamie; and Attorney General Herb Brownell and his wife.

The "kitchen debate" with Nikita Khrushchev. The savvy Soviet premier put Nixon on the defensive as they toured an exhibition of American economic accomplishment in Moscow. But in photographs like this, Nixon conveyed the message that he stood up to Khrushchev (under the baleful gaze of the then-little-known Leonid Brezhnev, right).

After Nixon had received the vice presidential nomination, Eisenhower adviser Herb Brownell took him to a World Series game in New York. Nixon's clamorous behavior in the stands—as seen here, at another ballgame with Pat and the girls—shocked Brownell, and left him wondering what lay ahead.

Nixon had a dedicated staff, led by Rose Mary Woods, augmented often by the volunteer "Miss Ryan." Here, Pat poses with the "vestal virgins," as they came to be known. From left to right: Loie Gaunt, Dorothy Cox, P. J. Everts, Pat, Woods, and personal friend Margaret Brock.

In 1958 Nixon traveled through Latin America and encountered anti-American crowds at several stops. The most violent protest came in Caracas, Venezuela, where his motorcade was attacked by a spitting, rock-throwing mob.

The Eisenhower-Nixon relationship was cinched in 1968, when Ike's grandson, David, married Nixon's daughter Julie. Here, in the viewing stands at the 1957 inauguration, David is seen gazing at his future wife, who is sporting a black eye from a sledding accident.

Wanting to be his own man, and urged by Mamie Eisenhower to protect her husband's health, Nixon limited Ike's campaign appearances in 1960. When Eisenhower joined the campaign trail, in the closing weeks of the election, he threw a scare into the Democrats and almost bore Nixon to victory.

Nixon had a cordial relationship with John Kennedy until the 1960 race, but came away from the contest believing that he had been cheated of the presidency by Democratic skullduggery and Kennedy's underhanded behavior. Nixon carried that resentment, and a damaging obsession with the Kennedys, for years.

Lyndon Johnson accused Nixon of treason when he heard how Dick had used Anna Chennault, a Republican fund-raiser, to persuade the leaders of South Vietnam to reject a promising peace deal on the eve of the 1968 election. Nixon's lawyers fought for years to keep the evidence buried in the archives, and his personal involvement was kept secret until the publication of this book. In this evocative photograph, Johnson and Nixon confer at the White House.

Nixon cinched one of the greatest political comebacks in U.S. history in 1968 by winning the presidency with 43 percent of the vote in a three-way race with Hubert Humphrey and George Wallace.

At the Republican National Convention in Miami he selected Maryland governor Spiro Agnew as his running mate. It was Nixon's first "presidential" decision, and one of his worst. Agnew was a crook who continued to accept bribes while serving as vice president.

Dick and Pat wave to the crowds, while riding down Pennsylvania Avenue on Inauguration Day 1969. They were met by antiwar protesters, who tossed debris and epithets at the limousine, causing the Nixons to withdraw inside the car for safety.

make it easier for Pat to travel with her husband. "If you feel that this will not take care of providing a good housekeeper, such additional help for the children and other expenses as will be falling on you from the household side don't hesitate to tell Herman, Tom or me because it is not going to be any serious problem to provide whatever may be reasonably necessary," Smith told Nixon. It led to loose talk in California that money was being raised to get Pat a maid.

SYNDICATED COLUMNIST PETER EDSON heard the rumors and resolved to inquire when he next met the candidate. His opportunity came on September 14, when Nixon and Edson appeared on *Meet the Press*. As they spoke after the show, Nixon was candid and urged the reporter to contact Smith for the details of the fund. Edson liked Nixon, though harboring "serious misgivings about his ability to be President in case anything should happen to General Eisenhower." On September 17, having interviewed Smith, Edson sent Nixon a draft of his story, scheduled for publication the following day.

"Mr. Smith was most cooperative, furnishing all information except the list of donors to the fund. I still think that should be published, to make this whole thing open and above board," Edson wrote. He signed his note, "My best wishes, and thanks for making this information available to me." The subsequent story was straightforward, and mildly damaging. NIXON AIDED FINANCIALLY BY RICH CALIFORNIANS, the headline said, describing the unnamed donors as "well-to-do Southern California political angels." It ran in afternoon newspapers around the country on Thursday, September 18.

Edson's version took a backseat, however, to a more lurid version of the tale, bannered on the front page of that day's *New York Post*. Correspondent Leo Katcher was one of several newsmen on the West Coast working for liberal publications that had been tipped by Warren loyalists. SECRET RICH MEN'S TRUST FUND KEEPS NIXON IN STYLE FAR BEYOND HIS SALARY, read the headline to the story. The copy was not as sensational, but it described the donors as "a 'millionaires' club devoted exclusively to the financial comfort of Sen. Nixon."

"Once the headline appeared, it . . . created a firestorm," Nixon remembered. The *Post*'s presentation was hideously inaccurate. There was no evidence that the Nixons were living in either great style or comfort. Pat had irregular help for gardening, child care, and housekeeping, in part because Dick was a workaholic—always away or at the office. The girls attended public school, and as often as not Dick's parents did the babysitting. The couple's new home would not get air-conditioning until 1953, when they bought their first window unit for the den. Their Oldsmobile was a two-year-old sedan.

The rules were looser then. Stevenson had his own $84,000 slush fund for political obligations, and used it to donate to other candidates, pay for entertaining, send Christmas hams to journalists, and supplement the salaries of his staff.* The Democratic vice-presidential candidate, Senator John Sparkman of Alabama, had his wife on his office payroll. And Eisenhower benefited from the lavish generosity of his wealthy golf and card-playing buddies, who, among their other gifts to the general, would build a house for his use at the Augusta National Golf Club in Georgia.

But only Nixon got the headlines when the wire services carried the story of the "secret fund" to newspapers around the country. Some gave it front-page treatment. Aside from the usual imperative of selling newspapers, journalists found that the commotion provided a useful opportunity to study Eisenhower and Nixon under pressure. Military leadership doesn't always transfer to political success: American history was littered with great commanders who failed as politicians. As much as anything, the controversy was to be a test of Eisenhower's judgment. In the week to come, Ike would lose or win the 1952 election.

NIXON WAS ABOARD the *Dick Nixon Special* when word arrived about the impending revelations. His first reaction was to dismiss it. "That's probably the Pete Edson story. There is nothing to worry about," he told his new press secretary, James Bassett. To be on the safe side, he called in Bassett, Chotiner, Bill Rogers, and Pat Hillings for a series of consultations. Eventually Chotiner wrote up a statement—"Facts Concerning Dana Smith Trustee Fund"—which was distributed to the press as the train neared Merced, in Northern California, at lunchtime that Thursday. The statement took a dig at Sparkman's wife, noted the high costs of representing California, and ended: "Surely the time has not come in America when a young man who has not had time to accumulate a private fortune should be barred from . . . representing the people."

Eisenhower, meanwhile, was crossing the farmlands of Nebraska on his own train, the *Eisenhower—Look Ahead, Neighbor!—Special,* where, like everyone traveling with the candidates, the press corps was getting

---

* About $750,000 in 2016, after factoring in inflation.

fragments of news—the biggest, that Democratic Party chairman Stephen Mitchell had called for Nixon to step down—from bundles of local newspapers tossed aboard at rural train stations. The two Republican campaigns, and their journalistic wolf packs, would spend most of Thursday and Friday in the western boondocks, rolling along through hundreds of miles of farms and fields, hardly speaking to each other, ensnared in speculation and rumor. By evening, the burgeoning story was causing "great concern" in the Eisenhower high command, his press corps reported. On Friday morning, Ike convened the first emergency meeting of his advisers and drafted a statement urging Nixon to release "all documentary evidence" of his innocence. The gist of the message was conveyed by a go-between, Senator Fred Seaton of Nebraska, in a phone call Nixon took from the train station in Chico. Ike's crusade was now enveloped in "a shadow of gloom," the newsmen reported.

The trouble for Ike was that the fund story cut against the grain of a campaign theme: Eisenhower had been blasting the Democrats for the Truman-era corruption in Washington. "The episode . . . threatened to demolish, with eloquent mockery, the more righteous pretensions of a campaign that had christened itself, without excessive modesty, a 'Crusade,'" Emmet Hughes, an Eisenhower speechwriter, recalled. The general's "aw shucks" manner was a priceless asset, and folks were catching a whiff of hypocrisy. "Corruption is the leading Republican argument," Eric Sevareid told his CBS radio listeners. "It seemed to be a winning argument. Now that weapon may be blunted." Ike had been quoting Ecclesiastes, telling his audiences that this was "a time to cast away" the old and bring in the new. The reporters gleefully asked: Was it not time "to cast away" Nixon?

In private, Ike's team was divided. The political professionals hoped to ride out the storm, knowing how disastrous it would be if Eisenhower's first "presidential" decision were exposed as a blunder. Another group, newcomers to politics but closer to Ike, were furious with Nixon and fretting about the hero's image. "The more idealistic and less experienced of the Eisenhower advisers wanted Nixon to vanish in a Wagnerian climax of flame and smoke," *Look* magazine reported.

For someone like Nixon, ever insecure, the next hundred hours were particularly hellish. One after another, his political patrons—Stassen, Dewey, Eisenhower—would abandon him, as his enemies closed in. "The rumors flew thick and fast as to this friend and that friend of Eisenhower's who felt it was imperative that I be dropped from the ticket," Nixon remembered. The Warren-Knowland wing of the California party "were particularly active in building up the Dump Nixon Movement," he recalled. "While they had paid the necessary lip service to my candidacy once I was nominated they did not appreciate the fact that I had refused to give my support to Warren from the beginning and had openly worked for Eisenhower in the pre-convention days as well as at the convention."

Nixon's instinct, throughout, was to fight back. He did so at Friday's first stop, in Marysville, a small town north of Sacramento, when a heckler shouted: "Tell them about the $16,000!"

"Hold the train!" Nixon ordered. He told a mostly supportive audience how "the Communists and crooks" were out to "smear" him. It felt good to lash out, and his aides were cheered by how the crowds reacted. Then word reached them that the Saturday morning editions of the *Washington Post* and the *New York Herald Tribune* would call on Nixon to step down. The knock from the *Post* was not particularly surprising; its editors never would like Nixon. The *Tribune* editorial was the "real blockbuster," Nixon recalled. It was the newspaper Bert Andrews worked for. It had helped Nixon break the Hiss case. Its editorial page was the voice of Wall Street Republicanism and the eastern establishment. Nixon considered its publishers to be "personal friends." Ominously, they were closer friends to Ike.

Nixon reeled as if "the roof caved in." Rogers was similarly shaken, while Chotiner raged at the "damned amateurs" who were playing "right into the hands of the enemy." If Nixon were forced to resign, the party would not recover and "Eisenhower will lose," Chotiner advised. Rose Mary Woods recalled Chotiner going days without sleep, and arguing on the phone, tears coasting down his face, for fairer treatment of Nixon. "Chotiner was the most solid and sincere friend that Nixon had at that time," the Amateur Earl Adams would recall.

This time, Pat was on Chotiner's side. She had watched it all unfold, and on Friday night, when her husband expressed his discouragement and wondered aloud if he should not step down, she told Dick to rally. "If you, in the face of attack, do not fight back but simply crawl away, you will destroy yourself," Pat said. "Your life will be marred forever and the same will be true of your family, and particularly, the girls." Her bracing talk was welcome. Nixon found the resolve to soldier on. "My emotional and mental and physical resources had been drained to a dangerous low point," he remembered. "Pat's insistence that I had to fight the battle through may have averted a rash decision."

—

SATURDAY BROUGHT THE strokes of a plan. The press was in full throat, baying, combing through records, searching for favors granted to donors, and giving credence to Democratic suggestions that Nixon could be prosecuted for tax evasion. "Here's a holy Joe that has been talking pretty big," Democratic chairman Mitchell taunted. "Now let him put up some facts." But from a variety of sources—on the Nixon train, in the Eisenhower campaign, and at Republican Party headquarters—an idea was aborning. Nixon could take his case to the voters. He could make an address to the nation. He could go on television.

"All we've got to do," Chotiner told him, "is to get you before enough people."

Nixon had now reached Oregon, where he was touched by the warm welcome he received from Governor Doug McKay. "I didn't like to see anybody kicked around when he is down," McKay told him later. "If you had the guts to fight it out I certainly should have enough guts to introduce you." When a heckler waved a sign about mink coats—a reference to Nixon's attacks on the Truman administration grafters—Nixon capably tapped the politics of grievance. His wife didn't own a mink, he told the crowd. They couldn't afford it. She wore a "good Republican cloth coat." But he was staggered to learn that Knowland had been called back from a trip to Hawaii to join Ike on the general's train. It seemed that his seatmate was auditioning to replace him. A "jostling, jeering crowd" in Portland shoved the Nixons and threw coins at them, hard enough "to cause us to duck," he would remember. A decade later, he recalled that weekend as "the dreariest and bleakest I was ever to experience in my political career."

Bassett, Nixon's new press aide, reported that 90 percent of the Eisenhower press corps believed that Nixon should, and would, be dumped. But Ike, in fact, was calm. In a letter to *Tribune* publisher William Robinson, he chastised his friend for the paper's "hair-trigger" reaction. There were elemental values of fairness at stake, the general said—principles more important than political expedience. "I am not willing to prejudge any man," Ike wrote. "I have had a sound regard for Dick Nixon, as a member of the United States Navy, as a strong congressman and senator, and as a man. I have had reason to believe in his honesty and character. As you know, I've admired him greatly." If there was "real wrong," Eisenhower promised, there would be "prompt and conclusive action by me." But Nixon deserved a chance. They should not "jump to the conclusion."

Arthur Summerfield, the chairman of the Republican Party, led a small but earnest band of Nixon's defenders on the *Eisenhower Special*. His aide,

Bob Humphreys, polled Republican leaders around the country, enlisting their support for a televised address. Eisenhower jogged from his train through a midday rain on Saturday to use a stationmaster's phone and confer with his old comrade-in-arms Lucius Clay, who, though no fan of Nixon's, advised Ike not to act precipitously. The press was looking for portents—peering through the windows of the stationmaster's office and reporting the shapes of Eisenhower's doodles (a "heavy black square" with dark lines through it) as he spoke with Clay—and so Ike called them in for an off-the-record chat. He would give Nixon the time to collect all the data and prove his innocence, Ike said, but make no mistake about it: his running mate needed to be beyond reproach. "Of what avail is it for us to carry on this crusade against this business of what has been going on in Washington if we, ourselves, aren't as clean as a hound's tooth?" he asked.

Privately, Ike knew the score. He told Sherman Adams, "If Nixon has to resign, we can't possibly win."

ON SUNDAY, THE running mates found time (and Ike the willingness) to talk to each other. Nixon had started the morning by slipping away from the hotel to attend a restorative Quaker service. He grew misty-eyed when his old law partner, Tom Bewley, and supporter John Reilly arrived from Whittier to announce that his hometown friends remained loyal. He slumped in a chair—dazed by the betrayal, arms listless at his side—when a telegram from Stassen arrived urging Nixon to step down and be replaced by Warren. And he sobbed after reading another telegram, this one from Hannah, pledging her love.

Chotiner and the others were worrying about Nixon's state of mind. He had read Ike's "hound's tooth" comment as "the presumption of guilt." Throughout the day, he was compelled to search for inner strength and composure. Yet work was never a chore for Nixon—it was an anodyne. "I will not crawl," he muttered to himself. His aides, in Oregon and in Washington, were given assignments: checking tax laws, sorting through HUAC files, and compiling profiles of the left-wing *New York Post* and its editor, James Wechsler, a former Communist.

SKIRL YOUR PIPES AND BEAT THE DRUM . . . WE'RE ALL WITH YOU, George MacKinnon told Nixon in a telegram from the staff in Washington.

Nixon kept to his schedule and attended a Sunday-night event at a local synagogue. "Never in the history of American politics has such a situation arisen," CBS radio advised its listeners. "The furor . . . has spread across the country." Nixon was back in his hotel room with a doctor who was treating his tension-torn neck muscles (Pat's own neck was so sore that she had already taken to bed), when the phone rang. It was Eisenhower.

"Hello Dick. You've been taking a lot of heat the last couple of days," Ike said.

"Yes," said Nixon.

"Has it been pretty rough?"

"Yes."

"You know," said Eisenhower, "this is an awful hard thing for me to decide."

"Well, General, you know how it is," said Dick, "but there comes a time in matters like this when you've either got to shit or get off the pot."

Nixon told Eisenhower that he would step down if that was what the general wished. But Ike dodged the responsibility.

"You've got a big following in this country, and if the impression got around that you got off the ticket because I forced you to get off, it's going to be very bad. On the other hand, if I issue a statement now backing you up, in effect people will accuse me of condoning wrongdoing," Ike said.

"I was out to dinner tonight with some of my friends and they just don't know what is to be done, but they thought some way you ought to get your story across to the country," said Eisenhower. "I don't want to be in the position of condemning an innocent man. I suggest that you ought to go on a nationwide television program and tell them anything there is to tell—everything you can remember. Tell them about any money you ever took."

A full financial scrubbing was a painful addition to the plan, and a signal from Eisenhower that some televised flummery would not suffice. This speech had to cauterize the wound.

"After the television, General, if you think I should stay on I think you should say so," Nixon pleaded.

Eisenhower dodged. "We ought to wait three or four days after the television show to see what the effect of the program was," Ike said. "Go on the television show, and good luck." They chatted a bit about the crowds they were drawing, and then Eisenhower rang off.

"Well, keep your chin up," said the general.

"Best of luck," said Nixon.

Long after midnight, Nixon addressed the *Nixon Special* press corps. Their dispatches broke the news: Nixon was suspending active campaigning to return to Los Angeles. From there he would make an unprecedented televised appeal to the nation. There was speculation he would resign. "Nixon has been thrown to the wolves," the wires reported one aide saying.

AFTER SIX YEARS in politics, Nixon had a settled speechwriting routine. It would vary little in the years to come. He would pull out his yellow pads and write an outline, adding and amending as he went. In time, the first outline gave way to another. Then another. The process of writing and rewriting sank the words into his memory. By the time it came to talk, he could recite without notes. He saw the text unreeling in his mind's eye.

The fund speech was born on the chartered airplane that carried him from Portland to Los Angeles on Monday. He decided on a three-part structure: a refutation of the allegations, the full financial disclosure Eisenhower requested ("Why do you have to tell people how little we have and how much we owe?" a miserably unhappy Pat asked), and then a pivot to offense, with a blast at the Democrats, and a pitch for Ike's election.

On an airline postcard from the seat-back pocket, Nixon scrawled a reminder to mention a black-and-white cocker spaniel that had been sent to Tricia and Julie as a gift. In a 1944 speech, Franklin Roosevelt had made his Scottish terrier Fala famous; now Dick resolved to do the same for their new puppy, Checkers.

He remembered, as well, the "Republican cloth coat" line he had used that week. From somewhere (maybe because it was cited by Whittaker Chambers in his memoir, *Witness*) he recalled a quip attributed to Lincoln—"God must have loved the common people. He made so many of them"—and decided it applied, and would resonate with his audience.

"And so it went," Nixon recalled, "thinking, dozing, scribbling until the plane arrived . . . at Los Angeles." There he stood on the hood of a car to thank a band of loyalists who had come to welcome him. It was times like this, he told them, that "one finds out who your friends really are." Wary of distractions, the campaign took a block of rooms at the Ambassador Hotel. Assembling the financial details was a necessary nightmare, for his critics were sure to pounce on any misstep. The learned faculty at Whittier College were called on to confirm the Lincoln quotation. Lawyers at Gibson, Dunn and Crutcher (Herb Brownell and Sherman Adams were just two of Ike's advisers who had friends at the firm) were hired to review Dana Smith's arithmetic, with aid from accountants at Price Waterhouse.

"I never worked harder in my life," Nixon recalled. The need to plunge a stake in the story grew dire as reporters dug up instances where Nixon's office had helped out contributors. Nixon knew, too, that the law firm's report would disclose that there was a second fund, of almost $11,000, that Smith had collected since the Chicago convention—the money to supply Pat with household help.

Nixon was grateful for the news reports that came on Monday, revealing details of Stevenson's fund, but he was wound awfully tight. "At times like this an individual is not controlled solely by intellectual considerations. His emotions are bound to have even more effect than they should," he would recall. "The attacks had worn me down. . . . The [Eisenhower] indecision. The way some of those I had thought to be my friends had been so quick to turn against me. The incessant hammering of the antagonistic press." He shared the outline of his speech with Rogers on a long walk they took, evading reporters.

ON TUESDAY, NIXON showed his audacity. He needed to end the speech by asking viewers to respond: the question was, to whom? If they wrote and called Nixon, the Democrats would surely accuse him of massaging the results. But if he asked folks to contact Eisenhower, he would be handing Ike's staff the power to manipulate the outcome. Nixon had settled on the Republican National Committee, led by friendly partisans, when he was called to the telephone. It was Tom Dewey. Nixon had to leave for the studio within the hour. But he assumed, correctly, that Dewey had a message from the high command.

"There has just been a meeting of all of Eisenhower's top advisers," Dewey said. "They have asked me to tell you that it is their opinion that at the conclusion of the broadcast tonight you should submit your resignation to Eisenhower."

Nixon was incredulous, devastated, and furious. They had thought it wise to interrupt his last-minute preparations with this one final knock? Were they *trying* to sabotage him? "What does *Eisenhower* want me to do?" he stammered.

Dewey hedged. Well, he hadn't actually spoken to Ike, the governor said, but he was sure from the men he spoke to that this word came from the top.

"It's a little late for them to pass on this kind of recommendation to me. I've already prepared my remarks," Nixon said. As his mind raced, Dewey rambled on with a proposal that he resign from the Senate as well, and vindicate himself in a special election. Nixon cut him off. He had to get to the studio.

"What shall I tell the group you are going to do?" Dewey asked.

"Just tell them that I haven't the slightest idea what I am going to do, and if they want to find out they had better listen to the broadcast," he said.

And with that, he slammed down the phone.

For the next half hour, Nixon moved in a daze—showering, shaving, and donning his suit. Because of Dewey's call, he could not finish memorizing his remarks: "I just hadn't had time to get it all in my head." He would have to carry notes onto the set.

No one spoke as Dick and Pat left their room and walked through the hotel lobby. He sat in the front of the Cadillac limousine, using his twenty-minute ride in the car to shuffle through the outline one more time. He had made the decision to defy Dewey, Ike, and the rest: he would not resign; he would fight to retain his spot on the ticket.

But the idea that the fight would end in victory, "I did not think, was possibly in the cards."

THE EL CAPITAN Theatre was on Vine Street, just up the hill from the storied intersection with Hollywood Boulevard. It was home to the mawkish reality show *This Is Your Life* and to the *Colgate Comedy Hour,* a showcase for comics like Abbott and Costello. For $75,000, the Republicans had strung together some sixty NBC-TV outlets, and hundreds of radio stations. The broadcast was slated for 6:30 to 7 p.m. on the West Coast, and 9:30 to 10 p.m. in the East. It was a fine time slot: Tuesday was the night that Milton Berle—"Mr. Television"—had his wildly popular show.

In 1950, Nixon had been introduced to a young Hollywood producer and director, Edward "Ted" Rogers. Intrigued by television and sensing its potential, he had questioned Rogers intently about the attributes of the new medium. Rogers had explained "the quantum jump of the visual sense over . . . audio" and the extraordinary "acceleration of impulse" that, advertisers were discovering, the medium stirred in an audience.

Nixon seemed "young, straightforward, energetic, not a poseur," Rogers remembered. There was "no deviousness" and "no fake, stylized quality to him. . . . You could laugh with him . . . there was an enormous eagerness to learn. . . . He was accessible. . . . open." When Nixon joined the Republican ticket, Rogers joined the staff as a media consultant.

Rogers's work was a marvel of improvisation. He'd hoped to have hours to stage and prepare Nixon for the broadcast but, in the end, got all of five minutes. At around 2 a.m. Monday, he had awakened John Claar, a TV director in Los Angeles, and told Claar to meet him at the Ambassador Hotel at daybreak. The team worked through the day and night, but Nixon refused to rehearse, or even meet the director.

"How the hell can I light a telecast, photograph a man, if I'm never going to see him before air?" the irate Claar demanded.

"I don't know how you're going to do it, but we will," Rogers told him. Someone remembered that a local ad salesman bore a striking resemblance to Nixon, and so the man was enlisted to stand in for the lighting checks and other technical preparations.

When Rogers asked Nixon how he would close the show, Nixon replied: "I don't know, but you'll know when I'm finished."

From an NBC lot, Rogers had chosen a stock desk and a bookshelf for the performance—"the library set," he called it—and, off to the side, an easy chair for Pat. There was no time to rehearse Nixon's movements—Rogers sketched a white circle on the stage and told him that as long as he stayed within it, the cameras would follow. The key was to be natural, he told Nixon—to be himself.

Pat and Dick retired to the dressing room for one last moment alone. "I just don't think I can go through this one," he confessed. He would forget the words she spoke, but never the expression in her eyes. "I seemed to sense she had far more confidence in my ability to do what had to be done than I had," he would remember, and it gave him strength. So did a quick prayer he murmured, with his head in his hands, just before the broadcast began: "God: Thy will be done, not mine."

Rogers brought him to his mark. "I watched the big clock in front of the camera turning into the final minute before air time," Nixon recalled. "The director brought down his hand and pointed to me." He stumbled in his opening, suppressed the urge to panic, carried on.

And then, as he spoke, Nixon realized that he had it nailed. The words were flowing. The argument was cogent. He stopped looking at his notes. The intense fatigue, the cost of not eating and hours of sleeplessness, fell away. "The tension went out of me," he recalled. "I felt calm, and in complete control of myself and my subject." He was onstage. He was acting. He could do this. And so Nixon proceeded, as Eisenhower aide Emmet Hughes would recall, to make "his dog, his wife, her clothes, his debts and his mortgages famous."

THE FIRST SEGMENT of the speech was perfunctory. Nixon opened like a lawyer, wooing a jury. He outlined the fund and its uses, displayed the

Gibson, Dunn and Crutcher and Price Waterhouse reports to the camera, and asked the viewers, as he had asked the crowds that week, if they would rather he spent their hard-earned money—the taxpayers' money!—on political expenses like postage, advertising, and his airfare home.

Then, with the drumroll that he was going to do something "unprecedented in the history of American politics," Nixon launched into the second segment of his talk. He gave the details of his family finances—mortgages, insurance policy, the two-year-old Oldsmobile, the money he owed to his bank and his parents—in terms with which the average couple could identify.

"Our family was one of modest circumstances, and most of my early life was spent in a store out in East Whittier. It was a grocery store, one of those family enterprises. The only reason we were able to make it go was because my mother and dad had five boys, and we all worked in the store.

"I worked my way through college, and, to a great extent, through law school. And then in 1940, probably the best thing that ever happened to me happened. I married Pat who's sitting over here. We had a rather difficult time after we were married, like so many of the young couples who may be listening to us. I practiced law. She continued to teach school."

He was now halfway through the broadcast. The camera panned to Pat for a moment. Her eyes never left her husband, seemingly—undoubtedly—riveted by the drama.

"In 1942, I went into the service," Nixon said. "Let me say that my service record was not a particularly unusual one. I went to the South Pacific. I guess I'm entitled to a couple of battle stars. I got a couple of letters of commendation. But I was just there when the bombs were falling."

Then came the detailed accounting. Money earned in public speaking. Their house in Washington. Net worth. "It isn't very much," he said, seemingly embarrassed, almost apologetic. "But Pat and I have the satisfaction that every dime that we've got is honestly ours."

Like a hot starting pitcher, Nixon was painting the black. "I should say this, that Pat doesn't have a mink coat. But she does have a respectable Republican cloth coat, and I always tell her she'd look good in anything." Now he paused, bowed his head, and brought his hand up to his brow, apparently searching for the words to make some awful confession.

"One other thing I probably should tell you, because if I don't they'll probably be saying this about me, too," he said. "We did get something, a gift, after the election." He had his audience's full attention for the moment that would give the speech its name.

"A man down in Texas heard Pat on the radio mention the fact that our two youngsters would like to have a dog. And believe it or not, the day before we left on this campaign trip we got a message . . . saying they had a package for us. We went down to get it. You know what it was? It was a little cocker spaniel dog in a crate that he'd sent all the way from Texas, black and white, spotted. And our little girl Tricia, the six year old, named it Checkers. And you know, the kids, like all kids, love the dog, and I just want to say this, right now, that regardless of what they say about it, we're gonna keep it."

If that corny ploy didn't drive his message home—*I* am one of *you* and *they* are screwing *us*—he tossed in the Lincoln quote to make the claim specific.

"It isn't easy to come before a nationwide audience and bare your life, as I've done," he said sorrowfully. "But I want to say some things before I conclude that I think most of you will agree on. . . . I believe that it's fine that a man like Governor Stevenson, who inherited a fortune from his father, can run for President. But I also feel that it's essential in this country of ours that a man of modest means can also run for President, because, you know, remember Abraham Lincoln, you remember what he said: 'God must have loved the common people—he made so many of them.'"

THE THIRD AND final element of the Checkers speech was the counterattack—upon *all* his tormentors. There were Truman, Stevenson, and the Democrats, who, Nixon said, had left the government riddled with Communists and corruption. There were the columnists and commentators who "were violently opposing me at the time I was after Alger Hiss." And then he fired a salvo—veiled but unmistakable—at Ike.

Stevenson and Sparkman were candidates for august offices, Nixon said. They needed to "come before the American people as I have and make a complete financial statement as to *their* financial history," he said. "And if they don't, it will be an admission that they have something to hide." There was, of course, another man running for august office that year. His name was Dwight Eisenhower. And by the end of the campaign this intensely private man would be compelled to expose his own finances to the press. Nor would he forget why.

Nixon had been sitting for more than twenty minutes. Now he stood up and moved beyond the desk—arms outstretched, fists clenched, daring his foes like a gladiator.

He spoke of the hope that Ike could settle the war in Korea, and read aloud a letter from the nineteen-year-old wife of a combat corpsman. She just knew that the general could end the suffering, and return her husband to her and the two-month-old son he'd never seen. She had sent in a check for $10. It was a check, Nixon told the audience, "I will never cash." And as bad as things got, he would prize that letter, which "no one can take away from us." As if anyone threatened to do so.

Finally, with a minute to go, Nixon showed his defiance. He ignored Ike's command—passed on by Dewey—to resign from the ticket. "I don't believe I ought to quit," he said, "because I'm not a quitter." His viewers should contact the RNC, he said, and he would abide by their decision. Not only had he refused to resign, he had taken the power from Eisenhower's hands and given it to the public and the party. A few last words about Ike—"A great man!"—and then, as Nixon was still speaking, the picture faded out.

Ted Rogers would remember the "absolute, emotionally charged silence in the studio during the entire telecast." He had emerged from the control room to squat by the camera and give Nixon his final cues. For those last three minutes "the tension . . . was almost stifling," he said. The producer and his crew were caught in the moment, and Nixon, in "a complete emotional daze," walked out toward the camera, as if to grasp the audience, and bumped right into the lens. Only then did he realize he was off the air. He turned away from those who tried to steady him and buried his face in the onstage drapes. He threw his notes on the floor. "I couldn't do it. It wasn't any good," he said, as Bassett and Chotiner embraced him.

"Let's get out of here and get a fast one," he told them. "I need it."

Nixon soon learned that he was wrong. He learned it from the teary eyes of the cameramen on the set, and the awe in the voice of the man who wiped away his makeup. He learned it from the cheers of the loyalists on the sidewalk, from an adoring crowd that now filled his hotel lobby, and the reports of swamped switchboards and overwhelmed telegraph lines all over the country. "In 30 minutes, by the exposure of his personality, he had changed from a liability to his party to a shining asset," *Time* reported. "He had established himself as a man of integrity and courage."

Sophisticates chortled. *Variety* called it "schmaltz." The traveling press had spent the thirty minutes making wisecracks, and griping about the lack of a text. Warren Olney, a Warren loyalist who would serve with Brownell in the Department of Justice, called it "an intolerable amount of corn" mixed with "tear-jerking remarks about the family dog." Walter Lippmann apologized to a foreign guest on behalf of the United States. And Lucius Clay "thought it was so corny that it would be an immediate flop." But then Clay found "the elevator boy crying and the doorman crying and I knew then I was wrong."

The Democrats had exploited the fund story "to the hilt," then California attorney general Edmund "Pat" Brown recalled, "but he overwhelmed us with that Checkers speech. . . . You've got to hand it to him." It was "as phony as a counterfeit dime but . . . very effective."

Nixon had looked young, honest, and earnest. His tabulation of accomplishment and debt had struck a chord with millions of postwar families, gathered in their suburban dens and living rooms. And they responded. Nine million televisions were tuned into the speech—the largest TV audience to that time. People wrote hundreds of thousands of telegrams and letters on his behalf. It was an astonishing act of self-resuscitation. "He . . . breathed into his own mouth," Bryce Harlow would remember. "Resurrected by his own hand."

"God help us if he ever turns into a force for evil," supporter Paul Hoffman told Rogers. "Television is so powerful, and he is so effective with it."

EISENHOWER WATCHED THE speech with his wife and staff in Cleveland before addressing a campaign rally. "Well that boy's got a lot of courage," he told them when it ended. Nixon reminded him of Patton, another quite useful but strong-headed subordinate, whom he had disciplined during the war. From fifteen thousand Republicans, gathered in the hall below him, Ike heard the chant: "We want Nixon! We want Nixon!" The band was playing "The Battle Hymn of the Republic."

Eisenhower sent a telegram to his running mate, congratulating him on a "magnificent" performance. But Nixon's insubordination had not gone unnoticed. "Nixon was particularly shrewd at the end of his speech," Brownell remembered. The "gambit took . . . control . . . away from the Eisenhower campaign" and placed it in friendlier hands.

And so Ike cuffed Nixon for his defiance. He told the nation's Republicans, via a statement, that the choice of keeping or jettisoning Nixon was not theirs, but his. And in his telegram to Nixon, the general let him know who was boss. They could resume the campaign just as soon as they met and Nixon made his report, and Ike reached a final, "personal conclusion." It wasn't over yet.

—

Ike's congratulatory message was lost in the tidal wave of telegrams. Nixon saw only the last part—summoning him to bend the knee—in a wire service story. "What more can he possibly want from me?" he asked, in anguish. After a historic performance that opened a half century of television's unrivaled domination of American politics—and will stand for all time among the most effective uses of the medium—Nixon succumbed to self-pity. "The point of greatest danger for an individual who is confronted with a great crisis is not in the period when he is preparing for battle or actually fighting the battle but in the period immediately after the battle is over. Then, at that time he will find himself emotionally and mentally and physically exhausted and it is then that the decisions he makes must be watched most carefully," he would explain. "For a week I had been through great emotional and mental strain. I had been forced to rein in my true feelings time and time again. The broadcast itself had required concentration more intense than I had ever been able to apply."

"I had decided in my own mind before the broadcast that at least when it was finished, my ordeal would be over," Nixon recalled. "And I was prepared to accept the verdict, whether it was favorable or unfavorable. But what I had not anticipated was that the terrible strain of indecision would not be lifted.

"I felt I could not stand even one more day of such indecision, let alone four or five days or a week. I just wanted the whole issue decided," he remembered. "I told Chotiner and the others in the room that if this broadcast had not satisfied the general, there was nothing more that I could do and that I would resign from the ticket."

Nixon dictated a telegram. (Chotiner collected it from Rose Mary Woods and tore it up.) They all were furious now, in the Nixon camp, and intent on ignoring Eisenhower's invitation. They headed for the plane to resume their campaign in Missoula, Montana. To hell with the general. Let Ike sweat.

As in Los Angeles, Nixon sought to burn off the tension by taking an unscheduled walk through the empty streets of Missoula that morning. Meanwhile, sound heads prevailed. Summerfield pleaded with Chotiner and secured an assurance from Ike and Adams (who had crowded into an Ohio phone booth to take the call) that Nixon would stay on the ticket. And Bert Andrews placed a call to Nixon from the Eisenhower train.

"Richard, you don't have to be concerned about what will happen when you meet Eisenhower. The broadcast decided that, and Eisenhower knows it as well as anyone else," Andrews said. "But you must remember who he is. He is the general who led the allied armies to victory in Europe. He is the immensely popular candidate who is going to win this election. He is going to be President, and he is the boss of this outfit. He will make this decision and he will make the right decision. But he has the right to make it in his own way, and you must come to Wheeling to meet him and give him the opportunity to do exactly that."

The Nixon entourage boarded a plane and flew to West Virginia, where Ike was waiting on what Nixon remembered as a cold, smoggy, stinking night. As they gathered their belongings and prepared to disembark, Nixon spotted Eisenhower on the tarmac.

"He's here!" Nixon said. "Ike . . . he's right here . . . outside the door." Before Nixon could put on his coat, Eisenhower had climbed onto the plane, the trademark grin in place.

"Dick—boy am I glad to see you," said the general.

"Ike—you didn't need to come way out here," Nixon told him.

"Why, Dick," said Eisenhower. "You're my boy."

Eisenhower put his arm around him. Nixon slumped. Ike "gently eased him into a seat, and began talking in reassuring tones about how the campaign would proceed," a radio newsman recalled. Pat reached over to comfort her husband. Eisenhower wiped his own eyes. There were tears "on all sides," the broadcaster noted, "then both men recovered and walked out of the airplane to greet the crowd."

Later that night, when it all was clearly, finally over—after Summerfield had reported to Ike that the RNC had voted 107 to 0 to keep Nixon on the ticket, Nixon saw Bill Knowland on the podium. "That was a great speech, Dick," his seatmate said.

"Oh, Bill," said Nixon, and at the sight of a familiar face, he lost his composure yet again ("I had not physical or emotional reserve left") and was crying on Knowland's shoulder when a news photographer captured the moment. It added one more unforgettable image to an already legendary week.

"It has been a tough one," Eisenhower told his brother Edgar. But to a pal Ike admitted, "There is nothing like adversity to bring out the best in a real man—and Nixon came through with flying colors."

A Candidate for the Little Man

I N ONE HALF hour of television, Richard Nixon had done more than save his career, he had reset the calculus of American politics.

For eighty years, from the end of the Civil War through the days of World War II, the Republican Party was known as a home for Babbittry, and a nest, its critics said, of swinish industrialists and Wall Street bankers. The Republicans could connect with the common folk by evoking the godly Lincoln, offering military heroes like Ulysses S. Grant and Teddy Roosevelt, or portraying the Democrats as dangerous radicals. But once the Democratic Party absorbed the Populists in the 1890s, there was little doubt, in the shorthand of American politics, about who spoke for the little guy. Franklin Roosevelt had championed "the forgotten man" and given unshirted hell to the "unscrupulous money-changers" and "financial oligarchies."

"I welcome their hatred," Roosevelt said, accepting the Democratic nomination in 1936. "I should like to have it said of my first administration that in it the forces of selfishness and of lust for power met their match. I should like to have it said of my second administration that in it these forces met their master."

Amid the postwar prosperity, however, the New Deal coalition was fraying. It was a disparate weaving, with its Ivy League intellectuals and big-city political machines, Catholics, Jews, and Negroes, and the segregationists of the "Solid South," who despised all the rest. Now it was Nixon who claimed a visceral connection with "the forgotten man," and the Democrats who—by nominating Adlai Stevenson—looked like elitists. With his Checkers talk, Nixon had struck a chord with white-collar salarymen and midlevel managers; midlands Protestants and striving Roman Catholics; aspiring young couples, the denizens of Levittown and its thousand imitations. As the centripetal imperatives of the Second World War receded, the centrifugal shoves of class and race revived, and

Nixon's speech added impetus to the Roosevelt coalition's unraveling. A man and a moment had arrived, together.

"The sophisticates . . . sneer," wrote columnist Robert Ruark, but Nixon's speech "came closer to humanizing the Republican Party than anything that has happened in my memory. . . . Tuesday night the nation saw a little man, squirming his way out of a dilemma, and laying bare his most private hopes, fears and liabilities. This time the common man was a Republican."

RUARK WAS NOT alone. Others saw the auguries of realignment. This was the year, 1952, that Whittaker Chambers published *Witness,* his autobiographical account of descent, recantation, and redemption. His gloomy embroideries resonated at a time when Albert Einstein was warning that "general annihilation" beckoned, *High Noon* was in the theaters, and *En attendant Godot* was about to debut in Paris. An excerpt from *Witness* ran in the *Saturday Evening Post,* which sold an extra half a million copies that week. It became a noir gospel for the right: a portrait of America emerging from its adolescence, confronted by evil—at home and abroad.

But the book was, as well, a manifesto for right-wing populism. There was "a jagged fissure," Chambers wrote, "between the plain men and women of the nation and those who affected to act, think and speak for them." He railed against the "musk of snobbism" and "barehanded rascality" of the "nicest people" from "socially formidable circles" that "ran through the Hiss case like rot through an apple." He warned of how, "from their roosts in the great cities, and certain collegiate eyries," the left "controlled the narrows of news and opinion." He laid claim to the silent mass of "my people, humble people, strong in common sense, in common goodness" who lived not in the elect precincts of Manhattan or its fancy suburbs, but "on the farms, on the streets, in homes, in shops." He likened the elites to the Dauphin's glittery knights at Agincourt, and ranked Nixon—"Nixie, the kind and good"—with King Hal's warriors for the working day.

The new divide was greater than "Hiss and anti-Hiss" or even "New Dealism *vs.* Taftism," historian Eric Goldman reported in *The Crucial Decade.* "More than ever, the conflict took on an aura of the highbrow and the heretical *vs.* God-fearing, none-of-your-highfalutin-nonsense, all-American common sense."

Nixie, the kind and good, was too cagey—had too fine a gift for political devilry—to miss so rich an opportunity. He knew how to reach the petit bourgeoisie, in part because he shared their background and their values, their discontents and rancor. "The Fifties were not the Eisenhower years but the Nixon years," the liberal columnist Murray Kempton would write, after the decade had run its course. They were the years "when the American lower middle class in the person of this man moved to engrave into the history of the United States, as the voice of America, its own faltering spirit, its self-pity and its envy, its continual anxiety about what the wrong people might think, its whole peevish, resentful whine."

When the *Saturday Review* asked a group of well-known folk to review *Witness,* it included Nixon. "I can hear now the epithets which will be directed against [*Witness*] in the drawing rooms, around the dinner tables, and during the cocktail hours among the 'better people,'" Nixon wrote. They would doubtless arch an eyebrow and dismiss Chambers as a "fat repulsive little creature who said . . . terrible things about a 100 percent certified gentleman."

The Republicans could capture the little guy, Nixon reckoned, if they could cast the Democrats as a distant elite—an effete establishment of lawyers, writers, and professors who dwelled in Georgetown, Cambridge, and the trendier neighborhoods of Manhattan, embracing the jaundiced values of the campus and the newsroom and rejecting old faiths in favor of modernity. The intellectual establishment had not endeared itself to Nixon when two dozen Ivy League professors—including Allan Nevins, Henry Steele Commager, Richard Hofstadter, Dumas Malone, Mark Van Doren, and Lionel Trilling—joined in a statement that scoured the Checkers broadcast as "an essentially dishonest and emotional appeal."

Nixon had played his part in earning enmity. He had questioned the patriotism of the liberal meritocracy when Hiss was convicted, in the speech he had mailed out to thousands of supporters. "Men like Alger Hiss . . . come from good families, are graduates of our best schools," he wrote. The mutual distrust would endure. Late in the decade, Rita Hauser, a young New York lawyer drawn to Nixon, was commissioned by his advisers to gauge the sentiments of East Coast intellectuals. She responded with a gloomy assessment. "The net feeling as to Mr. Nixon's campaigns is that they did dupe, and thus were 'dishonest' or lacking in campaign due process," Hauser wrote. "From this flows the strong feeling that Nixon is unprincipled, non-trustworthy, a man without a firm moral base."

Nixon's native opportunism freed him from convention, wrote political journalist William White, and "his antennae are remarkably acute—matchlessly acute among the national politicians." His appeal was "the quintessence of the modern spirit of revolt from the aristocratic principle of the leader. It is this quality of oneness with what ordinary people are thinking that gives him such an edge."

Polly Ryther was a fine example of the now-not-forgotten majority. She was a mother of three, a former schoolteacher married to a carpenter, and a Democrat overwhelmed by the emotions unleashed by Nixon's Checkers speech. Television had brought Dick "for a visit" to her living room, she told Pat in a letter written right after the broadcast.

"I watched your husband lay bare his soul on television and wept for you both," Ryther said. Dick was an "honest, common man" and "we ourselves are honest folks" and "could see nothing dishonest" about his fund-raising practices.

"After listening to your husband, seeing how a 'little' man could be for . . . the Republican party . . . and maintain his integrity . . . I now can see where there is hope for our country," she told Pat. "Keep fighting folks. There will be others fighting for you and with you. And some of us will be praying for your courage and strength to do what is right."

IKE HAD THE common touch—but in a gentler, more benevolent fashion. In the days before and after the D-Day invasion his fellow Americans had been charmed by the Supreme Commander with the winning grin: chain-smoking, reading Zane Grey westerns, corralling egotistical officers like General George Patton and Field Marshal Bernard Montgomery to whip the Nazis. The photographs of Ike, in his waist-length jacket, visiting with his paratroopers on the eve of battle were famous. Generations, contemplating the burden of leadership, would shudder at the message he wrote in the hours before the Twenty-Ninth Infantry took the bluffs at Omaha Beach, on the awful chance he might need it: "Our landings in the Cherbourg-Havre area have failed to gain a satisfactory foothold and I have withdrawn the troops. My decision to attack at this time and place was based on the best information available. The troops, the air, and the Navy did all that bravery and devotion to duty could do. If any blame or fault attaches to the attempt it is mine alone."

Ike had spent four years of war bringing order and unity to bickering allies. He was confident. He knew how to lead, and, from those seemingly endless mediations, he knew how to persuade, and to parcel out his charm. He was one of those rare military men who could transfer the fame of battle into political success. Korea needed solving, and Ike seemed the man to fix it, especially once he vowed, in mid-October, "I will go to Korea."

But the Communist threat still filled the headlines—Julius and Ethel

Rosenberg would die in the electric chair the following summer—and Nixon was dispatched by Eisenhower's managers to whip up voters' fears as a more respectable, temperate edition of Joe McCarthy. The temperate part did not come naturally. Brownell was flabbergasted at the sophomoric ardor Nixon displayed during a World Series game they attended in New York. The Yankees prevailed over the Brooklyn Dodgers in extra innings, leaving the raving vice-presidential candidate drained, and Brownell somewhat aghast. Nixon brought that same zeal to the campaign, lashing out at "Adlai the Appeaser"—who bore a "Ph.D. from Dean Acheson's cowardly college of Communist containment." The Republicans brought Nixon another primetime appearance on national television in mid-October, to scorch Stevenson for testifying as a character witness on behalf of Hiss at the spy's 1949 trial. He wasn't challenging Stevenson's loyalty, Nixon said piously, just his judgment.

In Texarkana, in late October, the "Tricky" side of Dick made its most consequential appearance when, with calibrated malevolence, he called Harry Truman and his colleagues "traitors to the high principles in which many of the nation's Democrats believe." Truman, Rayburn, and others were convinced that Nixon had accused them of treason—and never forgave him. Truman thought Nixon a "shifty-eyed goddamn liar" and Speaker Rayburn told associates that of all the men he served with in a half century in Congress, none had such a (and here the Speaker would vary the adjective) mean, devious, or hateful face as Nixon.

Nixon "didn't impugn their loyalty, he swears, but they thought so and tried to destroy him for it," Bryce Harlow recalled.

"He was tarring . . . with the widest brush, and you pay a price when you do that," Ted Rogers said.

Nixon's Northern California treasurer wrote to warn him how "a large group" of his former supporters now "seem to have lost faith in you" and were "expressing great concern should you ascend to the Presidency."

"They can understand that your stressing of internal security against the Communists was politically expedient during your contest with Mrs. Douglas and admit it had a place in the recent campaign but, when in their opinion you excluded almost every other subject, they seem to feel it is the only thing you know—that it has become a mania with you," the man wrote.

Nationally, Ike captured 55 percent of the popular vote to Stevenson's 44 percent, and took 39 of 48 states and 442 electoral votes. Stevenson even lost Illinois, and the Republicans clawed their way to narrow majorities in the House and Senate.

Nixon had no illusions about his role in Ike's victory; he knew the people had voted for a hero. As a gag one day he had switched places with a tall, skinny news reporter and watched, laughing, from the press bus as the newsman played his part, sitting next to Pat and waving to crowds that believed they were seeing the actual Nixon. Dick kept up his tradition of bolting on Election Day: he headed for the beach with Bill Rogers and played touch football with a group of Marines. Then he and Pat received the results in Los Angeles, at the Ambassador Hotel. Frank Nixon, ailing, was helped along by Aylett Cotton. "He didn't seem to show a great jubilation over his son's election," the Nixon aide recalled. "It was more or less of a tired, grim satisfaction."

The "Inquiring Photografer" [*sic*] from the *Washington Times-Herald* caught Tricia on the street outside the Nixon home.* "He's always away," Tricia told her. "If he's so famous why can't he stay home?"

THE VICE PRESIDENT elect remained exorbitantly sensitive and continued to suffer from wounds he attributed to the press. "His antipathy . . . was really very, very intense—etched into his mind and attitude," said James Keogh, a Nixon speechwriter and biographer. "It became a spiral: Nixon reflecting to the press he didn't like it; the press hitting Nixon's raw nerve. Just a real visceral feeling. . . . He could not excise himself of it. It would burn on him and burn."

The enmity between Nixon and the institutions through which American political leaders communicate would have profound consequences. It offers, as well, a window on the man. A turbulent childhood left Nixon craving order. In his teenage public speaking contests, he spoke against dissent. His Quaker upbringing left him with a profound sense of privacy. His insecurity left him vulnerable. The press was none of this—it was snoopy, chaotic, and irreverent. Nixon was "so goddamn shy that it was just painful for him," said Earl Mazo, a *New York Herald Tribune* reporter. "Newspaper men were all part of an inquisition to Nixon. . . . We were the representatives of a hostile world, a world trying to tear him down and find out what he wanted to hide—in a personal way. It wasn't really political. It was trying to reveal him to be a poor and clumsy boy. He was more that than anything else."

"He was never one of the boys. . . . He always had that sense that if

---

* The photographer's name was Jacqueline Bouvier, and in 1953 she would marry Dick's friend John Kennedy, who had just been elected to the Senate.

people knew him then they would not really like him," James "Scotty" Reston, the *New York Times* newsman, recalled. "He had so much to hide, and he would never give of himself, and reporters sense that and they push."

In his first campaigns, Nixon had learned how favorable coverage was for sale: by buying ad space in California newspapers, or kneeling to potentates like Kyle Palmer and the Chandlers. "Kyle allowed Nixon to think that Nixon could have special treatment—that he could have a kind of special deal," Pat Brown remembered. The effect was corrupting, and ultimately a disservice. It left Nixon with a cynical perspective—that the game was rigged, and newsmen were whores.

Nixon's suspicions were confirmed by the Hiss affair. He had come to Congress, courageously shouldered and capably performed a patriotic duty—only to be skewered by left-wing journals, columnists, and cartoonists. "In the Hiss days an aggressive and militant activity against Communism was very *de trop*," newspaper executive and Eisenhower confidant William Robinson would explain. "It was downright anti-liberal and put you in a very bad light at the Press Club bar." Nixon learned that, while journalists professed to revere fairness and truth, as mortals they also craved influence and power. His critics on the editorial pages of the *Washington Post* and other liberal newspapers would never forgive him for proving them wrong about Alger Hiss, Nixon thought, for he had not merely won, he had humiliated them when doing so.

"Without any doubt there is a hard core of 'hate Nixon' voters," Republican pollster Claude Robinson wrote Nixon. "We have talked about this and tried to analyze it, but possibly only a psychiatrist could figure it out. . . . The best theory that I can come to is that the liberal fringe has a guilt feeling attached to the Alger Hiss case and wishes to blame you for it."

Dick and Pat had arrived in Washington brimming with idealism, in awe of the historic mission that the city represented. The couple had a few happy months, going out to dinner or dancing at the Shoreham Hotel. Then Whit Chambers and Alger Hiss came along. "One thing I want to make clear to you," a vehement Pat would tell her daughter Julie. "The reason people have gone after Daddy is that no one could control him—not the press, not the lobbyists, not the politicians. He did what he felt was right, and from the time that became apparent in the Hiss case, he was a target."

For decades, many people of goodwill believed that Hiss, the compelling liberal icon, was brought down by trumped-up charges. They clung to the view of Nixon as Torquemada. "The Hiss case . . . never went away," aide Robert Finch recalled. "There was, for a long time, a corrosive effect. And there was genuine anger there, I mean real anger . . . real hostility, something that went so deep as to make a man embattled."

Nixon was a practical man and followed the advice that well-wishers gave him, to schmooze and carouse with the press. He invited reporters in for drinks in his office and showed up at the press club bar. But he was bad at small talk, and so awfully serious and awkward. "Nixon would call and say: 'Let's go face the enemy.' This would mean that he wanted to go to the National Press Club. There he would tease a drink in the bar, while trying hard to be 'one of the boys,' among reporters dedicated largely to his extermination," a friendly newsman, Walter Trohan, would recall. "These sessions did not help him."

"These newspaper guys just don't understand a guy that doesn't drink and chase women," Nixon told his law school classmate Lyman Brownfield.

THEN CAME THE Checkers episode, which stoked Nixon's conviction that he was held to a different standard. "Press men temperamentally and traditionally are skeptical and cynical," he would recall. But "when it is a public official who has been in what to most of them is the contemptible business of Red hunting, this feeling is particularly strong."*

Nixon had trusted Peter Edson and the other newsmen who made the initial inquiries about his political slush fund. But then he watched, scarcely comprehending, as one dishonest headline in a liberal tabloid triggered a national uproar. The scope and fury of the assault, the cruelty of his inquisitors, and the betrayal by those he thought were friends had seared the Nixons, bringing Dick to tears on more than one occasion and sending Pat, trembling, into seclusion with the Drowns.

Dick and Pat were horrified to hear from their advance men how photographers placed empty liquor bottles outside their hotel room during the crisis, hoping to frame a damaging photo when the Nixons emerged in the morning. Amid the celebrations on election night, Pat had stayed up toward dawn, gathering and washing the glasses from the victory party to keep the hotel maids from telling reporters how much alcohol was consumed.

---

* Nixon didn't like references to "the Checkers speech," which he thought belittling, and instead called it "the fund crisis."

"Never again was she to feel the same toward political life," Dick recalled. "She had lost her zest for it."

AFTER NIXON'S CHECKERS speech, the Republican ticket soared in the polls; reporters grew bored baiting Nixon, and the spotlight returned to Ike and Adlai. But a few commentators—just enough to keep him livid—stayed on Nixon's case. Herblock was a constant vexation. Nixon's attacks on Democratic "traitors" inspired a *Post* cartoon that coupled Nixon to McCarthy, with both men carrying brushes and buckets of tar. The chipmunk-cheeked Nixon of earlier cartoons now had a five o'clock shadow—the first step of his transformation into the sewer-dwelling miscreant of the many Herblock cartoons that followed. "It was the opportunist, the political thuggery in him," the cartoonist would explain years later.

It hurt. "You don't like to get up in the morning and see a Herblock cartoon showing you climbing out of a sewer," Nixon remembered. "Children grow up, and those images become seared onto their brains and in their minds and their souls." He had their home delivery of the *Post* canceled.

Drew Pearson was another tormentor. According to *Time* magazine, which put him on its cover in December 1948, Pearson was second only to the gossip columnist Walter Winchell in reach and earnings, with a broadcast audience of 10 million people and a column that appeared in six hundred newspapers. His "ruthless, theatrical, crusading, high voltage" style made him rich, the magazine noted, with an annual income of $350,000, a Georgetown mansion, and a Potomac waterfront estate. The liberal muckraker was a friend or admirer of Helen Douglas, Jerry Voorhis, Alger Hiss, and Pat Brown. His son-in-law, George Arnold, was a Democratic politician in California who passed on tips and rumors.

Nixon had barely learned how to traverse the Capitol before he was stung by Pearson and responded, in a letter to House colleagues in the summer of 1947, by denouncing the columnist as an "arch character assassin and truth distorter." So the game was on. Pearson flayed Nixon in 1952, skinning him several times a week. Some columns were on the mark. Nixon's office had indeed interceded with the State Department to help Dana Smith, the keeper of the slush fund, to wriggle out of a gambling debt incurred at a Havana casino. He had also helped Smith obtain a $500,000 tax break. And, yes, Nixon had fibbed when telling the nation, in the Checkers speech, that Pat was born on St. Patrick's Day. Her birthday was actually March 16. The columnist unearthed favors that Nixon's office had performed. Many were humdrum constituent services, but one intercession—for an unsavory Romanian industrialist named Nicolae Malaxa—reeked of influence peddling. Malaxa, whose entry into the United States was opposed by American immigration officials because of his years as a Nazi collaborator, had hired Nixon's old law partner, Tom Bewley, to help him acquire U.S. residence and federal aid to build a California pipeline factory. Bewley was promised what he described as "a substantial fee" if the plant was built, and he and Herman Perry were named officers and directors in the company. Nixon's office, not surprisingly, came to Malaxa's aid.

But other Pearson tales were riddled with errors. Nixon had not joined Smith at the gambling tables in Havana. He and Pat had not applied for a tax exemption reserved for low-income veterans (it was another couple named Nixon). And a letter purportedly showing how Nixon took a bribe from an oil company was found to be a forgery. "Nixon is being subjected to a continuing attack," *Look* magazine concluded. "He is the victim of apparent forgeries, admittedly false charges, innuendos not yet backed by fact."

"Drew . . . was capable of serious hyperbole and omissions of the truth when it suited his agenda," the columnist's legman, Jack Anderson, would admit. Pearson loved nothing more than "a protracted, ugly, bitter-end vendetta that rages for years and exhausts both sides, often bringing one to ruin." With Nixon, the columnist found his ideal match. A file in Nixon's office labeled "Smears" grew fat and multiplied.

"The campaign was quite rugged," Nixon wrote a former law partner, Henry Knoop, in late 1952. "The attacks which Drew Pearson and the left wingers made during the final two weeks of the campaign have done some damage."

THE EFFECT WAS cumulative, and lingering. Dubious accusations were picked up by other journalists, embroidered over the years, and repeated as fact in books and articles. "Some of the mud stuck," Nixon recalled. "Many people who under no stretch of the imagination could be called politically partisan . . . wondered whether there was 'something wrong' as far as my personal integrity."

Mazo was stunned when, at the end of the decade, he was offered a book contract to write a quick biography of the vice president. "I was personally a Democrat, like most reporters. And I despised Nixon," Mazo recalled. "I wanted to cut him up, but I wanted to do it honestly, so I started researching."

"I found out that so much of what I knew to be total fact, had rated as fact, even written as fact, was just total horseshit," said Mazo. "At least 50 percent of the accepted things about this man were total fabrications, just out of the whole cloth. Never happened. Never happened. They started in some column and they grew and grew and grew."

Washington reporters, in the abstract, recognize that chief executives employ vice presidents as their hit men so as to keep their own cuffs clean. They knew that, in the 1952 campaign, Nixon only did what Ike wanted. Yet many were "blinded by their emotional attachment to Stevenson," Nixon said. Adlai had his own way with a shiv. But he was witty and literate and protected by the reporters who covered him. "We all loved Adlai," Mazo said. Stevenson was "the only one who speaks with the voice of a philosopher, of a poet, of a true leader," James Reston confided to an associate later in the decade. Their attachment wasn't enough to turn journalists against Ike, the popular hero, but it was certainly sufficient to sic the press on the clumsy, beetle-browed Nixon.

John Kennedy was an expert manipulator and a keen observer of American journalism. He was stunned as he saw what happened to Nixon, and believed that his Republican colleague "was a victim of the worst that ever hit a politician in this country," Kennedy told a neighbor. The media's performance, he said, was "disgusting."

THE CHECKERS SPEECH, then, came as a revelation to Nixon. It showed him how to outflank the press. He could appeal to the voters directly, on television. "He saw that night what television can do and he was in awe . . . he was absolutely spellbound," Ted Rogers recalled. "He saw the ratings, and he was changed. He was the electronic man."

From then on, Nixon "didn't give a damn about the regular press," said Rogers. If the motorcade or the press plane were held up by an errant reporter, Nixon would say, "Fuck them. Let's go. They're the enemy. . . . We don't need them." The press, of course, picked up on it and responded. Nixon was hurt and infuriated when, after the controversy over whether or not he had called Truman a "traitor," reporters began carrying tape recorders to his campaign events.

To his admirers, Nixon was "a tough-minded young politician, a realist, a man of courage, who recognized that the first requisite of good lawmaking was getting elected," Bassett recalled. His enemies saw Nixon as "a gut-fighter, a groin-kicker, an unerring seeker-after-the jugular." Ultimately, Nixon's friends and family came to accept it. "Dick Nixon is a person people really like and admire or they hate his guts and there's no rhyme or reason for it. If you don't happen to like him you'll hear all the stories. And those become truths," said Bewley. "With Dick Nixon it is either black or white, there is no in between."

Nixon's closest advisers at that time—men like Rogers, Bassett, and Chotiner—all assigned wrenching changes in their boss's personality to this particular moment in his life. The anguish of the Hiss case and the agony of the fund crisis weighed heavily. The incoming vice president withdrew, trusted less, and looked with suspicion upon the world. And "a serious young man," said Bassett, "became a political megalomaniac."

McCarthy

JANUARY 20, 1953, was unseasonably warm for Washington. The president-elect and his running mate doffed overcoats for the ceremony. When Dwight D. Eisenhower took the oath of office, he was the first Republican to do so since Herbert Hoover. Those days of Babe Ruth and bootleggers seemed a geologic era away, supplanted by the great somber centralizations of the New Deal and the Second World War.

The transition of power was not especially graceful. Ike and Harry Truman were bickering over perceived affronts, and barely civil as they rode together to the Capitol. But Eisenhower could give a fine speech when the moment called for it, and this was such a day. He spoke of faith and hope and common purpose, but also of equality, and respect for all men, no matter their race or station. The Cold War brought nightmarish dangers, he told his countrymen. It was not yet time to rest. "Science seems ready to confer upon us, as its final gift, the power to erase human life from this planet," he said. The Communist legions were on the march. "Freedom is pitted against slavery; lightness against the dark."

Truman and Nixon slumped in front-row leather armchairs, flanking the new president. Having just turned forty, Nixon was the most youthful vice president in a century—the second youngest ever, younger than such prodigies as Aaron Burr, John Calhoun, and Teddy Roosevelt. He had revealed himself, as his aide William Arnold marveled, as someone with "a startling capacity" for identifying opportunities and transforming "unforeseen circumstance to his advantage." When he asked how that was, Nixon credited the biographies he had read of the lives of Teddy Roosevelt, Woodrow Wilson, and other great men. They had been bold; so, too, would he.

THE RELATIONSHIP BETWEEN the president and vice president was unsettled. "Arm's length . . . limited . . . tentative," Robert Finch recalled.

Nixon's age, of course, worked against him: he was from the Sad Sack generation—the shavetail *infanterie* that Eisenhower and his commanders led to victory in World War II. Dick had loaded cargo planes and played poker with his fellow grunts on bug-infested rocks like Green Island, while Ike's wartime contemporaries were titans like Churchill and Roosevelt.

Eisenhower had spent forty years in uniform, where the chain of command was inviolable. Junior officers were dispensable. Staff was staff. "He had for me, I believe, fulsome respect for my abilities and my integrity and similar political persuasion," Nixon would recall. "He considered me an important member of the 'team,' one who pulled his own weight. But there was little personal feeling between us. I gathered that I was considered a trusted lieutenant to the commander, but with the differences in our age and temperament, I was not a personal friend."

Longtime Washington hostess Lorraine Cooper, the wife of Republican ambassador and U.S. senator John Sherman Cooper, went further. "Nixon knew that Eisenhower did not like him, and disliked him for that," she told historian Arthur Schlesinger Jr. "Well, how could Eisenhower stand this tense, insecure, self-absorbed man, always looking for marks of favor? Eisenhower liked rich, self-assured, relaxed people. . . . The Nixons felt all the time that they were being ignored and left out."

Nixon did not get a West Wing office. Ike did not ask for his help in selecting the cabinet. The vice president was not included in the circle of advisers—John Foster Dulles, Herbert Brownell, Lucius Clay among them—who joined Eisenhower on the cruiser *Helena*, homeward bound from Ike's vaunted trip to Korea, to chart the course of the administration. Nixon did not have the tweedy heft of Dulles, the new secretary of state, or the legal savvy of Brownell, the incoming attorney general. Nor would he ever be one of "the Gang"—the coterie of businessmen who went fishing or played golf or cards with Eisenhower, joined him for drinks and charcoal-grilled steaks, with whom Ike blew off steam. Nixon was dour and awkward on the golf course and helpless with a fly rod. He was "intensely interested in the American political process and politics and he was a hard worker," Bryce Harlow recalled. "As personalities, though, they didn't blend well. Eisenhower would never have picked him as his favorite bridge partner." Said Brownell: "They were never pals."

Like many vice presidents, Nixon was viewed by the president's staff as a newcomer of unproven loyalties, if not—given the scars of the Checkers business—an outright encumbrance. They had chosen him because he was young, but when he did brash things—like embarrassing Brownell at Yankee Stadium—they grimaced. They were men of the East, or the midwest-

nds, and did not share the values of that accelerant, California.
White House chief of staff, and gatekeeper to the Oval Office,
an Adams, who thought Nixon should have stepped down during the early days of the fund flap.

"From his awareness of the hostility . . . there came the first stirrings of
emotions that would cloud much of Nixon's future relations with Eisenhower and the White House staff," Emmet Hughes recalled. "As these
sentiments persisted and evolved, they would inspire in Nixon much
detachment, some disparagement and a little distrust. And, in varying
degrees at different times, the White House would reciprocate."

And though Ike was never one to jettison skilled captains like George
Patton or Dick Nixon for a gaffe, the president kept a scorecard, and Nixon's insubordination in the Checkers episode had been noted.

On the other hand, Eisenhower had been appalled at Roosevelt's truly
negligent failure to keep Truman informed on momentous matters like
the Manhattan Project. At sixty-two (just a year younger than FDR when
he had died of a massive stroke), Ike was a former chain-smoker, worn
by years of stress and secretly suffering from ileitis, a chronic intestinal
disorder.* Duty demanded that he not leave the country unprepared. He
insisted that Nixon join him at the regular White House meetings with
congressional leaders, the cabinet, and the National Security Council. The
last was a new forum—a gathering of the administration's top military
and diplomatic leaders—that Truman had slighted but Ike relied on for
counsel and discourse.

Nixon was not someone to whom Ike confided his judgment of men,
or with whom he screened decisions. But when the president fled D.C.
for the fairways of Augusta or the cool of Colorado, he had Nixon preside
at the gatherings of the NSC and cabinet. He invited him to the White
House "stag dinners" with other Republican big shots. He did what he
could to ensure that his vice president would not someday arrive in the
Oval Office, like Harry Truman, unprepared and feeling "like the moon,
the stars, and all the planets had fallen on me."

NIXON HAD ONE valuable attribute—an expertise in practical politics—
that many of Ike's other advisers did not share. (The nickname for the
cabinet was "eight millionaires and a plumber.") In his dealings with Con-

---

* Also known as Crohn's disease.

gress, in his first six months in office, Eisenhower relied
master, Robert Taft. But then the Ohio senator was stricl
died on the last day of July, and Bill Knowland took ovei
ity leader. His talents in no way matched those of Taft,
became commensurately more important. With the Rep
tiny majorities in Congress, Ike needed Nixon's know-how.

In politics, however, strengths can double as weaknesses. Boldness is
perceived as ruthlessness. Genius lacks the common touch. Steadiness is
square. So it was with Nixon. The Checkers speech was a spectacular resurrection. But to many of the "the critical taste-making people" it was
"unbecoming, a misuse of television, too maudlin," journalist David Halberstam suggested to Ted Rogers, its producer. "It stayed with [Nixon] and
haunted him and in a way created an image of a man who was beneath
himself."

"Absolutely," said Rogers. "Even for Eisenhower."

For all that Ike valued and needed Nixon's thoughts on congressional
relations, the vice president still represented a class of people—professional
politicians—that the president viewed as a necessary evil.

"The one thing that we always had in the war was a burning and constant desire to win. That burning desire helped us to defy fatigue and
so filled our minds and hearts that there was no room for depression or
anything else. The big and almost single job was to determine what was
right—after that it was simply a matter of execution to which we gave our
full energies," Ike wrote his old wartime chief of staff, Walter Bedell Smith.
But in politics, the president discovered, "right, as opposed to expedient or
even subterfuge, is often at a disadvantage."

He was not a hack like Truman, Ike told his staff. He would not use
his office as a platform to launch partisan attacks. He valued individuals—
as he fancied himself—who brought skills learned in war or business to a
patriotic tour of duty in government. And Nixon was no Cincinnatus.

WITH REPUBLICANS CONTROLLING the Senate, Joe McCarthy was now
a committee chairman, free to lay on staff and set an agenda. Nixon was
inclined to help. Like other Republican Party professionals, he saw the
"Commie" issue as a major asset. ("There were [*sic*] gold in those hills,"
Nixon would recall.) It had won him a Senate seat, had helped them whip
Adlai, and could be wielded against the Democrats in the midterm elections in 1954.

cCarthy had come to Nixon's defense during the fund controversy, d Nixon had returned the favor by endorsing the senator for reelection. Yet Eisenhower, and many on his staff, viewed McCarthy and a half dozen other right-wing senators as political troglodytes. The president needed their votes, and didn't much like the leverage it gave them.

McCarthy was at a crossroads. It had been grand to lead the mob down the boulevards, dispensing brands and pitchforks and hunting for subversives, when the Democrats were running things. But now the Republicans were in charge. If McCarthy kept foraging for Communists, he would collide with Eisenhower appointees in the diplomatic corps and the national security agencies. Nixon and McCarthy met in Key Biscayne while on post-election vacations, and Nixon and Bill Rogers dined with McCarthy in Washington, urging the senator to moderate his behavior. But that was not McCarthy's nature. It would cost him the attention he craved. Instead of ferreting out Democratic malfeasance, as Nixon urged him, McCarthy chose to confront Eisenhower. "Nixon suddenly found himself in a unique position vis a vis Joe McCarthy," the vice president's friend and adviser James Bassett would recall. "It was one that would become increasingly uncomfortable, even painful."

In the first weeks of the new administration, McCarthy challenged three of Ike's appointees—former CIA director Walter Bedell Smith as under secretary of state, Harvard president James Conant as high commissioner for Germany, and diplomat Chester "Chip" Bohlen as ambassador to the Soviet Union—on the grounds that they were insufficiently militant in the war against Communism.

Nixon was all for chasing Reds. One of his first requests of the new president was for a $150,000 allowance so that now, with Republicans in control of the government files, they could find (and flaunt) the proof that Alger Hiss was a Soviet spy. Ike turned him down, but Nixon's colleagues at Republican headquarters and on the Hill were happy to pump the Red bellows. With farm prices sagging and other uncertainties, they absolutely needed to "save Communism" as an issue, Republican chairman Leonard Hall told the vice president.

Eisenhower bristled when McCarthy took after Smith, Ike's comrade-in-arms and wartime chief of staff. Nixon and Taft persuaded McCarthy to back off, and persuaded him, as well, to mute his opposition to Conant. But blood was spilt and Bohlen smeared when his name reached the Senate floor. McCarthy's acolytes had launched a purge of homosexuals in the State Department and spread rumors that Bohlen was gay. To get him confirmed, Eisenhower had to agree to share Bohlen's FBI file with the Senate.

THE THREE NOMINEES were ultimately approved. McCarthy didn't really care. "The bigger the target, figured Joe, the blacker the headlines," Bassett wrote. "It didn't matter whether you won or lost." And the senator had scented weakness in Dulles—who felt vulnerable, for his role in hiring Hiss at the Carnegie Endowment for International Peace. As the year progressed, McCarthy kept his focus on State. Two young aides, Roy Cohn and G. David Schine, toured the capitals of Europe at government expense, searching the public libraries at U.S. embassies for subversive books. Another young lawyer on McCarthy's staff—Robert F. Kennedy— hounded Western shipping firms that carried trade to China. McCarthy then proposed to investigate the Central Intelligence Agency. Again, Nixon wined and dined him. At the same time, in the White House councils, the vice president urged restraint. Cohn called it Nixon's "buffer" strategy. "A controversy would cause a very decided split among Republicans and could well lead to defeat for us in the 1954 election," Nixon explained to journalist Ralph de Toledano. "There may be a time when as a matter of principle the president may have to become involved in such a fight. But I think it is the responsibility of all of us to avoid it as long as we possibly can. It will give aid and comfort to no one but the Democrats."

And so Eisenhower and Nixon, committed to the proposition that bullies must be stopped abroad, truckled to the demagogue at home.

JOSEPH STALIN DIED in March, and Eisenhower took advantage of a Cold War thaw to make a plea for peace.

With continued hostility and a nuclear arms race, "the worst to be feared and the best to be expected can be simply stated," he said. The worst was atomic war, and the best was "a life of perpetual fear and tension" with "a burden of arms draining the wealth and the labor of all peoples."

"Every gun that is made, every warship launched, every rocket fired, signifies, in the final sense, a theft from those who hunger and are not fed, those who are cold and are not clothed," Eisenhower said. "This is not a way of life. . . . Under the cloud of threatening war, it is humanity hanging from a cross of iron."

In July, Ike announced the armistice that ended the war in Korea. With the help of an Indian diplomat, Eisenhower had sent a message to Moscow and Peking that the United States would not continue to bleed in Korea but would take decisive action, attacking the Chinese if necessary, with "no limit on weapons." It was a bluff. Eisenhower "probably didn't have the power to carry it out" without congressional approval, which he was not likely to get. "But it worked," he told Nixon, some years later.

The reviews of Ike's first six months in office were good, as were those for his vice president. Substituting for Taft and mollifying McCarthy, Nixon had recognized Ike's preference for "team" play and embraced a backstage role, the *New York Times* reported. "With the President's approval and backing, Mr. Nixon is acting as a catalytic agent in the immiscible compound of the legislative and the executive which the founding fathers set up to run the country," the newspaper advised. "He spends more time at the White House than any other occupant of the Capitol and more time at the Capitol than any other member of the Administration." There were rivals, jealously guarding prerogatives, at both ends of Pennsylvania Avenue, but "from all accounts the Vice President has thus far steered a canny course between the threatening shoals."

Ike was grateful. Losing Taft could be "quite a blow to me," Ike told his diary, after learning of his old foe's fatal illness. On the other hand, Taft was stiff, proud, and crusty. He was "far from being a Dick Nixon, who is not only bright, quick and energetic—but loyal and cooperative," Eisenhower wrote.

IKE NOW ADDED another brief to Nixon's portfolio. In October, at the president's request, Dick and Pat said good-bye to their girls and set off on a two-month tour of Asia and the Middle East. In schooling his apprentice, Eisenhower hoped to augment Nixon's knowledge of foreign affairs with firsthand experience. He wished, as well, to rally the nations on the Asian rim and to present the handsome couple as emblems of American dynamism.

The Nixons joined hundreds of guests at McCarthy's wedding to a twenty-nine-year-old congressional aide on September 29, and attended Earl Warren's swearing-in as chief justice of the U.S. Supreme Court on October 5. They then left for San Francisco, where their California friends gathered to salute them. They stopped in Hawaii, and a flower-filled suite in the Royal Hawaiian hotel, and toured Pearl Harbor. Pat was startled by the roar of cannon fire, then realized it was a nineteen-gun salute to her husband. When Dick headed off to a stag dinner (hosted by the ever sociable Kyle Palmer), Pat watched the local doyennes put on a "female frolic . . . quite risqué" with the male Hawaiian dancers. On October 10, laden with briefing books, the Nixons embarked on a specially outfitted Lockheed Constellation that would carry them to New Zealand and onward to Australia, Indonesia, Singapore, Malaya (now Malaysia), Thailand, Cambodia, Vietnam, Laos, Hong Kong, Taiwan, South Korea, Japan, the Philippines, Burma, Ceylon (now Sri Lanka), India, Afghanistan, Pakistan, Iran, and Libya.

"The excitement was high . . . but the thought of leaving Julie and Tricia dominated and saddened the day," Pat wrote in a diary on the day they left Washington. She read her daughters bedtime stories and "kissed them goodnight, knowing that it would be the last time in over two months that I would see them.

"The hour was black with sad thoughts because the loss of them made any thoughts of the thrill of traveling seem as a mere nothing," Pat wrote, then characteristically added: "But a job had to be done—so full force ahead."

Ahead they went, on a forty-thousand-mile, kaleidoscopic spin around the planet. They dined with emperors, kings, and dictators; were saluted by royalty and feted by the rich, yet took time to wander with the folk in the streets. Word spread, and crowds flocked to greet them. "The common man of Asia liked this big, friendly, informal, democratic, serious young American, and got the impression that he likes them," the *New York Times* reported. The Nixons rubbed noses with the Maori in New Zealand, gawked at the women wearing burkas in Afghanistan, and marveled at the wonders of the Hindu Kush, Angkor Wat, and the Taj Mahal. In India, with their insides churning after weeks of strange cuisine, they begged a meal of K rations from their U.S. military escorts—then smuggled out the scraps in Pat's suitcase lest their hosts, insulted, raise a stir. In Malaya and Vietnam, Nixon ventured into countrysides contested by insurgents, and on Thanksgiving Day in Burma he and Pat encountered a loud contingent of anti-American protesters, walked up to them, and disarmed them with friendliness. Pat toured hospitals, schools, and orphanages, and bristled in her diary at the near-universal maltreatment of women.

Nixon had serious diplomatic assignments to conduct in Taiwan and Japan and South Korea, where, at Ike's direction, he ordered President Syngman Rhee to forgo his dreams of invading North Korea. The vice president discussed the region's future with leaders like Achmed Sukarno in Indonesia, Norodom Sihanouk in Cambodia, Chiang Kai-shek on Taiwan, Jawaharlal Nehru in India, Mohammad Ayub Khan in Pakistan, and

Shah Mohammad Reza Pahlavi of Iran. Pat found the experience surreal at times. "You are only Pat Ryan from Artesia. What are you doing here?" she thought, battling self-doubt and the butterflies in her stomach on their visit with Nehru.

The most important legacies of Nixon's tour were the personal impressions he carried home. They would linger for years. After visiting Phnom Penh, Saigon, and Hanoi—and observing a French attack on a Communist-held hamlet near the Chinese border—he concluded that France's effort to retain its Southeast Asia colonies was doomed by arrogance and a fatal underestimation of the power of nationalism. The United States would have to help. He promised his hosts, "You shall not fight unaided."

Nixon took on a lifelong dislike of India's haughty leaders and embraced the cause of its rival, Pakistan, which wanted closer ties—and an arms deal—with the United States. The trip also marked the beginning of Nixon's long friendship with the shah of Iran, which would have lasting ramifications for both nations. If Nixon was struck with inspiration when gazing at China from across its border with Hong Kong, he did not record it. But a British diplomat in Singapore reported to his superiors that Nixon had pondered how the West might lure the Chinese from the Soviet Union's embrace.

The Nixons returned home ten days before Christmas. Ike and Mamie welcomed them with coffee in the White House. The NSC gave him a spontaneous round of applause after listening to his tour d'horizon. Caustic members of the council staff, impressed, stopped calling him "Junior."

"If I were assigned to write—for the NSC—a staff study of southeastern Asia, its important personalities, its problems, and suggested course of US action, I would take Nixon's report verbatim, interview Dick for half an hour to flesh out a couple of footnotes, and turn it in convinced this was the ultimate job of reporting," an NSC expert told a newsman.

Outside the administration, the reviews were as spectacular. Field Marshall Gerald Templer, the British high commissioner of Malaya, reported to Whitehall that Nixon was "an extremely nice man" with "charming manners" and "the reverse of everything one had expected after reading press reports of the American elections."

"He is easy in his conversations and got on extremely well with the many Asians that he met," Templer wrote. "I was really very impressed with Nixon indeed. He seemed to me potentially to be a much bigger man than Adlai Stevenson, who as you know stayed with us a few years ago."

The *New York Times* struck much the same note. It had kicked off its coverage by calling the trip "the most extensive and most important journey ever undertaken by any Vice President." It was a voyage that would "underline again the amazing comeback both in Presidential and public confidence Mr. Nixon has made . . . since the 'California fund' scandal threatened to . . . end his political career in disgrace." And after seeing Nixon's performance, the *Times* predicted, "Mr. Nixon will be able to influence United States foreign policy as has perhaps no other vice president."

ONE MIGHT EXPECT, after hearing such accolades, that the Nixons were gleeful. They were not. In fact, they were planning to abandon politics. Dick and Pat had found the life they wanted—free from the ligatures of Whittier, roaming the world, tilting with evil—and discovered its costs.

Dick still struggled with tension and anxiety. Pat was guilt-stricken at leaving her daughters, even in the care of Frank and Hannah. Tricia, in particular, seemed affected: she would slip into her grandparents' room at night to touch Frank's face and assure herself she'd not been abandoned.

Pat maintained her faith in Dick, but the attacks on her husband from liberal partisans "caused an irreparable crack in her idealistic view of politics," her daughter Julie would write. After returning from Asia, Pat ran into an old acquaintance, Alyce Koch, at a luncheon in Los Angeles. "I wish Dick would get out," Pat told her, "I wish he'd get out and make some money."

"There is precious little home life for the Nixons," a *Time* correspondent, sent to interview Pat, reported to his editors that January. "Pat has no intimate friends in Washington; her life won't allow it. . . . She put up the Christmas tree by herself, while Nixon was working. . . . One night last week, when Dick was resting in Miami, she stayed up until 3:30 a.m. getting caught up with her mail." Checkers was not housebroken, and ran off and got pregnant. The blinds were kept drawn to foil the gawkers who drove by, parked outside, or peered in the windows on Tilden Street.

They were always broke, Pat told their friends. Citing their monthly bills, Dick had turned down her plea to air-condition their home. They couldn't afford to replace their 1950 Oldsmobile. She worried that her family must always look perfect to the press. Her daughters couldn't just be little girls; spontaneity was taboo. "I have to change them and get them ready so that they look beautiful and attractive and clean for all the reporters," she told Koch. "I just wish we could stop this kind of life."

"I don't know of anyone who has so disciplined herself to endure a life she does not like," Dick's friend and teacher, Paul Smith, said of Pat. "I just hate it," she told a friend, when asked about her newfound fame.

THE LAURELS OF the trip wilted quickly. While Nixon was away, the maverick McCarthy had bolted the corral.

Before leaving Washington, Nixon had advised the cabinet to steer clear of the bully. McCarthy was cranky, drinking, and looking for trouble. He had been burned that summer when J. B. Matthews, his staff director, accused the mainstream American churches of nurturing subversives; it was a crazy, cockeyed blunder ("The largest single group supporting the Communist apparatus in the United States today is composed of Protestant clergymen," an article by Matthews began), and McCarthy's enemies seized the opportunity to pinion him.

Nixon, at first, tried to smooth things over. But prodded by Adams and the White House staff, he got caught up in their plotting. Hearing that McCarthy was about to sack Matthews, Nixon and Bill Rogers waylaid their old pal Joe, stalling until Eisenhower could publicly call—and so claim the credit—for Matthews's dismissal. For a moment, to the country, it looked like the president had put McCarthy in his place.

Then Nixon had left for the far side of the world, and McCarthy counterattacked, lashing out at Eisenhower's foreign policy and bombarding the institution dearest to the president's heart, the United States Army. His primary target was Fort Monmouth, a Signal Corps station in New Jersey. Among those in the crosshairs was an obscure army dentist, Major Irving Peress, who had been given a routine promotion and discharged, honorably, after his leftist sympathies were discovered. Acting as a Grand Inquisitor, McCarthy reviled army officers in a series of one-man hearings. The dentist, he said, was a threat to the Republic.

On his return, Nixon found Ike in a five-star fix. Of the trials that Eisenhower encountered in politics, McCarthy's behavior was the most difficult to abide. In his private correspondence, Eisenhower repeatedly conveyed his conviction that the way to curb a demagogue was to ignore him. And, given the separation of powers, the president had few levers to discipline a senator. He could try to rally public opinion, but an open clash would elevate McCarthy and tarnish the presidency. "I personally deal in principles, ideas and national purposes," Ike told a supporter. "I shall not demean this office by indulging in personal Donnybrooks."

McCarthy was the Republican Party's "Frankenstein monster"— a "Wisconsin wildman" whom "they themselves had allowed to grow,"

Bassett confessed to his journal. But Ike was firm. "He would not, said the President repeatedly and firmly, stoop to McCarthy's level. . . . So McCarthy's rampage continued."

Nixon, worried that the party could lose its marquee issue, was relieved at Ike's hands-off policy. He identified more with McCarthy—the farm boy graduate of a small Catholic college—than he did with the "tea drinkers" on Eisenhower's staff, who went to Ivy League schools and played effete games like bridge and tennis. And both Nixon and Ike were grateful when McCarthy agreed to stay out of an ongoing investigation of physicist Robert Oppenheimer.* "I am pretty sure that the President will not get into an open fight with McCarthy," Nixon told his friend Robert King. "I have done all that I can during the past year to avoid just that happening."

"The truth is mighty and will prevail," Eisenhower assured his friends. The bully would one day bring himself down.

Yet inside, Ike was fuming. "It is a sorry mess; at times one feels almost like hanging his head in shame when he reads some of the unreasoned, vicious outbursts of demagoguery," Eisenhower told a pal. McCarthy represented qualities—recklessness, self-promotion, and calumny—that Eisenhower abhorred. "He loathed McCarthy as much as any human being could possibly loathe another," Ike's brother Milton recalled. Eisenhower believed, as well, that the issue of Communist subversion was concocted, divisive, and exaggerated. When the Soviet Union and the Western democracies were allies during the 1940s, even Churchill had welcomed the help of the Communists, Ike told Brownell, and "any American could have been excused for statements or actions favorable to the Soviets during the war and even as late as 1948."

Eisenhower, moreover, was ashamed of his own behavior during the 1952 presidential campaign, when—at the urging of his political advisers—he had deleted remarks from a speech in Wisconsin that defended George Marshall from McCarthy's ludicrous charges. During the Truman years, as an envoy to China as it fell to the Communists, Marshall had participated in "a conspiracy so immense and an infamy so black as to dwarf any previous such venture in the history of man," McCarthy had alleged. And so, when the senator did overreach, Ike had the moment and the motive to respond.

---

* In an off-the-record appearance before an audience of newspaper executives that spring, Nixon spoke up for Oppenheimer, who was being stripped of his top-secret clearances for consorting with Communists before the war.

—

THE TURNING POINT arrived on February 18, 1954, when McCarthy called General Ralph Zwicker—Eagle Scout, West Point graduate, possessor of a Purple Heart and a Silver Star for the bravery he displayed on Omaha Beach on D-Day—before his committee to testify on the Peress affair. "Your honesty or your intelligence; I can't help impugning one or the other," McCarthy told Zwicker. The general was "not fit to wear that uniform," the chairman sneered. Zwicker didn't have "the brains of a five-year-old child." His testimony was "a disgrace to the army."

McCarthy's defamation of a U.S. fighting man rang throughout the military. Army chief of staff Matthew Ridgway and army secretary Robert Stevens were incensed. Stevens—a veteran of both world wars—forbade his officers to testify before McCarthy's committee.

Nixon tried to broker a truce, convening meetings between Stevens and the Senate's Republican leaders. Over a lunch of fried chicken with McCarthy and a contingent of Old Guard senators on February 24, Stevens thought he won a promise that his officers would be treated with respect. But McCarthy jolted him that evening, telling newsmen that he had given no guarantees and crowing that Stevens could not have behaved "more abjectly if he had got down on his knees."

"We were sure dumb," White House press secretary James Hagerty told his diary. "Someone let Stevens walk right into a bear trap." The headlines heralded the army's disgrace, and the overwrought secretary threatened to resign.

"Well, Dick, I see you're still smiling," Ike needled Nixon the next morning. The vice president appealed to McCarthy, who refused to compromise. Eisenhower backed Stevens, who breathed defiance at a White House press conference. McCarthy's response was to insult Ike, and to add to his slandering of General Zwicker as "stupid, arrogant or witless."

To his diary, Hagerty now noted: "President in fighting mood, has had it as far as Joe is concerned."

"This guy McCarthy is going to get into trouble over this. I'm not going to take this one lying down," Ike told his staff. "He wants to be President. He's the last guy in the world who'll ever get there, if I have anything to say."

Ike's aides had been stocking ammunition. Their most powerful ordnance was a chronology they had assembled of Roy Cohn's frantic efforts to get preferential treatment for his friend and former colleague David Schine, who'd been drafted into the army. The drama now hurtled toward its culmination. Spurred on by the White House, Republican centrists taunted the senator. "He dons his war paint," said Senator Ralph Flanders of Vermont. "He goes into his war dance. He emits his war whoops. He goes forth to battle and proudly returns with the scalp of a pink Army dentist." CBS correspondent Edward R. Murrow aired a special episode of his *See It Now* show, exposing McCarthy's bullying. The White House leaked the Cohn-Schine report, prompting a series of "Army-McCarthy" hearings, which fueled conjecture that Cohn was enthralled by lust for Schine. When McCarthy and his allies demanded to know where the report originated, Eisenhower threw a broad cloak of executive privilege over the matter and refused to let his staff testify.

McCarthy fired back. When attacking the Roosevelt and Truman administrations he had spoken of "twenty years of treason." Now he included Eisenhower in his indictment; there had been "twenty-one years of treason," he declared.

Ike? Treason? Tom Bewley wrote to Nixon, warning his former law partner that even in conservative Whittier, "McCarthy is now antagonizing people who have been loyal supporters."

NIXON WAS DEVASTATED. The cause of anti-Communism, which more than any other had carried him to power, was being discredited. It would never be so potent again. He had failed to keep the peace and now was perceived, after all his pleading with McCarthy, as at best ineffective, and at worst a knuckle-dragging twin.

"Mr. Nixon is an ambitious young man. He is supposed to be a smart politician. He seems to believe that for the sake of harmony Republicans should swallow their conscientious scruples against McCarthy-type smears," wrote Ike's good friends at the *Denver Post*. "Mr. Eisenhower is not a politician. But he has been forthright in his opposition to all that McCarthyism means. We believe that he has made more votes for the GOP by his attitude . . . than Mr. Nixon can ever make with his amoral talk about the necessity for appeasing Joe."

Even Nixon's work in the Hiss case was tarnished—lumped in with McCarthy's disreputable fantasies. "What could I do?" he asked de Tole-dano. "Joe wouldn't let up." Nixon's mood wasn't helped by news from the West, where his father had been taken from an airplane in Phoenix, pained by internal bleeding. Frank survived but recovered slowly, and his illness taxed Hannah's strength.

Nixon's troubles peaked when Ike insisted that Nixon walk point in the administration's offensive. Stevenson had sneered at the White House in a televised speech in early March—"A group of political plungers has persuaded the President that McCarthyism is the best Republican formula for political success"—and Eisenhower ordered his vice president to take to the airwaves and reply.

Nixon balked. There was no political mileage in attacking McCarthy; their friends on the right would see him as a turncoat. "This is one I can't win," he told de Toledano. Nixon viewed McCarthyism as a valid, if ineptly waged, campaign that he had no motive—moral, personal, or political—to obstruct. "I did my best to avoid this break," he told de Toledano, "not only because it would be harmful to the party and the administration, but because I felt it would be harmful to the cause of those [like himself] who had been engaged for years in the anti-communist fight."

Let this pass, Nixon asked the president. "I wasn't . . . eager to address the issue. After all, a lot of my friends were McCarthy's friends," Nixon would remember. "To divide the Republicans didn't appeal to me at all." Ike invited him to the White House and told him to smile, and be positive—and to give the speech. Nixon had to comply.

He retreated to a hotel for seclusion. Out came the yellow pads. His address was not eloquent, but it had its memorable moment.

"Men who have in the past done effective work exposing Communism in this country have, by reckless talk and questionable methods, made themselves the issue rather than the cause they believe in so deeply," Nixon said, in his most direct reference to McCarthy. He elaborated with a metaphor. "When you go out to shoot rats you have to shoot straight," he said. "When you shoot wildly, it not only means that the rats may get away . . . but you might hit someone else who is trying to shoot rats too."

The rodent metaphor was memorable and, some said, revealing. The "image of rats illuminated for an instant a black id," thought William Ewald Jr., one of Nixon's critics on Eisenhower's staff.

TAIL GUNNER JOE survived the rat speech, but not the Army-McCarthy hearings, which joined the growing list of television spectaculars, like the Checkers address or the Kefauver investigations. It was a spat among Republicans over the antics of Cohn and Schine, and neither side looked very noble. "Beginning on April 22, and running for 57 days, including 36 televised sessions, it became the American public's favorite daytime soap opera," Bassett reported in his journal. "The little red light was glowing and the cameras rolled."

The hearings reached a peak on June 9, with a performance by McCarthy that was instantly recognized, by everyone but him, as a ruinous blunder. He had acquired a damaging tidbit—a bygone membership in a left-wing lawyers' guild—about one of the young attorneys who worked with Joseph Welch, the counsel for the army. The senator raised it as Welch was interrogating Cohn. Welch's young colleague, said McCarthy, had been a member of a "Communist organization."

Welch had anticipated McCarthy's assault. He spoke with what seemed genuine sorrow. "Little did I dream you could be so reckless and so cruel as to do an injury to that lad," Welch told McCarthy. "He shall always bear a scar needlessly inflicted by you. If it were in my power to forgive you for your reckless cruelty, I would do so. I like to think I am a gentleman, but your forgiveness will have to come from someone other than me."

McCarthy shrugged it off, pressing his attack.

Welch stopped him.

"Let us not assassinate this lad further, Senator. You have done enough," Welch said. "Have you no sense of decency, sir, at long last? Have you no sense of decency?"

The television audience knew a bad guy when they saw him. Eisenhower had won his wager. Given the rope, the demagogue hanged himself. Cohn resigned. Flanders introduced a resolution to censure McCarthy for unbecoming conduct. After more weeks of hearings, and futile efforts by Nixon and others to broker a compromise, McCarthy was condemned by his peers—by a vote of 67 to 22—on December 2, 1954.*

Nixon played a role, leaking information that was damaging to McCarthy. It gave rise to the feeling among those on the right that Nixon was an opportunist, "fawning in front of anyone who could get him one step ahead," Cohn said.

Churchill had visited Washington that summer. It was a thrill for Nixon to sit and listen to Ike and his friend Winston and to discuss history, war, and politics with them. In his diary, he also reported Churchill's disparaging verdict on McCarthy. There was a right way and a wrong way to fight Reds, Churchill told Nixon, and McCarthy's methods were counterproductive. "I have done as much against the Communists as McCarthy has done for them," said Stalin's old nemesis.

---

* "It's no longer McCarthyism," Ike said. "It's McCarthywasm."

Tail Gunner Joe was never again a force in American politics. He drank himself to death and died, in 1957, at the age of forty-eight.

AFTER EIGHT YEARS, the Red Scare had run its course. Oppenheimer was still stripped of his security clearance. HUAC labored on. J. Edgar Hoover remained at the helm of the FBI. Yet the danger seen by George Kennan and Ike and others—that the fear of Communism would compel Americans to sacrifice the liberties they sought to defend—appeared to have passed. The primitives had lost.

As one ugly chapter of Cold War history drifted to its conclusion, however, another was beginning. And for all the evils of McCarthyism—for all the hatred and dissension and division it engendered—the coming epoch would be far, far worse. It would carve at the soul of America and poison its politics for more than fifty years. It would give Richard Nixon his greatest political prize, strip it from him, and consume him in its fury.

The rough beast arrived amid the death throes of its forebear. As McCarthy was staggering toward his end, in that spring of 1954, Eisenhower was weighing what to do about Southeast Asia.

When declaring Vietnam's independence in 1945, the rebel leader Ho Chi Minh had cited the American Declaration of Independence. He was a nationalist first, and then a Communist. Ho had studied in Moscow, but also lived a year in Brooklyn and admired Woodrow Wilson. He had led his nation against the Japanese in World War II when, during the fighting, his life was saved by an American medic. But Harry Truman and Dean Acheson had deferred to their European allies, who were struggling to retain their colonial possessions. The United States needed France to fight Communism in Europe, and the French price was America's help in subjugating Southeast Asia. "We want the French to stay there," Acheson told Congress. "And we are willing to help." Within a few years, the United States would be paying more than a billion dollars a year—three-fourths of the cost of the Indochina war.

After losing ninety thousand killed and wounded, the French strategy— to amass troops in a fortress near the Laotian border—had caromed. The garrison at Dien Bien Phu was besieged by the Vietminh armies led by General Vo Nguyen Giap, and likely to fall. Ike tested the appetite of Congress and America's allies for Western intervention. He warned, in March and April press conferences, that Vietnam's neighbors could topple like dominoes if France surrendered. He called it a matter of "transcendent importance." At NSC meetings on March 25 and April 6, he chastised

Defense Secretary Charles Wilson and Treasury Secretary George Humphrey when they questioned the need for American involvement. Nixon backed the president and made a case for rescuing the French to congressional leaders.

Their pleadings were not successful. Nobody wanted another war in Asia. The congressional leadership insisted that the United States intercede only as part of a multinational force—and Churchill was not inclined to spill British blood so France could keep a colony. Nor was General Matthew Ridgway, the U.S. Army chief of staff. If the United States went in alone, he told the president, it would need to send seven divisions—275,000 men—to beat the Vietminh. Eisenhower was stymied.

In April, Senator John Kennedy called to confer with his friend Dick. Nixon was "very bitter against the British" and worried that the administration had exposed itself to criticism for not doing enough to save Vietnam, Kennedy noted. But if the United States sent in troops, Nixon said, it could provoke a Chinese counterattack, and another Korea. The two men discussed partition, Vietnamese independence, and a coalition government, with Nixon rejecting every option. All they could do, the vice president said, was maintain support for France's doomed campaign.

In public, Nixon made one last attempt to light the way toward U.S. intervention. On April 16, he made the case before a group of newspaper executives. "If in order to avoid further Communist expansion in Asia and particularly in Indochina . . . we must take the risk by putting American boys in, I believe that the executive branch of the government has to take the politically unpopular position of facing up to it and doing it," he said, "and I personally would support such a decision."

Nixon had been assured that he would only be identified as a "high administration official," but European journalists ignored the agreement as, then, did their U.S. counterparts. His remarks spurred headlines around the planet and roused those opposed to intervention. Amid the uproar, Senator Edwin Johnson, a Democrat from Colorado, called it "Mr. Nixon's War" and described the vice president's efforts as "whooping it up for war."

"I am against sending American GI's into the mud and muck of Indochina on a blood-letting spree to perpetuate colonialism and white man's exploitation in Asia," the Colorado senator said.

If Nixon was trying to nudge Ike toward war, he failed; if he was floating the idea so Ike could get a read on Americans' response, he succeeded. The public and congressional reaction—68 percent of those surveyed in a Gallup poll opposed the use of U.S. ground forces—would inoculate the president from right-wing attack if Indochina was lost to the Communists. "The trial balloon, whatever it was . . . was more or less a lead balloon," Knowland remembered.

The French and Americans weighed their options, including the use of atomic weapons. Ike had not included Nixon in the private strategy sessions he conducted with his top military and diplomatic advisers that spring—he usually did not, in that first term—but he called Nixon to a late April briefing on the feasibility of a nuclear attack on the Vietminh. Ike was willing to rattle the saber—maybe even give the Bomb to France—but ultimately decided that atomic weaponry would not prove effective.

It was not the first or last time that the president, like Truman before him, considered using the nation's nuclear arsenal to extinguish a threat in Asia. A year later, when the Chinese bombarded Quemoy and Matsu—two small islands controlled by Chiang Kai-shek—Ike and Dulles and Nixon took turns threatening Mao with a nuclear response. "Tactical atomic explosives are now conventional," Nixon said in a Chicago speech, "and will be used against military targets of any aggressive force." Watching Eisenhower brandish—without detonating—nuclear weapons left a lasting impression on the vice president.

Ike's final option in Vietnam was "unilateral intervention"—going it alone—and he wanted none of that. In a stormy NSC meeting on April 29 he rejected a proposal by Harold Stassen, who was serving Eisenhower as a foreign policy adviser, that the United States land troops in southern Indochina. "It was all well and good to state that if the French collapsed the United States must move in to save Southeast Asia, but if the French indeed collapsed and the United States moved in, we would in the eyes of many Asiatic peoples merely replace French colonialism with American colonialism," Eisenhower told his advisers. "To go in unilaterally in Indochina or other areas of the world which were endangered amounted to an attempt to police the entire world."

"We should be everywhere accused of imperialistic ambitions," Ike said. The concept of leadership implied adherents. "Without allies and associates the leader is just an adventurer like Genghis Khan."

If they must have war with the Communists, better to have it out in a direct clash with the Soviets, the president said. Before he would allow the United States "to be exhausted in piecemeal conflicts," Eisenhower would ask Congress to declare war on the Soviet Union—to "leap over the smaller obstacles and hit the biggest one with all the power we had. Otherwise we seemed to be merely playing the enemy's game—getting ourselves involved in brushfire wars."

Nixon offered a middle way. He worried about American prestige and credibility—"the climate of opinion throughout the free world." Why not launch air strikes as the French waged war on the ground? Nixon suggested. The problem, Eisenhower told him, was that France was whipped, and intent on withdrawal. Ike knew the region; he had served in the Philippines before World War II. American air power alone would not succeed in Asia. He ruled out the use of American ground forces, and brought the meeting to an end.*

"The jungles of Indochina . . . would have swallowed up division after division of United States troops who, unaccustomed to this kind of warfare, would have sustained heavy casualties until they had learned to live in a new environment," Eisenhower wrote, a few years later. "The presence of ever more numbers of white men in uniform probably would have aggravated rather than assuaged Asiatic resentments. Thus, even had all of Indochina been physically occupied by United States troops, their eventual removal would have resulted only in a reversion to the situation which had existed before."

"The standing of the United States as the most powerful of the anti-colonial powers is an asset of incalculable value to the Free World," he added. "Thus it is that the moral position of the United States is more to be guarded than the Tonkin Delta, indeed than all of Indochina."

Ultimately, Eisenhower settled for an international peace conference. Dien Bien Phu fell on May 7. The next day, in Geneva, West met East.

China's representative, Zhou Enlai, was a key to the conference. He and Mao were happy to carve up Vietnam: it kept U.S. forces away from China's southern border and left China's age-old enemies—the Vietnamese—divided. So, like Korea, Vietnam was partitioned. Elections were promised. But the representatives of the new entities of North and South Vietnam had no illusions. This was but a pause in the struggle.

As NIXON HAD feared, the Republicans were riven and the Nixon brand blighted by McCarthy's demise. Nixon became a target of Walt Kelly,

---

* The Democratic Party leaders who, years later, would launch American intervention in Vietnam also recognized the danger in 1954. John Kennedy listed, as a prerequisite of victory, the support of an independent Vietnam and "a crusading native army with a dependable officer corps." Without it, U.S. intervention would be "dangerously futile and self-destructive." If the United States did not have the support of the Vietnamese people and a committed multinational coalition, it was a "lost cause," said Senator John Stennis of Mississippi. "To go in on a unilateral basis would be to go into a trap . . . from which there could be no reasonable recovery and no chance of victory."

creator of the comic strip *Pogo*. In one strip McCarthy (portrayed as a shotgun-toting polecat named Simple J. Malarkey) praised his sidekick Nixon (a badger known as Indian Charlie) as "the finest fryer . . . the most brilliant young man with a pan." In another, the two donned Ku Klux Klan–style hoods. Nixon was humiliated when the faculty at Duke University voted not to award him an honorary degree. Even Whittier seemed to spurn him: a proposal to name a boulevard in his honor was rejected by town officials, and when he came home to give the commencement address at the college, few students wanted to shake his hand. He reinforced his image as a hotheaded partisan when, in June, he traveled to Milwaukee for a speech on foreign policy. He lapsed into the old virulent rhetoric and blamed Dean Acheson for the loss of China and the wars in Asia.

Ike reproached Nixon, expressing his belief that this kind of hatchet work interfered with their goal of building a bipartisan foreign policy. They would clash on the matter several times in the course of their partnership. The president "had an almost obsessive hatred for the reputation-smearing raking over of the Truman and Roosevelt administrations for the mistakes and scandals of the past," Sherman Adams would recall.

Nixon's enemies were delighted. He took a pounding—in the press, and from Representative Emanuel Celler, the Democrat from Brooklyn, on the floor of the House. "The so-called Little Boy Blue, the vice president, espouses [bipartisan] flexibility," Celler told his colleagues, but after the Milwaukee speech Nixon's support for legislation would be its "kiss of death" for Democrats. Celler called Nixon a "hoax of a statesman" and—reaching into Broadway history for the model of an ineffectual vice president—lambasted him as a "naïve, inept, maladjusted Throttlebottom."*

William White, one of the shrewder analysts of power in Washington, would describe how Nixon looked in that first term as vice president, presiding in the Senate. He appeared "with the rather tight-lipped, over-tense and slightly perspiring manner of a desperately earnest man determined to make no slightest mistake, but not quite at home, and not likely to be."

IKE CLAIMED TO be fond of his vice president. In his private correspondence he told friends and family that Nixon was a "trusted adviser" with the qualities to make a fine president. He had brought Nixon into the loop on matters like Vietnam and listened to his commonsense questions and

---

* Alexander Throttlebottom was the model of a clueless vice president in the George Gershwin musical *Of Thee I Sing*.

advice at cabinet meetings. But that did not mean that Eisenhower could not be curt, impatient, or, as Nixon would famously report: "devious . . . in the best sense."

"Eisenhower . . . was very charming and warm socially, but he was a hard ass," Nixon would recall. "He had to be to lead the Allied victory in Europe." The president could be "petty" and "he held grudges."

De Toledano, the conservative writer whom the vice president befriended, described how Eisenhower played with his apprentice's head—pulling him in then pushing him away. Nixon would return from meetings of the National Security Council to his office on the Hill and "as much as he ever showed emotion you'd think he was on the verge of tears," de Toledano recalled. "His pride was bruised, not because he had in any way failed the President but because Eisenhower seemed to take a particular pleasure in ignoring Nixon's tremendous services."

De Toledano called Ike "a complete sadist." But the president's behavior also reflected his impatience—expressed in his diary and letters—with Nixon's sluggish growth as a leader. For all his otherwise admirable qualities, Nixon was too willing to settle for the role of partisan scrapper. Eisenhower was conservative, but he had wielded great power in a great cause and was comfortable expanding popular government programs like Social Security, or meeting challenges with government solutions—like federal aid to education, or construction of an interstate highway system. He had a strategic vision—of Americans of all political persuasions united in a great crusade, with Ike as its leader. Nixon worried about immediate tactical problems—saving Republican seats in the 1954 off-year election and advancing his own career. He aimed to rally the party faithful with attacks on the opposition. He was Frank Nixon's son. It's what he did. Ike searched for signs that Nixon had the grandness of vision, and spirit, to unite a great country. Failing to find them, he would gripe about Nixon's lagging "maturity."

Nixon did the grubby work for Eisenhower that Ike deigned not do. ("I have not, of course, ever—in my life—indulged in personal, public vituperation," Eisenhower wrote a friend.) But the president was not deluding himself. Nor was he a fool. He knew who sent Nixon out on the campaign trail to throw meat to the crowds. And at some level the president detested Nixon for reminding him that he, too, was in the sordid game of politics.

Nixon, rightly, thought it unjust. Ike floated above the fray, playing golf in Colorado, while he slugged it out with the Democrats and got pummeled by the press. At some level Nixon understood that this was the way that Eisenhower maintained his hero's pose. But it ate at him just the same—especially when, tired and snappish from a merciless travel schedule, he struck an off note, and there was Eisenhower, rapping his knuckles. It all left Nixon with a "dismal inner emptiness," Bryce Harlow recalled. Nor, try as they might, could Ike or Nixon completely forget the morbid constitutional reason for a vice presidency. At one White House meeting that summer, Arthur Summerfield dismissed a sixty-four-year-old Republican senator as "someone who could go like *this*," and snapped his fingers. "The president, who is 63, noticeably flinched. So did we, especially RN," Bassett recalled.

The word of Nixon's fluctuating status with the president inevitably spread in Washington. "Ever since his remarkably successful tour of non-Communist Asia last autumn, Vice President Richard M. Nixon has steadily squandered what seemed to be the most promising political reputation in the Republican Party," wrote Reston in the *New York Times*. Nixon's friends worried. "The impression, gladly fed by the opposition, is getting around that RN and the White House have *pffft*," Bassett told his diary. "The hatchet boys (and girls) are really at work." On the campaign trail, stressed out, subsisting on tomato soup and hamburgers, Nixon seemed morose. Bassett dispatched word to the White House that their champion needed reassurance. Ike responded with a note of gratitude and an invite to play golf when Nixon's schedule next took him through Colorado.

BASSETT, WHO HAD signed on to give public relations advice to the Republican National Committee, and joined Nixon on the campaign trail, recorded the year's events in the diary he titled "Ugly Year, Lonely Man." His portrait of Nixon is intimate, and gloomy. Instead of going home to Pat and the girls, Dick would pick Bassett up in his vice-presidential limousine and head out for drinks, dinner, and long rambling monologues.

> 19 August—Return to RN home . . . RN is living alone and obviously not liking it, with the mail strewn around like old gum wrappers, the TV on (how long?), ants teeming in the kitchen and a half eaten box of Shredded Wheat the only sign of food. "Have a 25-year-old scotch, boys," he said. Wearily we did, while RN, hair down, talked and talked. . . .
>
> "The zeal's gone. So's the idealism. That's why I've made up my mind to get out of politics. . . . I'm not going to be a candidate for P

or VP in 56," he went on. "I'm going out and make more goddamn money than anybody ever made."

Weird night. RN at one point said, "I'm too introverted to be in politics. I hate to backslap—or to be backslapped!" RN says he's going through all the proper motions of campaigning this fall, a rugged schedule, but his heart isn't in it. Yea: the VP was in a dark purple, somber mood.

In another "hair down" chat with Bassett, Dick spoke of how his gloominess was "intensified by the White House's almost obvious coolness." He was "too intense," Nixon said. "I feel things too deeply to stay in this business."

Pat agreed. "It all seemed so wonderful and glamorous when the nomination came at Chicago. . . . Then there was that awful 'fund' thing. And I have hated it ever since," she told Bassett.

Dick spoke of writing a book.

The title: *I've Had It.*

IN PART BECAUSE of Nixon's prodigious efforts—he campaigned in thirty states—the Republicans suffered just modest reversals in the 1954 off-year elections. Nevertheless, they lost control of the Senate for twenty-six years, and the House for four decades. Their postwar resurgence, fueled by the hysteria over Communism, faded. McCarthy and his kind had unearthed few Communist sympathizers in government, and not one more dangerous spy like Hiss. "McCarthy was hopeless. By the time he came along, there was no Communist left" in government, said Father John Cronin. But in the process, the witch hunters had injured thousands whose friends, political beliefs, or sexuality got them branded as "security risks." Some, like Marshall, were American heroes. Some were diplomats, or analysts, whose departure stripped the State Department of valuable expertise. Most, like Annie Lee Moss, a meek army typist whom McCarthy bullied, were only folks.

During and after the campaign, Ike had cautioned Nixon about appearing overly harsh. But Nixon's performance allowed Stevenson to coin another lasting moniker that journalists used. Nixon was "McCarthyism in a white collar," said Stevenson.

—

EARLY IN 1954, as they sat before the fireplace in their Tilden Street home, Dick had promised Pat that he would not run again. He vowed to "quit the game forever" and scribbled the date on a piece of paper that he carried in his wallet.

On his way back to Washington from that fall's campaign finale, Nixon seemed intent on keeping his promise. He handed the text of his talk to Chotiner. "Here is my last campaign speech," he told him. "You may like to keep it as a souvenir. I'm through with politics."

Nixon may have meant it.

Then Ike had a heart attack.

The New Nixon

I N THE EARLY evening of September 24, 1955, the growing band of reporters and cameramen outside the Nixon home on Tilden Street were roused from their muttering and smokes. Pat and Tricia had appeared at the front door: at last there might be something to report. The nation had been rocked that drizzly Saturday by bulletins conveying the news that Dwight Eisenhower had suffered a heart attack. The liberator of Europe, gravely ill, lay gasping in an oxygen tent in a hospital in Denver. At the age of forty-two, Nixon might well become president of the United States. As Pat and Tricia did their part to distract the newsmen, Nixon and Bill Rogers scooted out the kitchen door and across a neighbor's lawn to where Bill's wife waited in her Pontiac. "The coast was clear," Nixon recalled, "and we made it to the car in a run."

THE NIXONS HAD attended a wedding that Saturday. They did not know that Ike had quit on his twenty-seventh hole of golf on Friday, made it through dinner and an evening with friends, then been stricken around 2:30 a.m. The president had been in foul temper for much of that year— stressed by the crisis over Quemoy and Matsu, and the preparations for a summit meeting in Geneva. The summit had gone well, but Ike found it hard to gear back in the aftermath. "The veins stood out on his forehead like whipcords," his doctor recalled, when the president's round of golf on Friday had been interrupted by messages from Secretary Dulles.

Eisenhower's seventy-four-year-old physician had botched the diagnosis, declaring that the president was suffering from indigestion. It was not until 2:30 that afternoon—5:30 p.m. in Washington, twelve hours after his coronary—that the sixty-four-year-old president was taken to the hospital and the country informed. The Nixons had returned home. Pat was changing clothes and Dick had picked up the newspaper when the telephone rang at 5 p.m.

"Are you sitting down?" James Hagerty, the president's press secretary, asked Nixon. "The president has had a coronary."

Nixon's first reaction was, "Oh my God." He remained "in a momentary state of shock" for several minutes. He was "numb" and his thinking "disjuncted." *It might not be true . . . maybe it was a stomach problem . . . doctors could be wrong . . . people recover . . . they lead active lives . . . they must get Eisenhower expert care.* And then there was "the awesome thought," as Nixon recalled it. "The President might indeed die. . . . I would become President."

"With all my being, I prayed for the recovery of Dwight D. Eisenhower," he would remember.

Rogers had arrived in a cab; he found Nixon pale, red-eyed, stunned. They huddled in the den, with just moments to confer before the news swept the globe. Dick realized he had not told Pat. They walked into the kitchen and let her know what happened. She asked them not to frighten her girls.

Few moments speak about the Nixon marriage like this one. Nixon did not include his wife in his deliberations—or even, at first, his thoughts—after hearing of Ike's heart attack. And Pat's first reaction, upon learning the news, was to think of her children.

"I needed someone to talk this over with, someone with whom I could work out my own thoughts by verbalizing them and measuring them against thoughts and suggestions," Nixon would recall. That was not his wife—that was Bill Rogers. It was the same in other crises, Nixon would tell an interviewer, a few years later. What he most needed from Pat was for her to stay out of the way. "At a time like this, it is tremendously important that the people around me avoid showing their worry as much as possible in my presence," Nixon said. "It was essential that I be able to think clearly and that I not be distracted by the problems or worries that others might have."

THE NIXON PHONE would not stop ringing. Reporters arrived. Soon there were spotlights on the house. This was Washington at its most ghoulish. Even if Ike survived, Nixon was now "heir to one of the greatest responsibilities and political opportunities ever presented to so young a man in the history of the Republic," the *New York Times* would report the next morning. He was "in a better position than anybody else to get the Republican nomination" in 1956, "if, as seems almost certain, the stricken President retires at the end of his first term."

Nixon felt a target being pinned to his back. "My every move, gesture would be watched, interpreted and misinterpreted for the slightest sign that I was moving to 'take over,'" he'd remember. He needed space to think—thus the back-door bolt for the Rogers home in nearby Bethesda, where they met up with Jerry Persons, the White House liaison with Congress, and took calls from the president's staff, using the Rogers kitchen phone.

With Attorney General Brownell out of the country, Deputy Attorney General Rogers was called on for advice about a potential delegation of power. What did the Constitution say? "I haven't the vaguest idea," Rogers said. He suggested they call a scholar. "We can't do that," Nixon said. "If the vice president and the deputy AG don't know what the Constitution says, we will look like a couple of idiots." They searched the house and finally found a copy in the *Farmer's Almanac*.

The vice president got little, if any, sleep that night: he was suffering from hay fever and one of Rogers's sons was a ham radio enthusiast, tapping out Morse code up in the attic. Nixon lay in bed, mind racing, listening to the dots and dashes, thinking about how, in the days ahead, he would be "trodding on eggs." In the morning he borrowed a shirt from Rogers and joined Pat at church. Afterwards, he spoke briefly, and reassuringly, to a small group of reporters in his living room. (Pat, taking pity on those manning the stakeout, had ultimately opened her basement to them.) On Monday, Nixon and Rogers met with White House chief of staff Sherman Adams, Republican Party chairman Len Hall, and others to discuss the politics of a presidential illness. They agreed to curb all talk of 1956.

In the days that followed, Nixon showed sagacity and self-control. Ike improved, but faced unnerving setbacks. The president was weak, anxious, and depressed—consigned to bed for weeks. His aides and friends, worried and knowing their influence flowed from the president, eyed Nixon warily. The capital and its press corps fed on rumor.

Nixon, recalling the vacuum of authority that resulted after Woodrow Wilson suffered a stroke, "knew that those pitfalls must at all costs be avoided." The country and its adversaries must believe that the conduct of the government was in strong, sound hands. But it was a challenging balancing act, for he also recognized that "I must do nothing which could possibly be interpreted as a move toward usurping the duties and powers of the President." At one point the question arose: Who would "push the button" in a nuclear attack? "The problem was never searched to its end although probably if the alert came, most likely the decision . . . would have been made by me."

At the White House, the catchword was *team,* but there were a few unsourced hints, in the *Times* and elsewhere, that Nixon was being restrained by Adams and the other "Eisenhower Republicans." The cabinet officers concluded that Adams should fly to Denver and resume his role as Ike's Cerberus. Nixon, outgunned, did not resist. "Adams was Eisenhower's alter ego," Nixon would recall. "He was with him" during the recovery. "He was President, actually."

Eisenhower sent notes directing Nixon to lead the cabinet and National Security Council meetings, but reminding the vice president that Dulles had the authority to conduct foreign policy. The secretary of state was in postsummit talks; the last thing he needed was for Nixon to pop off about Communists. But Ike's caution wasn't necessary. The vice president was performing his duties with sensitivity—declining to take the president's chair, and consulting the White House staff and cabinet members in their offices, not summoning them to his.

"Throughout this whole terrible episode, your straightforward dignity and visible unselfishness and loyalty has been superb," wrote C. D. Jackson, a former White House aide. Nixon struck each chord with a display of tact and steadiness that bolstered confidence at home and abroad. Skeptics were converted. "Nixon is behaving like a model vice president," Jack Anderson reported in a memo to Drew Pearson. Dulles, reassuring a fretful world, was grateful.

Yet Nixon had been in Washington for nearly a decade. He was now a creature of the city and, like all the rest, ever mindful of the political repercussions. On October 3 Frank Jorgensen wrote with a proposal to secure the California delegation for the 1956 convention, and a list of nominees for a "Nixon for President" committee. California governor Goodwin Knight and Senator Bill Knowland, convinced Ike would retire, maneuvered to outflank Nixon. Rose Mary Woods kept detailed notes, and conveyed instructions, as Murray Chotiner, Kyle Palmer, and other loyalists plotted and schemed on Nixon's behalf. Father John Cronin, an unpaid adviser and speechwriter, sent Nixon a long memo in mid-October, outlining the steps he should take to clinch the Republican nomination. Cronin warned against cockiness, and endorsed stealth: "It is of the utmost importance that the President and his immediate advisers feel that your primary concern is to be of help in the crisis, without any signs of independent excursions for political ends."

Nixon felt confident. His vow to Pat to abandon politics was forgotten. Ike returned to Washington on November 11, to a joyous reception at National Airport. "The whole town was bustling with excitement," Nixon recalled. "The river sparkled blue in the late autumn sunshine and thousands of happy faces lined the streets of the nation's capital. Washington can be a beautiful place."

A BEAUTIFUL PLACE, sure—sometimes. For in the nation's capital, the cynics' hymn rings true, and no good deed does go unpunished. So Nixon soon discovered. Eisenhower emerged from postcoronary melancholy prepared to run for reelection—and ready to drop Nixon from the ticket.

Privately, to friends, Ike had long insisted that one term would be enough. "I shall never again be a candidate for anything," he told Swede Hazlett in 1953. And his friends were pleased to read the predictions that their old pal would retire. "But of course you won't run," Hazlett wrote Eisenhower on October 21. "And I'm glad of it!" As autumn turned toward winter, however, the thought occurred—to Ike, and even Mamie—that leaving a job undone could create more stress than staying. The challenge of a second term, while arduous, was stimulating and life affirming. Coronary patients need inspiration, and Ike had always been stirred by the summons of competition and the call of duty. He loathed the idea of turning the country over to "crackpot Democrats."

In early October, Nixon had visited Ike in the hospital in Denver. "It hurt like hell, Dick," the president told him, recounting the story of the heart attack. The clash with death spurred Eisenhower to consider his successor. Nixon always made the roster on the lists Ike made, but somehow never topped it. Eisenhower expressed his admiration for Nixon's deft performance during that fall's crisis but griped to others about Dick's *immaturity*. There was too much political hack in Nixon. Too much an opportunist. He had not *grown*.

A letter from Ike to Nixon that summer had captured Eisenhower's ambiguity. As he left for the Geneva summit, Ike had spelled out Nixon's duties, warned him against overreaching, and ordered him to be guided by Adams. "Dear Dick. I hope you will have a Cabinet meeting when I am gone. I would likewise hope that you would have the weekly [congressional] 'leaders' meeting," Eisenhower wrote. "Of course, if the majority of the individuals concerned would prefer to omit one of these meetings, I do not expect you to embarrass yourself by insisting on it."

The coronary accented Ike's misgivings. "Eisenhower's feeling for Nixon altered after his first hospitalization, and not because Nixon didn't behave with most scrupulous correctness, but simply because his . . . brush with death . . . had been so close that from then on he never could look at Nixon without thinking: This man may be President at any moment," Republican doyenne Clare Booth Luce, a journalist, congresswoman, and ambassador, recalled. "And when you look at your vice president, *sub specie aeternitatis,* thinking, 'My gosh, he can take my place,' you begin to see all the faults in him. . . . There was a cooling afterwards, in spite of the fact that Nixon behaved most correctly."

So NIXON WAS stupified when, on the day after Christmas, Ike invited him for a talk at the White House and suggested that, instead of serving their crusade as vice president, he spend the second term in the cabinet. It would be good for him, Eisenhower said. Nixon would get executive experience, running the Pentagon or another big department.

There was sense in the suggestion. William Howard Taft and Herbert Hoover had claimed the White House from cabinet posts, while the last vice president to succeed a healthy president was Martin Van Buren in 1837. Nixon had never run anything bigger than his office staff. Riding herd on the joint chiefs, defusing interservice rivalries, and signing off on weapons procurement was a big step up from hounding Rose Woods to keep up with the mail. He would look like a young executive, instead of Ike's hatchet man. As the weeks passed, Eisenhower would sweeten the deal, having Dulles dangle the secretary of state's job as well.

Yet Nixon realized—as Eisenhower should have, must have—how perceptions had been skewed by the president's heart attack. By shifting his vice president to the cabinet, Ike would be signaling that he doubted Nixon's capacity to assume the office in perilous times. That, at least, is how the press and public would interpret the move. Of course, Eisenhower told Nixon—in a moment that seems calculated to shame the vice president— the smart play might be to stay on, wagering that a sexagenarian with a bad heart would not survive until 1960. "I can only assume that if he puts it this way, this must be his way of saying he'd prefer someone else," Nixon told Hall, the Republican Party chairman.

Nixon was correct. Hall knew well what Ike preferred. The president had summoned him to the Oval Office to consider alternatives. What about Ohio governor Frank Lausche, a Democrat and a Catholic? They would make political history. Or Robert Anderson, a conservative Texas Democrat, former secretary of the navy and presidential envoy to the Middle East, whose abilities Eisenhower was forever applauding?

It was 1952, redux. Ike wanted Nixon gone—but was leaving it to him to cut his own throat, to minimize the political cost. Those wounds had never fully healed, and Nixon, always sensitive, insecure, and wary, smelled a trap—set, probably, by Adams, Clay, and others. Nor was Nixon's humiliation yet complete, for his torment became public spectacle. He was snubbed when Ike gathered his top political lieutenants to a dinner and discussion of the 1956 campaign. "Ike went along" with Nixon's enemies. "If the fellows could organize [the coup], it was alright with him," said Hall's deputy, Lou Guylay, summing up the vice president's stretch in purgatory.

As was often the case when the topic was Nixon, the president displayed ambivalence when talking to the press. At the end of February, after Eisenhower declared himself a candidate for a second term, he was asked if Nixon was his choice as a running mate. It would be presumptuous to dictate the party's decision before he actually won its nomination, Ike replied—an obvious dodge. When asked again, a few weeks later, the president said that Nixon would have to "chart out his own course." Whatever Ike meant by that, it was no endorsement. Eisenhower summoned Anderson and dangled the vice presidency. Anderson turned him down. It just wouldn't work, the Democrat told the disappointed president. The Republican Party would never accept him as Ike's successor.

Nixon's friend and future rival, Senator John Kennedy, was struck by Ike's treatment of the vice president. Eisenhower "won't stand by anybody," Kennedy told Arthur Schlesinger. "He is terribly cold and terribly vain. In fact, he is a shit." Nixon was in "absolutely indescribable anguish," Bryce Harlow recalled. The tension showed. Nixon was in and out of hospital beds, complaining of stress, drinking, popping uppers and downers, and fleeing to Florida for therapeutic outings on Rebozo's boat. During one long escape from Washington, using Woods as a conduit, Nixon reported to Hutschnecker on his progress. He was having "up and down" periods, he complained, even on vacation. "On Wednesday which was the 8th day here I did not feel so hot." Hard work, or forced relaxation—his anxiety persisted. "I don't see any relation to how you feel to what you do."

"I did a little experiment on the mail. It didn't go badly at all but I am still not to the point where reading and mail does not bother me some," Nixon reported. "I am not yet to the point where I could get a speech out. I did not spend more than half hour doing the mail and at the end of the time I felt edgy." He was taking Equinal for his anxiety, and Dexamyl, an amphetamine then prescribed for depression and anxiety, and Doriden to sleep. "In the evening if I have two or three drinks I feel good," he told the doctor. "Do you think that should be knocked off or reduced?"

Hutschnecker replied, via Woods, that "the absence of an immediate goal at this time is bad. He cannot build. He doesn't know which way to go. This in itself is a deadly state of frustration." He warned Nixon against becoming reliant on the drugs, and of the effects of mixing the medicines and alcohol. "The danger of these other things" is that "it causes something like a mental depression. You become listless. We want a state of relaxation but not this other listlessness," Hutschnecker said. And "if very tense and you take another drink I am afraid you would lose control."

Eisenhower "never liked me. He's always been against me," Nixon muttered to Hall. But he refused to crawl, and Ike dared not to fire him—especially after Nixon's allies organized public displays of affection from the voters in early primary states. In New Hampshire, where Senator Styles Bridges was an enemy of Sherman Adams, and so a friend to Nixon, an orchestrated write-in campaign gave Nixon more than twenty-two thousand votes.

Finally, in late April, Nixon decided he'd had enough. He drafted notes of withdrawal, and word made its way, as he knew it would, to Hall and others. Consternation ensued. Hall confronted Ike, then told Nixon to drop the Eeyore act. Nixon requested an appointment, formally informed Eisenhower that he wanted to stay on the ticket, and Ike made a show of being pleased. But instead of posing with Nixon, the president sent Hagerty out with the news.

So IT WAS settled, until it wasn't.

In June, Ike was stricken with stomach pains. After years of wrong guesses, his doctors diagnosed this recurring ailment as ileitis—and, in a hurried predawn operation, removed an obstructed segment of the president's intestine. Once again, the spotlight was on Nixon. Did the nation want him a heartbeat from the presidency? Harold Stassen saw an opportunity, met with Eisenhower, and launched a "dump Nixon" campaign in July. Ike let it drag on. "There has always been an almost visible unease in the President's handling of the Nixon question," wrote Richard Rovere in *The New Yorker*. Right up to the convention, "he was careful not to foreclose the possibility of another Vice-Presidential candidate."

In the end, the Republican delegates chose Ike as their nominee and Nixon as his running mate and potential successor. After seven months as the presidential piñata, Nixon had survived to claim the prize. But there was little celebration. And in keeping with that sour spring and summer, Frank Nixon's dying tugged his son away from the Republican convention in San Francisco. Dick flew to Whittier, where, in this most painful hour, the press revealed the scale of its antipathy for Nixon and earned, in the process, a little more of his. To make sure that the family was not faking things for sympathy, the reporters appointed one of their own to visit the sickroom and satisfy them that Frank was indeed on his deathbed. Nixon agreed to let them do it. On the deathwatch with his boss, as they listened to Frank's last gasps, Jim Bassett was struck by Nixon's dissociation. Dick flew back to San Francisco, made his acceptance speech, and launched the campaign. He was back a few days later and was there, on September 4, when his father succumbed. Hannah was stoical. She "put her little head down, and said her prayers, grit her teeth together and that was it," Evlyn Dorn, Nixon's old Whittier secretary, would remember.

THE PROSPECTS WERE good for Ike that fall. The decade had taken a turn toward the better. The consumer culture blossomed; the economy roared. "The U.S. is more prosperous than ever before," *Time* cheered. Europe and Japan were rebuilding; China still hid behind its bamboo curtain. The United States might face competition for economic primacy one day, Ike told a friend, but there was nothing to worry about at the moment. Americans made their own steel, cars, telephones, and televisions. Labor asked for better wages and benefits, and management shrugged, nodded, and headed for the golf course. The autos on the highways were massive, finned behemoths, powered by guzzling V8 engines. Gasoline was a quarter a gallon. The baby boomers would remember their childhoods as Happy Days. Or, at least, the white kids would.

The Democrats chose Stevenson again. He offered no persuasive rationale for change. Americans still loved Ike. And so Nixon became the opposition's target. In a speech in California in October, Stevenson described "Nixonland" as "a land of slander and scare; the land of sly innuendo, the poison pen, the anonymous phone call and hustling, pushing, shoving; the land of smash and grab and anything to win." The "Nixonland" speech was written by economist John Kenneth Galbraith. "This is the kind of speech that can only lose us votes," Stevenson told him, reviewing the text and thinking it too harsh. Upon reflection, Stevenson changed his mind. "I suppose we might as well tell the truth about the man," he said.

On the eve of the election, apologizing for the "distasteful" chore (then proceeding nonetheless), Stevenson raised the probability that Ike would die in office. "Every piece of scientific evidence we have, every lesson of history and experience, indicates that a Republican victory tomorrow would mean that Richard Nixon would probably be President of this country within the next four years," Stevenson told his countrymen. "I say frankly, as a citizen more than a candidate, that I recoil at the prospect of Mr. Nixon as custodian of this nation's future, as guardian of the hydrogen bomb, as representative of America in the world, as Commander in Chief of the United States armed forces."

As America voted, the world was in the grip of crises: a Soviet crackdown in Hungary, and a war between Egypt and three nations—Great Britain, Israel, and France—over the Suez Canal. Dulles had been stricken with cancer. But the voters had had months to digest their choice, and to conclude that Ike's health was a better risk than Stevenson's deficiencies. On Election Day, Eisenhower won a spectacular victory, triumphing everywhere but in Missouri and deepest Dixie and chiseling, once again, at the "Solid South." Of the eleven states in the old Confederacy, Ike carried Texas, Florida, Virginia, Louisiana, and Tennessee.

NIXON CAMPAIGNED IN a DC-6, with his usual frantic energy, in thirty-six states. He had wooed reporters, holding more than fifty press conferences, resolved to counter the "horror image" of a gutter-dwelling hatchet man. His trademark anti-Communism was shelved in favor of "a non-polemical, balanced discussion, with no comments on Democrats as such, no figures of subversives purged from government etc.," as an internal campaign memo put it. He would reach out to academia and the churches, publicize his support for civil rights, and seduce the pundits. The goal was to get his audiences thinking: "Here is a sound, thoughtful, mature, statesmanlike approach. Surely we have nothing to fear from such leadership, should Providence decide to shorten the life of our President."

"We had to show the country that he didn't have horns," one aide said. But it was tricky, said *The New Yorker*—like dressing Marilyn Monroe as Mother Hubbard, while keeping the erotic sizzle. Nixon "has lately been laboring with great zeal to remove any possible reasons for being unloved," wrote Rovere from Washington. "There are some people here who think that the new Nixon is an authentic creation."

There were cracks in the veneer. When his staff scheduled his appearance before a group of antagonistic student editors at Cornell University, Nixon returned to his airplane and exploded in anger. "He went for me like a caged animal," Ted Rogers recalled. "He was shouting at me; screaming at me; [they] had to pull him off." Morale sank, there were murmurs of mutiny. Bassett confronted Nixon. "What scares the hell out of me is that you would blow sky high over a thing as inconsequential as this," he told his boss. "What in goddamn would you do if you were president and get into a really bad situation?"

Though witnessed by the press, the incident was not publicized. And in the end, the strategy worked. Newsmen wrote about his "maturity." Stevenson griped that the "new Nixon" had "put away his switchblade" and "now assumes the aspect of an Eagle Scout."

Nixon took the oath of office for a second term on January 20, 1957, in a near-empty East Room of the White House. Senator Bill Knowland, the Republican leader, swore him in, then Chief Justice Warren administered the oath to Eisenhower. (Had the Californians been outfitted with rapiers, the day may well have ended in Shakespearian slaughter.) Pat stood at Dick's side, as Hannah, Julie, and Tricia watched. Then they all walked over to the dining room for sweet rolls and coffee. It was a Sunday, the Lord's Day, and the speeches and pomp were postponed for Monday, when news photographers captured the president's grandson David stealing an enthralled look at Julie as they stood in the reviewing box at the inaugural parade. He was fascinated by the black eye she sported after a sledding accident that week. They would marry in 1968.

Dick and Pat bought a new house—a lavish twenty-one-room stone dwelling that was better suited for entertaining than their previous residence—with three bedrooms and quarters for the maid. They enrolled their daughters in an elite private school. If all went well, Dick would declare his own candidacy for the presidency in thirty-six months. His second term would be dedicated to that end. He turned ceremonial duties into vote-getting opportunities, survived the machinations of his rivals, and kept in Ike's good graces. With Taft, McCarthy, and Dulles gone, the president and vice president towered over their party, and drew closer together.

IKE SOON HAD the Nixons traveling. In March they were dispatched to Africa, where, while attending the ceremonies celebrating Ghana's independence, Nixon met the Reverend Martin Luther King Jr. The young civil rights leader urged Nixon to speak out against segregation. Keeping the peace and preserving prosperity were Ike's primary orders of business. But just as McCarthyism had posed a moral challenge in their first term, the aborning of a great civil rights movement would test Eisenhower and his vice president in their second. In each case, Ike dodged confrontation for as long as possible, putting his faith in calm, steady progress and the goodwill of the American people. In both instances, gradualism would fail, and he would be compelled to take a more muscular stand. And Nixon? He had dragged his feet in the war against McCarthy, but on civil rights he would lead the way.

The Desolate Night of Man's Inhumanity

T HE AFRICAN AMERICAN struggle for justice dated back to the founding of the Republic; to the abolitionists of the early nineteenth century; to the 180,000 black troops who helped end slavery with their service in the Union Army; to the sorrows of Reconstruction and an abominable Supreme Court decision—*Plessy v. Ferguson*—which upheld segregation in 1896. A few black leaders and white liberals nurtured the flame in the early twentieth century, but a Congress dominated by southern Democrats refused to pass laws against lynching, protect black voting rights, or guarantee fair housing and employment opportunities.

The Second World War, with its rapacity for manpower, invigorated the movement for civil rights. Thousands of black families moved north to work in the factories. There they purchased property in New York, Chicago, Detroit, and other cities, packed the schools, and exercised their right to vote. A million African Americans proved themselves in uniform, many on vital combat missions. And when the war was over, having bled to defeat the racial supremacists overseas, blacks north and south were in no mood to genuflect to bigots at home.

The revitalized movement coursed on three tracks after the war— through the courts, in Congress, and in acts of public protest that transformed streetcar lines, lunch counters, buses, and schools into battlegrounds for freedom. The New Deal's social programs had lured millions of black Americans into Democratic ranks, and Harry Truman had issued the order to desegregate the armed forces, but the first concrete gains, in all three venues, took place in the Eisenhower-Nixon years. A Republican president, a Republican attorney general, a Republican chief justice, and a coalition of Republicans and northern Democrats in Congress responded to the call of conscience and the insistent courage of civil rights activists. And in the councils of the Eisenhower administration, Richard Nixon was a champion for equality.

The initial waves of success crested when, after the Warren Court's

1954 ruling against segregation in *Brown v. Board of Education,* Congress passed the 1957 civil rights bill and Eisenhower dispatched the 101st Airborne Division to Arkansas to escort nine black children to class at Little Rock's Central High School, putting the White House and the federal government, adamantly, on the side of justice. "America's heart goes out to you and your children," Eisenhower wrote the parents of the Little Rock students. "In the course of our country's progress toward equality of opportunity, you have shown dignity and courage in circumstances which would daunt citizens of lesser faith."

IKE DIDN'T GET there quickly. He was a product of his times, a cautious soldier for the cause. He had sped black troops into combat to stop Hitler's last offensive in the Battle of the Bulge. But when asked to testify as an army spokesman in 1948 on the question of desegregation of the armed forces, General Eisenhower had urged Congress to go slow. "If we attempt merely by passing a lot of laws to force someone to like someone else, we are just going to get into trouble," he said. When he ran for the presidency in 1952 he bowed to southern sensibilities (and won four southern states) by opposing the civil rights issue of the moment, the call for a federal fair employment commission. Having served in a segregated army, often in the South, he foresaw the wrenching effect of desegregation and, like any political leader, wasn't beyond hoping that this cup might pass.

"I was sitting in the audience . . . yesterday when you said we must have patience," civil rights hero Jackie Robinson, who had broken the color bar in major league baseball, chided the president in a letter. The nation's 17 million black citizens "cannot do what you suggest and wait for the hearts of men to change," Robinson told him. "You unwittingly crush the spirit of freedom in Negroes by constantly urging forbearance."

When it came to settled law, Ike did his duty. He took Truman's order to desegregate the armed forces and made it happen—even on the South's military bases, where squads of men went to work on weekends, painting over the "whites only" signs and presenting their comrades with a fait accompli on Monday morning. The federally administered District of Columbia and the Veterans Administration's facilities were desegregated. And when the Supreme Court delivered the *Brown* decision, outlawing segregation in the public schools, the president swallowed his disapproval and enforced the ruling.

Ike didn't like the *Brown* decision. He told his secretary, Ann Whitman, that he would have preferred a more gradual approach, with the desegregation of graduate schools first, then colleges, and then the public secondary and elementary schools.

"As you know, the reason I so earnestly support moderation in the race question is because I believe two things," he wrote Atlanta newspaper editor Ralph McGill. "The first of these is that until America has achieved reality in the concept of individual dignity and equality before the law, we will not have become completely worthy of our limitless opportunities. The second thing is that I believe that coercive compliance is, by itself, powerless to bring about complete compliance . . . when in any extensive region the great mass of public opinion is in bitter opposition. This generalization was true under the carpet-bagging government of the South, under the Prohibition Amendment and the Volstead Act, and it is still largely true within the four states . . . in the deep South."

Eisenhower yearned for consensus, and infuriated civil rights leaders by lumping them with white supremacists as "extremists." But as time went on, and he witnessed the South's unyielding hatreds, the president found himself drawn, against his wishes, into a more militant role. He did not sound a moral trumpet. But his judicial appointees were fearless and superb, and the rulings they made did it for him. And Ike's two civil rights bills—though stripped of key powers by the Democratic Congress—were models for landmark legislation that followed.

LIKE IKE, RICHARD NIXON was a man of his times. He had attended law school below the Mason-Dixon line, joined a segregated navy, and served in an almost lily-white Congress.* The deed to his home in Washington, D.C., bore a typical (unenforceable) covenant that forbade its sale to blacks or Jews. He was advised by Father Cronin to "take a middle ground," on civil rights, "between those who would do nothing and those who try to change everything overnight." But his Milhous forebears were disciples of Lincoln, and his great-grandfather Nixon had given his life at Gettysburg. The Quakers of Whittier were not so singularly committed to social justice as their Eastern counterparts, but they practiced the brotherhood

---

* The House had two black congressmen—William Dawson of Chicago and Adam Clayton Powell Jr. of New York—when Nixon was a representative. There were no black senators when Nixon served in the Senate.

they preached. In an era when few social clubs in the United States were integrated, the Orthogonians of Whittier College had welcomed black members.

Dean Triggs, a club founder, remembered that Nixon "was one of the guys that was a believer in bringing a Negro into this group." It was "unheard of" at the time, but Nixon "felt very strongly" that no one should be denied "because of the color of a man's skin . . . that he was just as good a man as anybody else." Years later, as vice president, Nixon intervened to help William Brock, a black Orthogonian who had lost a security clearance. "It gave me a feeling of pride to know that I was . . . closely associated with a man who, although having soared to the very pinnacle of success, still remembers and offers a helping hand to an old classmate," Brock wrote him.

There were many such stories. As a young lawyer in Whittier, Nixon had defended a family of gypsies who were being hounded by the authorities. In the 1946 campaign, Nixon spoke out on behalf of black Americans and was awarded a membership in a local NAACP chapter. One of his earliest celebrity supporters was Kenny Washington, a football star at UCLA who integrated the all-white National Football League—and hosted the election eve party for Nixon and his aides at his home in 1950. When Whittier's black shoeshine man visited the Capitol with his daughter, Nixon braved the stares and took them to lunch in the Senate restaurant. "She is a very pretty and intelligent girl," Nixon reported to Tom Bewley. "It renews your faith in the country to realize that the daughter of a barber shop bootblack could get a Master's Degree from Columbia, standing in the higher percentage of her class."

At the Republican convention in 1952, Nixon struck up a friendship with Jackie Robinson, who had broken the color bar with the Brooklyn Dodgers in 1947. In the years to follow, Pat and Dick would invite Robinson, E. Frederic Morrow—the first black American to hold an executive position in the White House—and other African Americans to dinners at their home. The Nixons also attended a party held by black journalist Ethel Payne—the first time, in the memory of black Washingtonians, that a vice president had socialized in an African American home. Arriving early and staying late, "you and Mrs. Nixon created an atmosphere of relaxed informal friendliness that everyone thoroughly enjoyed," wrote Val Washington, the director of minority affairs for the Republican Party.

In 1953, Ike placed Nixon in charge of a presidential committee on government contracts, whose job was to raise awareness about employment practices. It held hearings in the South and elsewhere, and required that Nixon get on the phone with corporate executives, lobbying them to hire African Americans. At one point, the committee produced a movie about black America, which was shown to Nixon and his staff. When the lights came up, his aide Bob King was startled. The vice president was all choked up, his eyes brimming with tears.

From the vantage point of more than half a century later, Nixon's actions may seem like token steps—but they were steps that not many white Americans were taking. Like Ike, Nixon counseled patience. And like Ike, he believed it would take decades for the unskilled millions of black Americans to match—in education, experience, networking, and corporate know-how—the talents of the white majority. Like Ike, his commitment was subject to political expediencies, but it was genuine nonetheless.

"It is altogether possible that he has no basic racial prejudice," said the impressed Reverend Martin Luther King Jr., in a letter to an inquiring reporter.

EISENHOWER'S POLITICAL PROBLEMS with civil rights were, to a significant extent, of his own making: he insisted on appointing men of high principle to the Department of Justice, the Supreme Court, and the federal courts in the South. Chief Justice Warren, Attorney General Herb Brownell, and federal judges like Elbert Tuttle, John Minor Wisdom, Simon Sobeloff, and Frank Johnson shared the qualities of integrity and courage, and a keen sense of justice. Ike recognized the political benefit of posing as a captive of events, and harbored his own reservations, but he had plenty of opportunities to reverse course on civil rights, and never did. After the *Brown* decision (which spurred 101 senators and representatives, all but two of them Democrats, to sign a "Southern Manifesto" in defense of segregation), Eisenhower chose two northerners, John Harlan and William Brennan, as his next two appointees to the Supreme Court, where they were exponents for civil rights.

Brown II, requiring that the schools be integrated "with all deliberate speed," was handed down in May 1955. That summer, the Reverend George Lee and Lamar Smith, black participants in voter-registration drives, were shot and killed in Mississippi—Smith in the light of day, on the courthouse square. In August, Emmett Till, a fourteen-year-old boy from Chicago on a visit to Mississippi, was tortured and shot and his body dumped in the Tallahatchie River for talking fresh to a white woman. His murder inspired rage across black America. In December, Rosa Parks declined to give up her seat in a blacks-only row of a Montgomery, Alabama, city bus. When she was arrested, the city's black residents staged a yearlong boycott, led by the charismatic young Reverend King. "If we are wrong, justice is a lie," King told the boycotters. The racists responded by bombing his home. But the Warren Court came through again, outlawing segregation on public transit.

Though no one could foresee it—not then, when the laws of human nature and social order seemed so implacable—Parks's act of defiance was like the first tiny fissure that triggers an avalanche. The fissure became a rift, the rift a crack; the crack crept, then raced and branched until, with a roar, the whole great mass of American complacency crumbled. The enormous release of energy broke the norms of not just race, but of age and gender and sexual orientation. It transformed literature, music, education, art, and politics. It terrified many, inspired others, destroyed more than a few. When it was over, America had changed, almost beyond recognition.

TOWARD THE END of 1955, Brownell asked his aides to draft a civil rights bill. The Justice Department needed legal tools to investigate cases like the Till lynching, to guarantee the right to vote, and to enforce desegregation of schools and campuses. After considerable wrangling with the White House, the resulting legislation had four segments. Part I set up a Civil Rights Commission to investigate discrimination; Part II established a civil rights division within the Justice Department; Part III gave the federal government the authority to file suit, seek injunctions, and win contempt charges in a range of civil rights cases; Part IV contained specific protections for voting rights. In cabinet meetings, where others were skeptics, Nixon backed Brownell.

The package was introduced late in the 1956 session, passed the House, and stalled in the Senate. The Democrats accused the wily attorney general of an election-year ploy. No doubt, in part it was. "From a vote-getting standpoint, the South appears lost, whereas large Negro voting groups in states with heavy electoral votes can be most important," Father Cronin wrote, memorializing what Nixon had told him at a meeting in October 1956. Nixon campaigned in Harlem that fall, and in a speech at the Al Smith dinner in New York—an event dedicated to fellowship—he predicted: "Most of us here will live to see the day when American boys and girls shall sit, side by side, at any school—public or private—with no regard paid to the color of their skin. Segregation, discrimination and prejudice have no place in America."

Eisenhower endorsed Brownell's legislation, promised to push for its passage if reelected—and increased his share of black votes in the northern cities. The focus fell, once more, on Congress.

NIXON'S INITIAL CONTRIBUTION to the passage of the 1957 civil rights act came at a key parliamentary juncture—the moment when Congress convened in January.

The South was nothing if not resourceful. For decades, southern voters had been electing Democrats to the House and Senate and sending them back, year after year, so they could accumulate power through seniority. Many became chairmen, happy to inter civil rights measures in their committees. The ultimate line of defense was in the Senate—where a historic wariness of imperious majorities led to a requirement that two-thirds of the senators need vote to end debate before the Senate could proceed with a roll call. As long as the southerners remained united, they had enough votes to keep arguing—to filibuster and talk a bill to death. Because of its rules the Senate was, as William White wrote in his book *The Citadel,* "the South's unending revenge upon the North for Gettysburg."

"The Democratic Party got away with that for a long time. They could have the semblance of liberalism—pro–civil rights and all the rest—the commitment, the pledges, the platforms, the enunciations on the part of northern leaders and liberal leaders," a future party chairman, Lawrence O'Brien, would recall. "But the reality was it hadn't resulted in any mean ingful action."

The Senate governed itself and, theoretically, could revise the number of votes needed to end a filibuster. But the South had the shelter of a parliamentary haven, for the rules could be changed by majority vote only at the very beginning of a Congress—otherwise, it took a seemingly unachievable two-thirds tally. And since a third of the senators are elected at one time, the southerners opportunely contended that the Senate was a continuing body, perpetually in session. The filibuster would live on— unless Vice President Nixon, sitting in the chair, presiding over the Senate, would issue a ruling that said otherwise.

For a politician with national ambitions, the payoff was uncertain. Ike had carried Texas, Virginia, Florida, and other southern states—and Nixon would infuriate white southerners if he ruled against the filibuster. Nor would southern blacks, barred from the polls, be able to express their gratitude.

Up north, it was different. "The Negro vote is the balance of power in so many important big states that one almost has to have the Negro vote to win a presidential election," King advised Nixon. But though they helped give Eisenhower his 1956 landslide, the black voters in the northern cities were largely registered as Democrats. It remained to be seen if Eisenhower's popularity in African American wards was transferrable to another Republican.

So virtue would be its own reward; that, and whatever contribution a virtuous act would make to the perception of a "new" Nixon. He gave it much thought—had a eureka moment and rose from his bed to write out his decision—and did the right thing. When Congress convened and the civil rights forces offered a motion to adopt new rules, Nixon issued an advisory opinion that the Senate was convening as a fresh body and could change the rules via a simple majority vote.

It was a "thunderstriking" moment, *Time* declared. The southern leaders were forced to scurry, and with considerable arm-twisting Majority Leader Lyndon Johnson of Texas and Senator Richard Russell of Georgia rounded up fifty-five votes to table the motion. But that was fifteen votes less than the South had commanded the last time the Senate voted on the filibuster. The southerners had been put on notice—shown what could happen if they continued to abuse the privilege. Russell holstered the tactic, and civil rights leaders called the day "historic."*

Nixon had declared himself. No other administration official, save perhaps Brownell, would match the vice president in the effort he now invested in the bill.

"I am coming to believe that Nixon is absolutely sincere about his views on this issue," King wrote a newsman. "It is my humble opinion that much of the tension in the South and many of the reverses that we are now facing could have been avoided if President Eisenhower had taken a strong positive stand on the question of civil rights and the Supreme Court's decision as soon as it was rendered in 1954. His popular appeal could have made it possible for him to speak to the conscience of this nation on this pressing moral issue. Nixon, I believe, would have done that."

King elaborated. Like many, he had found Nixon's behavior in office more impressive than expected.

"I must admit that I was strongly opposed to Vice President Nixon before meeting him personally. . . . I remembered his statements against Helen Gahagan Douglas and also the fact that he voted with the Right

---

* The predictions of the filibuster's demise were premature. Nixon issued his opinion again in 1959, but again the Senate declined to abandon the filibuster, and it continues to be used, with even greater frequency, today.

Wing of the Republican Party. These were almost unforgivable sins for me at that time," King noted. "After meeting the Vice President, however, I must admit that my impression somewhat changed. I have frankly come to feel that the position and the world contacts of the Vice President have matured his person and judgment. Whether he can have experienced a complete conversion, I cannot say. But I do believe that he has grown a great deal."

Nixon was "a very personable man" with "one of the most magnetic personalities that I have ever confronted," King said.

"There is a danger in such a personality, and that is that it will be turned on merely for political expedience when at bottom the real man has insincere motives," he wrote. "I hope this is not the case with Nixon. He has a genius for winning people . . . for convincing one that he is sincere. . . . If Richard Nixon is not sincere, he is the most dangerous man in America."

Despite rigorous opposition, the civil rights bill passed the House—with 167 Republicans and 118 Democrats voting for it—in June. Again, Nixon was called upon to make a controversial ruling. Once more, he did so—allowing the bill to move directly to the Senate floor, escaping the grave that had been dug for it in the Senate Judiciary Committee by Chairman James Eastland, a Democrat from Mississippi. And this time the Senate sustained Nixon's ruling, 45 to 39. "The outer buttresses of the great dam had crumbled," historian C. Vann Woodward wrote. "For the first time since 1875 an elaborate civil rights bill was before the Senate."

"Once more it was Richard Nixon who saved the day for the civil rights forces," wrote Denton Watson, the biographer of the NAACP's chief lobbyist, Clarence Mitchell.

Two Republican presidential hopefuls—Nixon and Minority Leader Bill Knowland—were now shepherding the legislation, and wooing black voters in Electoral College giants like New York, California, Illinois, and Pennsylvania. But the leading Democratic contenders—John Kennedy and Lyndon Johnson—were jockeying for the support of the Solid South, and supporting eviscerating amendments. They both voted to consign the bill to Eastland's abattoir. To enlist others, Johnson dangled committee assignments, labor support, and, to western Democrats, southern votes for a federal water and power project.

Launching the floor debate, Russell attacked Part III as a dictatorial "devil's broth"—an "instrument of tyranny" insidiously disguised as a voting rights measure, which would give the federal government vast new powers to "put black heels on white necks." When asked by the press if Russell's charges were accurate, Eisenhower dismayed the civil rights forces by declaring that he "didn't completely understand" just what the bill would do and invited the senator to the White House to explain it.

It was a hideous blunder. It "essentially killed us," said Howard Shuman, a Senate aide on the civil rights side. Republican support for Part III crumbled. At his next press conference, Ike pulled the plug on that section of the bill. You don't want to go "too far too fast," he said.

"President Eisenhower never showed anything that I would regard as interest in the civil rights legislation," Brownell's deputy Warren Olney would remember. "He thought of himself as sort of a reconciler of the people who were favoring integration . . . on the one hand, and those southerners who were talking about massive resistance on the other. He was trying not to give offense to either side. Well, I believe that this was really a tragic mistake." Had the president showed more leadership, "the history of this issue might have been very, very different. But he didn't do that."

WITH EISENHOWER WAVERING, Russell now focused on gutting Part IV. He and his southern allies portrayed the bill as a constitutional apostasy which, in voting rights cases, would deprive defendants of their right to a jury trial. Left unspoken was the deplorable reality: southern juries invariably sided with white offenders, even in open-and-shut cases like the lynching of Emmett Till. But with the votes of Kennedy, Johnson, and moderates of both parties the southerners prevailed and a requirement for jury trials was added to the measure. Kennedy had "toppled over like a ten pin" as Johnson "cracked his whip and marshaled his forces to cut the guts and heart out of the bill," the African American journalist Ethel Payne reported.

Nixon seethed. Ike (at last) fumed. The press was portraying Johnson as a mastermind, Russell the victor, and Eisenhower a befuddled loser. Knowland, whose performance had ranged from dismal to inept, was said to have broken down and wept. In describing the eviscerated legislation, one supporter quoted Lincoln: it was soup made from the shadow of a crow that starved to death.

At first Nixon suggested that Ike abandon the legislation, return the next year with a stronger bill, and blame the demise of the 1957 version on the Democrats. But after a moment's reflection, Nixon and Brownell and the civil rights leaders opted to take what they could get. And with Eisenhower's assistance, the jury trial loophole was abridged in the last rounds of negotiations. The bill's passage represented a significant victory, said Mitchell, the NAACP's top lobbyist. "At last, the Congress has assumed some of its responsibility in the field of civil rights," he wrote Nixon. "Your ruling . . . opened a door that long had been closed."

King agreed. "After considering all angles I have come to the conclusion that the present bill is far better than no bill at all," he told Nixon. "This could be a powerful incentive in changes in behavior and attitude. . . . Civil rights legislation is urgent now, and the present limited bill will go a long way to insure it."

Indeed, in the years to come the new U.S. Civil Rights Commission would tour the South, exposing injustice, and the new Civil Rights Division would flourish. But most of all, having handed the South its first such defeat in eighty-two years, the United States Congress had broken a barricade and taken a stand for black Americans. The coalition of moderate Republicans and liberal Democrats would assemble again and pass landmark statutes—the Civil Rights Act in 1964 and the Voting Rights Act in 1965—in an evanescent moment of purpose and national unity. Russell may have won this day, but he'd only purchased time. The civil rights forces would get Part III, and more—and next time Lyndon Johnson would be on *their* side, exploiting the memory of the martyred John Kennedy. The South's hold on the Congress was crumbling—one more rockslide in the era's many.

NIXON HAD BEEN guided, in his dealings on the bill, by King's advice. In June, they met at Nixon's office in the Capitol. "The Vice President was very much impressed with Reverend King, and thinks the President would enjoy talking to him. He is not, he says, a man who believes in violent and retaliatory pro-Negro actions, but sponsors an evolutionary but progressive march forward," wrote White House aide Max Rabb to Sherman Adams. It was a welcome endorsement for King, whose prominence had alienated some older civil rights leaders.

After seeing Nixon's work in the legislative wrestling that summer, King returned his compliments. "Let me say before closing how deeply grateful all people of goodwill are to you for your assiduous labor and dauntless courage in seeking to make the Civil Rights Bill a reality," King said. "This is certainly an expression of your devotion to the highest mandate of the moral law. It is also an expression of your political wisdom. . . . With men like you occupying such important positions in our nation I am sure that we will soon emerge from the bleak and desolate night of man's inhumanity to man to the bright and glittering daybreak of freedom and justice for all men."

The press agreed. "Through the fight," *Time* reported, "Vice President Nixon punched hard for a meaningful bill." But the most reliable indicator of Nixon's effectiveness may have come from Russell, who caustically predicted on the Senate floor that, with the 1960 election just over the horizon, Nixon would continue to press the administration "to apply the great powers of the law to the Southern states at such places and in such time and manner as the NAACP, of which the Vice President is the most distinguished member, may demand."

IT DIDN'T TAKE long for Ike to discover just what he lost when he helped the Senate strip Part III from the bill. Brownell had fashioned that section as a tool chest—with an array of legal remedies that would give the president options. When Governor Orval Faubus deployed his state's National Guard to bar the doors of Central High in Little Rock—just a week after Eisenhower signed the stripped-down act—Ike had but one blunt instrument to enforce the Constitution, and that was the U.S. Army.

Eisenhower had met with Faubus and announced to the nation that the crisis was over—the governor would obey the law. But on September 24, after discovering that Faubus had deceived him, the furious president federalized the Arkansas guard and dispatched the 101st Airborne to protect the black children from a violent, ugly racist mob. Ike believed in the persuasive impact of overpowering force: eleven thousand soldiers were involved. What Russell most feared had happened: federal troops had seized control of southern streets and institutions, intent on mingling the races.

Ike regretted how he'd been compelled to use force by the obdurate southerners, but not that, as president, he had fulfilled his duty to enforce the law. Early in October, he invited Nixon to play golf with him, while warning his vice president that their plans might be spoiled. "Mine are necessarily so uncertain because of the stupidity and duplicity of one called Faubus," the president wrote.

RUSSELL HAD ONCE confided to a friend that he hoped to save segregation for two hundred years. His summer successes seemed like Pyrrhic victories now. Whatever moral high ground he had claimed in the Senate debate was squandered in the Little Rock showdown, when he sent a crazed, boorish telegram to the White House, accusing Eisenhower, the liberator of Buchenwald and other Nazi concentration camps, of applying "strong armed totalitarian police state methods . . . copied from the manual issued the officers of Hitler's storm troopers" against "inoffensive and peaceable American citizens."

Eisenhower addressed the nation on television. The country, having witnessed the president's patience, and hearing his call for justice, sided against the South. Ike was acting like Lincoln's heir. The civil rights of black Americans would be protected, with rifles and bayonets if necessary. "The alternative to supporting the law in such a situation is to acquiesce in anarchy, mob rule and incipient rebellion," Eisenhower scolded Senator John Stennis, a Democrat from Mississippi.

Nixon backed Ike. The president may have saved the Little Rock children from a gruesome lynching, Nixon told a conference of journalists. In the struggle for the rights of black Americans, "there is, here, a very real moral issue," he said. Ike had done his duty, saving the country from constitutional chaos.

Nixon's fealty was not without cost. He had gone too far for some of his supporters, who were looking, as he was, toward the 1960 election. Nixon "has a good chance of picking up a lot of convention votes in the southern block, but such statements will make it hard for those who wish to support him to do so," a Florida Republican griped. "He could have let Ike take the rap on this one down here and save a lot of good votes that he might need."

15

The Field of Pending Battle

I T IS DIFFICULT to choose one day, or event, that marks the beginning
of the paroxysm known as "the Sixties." The Montgomery bus boycott
and the fall of Dien Bien Phu were foreshocks of seismic events to follow. The Little Rock crisis was another such temblor. Elvis Presley ruled
the pop charts that summer, and Jack Kerouac's Beat classic *On the Road*
was published. Yet if one had to pick a moment that "forever separates the
old from the new"—as an NBC commentator declared at the time—it
might well be the evening of October 4, 1957. Ike was at Gettysburg, preparing for his fifth round of golf that week. Millions of his countrymen
were at home, watching the debut of *Leave It to Beaver,* a candied TV portrait of American life. But high above, orbiting the earth every ninety-six
minutes, was a silver Russian beach ball, singing *beep beep beep* in the key
of A-flat, at eighteen thousand miles an hour.

The Soviets called it Sputnik. Earth's first man-made satellite wasn't
much—its main component was batteries, to power the radio transmitter.
It lasted just a bit more than three months before succumbing to gravity
and burning up on reentry. Its true impact was political. The empire build-
ers in the air force had been spreading fear about a "bomber gap." Now
the Pentagon doomsayers—joined by Democratic senators (and presidential hopefuls) Lyndon Johnson, Stuart Symington, and John Kennedy—
alleged an ersatz "missile gap."

The Soviet Union had proven it could launch a heavy payload with an
intercontinental ballistic missile (ICBM). If the Soviets could put a satellite in orbit, they could soon drop a warhead on Washington or New York.
American prestige suffered. So did Ike's aura as a military genius. The
Eisenhower epoch was discredited. The intellectual elite, and its subscrib-
ers in the press, now cast the "happy days" as a slough of somnolence and
complacency. The Eisenhower administration, wrote one liberal critic, was
"a bowl of tapioca," bathed in a "gangrenous sunset."

"We are in a race with the pace of history," James Reston wrote in the

New York Times. "But in the last five years the president has gradually drifted apart from the intellectual opinion of the country, [and] filled up his social hours with bantering locker-room cronies." The argument was underscored in November, when the president distressed his wife and aides with incomprehensible mutterings. Unable to find the right words, he flailed at his bedclothes with his fists. He had suffered a stroke. Once more, Nixon received a chilling phone call. Again, the prognosis looked glum. "The severity of his stroke was considerably greater than people generally were aware," Nixon would recall. "He had enormous difficulty in speaking and the more his inability to articulate frustrated him, the worse the problem became."

"You may be president in the next twenty-four hours," Sherman Adams told Nixon. With Secretary of State Dulles, Nixon discussed their options if Ike were incapacitated. The president was thinking the same thoughts, and intent that only he make the decision to cede power. Ike's old comrade-in-arms, Lucius Clay, arrived to look out for Eisenhower's interests and, he later admitted, to quash any move by the vice president to take control. "This is the concern that I had," Clay recalled. "I can't say that I had any foundation for it, but this was a concern that I had." *

Ike made a strong, quick recovery, and Nixon again won fine reviews for his deft performance as an understudy. But it all added up: Sputnik, the missile gap, Ike's sixty-seven years, and the reputed demise of American vigor. "It is the part of realism to concede a high degree of foundation for these doubts and fears," Father Cronin warned Nixon. "In spite of high prosperity, there is a mood of uneasiness in the nation . . . a feeling that we are drifting into dangerous situations without clear leadership or a plausible program."

"What people want at this moment is HOPE," Adela St. Johns wrote Nixon. "HOPE that there is a chance we may live on—grow—be better—reach peace—the Aquarian Age."

It was time to get the country moving again, the Democrats argued—none so urgently as John F. Kennedy.

KENNEDY WAS, IN many ways, Nixon's opposite. He was rich, a playboy, charming, and Harvard educated, and an accommodating press concealed his more disreputable characteristics. The two men shared enough

---

* This third health crisis prompted Eisenhower to fill a gap in the Constitution, which then had no provisions for presidential disability. On February 5, 1958, Ike drafted a letter outlining the conditions under which he would declare Nixon, or Nixon could declare himself, acting president. The Twenty-fifth Amendment, adopted in 1967, formalized the process.

attributes—demanding fathers, distant mothers, the death of siblings, navy service in the South Pacific, a thirst for glory—to forge a friendship. "Poor brave Jack is going to die. Oh God, don't let him die," Nixon had prayed when Kennedy dodged death on an operating table in 1954. Four years later, he told Christian Herter Jr., a former aide, that he could not campaign for him in the Massachusetts attorney general race because Kennedy was running for reelection to the Senate that year. The press would expect him to endorse Kennedy's Republican challenger, said Nixon, and he would not do it. "I know Kennedy," Nixon said, "and I have a fairly high regard for him. It would be difficult for me."

The Kennedys had fewer scruples, and targeted Nixon's top strategist for ruin. Murray Chotiner was subpoenaed, hauled before a Senate committee, and grilled by Robert F. Kennedy, the committee counsel and the senator's brother, over charges that he traded on his access to Nixon to attract high-paying, unsavory clients. Evidence of influence peddling was there, and embarrassing, though not provably illegal. Nixon cut Chotiner loose, and he was blacklisted in national politics. In the 1960 presidential campaign, Nixon would be without the help of a most valuable adviser. Chotiner had outlived his usefulness.

Ralph de Toledano had a similar experience. After years of serving as friend, friendly biographer, and admiring *Newsweek* columnist, he was startled to hear how his friend Dick had shrugged when the magazine's editors, intent on firing de Toledano but worried they might anger the vice president, ran the decision by Nixon. De Toledano told the tale to Whittaker Chambers, who was also feeling discarded. "I have only contempt for an expediency which is . . . empty, brittle and not fed and tempered by a true human understanding where friends are concerned," Chambers said. Nixon's betrayal of his friends was not just cruel, it was self-defeating. "My anger," said Chambers, "burns on a wick of disrespect for what I consider his failure."

JOHN KENNEDY HAD notable political impediments. He was young—he turned forty in May 1957 and his wife Jacqueline twenty-eight in July— and a Roman Catholic. His health was suspect, his womanizing known in political circles, and his record in Congress underwhelming. Liberals scorned his pallid stance on civil rights. His father, Joe, a corsairing businessman, had disgraced himself when prescribing appeasement in the face of Nazi aggression while serving as the U.S. ambassador to Great Britain before World War II. After the war, Joe and the family had embraced Joe McCarthy.

But when Adlai Stevenson left the choice of his running mate up to the Democratic convention in 1956, Kennedy had mounted a spirited, improvised campaign and almost snatched the prize. The experience persuaded Joe and Jack and Bobby that the impediments were surmountable.

For Kennedy, Sputnik's beeps were manna. Ike had seemed impregnable on the issue of national security. Now the Democrats could attack from the right, alleging that the doddery old general had left the country vulnerable. Nixon immediately perceived the danger. At the NSC meeting on October 10, after listening to CIA director Dulles minimize the Soviet achievement, and to Ike pronounce his satisfaction with the U.S. space program, Nixon proffered a splash of reality, warning his colleagues to ready themselves for a political inquisition. Things got worse before they got better: the Vanguard rocket, billed as the American reply to Sputnik, climbed feebly for a few feet and then blew up on its launchpad in December.

The United States ramped up production of nuclear weapons, compiling seven thousand new warheads a year in 1959 and 1960, and another five thousand in 1961. But in private, and in off-the-record sessions with select commentators, Nixon was fuming. Ike declined to authorize big boosts in spending for conventional weapons; in his farewell address, the president would famously warn against the ravenous appetites of the "military-industrial complex." The administration was plodding along like a "caretaker," Nixon told Cronin. Its motto might as well be: "Things are good—let's don't rock the boat." Elliot Richardson, then an acting cabinet secretary, recalled days when Nixon would rise from a cabinet or legislative leaders meeting "literally shaking with tension" over "decisions being made by the president that [Nixon] saw as undercutting his chances for election in 1960."

In an airplane ride with reporters and members of his staff, Nixon took a couple of drinks—stiff shots poured by aide Don Hughes—and launched into a tirade. The president was an idiot, cruel and ungenerous, who had subjected him to gross indignities, Nixon said: a tin god who had duped the American people. Only he, Richard Nixon, could change all that by being elected president. "He was blind drunk," another aide, Charles Lichenstein, recalled. "It showed how insecure he was."

—

NIXON'S MARCH TO the Republican nomination was marked by arduous ascents, mortifying slips, and ensuing demonstrations of resiliency. His first big break verged on tragedy. A humdrum tour of Latin America was transformed in the spring of 1958 when a mob in Caracas, Venezuela, attacked his motorcade.

Dick and Pat had left National Airport on April 27, a chilly and drizzly day. "We'll see you in three little ol' weeks," Julie told them. In Uruguay, there were anti-Nixon demonstrations. "This caused me no real concern at first. After all, every country . . . has some crack pots, Communists, and other breeds of America-haters," he recalled. By the time they arrived in Peru, the "crack pots" had organized. At a welcoming reception at the American embassy, Nixon was informed that a hostile mob was going to confront him at the University of San Marcos the next day. The U.S. ambassador outlined the vice president's choices. If Nixon fled, the United States could be disgraced. If he plunged ahead, he might win points for bravery, but could spark a violent confrontation, for which he would be blamed. "It was a momentary feeling of unreality," Nixon remembered. "In the Great Hall just a door away . . . the elite of Lima was gaily dancing, chatting, nibbling and sitting. The laughter and occasional wisps of chatter flowed into the room where my associates and I sat so solemnly, analyzing the field of pending battle."

Nixon found it hard to sleep. "In the crisis syndrome," he recalled, "the arduous process of deciding which course to take, what to do, is exceeded only by the aftermath of battle as a time of trial and mental torment." (In later years, he melodramatically likened this night to the "tortures of the damned" that Eisenhower suffered before ordering the D-Day landings.) Ultimately, Nixon decided to confront the leftist protests. "Under no circumstances should any American official ever fawn," he concluded. The leader of his Secret Service detail, Jack Sherwood, gulped and gave the orders to proceed.

At San Marcos, Nixon left his limousine and, with Sherwood, some of the local police, and Vernon Walters, his interpreter, strode into a shrieking, sign-waving crowd. "I want to talk to you," the vice president shouted. The crowd at first gave way; then its organizers regained command. "Mr. Vice President, they are throwing some stones and fruit at us," Walters told him. "I know," Nixon replied. "Our exit has to be slow and dignified." A rock broke one of Sherwood's front teeth. Another glanced off Nixon's shoulder. They backed away.

"By now I was excited, of course, I felt the excitement of battle," Nixon remembered. "I stood up in the back of my convertible, with Sherwood holding my legs to keep me from falling, and I shouted to be heard above the melee: 'You are cowards! You are afraid of the truth!'"

The American correspondents in Nixon's entourage wrote glowing reports, and Eisenhower cabled his congratulations. U.S. ambassador Theodore Achilles, a career diplomat, wrote to Nixon: "I again express my deep regret at having to recommend your exposing yourself to such unpleasantness and possible danger, but I would certainly do it again, and with more certainty than before, now that I have seen how you handled it. . . . No one who was with you . . . as the correspondents and I were, could help having a profound admiration."

Later, however, Nixon succumbed to the day's "emotional strain." After hearing that two State Department aides had objected to the San Marcos visit, he lost control, summoned them to his room, and reviled them for timidity. He told them to "act like Americans" and "not put their tail between their legs every time some Communist bully made a threat." His rage was "uncalled-for," he would later admit. He could never satisfactorily explain it to himself. They had worked hard and "should have been praised, not censured."

NIXON AND HIS entourage moved on to Ecuador, Colombia, and Venezuela. Two days before landing in Caracas, Nixon received news that the CIA had picked up rumblings of an assassination plot. On May 13, a loud crowd at the airport welcomed him to Venezuela. "Mr. Vice President, they're not friendly," the interpreter told him. Demonstrators showered them with spit from a balcony and a nearby barrier as the couple stood at attention for the Venezuelan national anthem. Dick had been spit on in Peru, "but now Pat was having to submit to this filthy indignity, and this second baptism for me was far worse than the first," he recalled. "If the sky wasn't so clear and the day so bright you might have thought it was raining." Nixon resolved to burn his suit. Pat's dress was blotched; Sherwood, furious, threw an elbow at a protester. Pat reached across a barricade, and gently took a young woman's hand. Astonished, seemingly abashed, the girl ducked away.

Nixon was scheduled to lead a wreath-laying service at a statue of Simon Bolivar, but on a broad city boulevard his caravan of limousines (some rented from a local funeral parlor) was brought to a halt by a roadblock. "Things began to happen," he remembered. "Here they come," said Sherwood.

Dozens of demonstrators rushed the cars, some shouting *"Muera*

Nixon!" Glass from a shattered window showered the passengers and caught the Venezuelan foreign minister in the eye. The driver needed the windshield wipers, to see through all the spittle. "The hate on their faces was unbelievable . . . they were out to kill us," Hughes recalled.

Nixon laughed, in spite of himself, when an AP cameraman on the flatbed truck ahead of them used his camera to club a protester back onto the street. One car back, Pat tried to comfort the near-hysterical wife of the Venezuelan minister. The Secret Service detachment ran beside the cars, shoving the protesters away. "Many were clearly teenagers. Mostly boys, a few girls. But they all had a look of unadulterated hatred," Nixon remembered. "And interspersed through the youngsters were the tough case-hardened Communist operatives." The auto began to rock. Sherwood and another agent pulled their guns. "I think we'll have to get some of these sons of bitches," Sherwood said. No, said Nixon. Not unless they pulled him from the car. "If it got that bad, I knew it all would be lost anyway," he recalled.

And then, like cavalry arriving, the Venezuelan police cracked the traffic jam. The press truck and the cars lurched into an open lane and sped away. Safe in the courtyard of the American embassy, guarded by Marines, Dick and Pat looked at each other, and took stock. "There was no great emotional reunion," Hughes recalled. "Just an . . . 'Are you okay?' 'Yes, are *you* okay?' . . . sort of a situation." Hughes was more ebullient. "This is American soil," he told them, "and a little bit of heaven."

Only later, away from the press and the embassy officials, did the Nixons reveal their fear to each other. "That's when they realized it was a near-death experience," their daughter Julie recalled.

THE PRESS ACCOUNTS from Lima and Caracas had portrayed the vice president as cool under fire, defending his nation's honor. Nixon was thrilled by the warmth of the crowd—led by Ike himself—that assembled at National Airport to welcome him back to Washington. The story claimed the cover of *Life*, seized the imagination of his countrymen, and fueled Nixon's climb in the polls. Upon hearing the reports from Caracas, Eisenhower had alerted the military and sent troops, planes, and warships into the Caribbean to guarantee the vice president's safety; now he and Nixon shared a convertible, waving to the 100,000 who crowded the airport and lined the route to the White House. Nixon was a genuine hero.

"My God, what a fantastic occurrence," Ted Rogers, his media adviser, wrote him. A few columnists had carped that Nixon should never have placed himself in such danger. "But they don't amount to a hill of beans compared to the way your actions and attitudes captured the public's need for leadership and decisiveness."

As sweet was the spring, so rank was the fall. The 1958 election was a debacle for the Republicans—reversing all the party's postwar gains and leaving it dispirited and outnumbered to an extent not seen since Franklin Roosevelt's first term. The furor over Sputnik had been followed by a mid-term recession, rising unemployment, trouble in the farm belt, and reports of corruption at federal agencies. The last claimed Sherman Adams, accused of accepting a vicuna coat and other gifts from Bernard Goldfine, a New England businessman. Eisenhower could not bring himself to fire his chief of staff, so Nixon and others were dispatched to urge Adams to fall on his sword. Nixon detested personal confrontations. Taking his turn at telling Adams to leave was, he recalled, "the most difficult single assignment I undertook" for Ike.

The November verdict—"a shellacking," Nixon called it—was especially sour for the vice president. The Republicans lost forty-eight seats in the House and thirteen in the Senate, as well as both Senate seats in the new state of Alaska. He had seen it coming, but decided that trying to minimize the Republican losses was a better gambit than standing clear of the train wreck. For the fourth time in six years, Nixon had campaigned at a furious pace, barnstorming the country on behalf of Republican candidates, earning their gratitude and that of precinct leaders, state chairmen, and national committee members. But the currents were against him, most notably in California, where self-destructive scheming cost the party dearly.

It was known as the Big Switch. Bill Knowland's ambition, suspect judgment ("In his case there seems to be no final answer to the question 'How stupid can you get?'" Ike wrote in his diary), and wandering eye were the proximate causes. The senator believed that the governor's mansion offered a better road to the White House than the Senate, and he and his capricious wife, Helen, wished to return to California, in part to save their marriage. The state, however, already had a Republican governor—Goodwin Knight—with his own outspoken wife and presidential designs. The three men—Knight, Knowland, and Nixon—had jockeyed throughout the Eisenhower years, most notably in the weeks after Ike's heart attack, when Knight and Knowland maneuvered to block Nixon's presumed succession as the party leader, and "Ike and Goodie" buttons were spotted in Sacramento.

In the fall of 1957, Knowland declared that he would run for governor, regardless of Knight's plans. The decision was imperious, and disastrous. To forestall a destructive primary, Nixon and newsman Kyle Palmer coerced Knight to run for the now-open Senate seat instead. The governor resisted until the state's Republican donors threatened to cut off his campaign funds. It was all played out in public, with arch salvoes from Mrs. Knight and Mrs. Knowland, who observed that Goodie had "a macaroni spine." Amid the antics, Knowland endorsed a right-to-work initiative that was anathema to unions. Propelled by organized labor, and the listing economy, Attorney General Edmund "Pat" Brown whipped Knowland by a million votes, and Knight lost the Senate race by almost as great a margin. The Republican Party, regnant in California for decades, was decimated. Nixon could console himself—two rivals, after all, had plunged daggers in each other's throats—but he now faced a struggle to win his own state in 1960. "They just pulled the rug from under Knight," Brown happily recalled. "Mrs. Knight hated Knowland and she hated Nixon. There was awful hatred in that Republican Party. Everybody hated everybody." Nixon's mood wasn't helped when he slipped on the ice (again) that winter and cracked two ribs.

The Republicans took one sip of cheer from the 1958 results—but even it was ashes to Nixon. In a contest of robber baron offspring, the bon viveur, arts patron, and presidential aspirant Nelson Rockefeller defeated Averell Harriman and won election as governor of New York. Nixon's rival for the Republican nomination was no longer the plodding Knowland but "Rocky"—a charismatic extrovert whose name was synonymous with limitless wealth, and who joined in the complaints about the administration's lethargy. "Bets at even money are already being made that the vice president is through and that the 1960 Republican nomination is Mr. Rockefeller's," wrote Richard Rovere in *The New Yorker.* Nixon was especially galled when Rockefeller flew to a family ranch in Venezuela for a post-election vacation. During Nixon's trip to Caracas, Rocky had cabled his support. Now he told the Latin American press: *"No tengo nada que ver con Nixon."* ("I have nothing to do with Nixon.") The episode and its author were inscribed in Nixon's book of grudges.

"As 1958 came to a close Dick Nixon had grievous doubts about whether it was possible for him . . . to win in 1960," Robert Finch recalled. And "at this moment, when Dick Nixon was still in the throes of his own personal decision and without any semblance of a personal organization, Jack Kennedy had been moving in an organized fashion for over two years."

THEN, AS SUDDENLY, Nixon was summiting. At talks in Geneva, the Soviet Union and the United States had agreed to host world's-fair-style "exhibitions" of each other's cultural, economic, and scientific achievement. High-ranking Soviet ministers attended the opening of their pavilion in New York in the summer of 1959, and Nixon was dispatched to launch the American display in Moscow.

Ike gave Nixon no authority to negotiate. Nor were one-on-one sessions with Nikita Khrushchev so singular: the Soviet premier had recently spent eight hours with Senator Hubert Humphrey, a Democrat from Minnesota. And when Milton Eisenhower joined the trip, it looked like the president sent his brother to babysit. Still, this was no small opportunity for a prospective presidential candidate. These were not Third World despots: this was the Kremlin, Red Square, the Soviet Union—the heart, brain, and brawn of the international Communist conspiracy. KNOCK THEM DEAD IN RUSSIA, Ted Rogers cabled. PUBLICITY AND BUILD UP HAVE BEEN EXCEPTIONALLY WELL RECEIVED EVERYWHERE I HAVE BEEN. THIS IS MOST IMPORTANT TRIP OF YOUR LIFE. Nixon's luck held. He was there "to extend the usual social courtesies," he would remember, but "what caught and held the interest of the world was a series of bizarre circumstances which ran the gamut of high drama to comic opera."

Nixon did his usual iron-assed cramming for the trip, and a second jetliner packed with the press followed along to Moscow. He found sleep difficult the first night, and slipped away just after dawn to roam a farmers' market with Sherwood and a Soviet police interpreter. His first meeting with Khrushchev set the tone of their talks: he found the premier fondling a model of a Soviet rocket, like Charlie Chaplin toying with a globe in *The Great Dictator.*

Khrushchev was as Nixon's briefing books described him: a burly peasant who displayed shrewdness, brutality, and stamina in his turbulent ascent, during which he had survived the rigors of the coal mines, the Russian Revolution, the death of his wife, Stalin's purges, and the siege of Stalingrad. His behavior toward the West zigzagged from sweet talk to bluff to confrontation as the need to maintain power in the chum-bloody waters of the Soviet Union required. Khrushchev had played on Soviet paranoia to outmaneuver rivals—then renounced Stalinism and Stalin's crimes. He had shown signs of reason at Geneva—then crushed the Hungarian revolt. He was a proud, insecure, emotional man, threatening to send Soviet tanks into West Berlin. His tantrums and tirades—from a leader equipped with a nuclear arsenal—had the intended effect of unnerving Western foes.

Nixon had been briefed on 132 topics. Yet "all the briefings in the world could not have prepared me for Khrushchev's unexpected, unpredictable conduct," he recalled. The premier's opening salvo was typical—a graphic complaint about Congress's passage of a "captive nations" resolution, calling for the liberation of Eastern Europe. If the United States wanted constructive talks, he told Nixon, it should not pollute the terrain. "People should not go to the toilet where they eat," said Khrushchev. "Fresh shit stinks."

The official record excised the remark, as well as Nixon's riposte: "The Vice President noted that he had also grown up on a farm and that he knew that if anything smells stronger than horse shit it is pig shit. To this Mr. Khrushchev replied that human shit smells worst of all."

The two men then toured the American exhibition, where a young TV executive lured them onstage for a demonstration of that newfangled contrivance: color television. "We found ourselves by accident . . . with literally millions of potential viewers," Nixon recalled. Khrushchev was in his element, hamming it up for the Russian onlookers, lecturing the vice president, and at one point, mockingly, waving bye-bye to vanquished capitalism. Nixon was unscripted and unsure. Ike had given him explicit orders: he was there to cut ribbons, not to brawl. "Nixon's reputation for being a tough bargainer who could 'stand up to the Russians' was in danger of being forever dissipated," recalled William Safire, a New York PR man (and future Nixon speechwriter) who witnessed the scene. "He was getting clobbered." Shaken, the vice president broke into a flop sweat and ineffectively parried the premier's tough critiques. "Khrushchev," Nixon remembered, "knocked me out of the ring."

Nixon didn't do *that* badly—or really that much better when, a few minutes later, he and Khrushchev resumed their debate at an exhibit of a "typical" American kitchen. But he caught a huge break from the U.S. press corps, who were rooting for their guy in this match of heavyweights, and awarded this round of what came to be known as the "kitchen debate" to Nixon. The photographs sealed the verdict. The two leaders had been wagging fingers at each other all day, but the front pages in America showed Nixon jabbing Khrushchev's chest or chopping with his hand to emphasize a point. They made Nixon look strong, like he had bested a flummoxed Soviet tough guy.

Nixon could not know this at the time, of course. As they moved from the kitchen display, "I felt actually physically weak" from tension, he would remember.*

Khrushchev disliked Nixon, the renowned anti-Communist, but displayed a wary regard for his political gifts. The vice president was "exceptionally able," but "a man who never stands on one point," Khrushchev told the U.S. ambassador. "You never know where you are with him." To the extent that the Soviets could influence American voters, they would spend the next decade trying to keep Nixon from the Oval Office.

The next day, Khrushchev took Nixon boating on the Moscow River, stopping to greet crowds of swimmers and sunbathers and shouting, "Are *you* captives?" When their boat got stuck on a sandbar, the premier simmered, and Nixon wondered if the craft's pilot lived to see another dawn. But at lunch at his dacha outside the city, the Soviet leader displayed his self-control. "He likes both his food and his liquor," Nixon recorded. "But just as his famed temper is his servant and not his master . . . he hardly touched the array of vodka and wine glasses which were in front of him during the course of our four-hour luncheon, and though the subjects we discussed were of the greatest importance he never raised his voice once."

Nixon went on to tour the country—from Leningrad to Siberia to the Urals. He was given half an hour on Russian television to address the Soviet people. He resisted the temptation to lash back at the hecklers planted by the government along the way whose aim, he told Ike, was "to provoke me into some angry and ill-considered reactions." It was Khrushchev's aim as well. When Nixon spoke about his boyhood and the Nixon market, Khrushchev spat on the memory. "All shopkeepers are thieves," the premier said. Nixon's sole misstep (after cautioning his staff to watch how much they drank) was to take too much vodka at an embassy reception following his speech, and reveal his lack of self-confidence, again, by boorishly badgering the other guests for compliments.

"He was pleading for reassurance and, as nearly always happens, the confirmations and slightly sycophantic replies and comments from his staff did not help," a U.S. diplomat, Vladimir Toumanoff, recalled. "His insecurity was too deep, he was too intelligent, and I surmise he had repeated the same scene too many times and for too many years to fool himself. His anxiety seemed to increase."

---

* Khrushchev's antic exchanges with Nixon at the color television exhibit, not the model kitchen, were what Americans saw on television at home. Safire later claimed credit for orchestrating the rematch at the famous kitchen and for helping photographers take the pictures.

Dick and Pat capped their tour with a stop in Poland on their way home, where hundreds of thousands of cheering and adulatory Poles showered them with flowers. Aside from the Cold War theatrics, Nixon's trip added little to the state of U.S.-Soviet relations. Its chief legacy was political. Nixon had come across as bold and statesmanlike.

Nixon was now "the first guy from the Free West to stand up and bark back at Khrushchev," Ted Rogers wrote. "I assure you it built the path to the White House. I know it. I feel it."

ROCKEFELLER WASN'T HAPPY with Nixon's success, and the sniping between the two led an irritated president to cuff his two ambitious cubs. He suggested that Rocky take the second spot on the Republican ticket in 1960, in return for a promise that Nixon would serve one term as president and then back Rockefeller in 1964. Ike was trying to remain neutral, telling the White House press "there is a lot of darn good men" who could succeed him. Once more, he pined for Bob Anderson.

The Rockefeller campaign organization was "a thing of political wonder, large enough to make even the Kennedy operation seem a Montana roadshow," wrote journalist Theodore White. The Eastern press adored Rocky, he made friends easily, and there were grassroots Citizens for Rockefeller Clubs "that seemed ready to sprout, fully armed, like dragon seed, across the country." Nixon had earned the right to run, Rockefeller would say, sotto voce, to the Republican grandees. But it was unfair, and a sad, sad thing, that poor Dick just "can't be elected."

But then Rocky, after testing the waters for most of 1959, withdrew from the race at Christmastime. Nixon and his team were "completely dumbfounded," Bob Finch remembered. They had spent much of the previous year inching leftward and otherwise preparing for the governor's challenge. When Finch called Nixon with the news, the vice president was "incredulous."

Rockefeller was a realist. Nixon had a six-year head start, traveling 100,000 miles selling Ike and Dick, riding on a smile and a shoeshine—RON (Remain Overnight) in Nashua, Duluth, or Pocatello; pocketing chits at Lincoln Day dinners and election-year rallies; scotch and steaks with donors; hallways, highways, runways—until he had memorized the suites in the best hotels and the acoustics of the auditoriums and the names of the county chairmen's wives. There was just one way for Rocky to break Nixon's ties with the regulars—he had to whip Nixon in the primaries. And this, Rockefeller had ultimately concluded, was not possible. "Every poll we had" showed Nixon defeating the governor in New Hampshire and the other presidential contests, Finch recalled. And so Rocky was out.

Nixon had no other Republican rivals. There was energy and restlessness on the right, where remnants of the Old Guard were teaming with militant Sunbelt conservatives, East Coast anti-Communists, and tax-hating suburbanites. The movement had a champion—Senator Barry Goldwater of Arizona—but the revolution was still years away from ripe. Nixon recognized the energy and would spend years trying to tap it without being subsumed.

"The problems you raise are, of course, the burdens that the moderate in politics always has to bear," he wrote a Texas professor. "It is so very easy to adopt an inflexible, doctrinaire attitude at either end of the political spectrum, and so difficult to try and balance what is theoretically desirable with what is practically possible. Yet this balancing-act, it seems to me, is precisely the role of the creative political leader—the man who wants to be true to basic principles, and also to win elections and get things done."

SO NOW THE action was with the Democrats, where John Kennedy used his charm and good looks, his father's riches, and an array of ruthless tactics (having Franklin Roosevelt Jr. accuse Kennedy rival Hubert Humphrey of dodging military service in World War II) to defeat the Minnesota senator in the Wisconsin and West Virginia primaries. With money, muscle, and nerve, Kennedy and his lieutenants corralled the party's big-city bosses and enough northern and western delegates to hold off an eleventh-hour challenge from the South's champion, Lyndon Johnson.

After losing to Kennedy on the first ballot at the party's Los Angeles convention, Johnson surprised everyone by accepting JFK's offer to be his running mate. It was a most consequential development—and awful news for Nixon, who had hoped to follow Eisenhower's lead and steal Texas and other southern states from his foes. The Democrats now had a presidential candidate who could sing one song on race and faith in liberal, Catholic, and African American precincts up north—while his running mate roamed the South, winking at white Protestant Democrats, assuring them they had nothing to fear, and bawling, as he did in one Virginia town, "What's Dick Nixon ever done for Culpeper?"

Karma can be cruel. A factor in Johnson's acceptance of the second spot was his mentor Sam Rayburn's intense dislike of Nixon ("that ugly fellow with the chinquapin eyes"), who, the Speaker believed, had branded him, Harry Truman, and other Democrats as traitors. Alas, for Nixon,

Nelson Rockefeller did not nurture such hatreds—or party loyalty. When Nixon tried to match Kennedy's coup, entreating Rockefeller to take the vice-presidential nomination, thus securing New York and perhaps other northeastern states for the Republicans, Rocky turned him down.

THE COLD WAR tensions had relaxed in early 1960. Americans recoiled from Khrushchev's alarming behavior, but Ike knew how much of it was just bravado. The CIA's top-secret U-2 spy planes had kept him informed on the Soviet Union's actual capabilities. As he joined Khrushchev at a summit meeting in Paris in May, Eisenhower knew the "missile gap" was a myth. But Ike had been imprudent, ordering one last U-2 mission. The Soviets shot down the plane and captured the pilot, and Khrushchev used the episode to humiliate the American president.

The U-2 incident was a setback for Nixon. It gave credence to Kennedy's clamor for change—and Rockefeller an excuse to return to the race. The governor had a pie-eyed dream that, using polls proving that "Dick can't be elected," he could stampede the delegates. It went nowhere. ("Rockefeller's behavior is simply inexplicable—what a tragic waste of a valuable political property," Finch wrote a friend.) On the eve of the Republican convention, the sullen New York governor agreed to meet with Nixon. They dined on lamb chops at Rockefeller's Fifth Avenue home, where Rocky rejected Nixon's offer of the vice-presidential nomination and gave him a list of changes he would have to make in the Republican platform to win the governor's endorsement. Two were consequential: a demand for more defense spending, which infuriated Eisenhower, and a strong civil rights plank, which, along with Rockefeller's general mien and big-government philosophy, enraged the right. The press called it "The Compact of Fifth Avenue." Goldwater called it "Munich."

"I didn't sleep for two nights trying to hold everything together," Leonard Hall recalled. "I called Nixon, cussed him for kicking his own friends in the stomach."

The necessary soothing of irate delegates was, in due course, accomplished. Goldwater showed patience and class, declined to split the party, and endorsed Nixon. (In his own address to the delegates, Rocky hailed the nominee as Richard *E.* Nixon.) Nixon chose Henry Cabot Lodge as his running mate and gave what Ted Sorensen, JFK's wordsmith, called a "brilliant" acceptance speech. But just before Labor Day, Nixon fell victim, once again, to Eisenhower's thoughtlessness. When asked at a press conference to name an important contribution that Nixon had made to a presidential decision, Ike replied: "If you give me a week, I might think of one."

It was a "debilitating, painful and depressing rejection by an authoritative father figure," Dr. Arnold Hutschnecker, the physician Nixon consulted about tension-related and psychosomatic illness, would recall, and a fresh cause of discord between the president and his insecure apprentice.

"Eisenhower was not deliberately snubbing Nixon," said Herb Brownell, but added, "I don't think Nixon was ever convinced of that."

16
———

Nixon vs. Kennedy

A S HE LEFT the Republican convention in Chicago for his fifth national campaign (1952, 1954, 1956, 1958, and 1960) in nine years, Richard Nixon had a narrow lead in the polls, formidable assets, and major deficiencies. With no military idol atop the Republican ticket, there was every reason to think that the Eisenhower landslides were aberrations, and that the 1960 election would be more like that barnburner, Truman vs. Dewey in 1948. "For our ticket to win it was necessary to get eight to ten million Democratic votes, plus between 55 and 60 percent of the independent vote," campaign director Robert Finch recalled. Ike had done it. Could Nixon?

Nixon's most appealing attribute was experience. For eight years he had participated in cabinet meetings, served on the National Security Council, and kept the Cold War secrets. He was forty-seven—young enough to match the vigor of the forty-three-year-old Kennedy—yet he had roamed the world, consulting with foreign leaders, and faced off against Communists in Caracas and Moscow. His aides, and the journalists they cultivated, repeated the theme, again and again and again. The ratcheting tensions that followed the U-2 incident reminded voters of the need for seasoned leadership. In October, Khrushchev visited the United Nations, took off his shoe, and pounded it on his desk in anger. The Nixon campaign goal, his pollster Claude Robinson advised, was to "help voters make up their minds that Kennedy is immature and that in this time of crisis the country is better off by calling on the experience of Nixon-Lodge."

The flip side of experience is monotony. Ike turned seventy in 1960 and became the oldest man to serve as president to that time. The miniskirt and the Beatles were beyond the horizon and *Father Knows Best* would win an Emmy that year—but signs of political and artistic restlessness were starting to seep into mainstream culture. Americans read Ian Fleming and danced the twist, and the mad men in the ad game pitched "Now it's Pepsi, for those who think young." In an age of cool, Nixon was not.

"I had a great advantage from being Vice President and being able to use the argument of experience," Nixon recalled. And yet "there was a corresponding disadvantage in being required . . . to stand for the status quo." He would make that stand, mostly, alone. The ranks of Republican leaders had been ruinously thinned in the 1958 fiasco. Nor had Ike done the arduous, often tedious work of building the Republican Party. Indeed, he had mused about starting a centrist third party and leaving the right behind. "The spectacular non-transferability of the Eisenhower name and 'magic' had been conclusively demonstrated in '56 and '58," a Nixon campaign analysis noted. In 1950, there had been thirty Republican governors, and the party controlled twenty-six state legislatures. After the 1958 election, there were just fourteen Republican governors, and only seven Republican-controlled legislatures. "Because of the Electoral College system, the premium is on state party organization and control of state election machinery," read the campaign analysis. "No Republican candidate since 1936 faced a worse situation."

"Our people are discouraged, disillusioned and terribly pessimistic," Nixon's former aide, Pat Hillings, warned.

The Republican Party was still the vehicle of Business, and while that guaranteed a sufficient treasury, it tilted the party's agenda away from working families. The Democrats had a three-to-two advantage in registered voters, and Republicans found it hard, in many areas, to find the bodies to perform such basic duties as distributing literature, policing the local election procedures, and guarding the polls.

There was passion in the grassroots conservatives who had started to rally around Goldwater. The Arizona senator was traveling around the country with his new book, the bestselling *The Conscience of a Conservative,* signaling followers that it was better to lose in a holy cause than to compromise their principles. Someday, said businessman Justin Dart, a prominent California conservative, those folks might join with mainstream Republicans and compose a mighty movement. But as for 1960, Dart told a writer, "I can assure you that next door to nothing has been done of any substance to initiate an organization with enough virility, enough magnitude, enough professional backing to do anything except guarantee another disaster."

The future was in the Sunbelt and suburbs. But while California was still growing at a torrid pace, the rest of the South and Southwest lagged behind, as the marvels of central air-conditioning spread slowly through the intemperate regions. In the 1960s, the Electoral College would look very much like those that graced Roosevelt and Truman with victory.

Newcomers had brought ten new electoral votes to California from 1932 to 1960, mostly at the Northeast's expense. But the Rust Belt giants of New York, Ohio, Pennsylvania, Michigan, and Illinois—along with Texas and California—would still decide the 1960 election. Suburban sprawl had diluted the clout of Democratic bosses, but their urban machines were formidable. And even Nixon's home state, thanks to the 1958 debacle, would pose a challenge.

Rockefeller's withdrawal cut both ways. Without a Republican opponent, Nixon had watched glumly as Kennedy commanded the headlines that spring, tacking victory onto victory, and building excitement. Nixon's own campaign polling showed him beating all the other Democratic candidates by double digits, but losing to the "charismatic" Kennedy.

"What happens is in the lap of the Fates," Nixon liked to say. The hags were mischievous from the start, handing Kennedy the kind of breaks that Nixon had gotten against Jerry Voorhis and Helen Gahagan Douglas. In late August, Nixon banged his knee on a car door while campaigning in North Carolina, and a staph infection put him in a hospital for twelve days. Meanwhile, the TV lords, good government types, and the Democrats in Congress had conspired to have Kennedy and Nixon stage historic, televised debates. Nixon remembered what he learned in 1946—that unknown challengers inordinately profit from such face-offs. But he feared he would look craven if he declined and was convinced he could defeat his foe in a showdown. And so he agreed.

The economy betrayed Nixon as well. When the White House refused his requests to stimulate commerce with more federal spending, unemployment inched up, signaling a coming recession. Joblessness rose by more than 450,000 in the weeks before the voting. "When you have good times you don't have the credit, but when they get bad you get all the blame," his economic adviser Arthur Burns warned Nixon. "The decline in government spending this year . . . is just plain stupid."

Nixon and Leonard Hall, the former Republican Party chairman who was advising the vice president, made a personal appeal to Ike to have the Pentagon order military aircraft and help the slumping California aerospace industry. The president declined. "That goddamned old fool," Nixon fumed to Hall when they left. "If I had been sitting in that chair and wanted to keep my successor there I'd spend the whole goddamned treasury."

The issue of the candidates' religious beliefs also commanded attention as the fall campaign began; the conventional wisdom held that Kennedy would be wounded by the anti-Catholic bias that had doomed New York governor Al Smith's presidential campaign in 1928. But the sixties were not the twenties. This was the age of rights and freedoms. Anti-Catholic prejudice, while not as virulent as the bigotry against Jews and African Americans, was serious stuff for Catholic voters, and Kennedy had proven, in the Democratic primaries, that he could tap tribal loyalty at a rate that more than compensated for the votes he lost among Protestants. No one, Kennedy told his audiences, had asked his brother Joe what church he attended before he flew the mission that claimed his life in World War II. Nixon's old law partner, Henry Knoop, wrote to warn Nixon that if bigoted Protestant clerics continued the "vicious, senseless anti-Catholic propaganda" then "many Catholics who actually prefer you will vote for Kennedy in the spirit of revenge."

The Kennedys stoked the bunker mentality. "I don't believe there is such a thing as a 'Catholic vote,' but I think there is a concerted campaign going on right now to create one," said Al Smith Jr., a Nixon supporter. The obvious countermove for Nixon was to drive up the Protestant turnout by stirring fear about Kennedy's faith. But this he declined to do. It went against the lessons of religious tolerance he had been taught at Whittier College, and in the Quaker meetinghouse—and could resurrect memories of Tricky Dick.

THE GENERAL ELECTION played out in stages. August was a draw, with Nixon lying in a hospital bed and Kennedy mired in a special summer session of Congress. The first transformative event occurred on the night of September 12, after Norman Vincent Peale and a group of Protestant leaders made headlines with their warning that a Catholic president would do the Vatican's bidding. Kennedy confronted the religious issue before a ministerial conference in Houston. He seemed the soul of reason, and his inquisitors looked like pinched, sour roundheads. The Kennedy campaign took the film from the showdown, bought TV time, and showed it again and again. California Democrats then charged that the pastor of Nixon's East Whittier church had also endorsed "scurrilous literature" that maligned Catholicism. They called on Nixon to repudiate the pamphlet. Another day passed, and Senator Henry "Scoop" Jackson of Washington, the national Democratic Party chairman, claimed that the Nixon campaign had prompted Peale's attack. Jackson demanded that Nixon repudiate the injection of "religious hate" into the election. Protestant clerics were spreading bigotry, in person and through the mails, he said. "Religion has become an issue."

Peale later wrote to Nixon, apologizing for "my terrible stupidity in allowing myself to get into a position where they could so misrepresent and distort." The evangelist Billy Graham wrote too, to warn Nixon that "the open attacks by Protestants" were "having the effect of solidifying a much stronger Catholic vote than I anticipated." The Democratic campaign was itself printing anti-Catholic hate mail, Graham conjectured, to put Catholic voters in a state of siege and "make a martyr out of Kennedy." He urged Nixon to "concentrate on solidifying the Protestant vote" and profit from a polarized electorate. Nixon declined. "I know what those cocksuckers are doing to me," Nixon told journalist Earl Mazo. "But how do you answer that stuff?" Besides, if he whipped up Protestant bias, it would only alienate more Catholics.

As the weeks passed, Graham's fears seemed overstated. "Contrary to rumors, Catholic support of the Nixon-Lodge ticket appears to be rising" and "bigotry may have less influence than one might think," Nixon's pollster, Claude Robinson, informed him in October. Nixon was not completely persuaded. "The religious issue helped Kennedy more than it hurt him," he concluded, in a post-election memo. Nixon got just 22 percent of the Catholic vote, according to Gallup—a record low for a Republican.

When dealing with the religious issue, and other breaking developments, Nixon walled himself off. "The vice president has no kitchen cabinet or small elite circle of close advisers," Finch told a room of Republican officials. "He is his own campaign manager."

On major decisions—to debate, to parlay with Nelson Rockefeller in New York, to keep his rash pledge to campaign in all fifty states—Nixon consulted few, if any, aides. His dinner with Rockefeller was "totally . . . his own" decision, Finch recalled. "It was never even discussed as a remote possibility" and created "terrible havoc" in the party and the campaign.

"You could have taken the key to the Republican National Committee and locked up the office and thrown the key in the Potomac and shipped all 175 employees off to the Virgin Islands and saved money, for all the good we did the campaign, for all that Nixon listened," Lou Guylay, the RNC publicity director, recalled. "Nobody could get through to Dick to talk to him. . . . He had to run everything himself. It was he who had to decide down what street at what hour the campaign would go." Nixon's attitude was "I know the answer," Frank Jorgensen, the Amateur, recalled, lamenting the changes in his old friend Dick. "This is the arrogance that the position breeds, that power breeds."

Over time, Finch and Hall were shoved aside, and H. R. "Bob" Haldeman—whose self-serving dedication to letting Nixon be Nixon was pleasing to the candidate—gained influence. Haldeman was a third-generation Californian, a graduate of UCLA, and an adman with the J. Walter Thompson agency. A somewhat cheerless Christian Scientist, known for his crew cut and thick-soled shoes, he had worked as an aide for Nixon in 1956 and 1958 and as chief of the advance team (nicknamed the "frogmen" for their leaps from one event to another) in 1960. Though he in many ways was the beneficiary, Haldeman came to see Nixon's need for dominance as a serious flaw, stemming from "incredible self-doubt" and insecurity. "Like the old adage that the lawyer who handles his own case has a damn fool for a client," said Haldeman, "the politician who manages his own campaign has a damn fool for a client. . . . He had no management skill."

Serving as both candidate and manager often left Nixon dead on his feet. He barely slept during the Chicago convention, and he and the staff were relying on their "jolly pills" to complete each day's schedule. After one event, in Fresno, Don Hughes found Nixon literally asleep on his feet. As Hughes put the exhausted candidate to bed, Nixon opened one eye and said, "It will be alright . . . God is on our side." On other nights, Haldeman found Nixon missing from their hotel, and would track the sleepless candidate to "flea-bitten" coffee shops. The strain brought on the now-familiar eruptions of anger. In Iowa, Nixon vented by violently kicking the car seat in front of him. Its enraged inhabitant, the loyal Hughes, left the broken seat, and the car, and stalked off down the road. At an otherwise successful telethon in Detroit on election eve, Nixon once again lost his temper, and struck aide Everett Hart. Furious, Hart quit the campaign. "I was really mad," Hart recalled. "I had had a rib removed where I had had open heart surgery, and that is where he hit me."

As NIXON BECAME mired in details, his campaign suffered accordingly. "RN wants, as always, to hold all the reins in his own hot li'l paws," aide James Bassett confided to his wife. "Ergo: he has to make all the decisions, most of which ought to be handled by somebody with delegated authority; and since he's literally on the dead run all day . . . you can't get to the guy FOR the necessary decisions."

"My problem . . . is that I simply haven't had in all fields people of enough competence that I could delegate important responsibilities to them," Nixon would later insist.

Maybe. Had Chotiner been there, he would doubtless have confronted Nixon—and told him to focus on being the candidate. Instead, Nixon was constantly meddling. He sent out one memo, referring to an earlier memo, about how he was to be introduced at rallies. "At least a year ago I sent out instructions that we were to send out guidelines for introductions which would not go into the fact that I graduated from grammar school at the age of 12 and/or that crap," Nixon told Finch. "I want a report on this.

"Pick out the best terse ideas that ought to be included in an introduction. For example, my experience, my handling of myself in South America, my tough-mindedness in dealing with Khrushchev—just a few points, you can throw in the fact that I worked my way up from modest circumstance in the great American tradition," Nixon wrote. "I don't want to go into another meeting in the next six months which has one of these stupid introductions which goes into my biography from Whittier on. I don't want this to happen again."

A few weeks later he was nitpicking again. "I do not think it is effective to say at the end of a program—'Vote for Dick Nixon on election day.' I would prefer to have it Richard Nixon," he wrote Finch. "I realize there are times when the less formal salutation should be used but when referring to how people vote you should use the name that they are going to see on the ballot. The Dick Nixon in this case sounded somewhat flip and undignified."

Striving for control, Nixon called a meeting with Finch, Haldeman, and others and directed them to end all receptions, photographs, and rope-line handshaking after his speeches. He would no longer greet workers at factory gates; share meals with supporters; join corn-husking contests or other campaign standards at state fairs; take meetings with donors ("Only to be done if really big money is involved and essential"); or spend nights at private homes. There was "too much emphasis" on getting people to attend his speeches. "The emphasis should be on the coverage for television rather than the live audience," he told his aides. And "as a basic rule, we will work the good areas . . . not go across the tracks."

In Henry Cabot Lodge, Nixon had chosen a Brahmin viscount for a running mate, who napped each afternoon and conducted a gentlemanly—some said lethargic—campaign. Father Cronin wondered if Nixon *wanted* to lose.

Burying the Old Nixon, without losing his dynamic qualities, was a tricky enterprise. "You are more than the Vice President," Finch told him, urging him to become more aggressive. "You are an active candidate for the Presidency. . . . To beat Kennedy is not enough. *You must clearly overshadow him* in Knowledge. Confidence. Desire to lead."

But Nixon was getting conflicting advice. Pollster Robinson urged the candidate to tone down his campaign. "I hope to God we don't go off the track," the pollster wrote. "I know some of the people are asking for red meat" but Nixon had "to get Democrats and Independents to come over the line." If he got "too rough" his foes will "flood the country with this Tricky Dick thing."

Nixon didn't know who he was, or who to be, and it began to show. He became "preoccupied with changing his image," said Guylay. A "prissiness came into his face. It contributed to this image of weakness, of vacillation, and timidity . . . this constant apprehensiveness."

"Nixon must always be thinking about who he is," Kennedy told a friend. "That is a strain. I can be myself."

THE NEXT TURNING point—and the single most important event in the 1960 presidential contest—was the first televised debate, which took place on September 26 in Chicago. Neither man stumbled—there were no harmful gaffes to be played and replayed on the next day's news. They both displayed command of the subject: domestic affairs. The panel of reporters challenged Nixon's claim of experience by tossing Ike's comment— *Give me a week and I might think of one*—in his face, but he fielded it well. Nixon's fans, and many radio listeners, believed he won. In fact, Nixon lost not only the debate but probably the election. Television had betrayed him.

In the ten years since Nixon ran against Helen Douglas, the percentage of American households with television sets had leaped from 11 to 88 percent. The tubes glowed for four or five hours a night. "It is now possible for the first time to answer an inquiring foreign visitor as to what Americans do in the evening," wrote Theodore White. "The answer is clear: *they watch television.*" The audience for the first debate was some 70 to 80 million people, in a country with 107 million adults.

Playing at inside baseball, reporters queried the new crop of industry analysts, who zeroed in on cosmetic causes for Kennedy's victory. Nixon's makeup molted. The lighting in the studio was bad. His clothes were not dark enough, and ill fitting. His hair was cut too short, accentuating his receding hairline. He fidgeted in his chair. His eyes darted furtively. He was captured on camera using a handkerchief to mop up the sweat on his upper lip and chin.

There were reasons for most of this. Nixon had not broken away from his crushing campaign schedule to adequately rest and prepare. "I was told to brief him on the most important telecast of his life while riding over to the studio in an automobile," Ted Rogers would marvel. Nixon spurned a professional makeup session, thinking he would look feminine. Egged on by the Kennedy campaign, the CBS crew caught him in unflattering reaction shots. And he was still a recovering hospital patient. "I felt like the wrath of God," Nixon told a confidant. "No one knows what that knee did to me—those antibiotics—I lost eight pounds." Nixon had spent twelve days in the hospital, took on a brutish schedule to catch up on his fifty-state promise, caught a cold, was running a fever, and then banged the infected knee again when emerging from his car at the studio. His face went pale with pain. He could have used his illness as a reason to cancel or postpone the debates, but did not.

Yet more than lousy makeup cost Nixon the election. He would recoup for the next three debates, be better prepped, drink his milk shakes, recover the lost weight, and more than hold his own onstage. But the novelty and mystique of the later showdowns, and the number of viewers who watched them, did not match that of the first encounter. And in that initial face-off, Kennedy dominated. He showed he was the equal, at very least, of the awkward man with whom he shared the stage. Yes, Kennedy was tanned and rested and coiffed and elegant. But mostly he won because he was better. Kennedy spoke, intently, to the viewer. He stayed on the offensive. He did just enough parrying to meet the conditions of "debate," but turned his opening and closing statements, and his answers to most questions, into mini-variations on his campaign theme.

"If we meet our responsibilities I think freedom will conquer. If we fail, if we fail to move ahead, if we fail to develop sufficient military and economic and social strength here in this country, then I think that the tide could begin to run against us," Kennedy said in his closing comments in that first debate. "I don't want historians, ten years from now, to say these were the years when the tide ran out for the United States. I want them to say these were the years when the tide came in; these were the years when the United States started to move again. That's the question before the American people, and only you can decide what you want, what you want this country to be, what you want to do with the future. I think we're ready to move. And it is to that great task, if we're successful, that we will address ourselves."

Nixon, in contrast, spent much of the night agreeing with Kennedy (to demonstrate how the "new Nixon" was no hatchet man) or on the defensive, sticking up for the Eisenhower administration's "programs"—he used the word a dozen times in his opening statement—with meandering jargon and statistics.

"I think it is well to put in perspective where we really do stand with regard to the Soviet Union in this whole matter of growth," Nixon said in his own closing moment. "The Soviet Union has been moving faster than we have. But the reason for that is obvious. They start from a much lower base. Although they have been moving faster in growth than we have, we find, for example, today that their total gross national product is only forty-four per cent of our total gross national product. That's the same percentage that it was twenty years ago. And as far as the absolute gap is concerned, we find that the United States is even further ahead than it was twenty years ago. Is this any reason for complacency? Not at all. Because these are determined men. They are fanatical men. And we have to get the very most out of our economy. I agree with Senator Kennedy completely on that score."

It was an awful conclusion, which no amount of makeup could have saved. A college debate judge might have tallied the points and declared the match a draw, for Nixon had performed like the captain of the Whittier College debate team. But the truth was that, by the end of the night, the American people had scrutinized Kennedy and concluded he was Nixon's equal. According to the Gallup Poll, 43 percent of those surveyed thought Kennedy won the debate, with 29 percent saying it was a toss-up and 23 percent handing it to Nixon. "Kennedy was brimming with confidence, glib, full of bounce. The vice president, people thought, looked tired and less self-assured," wrote pollster Robinson in an internal campaign analysis. Kennedy had answered the questions about youth, stature, and experience. He had stared down the man who stood up to Khrushchev.

Robinson had assured Nixon, before the debates began, that the vice president would make Kennedy seem like a valedictorian "at Podunk College." And in the course of the four televised face-offs, Kennedy did come across as "the shy young sheriff," that early scholar of the medium, Marshall McLuhan, told an interviewer. But Nixon, "with his very dark eyes that tend to stare, with his slicker circumlocution, has resembled more the railway lawyer who signs leases that are not in the interests of the folks in the little town."

The voters had gotten the "demonstration through visual contrast" that

Robinson had forecast—but not the results the Nixon team expected. On October 25, after the four debates were over, Ted Rogers described their cumulative effect in a confidential memo to Finch and Hall. "People want more than just another man as their leader. They want a hero, a father image, a king," Rogers wrote. After the showdown with Khrushchev in Moscow and his coronation at the Republican convention, Nixon had achieved that status. "Since then, this hero image has been methodically destroyed."

"Kennedy went into those debates having nothing to lose. The public had no clear image of him. But they do now. They know Kennedy as the man who can stand up to RN," Rogers wrote. The debates "provided the cast and stage to make Jack Kennedy a star. Some will argue RN 'won' some of the later debates. This was a Pyrrhic victory at best. While we've been occupied with formats, 'image' and presentation," Kennedy was "killing off our hero."

THE DEBATES ENDED on October 21. In that four-week stage of the campaign, Kennedy had transformed a few-point deficit in the Gallup poll into a slim advantage—which a fawning press corps viewed as a portent of a coming landslide. With all the advantages of a Democratic candidate—the urban machines to gin up turnout; the lead in registration; the aid of liberal-leaning reporters—the contest looked like it was all but over. But Nixon would not surrender. He campaigned like a berserker in the last two weeks; his party rallied round him and, with Eisenhower's help, eclipsed the Democrats in news coverage and outspent them on televised advertising.

The trend lines in the polls switched direction. Nixon was closing—to within a point. Kennedy grew sick with the thought that, like Truman in 1948 (or Bill Mazeroski, whose walk-off home run for the Pittsburgh Pirates sent the New York Yankees wailing to baseball Hades that fall), Nixon would win it in the last turn at bat. But the Fates threw Nixon a final curve. He chose not to swing. The election results were so close—possibly the closest ever, depending on how they are measured—that his failure of nerve, or what he called scruples (as if any survived in either candidate in the last week of the election), may have cost him the presidency. For, after all the talk about Youth and Religion, it was Race that ruled the final innings.

BACK IN THE spring, when the campaign began, the civil rights issue was gnarled as ever. The Solid South had not been truly solid for Democrats since the election of 1944, and with a Catholic leading the Democratic ticket in 1960, and blacks agitating for rights, the Republicans were presented with a Faustian bargain. "The prospect for the Republican high command is . . . tantalizing in the extreme," White reported. "If they adopt a civil rights program only moderately more restrained than the Democrats', the South can be theirs for the asking; and with the South, if it comes permanently to Republican loyalties, could come such solid addition of electoral strength as would make Republicans again, as they were for half a century, the majority party of the nation."

For months, Nixon resisted. The Republican Party plank on civil rights did not cater to the South: it was, in fact, progressive. It was a given that both parties would contest Texas, with its 24 electoral votes, but the remaining ten states of the old Confederacy contained just 104 votes in the Electoral College, and unaffiliated segregationists, running slates of electors, would claim some of those. With 270 electoral votes needed to win, the price could be too high to pay if Nixon or Kennedy, targeting votes below the Mason-Dixon Line, alienated black voters in crucial states like New York (45 electoral votes), Illinois (27), Pennsylvania (32), Michigan (20), and Ohio (25). Nixon's record on civil rights was more than sound; he had backers like Jackie Robinson and the Reverend Martin Luther King Sr. He hoped to take a third or more of the black vote, with enough in New York, Chicago, and other cities to prevail.

But then there was this: Nixon had pledged to compete in all fifty states, and he had been thrilled to draw big, enthusiastic crowds when he visited Georgia, Alabama, and North Carolina. Like Kennedy, he had visions of carrying Texas and states in the outer South. And so both candidates entered the final weeks trying to finesse the issue—to have it both ways—unless an unforeseen development forced their hand.

THE UNEXPECTED MOMENT arrived on October 19 when Martin Luther King Jr. was arrested at a sit-in in the Magnolia Room, a segregated upscale department store restaurant in Atlanta. Five days later, a state judge used an old traffic ticket as an excuse to sentence King to four months of hard labor at the state penitentiary in rural Reidsville. He was taken away at night, in shackles. King's pregnant wife, Coretta, family, and associates were seized with the terror that he would be murdered en route to the prison or in his cell. It was not an unreasonable fear.

Nixon had the opportunity to intervene. Jackie Robinson, Clarence Mitchell, and Fred Morrow, Nixon's black associate from the Eisenhower

White House, urged the campaign to reach out to Coretta King. But they could not persuade the candidate. Nixon privately requested that Attorney General William Rogers look into the case, but the White House declined to give its consent. The public response of the campaign was perfunctory: "No comment," said a spokesman. Robinson shed tears of frustration, but Nixon remained mute. In a letter to the ballplayer, Nixon dismissed the idea of interceding as "a grandstand play."

"I just didn't realize such a call could swing an election," Nixon would recall. "The Democrats whipped up a fury in the Negro areas. I was painted a villain, and my entire record was erased within a few weeks."

Kennedy, prodded by brother-in-law Sargent Shriver, called Coretta King to comfort her. ("What the hell, that's a decent thing to do," he told Shriver.) When campaign manager Robert Kennedy heard, he took Nixon's tack and cursed Shriver and others for interfering. "This election may be razor close, and you have probably lost it for us," he said. But as the hours passed, Bobby found his sense of outrage, or remembered a Kennedy maxim—in for a dime, in for a dollar. John Kennedy appealed to Georgia's Democratic governor, who laid the groundwork for brother Bob to telephone the Georgia judge. And on October 27, twelve days before the election, King was freed.

The Kennedy campaign followed up, targeting black precincts with a blue-tinted brochure headlined "NO COMMENT" NIXON VERSUS A CANDIDATE WITH A HEART, SENATOR KENNEDY. The deep-pocketed Kennedys had already secured the support of the North's most prominent black bosses: Democratic representatives William Dawson of the South Side of Chicago and Adam Clayton Powell Jr. of Harlem. And there was no exaggerating the King family's gratitude. "I had expected to vote against Senator Kennedy because of his religion," King's father, a well-known Baptist minister, declared. "But now he can be my President, Catholic or whatever he is. It took courage to call my daughter-in-law at a time like this. He has the moral courage to stand up for what he knows is right. I've got all my votes and I've got a suitcase and I'm going to take them up there and dump them in his lap."

Nixon would come to tell a story of how, a few days after the election, his African American driver John Wardlaw described the sea change in the black community: "They were all friendly until Kennedy called the judge, and then they all changed."

Nixon came to regret his faintheartedness. "I could have become president. I needed only 5 percent more votes in the Negro areas," he told a writer for *Ebony* magazine in 1962. He was paying a price, as well, for years of Republican Party neglect. "We had no organization in the Negro areas. We had only a handful of Negro Republicans and in many cities the groups were very weak." And he might have, he admitted, campaigned harder in black neighborhoods. It is reasonable to suggest that the black votes for Kennedy were factors in his victories in Illinois, the Carolinas, Michigan, New Jersey, and Texas, and perhaps Pennsylvania.

Through much of the fall, Kennedy's pull among black voters was in keeping with Stevenson's 1956 performance, pollster Lou Harris reported, at about 62 percent. But then, with the oncoming recession and the King incident, "the Negro vote soared for Kennedy" in both the North and the South in the final days. It was "the most dramatic upturn for the Democrats on the presidential line," Harris wrote, with double-digit gains or better in New York City, Chicago, Memphis, and Atlanta and rural areas of Texas and Virginia. "Their Martin Luther King gambit paid off handsomely," William Safire reported to Finch, in a postmortem analysis of the campaign.*

By choosing Lyndon Johnson as a running mate, and making that phone call to Coretta King, Kennedy had done a better job straddling the issue of race than Nixon. He got the big turnout he needed in the northern cities but, with Johnson's help, still carried seven of the eleven Confederate states—including Texas, Georgia, the Carolinas, and Louisiana.

Robinson was crushed, and King came away from the election with a new opinion of Richard Nixon. "I had known Nixon longer. He had been supposedly close to me, and he would call me frequently about things . . . seeking my advice," King would recall. "And yet, when this moment came, it was like he had never heard of me, you see. So this is why I really considered him a moral coward and one who was really unwilling to take a courageous step and take a risk."

IT IS HARD to apportion the import of each factor in Nixon's defeat, but his final regret involved Eisenhower. This much is clear: First, that Nixon wished to star on his own in 1960, for personal and political reasons. Next, that Eisenhower wished to do more on Nixon's behalf and thought Nixon was an egotistic fool for spurning his help. And last, that when Eisenhower did hit the campaign trail—with great success—Pat and Dick were asked by Mamie Eisenhower and the president's doctor to limit Ike's participa-

---

* The Gallup organization put Nixon's final share of the black vote at 32 percent.

tion. And so the partnership ended much as it began, and had endured: with hard feelings and miscommunication.

"It got under Nixon's skin that people might say he won the campaign as Daddy's boy. He wanted to win on his own," said Clare Booth Luce, the Republican grande dame. "It was a little stupid of him, because when you're running for the Presidency of the United States you certainly wouldn't scorn the help of the Lord Almighty and you shouldn't scorn the help of the present incumbent. . . . And this also offended Ike."

"What the hell was it?" Eisenhower asked Earl Mazo. "Did the SOB think I was going to steal the limelight from him?" To Leonard Hall, the president performed a cruel Nixon imitation and said that Nixon "doesn't look like a winner to me. . . . When I had an officer like that in World War II, I relieved him."

But Mamie's fears about her husband's health were well grounded. In mid-October, while on a speaking trip to Detroit, the president had picked up a union pamphlet and become so enraged at the political slanders listed therein that his doctor had to treat him for a prolonged attack of arrhythmia.

Whatever the cause, Eisenhower's abbreviated schedule cost Nixon dearly. The president was "knocking our block off," Kennedy told a friend. JFK had an awful feeling, like he was "standing on a mound of sand with the tide running out." No one was more grateful than Kennedy when Ike's appearances were curtailed.

THE 1960 ELECTION had its share of chicanery. J. Edgar Hoover had the FBI spy for Nixon, funneling him damaging information about Kennedy and Rockefeller. There was intrigue, throughout, about Kennedy's health. He suffered from Addison's disease, an adrenal disorder, but publicly denied it. In July, someone broke into his doctor's office. A few days later, at the Democratic convention, the Johnson forces charged Kennedy with concealing the illness. The Nixon campaign waited until the last week of the election and then schemed to have Eisenhower raise the issue. White House press secretary James Hagerty called it a "cheap, lousy, stinking political trick," and the president declined to go along. Instead, the campaign enlisted FDR's son, John Roosevelt, to stir up fears about Kennedy's health.

Kennedy gave as good as he got. His campaign was the conduit for a damaging, mostly accurate story that surfaced near Election Day, of how Nixon's brother Donald, short on cash and in danger of losing his "Nixonburger" restaurant business, had secretly borrowed $205,000 from the billionaire Howard Hughes, with the family's East Whittier homestead as security. After weeks of conniving on all sides, Kennedy's operatives leaked documents obtained from an aggrieved Hughes associate to Drew Pearson, who published the tale and alleged that Dick had intervened on the billionaire's behalf with federal regulatory agencies. Nixon viewed the story, then and later, as quite damaging, and his campaign thoroughly bungled its handling of the episode—denying and retracting for days—thus calling attention to the muckraker's revelations.

As HE NEARED Election Day, Nixon still had a chance. On October 28, pollster Robinson told him that they held a secure lead in states with 130 electoral votes, mostly in the West, Midwest, and outer South, and that Kennedy had clinched states with 151 votes, including New York, much of the Northeast, and the inner South. There were several errors on Robinson's scorecard, but the gist of it was correct. The contest would come down to nineteen states where the candidates were tied or within one or two points, including the decisive battlegrounds of California, Ohio, Texas, Illinois, Pennsylvania, and Michigan. With 269 electoral votes needed to win, Nixon would have to split the smaller states with Kennedy and take four of those six big ones. Organized labor was strong in Pennsylvania and Michigan, and so "California, Texas, Ohio and Illinois are the key to a Nixon victory," Robinson wrote.

Nixon put the final, thoroughly wasteful, touch on his fifty-state pledge by flying to Alaska on the weekend before the election. Bassett saw it as a totem of the whole 1960 campaign. "The one guy most responsible . . . perhaps the only guy, is The Candidate himself," Bassett wrote his wife. "When loners insist on lone-ness, and shun advice—even reject it out of hand—and fail to make use of their considerable resources available . . . then, by golly, they suffer also the penalties of being loners. No ONE man can be all things, even to himself. And when his brain tires, and his temper shortens, then the alone-ness is magnified rather horribly. . . . You know what I mean. We've seen it operating. And it is a little scary, isn't it?"

After an election eve telecast with Eisenhower and Lodge in Chicago, Nixon flew to California in the predawn hours of Election Day—where twenty-five thousand people met him at the airport with fireworks and torchlights. He and Pat got two hours to rest before leaving for Whittier to vote.

Nixon had asked that their motorcade include a convertible. After they voted, he sent Pat back to Los Angeles and he and Don Hughes, accompanied by a driver and a Secret Service agent, took off in the ragtop. "Shake them," Nixon told his driver. Speeding through the side streets of Whittier, they ditched the press corps. Nixon set the rules. There would be no talk of politics, or of the election. "Let's head for the beach," he said.

Sitting in the front passenger seat, Nixon kept up a running travelogue as they motored along the coastline—the four men chuckling at the double takes of motorists who pulled up next to them at stoplights. The candidate was relaxed. The ordeal was over. They had done all they could. "Let's go to Mexico! Let's go down to Tijuana and have some Mexican food," he said. So they did. After lunch, heading home, they stopped at the mission at San Juan Capistrano, where Hughes, a Catholic, lit a candle.

The first clue to the results were the returns from Connecticut. Ike had carried the state handily in 1956 but at 8 p.m. in the East—5 p.m. on the West Coast—it appeared that Nixon lost it by ninety thousand votes. As the other Eastern precincts reported their totals, Kennedy's lead in the popular vote swelled to two million votes, and New York and Texas fell to the Democrats. Nixon won Ohio, and California was so close that the absentee ballots would make the difference, but the media was predicting a Kennedy victory. Julie was inconsolable, and Pat and Tricia struggled to keep from breaking down in public. The pathetic Don Nixon feared that people would blame him—"It's all my fault," he said—for trading on his brother's influence with Howard Hughes. Just after midnight in Los Angeles, Nixon appeared before the cameras at the Ambassador Hotel and, while not conceding, admitted: "If the present trend continues, Senator Kennedy will be the next President."

Across the continent, in Hyannisport, Nixon's remarks were a buoying respite on a night where glee had turned to gloom. In the hours after midnight, Kennedy's lead in the popular vote had dissolved like spindrift on the strand. The *New York Times* stopped the presses to change its headline from KENNEDY ELECTED PRESIDENT to KENNEDY IS APPARENT VICTOR. It was going to be one of the closest elections ever. California would not be awarded (to Nixon) for days, and Hawaii was decided, in a recount, by 115 votes.

Pennsylvania and Michigan fell to Kennedy. And then-mayor Richard Daley of Chicago called, to tell him, "Mr. President, with a little bit of luck and the help of a few close friends, you're going to carry Illinois." As Reston captured the night's drama in the *Times*, "At one point Mr. Nixon pulled ahead . . . until a last batch of Chicago votes was produced." Until noontime on Wednesday, when Kennedy was declared the winner in Minnesota, there was still a chance the election could be thrown to the House of Representatives. But with Minnesota gone, Nixon conceded.

So ended the tightest election in American history. Both candidates had gone to bed not knowing who won. Across the country, Kennedy would get some 34,221,000 votes, and Nixon 34,108,000. Nixon had lost by less than 1 percent.

Wilderness

R ICHARD NIXON HAD won more states, and captured more congressional districts, than John Kennedy. But Kennedy took the popular vote by a lash, and prevailed with a majority in the Electoral College. If twelve thousand people in Illinois, Nevada, New Mexico, Hawaii, and Missouri had voted Republican instead of Democratic, Nixon would have been president.

The air was rife with *ifs*. "I can think of a hundred things I could have done or said that might have changed the result," Nixon wrote to Norman Vincent Peale.

If the Soviet missile had missed the U-2 . . . *If* Ike had juiced the economy . . . *If* Rockefeller had joined Nixon on the ticket . . . *If* Nixon had not hurt his knee . . . *If* Eisenhower had done more on the campaign trail . . . *If* Nixon had responded to King's arrest . . . *If* Nixon had forsaken his fifty-state pledge . . . *If* the Republicans had guarded the polling places in Illinois and Texas.

That last was the most intriguing *if*: Did the Kennedys steal the presidency? Had Nixon actually won? As the stories came in from around the country, Nixon came to believe it.

TEXAS WAS WORTH twenty-four electoral votes. More than 2.3 million votes were cast there, and Kennedy won by forty-six thousand. The Democrats profited from the crude behavior of Republican right-wingers who ambushed Lyndon and Lady Bird in the lobby of the Adolphus Hotel in Dallas a few days before the election, cursing and spitting and jostling the Johnsons. It was an ugly scene, and LBJ knew to exploit it. Texan pride was at stake, he declared, and Democrats responded on Election Day. And though the cocklebur preachers condemned the papist Kennedy from their pulpits, the state's Latinos showed compensatory ardor for a fellow Roman Catholic.

But while Kennedy's margin of victory seemed formidable, Texas Republicans had grounds to question the results. Twelve years earlier, "Landslide Lyndon" had been elected to the Senate by 87 votes with the help of the Mexican Americans who lived along the Rio Grande and voted as the local Anglo bosses and their *pistoleros* instructed. In some districts, the *jefes* saved the voters the trouble of voting. One precinct—Box 13—had provided the decisive margin by giving Johnson 200 new votes, "votes that were cast in alphabetical order and all in the same handwriting six days after the polls were closed," noted Johnson biographer Robert Caro. In the years that followed the 1948 election, Johnson had maintained his alliance with George Parr, the region's most powerful boss, and helped rescue him from a prison stretch for mail fraud. In 1960, Box 13 went for Kennedy over Nixon by 1,145 to 45, and the nine counties controlled by Parr and his fellow bosses gave the Kennedy-Johnson ticket almost 80 percent of their votes. The resultant plurality of 21,691 votes was almost half the margin of the Democratic victory.

Nor were the border counties unique. In rural Angelina County, north of Houston, 86 voters qualified for ballots in Precinct 27. The official results: 147 for Kennedy, 24 for Nixon. Texas had a new "negative ballot" that year, in which the voter was asked to cross off the names of candidates he or she did *not* want elected. It led to much confusion, and to temptation in the countryside—where paper ballots were used—for election judges to reject the opposition's ballots as flawed, while accepting their own side's votes as valid. "The illegal votes which were counted preponderated heavily in favor of Kennedy," the Republican state chairman, Thad Hutcheson, informed Nixon.

IN CHICAGO, ELECTION fraud was a work of art, a tradition dating back to the days when the faro games and bordellos ran all night and such esteemed public servants as Michael "Hinky Dink" Kenna and John "Bathhouse" Coughlin packed the polling places with tramps, repeaters, and mattress voters. (At one precinct the voters handed their ballots through a hole in the door, and were wise to remove their rings or cuff links before doing so.) The cheating blossomed in 1960, as Ben Adamowski, a Republican state's attorney, challenged Mayor Daley's machine. Electing presidents was all well and good, but the prospect of a hostile local prosecutor really set the boys to work. Illinois Republicans wrote Nixon to alert him that, as Representative Les Arends told him, "We wuz robbed!" Said Arends: "I sincerely believe in my heart that you were elected, but the votes weren't counted that way."*

Kennedy took Illinois by nine thousand votes. Claude Robinson, the Nixon pollster, expected they would lose Chicago's Cook County by from 250,000 to 290,000 votes, which would have to be made up elsewhere in the state. But the election night results gave Kennedy a 320,000-vote victory in Cook County—too much for the downstate Republicans to overcome. The city's newspapers reported that, in the hours around midnight, the counting of votes in Chicago had ominously paused—as if Daley was waiting to see how the Republicans were doing elsewhere, so that the mayor's machine could adjust its totals.

THEODORE WHITE CALLED it "the night of the gnomes" and reported that "no one will ever know precisely who carried the majority of 1960, for on that night political thieves . . . were counterfeiting results all across the nation." In Illinois and Texas, White would conclude, Democratic "vote-stealing had definitely taken place on a massive scale."†

With the help of local Republicans, the newspapers in Texas and Illinois—and the *New York Herald Tribune*'s Earl Mazo—were soon collecting anecdotal evidence like the Angelina County, Texas, results. It was not hard to find vacant lots that served as addresses for Chicago voters, or Illinois Democrats whose devotion to the political process had apparently survived their deaths. Daley's furious battle to unseat Adamowski had, beyond doubt, inspired such creativity, and the mythos of a historic larceny was born. "We won, but they stole it from us," Nixon told Eisenhower speechwriter William Ewald Jr. Tricia and Julie donated their Christmas money to a Nixon recount committee. Pat remembered the time as "a nightmare—tenseness everywhere . . . the girls hearing far too much ugly discussion."

"I was in a state of numbness, with faith in the 'right' shaken to the point I could not discuss the situation anymore," Pat wrote a friend.

Proving the theft was something else. The votes in a presidential election are immediately counted, quickly announced—and certified just a few

* Suburban do-gooders, outraged by the reports of fraud, canvassed the city's neighborhoods for evidence of wrongdoing. Among them was a thirteen-year-old Young Republican whom Americans would come to know as Hillary Rodham Clinton.
† White's panegyric account of Kennedy's victory, *The Making of the President 1960* (Atheneum, 1964), omitted reports of voting fraud. His comment about "the night of the gnomes" is from a later book, *Breach of Faith: The Fall of Richard Nixon* (Atheneum, 1975).

weeks later. For Nixon and Ike and their fellow Republicans, the initial outrage gave way to more sobering analysis. Illinois offered Nixon his most promising opportunity to prove fraud, but even if he managed to have Kennedy's nine-thousand-vote victory invalidated, the state's twenty-seven electoral votes would not be enough to give Nixon the White House. The forty-six-thousand-vote margin in Texas was as forbidding. Nor would Democrats stand by and watch their prize be taken. There would be precincts, counties, and states where the Democrats could challenge Nixon majorities as well, including California, where Nixon's margin of victory was much smaller than Kennedy's margin in Texas. In one Chicago precinct, a partial recount showed, a malfunctioning voting machine had cost Kennedy some 190 votes. Another recount, in Hawaii, shifted that state's three electoral votes from Nixon to Kennedy.

The procedure for contesting election results varied widely by location, and seemed labyrinthine at best. In Missouri, a challenge had to be settled by the state legislature—which wasn't scheduled to convene until the following year. A purposeful attempt to reverse the outcome would divide the country and submerse the government in uncertainty and rancor. And so Nixon gave up the quest. With Joseph Kennedy and Herbert Hoover acting as the duennas, Nixon and Kennedy met in Florida on November 14, where Nixon assured the president-elect that he accepted the results.

Nixon was wise to do so. He was still young, his future was bright, and he did not want to be cast—just when he seemed to have moved past the "Tricky Dick" stuff— as a poor loser. Moreover, his party's challenges in Texas and Illinois were going nowhere. In Texas, the Republicans appealed to a Democratic attorney general, who turned them down, and to a federal judge, who rejected their claim, and the Democratic-controlled election board, which gave them no relief. In every case, the officials cited a lack of evidence. In Illinois, the U.S. attorney, a Republican appointee, proclaimed the election as "relatively clean." Good government groups had staked out hundreds of precincts on Election Day, and found chaos and confusion, but little proof of fraud. The Republican-controlled state election board and a special prosecutor's investigation suggested that Nixon was counted out of hundreds of votes—but not victory. Scholar Edmund Kallina concluded in a book-length study that, though Adamowski's candidacy was doomed by chicanery, it is not possible to "assert with confidence that Nixon was swindled out of Illinois's electoral votes."

In early December, Nixon called Mazo in for a talk. The *Herald Tribune* had published several stories alleging fraud, and Nixon wanted it stopped. "Earl," he said, "these are interesting articles you are writing—but no one steals the presidency of the United States. . . . Our country cannot afford the agony of a constitutional crisis."

NIXON HAD NEVER lost an election. His reaction was, as in the Checkers episode, or the "dump Nixon" days of 1956, to cloak the hurt and trudge ahead. "You're physically drained, emotionally drained, mentally drained," he would recall. Winners are revived by victory, but "when you lose, you become more and more numb."

Within days he had aides writing memos, analyzing the causes of the 1960 loss and drawing up blueprints for a rematch. He turned down Kennedy's offer of a diplomatic post, graciously presided, as vice presidents do, at the ceremonial declaration of the Electoral College results, and made one last visit to the Capitol—a private citizen now—on the night of the inauguration. Restless, wandering, alone, he listened to the song and laughter and watched "the ladies in their marvelous ball gowns trying to get through the snow, stepping over the gutters with the help of their escorts, all in white tie and tails." The previous evening, in his last hours in office, he had gone out on his balcony with its view of the Mall and the Washington and Lincoln memorials, alight in the falling snow. A thought "rushed into my mind—not consciously, but then it seemed almost to overwhelm me. . . . *I'll be back.*"

That was how Nixon recalled it. Campaign adviser Leonard Hall remembered another moment, when Nixon was presented with a farewell gift from his staff. In thanking them, he tried to tell the story of how Julie had come into his room on the morning after the election and asked, "Did we win, Daddy?" Nixon halted his remarks, waged a losing battle with his emotions, and left the room.

Pat was stricken too. The nation had watched her struggle to maintain her composure when standing by Dick's side on election night. A friend found Pat weeping in her room. "Now I'll never get to be First Lady," she said. From the vantage of the winner's circle, Jackie Kennedy looked in horrified fascination at the fate she so narrowly avoided, and drank in the reports from their mutual friend, Senator George Smathers, who described Pat as "exhausted . . . lying like a cadaver . . . with this bitter desperate face . . . terribly bitter." She was not entirely unsympathetic to Pat—"You could see she could be rather New York chic when she wanted," Jackie would say—but aghast at how the strictures of politics had turned the Nixons into paper dolls: "You know, Pat and Dick." The friendship was over. If he had any regrets over the heavy-handed conduct of his campaign,

John Kennedy didn't express them, and he justified his tactics by telling friends how Nixon had "no taste" and "no class."

Nixon was seared, his daughter Julie recalled, by a contest that was "so close; so hard-fought," in which an opponent "out-cheated" them. He left 1960 with a sore mistrust of the Kennedys, a swollen sense of grievance, and a consuming resolve to never be outdone by a rival's dirty tricks again.

It wasn't just the thievery in Illinois and Texas. Nixon simmered over the Kennedys' manipulation of religion and chewed on how the establishment had come to the senator's aid when Kennedy appeared vulnerable on the issue of defending Quemoy and Matsu, and how old-school diplomats like Chester Bowles and Christian Herter had urged Nixon, in the interest of national security, to let Jack slip the gaffe.

Nixon was angry as well, and cynical, about the black voters who abandoned him. He and Ike viewed African Americans as ingrates—addicted to the Democratic Party's social programs. Southern whites seemed a more auspicious quarry, and Nixon's ardor for the civil rights movement waned.

Then there was the campaign press corps, which, as any sentient being recognized, had skewed their reporting in favor of Kennedy. *Time* called it the most adoring coverage "in modern history." White, in *The Making of the President 1960*, described the newsmen as "devoted admirers" of Kennedy, "marching like soldiers of the Lord to the New Frontier." Russell Baker, who covered the campaign for the *New York Times*, recalled how "a depressing number of really fine reporters lost their skepticism and went ga-ga" for the Kennedys.

The members of the press were "suckers for style," Nixon would conclude. "In Kennedy, they saw somebody they would like to be. . . . He was a 'Stevenson with balls,' and . . . attracted the people who wanted a young courageous man in the presidency and yet one who was smooth and graceful. Basically . . . the mark of royalty." Nixon, on the other hand, had salted his speeches with self-pity, like his maudlin account of the pony that his parents could not afford to buy his dying brother Harold, lest they deprive the other boys of food and shoes. The reporters didn't just root for Jack— they heckled Dick. "They were outspoken in their hatred and contempt," wrote a conservative newsman, Willard Edwards of the *Chicago Tribune*. "It was an extraordinary hostility." And so the cycle of enmity persisted. At a campaign rally in Spokane, a journalist in the front row made fun of Nixon's involuntary expectoration ("That's right. Spit at 'em, Dick!") during a speech. "Get me the name of that reporter!" Nixon raged. "We're going to get that guy!"

The best of statesmen rage, and draw up lists of journalistic enemies—but recognize that criticism comes with the territory. Kennedy could curse the press, tap their phones, keep his private blacklist, and pitilessly crush a foe; but with the confidence bestowed by wealth, good looks, and breeding, he didn't let the censure get to him. The storms passed, the tempests eased by irony or humor. Nixon did not have that quality.

Nor could Nixon place all the blame on others. During a post-election break in Florida, Hall reminded him how he had vowed, early in the campaign, never to debate the Democratic candidate. ("Young Jerry Voorhis was a damn fool to accept my offer to debate in California," Nixon had told his staff.) As they cruised on a millionaire's boat, Hall demanded: "Goddamn it Dick, tell me what changed your mind."

Nixon stared at the sky.

"Didn't answer. The rain started to come down a little bit," Hall recalled. "He still stood out there, looking at the sky."

A few months later, Nixon wrote: "Leaders are subject to all the human frailties: they lose their tempers, become depressed, experience the other symptoms of tension. Sometimes even strong men will cry."

The Eumenides had one last dart. Nixon sent a cast of Abraham Lincoln's hand as a thank-you gift to a hundred or more of his supporters. The casting was defective, and when the recipients opened the package, most found the memento in shattered pieces.

THE NIXONS PACKED up and moved West—the place you go, the novelist said, "when the land gives out and the old-field pines encroach . . . when you look down at the blade in your hand and see the blood . . . when you are told that you are a bubble on the tide of empire." Dick bought a Starfire convertible. He became a member and scored a hole-in-one at the Bel-Air Country Club. He and Pat rented a mansion from a Hollywood director, on Bundy Drive in Brentwood, where the news photographers covering the great Bel Air fire of 1961 found him on the roof with a garden hose, wetting down the shakes, as around him the homes of movie stars were burning.

Nixon had several choice offers but ultimately accepted a position with the Los Angeles law firm of his friend Earl Adams. It allowed him time to write and travel, keep his hand in politics, and earn $350,000 that year. He and Pat designed and built a new hillside home in Trousdale Estates in Beverly Hills, with a swimming pool, four bedrooms, seven bathrooms, quarters for the hired help, and a spectacular view of Los Angeles, twin-kling at night like a phosphorescent sea. Julie, fourteen, performed a water ballet for a visiting J. Edgar Hoover. Tricia, sixteen, started dating. "Isn't she too young?" asked Dick. "You've got a lot to learn," said Pat. They put the girls in a private school, hoping they'd escape the taunts they had sometimes heard in Washington. "If these two were boys, I would say: 'Let them get in there and slug it out.' But if girls are going to grow up gracious and feminine," said Dick, "they should not develop strong dislikes at an early age."

By summer Nixon had begun a new project: *Six Crises,* a memoir. His assistants gathered the facts and records and Dick, after scrawling outlines on his yellow pads, dictated 1,200 pages of narrative, which were tran-scribed, honed, and rewritten by a team of researchers and ghostwriters. Nixon found it taxing work. Subsisting on Grape-Nuts and frozen TV dinners, he searched for a muse in the house of a friendly developer in a desert community called Apple Valley; a downtown hotel room; and a beach home in Malibu where, deep in thought as he hiked the shore, he lost track of Checkers, and had to trot a mile back to find her. He decided that he detested writing and called the book his seventh crisis.

"This was my first effort in the literary field and probably my last," Nixon wrote Ike. "It was the hardest work I have ever done from the standpoint of concentration and discipline required." Years later he would remember that "as usual, the ones who suffered most, and most silently, were my fam-ily. . . . I was almost ten pounds underweight from strain and fatigue, and I became short-tempered at home and at the office."

Six Crises was a fine first effort, mostly accurate, and a deserved best-seller. Nixon, of course, was the hero of his story, and some who had helped him on his way, like HUAC aide Robert Stripling, felt short-changed. But Nixon showed some ankle, and the six crises—the Hiss case, the Check-ers speech, Ike's heart attack, Caracas, the Kitchen Debate, and the 1960 campaign—were inherently gripping. Nixon unveiled his feelings—not only of triumph, but also of depression, intemperance, and despair. "I am trying to delve deeply into what, for lack of a better term, I would describe as the 'anatomy' of crisis," he wrote to two Northwestern University schol-ars of political behavior.

The publication of *Six Crises* in 1962 was accompanied by its own little intrigues. To make sure it hit the bestseller lists, Nixon ordered aides to buy one thousand copies from the bookstores that reported sales to the New York newspapers. When the Book of the Month Club failed to select the book, Nixon had Haldeman set out to prove that it was biased against conservatives: aides were ordered to take the names from the club's selection board and "have all of their records checked against the Un-American Activities file."

The book was dedicated to Pat, with the note: "She also ran." And if some caught a double meaning in the phrase (for Pat was an also-ran to her husband's career), he doubtless encouraged it when defining the secondary place of loved ones in a man's quest for happiness: "What counts is whether the individual used what chances he had. Did he risk all when the stakes were such that he might win or lose all? Did he affirmatively seek the opportunities to use his talents to the utmost in causes that went beyond personal and family considerations?" he wrote. "A man who has never lost himself in a cause bigger than himself has missed one of life's mountaintop experiences. Only in losing himself does he find himself."

SIX CRISES PITTED Nixon against Kennedy once more—in a short but nasty brawl over Cuba.

Fidel Castro had seized power on the island in January 1959, and Nixon had been one of the first administration officials to meet the Cuban leader. Though he recognized Castro's charisma, he concluded in a memo to Eisenhower that "Castro is either incredibly naïve about Communism or is under Communist discipline." (For his part, Castro left the meeting bristling. "This man has spent the whole time scolding me," he said.) Eisenhower had authorized CIA operations that led to coups d'etat in Iran in 1953 and in Guatemala in 1954. To keep the Red virus from spreading through Latin America, he ordered Langley to devise a covert plan to overthrow Castro as well. The president had two preconditions for a revolt: it must be led by a genuine Cuban democrat, and it must be carried out with no telltale U.S. fingerprints. The plan called for infiltration and guerrilla warfare; there was no mention of invasion. Robert Cushman, Nixon's national security aide, was continually updated and kept his boss informed.

At some point in 1960, the CIA went further, and launched a series of schemes to murder Castro—in the most risible of their plots by employing Mafia hit men. There is no evidence that either Nixon or Eisenhower knew of the assassination plans. On the other hand, such matters would not likely be discussed in recorded conversations. "Only the good Lord knows whether President Ike knew about it or whether Vice President

Nixon knew about it," Cushman recalled. "I would say the odds are that he didn't know."*

Nixon had hoped that Cuba would be liberated before the 1960 election. Kennedy, after being briefed on the administration's policy by the CIA, feared the boost it might give his opponent, taunted the Republicans for "losing Cuba," and called for aid to Cuban rebels. ("Of course, we don't say how we would have saved Cuba," Kennedy mused to speechwriter Richard Goodwin. "What the hell, they never told us how they would have saved China.") Nixon was in a bind: he could not tell the public the truth, but felt the need to say something. So he denounced Kennedy for recklessness.

The episode had little, if any, impact on the 1960 results. But Nixon gnawed on the thought that Kennedy had behaved dishonorably by using information the CIA provided: another case of Ivy League elitists aiding each other at his expense. When writing about the 1960 campaign in *Six Crises,* Nixon put his pique into print. The White House loudly denied the accusation. It was a teapot tempest, except that the topic was now quite a sore spot for John Kennedy. In April 1961, having met none of Eisenhower's conditions for success, Kennedy had ordered the CIA to proceed with an invasion at the Bay of Pigs, on Cuba's southern shore. A brigade of 1,500 exiled Cubans landed on a beach surrounded by mangrove swamps. Many fought bravely, but short on air cover and ammunition, they were crushed by Castro's counterattack.

It was a first-class disaster. Kennedy, desperate for bipartisan support, had invited Nixon to the Oval Office and explained how he had refused to allow U.S. armed forces to intervene and save the Cuban rebels because he feared a Soviet countermove in Berlin. Nixon considered it a failure of nerve and urged Kennedy to find a pretext to invade.

As *Six Crises* made its way onto the bestseller lists, Nixon's thoughts returned to politics. He could run again for president, but the Republican Party was a shambles and seemed destined to be cleaved by a showdown between Nelson Rockefeller and Barry Goldwater. It was better, Nixon

---

* Nixon was briefed about the CIA plan to overthrow Castro, and another to dose the Cuban leader with a drug that would make him behave in an "irrational manner." But "by no stretch of the imagination was Nixon 'the architect of the Bay of Pigs,'" said a long-secret study of the misbegotten invasion released by the CIA in 2011. And "the fact that he heard about the drug in the course of a briefing will not be construed to make him a member of a conspiracy to assassinate Castro."

thought, to let the bruised victor of that contest lose to Kennedy, leaving Nixon as the centrist who could reunite Republicans and win in 1968. He considered various platforms—senator? governor? citizen statesman?—from which to make his comeback.

The Republican hierarchy, from Eisenhower down, urged Nixon to challenge California governor Pat Brown in 1962. Who better to repair the damage left by the Big Switch than Nixon? California would give him a formidable base. And while Brown was more than competent in the business of building schools, roads, and water projects, he was not a slick campaigner and had irritated many voters by granting a stay of execution to a notorious rapist, Caryl Chessman, just as crime rates were starting to soar.

The downsides for Nixon were few, but far from insignificant: he very well might lose, and he did not want the job. As small as Kennedy's margin was in Illinois and Texas, Nixon's margin in California—thirty-six thousand votes—had been just as slim in 1960. There were 1,360,000 more Democrats than Republicans in the state, and his ability to win the support of independents was hobbled by the memories of his old campaigns. To many California Democrats, he was still a loathsome trickster. Brown, meanwhile, had lost weight, quit drinking, and primed his soul for battle at a spiritual retreat.

Nor was it clear, to Nixon or the voters, just what he would do as governor. He saw himself as a crusader. He had no experience as an administrator and didn't much care to acquire it. Rocky had promoted a bold program in Albany and alienated the right by raising the taxes to pay for it. To be stuck in Sacramento, far from the enthralling play of international affairs, scrapping with the legislature over smog and storm drains, was an unappealing option. How could anyone who had served on the National Security Council get excited about disposal of sewage in Los Angeles? he asked his advisers. He found Californians self-absorbed and listless, and missed the action of the nation's capital. "When you aren't around people whose conversation is stimulating, you begin to rot," he griped.

Nixon wrote to Eisenhower, listing his concerns. Sacramento was "so far away from the centers of national and international news media that I simply do not believe it would be possible for me . . . to speak at all constructively," he said. "My entire experience in government has been in national and international affairs. I think the problems which governors have to handle are immensely important but my interests simply are in other fields."

His wife, his longtime adviser Bob Finch, and others agreed. "If you run, it will be a terrible mistake," Pat said. "We've just been through a campaign. We're just getting back on our feet. We owe time to the girls. We owe time to ourselves." At a tense family conference, with their daughters in tears, she refused to campaign with him. But Ike and the party prevailed. And, in the end, Pat agreed to go along. The spirit of halfheartedness would linger, and hurt him, as he made the race.

NIXON ASSEMBLED A team of young professionals to run his campaign. Their names, soon enough, would become familiar to the American public. Bob Haldeman, the young executive on leave from the J. Walter Thompson advertising agency, became the campaign manager, filling the campaign manuals with public relations and marketing theory. He had led the advance team in 1960, and he tapped that pool of talent for another recruit—his old friend John Ehrlichman, whom he had met when they were students at UCLA. Lawyer Herbert Kalmbach, young Dwight Chapin, and fund-raiser Maurice Stans signed on. The prodigal son, Murray Chotiner, was quietly welcomed back and given a portfolio for fundraising and skullduggery.

Still sore about Kennedy's larceny, Nixon ordered his staff to be aggressive. "We cannot allow the situation to develop where they are stirring up trouble all the time and we are not," he said. He asked for lists of enemies in the press. He called for a "completely independent organization for counterattack and counter intelligence" to conduct "everything from getting information surreptitiously to heckling."

"We have to have some of these other candidates tailed and tapped," Nixon told his aides.

Chotiner suggested that Nixon tour the state, as he did in the 1950 Senate contest, to reacquaint himself with the voters and "reestablish your reputation as the old fighting campaigner." But Nixon resisted. His great asset was his "stature," he said. He would not campaign, he told Chotiner, like "a common John Doe." The haughtiness fueled the notion that Nixon was in the race for himself, and not for California. "He was always talking too much about national issues," Nixon's press aide Herb Klein remembered, "not about the streets of Shasta."

Len Hall and others urged Nixon to get a more seasoned hand to run the campaign—someone who could keep him focused on the big picture and give unvarnished advice. Haldeman, the yes-man, was not that guy.

"Haldeman's appointment has not been received well" in New York and Washington, Hall wrote Nixon. "I am going to repeat for the hundredth time that you just can't do everything yourself and Haldeman's appointment indicates that you expect to."

Indeed, Haldeman was deferential to a fault. ("Obsequious with people above him and at times tyrannical with people under him," Nixon White House aide Charles Colson would later report.) When Nixon sent Haldeman notes on, say, the proper application of bumper stickers, the campaign manager would stop what he was doing and compose and distribute a memorandum to his troops, rather than suggesting that the candidate might make better use of their time. When Nixon fell back on an old standard—suggesting that Brown was soft on Communism—Haldeman tagged along. The campaign doctored photographs and dispatched a duplicitous mailing to Democratic voters, and got caught and hauled into court.

"The people knew that I was a practicing Catholic. . . . they just didn't believe that Pat Brown was a Communist," the governor recalled. If Nixon "had stuck to the issues and his own worldwide experience and leadership against the weak, vacillating Brown and laid off the Communism, I think he could have beat me." Instead, Brown cited the Red bashing as proof that the Trickster had not changed. *Falsus in uno, falsus in omnibus,"* Brown said. "I just argued that to beat all hell."

IT WAS A nasty campaign on both sides. "We used everything we could," Brown would admit. The Kennedy Justice Department investigated Don Nixon's ties to Howard Hughes. The Democrats sent a lawyer to visit mobster Mickey Cohen in his cell at Alcatraz, where, undoubtedly swayed by the possibility of clemency, he signed an affidavit linking Chotiner and Nixon to organized crime. A Democratic prankster named Dick Tuck made his bones in this campaign, trailing Nixon through the state, tossing sand in the Republican gears. Conspiring with Drew Pearson, Brown revived the story of the "Nixonburger" folly, and Tuck had signs printed in Chinese and held behind Nixon at a Chinatown rally: WHAT ABOUT THE HUGHES LOAN? A decade later, Nixon would testify, under oath, that he believed his campaign was bugged.

It was "dirty campaigning," Lucien Haas, the governor's press aide, conceded. "When you got into a campaign, especially with a guy like Nixon whose guts we hated, it was easy to get combative. You're not running against a nice guy. You're running against a first-class son of a bitch."

NIXON QUASHED THE talk about the Hughes loan in a winning performance when he and Brown debated before an audience of editors and publishers in early October. It was a replay of the Checkers speech:

> Six years ago, my brother was in deep financial trouble. He borrowed $205,000 from the Hughes Tool Company. My mother put up as security for that loan practically everything she had—a piece of property which to her was fabulously wealthy and which now is producing an income of $10,000 a year to the creditor. My brother went bankrupt six years ago. My mother turned over the property to the Hughes Tool Company....
>
> I had no part or interest in my brother's business. I had no part whatever in the negotiation of this loan. I was never asked to do anything by the Hughes Tool company and never did anything for them. And yet ... Mr. Brown, privately, in talking to some of the newsmen here in this audience, and his hatchet men, have been constantly saying that I must have gotten some of the money—that I did something wrong.
>
> Now it is time to have this out.... I went to Washington for 15 years with a car and a house and a mortgage. I came back with a car and a house and a bigger mortgage.

The governor was doing the smearing, Nixon said. Brown was the slippery politician. He challenged him to deny it:

> I have made mistakes, but I am an honest man. And if the governor of this state has any evidence pointing up that I did anything wrong in this case, that I did anything for the Hughes Tool Company, that I asked them for this loan, then instead of doing it privately, doing it slyly, the way he has.... Now he has a chance. All the people of California are listening on television. The people of this audience are listening. Governor Brown has a chance to stand up as a man and charge me with misconduct. Do it, sir!

Brown backed down. "I never said anything about it other than in casual conversation from time to time," he quibbled.

NIXON SURGED AHEAD in the polls, then fell behind, but was making what looked like a winning sprint to the finish when Kennedy appeared on national television on the night of October 22 to announce that Khrushchev had installed ballistic missiles in Cuba. Nixon watched the speech in an Oakland hotel room, turned to an aide, and said, "I just lost the election." The most dangerous of the Cold War crises dominated the news, and Nixon's opponent profited. Brown flew to Washington, where he was photographed at the White House consulting on civil defense. The missile crisis snuffed Nixon's chances. For years he would mutter that Kennedy timed it to defeat him.

Nixon was hurt, as well, by desertions from the right. Discarding the advice of his Southern California friends, he had launched his campaign with an attack on a group of reactionary crazies (even J. Edgar Hoover thought them "wild-eyed people of the right") who called themselves the John Birch Society. They had made their name by libeling Eisenhower, Earl Warren, and others as traitors. "I thought it was time to take on the lunatic fringe," Nixon wrote Ike.* It was the right thing to do, and attuned to Nixon's need to capture votes from Democrats and independent voters. "I am glad that you had the political courage to brand the Society for what it is . . . a neo-Fascist organization which certainly poses a real threat to the Republican Party," the GOP adman Elwood Robinson told Nixon. The newspapers hailed Nixon's valor. Yet many in Southern California's conservative movement viewed Nixon's action as an assault on the Cause and worked hard for Los Angeles assemblyman and former USC fullback Joe Shell, who took a third of the vote from Nixon in the Republican primary. "We will do everything we can to help you win in November," wrote Walter Knott, the proprietor of Knott's Berry Farm, to Nixon. "But it would make our work much easier in Orange County if you would lay off the Birch Society and refrain from depreciating [sic] the conservative movement."

Nixon's response was "I don't need those people." But an internal campaign analysis noted the risks. "The high degree of enthusiasm and dedication among the . . . Shell camp during the primary was the belief . . . they were carrying the conservative banner," it said. "Dick Nixon's nonextremist positions won't serve . . . to provide the sort of 'cause' calculated to inspire fanatic enthusiasm."

"It was a brutal, bloody primary and the Joe Shell forces never did sup-

---

* In 1952, he had written a similar note to Eisenhower, saying he was "ashamed" at California's facility for attracting "so many crackpots."

port Nixon in the general election," Patricia Reilly Hitt, then a young supporter from Whittier, recalled. To centrist Republicans like herself, the burgeoning conservative movement was "a monster," she said, chock-full of "bitter, nasty, hate-filled" people.

The Birchers' main target was Warren, but the enemy of an enemy isn't always a friend, at least not for the chief justice, who saw the opportunity to avenge himself on the man he called "Tricky."

Warren came to California, posed at photo ops with Brown, and extolled the governor's stewardship. His son, Earl Warren Jr., campaigned against Nixon. The chief justice "felt that Nixon double crossed him in 1952," Brown remembered, and when Warren "hated people, he hated them." After the campaign was over, and Nixon had lost by almost 300,000 votes, Warren "laughed and laughed and laughed," said Brown.

AND THERE WAS, again, the press. In Nixon's years away from California, the media had undergone its own transformation. Kyle Palmer fell fatally ill. The cascade of television-watching newcomers diluted the influence of the old newspaper barons. The Chandlers turned the *Times* over to their son, Otis, who brought in professional newsmen, owing no allegiance to Nixon. The California press corps knew the state and its issues, believed that Nixon was using the governor's office as a stepping-stone, and bridled at his haughty expectation that they owed him a free pass. They met him with skepticism, and sometimes hostility. He returned the favor, labeling the newsmen as prostitutes or hatchet men. "You had a very combative set of . . . tough political reporters," Lucien Haas recalled. "I knew them well. I knew that they were liberal Democrats, most of them. . . . A lot of them were very careful to disguise it . . . [but] it crept out, especially when you had candidates like Nixon whom they didn't like. So I don't doubt for a minute that it was reflected in their writing."

Nixon spent election night at the Beverly Hilton Hotel in Los Angeles. There was drinking, and little sleep. As the day dawned, and defeat set in, he resolved not to meet the press. Screw them. Why give them the satisfaction? Herb Klein was dispatched to the filing room to read a statement from the candidate.

But as Nixon went to leave the hotel, old friends Jack Drown and Ray Arbuthnot cornered him and told him that fleeing would look cowardly. It would give the reporters another excuse to bash him. Nixon reversed course and climbed into an elevator. "As we came down you could almost see the temperature boiling," Drown recalled. "He was working himself up."

At the podium, Klein had just announced that the candidate would not appear when Nixon arrived and nudged him out of the way. "Now that Mr. Klein has made his statement, and now that all the members of the press are so delighted that I have lost, I'd like to make a statement of my own," he declared.

What followed was less awful than it sometimes was portrayed, yet as revealing. It was not a tirade, but a fifteen-minute struggle. The sides of his personality warred with each other—idealist versus cynic, father's son versus mother's boy, trickster versus statesman—for all to see. "I congratulate Governor Brown," Nixon began. "I believe Governor Brown has a heart, even though he believes I do not. I believe he is a good American, even though he feels I am not." His cousin, the novelist Jessamyn West, was stunned as she watched the performance. It was as if the Frank and Hannah sides of him were warring for control. Others saw Captain Queeg ranting about the missing strawberries in the climactic scene from *The Caine Mutiny*.

"For sixteen years, ever since the Hiss case, you've had a lot of fun—a lot of fun—that you've had the opportunity to attack me," said Nixon. "I leave you gentlemen now and you will now write it. You will interpret it. That's your right. But as I leave you I want you to know—just think how much you're going to be missing. You don't have Nixon to kick around anymore because, gentlemen, this is my last press conference."

Pat Hitt, standing behind the cameras, had tears on her cheeks as Nixon poured his guts out. "He looked just terrible," she recalled. "He'd been up all night and what was to him his whole life was lying in a shambles at his feet." Part of her—the political professional—wanted to stop him. "The guy was unglued and he was going to say what he felt and what he thought, and not what was . . . politically expeditious." But as she stood there watching, the loyalist in her took over. She shared his fury and clenched her fists. She found herself thinking, "Attaboy, Dick. Give it to them."

CHOTINER AND DROWN drove Nixon home, to his family at their dream house in Trousdale Estates. He brushed past the girls at the door. Dick and Pat quarreled, and the Drowns took Julie and Tricia away to stay at their home. Dick left for the Bahamas, without Pat. He hung out on the beach with Rebozo and friends. She and her daughters did not join him until Thanksgiving.

On the evening of the "last press conference," Kennedy and Brown compared notes over the telephone. The president had done what he could to hammer a stake through Nixon's heart. "I killed him, all you have to do is bury him," Kennedy said. The White House taping system caught their gloating.

"I'll tell you this. You reduced him to the nuthouse," the president told Brown. "God, that last farewell speech of his . . ."

"I don't see how he can ever recover," said Brown. "This is a peculiar fellow. I really think he's psychotic. He's an able man, but he's nuts. Like a lot of these paranoiacs."

On *Air Force One* a few days later, while returning from Eleanor Roosevelt's funeral, Kennedy and Chief Justice Earl Warren laughed like schoolboys as they huddled together, reading aloud from press clippings about Nixon's demise.

THE 1960 DEFEAT had been "shattering" for Nixon, Haldeman recalled. "The defeat in '62 was even more shattering, because it was more disgraceful. . . . He lost to Pat Brown, a man for whom he didn't have overriding respect . . . and he lost by a big margin."

"There is an element of tragedy in Richard Nixon's farewell," wrote James Reston. "Two years ago he was within 100,000 votes of the American Presidency and today, unelected and unmourned, he is an unemployed lawyer in Los Angeles. No wonder he slammed the door as he went out."

ABC News ran a prime-time special called *The Political Obituary of Richard Nixon*. Alger Hiss was among those interviewed. For the Chandlers, and many others, this was overkill. Employing a Soviet spy as a commentator was an "obscenity," the *Los Angeles Times* said.

"For years the liberals have been panting for the Walpurgis Night when they would all dance on the grave of Richard Nixon," read the *Times* editorial. "They performed the first of their ghoulish revels on Sunday night and it was so thoroughly in the medieval crossroads-and-gibbet spirit that even some seasoned Nixon haters must have hurried away to be sick."

Few, however, contested the network's thesis.

"I thought," said Brown, that "he was as dead as Kelsey's nuts."

The Greatest Comeback

JOHN KENNEDY WAS shot and killed while riding in an open car through Dallas on November 22, 1963. His motorcade slowed as it made a turn before the Texas School Book Depository building, from where Lee Oswald, a deluded Communist, consigning all the rage at his shabby life to a mail-order rifle and his Marine Corps marksmanship, fired three times from a sixth-floor window, hitting the president in the throat and skull.

Nixon had left Dallas that morning, after speaking to a group of soft-drink bottlers. He had landed at Idlewild Airport and was in a taxi, heading toward his new Manhattan home, when a pedestrian cried out the gruesome tidings. The doorman at his building confirmed it. His rival was dead, the fetch dispelled. Hannah Nixon heard the news in California. Her first thought was that, save for a few thousand votes, it would have been Richard in that car, and Pat beside him, splashed with gore.

That was Jacqueline Kennedy's thought as well. She knew how Nixon's ambition would draw him back to the devouring swirl. He had written to her, with some grace, on November 23, recalling "the hand of fate" that had brought them all together, and the "mystique of the young at heart" that Jackie had displayed in the White House. The widow was no political naïf. She knew what must be. She tried, all the same, on her black-bordered note cards, to forewarn him of how splendor can turn to horror, and blood mix with roses on a warm Texas day. "You two young men—colleagues in Congress, adversaries in 1960—and now look what has happened," she wrote. "I know how you must feel—so long on the path—so closely missing the greatest prize—and now for you, all the questions come up again and you must commit all you and your family's hopes and efforts. . . ."

"Just one thing I would say to you—if it does not work out as you have hoped for so long—please be consoled by what you already have—your life and family," she wrote. "We never value life enough when we have it."

—

NIXON HAD MOVED to New York in June 1963, to lay him down and bleed awhile. With the help of admiring corporate chiefs, who let it be known that their legal business would follow, he had brought his name and rainmaking potential to a Wall Street law firm that was then retitled Nixon, Mudge, Rose, Guthrie & Alexander. Los Angeles was a land of lotus-eaters. But "New York is very cold and very ruthless and very exciting," Nixon told the *Los Angeles Times*. "It is a place where you can't slow down."

The Nixons sold the Trousdale house and bought a twelve-room co-op overlooking Central Park in the Fifth Avenue building where Nelson Rockefeller lived. Dick forswore politics—he was "taking the veil," he insisted. He and Pat and the girls went on a six-week tour of Europe and the Holy Land. They dined out and went shopping in Manhattan, and tapped their feet at Broadway shows (*Hello, Dolly!*). Tricia attended Finch College, and Julie went to Smith; both were debutantes. Nixon joined two elite suburban country clubs and threw a big annual Christmas party, where he entertained the guests, playing carols on the piano. Pat was delighted, as their friend William Safire recalled, that "the hatred heaped on her family was over." The Nixons dined at "21" with Bill Rogers and his wife, and toasted their escape from politics.

"Daddy is nice and busy and seems happy," Julie wrote in her diary. "He tries hard to have a fun 'family life.'"

Nixon sampled litigation and took a privacy case to the U.S. Supreme Court. He discovered that his destiny was not corporate law, finding it "degrading" and "terribly difficult" to solicit and represent businessmen. But one top client, Pepsi-Cola, sought new markets overseas, and so its interests jibed with his. He could roam the capitals of Europe and Asia, visiting American ambassadors and foreign leaders, quizzing them, sometimes for hours, and recording their answers on his foolscap pads. On a trip to Finland, he impulsively hopped the train to Moscow to knock on the door of an old foe. A housekeeper informed him that the ousted Premier Khrushchev was not in.

MUCH OF WHAT Nixon discussed with his international acquaintances concerned Southeast Asia. In the months after the Cuban missile crisis, hope had subdued dread for a time. The Soviets and Americans sidled back from the verge of war and signed an agreement banning aboveground nuclear tests. But the Cold War endured, and Kennedy's presidency was an unfinished portrait when he died. The CIA assassination plots in Cuba and elsewhere continued—on taking office, Lyndon Johnson was stunned to find that "we had been operating a damn Murder Inc. in the Caribbean," he told a former aide—and there were sixteen thousand U.S. troops in Vietnam.

In the years since the fall of Dien Bien Phu, the Communists had consolidated their hold on the North and worked to undermine the government of South Vietnamese president Ngo Dinh Diem. In the United States, there was a broad bipartisan consensus—from liberals like Congressman Tip O'Neill to conservatives like Cardinal Francis Spellman and Senator Barry Goldwater—that Southeast Asia must be saved from the Communist colossus that seemed poised to swallow all of Asia. Nixon's 1960 running mate, Henry Cabot Lodge Jr., signed on as John Kennedy's ambassador in Saigon.

"We were wrong, terribly wrong," Robert McNamara, the secretary of defense for Kennedy and Johnson, would confess. "I saw Communism as monolithic . . . in hindsight, of course, it is clear that they had no unified strategy. We also totally underestimated the nationalistic aspect of Ho Chi Minh's movement. . . . We failed to analyze our assumptions critically. . . . The foundations of our decision making were gravely flawed."

The war was fought for "prestige" and "credibility." Vietnam was of peripheral interest, with few strategic assets, but its fall to the Communists, it was said, would persuade other nations that Americans were fainthearted. In the ranks of the New Frontier, a few saw that the argument was a trap: that the United States, like France before it, would be snared in a land where the springs of nationalism fortified the enemy, and only a massive, indiscriminate expenditure of high explosives amid the civilian populations might deliver a stalemate, at best. Where was the prestige in that? And when the thought occurred that America's stature might actually be enhanced if the United States showed good sense, cut its losses, and withdrew, the political price was thought too high. The "loss" of China had helped bring on Joe McCarthy, and the Red Scare of the 1950s. Losing Vietnam, the New Frontiersmen told each other, could cost them their careers.

And so Kennedy had gone to war—hiding behind the fiction that U.S. "advisers" would not take combat roles. Nixon was an enthusiast. He backed Kennedy "to the hilt," he said. But the fighting did not go well. Searching for a scapegoat, Kennedy and his advisers settled on Diem. He was an aspiring dictator, from the Roman Catholic minority, something of a mystic, and empowered by a clique that used terror to maintain its grip on power. In the summer of 1963, Buddhist monks began to immolate themselves in protest of the regime's cruelty; they burned, serenely, as photographers recorded the scenes for American newspapers. Kennedy and Lodge gave their blessing to a military coup, during which Diem and his brother were murdered.

Three weeks later, Kennedy was shot. In the great keening that followed the assassination, Johnson and his legislative captains moved the stalled liberal agenda—Medicare and Medicaid, the Civil Rights Act of 1964 and the Voting Rights Act of 1965, federal aid to education, a war on poverty, and a Keynesian tax cut—through Congress. "These are the most hopeful times in all the years since Christ was born in Bethlehem," Johnson declared at the lighting of the national Christmas tree in 1964. Americans were united, to a degree "unmatched in the history of freedom," he said.

But the inherited agenda included Vietnam. In August 1964, using an unverified clash between American and North Vietnamese warships in the Gulf of Tonkin as a pretext, Johnson asked Congress for broad war-making powers. The vote in favor was 416 to 0 in the House, and 88 to 2 in the Senate. Campaigning for election, LBJ promised that he would not "send American boys nine or ten thousand miles away from home to do what Asian boys ought to be doing for themselves." This was a lie. By the end of 1965, there were 184,000 American boys in Vietnam, twice that were on the way, and Johnson had launched "Rolling Thunder," a bombing campaign that would exceed, in tons of high explosives, those of all previous wars combined.

A few, mostly pacifists and elements of the liberal intelligentsia, dissented. Protests gripped the campuses at Berkeley and elsewhere. And as the butcher's bill soared, the loss in prestige was commensurate. In the end the United States would implore Moscow and Beijing, the enemies it had hoped to chasten, to release it from its pain. A war waged to avoid humiliation would end in mortification, rout, and retreat. The unity of the early 1960s would give way to decades of hatred and division.

As HE ROVED the political wilderness, Nixon had taken to studying philosophy, reading or rereading Edmund Burke and Machiavelli, and a favorite, Friedrich Nietzsche, who advised: "What does not destroy me makes me stronger." He agreed. It was struggle that gave life meaning, he believed, not material comforts.

Friends had urged him to remain in public life after the 1962 disaster, from Jackie Robinson ("You are good for politics; good for America. . . .

Do not let the critics cause you to give up your career") to Billy Graham ("There are few men whom I have loved as I love you. . . . It would be the greatest tragedy I can think of for you to turn to drink or any of these other escapisms").

Kennedy's assassination corroded Nixon's resolution to sit out the 1964 election. Within days he had canceled a pending book contract and was meeting with his political advisers. Over martinis, a friend sought to talk him out of it and asked why he would subject himself to the strain and toil. "I know the fucking Commie mind. But they don't know mine," Nixon replied. "I really think I could do something. I really believe I could make a contribution to peace."

He could not resist the itch when Goldwater was defeated by a write-in vote for Lodge in the New Hampshire primary, and hostile Republicans told Rockefeller just how they felt about his divorce and remarriage to a woman who abandoned her four children for him. Nixon let it be known he was available—as an anyone-but-Goldwater candidate or a peacemaker palatable to all segments of the party. He connived to have his name entered as a write-in candidate in the presidential primaries, took a high-profile tour of the battleground states, and embarked on a twenty-four-day trip through Asia, visiting Saigon, accusing Johnson of timidity, and recommending that the United States rain more bombs on Vietnam. Senator J. William Fulbright, the Democratic chairman of the Foreign Relations Committee, had called for a reexamination of American policy toward China. In a stop in Hong Kong, still the hawk, Nixon called it "naïve, woolly-headed thinking."

The Republicans convened in San Francisco, and Nixon brought a squad of aides, who manned a war room in case the delegates became deadlocked. There was a flicker of hope when the Rockefeller and Goldwater forces clashed, and Nixon's men rushed to the hall. But the right had the convention in hand. The best Nixon could do was deliver a glowing endorsement of Goldwater, and then grow "almost physically sick," he would say, as he listened to the nominee declare: "Extremism in the defense of liberty is no vice."

Journalist Robert Novak summed up Nixon's thrashings in an article for *Esquire:* "Each one of his carefully calculated moves in 1964—most of them shrouded from public view—was followed only by his own further political deterioration. When it all ended . . . he was a fallen idol." In keeping with the theme, the magazine's editors added a précis—a quote from a nineteenth-century English poet that thoroughly irritated Nixon:

Look in my face; my name is Might-have-been;
I am also called No-more, Too-late, Farewell.

In fact, Novak underestimated Nixon's determination. As Rocky and others sat on their hands that fall, he barnstormed for the ticket, harvesting the gratitude of both the moderate Republicans who were trying to escape the tide—and conservatives who were joyously drowning in the cause. When the storm had passed, the journalist Tom Wicker wrote, it was Richard Nixon who bobbed to the surface, like Ishmael on Queequeg's coffin.

On his fifty-second birthday, Nixon sat in his New York study and drew up a list of resolutions for 1965 (*Set great goals . . . Daily rest . . . Brief vacations . . . Knowledge of all weaknesses . . . Better use of time . . . Begin writing book . . . Golf or some other kind of daily exercise . . . Articles or speeches on provocative new international and national issues*). Then he put down his yellow foolscap, turned out the light, stared into the fire, and began to plot his march to the presidency. He would waver, sometimes, in the next three years, mostly when he considered the impact—the "emotional disaster"—that another campaign could have on his family. But ultimately he reached the conclusion "that politics was not just an alternative occupation for me. It was my life."

HANNAH NIXON SPENT her final years in California, far from her famous son. Cozy Whittier had been reshaped—engulfed by suburban smog and sprawl. She filled her small home with mementos of his political life and retained her work ethic as long as she could—frustrating Dick by refusing nursing care.

"I think it is a fine trait that you do not want to spend money unnecessarily and that you have the kind of pride and a sense of individual responsibility which makes you resist having anybody full-time to take care of you," Nixon wrote her in a long, reasoned letter. But "since you obviously seem to prefer to be in your own home—an admirable and understandable instinct—you must now have the help that is necessary. . . . We all want you to use your money for that purpose and not store it up in the bank."

Nixon was seized by grief when Hannah died, after a final stretch in a nursing home, in September 1967. Her last years were painful, and she would cry out, "Richard! Richard!"

"I expected it but was not prepared for it," Nixon confided in a letter to his friend Jack Drown: the news of her death; the long flight west; the little Quaker church across the street from the site of Frank's store; the sight of Hannah in an open casket; and the intrusive photographers and reporters, which he "deeply resented." He regretted he had not visited her more. "Only after the funeral services did the pent up emotion burst forth," he wrote. Leaving the church, he wept in the arms of Billy Graham. Dick and Pat did not linger, but went straight to the airport from the cemetery.

Nixon would miss Hannah's presence in his life. His idealized vision of her kept his wayward instincts in check and inspired his nobler yearnings. "For weeks" after her death, he told Drown, "I could think of little else."

NIXON ASPIRED TO geopolitical genius, but his stance on Vietnam in the early 1960s was never more than ordinary. Until the polls showed a rising public discontent, his was a loud, insistent voice for escalation. For Nixon, like most men of his generation, the lesson of Munich was immutable. "What had been true of the betrayal of Czechoslovakia to Hitler in 1938 was no less true of the betrayal of South Vietnam to the Communists," he insisted.

Again and again he called for more: more time, more troops, more bombs. On his trips to Saigon, he opposed proposals for a negotiated settlement and declared that anything short of absolute victory "would be a defeat or a retreat," for which the Democrats should be held accountable.

"Mr. Nixon is playing a political game with a situation that ought to be put on a higher plane," the New York Times scolded.

Nixon's cynicism revealed itself on a visit to Saigon, when he was invited to dine at the home of retired general Edward Lansdale, a counterinsurgency expert who believed that, in order to prevail, the Saigon government needed to be more responsive to the people. Among the guests was an acolyte of Lansdale named Daniel Ellsberg.

"What are you up to?" Nixon asked Lansdale.

"Trying to make the coming elections the most honest Vietnam has ever had," Lansdale replied.

"Honest, yes," Nixon said, "as long as you win."

In 1966, Nixon again took to the road, campaigning for Republican congressional candidates across the country. It was his ninth major campaign in sixteen years, and this one yielded victory.

On the eve of the election, Johnson traveled to the Philippines to confer with Asian leaders and proposed a cease-fire, with the mutual withdrawal of American and North Vietnamese forces from South Vietnam. Nixon opposed the president, and the plan. "Communist victory would most certainly be the result," he said. It prompted a rebuke from Johnson, who called Nixon a "chronic campaigner" who would get men killed to sate his ambition.

Nixon was delighted. Johnson's tantrum had raised Nixon's stature, and shown that he could rankle the president he expected to challenge in 1968. He was given a half hour on NBC to respond, and starred on an ABC Sunday talk show. He accused Johnson of "cheap political demagoguery"— capping the episode with a winning reference to his own 1962 meltdown. He felt for Johnson, Nixon said, with practiced unction: "I think I can understand how a man can be very, very tired and how his temper can then be short."

The Republicans scored in the off-year elections—gaining forty seats in the House and three in the Senate—for which Nixon earned much of the credit. "We won! We won!" he told his entourage, ecstatic on election night. "Let's go to El Morocco and have some spaghetti!"

Nixon was now the leader of the loyal opposition. "Lazarus laughing," wrote columnist Murray Kempton.

Attention was paid. Nixon was "forever and to everyone, a mystery," Theodore White wrote in his journal. "The new Nixon and the old Nixon. A man plucked apart by the press: his eyes are beady, his nose is a ski slope, his brow is what? And is he a sneak? Over and over again, the prying at the character."

In 1967 the number of American troops in Vietnam soared toward 500,000, and 100 died each week. "We face more cost, more loss, and more agony," Johnson said, in his State of the Union address. "For the end is not yet."

JOHNSON HAD SOUGHT to fight war on the cheap, both in means—the government ran a deficit—and manpower, as he ducked the politically volatile act of calling up the reserves. But the draft, inequitably administered and tapping 350,000 young men a year, brought the reality of war to middle America. So did the returning casualties. So did the increasingly skeptical coverage of the combat correspondents in Saigon. And so, with the help of the new communications satellites launched in the early sixties, did the nightly television news. By the end of 1967, rebellious liberal Democrats and heartfelt college kids were flocking to New Hampshire to campaign for an antiwar candidate, Senator Eugene McCarthy, a Democrat from Minnesota.

Johnson's government issued buoyant accounts of military success. Intelligence analysts who questioned the pronouncements found that their reports were rewritten, or ignored, by superiors. As 1967 turned toward 1968, the CIA detected signs of an imminent enemy offensive, to coincide with the upcoming Tet holiday. American commanders shifted their forces toward the northern and western borders, but as the North Vietnamese froze the U.S. soldiers in place at far-flung outposts like Khe Sanh, the Viet Cong struck behind them, in the cities. The ancient capital of Hue fell, and three thousand political and civic leaders were massacred by the Communists. Suicide squads attacked American installations in the heart of Saigon. Bay Tuyen and Ut Nho, who led seventeen other Communist guerrillas into the U.S. embassy compound—breaching the wall, besieging the building, and killing five guards before being cut down by American reinforcements—may have struck the war's single, most telling psychological blow. Their audacious assault was repeated throughout South Vietnam, as over one hundred cities, towns, and hamlets came under attack. The news of Nixon's announcement for the presidency, on February 2, 1968, shared the front page of the *New York Times* with a photograph of a Vietnamese police chief using a shiny, snub-nosed revolver to peremptorily execute a Viet Cong captive amid the chaos in Saigon.

Johnson's credibility had been said to have a gap; now the gap was a gulf. The Pentagon said that it would need another 206,000 troops to win the war, on top of the 525,000 already authorized. Young men—and their girlfriends and families—did the math. On March 12, McCarthy won 42 percent of the vote in New Hampshire. By St. Patrick's Day, Robert Kennedy—whose loathing for Johnson was reciprocated—had joined the race.*

The impact of the General Offensive and General Uprising, as the North Vietnamese called the Tet attacks, transformed the war. Hanoi had hoped to spur a popular uprising and topple the government of South Vietnamese president Nguyen Van Thieu. It didn't happen. American firepower proved decisive, and the Viet Cong were depleted as a fighting force. But from tactical defeat came strategic victory. America's will had been broken.

---

* LBJ got 49 percent of the vote in the Democratic primary, and McCarthy 42 percent. When GOP crossover votes were included, Johnson beat his challenger by just 230 votes.

A new defense secretary, Clark Clifford, reported to Johnson that the nation's political and business leaders wanted no more of this "hopeless bog." A bipartisan skein of "wise men"—elder statesmen from previous administrations—now urged the unnerved president to give up hope for victory and barter for what he could salvage. On March 31, in a nationally televised speech, Johnson halted the bombing in much of Vietnam, called for peace talks, and announced he would not run for reelection.

"I've come to the conclusion there's no way to win the war," Nixon told speechwriter Richard Whalen. "We can't say that of course—in fact, we have to seem to say the opposite, just to keep some degree of bargaining leverage," but the war "can't be brought to a successful military conclusion."

Nixon became a peace candidate, promising the troubled electorate that he would bring his skill and know-how to the pursuit of an honorable settlement. "It is essential that we end this war," he declared. He, like Chamberlain years before, promised "peace with honor." Nixon would find it just as difficult to achieve.

HISTORY WAS MOVING in vertiginous leaps. Among the war's critics was Martin Luther King Jr., who saw the conflict through a moral perspective—the U.S. government, he said, had emerged as "the greatest purveyor of violence in the world"—and a racial lens: white versus yellow, with black soldiers doing a disproportionate amount of the killing and dying.

The freedom rides and sit-ins—even the arduous enactment of the landmark legislation in the early 1960s—had turned out to be the easy part of the civil rights movement. The task of bringing real and equal opportunity to schools, neighborhoods, factories, and municipal workforces was moving with far less than deliberate speed. A white fireman in Newark or a family in South Boston may have shrugged, or sympathized, when black protesters were suppressed by fire hoses, bombings, and police dogs in Alabama. But when asked to share the PTA, the factory floor, or city hall with black neighbors, whites up North acted much like those down South. The racist governor of Alabama, George Wallace, preying on prejudice, had entered the presidential primaries in 1964 and won 34 percent of the Democratic vote in Wisconsin, 30 percent in Indiana, and 43 percent in Maryland. The word *backlash* entered the political lexicon.

African American expectations, climbing for decades, sired eruptions of frustration. There were race riots in Harlem, Bedford-Stuyvesant, Rochester, and Philadelphia in 1964, and the following summer—five days after Johnson signed the Voting Rights Act—a routine drunk-driving stop triggered a riot in the Los Angeles neighborhood of Watts, in which thirty-four people were killed. The summer of 1967 saw more riots, and similar death tolls, in Newark and Detroit.

At the same time, throughout that decade and the next, the crime rate in the country surged—with a doubling of reported murders, rapes, assaults, and robberies. In part the result of a more youthful population— young men and women of the Baby Boom were using more drugs, having more illegitimate children, and committing more crime than their staid, older counterparts—the epidemic struck the cities with a special ferocity.

To the average white voter, "the Negro, for whom the past fourteen years represented a unique era of progress, showed himself to be, not only ungrateful, but sullen, full of hate and the potential of violence," warned Harry McPherson, an aide to Johnson, in a memo to the president. "The crime rate continued to rise; the number one 'public' problem for millions of people became physical fear; the administration seemed unable to do anything about this; or in the eyes of some whites, it was unwilling to offend the Negroes upon whom it depended for votes."

All was but prequel to the outrage, grief, and violence that followed King's assassination, on a balcony at the Lorraine Motel in Memphis, on April 4, 1968. The country was still staggering from Johnson's abdication— now it watched as the Eighty-Second Airborne fixed bayonets and deployed machine guns to guard the White House and the Capitol from the mobs that were torching the nearby business district. After some deliberation— remembering Kennedy's call to Coretta King in 1960, but certain that a similar gesture would be scorned as expedient in 1968—Nixon made a private visit to the widow and her family in Atlanta. He attended the funeral, as well, though it "won no votes," he told Haldeman, upon his return.

America was reeling, and the battering was not nearly done. After quoting Aeschylus to a devastated audience of black Americans on the night that King was murdered, Robert Kennedy was himself gunned down on June 5, as he left the celebration of his victory in the California primary. In six months, a liberal movement that had been "Clean for Gene" in New Hampshire, boasted of its "flower power," or rallied for a Kennedy restoration had been eviscerated. Radicals and nihilists took over. "The New Left seems to have read nothing and relies entirely on the proposition that feeling and acting are all that matter; the deed will eventually produce the doctrine; the act of revolution will lead to the program," Arthur Schlesinger Jr. wrote in his diary. The furies peaked at the Democratic convention in Chicago in August, where the brutality displayed by Mayor Daley's cops, gassing and beating the demonstrators in the streets outside the convention hall, was matched by a raw show of power within, as Johnson and his captains stifled dissent and ensured that Vice President Hubert Humphrey received the Democratic nomination.

Nixon never liked Robert Kennedy. He referred to him as "the little sonofabitch" and marveled at how a new Good Bobby had replaced the old Ruthless Bobby in the press. "Why does he get to be mean, and why do I have to be so nice?" Nixon asked. He had welcomed Kennedy's entry into the race only because it would split the Democrats. Yet the Nixons were rocked by the second Kennedy assassination. "That poor boy died," Pat told Dick, through tears, after hearing the news that Kennedy had succumbed to his fatal wound.

In an advertising studio in New York City, the imagery of that hellish year—riots, fires, mobs, guns—was assembled as montage, to be streamed into American living rooms. The bacchanal of violence was followed by the name of a man—*Nixon*—who promised to restore order. *This time,* urged the ads, *vote like your whole world depended on it.*

As THE WORLD went mad around him, Richard Nixon had shown touch and timing in his campaign to claim the Republican nomination. The ever-loyal Rose Mary Woods had followed Nixon to California, and back to New York, and was with him as personal secretary. His new law partner Leonard Garment, an accomplished litigator and jazz musician, signed on in the throes of a midlife crisis. Old hands Haldeman, Ehrlichman, and Finch had returned to day jobs but remained on call. The first outsider to be hired was Patrick Buchanan, whose bluff combativeness masked degrees from Gonzaga High School, Georgetown University, and the Columbia University graduate school of journalism. Buchanan was a jack-of-all-trades: body man, speechwriter, and liaison with the press. For a decade, he would also serve as Nixon's bridge to the conservative movement.

John Sears and Tom Evans, young lawyers with Nixon's firm, were drawn into the campaign, as were a mix of former aides and friendly advisers that included Charlie McWhorter, Peter Flanigan, Maurice Stans, Pat Hillings, John Whitaker (who made the odd suggestion that Nixon might consider a trip to China), and William Safire. Dwight Chapin, a Haldeman protégé, joined as the new body man. Raymond Price, the former editor of the editorial page for the now-defunct *Herald Tribune,* was recruited as a speechwriter, and in 1967 a new partner—John Mitchell—joined Nixon's firm. In time, he became the campaign manager.

Another desk in Nixon's outer office was reserved for "Miss Ryan," who helped Woods with her work, swapped cigarettes with Buchanan, and dreaded what lay ahead. Over Christmas break in 1966, her benumbed mother had told Julie "flatly, almost tonelessly," that she could not endure another presidential campaign. Tricia was dismayed, unable to sleep at the prospect. In the summer of 1967 Pat fled, alone, to California for three weeks with the Drowns. Like many of Dick's friends, they were invested in his comeback. His lifelong dream was in his grasp, they told her. How could she oppose him? By the time the calendar turned again, Pat and her daughters had made "the awful decision" to support him one more time. Their lives would be hell, either way. "If I had to practice law the rest of my life," Nixon was telling friends, "I would be mentally dead in two years and physically dead in four."

NIXON'S GREATEST OBSTACLE was the "image of a loser" that lingered from the 1960 and 1962 campaigns, White noted. To confront the perception, Nixon entered all the Republican primaries. "If we can lick the can't-win thing we've got it made," Price told the boss in a campaign memo.

The general election would present a different challenge. Could the newest new Nixon countermand the old caricature?

"We have to deal with . . . not the facts of history, but an image," Price advised. For many years the old Nixon had been "fashionable to hate . . . particularly in many of the Best Circles. . . . Whatever the strange complex of passions that went into the hysterical anti-anti-Communism of the postwar and McCarthy years; whatever the emotional response of those who disliked his style . . . he was viewed as a partisan figure first, a national figure second; as devious and unfair in his debating tactics—a master of unsupported innuendo."

And so Dick campaigned as "Nixon as nice guy" (as he scornfully put it in private), a contrivance "to placate the Eastern Establishment press." And it worked.

Moderates and conservatives—even card-carrying liberals—were shaken by the violent twists of 1968. Humphrey seemed a gasbag and Wallace an abomination. Nixon came across as a reassuring, stolid centrist, with foreign policy experience that might give him an edge and bring sense to the shambles in Southeast Asia. He spoke movingly of the need for "the lift of a driving dream" that would invigorate America.

"Nixon now appears to be a softer, more mellow, more self-confident, more amusing well-to-do lawyer-statesman," White wrote in his notes. "There is this perplexity in me . . . of why I find him a good man now." Walter Lippmann, the nation's foremost liberal columnist, endorsed him as a "maturer and mellower man." A young navy officer named Bob Woodward cast his vote for Nixon, convinced he was the candidate who could end the war.

"For years I've regarded his very existence as a monument to all the rancid genes and broken chromosomes that corrupt the possibilities of the American Dream; he was a foul caricature of himself, a man with no soul, no inner convictions, with the integrity of a hyena and the style of a poison toad," wrote the counterculture journalist Hunter Thompson. But after getting Nixon's "nice guy" treatment in a car ride in which they shared their passion for pro football, Thompson reported that "I came away convinced that Richard Nixon has one of the best minds in politics. . . . This new model might be different. . . . The 'new Nixon' is more relaxed, wiser, more mellow."

Dick Schaap, a gifted feature writer, was assigned to write on Nixon for *New York* magazine, that tout sheet of hip. He had expected to find the Old Nixon, the one whose "name was invoked to frighten little liberal children." But Nixon "fell short of being the personification of evil," Schaap confessed. He now seemed like an appealing underdog, "in the grand style of the New York Mets." The left had "lost faith . . . after offering their hearts to Lyndon Johnson," Schaap explained. "Instead of seeing opposing views as black and white now, they see them more often as black and grey." So what if Nixon used racial code words like *law and order.* "Nixon is merely playing the game," Schaap wrote. "And if it is a dirty, degrading game—and it is—he did not invent it."

The emblematic Nixon, the personification of middle America ("We are all of us Nixon, and he is us," said Gore Vidal), reemerged in the pages of glossy magazines. Not as a herald of "peevish, resentful whine," as Murray Kempton had put it a decade earlier—this time as a symbol of grit, tenacity, and hope. But mellowed.

Harper's dispatched novelist Norman Mailer to cover the campaign. He was struck, first off, by the loveliness of Nixon's daughters. Tricia was "gentle, bemused, a misty look to her face but incontestably a beauty" with a complexion of "alabaster and ivory." Julie was "brown-haired, apple-cheeked, snub-nosed . . . healthy, genial, a perfect soubrette." Mailer confessed that "nothing in his prior view of Nixon had ever prepared him to conceive of a man with two lovely girls." When Nixon joined his family at the scene, the author asked, "Was it even possible that he was a good man, not a bad man?"

Mailer retained a suspicion that the latest Nixon was an artifice—that "the young devil had reconstituted himself into a more consummate devil, Old Scratch as a modern Abe Lincoln." But he prayed it was not so. "It might even be a measure of the not-entirely dead promise of America if a man as opportunistic as the early Nixon could grow in reach and comprehension and stature to become a leader," Mailer wrote. "For if that were possible in these bad years, then all was still possible, and the country not stripped of its blessing."

THE CHALLENGE TO Nixon's nomination came from a skulk of moderate Republicans led by Rockefeller and Governor George Romney of Michigan, and (after defeating Pat Brown in 1966) the newly minted governor of California, Ronald Reagan. Rocky had no friends on the right, and while conservatives loved Reagan, many in the party still winced at the memory of the Goldwater debacle and believed the former movie star lacked gravitas and experience.

That left Romney. Nixon had taken stock of him during the 1964 campaign and come away thinking that Romney lacked both brains and guts. In one of his shrewder political maneuvers, Nixon declared "a holiday from politics" in 1967, went globetrotting, and let the spotlight swing to the Michigan governor. "Let them chew on him for a while," Nixon told Buchanan. Sure enough, Romney plummeted in the polls after declaring that he had "changed his mind" on the Vietnam War. His previous support was the result of a Pentagon "brainwashing," he explained. As Gene McCarthy was said to have remarked, "a light rinse would have been sufficient."

Romney quit the race two weeks before the New Hampshire primary, handing Nixon the big victory he needed to give the lie to his reputation as unelectable. As in 1960, he was seen as a pragmatist—tolerated if not especially loved by the antipathetic wings of his party, but a hero to its middle, with a fat wad of IOUs pocketed in all those years of Podunk rallies and peas-and-chicken Lincoln Day banquets. He appeared to have clinched the Republican nomination before a single vote was cast, unless Rocky and Reagan were to join in a cynical stop-Nixon alliance.

Which of course, this being the annus mirabilis of 1968, is what happened.

—

Rocky had the newspapers' regard, a credible patter, New York's delegates, and the cash to stage a show. But, typically, he had wavered—renouncing the race in winter, then changing his mind in spring. The bigger threat was Reagan. The fifty-seven-year-old California governor was Goldwater without the crust—a herald of conservatism whose sunny, almost mystical surety inspired his followers and disarmed doubters. The right might appear quiescent, but a flame still danced in millions of hearts, and Reagan had the gifts to fan it.

Nixon recognized this. No Republican candidate could "stray too far from the right wingers," he told an aide who had been prodding him to move leftward. The conservatives could swing a presidential primary or, if inadequately courted, stay home and doom a candidate in the general election. "The far right kooks are just like the nuts on the left," he said. "They're door bell ringers and balloon blowers [and] they turn out to vote."

The key to stopping Nixon, for Reagan, was the South. The Republican Party's growth in the region had been slow but ceaseless in the postwar era as the Democratic Party, after years of failing to address the evils of segregation, broke apart over race and fumbled its hold on a region it had ruled since the days of Reconstruction. Eisenhower had taken Virginia, Tennessee, Texas, and Florida in 1952 and added Louisiana in 1956. Nixon almost matched him in 1960, winning Florida, Virginia, and Tennessee, and coming close in Texas and the Carolinas.*

"Ike's campaign was really the first campaign that made a two-party area out of the South," former GOP chairman Leonard Hall recalled. Young veterans home from World War II, chafing at the way that the Democratic courthouse gangs kept a grip on their communities, had looked to General Eisenhower's party as a more inviting outlet for their ambition. By 1968, Republicans like John Tower and George H. W. Bush of Texas, Linwood Holton of Virginia, and Howard Baker and William Brock of Tennessee were taking advantage of the Democratic disarray, and corralling converts in the growing southern middle class.

The Republican Party found it as difficult as its rival to deal honorably with the issue of race. It sipped from exhilarating bigotry in 1964, when

* Republican Herbert Hoover took five states of the old Confederacy from the Roman Catholic Democrat Al Smith in 1928, before Franklin Roosevelt's political gifts and the effects of the Depression restored order.

the Goldwater campaign, championing opposition to the Civil Rights Act, broke the Democratic lock on deepest Dixie, carrying South Carolina, Georgia, Alabama, Mississippi, and Louisiana in the teeth of the Johnson landslide. The scale of the backlash was stunning: Goldwater reaped an astonishing 87 percent of the vote in Mississippi and 70 percent in Alabama. In Leake County, in central Mississippi, where Nixon had earned just 9 percent of the vote in 1960, Goldwater won with 96 percent. The 1964 results gave the southern delegations disproportionate clout at the 1968 convention. If Reagan could stir enough emotion and start a stampede, Nixon might fall short on the first ballot.

But as the South was the key to the nomination, so the key to the South was Strom Thurmond—and Nixon had that key tucked in his pocket. The South Carolina senator had evolved some since the day in 1948 when he and his Dixiecrats stormed out of the Democratic convention to protest the platform's modest nod to civil rights ("Racial and religious minorities must have the right to live, the right to work, the right to vote and full and equal protection of the laws"). In 1964, Thurmond switched parties and became a Republican. He still cared about segregation, but not exclusively. He was a dedicated anti-Communist, and military spending was an economic mainstay in his state. So was the textile industry, protected by federal trade rules.

Mostly, Thurmond wanted to win. He had seen what happened in 1964 and dreaded the prospect of four more years of liberal programs, liberal taxes, and liberal appointees to the federal bench. Nixon could unite the Republican Party and was willing to make the necessary genuflections. Forgotten was their warring over the 1957 civil rights bill—when Nixon had defied the segregationists, and Thurmond had waged the Senate's longest filibuster. "Strom is no racist," Nixon told reporters on a visit to South Carolina in 1966. "Strom is a man of courage and integrity." The South needed sympathy and understanding, Nixon said. Southerners "didn't want to be treated like national pariahs, they wanted recognition, their right to be heard," he told White.

That was enough for Thurmond, who sealed the deal and endorsed Nixon at a summit of southern Republicans in June. And, in the end, it was good enough for the South. An enterprising reporter from the *Miami Herald* smuggled a tape recorder into Nixon's closed-door meeting with southern delegations at the Republican convention. He was going to be a "national" candidate, Nixon said, considering the feelings of *all* regions. He promised to appoint conservative judges, keep America strong, and govern with moderation.

The first question raised by the delegates concerned compulsory busing—the newest formula for mixing the races. Integrating schools in the rural South was a relatively straightforward task, but pulling black students from the poorer sections of Richmond, Charlotte, or Atlanta—or Detroit, Boston, or Los Angeles—and busing them to white neighborhoods was a politically explosive, expensive, and dubious proposition. Often, it spurred a "white flight" that undercut support for public school systems. In Boston, the number of white students in the public schools dropped from forty-five thousand in 1974 to sixteen thousand in 1987. Even among black parents, in public opinion polls, the remedy barely won majority support. And for the southern and working-class whites Nixon was courting, busing was anathema.

"My feeling is this: I think that busing the child—a child that is two or three grades behind another child—into a strange community . . . I think you destroy that child," Nixon told the southern delegates. The country certainly needed to get about the business of "building bridges to human dignity" but not "try to satisfy some professional civil rights group, or something like that, that we will bus the child from one side of the county over to the other."

His opposition to busing was Nixon's sole explicit pitch on race to white southerners (and their northern kin) in the 1968 campaign. If John Kennedy and Lyndon Johnson had—somewhat slowly in Kennedy's case and more enthusiastically in Johnson's—aligned the moral authority of the presidency with the cause of civil rights, Nixon would return to Eisenhower's policy of enforcing the law, and little more.* But he made no blatant racist appeals. No son of Hannah Nixon would endeavor to "out-nigger" the Democrats, as Wallace had once, so felicitously, described his own strategy.

Nixon had supported the Civil Rights and Voting Rights Acts, and in 1968 he endorsed the Fair Housing Act. He would not compete with Wallace in the core states of the Confederacy. "Forget the Goldwater South," Nixon told his aides. "You can't just echo Wallace," he said. "You've got

---

* "He has unlimited power to express the moral sense of the people," the disappointed White House aide Arthur Schlesinger Jr. wrote about President Kennedy and civil rights in a May 8, 1963, diary entry. "In not doing so, he is acting much like Eisenhower used to act when we [liberals] denounced him so."

to be more sophisticated." What came to be known as "Nixon's southern strategy" was, in fact, discreet. He kept with Bush, Baker, Brock, and
other moderates, relying on a message that was low-tax and pro-business,
stressed national defense, lauded traditional values, opposed busing, and
targeted Southern suburbs—and ethnic neighborhoods in northern
cities—with calls for law and order.

Haldeman recorded Nixon's private thoughts during a meeting in July.
"RN has emotional access to lower middle class white—not fair [to call
them] racist—but concerned re crime & violence, law & order," Haldeman wrote in his notes. The Roman Catholic minorities—"Irish, Ital, Pole,
Mex"—were "afraid of Negroes," and should be targeted after the convention. "Need stronger N position on this operationally—must do something," Nixon told Haldeman. "Must dry up Wallace vote."

"Law and order" was a legitimate issue—and a euphemism. The violent
crime rate doubled in the 1960s. Any dutiful candidate for office, responding to the public's yearnings in 1968, had to condemn violence and call
for the reassertion of authority. Not to do so, in a year so drenched in
death, blood, and lawlessness, was political malfeasance. Robert Kennedy,
a case in point, campaigned as a crime-busting attorney general. In the
Indiana primary, Kennedy sought "to identify himself with the yearnings
of the great centrist majority" and spoke like "a reconditioned Barry Goldwater plugging for 'law and order,'" *Newsweek* reported. While debating
Gene McCarthy in the California primary, Kennedy chided his opponent
for suggesting that low-cost housing be built outside the ghettoes. "You
say you are going to take ten thousand black people and move them into
Orange County . . . where their children can't keep up with the schools,
and where they don't have the skills for jobs," said Kennedy. "It is just
going to be catastrophic."

In a memo to Nixon's campaign managers, a number-crunching wun-
derkind named Kevin Phillips identified the guiding dynamic of the 1968
election as the "law and order/Negro socio-economic revolution syndrome."
There was no need for explicit racial appeals. "In the public perception, all
these things merged," wrote political scientist James Sundquist. "Ghetto
riots, campus riots, street crime, anti-Vietnam marches, poor people's
marches, drugs, pornography, welfarism, rising taxes, all had a common
thread: the breakdown of family and social discipline, of order, of concepts
of duty, of respect for law, of public and private morality."

Nixon was what stood, his supporters told themselves, between Wallace and the presidency. While there was doubtless an element of rationalization in this, to his aides he was Horatius, astride the bridge and holding off barbarians of all complexion.

"We are dealing with large numbers of Negroes who harbor . . . a suicidal and blindly destructive hatred of the white-dominated society," Richard Whalen wrote in a memo to Nixon. "If their hate cannot be extinguished by concrete gestures of help and sincere words of hope, then it must be extinguished by force." For the real danger was on the right, said Whalen. If responsible men like Nixon did not assert control, demagogues could seize power. "If and when this under-class erupts in full fury, the popular support for equally savage repression will cast up a new breed of leader—Wallace is the first."

Whalen was a conservative, but more than a few liberal intellectuals shared his fears. "We would be hiding our heads in the sand," columnist Walter Lippmann wrote, "if we refused to admit that the country may demand and necessity may dictate the repression of uncontrollable violence. . . . It is better that Mr. Nixon should have the full authority if repression should become necessary in order to restore peace and tranquility at home. . . . Repression of some sort may be unavoidable."

And so in his speeches, and magazine articles like "What Has Happened to America?" and "If Mob Rule Takes Hold in U.S.," Nixon restated the winning thesis from all those teenage speaking contests back in Whittier: that liberty is not a ticket for license, violence, and chaos. The majority had its rights. "There can be no progress without order, no freedom without order, no justice without order," he said.

It was enough to cost Nixon, among other things, the support of his old friend Jackie Robinson. Yet Nixon took pains not to inflame. He was offering calm and accord—not further division—to fretful Americans. The intentional polarization came later—during his presidency. The rioters portrayed in the Nixon campaign ads were white, and the villains that he denounced in his speeches were pornographers, dope peddlers, permissive judges, and the dons of organized crime—not ghetto children. His was a campaign of "social stolidity," not racial passion, noted political scientists Richard Scammon and Ben Wattenberg. He stood for stability, for "stopping history in mid-dissolution," wrote Garry Wills, who followed Nixon as he campaigned that year.

In decades to come, Nixon's liberal critics would dismiss the previous one hundred years—in which such progressive icons as William Jennings

Bryan and Franklin Roosevelt declined to support anti-lynching measures and other civil rights remedies for fear of offending the Democrats of Dixie—and start the clock on the political exploitation of racism with the 1968 campaign. There was some of that, but Nixon also spoke with insight and decency. In a national radio address, he asked: "Are we to become two nations, one black, one white, poised for irrepressible conflict?"

"The answer is no," Nixon said. "Only if we can light hope . . . can we have peace," Nixon said. "We must move with both compassion and conviction to bring the American dream to the ghetto."

And to an audience in a prosperous Philadelphia suburb, Nixon said: "You are fortunate people, but you know that in the great cities of America there is terrible poverty. There are poor people. There are people who haven't had a chance—the chance that you've had."

"You can't be an island in the world," Nixon told them. "You can't live in your comfortable houses and say, 'Well, just as long as I get mine, I don't have to worry about the others . . .' This isn't going to be a good country for any of us to live in until it's a good country for all of us to live in."

It was a rhetorical tightrope, but few were as accomplished as Nixon at walking the wire.

Still, there was a moment, at the Republican convention, when loud rumor spoke: Reagan was on the move; the South was up for grabs; Nixon would be stopped. Campaign manager John Mitchell conveyed his fear to Nixon that a "southern rebellion" was "on the brink of becoming serious." The South was "up in arms" at reports that the liberal senator Mark Hatfield of Oregon or New York mayor John Lindsay was to be Nixon's running mate. "All we need is just one break—one state switching to Reagan—and we've got him," the governor's delegate hunter, Clif White, told the press.

But Thurmond stood for Nixon like Jackson at Manassas, assuring the delegates that the South would be consulted on the choice of the vice-presidential nominee. Goldwater, remembering who had campaigned across the country for him in 1964, backed Nixon. And Nixon dispatched Mitchell to see Peter O'Donnell, the Texas state chairman, with messages to "cool off the southerners." They should know, Nixon said, that in choosing a running mate he would not "ram someone down your throat." They should also know that Nixon, like Eisenhower, "will bring peace" on civil rights and "lay off pro-Negro crap," Nixon said.

Nixon, moreover, still had that bag of IOUs. "I was the southern chairman for him in 1968," Brock recalled. "I worked the country for him—in part because I owed him. He came to me [in Brock's early campaigns] when nobody else would come. And I appreciated that." In years gone by, Mississippi's Clarke Reed had called on both Reagan and Nixon to help build the Republican Party in his state. Nixon had shown up, Reagan had not. "Perhaps you had better try where you have a few favors owing," Reed told the California governor.

The rebellion fizzled. In 1964, the conservatives "had our shot at a candidate who totally met our qualifications and that candidate got six states," Louisiana committeeman Tom Stagg told reporters. "We've had our druthers. Now shall we win one?" Reagan retired from the field, looking toward another day. Rockefeller slunk home: his third campaign for the presidency had ended like the others.

The South got its deserts when Nixon chose Maryland governor Spiro Agnew, a handsome mediocrity from a border state, as his running mate. Ward Just, writing for the *Washington Post,* said that Agnew's selection was to be regarded as "perhaps the most eccentric political appointment since the Roman emperor Caligula named his horse a consul." Even given the tinseled folderols of politics, Nixon showed a special chutzpah when hailing Agnew as "a statesman of the first rank."

The selection of Spiro Agnew revealed Nixon at his worst. It was a cynical nod, a race-baiting wink—and a catastrophic blunder. It was Nixon's first "presidential" decision—the choosing of a running mate—and a disaster. "What appealed most to Nixon was Agnew at his public worst—administering a demagogic public tongue-lashing to black leaders in Baltimore after the riots following the death of Martin Luther King," wrote Robert Novak. Meanwhile, "in the absence of any vetting process, nobody suspected that Agnew was one of the most crooked politicians in America."

NIXON SHOWED BOTH calculation and refinement in the acceptance speech he had crafted in seclusion on the Atlantic shore at Montauk, New York, in the week before the convention. Once again, he aimed his remarks at his "forgotten" Americans. Over the years, he would call them the "silent center," or "the great Silent Majority" and, later on, the "New American Majority." They were soldiers in a conservative revolution that began in opposition to the New Deal during the Taft and Eisenhower years, flared with Goldwater in 1964, swelled in the Nixon era, and triumphed at century's end. They were self-made men "in an age when self-made men were not honored for the agony of their creation," Wills wrote. They were those whom Nixon relied upon in 1946 ("Richard Nixon is one of us"), and those he aimed the Checkers speech toward in 1952.

The great silent majority lived south of the Potomac and west of the Appalachians, or in tight-knit ethnic neighborhoods in northern cities. The nation's advertising agencies, pitching soft drinks and automobiles, depicted them as steadfast, the salt of the earth, driving Chevys, hunting and fishing, watching NASCAR or the NFL, or playing summer softball. They donned their best clothes and went to church on Sundays; bowed their heads, held hands, and said grace before dinner. They gave their time to the Boy Scouts, the Rotary, and the Jaycees. They honored Old Glory. They laughed with Bob Hope and cheered John Wayne. Their sons volunteered to fight in Vietnam. It is no accident that the painting of Richard Nixon that hangs in the National Portrait Gallery in Washington is one by Norman Rockwell. "The Irish, Italian, Polish Catholics of the big cities—these are our electoral majority—they, and the white Protestants of the South and Midwest and rural America," Buchanan advised his boss.

Nixon "emotionally related to these people," said aide Tom Huston about those Americans that H. L. Mencken, in one of his less acidic appraisals, called "the plain folk." Nixon was "a guy who never should have been an effective political figure in terms of personality . . . but in his gut he understood the middle class and the working middle class," said Huston. "He understood when they felt they were being put upon, because he felt he had been put upon." The candidate and his supporters shared that sense of grievance: that others were being handed what they had worked so hard to come by. His childhood was "pretty tough," Nixon would recall, "particularly compared with . . . most young people, including those living in ghettoes, who were supposed to be deprived."

In the realignment in American politics in the late twentieth century, Nixon was a key transitional figure. He and his "forgotten" felt besieged in 1968. They could not relate to those other Americans, restless in affluence, collecting on campuses from Cambridge to Berkeley, in the newsrooms of Manhattan or the lanes of the Hollywood hills, who found not comfort but witless conformity in hallowed ways and tradition. The chic cheered liberation. They wore their hair long, sampled recreational drugs, and embraced new sensibilities of fashion, sex, music, film, and art. Their movies honored outlaws—*Bonnie and Clyde, Cool Hand Luke, The Graduate*—and they seemed to have limitless depths of sympathy for those who opposed the System. They had first marveled at, then embraced, the civil rights movement, and moved from there to support an array of new rights—for women, gay Americans, atheists, artists, criminal defendants, and welfare recipients. "The man who works hard, pays his taxes, rears his children—the man who has always been the hero of the American folk mythology—now finds himself living in an era where the glorified man is the antihero: morose, introspective, unconcerned with God, country, family or tax bill," Scammon and Wattenberg noted.

The nightly TV news conveyed unsettling imagery. Much of it—the separatist rhetoric and assassination of Malcolm X, the march of Black Panthers, the taunts of Muhammad Ali—worked like bellows on old racial fears. Others—the sniper Charles Whitman's murderous spree from a tower at the University of Texas, the killing of student nurses by Richard Speck in Chicago—were terrifyingly random. "There was a sense everywhere, in 1968, that things were giving. That man had not merely lost control of his history, but might never regain it," wrote Wills. And as the cities burned, and the antiwar cadres moved from flowers to arson and TNT, the fear and anger in the midlands grew. Nixon "knew a lot about America," Democratic speechwriter Richard Goodwin recalled. "He could reach, with uncanny intuition, the buried doubts, the secret dreads, the nightmare panic of the threatened soul."

"Peace in the family" had been Nixon's mantra for the Republican primaries. Now it was time to launch the "crusade," he told his aides. The targets in the general election, Nixon said, were angry and resentful low- and moderate-income white suburban voters, many working blue-collar jobs. He and his samurai called them "the gut vote." And his acceptance speech, as *Time* put it, was a masterful mix "of carefully balanced political calculation and genuine personal warmth" aimed at the "nice people," as one Republican senator called the delegates, who had "never ridden a subway."

As we look at America, we see cities enveloped in smoke and flame. We hear sirens in the night. We see Americans dying on distant battlefields abroad. We see Americans hating each other; fighting each other; killing each other at home.

And as we see and hear these things, millions of Americans cry out in anguish. Did we come all this way for this? Did American boys die in Normandy, and Korea, and in Valley Forge for this?

Listen to the answer to those questions.

It is another voice. It is the quiet voice in the tumult and the shouting. It is the voice of the great majority of Americans, the forgotten Americans—the non-shouters; the non-demonstrators.

They are not racists or sick; they are not guilty of the crime that plagues the land. They are black and they are white—they're native born and foreign born—they're young and they're old.

They work in America's factories. They run America's businesses. They serve in government. They provide most of the soldiers who died to keep us free.

They give drive to the spirit of America. They give lift to the American Dream. They give steel to the backbone of America. They are good people, they are decent people; they work, and they save, and they pay their taxes, and they care.

Nixon promised to bring the good and decent people peace. Not just any peace—not some turn-tail retreat. But peace with honor. For the good and decent people, he said, had been betrayed by their leaders.

When the strongest nation in the world can be tied down for four years in a war in Vietnam with no end in sight . . .

When the richest nation in the world can't manage its own economy . . .

When the nation with the greatest tradition of the rule of law is plagued by unprecedented lawlessness . . .

When a nation that has been known for a century for equality of opportunity is torn by unprecedented racial violence . . .

And when the President of the United States cannot travel abroad or to any major city at home without fear of a hostile demonstration—then it's time for new leadership for the United States of America. . . .

To them Richard Nixon said: I am one of you. In his own climb to the pinnacle, in his great fall and rise again, he cast himself as an emblem of the American Dream, which he vowed to replenish in a Nixon presidency.

Tonight, I see the face of a child. He lives in a great city. He is black. Or he is white. He is Mexican, Italian, Polish. None of that matters. What matters, he's an American child.

That child in that great city is more important than any politician's promise. He is America. He is a poet. He is a scientist, he is a great teacher, he is a proud craftsman. He is everything we ever hoped to be and everything we dare to dream to be.

He sleeps the sleep of childhood and he dreams the dreams of a child. And yet when he awakens, he awakens to a living nightmare of poverty, neglect and despair. He fails in school.

He ends up on welfare. For him the American system is one that feeds his stomach and starves his soul. It breaks his heart. And in the end it may take his life on some distant battlefield.

To millions of children in this rich land, this is their prospect of the future. But this is only part of what I see in America.

I see another child tonight.

He hears the train go by at night and he dreams of far away places where he'd like to go.

It seems like an impossible dream.

But he is helped on his journey through life.

A father who had to go to work before he finished the sixth grade, sacrificed everything he had so that his sons could go to college. A gentle, Quaker mother, with a passionate concern for peace, quietly wept when he went to war but she understood why he had to go. A great teacher, a remarkable football coach, an inspirational minister encouraged him on his way.

A courageous wife and loyal children stood by him in victory and also defeat.

And in his chosen profession of politics, first there were scores, then hundreds, then thousands, and finally millions worked for his success.

And tonight he stands before you—nominated for President of the United States of America.

My fellow Americans, the long dark night for America is about to end.

It was, indeed, a long night. At 1:30 a.m., Safire was summoned to Nixon's suite, where he found the candidate in a familiar pose: coming down from a big moment, nursing a drink, wanting to talk, running on adrenaline after almost no sleep in thirty-six hours. "None of them could write a speech like that," Nixon said of his Establishment critics, "and they hate me for it." An hour passed, Safire told his diary, and Nixon was "nodding, eyes closing, holding on to the same drink"—with his insecurities on full display. "They won't like the speech, will they?" Nixon asked. "The *New York Times* and those boys. Fuck 'em."

Rockefeller and Lindsay were elitists, he said. They could not speak to the American heartland about an "impossible dream." But he and "Ike could give a speech like that. We both started with nothing. We're emotional," Nixon said. "They call me intelligent and cool and no sincerity and then it kills them when I show 'em I know how people feel."

It was after 3 a.m. when Safire said good night, leaving the candidate dazed with fatigue, leaning against a wall, still too wired to sleep, and asking the Secret Service if there wasn't someplace open where he could get a sandwich and a glass of milk.

NIXON HAD LEARNED some, in his fifty-five years. He had given much thought to presidential candidacy, analyzed the flaws of his 1960 campaign, and taken steps to correct them. For the general election, he handed Mitchell and Haldeman authentic authority. Nixon could not resist the urge to dash off memos on the conduct of the operation ("We need to mention crime in every speech"), but he tried not to be the candidate who carped over every last detail.

The campaign tried, in return, to maintain a comfortable, controlled climate. Nixon's schedule was detailed, the operation crisp. "We should continue endeavoring to keep the day of telecast uncluttered for RN . . . and provide him with sufficient time at the studio to be alone for ten minutes, in a cool room, collecting his thoughts, just prior to air," one memo noted.

The primary target was not the political bosses, or the press, or the crowds—it was those at home, watching television. Looking back at past campaigns, Haldeman asked, in a memo to Nixon: "What happens to the candidate in this process? He becomes punchy, mauled by his admirers, jeered and deflated by his opponent's supporters (and paid troublemakers), misled by the super-stimulation of one frenzied rally after another. He has no time to think, to study his opponent's strategy and statements, to develop his own strategy." Unconsciously borrowing some totalitarian imagery from the likes of Aldous Huxley and George Orwell, Haldeman argued that "the time has come for political campaigning . . . to move out of the dark ages and into the brave new world of the omnipresent 'eye.'"

Haldeman took it even further after Robert Kennedy was shot, when he suggested that Nixon abandon *all* personal appearances. "Eliminated would be all rallies, large public functions, press-the-flesh campaign techniques, plunging through crowds, whistle-and-prop stops," the adman wrote. "Instead, utilize the mass communications media." They never went quite that far, but Haldeman and his aides exercised their beliefs about television that fall. Nixon's schedule would be culled to produce one newsworthy event per day. Their rested candidate could then perform at his best—relaxed, on his feet, projecting authenticity.

"The greater the element of informality and spontaneity the better he comes across," Price wrote. "We have to capture and capsule this spontaneity—and this means shooting RN in situations in which it's likely to emerge, then having a chance to edit the film so that the parts shown are the parts we want shown." The discussion led them to notably effective "man in the arena" events. The campaign staged ten hour-long TV shows in which Nixon stood on a circular stage, enveloped by the audience, and fielded questions from a panel of voters.

"The look has guts," producer Roger Ailes told his colleagues. "The subliminal message of the 'arena' works."

"Even if a viewer is not in favor of Richard Nixon, by 15 minutes into the program he almost subconsciously begins to root for him because of the odds. . . . he's alone. . . . he's standing while all others are comfortably seated. . . . he has no place for notes . . . he is surrounded by people looking into the pit at him, and most people would think of that as a nightmare," Ailes wrote. "The feeling is that anyone who can do that on 'live' television, keep his cool, and not be stuck for an answer must certainly be admired."

Color television helped Nixon by restoring flesh tones; so did tanning sessions and expertly applied makeup. Spotlights were aimed at the shadows of his eyes. Nixon had a phobia about being televised from his left: the cameramen were so instructed, and the studio was chilled, to cut down his perspiration. Pat and the girls were seated in the audience, for moral support and homey appeal. The questions were not screened, and he took inquiries that ran the gamut: from anti-Semitism to civil rights, the Vietnam War, and relations with the Soviet Union.

"The response is to the image, not to the man," Price wrote. "It's not what's there that counts, it's what's projected."

"Reason pushes the viewer back, it assaults him, it demands that he agree or disagree," noted Nixon speechwriter William Gavin. "Impression can envelop him, invite him in, without making an intellectual demand."

NIXON STARTED THE fall campaign with a huge lead over his challengers. In early September he was dreaming of a landslide, of a size and scope that would give Republicans control of Congress. A young aide, Alan Greenspan, crafted an Election Day simulation, based on the polls, that had Nixon winning 461 electoral votes, to 11 for Humphrey and 66 for Wallace, who was running a third-party crusade on the American Independent

Party ticket. The Nixon campaign went into a tuck. It suffered, one aide recalled, from "platitudinous wishy-washiness." It became, Buchanan said, "programmed, repetitious and boring."

Nixon knew it would not last—that blue-collar Democrats siding with Wallace would return to the Democratic Party if its nominee showed the slightest hint of life. Humphrey did so in a speech in Salt Lake City on September 30, when he opened a sliver of daylight between his position on Vietnam and that of the Johnson administration. The press craved a contest and—reverting to form at the thought of a Nixon landslide—hailed Humphrey's tiptoe as a defining act. Liberal donors reached for their checkbooks, and Humphrey's campaign manager, the skilled Lawrence O'Brien, got the wheezing party machinery chugging. Labor leaders reminded their rank and file of the causal connection between higher wages and electing Democrats.

After Johnson withdrew from the race to focus on making peace, Nixon had been pleased to declare a self-imposed moratorium on commenting about the Vietnam War. "Non-specificity is desirable," Phillips advised his candidate. "No articulate or definitive position should be taken viz the war in Vietnam . . . the lack of an ideological position helps make RN a rallying point for a cross-section of voters disgusted with the war. . . . RN must paint himself as a responsible, experienced peacemaker in the Eisenhower-Korea vein, labeling HHH as an architect of past war policy and implying that . . . Wallace . . . is inexperienced and trigger happy."

But Nixon's silence stretched into the fall. Mark Hatfield remembered how, four years earlier, Johnson had misled the voters. The senator chided Nixon for peddling a pig in a poke. "In 1964 the American people—trusting the campaign promises of the Democratic presidential candidate—thought they were voting for peace, only to have their trust betrayed," Hatfield wrote in a Republican Party publication. "Caution growing out of a sense of responsibility should not be confused with caution growing out of political calculation. The Paris peace talks should not become the skirts for timid men to hide behind."

Nixon spurned Hatfield and other critics and stuck with the palliative of "peace with honor." Wallace assisted in his own destruction, reminding the electorate of his incompatibility for the Oval Office by naming retired air force general Curtis LeMay as his running mate. As Wallace stood by glumly at a press conference, the hawkish LeMay recited paeans to nuclear warfare. Wallace had to step in and stop him, and LeMay belatedly recognized his mistake. He had not intended to come across "as a drooling idiot whose only solution to any problem is to drop atomic bombs all over the world," he told the press. "I assure you I'm not." Soon Michigan, New York, and Pennsylvania were sliding back into Democratic hands, as Humphrey began closing a 15-point gap in the polls.

THE NORTH VIETNAMESE, meanwhile, had suffered grievously in the Tet Offensive. Their Soviet quartermasters, preferring to deal with a President Humphrey, pressed them to be pliable. To better Humphrey's chances, and keep Nixon from the White House, Soviet premier Alexei Kosygin wrote to Lyndon Johnson, offering a deal that summer. If Johnson would halt all bombing of North Vietnam, Moscow would compel Hanoi to engage in constructive talks. "I and my colleagues believe—and we have grounds for this—that a full cessation by the United States of bombardments . . . could promote a breakthrough," Kosygin promised. The odds had never looked better for a settlement of the war, which had already claimed 30,000 American lives.

In 1966, Johnson had made an election-eve dash to Manila to hype the prospects for peace. Now, after a postconvention briefing at the LBJ Ranch, in which Johnson told Nixon there was cause for optimism, "I knew what was coming," Nixon recalled. Big events, like a breakthrough in Southeast Asia, could "change people," he feared. "Events could cut down a lead as big as ours."

The Nixon campaign had moles within the Johnson administration— Harvard's Henry Kissinger was a particularly indiscreet visitor to the American delegation in Paris—and so was not surprised when, five days before the election, Johnson announced a bombing halt to spur negotiations. With Moscow pressing Hanoi, LBJ and his advisers believed they had a genuine opportunity to end the war. On October 28, after leaving a dinner meeting at the White House, Johnson's national security adviser, Walt Rostow, composed a late-night letter to the president. "There were four people in that room at dinner tonight, aside from yourself, who have lived Vietnam, with all its pain, since January, 1961: [Secretary of State Dean] Rusk, [General Maxwell] Taylor, [General Earle] Wheeler and myself. All of us know that, with all its uncertainties, we have the best deal we now can get—vastly better than any we thought we could get since 1961," Rostow wrote. "If we go ahead we know it may be tough. But with military and political determination we believe we can make it stick. . . . None of us would know how to justify delay."

But Nixon was distressed. After 1960, he put nothing past his enemies. "To him, it was a very personal thing," aide Tom Huston recalled.

So began "the Chennault affair."

THE KEY TO a settlement was the Communists' inalterable demand that they hold an ascending share of power in South Vietnam. Doves like Kennedy and McCarthy had been willing to entertain the possibility of a coalition government with the Viet Cong. But persuading President Thieu to participate would never be an easy task—and likely impossible once Nixon urged him to resist.

Nixon employed Anna Chennault and South Vietnamese ambassador Bui Diem as conduits to let Thieu know that Saigon would get a better deal if he helped elect a Republican president. Anna was the China-born widow of Claire Chennault, the U.S. general who organized the Flying Tigers, a squadron of American pilots that battled the Japanese in China during World War II. She was a noted hostess, a Nixon fund-raiser, and a grandee of the China lobby, with friends in the palaces of Asia. Some called her the Dragon Lady; others, the Little Flower. It did not take much to persuade Thieu. He dragged his feet, the press headlined his intransigence, and soon Johnson's plan was looking like an election-year Hail Mary.

"We could stop the killing out there," Johnson insisted to his friend Everett Dirksen, the Republican leader in the Senate. "But they've got this . . . new formula put in there—namely, wait on Nixon. And they're killing four or five hundred a day waiting on Nixon."

The political *pop!* of the bombing halt was sapped by Thieu's obstruction. Haldeman's notes from the 1968 campaign show how Nixon personally directed the skullduggery—conducting backstage negotiations with a foreign country in violation of U.S. law.*

"Keep Anna Chennault working on SVN," Nixon ordered Haldeman, at the peak of the intrigue.

In the background, in their midnight telephone conversations, Haldeman could hear Nixon playing the *"Victory at Sea* album—loud."† Nixon gave him Chennault's latest report on how the Thieu government and the

---

* "Nixon never admitted this," Kissinger wrote in his memoir, *Ending the Vietnam War.* "It would have been highly inappropriate if true." Under federal law, which bans private citizens from undercutting the government by negotiating with foreign powers, Nixon's actions were potentially felonious.

† Nixon loved, and often played, his recording of the rousing Richard Rodgers and Robert Russell Bennett score to *Victory at Sea,* a 1950s documentary on World War II.

U.S. commander in Saigon, General Creighton Abrams, had reacted to prospects of a bombing halt: "D. Lady says Abrams screamed like stuck pig." Elsewhere in his notes Haldeman reports Nixon asking, "Any other way to monkey wrench it? Anything RN can do" as well as Nixon's suggestion that Rose Woods call Louis Kung, another nationalist Chinese figure, and get him going "on the SVN—tell him hold firm."

A NEW YORK businessman who chanced upon the plot alerted the White House to Nixon's machinations. The U.S. government eavesdropped on communications to and from the South Vietnamese embassy in Washington and Thieu's office in Saigon. Johnson had "the Dragon Lady" placed under surveillance. The FBI traced the phone calls made by Agnew's campaign staff.

Some of the wiretaps brought fruit. "Anna Chennault contacted Vietnam Ambassador Bui Diem," a report noted, "and advised him that she had received a message from her boss . . . which her boss wanted her to give personally to the ambassador. She said the message was that, 'Hold on. We are gonna win. . . . Please tell your boss to hold on.'"

Transcripts in hand, Johnson blamed Nixon for strangling a chance for peace. He lashed out in a November 2 telephone call with Dirksen.

"I'm reading their hand, Everett," Johnson told his old friend. "This is treason."

"I know," Dirksen said sadly.

But Johnson did not have Haldeman's notes—or other conclusive evidence of Nixon's personal involvement. And Nixon, alerted to Johnson's rage, denied it all in a November 3 call to the president.

"My God, I would never do anything to encourage . . . Saigon not to come to the table," Nixon assured Johnson. "Good God, we want them over in Paris. We've got to get them to Paris or you can't have a peace."

Rostow urged Johnson to "blow the whistle" and "destroy" Nixon. But to expose the Republican campaign's perfidy on the eve of the November 5 election, Johnson would need to disclose the surveillance of both a wartime ally *and* the domestic political opposition. The scandal would taint the next presidency and cause, perhaps, a fatal break with South Vietnam, and neither Johnson nor Humphrey was willing to pay that price. Nor did Johnson have proof of Nixon's direct involvement. A skeletal version of the Chennault affair leaked quickly, but the documents and White House tapes that confirmed the tale were locked away at the Johnson presidential archives; some would be sealed in what came to be known as "the

X envelope." And Haldeman's notes confirming Nixon's culpability were kept secret by Nixon and his lawyers for decades.*

THE DROVES OF variables forestall a conclusion that Nixon's meddling cost the United States an opportunity to end the war in the fall of 1968, saving tens of thousands of American and Vietnamese lives and four years of excruciating political division at home. The stubbornness displayed by both North and South Vietnam in future negotiations, and history's analysis of the internal political machinations and external pressures at play in Saigon and Hanoi, preclude so ready a judgment. "Probably no great chance was lost," wrote the Democratic national security expert William Bundy in a book-length examination of Nixon's foreign policy.

But Bundy wrote with hindsight. What can also be said is that Thieu's foot-dragging was encouraged by signals sent by Nixon and shut a window that, with the help of the Soviet Union, Johnson and his aides believed they had opened. For them a moment of genuine hope—improbable perhaps, but nevertheless hope—was stolen. Given the lives and human suffering at stake, and the internal discord that was ripping the United States apart, it is hard not to conclude that, of all of Richard Nixon's actions in a lifetime of politics, this was the most reprehensible.

BY HOOK AND crook, Nixon survived Johnson's machinations. Humphrey closed the race at a startling pace once the bombing halt gave the Democrats something promising to say about the war. The blue-collar workers of Michigan and Pennsylvania and the peaceniks of the college towns, tony suburbs, and silk-stocking districts returned to the Democratic Party. Nixon's advisers had hoped for "a November 1 crest—then a few days of statesmanship and rest." Instead, October went to Humphrey.

Nixon parried by playing on the public's well-earned suspicion of LBJ. "I am . . . told that this spurt of activity is a cynical, last-minute attempt by President Johnson to salvage the candidacy of Mr. Humphrey," said Nixon, channeling Uriah Heep. "This I do not believe."

It was a visit from "the familiar Nixon of old . . . managing with artful rhetoric to convey a vicious and false accusation without taking responsi-

* From 1974 until his death Nixon battled in court, successfully, to control his White House personal and political files, which were seized by the government after the Watergate scandal. They were not released until 2007. The author found Haldeman's notes on the Chennault affair while conducting research for this book.

bility for his words," O'Brien said. The "old Nixon" had made an appearance, Bundy noted, mixing "maximum innuendo" with "pious dissociation." On the telephone, Johnson complained to Dirksen that "Dick's statement was ugly . . . that he had been told that I was a thief and a son of a bitch . . . but he knew my mother and she really wasn't a bitch."

But Johnson's credibility was suspect. The news of Thieu's intransigence and the skepticism that Nixon fanned—that the peace offensive was no more than a political ploy—fed the voters' existing distrust for the Johnson-Humphrey team. And as Wallace faded, the conservative vote in the "peripheral South" moved to Nixon. And Humphrey's tide stopped just short of victory.

DICK AND HIS family took separate suites at the Waldorf Astoria in New York on election night. He chose to be alone, to face the emotional ups and downs without Pat and the girls at his side. On the airplane east that day, he had warned them that the election would be close, and that they might lose. The bombing halt had hurt that much.

Haldeman, only, was allowed to carry him reports, which Nixon toyed with on a legal pad. The early returns confirmed the news that Nixon had seized big chunks of the Wallace vote on the perimeter of the South— giving him states like Tennessee, the Carolinas, Florida, and Virginia— but that the blue-collar voters in New York, Pennsylvania, and Michigan were indeed returning to Democratic ranks. By midnight, Humphrey had taken a tiny lead in the popular vote. It would come down, as in 1960, to California, Ohio, Texas, and Illinois. At 6 a.m., when the newscasters reported that Mayor Daley was holding back votes in Chicago, Pat went into her bathroom and threw up.

But this was not 1960. New York, Pennsylvania, and Texas went to Humphrey, but Ohio and most of the Midwest, the border South, and almost all the West chose Nixon. And this time Nixon's campaign had taken precautions to safeguard the voting, especially in Illinois. Outside Chicago, Republican election judges withheld their results, as the Nixon campaign taunted Daley, daring him to release his precincts. Finally, he did so. It wasn't enough. Nixon had clinched Illinois, and the White House.*

* The southern strategy was never so crucial to Nixon's general election hopes as it was to his primary campaign. The 1960 U.S. census determined the allocations of votes in the Electoral College in 1968, and the historic growth of the Sunbelt had barely begun to register. It was only as air-conditioning made the South and Southwest more habitable (fewer than one in five southern homes had air-conditioning in 1960; almost three in four

Nixon invited his staff in to celebrate. He spotted Chotiner. "Murray, whatever made you put out those vicious pink sheets?" he asked.

Chotiner replied, "Mr. President, you know I had a pretty good reputation until I joined up with you."

His aides recalled the moment: it was the first time someone addressed Richard Nixon as "Mr. President."

THE NIXONS WENT home, to find a nearly empty refrigerator and the president-elect's valet, Manolo Sanchez, out for the afternoon. So the family celebrated with canned soup and scrambled eggs. Then Dick went into his study, put *Victory at Sea* on the stereo, and cranked it so loud, he said later, that "everybody on Fifth Avenue . . . could hear it," five stories below. The glow of the bombing halt had faded just in time. "If the election had been one day earlier, we would have lost," Price recalled. Nixon would take office with but 43 percent of the vote in the three-way race. It was a Goldilocks victory. On November 5, he had won by just enough.

Johnson swallowed his disappointment and offered the Nixons a presidential aircraft to fly them to Florida for a brief vacation. Pat and Dick climbed aboard and, away from the prying eyes of the press, "they turned to each other," Julie recalled. "Simultaneously, they embraced, and my father swung Mother around in a pirouette."

---

enjoyed it in 1980) that those regions boomed and assumed far more important roles, with increased clout in Congress and many more votes in the Electoral College. Of the 301 electoral votes Nixon collected in 1968, just 57 came from the South, and most of them were from states (Virginia, Tennessee, Florida) that Republicans had carried in 1952, 1956, and 1960. Deepest Dixie stuck with Wallace.

Nixon's War

O N A CHILL winter day in the last year of the 1960s, Richard Nixon joined the roll of Cold War presidents, with unprecedented destructive might at his command and the duty of resisting, in China and the Soviet Union, two truculent giants whose proficiency in slaughter during World War II, and tyrannical behavior since, spoke of their belief that life was a negligible commodity.

Communism dominated Nixon's thoughts. Time had barely blinked since JFK and Khrushchev did their danzón over Cuba. The Soviets had launched a furious attempt to catch up to the United States by whatever standard—missiles, warheads, megatons—supremacy was measured. The Americans still held a superior arsenal, but the Soviet Union had enough nuclear weaponry to make "victory," as Eisenhower had once told his commanders, a meaningless concept. Together, the two superpowers amassed more than thirty thousand nuclear warheads, with the explosive power of a million Hiroshimas.

The latest Soviet leaders were thuggish opportunists. Their armored columns had swept into Czechoslovakia that summer, crushing the liberalization movement known as the Prague Spring. The Iron Curtain, the Gulag, and the Wall endured. West Berlin was still encircled. Reds were making mischief in the Middle East and Latin America, and North Vietnam was bleeding the United States in Asia. The Chinese were in the grip of the Great Proletarian Cultural Revolution—a time of internal frenzy and of purges, launched by Mao Zedong to purify his reign, in which hundreds of thousands of people died.

DEFYING THE CLOUDS, figurative and literal, the new president made his entrance on the east side of the Capitol to the shout of golden trumpets. Nixon was, and would stay for weeks, exhilarated at being president. "Expression on his face was unforgettable, this was the time!" Haldeman wrote in his diary. "He had arrived, he was in full command, someone said he felt he saw rays coming from his eyes."

"I was a happy man," Nixon would remember. He had just turned fifty-six, and the grail was in his grasp. It was a time of "charmed innocence," Henry Kissinger wrote. Nixon "had arrived at last after the most improbable of careers and one of the most extraordinary feats of self-discipline. . . . He seemed exultant, as if he could hardly wait for the ceremony to be over so he could begin to implement the dream."

Nixon swore the oath of office on two brown leather Milhous family Bibles, held open by Pat to Isaiah 2:4. ("They shall beat their swords into plowshares and their spears into pruninghooks: nation shall not lift up sword against nation, neither shall they learn war any more.") The new president then delivered a fine, generous inaugural address. "We cannot learn from one another until we stop shouting at one another—until we speak quietly enough so that our words can be heard as well as our voices," he told his countrymen. "No man can be fully free while his neighbor is not. To go forward at all is to go forward together. This means black and white together, as one nation."

So do presidencies begin: with hope and zeal, even—maybe most so—in the direst times. The muscle of political victory intimidates, and in the Cold War years it was thought unseemly for the opposition to rebel too soon. The left had been dismayed by the catastrophes of 1968, and was quarreling with itself. Nixon would have a breath of honeymoon.

DICK AND PAT's joy had been sweetened that Christmas when their younger daughter married Ike's grandson, David Eisenhower, in an old-fashioned ceremony conducted by Norman Vincent Peale at his Marble Collegiate Church in New York City. "Julie Nixon: Bride of a Nostalgic Era," said the *Washington Post*, with a sniff of disapproval.

Dick had handled the news of the engagement poorly, Julie recalled—"In his shy way my father seemed pleased, but he did not say much"—leaving her hurt and fearing that he disapproved. In fact, he was stunned at losing her and regretted all the time that his political career had taken him away. Prodded by Pat, he slipped a note beneath Julie's door. "I suppose no father believes any boy is good enough for his daughter," he wrote. "But I believe both David and you are lucky to have found each other." The reception was at the Plaza Hotel. In his toast to the newlyweds, Nixon noted that *Apollo 8* was halfway to the moon. From there its crew would take wondrous photographs of Earth rising over the lunar horizon. That ugly year, 1968, ended with a hint of possibility.

To Theodore White, who interviewed Nixon that winter, the incoming president seemed confident and relaxed. "Above all: the new sense; I'm boss. I run things," White jotted in his notes. "What a strange cool person he has become . . . a very much enlarged presence." The problems of the first weeks in office were trifles: they could not get the White House fireplaces to draw (Nixon liked a crackling fire—even in warm weather, when he would compensate by turning on the air-conditioning), nor the president's new dog, an Irish setter named King Timahoe, to lie at Nixon's side. ("Still trying to get Tim by his desk," Haldeman informed his diary on February 3. "Dog biscuits are starting to work.") Nixon's first use of the presidential shower did not go well; outfitted by Johnson with an array of jets, controls, and showerheads, it "nearly flung me out of the stall," he would recall.

To the side of his desk in the Oval Office, LBJ had a cabinet for the wire service ticker tapes and a long credenza containing three built-in television sets—one tuned to each major network. Nixon had it all dismantled and replaced with a stand of flags. Johnson had a secret tape-recording system; it too was removed. A presidential desk made of timbers from HMS *Resolute*, a gift from Queen Victoria, was too closely identified with Kennedy to suit Johnson or Nixon. Instead, Nixon called to the Capitol for the desk he had used as vice president, which he mistakenly believed had been Woodrow Wilson's. On a table behind his chair, Nixon placed photographs of his girls and, in time, a bust of Lincoln. He slept in the bedroom used by Lincoln, Wilson, Roosevelt, Truman, Eisenhower, Kennedy, and Johnson.

Within weeks Nixon was taking *Air Force One* to Europe, conferring with French president Charles de Gaulle, the pope, and Queen Elizabeth and gallantly defusing any awkwardness over the recent appointment of a Nixon critic as the British ambassador to Washington. "You can't guarantee being born a lord," said an appreciative Prime Minister Harold Wilson, after Nixon's deft performance at 10 Downing Street. "It is possible— you've shown it—to be born a gentleman."

Nixon "sailed joyously off," the veteran adviser Bryce Harlow recalled, "as most new presidents do, loving the world and reaching out for the whole world to love him. Filled with the sweetness of victory, they yearn to serve everyone well and faithfully and they are determined to be reasonable and get along with everybody. They are going to do great things . . . arm-in-arm with everyone. That's the way it starts."

But as his limousine made its way down Pennsylvania Avenue under gunmetal skies on inauguration day, there was little joy or sweetness and no quiet voices among the scores of long-haired, blue-jean-wearing protesters who surged toward the motorcade, pressing against the lines of police, tossing objects and epithets at Nixon. "Ho, Ho, Ho Chi Minh. N-L-F is gonna win," they chanted. "One. Two. Three. Four. We don't want your fucking war."

Julie saw it coming. "I dread his future task of ending the war," she confided to her diary. "It will be hell on earth."

Nixon was the fifth of the nine Cold War presidents, a pivotal figure with jaw-dropping audacity and a geopolitical vision. Seizing on a split between Moscow and Beijing, the grocer's son would stoke the historic forces that were undermining the Soviet empire and lay a foundation for a less dangerous, more stable, multipolar world order. But Vietnam would devour him. The signs were there, that very first day, on Pennsylvania Avenue.

HEINZ ALFRED KISSINGER was the most significant (and the most devious, bright, and compelling) individual that the new president brought with him to Washington. As the new national security adviser, he met Nixon's wishes and devised a structure to vest control of national security and foreign policy in the White House, not the State Department or the Pentagon. The Harvard professor was alternately witty, insecure, arrogant, obsequious (to Nixon), a charmer of the press, and a despot to his staff. Like Haldeman, he would provide historians with splendid accounts of the Nixon presidency. He had come to Nixon's notice as a Rockefeller man (for Rocky gathered talent like Nixon collected figurines of elephants), fluent in the liturgies of nuclear weapons and the balance of power. Kissinger had shown his usefulness, a taste for intrigue, and a certain moral flexibility by leaking the Johnson administration's peace plans to the Nixon campaign in the fall of 1968, despite his expressed belief (when advising Rockefeller) that a Nixon presidency could be disastrous.

Kissinger was a native German whose Jewish family had fled Bavaria before the Holocaust and settled in New York in 1938, when Heinz was fifteen years old; it was there he began to call himself Henry. He returned to Europe with the U.S. Army during World War II and served in the Battle of the Bulge and the conquest of Germany as a member of the counterintelligence corps, pitted against Nazi saboteurs and Gestapo spies, for which he was awarded a Bronze Star. He helped liberate a concentration camp, though not the ones in which his grandmother, aunts, and uncles and a dozen or more members of his family died. From all this, he emerged dually wedded to order and to liberty: coldhearted in his calculations, but convinced that his adopted land was the guardian of freedom in a world of totalitarian evils.

Nixon and Kissinger viewed themselves as principled realists. They would not fall for dreamy, Wilsonian "moral exuberance" (as Kissinger liked to call it) and travel the world sowing expectations, or crying about human rights. But neither would they abandon their goal of "a new equilibrium," and a peace that could endure for twenty or thirty years.

Nixon recognized Kissinger's qualities and convictions, forgave some, and shared many. Taking him on was a bold and consequential decision. "Here was Nixon from California; conservative, anti-Communist Republican from the grassroots of America, . . . distrustful and disdainful of the elite, the establishment, the northeast Ivy League and, frankly, with a heavy dose of anti-Semitism," recalled Winston Lord, an aide to the two men. "And who does he pick . . . but Henry Kissinger, a Jewish immigrant from Harvard who had worked as a close advisor to Nelson Rockefeller—Nixon's strongest opponent. So it was an amazing choice."

Nixon and Kissinger viewed the war in Southeast Asia as a shackling impediment to America's role as watchman of liberty and leader of the West. It was "a short term problem," Nixon believed, that should not serve as an obstacle to greater deeds. As early as 1965, after returning home from a fact-finding trip to Vietnam, Kissinger had been asked by Clark Clifford, an adviser to Lyndon Johnson, if South Vietnam was worth saving. "I said I had great sympathy for the difficulties of the president," Kissinger told his diary, but the fate of the Vietnamese people was "no longer the issue." What mattered was "the future world position of the United States."*

The heavyweights in Nixon's cabinet were his friends John Mitchell, who took over as attorney general, and William Rogers, who had advised Nixon since the days of the Hiss case and served Eisenhower as attorney general, and was now installed as secretary of state. When he could not persuade Senator Henry "Scoop" Jackson, a Democrat from the state of Washington, to lead the Department of Defense, Nixon settled on Representative Melvin Laird, a Republican from Wisconsin who (unlike Rog-

---

* The opinion was widely shared. In November 1964 John T. McNaughton, a top aide to Defense Secretary Robert McNamara, had quantified the aims of U.S. involvement in Vietnam in a document later included in the Pentagon Papers. Avoiding "a humiliating U.S. defeat" that would damage "our reputation as a guarantor" came first, and was judged by McNaughton and his colleagues as 70 percent of the reason for the war. To the U.S. policy makers, the publicly avowed goal of allowing "the people of SVN to enjoy a better, freer way of life" supplied just 10 percent of the rationale.

ers) would prove himself Kissinger's equal in bureaucratic intrigue. The cabinet chiefs were all male and white. "I seriously doubt if jobs in government for women make for many votes from women," Nixon told Robert Finch, the new secretary of health, education, and welfare.*

Haldeman served as chief of staff and Ehrlichman as White House counsel and, later, head of domestic policy. Their influence—and control of access to the president—would earn them the nickname "the Berlin Wall." Back in the wilderness years, Nixon had gathered an eclectic array of advisers who "ran around without much adult supervision," Leonard Garment recalled. But in the course of the 1968 campaign most of them fell from grace as Nixon turned to Mitchell, Haldeman, and Ehrlichman, a triumvirate who competed "to see who was the toughest, most effective manager." Garment himself was left out of the first round of appointments; he eventually joined the White House staff as a special consultant with a vague portfolio.

Haldeman and Ehrlichman were pals—fellow Christian Scientists and classmates at UCLA—who had come up through the ranks of campaign advance men. They and their unseasoned entourage, all still in their twenties—Larry Higby, Gordon Strachan, Dwight Chapin, Egil Krogh, and press secretary Ron Ziegler—were marketers, not ideologues or policy wonks. Their job was to manage things for Nixon, not to pursue some cause or partisan purpose. "They are so straight they are deviant," Daniel Patrick Moynihan, a wry Democrat who joined the White House staff, would say. They never forgot what Nixon craved: a controlled clime, and time and room to think, and plot, and brood, mostly about foreign policy. Haldeman designed a system in which access to the Oval Office—by people or paper—was funneled through his office. It was efficient and met its goal; it was also blind and mechanical. Buchanan called it "Prussian . . . a corporate or paramilitary pyramidic structure." It had the effect, Garment would conclude, of negating Nixon's goodness—of banning entrance to that "profoundly emotional, thoughtful interior . . . the walled garden of Nixon's soul."

"MR. NIXON'S STRENGTH was not his being gregarious," said James Schlesinger, a White House aide who would rise, in the course of the

---

* In his second term Nixon named a woman—Anne Armstrong—as a counselor, and gave her cabinet rank.

administration, to the cabinet. From the days of his childhood, with that bullying father, Nixon had come to abhor interaction or, worse, confrontation. With drive and determination—"an introvert in an extrovert profession," as he described himself to Garry Wills—he had mastered the glad-handing needed to reach his goals. Now, as president, secure within the walls of the Executive Mansion, he had the ability, and the excuse of pressing duties, to duck the interpersonal relationships he found difficult—with Congress, aides, and family.

The president and his family would often communicate, noted aide Frank Gannon, like actors in a Tolstoy saga—slipping notes under doors or leaving them on pillows, or having intermediaries convey awkward news. Nixon found the Oval Office insufficiently womb-like, and as the first months of his presidency passed by, he fled to an aptly named "hideaway" in the Executive Office Building, to a snug sitting room off the Lincoln Bedroom, and to even more private retreats at Camp David in Maryland, San Clemente, California, or Key Biscayne, Florida. When they proved too populous, he sought the near-total seclusion of a private cay in the Bahamas owned by Robert Abplanalp, a wealthy friend and supporter. There, Nixon walked the beach alone.*

The president was still shy and clumsy with strangers. He did spontaneity poorly. When introduced to Alexander Butterfield, the aide who would control the flow of paperwork to and from his desk, Nixon made a guttural sound, flapped his hands, and failed to find a word to say. The relief in Nixon's voice was manifest when, at the end of a meeting with strangers, he pawed through his desk for the golf balls ("Everybody who gets in here gets loot!"), cuff links, and other presidential trinkets he distributed as souvenirs. He insisted on structure and tempo. Many years later, Chapin remembered a morning he awoke and found his arm black and blue, from where Nixon clutched it as a group of people had unexpectedly closed in on them the day before.

"I want it clearly understood by the entire Congressional Staff that I cannot and will not intercede with individual senators in order to enlist their votes," Nixon told Haldeman. In a memo to Ehrlichman he extended the ban to the House. The arc of the American presidency yields few more shortsighted decrees.

* Abplanalp was the inventor of the aerosol spray valve. Like Rebozo, he was prized for his discretion. Both were self-made men who put their fortunes at Nixon's disposal. Nixon prized the waterfront properties because "the ocean has great powers of relaxation for him," Rose Mary Woods recalled.

Aides learned not to argue, or to contradict Nixon. Those who pressed their case, even when he ultimately ruled in their favor, could find themselves banished. He built labyrinthine back channels to evade the experts at State and Defense, with the predictable result that components of his administration often worked at cross-purposes, and incensed bureaucrats leaked and undermined him. He and Kissinger repeatedly evaded, lied to, and humiliated Rogers. They would "conceal, sometimes by simple silence, more often by articulate deceit" and thus "created a system," recalled Admiral Elmo Zumwalt, a chief of naval operations during the Nixon years, "in which leaks and spying were everyday and essential elements."

PEACE WAS THE aspiration of the lonely soul; peacemaker the yearned-for appellation: Nixon still harbored his bold romantic dreams. His spirits would soar when he mingled with giants like Eisenhower, de Gaulle, or Mao—he'd scrawl notes on little scraps of paper to commemorate the moment, and painstakingly preserve them. He longed to be the hero of his life and read ceaselessly of history, and biographies—of Lincoln, Wilson, Disraeli, and others. And when, the next day, he and Kissinger were chewing on a problem, Nixon would reach back to his reading and find a lesson in Napoleon's tactics in the battle of Leipzig, or Churchill's account of a Western Front offensive.

"He wanted to be a great man," said Pat Buchanan, summing up the boss in seven words. And, in many ways, Nixon was equipped for the quest. Few of his contemporaries could size up the political landscape, identify the popular disposition, and devise tactics like Nixon. He was a thoroughbred, said Ehrlichman: trained for a mission and performing superbly. "There are people who are . . . head and shoulders different than the run of ordinary mortals," said Haldeman. "He was one of them."

The racehorse had his quirks. It was part of his decision-making process to spend vast chunks of time in conference with a very few close advisers, examining all sides of the issue, asking questions, posing answers—playing the devil's advocate. Nixon came to a decision "crabwise," said Kissinger. He would "turn the same rock over a dozen times . . . come back to it two weeks later and turn it over another dozen times," said Ehrlichman. The president was like "a dog who is getting ready to lie down," Haldeman said. "He's trying to decide how he's going to settle . . . and he makes these circles and circles. Now finally, somehow, just the right thing develops and he settles down and lies down."

In the evenings, Nixon would nestle in his armchair by a fireplace, prop his feet on a hassock, and cover his yellow foolscap with admonitions. *"Hard work-Imagination-Compassion-Leadership,"* he would write. *"Cool-Strong-Organized-Temperate . . . Excitement-Joy in Life-Sharing. Lift spirit of people-Pithy, memorable phrases."* Nixon rarely took off his tie and liked to relax in smoking jackets. "He . . . spent long hours pondering things—meditating," said Butterfield. For background Nixon would play stirring romantic music on the stereo—Beethoven's Ninth Symphony, Rachmaninoff concertos, or that old favorite, the score from *Victory at Sea.*

Nixon could be humble—covering a White House ottoman with a towel to keep it clean—or imperious: ostentatiously standing beside *Marine One,* tapping his foot, when Pat was a few moments late. He hated being delayed. After one fund-raiser, when the fat cats scheduled for a grip and grin were tardy, his staff—aware of his building wrath—grabbed a random group of salesmen from a nearby hallway and steered them into Nixon's suite. The conventioneers were "flabbergasted, bug-eyed, stuttering but thrilled," Safire recalled. "The president never knew."

Nixon found virtue in his solitary ways. "It has been my experience . . . that the social lunch, the social dinner or the social cocktail hour is one where there is a great deal of talk and many promises but very little follow-through," he told Haldeman, looking back with satisfaction halfway through his term. "I have accomplished . . . the simple expedience of not wasting two hours in the middle of the day with social or business lunches and of having breakfast with someone else only when [it] serves a necessary purpose. . . . For example, in over two years in the White House I have had lunch in the Residence on only two occasions—once for the King of Belgium."

By removing his middle initial from his official signature, Nixon discovered, he could cut a second or two. Over four years, he told Haldeman, "that's a real time-saver!"

His lunch was the same, almost every workday: a ring of canned pineapple, a scoop of cottage cheese flown in from his favorite California dairy, some crackers, and a glass of skim milk. He exercised by running in place. Sometimes at night he would bowl alone.

AT FIRST, NIXON expected his cabinet secretaries to forge the administration's policy. He quickly discovered how his own reputation and political fortunes rested on their performance and, after a few minor disasters, ordered Haldeman and the White House staff to seize the reins. Athens gave way to Sparta.

Haldeman supplanted even Rose Woods, one of several intimate aides and advisers—like Finch, Garment, and Chotiner—who had roles in the administration but lost their special access to Nixon. She knew her man and was wise enough to not blame Haldeman. "Go fuck yourself!" she had told the president-elect, throwing a pile of papers onto his desk, after being informed she would no longer serve as the empress of access.

In time, even Nixon's family grew to resent Haldeman. His disrespectful attitude toward Pat did not help—he bullied her staff and called her "Thelma" behind her back—but Haldeman was a convenient target for those who were hurt when Nixon pushed them aside. He did little that Nixon did not know, and approve.

A president's most important asset is "the ability to concentrate on those subjects in which what he says or does can make the difference and to delegate to others all other subjects," Nixon told his chief of staff. "With regard to delegation, I am exactly the opposite of [Grover] Cleveland. Cleveland read every bill . . . he got so enmeshed in details that he could not take the long view."

Nixon was a dexterous liar, but even for him this was an egregious whopper. He puttered—endlessly—with the trappings of the presidency, enmeshing himself in detail as a balm for his soul, instructing Haldeman and the others on matters of art, music, pomp, and cuisine.

"Any individual can only focus on the weightiest matters for certain lengths of time. . . . You need a diversion," Haldeman would explain. "For some people it's exercise; for some people it's sex; for some people it's reading Western novels" and for Nixon "it was sitting talking about things that don't matter very much."

"The rule regarding no luncheons has been modified," began a typical memo, conveying an instruction from Nixon to the staff. The protocol for dinner guests was modified as well. Dining out was a whole other ball game. "The President is concerned that we are not handling the tipping process properly," Haldeman wrote. "The head waiters involved in overseeing the seating, etc., should get $10, the wine steward should get $5, and the waiter serving the President should get very substantial tips totalling about 25 percent of the check. It is perfectly proper to sign the check itself, because as you know, frequently the restaurant will compliment it, but always the tips should be given in cash and should be generous."

Pat was in charge of social events, decorations, and furniture—and would do a fine job with the White House curators, acquiring historic furnishings for the mansion. She got memos too. Five days after the inauguration, "The President" dispatched a memorandum to "Mrs. Nixon" saying, "With regard to RN's room, what would be most desirable is an end table like the one on the right side of the bed which will accommodate *two* dictaphones as well as a telephone. RN has to use one dictaphone for current matters and another for memoranda for the file which he will not want transcribed at this time. In addition, he needs a bigger table on which he can work at night." Needless to say, Pat had her own bedroom.

Nixon issued a presidential directive banning the soup course at state dinners. The purported goal was to trim the evenings' length, but word soon spread that he'd fumbled a spoon and spilled soup on his white shirt. The steaks served on the yacht *Sequoia* were too thick, he decided. The canned music played in the residence dining room should be replaced with tunes from the Nixon record collection. The chairs in the Cabinet Room were too hard. LBJ's shower was redesigned. An ice machine was junked because the president preferred his ice cubes without holes. "When the oval room is re-done I would like to have the coffee table in front of the fireplace replaced by one that does not block the view of the fireplace from the desk," he wrote Haldeman. The portrait of George Washington needed to be higher, and a better clock acquired. Television cameras should be banned from fund-raisers: donors were "rich and fat and drunk and dumb," Nixon said. "You want to get on TV with the real people, not these sodden looking bastards."

The Nixon campaign bumper stickers needed improving. "The President wants his phone redesigned," Haldeman told the staff—and an inventory conducted of the presidential golf bags. There was little golf, but when there was golf there would be absolutely *no* golf at country clubs that allowed photographers on the links. Nor was he ever to have a caddie—he found the relationship excruciating. The meddling with minutiae didn't end at the water's edge. "I want a check made with regard to the incredibly atrocious modern art that has been scattered around the embassies around the world," Nixon wrote. "This Administration is going to turn away from . . . offbeat art, music and literature."

It was Nixon who reclaimed the disused White House Map Room—where Franklin Roosevelt had given his fireside chats and tracked the Allied armies' progress during World War II—and had it returned to its previous eminence. He had the White House indoor swimming pool (where FDR had exercised his withered body, and JFK his libido) converted into a modern pressroom. After viewing the public bathrooms in Yugoslavia, the president ordered an upgrade for the facilities along the

National Mall. And it was he who, after seeing how the honor guards were dressed in the capitals of Europe, commanded that the White House sentries be refitted in costumes more suited for Freedonia.

"The only more unkempt . . . security people than the ones at the White House were the ones in the Congress," he would explain. "It's really disgusting to see these overblown fat people that are basically political hacks running around there . . . and that's the way the White House looked." But Nixon was universally mocked when the sentries made their debut in gold-braided white tunics and stiff, peaked short-brimmed hats. The costumes were quickly abandoned and donated to a marching band.

Nixon's idiosyncrasies were generally harmless. But one of the president's quirks proved catastrophic. As the pressures and demands of the office built, he would seek relief by issuing menacing commands to his aides—leaving them to decide which ones to obey, and which to ignore. He had ratified the process in writing during the transition period before inauguration day. "There may be times when you or others may determine that the action I have requested should not be taken," Nixon wrote Haldeman. "I will accept such decisions but I must know about them."

Ehrlichman likened Nixon's rants to the Queen of Hearts in *Alice's Adventures in Wonderland* ("Off with their heads!"), and, indeed, the results sometimes were comical. "That's an order. No discussion. Unless of course you disagree," the president told Ziegler. After Nixon banned his staff from eating at the White House congressional breakfasts, some aides obeyed him and others (assuming, correctly, that he did not really mean it) dug into the sausage and eggs. The unfed staffers fumed for days.

Most of the decrees were innocuous—banning a newsman from *Air Force One,* or threatening to cut off federal funds to an offending university—but others, like bombing Damascus after a Middle East skyjacking, could carry real import. "He had certain hot buttons and if you inadvertently trip that wire, it was going to set off an explosive reaction," aide Tom Huston recalled. "He had a dark side and . . . what he really expected from the people around him was to recognize this and . . . when he came out with one of these goofy ideas to basically let it fester for a while until he got through it and would re-think it."

"Oh hell, Bill—you know me better than that," Nixon told Rogers, after the secretary of state waited a while, then double-checked with Nixon on a presidential order to fire all the department's personnel in Laos. Nor was

Damascus bombed. But of all the peculiar features of the Nixon presidency, this was the most dangerous. It may have let him exorcise his demons and feel powerful by calling down destruction upon an enemy—to relieve "his fevers," as Garment put it—but eventually a sycophant was bound to take the president seriously.

That individual arrived in 1969. As the hours he spent listening to the presidential cud-chewing dragged by, Haldeman had begun to fret—he had work that needed to get done—and by the end of their first year hired a Massachusetts Republican operative, Charles Colson, as a counselor to the president, with a political portfolio. "I welcomed Colson, because I saw Colson as an opportunity for someone else to sit and listen to all that BS from the president," Haldeman would recall. It was a fateful decision: Colson was hard-nosed, pushy, and aspiring and saw in Nixon's meaner appetites a pathway to advancement. "I brought out the dark side of Nixon," Colson recalled, though "you didn't need to work very hard to bring it out—it was always close to the surface." The president was "a gut fighter. . . . His first reaction was to fight back . . . to get even."

Haldeman and Ehrlichman had years of experience saving the "mad monk," as they nicknamed Nixon, from himself. Kissinger and Laird learned to do so quickly. But Colson "vigorously stirred up the demons," Garment said. John Mitchell was no softie, but "that fucking Colson is going to kill us all," he marveled aloud. When Ray Price asked him just who Colson's constituency was, Mitchell replied: "The president's worst instincts."

NIXON'S CARDINAL CHALLENGE was direct: to bring the Vietnam War to a satisfactory conclusion. "Don't ever—no matter what facet of the Nixon presidency you consider—don't ever lose sight of Vietnam as the overriding factor in the first Nixon term," Haldeman would instruct. "It overshadowed everything, all the time, in every discussion, in every decision, in every opportunity and every problem."

Nixon thought he could bring the war to an honorable end in a matter of months. "I trust that I am not confronted with that problem when you speak of years," he told the country in a March 4 press conference. But it took six years, and the end was far from honorable. Retreat became rout, the cost in additional lives ran to the hundreds of thousands, and any prestige saved came charily, if at all, from a world agape at America's appetite for torment.

Nixon never *said* he had a secret plan to end the war; but in fact he did. The secret plan was to win. Not win in the sense that he imagined the North Vietnamese surrendering, as the Japanese had, on the deck of an American battleship. His goal was to wound and stay Hanoi long enough for Saigon to build institutions—an army, a government—and survive for at least a time on its own. In the meantime, he would mollify the American public by ending the draft, reducing casualties, and withdrawing troops. During the campaign he had called it "ending the war and winning the peace."

Five days into office, Nixon outlined his thoughts in a meeting with his foreign policy team. "We talk hard in private, but with an obvious peaceful public stance, seeking to gain time . . . giving the South Vietnamese a chance to strengthen the regime . . . while punishing the Viet Cong," he told the NSC. "Within three or four months bring home a few troops unilaterally . . . as a ploy for more time domestically, while we continue to press at the negotiation table for a military settlement."

Nixon and Kissinger summarily dismissed a different choice: an immediate withdrawal of U.S. forces under terms that would lead to the unification of Vietnam under a Communist government. This course had its appeal. He could blame his predecessors for losing the war, and there were precedents for such action, set by the French in Indochina in 1954, and by de Gaulle when the French withdrew from Algeria in 1962.

"Had we traded a unilateral withdrawal for our [POWs] when we still had over a half million men in Vietnam, I have absolutely no doubt we could have gained [a peace] agreement," wrote George Ball, a former top State Department official and leading establishment critic of U.S. policy, in his memoirs. "For South Vietnam, the final outcome would have been no different from what finally occurred.

"For America, the difference would have been profound," Ball said. "We would not have lost an additional twenty thousand young American lives and would not have killed at least six hundred thousand Vietnamese. We would have avoided the opprobrium attached to our bombing of Laos and invasion of Cambodia and saved far more of our reputation than we finally salvaged." At home, "we would have halted the building up of a catastrophic social eruption that left a lasting scar."

America's allies in South Vietnam might have been evacuated, and bloodshed minimized. Cambodia, in particular, may have escaped the grisly torment that lay ahead. American prestige could recover, perhaps improve. "There is more respect to be won in the opinion of this world by a resolute and courageous liquidation of unsound positions than by the most stubborn pursuit of extravagant or unpromising objectives," George Kennan had told Congress in 1966.

Nixon failed to dare. He lacked the imagination, could not free himself from the Cold War canon. And if he was not prepared to quit, neither was much of the country. As late as November 1970, in the liberal stronghold of Massachusetts, two-thirds of the voters in a statewide referendum rejected a proposal for immediate withdrawal. Nixon felt for those in South Vietnam who had put their faith in the United States. He and his countrymen believed, as well, that they had an obligation to the families of Americans killed or wounded in combat. And "credibility" ruled his thinking. "What is on the line is more than South Vietnam," Nixon told a meeting of the Cabinet and the NSC. "If we fail to end the war in a way that will not be an American defeat, and in a way that will deny the aggressor his goal, the hawks in Communist nations will push for even more and broader aggression."

The other states of Southeast Asia—like Thailand, Malaysia, and Indonesia—had made huge strides, building free-market economies. They needed time and breathing room. And "what concerns me more than anything else is what happens to the U.S. If a great power fails to meet its aims, it ceases to be a great power. When a great power looks inward, when it fails to live up to its commitment, then the greatness fades away," he said. Nixon was no man for faded greatness.

When the Cabinet and his aides applauded these remarks, he said, apologetically, "I really didn't mean to make a speech."

NIXON'S MODEL WAS Eisenhower, who had brought an end to the fighting in Korea. In the years as vice president he'd had a courtside seat from which to watch the great commander work. Now, trying to settle another war on the perimeter of Asia, he drew on that experience and employed Ike's tactics.

Soon after his election in 1952, Eisenhower had sent word to Moscow and Beijing that the United States would use *all* means to end the stalemate in Korea. The Communists could not be sure that the unsparing hero who had sent his army onto Omaha Beach and supervised the air assault on Germany was bluffing, and the ruins of two Japanese cities bore witness to America's willingness to use the Bomb. So the war in Korea came to an end.

"It is absolutely urgent," Nixon now told Kissinger, "that we find new ways to increase the pressure militarily."

"We will bomb the living bejeezus out of North Vietnam," he'd tell his adviser, "and then if anybody interferes we will threaten the nuclear weapon."

Yet Nixon was not Eisenhower, and this was 1969, not 1952. The Chinese had become a nuclear power, and the Russians possessed a fearsome arsenal. Neither would be easily bluffed. The North Vietnamese recognized that the United States was divided and had watched how the anti-war movement terminated Lyndon Johnson's presidency. They reasoned, correctly, that only a maniac would light a nuclear conflagration over a backwater like Indochina.

And so Nixon took on a role for which, given his reputation as a snarly anti-Communist, he thought he was well suited. "They'll believe any threat of force that Nixon makes because it's Nixon," he had told Haldeman in a walk along a beach during the campaign. "I call it the Madman Theory, Bob. I want the North Vietnamese to believe I've reached the point where I might do *anything* to stop the war."

Nixon ordered his aides to shake their heads during their encounters with Soviet diplomats, and to worry aloud that: "I'm sorry . . . he is out of control . . . you don't know the man" or that "Nixon is . . . a dramatically disjointed personality . . . capable of barbaric cruelty . . . [and] more than a little paranoid."

There were carrots to be offered with the madman's stick, for Nixon hoped to enlist the Soviet Union in his search for an exit from Vietnam. It was another prime feature of the "secret" plan.

The Soviets were happy watching Washington flail at its tar baby, and supplied the ordnance that let Hanoi keep fighting. But Southeast Asia was just one corner of the world. The Soviet Union had a wide range of objectives, at home and abroad, that Nixon could help them meet. With Nixon's approval, Kissinger held secret talks with the Soviet ambassador, Anatoly Dobrynin. The two met in the Map Room on the first floor of the East Wing. Progress on trade, or in talks to ease the expense of the arms race, would be tied to the Soviet Union's willingness to pressure Hanoi. It was to be known as "linkage."

American honor did not require that South Vietnam stay free forever, Kissinger assured Dobrynin—only long enough for the United States to leave with its banners waving. If the North eventually triumphed, and South Vietnam went Communist after "a fairly reasonable interval"—

well, that would be acceptable, Kissinger said. When Dobrynin seemed unmoved, Kissinger tried threats. Ultimately, Nixon joined them—loaning the ambassador a yellow legal pad and telling him, "You'd better take some notes."

"The humiliation of a defeat is absolutely unacceptable," Nixon told Dobrynin. "We will not hold still for being diddled to death in Vietnam."

The president played a China card, assuring the Soviets that America's willingness to deal with the Chinese would not be directed against the Soviets—thereby confirming that it was.

But it was always a tricky, contradictory, maybe foredoomed business—to talk peace at home and thump one's chest abroad.

"We must convince the American public that we are eager to settle the war, and Hanoi that we are not so anxious that it can afford to outwait us," Kissinger said. In the summer of 1969, Nixon announced the withdrawal of sixty thousand U.S. soldiers. "What incentive did North Vietnam have to give up positions to get a US withdrawal when they were going to get a US withdrawal anyway?" asked NSC aide Winston Lord. "There was always a tension concerning our major bargaining chip."

To DEMONSTRATE HIS resolve, the madman ordered a military assault that later became grounds for an article of impeachment.

Ten weeks into his presidency, upon the advice and with the support of his military commanders, Nixon ordered the air force to start bombing the Communist camps and supply lines in Cambodia, a neutral nation whose sorry fate was to share a border with Vietnam. From beneath the shelter of its jungle canopies, the enemy had planned, refitted, and staged offensives. Hundreds of Americans were dying every week. Nearly half of all the casualties in the Nixon years were suffered in the first six months of 1969.

The military rationale for the bombing was sound: Saigon was just forty miles away. The targeted areas were lightly populated, and the North Vietnamese honored no borders when using neutral Laos and Cambodia to funnel men and matériel into combat. But Nixon kept the bombing secret: the military maintained phony records to disguise the air assault from all but a handful of men on Capitol Hill. And the lasting infamy of the "Menu" attacks, as they were called (the Breakfast campaign was followed by Lunch, Snack, and so on) was that they further destabilized—with, ultimately, horrific effects—a nation striving to stay out of war.

The air force had been using high-altitude, B-52 Stratofortresses in

Southeast Asia since 1965. The swept-wing BUFFs* had begun life as delivery vehicles for nuclear weapons, but with modified bomb bays and new wing racks carried twenty-seven tons of high explosives. A cell of three bombers could saturate a strip of land a mile long and half a mile wide with 500- and 750-pound bombs. Inside that box, generally without warning, human beings, animals, machinery, and structures took a hellish pounding. American troops, entering the bomb zone after the strikes, found no-man's-lands of moonlike craters, splintered and uprooted trees, and enemy soldiers wandering in a daze, coated by blood, with shattered eardrums and internal hemorrhaging. The B-52s were devastating weapons when used against concentrations of Communist troops and prized for shattering enemy morale, but were costly and inexact tools for jungle warfare. The bombs rained from thirty thousand feet. The danger to civilians was plain.

Nixon and Kissinger would absolve themselves from responsibility for the chain of events that followed and culminated in the reign of the Communist Khmer Rouge. Bombing Cambodia in the 1970s was like bombing occupied France in 1944, Nixon argued. They were bombing the enemy, not the populace. "We did not know at that time that the Khmer Rouge were genocidal murderers," Kissinger would tell newsman David Frost. "This went beyond our imagination." Nor, the two men argued in their memoirs, did the bombing have the perverse effect of driving the Communist forces farther into Cambodia, sowing chaos and involving the Cambodians in the greater conflict.

While in office, however, the president and his adviser thought otherwise.

"We bombed the hell out of those sanctuaries," Nixon recalled, in 1972.

"It led to the collapse of Cambodia because it pushed the North Vietnamese deeper into Cambodia," Kissinger said. "And as a result . . ."

"That triggered Cambodia," Nixon said.†

THE NEWS OF the Menu bombing raids broke in a front-page story in the *New York Times* on May 9. Kissinger exploded in fury, and he and Nixon called in J. Edgar Hoover, whose agents installed wiretaps, over

---

* Big Ugly Fat Fuckers.
† Nixon ordered more bombing of Cambodia after the North Koreans, in April, shot down a U.S. spy plane, killing thirty-one Americans. He did not want to appear weak but shied away from a confrontation that could reopen the Korean War, and so chose to punish the Communists in Cambodia.

time, on the telephones of four news reporters and thirteen administration officials—including Nixon loyalists like John Sears and William Safire—suspected of leaking. When Hoover balked at bugging columnist Joseph Kraft, the White House had a private investigator complete the task.

Six months on the job, and the president's men were flouting the law. The surveillance yielded little but gossip and traces of bureaucratic jockeying. Nixon and his aides, with a revealing degree of self-consciousness, at long last packed the transcripts up and locked them in a White House safe, where their faint *tick, tick, tick* was, for a time, forgotten.

By EXTENDING THE bombing into Cambodia, Nixon had sent a signal to Hanoi. But the message was mixed. The madman had demonstrated his readiness to escalate—yet by doing so covertly, he'd confirmed that the public appetite for war was not limitless.

"The fundamental problem is time," Kissinger said. If the Nixon administration did not show progress by the midterm elections in 1970, the doves would score gains and Congress could order its own withdrawal by cutting off funding for the war. "If we had no elections, it would be fine," Nixon told the NSC. "The reality is that we are working against a . . . clock."

That summer, to buy more time and reassure the public, Nixon publicly embraced a plan designed by Defense Secretary Laird to replace the front-line U.S. fighting forces with South Vietnamese troops. It came to be called Vietnamization. Nixon set the terms with President Thieu at a meeting on Guam and, almost parenthetically, outlined what came to be known as the "Nixon doctrine." The United States would no longer do the fighting for those who would not defend themselves, he informed the press. The U.S. military was not deluded by Vietnamization and what it signified. Nixon's commanders recognized that, without American combat forces, South Vietnam's survival was "highly uncertain," Kissinger wrote. The decision had been made that "victory was impossible."

As THE FALL of 1969 arrived, Dobrynin reported to Moscow that Nixon was growing angry, sarcastic, paranoid, and agitated: "Events surrounding the Vietnam crisis now wholly preoccupy the U.S. president. . . . To all appearances, the fate of his predecessor Lyndon Johnson is beginning to really worry him. Apparently, this is taking on such an emotional coloration that Nixon is unable to control himself."

Dobrynin's description was attributable, in part, to the madman act.

But Nixon's hopes for ending the war in months, the president now realized, were preposterous. "I underestimated the willingness of the North Vietnamese to hang on," he would recall.

That defective calculation was not unique to Nixon. Since 1945, America's leaders had failed to recognize the North Vietnamese capacity for sacrifice. The Americans wanted to believe that the North could be reasoned with, and that Hanoi's willingness to carry on its war was finite, that at some point its Politburo would see the light and cut a deal, and the United States could go home with pockets full of prestige, leaving Saigon in safe hands. It was folly—wishful thinking of the worst kind. For all his tough talk, over so many decades, about Communist fanatics, Nixon had underestimated his enemy's resolve.

The negotiations that Johnson had opened with the North Vietnamese in Paris remained deadlocked, but in the summer of 1969 Hanoi agreed to parallel secret talks between the two nations. Nixon's terms were nonviable: he insisted that the North must leave the Saigon government intact. But the North Vietnamese attended the sessions with but one objective in mind—to orchestrate the South's capitulation. The losses suffered in the Tet campaign had not destroyed the Politburo's determination. Like George Washington's army, they didn't have to win—just keep from losing, and exhaust an empire's will.

"Any incentive for the enemy to negotiate is destroyed if he is told in advance that if he just waits for 18 months we will be out anyway," Nixon told the nation, in a September press conference. He was arguing against a fixed timetable, as members of Congress suggested—but he might as well have been talking about his own strategy. If the Americans were leaving, the Communist leaders in Hanoi calculated, why make concessions?

"We have won the war," the North Vietnamese negotiator, Le Duc Tho, told Kissinger when they met. "You have lost the war. . . . You have not realized this objective reality."

ON THE HOME front, Nixon faced a striking divide between the World War II generation and their children, who had not endured the hardships of war and depression that molded their parents.

In the course of a long drive through Virginia back in 1954, Eisenhower and Nixon had discussed the morality of war and, specifically, the Allied strategic bombing campaigns. It had been immoral to slaughter civilians, Eisenhower conceded, yet justified by the evil of the enemy. The barbarism of Nanking, the Blitz, and Treblinka warranted the incineration of Dresden and Nagasaki.

Neither Kennedy nor Johnson had challenged the canon, and neither would Nixon. Before Congress cut off funding for the bombing in the summer of 1973, the United States dropped more than 7.5 million tons of bombs on Laos, Cambodia, and Vietnam—the equivalent of one hundred A-bombs, and more than three times the 2.1 million tons of explosives sown by American bombers during all of World War II.

"Just remember you're doing the right thing," Nixon would tell his aides. It was how he always comforted himself "when I killed some innocent children in Hanoi."

The air force alone flew more than *five million* sorties. There were areas of Southeast Asia—along the Cambodian border, or in Quang Tri province in South Vietnam—where the statistical pinpoints marking a bombing raid were too many to distinguish and blended into long, wide swaths of color on the maps.

Midway through the first term, a reporter would rise at a presidential press conference and challenge Nixon on the morality of such a war. Nixon handled the encounter calmly, but in the Oval Office he stormed and raged.

"I visited Germany. I stood on top of a ruined building in Essen and for miles around everything was flattened. Hundreds of thousands of civilians were killed by American bombing. I saw the same thing in Berlin. I saw the tragedy in Dresden," he told Kissinger and Haldeman. "Would it have been more moral to let Hitler conquer Europe and lead the world?"

"Would it be moral to allow a Communist takeover and have the bloodbath in South Vietnam that they had in North Vietnam where 50,000 of our good Catholic faith of Danang were murdered [and] 500,000 were starved to death in slave-labor camps?" he asked. He pounded the desk. "How many? In the atomic bombings of Nagasaki and Hiroshima? . . . At least a million Americans would have died going into the Japanese homeland. . . . Was it more moral?"

"War is immoral because people are immoral, and they're aggressive all over the world. Hitler was a vicious son of a bitch and somebody had to stop him," Nixon said. "The North Vietnamese are bastards."

For most of Nixon's generation, that was the moral calculation. But many of their children, not steeped in the mythos of Munich and Pearl Harbor, saw things differently. An industrial titan, reaching halfway around the world to intercede in a civil war, using modern armaments, defoliating chemicals, napalm, and strategic bombers on a primitive, rural society? ("It became necessary," one air force officer would say, "to destroy the town to save it.") Where was the morality in that?

"With the battle cry of upholding our reputation, we degraded ourselves," Ball would conclude. "No friendly nation applauded our massive use of B-52s. . . . The vision of the world's most powerful nation smashing up the people and meager assets of a tiny, backward country was not only unedifying, it evoked charges of colonialist, imperialist, capitalist brutality. Moreover, it damaged our own self-esteem since, as the bombing grew more indiscriminate and desperate, our own vision of our country as strong, generous [and] human . . . was sadly diminished."

With Vietnamization, Nixon could draw down the American force. But the draft boards were still summoning record numbers of young men. And as fall arrived, as the colleges welcomed the students back, the peace movement quickened. "Our job is to call down justice like rolling waters," the Reverend William Sloane Coffin, the chaplain from Yale, informed Kissinger. The antiwar groups made plans for a monthly series of demonstrations— vigils, teach-ins, and other peaceful protests—to begin on October 15. The first, the Moratorium, went exceedingly well—with national television coverage and two million protesters around the country. "The young white middle class crowds were sweet-tempered and considerate: at times even radiant," Moynihan wrote the president. Some of those protesting in the streets of Washington were children of Nixon aides. The next event, the Mobilization scheduled for November 15, called for a candlelit march past the White House, and the reading aloud of the names of the dead.

Nixon was now headed for a confrontation, like LBJ before him, with the most formidable peace movement in U.S. history. His worried aides circulated a column by newsman David Broder. "It is becoming more obvious with every passing day that the men and the movement that broke Lyndon B. Johnson's authority in 1968 are out to break Richard M. Nixon in 1969," Broder wrote. "The likelihood is great that they will succeed again, for breaking a President is, like most feats, easier to accomplish the second time around."

Moynihan warned his colleagues that they needed to prepare themselves, because Nixon "is going to be the 1st Pres to lose a war," Haldeman noted. Since defeat was inevitable, Moynihan contended, they should end the fighting now, while it was still "LBJ's war." Their hour of opportunity was drawing to a close. If they toughed it out much longer, Moynihan said, it would be "Nixon's war."

Nixon promised further withdrawals, but at his urging the Pentagon also readied a comprehensive plan to punish North Vietnam. If Hanoi didn't budge, it would face "measures of great consequence and force," he wrote Ho Chi Minh that summer. In the early versions of Operation Duck Hook, as it was conceived, Hanoi would be bombed, dikes destroyed, harbors mined, and tactical nuclear warheads readied to close off key supply routes. To deter Soviet or Chinese interference, America's nuclear forces around the world would be placed on alert.

In the end, Nixon blinked. Worried that escalation would rip the nation apart, he rejected all the Duck Hook options, save the worldwide alert. He needed to show Hanoi that America stood behind him, and streets filled with rioters and burning college campuses would not do that. Instead, he took to the airwaves on November 3 and appealed to his forgotten Americans. He called on "the great Silent Majority," and asked them for more time. Nixon outlined the steps he had taken to negotiate, Hanoi's continued obstinacy, and the dangers of a precipitous withdrawal. Noting how the Communists had massacred three thousand civilians in Hue during the Tet Offensive, he warned that "these atrocities of Hue would become the nightmare of the entire nation" if the United States fled.

"The first defeat in our nation's history would result in a collapse of confidence in American leadership," he added. "A nation cannot remain great if it betrays its allies and lets down its friends."

"Let historians not record that when America was the most powerful nation in the world we passed on the other side of the road and allowed the last hopes for peace and freedom of millions of people to be suffocated by the forces of totalitarianism," Nixon said. "I pledged in my campaign for the Presidency to end the war in a way that we could win the peace. . . . The more support I can have from the American people, the sooner that pledge can be redeemed; for the more divided we are at home, the less likely the enemy is to negotiate at Paris.

"Let us be united for peace. Let us also be united against defeat. Because let us understand: North Vietnam cannot defeat or humiliate the United States. Only Americans can do that."

THE "SILENT MAJORITY" speech was a brilliant piece of political communication—one of those very few speeches, as Nixon liked to say, that changed history. Telegrams flooded Washington, sustaining Nixon's leadership and bolstering his confidence. His standing in the polls soared. With the stepped-up bombing and the troop withdrawals he'd ordered, the American casualty rate in Vietnam was shrinking, and in late November, Nixon signed a law replacing the current draft system with a lottery: those who drew high numbers would no longer have a personal stake in the debate over the war.

He was buying time, but at what cost? Americans were shaken when journalist Seymour Hersh broke the news of how U.S. soldiers had massacred hundreds of South Vietnamese villagers—including women, children, and infants—at a hamlet called My Lai in 1968. The atrocity took place before Nixon took office, but rather than seeking justice—as he promised the American people in a December 8 press conference—his response was to direct his aides to use the necessary "dirty tricks" and discredit the army witnesses who had intrepidly refused to participate in a cover-up.

The inauguration theme—"Forward Together"—was shelved. Vice President Agnew was dispatched to libel antiwar leaders as an "effete corps of impudent snobs who characterize themselves as intellectuals," and to upbraid the network commentators who had criticized the president's speeches. Nixon would divide, to rule.

The Mobilization in November fed the siege mentality. The candlelit march from Arlington past the White House to the Capitol went on through the rainy night, and into a brilliantly sunny, cold windy day. Nixon's staff—huddled inside the White House, protected by paratroopers, and isolated from the demonstrators—was shaken, more so when the marchers paraded down Pennsylvania Avenue, banners waving like a Napoleonic army, and it became clear that some 500,000 had gathered that weekend.

Kissinger had chided the North Vietnamese negotiators in Paris for seeking to polarize Americans over "Nixon's War." Now the president had done precisely that.

20

Not Fish nor Fowl

O N JANUARY 20, 1970—the first day of his second year in office—
Richard Nixon donned his overcoat and was on his way out of
the Oval Office when he paused to open a silver cigarette box.
Not for a smoke: it was a gift from an admirer that played "Hail to the
Chief" when the lid was lifted. "Got that box just a year ago," he said
to Bob Haldeman and Rose Woods, as the now-familiar notes filled the
darkened room.

The first twelve months of Nixon's presidency had been remarkably
consequential. Vietnam alone would have made them so. But in the Nixon
era—in those days before Ronald Reagan would inaugurate his presidency
with the declaration that "government is the problem" and Bill Clinton
would proclaim that "the era of big government is over"—there was still
the presumption that Americans wanted an activist government addressing the nation's ills. And Nixon had met that goal.

Growth alone required it: the country was doubling in population,
from 140 million individuals during World War II to 281 million at
the millennium, with tens of millions migrating to Southern California,
Arizona, and the states of the old Confederacy. The newcomers needed
highways, classrooms, and health care; their businesses, cars, and homes
devoured open space, swilled energy, and clogged the air and water with
waste. Americans were rubbing elbows with each other like never before.
Much of the so-called "activist" government, raged at by business interests
and conservative politicians in the second half of the century, was an inevitable response to the growth that they otherwise cheered or, in the case of
immigration, ardently promoted for cheap labor.

As he prepared to take office, Nixon had told Theodore White that he
planned to focus on foreign affairs, for when it came to domestic policy,
the cabinet and Congress could run the country. Even had he wanted to
dismantle the popular achievements of the New Deal or the Great Society,
there was no constituency on Capitol Hill, or in the federal bureaucracy, for

such action. The Republicans had whittled down the Democratic majority in the two elections since Lyndon Johnson's 1964 landslide, but there were still 57 Democrats and 43 Republicans in the Senate, and 245 Democrats and 192 Republicans in the House. Nixon was the first first-term president since Zachary Taylor, in 1849, to take office with both houses of Congress in the hands of the opposition party.

Nixon needed to hoard political capital for Vietnam and other foreign policy tests—"I knew that in order to get the enemy to take us seriously abroad, I had to have enough support at home," he would recall. He had no taste for battling the Democrats over social welfare bills, a battle in which his only weapon was the bludgeon of a veto. Nixon "didn't give a damn" about the finer points of domestic policy, said aide Tom Huston. "All he wanted to do was to keep the sharks away."

And so many progressive measures, crafted with the help of his administration, made their way to Nixon's desk, where he acquiesced, signed his name, and took his just share of the credit. He was no ideologue. "Elections are not won or lost by programs," he told Haldeman. "They are won or lost on how these programs are presented to the country . . . how all the political and public relations considerations are handled." He governed with the "practical" liberalism he had promised California voters in 1946 and watched Ike employ in the 1950s. Keeping with tradition, Nixon sent a message when choosing the portraits of three presidential muses to hang in the Cabinet Room. He chose Dwight Eisenhower, Woodrow Wilson, and Teddy Roosevelt.

Nixon sought to look like a man of reason bringing commonsense solutions and reform to Washington. He did that, and much more, as he and the many talented individuals he brought into his administration joined with the Democratic Congress and left their mark. "The size of government under Nixon grew immensely," economist Alan Greenspan recalled. "His reasoning was always, 'Well if we don't do it, they'll do more.'"

IN COPING WITH the presidency's demands, Nixon often fell back on the lessons he had learned as Eisenhower's understudy. Ike was the leader with whom he had apprenticed; it was the presidency he had known up close. "He was a great admirer," aide James Schlesinger recalled. "He would frequently cite what Eisenhower felt about this or that."

Like Ike, Nixon sought to govern from the center, installed his campaign manager as attorney general, and chose a deliberate pace when dealing with civil rights. His initial plans to end the Vietnam War were based largely on how Ike wrapped up the Korean conflict. Like Eisenhower, Nixon made strong claims of executive privilege, employed the CIA to mount coups overseas, sought détente with the Soviet Union, and flirted with the notion of replacing the GOP with a new centrist majority party. They both considered dumping their vice president and running for reelection with a Texas Democrat on their ticket. Ike added the phrase "under God" to the Pledge of Allegiance—Nixon stuck a U.S. flag pin on his lapel, and for decades American politicians failed to do so at their peril.

Their differences were as telling. Ike was a people person, and Nixon was not. Ike liked to mix and meet. The social obligations of the presidency were chores for Nixon. "I would like to invite, even though I don't like most of these people, Johnny Carson, Merv Griffin and Mike Douglas . . . for Evenings at the White House," he told Haldeman, referring to three talk-show hosts. "This could pay off in great measure for us." Sunday church services were staged, not for worship, but "to use . . . as a political opportunity." Nixon invited Johnny Cash and other country-western stars to perform at the Mansion "not because I particularly liked Country music—it really doesn't appeal to me that much—but because I realized most other people and my Silent Majority did." When he hosted a reunion of his college classmates at the White House, Nixon told Haldeman to arrange a musical performance or religious service. "This would be better than a reception for them alone where I would have to get into too much conversation," he said. Ike endured the White House press corps as a bothersome but inevitable complication of life—a nuisance, like black flies. Nixon was forever fuming. When a speechwriter commented on the "excellent" press that the president was receiving in the honeymoon period, Nixon replied, "You don't understand, they are waiting to destroy us." He had been president less than four weeks.

"Eisenhower's tendency . . . was to calm a crisis; Nixon's to play it up," said Stephen Ambrose, who wrote multivolume biographies of both men. "Ike's instinct was to put salve on a wound after a political dispute, Nixon's to rub in some salt. Eisenhower liked, respected and worked effectively with the Establishment; Nixon hated and scorned it."

But the old general's influence was always there—even more so after the Nixon and Eisenhower bloodlines were joined by Julie's marriage. In the spring of 1969, after hearing that Ike, worn down by a spate of heart attacks, had succumbed, Nixon turned away from his aides, trembled, and fled the room to weep, alone. When the Oval Office floor was torn up by remodeling, Nixon preserved the boards pitted by Ike's golf spikes, and sent fragments as mementos to Eisenhower's old friends and aides.

LIKE EISENHOWER, NIXON entered office with expansive notions. Haldeman was told to cast a wide net, and newsman Mike Wallace, scholar Doris Kearns, Kennedy speechwriter Richard Goodwin, and other liberals were considered for positions on the White House staff. Civil rights leaders Roger Wilkins and Whitney Young were offered jobs in the Nixon administration, and Freedom Rider James Farmer took one. A Democrat—Scoop Jackson—was Nixon's first choice for secretary of defense. Jackson turned Nixon down, but Harvard professor Daniel Patrick Moynihan, a Kennedy Democrat, took a job as a presidential adviser on urban affairs. Kissinger sowed the National Security Council offices with bright Ivy Leaguers like Anthony Lake, Winston Lord, and Morton Halperin. The cabinet had its share of duds, but talents like George Shultz and Elliot Richardson bloomed as skilled, principled administrators. Men like Len Garment and Ray Price were "warm, decent, humanitarian liberals," Nixon told Haldeman. "We need such men on our staff because they give leaven to the hard-nosed people like Buchanan." Within the Nixon White House, there were learned debates, and dollops of wit. One Price memo on youthful unrest was as gentle, forgiving, and perceptive a statement about America's alienated children as any White House aide ever wrote about an administration's political foes.*

The problem with the right-wingers, the president told Haldeman, is that "they have a totally hard-hearted attitude where human problems and any compassion is concerned."

Nixon found Moynihan a particular treat. In 1969, the ebullient professor led the drive for the Family Assistance Plan, a welfare reform with a work requirement that guaranteed a basic annual income, day care, and training for the jobless. "For two weeks' growth in the Gross National

---

* The list of prime movers in American politics and government who cut their teeth with Nixon includes George H. W. Bush, William Rehnquist, Alan Greenspan, Henry Kissinger, George Shultz, Dick Cheney, Donald Rumsfeld, William Ruckelshaus, John Warner, James Baker, Colin Powell, Antonin Scalia, Henry Paulson, Roger Ailes, Paul Volcker, Pat Buchanan, David Gergen, John Lehman, Lamar Alexander, Richard Darman, Frank Carlucci, Caspar Weinberger, Alexander Haig, and Robert Bork. Speechwriter William Safire became a *New York Times* columnist; Brian Lamb went on to found C-SPAN, and press aide Diane Sawyer emerged as a TV news star. Leon Panetta was fired for his liberal zeal, switched parties, and served as White House chief of staff, secretary of defense, and director of the CIA.

Product you can all but eliminate family poverty in America. And make history," he promised Nixon. After hearing Moynihan's ideological rival, presidential counselor Arthur Burns, complain that the plan did not fit Nixon's conservative philosophy, aides chuckled.

"Don't you realize the president doesn't have a philosophy?" Ehrlichman asked Burns.

When a commission led by William Scranton (Yale '39) concluded that the blame for campus rioting should be placed on the authorities, Moynihan arraigned the assessment as a Harvard man would. "The men with balls in this business," he began, "just aren't buying that curious form of narcissistic transfer whereby middle-aged Yalies agree that there is nothing on God's Greening Earth so beautiful as a young Yalie—especially in those fleeting moments when the morning sun catches those long flowing locks illuminating, as if from some inner source, the subtle, raptured irregularity of prayer beads worn in quest of, yet somehow also in testament to, a fundamental unity with all things."

Moynihan's mischievousness was not without cost. A January 1970 memo he wrote, accentuating the quiet progress being made in black America and ridiculing the attention being given by Manhattan liberals to radicals like the Black Panthers, suggested that the White House would be well advised to lower the temperature of the national debate on race and treat the plight of African Americans to some "benign neglect." The memo was leaked to the press and the phrase misconstrued by Nixon's foes, then and ever after, as evidence of bigotry.

THE PRESIDENT ENDORSED Moynihan's policy innovations, and other liberal measures, not just because they were good politics but also "for personal psychological reasons," Burns concluded. Nixon "wanted to think of himself as a great innovator, a bold man, creative, a man of ideas. He needed that.

"He is not a strong man," Burns found. "He is a man of great intelligence and ability but he lacked self-assurance."

Whatever the case, the president's pen stayed busy. Tax reform for low- and middle-income individuals, increased aid for education, a bigger food stamp budget, a 20 percent hike in Social Security payments, and the new annual cost-of-living allowances became law with his approval during his first term.

Nixon signed the Occupational Safety and Health Act, creating a federal agency to police unsafe workplaces. He declared a war on cancer, with a massive infusion of medical research money. He asked Congress to double federal funding for the arts. Nixon presided over the glorious final stages of Project Apollo, with the moon landing on July 20, 1969, and the birth of the space shuttle program.*

Nixon gagged at the potential effect on collegiate football and other big-time men's athletics, but he okayed the requirement that women athletes have access to equal funding when he signed a higher education act with the far-reaching Title IX, banning gender discrimination in education and giving millions of young women the opportunity to demonstrate dash and skill on the playing field. The Nixon administration ended the draft, created a volunteer military, and approved a drop in the voting age from twenty-one to eighteen. A "new federalism" policy proposed to return federal revenue to the states.

Nixon's "self-determination" policy—reversing decades of government coercion forcing Native Americans to assimilate—made him an honored figure on many Indian reservations. Indian country was not immune to the spirit of the sixties, but in a series of sometimes violent disputes with young militants—the 1969–1971 occupation of Alcatraz, the seizure of the Bureau of Indian Affairs in Washington in 1972, and the 1973 "siege" at Wounded Knee—Nixon's lieutenants helped bring the crises to a close with a minimal loss of life.

The White House staff showed intellectual spryness. Senator Edward Kennedy, a longtime advocate for a federal health insurance program, would come to rue his opposition to Nixon's health care plan, which was based on the private market, with mandated coverage, augmented by public subsidies. It would return, in somewhat altered form, as the Affordable Care Act, and be enacted by Democrats in the first term of Barack Obama.

Some of his supporters growled. "Richard Nixon? Man on the make; ashamed of and constantly running away from his past; manipulator; unsure of his convictions; tactician instead of strategist.... That is the public impression," warned Douglas Hallett, a young aide to Charles Colson. Midway through the first term, Buchanan composed a long memo to Haldeman entitled "Neither Fish Nor Fowl" describing, with alarm, Nixon's image as a "political transient" who governed like the "bubble in the carpenter's level."

"We suffer from the widely held belief that the President has no Grand

---

* Though he had played no role in the process (and had no notion of the transformative changes to come), the Internet was born on Nixon's watch, when scientists at UCLA and other western universities coupled the first nodes of ARPANET, its federally funded precursor.

Vision that inspires him, no deeply held political philosophy that girds, guides and explains his words, decision and deeds," Buchanan wrote. For better or worse (and Buchanan definitely saw this as worse), "the President is viewed as the quintessential political pragmatist, standing before an ideological buffet, picking some from this tray and some from that."

NIXON STAYED RESOUNDINGLY square, but did not choose to exploit many of the divisive issues—like gun control, gay rights, and abortion—that would come to preoccupy cultural conservatives. In Nixon's first term, they "weren't even on the table," Huston recalled.

"On abortion—get the hell off it," the president told his aides. "Just say it's a state matter and get the hell off it." Over time, Nixon's Supreme Court appointees—particularly William Rehnquist—would leave a lasting legacy, turning the high court, and American jurisprudence, in a rightward direction. But it was a Nixon appointee—Harry Blackmun—who wrote the opinion in *Roe v. Wade,* establishing a woman's right to terminate a pregnancy.

Abortion encouraged permissiveness, Nixon believed, but "there are times when abortions are necessary. I know that—you know . . . between a black and a white," he told Colson.

"Or rape," Colson said.

"Or rape. . . . You know what I mean. There are times."

Nixon would never admit to watching commercial television, but he sometimes chanced upon shows or scenes, he'd tell his aides, while surfing the channels for a sporting event. Midway through his first term, he caught an episode of *All in the Family*—a comedy that lampooned both the silent majority and the woolly-headed left and, on this occasion, was making the case for tolerance for gay Americans.

"I do not mind the homosexuality. I understand it," Nixon told Haldeman and Ehrlichman. "We all have weaknesses and so forth and so on."

"Nevertheless, the point that I make is that, goddamn it, I do not think that you glorify on public television, homosexuality . . . even more than you glorify whores," he said. "What do you think that does to kids?"

Nixon followed with a classic rant about the deleterious influence of sexual license on the Catholic Church, the Roman Empire, France, Great Britain, and elsewhere. The West, with permissiveness and drug use and alternate lifestyles, was suffering from a fatal decadence, he said. "Let's look at the strong societies. The Russians. Goddamn it, they root 'em out. . . . You think the Russians allow dope?"

"Homosexuality, dope, immorality generally—these are the enemies of strong societies."

"The upper class of San Francisco is that way. . . . I don't even want to shake hands with anybody from San Francisco," Nixon said. "Decorators. They've got to do something . . . but goddamn it we don't have to glorify it."

"You know one of the reasons fashions have made women look so terrible is because the goddamned designers hate women," Nixon theorized, though "now they're trying to get in some more sexy things coming on again."

"Hot pants," said Ehrlichman.

"Jesus Christ," said Nixon.

The president viewed the gay rights movement as a brew of political hemlock. When Rita Hauser, a lawyer and liberal supporter from New York, publicly suggested that homosexuals might marry, Nixon told his aides that Hauser had doomed her chances of winning an appointment to the bench.

Yet he was not without foresight. "Maybe in the year 2000," he said, when pondering gay marriage.

Nixon's more libertarian leanings were generally subject to changes in the political breeze. When pollsters showed that the public was increasingly alarmed about the increase in drug use in the inner cities, among the troops in Vietnam, and on college and high school campuses at home, Nixon launched a national "War on Drugs." It was "the single greatest opportunity we have by a thousand-mile margin," he told his aides after studying the polls.

The drug war had some early success—the efforts to combat heroin abuse in the District of Columbia, using methadone treatments, were particularly noteworthy. But as implemented and augmented by opportunistic Congresses, governors like Nelson Rockefeller, and Nixon's successors—notably Ronald Reagan and Bill Clinton—the "war" on drugs and the battle for "law and order" would metastasize, yielding punitive measures like mandatory minimum sentences, no-knock raids, and other relaxations of defendants' rights. When Nixon launched his "war," American prisons held 200,000 inmates. In the decades to follow, a country founded on the principles of individual freedom achieved the disgraceful distinction of becoming the world's greatest prison state—with more than two million people incarcerated. By 2015, with less than 5 percent of the planet's population, America had 25 percent of the world's prisoners. The cost of jailing those men and women reached $80 billion a year and the effect on African American families and communities—where one out of three young black men could expect to be imprisoned at some point in his life—was appalling.

EIGHT DAYS AFTER Nixon's inauguration, a blowout on an offshore drilling platform dumped 100,000 barrels of oil into the Pacific Ocean off Santa Barbara, fouling the beaches and slaying birds and marine wildlife. The black goo spread along the California coastline as far south as Catalina. Shorefront residents were evacuated, lest they become sick from the fumes. It was the largest oil spill to that time in America and captured national attention just as the injured environment was emerging as a potent issue in American politics.

The president flew to California and surveyed the scene by helicopter; he told the traumatized Santa Barbarians that the disaster had touched the conscience of the nation. The percentage of Americans who rated the environment as their number one concern in the White House polls soared from 1 to 25 percent in months. It was "a political hurricane," said aide John Whitaker, and two Democratic presidential hopefuls—Senators Scoop Jackson of Washington and Edmund Muskie of Maine—were angling for the movement's support.

Nixon was not averse to a Teddy Roosevelt sort of environmentalism, preserving natural resources for future generations. Russell Train, a well-known conservationist, had chaired Nixon's transition task force on the issue and been appointed undersecretary of the interior. Ehrlichman, a land-use lawyer from Seattle, was supportive of the cause, as was his deputy Whitaker, a native of British Columbia, and Moynihan—who (in 1969!) alerted Ehrlichman to the "apocalyptic" dangers of global warming. By May there was a new White House environmental council. In July Nixon gave a ringing endorsement, and a pledge of federal support, to population control. In September the administration announced its opposition to construction of a new South Florida airport close by the Everglades. And on New Year's Day, 1970, Nixon signed the National Environmental Policy Act—the far-reaching law requiring environmental impact statements for large-scale federal actions.

He was just getting started. Nixon appointed Train as chairman of the newly established Council on Environmental Quality. And, as the nation prepared to mark the first Earth Day that spring, the Nixon administration sent a wide-ranging environmental message to Congress, with thirty-seven proposals to heal the earth and preserve its gifts. "No president before—or since—has offered such an extensive, coordinated legislative agenda" to protect the environment, scholar J. Brooks Flippen wrote in 2000. The Environmental Protection Agency (EPA) was established by executive fiat and placed in the capable hands of William Ruckelshaus. When Ruckelshaus moved on, Train succeeded him. With a stroke of Nixon's pen, the National Oceanic and Atmospheric Administration (NOAA) was born. The smog-killing capstone of the environmental movement emerged from Congress as the Clean Air Act of 1970. Nixon signed it and his EPA followed up with tough automobile emission and air pollution standards. He harked back to his childhood and, recognizing the political wisdom of offering benefits to working-class voters, ordered federal agencies to shed surplus properties—which were transformed into parks, for families to enjoy.

THESE WERE BANNER years, with worthy achievements, yet Nixon had a pervasive feeling that his record was not yielding commensurate rewards. No matter how deftly he played the game, he could not match the Democrats at catering to the environmentalists. "Some of these people are nuts," he told Barry Goldwater. America's business community was a formidable counterweight, and Nixon's commitment to U.S. leadership in high technology led him to endorse projects like the environmentally dubious Super Sonic Transport (SST). "We shall continue to do environment [events] once a month for *defensive* reasons," Nixon would write in the summer of 1971. "But *not* at the cost of jobs."

Sensing a change in momentum, Whitaker made the argument that the president should stay the course.

"I presume your basic reaction to the environment issue is that it is media created and may soon peak out and appeals only to the liberals you can't reach anyway in '72," he wrote Nixon. "Therefore, you have formed a basic conclusion that pushing too hard on the environment is a bad trade-off in terms of alienating your 'natural constituencies,' the rural heartland people and the businessman."

But the movement was more than just a few extremists, Whitaker contended. "It is my firm conviction, backed up by all the polling data available, that the backbone of those concerned with the environment is white, middle-class, suburban American and that housewives are a major component. To equate this group with a sort of wild-eyed radicalism is erroneous and politically harmful," he argued. "It follows the tactic of polarization of the issue—a certain guarantee of extremism on both sides."

Nixon relented, and maintained his bona fides with the movement by signing legislation to regulate pesticides, to police ocean dumping, to protect marine mammals, and to safeguard coastal zones and shorelines. But evidence of an approaching energy crisis caused a further recalibration of priorities. To the dismay of the environmentalists, he backed the proposed Alaska Pipeline and, in late 1972, vetoed the Clean Water Act, which he claimed was too costly. Congress disagreed and overrode the veto.

As a motivating issue for American voters, the fate of the environment had flashed from spark to conflagration in a matter of months; then settled into a steady flame. Nixon's interest in the issue followed the course of the public's passion and left an abiding legacy. In 2012, the leaders of major environmental organizations—the Sierra Club, Greenpeace USA, Friends of the Earth, and others—were asked in a poll to name the U.S. president who did most for the environment. Nixon trailed only Teddy Roosevelt in the results.

WITH A SHAPE-SHIFTER like Nixon, little was indelible. The campaign to clean up the environment was one of several causes for which he launched creative initiatives—then retreated as time passed, the country returned to its tory predilections, and his reelection campaign beckoned. He found it most irritating when he did not receive the political mileage he was due, because rancorous liberals and unappeasable liberal-leaning commentators kept carping about his performance. "During those first few years of Nixon, there was some damn good government. But Nixon couldn't get any credit for it," Moynihan recalled. "The press and others just kept denying it, denying it, and he gave up. He gave up trying."

Moynihan and Burns clashed. The concept of the White House as a policy salon, with aides engaged in intellectual jousting, was far too messy to last under Haldeman, no matter how "bright and sparkly and exciting and interesting and entertaining" (as Huston put it) the president found Moynihan, or how often Moynihan whispered in Nixon's ear that he could be another Disraeli—ushering historic emancipations in conservative guise.

Without powerful sponsors, many of the Nixon administration's more progressive innovations lost traction in Congress, were abandoned, or failed. Moynihan moved on, and Burns went off to chair the Federal Reserve; Ehrlichman took over domestic policy and consolidated the staff.

As Nixon turned rightward for the 1970 and 1972 elections, the White House liberals were swimming upstream.

The president's warring priorities, and internal conflicts, showed themselves in an outburst before his aides, in the summer of 1971. "I am not a liberal," Nixon raged, "I am a conservative!"

"We don't do a goddamn thing right around this place in terms of accomplishing anything. On the domestic scene we haven't fired the right people, we're still screwing around on permissiveness on the welfare thing, we're just giving more food stamps to loafers—all the things that are wrong—and we're just running the chaos a little better," he griped.

"I am opposed to these goddamn liberal plans. I'm simply against them and all I get in front of me is some other liberal initiative. The environment and all that bullshit.

"We're spending hundreds of millions of dollars on the food stamp program," Nixon said. "It's wrong, it's wrong. We're playing a game in which we don't gain a goddamn thing. And we're doing the wrong thing for the country. Oh, we can say—'We're keeping the issues from them.' Bullshit."

Nixon had not forgotten how Joe Shell and the Birchers had damaged his campaign in California in 1962. A few weeks after Moynihan announced that he was departing, Haldeman recorded Nixon's Machiavellian instructions about the Family Assistance Plan in his diary: "Wants to be sure it's killed by Democrats and that we make big play for it, but don't let it pass, can't afford it." The plan passed the House but died in the Senate.

The president "was an almost completely political animal. He was neither moral nor immoral, but was amoral," said Farmer, the civil rights leader who worked on Robert Finch's staff at the Department of Health, Education, and Welfare. "I don't think right or wrong entered into it."

"Nixon would have been recorded as being a very great president had it not been for that fatal character flaw," said Farmer. "He did not believe in anything."

When Farmer was preparing to leave government, he met with the president before seeing the press. Nixon asked him for his continued support for the Family Assistance Plan and vowed that in the next Congress he was going to fight for it "tooth and nail." There would be "blood on the floor," the president promised, and Farmer so assured the media. "But there was no blood on the floor and he didn't fight for it," Farmer recalled. "because it was not politically expedient for him to battle for it at the time."

—

SPENDING MONEY WAS easy work. Nixon's chief domestic challenge—the continued integration of America's schools, neighborhoods, and work sites—was not. Confronted with that duty, he trudged ahead, fixed in his commitment but mindful, ever, of the political cost. The Nixonian solution: to take actions that were "operationally progressive," as Leonard Garment put it, "but obscured by clouds of retrogressive rhetoric."

In polarized times, Garment argued, no more can be asked of a chief executive. Perhaps. Successful presidents must be, first and foremost, effective political leaders who nourish and conserve support. But the Nixon administration's concrete achievements—the initiation of affirmative action as a remedy for generations of mistreatment of women and minorities, and the historic gains made in desegregating southern schools—must be measured against what damage the president did to the cause of civil rights with his cynical romancing of voters who remained in the grip of prejudice.

"The political message that was going forth," said aide Sallyanne Payton, an African American legal scholar on Nixon's staff, "was one . . . of nods and winks."

"The subliminal appeal to the anti-black voter was always in Nixon's statements and speeches on schools and housing," Ehrlichman agreed. "He was never as blatant as George Wallace or Lester Maddox, but he delivered a clear message that was hard to miss . . . [presenting] his views in such a way that a citizen could avoid admitting to himself that he was attracted by a racial appeal."

Nixon reverted to Eisenhower-era rhetoric, equating civil rights leaders who wanted "instant integration" with bigoted extremists who were preaching "segregation forever." They were each "extreme groups," the president declared. Over time, the president of the United States gave credence to the feelings, shared by millions and fanned by Wallace and his kindred, that blacks were ingrates, offenders, and welfare chiselers handed unfair advantages by dizzy Democrats at the expense of hardworking, law-abiding citizens.

It was during the Nixon years, said Payton, that the cause of civil rights lost an invaluable asset—"the moral presence of the presidency."

SINCE 1957, WHEN Ike dispatched the 101st Airborne to Little Rock, the South's segregationists had given ground grudgingly, compelled by teargas and bayonets. After 160 U.S. marshals were wounded—28 by gunfire—it took twenty thousand troops to suppress an armed insurrection against integration of the University of Mississippi in 1962. Then-governor Wallace won his first taste of national fame by standing in the "schoolhouse door" at the University of Alabama the following year.

In the Johnson years, the civil rights movement had focused its energy on Capitol Hill and enactment of landmark civil rights, voting rights, and open housing legislation. Officials at the U.S. Department of Health, Education, and Welfare, by threatening to cut off federal funds to segregated school districts, made just limited progress integrating southern classrooms. Delays were granted, and deadlines extended, as the federal government bowed to the argument that the South needed time. When Nixon took office—sixteen years after the *Brown v. Board of Education* decision—the overwhelming majority of the region's black children still attended segregated schools.

The Supreme Court, in no-nonsense decisions during 1968 and 1969, ordered the South to change its ways.* The task of enforcing the rulings fell to the incoming president, who would otherwise have chosen to follow Johnson's more deliberate pace. On no domestic issue was President Nixon's behavior so revealing. His efforts to fulfill the nation's obligation to black Americans, while simultaneously securing the votes of disgruntled ethnic voters and white southerners, offer a prism through which to watch convictions meld with calculation.

"The laws have caught up with our conscience," Nixon told the nation in his inaugural address. "What remains is to give life to the law." But most of the initial steps that he took to breathe life into law were not promising—in his first two years in office he begged the courts for more time; shifted the task of integrating schools from the more militant staff at HEW to Attorney General Mitchell and the Department of Justice; fired the HEW civil rights director, Leon Panetta; removed Finch as department secretary; put Spiro Agnew in nominal charge of school desegregation; and proposed dilutive changes in the Voting Rights Act. Harry Dent, a longtime aide to Strom Thurmond, joined the White House staff, and Nixon assured southern lawmakers that he knew how much he owed the "thin gray line" who had helped him clinch the nomination and win the 1968 election. There had been "promises made," Garment recalled, to "lighten the load" of court-ordered desegregation.

The Nixon administration's retreat brought a storm of criticism upon the White House, even from within. "There is an unstated attitude (almost

---

* *Green v. Kent County* (1968) and *Alexander v. Holmes County* (1969).

a policy) of disregard toward blacks brought about by a political concern for white votes," Lamar Alexander, a young White House aide and future Tennessee governor and senator, complained to his boss Bryce Harlow. "As a result, we generally think all white, ignore black."

Nixon was fulfilling his southern strategy, his foes said—trading the future of black children for political advantage in the South. The well-sourced columnists Rowland Evans and Robert Novak predicted that Nixon would push for only "token integration" and take "the first serious backward step from racial integration by any national administration in a generation."

As was often the case, the cause of Nixon's backtracking on civil rights was a brew of personal resentment and political opportunism. The young man who attended integrated clubs and parties and called Jackie Robinson and Martin Luther King Jr. friends had grown into an aggrieved and more calculating politician, who had come to the conclusion, along with Eisenhower, that black Americans, dependent on Democratic social programs, would not support Republican candidates.

Nixon felt betrayed by the cuff he got from black voters in his race against John Kennedy. In his private roll calls of perceived enemies, African Americans never ranked as high as liberal Jews, but in his rants about race and ethnicity (Jews were obnoxious, the Irish were mean drunks, Mexicans were thieves) he stirred in theories of black inferiority. "Most of them basically are just out of the trees," he told one young appointee, Donald Rumsfeld.

"I have the greatest affection for them, but I know they ain't going to make it for five hundred years," Nixon told Ehrlichman and Haldeman. "The Mexicans are a different cup of tea. They have a heritage. At the present time they steal, they're dishonest . . . [but] they do have some concept of family life, at least. They don't live like a bunch of dogs, which the Negroes do live like."

It wasn't just off-the-cuff, Oval Office rambling. Toward the end of his first term, Nixon put his thoughts on race to paper.

"Segregated white education is probably superior to education in which there is too great a degree of integration of inferior black students with the white students," Nixon wrote in a memo to his senior aides. Minority students and teachers "dragged the others down with them."

He challenged the basic tenets of the *Brown* decision. "Busing black children from poor families to richer white schools will have little effect on how they learn," he contended. "I believe there may be some doubt as to the *Brown* philosophy that integrating education will pull up the Blacks and not pull down the Whites."

During the 1968 campaign, Nixon had promised the South that he would oppose school busing for racial integration. After the Supreme Court, in a 1971 decision, authorized cities and counties to use the practice to end the segregation of their school districts, Nixon endorsed constitutional amendments to ban court-ordered busing and the "forced" integration of housing in all-white neighborhoods. All the while, he denied any overt political motivation. "There is nothing that disturbs me more than to have to appear before the country as a racist," Nixon wrote his aides. "My feelings on race, as you know, are if anything ultra-liberal."

Busing was a virulent issue that drove a wedge into the New Deal coalition, splitting liberals and minorites from blue-collar workers and suburbanites, and so spurred plenty of hemming and hawing from Democrats.

"Wherever large numbers of lower middle class whites live in close proximity to blacks the existence of busing or the threat of busing is . . . an absolutely decisive issue," aide Charles Colson counseled Nixon.

"If we handle it properly, the Democrats will be stuck," Colson said. "If we are clear and hard their waffling will only compound their problem." The White House needed, Colson advised, to "exploit the hell out of it."

And so, throughout his first term, Nixon urged his aides to "exploit the hell" out of the divisions caused by the court-ordered remedy. "The President feels that it is imperative that all of our candidates . . . put their opponents on the spot regarding busing," Haldeman told Chotiner and Dent. "Each candidate should hit his opponent on this and force them to take a position for or against" busing. The Democrats will "lose either way."

THE WHITE SOUTH, of course, presented a tantalizing opportunity for Nixon's and his party's strategists. Wallace had, for the moment, corralled the hard-core racists of deepest Dixie, but voters in Florida, Texas, Virginia, the Carolinas, and Tennessee, and growing urban centers like Atlanta, were golden tickets to political prosperity, and seemingly up for grabs.

The civil rights movement, in the late 1960s, had grown more militant and off-putting to many white Americans. The photographs of nonviolent martyrs in Birmingham and Selma—being beaten by state troopers, bitten by police dogs, or tossed by fire hoses as they fought for their rights as citizens—had given way to images of "black power" advocates like Stokely

Carmichael, defiant sports figures like Muhammad Ali, and the gun-toting revolutionaries of the Black Panther Party.

The movement had shifted its agenda, as well. With the fundamental rights of citizenship now legally secured, civil rights leaders like King had pressed for economic benefits and tax-supported social programs, irritating the white working and middle class, who were starting to chafe at rising income and property taxes. In the year before his death, King joined the opposition to the Vietnam War, yet another polarizing issue.

Blue-collared white voters in the cities and working-class suburbs of the North had grown as tired of liberal philosophizing and black militancy as their southern counterparts, especially when the courts' assault on de jure integration expanded to include the de facto segregation north of the Mason-Dixon Line. Political leaders like Anthony Imperiale in Newark, Frank Rizzo in Philadelphia, Sam Yorty in Los Angeles, and Louise Day Hicks in Boston tapped strong reactionary currents outside the South.

In what soon became known as the Rust Belt, the promise of a well-paid union job at the local factory was fraying, adding to the fears that Wallace stirred about social disorder, race, and violence. As complacent American corporate executives and union leaders watched, first Europe, then Japan, and then Korea and other Asian nations elbowed their way into the international economy, building factories and stocking assembly plants with low-wage workers and modern machinery. The 1970s would witness an acute contraction of the U.S. steel industry, matched by equally worrisome declines in the manufacturing of automobiles, electronics, and other goods.

The huge majorities that Lyndon Johnson enjoyed in the wake of his 1964 landslide eroded: Democrats lost fifty-two House seats in the 1966 and 1968 congressional elections, and eight seats in the Senate.

The era's two hot books on politics—*The Real Majority,* by Richard Scammon and Ben Wattenberg, and *The Emerging Republican Majority,* by the young Nixon enthusiast Kevin Phillips—heralded the prospect of electoral realignment based on what was politely referred to as "the social issue." Nixon was fluent in the ideas expressed in both volumes. "Have you read the Scammon book?" he would quiz his aides.

The Real Majority proposed that the bellwether American voter was a forty-seven-year-old housewife, married to a blue-collar worker, from a middle-American city like Dayton, Ohio. "To know that the lady in Dayton is afraid to walk the streets alone at night, to know that she has a mixed view about blacks and civil rights because before moving to the suburbs she lived in a neighborhood that became all black, to know that her brother-in-law is a policeman, to know that she does not have the money to move if her new neighborhood deteriorates, to know that she is deeply distressed that her son is going to a community junior college where LSD was found on campus—to know all this is the beginning of contemporary political wisdom," the authors wrote.

For Nixon and his aides, the temptation was irresistible. The "great Silent Majority" could be swayed not just on law and order, Vietnam, and patriotism, but on that most potent issue, race. Colson's office weighed the payoff of turning white against black using "symbolically laden messages . . . in a calculated but carefully contrived form of polarization." They would portray Democrats as "the party in favor of sacrificing the majority of Americans . . . to appease a racial minority."

Michael Balzano, a Colson deputy, proposed in a 1971 memo to Nixon that the president transmit the following message to disgruntled white voters: "Today, racial minorities are saying that you can't make it in America. What they really mean is that they refuse to start at the bottom of the ladder the way you did. They want to surpass you . . . [and] they want it handed to them. . . . You worked the menial jobs to get where you are—let them do it too."

Balzano knew what he was proposing—an intentional rending of American society along racial lines, for political profit. "caution-danger," he wrote. "With respect to the calculated polarization described in this paper, absolute secrecy cannot be overstated" or "there would be no way of calculating the damage to the Administration." The capitalization is his.

Colson and Balzano had many intellectual allies in the Nixon administration. "All the talk about Republicans making inroads into the Negro vote is persiflage. . . . the Republicans are never going to get more than 10 to 20 percent of the Negro vote," said Phillips, who had been assigned to Mitchell's staff at Justice after serving as a campaign strategist. But that was okay, he told a reporter. "The more Negroes who register as Democrats in the South, the sooner the Negrophobe whites will quit the Democrats and become Republicans. That's where the votes are."

"There is a legitimate grievance in my view of white working class people that every time, on every issue, that the black militants loud-mouth it, we come up with more money, whether for their colleges, for civil rights enforcement, for ghetto schools, for new appointments," Pat Buchanan advised his boss. "The time has come to say—we have done enough for the poor blacks; right now we want to give some relief for working class ethnics and Catholics—and make an unabashed appeal to these patient working people."

The result, said Ehrlichman, was that Nixon juggled competing demands. The courts were insisting on one thing; the voters clamoring for another. "A lot of our time was spent in reconciling the so-called Southern Strategy of Nixon's, which cracked the South for the Republicans . . . and the requirements of law," he would recall.

A RUSH OF retirements on the U.S. Supreme Court gave Nixon an early opportunity to pay back his debt to the South. But in November 1969 the Democrat-controlled Senate rejected Nixon's nomination of federal judge Clement Haynsworth of South Carolina to the Court.* Both the next nominee—Judge G. Harrold Carswell of Georgia—and his confirmation process were as disastrous. Democrats and liberal Republicans spent the spring of 1970 exposing Carswell's racist past and general mediocrity, prompting Senator Roman Hruska, a Republican from Nebraska, to defend him in nigh-legendary terms.

"There are a lot of mediocre judges and people and lawyers. They are entitled to a little representation, aren't they?" Hruska asked. "We can't have all Brandeises, Frankfurters and Cardozos." Perhaps not, but the Senate decided that excellence was not so bad a grail, and maybe it would be better if the next Supreme Court justice was not a segregationist. Carswell was rejected on April 8.

Nixon used the defeats of his two southern nominees to forge a common identity with the voters in Dixie. He may well have salvaged more support than he'd have gained had the two men been approved. "As long as the Senate is constituted the way it is today, I will not nominate another southerner and let him be subjected to the kind of malicious character assassination accorded both Judges Haynsworth and Carswell," the seemingly furious president told the nation. "I understand the bitter feelings of millions of Americans who live in the South about the act of regional discrimination that took place."†

* The Haynsworth defeat was, in part, payback for the role that Republicans played in the fall of 1968, employing hardball tactics to stop LBJ's selection of Abe Fortas to succeed Earl Warren as chief justice. Not wanting Nixon to choose his replacement, Warren had announced his retirement. But once Fortas was blocked, the choice fell to Nixon, who named Warren Burger.
† Within a week, House Republican leader Gerald Ford, with information supplied him by the Nixon administration, had launched a defamatory campaign to impeach liberal justice William Douglas. It did not succeed.

—

EVENTUALLY, JUSTICE HARRY Blackmun of Minnesota was unanimously confirmed, joining his friend Chief Justice Warren Burger on the court. The next two men that Nixon named (he disregarded Pat's lobbying for a female nominee)—Lewis Powell of Virginia and William Rehnquist of Arizona—were militant conservatives. Over time, Nixon's appointees to the federal courts would reverse the leftward drift of the Warren years on an array of issues, including civil rights. "Equality was no longer the pole star," wrote Michael J. Graetz and Linda Greenhouse, in their study of the Burger Court. Given Rehnquist's long and influential tenure, his appointment would be as far-reaching, and consequential, as any Nixon made. Rehnquist would serve from 1972 to 2005. After being raised to chief justice by Ronald Reagan in 1986, he led the court on a rightward course, narrowing previous rulings on defendant rights, abortion, affirmative action, and other issues.

When it came to ending segregation, Nixon assured Senator Richard Russell of Georgia, the key was "to do what is legally required, but not to be evangelic."

AND YET. IF Nixon's behavior on the rights of black Americans reflected his political calculations, it also showed the striations in his character. He would not have gotten to be president without that streak of Frank Nixon's feistiness: after years of rising in a cutthroat business with no cause to carry him but his own wits, gall, and footwork, Nixon was crafty and expedient. He was a son of Southern California conservatism, with an old-fashioned veneration of values like property, order, work, and duty. But he was, as well, Hannah Nixon's boy—a sensitive man, raised in the Quaker faith, with a feel for underdogs and outsiders.

The politics were treacherous "through which he had to weave his way," said Garment. But "his gut was on the right side. He wanted to see something done. He knew this was a measure of his administration."

When they were allied in the cause of civil rights during the 1950s, King had expressed concern that Nixon's protean talents could make him "the most dangerous man in America." Nixon was now proving himself, if not dangerous, then certainly conniving. He was an improviser, with no firm ties to the liberal order of his day, yet no particular wish to destroy it. The issue of race was an obstacle to negotiate, like other domestic matters; to be faced, in its guises, with responses handy and dependent on the moment, while he chased his fancies of History and Peace. When the Supreme Court called for immediate action on integration, Nixon the idealist responded, as did the boy who followed the rules, and also the conniver who, recognizing inevitability, still tried to wring what advantage he could. He would obey the courts. But he would do so from behind a blind of rhetoric, assuring the South that their common foes were compelling him to take action. "What Nixon brought to Thurmond, and to the South generally, was an empathy," said Huston. He let the southerners know that "this whole thing is very disquieting. It's disrupting. We're talking about uprooting an entire society and its norms." That was half the message— the half that the press, the left, and the civil rights groups heard. The second part of the message, which was not heard, or was heard and dismissed, was "I'm going to get it done."

"We will carry out the law," he vowed, in a December 8, 1969, press conference. That was a promise he kept.

NIXON'S FUNDAMENTAL DECLARATION on civil rights, a white paper prompted by the federal court orders on school desegregation and released in March 1970, was unequivocal in its condemnation of race-based exclusion. "Deliberate racial segregation of pupils by official action is unlawful wherever it exists," Nixon said. "In the words of the Supreme Court, it must be eliminated, 'root and branch'—and it must be eliminated at once."

There was more than principle at stake. The last thing Nixon wanted was another Little Rock, or a fusillade of gunfire like that which accompanied James Meredith's enrollment at Ole Miss. Nixon and his political advisers wanted to attract a modest percentage of black voters in both the South and North in his reelection campaign, and they recognized that, for the electorate at large, they needed to maintain their image as problem-solving moderates. There was a need to stay free of "racist taint," Dent said, and provide "leadership to desegregate without bullets, blood and bitterness."

The key, Nixon concluded, was to find reasonable southerners, white and black, who would join to carry out the now-inevitable integration of their public schools. To meet the Supreme Court's mandates, George Shultz, with help from Garment and Moynihan and others, created local advisory committees in seven southern states* and, without fanfare, enlisted black

* Alabama, Arkansas, Georgia, Louisiana, Mississippi, North Carolina, and South Carolina.

and white citizens to sit down and find ways for their children to share classrooms. As the first day of the 1970 school year neared, Nixon personally joined the effort: meeting with the state committees in the White House, playing on southern pride, and keeping the weaponry that they knew he possessed—the ability to cut off federal funds for their school systems, or to go to court for judicial orders—oiled but holstered.

Working their way across the map of Dixie, Nixon and his aides honed their choreography until they had the "program" down, Shultz recalled. "We recruited these groups . . . we'd invite them up to Washington and we'd sit them in the Roosevelt Room [across the hall from the Oval Office] and open up the discussion. And the first group was from Mississippi and of course they started arguing."

Shultz would let the participants bicker, until "they had gotten it out of their system a little bit." Then John Mitchell would arrive, on cue, and play the tough cop—informing the visitors that they had not a jot of wiggle room: the law was the law.

"It's been an interesting discussion about the merits, but the discussion's kind of irrelevant," Shultz would say. "The point is, it's going to happen and you may like it, you may not like it, but it's going to happen. So the question is: How do you manage it?"

Nixon's aides had a trove of money, approved by Congress, which was offered to the locals to sweeten things. And when he thought the moment was right, Shultz would bring the group into the Oval Office, where the president would play on their awe, patriotism, and sense of history.

"Here we are in the Oval Office. Think of the decisions that have been made here," Nixon would say. "And we're involved in another great decision for our county. I've made my decision. But in a country like ours, that's not enough. People make decisions in states and communities and neighborhoods if this is going to work."

"President Nixon was magnificent," Shultz recalled. "People went out of there on Cloud Nine . . . inspired."

Nixon's allotment of his time, and the always unwelcome task of personally pleading, reflected his commitment to the cause, and the importance with which he weighed it. His performance with the seventh delegation to get the treatment—the Louisianans—was perhaps the most impressive. After six successful performances in Washington, Shultz had taken the show on the road and discovered that, without the majesty of the White House to awe them, the black and white leaders gathered in a New Orleans hotel conference room were more resistant. When the president arrived,

Shultz confessed to him: "Always before it was all teed up, but you've got to tee it up yourself this time because we're not quite there."

Agnew had warned Nixon that something like this might happen. "When the schools open, there will be blood running through the streets of the South, and if you go, this will be blood on your hands," Shultz remembers the vice president saying. "This is not your issue. This is the issue of the liberals who have pushed for desegregation. Stay away." Southern Republican leaders had added their words of caution. "It will become Nixon's integration," a worried North Carolinian warned the White House.

But if Nixon was irritated by the unexpected change in the scenario, and the challenge he now faced to "tee it up," he didn't let it affect his performance. "He came in . . . and turned it around," Shultz remembered. "I had a lump in my throat." Nixon persuaded the Louisianans to cooperate, and then stood with the representatives of both races, from all seven states, before the television cameras. "The transition will be orderly and peaceful," the president told the nation. "This is one country, and one people."

"It will be harmful politically," Nixon had told Ehrlichman before heading to New Orleans, "but it will help the schools so we'll do it."

"I WANTED TO bring the South into this Union. Back into this country," Nixon told newsman David Frost in 1977. "Instead of making a grandstand play out of it, I did it quietly, with persuasion and with great effect." In his memoir of the Nixon years, speechwriter William Safire summed up the policy as "Make-it-happen, but don't make it seem like Appomattox."

"It worked," wrote Dean Kotlowski, a scholar of the era. "A confluence of presidential leadership, federal persuasion, Supreme Court rulings, Justice Department lawsuits, and the threat of HEW denying holdout districts federal aid broke white southern resistance."

"Out of a total school population of 3 million, only 186,000 African American children attended desegregated schools in the South prior to 1969. During autumn 1969, after the Nixon administration began to desegregate schools via litigation, 600,000 southern blacks entered desegregated schools" and by the end of 1970 "two million more African Americans were attending desegregated schools," Kotlowski wrote. "In this sense, Nixon was the greatest school desegregator in American history."

The budget bureau was put on notice, and congressional appropriators cooperated. During Nixon's first term, the funds available for the enforcement of civil rights, including the inducements for integrating school districts, leapt from $75 million to $2.6 *billion*. Early in the Nixon years, Mitchell had met with a group of civil rights activists. "You will be better advised," he told them, "to watch what we do instead of what we say."

And so Nixon's record on race is textured. "The standard indictment," wrote scholar Hugh Graham in 1987, "cannot account for the counterfactuals."

"Mr. Nixon was elected on a tide of reaction," said Payton, one of the few women, and African Americans, on his staff. "There was a good deal of space to the political right of him that he might have occupied, but did not.

"There was, predictably, a great deal of symbolic political activity directed at wooing the most discontented whites. But Mr. Nixon was no counterrevolutionary. Nor was Mr. Ehrlichman, nor Mr. Shultz. There is no villain in this piece," Payton said. "Indeed, some conservatives have never forgiven Mr. Nixon for being so sensible."

THE NIXON ADMINISTRATION's success at ending de jure segregation was not enough for civil rights activists, liberal members of Congress, and editorial writers who wanted to eliminate de facto segregation, in North and South, by busing schoolchildren across district lines or using court orders to integrate segregated neighborhoods. And so, Nixon received little credit for the revolution that he brought to the southern schools. Though he'd usually rant about media bias, in this case he was content to remain a quiet hero.*

"When this Administration comes up for re-election in 1972, desegregation will have been completed, killing the idea that the Administration has sold out to the South," Dent advised Nixon. But "we should insure that whatever blame emanates from the South is placed elsewhere." At all costs, they needed "to keep the fallout falling" onto the federal judiciary, civil rights groups, and northern liberals.

---

* The telling exception was among southern blacks, who gave credit to the president and handed Nixon a positive rating in a 1971 Gallup poll; 42 percent approved of the job Nixon was doing, and just 40 percent disapproved.

"The public schools in the South ended up more integrated than the public schools in Michigan," Moynihan recalled. "But at the time, nobody would say Nixon had done it. And, of course, he wouldn't say he had done it. He didn't want credit for it. He wanted to carry South Carolina. He wanted Strom Thurmond to say this is a good ole boy."

THE WHITE HOUSE took other unheralded steps toward racial equality. When southern hard-liners sought to dodge integration by enrolling children in segregated private academies, Nixon ignored the wishes of Thurmond and others and rejected the suggestion that the all-white private schools should have tax-exempt status. "Federal aid to schools deliberately segregated on racial grounds is wrong constitutionally, and morally," Harlow had advised. "The South will respect him for it, angered though it will temporarily be."

In 1970, Harlow was asked to explore the possibility that Virginia senator Harry Byrd, a noted segregationist, might join the state's Republican Party. After consulting with Republican governor Linwood Holton, Harlow reported: "Senator Byrd would bring in the red necks if he joined the party now, and this would destroy what we have been doing extremely well in Virginia. The present Republican Party in Virginia has no desire to befoul its ranks with white supremists."

If the South came to see him as "the goddamnest integrationist there is," Nixon told his aides, so be it. In early 1969, he created the Office of Minority Business Enterprise to encourage black, Latino, and American Indian entrepreneurs by setting aside federal contracts for minorities. And when Shultz and his African American deputy, Arthur Fletcher, presented the president with the first broad affirmative action plan—a muscular proposal called the Philadelphia Plan to integrate construction firms and other federal contractors—Nixon endorsed it, and defended it in Congress and the courts.

Nixon did not invent affirmative action. And, as with everything Nixon did on civil rights, there was a political component to his proposal. He savored, Ehrlichman recalled, how the Philadelphia Plan drove a wedge between two Democratic constituencies: minorities and labor. But whatever his motives, Nixon played the critical role in launching affirmative action, and two of his Supreme Court appointees a key part in preserving it. "In order to get beyond racism, we must first take account of race. There is no other way," wrote Blackmun, concurring with the ruling decision, written by Powell, in the case of *University of California v. Bakke* in 1978. "In order to treat persons equally, we must treat them differently."*

"You're not going to solve this race problem for a hundred years. Intermarriage and all that, assimilation, it will happen, but not in our time," Nixon told his aides.

"That's why I hit this minority enterprise thing so hard—sure, [the liberals] laugh at it—but better jobs, housing, Negroes moving to Scarsdale." He turned to Haldeman. "That's the only way they're going to get into Palisades High and Whittier High."

NIXON KNEW HOW artful was his treatment of race. At the 1970 Gridiron Dinner, he confessed it with a wink, while giving the club members and guests one of Washington's legendary performances. The white-tied swells were surprised when two pianos materialized on the Gridiron stage, so that Nixon and Agnew could perform as a duo, and everyone laughed when, no matter what song Nixon played—"Home on the Range" or the "Missouri Waltz" or "The Eyes of Texas Are Upon You"—Agnew drowned him out with "Dixie."

But one of the finest events in the Nixon White House—the one at which the president seemed to enjoy himself the most—was the April 29, 1969, celebration of Duke Ellington's seventieth birthday, a party packed with black jazz musicians, at which Nixon exchanged hugs and kisses with Ellington, awarded him the Medal of Freedom, and sat down at the piano to serenade the great bandleader and composer with a presidential rendition of "Happy Birthday."

It was an especially fine moment for the Washington-born Ellington, whose father had, on at least one occasion, worked in the mansion as a butler.

* The Bakke case is 438 U.S. 265 (1978).

Drawing the Sword

THE FLAG-DRAPED CASKETS kept coming home. In March 1970, Nixon's second year in office, the pro-Western leaders of the Cambodian military staged a coup, overthrowing the neutralist Prince Sihanouk and prompting the North Vietnamese and the home-grown Communist Khmer Rouge to march upon Phnom Penh. Events drew Nixon into crisis mode. That spring would produce some of the most emotionally charged and dramatic moments of his presidency.

There were already signs that the strain of the office, and the belligerency of his enemies, had begun to unsettle the president, dispelling the "mellow" Nixon of 1968 and unleashing the self-injurious behavior of old. In Haldeman's diary, the president's dark moods were making more frequent appearances. The Middle East was roiling, and the Soviets were exploiting the turbulent state of affairs to send arms and advisers to the Arab states. At home, the discord continued: fearful of clamorous protests, the Nixons were forced to cancel plans to attend Julie's graduation from Smith College.

"I truly think the day will be a disaster if he comes," Julie told Ehrlichman. "The temper up here is ugly." The leader of an antiwar rally led an audience of ten thousand in a chant of "Fuck Julie and David." When the couple moved to Washington, Pat and Dick came to their apartment for dinner. So did the protesters. "Julie cried. P left abruptly, really too bad . . . tough on the family," Haldeman noted in his diary.

Nixon was finding enemies everywhere: among liberals, the bureaucracy, on Capitol Hill, and in the press. "We can have peace. We can have prosperity. We can have all the blacks screwing the whites," and still not get credit from the liberal establishment, he complained. His orders sometimes sounded like the mutterings of a paranoid. He had his staff comb through the microfilm at the D.C. public library and compile every Drew Pearson column dating back to 1946 that mentioned his name. "Agnew must be warned," Nixon had told Haldeman and others, back during the campaign. "A candidate has *no* friends in the press—they are all enemies." He underlined the word *no* four times.

"Was Nixon paranoid? Yes," said aide Dwight Chapin. "But he also had the right to be."

"To understand Richard Nixon you have to look at what happened to that man at each step of his ascent to the White House," Chapin said. "He took on this self-survival . . . cloak, and that led to other things happening. The we vs. them."

A snarl of incitements spurred Nixon on. His goals were grandiose, and the lessons of his youth never left him—of an uncaring world's unfair dispersal of riches, good looks, and popularity; its random distribution of grief, and the need for unrelenting fortitude. And when he was frustrated, his fragile sense of worth was threatened, and often he lashed out.

Nixon's visitors were spared the ugliness. Representative Jim Wright, a Democrat from Texas, sized up the president in a sympathetic entry to his diary. "He is a cold customer," Wright wrote. "He gives the impression of aloofness and austerity. . . . He retreats behind a wall of privacy remarkable for a modern president."

But "he may be . . . a sensitive person," Wright reported. "The public doesn't love him, and this knowledge must bother him."

If Wright and other official callers missed Nixon's eruptions, subordinates were fair game, and frequently astonished by his crude, profane outbursts. After witnessing that side of Nixon during a 1968 campaign meeting, Alan Greenspan had spurned an invitation to join the administration. "He has enormous hang-ups. He is unable to get close to people," George H. W. Bush wrote his sons. "It's almost like he's afraid he'll be reamed in some way."

Doubt gnawed at Nixon. Victory could not console him. He looked at the dominoes that had toppled—the assassinations of John and Robert Kennedy, the collapse of Johnson, Rockefeller, and Romney, the split in the Democratic Party—and viewed his success as adventitious. Early in his presidency, on a trip to California, Nixon slipped away from the White House press pool and, with a single Secret Service agent as a driver, took Henry Kissinger and Bebe Rebozo on a tour of Yorba Linda and Whittier. "As he was talking softly and openly for the first time in our acquaintance, it suddenly struck me that the guiding theme of his discourse was how it had all been accidental," Kissinger would recall. "There was no moral to the tale except how easily it could have been otherwise. . . . He never was certain that he had earned it. . . . He could not find the locus of his achievements."

Work was his medication. So was risk. The arduous quest for the presidency and the all-consuming exercise of its powers furnished relief. "He had no personal ability to get control," his television adviser, Roger Ailes, recalled. "He has to live in a drama—in a Western: Nixon against the world." Another aide, years later, came to the conclusion that Nixon sought crises like a gambler craves the game. "He needed to tempt self-destruction," said Monica Crowley. "He courted controversy intention-ally . . . the thrill was in those few breathtaking moments when the dice were in the air."

Kissinger once posed the question: Given what this needy and imper-fect boss still managed to attain, what greater deeds might Nixon have accomplished if someone only loved him? But Elliot Richardson, who knew Nixon from the Eisenhower years and would serve him in several cabinet positions, suspected that an emotionally nourished Richard Nixon would never have achieved as much: "You could well say he never would have been president if he hadn't had that basic core of insecurity."

Discipline was paramount. It allowed Nixon to perform at high levels and surpass the flaws in his character. "I have a fetish about disciplining myself," he once said. "It is important to live like a Spartan," Nixon told another journalist. "The worst thing you can do in this job is to relax, to let up."

But self-restraint exhausted Nixon, and made him appear phony and uncaring. The fear of losing control left him tense, and tension fed grace-lessness. "I can't really let my hair down with anyone," he had once con-fessed to Stewart Alsop. "Not even with my family."* What love he earned flowed from admiration, or empathy from those who felt protective of the man. "He is a shy man, and he needs compassion," Kissinger told an old friend from Harvard that spring. The mean and the cruel—and those to whom he, in turn, was mean and cruel—reserved, for Nixon, a special hatred. And so did he for them.

"He was conscious every minute of self-discipline, therefore he couldn't relax," said Haldeman. "Such a man, in the pressures of the political world, would see enemies—most of them real—everywhere; would be unable to defeat those enemies by a normal 'easy' attitude that inspires popularity, would despair at his lack of natural charisma and realize that if he was to win he would have to attack and destroy."

In the best times, Nixon kept his dreams and resentments in balance. But in the crucible of a Cold War presidency, "Nixon's character began

---

* In another version, Alsop quotes Nixon saying, "Not even with Pat."

to change," Chapin recalled. "He cannot . . . does not . . . make good decisions when it's personalized and he is under attack politically. If it is abstract—China and Russia and the world today . . . he's brilliant. Brilliant strategist. But boy when you get in tight and close and everything else and you're fighting him and you're fighting his people and you're coming at him and its them vs. we—he starts falling apart."

PAT HELPED, AS she could. But the new First Lady had undergone her own difficult first year. She seemed lost or glum, fretted about letting Dick down, and focused on familiar tasks she knew she could accomplish—like answering her mail.

"The West Wing wanted the First Lady to be quiet, not to make waves, to go to tea parties, to be seen but not heard," said Sheila Weidenfeld, a television journalist in the Nixon years and a future First Lady's press secretary. Pat Nixon "wasn't allowed to be. She wasn't allowed to express an opinion," said Weidenfeld. "If she had married somebody else who made her feel more secure in herself, she might have had a happier life."

"She was . . . afraid to say anything—afraid of what the outcome would be. Would she say something wrong? Would this effect something? Would they scream and yell? She had no support whatsoever," said Weidenfeld.

Nixon wanted his wife to stay in her place. "Good," he wrote, when the press noted how she shied from controversy. "We don't want her to become like Eleanor Roosevelt."

Now, more than ever, it seemed like Dick and Pat worked as partners in a family business—each with duties that engulfed their relationship. After dinner or White House social events, the president and his wife retreated to their separate desks to put in extra hours of work. The demands and constant scrutiny limited their ability to relax and enjoy the whirl.

"The President does not dance," wrote Pat's press secretary, Constance Stuart, to another White House aide. "He never has and he and the Mrs. have an agreement that even though she loves to dance, she doesn't want to get stuck dancing if he isn't. So, neither of them do."

Pat didn't fit in with the boys—Abplanalp and Rebozo—and was often left alone, and bored, in Key Biscayne or didn't make the trip to Florida, or Camp David, with Dick at all. Stuart alerted Haldeman to remind the Boss that the Nixons' thirtieth wedding anniversary was approaching. "Pearls are the traditional gift for thirty years of wedded bliss," she noted.

The staff witnessed signs of coldness. "I don't have a lot to talk with my wife about at dinner and I find I don't have anything to talk about to the guest's wife," Nixon told Haldeman, reviewing the seating arrangements for state dinners. "I hate it."

It was to Haldeman that Nixon left the onerous duty of telling Pat, or Rose or Julie or Tricia, that "the president doesn't have time to see you." Even a veteran political wife like Pat could not adjust to the all-consuming obligations, big decisions, and tide of data that were swamping her husband. "It was hard for Pat Nixon in lots of ways," Haldeman recalled. There were no Judith Exners or Lucy Mercers: the presidency was Nixon's mistress. She was "the wife of a man who was totally absorbed in his work," said Haldeman.

"While he always loved and respected her, his profound introversion and selfish decision-making kept their relationship out of balance," wrote John Taylor, who ran the former president's office after the Nixons left the White House. "Too many instructions to several generations of aides began with the words, 'Call Mrs. Nixon and tell her that. . . .'"

After watching the Nixons interact on a presidential trip to Texas, Ailes warned Haldeman that "it is important for the President to show a little more concern for Mrs. Nixon as he moves through the crowd. At one point he walked off in a different direction. Mrs. Nixon wasn't looking and had to run to catch up. From time to time he should talk to her and smile at her. Women voters are particularly sensitive to how a man treats his wife in public."

The press saw Pat as a cipher or a victim, robotic, or as a woman who had subjugated her independence in a Faustian bargain for wealth and comfort. "She had been through a lot, so, consequently, she rather expected things to be as they were. She expected them to be rather bad, and they were," Nixon recalled, bristling at the criticism.

Some of the damage was self-inflicted, by the controlling White House staff. "Too often they come across as actors in the plot," said a Nixon public relations adviser, confidentially weighing in on the role of Pat, Tricia, and Julie. "Like the president himself they are the victims of complicated programming that stifles their warm and genuine appeal."

Helen Thomas, the White House correspondent for UPI, came to regret that she did not tell Pat how much she admired her. "She was a real human being, a great human being," Thomas recalled, but one who had "learned in the years of politics that the quieter you are, the better off you are."

Then, in the spring of 1970, Peru was struck by a massive earthquake. It was one of the deadliest natural disasters of the twentieth century, killing sixty-six thousand people. Pat offered to visit the shattered country, and

Nixon seconded the suggestion with enthusiasm. She roamed far beyond Lima, to the most ravaged districts, hugging the homeless and consoling the wounded. It was a humanitarian and diplomatic triumph that showed Pat she could make a difference, and propelled her into a more confident role as First Lady.

"As you know we have tried hard . . . to project 'color' about you, to portray the human side of the President, the personal warmth, the compassionate, considerate qualities that you have," Colson wheedled in a memo to the president. "Because of the hostility of the media, it has been an exceedingly difficult, frustrating and not especially successful undertaking.

"Mrs. Nixon has now broken through where we had failed. She has come across as a warm, charming, graceful, concerned, articulate and most importantly—a very human person," Colson wrote. "It would be hard to overestimate the political impact. . . . She is an enormous asset."

IN APRIL, AN oxygen tank on the *Apollo 13* spacecraft exploded, putting the lives of three astronauts in jeopardy. The country and its president faced a week of anxiousness and worry: Would those brave men suffocate in space, as Earth listened in on their deaths? Nixon was as tense as anyone and, relieved when the heroes returned safely, ordered celebratory drinks. By 3 p.m. the commander in chief, Haldeman noted, was hammered and snoring.

It was during that week, on a trip to Hawaii to welcome the heroic astronauts home, that a briefing from his Pacific commanders persuaded Nixon that he needed to take forceful action to save Cambodia. The president seemed "overwrought" and "increasingly agitated," Kissinger recorded, but his reasoning was sound. If the Communists seized the rest of Indochina, South Vietnam appeared doomed.

"Do you think there's a prayer for Vietnamization if Cambodia is taken over?" Kissinger asked Rogers.

"Yes," said Rogers. It would be a setback, but the South could survive.

"You're entitled to your opinion," Kissinger told him.

The initial plan was for the South Vietnamese Army, supported by U.S. artillery and aircraft, to go into Cambodia and attack the North Vietnamese military headquarters and ordnance depots at a salient called the Parrot's Beak. Nixon proposed to double the mission, adding thirty thousand American troops to cross the border and sweep through a second Communist sanctuary known as the Fishhook. At a meeting of NSC officials, Agnew had recommended that the administration stop "pussyfooting," and Nixon, not to be outdone at manly chest-beating, expanded the scope of the invasion. He fortified his nerves with viewings of the motion picture *Patton* and cocktail cruises on the White House yacht *Sequoia* with his family, Rebezo, and aides. On May 1, as the boat approached Mount Vernon, Nixon punched the air and told an aide that he wanted the national anthem "blasted out." He and Bebe, Pat and David and Julie stood at attention in the bow while a recording of "The Star-Spangled Banner" played. "It was a lonely time for him," his military aide, Jack Brennan, remembered. "I had never seen him appear so physically exhausted."

"Historians rarely do justice to the psychological stress on a policy maker," Kissinger noted. Nixon was raging, hanging up on aides, and increasingly huddling in his hideaway office in the Executive Office Building, "reflecting, resenting, collecting his thoughts and his anger."

"Don't worry about divisiveness—having drawn the sword, don't take it out—stick it in hard," Nixon told his staff. "Hit them in the gut."

THE CAMBODIAN INCURSION was marginally successful, in that it disrupted the Communist command, bought Nixon more time, and demonstrated that the South Vietnamese could put up a fight. "After 1969 the war in Vietnam had turned into a race between our withdrawals, the improvement of the South Vietnamese Army, and the ability of Hanoi to interrupt the process by launching offensives," Kissinger wrote. The incursion secured the border for most of 1971.

The gains, however, were not commensurate with the cost. The purpose of the mission was not, as many in the peace movement charged, to open a new front, escalate the fighting, and involve all of Southeast Asia in the conflagration. Quite the opposite: the offensive was limited in scope and designed to provide time and cover for Vietnamization. But it *looked* like Tricky Dick was expanding the conflict—after promising the country he would wind it down. His April 30 speech announcing the incursion was not so calm and reasoned as the silent majority address; he looked tense and had to pause to wipe the sweat from his upper lip. "If, when the chips are down, the world's most powerful nation, the United States of America, acts like a pitiful, helpless giant, the forces of totalitarianism and anarchy will threaten free nations and free institutions throughout the world," he said.

Drafted with the help of the pugnacious Buchanan, Nixon's speech was deceptive (falsely claiming that the United States had always "scrupulously" respected Cambodian neutrality) and gratuitously confrontational. So was the president's comment, recorded by the press as he left the Pentagon the next day, that college students who opposed the war were pampered and ungrateful "bums." It reflected his lifelong prejudice against the sons and daughters of the Ivy League but was difficult to apply to the hundreds of demonstrations that had erupted throughout the country, at institutions like Notre Dame, the University of Virginia, or Kent State—an Ohio university with a student body drawn from the working and middle class. During a weekend of unrest at the college, in which arsonists torched the ROTC building, Governor James Rhodes dispatched the Ohio National Guard to restore order, with live ammunition and predictable results. On May 4, the raw, tired, taunted guardsmen fired into a crowd of protesters. Four students died, nine were wounded. Several were just spectators; others had been walking to class.

Nixon was stunned. "I could not get the photographs out of my mind," he recalled in his memoirs. "I could not help thinking about the families, suddenly receiving the news that their children were dead."

"I thought of my own daughters . . . of their learning to talk and to walk, and their first birthdays, and the trips we took together, going to the ballgame . . . and to the circus . . . getting them through the teenage years, getting them through college and then—*whoosh*—all gone."

But publicly, his response was unyielding, even cruel. "When dissent turns to violence it invites tragedy," the White House statement said.

Nixon's pose crumbled in the face of the resultant, "profoundly unnerving" uproar, Kissinger recalled. Across the nation, higher education ground to a halt, as campus after campus suspended classes or was closed by student strikes. Three members of Nixon's NSC staff resigned. The atmosphere was "absolutely poisonous," aide William Smyser recalled. "We were not only fighting the North Vietnamese, we were fighting the Americans."

EISENHOWER, KENNEDY, AND Johnson had all suffered moments when the stupefying strain in their lives—the knowledge that a blunder could leave hundreds of millions dead, and civilization in radioactive ruin—led them to episodes of rage or sorrow, use of drugs or alcohol, stress-induced illness, or bizarre behavior. The spring of 1970 saw Nixon's visit to that sort of Gethsemane.

It was a "paradox," Garment said. When wounded, Nixon was both strengthened—in that he drew renewed confidence from surviving—and weakened, in that he just could not forgive, or forget, or bring a halt to his self-destructive gnashing. "This man had real demons," Gerald Ford remembered.

Nixon's national security adviser and later secretary of state, Henry Kissinger, was a fawning but talented courtier who avoided the crimes of Watergate.

Nixon's aides strove to keep the volatile president happy. Charles Colson (left) was a provocateur who fed Nixon's baser instincts. H. R. "Bob" Haldeman (center) and John Ehrlichman (right) clung to power by giving Nixon a "Berlin Wall" that blocked outsiders. All three were sentenced to prison.

The newly elected president spent hours alone or with his staff, and Pat felt swamped by her duties as First Lady. But by the time Nixon ran for reelection, she was a major political asset, as were their daughters.

The need to humanize the introverted president led to a Florida photo shoot. Here Nixon stands on the beach with his friend Charles "Bebe" Rebozo and the family's Irish setter, King Timahoe. "A nation of dog lovers can't hate a man who loves dogs," a political consultant advised the president.

Tricia Nixon's wedding to Ed Cox captivated television viewers. Before and after the ceremony, however, Nixon raged at his enemies. "I get a lot of advice on PR and personality and how I've got to put on my nice-guy hat and dance at the White House, so I did it," he told his cabinet. "But let me make it clear that's not my nature."

"Don't ever lose sight of Vietnam as the overriding factor in the first Nixon term," Bob Halde-man would instruct. "It overshadowed everything, all the time, in every discussion, in every deci-sion, in every opportunity and every problem." More than twenty thousand U.S. soldiers, and hundreds of thousands of civilians, died on Nixon's watch. He was captured by photographers visiting with soldiers in the field (top left). In the evocative photograph immediately above, he reviews the troops at a fog-cloaked ceremony. His conduct of the Vietnam War led Nixon (seen at a press conference, top right) into conflict with his old foes in the media. "The press is the enemy. The press is the enemy. The press is the enemy," Nixon recited to his aides.

The opponents to the Vietnam War organized monumental antiwar demonstrations in Washington. The administration circled the White House grounds with buses, at one point, and troops were billeted in the Old Executive Office Building, in case it became necessary to defend the grounds.

Nixon sought to capitalize politically by polarizing the country. He and his aides got a hoped-for confrontation with rock-throwing protesters in San Jose during the 1970 campaign, but Nixon's grim response in Phoenix, seen here and televised nationwide on the eve of the balloting, was politically catastrophic overkill.

Nixon and Henry Kissinger are heard on the White House tapes discussing the most politically advantageous time for ending the Vietnam War. Critics saw raw opportunism when Kissinger announced, at a White House briefing just days before the 1972 election, that "peace is at hand" in Southeast Asia. It wasn't.

Richard Nixon had a peculiar personality, and the joys of relationships and relaxation did not come easy. He and Pat enjoyed the trappings and thrills of the presidency (above), but Dick had to work hard at relating to the voters. Here he is seen bowling at the White House, hosting rock star Elvis Presley in the Oval Office, and banging at the piano at the Grand Ole Opry in Nashville.

Nixon's February 1972 trip to China was indeed "the week that changed the world." Here he is seen shaking hands with Zhou Enlai (left) and reviewing troops at the Beijing airport upon his arrival (right). Nixon was preparing for a nap when word arrived at his villa that Mao would see him. The two old Cold War adversaries chatted happily in Mao's home (below) and agreed that a right-wing president had more freedom to negotiate with Communists. In other words, only Nixon could go to China.

Pat was enchanted by the giant pandas at the Beijing Zoo (left) and, at a banquet later with Zhou Enlai, pointed at an illustration of the bears on a cigarette package. Said Pat: "They're so adorable. I love them." Said Zhou: "I'll give you some." Said Pat: "Cigarettes?" "No," said Zhou: "Pandas." At right, Dick and Pat visit the Great Wall.

From one of the Watergate burglars, the police obtained a key piece of evidence linking the Nixon administration to the crime: an address book (above) with the White House ("WH") phone number of ringleader "HH" (Howard Hunt). John Dean, the White House counsel (top left), was the first Nixon intimate to tell what he knew about the Watergate break-ins and the other "White House horrors" to federal prosecutors. Dean's testimony played a key part in the eventual convictions of John Mitchell (top right) and other Nixon aides.

As the Watergate crisis deepened, Nixon fought to save his presidency by playing a trump card: his expertise in foreign affairs. Here he is seen on his June 1974 trip through the Middle East—in a parade (above) and a meeting with Egyptian president Anwar Sadat (at right)—and in the seaside library of his home in San Clemente, during summit talks with Leonid Brezhnev (below).

In the first week of August 1974, the Republican leaders in Congress brought Nixon the news: the party had deserted him, and his old friends and allies would vote to impeach and convict him of the crimes of Watergate. Here, from left to right, Senate minority leader Hugh Scott of Pennsylvania, Senator Barry Goldwater of Arizona, and House minority leader John Rhodes of Arizona address the press outside the White House, after giving Nixon the bad news.

Pat Nixon came to hate this photograph of the Nixon family (left) taken on the night before Dick announced that he would resign the presidency. "Our hearts were breaking and there we are smiling," Pat would tell her daughter Julie. After the formal posing was over, the photographer caught Nixon and Julie in a sorrowful embrace (right).

Over Pat's objections, Nixon allowed the press to cover his farewell to his staff, in the East Room of the White House on August 9, 1974, the day he resigned the presidency. It was an unforgettable, perhaps unmatched, moment in American history. The president and his family and aides struggled to control their emotions. "Only if you have been in the deepest valley can you ever know how magnificent it is to be on the highest mountain," Nixon told them. Be strong, he urged them. "It is only a beginning, always."

As exiles, the Nixons retreated to La Casa Pacifica (left), their estate on the Pacific coast in California, pictured below. In time, they returned to the East Coast (right), to be closer to their daughters and grandchildren.

To help pay his massive legal bills, Nixon wrote his memoirs and agreed to appear in a series of televised interviews with David Frost (pictured together). "I gave them a sword," Nixon said of his political enemies. "I let down the country."

He lived for almost twenty years after leaving office, succumbing to a stroke in 1994, less than a year after Pat Nixon's death in 1993. Her funeral, above.

On August 9, 1974, Richard Nixon became the first U.S. president to resign in disgrace.

On the night of May 8, Nixon held a prime-time press conference, assuring Americans that the U.S. forces in Cambodia would withdraw soon and that he would keep his promise to bring home another 150,000 troops from Southeast Asia. In the Parrot's Beak and the Fishhook, "we have bought at least six months, and probably eight months of time," he said. Afterward, wired from the performance, and "agitated and uneasy" from the week's events, he worked the telephone long past midnight, consulting with aides, advisers, and reporters. He was facing an emotional crisis as real as that confronting the country. Unable to sleep, he put Rachmaninoff on the stereo and awakened his valet, Manolo Sanchez. Sometime after 4 a.m., he decided to show Sanchez the glories of the Lincoln Memorial at night.

"Searchlight is on the lawn!" a White House guard reported, using the president's Secret Service code name. (Nixon would recall with satisfaction that "I've never seen the Secret Service quite so petrified with apprehension.") Nixon, Sanchez, and the presidential physician, Dr. Walter Tkach, got in a car and left the White House. A few minutes behind them, in a second auto, was the frantic Egil Krogh, the White House aide who was on duty that night. The Lincoln Memorial steps, rising above the Mall, were a rendezvous for students assembling for that day's demonstrations. "Perhaps the major contribution I could make to them was to try to lift them a bit out of the miserable intellectual wasteland in which they now wander aimlessly," Nixon told Haldeman later that week. Some of the students gathered round, and he awkwardly tried to connect. His feelings surfaced in zoetropic flashes. Peace and war were on his mind that night, the lesions of his childhood, his mother and her death.

"My goals in Vietnam were the same as theirs—to stop the killing and end the war," he would remember. He spoke about his own generation, about Munich and Chamberlain and Churchill, and the need to deal with Russia and open China. "It was not just a drop by . . . he had no talking points," Krogh recalled. "His manner was intense—trying to reach out into them, to communicate with them. I've never seen him do it like this before. . . . He was trying to empathize with them as best he could."

"I hope you realize that we are willing to die for what we believe in," one student demonstrator told the president.

Of course, Nixon responded. "Many of us when we were your age were also willing to die for what we believed in," he said. "The point is, we are trying to build a world in which you will not have to die for what you believe in."

Trying to "draw them out," Nixon asked about their college football teams and spoke of his own days at Whittier College; about surfing, the environment, the plight of the American Indians, and the rewards of traveling through Europe and Asia. It was important to understand, he said, that amid the material comforts of life, it is "the elements of the spirit that really matter."

Streaks of rose above the Capitol signaled the approach of day. As he returned to his limousine, Nixon ran across Bob Moustakas, a tall and portly bearded longhair from Detroit who, by self-admission, was not looking his best after a long drive to Washington, in which mood-altering substances were consumed. Moustakas had a camera, and Nixon called on Tkach to take their picture. The mood was not hostile, Moustakas later recalled, but it was stilted—like that of a high school party, in which the host's parents came down to the basement rec room to make small talk. As they posed and chatted, Nixon assessed Moustakas, and told him how, in China, the children were culled at an early age and sent off on different tracks, toward professional, academic, or manual labors. The system was flawed, Nixon said, for it missed "late bloomers." Then he patted Moustakas on the back, as if to say, there is hope for you yet.

The failure of the Lincoln Memorial visit was "a great shame," said Ehrlichman, because "that was an opportunity for some reconciliation that didn't take place." Nixon and the students "just never reached each other." Ehrlichman had a similar experience when he brought a small group of Kent State students to meet with Nixon in the Oval Office. Intimidated by the setting, they grew tongue-tied in the president's presence.

NIXON WAS NOT finished roaming. To the Capitol they drove, where he tried to show Sanchez the Senate and his old vice-presidential office and, finding the doors locked, settled on taking him into the House chamber and ushering him up to the rostrum, to stand where the Speaker wields the gavel and deliver a speech that Nixon applauded. In Statuary Hall, as the president made his way back to the car, a cleaning lady caught his attention and asked him to sign her Bible. He did so and urged her to read it faithfully. "Most of us don't read it enough," he said. And then, holding her hand, he stammered with some emotion, "You know, my mother was a saint. She died two years ago. She was a saint. You be a saint too."

Frenzied aides, who had rushed into town from their homes in the suburbs ("Weirdest day so far," Haldeman confided to his diary), caught up to Nixon at the Capitol. He decided to take them to breakfast. To the

Mayflower, he told his driver. The presidential entourage arrived at the hotel restaurant, sat down, and gave their orders to the startled waitresses. Nixon remembered how, as a young politician in the 1950s, he liked their corned beef hash and eggs. Finally, with morning well under way, and groups of demonstrators tromping the streets, Haldeman and Krogh persuaded Nixon, with more than a little difficulty, that it was not safe to walk back to the White House. He got back in the car, passed through a ring of buses parked end to end around the mansion grounds, and the gates of "this great white jail," as Truman called it, shut behind him.

"I am concerned about his condition," Haldeman confided to his diary. "The decision, the speech, the aftermath killings, riots, press, etc.; the press conference, the student confrontation have all taken their toll, and he has had very little sleep for a long time and his judgment, temper and mood suffer badly. . . . He's still riding on the crisis wave, but the letdown is near at hand and will be huge."

Kissinger was worried as well. "He was prepared to make decisions without illusion. Once convinced, he went ruthlessly and courageously to the heart of the matter," the national security adviser recalled, "but each controversial decision drove him deeper into his all-enveloping solitude."

NIXON WAS NOT a mirthless man. Prowling a hotel hallway in his bathrobe one night during the 1968 campaign, he had come upon an aide who was escorting a young lady to his room. "Mike, we don't have to get those votes one at a time, you know," he said. When Elvis Presley arrived at the White House, hoping to visit with Nixon, the president played along and welcomed him into the Oval Office. He gave Presley a federal narcotics agent's badge, accepted a Colt .45 pistol from the singer, and posed for a very famous photograph.

Nixon loved to watch movies and remained a dedicated sports fan. The White House tapes capture a Sunday on which Pat dispatched Julie to convey the word that dinner was getting cold, as the president watched the Washington Redskins make a thrilling second-half comeback against the Dallas Cowboys. (Nixon: "Hit him, hit him, goddammit!" Julie: "Uh-oh.") He made the effort, in the midst of his schedule, to research and compile lists of the greatest baseball players (pre– and post–World War II). "He's spending an incredible amount of time today on the whole thing. Working out all the little details. . . . Kind of fascinating and not just a little amusing," Haldeman told his diary.

But recreation was submitted to the test of efficiency. "A swim, which may take an hour, in the surf, a walk on the beach, bowling for an hour may not give me as much pleasure as four to five hours on the golf course might give me, but I have no feeling of shortchanging my greater responsibilities," he informed his aides in a memo on his personal habits. "A ride on a boat in the Florida Keys or in the Bahamas for an hour is also enormously refreshing and does not consume so much time that I feel guilty."

A White House public relations consultant, in a twenty-seven-page memo on mystique making, advised the staff to make Nixon seem more human. "It is great to eat cottage cheese," the PR man wrote. "But it's better to emphasize his passion for good red meat, hot dogs . . . and pizza pies—even if he doesn't like them . . . he has to get the message across that he's as vulnerable to the tempting little sins of life as the rest of mankind."

The adviser suggested that they go to work promoting the president's relationship with King Timahoe. "A nation of dog lovers can't hate a man who loves dogs," the consultant wrote. "To the broad American public, the companionship between a man and his dog is still a changeless image of trust and devotion." Nixon posed for photographs with the Irish setter, but he had no more time for King Timahoe than he did for pizza or golf.

"Timahoe spent all the time with Manolo and really didn't know who the president was," said aide Steve Bull.

"He had no hobbies. The presidency was his hobby," said Butterfield. "He meditated, he thought, he pondered. He worked on his yellow pad."

Nixon and Rebozo would sit in silence as Rebozo's boat cruised the turquoise waters off Florida. Or Nixon would take long walks, "all by himself, thinking and meditating," along the beach of Bob Abplanalp's private island in the Bahamas. "The great classic remark about Bebe was that Richard Nixon really most preferred to be alone," said Haldeman, "and that's why he spent so much time with Bebe Rebozo."

Nixon recognized the limits of his relationship with Rebozo. "I do not have a friend in the world," he told his cousin Jessamyn. He was barely more generous in a conversation with Lyndon Johnson. "Old Bebe is a great guy to have around," Nixon told his predecessor. "He cheers people up . . . he never brings up any unpleasant subjects." It was Bebe's job to be "a sponge" for Dick, Pat said.

Why did his brother so like the beach? Ed Nixon was asked. It was the "white noise" of the waves, he replied. It left Dick alone to think.

NIXON'S WHIMS WERE bafflingly fickle. Kennedy's ghost seemed to haunt him, and evoked wildly varying responses. He excised a reference to the

"Battle Hymn of the Republic" from the draft of one speech because, he told Safire, it was "a Kennedy song" played at Robert Kennedy's funeral. After spotting photographs of JFK in an office in the Executive Office Building, Nixon ordered Butterfield to search the place for Kennedy likenesses, to have them removed—and to investigate the loyalty of the employee with the offending pictures. Butterfield complied, checking the worker's name against FBI, CIA, and HUAC security files, and reported back to Nixon when the walls were properly purged.

When gushing coverage of the new John F. Kennedy Center for the Performing Arts was cited in a White House news summary, Nixon scrawled a note to Haldeman complaining about the "orgasm over this utter architectural monstrosity." Despite a personal appeal from Rose Kennedy, Nixon declined to attend the official opening of the center. The next day, he quizzed Haldeman about the ceremonies, which included the debut of the musical work *Mass* by Leonard Bernstein. "I just want to ask you one favor," Nixon told Haldeman. "If I'm assassinated, I want you to have them play 'Dante's Inferno' and have Lawrence Welk produce it." Even reelection failed to ease his insecurity. "I don't want to go to the [Kennedy] Center for *anything* at any time unless it is an event I *have to* participate in," he told Rose Woods, two weeks after his landslide victory in 1972.

And yet. A year earlier, in deepest secrecy—even the White House photographer was banned—Nixon and his family hosted Jacqueline Kennedy Onassis and her children, John and Caroline, at the White House so that the family could view the newly finished official portraits of JFK and his First Lady. An air force jet flew the Kennedys to Washington, where Pat, Julie, and Tricia joined Nixon to welcome them to the White House, introduce them to the family dogs, and show them through the West Wing and the residence. Dick uncorked a bottle of his best Bordeaux at dinner. They all laughed ruefully at how sick they got of the smell of paint during campaigns, because hotel managers inevitably had their rooms repainted just before they arrived. At one point, Nixon would recall, Jackie murmured: "You know, I always lived in a dream world."

"Can you imagine the gift you gave me?" she wrote in her thank-you note a few days later. "To return to the White House privately with my little ones while they are still young enough to rediscover their childhood— with you both as guides, and with your daughters, such extraordinary young women. . . . Thank you with all my heart. A day I always dreaded turned out to be one of the most precious ones I have spent with my children."

The Kennedy children wrote thank-you notes as well, and Nixon replied with long handwritten letters.

"You told us your favorite subject was history but that a poor teacher this year had somewhat dampened your interest. I know a teacher can make a great difference but I hope your enthusiasm for history continues," he told Caroline. "History is the best foundation for almost any profession—but even more important you will find the really most fascinating reading as you grow older is in history and biography. As far as the teacher is concerned, I recall that some of the teachers I thought at the time were the worst (because they graded so hard) were actually the best."

To John, who had sat on the bed in the Lincoln bedroom and made a wish (to do better in school), Nixon wrote, "I was glad your wish which you made in the Lincoln bedroom became true—when you need another one like that—come back to see us."

Nixon did many generous things like that—writing a consoling letter to the son of Senator Thomas Eagleton when the senator's mental illness was disclosed; telephoning cancer victims or the families of Vietnam heroes; dropping a note to a congressional aide caught up in scandal; being "nicey-nice," as he called it, to the families of the cabinet officers and the White House staff and servants; consoling Butterfield's daughter when she was hurt in a car accident. He was delighted, while touring storm damage in Wilkes-Barre, Pennsylvania, to drop in at a wedding ceremony that he chanced upon, and pose with the startled bride and groom. He invited Lee Simmons, the black steward on *Air Force One,* and his wife to be presidential guests at a White House state dinner. Senator Robert Dole of Kansas, a battle-scarred veteran of World War II, was moved by how Nixon always took care to extend his left hand when greeting Dole, whose right arm had been shattered in combat. "Didn't mean a thing to anyone else but me," Dole recalled. But to Dole it meant a lot.

Nixon would insist on keeping such acts of generosity secret, for that was what made "the whole warmth business" real, he told Haldeman. But then he would complain in long cranky memos about his "crafty, cold" image, and how his kindnesses never were leaked to the press. "We have been utterly deficient about creating that mystique," he griped.*

---

* When Nixon was vice president, Jim Bassett found him with a doll he was taking to an ailing little girl. When the aide suggested that they warm up Nixon's image by having photos taken at the presentation, Nixon promised to castrate him—"I'll cut your balls off"—if even a hint of the event appeared in the press. Yet the anecdote was preserved, and leaked a few years later to biographer Earl Mazo.

NIXON WAS A man of his era, and men of his age and stature were expected to have a sophisticated acquaintance with alcohol. During the vice-presidential years, Nixon told his doctors, he had two or three drinks a night. Like FDR before him, he took pride in mixing the martinis, or pouring thirty-year-old scotch for his guests. He came to detest champagne but developed a taste for French wine over the years, and sometimes had the stewards covertly pour him better vintages than his guests were being served.

Most presidents of his era enjoyed their cocktails. Bess Truman had to school the White House butler on the way that she and Harry preferred their old-fashioneds: double bourbons, basically, with nothing but a hint of fruit and sugar. Ike liked a couple of scotches before dinner, Kennedy his daiquiris. Lyndon Johnson got rip-roaring drunk during the 1960 campaign, and Jerry Ford had to be warned by his staff to cut off his lunchtime martinis. The columnist Robert Novak described a typical working lunch with a Nixon White House aide—three double bourbons before the meal and another during it. Haldeman and Ehrlichman were Christian Scientists, but Pat Moynihan ("Alex, c'mon, let's have a belt") and Alexander Butterfield were known to share a drink at day's end in the West Wing, and Ken Clawson, a communications aide, treated reporters to off-the-record briefings called "Cocktails with Clawson."

That said, Nixon was known to overindulge. "I don't think that it should be exaggerated," said Winston Lord, an NSC aide. "However, there is no question that he had a problem." Nixon could not hold his booze in the best of times. "He never could handle liquor," his former press secretary Jim Bassett said, "and you had to be very careful with him about that." On several occasions—the *Apollo 13* drama, a banquet in China, an evening during the Yom Kippur War, a flight back from Denver—his aides reported that he drank to excess. Nixon's daughter Julie and friend Billy Graham both acknowledged it after his presidency.

Ehrlichman, after watching a sodden Nixon make a clumsy pass at a young lady in 1964, had made him promise to lay off the stuff before agreeing to work for him. Garment remembered instances during the 1968 campaign when his exhausted friend—after a drink or a sleeping pill or both—would call him late at night and ramble on and on until Morpheus claimed him in midconversation. After one such phone call, in which Nixon passed into slumber, an inexperienced, panicky Colson called Manolo Sanchez, thinking the president had a stroke or a heart attack. Nixon apologized the next day; sleeping pills and jet lag had caught up with him, he said.

A beer and a sleeping pill, and Nixon began to mumble, Price recalled. Two drinks and "his voice would become slurred," said Safire. "He would reminisce . . . open himself up." On a private jet to Florida during the 1968 campaign, Nixon had downed a quick scotch or two and began to cry as he spoke to his aides of Frank and Hannah, Arthur and Harold. "People don't know me," he pitiably told his staff.

Three drinks? "He couldn't handle it," said veteran California strategist Stu Spencer. "He really got paranoid when he got three drinks in him. There are things I'm not even going to discuss that were said, but they were the result of drinking. He could not handle drink." His White House tapes capture the tinkling of ice cubes on several occasions in which Nixon, coming down from the high of a nationally televised address or a prime-time press conference, starts slurring his words while polling friends and advisers on his performance. "When I talked to the president he was loaded," Kissinger told a colleague, explaining why Nixon could not take a phone call from the British prime minister during a Mideast crisis.

Insomnia was a long-standing problem. Nixon augmented his prescription sleeping pills with Dilantin, an anti-seizure drug recommended by a friend, the businessman Jack Dreyfus, who championed the drug for an unintended use: to combat depression. The slurring of speech was one potential side effect.

Nixon "took all those sleeping pills that would give him a low in the morning and a high in the evening," said his spiritual counselor, Billy Graham. The president's failures could be blamed on "sleeping pills and demons," said Graham. "All through history, drugs and demons have gone together. . . . They just let a demon-power come in and play over him."

"P looped," Ehrlichman wrote in his diary after visiting with Nixon the night of the president's speech on Cambodia.

As the midterm elections of 1970 approached, Nixon faced an unforgiving calculus. For Vietnamization to succeed, he had to stave off the Communists, but every action he took to do so—bombarding Laos, invading Cambodia, bombing sites in southern North Vietnam—stirred the fears of the public back home, lacing steel through the backbones of the antiwar members of Congress.

From government infiltration and intimidation, changes in the draft laws, internal bickering, or simple exhaustion, the peace movement sagged after the deaths at Kent State. But the uproar over the Cambodian incursion had heartened the opposition on Capitol Hill, and by a 57–38 vote, the Senate approved a measure introduced by Senators Frank Church, a Democrat from Idaho, and John Sherman Cooper, a Republican of Kentucky, prohibiting U.S. military action in, and aid to, Cambodia after June 30.

The House refused to go along, and the Senate soundly rejected another amendment (offered by Senator George McGovern, the Democrat from South Dakota, and Republican Senator Mark Hatfield of Oregon) to cut off funding for *all* military action in Southeast Asia. But the hourglass had been turned. It was only a matter of time before the rebels in Congress succeeded. "The president's personal relations with Congress have deteriorated gravely," Bryce Harlow warned. Hanoi took heart.

Nixon's critics missed "the vastness of the things that he had to deal with . . . they miss the challenges of the political environment in which he had to try to get something done and of the international environment," Ray Price would remember, seeking to justify what followed. "In that office you have to do a lot of things you otherwise wouldn't do in order to get the important things done. You have to make a lot of compromises. You have to, in some cases, sacrifice a lot of virtue."

Identifying enemies, and offering battle, were among those things that Nixon did best. The events of the spring of 1970 left him feeling beleaguered. The face he showed to his foes, for the rest of his presidency, would be one long contorted snarl.

In 1969, Nixon had dispatched Spiro Agnew to lambaste the network news executives ("a small and unelected elite") and American intellectuals who opposed the war. The vice president had urged Americans to "separate them from our society with no more regret than we should feel over discarding rotten apples." Now Agnew took to the stump again, railing against Nixon's critics ("nattering nabobs of negativism") and liberals ("radic-libs") and stoking the nascent culture wars. "How do you fathom the thinking of those who work themselves into a lather over an alleged shortage of nutriments in Wheaties," Agnew asked, "but who cannot get exercised at all over a flood of hard-core pornography?

"Dividing the American people has been my main contribution to the national political scene," Agnew would come to boast. "I not only plead guilty to this charge, but I am somewhat flattered by it."

Nixon's foes were as determined. There might be "somewhat fewer of them," but "those who distrust the Presidency do so with greater intensity than before," Moynihan advised. "Do not doubt that there is a struggle going on in this country of the kind the Germans used to call a *Kulturkampf.* The adversary culture which dominates almost all channels of information transfer and opinion has never been stronger, and as best as I can tell it has come near to silencing the representatives of traditional America."

Pat Buchanan wrote a thirteen-page memo to Nixon, urging him to engage in "heated political warfare, of not cooling off our supporters but of stirring the fires" as they were now "in a contest over the soul of the country" with their liberal enemies in Congress, the press, and the universities. "It will be their kind of society or ours; we will prevail or they shall prevail."

White House aide Tom Huston ("I was a conservative hard liner . . . I mean, I was a hard core conservative") drafted an organizational plan for government intelligence agencies, to improve upon the performance of FBI Director Hoover, who was deemed too timid in his dotage to adequately suppress the radicals. The "Huston plan," as it became known, explicitly authorized wiretapping, clandestine mail openings, and break-ins, and acknowledged that such measures were illegal. Nixon approved it—it was rescinded only because Hoover and Mitchell objected.

After several hundred construction workers went on a rampage in downtown Manhattan, beating antiwar protesters and other young people on what came to be known as "Bloody Friday," the White House helped organize hard-hat demonstrations. A hundred thousand marched in New York. Nixon welcomed a group to Washington, and accepted a helmet of his own. The offensive continued through the fall election, as Nixon joined Agnew on the stump, and the two of them blistered the Democrats for encouraging a climate of riot and disorder.

On October 29 the president was the target of a rowdy demonstration in San Jose. He and Haldeman were hoping to turn the incident into an evocative confrontation ("If anybody so much as brushes against Mrs. Agnew, tell her to fall down," Nixon told his aides), and the president climbed atop his limo to defy the rock-throwing protesters.* He followed that performance with an ill-tempered speech from a poorly lit airport hangar in Phoenix that his aides chose to televise as the Republican curtain-closer for the fall campaign:

---

* Nixon urged Agnew to ignore the Secret Service and confront demonstrators. "If an egg is thrown and hits the Vice President—all the better," Nixon ordered Pat Buchanan to tell Agnew. "If the Vice President were slightly roughed up by those thugs, nothing better could happen for our cause." He concluded, "Buchanan, You should kick them in the groin—or any other place you can find where it hurts worse."

Let's recognize these people for what they are. They are not roman-tic revolutionaries. They are the same thugs and hoodlums that have always plagued the good people. . . .

For too long, and this needs to be said and said now and here, the strength of freedom in our society has been eroded by a creeping permissiveness in our legislatures, in our courts, in our family life, and in our colleges and universities.

For too long, we have appeased aggression here at home, and, as with all appeasement, the result has been more aggression and more violence. The time has come to draw the line.

Nixon looked awful—too "hot" and mean for television—and Senator Edmund Muskie of Maine, responding with calm dignity from his homey living room Down East, made a far better impression for the Democrats, becoming an instant front-runner for his party's presidential nomination in 1972.

The Election Day results were mixed, but Nixon's foes on Capitol Hill were emboldened. In March 1971 the Democratic caucus in the House went on record, demanding a "date certain" for withdrawal from Vietnam. William Timmons, the White House congressional liaison, warned the president that it was just a matter of time before Congress cut off funding. The loss of leverage "will murder us with the North Vietnamese," Kissinger noted.

In the early months of 1971, Nixon approved the installation of a secret White House tape-recording system to memorialize his decision-making process for posterity. It quickly captured the president ordering his aides to target Muskie, Ted Kennedy, and other Democratic rivals, Jews, liberal donors, journalists, and media organizations for harassment, sabotage, and surveillance. "Politics over the next two years is not a question of bring-ing in the blacks, and liberal senators, and making them feel that they are 'wanted,'" Nixon told Haldeman. "It is going to be cold steel."

The Road to Watergate

O N THE SUNDAY morning that sired the flames that came to claim his presidency, Richard Nixon stirred slowly. The guest rooms at the White House were packed with relatives and friends who had gathered for Tricia's wedding to Edward Cox, staged on the previous afternoon amid the blossoms in a misty Rose Garden. The ceremonies had been a delight: "a fairyland" to rival Christmas, an enchanted Rose Woods told the president. Even Nixon danced. As the orchestra played the sentimental standard "Thank Heaven for Little Girls" he twirled Tricia, Julie, and Pat at an East Room reception for four hundred guests. It was his first turn on the dance floor in the White House, and he seemed to enjoy himself. He grabbed the hand of Lynda Bird Johnson and whirled her about as well. "All of us were beautifully, and simply, happy," he recalled. It had met the wish he conveyed to the newlyweds: "The day indeed was splendid."

On the night before the wedding, Nixon slipped a note beneath Tricia's door. "Today is the day you begin a long and exciting journey. I want you to know how proud I have been of you through the years—some of them—pretty difficult for you I'm sure," he wrote. And because of who he was, what Frank and Hannah and time had made him, he spoke of the nobility of struggle. "The years ahead will be happy ones because you will make them so," he told his daughter. "Your strength of character will see you through whatever comes."

The Nixons rifled through the wedding coverage in the Sunday morning newspapers. The *New York Times* was properly reverent, describing Tricia as "ethereal . . . beautiful" and "floating in organdy" to the altar. But the writers at the *Washington Post,* the president concluded, had been snide. He got Ron Ziegler, his press secretary, on the phone. The newspaper, an irritant of twenty years, was to be banned from White House social events, Nixon decreed. "They're never to be in the White House again," he said. "Never! Is that clear?"

"I just don't like that paper," said the wounded father of the bride. "They don't care if it hurts."

Nixon asked Ziegler to ready a tape of the TV coverage for the First Family to watch. The networks had given lavish attention to the ceremony; their commentary was deferential and the ratings superb. The president had made a special effort to stand up straight, and he cut a dashing figure in his cutaway suit. Even the combative CBS correspondent, Dan Rather, was respectful. Nixon would nag his staff, in the coming days, to lobby the network chiefs and have the show rerun as a prime-time special. "Women all want to see the damn thing," he'd tell Haldeman, in a conversation captured on the new taping system. "If it were the Kennedys it would be rerun every night for three weeks, you know."

Politics aside, it was a bittersweet and unsettling moment. His girls were gone. Julie was married to David Eisenhower, and now Tricia was departing for a new life as the wife of Ed Cox, a Princeton graduate attending Harvard Law School, described by the *Times* as "tall, fine-boned and handsome . . . the scion of Easterners whose ancestors go back to . . . the American Revolution." It was almost noon before Nixon could push the personal aside, settle into his hideaway office in the Executive Office Building, and check in on the world.

THE DAY WAS June 13, 1971, and Nixon was primed to incite turmoil. In later years he would mark this spring as the nadir of his first term, a moment when his troubles were "so overwhelming and so apparently impervious" that he feared they had extinguished his chances for reelection. The war dragged on. His approval rating had plummeted; less than half the country thought he was doing a good job. The Senate was voting on a series of measures to halt funding for military operations in Southeast Asia. The economy was uncooperative: "If the prospects are that dire," Nixon told George Shultz, after getting a gloomy report on growth and employment, "maybe we all better turn in our suits and run for the hills."

"Unless he acquires some new assets and divests himself of some old liabilities, his defeat seems probable," Richard Rovere wrote in *The New Yorker*. In the Oval Office on Saturday, fretting as he waited for the rain to lift and give Tricia the outdoor wedding she hoped for, Nixon had raged, sequentially, about his enemies. It was a hardy list that included the "long-haired, dirty looking" protesters; the eastern establishment; feminists;

teachers' unions; Jews ("Goddamn, they are a vicious bunch"); African Americans ("We don't do well with blacks. . . . We don't want to do so damn well with blacks"); the "softies" of the Ivy League; the "ass kissers and butter uppers" in the bureaucracy; and the "lousy dirty . . . cowardly bastards" in the press.

And TV host Dick Cavett, a boyish, sly Nebraskan whose talk show catered to sophisticates.

"We've got a running war going with Cavett," Haldeman said.

"Is he just a left-winger? Is that the problem?" Nixon asked.

"Yeah," said the chief of staff.

"Is he Jewish?" asked the president.

"I don't know," said Haldeman. "He doesn't look it."

NIXON'S PROSPECTS NOW rested with three transformative initiatives: the secret Vietnam peace negotiations; the back-channel talks on a strategic arms limitations treaty (SALT) and other issues with the Soviet Union; and an opening to China. The prospects for a stunning turnaround were tantalizing—and thereby terribly stressful. His thoughts about achieving a breakthrough with China reflected his general mood. "Nixon was excited almost to the point of euphoria about the prospect before us," Kissinger recalled. "But he also was assailed by his chronic anxiety that no enterprise of his would ever come to a totally satisfactory ending."

Alone in the Oval Office, the president and his national security adviser had shared their private hopes.

"By the end of the summer," said Kissinger, "we will know whether we have broken Vietnam."

"Or SALT," said Nixon.

"Or SALT," said Kissinger.

"Or China."

"Or China."

"In terms of achievements," Kissinger said, "who has had a three-year period like this? If you had said . . . that you would get 400,000 troops out of Vietnam in two years, open the way to—of a visit to Peking, a visit to Moscow, a SALT agreement. . . ."

"That'd be incredible, wouldn't it," Nixon said.

"They would have said, 'That's insanity!'" said Kissinger.

—

So THINGS STOOD that Sunday when, at 12:18 p.m., a voice-activated tape machine captured the conversation as a White House operator connected Nixon to his deputy national security adviser, General Alexander Haig, who conveyed the disappointing news that some twenty Americans had lost their lives in Vietnam that week. It was a tenfold drop, and more, from the weekly totals of the late 1960s, but not as much as the president hoped.

Nixon, distracted, asked: "Nothing else of interest in the world today?" And Haig, eager adjutant, struck the match. The "goddamn *New York Times*" had published "an expose of the most highly classified documents of the war," Haig said. It was "a devastating security breach of the greatest magnitude of anything I've ever seen."

THEY WOULD COME to be called the Pentagon Papers—a top-secret and politically "sensitive" seven-thousand-page study smuggled out of official hands, painstakingly copied, and given to the *Times* by defense analysts Daniel Ellsberg, Anthony Russo, and a tiny band of helpers. Commissioned by a repentant Robert McNamara, in one of his last acts as secretary of defense, the forty-seven volumes traced the U.S. government's blunders and duplicity in Southeast Asia.

According to the *Times'* front-page story:

Four succeeding administrations built up the American political, military and psychological stakes in Indochina, often more deeply than they realized at the time, with large-scale military equipment to the French in 1950; with acts of sabotage and terror warfare against North Vietnam beginning in 1954; with moves that encouraged and abetted the overthrow of President Ngo Dinh Diem of South Vietnam in 1963; with plans, pledges and threats of further action that sprang to life in the Tonkin Gulf clashes in August, 1964. . . .

The United States had gone to war, wrote reporter Neil Sheehan, not to save the South Vietnamese people, but to maintain "the power, influence and prestige of the United States . . . irrespective of conditions in Vietnam."

Ellsberg, a summa cum laude graduate of Harvard, defense scholar, and former Marine who had helped craft military strategy during the Kennedy and Johnson years, had been transformed by the two years he spent as a counterinsurgency expert in Vietnam, where his tutors were mavericks like

Edward Lansdale and John Paul Vann, veterans who knew the terrain and fed his skepticism. Kissinger had admired Ellsberg, and invited him to help frame the administration's options on the war in late 1968 and early 1969.

From his contacts in government, Ellsberg learned how Nixon's policy for Vietnam had progressed from a swiftly negotiated peace to the prolonged process of Vietnamization, in which American draft calls and casualties receded but people in Asia kept dying, and the bombing went on with no end in sight. Ellsberg thought it immoral. He hoped that by leaking the Pentagon study to Congress and exposing the U.S. government's record of deceit, he could present Nixon with a politically palatable path home: the president could blame the Democrats for taking America into the morass, declare that the war was unwinnable, and withdraw.

From the fall of 1969, for more than a year, Ellsberg had trudged around Capitol Hill sowing top-secret chapters from his briefcase, trying to persuade antiwar lawmakers like Senators William Fulbright and George McGovern to hold hearings, or stage a filibuster, or read the secret papers into the *Congressional Record*. None summoned the grit to do so. "The Democrats I talked to were good Democrats," Ellsberg recalled. They saw the political profit in making it Nixon's War and had "no interest in pulling McNamara in front and confronting him with lies that he had made." By the time Ellsberg approached the *Times* in March 1971, his expectations had plummeted. Nixon was extending the war into Cambodia and Laos, not seeking a rationale to quit. The study's publication, he believed, might at best cause a minor stir—"close to zero." He could not have been more wrong.

At first, it unfolded as Ellsberg predicted. The papers were "a tough attack on Kennedy" and "brutal on President Johnson," Haig told Nixon that Sunday morning. "They're gonna end up in a massive gut fight in the Democratic Party on this thing."

A few hours later, Kissinger agreed. "This is a gold mine," he told Nixon. "It pins it all on Kennedy and Johnson." The content was dated—the study ended in early 1968—and posed no true threat to national security. As Haldeman wrote in his diary that evening, "The key now is for us to keep out of it, and let the people that are affected cut each other up."

But in the course of the next forty-eight hours, Nixon commandeered the gut fight, plunging almost madly into a historic confrontation with the press. In doing so, he gave the grateful Democrats the opportunity (it fell like divine favor on a party riven by Vietnam) to make Nixonian "repression" the story. And as the press rallied to the side of the *Times* and the courts ruled against him, Nixon worked himself into a frenzy—launching the calamitous initiatives that would grow, it would be said, like a cancer on his presidency.

"Strategic retreat is the hardest thing in all military campaign history," said the old jazz musician Len Garment, riffing on the Nixon presidency. "A strategic retreat: with large masses of people. Men. Armor. Horses. Snow. Demonstrators. Tear gas. Exploding academic buildings. Russians. Tough stuff. Napoleon's retreat from Moscow was disorderly—he got out of there but was savaged along the way. So Nixon managed it pretty well until the Pentagon Papers and other mounting frustrations. Then it blew up. Nixon blew up. Lost his cool. And you had a couple of people like Charles Colson and his band of merry men taking instructions that were meant to be denied and running with them like crazy."

NIXON'S FOES WERE legion. In late April and early May, hundreds of Vietnam Veterans Against the War had led antiwar protesters into Washington. The veterans camped on the Mall and tossed their medals and ribbons over a fence at the Capitol. Thousands of other demonstrators vowed to shut the government down via acts of civil disobedience. Some rampaged through the city, vandalizing property and confronting police. The authorities responded with illegal mass arrests, filling outdoor holding pens with detainees. To Nixon's fury, the White House press corps took the side of the demonstrators, grilling him at a June 1 news conference about the threat to civil liberties.

The grilling would have been tougher yet if the reporters had heard Nixon's conversation with Haldeman, in which the president of the United States encouraged the White House chief of staff to enlist thugs from the Teamsters union to beat up protesters.

"They've got guys who'll go in and knock their heads off," Nixon said.

"Sure. Murderers," said Haldeman. "They're going to beat the shit out of some of these people. And, uh, hope they really hurt them. . . . smash some noses."

America's grand strategy—to contain Soviet aggression until Europe and Japan could reemerge as great, countervailing powers—was succeeding. Indeed, the independent-minded Europeans and industrious Japanese were now presenting challenges of their own to American economic and diplomatic primacy. But the other danger that George Kennan warned about—that Americans would lose their way in the long twilight struggle—had shown itself as well.

The government that Nixon inherited was steeped in arrogance, luxuriant in sin. For more than a decade, under Eisenhower, Kennedy, and Johnson, it had spied on its citizens, suppressed dissent, and overthrown overseas regimes. Antiwar and civil rights groups had been infiltrated, framed, bugged, and assaulted by agents of their government. The Nixon administration had embraced the tradition, harrying John Lennon, the Black Panthers, and Muhammad Ali, and rounding up a cross-section of "the usual suspects"—a band of antiwar leaders who came to be known as the Chicago Eight—to be prosecuted for the violence at the Democratic National Convention in 1968. "The fact of the matter is that there is a little bit of the totalitarian buried somewhere way down deep, in each and every one of us," Kennan had warned. The military-industrial combine prospered, the state flourished, and the tentacles of surveillance crept through society. "I have destroyed him with the weapons I abhorred, and they are his," says the spy George Smiley of a Soviet counterpart, at the climax of one of John le Carré's admonitory Cold War novels.

AN ARRAY OF motives now led Nixon to join the brawl over the Pentagon Papers. There was his old-fashioned sense of duty, for one thing; he would not be a proper steward of his office if he just sat by as seven thousand pages of classified material was splashed across the pages of the *Times*. "If they're going to fight the presidency, they're going to fight the president," he declared.

Secrecy was an essential component in war and diplomacy. "It really involves the ability to conduct government. How the hell can a president . . . do anything?" Nixon said. "How can they make a contingency plan if it's going to be taken out in a trunk and given to a goddamn newspaper?" The United States was very much at war; the secret Paris peace talks and his diplomatic initiatives with Russia and China were both radical and profound—and dependent in their unfolding on the legroom granted by confidentiality. "This is treasonable action," Nixon told Kissinger. "What kind of people would do such things?"

"We were obsessed with secrecy," Nixon would remember. "I was paranoiac, or almost a basket case."

The release of the papers posed a challenge, as well, to Nixon's plans for a "peace with honor" that would sustain American prestige. Though the study targeted Democrats, its tales of official error and deception would erode the already flagging support for the war.

"To the ordinary guy, all this is a bunch of gobbledygook. But out of the gobbledygook comes a very clear thing: you can't trust the government; you can't believe what they say; and you can't rely on their judgment," Haldeman advised the president. "The implicit infallibility of presidents, which has been an accepted thing in America, is badly hurt by this, because it shows that people do things the president wants to do even though it's wrong, and the president can be wrong."

The president agreed. "You cannot justify continuing a war you got into by mistake," he told Haldeman. "You've given away the whole game."

PARANOIAC WAS AN apt description of his mood and mind-set. Nixon saw Ellsberg's actions as part of "a conspiracy" aiming to bring him down— a follow-up to the May Day protests and the next step in a plot to swing support in Congress for the end-the-war resolutions. Word came from John Mitchell that the Pentagon Papers were only the nose of the beast. The theft of documents was not limited to military history: there was pilfered paper, afloat on Capitol Hill, from the Nixon years as well. What did his adversaries possess? Proof of the Menu series—the secret bombing of Cambodia—heretofore concealed by falsified records? The Duck Hook plans for attacking Hanoi, mining Haiphong harbor, bombing the dikes, and brandishing nuclear weapons?

"If this thing flies," warned Kissinger, "they're going to do the same to you."

"They'll have the whole story of the Menu series," Nixon said.

The members of Congress were measuring him, he believed, and so were the newspapers. Nor would the Soviets, Chinese, and North Vietnamese show much respect for an American president who couldn't keep secrets, or control pissants like Ellsberg.

Nixon's final motivation led down to the cellar of the presidential psyche. The adversaries in this fight—the press, the liberals, the smart-ass Ivy Leaguers—were his ancient foes. He ached to give them a good kick. "Believe me," he told Colson, excitedly, "The *New York Times* can be discredited indefinitely as a result of this." It is "the same media that supported Hiss," Nixon told his aides.

It would have been stunning had Frank Nixon's son dodged the battle. Like the scorpion in the fable, riding a frog to cross a river, lashing out was Nixon's nature. His actions were reflexive, heedless of the peril in which he himself would drown.

—

AT NOON ON Monday, Nixon was still advising his aides to "stay out of it." But that night he spoke to Ehrlichman and Mitchell, who sought his permission to put the *Times* on formal notice: the paper could be prosecuted under the federal Espionage Act if it continued to publish state secrets.

Sipping a drink, the president mused, "Hell, I wouldn't prosecute the *Times*. My view is to prosecute the Goddamn pricks that gave it to 'em." But Mitchell told him that the administration would look "silly" and "foolish" if it failed to act against the newspaper. So Nixon gave his blessing. "He's a strong man, that Mitchell," Nixon told Kissinger after the conversation with the attorney general ended. "A lot of people will say this is trying to suppress the press and the rest. But so be it. We'll go down fighting." The decision made, he went bowling.

The *Times* ignored Mitchell's warning. And so, on Tuesday, the Justice Department urged the federal courts to suppress the newspaper's continued publication of the study—the first time a U.S. government had ever demanded such "prior restraint." A judge in New York granted an initial restraining order. "It's one of those fights . . . we had to make, and by God it's one I enjoy," Nixon told Mitchell. He was warming to the task. "These bastards have gone too far this time."

THINGS WENT SOUTH quickly. Johnson and the Democrats were, wisely, lying low. The press and public—with mounting disapproval—focused on "the wicket of suppression," as Mitchell put it. "People believe that we are covering something up," Colson told Haldeman. By Thursday night, Nixon realized the fix he was in. "It's all blurred," he groaned, his voice filled with frustration.

The nation's editors—roaring "I am Spartacus!"—rallied around the *Times*. The *Washington Post* was the first into the breach, carrying on for the muzzled *Times* and publishing more secrets from Ellsberg's cache. When Mitchell's lawyers won another order, restraining the *Post,* the *Boston Globe,* and then sixteen more newspapers across the land, commenced their own defiant publication of the Pentagon's study.

The courts, too, rebuffed Nixon. After a series of preliminary skirmishes, the Supreme Court took the case on an expedited basis, and in a six-to-three decision on June 30 handed him a humiliating defeat. It was the duty of a free press "to prevent . . . the government from deceiving the people and sending them off to distant lands to die," wrote Justice Hugo

Black in a majority opinion. The restraining orders were "a flagrant, indefensible and continuing violation of the First Amendment."

A SWARM BESET him. Nixon had seized a relatively minor incident, injurious to his rivals, and transformed it into a political crisis that left him stung and blinded. He kicked wildly in pain.

At first he focused on Ellsberg. In a manic scene in the Oval Office, Kissinger and Haldeman and Ehrlichman whipped themselves and the president into ascending states of wrath about this left-wing troublemaker. Kissinger was defensive—he shared Ellsberg's Ivy League pedigree and Jewish heritage, and had brought Ellsberg into the administration's councils. He layed it on, dissembling about their relationship and slandering the whistle-blower as a war criminal and a sexual deviant. Together, the president and his advisers toured the realm of grievance, stopping to traduce the Kennedys ("How about the fact that . . . Kennedy conspired in the murder of Diem?"), the liberal establishment, the bureaucracy, and the press. "They've thrown the sword down," Nixon vowed. But "they made one mistake. . . . Never strike a king unless you kill him. They struck and did not kill. And now we're going to kill them."

HALDEMAN REPORTED THAT their antagonists at the Brookings Institution, a liberal think tank, were sitting on a heap of secret files. Some dealt with the bombing halt on the eve of the 1968 election, he told the president. They pondered what the press would do with news of the Chennault affair.

"Bob? Now you remember Huston's plan?" Nixon said, referring to Tom Huston's proposal to expand the use of black-bag jobs and other illegal counterintelligence tactics. "I want it implemented on a thievery basis. Goddamn it, go in and get those files. Blow the safe and get it."

To Kissinger, Nixon said: "I don't give a goddamn about repression, do you? I don't think we're losing our soul. If we do, it'll come back."

Colson drew the assignment, and he and his flunkies concocted a plan to start a fire at Brookings and ransack the building in the resulting chaos. When White House counsel John Dean heard of it he flew to California, where Nixon and his aides had relocated to "the western White House" in San Clemente. Dean reminded Ehrlichman that arson was a felony, and if someone died in the conflagration, the president of the United States could be charged with murder. Ehrlichman picked up the telephone and squashed the scheme.

ELLSBERG'S ANCESTRY WAS Jewish, though he practiced no faith and had been raised by Christian Scientists. It was enough to evoke Nixon's latent anti-Semitism, which was fed in turn by Haldeman and others.

In early July, analysts at the Bureau of Labor Statistics advised the press that some good economic news might only represent a statistical quirk, and Nixon ordered Haldeman to conduct a head count of the Jews at the agency: "There's a Jewish cabal, you know."

"The government is full of Jews," the president told his chief of staff. "Most Jews are disloyal. You have a Garment and a Kissinger and, frankly, a Safire and by God they're exceptions. But Bob, generally speaking you can't trust the bastards. They turn on you."

"All Jews. Every one is a Jew," said the president, reviewing the list of suspects in the Pentagon Papers case. And when the courts ruled against him, he railed about "the damn New York Jews" and "the Washington kikes" on the federal bench.

"It is part of the background, the faith and the rest. We would probably be that way if we were a persecuted minority concerned about suppression, police state etcetera," Nixon told a gathering of his aides. "They always come down that way . . . you just can't find any who don't."

"Well at least the Supreme Court ruled yesterday that the Jews couldn't get into our golf clubs," Attorney General Mitchell reassured him.

NIXON VIEWED SENATOR Edward Kennedy as a likely opponent in 1972. With remarkable moral agility, he ordered his aides to covertly circulate the Kennedy administration chapters of the Pentagon Papers—the very material they were asking the courts to keep wrapped in the mantle of national security. "Leak it to some other paper," Nixon said, and with no apparent irony added: "The public is entitled to know."

If his enemies wanted disclosure, Nixon would give them disclosure. He ordered up a "declassification project" in which evidence of transgressions by Democratic presidents—Roosevelt's responsibility for Pearl Harbor, John Kennedy's actions in the Bay of Pigs, Johnson's intervention in the Dominican Republic, and the like—would be excavated from government files. He needed "a small group of tough guys" to do it. "I really need a son of a bitch like Huston who will work his butt off and do it dishonorably. . . . I'll direct him myself."

"They are using any means," Nixon told Haldeman and Kissinger. "We are going to use any means."

Colson had just the man: a retired CIA agent named Howard Hunt, whom he knew from Brown University alumni gatherings. Hunt was versed in tradecraft and dedicated to the cause; he was hired as a White House consultant in the first week of July. When he couldn't unearth proof that Kennedy had ordered Diem's assassination, Hunt forged State Department cables, which Colson peddled to *Life* magazine.

Nixon came up with another assignment for his "tough guys" after hearing that the FBI investigation of Ellsberg had been tempered by Hoover's warm relationship with toymaker Louis Marx, the suspect's father-in-law. They would smear Ellsberg themselves. "Convict the son of a bitch in the press. That's the way it's done," he told Haldeman, Colson, and Ehrlichman. "I need a man—a commander—an officer in charge here at the White House that I can call when I wake up, as I did last night, at 2 o'clock in the morning and I can say I want to do this, this and this. . . . A guy, also, who will have the initiative to go out and do a few of these things" on his own.

Thus was born the Special Investigations Unit. Nixon plucked David Young, thirty-two, from Kissinger's office, and Egil Krogh, thirty-one, from Ehrlichman's staff, and gave them the duty of plugging leaks and discrediting leakers. Lacking any expertise in black ops, Krogh brought on an erratic former FBI agent whom the Treasury Department was thrilled to dump on the White House: G. Gordon Liddy. They were given a wad of money, high-tech toys, and a room on the ground floor of the Executive Office Building (EOB). They called themselves the Plumbers. Soon Colson sent Hunt to join them. Ehrlichman telephoned the CIA, instructing the agency to give Hunt "carte blanche."

It was an awful notion. The very last thing Richard Nixon needed was "tough guys" like Hunt and Liddy, inadequately governed by spaniels like Colson, Young, and Krogh, who would salute Nixon at 2 a.m. or "go out and do a few" dirty tricks on their own.

Haldeman had constructed, and lovingly maintained, an administrative engine to produce accountability. Low-level aides were inculcated with the need to follow orders and report back on their progress. No detail was too insignificant: when the campaign song needed approval, or the gardener at San Clemente got a five-dollar-a-week raise, Haldeman was consulted.

But now Haldeman was weary; he wanted to spend more time on the big picture, on foreign affairs. He was tired of rushing across West Executive Drive to keep tabs when he heard that Nixon was hunkered in the EOB hideaway, scheming with Colson. Kissinger was overworked. Ehrlichman had come to Washington with ideals, but his sardonic disposition had given way to full-dosed cynicism as he dealt with the members of Congress, whom he viewed as lazy, mercenary drunkards.

And Nixon? He turned a corner in those last days of spring and the first of summer in 1971. In the crucible of the presidency, with his adversaries gloating and his reelection imperiled and that trinity of foreign policy initiatives still at play, Richard Nixon cracked. By mid-July, he would leave the Ellsberg disaster behind. His duties would draw him on, to triumphs in China and Moscow, a reordering of the international monetary system, and a peace deal for Vietnam. But he had left an indelible impression on his lieutenants. Colson and the others had discovered that the way to presidential favor, as a federal prosecutor would later describe it, "was to bring the dead mouse to his door." And there was to be no quarter, no scruples. *They are using any means; we are going to use any means.*

"This is the time men have to be strong," Nixon told his aides. "I don't have contempt for strong men that disagree with me—like the Communists. I respect them.

"I have utter contempt for the so-called . . . intellectuals who put themselves on a high moral plane and are just weak."

"Weak, selfish and cowardly," Kissinger chimed in.

"Clowns, dilettante intellectuals . . . who bite us like sand flies," said Nixon.

Dispatching his men to war on the elite, Nixon recalled conservative senator William Jenner's description of the diplomat Averell Harriman: as thin as piss on a rock. "You're the rock," Nixon told his aides. "They're the piss."

HALDEMAN'S MACHINERY SPUTTERED and failed. With Nixon's hot breath on their necks (an exhalation that reached the scalding point when the *Times* followed up the Pentagon Papers with a leak of the administration's strategy in the SALT talks), Colson and Ehrlichman put the spurs to Young and Krogh. The earnest young men consulted their tough guys and concocted a plan to discredit Ellsberg. Among other measures, it called on the CIA to manufacture a psychiatric profile of the whistle-blower. When the agency's work appeared halfhearted (it was), Hunt and Liddy drew CIA disguises and equipment and jetted off to Los Angeles to case the Beverly Hills offices of Ellsberg's psychiatrist, Dr. Lewis Fielding. If the CIA would not smear Ellsberg, they would break into his doctor's office, rifle the files, and do it themselves.

The wannabe James Bonds left a trail of botch and bungle. With a camera borrowed from the CIA, Hunt took photographs of Liddy posing outside Fielding's office and, after returning to Washington from their scouting trip, gave the film to the agency to develop. Of course the spooks made copies, which sat ticking in the files. The duo then returned to L.A. on Labor Day weekend with a squad of Hunt's old Castro-hating associates (he had been a player in the Bay of Pigs fiasco, which Colson had inexplicably identified as a virtue) and a satchel of burglary tools. They broke windows, jimmied locks, and threw files and pills around Fielding's office—to make it look like a routine, drug-related crime—but failed to find the proof they wanted to defame or blackmail Ellsberg.

Ehrlichman and Krogh were stunned when they reviewed the report, and the photographs of Fielding's trashed office, that Hunt and Liddy submitted. Ehrlichman had signed off on a "covert" operation with the express caveat that it not be traced to the White House. He later claimed that he thought the Plumbers would obtain Ellsberg's file through more subtle means, like bribing a nurse.

To give Nixon the desired deniability, Ehrlichman did some tap dancing when he, in turn, reported to the president. The White House tape recorders captured the conversation, which rather spoiled his ruse. "We had one little operation. It's been aborted out in Los Angeles, which, I think, it is better that you don't know about," Ehrlichman told Nixon in September. "But we've got some [other] dirty tricks under way."

HUNT AND LIDDY were not reprimanded for their bungling in the Fielding burglary. After all, the president wanted tough guys. Instead, in a classic bureaucratic adjustment, they got made somebody else's problem. The unhappy dupe was Jeb Magruder, the young deputy director of the Committee to Re-Elect the President, the new Nixon campaign organization. Young and Krogh continued their work on high-level security projects, but Liddy was shipped to the CRP—or CREEP, as it was known—to serve as its counsel, with the continued responsibility of gathering dirt on Nixon's foes in the Democratic Party and the antiwar movement. (Haldeman and

Mitchell feared that yippies and Weathermen might descend on the GOP convention in Miami, as they had in 1968 on Chicago.) Liddy recruited Hunt, who brought along the anti-Castro crew. Different address, different boss, but the boys were still in business.

Much later, Nixon would wonder how Liddy and Hunt survived the Ellsberg debacle. Ehrlichman "probably thought, these crazy bastards, get them out of here" and had them shipped to CREEP, the president concluded. And so the fault for what followed must lie with Haldeman. "I would never say this to him, but it was Bob Haldeman giving Jeb Magruder the enormous responsibility he did over there at the campaign," Nixon decided, "and Magruder then taking the Liddys and Hunts and that bunch of jackasses."

As HE STARTED his reelection campaign, in 1971, America had made up its mind about Richard Nixon, and his singular disposition. Few didn't have an opinion. There were unrelenting enemies, of course, old Lefties who never would forgive what he did to Alger Hiss or Adlai Stevenson; diehard sixties types, marching against the war, or for an ever-expanding catalog of rights and liberties; and Kennedy acolytes, for whom Nixon would always be a usurper. Much of the Democratic Party, and many in the capital's press corps, fit into one or more of these categories. As much as he hated them, they detested him.

And then there were his followers, who saw in Nixon—self-made, patriotic, square—the personification of all that was righteous in the United States of America, and just the man to return the nation to its old-time values. They were center-right Republicans; Sunbelt and business folk; Babbitts of the heartland and the hard-hatted *proletarii* of the cities. They were willing to forgive almost anything. For true believers, on both sides of the ideological divide, Nixon was emblematic—a Rorschach test that revealed what you thought about the cultural transmutations of the times.

Up close, things were more muddled. Advisers who glimpsed the ugly facets of Nixon's personality had to work out their feelings. Some saw the sad boy inside the lonely man, felt sympathy, and forgave the viciousness. Some were careerists and accepted the boss's animosities as his due. Still others, feeling under siege themselves, excused his hateful tantrums as rightful responses to vile, implacable foes. They were warriors, there to follow orders.

From the beginning of his presidency, the White House staff had toiled to meet Nixon's appetite for political intelligence and subterfuge. They were still unpacking when in March 1969—a few weeks after the inauguration—Ehrlichman hired Jack Caulfield, who had handled security for the 1968 campaign, as an in-house private eye. When the White House wanted the telephone of columnist Joseph Kraft tapped, it was Caulfield who oversaw the arrangements. When the news broke of Ted Kennedy's calamities on Chappaquiddick, it was Caulfield who dispatched a sidekick—another former New York City policeman, Anthony Ulasewicz—to pose as a journalist and shadow the investigation. Ulasewicz's salary and expenses were off-the-books: paid through Nixon's lawyer and political fund-raiser, Herb Kalmbach. In the course of three years, Kalmbach spent more than $130,000 on the operation, which covered assignments in twenty-three states.

It wasn't enough for Nixon. Throughout that woeful spring of 1971, he had anxiously mulled the 1972 campaign. Kennedy and Muskie—even Humphrey—looked formidable, and Wallace represented, once again, a potential claim on the silent majority. The polls showed Nixon losing in a three-man contest.

Nixon grew agitated: the "little boys" on his White House staff didn't know how to play the game, he decided, and he would have to coach them.

"I want, Bob, more use of wiretapping," he told Haldeman in May. "Why don't you put your money . . . on surveillance and so forth . . ."

"Maybe it's the wrong thing to do, but I've got a feeling that if you are going to start, you have to start now," Nixon said. "Maybe we can get a real scandal on any one of the leading Democrats."

"Scandal or improprieties," Haldeman echoed. "The leading Democrats."

"Now you're talking," said Nixon.

By the first snows in New Hampshire, the White House was hip deep in sabotage and surveillance. Nixon had Butterfield place a mole in Kennedy's Secret Service detail. Colson sent a private detective to tail Kennedy in Paris and leaked photographs of the senator with various women. To confuse their enemies, Colson staged a phony write-in campaign for Kennedy in the first primary state. Chotiner had a man masquerading as a newspaper reporter, under the code name "Chapman's Friend," collecting information on the Democratic field. Magruder was supervising "Ruby I," a spy who had infiltrated the Muskie campaign and was copying sensitive documents—including the floor plan of its headquarters, a prerequisite for bugging. Bart Porter, one of Magruder's assistants, was managing "Sedan Chair I" and "Sedan Chair II," operations to infiltrate or disrupt Democratic campaigns, which ultimately landed a mole in McGovern's inner council. Dean and Caulfield were collecting enemy lists and pressing the IRS to target Democratic donors. Ulasewicz sought to penetrate the campaign of a long-shot Republican peace candidate, Representative Pete McCloskey of California. And Hunt, under "Ruby II," was running a spy in McGovern headquarters.

With Nixon's direct approval, Dwight Chapin and Gordon Strachan called on a college buddy, Donald Segretti, to orchestrate the biggest dirty trick campaign of all. They yearned to imitate Dick Tuck—the Democratic prankster who had roused such admiration and hilarity in the press over the years staging stunts at Nixon's expense. Segretti was put on Kalmbach's payroll and ran two dozen agents in eleven states. They were told to target Muskie, who was seen as Nixon's likely opponent. Many of the tricks were harmless: releasing mice at a Muskie press conference, staging "Gays for Muskie" pickets, hiring a female college student to run naked by the senator's Florida hotel screaming "Senator Muskie, I love you!," and ordering huge quantities of pizzas, or limousines carrying baffled African diplomats, to arrive unbidden at a Muskie campaign dinner. Other capers, like the forgeries they produced on counterfeit stationery, spreading racial and sexual slurs to divide the Democrats, were unlawful. "Nixon had always had this rinky-dink crap pulled on him," Chapin recalled. "That's what they asked me to do . . . that's what I did."

One scheme was spectacularly successful. The White House knew that if George Wallace campaigned as an independent candidate in 1972, he could pull aggrieved voters away from the president. He had to be neutralized. And so, when Wallace ran for governor in 1970, Nixon's political team consigned $400,000 in cash to underwrite a challenger in Alabama's Democratic primary. Wallace had to resort to ugly race-baiting and just barely survived. The president followed the contest closely.

Nixon's men then turned to the IRS and the Justice Department, which mounted an aggressive investigation of Wallace's brother Gerald and other cronies for political corruption and tax evasion. "Those damn IRS boys," Gerald Wallace told a friend. "I think they've got me." But in January 1971 the Nixon administration announced that it was ending the investigation. The very next day George Wallace announced that he would run as a Democrat, not an independent, that year. He would be Muskie's problem, not Nixon's.

"Deal! Shee-it!" Wallace said dismissively, when asked if he and Nixon had agreed to defuse the threats they posed to each other. Others thought differently. "There was motive and opportunity," wrote Wallace biographer Dan T. Carter.

By the fall of 1971, it was hard to find a White House aide with a political portfolio who wasn't involved in a dirty tricks campaign, and inevitably they began to tumble over each other. Strachan, a dutiful lieutenant, prodded Haldeman to confer with Mitchell and bring order to the chaos surrounding "covert activities." The two chiefs turned down one proposal, called "Operation Sandwedge," that would have set up a private investigative agency, run by Caulfield, Rose Woods's brother Joe, and others. Dean and Magruder now saw their opportunity to rise in Nixon's graces. They set to work on a million-dollar project called "Gemstone," and put the lamebrained Liddy in charge. His plan was rife with burglary, bugging, and blackmail and, in its early iterations, with prostitutes, spy planes, thuggery, and kidnapping. Maybe that is too hard on Liddy. After all, when he presented this abomination to the attorney general of the United States, in his offices in the U.S. Department of Justice, with the counsel to the president at his side, using charts prepared by the Central Intelligence Agency, Liddy was not fired or scolded. Mitchell told him to come back with something a little cheaper.

On behalf of the succession of Cold War presidents—who had conspired to keep the knowledge from a contentedly oblivious public—the FBI, the CIA, and other agencies had employed such tactics, and worse, for decades. Stashed in the government's files were records of the massive surveillance programs aimed at the American public, hundreds of "black bag" jobs, CIA drug experiments conducted on unsuspecting citizens, and the attempted assassinations of foreign leaders. The Kennedy administration had authorized the FBI's surveillance of Martin Luther King Jr., recording his extramarital affairs. When civil rights demonstrators threatened to disturb Lyndon Johnson's coronation at the 1964 Democratic convention, he had sent the FBI to eavesdrop—and then called on the bureau in the Chennault affair. "The violations of civil liberties were much greater in magnitude" during previous administrations, Moynihan would argue. But "God help the man who had done small things at the end of a long sequence of big things—when the people are finally sick of it."

What Nixon failed to see was that, as the long-haired blue-jeaned kids in the streets could have told him, the times were indeed changing. Vietnam had shattered the Cold War consensus, polarized a generation, and primed Americans to mistrust presidents ("Don't follow leaders, watch the parking meters"). Nixon's wily old pal J. Edgar Hoover read the tides of public sentiment and balked when he was asked to do what he had done for other chief executives. So Nixon brought the black ops into his White House, to be run by sycophants and klutzes. Predictably, the distinction between national security and political expediency eroded.

You could trace it back to that morning after Tricia's wedding, Garment said. "That's a straight line, from there to the Plumbers to the crazy people—to Hunt, to Liddy—and then everybody climbing aboard the good ship, Let's Get Rid of Nixon. And Nixon collaborated in his own demise. That is why the story is so interesting."

"Who will rid me of this meddlesome priest?" mused Henry II, and a knight seeking royal favor murdered Archbishop Thomas Becket in the cathedral at Canterbury. Did Richard Nixon order every breach of the law? No. But in May 1971 he called for the wiretapping of his Democratic foes. And in June he instructed Haldeman and Colson: "You've got to really have a sophisticated assault upon the Democrats. Humphrey must be destroyed. Muskie must be destroyed. Teddy Kennedy must be." It wasn't hard for Nixon's knights to know what the sovereign wanted. Nixon's mutterings led not to Canterbury, but to Watergate.

The Week That Changed the World

HAVING PAVED THE road to hell, Nixon went to China. His agitation in the Ellsberg mess had been stoked by the stress of waiting for the outcome of his diplomatic maneuvering.

Europe was uniting, China was stirring, and upon the horizon, Nixon saw a revived Japan. The Russians seemed calmer, but that was a reflection of strength and confidence: in the nuclear arms race, the Soviet Union had caught up to the United States. In all this, Nixon groped for opportunity. For a bold enough statesman, the grail of a stable international order, with an array of counterbalancing powers, seemed within reach.

"Everything is linked," Nixon told Kissinger and ambassador Kenneth Rush. "It's . . . part of a grand scheme." It would determine "where our kids are going to be, 25 years from now."

On July 6, thinking aloud at a conference of editors in Kansas City, Nixon spoke of the great changes in the postwar era, and how the end of American preeminence was "not a bad thing." He sketched his vision of a pentagonal multipolar world "within our time" that would be dominated by five great "superpowers": the United States, the Soviet Union, Japan, Western Europe—and China.

"The doors must be opened and the goal of U.S. policy must be . . . ending the isolation of Mainland China and a normalization of our relations," Nixon said. "Looking down the road—and let's just look ahead 15 to 20 years—the United States could have a perfectly effective agreement with the Soviet Union for limitation of arms; the danger of any confrontation there might have been almost totally removed. But Mainland China, outside the world community, completely isolated, with its leaders not in communication . . . would be a danger to the whole world."

Nixon had been scheduled to speak about domestic policy and politics that day; no doubt that's why the White House press corps and his countrymen missed the import of his tour d'horizon. On the far side of the world, the Chinese did not. Zhou Enlai studied those words carefully, annotating the text.*

Three days later, the press was informed that Kissinger had suffered a stomachache—a touch of "Delhi belly"—and retired to his bed in Pakistan, where he had stopped on what the White House was calling a routine fact-finding trip through Indochina, Southwest Asia, and on to France. His airplane remained on the tarmac for all to see, and his motorcade took off for a cool mountain refuge, where Kissinger could rest away from the heat of Islamabad. It was a ruse. In fact, Kissinger was heading to China. He had grabbed a hat and dark glasses, left his guesthouse in the predawn hours, and boarded a jet for Beijing.

No SAUL-LIKE MOMENT of enlightenment led Richard Nixon to China. Lyndon Johnson, Nelson Rockefeller, and Hubert Humphrey were among a number of American leaders who teased themselves in the 1960s with dreams of a diplomatic breakthrough. But the hardened dogma of the right was to treat "Red China" as a pariah, a policy reinforced by the influential China Lobby, and sustained by periodic reports of the Communist Chinese purges and atrocities. And so American diplomats, and Asian leaders, had been surprised when they hosted Nixon during his "wilderness years," and he pressed them with questions about rapprochement with the Communist colossus.

In 1967, Nixon had stayed two nights with Ambassador Marshall Green in Indonesia. After a diplomatic dinner party, Nixon took out a tape recorder, and the two men talked long into the night. On the drive to the airport, as Nixon was leaving, Green asked him what he would do with his tapes and notes. Nixon said he would have his secretary transcribe them, so he could have the information for his files.

"I had thought of Nixon as vice-president, as having been ultra-right wing—a China firster . . . a man I had been prepared to dislike because of his connections with [Joe] McCarthy, who had done such disservice to the Foreign Service," Green recalled. "But he was very different: he was open-minded, with a very clear understanding of the interrelationships between the great powers. He seemed to be remarkably enlightened, not only about the world in general, but with particular reference to China and the Soviet Union."

---

* Zhou studied his adversaries. He would later tell Kissinger that he watched the movie *Patton* to gain insight into Nixon's mind.

In October 1967 Nixon published an essay—"Asia After Vietnam," written with the help of Ray Price—for the journal *Foreign Affairs*. It alerted Americans to great changes taking place on the far side of the world.

"The war in Viet Nam has for so long dominated our field of vision that it has distorted our picture of Asia," Nixon wrote. "A small country on the rim of the continent has filled the screen of our minds; but it does not fill the map. Sometimes dramatically, but more often quietly, the rest of Asia has been undergoing a profound, an exciting and on balance an extraordinarily promising transformation."

The great isms—Communism, totalitarianism, colonialism, and even anticolonialism—were giving way to "the age of computers and cybernetics" in which independent Asian countries no longer seek to subject their citizens, but to liberate them and to prosper from their creativity, Nixon wrote. "The 'people,' in the broadest sense, have become an entity to be served rather than used," he said. "In much of Asia, this change represents a revolution of no less magnitude than the revolution that created the industrial West."

"Governments are consciously, deliberately and programmatically developing in the direction of greater liberty, greater abundance, broader choice and increased popular involvement in the processes of government. Poverty that was accepted for centuries as the norm is accepted no longer," Nixon wrote. The West, he contended, was winning. The American mission in Vietnam had not been wasted; the lives lost there had "bought vitally needed time for governments that were weak or unstable or leaning toward Peking as a hedge against the future—time which has allowed them to attempt to cope with their own insurrections while pressing ahead with their political, economic and military development."

Across these great changes, China threw its shadow. Now was the time for the West to act. "We simply cannot afford to leave China forever outside the family of nations, there to nurture its fantasies, cherish its hates and threaten its neighbors," Nixon wrote. "There is no place on this small planet for a billion of its potentially most able people to live in angry isolation. . . . The world cannot be safe until China changes. Thus our aim, to the extent that we can influence events, should be to induce change."

Mao read the article, and passed it along to Zhou.

"IF I AM elected president," Nixon told Theodore White in early 1968, "the first thing I'll do is get in touch with Red China." In a decade or two it would be impossible to run the world without its collaboration. Perhaps the means, he mused, were "to play Russia and China off against each other."

Once in office, Nixon wasted little time. In his second week as president he wrote to Kissinger, who had submitted a gloomy report on the status of low-level discussions between American and Chinese diplomats in Warsaw. Nixon wanted to resuscitate the talks. "I think we should give every encouragement to the attitude that this administration is 'exploring rapprochement with the Chinese.' This, of course should be done privately and should under no circumstances get into the public prints," Nixon told Kissinger. "However, in contacts with your friends and particularly in any ways you might have to get to this Polish source, I would continue to plant the idea."

As Rockefeller's foreign policy adviser, Kissinger had proposed that the United States form "a subtle triangle" with China and the Soviet Union. But with Vietnam and the Russians on Nixon's plate, the task of crafting a diplomatic opening with the Chinese seemed awfully far-fetched. "Our leader has taken leave of reality," Kissinger told his aide, Alexander Haig.

Though not widely recognized at the time, the Soviet Union's 1968 invasion of Czechoslovakia was a Cold War turning point—not for how it affected Europe, but for how it spooked Mao and his colleagues in Beijing. The Soviets had proclaimed the right to curb ideological deviancy in Communist states and used the Red Army to suppress the Czechs. The Americans might be jackals, but California was five thousand miles away. With the Soviets, Mao shared a border. An uneasy border. In 1969, Soviet and Chinese frontier guards had waged running gun battles along the Amur and Ussuri rivers. Soldiers on both sides died as the fighting escalated into mortar and artillery duels and amphibious assaults. There were massive military buildups: soon more Soviet armor faced south and east than west. The Chinese tested H-bombs in the wastelands along the border. A Soviet diplomat reached out to an American counterpart, inquiring if the United States would join in a preemptive attack on China's nuclear weapons program.

"China looked around and saw itself surrounded by potential enemies," Nixon would remember. "To the north was the Soviet Union, with troops aligned on the border. To the south was India, friendly with the Russians, and a potential nuclear power. To the northeast was Japan, an economic powerhouse and a traditional enemy. But across the Pacific, the Chinese saw the United States: an ideological opponent but with interests opposed to those of the Soviet Union, its most serious and immediate threat. So the

Chinese saw the benefits of working with us. They had to choose between ideology and survival. They chose survival."

Mao had given four Chinese marshals—trusted soldiers of the revolution—the task of assessing China's defense. The Soviet "revisionists," they reported, represented "a more serious threat to our security than the U.S. imperialists." Moscow was planning "an anti-China ring of encirclement." An approach to the United States had to be handled delicately, they warned their old leader, lest it leave the U.S. "sitting on top of the mountain [watching] a fight between two tigers." But a "tactical" accommodation with the Americans "may bring about results of strategic significance." Nixon "hopes to win over China," one of the marshals wrote. "It is necessary for us to utilize the contradiction between the United States and the Soviet Union in a strategic sense, and pursue a breakthrough in Sino-American relations." It was important enough, even, to put the contested status of Taiwan, and the fate of Chiang Kai-shek's island republic, on a back burner.

"Policy emerges when concept encounters opportunity," Kissinger would recall, sounding more than a little like a fortune cookie. On his first overseas trip as president, Nixon talked about China when meeting with Charles de Gaulle in Paris. They were in agreement—the West could not let China "cook in their own juice," the French leader told him. That summer, Nixon conveyed messages of friendship to China via the leaders of Pakistan and Romania, who had contacts with Beijing.

Soon both sides were making small, symbolic gestures, each unsure if the other was catching its drift. The U.S. Navy scaled back its presence in the Taiwan Straits. The Chinese released captured American yachtsmen. In December 1969, the impatient American president ordered the U.S. ambassador in Poland to convey a more direct message to his Chinese counterpart. In Warsaw, at the unlikely setting of a Yugoslav fashion show, Ambassador Walter Stoessel chased down a startled Chinese diplomat, who conveyed the news to Beijing. "We have found the door," Zhou told Mao. "It is time to knock."

The American invasion of Cambodia in the spring of 1970 cooled the budding relationship. But Nixon and Mao kept thumping on the door. "If there is anything I want to do before I die, it is to go to China," Nixon told *Time* magazine. "If he wishes to visit Beijing, tell him to come," Mao told a *Life* correspondent. "Only Nixon, not the leftists or the centrists, can solve the problems we are now facing."

The breakthrough came in the spring of 1971 when the U.S. table tennis team, competing against the expert Chinese and others at the world championships in Japan, brashly invited themselves to China. Mao liked the idea. On April 12, the American athletes landed in Beijing, where the Chinese welcomed them warmly. Then, late in the afternoon of April 27, Kissinger got word that the Pakistani ambassador would like to see him. Ambassador Hilay delivered a two-page handwritten account of a message that Pakistani leader Yahya Khan had received from Zhou. "The Chinese Govt reaffirms its willingness to receive publically in Peking a special envoy of the President of the US (for instance, Mr. Kissinger) or the US Secy of State or even the President of the US himself for a direct meeting and discussions," it said.

The Americans fired back their acceptance, and confirmation arrived, again via Pakistan, on June 2. "Chairman Mao Tse Tung has indicated that he welcomes President Nixon's visit and looks forward to that occasion when he may have direct conversations with His Excellency the President," Zhou wrote. China would welcome Kissinger as a secret envoy, to plan the historic visit. "This is the most important communication that has come to an American President since the end of World War II," the national security adviser told his boss.

KISSINGER'S SECRET MISSION was the stuff of thrillers, and not without a touch of farce. A British newsman, dropping his mother off at the airport, stumbled onto Kissinger and his entourage—but could not persuade his editors that he was neither drunk nor crazy, and lost his scoop. At the State Department, hearing reports of Kissinger's illness, Marshall Green joked that he was more probably sneaking into China. Immediately, it dawned on Green that he might have guessed the truth; he shuddered, left his colleagues, checked with Rogers (who paled, and confirmed it), and returned to swear the others "to utter secrecy." Kissinger, meanwhile, had left behind his shirts, forcing him to borrow supersized substitutes from a husky aide. On this historic visit, the first by an American diplomat since 1949, he shuffled about the Chinese capital looking a bit like a penguin.

Kissinger's party remembered the comic touches, but also how stirred they were soaring over the snowcapped Himalayas that near-perfect morning, high above the trade routes of antiquity, a happy few dispatched to cheat grim-visaged war. Kissinger felt a regained capacity for wonder and discovery, "the quality that in one's youth made time seem to stand still; that gave every event the mystery of novelty; that enabled each experience to be relished because of its singularity." Their code name for the trip was Polo.

The Americans arrived a little after noon that Friday and were taken to the Diaoyutai, a compound of lakes and trees that long ago served as the imperial fishing hole but now was a guarded enclave for important foreign visitors. Zhou joined them at 4:30 that afternoon and stayed for most of that first night, and much of the next two days. "His gaunt expressive face was dominated by piercing eyes, conveying a mixture of intensity and repose," Kissinger recalled. He filled the room "not by his physical dominance" like de Gaulle, but by an air of "controlled tension, steely discipline, and self-control, as if he were a coiled spring." Given the state of the world in the early 1970s, the Chinese-American rapprochement was inevitable, Kissinger would conclude. But "that it should occur so rapidly and develop so naturally owed no little to the luminous personality and extraordinary perception of the Chinese premier."

Zhou was the son of a mandarin. As a young man he had identified Communism as the optimal vehicle for Chinese resurgence, joined the revolution, and survived the Red Army's storied 1930s retreat—the Long March—the civil war with Chiang Kai-shek, and all that followed.

There were sporadic breakdowns of the premier's self-control, Kissinger would discover, when Zhou and the other Chinese leaders revealed the emotional and intellectual toll that they were paying in lying down with the running dogs. There was a "certain brooding quality," and an "occasional schizophrenia," in Zhou's behavior, evoked by this troubling need for "dealing with arch capitalists," Kissinger wrote.

"These were men in some anguish," he reported. "Yet their long history of past suffering gave them an inner confidence that was reflected in a certain largeness of spirit. There was none of the Russian ploymanship, scoring points, rigidity or bullying."

The ideological contradiction was real on the American side as well, but apparently not as wrenching. They were realists, Kissinger told Zhou, accepting the imperative of defending national interests in a time of transformative change. Nixon's long hatred of Communists could, in fact, be employed: it would arm their venture against right-wing opposition in America. As Mao had said: only Nixon could go to China.

Two days later, anxiously awaiting word in San Clemente, Nixon received the prearranged code word—Eureka—that signaled success. In three days of roast duck and banter, of philosophy and history, Taiwan and Vietnam, cabbages and kings, Kissinger and Zhou had reached agreement on a summit. They struggled only over the question of face: each wanted the other to seem the supplicant. (Nixon had begged an invitation, Zhou would later tell colleagues, like a whore at the door.) The final formulation of the announcement was suitably clever: "Knowing of President Nixon's expressed desire to visit the People's Republic of China, Premier Zhou Enlai . . . has extended an invitation."

Kissinger composed a twenty-seven-page report on his trip for Nixon, describing the Chinese as "tough, idealistic, fanatical" but with the "inward security" needed to negotiate. Unlike the Russians, who gave tiny slices of concessions over an extended period of time, the Chinese cut right to a reasonable bottom line: "They concentrated on essentials; they eschewed invective and haggling." The future would require "reliability, precision, finesse," Kissinger concluded. But "if we can master this process, we will have made a revolution."

Nixon, driving his golf cart, welcomed Kissinger at the San Clemente helipad in morning sunshine on July 13. They huddled in his study above the beach to assess the revolution. The opening to China held all sorts of possibilities, they agreed, but the immediate payoff was psychological: American pride and confidence would be restored, and the North Vietnamese dismayed, to a commensurate degree. They had bought more time to win the war, and room to employ more brutal tactics without fear of Chinese intervention.

Haldeman joined them and the talk turned toward domestic politics. It was clear that the modest visit proposed by the Chinese—a delegation comprised of Nixon, Rogers, Kissinger, "a couple of aides," and ten or so reporters—was not what the White House image makers had in mind. Someone would need to educate Zhou: planeloads of Americans would be coming. In announcing the breakthrough, however, Nixon and his aides made the decision that less was more. At midafternoon on July 15 the White House issued an enigmatic bulletin announcing that Nixon would make a "major statement" on prime-time television that night. At 7:30 p.m. Pacific time, Nixon spoke for but seven minutes from the NBC studios in Burbank. "I will undertake what I deeply hope will become a journey for peace," he said.

Then the exuberant president did something he very rarely did, breaching his personal protocol to take staff—Kissinger, Haldeman, Ehrlichman, and others—to Perino's Restaurant on Wilshire Boulevard, a now-fading hot spot whose plush peach-colored booths and red velvet barstools had, for decades, cuddled the fannies of California pols and Hollywood's movie stars. Nixon "reveled in an unchallengeable triumph," Kissinger recalled, accepting the good wishes of fellow diners and lingering in the foyer after a fine wine (Château Lafite-Rothschild 1961), beef, and crab, not wanting the evening to end.

"There was a mutual shyness; Nixon was always ill at ease with strangers, and the other guests were not comfortable in approaching," Kissinger recalled. "In his hour of achievement Richard Nixon was oddly vulnerable, waiting expectantly for recognition without quite being able to bridge the gulf by which he had isolated himself from his fellow men."

AMERICANS WERE STUNNED by the news of the opening to China. Millions were delighted. The Taiwanese were not.

Before Kissinger left on his trip, Nixon had instructed his aide to be tough with Zhou and Mao. He told his adviser to provoke "fear" in the Chinese by describing Nixon as the madman who might join with China's rivals—the Russians, the Japanese, and the Taiwanese—in unspeakable acts. But in his very first discussion in Beijing, Kissinger had accepted China's precondition to a Nixon-Mao summit: he renounced the Taiwanese independence movement and a "two China" policy, and promised Zhou that the United States would "not stand in the way" of a "political evolution" that would gratify the Communists at the expense of Taiwan's freedom.

The sudden change in U.S. policy didn't sit well with the right. Nixon had been Taiwan's stalwart defender. Now, "he turned around, with cool precision—a politician without any principles at all ... [and] proceeded to double-cross them," said William Rusher, publisher of the *National Review*. It was one of "the greatest historical double-crosses of all time."

In public, Nixon and Kissinger downplayed the adjustment in American policy toward China. In private, they did not delude themselves.

"Taiwan, except for the sentimental thing, is really the least significant" American interest, Kissinger told the president.

"I'm afraid it is. I'm sorry," Nixon replied.

"It's a heartbreaking thing. They're a lovely people," said Kissinger.

"I hate to do it," said Nixon. "I hate to do it. I hate to do it. . . . They have been my friends."

But the China game was a linchpin. The China game proved that Americans still had vigor, audacity, and imagination. The China game strengthened Nixon's hand in seeking an "honorable" end to the Vietnam

War. The China game empowered the Russia game. It could pave the way for a generation of peace. To illustrate his vision to German chancellor Willy Brandt that summer, Nixon held up his hand and ticked off the five fingers—the United States, Europe, the Soviet Union, China, and Japan— that coming together made a fist. His goal was "to see that these five can develop a live and let live attitude," Nixon said.

So Taiwan was collateral damage. On June 30, Nixon had given his instructions to Walter McConaughy, the U.S. ambassador, who was about to leave to brief the Kuomintang.

"They must be prepared for the fact that there will continue to be a step-by-step, a more normal relationship with . . . the Chinese mainland," Nixon said. "Not because we love [the Communists] but because they're there . . . and because the world situation has so drastically changed. . . . Our failure to move would . . . prejudice our interests in other areas that are overwhelming."

Taiwan would survive, and prosper. But the immediate consequence of the change in U.S. policy was a minor diplomatic catastrophe: the United Nations voted to eject Taiwan and accept the mainland government as China's representative.

The Japanese were only slightly less distressed. In deference to the United States, Japan had shelved plans for its own rapprochement with China, and Nixon's surprise announcement caused Prime Minister Eisaku Sato a serious loss of face. The Japanese had hardly recovered their composure when the United States followed with another "Nixon Shock"—a monetary coup that rocked not just Japan, but all the world economies.

÷

IT HAD TAKEN Nixon months to find the proper ancillaries, but in Federal Reserve chairman Arthur Burns and the new treasury secretary, former Texas governor John Connally, he had finally installed allies at the levers of economic policy. On Sunday night, August 15, the president commanded prime-time television (preempting *Bonanza*) with the summer's second stunning announcement: he would treat the ailing American economy with a dose of measures that included wage and price controls, a tax on imports—and suspension of the Bretton Woods Agreement, which had governed world trade for more than twenty-five years. The United States was scrapping the gold standard, Nixon said, for a yet-to-be-determined substitute. The golden postwar era was officially interred.

Nixon was responding to two economic predicaments; one at home, the other overseas. The chief culprit on the home front, as with so many other issues, was the costs of the Vietnam War. Nixon, like Lyndon Johnson, had conspired with the Democratic Congress to pay for the war with borrowed funds: they declined to make meaningful cuts in popular domestic programs and ran up budget deficits. The Fed tried to curb the resulting inflation via a measured tightening of the money supply—a process called gradualism. Gradual or not, it helped bring on a recession and contributed to Republican reversals in the 1970 election.

With his own reelection campaign under way, Nixon grew increasingly anxious. He recalled how the Federal Reserve, taking the safe route, had driven the economy into recession in 1960 and given a boost to Kennedy. "You have to consider the political timing," Nixon had ordered his White House advisers soon after taking office. "Whenever political considerations are not present we can afford to look at things purely from an economic standpoint. But that will not be often."

"I remember '58," Nixon told them. "We cooled off the economy, and cooled off 15 senators and 60 congressmen at the same time."

So NIXON COERCED his new Fed chairman to get the economy chugging. He was not subtle. "The President looked wild; talked like a desperate man . . . released a torrent of resentment against me," Burns told his diary, after a confrontation in March 1971. "I am convinced that the President will do anything to be re-elected   There were moments during this meeting when I felt that the President was going mad. . . . I left with a deeply troubled mind."

"We've got to keep Arthur's feet to the fire on the money supply," Nixon told his aides. "By God, we have got to put his feet to the fire." Conspiring on a cocktail cruise on the *Sequoia,* Nixon ordered Colson to leak word that Burns, while preaching restraint to American firms and families, was bucking for a pay raise. "Let's teach Arthur something [so] that he'll learn to be more cooperative," Nixon said.

Envoys were dispatched to threaten Burns. He would not be reappointed, they said, or the White House would neuter him by packing the Federal Reserve Board with tamer appointees. Burns had another confrontation with Nixon. "His features became twisted, and what I saw was uncontrolled cruelty," the chairman wrote in his diary. "While my heart was filled with sadness for him, I was seized suddenly with fear for the safety of our country, which depended so heavily on this insecure man."

Several of Nixon's advisers—including George Shultz and economist Milton Friedman—told the president that gradualism was working and a sound recovery lay ahead. They urged him to stay the course. But Burns was not so sure. Economists were confronting a new phenomenon— stagflation, they called it, a coupling of unemployment and inflation— that didn't respond like the traditional business cycle. "What the boys that swarm around the White House fail to see is that the country now faces an entirely new problem—namely, a sizable inflation in the midst of a recession," Burns noted. He warned Congress: "The rules of economics are not working the way they used to."

Fretting about inflation but needing to help Nixon get reelected, Burns seized on a wage–price freeze as the only way out. It violated conservative doctrine, but they could goose the economy and still control the cost of living. With remarkable facility, Nixon and Connally abandoned their previous opposition to government controls and made plans for a grand announcement when Congress returned in September.

THE OTHER QUANDARY had a golden hue. Since 1944, when the nations of the West gathered at a resort in Bretton Woods, New Hampshire, and hammered out a system of fixed exchange rates, the gold-backed U.S. dollar was the rock on which bankers built the church. It remained so as Western Europe and Japan recovered from the ruins of World War II with rebuilt factories, and emerging nations offered new markets, spurring American investors, consumers, and corporations to spend dollars overseas. Offshore vaults were soon chock with "Eurodollars," and the list of foreign-made products that threatened U.S. industries—automobiles, cameras, televisions, textiles, shoes, pianos—grew longer with each passing year. America was poised to run its first trade deficit. Everybody winked, but the dollars in foreign banks far exceeded the gold the United States held in its depository at Fort Knox.

From the earliest days of his administration, Nixon had been warned that a reckoning was coming. To some degree, he welcomed it. Now was the time to reform the international monetary system and strike back at the "gangsters" and "vampires sucking the blood out of every transaction," he said. He worried, as well, about American competitiveness. It was a primary factor in his push for development of supersonic transport aircraft and NASA's space shuttle program. But while Treasury had drawn up plans to "close the gold window" and allow currencies to "float" in a system of adjustable rates, it would be a wrenching change, and inertia had ruled in the absence of a crisis. Nixon put monetary reform on a list of issues he handed to Haldeman, about which he was not to be annoyed.

The world did not cooperate. A reckoning arrived in August, when a run on gold yanked Connally back to Washington from a Texas vacation. Congenitally disposed toward the bolder course of action, Connally and Nixon gathered their top advisers and flew off to Camp David for secret rites: they would marry the death of the gold standard with the birth of wage and price controls.

VARIOUS TAX AND spending cuts filled out the package, the most important of which was a new 10 percent tax on imports. In league with a devalued dollar, the border tax would raise the costs of imports, create jobs at home, and please the worried electorate. With the progress he was making on foreign affairs, Nixon believed that the lunch-bucket issue was all the Democrats had left, and he meant to deprive them of it. As "a political matter . . . our primary goal must be a continued upward surge in the domestic economy," Nixon said. "We must not, in order to stabilize the international situation, cut our guts out."

This was no time for Churchillian sacrifice. "Blood, sweat and tears? Hell no," said Nixon. He wanted "one big bold play . . . the whole damn thing at one time," and that is what he got: by far the most momentous intrusion by an American president in the U.S. economy since Roosevelt and the Great Depression. "Goddamn it, my view is why be bound by all that stuff in the past?" he said.

Nixon choreographed the conclave at Camp David. His advisers broke into teams and (cloaked in commemorative windbreakers supplied by the ever-thorough Haldeman) hammered out the details. Safire was along to write the speech, but Nixon arose at 3:15 a.m. on Saturday, crafting it himself. He didn't want it "brittle and beautiful, but brutal and effective." That night he lit a fire in his cabin and sat in the darkened room, where Haldeman found him staring into the flames, lost in one of his "mystic moods." All summer he had been talking about the spiritual bankruptcy of the elites, and the gutsiness of working men and women. The American spirit needed rallying, Nixon said. "We must try to be what it is in our power to be."

Burns and Safire, on a midnight walk, discussed the performance of their chief. "He's a President now," Burns said. "He has a noble motive in foreign affairs to reshape the world—or at least his motive is to earn the fame that comes from nobly reshaping the world."

Nixon's speech was a triumph. The stock market rose by thirty-two points, its largest one-day gain to date. He leaped past Senator Edmund Muskie, the Democratic front-runner, in the polls. PREZ CHANGES ECONOMIC GAME PLAN, read the headline in *Variety*. NEW SCORE IS DOW 32, NIXON 72. Returning from a negotiating session with the North Vietnamese in Paris, Kissinger found the president "elated," trending toward "euphoria."

"He saw himself as revolutionizing international economics as he had already transformed international diplomacy," Kissinger recalled. "He reveled in the publicity coup."

There was one down note. The president felt the need to exhort his fellow Americans to rise above a worrisome mood taking hold even in the heartland—a feeling that Kissinger called "malaise."

The calm of the fifties and the electric thrills of the sixties had been replaced by a sullen feeling—befitting the coming decade of shortages, defeat, doubt, and limits. Vietnam could do that to a country. Nixon sensed it: no politician so acutely tuned to the spirit of the common folk could not. Taking a page from Franklin Roosevelt, he tried to inspire, challenging Americans to "snap out of the self-doubt." He would not be the last U.S. president to do so.

WHAT STARTLES, IN retrospect, is that Nixon and Connally had no blueprints for what came next—no replacement for Bretton Woods, no long-term fix for stagflation. They were improvising, making it up as they went along, eking it out to November 1972. "Are we going to build a new world in sheer bluff and bombast?" Burns asked his diary.

Memos flew about the government. "As the shock effect of August 15 wears off and other countries develop their negotiating strategy, defining where we want to go becomes increasingly essential," Kissinger warned Nixon on September 20. "What exactly do we want others to do?"

For Connally, an LBJ Democrat with an ear for what played with the voters, inculpating foreign bankers was enough. At first, Nixon agreed. "Between now and the election . . . there must be one paramount consideration," he told Connally and Burns on September 11. "And that paramount consideration is not the responsibility of the U.S. in the world.

"I want to do the responsible statesmanlike thing, but not now," said Nixon. "That means, frankly, playing the international thing to the hilt politically."

But America's trade partners outwitted Connally in the negotiations over a new monetary regime, and Kissinger got an earful from the allies. When the financial standoff threatened to bring on a worldwide recession, for which Nixon would be blamed, Kissinger was summoned to save things. "Even in my most megalomaniac moments," Kissinger recalled, he would not claim expertise in economics. The subsequent arrangement of fixed exchange rates—the Smithsonian accord of December 1971—would collapse, and the world resorted to a network of floating currencies in 1973. The U.S. trade deficit continued to soar, and the world suffered "crises and panics even more dramatic," Kissinger recalled.

At home, the wage and price freeze proved, as predicted, a popular and effective measure—temporarily. College students reveled in ninety-eight-cent six-packs. Homemakers purchased steak. Inflation was held to 3 percent, and the unemployment rate dropped to 5.5 percent by Election Day 1972.

But the freeze just kicked the can down the road, as the Federal Reserve, Congress, and Nixon's budget mavens madly pumped money into the economy. Not all was one-shot stimulus: some of the spending measures—like the Social Security cost-of-living raises authorized in 1972—bore mammoth long-term costs. Steam was building in the boiler. Someday it must explode. "Sooner or later," wrote Milton Friedman in his August 30 column for *Newsweek,* "it will end as all previous attempts to freeze prices and wages have ended . . . in utter failure and the emergence into the open of the suppressed inflation."

Opting for the short-term political payoff, Nixon made a choice that would haunt him. The time would come to "answer for Santino"—to borrow a line from *The Godfather*—and it arrived when he could least afford it. Like the shady campaign tricks being staged by CREEP, Nixon's economic maneuvering helped clinch his reelection. But afterwards, as the wage and price controls were lifted, the cost-of-living for American households rose by almost 10 percent in 1973 and by more than 12 percent in 1974—the worst peacetime inflation in the nation's history.

Irate over Nixon's support for Israel, the Arabs played their oil card. The price soared from $1.77 to $10 per barrel. Unemployment began to climb as America slid into a recession that lasted into 1975. The gross national product fell by more than 2 percent per capita. And Wall Street saw through Nixon's shenanigans. The stock market went into a long slump in December 1972, losing almost half its value over the next two years. In those crucial months during 1973 and 1974, as the Watergate scandal peaked and the Democrats strove to reverse the results of the 1972 election, the economic turbulence would thoroughly corrode Nixon's public support. The kick had been terrific; the hangover was a killer.

÷

KISSINGER'S ALARM OVER Connally's trade war was not the only reason that Nixon, having wrung what domestic political benefits there were from the monetary dispute, sued for peace with the European allies as fall turned toward winter. His trip to China was on the horizon, and he wanted to build toward the historic visit with a series of headline-grabbing consultations with the leaders of France, Great Britain, and West Germany—not get bogged in mind-numbing haggling about exchange rates.

Besides, the world had served up more good news. In August, Nixon had received a message from Leonid Brezhnev—an invitation to visit Moscow for another election-year summit, to conclude the strategic arms negotiations. "If they only knew what the hell was coming up, they'd be in here panting for that summit," Nixon had said about the foot-dragging Russians back in June. He was right. Within days of announcing the opening to China, Nixon heard from Dobrynin, and the formal letter from Brezhnev followed.

"Here we kick the Russians in the teeth—and they invite us," Nixon grinned.

Nixon announced the Moscow trip on October 12. The monetary crisis was in full sway. The UN was expelling Taiwan. The South Vietnamese were busy rigging their elections. And there was the usual domestic political skullduggery: an aborted attempt by Nixon to force J. Edgar Hoover to retire, and a presidential commutation of labor leader Jimmy Hoffa's prison sentence. The conventions of narrative require that events be taken sequentially, but crises don't stand in line. And slithering through the whole of 1971, an ugly dispute between India and Pakistan clamored for attention until, in December, Nixon stumbled into a perilous showdown with the Soviet Union, endangering the Moscow summit and testing the new relationship with China before it was much of a relationship at all.

THE WELLSPRING OF tragedy was the familiar negligence of an imperial power, vanquished by nationalists, going home and leaving ancient grievances, arbitrary boundaries, and Cold War intrigue to exacerbate the chaos.

In this case it was not France, as in Indochina, but Great Britain in Southwest Asia.

India won its independence from the British in 1947, but in the blood-soaked partition that followed, the Muslims of West Pakistan had been separated by one thousand miles of Hindu India from the Muslims of East Pakistan. To compound the mess, the two Muslim peoples came from very different ethnic backgrounds (they were Bengalis, mostly, in the East and Punjabis and others in the West) and had little in common save their faith. Pakistan had staggered along, a minor player in the postwar era until its leader, Yahya Khan, made himself so useful as the conduit between Nixon and Mao.

Nixon liked Yahya, but Yahya came with baggage. Though East Pakistan was smaller in territory, it had a larger population than its more sophisticated western counterpart and felt snubbed and exploited by the powers in Islamabad. The East's leaders built a political movement, pushed for autonomy, and—infuriated by the government's sluggish response to a cyclone that devastated their homeland in 1970—amazed the world when they won enough seats to take control of the Pakistani parliament.

Determined to keep the country intact, with the center of power in West Pakistan, Yahya and the Pakistani military launched a crackdown on Bengali political leaders, press, intellectuals, and militias in March 1971. Thousands were gunned down in the cities of East Pakistan, and as the army moved to take control of the countryside (singling out the Hindu minority for special persecution), millions of refugees fled into India. Two hundred thousand people died in the first six months of violence. American diplomats in India and Pakistan had warned Washington of what was coming, and resounded the alarm when the "reign of terror" got under way. They headlined their cables SELECTIVE GENOCIDE. The U.S. ambassador to India, former Republican senator Ken Keating, wrote: "Shocked at massacre by Pakistani military in East Pakistan, appalled at possibility these atrocities are being committed with American equipment." Nixon chose not to intervene.

Could Nixon have stopped the carnage? No. At least not in those first, horrific nights and days. As the world learned in Biafra in 1969, and later in Rwanda and Bosnia, ancient ethnic and tribal hatreds are among the most resistant to statecraft. A "bloodbath" was looming, warned Under Secretary of State Alexis Johnson, a veteran diplomat, in a meeting chaired by Kissinger three weeks before the crackdown, but "we have no control over the events which will determine the outcome, and very little influence." Another veteran State Department official, Christopher Van Hollen, advised that the United States could lose what influence it had if it applied too much pressure: "West Pakistan is very suspicious that we are supporting a separate East Pakistan state. If we tell Yahya to call off the use of force, it will merely fuel this suspicion."

The United States had few carrots; it had abandoned the arms trade with Pakistan and India after their 1965 war, and a few million dollars in spare parts represented its only hooks in the Pakistani military. Nor, given their record in the months that followed, is it likely that Yahya and his generals would have bowed. The Pakistanis saw themselves in an existential crisis and had dispatched one of their cruelest generals to East Pakistan to choreograph the slaughter. They had no fear that the United States, mired in Vietnam, would intervene militarily. India might, but even when staring at war with their massive and powerful neighbor, Pakistan's leaders refused to budge—not even to negotiate with the imprisoned separatist leader Mujibur Rahman. If they were going to lose East Pakistan, they would do so fighting. Under such circumstances, "I can't imagine that they give a damn what we think," Kissinger told his colleagues. The CIA and the State Department representatives agreed.

EVEN AS A gesture, should Nixon have done more than he did? Yes. Kissinger would later concede that there was "some merit" to "the charge of moral insensitivity" in the Nixon White House. As the crisis wore on, and the massacres turned to bloody civil war, it is conceivable that vigorous protest by the United Nations, universal condemnation, and the prospect of an international peacekeeping force may have given Yahya pause and saved lives. "No single Western country has much influence on the situation," the CIA said, "but general Western disapproval may make the government in Islamabad less certain of the wisdom of present policies and more amendable to pressures for change."

Nixon did close to nothing. On March 28, the first reports of the "reign of terror by the Pak military" were raised at the White House. "Is the present U.S. posture of simply ignoring the atrocities in East Pakistan still advisable or should we now be expressing our shock at least privately to the West Pakistanis?" an aide asked Kissinger.

Nixon gave the answer: "I wouldn't put out a statement praising it, but we're not going to condemn it either," he said.

The president clung to this policy, even when the more conservative of the two U.S. ambassadors on the scene, Joseph Farland in Islamabad, urged Nixon to intercede. "We do not believe army over long run can hold East by bayonet," Farland wrote Washington on April 6. "Yahya's action . . . is a self-defeating step which in time will land Pak army into a hopeless morass. . . . [It] has probably made inevitable the thing he is ostensibly seeking to prevent in the long term; the disintegration of Pakistan." Farland suggested that a presidential message, delivered to Yahya, might "hopefully give Pak military some pause." The "human and political problems" then emerging "argue cogently for less reluctance on our part about using our influence."

The American response was muted. And when India—grappling with millions of refugees, who were sick and dying in camps swept by cholera and other diseases—threatened Yahya, Nixon famously ordered U.S. policy to "tilt toward Pakistan." American diplomats who had raised the humanitarian alarms, and sent a bold letter of dissent to Washington, were mocked and punished.

"This will be only one blip in the battle and then it will go on and on and on," Nixon said, over the phone from San Clemente, after Kissinger had informed him that Yahya had taken control of East Pakistan. "It's like everything in the period we live in—isn't it?—since World War II—where revolution in itself, independence, is a virtue, which of course it never was. That wasn't true at the time of the French Revolution either and it isn't any more true today. The real question is whether anybody can run the goddamn place."

THERE WERE REASONS for Nixon's cool-bloodedness. The exonerative explanation was China.

Yahya had started his campaign of terror on March 25. The United States and China were then resuming their long-distance flirtation. The Ping-Pong team got its invitation on April 6, and it was April 27 when Zhou—using Pakistan as an intermediary—sent Nixon the handwritten note inviting an American envoy "or even the President" to visit China. At Zhou's suggestion, it was Yahya who managed the negotiations that led up to Kissinger's Beijing visit, and Yahya who helped orchestrate the secret trip, and Pakistan that served as the point of departure.

The China game needed Yahya. "That is the last thing we can afford now—to have the Pakistan government overthrown, given the other things we are doing," Kissinger told Nixon on May 23. Yahya must be "kept afloat for six more months," Kissinger told Farland. "All we need is six months." And all this time the Pakistani army was crushing East Pakistan.

It came down to a stony reckoning: Were the lives of several hundred thousand Bengalis worth more than what a new world order, and stability in the nuclear era, might offer to billions of human beings? In June, Ambassador Keating flew to Washington and warned Nixon that East Pakistan's Hindu population was facing "a matter of genocide." The China initiative was still secret. "There are some other major considerations . . . reasons we can't go into," the president told Keating. "What we have to do, Ken, is to find a way to be just as generous as we can to the Indians, but . . . we do not want to do something that is an open breech with Yahya. . . . We've got to take up here, for reasons that go far beyond India-Pakistan relations, another position." And so America took a hands-off course.

It is not that nothing was done. Under Nixon's direction, the United States authorized more aid for the Bengali refugees than all the other nations of the world combined—preventing a famine that, as CIA director Richard Helms put it, would "make Biafra look like a cocktail party." With varying effectiveness, the U.S. government moved to cut off military aid to Pakistan. American planes participated in an emergency airlift of refugees. And the United States urged Pakistan's leaders to negotiate with the separatists. But Nixon's response to Yahya was "not exactly strong," Kissinger would admit. On the bottom of an April 28 memo from Kissinger offering policy alternatives, the president wrote: "To all hands. Don't squeeze Yahya at this time." He underlined the word "don't" three times.

TYPICALLY, WITH RICHARD NIXON, his own resentments played a role in the Indo-Pakistani war that followed. Kissinger told Keating that, though crafting foreign policy based on personal relationships was a prescription for failure, Nixon had a "special feeling" for Yahya, and an innate dislike for the Indians. "One cannot make policy on that basis . . . but it is a fact of life," he said.*

Nixon's warmth for Pakistan dated back to his vice-presidential trips, and then his wanderings in the wilderness years, when the Pakistanis had welcomed him with honors and regard. He found them appealingly frank and down-to-earth. The Indians were another story. The Nehru dynasty—

* Kissinger's own view was that "Yahya and his group would never win any prizes for high IQs."

Jawaharlal Nehru and his daughter, the current prime minister, Indira Gandhi—were haughty and treated Nixon like a grocer's son. From their rung below the great powers, the Brahmins had adopted the pose of moral scold, criticizing the Cold War antagonists for their militancy while claiming leadership of the "non-aligned" world, thus clenching power by denouncing it. False piety was a Nixon trick: he didn't much like it used against him. "Nixon and Mrs. Indira Gandhi," Kissinger wrote, "were not intended by fate to be personally congenial. Her assumption of almost hereditary moral superiority . . . brought out all of Nixon's latent insecurities."

"Even apart from the Chinese thing, I wouldn't . . . help the Indians," Nixon told Kissinger. "The Indians are no goddamn good." In private, Nixon called Gandhi "that bitch," a "goddamn woman," and "the old witch" and sputtered ugly things. "The Indians need—what they really need—is a mass famine," he said.

Meanwhile, at home, those siding with India included a roster of Nixon enemies—the State Department and its Ivy League diplomats, Ted Kennedy and other Senate Democrats, and the liberal press. Kennedy, who chaired a Senate subcommittee on refugee affairs, toured the dismal camps of Bengal in August—when the number of refugees was more than halfway toward its eventual peak of 10 million—tailed by a pack of television cameras and reporters, ratcheting up American public opinion against Pakistan, and leaving the president fuming.

Though India was certainly struggling to cope with the tide of refugees, Nixon suspected—not without reason—that Gandhi was employing the humanitarian crisis as a curtain for aggression. Her motive "was to destroy Pakistan," he told Kissinger. India armed the East Pakistan resistance, trained Bengali guerrillas, and supported their raids with artillery fire across the border. There could be no peaceful settlement until the Indians "stop screwing around in East Pakistan," CIA director Helms advised.

Gandhi's generals were waiting for November, after the monsoon season, when India's armored columns could maneuver on dry land and the Himalayan passes would be blocked with snow, preventing Chinese intervention. They planned to dash for Dacca, the East Pakistan capital, while holding off Yahya in the west. Then, after liberating East Pakistan, India would shift all its forces to the western border and complete the defeat, humiliation, and dismemberment of Pakistan. To help keep China, the United States, and the United Nations from interfering, Gandhi played a red ace. In August she signed a Treaty of Peace, Friendship, and Cooperation with the Soviet Union.

In their minds, the treaty gave Nixon and Kissinger absolution for what guilt they may have felt for sustaining Pakistani barbarity. Americans in the Cold War tolerated many cruelties in response to a Communist threat.

On November 4, Gandhi visited Washington and met with Nixon for a final round of talks. It went as expected, given their mutual disregard. Nixon didn't want to give India a pretext for going to war with Pakistan, and so his toast at the state dinner was gracious, and his conversation free of overt insults. Instead, "we worked her around . . . I dropped stilettos all over her," Nixon boasted to Haldeman. But as Gandhi left, the president had no doubt that India would find its own excuse for action. She sent columns of tanks and troops into East Pakistan and Yahya, provoked, attacked India from the west on December 3.

Nixon, at first, kept to the sidelines. The United States took the issue to the United Nations and won a lopsided vote in the General Assembly condemning India. But then, though they had predicted it for months, the reality of an Indian victory began to grate on Nixon and Kissinger. As the Indian columns closed on Dacca and Indian bombers set the oil tanks of Karachi blazing, Nixon grew increasingly agitated. The CIA sent him a report from a source in Gandhi's government: the prime minister had vowed to keep her armies moving until East Pakistan and parts of Kashmir were liberated and the "Pakistani armored and air force strength are destroyed so that Pakistan will never again be in a position to plan another invasion of India."

"This woman suckered us," the president said. "She is going to pay." Kissinger egged him on. This was a case of naked aggression, he told Nixon. A rape of Pakistan. An ally dismembered. A watershed moment in the Cold War. Yahya would be forced from office, Kissinger said. Iran and Indonesia would turn toward Moscow. Israel was in peril. American prestige was at stake. Mao would never trust us, and the China game would be lost. This was Suez. It was Czechoslovakia. It was Nixon's Rhineland. The Soviets were humiliating the United States of America.

"We're in the position where a Soviet stooge, supported with Soviet arms, is overrunning a county that is an American ally," said Kissinger, casting it as a Cold War showdown, as if the whole sorry saga had been orchestrated by Moscow. "The major problem now is that the Russians retain their respect for you."

"We have only one hope now: to convince the Indians that the thing is going to escalate," Kissinger counseled. "We've got to scare them. . . . And to convince the Russians that they're going to pay an enormous price."

They could fail. Lose the Moscow summit. Maybe both summits.

There was "a high possibility of disaster," said Kissinger, but "at least we're coming off like men."

NIXON PLUNGED INTO madman mode. He sent a stark note to Brezhnev and called in a Soviet minister, warning that unless the Indians drew back from West Pakistan, the United States would take action that could lead to a military confrontation with the Soviet Union. To reinforce the threat, he sent the USS *Enterprise,* a nuclear aircraft carrier, and its battle group into the Bay of Bengal. He dispatched Kissinger to New York to meet with a Chinese official and urge Zhou to march troops south toward India. "A movement of even some Chinese toward that border could scare those goddamn Indians to death," Nixon said.

It was then illegal to send arms to Pakistan, or to use a third country to launder such a transaction. Nixon did so anyway, conspiring with Jordan, Iran, and Israel to have American-made fighter planes shipped from Jordan and Iran to Pakistan.

"We'll just close our eyes. Get the goddamned planes in there," said Kissinger.

"Is it really so much against our law?" Nixon asked.

"What's against our law is not what they do, but our giving them permission," Kissinger explained.

"We give the permission privately," the president said.

"That's right," said Kissinger.

"Hell," said Nixon, "we've done worse."

THE CRISIS PEAKED on December 12, with apocalyptic rumblings in the Oval Office. Nixon and Kissinger met that morning to compose a warning, to be sent to Brezhnev on the crisis hotline, to get his Indian clients under control or meet "frightening consequences."

A sign had come from Beijing. "They're going to move" against India, Kissinger predicted.

If the Chinese skirmished with the Indians, Nixon said, the Russians might feel compelled to attack China. The United States would side with China. And that could start World War III.

It was a terrifying thought. But "if the Soviets move against them, and then we don't do anything, we'll be finished," Kissinger advised.

"So what do we do? Start lobbing nuclear weapons in?" Nixon asked.

"Well, if the Soviets move against them and succeed, that will be the final showdown," said Kissinger. "If they succeed, we'll be finished. We'll be through. . . . What we are now having is the final—we may be looking right down the gun barrel."

Nixon pictured a world dominated by Russia, with a cowed China and "600 million Indians, the balance of southeast Asia terrorized, the Japanese immobile. The Europeans, of course, will suck after them, and the United States [left as] the only one" willing to defend freedom.

It represented "a change in the world balance of power of such magnitude," said Kissinger, that American security would be threatened "forever—certainly for decades."

The president drew a deep breath.

"Russia and China aren't going to go to war," Nixon said hopefully.

"I wouldn't bet on that, Mr. President," said Kissinger. "The Russians . . . are not rational on China."

THE CONVERSATION IS jolting: more so when one considers that the Russians weren't the only ones whose rationality was under scrutiny. The chairman of the Federal Reserve was confiding to his diary that, after witnessing Nixon's rages and insecurities, he feared for the country. And Nixon was telling aides that Kissinger might need psychiatric care.

Trying to juggle the China venture, the Vietnam peace talks, the channel with Dobrynin, the negotiations on the gold standard, and the India-Pakistan war, the volatile national security adviser seemed "to have lost his senses," one State Department hand reported to Haldeman. Nixon himself was shocked after hearing how Kissinger "ranted and raved" at his colleagues, and wondered aloud if "Henry's gotten past the point of basic stability" and should be eased out.

In the first week of December, Kissinger had stormed into Haldeman's office, thrown a "monumental" tantrum, and announced that he was going to resign. Nixon "feels, as do I now, that there's more to this than just India-Pakistan, and that there may be a personal problem," Haldeman told his diary. The president and his chief of staff pondered Kissinger's mental and emotional well-being all that month and the next, weighing reports that Kissinger was tired and overworked, nervous, uptight, depressed about botching the India-Pakistan crisis, and obsessed by his struggle for glory with Rogers and the State Department.

It was only after Haldeman threatened to bar Kissinger from the China trip and Nixon shut him out of a meeting with French president Georges Pompidou that the national security adviser's behavior improved. "Ego is something we all have, and then you either grow out of it or it takes you over," Nixon told Safire. "I've grown out of it. It's really a compensation for an inferiority complex. Henry has that, of course."

THE PROSPECT OF nuclear war tugged both sides back from the brink. The CIA reported that Gandhi and Brezhnev shared Nixon's fear that a runaway crisis could bring the great powers into conflict, much as in 1914 the world had drifted into World War I. The Russians pressured the Indians to accept a UN cease-fire resolution as soon as Bangladesh—the new nation that emerged from East Pakistan—was liberated, and Brezhnev guaranteed Nixon that India would not dismember West Pakistan. Gandhi prevailed over a more militant clique in her cabinet who wanted to seize parts of Kashmir, and the fighting came to an end in mid-December. Nixon's willingness to risk war with the Soviet Union was "a heroic act," the obsequious Kissinger told his boss. Ignored or forgotten were Yahya's refusal to honor the results of Pakistan's 1970 election, the genocidal crackdown in East Pakistan, the 10 million miserable refugees foisted upon India, and the fact that Pakistan had begun the war. In their minds, Nixon and Kissinger had stared down Hitlers.

"I had to do it," the president replied. "The whole government, the whole American establishment would say, well, don't start any trouble." But his "ultimatum" to Moscow had done the trick. Given the choice of playing Chamberlain or Churchill, Nixon said, he had chosen the role of bulldog. The balance of power was preserved. The Chinese now knew there was a man in the White House.

THE SOUTHWEST ASIAN drama had an epilogue. The holidays found Nixon coping with the biggest leak of government secrets since the Pentagon Papers: the explosive details of the "tilt" toward Pakistan, contained in secret transcripts published by Jack Anderson, the inheritor of Drew Pearson's column.

Anderson never confirmed it, but one of his sources was most likely Charles Radford, a lowly navy yeoman who worked in the military liaison office at the NSC and had also been passing documents to Admiral Thomas Moorer, the chairman of the Joint Chiefs of Staff. The chiefs, like the rest of official Washington, found themselves frozen out by Nixon's use of secret channels and were not above spying to see what they were missing. Radford had rummaged through Kissinger's briefcase and burn bags, and given the chiefs an early heads-up on the rapprochement with China and other foreign policy initiatives.

Nixon was confronted with a choice: he could purge the armed services leadership, or swallow the insult in the interest of maintaining the military's cooperation on Vietnam, SALT, and other matters. They had caught a skunk, Ehrlichman told the president, and they had to handle it carefully.

"What we're doing here is . . . excusing a crime," Nixon said, but "the Joint Chiefs, the military . . . cannot become our enemy. . . . We cannot weaken the only part of the government that for philosophical reasons supports us." Radford was transferred far from Washington, and no action was taken against the chiefs. The ultimate result was to give the tension rods another twist at the White House, where things were already as taut as a drumhead.

÷

AIR FORCE ONE left Washington on February 17, 1972. It stopped in Hawaii, Guam, and Shanghai (to take on a Chinese navigator) and landed in Beijing at precisely 11:30 a.m. local time on February 21—10:30 p.m. on the East Coast of the United States, ideal for Sunday-night prime-time television coverage. As was planned, Nixon and the First Lady strode down the steps alone (an aide had deliberately blocked the aisle, keeping Kissinger and any other would-be glory hounds aboard the airplane), and Nixon thrust out his hand to Zhou. It was a symbolic gesture, a declaration to the Chinese and the world that Nixon was not John Foster Dulles, who had famously snubbed Zhou at the Vietnam peace conference in 1954. Zhou shook the president's hand, and after a brief ceremony, the Nixons traveled by motorcade through cleared streets and empty sidewalks to their guesthouse. Amid the men in their somber colors, Pat stood out in a bright red coat.

The first riddle that Nixon confronted was resolved almost immediately. There had been nods of assurance, but no express promise that Mao would meet with the president. The Chinese leader was said to be in poor health; or perhaps he was hedging. But Nixon had just arrived at his villa, and was preparing to take a shower, when the word came that Mao would receive them.

Among the first furnishings that the Americans saw at Mao's home was a promising symbol: a Ping-Pong table. After posing for photographs, the U.S. delegation—Nixon, Kissinger, and NSC aide Winston Lord—sat down in a long arc of armchairs in a book-lined study with Mao, Zhou, and their interpreters.*

"I like rightists," Mao told Nixon.

"Those on the right can do what those on the left talk about," Nixon replied. His bona fides as an anti-Communist were beyond challenge. Only Nixon could go to China.

Mao sighed, and made a somewhat chilling reference to his own internal opposition. There had been "a reactionary group," he told the American president, which "got on an airplane and fled." Nixon knew that defense minister Lin Biao had been killed in a plane crash. He presumed it was not accidental.

He and Nixon should talk philosophy, said Mao, and leave the details of the "troublesome" issues to Zhou. But this much he would say: "The question of aggression from the United States or aggression from China is relatively small." There was no "major issue" to prevent the establishment of a peaceful and cooperative relationship. The problem of Taiwan would be solved by the immutable tides of history.

Mao and Zhou laughed aloud at the notion of Americans giving serious consideration to the rhetoric about Western devils and jackals that filled the Chinese newspapers and wall posters. "Generally speaking, people like me sound a lot of big cannons," Mao said.

Before leaving Washington, Nixon and Kissinger had huddled with the French man of letters André Malraux, who knew and had spent time with Mao. They would be dealing with a very special man, Malraux said—a visionary who now glimpsed the grave, and wanted to use his remaining time to preserve his creation beyond his death.

"The Chairman's writings moved a nation and have changed the world," Nixon told Mao.

"I haven't been able to change it," Mao sighed. "I've only been able to change a few places in the vicinity of Beijing."

THE CHITCHAT BETWEEN Mao and Nixon lasted an hour, and set the tenor for the visit. Nothing of great substance was decided, but their face-to-face meeting was extraordinary, bordering on the surreal. The photographs of the two archenemies grinning and shaking hands flashed around

---

* Rogers did not attend, and to keep the secretary of state's nose from getting too out of joint, Lord was cropped from the photographs released to the media.

the planet, sending signals—from Tokyo to Hanoi to Moscow, and to voters in the United States—in a way no dispatch or communiqué could. By embracing realism in that initial session, Mao had all but decreed that the summit would be a success; the talks would have a minimal dose of ideological or geopolitical posturing. Barring some trick—the Chinese were subtle, Kissinger kept telling his boss—Nixon had secured his diplomatic triumph.

At the opening dinner that evening, Nixon quoted Mao: "Seize the day, seize the hour."

"What legacy shall we leave our children? Are they destined to die for the hatreds which have plagued the old world, or are they destined to live because we had the vision to build a new world?" Nixon asked. "This is the hour, this is the day."

AND SO THE trip played out on cue. The U.S. press toddled along, agog, as Nixon walked the Great Wall ("This is a great wall," he said) and viewed the Ming tombs. They recorded Pat's delight at seeing the pandas in the Beijing zoo. At a dinner with Zhou, Pat pointed at the portrait of a panda on a pack of cigarettes.

"They're so adorable. I love them," she said.

"I'll give you some," said Zhou.

"Cigarettes?" she asked.

"No, pandas," said her host.

There was toast upon toast, often with mao-tai, an incendiary brandy. (Upon returning home, Nixon sought to determine just how flammable the liquor was, and almost set the First Family on fire.) The Chinese pushed the Americans in the final negotiations of the summit communiqué, but not impolitely. When the State Department took its revenge for the White House imperiousness—Secretary Rogers and Assistant Secretary Green found a flaw in the communiqué that required an eleventh-hour renegotiation with the Chinese—Zhou handled it with grace. (More grace than Nixon, who raged around his suite in his underwear.)

There were few reminders of the twenty years of vitriol since the People's Army and MacArthur's soldiers had slaughtered each other in Korea, though the Nixons did sit through a revolutionary ballet chosen by Mao's hard-liner wife Jiang Qing called *The Red Detachment of Women,* in which the dancers twirled rifles with fixed bayonets. At Zhou's suggestion, the Shanghai Communiqué included a frank statement of ongoing differences, freeing both sides from charges that they had sold out their principles.

As they rode to the airport on the president's last day in Beijing, Nixon and Zhou got to talking about loss and adversity.

"I said to Zhou that I found that I had learned more from defeats than from victories," Nixon noted in his diary. "And that all I wanted was a life in which I had just one more victory than defeat."

At 3 a.m., sleepless, on his final day in China, Nixon called Haldeman and Kissinger to his room in Shanghai.

"Nixon talked about his accomplishments, asking for confirmation and reassurance," Kissinger recalled. "We gave him both, moved in part by an odd tenderness for this lonely, tortured and insecure man."

"It was easy to give Nixon the reassurance he wanted," said Kissinger. "He had indeed wrought a genuine historic achievement. He had thought up the China initiative . . . he had fostered it, had run the domestic political risks of going it alone and had conducted himself admirably during the journey."*

CHINA HAD ACHIEVED its first, second, and third priorities: Mao had played "the American card" as a counterweight to the Soviets, obtaining U.S. intelligence reports and other aid in his struggles with the Soviet Union; the United States changed its policy toward Taiwan (though fifty years later, Taiwan was still independent, free, and prosperous); and America remained involved in Asia, with enough presence to restrain China's rivals in India, the Soviet Union, and Japan without threatening China itself.

Nixon got mixed results when it came to America's priorities, which he had listed on a yellow pad during the trip on *Air Force One*. He had taken a giant first step toward integrating China in a new international order, where an array of great powers would bring balance and stability to world affairs. Taiwan, Malaysia, Indonesia, South Korea, and other free states would grow and prosper in a region free of Chinese military threats and insurgencies. And Nixon had successfully played "the China card" with Moscow. Alarmed at the prospect of being caught between the hostile Far East and the determined West, the Soviets showed renewed interest in a nuclear arms treaty and otherwise moderated their behavior.

But Nixon's scheme to use great power diplomacy to bring an end to the Vietnam War—his top priority on that legal pad—had met with only

---

* To this account of Nixon's insight (reflecting, of course, his own insecurities) Kissinger then added: "I had reached the same conclusion independently."

partial success. The Chinese and the Soviets were competing for leadership in the Communist world, and both feared an upbraiding, at the hands of the other, for selling out their comrades in Hanoi. They would advise the North Vietnamese to be patient, to let the Americans withdraw, and to let the forces of history hand them Saigon in good time—but neither would cut off the flow of arms, ammunition, and other supplies that sustained the North's offensives. In the end Nixon got the necessary minimum of what he wanted: the two Red titans would fuss and raise pro forma objections, but not intervene as he ratcheted up the military pressure on Hanoi and fought his way out of Vietnam.

Nixon's China initiative was both wildly idealistic and profoundly practical. One of its least-noted benefits was as a demonstration—to Americans at home and observers abroad—that the United States had not lost all its creativity and spirit in the paddies and highlands of Vietnam. The opening to China was like the other historic voyage to a mysterious, forbidding terrain during Nixon's presidency, the Apollo moon landing—they were proof that, whatever its troubles, American democracy could still reach into the ranks of farmers, tinkerers, and grocers' sons and produce men and women with vision, drive, and ability. If the man, in this case, was a gloomy self-tortured sourpuss, so be it. "It was not one of the least ironies of the period that it was a flawed man, so ungenerous in some of his human impulses, who took the initiative," said Kissinger. At a closing reception in Shanghai on February 27, soaring on mao-tai and the bliss of fulfilled dreams, Nixon hailed "the week that changed the world."

It was, if anything, an understatement.

A Third-Rate Burglary

As RICHARD NIXON and his entourage toured the Great Wall, swapped toasts with Zhou Enlai, and gaped at the wonder of the People's Liberation Army band playing "Turkey in the Straw," Gordon Liddy was growing increasingly agitated. He had been led to believe by John Dean and Jeb Magruder that the White House wanted an "all-out, full capability, offensive and defensive intelligence service with sophisticated clandestine collection techniques and covert actions." Yet no one would pull the trigger.

It was characteristic of Liddy to think with such grandiosity. He was forty-one, hoping to climb in a second Nixon term. He was also a right-wing zealot, with a fixation for Nazi regalia and a kinky kind of Nietzschean philosophy. Liddy peppered his conversation with German idioms and organized a White House screening of the Nazi propaganda film *Triumph of the Will*. He would title his autobiography *Will* and boast of how he conquered fears by eating a rat, or by binding himself to the top of a tree in a violent thunder and lightning storm. He built his resistance to pain by holding his hand over a flame until the mutilated flesh needed surgery. He boasted of the men he had beaten, or threatened to kill, and declared himself free from ordinary legal and moral restraints.

"I was under no illusion about . . . legality," Liddy recalled. "Although spies in the enemy camp and electronic surveillance were nothing new in American presidential politics, we were going to go far beyond that. As far as I was concerned, anything went."

Howard Hunt was not as crazed as Liddy, though his emotional deterioration in the coming months would be more profound. His talents as a spy are best reflected in the fact that he played leading roles in two of the Cold War's biggest debacles—the Bay of Pigs invasion and Watergate. "There was some question at various times during his employment about how well he carried out certain assignments," CIA director Richard

Helms would recall. "There was a tendency sometimes for him to get a little bit carried away."

At fifty-three, Hunt was twelve years older than Liddy; he was a literary man, a romantic, and intellectually more sophisticated. But he was floundering at midlife. His consultancy at the White House was nearing its end. To save a few dollars he declared nonresident status at his Maryland country club and had his dues mailed from Florida to sustain the fiction. Hunt was "totally self-absorbed, totally amoral, and a danger to himself and anybody around him," said Samuel Hart, a longtime U.S. diplomat. "Howard went from one disaster to another . . . until he hit Watergate, and then it exploded on him."

Two "good healthy right-wing exuberants," as Charles Colson would call them. Given that he was a CREEP employee, Liddy had been ordered to insulate the Nixon campaign by hiring autonomous agents—cutouts, in the trade—to carry out his black bag jobs and other covert ops. But such humdrum work did not suit his swashbuckling self-image or slake his thirst for thrills, fine hotels, gunplay, and champagne. He insisted on going along and bringing Hunt—who had an office just down the hall and up the stairs from Nixon's EOB hideaway—as his sidekick. They compounded the sin by recruiting as their wireman James McCord—the chief of security for the president's reelection committee.

Like Hunt, the forty-seven-year-old McCord had worked at the CIA and been given early retirement. Like Hunt and Liddy, McCord would act erratically under pressure. Indeed, the blundering of these three misfits was so egregious that conspiracy buffs would prosper through the years offering alternate theories for their antics. They couldn't have been this witless, could they? Sadly, it was so. Haldeman long bewailed his failure to recognize that young chancers like Magruder, Dean, and Krogh were too callow to serve as effective managers and so unleashed, on a rolling deck, a careening cannon like Gordon Liddy.

In the spring of 1972, Liddy and his men went to war, equipped with their own twisted brand of patriotism, and an order of battle that traduced the principles—freedom of speech, the rule of law, liberty from unwarranted searches—of the democracy they claimed to revere. "To permit the thought, spirit, lifestyle and ideas of the Sixties movement to achieve power was. . . . unthinkable, an unspeakable betrayal," Liddy wrote. He remembered his days in the army and the red "Battle Override" switch that armed his anti-aircraft battery for combat. The sixties were a time of "rioting, burning cities . . . bombings," he wrote. "I knew that what had happened to Richard Nixon in 1960 and to Lyndon Johnson in 1968 could not be permitted to happen again. With an ice-cold, deliberate certainty I knew exactly what I was going to be doing in 1972 and it was damn well about time: we were going to throw the Battle Override."

So THEY BROUGHT in thugs to rough up antiwar demonstrators. They took over the daily management of Donald Segretti and other campaign tricksters. Colson added a bit of further intrigue when Jack Anderson revealed that Dita Beard, a lobbyist for the International Telephone and Telegraph company, had alleged that the firm promised $400,000 to the Nixon campaign in return for a favorable ruling in an antitrust case. Hunt donned a disguise, flew to Denver, and slipped into Beard's hospital room to persuade her to recant.

The ITT scandal was a major diversion for Mitchell as he tried to perform the overlapping duties of attorney general and campaign manager. Nixon had personally intervened in the case, threatening to fire the chief of the antitrust division. "The IT & T thing—stay the hell out of it. . . . Drop the goddamned thing," the president told Mitchell's deputy and successor at Justice, Richard Kleindienst.

Though no quid pro quo was ever cinched, their overarching denials of improper behavior put Mitchell and other Nixon aides in jeopardy. The Senate Judiciary Committee held weeks of hearings, at which Mitchell felt compelled to lie under oath. He faced yet another distraction in the unruly behavior of his wife, Martha, who had spent time in a hospital for her emotional disabilities and drunken antics.

ALL THAT SPRING, as Mitchell's troubles mounted, he was weighing the Gemstone plan. Liddy had pruned the operation, taking out the houseboat for hookers, the Mob hit men, and other flourishes, but leaving in bugging, blackmail, and burglary. The price tag had dropped from $1 million to $250,000. Colson and Haldeman were pressing Magruder for action, and he added Gemstone to the agenda when he flew to Key Biscayne to confer with Mitchell, who was on vacation, on March 30. When Magruder returned to Washington a few days later, he notified his CREEP colleagues and the boys in Haldeman's office that Liddy was in business.

"Intelligence—Gordon Liddy's intelligence operation proposal . . . has been approved," aide Gordon Strachan wrote to Haldeman on April 4.

"Now that Liddy will begin receiving this political intelligence information, you may want to cover with Mitchell, who should be charged with the responsibility of translating the intelligence into an appropriate political response." The fate of Richard Nixon's presidency now rested in the hands of a lunatic with a $250,000 budget, delusions of grandeur, and lax supervision.

The first task was recruiting. To help him with the bugging, McCord enlisted Alfred Baldwin, whose name he plucked from a directory of former FBI agents. Hunt called up the CIA, asking for the names of fellow retirees who might need a paycheck. He ultimately contacted the team of Castro-hating mercenaries—"the Cubans," as they came to be called—that had broken into the office of Ellsberg's psychiatrist the previous summer. This time, they were told they would be looking for evidence that Castro was secretly funding the Democrats.

Since Muskie was leading the Democratic pack, McCord rented an office to use as a listening post near the senator's campaign headquarters on K Street in downtown Washington. But Muskie faltered in the New Hampshire primary, and again in Florida and Wisconsin that spring. In May, George Wallace was wounded by an assassin and dropped out of the Democratic race. That left George McGovern atop the field.

NIXON WAS NOT too distracted with the Vietnamese, the Chinese, and the Russians to follow developments in the Democratic primaries, and McGovern's rise offers a revealing glimpse of how Nixon's impulses coursed along the White House synapses, from the president down through Haldeman's office to Liddy and the gang.

On April 5, worried that McGovern was a stalking horse for Ted Kennedy, Nixon told Haldeman to "be sure we have a [McGovern] plant." Haldeman then ordered Strachan to have Liddy shift his sights from Muskie to McGovern. Strachan called in Liddy, who had just gotten the go-ahead for Gemstone, and instructed him accordingly.

Liddy's team responded. Hunt shifted one of their clandestine operatives—a young man named Thomas Gregory—from the Muskie campaign to McGovern headquarters on Capitol Hill. McCord and Liddy cased the building, and Liddy used a pistol to shoot out inconvenient streetlamps. They tried, on four occasions, to gain entrance and install listening devices, but each attempt failed due to harebrained planning.

Liddy resolved to bide his time and try again, in June. In the meantime, he was feeling the need to produce results. He was burning through money and had nothing to show for it. There were plans to infiltrate McGovern's command suite and bug DNC chairman Lawrence O'Brien's rooms at the Democratic convention in Miami, but it would not convene for weeks. Their remaining target was the Democratic Party headquarters at the Watergate office complex.

The Watergate was never at the top of their list. On the other hand, it was not an insignificant objective. Once McGovern was nominated, his campaign would take command of the Democratic Party. Bugs planted in the DNC headquarters in May, functioning throughout the summer and fall, could provide "a wealth of information" of all kinds, Liddy believed.

There were rumors that the Democrats were involved in staging demonstrations at the Republican convention, and that the DNC had entered into a kickback scheme with Florida vendors to help fund its own convention in Miami; if Liddy could find evidence of that kind of skullduggery, he could run the Democrats through the same kind of hell that the White House had suffered over ITT. When accused of misbehavior, Nixon and his team often went looking for a comparable offense on the Democratic side to argue that they were victims of a double standard. The ITT scandal had hinged on the firm's proposed funding of the Republican convention; if Liddy could nail their foes on the financing of the Democratic conclave, it would be twice as sweet.

And the Watergate, of course, contained Lawrence O'Brien's office, files, and telephone.

O'BRIEN, FIFTY-FOUR, WAS the Democratic Party's most effective operative, respected and well regarded by all its varied constituencies. The son of an Irish immigrant, steeped in politics in the hardscrabble wards of Springfield, Massachusetts, he ran John Kennedy's Senate and presidential campaigns, then served as national director for Lyndon Johnson's landslide in 1964 and Hubert Humphrey's challenge to Nixon in 1968. "We were completely outgunned by O'Brien not only in this campaign [1970] but in 1968," Nixon told Haldeman. "We must not let this happen again."

For more than a year after learning that O'Brien had been working as a public relations consultant for Howard Hughes, Nixon had been badgering his aides to expose the relationship. "It would seem that the time is approaching when Larry O'Brien is held accountable for his retainer with Hughes," he told Haldeman.

O'Brien was "giving us a rough time," Nixon would explain to the Watergate grand jury. "He was the only effective pro that McGovern had working for him and was worrying us."

"The Howard Hughes organization at that time was under intensive public investigation as well as private, with regards to payoffs," Nixon testified. "And here Larry O'Brien had his hand in the till."

John Dean was assigned the matter and discovered to his horror that the Hughes connection was a roiling tar pit—something to be skirted at all costs. In the fall of 1970, an internal struggle in the Hughes corporate hierarchy had reached a climax, and Robert Maheu—a wily businessman who had helped the CIA recruit the Mafia for the assassination plots against Fidel Castro—was forced out as the operating officer of the billionaire's Las Vegas hotels and casinos.

Maheu's "tentacles touch many extremely sensitive areas of government, each one of which is fraught with potential for Jack Anderson type exposure," the White House private investigator, Jack Caulfield, reported to Dean. The list of "skeletons from the closet" included an array of ties between Hughes and Nixon and various presidential friends and relatives. "There is a serious risk here for a counter scandal if we move precipitously."

Bebe Rebozo, citing the "delicacy of the relationship as a result of his own dealings" with Hughes, also urged Dean to tread carefully. "Matters went from bad to worse in the Hughes organization, and I felt that sooner or later this matter would come up and be misunderstood," Rebozo would testify. "The concern was principally any disclosure that the president had received Hughes money. . . . I didn't want to risk even the remotest embarrassment about any Hughes connection. . . . I was convinced that it cost the president the 1960 election." There was another ongoing cause for concern, as the IRS was then examining Hughes and his dealings with Rebozo, Maheu, O'Brien, and the president's brother Donald.

Maheu had friends in the news business and, sure enough, Anderson was soon breaking stories of Hughes-related scandals. In August 1971, Anderson wrote of $100,000—in $100 bills from the Silver Slipper casino—that Hughes gave to Nixon via Rebozo, who had stashed the cash in a Florida safe-deposit box. Nevada publisher Hank Greenspun was poking around, trying to confirm a tip that Nixon spent the money on home improvements. In January 1972, Anderson was at it again, reporting how Don Nixon had renewed his financial ties to the Hughes operation. The worried president then ordered the Secret Service to bug his brother's telephone.

The Hughes connection was added to Liddy's agenda. At Magruder's direction, Liddy and Hunt met with Hughes officials and explored the notion of burglarizing Greenspun's safe. The two sleuths lunched with a retired CIA poison expert, exploring ways to assassinate Anderson. And Liddy was assigned to investigate the findings of a new book on the Hughes-Nixon loan and report back to Mitchell, Ehrlichman, and Haldeman. There was plenty that Nixon wanted to know about Lawrence O'Brien and what he may have learned while on the Hughes payroll.

And so, throughout the month of May, as they schemed to bug McGovern headquarters, Liddy's team also plotted to break in at the Watergate. After their usual series of inept attempts (Hunt spent one night hiding in a closet, emptying his bladder in a liquor bottle), they entered the Democratic offices on the night of May 28, rummaged through files, took photographs, and installed two listening devices. The bug on O'Brien's line failed to function. Another tapped phone offered little but some prurient conversations, in which DNC employees gossiped and scheduled assignations.

Liddy was chastised for his failure, and he summoned the Cubans back to the capital. It speaks volumes about his judgment that, to save a few dollars, he now scheduled a late-night double feature: they would fix the malfunctioning bug at the Watergate, photograph hundreds of documents from the DNC files, and still, he proposed, have the energy, composure, and time to drive to Capitol Hill, break into McGovern headquarters, and install listening devices there. At 2:30 in the morning on Saturday, June 17, clad in business suits and blue surgical gloves, toting burglar tools, listening devices, cameras, and forty rolls of film—and having left a trail of taped-over door locks for security guards to find and the police to follow—McCord and the Cubans were surprised and arrested in the DNC offices at the Watergate by a plainclothes squad of Washington, D.C., detectives.

Hunt and Liddy panicked. They fled their Watergate listening post, leaving ample incriminating evidence behind, and dithered until almost noon before Liddy called his superiors. By then the police had identified McCord and, persuaded by the wiretapping apparatus that this was a violation of federal eavesdropping statutes, summoned the FBI.

THERE WAS NEVER a thought that they would not cover it up. It was for the greater good, Mitchell would argue: ill means to save a noble end. In perilous times, with a radical Democrat as the alternative, the world needed Richard Nixon in the White House. And so they strove, in Mitchell's words, "to keep the lid on through the election."

Nixon, Haldeman, and Mitchell were out of town that weekend. After the rigors of winter and spring, with the Democrats intent on self-destruction, the president had opted for some rest and relaxation. On Friday, June 16, after presenting the Presidential Medal of Freedom to the family of the late John Paul Vann for his service in Vietnam, Nixon had taken off for the Caribbean. As Haldeman and others lay on the beach in Key Biscayne, Nixon communed with Rebozo and Abplanalp in the Bahamas. Dean was on a Far East junket. And the campaign team—Mitchell, Magruder, and others—were encamped at the Beverly Hills Hotel on Sunset Boulevard, dallying with film stars at a Hollywood fund-raiser and having a tête-à-tête with Governor Reagan. It was while breakfasting in the pink-arched Polo Lounge on Saturday that Magruder got Liddy's phone call, with its tidings of disaster.

Too late, Magruder told Liddy to find Kleindienst and inform him that Mitchell wanted the investigation throttled. Liddy caught up with the new attorney general at the Burning Tree golf club in Maryland. It was obviously, even to Liddy, a fool's errand. The police had been on the case for almost twelve hours; they were now securing search warrants for the burglars' rooms at the Watergate Hotel. There they would find address books with "H Hunt WH" and a White House telephone number—and Hunt's six-dollar check to his country club, which he had given to the Cubans to mail.

The time for throttling had passed. "Fuck what happens to me! What happens to *the President* if I do a damn fool thing like that?" Kleindienst told Liddy. Unfortunately for Nixon, the attorney general didn't carry the thought any further. He didn't summon the FBI and share what he had just learned about Mitchell and CREEP, nor did he think to use his authority as the nation's top law enforcement officer to have Liddy frog-marched to jail. Kleindienst might have performed the necessary triage and saved the presidency then and there. He did not.

Hunt fled town. Liddy met with Dean on a park bench near the White House, and then with Mitchell's closest aides—Robert Mardian and Fred LaRue—at LaRue's apartment in the Watergate. In the course of those conversations, Liddy passed on word of his other illicit activities—the "White House horrors," as Mitchell came to call them—a list topped by the burglary of Daniel Ellsberg's psychiatrist's office.

HAD THE PRESIDENT's men come clean at this point—before Nixon got back to Washington and was sucked into the cover-up—the scandal would still have enveloped Mitchell, Haldeman, Ehrlichman, and a bundle of lesser aides. Most had joined the walking dead at the instant that Frank Wills, a security guard at the Watergate, found the tape on the stairwell doors. Yet given Nixon's resourcefulness, and George McGovern's flaws, the president may well have survived.

Wallace, bound to a wheelchair, was not running as a third-party candidate, ceding the silent majority to Nixon. And McGovern's party was savagely divided. The AFL-CIO's George Meany, aghast at the rad-lib poseurs who had usurped the Roosevelt coalition, would sit out the election. So would Mayor Daley, whose creative approach to electoral arithmetic had been so helpful to John Kennedy in 1960. The Democratic convention in Miami was chaotic: an unruly spectacle of New Left posturing for those who cared to watch. McGovern missed television's window for his acceptance speech: he took the podium at 2:48 a.m., when viewers had long since turned their television sets off and gone to bed.

The Nixon and Wallace voters had made up almost 57 percent of the electorate in 1968. Now they were primed to reelect the president. The "forgotten American," *New York Times* columnist Tom Wicker wrote, has "fled the approach of the ghetto . . . to establish himself in the suburbs and small towns. He worries about crime, immorality, unrest, prices and taxes."

"He is not 'against' blacks, but thinks they are getting too much, too fast, for too little effort, and he can prove that their presence in the neighborhood lowers hard-earned values and in the schools destroys long-established standards," Wicker wrote. "He fears that welfare damages character and costs too much, thinks that a hardline police policy would deter crime and violence, and believes that his own children do not play around with pot, drugs . . . or pre-marital sex. He is fed up with a war that is not being won, but shocked at the notion of an American defeat. And he is inclined to agree with J. Edgar Hoover that justice is only incidental to the maintenance of order."

This was not the McGovern constituency.

In a slapdash decision, McGovern chose Senator Thomas Eagleton of Missouri as his running mate—a man whom neither he nor the American public knew much about, but of whom, the candidate's advisers had been warned, there were rumors of drinking and depression. Eagleton would be dumped from the ticket after acknowledging that he had received electric shock treatments for bouts of mental illness. Nixon, remembering the hurt he had suffered during the fund crisis, wrote Eagleton's son a kindly note—even as his aides asked reporters: "How could McGovern be trusted, after putting a crazy man on the ticket?"

Victory seemed assured. The cover-up, in retrospect, was ruinous over-kill. Even had Nixon lost in November, he would have at least departed the White House in dignity, his foreign policy achievements intact and his own hands clean. Instead, Nixon's worst instincts, and those of his aides, betrayed him. The shredders worked overtime in the White House and at CREEP, destroying memos, photographs, the wiretap logs—even hotel soap wrappers, and $100 bills. In the fireplace of his suburban home, Magruder burned the Gemstone files, fretting that a neighbor might summon the fire department. Dean destroyed evidence from Hunt's safe and, with Ehrlichman, ordered L. Patrick Gray, the acting director of the FBI, to make sure that embarrassing records of the Plumbers' activities never saw "the light of day." Gray hid the files for six months and then burned them with his Christmas trash.

Dean sat in on the FBI's interviews of CREEP personnel, an intimidating presence who annoyed the federal agents. And Nixon's personal lawyer, Herbert Kalmbach, was summoned from California and assigned the task of orchestrating the collection and payment of hush money. If they kept their mouths shut, the burglars were told, they would serve a brief sentence in a minimum-security prison and then be freed through an act of presidential clemency. In time, the hush-money scheme would drag Haldeman, Mitchell, Dean, LaRue, Strachan, and others into further legal jeopardy. They called it "containment." The legal term was "obstruction of justice," and it was a criminal act.

Taken in its entirety, the historical record—months of hearings, thousands of documents, four thousand hours of White House tape recordings—speaks to the conclusion that Nixon did not know beforehand about the break-ins at the DNC. In the taped conversations, he sounds genuinely baffled. The early months of 1972, when the Watergate burglary was conceived and carried out, were a particularly hectic time, with the trips to Beijing and Moscow and a massive spring offensive by North Vietnam. It is not difficult to accept Nixon's assertion that he wasn't minding the store at CREEP. "It is one of the weaknesses I have—and it is a strength in another way—I am quite single minded," he would one day tell the Watergate grand jurors. "Some people can play cards and listen to television and have a conversation at one time. I can't. I do one thing at a time."

In May 1971 Nixon had ordered Haldeman to begin "more use of wiretapping" of his Democratic foes. One might expect that the dutiful chief of staff kept the boss apprised. On the other hand, Nixon's aides had the custom, as Ehrlichman had shown in the Ellsberg case, of trying to insulate Nixon when a "little operation" was under way. In that first week after the arrests at the Watergate, Haldeman maintained the practice, only hinting to Nixon of the White House horrors, calling them "fringe bits of pieces that you don't want to know."

Winks gave the president a measure of protection. But there was a downside to deniability. If Nixon was never fully informed, he could not apply the full force of his intellect, instincts, and experience to the crisis. He could not make an informed judgment of whether an aide, from fear and self-interest, was trimming the story. And even Haldeman, his most loyal and intimate associate, would dissimulate, change subjects, tiptoe to the edge of truth, and dance back. Nor, with his distaste for confrontation, did Nixon ever brace his old friend Mitchell, demanding a full account. "There started the tragedy," Nixon said later.

Nixon knew, and reminded his aides until they grew tired of hearing it, that it was the cover-up, not the crime, that had brought down Alger Hiss. The traitor had gone to prison for perjury, not espionage. And so, Nixon said, Liddy and the burglars could not be protected. "The truth, you always figure, may come out," Nixon told Haldeman. "You're a hell of a lot better doing that than to build another tissue around the goddamn thing."

But that was for groundlings. As the FBI aimed higher, Nixon wavered, and perjury showed a certain appeal. Maybe Magruder had to be sacrificed—but if so, did he have to admit to ordering the wiretaps? That would surely look bad. And Mitchell? Well, he would rather lose the election, the president told Haldeman, than have John Mitchell prosecuted. "It would destroy him," Nixon said.

FINALLY, THERE WAS this: Watergate was a political struggle, with tactics and enemies old and fierce. A decade before, at the start of the 1960 presidential campaign, veteran Secret Service agent John Sherwood had written a memo outlining the division of duties between the Secret Service detail and Nixon's staff. Item number 6—"Dirty Tricks Department"—warned what the campaign could expect from the Kennedys. The customary chicanery of American politics, Sherwood wrote, included spying, blackmail, "come-on girls," saboteurs, hecklers, and bugged hotel rooms.

Now O'Brien was savaging Nixon in the press, readying a civil suit against CREEP, and scheduling depositions. The Democrats shared a lawyer—Edward Bennett Williams—with the *Washington Post,* whose pages were rife with insinuation. The *Post's* editor, Benjamin Bradlee, was a Kennedy confidant, and its staff was thick with Nixon haters. In the Senate, Ted Kennedy chaired a Judiciary subcommittee whose staff was breaking trail for the investigations that followed. To the liberal establishment, "Nixon is a low-brow, not very thoughtful, low-quality, mid-1930s Depression-influenced, out of date man-on-the-make," aide Doug Hallett advised Haldeman. "Poor boy made good, he reflects all the worst aspects of American conservatism—a bigoted, reactionary, unfeeling, unhumanistic make-it-or-else philosophy."

It was shaping up as "Us Against Them," another gut fight—a Pentagon Papers redux. There was no way Frank Nixon's son would stay on the sidelines. It was not his nature.

NIXON LEARNED OF the arrests sometime that weekend, probably from a Sunday-morning newspaper he found on the kitchen counter at Key Biscayne after returning to Florida from Abplanalp's island hideaway. The reports of the president's reaction—his own and those recorded by his friends—were alike in insisting that he shrugged it off as a dumb, silly episode. "My God, the committee isn't worth bugging in my opinion—that's my public line," Nixon told Haldeman. The outlier was Colson, who said Nixon was so outraged that he threw an ashtray across the room.

A passing hurricane delayed *Air Force One's* return to Washington until Monday night. Nixon brooded about Colson those first few days, fretting that in their conspiratorial chats he had given his eager attendant enough rope to hang them both. It was dawning on Nixon that the taping system "complicates things." But having watched Truman and Eisenhower hold off Congress on the principle of executive privilege, Nixon felt confident. The tapes were his. No one would hear them without his permission.

Haldeman had, from the first, a sound understanding of the perils they faced. The smart play was to cut their losses: saddle the blame on misguided underlings and keep the scandal away from the president. The bedeviling complication, he immediately recognized, was that Liddy and Hunt had drifted through the White House like vectors of disease, contaminating things on their way to CREEP. Ehrlichman was tainted by the Ellsberg case; Dean by the meetings on the Gemstone plan; Haldeman by Strachan's liaison with Liddy and Magruder.

They needed to take action; to do "something . . . other than just sitting here and watching it drop on us bit by bit," Haldeman urged Nixon on Wednesday. "The problem is that there are all kinds of other involvements, and if they [the press, the Democrats, the FBI] started a fishing thing on this they're going to start picking up tracks." They had to "get one jump ahead of them and hopefully cut the whole thing off and sink all of it."

Nixon resisted, showing signs of denial. "I think the country doesn't give much of a shit about it," he assured his chief of staff. "Now, everybody around here is all mortified by it. It's a horrible thing to rebut. And the answer, of course, is that most people around the country think that this is routine, that everybody's trying to bug everybody else. It's politics. That's my view. The purists probably won't agree with that, but I don't think they're going to see a great uproar in the country about the Republican committee trying to bug the Democratic headquarters."

Haldeman nudged back. Okay. If no one in the country cares, then why not throw Liddy to the wolves? "It'll all tie back to Liddy," Haldeman proposed, "and he says, 'Yeah, I got the money and I paid them the money and I told them to bug the place and I was going to be a hero.' Then we ask for compassion: This is a poor misguided kid who read too many spy stories, a little bit nutty, and obviously we'll have to get rid of him, we made a mistake in having him in there, and that's too bad."

Sever. Cauterize. "Cut our losses and get out of this damn thing," said Nixon, warming to the notion.

But Liddy was "nutty" and unreliable. And giving up Liddy meant giving up Hunt, and giving up Hunt drew the bloodhounds toward Colson. And Colson, squirming, had a better idea.

They could blame the CIA.

"I think that we could develop a theory as to the CIA if we wanted to," he told Nixon.

All that first week, Nixon breached his constitutional duty. Article II is explicit: the President "shall take care that the laws are faithfully executed." Instead of the Constitution, he sought to preserve, protect, and defend Richard Nixon.

Crimes were committed? It's politics.

The FBI was searching for Hunt? Have him disappear.

Liddy was involved? Muzzle him.

Mitchell knew? Cover it up.

"Mitchell's concern is the FBI, the question of how far they're going," Haldeman said on Wednesday. "He's concerned that that be turned off."

"It's got to be done," the president replied.

—

Nixon's decision to take his aides' advice and bring the CIA into the cover-up is startling in its demonstrable foolishness. He could not have found a less reliable ally.

After twenty-five years of Cold War iniquities—illegal domestic surveillance, assassination plots, alliances with tyrants and mobsters—the CIA was a monster, loyal to itself. Nixon recognized that rogue temperament but believed he knew enough of the CIA's secrets to bring director Helms to heel. And, indeed, the agency's headmen had carried out many demeaning tasks demanded by the White House—giving Hunt his silly gadgets and Liddy his Gemstone charts, loaning them a camera and developing their film from the Ellsberg caper, and sharing files on the president's foes. But all that time, out at Langley, they were building a record: phone calls were taped, memcons written, photographs copied. And Hunt, McCord, and others had been reporting, with varying degrees of formality, to their old pals. The CIA was not surprised to hear that the Plumbers screwed the pooch. The agency knew all about Liddy and the boys, and what they were up to. "Nixon and Helms have so much on each other that neither one of them can breathe," Senator Howard Baker would conclude. It was not a relationship on which to rest a presidency.

Before Nixon ever heard of Watergate, Helms had called the FBI and told them: "This was not our operation." But considering the burglars' long-standing ties to the CIA, the fancy equipment and sequential hundred-dollar bills, and the evidence they discovered of a money-laundering scheme that Liddy had run for CREEP through Mexico, the FBI agents could not help but wonder. And that gave Haldeman, Mitchell, and Dean an opportunity, they thought, to strangle the investigation in its infancy.

"On the . . . Democratic break-in thing, we're back . . . in the problem area because the FBI is not under control, because [acting director L. Patrick] Gray doesn't exactly know how to control them, and . . . their investigation is leading into some productive areas," Haldeman told Nixon on Friday morning, June 23. The FBI had found the photo shop where the burglars had their film developed and discovered the bank that was used to wash funds. "They've been able to trace the money," Haldeman said. "It goes in some directions we don't want it to go."

Haldeman proposed that CIA deputy director Vernon Walters, Nixon's chosen man at the agency, should be told to call Gray and say: "Stay the hell out of this."

"All right, fine," Nixon said. "Right. Fine. . . . All right, fine."

"They should call the FBI in and say that we wish for the country, don't go further into this case, period!" Nixon said. "And that destroys the case."

If Helms resisted, Nixon told Haldeman, they should remind the CIA director of Hunt's involvement in the Bay of Pigs fiasco: "The Cuban thing." To scrape that scab would harm the CIA, and harm America, Nixon said. "Play it tough," he told Haldeman. "That's the way they play it, and that's the way we are going to play it."

Helms and Walters were summoned to the White House. Haldeman explained the president's concerns. Walters spoke to Gray. And Gray told his agents not to follow the money.

In the days to come, Dean would press Walters again and again for help in containing the scandal. And each time Walters would write memos to his files, where they added to the growing collection of unexploded ordnance, stored around the city.

And down in the White House basement, in the closet below the stairs, a technician removed the June 23 reel from the hidden tape recorder and carefully marked it, and its incriminating conversation, for preservation. One day they'd call it "the smoking gun."

DEAN BECAME THE "desk officer" for the cover-up. As the White House counsel, he claimed access to the FBI interviews and reports, and regularly consulted with the Justice Department officials overseeing the case. He was thirty-five years old, with longish blond hair, drove a sports car, and was viewed around the White House as a swinging bachelor type. He had won Haldeman's confidence and glimpsed the way to climb above his routine legal duties by providing analyses and timely intelligence on the antiwar movement and the administration's liberal critics.

Mitchell had never liked Ehrlichman or Colson, and only tolerated Haldeman. Under pressure, in the days after the arrests at the Watergate, the president's team broke asunder, with Mitchell, Kleindienst, Mardian, and LaRue off in a CREEP camp and the others staked out in the White House. One of Dean's major assets was that, operating from his own little duchy in the counsel's office, he could shuttle back and forth.

Dean had the leash to make on-the-ground decisions, but his work was overseen by the Mitchell camp, and managed by Haldeman and Ehrlichman, who were nagged by Nixon to keep a close watch on the cover-up. They directed Dean, debriefed him, and kept the president up to date. If Nixon was going to break the law—and while they may have had an inadequate understanding of the obstruction-of-justice statutes, the president and his aides certainly knew what perjury was—he was not about to place his presidency, his legacy and liberty, in the hands of a twerp. He wanted proven loyalists. "John Dean is watching it on an almost full-time basis and reporting to Ehrlichman and me on a continuing basis," Haldeman assured the president.

Later on, when the cover-up collapsed, Senator Howard Baker, who had a gift for pithy encapsulation, would reduce the issue to: "What did the president know, and when did he know it?" The answer is that Nixon knew it all, and he knew it all along.

On June 30, two weeks after the arrests, Haldeman told Nixon that the federal prosecutors in the case were pushing ahead; Nixon suggested that the CIA be sent "to see them too."

In the same conversation, Haldeman told Nixon that Liddy would take the fall. "We'll take care of him," Nixon promised.

"We'll wait a discreet interval and pardon him," said Haldeman. "After the election."

"Sure," said Nixon.

On July 19, Ehrlichman briefed Nixon and confirmed to the president that Haldeman, Magruder, Mitchell, and Dean had all been involved in the Gemstone planning. Magruder might have to perjure himself—to "rationalize a story which doesn't lead to his conviction"—Ehrlichman said.

Nixon voiced his alarm at resting their defense on such a weak reed as Magruder. He might crack on the stand and implicate Mitchell.

"Too much rides on this," the president warned Ehrlichman. "You cannot put John Mitchell in this thing."

He and Bob were on it, Ehrlichman told the worried president. "Dean has been admonished not to contrive a story that's liable not to succeed."

On August 1, Haldeman assured Nixon that Magruder would lie convincingly on the stand. Their greater fear, the chief of staff said, was that dumb Magruder would then blab to someone before the five-year statute of limitations expired.

"That's right," Nixon said.

The talk turned to Hunt and the burglars.

"Hunt's happy," said Haldeman.

"At considerable cost," Nixon said.

"Yes," said Haldeman.

"It's worth it," said Nixon.

"It's very expensive," Haldeman noted.

"That's what the money is for," said Nixon. "They have to be paid. That's all there is to that. They have to be paid."

They still had a problem at Justice, where the prosecutors and FBI agents investigating Watergate had come to believe that Magruder was lying, Haldeman informed Nixon. So Ehrlichman had called Kleindienst in and ordered him: "For God's sake, turn it off."

It worked. A day later, Haldeman reported to the president, "Kleindienst has now ordered Gray to end the investigation." And once again, and again on August 4, and yet again on August 16, Nixon and his aides discussed the content of Magruder's perjury.

THE CIA PLAY did not last long. Gray could not control his agents: he would storm and stamp, but they pushed back. On July 6, after Gray and Walters shared their mutual fear that the route they were traveling could land them in a prison cell, the FBI director called Nixon to warn him that he was being badly served by his White House aides. They were hiding something, and it could "mortally wound you," Gray said.

"Pat," said Nixon to Gray, "you just continue to conduct your aggressive and thorough investigation."

But the next day, the president was back at it—telling Ehrlichman that Helms and Walters needed to know that there could be "grave consequences" if the Watergate investigation unearthed uncomfortable facts about the Bay of Pigs, the Diem assassination, and other secrets kept by Hunt. "All will blow," Ehrlichman wrote in his notes. "Can't have this followed up."

A few days later, Nixon told Haldeman to find another candidate to lead the FBI. Gray was unreliable. What about the deputy director, Mark Felt? He was ambitious. He would play ball.

"We ought to throw some tests at Mark Felt," said Haldeman. "We could put some real sticky wickets to him and see how he bounces."

WHAT NIXON DIDN'T know was that Mark Felt knew a young reporter on the Metro staff at the *Washington Post,* and that they were meeting, late at night, in a parking garage across the river. The reporter's name was Bob Woodward. He and his colleague, Carl Bernstein, had many sources. Felt was the one they called Deep Throat.

Felt was an FBI loyalist. Like many, he had bristled at the threat that a political appointee like Gray posed to the bureau's independence. Felt was ambitious, as well, and thought *he* should have been named to succeed J. Edgar Hoover. So he set out to undermine Gray: to show the country that Gray was a tool, and to demonstrate to Nixon that his tool was undependable. He almost pulled it off.

With sources like Felt, the *Post* and a handful of other journalistic stalwarts kept the Watergate scandal alive through the summer and fall of 1972. *Time* magazine put a dogged crime reporter, Sandy Smith, on the story. Jack Nelson and Ron Ostrow of the *Los Angeles Times* were the first reporters to get to Alfred Baldwin and to print his inside tale of the Watergate break-in and wiretapping. Walter Cronkite infuriated Nixon by devoting huge chunks of the CBS evening news, on two successive nights in October, to the scandal. And the *New York Times* would hold its own once Seymour Hersh was assigned to the Watergate beat, and wrote the first account of hush money payments to the burglars.

The *Post,* which led the pack, was drawn to a terrific story—five bumbling burglars in business suits caught bugging a party headquarters—in a town where politics was the hometown racket and the newspaper's contacts with local and federal law enforcement gave it a jump on its rivals. Bradlee and his colleagues were moved by ambition, animal spirits, and competitive zeal. But they were longtime Nixon loathers as well—and representative of the general acrimony toward the president in the Washington press corps. "As a kid who grew up with Nixon being the bête noire in the Hiss case and Helen Gahagan Douglas," managing editor Howard Simons would admit, "I carry all that with me still."

Bradlee was no ideologue. He was a navy veteran who was proud of his wartime service in the South Pacific: the liberal purists on his staff thought him too ambivalent about Vietnam. His gripe with Nixon was attitudinal, if anything. He was Cool, of the East, the Ivy League, Georgetown—all that Nixon had come to identify as enemy territory. Above all, Bradlee was a Kennedy coat holder. The junior senator from Massachusetts had bought a house down the street from the journalist in Georgetown in the 1950s, and the men and their wives had become fast friends. Kennedy and Bradlee were "intelligent but hardly intellectual, long on vision and wit, short on temper and attention span," *The New Yorker*'s David Remnick would note. "They shared a sense of privilege and fortune; they shared

Harvard, the war and an understanding of class; and they shared a penchant for gossip, detachment, irony and courage." They also shared an eye for women, and the editor—in those days when men's sexual adventuring was off-limits in public discourse—had no problem squelching the news that Kennedy, as president, had been sleeping with Bradlee's sister-in-law.

Bradlee had covered the 1960 presidential campaign for *Newsweek*. "However much I had tried to be fair and objective in my reporting . . . I wanted Kennedy to win," he wrote in a 1975 memoir. "It wasn't that I didn't like Richard Nixon. . . . I just didn't know him. I never got close to understanding him. I never got behind that stagy, programmed exterior to anything like an inner man that I could understand, or laugh with." If it ever occurred to such professed admirers of courage as Bradlee and Kennedy to weigh the guts it took for Nixon to climb to their elite level of hereditary advantage, or the toll that was enacted on that emotionally starved personality along the way, they did not record it. Early in his presidency, Nixon had tried calling Bradlee on Saturday mornings to shoot the breeze as Kennedy had. "It was most uncomfortable, awkward," Bradlee would recall. He concluded that Nixon's staff had put him up to it. "I didn't give a shit" and it showed, said Bradlee. "He tried it two more times and then realized it was a bad, bad idea."

The White House turned to more muscular means of persuasion. Colson oversaw a campaign to challenge the *Post* company's television licenses in Jacksonville and Miami, and met secretly with the Wall Street investment bankers who had taken the company public and were worried that its stock was hurting. He promised that the White House would relent if Bradlee were fired, the editorial page was more supportive, and the *Post* "started putting the Watergate case back inside the paper where it belongs." Publisher Katharine Graham felt the pressure. There were many days, she would recall, of cold terror—days she feared she would lose her newspaper.

What Woodward and Bernstein had were youthful ambition and legs. Their competitors worked the phones. But the two *Post* reporters—divorced or single, toiling round the clock—showed up at the homes of CREEP employees at night, where they pried tiny bits of information out of tense and frightened people. The elders in the Washington press corps just could not believe that accomplished pros like Nixon, Haldeman, and Mitchell had countenanced such a train wreck. But the fear that Woodstein sensed on those doorsteps on those summer and autumn nights—and Felt's assurances—kept them going when the trail went cold.

The FBI was faring better. In the bushel of clues left at the scene on June 17 were the records of Baldwin's phone calls home to Connecticut.

The bureau soon had him in hand, and with him an insider's account. A few CREEP employees, to ease their conscience or stay out of jail, gave investigators a rundown of the organization's structure—who had what authority and how the money flowed. But Mitchell's perjury, the lies told by the baby-faced Magruder, and Liddy's refusal to say anything at all stymied the investigators.

On September 14, U.S. attorney Earl Silbert announced that no higher-ups would be put on trial—only Liddy, Hunt, McCord, and the Cubans. The following morning Nixon welcomed Haldeman and Dean to the Oval Office and praised them for their efforts.

"Well, you had quite a day, didn't you? You got Watergate on the way," the president told Dean. "The way you've handled it, it seems to me, has been very skillful . . . putting your fingers in the dikes every time that leaks have sprung."

"This is war," Nixon added. "We're getting a few shots and it will be over, and we'll give them a few shots and it will be over. Don't worry. I wouldn't want to be on the other side right now."

Dean told the president that he had been "keeping notes on a lot of people" who had acted as Nixon's enemies.

Good, the president told him. "We have not used the power in this first four years, as you know. . . . We haven't used the Bureau and we haven't used the Justice Department, but things are going to change."

"That's an exciting prospect," the counsel said.

A Fairly Reasonable Interval

Watergate was something Nixon needed to address before the 1972 election. So was the Vietnam War. In each case, he fashioned a strategy that would see him through Election Day—and not much further. In each case he would declare victory, knowing that the tactics he used to get across the finish line were patchwork fixes. The Watergate investigations were dormant—not dead. The North Vietnamese were neither.

In the dry-weather months of early 1971, Nixon and Kissinger had put Vietnamization to a test, sending the South Vietnamese Army into Laos to cut the Ho Chi Minh trail. Many of the South Vietnamese troops fought bravely, but despite the assistance of American airpower, the Lam Son 719 operation was a fiasco. President Thieu's hold on power was fragile, and he feared the loss of popular support if the army suffered a demoralizing number of casualties. So he hedged his bet: his soldiers advanced cautiously, took heavy losses, and left Laos in a hurry.

Nixon sensed danger. His silent majority tolerated the ongoing war in Vietnam because U.S. troops were coming home. But his preferred deadline for ending American involvement—the 1972 election—seemed sure to arrive before the South could adequately defend itself. He could cut a deal with Hanoi for the return of U.S. prisoners of war, pack up, and go home—but if Saigon then fell, Americans would ask: What did we buy with four extra years, and twenty thousand additional lives?

Nixon anticipated the kinds of attacks he would hear: "You can say, 'He was wrong. He continued this war for four more years when we could have bugged out four years ago—and still we lost. . . .' That's one game you could play," he said. "If I were [an opposing] politician," he said, "I'd play that game."

And so Nixon capitulated. In their quest for a deal, he and Kissinger dropped the United States' long-standing demand that the North Vietnamese and Americans make a simultaneous withdrawal from the South.

The United States would still depart, but Hanoi could keep its troops in place. The war had been fought to secure South Vietnam; now much of the country had been abandoned, and the rest was likely doomed.

The two sides were bound for a solution that Kissinger had suggested to Dobrynin in 1969, to Zhou Enlai in Beijing in July 1971, and to Soviet foreign minister Andrei Gromyko in May 1972. If the Communist giants would restrain the North Vietnamese and ensure that Saigon survived for a "fairly reasonable interval," Kissinger had promised Dobrynin, the United States would leave Vietnam to its fate. "We want a decent interval," Kissinger wrote in his briefing book for the China trip. "We are prepared to leave so that a Communist victory is not excluded," he told Gromyko.

Settling for a "decent interval" would fulfill Nixon's campaign promise. There would be peace, with a modicum of honor. America would save face, and the costs of four more years of war could be defended. But it was still bitter medicine. Seen in its worst light, it was a cynical abandonment of an ally and a cause that Nixon and his predecessors, time and again, had pledged to defend.

NIXON DID NOT forfeit all hope that South Vietnam, with U.S. aid, might find the strength to survive. The president's estimation of South Vietnam's fighting prowess varied with the circumstances, but he spoke with more optimism than Kissinger.

"The South Vietnamese are not going to be knocked over by the North Vietnamese—not easily," the president told his adviser in March 1971.

But after witnessing the performance of the South Vietnamese Army in Laos, Nixon lowered his expectations. He drew a new bottom line: that the South not collapse before the 1972 election.

"Our problem is that if we get out," said Kissinger, "after all the suffering we've gone through . . ."

"We can't have them knocked over brutally," said Nixon.

". . . we can't have them knocked over brutally—to put it brutally— before the election," Kissinger said.

"That's right," said the president.

NIXON WEIGHED THE consequences of a North Vietnamese victory on American prestige. Kissinger reassured him that the South Vietnamese were expendable. If Saigon could hang on for a few years, or even months, its failure would be its own.

"I look at the tide of history out there, South Vietnam probably can never even survive anyway," Nixon told Kissinger. "Can we have a viable foreign policy if a year from now or two years from now, North Vietnam gobbles up South Vietnam? That's the real question."

"If a year or two years from now North Vietnam gobbles up South Vietnam, we can have a viable foreign policy if it looks as if it's the result of South Vietnamese incompetence," Kissinger replied. "If we now sell out in such a way that, say, within a three- to four-month period, we have pushed President Thieu over the brink. . . . our opponents will say we should've done it three years ago."

"I know," said Nixon.

"So we've got to find some formula that holds the thing together a year or two after which—after a year, Mr. President, Vietnam will be a back-water. If we settle it, say, this October—by January 1974 no one will give a damn."

In his diary, Nixon returned to a favorite theme, how the decadence of the West—its focus on comfort, pleasure, and intellectual self-indulgence—bred materialism and corruption, and undermined it in its wars against the Communists.

"If we fail it will be because the American way simply isn't as effective as the Communist way," he wrote. "We give [South Vietnam] the most modern arms, we emphasize the material to the exclusion of the spiritual and the Spartan life, and it may be that we soften them up rather than harden them up for the battle. On the other hand the enemy emphasizes the Spartan life, not the material, emphasizes sacrifice and, of course, with the enormous Soviet technical help on missiles, guns, etc. they have a pretty good advantage."

UPON HIS RETURN from China, Nixon discovered that his televised showmanship had delivered the hoped-for political bonanza. His ratings in the polls leapt. And, as the spring of 1972 arrived, he turned to the second of his three big goals—a summit in Moscow to sign treaties limiting nuclear arms.

The Soviets had peered inward in the Brezhnev and Kosygin era, and what they saw was troubling. The citizens of the United States, Western

Europe, and Japan were reaching levels of achievement and prosperity that left the peoples behind the Iron Curtain envious and restless. The U.S.S.R. needed access to trade and technology, and relief from the costs of the arms race.

The Soviet Union "is trying to sustain a world power competition with the US on an economic base half that of the US. While this had been managed by reliance on a highly-centralized and inflexible command economy, the resulting strains are serious and have been increasing," the CIA advised Nixon. "In strategic weapons the US is now moving to new generation systems which will demand further strenuous efforts—and added economic burdens—if the Soviets wish to keep pace."

The Soviet Union's economic concerns would not stop it from stirring trouble in the Middle East, or the Third World, when the opportunity arose. Nor did the Soviet leaders abandon their costly arms buildup. Nor did they offer substantial help to Nixon on his top priority, the withdrawal from Vietnam. And yet, these were Russians who were willing to deal. Their response to Nixon on Vietnam was similar to that proffered by the Chinese: they would not abandon Hanoi, but would limit their response to pro forma protest when Nixon ratcheted up the violence.

The back channel with Dobrynin was the essential vehicle for Soviet maneuvering. The ambassador would meet with Kissinger in the Map Room, where they bartered in the comfort of confidentiality. Their conversations could be frustrating, yet both sides could at least communicate and explore, explain motives, and modulate fears. There was plenty of business to conduct in this détente. The Israelis and Arabs still lived with their hands around each other's throats. The postwar map of Europe was still not settled, with outstanding questions on the unification of Germany and the status of Berlin. And though the conversation had been interrupted by the Soviet invasion of Czechoslovakia, the two superpowers had maintained a dialogue on strategic arms with a summit meeting between Soviet premier Alexei Kosygin and Lyndon Johnson in Glassboro, New Jersey, in 1967 and the signing of an international nuclear nonproliferation treaty in 1968.

Nixon maintained that progress toward the Soviet Union's goals on arms and trade must be tied to its behavior in other trouble spots: the policy called "linkage" that Dobrynin and his bosses resisted. To squeeze Moscow, Nixon had spent valuable political currency to win congressional approval of an antiballistic missile (ABM) system (by one vote in the Senate, in August 1969) and proceeded with research on intercontinental ballistic missiles (ICBMs) that could carry multiple, independently targetable warheads (MIRVs). The Soviets lagged behind the United States on ABM and MIRV technology but were reaching parity in the size and number of nuclear warheads deliverable by missile. The outlines of a deal were there. The United States might be able to trade its technological edge for caps on the Soviet Union's cruder but powerful arsenal.

The SALT negotiating sessions had begun in Helsinki at the end of 1969, and conceptually the way was clear. "We would freeze our ABM— which Congress was in the process of killing—in exchange for a Soviet freeze on offensive weapons that they were still building," Kissinger recalled. Almost simultaneously, the election of Willy Brandt as the new West German chancellor bode well for reductions of tension in Europe. His policy of *Ostpolitik*—trading recognition of East Germany and the ratification of postwar boundaries for a settlement guaranteeing the security of Berlin—led West Germany to a treaty with the Soviet Union. With the help of the United States and other NATO powers, that longtime Cold War hot spot was quenched.

Nixon struggled to maintain his bargaining edge, as the Democratic Congress threatened to cut the funding of new weapons systems. Like the North Vietnamese, the Soviets were loath to make concessions for objectives that Nixon's political opponents might hand them anyway. Meanwhile, Moscow continued to meddle. The Soviet Union sent its best surface-to-air missiles and MiG-21 fighter jets to Egypt, and ten thousand military personnel to maintain them, and dispatched nuclear-armed submarines to visit Cuba. As Nixon clashed with his domestic opposition over Cambodia and the 1970 election, Russian pilots tangled in dogfights with Israeli jets, and Syria, a Soviet client, invaded Jordan. Nixon dispatched three U.S. aircraft carriers to the eastern Mediterranean and put the Eighty-Second Airborne on alert and, ultimately, the Syrians stood down.

Despite such provocations, Nixon continued to covet the political payoff of a Soviet-American summit. "An American President to visit Russia," he marveled. "Do you realize what that's going to be? The damnedest show you ever saw." The dismay of his liberal foes was never far from Nixon's thoughts. "By God, if we can get this SALT thing, this will really make these bastards look like a bunch of cheap politicians and cowards," he said.

Nixon's trip to China helped bring an end to Soviet procrastination. From his very first meetings with Kissinger, in the spring of 1969, Dobrynin had revealed his country's attentiveness to prospects of a Sino-American alliance. Kissinger assured the Soviets that the U.S. approach to China was no threat to Moscow, but that was "the conventional pacifier of diplomacy by which the target of a maneuver is given a formal reassurance intended to unnerve as much as to calm, and which would defeat its purpose if it were actually believed," he said.

"We've got their paranoia working for us," Kissinger reported to his boss.

"They really think I'm a tricky bastard. And they're right," Nixon said.

When the news of Nixon's trip to Beijing broke, the Soviet leaders immediately invited him to an election-year summit. A few months later, the four governing powers—the United States, Great Britain, France, and the Soviet Union—reached an agreement securing West Berlin as a free city. Another month passed, and Nixon told his pleased countrymen that he would visit Moscow in May 1972.

"One more. We've got two out of three, now," he told Kissinger.

NIXON SPOKE TOO soon. Another dry season had arrived, and the North Vietnamese caught him off guard with a massive election-year assault. On March 30, just a few weeks after Nixon returned from China, the North sent armored divisions south across the Demilitarized Zone, and infantry across the Laotian and Cambodian borders. In the Christian world, it was Holy Week, and the attack became known as the Easter Offensive.

"We are determined and will throw everything we have into this effort," the North Vietnamese Politburo cabled its southern forces. "The enemy also knows that this offensive will be decisive in determining the outcome of the war. . . . He will take ferocious countermeasures. We need to be on guard against the possibility that the enemy might employ even more powerful and brutal weapons in response to our attacks, because Nixon is a very daring individual who might take that risk, no matter what the consequences. We should not underestimate him."

Hanoi put twelve divisions into the battle. The South Vietnamese Army fought capably in defense of its homeland, but bad weather deprived its troops—which by now far outnumbered the last remaining American ground forces—of U.S. air support. A provincial capital fell, another was encircled, fleeing soldiers and refugees jammed the roads, and the South's resolve wavered. Nixon faced another crisis, equal to any of his presidency. The U.S. election was six months away. If he met the North Vietnamese invasion with "brutal weapons"—bombing Hanoi and Haiphong and mining Haiphong harbor—he could lose the Moscow summit and suffer the same kind of politically costly rebuff that Khrushchev had handed Eisenhower in the U-2 crisis.

It might be better to cancel it himself. "I just can't see myself being in Moscow toasting the goddamn Russians, signing the SALT treaty in the Hall of St. Peter, when Vietnam is under serious attack," he told Kissinger. "We cannot go to the summit while Russian tanks and guns are kicking the shit out of us in Vietnam."

If South Vietnam collapsed, the price he would pay in November could be fatal. "We can lose the summit, and still not lose the country. But we cannot lose this war without losing the country," Nixon said. "Having started on that proposition, what do you have to do? For once, we've got to use the maximum power of this country against a shit-ass little country to win the war."

It was no easy trade-off. Critics would howl if he sacrificed SALT and the Moscow summit. He would lose his prized status as peacemaker. So he immersed himself in the details of battle, and for weeks the mood in the Oval Office matched that in the days of rage over the Pentagon Papers, or the state of siege during the Cambodian invasion.

When Kissinger traveled to Moscow for secret talks, Nixon (ensconced at Camp David with Rebozo and their martini recipe) cuffed his national security adviser in long-distance missives. He stormed at the weather, the air force, and his commanders in Vietnam.

"I want everything that can fly, flying. . . . Good God! In the Battle of the Bulge they were able to fly even in a snowstorm," he said. "The Air Force has got to take some goddamn risks, just like the Air Force took some risks in World War II."

The U.S. commander, General Creighton Abrams, was to be "braced" and informed that his career was on the line. "He's fat," Nixon griped. "He's shown no imagination. He's drinking too much."

"I want you to get an order to him that he's to go on the wagon through-out the balance of this offensive," Nixon instructed Admiral Moorer, the chairman of the Joint Chiefs. Abrams, a brilliant tank commander in World War II, threatened to resign.

At night, instead of watching *Patton*, Nixon searched for inspiration in the works of Winston Churchill. He compared the fighting in Vietnam ("Hue is like Verdun . . . you can't lose Hue") to the struggle on the Western Front in World War I. At times, he seemed to exult. The Communists had emerged from the jungles—they were out there in tanks, where the B-52s and F-4 Phantoms could hit them. Nixon ordered the Pentagon to send more warships and more aircraft—six aircraft carriers assembled on Yankee Station in the South China Sea—for what he now believed was the decisive showdown. For the first time in the Nixon years, the B-52s ventured far to the north, braving the surface-to-air missile batteries to pound targets around Haiphong and Hanoi.

"Henry, this gives us one hell of an opportunity, an opportunity to really clobber them, something we've been wanting to do," he said. "By God, they have walked into it."

If it wasn't "the last gasp," then the North Vietnamese were not human, said Nixon. And "they are not supermen."

Be strong, the president told his commanders. They would blockade the port of Haiphong, cutting off the North's supplies, and then "systematically destroy everything that you possibly can that's already there," he told Moorer. On May 8, after much agonizing, Nixon ordered the mining of Haiphong harbor and the bombing of heretofore off-limits targets in Hanoi. The code name was "Operation Linebacker." If they hit Russian cargo ships, or Chinese personnel, or North Vietnamese civilians, so be it.

"What I am directing is bombing, all out," Nixon told Moorer. "You are to hit, in terms of your bombing, North Vietnam. . . . You are to aim for military targets. You are not to be too concerned about whether it slops over. . . . If it slops over, that's too bad."

"Slop over" was a euphemism for dead Vietnamese civilians. John Connally was at hand to give Nixon absolution.

The president had summoned the Treasury secretary from his home in Texas because he had "animal-like decisiveness," Nixon told Kissinger, "which I also have, except I have through many years, I've put much more layers of subtlety on it."

"You're much more subtle," Kissinger told him.

Connally assured Nixon that the United States had been too punctilious in its bombing campaigns. "We bomb North Vietnam, yes, but it's been targets, uh, highly selective targets and so forth. There's been no devastation. People in North Vietnam have been relatively free of the fear of retribution!"

"Civilians, that's right," said Nixon.

"Civilians," said Connally. "And the fear of retribution is a powerful motivating force and we've let them go ten years without it."

"Don't worry about killing civilians, go ahead and kill 'em," Haldeman said, elaborating on the Connally thesis. "People think you are now."

"That's right," said Nixon.

"So go ahead and kill some," Haldeman said. "Henry says, 'Jesus, you'll have all these pictures of dead bodies.' A dead body is a dead body. There's pictures of dead bodies everywhere right now. . . . Nobody knows who the hell's body they are or who killed them."

"Not going to worry about it," Nixon said.

"Don't worry about slop over," said Haldeman.

Americans would forgive Nixon for killing civilians, Connally promised the president, but he would not be forgiven if he lost the war.

"The thing that's troubling the American people is that the United States has for a number of years been leading from weakness," the Texan advised. "The American people are highly competitive. They don't wanna lose. They don't even wanna have a draw."

Nixon would not let Saigon fall. If need be, he told Kissinger, they would wave their most fearsome spear.

"I'll destroy the goddamn country, believe me, I mean destroy it. And let me say, even the nuclear weapon if necessary," Nixon said. "We will bomb the living bejeezus out of North Vietnam, and then if anybody interferes we will threaten the nuclear weapon."

It was a reprise of the madman act.

"As far as anybody else is concerned you must give the impression of being on the verge of going crazy," Kissinger told him.

"Oh, absolutely," Nixon said. "I've got everybody so scared then. Go berserk. Worry them."

It is said that the Watergate break-in was an act of folly because by the time the burglars were arrested Nixon had triumphed in Moscow and Beijing, the radical McGovern had clinched the Democratic nomination, and Nixon's reelection was assured. But until the Easter Offensive was defeated, and the Russian summit secured, the White House was still caught up in the fear that the Democrats would coalesce around Senator Edward Kennedy. In mid-April, as Jeb Magruder and Gordon Liddy were plotting to break into the Watergate, Nixon was weighing the ugly prospect of defeat in Vietnam—and the fall election.

"Sitting in this chair could be somebody else," he told Kissinger. The president shuddered at the loss to U.S. foreign policy if his genius was replaced by the "up and down" Kennedy or the "lightweight" Ronald Reagan.

"I have to leave this office as strong as I possibly can because whoever succeeds me, either because of lack of experience or because of lack of character or guts, heading a weaker United States would surrender the whole thing," he told Kissinger.

It was, as the Duke of Wellington said after the battle of Waterloo, "the nearest run thing." The American B-52s, used for close-in support to devastating effect—when Abrams could wrestle them and their fighter escorts away from Nixon's preferred pounding of North Vietnam—disrupted the Communist attacks and saved South Vietnam from toppling. The mining of the approaches to Haiphong harbor cut into the Soviet supply line. Moscow's envoys protested the deaths of Russian seamen, but the summit was not canceled. Nor were the SALT negotiations, and Brezhnev made the final concessions—on submarine-launched missiles—that clinched a deal.

Hanoi seemed isolated by Nixon's great power diplomacy. But America's victory in the Easter Offensive carried an unsettling lesson. Without the protection of U.S. airpower, it was clear that the South could not survive. The prescient Al Haig warned the president that while the South Vietnamese "are good in defense if they have a good strong position," they did not have the nerve to conduct a fighting withdrawal. And the North Vietnamese, having seized more territory in the South, were "in there to hold . . . get their infrastructure built back and to destroy pacification and Vietnamization." Under the terms of the latest U.S. peace proposal, the North would maintain control of the land it had seized in the southern countryside. The map of South Vietnam, with the Communist enclaves marked and shaded, now looked like a leopard's skin.

"We shouldn't fool ourselves," Haig said. The only guarantee of Saigon's survival was to kill the one hundred thousand North Vietnamese soldiers then at large in the South.

"One hundred thousand is a lot to wipe out, Al," said Nixon.

"Yes," said Haig.

÷

THE MOSCOW SUMMIT, in the final days of May, was marked by random oddities—Nixon leaving his Kremlin quarters in the predawn hours to ramble around Moscow, and the president's "kidnapping" by Brezhnev, who hustled him away from the alarmed American entourage to a riverside dacha where the Soviet leaders alternately harried Nixon about Vietnam (to manufacture a record they could show to their revolutionary brethren in Hanoi) and wooed him with toasts of cognac.

The ABM and SALT treaties were evidence, in themselves, of decreasing Cold War tensions. They were also, in the context of the time, good deals for the United States. The Soviets were determined to catch up to the Americans in the nuclear arms race,* while the cost of the Vietnam War and domestic political pressures had stalled the Pentagon's own strategic weapons programs. By freezing the race at a moment of parity, Nixon's team won a five-year window for further negotiations, while retaining the bargaining chips of MIRV technology, new Trident nuclear-armed submarines, and other strategic arms.

The reviews were raves, especially when Nixon stepped off *Air Force One* at Andrews Air Force Base and, with a dramatic flourish, took the presidential helicopter directly to the U.S. Capitol to address a joint session of Congress. Nixon seemed unbeatable—with only a settlement of the Vietnam War standing between him and exalted status in the top rank of American presidents.

WITH THE EASTER attacks blunted, the military situation deadlocked, and Election Day approaching, the North Vietnamese concluded that the American president would be willing to cut a deal that they, at last, would accept. Hanoi's armies had suffered dearly, and Nixon's trips to Beijing and Moscow had the North Vietnamese worrying about the fealty of their allies. But the rulers in Hanoi were nothing if not patient. Once the Americans departed, their armies could rearm and regroup and sweep south at a time of their choosing. China's advice to Hanoi, Winston Lord would recall, was "Wait them out. In a few years Saigon will fall in your laps."

Nixon had long been skeptical about negotiations. "The North Vietnamese are not gonna deal; they never were," he complained to Haldeman. "They were diddling Henry along." But in August, Kissinger's antennae quivered: his North Vietnamese counterparts had augmented the quality and sweetness of the snacks they served at tea breaks. By late October, he and negotiator Le Duc Tho had reached an understanding. "The situation is now ripe," Tho told his counterpart.

Each side accepted the stalemate. Hanoi dropped its demand that Thieu be deposed, and the United States agreed to let the North Viet-

---

* Like many of Nixon's accomplishments, the prospects for détente and strategic arms limits were wrecked by his folly in the Watergate scandal. His policies were discredited by foes at home, and the Soviets saw him as a weakened leader who could not deliver. Both nations soon exploited the MIRV loophole to trigger a new and dangerous phase in the nuclear arms race.

namese armies and the Viet Cong keep the territory they held in South Vietnam. Thieu still ruled the major cities, but his American protectors were leaving him besieged, the country suffused with enemy forces.

"Thieu says that, sure . . . these proposals keep him going, but somewhere down the road he'll have no choice except to commit suicide. And he's probably right," Kissinger told Nixon. "We have to be honest . . ."

"Right," said Nixon.

". . . among ourselves," said Kissinger.

The "morality" worried him, Nixon said. "We don't want him to—him personally or the 17 million South Vietnamese collectively—to commit suicide . . . or to be murdered."

Kissinger reassured him. They had done all they could. "Everything that we ever planned for is happening. The Russians are pressing them. The Chinese are pressing them. . . . I actually think we can settle it. On terms."

"On our terms," said the president, "but not Thieu's."

"On close to our terms," said Kissinger. "And I also think that Thieu is right, that our terms will eventually destroy him."

"You're convinced of that, Henry?"

"Given their weakness, their disunity, it will have that consequence."

"And their fear. Fear. Fear," said Nixon. "They're scared to death of those people—the North."

But Nixon had run out of time. They were out of options. "As I look down the road, I think there is one chance in four," said Kissinger, that South Vietnam would survive.

"Well, if they're that collapsible, maybe they just have to be collapsed. That's another way to look at it," said Nixon. "We cannot keep this child sucking at the tit when the child is four years old."

ON OCTOBER 12, Kissinger returned from Paris and met with Nixon in the president's EOB hideaway. He and Tho had reached an agreement.

"You got three out of three," Kissinger told Nixon. Beijing. SALT. Vietnam. The president was incredulous, then skeptical, then excited, then exultant.

He "told Manolo to bring the good wine, his '57 Lafite Rothschild, or whatever it is, to be served to everyone," Haldeman told his diary. "Usually it's just served to the president and the rest of us have some California Beaulieu Vineyard stuff."

"Peace is at hand," Kissinger assured the nation on October 26—but

Election Day passed without a deal. As in 1968, Thieu was showing mettle and refusing to sign on.

"You should not underrate the substantive justification for Thieu's intransigence," Haig advised Kissinger. "Hanoi has made political concessions in return for an improved de facto security situation on the ground which would enable them to maintain a strong presence in South Vietnam backed up by their divisions from the North. This is combined with the fig leaf of an agreement."

Kissinger acknowledged it. The U.S. goal was "honor," but "Thieu's problem was survival."

At home, the urge to be done with Vietnam was overwhelming. Even the hawks in Congress—Senators John Stennis, Barry Goldwater, and others—threatened the obdurate South Vietnamese president with the loss of U.S. military and economic assistance.

"The fat is in the fire. It is time to fish or cut bait," Nixon ordered Kissinger to tell Thieu. The "option of . . . continuing the war is simply not open. The door has been slammed shut hard and fast by the longtime supporters of the hard line in Vietnam in the House and Senate who control the purse strings."

Congress had adjourned and would not convene until after the Christmas holidays. Nixon had a window. When the North Vietnamese refused to tailor the agreement to mollify the South, he resolved to loose the B-52s on Hanoi. He needed to show both sides: it was time to end it.

÷

KNOWING WHAT LAY ahead—with Watergate and Vietnam—spoiled Nixon's reelection victory for him. It was a landslide matched by few others in American history, depending on how one measured things. Only Massachusetts, and the District of Columbia, voted for McGovern. Nixon took nearly 61 percent of the popular vote.*

And yet, for the president, the hour was strangely sour. Billy Graham and the newspaper fortune-teller Jeane Dixon had rattled him with premonitions of danger. He had noted, walking the beach at San Clemente

---

* Nixon's margin of 18 million votes was the largest in American history, and the percentages of his margin of victory, popular vote, and Electoral College votes have been exceeded by very few presidents, before and since. He was the first presidential candidate to carry forty-nine states, and the sole one until Ronald Reagan lost only Minnesota (and the District of Columbia) in 1984.

on election eve, that "the tide was out further than I have ever seen it—a real ebb tide" and wondered in his diary, like a latter-day Macbeth, about what such portents signified.

On Election Day, he was subdued as he traveled back to Washington to receive the returns at the White House. "I am at a loss to explain the melancholy that settled over me that night," he would recall. The cap on a front tooth snapped off, a painful irritant amid the celebration. But there was also "a foreboding," Nixon said. Kissinger thought him "grim and remote as if the more fateful period of his life still lay ahead."

Nixon seemed to search for things to spoil the moment. He griped about his opponent's concession speech, in which McGovern called for an end to the violence in Southeast Asia.

McGovern, "to the last, was a prick," Nixon grumbled. "Don't you agree?" he asked Kissinger.

"Absolutely," said the aide. "He was ungenerous."

"Yeah," said Nixon.

"He was petulant," said Kissinger.

"Yeah," said Nixon.

"Unworthy," said Kissinger.

"Right," said Nixon. "As you probably know, I responded in a very decent way to him."

"Well, I thought that was a great statement," said Kissinger. At their hour of triumph, he stoked Nixon's paranoia. "Year after year the media were harassing you. All the intellectuals were against you and you've come around. . . ."

"That's right," Nixon said.

"And had the greatest victory," said Kissinger.

NIXON'S MOOD WAS no better the next morning, when he summoned the White House staff to the Roosevelt Room, spoke about "dead wood" and "exhausted volcanoes," and left them to the icy Haldeman, who demanded their resignations. "Sweet Old Bob, as he called himself," said Buchanan. "The initials fit."

Nixon "wanted the second term to have creativity and energy. That was the theory of it, but it was done in an appallingly brutal" and "cruel" manner, said George Shultz. "A mood of gloom pervades the White House," Evans and Novak soon told their readers. "The President's attempt to revive the Administration with new faces has been a total flop."

Nixon left for Camp David, where he would spend most of the rest of

1972, brooding. "A new group of Nixon loyalists . . . is an urgent necessity," he told his diary. His girls and their husbands were away. He and Pat were "more and more lonely."

Watergate lingered like Banquo's ghost. As the president was planning the bombardment of Hanoi, he got worrisome news from Haldeman about the cover-up. On December 8, a United Airlines jet carrying Howard Hunt's wife, Dorothy, crashed on landing at Midway Airport, in Chicago, killing forty-three people. Some $10,000 in $100 bills was found in her purse. Nixon expressed sympathy, then worried aloud that the cash would be traced. It could be some of the "payoff money," Haldeman acknowledged. Hopefully, he told the president, the Hunts had been "smart enough to wash it."

"There is something rancid about the way things are going," Ehrlichman warned Haldeman in a memo.

÷

BACK IN OCTOBER, when they thought peace was "at hand," Nixon had told Kissinger that he would pay $10 billion in reparations to the North.

"I'd give them everything because I see those poor North Vietnamese kids burning with napalm and it burns my heart," the president said. "I feel for these people. I mean they fought for the wrong reasons but damn it to hell . . . I just feel for people that fight . . . and bleed, and get killed."

It was a different Nixon who said, on December 14, that "I will do things that are goddamn rash as hell, 'cause I don't give a goddamn what happens. I don't care. I don't really care." The bombers would fly on every day but Christmas Day. There would be more slop over. The press might "cry buckets of tears," but the average American "doesn't give a damn," he said.

"Now that we've crossed the Rubicon, Mr. President, the only thing that we can do is total brutality," said Kissinger. Each wave of B-52s, he informed Nixon, would be "like a 4,000-plane raid in World War II."

The shades of old hatreds resurfaced.

"Never forget, the press is the enemy," Nixon told his aides. "The press is the enemy. The press is the enemy. The establishment is the enemy. The professors are the enemy. Professors are the enemy. Write that on the blackboard 100 times and never forget it."

FOR TEN DAYS, before and after Christmas Day, the United States Air Force and Navy launched more than 3,400 sorties against North Vietnamese ports, oil depots, power stations, and other targets. It was a ghastly time to bomb, but Nixon needed to get it done while Congress was out of town. More than 1,500 civilians were killed, and hundreds more wounded. Fifteen B-52s were shot down. But the Politburo in Hanoi relented, talks resumed, and a deal was quickly struck.

"Though padded out with technical and political provisions, it was, in practical terms, nothing more than we could have obtained four years before," George Ball reckoned.

ON JANUARY 23, 1973—three days after Nixon's inauguration—the Paris Peace Accords put an end to this stage of the Vietnam War. The U.S. forces stood down, and the North Vietnamese released the American prisoners of war. To persuade Thieu to sign the accords, Nixon made explicit, secret promises to employ U.S. military power "with full force" against North Vietnam if Hanoi violated the agreement. They were promises that he knew could not be met without public and congressional approval—an uncertain, if not altogether dubious, prospect. And since they were secret, they would have no deterrent effect on Hanoi.

"There are at least two words no one can use to characterize the outcome of that two-faced policy," recalled Admiral Elmo Zumwalt, then the naval chief of operations. "One is 'peace.' The other is 'honor.'"

Nixon and Kissinger had no illusions about the North Vietnamese, but "we thought that, on balance, they would choose to respect the agreement in their own self-interest, biding their time and postponing action," said Winston Lord. "The Saigon government would have a fair chance to compete with the Hanoi government and to prevail. If the South Vietnamese didn't succeed in this effort, in effect it would be the fault of the Saigon government, through corruption and a lack of democracy."

"That was our rationale. We knew we were running some risks, but it was the best we could get," said Lord.

The fighting had lasted for most of three decades, from the days when Harry Truman agreed to underwrite a French colonial war: 58,000 Americans were dead; 300,000 were wounded. The death toll for the Vietnamese, Laotians, Thais, and Cambodians was in the millions, and far from final.

"The people of South Vietnam have been guaranteed the right to determine their own future," Nixon told the country. But for most of the spring and summer of 1973, Kissinger was preoccupied with cease-fire violations, and Nixon feared that the decent interval might come to an end too quickly.

"We've got to do everything we can to see that it sticks for a while," he told Haldeman. "As far as a couple of years from now, nobody's going to give a goddamn what happens in Vietnam. . . . Not one damn degree."

A few days after the second inaugural, Ehrlichman ran into Kissinger in a West Wing hallway.

"How long do you figure the South Vietnamese can survive under this agreement?" Ehrlichman asked the national security adviser.

"If they're lucky they can hold out for a year and a half," Kissinger told him.

A SERIES OF lethal wounds contributed to the death of South Vietnam. The first had been administered by Nixon and Kissinger in 1970 and 1971 when they made the diplomatic concession to let the North Vietnamese maintain an army on South Vietnamese territory.

The second was suffered in the spring of 1973 when Nixon, intent on getting the POWs home, passed up an option to punish the North for its violations of the Paris agreement. "The normal Nixon would have been enraged beyond containment," Kissinger recalled. "But Watergate Nixon continued to dither."

As did Kissinger. "I did not see how I could urge Nixon to put his diminishing prestige behind the new prolonged bombing campaign that the situation required," he reported. "Thus sooner or later South Vietnam would have to cope with the full fury of the unimpeded North Vietnamese buildup."

The third—the coup de grace—came when Congress approved legislation that prevented U.S. military operations without its specific consent. The public was weary of war, and the Pentagon wanted to spend its peace dividend on new weapons systems. Nixon could have vetoed the legislation and taken his case to the American people. Instead, he signed it. On August 15, 1973, the legal authorization for U.S. military operations in Southeast Asia ended.

"I knew at the time Vietnam was lost. I knew it, and I told it to Henry and he knew it, and it was done by the president's own people," Haig recalled.

BY THE SPRING of 1974, the North Vietnamese had doubled the size of its army in the South, and open warfare resumed. When the dry season arrived the next winter, Hanoi launched a probing attack. Thieu tried to consolidate his forces, and have them fall back around Saigon. As Haig had foreseen, the South Vietnamese Army was not up to the task of a fighting withdrawal. It crumbled and panicked. Thieu fled, the government fell, and on April 30, 1975, Vietnam became one, united, Communist country.

"The interval ended up not being as decent as we wanted it to be," said Kissinger aide John Negroponte.

Richard Nixon was not in the White House to watch South Vietnam expire. He was not the first president to lose a war after all. For by then his presidency had become, as he would note, the final American casualty.

Cancer on the Presidency

WHILE NIXON CRUSHED McGovern, bombarded Hanoi, and issued decrees from his Catoctin mountaintop, the Watergate burglars were confronting their imminent incarceration. The Cubans were stoic. Gordon Liddy seemed to welcome it. The weak links were Howard Hunt and James McCord. A good defense attorney could have warned the president of the threat they posed to his presidency. The attitude in the Oval Office, and throughout the Nixon White House, was to hope it all would go away.

Hunt wanted money. The father of four children was about to be imprisoned for what could be a long time. He and his wife had helped orchestrate the hush money scheme with scenes from a third-rate spy novel: anonymous telephone calls and secret code names, bundles of cash in airport lockers, and other hugger-muggery. Tony Ulasewicz, the bagman, spent so much time at pay phones that he took to wearing a change machine on his belt.

The paymaster, Nixon lawyer Herbert Kalmbach, grew increasingly queasy, and after being warned by Ulasewicz that they had moved beyond the "kosher," announced that he was quitting the team. In September, he burned the cryptic record of his disbursements in an ashtray as John Dean and Fred LaRue watched. This sucked Bob Haldeman deeper into the plot, as he now had to authorize the use of the White House campaign slush fund for cash. By the time they ended, in the spring of 1973, the hush money payments would reach $429,500.* The Cubans received very little of it; the lion's share went to the Hunts and the lawyers.

It wasn't enough for Howard Hunt, who believed that the White House had an obligation to maintain his family's middle-class lifestyle, and that Nixon and his men should conduct themselves like the Marines, and not leave a man on the field of battle. He pestered Chuck Colson for more money and a pardon, and grew blunt with his demands.

---

* Almost $2.5 million today, accounting for inflation.

"Commitments that were made to all of us at the onset have not been kept," Hunt told Colson in mid-November. "This thing must not break apart for foolish reasons."

"I agree. Yeah. Oh no, Christ no," Colson said.

"After all, we're protecting the guys who . . . were really responsible," said Hunt. "Surely your cheapest commodity available is money."

Hunt followed his phone call with a memo to CREEP officials.

"The Watergate bugging is only one of a number of highly illegal conspiracies engaged in by one or more of the defendants at the behest of senior White House officials," he wrote. As an author, he had particular leverage: a publisher would pay plenty for his story.

Dorothy Hunt's death desolated her husband. He sent a letter to Colson, damning the fecklessness of those who deserted their friends in times of need. "There is a limit to the endurance of any man," Hunt said. He sent word through his lawyer: he wanted $132,000 to pay legal fees and support his family while he wasted in prison or he would expose the "seamy things" he had done for Richard Nixon.

Colson passed Hunt's letter to Dean with a cover note: "Now what the hell do I do?" He raised the issue of executive clemency with the only man who could grant it. "Colson told me . . . that he had tried to do everything he could to keep Hunt in line from turning state's evidence," Nixon confided to his diary. "After what happened to Hunt's wife etc. I think we have a very good case for showing some clemency."

The president now took a more active role in the hush money operation. After John Mitchell solicited funds from Tom Pappas, a wealthy Greek American, and a friend of the right-wing junta in Athens, Haldeman passed word to Nixon that Pappas wanted the compliant U.S. ambassador to Greece reappointed. They needed to keep Pappas happy, Haldeman told the president, for "the continuing financial activity in order to keep [the defendants] in place."

Nixon replied: "Good. I understand. No problem."

Said Haldeman: "And he's able to deal in cash." Pappas was invited to the Oval Office and got a personal thank-you from the president. The ambassador stayed on.

McCord was another sticky wicket. As he drew nearer to his prison cell, the wireman began to wobble, concocting apocalyptic fantasies about the threat posed by Nixon and Watergate to his beloved CIA. "Every tree in the forest will fall," he warned Jack Caulfield, the White House private detective. "It will be a scorched desert," if the White House tried to pin the scandal on the agency. Caulfield was assigned to reason with him. McCord, too, was offered a blurry promise of clemency. But Nixon and his aides failed to take the danger seriously, assuring one another that McCord's knowledge was mere hearsay—he knew only what Liddy had told him. Not for the last time, they deluded themselves. Hearsay may be banned in court, but it was more than fair game for congressional investigators and their confederates in the press.

A step up the ladder was Jeb Magruder, who lied under oath when the Watergate burglars went on trial in January. U.S. District Court judge John Sirica, after reading the *Washington Post* coverage that fall, was determined to get the full story. He badgered prosecutors, grilled witnesses from the bench, and declared that he would use his sentencing power to compel the defendants to name culpable higher-ups: if not, they could rot in prison. The judge left a deep impression on Hunt and McCord. They were agitated, and so was Magruder, who knew he was the ideal fall guy and incessantly looking to the White House for reassurance.

And then there was John Dean, who was trying to cope with the disconcerting news that the CIA had given the Justice Department copies of the photographs Hunt had taken on his trip with Liddy to case the office of Ellsberg's psychiatrist, Dr. Lewis Fielding. It was only a matter of time, Dean feared, before the FBI put two and two together, and the Fielding burglary was also exposed as a White House caper. Dean's jitters turned to tremors when Pat Gray, in his confirmation hearings as FBI director, described how Dean had hobbled the bureau's investigation. John Dean was now where he did not want to be: out of the shadows, on the front pages, in the glare of congressional scrutiny.

THE WATERGATE COVER-UP had entered its final stage. It had lasted just long enough for Nixon to win reelection, and take his oath of office for a second term. As Nixon gave his inaugural address on January 20, he had nine weeks in which to meet his wish, expressed to aides in the weeks after the election, that they "clean the skirts" of the stains of Watergate. He failed to take advantage of the opportunity. Each time he faced the choice—to come clean and "box it," as Haldeman put it, or to do nothing and hope that time would "fade it away"—the president chose not to act at all.

Nixon and his men suffered from a shortage of imagination, and an excess of wishful thinking. It was so much nicer to believe that, with the historic election victory, their replenished powers, and the resources of the White House at their command, they would somehow skate by. "The country is bored with it," Colson assured Nixon. "The public respects you for hanging tough," Kissinger said. "Perjury's an awful hard rap to prove," Nixon told Dean. No, it wasn't. Nixon was apt, throughout the scandal, to tell his aides to read the chapter on Alger Hiss in *Six Crises*. He'd have been better served to read it himself.

ON MARCH 21, an overwrought Dean summoned the grit to give Nixon an account of where things stood. The cover-up was crumbling, the counsel said. "We have a cancer—within—close to the presidency, that's growing. It's growing daily. It's compounding, it grows geometrically now," Dean told him. "We're being blackmailed . . . people are going to start perjuring themselves very quickly that have not had to perjure themselves to protect other people. And . . . there is no assurance . . ."

"That it won't bust," Nixon said, finishing the thought.

They needed to find a way "that this can be carved away from you, so that it does not damage you or the presidency," Dean said. "Some people are going to have to go to jail. . . . I could, for one."

But Nixon shied from the prospect of a public burning. It would take years, if ever, for a president to recover from such a spectacle. And he was more entangled than Dean suspected. There was little that Nixon heard in Dean's "cancer on the presidency" talk that the president did not already know. It did not matter that Nixon, personally, had not ordered Liddy's team into the Watergate: he had conspired with Haldeman, Ehrlichman, and Colson about wiretaps, dirty tricks, break-ins, hush money, clemency. Could he count on a dozen frightened men—from the Cubans up through Haldeman—to protect him? With a hanging judge and zealous prosecutors dangling deals? No.

They had to buy time, Nixon told Dean. Hunt's immediate demands must be met. "You could get a million dollars, and you could get it in cash. I know where it could be gotten," the president told his counsel. After Dean left the Oval Office, Nixon checked with Rose Woods on the status of his own private slush funds, which totaled some $200,000.

NIXON WORRIED THAT his own involvement in the cover-up left him vulnerable. He explored, with his aides, the notion of full disclosure.

"We've been over this a number of times," Ehrlichman told the president. "There's no way to do an effective job of disclosure. . . . It's the nagging loose ends, the little inconsistent fact—the unassailable piece of evidence that wasn't included is always the thing that bites in the end."

"So you have to make it more general," said Nixon.

"You have to make it more general," Ehrlichman nodded, "and when you make it general then it's a cover-up."

NIXON AND HIS aides were still thrashing about when Sirica read a letter from McCord aloud in court on March 23.

"There was political pressure applied to the defendants to plead guilty and remain silent," McCord wrote the judge. "Perjury occurred during the trial. . . . Others involved in the Watergate operation were not identified." Sirica handed out severe "provisional" sentences: Hunt and the burglars would get thirty-five to forty years in prison—unless they talked.

McCord left the courthouse, heading straight for Capitol Hill. In February, the Senate had voted, 77 to 0, to establish the Select Committee on Presidential Campaign Activities to investigate the Watergate scandal, to be chaired by Senator Sam Ervin, a North Carolina Democrat. Jolted by Sirica, McCord told his story to the committee staff, and then to the senators in a private session. He knew little more than what Liddy had babbled, but that was more than enough. Within days, reports of the Gemstone planning were leaked to the press, publicly linking Dean, Magruder, and Mitchell to the Watergate break-in. The frenzy was on. "Watergate was a bloody body in the water. And every other newspaper became a shark," the *Washington Post* managing editor, Howard Simons, remembered. "They would take a bite and swallow it without chewing."

AFTER HEARING DEAN propose that they all confess and save the presidency, Haldeman and Ehrlichman caucused and came up with a better solution: They would pin it on a fall guy. Dean could be a tasty "hors d'oeuvre" but only a "big fish" would sate their foes: they would offer up Mitchell. But though they talked tough with each other, they balked at confronting their old comrade.

Nixon's attempt at belling the cat was typical. Instead of chastising his old friend, Nixon rambled on about the fund episode and Ike's abandonment of Sherman Adams, the White House chief of staff who accepted a vicuna coat and other improper gifts from an industrialist under investigation by the government.

Nixon vowed not to betray Mitchell in the same cruel manner.

"Eisenhower. That's all he cared about. He only cared about—Christ, 'Be sure he was clean.' Both in the Fund thing and the Adams thing. But I don't look at it that way. And I just—that's the thing I am really concerned with. We're going to protect our people if we can," Nixon said.

"I don't give a shit what happens. I want you all to stonewall it, let them plead the Fifth Amendment, cover-up or anything else," the president told Mitchell. "On the other hand, I would prefer, as I said to you, that you do it the other way. And I would particularly prefer to do it that other way if it's going to come out that way anyway."

Mitchell could be forgiven for not complying.

NIXON WASTED HOURS of plotting with advisers—like Ehrlichman, Haldeman, and Colson—whose self-interest was contending with their loyalty.

"I was working from all kinds of misleading information from everybody else," Nixon would recall. "Dean would come in and tell me one thing, Haldeman another, Ehrlichman another. . . . I'd make decisions based on what they were telling me, but they all had their own agendas and their own asses to protect."

There were too many sparks in the wind. McCord had fingered Magruder, who was sure to be called before the grand jury and the Senate. Magruder needed a collaborator and asked Dean to join him in perjury. Dean, though pressed by Haldeman and Mitchell, refused to do so.

Thus ended the cover-up. Dean and Magruder took stock of the deteriorating situation, and went out and hired lawyers. "Nixon thought I should lie for him. I should fall on the sword. . . . I should go to jail indefinitely so he can continue to be who he wants to be," Dean said. "I didn't see it that way."

Revelations now arrived like salvoes of fireworks; no sooner had one report begun to fade than another wondrous bang took its place. The headlines told the story—WATERGATE SPY SAYS DEFENDANTS WERE UNDER "POLITICAL PRESSURE" TO ADMIT GUILT AND KEEP SILENT . . . MCCORD TELLS SENATE UNIT OF NEW WATERGATE NAMES . . . WATERGATE JURORS HEAR HUNT . . . MCCORD REPORTED TO LINK MITCHELL TO BUGGING PLOT . . . MITCHELL ON STAND FOR THREE HOURS . . . GRAY SAYS HE DESTROYED FILES . . . GRAY QUITS THE FBI—rising in a crescendo toward a roaring finale.

Max Friedersdorf, the White House congressional liaison, offered another metaphor. "It was," he said, "like an ink blot spreading."

NIXON SOUGHT TO distance himself, tried to escape the headlines, the anxiety, and the sleepless nights, restlessly roving to and from the White House, Key Biscayne, San Clemente, and Camp David. He and his men readied one final ruse: they would announce that the president had personally cracked the case, and pin the break-in on Magruder and Mitchell and the cover-up on Dean. But before they could do so, Dean and Magruder arrived in the offices of the U.S. attorney, offering to testify in return for favored treatment. Right behind them, LaRue led a line of others.

The White House heard of Magruder's impending treachery on Friday, April 13. The next night—as Nixon and his men feigned goodwill toward the baying hounds at the White House correspondents' dinner—U.S. attorney Earl Silbert alerted Henry Petersen, the head of the criminal division at the Justice Department, that Magruder and Dean were starting to sing.

Petersen called Kleindienst, and the prosecutors all gathered at the attorney general's home, reviewing the libretto until dawn. That Sunday afternoon, a distraught Kleindienst slipped into Nixon's hideaway office to inform the president that Haldeman and Ehrlichman had been implicated in the cover-up. He and Petersen urged Nixon to jettison his Berlin Wall. He wouldn't fire an aide on the basis of a snitch's testimony, Nixon replied. "What you have said, Mr. President, speaks very well of you as a man," Petersen said. "It does not speak well of you as a president."

PETERSEN, A REVERENT civil servant, was dumbfounded by Nixon's response when the president was informed, several days later, that Dean had told the prosecutors about the burglary of Ellsberg's psychiatrist.

"I know about that. That's a national security matter," Nixon told Petersen. "You stay out of that."

Ellsberg was then on trial in Los Angeles. Fairness required that the judge be told. Petersen and Kleindienst wrestled with their consciences and concluded that they had to defy the president, even if it meant resigning. Nixon backed down. The judge was alerted, announced the news in court, and, after unearthing further government misconduct, dismissed all charges against Ellsberg. The saga of the Pentagon Papers came to a close with the president, not the whistle-blower, as the premier casualty.

—

On April 17, Nixon made a last attempt to get ahead of the Watergate story, with a public declaration that his personal "investigation" had resulted in "major developments" and "real progress . . . in finding the truth." He was trying to pull away from Haldeman and Ehrlichman—but slowly, for they knew so much. He needed to ease them out, with a minimum of hard feelings. The "separability," as he called it, took two weeks.

Nixon begged Secretary of State Bill Rogers to fire the two men, but Rogers refused to do it. Haldeman and Ehrlichman had earned a face-to-face dismissal. On Sunday, April 29, the two aides were summoned to Camp David, carried to the presidential retreat by helicopter, and called in, individually, to see Nixon. He sobbed and told them how he had prayed to God to take his life, so that he would not awake that morning. Haldeman took it better than Ehrlichman, who urged Nixon to resign. "Just explain all this to my kids, will you?" Ehrlichman said. "I still feel I have done nothing that was without your implied or direct approval."

Kleindienst was the other casualty. He had been planning to return to a private law practice for some time; now Nixon told him that his resignation would be lumped in and announced with the others on Monday. The attorney general wept in shame, but agreed. Stunned by Kleindienst's sacrifice, his successor, Elliot Richardson, told him: "I wouldn't have done what you just did for anybody."

Nixon's televised address that Monday night was graceless. "There can be no whitewash at the White House," he said.

"The easiest course would be for me to blame those to whom I delegated the responsibility to run that campaign. But that would be a cowardly thing to do," the president said, in a now-familiar Nixonian dodge. In fact, he was doing just that.

The speech had all the hallmarks of the Cambodia address, or the "Silent Majority" broadcast. Dick got a haircut from the White House barber. The Oval Office was chilled to limit the president's perspiration. And, afterwards, sipping a drink, he worked the phones, seeking feedback. By the time he called Haldeman he was maudlin, slurring words, awash in self-pity. More than an hour had passed, and only one member of the cabinet had called, the president said. "All the rest, you know, are waiting to see what the polls show. Goddamn strong cabinet, isn't it?"

Haldeman tried to console him. The switchboard had been told to screen his calls. The lines were no doubt jammed.

"No, no, no. They know. They know. They know who to call, you know. They know they can get through," the president said.

His pain poured out. "You're a strong man, goddammit. And I love you," Nixon told his ex–chief of staff. "And, you know, I love John and all the rest, and by God keep the faith. Keep the faith. You're going to win this son of a bitch."

Shyly, pathetically, he asked Haldeman to make some calls—"like the old style"—and gauge the public reaction to the speech. "Would you mind?"

Haldeman demurred, and Nixon backed off. "No, I agree," he said. "Don't call a goddamn soul. The hell with it."

"God bless you boy. God bless you," Nixon murmured, as he said good-bye. Speaking slowly, he offered a glimpse of his tortured self. "I love you," he said, "like my brother."

THROUGHOUT THAT AWFUL spring, Nixon walled out Pat. "My father was more tense and uncommunicative than I ever remembered him," Julie recalled. "He had withdrawn into his own world and away from the family."

Nor did Pat pry. "Because both my parents were very private people, their relationship was a delicate, polite one that did not allow for much second-guessing," Julie remembered. Nixon may simply have felt too ashamed to tell his girls how much trouble he was in.

On May 25, after hosting the families of the Vietnam prisoners of war at a gala dinner, the president was struck by "an almost physical force" of dread. He called Julie and Tricia to the Lincoln Sitting Room. "Do you think I should resign?" he asked. "Don't you dare!" they replied.

"An evening representing a great historical and personal achievement for Daddy" had been "marred by a great personal tragedy," Tricia told her diary. "Man lives in the hope of perfection, but lives in the reality of imperfection in himself and in those around him."

TWO YEARS HAD passed since Richard Nixon began to forge the sword he gave his enemies. The demands of his office were relentless, and he'd added to the duress with his own audacity. It should not surprise that he cracked—or that, when it happened, the fissures spread along long-familiar faults.

In a conversation with newsman Stewart Alsop, Kissinger marveled at what Nixon had brought upon himself.

"All his life he's been assailed by the fear of the horrible disasters—now everything that can possibly happen to him has happened," Kissinger said. "In an attempt to stave off the worse, it's all been brought on."

All around Washington, such conversations took place. In a private lunch at the Federal Reserve, Moynihan and Burns looked to Freudian theory for an answer. "Repressed homosexuality; sense of deprivation—a castration sense," they speculated.

"I sometimes had the impression that he invited crisis and that he couldn't stand normalcy," Kissinger said later. Nixon had written in *Six Crises* how extremity can relieve a troubled man, by demanding "creative action" that eclipses doubt and self-destructiveness. "By an act of will, he refuses to think of the reasons for fear and so concentrates entirely on winning the battle."

Maybe, friends like Garment wondered, destruction was what Nixon wanted: Nixon knew he wasn't likable. He didn't like himself. He didn't deserve to be happy. Perhaps he sought to be caught. "The witch was for burning," as Garment said. "He may have even wanted to be gotten."

Kissinger shared the sentiment. "Triumph seemed to bring no surcease to this tortured man," he would write. "It was hard to avoid the impression that Nixon, who thrived on crisis, also craved disasters."

But there were plenty to help Nixon into the tumbrel.

The president "was sardonic about all kinds of agencies of government," CIA director Richard Helms said. "His attitude was that the only bright, really intelligent fellow in town was himself. . . . He was constantly disparaging everybody else about their abilities."

Nixon was more than just disparaging; he had plans to reorganize the government, threatening organizations like the FBI and the CIA, whose files were crammed with material that could embarrass and incriminate the president and his aides. He had tried to make the bureau more compliant by replacing Hoover with a toady. And in May, Nixon had written Haldeman: "One department which particularly needs a house-cleaning is the CIA. The problem in the CIA is muscle-bound bureaucracy which has completely paralyzed the brain and the other is the fact that its personnel, just like the personnel in State, is primarily Ivy League and the Georgetown set." He told Haldeman to study "how many people in CIA could be removed."

The judiciary was not exempt, either. Nixon schemed to put an end to the lifetime tenure of federal judges.

"It seems as if Nixon . . . decided at some level of deliberation to raise the stakes and take on the whole world of Washington in his last and greatest crisis," Garment wrote. "When Nixon's opponents saw the administration caught up in the act of lawbreaking and cover up, they descended on the case with a fire born of years."

Congress led the cavalcade. Its members were proud, independent operators who had forged their own careers. They had always bridled when Colson or Haldeman or Ehrlichman issued orders from the White House, as if congressmen were mere shills for the president. "I detested them," said Representative Gerald Ford of Michigan—who was the House Republican leader at the time. "I resented the way they treated Congress."

Had the president paid less attention to the size of his landslide, and spent more time and money helping Republican candidates for Congress in 1972, then the Senate and the House—with fewer Democrats and fonder Republicans—might have been firebreaks, rather than pyres, in what was to come. But until Nixon's landslide was assured, CREEP had declined to invest in the congressional races. "Anything we do in behalf of House and Senate candidates must be *very low profile*," Nixon ordered Haldeman, who then wrote across the memo: "We do *nothing* at this point."

In the end, the Republicans lost two Senate seats and peeled only enough seats away from the Democrats to leave the House with a more militant majority. It was peppered with staunch liberals like Representatives Ron Dellums of California, Patricia Schroeder of Colorado, Robert Drinan of Massachusetts, and Bella Abzug of New York, and led by a new majority leader, Representative Thomas P. "Tip" O'Neill of Massachusetts, a left-leaning giant who had replaced the more malleable Representative Hale Boggs of Louisiana, whose airplane had gone missing on a campaign trip to Alaska. "There can be no question that the House leadership will be far more liberal," William Timmons, the White House liaison to the Hill, warned the president. Boggs's disappearance was bad luck for Nixon, who recognized O'Neill as an "astute, tough, ruthless politician," an "all-out dove and a vicious bastard." O'Neill, for his part, thought Nixon was extremely bright, but "the wrong type of man"—suspicious, resentful, a loner—to lead the country. Speaker Carl Albert was a weak individual who tried to get along with everyone. O'Neill, who had inherited John Kennedy's seat in Congress, with its Nixon-loathing constituency (it included Harvard University, Cambridge, Brookline, and parts of Boston over the years), was more representative of the combative majority in the Democratic caucus.

"All the ingredients are present, and the timing right, for a somewhat historic confrontation with executive power and its . . . usurpation of congressional prerogatives," Representative Jim Wright, the House Whip, wrote O'Neill on the eve of Nixon's second inauguration. "Let's assume the initiative. . . . Congress could keep a left jab in his face all the time. Let's keep *him* off balance."

"You have done a fine job in your letter," O'Neill replied. "The Speaker and I have been speaking to the same points and making plans."

The White House and Congress plunged into constitutional struggles over the president's power to wage war, impound appropriated funds, and restrict congressional access to White House aides and documents—an "executive privilege" that Eisenhower and Truman had pushed to extremes in the postwar years, and that Nixon presumed was settled law.

The Senate had its own torch-and-pitchfork crew. Edward Kennedy had used an obscure Judiciary subcommittee to fan the fires through the fall and winter. But he was too obvious a partisan, and too tainted by scandal, to conduct an inquest. He had dispatched his leads, and best investigators, to the Ervin committee, then joined with his fellow Democrats to make Pat Gray's confirmation hearing an inquisition.

AFTER KLEINDIENST RESIGNED as attorney general, the Judiciary Committee exacted a promise from his successor, Elliot Richardson, to appoint a special prosecutor. Richardson was from Massachusetts, a Harvard man, and he plucked Archibald Cox from Harvard Law School to lead the Watergate Special Prosecution Force. Cox had been John Kennedy's solicitor general. Both Edward Kennedy and Robert Kennedy's widow, Ethel, attended the swearing-in. The WSPF, the Ervin committee's staff, and the staff of the House Judiciary Committee would be dominated by Ivy Leaguers of liberal persuasion, many of whom were veterans of the Kennedy administration or campaigns. Eight of the dozen senior attorneys on the WSPF, to cite the most obvious example, had worked for RFK when he was attorney general. The Ervin committee, Pat told her friend Helene Drown, was "a snake about to devour people."

The media, its rancor fanned by Nixon's spite, Agnew's rhetorical affrays, Colson's behind-the-scenes bullying, and the Pentagon Papers showdown, smelled blood. The *Washington Post* won a Pulitzer Prize for its groundbreaking work on Watergate and was now racing an aroused *New York Times* for each day's leaks. *Time* magazine had forty Watergate-related covers. The three major television networks planned gavel-to-gavel coverage of the Watergate committee hearings, and PBS followed up with taped prime-time shows at night. Nixon-baiting journalists—Dan Rather was the most prominent example—made names for themselves. Watergate had become, as writer David Halberstam put it, "the great national detective thriller."

Nixon's aides were staggered. "If I had to depend for my information on the *Washington Post,* the *New York Times* and CBS, I'd hate the son-of-a-bitch too," speechwriter Ray Price told a friend.

MAY WAS ANOTHER horrid month. Ehrlichman's role in the Fielding break-in became public—as did the "national security" wiretaps and details of the Huston plan to harass radicals.

"Have I been a fool or a whore or both? Or perhaps something quite different; something to be forgiven," Moynihan wrote a friend, unnerved at what he was discovering about his old colleagues; grateful that they had not trusted him enough to include him in their plots; and saddened at how their accomplishments, like school desegregation and the Family Assistance Plan, were stained. "They were not berserk. They merely let themselves get involved step by step into something that got out of control, whereupon they tried to cover up and thereupon came catastrophe."

The Watergate committee launched its hearings in midmonth, laying a foundation with McCord, Ulasewicz, Caulfield, and other enthrallingly Runyonesque witnesses. It was great public theater. Elsewhere on the Hill, the closed-door hearings of other Senate committees provided the first evidence of Nixon's involvement in the cover-up.

In June 1972, Vernon Walters had written a series of memcons to his files detailing the attempts by Haldeman, Ehrlichman, and Dean to use the CIA to quash the FBI's investigation of the Watergate break-in. Walters was a Nixon loyalist. He had been with Nixon in Caracas. He had participated in the secret Paris peace talks with Kissinger and helped in the opening with China, and been rewarded with the job of deputy director of the CIA, where the White House considered him its guy in Langley. But Walters's knowledge and experience—with Nixon, and of the ways of Washington—had spurred him to write the self-protective memos ("Notes to refresh my memory, if I should need it," Walters called them) when the White House ordered him to impede the FBI's investigation.

The *New York Times* acquired the memcons, which recounted, among other things, how "Haldeman said the whole affair was getting embarrassing and it was the President's wish that Walters call on Acting [FBI] Director L. Patrick Gray and suggest to him that, since the five suspects had been arrested, this should be sufficient. . . . Haldeman then stated that I could tell Gray that I had talked to the White House and suggested that the investigation not be pushed further."

In June—after a momentary suspension of the hearings while Soviet premier Brezhnev met with Nixon in Washington and San Clemente—the Watergate committee welcomed John Dean. For five days the country was riveted as, dressed and coiffed like a straitlaced junior partner, with his blond wife sitting primly behind him, he dispassionately detailed the White House horrors and Nixon's attempts to conceal them. "He was going further than we had gone," Bob Woodward recalled. "What Dean said was Nixon was at the center and involved."

Yet the conversations recounted in the Walters memcons were hearsay. And while Dean had given direct testimony, it was his word against Nixon's. As the hearings progressed that summer, Haldeman, Ehrlichman, and Mitchell took their turns, confessing some sins but defending and protecting the president. By autumn, the show seemed stale; the public was tired of overheated antics. "Barring some new sensational revelations, it would appear that the tempest . . . has passed its peak," a Republican pollster told the White House. "We've survived it," Nixon told Kissinger.

But there was, it turned out, a way to verify Dean's testimony. The Watergate committee had stumbled on the secret in July. Nixon had been taping himself. The tapes would tell the story.

The Final Days

T HE WATERGATE SCANDAL had been distilled to a single essence: a furious tug-of-war between Archibald Cox and Richard Nixon over the White House tapes.

Electronic record-keeping was a long-standing practice at the White House. It kept track of the decision-making process for historical accuracy, bureaucratic accountability, and political indemnity. Franklin Roosevelt had a microphone in the Oval Office, with aides in the basement transcribing what was said. Ike used tape recorders and had Ann Whitman, his personal secretary, listen in and make notes on his meetings and phone calls. John Kennedy had tapes spinning during times of crisis. And Johnson, who had a taste for gadgets, taped hundreds of conversations that he toted with him when he left for Texas.

Nixon had ordered Haldeman to dismantle Johnson's taping system. So Kissinger had secretaries listen in and make transcripts of phone calls, and Haldeman and Ehrlichman and other aides kept reams of notes of their conversations with the president. Ultimately, it seemed easier to bring back the machinery. Nixon's predecessors used a manual switch, taping only the conversations they chose. The efficient Haldeman (knowing that Nixon was something of a stumblebum) made the system noise-activated: everything got recorded, right down to the scratch of pens, the rattle of cutlery, and the tinkling of ice cubes.

"It never occurred to me that anyone in his right mind would install anything so Orwellian as a system that never shut off, that preserved every word, every joke, every curse, every tantrum, every flight of presidential paranoia, every bit of flattery and bad advice and tattling by his advisers," Alexander Haig would marvel. The secret was closely held—not even Kissinger and Ehrlichman knew they were being taped. And though Nixon and Haldeman were aware the machines were running, they generally dropped their guard. It would be mentally exhausting, obviously contrived, and of dubious benefit to try to manipulate every conversation. Besides, they thought, no one would ever hear the tapes but Nixon.

The president had a window to destroy the tapes after White House aide Alexander Butterfield, a custodian of the system, alerted the Senate to their existence in July. Nixon was being treated for pneumonia at the Bethesda naval medical center and heard competing arguments from his hospital bed. His Watergate counsel, Fred Buzhardt, urged him to destroy the recordings. They had not yet been subpoenaed. And though Nixon faced a partisan Congress, no Senate would convict a president for destroying his personal records. Impeachment was a political act. The sole precedent—the trial of Andrew Johnson by the Radical Republicans in a Reconstruction Congress in 1868—had so tarnished the process that the country swore off it for a hundred years. Impeaching a Cold War president for liquidating his private tape collection? Not likely.* Len Garment, now acting as a general White House counsel, argued the other side. Though the tapes were not yet subpoenaed, there was case law to say that their destruction would still be viewed as an act of obstructing justice. And burning the tapes would seem, to the public, like an admission of guilt.

Nixon leaned toward Garment. Having watched Truman and Eisenhower make and sustain bold claims of executive privilege, Nixon believed the courts would respect his presidential prerogative and rule his way. Keeping the taped record could prevent Dean, Haldeman, Ehrlichman, and other desperate aides seeking prosecutorial favor from lodging false accusations against him. And besides, the tapes were the record—the certification, for himself and others—of his accomplishments. Nixon prized his tough and, he thought, noble decisions on Vietnam, China, and the Soviet Union—and planned, with the selective use of the recorded conversations, to buff his image for history in his memoirs.

So Richard Nixon didn't burn the tapes. And Archibald Cox filed suit in Judge John Sirica's court for the recordings that could prove, or disprove, John Dean's testimony.

THE AUTUMN OF 1973 then unfolded like an overheated screenplay, with violence, scandal, bloodshed, and intrigue—all building toward a third-act conflagration.

---

* The constitutional requirement—"high crimes and misdemeanors"—is nebulous. In practical terms (as Republican lawmakers would demonstrate in 1998), the phrase is most accurately read as "whatever Congress believes it can get away with."

Nixon did not worry too much about impeachment while Spiro Agnew was his successor.* To the Democrats in Congress and their allies in the media, the vice president had most of Nixon's flaws and none of the president's gift for foreign affairs that, even they had to admit, was making the world a safer place. But Nixon's luck was running in but one direction now. A federal corruption probe in Baltimore had unearthed reports that Agnew had taken bribes, as governor of Maryland, from consulting firms doing business with the state. By summer's end, Elliot Richardson and Henry Petersen had reviewed the case and confirmed it was true. Indeed, Agnew had continued to accept the envelopes of cash while serving as vice president—at least one $10,000 payoff had been delivered to him in his office at the White House. The news of Agnew's crimes broke in August. For two months, he flopped about like a gaffed fish. On October 10, he pleaded no contest to a federal indictment and resigned. The deal kept him out of prison.

Under the Twenty-fifth Amendment to the Constitution, which had been passed in the wake of Ike's illnesses and Kennedy's murder, Nixon had the duty of appointing a new vice president, to be confirmed by Congress. John Connally topped his list, which also included Nelson Rockefeller, Ronald Reagan, and others. But the president was no longer so strong as to choose his own successor. "We simply cannot afford another . . . imbroglio, ending in defeat," Ray Price warned Nixon. "The nomination of John Connally could trigger a disaster. It would be bitterly divisive among Republicans and an open invitation to the Democrats on Capitol Hill to play the crassest sort of politics, and by doing so cripple if not topple the Presidency.

"They'd comb every inch of his past and I can't believe that in 20 or whatever years of acquiring millions while in Texas as a protégé of Lyndon Johnson, there isn't something that could be unearthed," Price wrote. "In the course of the confirmation hearings every dead cat in the Southwest would be dragged across the hearing-room floor."

Price was right. The Democrats vowed to block Connally and persuaded the president to name Gerald Ford, the House minority leader, instead. Ford was a man of the House, and popular in the cloakroom. He offered Nixon no "impeachment insurance." But as a friend of Nixon's for more than two decades, a colleague in the Chowder & Marching Club, and a good and decent man, he had his own appeal to a president starting to envision a day when he might need clemency himself.

* In 1969, Nixon and Ehrlichman had jokingly called Agnew "the assassin's dilemma."

In a stunning sign of just how fiercely the partisan fires were raging, a gang of House liberals urged Speaker Albert to stall Ford's confirmation until they could impeach Nixon—and make Albert, Majority Leader O'Neill, or another Democrat, like Ted Kennedy, the president. "Get off your goddamn ass, and we can take this presidency," Representative Bella Abzug of New York told the diminutive Speaker, poking him in the chest. Ted Sorensen, the longtime Kennedy hand, sent the Speaker a twenty-page "contingency plan" for a Democratic takeover, complete with suggestions for an inaugural address. Neither Albert nor O'Neill, however, had an interest in entering the history books as the blackguard leaders of an antinomian coup d'etat, and Ford was confirmed.

IF WASHINGTON NEEDED additional tension, the Russians were happy to oblige; it was not beyond Nixon's partners in peace to take advantage of his weakened condition. On October 6, a Jewish holy day, the Egyptians and Syrians launched surprise attacks, driving the Israeli forces back from the Suez Canal and the Golan Heights in what became known as the Yom Kippur War. The Soviet Union, seeing an opportunity to extend its influence in the oil-rich Middle East, provided the attackers with military advisers, anti-aircraft missiles, arms, and other matériel.

"The Israelis must not be allowed to lose," Nixon told his aides. He ordered them to send tanks, jet fighters, and ammunition to the embattled Jewish state. The American airlift conveyed a thousand tons a day. When diplomatic red tape slowed the process, the president erupted. "Do it now!" he ordered Kissinger. The United States was saving Israel, and no tiptoeing would quell the Arab anger. "We are going to get blamed just as much for three planes as for three hundred," Nixon said.

It was one of those times, Nixon told Kissinger, that showed "what we are here for." The crisis was downright liberating. Watergate "gave him the composure of a man who had seen the worst and to whom there were no further terrors," Kissinger recalled. "He probably welcomed staking his future on defending the interests of free peoples ... rather than on the outcome of a sordid litigation over events that had clearly gotten away from him."

AMID ALL THIS—AS Agnew left office in ignominy and shame, Ford was chosen as vice president, and the Israelis and Arabs waged war—Nixon resolved to fire Cox.

Nixon had supported Richardson's selection of a special prosecutor: initially, he did not believe that the bow-tied former solicitor general would join in a plot to get him. When Cox went to court to obtain tapes, including the "cancer on the presidency" recording, Nixon had second thoughts, and his ire swelled to outrage when Cox's staff started poking into matters that had nothing to do with the Watergate break-in. "He is deliberately going into extraneous issues. He cannot be allowed to get away with this," Nixon told Alexander Haig, the new White House chief of staff, that summer. "As Special Prosecutor he is derelict in his duties in trying to conduct a partisan political vendetta."

Cox's troopers indicted former White House aide Egil Krogh for perjury in the Ellsberg caper and rummaged through Nixon's income taxes, real estate purchases, and financial dealings with Bebe Rebozo. The special prosecutor rejected the advice of a federal appeals court and turned down White House offers to compromise on the tapes, including one plan that won the support of Senator Sam Ervin. Even Cox would publicly wonder if he had gotten "too big for my britches—that what I see as principle could be vanity." But on he marched. Nixon told Haig to prepare: they would order Cox to drop his demands, and if he refused they would fire him.

After several fruitless days of negotiation, marred by charges of bad faith on both sides, Nixon summoned Richardson to the Oval Office—where the attorney general, after refusing to sack the special prosecutor, resigned. Richardson saw it as an act of conscience and shared this quotation from the *Iliad* with Cox: *Now, though numberless fates of death beset us which no mortal can escape or avoid, let us go forward together, and either we shall give honor to one another, or another to us.* It was that kind of weekend. Richardson's deputy William Ruckelshaus likewise, nobly, fell on his sword. This left Solicitor General Robert Bork to dismiss Cox.

It was October 20, a Saturday night. The White House announced that the office of the special prosecutor "has been abolished." As reporters and Cox's outraged staff stood there watching, federal agents secured the prosecutor's files. "Firestorm" was the universal, and fitting, description of what followed. "The country tonight is in the midst of what may be the most serious constitutional crisis in its history," newsman John Chancellor told NBC's viewers, interrupting the usual prime-time lineup with a special report. It went down in history as the Saturday Night Massacre. "You will be returning to an environment of major national crisis," Haig cabled Kissinger, who was on his way home from negotiations on a Middle East cease-fire. "The situation is at a state of white heat. . . . An impeachment stampede could well develop."

Nixon, "taken by surprise by the ferocious intensity" he had stirred, was compelled to capitulate. "For the first time I recognized the depth of the impact Watergate had been having on America," he recalled. "I suddenly realized how deeply its acid had eaten." He announced he would release the requested tapes.

On the Tuesday after the Massacre, Tip O'Neill called on Congress to "examine its constitutional responsibilities." The House proceeded toward impeachment. Julie wrote on her calendar: "Fight. Fight. Fight." Nixon could be heard at the piano, alone, at night. He played "Rustle of Spring," his mother's favorite. The mood in the capital shifted—away from the thrill of the chase and the marvelous jolts of fresh disclosure that had filled the spring and summer. A wretched despondency set in. "You definitely felt an emptiness . . . all these things—because it wasn't us. These things don't happen in America," White House reporter Helen Thomas would recall. "It was darkness at noon . . . as inexorable as a Greek tragedy," and the president, she said, was "like a dead man walking."

LEON JAWORSKI, AN experienced Texas lawyer (and friend of Lyndon Johnson), was named by Nixon as a new special prosecutor. The tension in the capital seemed to abate. The Soviet Union, however, was still stirring things in the Middle East. "The Soviets are playing," Kissinger warned Haig. "They find a cripple facing impeachment."

After rallying from its initial defeats in the Yom Kippur conflict, Israeli armored columns were chasing the Syrians down the road to Damascus and had crossed the Suez Canal into Egypt. An Egyptian army was encircled, and dying, in Sinai. Leonid Brezhnev proposed to save the Arabs, if not via a partnership with the United States, then (he told Nixon in a message on the Cold War "hotline") by intervening unilaterally. It was a "piss swisher" of a message, Admiral Moorer, the chairman of the Joint Chiefs, said. Either option would expand the Soviet footprint in the Middle East.

Nixon had played a direct role in the war's early days, ordering Kissinger and Defense Secretary James Schlesinger to keep Israel resupplied, no matter the political or geopolitical costs. In reply, the Arabs used their oil as a weapon, hiking American gasoline, industrial, and home heating bills—fueling inflation and wounding the U.S. economy.

On the night of October 24, however, Nixon was absent: preoccupied with Watergate—"down, very down," said Haig—and bunkered in the White House living quarters. On a previous occasion during the crisis, Kissinger had complained to aides that Nixon was not focused and was drinking heavily. Shortly after 7 p.m., the president called Kissinger. He was "as agitated and emotional as I had ever heard him," the secretary of state would recall. "We were heading into what could have become the gravest foreign policy crisis . . . with a president overwhelmed by his persecution."

Nixon ranted about his enemies. "They are doing it because of their desire to kill the president," he told Kissinger. "And they may succeed. I may physically die."

Nixon was not present in the White House Situation room that night, when Kissinger and the others ordered a readiness alert, the aircraft carriers *John F. Kennedy* and *Franklin Delano Roosevelt* were dispatched to the eastern Mediterranean, and the troopers of the Eighty-second Airborne were told to be ready for war. Haig had shuttled to the upstairs living quarters, and told the others that he'd informed Nixon of what was being done.

"We have to go to the mat on this one," Kissinger told Haig, a few moments before 10 p.m. "Should I wake up the president?"

"No," said Haig.

The next morning, October 25, Americans woke to the news that the U.S. nuclear weapons forces had been moved to DEFCON III, a status of high alert, to keep the Russians from intervening.

The Soviets took a step back. "Nixon is too nervous," Brezhnev told his colleagues. "Let's cool him down."

The Soviet Union endorsed the idea of a United Nations peacekeeping force, and Kissinger worked the phones—bullying Jerusalem until Cairo, Damascus, and the encircled Egyptian army were safe. The fighting ended badly for Sadat, but he had claimed a great psychological victory, whipping Israel in the opening round, restoring Arab pride, and claiming an equal footing for talks that eventually led to peace.

In the days that followed, Nixon boasted of how the showdown was as dangerous as any since the Cuban missile crisis. "Even in this week, when many thought the president was shell-shocked, unable to act, the president acted decisively," he told the press. "The tougher it gets, the cooler I get."

His aides let Nixon have his day but didn't hesitate to express doubts when they reminisced years later. Bill Rogers had left office in September, and Kissinger was now serving as both national security adviser and secretary of state. "Nixon no longer had the time or nervous energy to give consistent leadership," he recalled. "He was too distracted to shape the decisions before they reached him."

Congress sensed weakness. It carved away at executive authority with the War Powers Resolution, passed over Nixon's veto on November 7, which trimmed his ability, and that of future presidents, to take the country into undeclared wars.

It was about then, Fed chairman Arthur Burns said later, that he and Kissinger would meet and "Kissinger became very forceful in saying Nixon should go."

"What happened to President Nixon is a human tragedy," Kissinger would marvel in a later conversation with a newsman. "When I say tragedy, it doesn't mean that it wasn't undeserved. . . . It was like one of those Greek things where a man is told his fate . . . and fulfills it anyway, knowing exactly what is going to happen to him."

NIXON TOOK ANOTHER awful beating when the news became public that two of the disputed tape recordings were missing and another had an eighteen-and-a-half-minute gap. Haig suggested that an unknown "sinister" force was responsible. The missing segment had been wiped out by repeated erasures, a panel of experts told Judge Sirica. Nixon denied he'd done it, and Rose Mary Woods stepped forward, with contortions worthy of a gymnast, to demonstrate how she might have inadvertently erased the tape. The *New York Times,* the *Denver Post,* and Nixon's old cheerleader, *Time* magazine, led a cavalcade of news organizations calling on Nixon to resign. To salt his wounds, word came from Sweden that Kissinger and North Vietnamese negotiator Le Duc Tho had been given the Nobel Peace Prize, for ending the Vietnam War.

Collateral issues injured Nixon as well. The press and Congress questioned the need for $100,000 in taxpayer-funded improvements at San Clemente and Key Biscayne. The ITT scandal was reexamined, and the administration's finagling with milk subsidies. Newspapers in Baltimore and Providence reported how Nixon shaved his federal income-tax payments through ornate deductions, including a $576,000 write-off for the donation of his vice-presidential papers to the National Archives. (It didn't help Nixon when an aide was found to have backdated the deed.) The president had paid but $792 to the IRS in 1970 and $878 in 1971, and an examination by the congressional Joint Committee on Internal Revenue Taxation determined that he owed $476,000 in back taxes and interest. At a gathering of the nation's editors in Disney World in mid-November, Nixon felt the need to assure them: "People have the right to know whether or not their president is a crook. Well, I am not a crook."

—

ON JANUARY 5, Nixon met the new year with a note to himself. "Above all else: Dignity, command, faith, head high, no fear, build a new spirit, drive, act like a President, act like a winner. Opponents are savage destroyers, haters. Time to use full power of the President to fight overwhelming forces arrayed against us."

He had so little quit. But Nixon's family saw through his bravado. "Something Daddy said makes me feel absolutely hopeless about the outcome," Tricia wrote in her diary. "He has . . . repeatedly stated that the tapes can be taken either way. He has cautioned us that there is nothing damaging on the tapes; he has cautioned us that he might be impeached because of their content. Because he has said the latter, knowing Daddy, the latter is the way he really feels."

Politically, things looked grim. "We are dying by inches," Buchanan told Nixon. "Our margin for error has disappeared; our reservoir of credibility with the American people dried up."

ARTHUR BREMER, WHO shot George Wallace in May 1972, had trailed Nixon to an event in Ottawa, Canada, in April of that year but turned his attention to Wallace after concluding that the security around the president was too tight. "You can't kill Nixie boy if you ain't close to him," Bremer wrote in his diary. He called his journal, "My diary of my personal plot to kill by pistol either Richard Nixon or George Wallace."

On the morning of February 22, 1974, an unemployed salesman named Samuel Byck arrived at Baltimore Washington International Airport with a stolen pistol, and a crude homemade firebomb in his briefcase. He had spent much of his time in recent days, and on the drive from his home in Pennsylvania, speaking into a tape recorder. In a calm voice, he outlined plans to hijack an airliner and, as the plane soared over the nation's capital, to seize the controls and steer the jet into the White House, where the Nixons had just returned from a trip to Florida. It was better to live "one day as a lion," Byck said, than go on in failure. "My death will be Watergate connected," he muttered. The government was run by "cheats" and "thieves," he said, and "I will cleanse it by fire."

The Secret Service knew Byck: he had been writing threatening letters and parading before the White House with protest signs and, on Christmas Eve, in a Santa Claus suit. But the authorities judged him harmless. Far from it. He breezed into the terminal with his little arsenal and approached Gate C, where a Delta Airlines DC-9 was preparing to shove off for Atlanta. Byck shot and killed a guard and then stormed down the ramp to the cockpit, where he ordered the crew to "Fly this plane out of here!" When they stalled, he shot the copilot, turned to the pilot, and said, "The next one will be in the head." When the pilot tried to reason with him, Byck shot him too. He then ordered a terrified female passenger to fly the plane. "Emergency. Emergency," the wounded pilot radioed. "We're all shot."

Byck's plot ended when a moonlighting local policeman working airport security fired at him through an airplane window. Wounded twice, Byck ended matters by raising his gun to his temple and pulling the trigger. The airport shootout was well covered in the media, except that the U.S. government refused to disclose that Nixon was Byck's target. It would not do so until 1987, for fear of inspiring copycat hijackers.

SPRING ARRIVED. IN April, Nixon made a final, futile attempt to turn things around. In a televised address, he announced that he was releasing more than 1,300 transcribed pages, from forty-six tapes, to Congress and the public. With a pile of volumes stacked beside him, he looked like an encyclopedia salesman. The public was riveted by the transcripts—two paperback editions sold three million copies in a week. As with every release of Nixon tapes, journalists focused on the salacious and sensational. The president would have been better served had he left the curse words intact—the repeated citation "expletive deleted" left too much to the imagination. And the White House editing of the tapes was clumsy—it allowed the House Judiciary Committee, leaking its own transcripts as it pondered impeachment, to show how Nixon made self-serving deletions.

Three years of caustic revelations had passed since Haldeman had warned Nixon that the publication of the Pentagon Papers would corrode Americans' faith in government. The My Lai trials and the Watergate hearings had added to that corrosion. But the raw, cynical exchanges captured by the transcripts were like nothing the silent majority had ever heard. "This thing is hemorrhaging terribly," Buchanan told Haig. The Watergate tapes, with their crudity and cruelties, interred Nixon's image as an upright, righteous son of the heartland. "Sheer flesh-crawling repulsion. The back room of a second-rate advertising agency in a suburb of hell," wrote columnist Joseph Alsop. "A shabby, disgusting, immoral performance," said Senate Minority Leader Hugh Scott.

Pat stopped reading the newspapers. "If there is a hell on earth," Rose Woods told Julie, "we are living through it now." With her mother's encouragement, Julie began to campaign on her father's behalf, taking speaking engagements around the country. When Nixon suggested that she not be so involved, she replied, "But, Daddy, we have to fight." Mel Laird and Bryce Harlow, two old comrades and former aides who had joined the White House staff to help right the ship, quietly left the administration, angry that Nixon had lied to them. Vice President Ford felt betrayed.

The Judiciary Committee subpoenaed more tapes, including those of the June 23, 1972, conversations. The White House resisted, and the case went to the U.S. Supreme Court. As the Judiciary Committee prepared for impeachment hearings, the news leaked that Jaworski's grand jury had named Nixon as an "unindicted co-conspirator." The Nixon administration drifted, rudderless, heading for the rocks.

NIXON SOUGHT RELIEF in foreign affairs. On June 10 he left for Europe and the Middle East. The pictures from Cairo, of hundreds of thousands of Egyptians cheering Nixon and Sadat, were almost matched by the grand welcomes from the heads of state of Saudi Arabia, Israel, Syria, and Jordan. A growing pain in Nixon's leg was diagnosed as phlebitis, a dangerous vascular condition, for which patients should rest and keep the affected limb elevated. Nixon insisted on continuing the trip, despite the long hours he was facing—standing and sitting—in the Middle East. "The purpose of this trip is more important than my life," he told his doctor, Walter Tkach. He gave a similar explanation to the Secret Service, who were aghast at the idea of Nixon touring Egypt in an open car with Sadat.

The president and his entourage returned to the United States just long enough to repack and were off to the Soviet Union for his third summit meeting with Brezhnev. As in their first two meetings, at which Nixon had presented the Soviet leader with a Cadillac and then a Lincoln Continental, Nixon brought along a car: this time a Chevrolet Monte Carlo. The best that can be said for the summit is that, despite his eagerness to play peacemaker for the people back home, Nixon made no damaging concessions.

Nixon's family continued to stand by him. After the House minority leader, John Rhodes, suggested to a reporter that Nixon might want to resign, he received a frosty greeting from Pat when they ran into each other at a reception.

"Oh yes," she said, as they posed for a photograph. "Let's smile as if we like each other."

"Mrs. Nixon. It isn't the way you heard it," Rhodes told her.

"Yeah. That's what they all say," Pat responded.

—

THE JUDICIARY COMMITTEE hearings were, for the most part, theater to sustain an existing consensus: it was time for Tricky Dick to go. When the political establishment reaches a conclusion—as happened in Washington in the weeks after the Saturday Night Massacre—it takes an intense contravening force to shatter the consensual judgment. In Nixon's case, the subsequent months had borne only reinforcing evidence.

"Teddy Roosevelt used to talk about 'standing at Armageddon, doing battle for the Lord,'" a frustrated White House aide, Ken Khachigian, warned Haig. "We are standing at Armageddon, but we are not doing battle. . . . Now is the time to draw the partisan lines. . . . We cannot allow the articles of impeachment to be enshrined in respectability and legitimacy. They are producing a bastard product of dubious parentage conceived in clandestine back room trysts."

There were sufficient conservative Democrats and Republicans to defeat two articles of impeachment—on the bombing of Cambodia and alleged tax evasion. But the counts on obstruction of justice and abuse of power passed by big, bipartisan margins. So, by a narrower vote, did an article damning Nixon for refusing to honor congressional subpoenas. "I was getting dressed" after a swim in the Pacific, Nixon would recall. "That was how I learned that I was the first President in 106 years to be recommended for impeachment: standing in the beach trailer, barefoot, wearing old trousers, a Banlon shirt and a blue windbreaker emblazoned with the Presidential Seal."

That night, in his diary, Nixon wrote of Pat: "God, how she could have gone through what she does, I simply don't know."

As THE JUDICIARY Committee was debating impeachment, the Supreme Court—as yielding to popular consensus as any of the capital's institutions—had handed down its ruling in *United States of America v. Richard Nixon.*

The former chief justice, Earl Warren, had suffered a heart attack in early July. In the hours before his passing, Justices William Douglas and William Brennan visited him in his hospital room, where Warren grabbed Douglas by the hand and told them: "If Nixon is not forced to turn over tapes of his conversations with the ring of men who were conversing on their violations of the law, then liberty will soon be dead in this nation."

They assured him that the court would rule against his old enemy. Warren died a few hours later.

Judges "do not stand aloof and chill on . . . distant heights," Justice Benjamin Cardozo once wrote. "The great tides and currents which engulf the rest of men do not turn aside in their course and pass the judges by."*

THE SUPREME COURT's decision, delivered on July 24, was unanimous. The court recognized a doctrine of executive privilege but concluded that it did not apply in Nixon's case, where the issue was one of criminal behavior. The president would have to release more tapes.

Robert Bork received a phone call from Haig: the president was thinking of defying the Court. "That is instant impeachment," Bork told him. There was no wiggle room. The decision was unanimous, with three Nixon appointees joining the others against him and Chief Justice Warren Burger writing the opinion. All along, Nixon had it right. He was alone. "If you're a nice guy and make a mistake they'll forgive you," said his last treasury secretary, William Simon. "But if you are a prick, they're going to step on you and not let up."

After hearing of the ruling, one of Nixon's first calls was to Buzhardt. "There may be some problems with the June 23 tape, Fred," he said.

On Tuesday, August 6, Washingtonians awoke to read, in the lead story of that day's *Post*, a Woodward and Bernstein story that began: "President Nixon personally ordered a pervasive cover up of the facts of Watergate within six days after the illegal entry into the Democrats' national headquarters." The transcript of the June 23 tape, the smoking gun, was now public.

"THIS IS IT. It's all over," said Rhodes, remembering his reaction. "There was the smokin' gun. He had it in his hand. . . . My mind at that moment was made up. I would have to vote for impeachment. . . . There was no chance of saving it."

Haig had already begun to orchestrate Nixon's departure from office, quietly showing the transcript of the June 23 tape to leaders of Congress, Nixon's closest aides, and cabinet officers. Some were furious to discover

---

* Peter Finley Dunne's fictional barkeep, Mr. Dooley, put it this way: "No matter whether th' constitution follows the flag or not, th' supreme coort follows th' iliction returns."

that Nixon had listened to the recording that spring, and not warned them of its contents. Kissinger was told, and so was Ford—and Haig asked the vice president if he was ready to become president.

On Friday, August 2, Nixon warned Julie, and she told Pat and the others, that he might have to resign. The family spent their final weekend at Camp David, nursing the wistful hope that the country would not find the June 23 conversation *too* incriminating. The transcript was released to the public on Monday evening, with a statement from the president asking the American people to put his sins in context. That was something they were well prepared to do—but not to Nixon's benefit.

He vacillated in his last seventy-two hours in office, as his family urged him to continue the fight. At times, as when he conducted his final cabinet meeting on Tuesday, he sounded downright cocky. ("All that talent—all those flaws," Caspar Weinberger, the secretary of health, education, and welfare, whispered to James Schlesinger. "No morality," George H. W. Bush thought. "Caring for no one and yet doing so much.") But Nixon had been thinking about resigning for more than a year, and that evening he began working on a farewell address. Rose Woods was dispatched to the residence to tell Pat and Tricia and Julie that his enemies had at last unhorsed him. When he retired for bed in the early morning hours of Wednesday the 7th, he found a note from Julie on his pillow.

> Dear Daddy—
>   I love you. Whatever you do I will support. I am very proud of you.
>   Please wait a week or even ten days before you make this decision. Go through the fire just a little bit longer. You are so strong! I love you.
>   Julie
>
>   Millions support you.

HAIG WORRIED THAT Nixon might harm himself. "You fellows, in your business, you have a way of handling problems like this," Nixon had told him. "Somebody leaves a pistol in the drawer." On Capitol Hill, the congressional leaders fretted about his mental state. At the Pentagon, Schlesinger had similar concerns. To ensure against a military coup, a nuclear Götterdämmerung, or some other frantic act, the secretary of defense instructed the Joint Chiefs that any eleventh-hour orders from the White House must be vetted by the chain of command.

On Wednesday afternoon, Republican leaders Barry Goldwater, Hugh Scott, and John Rhodes arrived at the White House, and met with the president in the EOB. Nixon didn't have a prayer, they told him. Not in the House. Not in the Senate. He would certainly be impeached and convicted. Nixon took the news calmly, bid them good-bye, and left the Oval Office for the residence, where his family had gathered in the Solarium.

"We're going back to California," he told them. They ate dinner off trays and then posed, smiling through tears, for Ollie Atkins, the presidential photographer. Pat hated the picture. "Our hearts were breaking and there we are smiling," she said. As the group broke up, Atkins snapped a final shot, of Julie and her father in each other's arms.

THE FINAL HOURS had more than their share of Shakespearean scenes. Nixon choking back sobs and rushing from the room after telling a group of his old friends from Congress, "I hope you won't feel I have let you down". . . . The leaders of the House and Senate leaving Nixon and hearing, from the crowds outside the White House gates, the people singing "God Bless America". . . . Nixon asking Kissinger to join him on his knees in prayer in the Lincoln bedroom. . . . The president's televised address, announcing his resignation, to spare the nation further pain. . . . Pat working throughout the night, packing their things for the trip to California.

"There are worse things than jail," Nixon told Garment, in one of the dozens of late-night telephone calls he made after his Thursday-night speech. "There is no telephone there. There is, instead, peace. A hard table to write on. The best political writing in this century has been done from jail."

But no scene in a career of astonishing spectacle, not Checkers, not Caracas, not the first debate with Kennedy or the last press conference in 1962—nor even the predawn visit to the Lincoln Memorial—was as memorable as Nixon's farewell talk to the White House staff on Friday morning. The actor met the moment. It may well have been the most raw, acutely painful, and unforgettable speech in American political history.

"Do not trip over wires. Stand on name marker. Reach for Mama's hand. Hold it. Applause. Daddy is speaking. People are letting tears roll down their cheeks. Must not look. Must not think of it now," Tricia wrote, recounting the moment in her diary. "The real Nixon was being revealed as only he could reveal himself. By speaking from the heart people could finally know Daddy. It was not too late."

Nixon began with a dig at the press. Then segued into the old fib about Frank selling the lemon ranch before oil was discovered on the property. He tried, one more time, to tell them who he was. How lonely. How alone. "Nobody will ever write a book, probably, about my mother," he said. "Well, I guess all of you would say this about your mother. My mother was a saint. And I think of her, two boys dying of tuberculosis, nursing four others in order that she could take care of my older brother for three years in Arizona, and seeing each of them die, and when they died, it was like one of her own. Yes, she will have no books written about her. But she was a saint."

His insecurity danced across the stage. "I had a little quote in the speech last night from T.R.," he said. "As you know, I kind of like to read books. I am not educated, but I do read books."

Then came proof of his astonishing resilience. "We think that when someone dear to us dies, we think that when we lose an election, we think that when we suffer a defeat, that all has ended," he said. "Not true. It is only a beginning, always.

"The young must know it; the old must know it. It must always sustain us, because the greatness comes and you are really tested when you take some knocks, some disappointments, when sadness comes, because only if you have been in the deepest valley can you ever know how magnificent it is to be on the highest mountain."

There was "a faded doom" about the man, Kissinger thought. Many in the audience were weeping. And in the end, from Richard Nixon, came words as wise as any ever spoken in the great old house. Rich in self-knowledge, purchased at a price: "Always remember, others may hate you—but those who hate you don't win unless you hate them, and then you destroy yourself."

DICK AND PAT made their way out to the South Lawn, walked down a long red carpet, shook hands with a funereal vice president, and climbed the steps of the presidential helicopter, *Army One*. At the last, Nixon turned and, grimacing, gave one sweeping, defensive wave, as if to ward off unquenchable grief. Then he thrust his arms skyward, flashing the trademark V's for victory, turned, and entered the helicopter.

Army One lifted from the lawn, rose above the muggy capital, the National Mall dimmed in a summer morning's haze. Below, L'Enfant's grand boulevards and Brumidi's halls and corridors pulsed with visionaries, parvenus, and hustlers; with dreams and scheming; with avarice, ambition, rivalry, and purpose. The chopper soared over statues of heroes, and monuments to great statesmen whose ranks, with such American audacity, the awkward grocer's boy had presumed to join, had come so near, only to fall. "It's so sad," Pat said, to no one in particular.

They spent the flight to California alone, each in his or her cabin on *Air Force One*. The president had a cocktail. At noon, when they were somewhere over Missouri, the resignation took effect.

Exile

RICHARD NIXON'S ELBA was a seaside mansion with a swimming pool, gardens, three-hole golf course, and a study overlooking the ocean, where, as he liked to tell visitors, he had once plotted the fate of the world with Leonid Brezhnev. Just north, jutting into cerulean waters, was Dana Point, where he had proposed to Pat so many years before. To the south were a Coast Guard station and a sprawling Marine base, with a private beach where he could swim. He left office with a generous six-month transition fund and the pensions and allowances due a retired chief of state. It is fair to say that nine out of ten of his fellow Americans, and a higher percentage of the citizens of the world, would see La Casa Pacifica as heaven. For Nixon it was hell. "Humiliation after the shame of humiliation," said his White House press secretary, Ron Ziegler, who went with him to California. Nixon did not find, or seek, peace there. He did not apply his talents to mankind's business. He did not make amends. He did what he was best at. Driven by his complex will, and his thick catalog of resentments, he campaigned. Not for public office, a cause, or some altruistic purpose—but for his own exculpation, and place in history. "There are all kinds of prisons," Bob Haldeman's wife, Jo, would say.

IT'S PERHAPS TOO much to ask that Nixon should have given more to the world in the last two decades of his life. It would take a Christlike figure to forgive what had been done to him, and Nixon was never that. Nor, at the start, would anyone have let him make much of a contribution. In Washington, there were those still yearning to drag the corpse through the dust down Pennsylvania Avenue: young prosecutors who wanted to make their mark by putting an ex-president behind bars, and members of Congress seeking to cut the funds due a retired chief of state. Longtime aide and friend Bob Finch was among those who visited Nixon in his first weeks of exile. He found no sign of atonement, no recognition of his crimes, only anger in Nixon, at how he had been crucified for "mistakes."

Nixon admitted few visitors. But Pat Buchanan and Ray Price came, as did Ken Clawson, from his White House communications team, who recorded an atypical moment of self-awareness by his former boss. Sitting in his office, ranging back over his years in politics, Nixon described how the candle had come to singe the moth.

"What starts the process, really, are laughs and slights and snubs when you are a kid," Nixon said. "But if you are reasonably intelligent and if your anger is deep enough and strong enough, you learn that you can change those attitudes by excellence, personal gut performance while those who have everything are sitting on their fat butts."

"Once you learn that you've got to work harder than everybody else it becomes a way of life as you move out of the alley and on your way," Nixon mused. "In your mind you have nothing to lose so you take plenty of chances, and if you do your homework many of them pay off. It is then you understand, for the first time, that you have the advantage because your competitors can't risk what they have already."

Nixon rested his aching leg on the desk.

"It's a piece of cake until you get to the top," he told Clawson. Then "you find you can't stop playing the game the way you've always played it because it is part of you and you need it as much as an arm or a leg.

"So you are lean and mean and resourceful and you continue to walk on the edge of the precipice because over the years you have become fascinated by how close to the edge you can walk without losing your balance," Nixon said.

Clawson interrupted. "Only this time there was a difference."

"Yes, this time there was a difference," Dick said softly. "This time we had something to lose."

The staff marveled at Nixon's perseverance. He kept up his personal appearance, came to his office each day, and wore a jacket and tie to maintain standards. "Any other person would have walked out into that ocean," a loyal secretary, Marje Acker, said.

AFTER A MONTH of misery, Nixon's first good news arrived on a Sunday in September when Gerald Ford, knowing the huge political cost he would suffer for his action, granted him a presidential pardon. The first question asked of Ford, by his friend Tip O'Neill and others, was if the pardon was the payoff in a deal to get Nixon to resign.

With Nixon's approval, Al Haig had gone to see Ford in the final days—Haig went alone, and under an assumed name in the appointment book—and proposed that, if Nixon resigned, President Ford might pardon him. Ford was amenable. And Haig, doubtless, reported back to Nixon.

There was no quid pro quo, Ford would insist, under oath before Congress. But his testimony skirts the old political maxim: "Never write when you can speak, never speak when you can nod." And nods—feelers, understandings—had greased Nixon's departure. "I told him he would be pardoned if he resigned," said Mel Laird, a good friend of both presidents, many years later. But it was a prediction, Laird said, not a proffer.

After taking power, Ford had dispatched attorney Benton Becker to San Clemente with conditions: Nixon needed to recognize that, under law, accepting a pardon was an admission of guilt, and he must make a statement of contrition. "No question about it," Ford would recall. "If I had been a member of the Senate following House action, based on the evidence I know, I would have voted to convict."

These were bitter herbs for the ex-president. Nixon, in return, wanted control of his presidential tapes and papers—which Ford, under pressure from the press, Congress, and the special prosecutor, had secured and retained. The negotiations were not pretty, or final—Kissinger would intrude, Congress would respond, and the legal status of the tapes and documents would remain in dispute for twenty years—but Nixon ultimately acceded.

He was "wrong" in his handling of the Watergate scandal, Nixon admitted, and fair-minded people could consider his actions "intentionally self-serving and illegal." For years, it was as far as he would go. The tapes reeked of felonious behavior, but only at the end of his life would he acknowledge to an aide that ordering the CIA to obstruct the FBI investigation of Watergate was both stupid and illegal. He never would say publicly, "I broke the law." Only by accepting the pardon did Nixon confess.

It was, he told Pat, "the most humiliating day of my life." Before leaving San Clemente, Becker was summoned one last time, so that Nixon could give him presidential cuff links. Nixon apologized for the meagerness of the souvenirs and waved at the walls of his cheapjack annex office. "I wanted to give you something," he lamented, "but they took it all away from me."

The inferno that followed Ford's announcement rivaled that which accompanied the Saturday Night Massacre, spoiling his chances to be elected on his own. ("The son of a bitch pardoned the son of a bitch," Carl

Bernstein told Bob Woodward.) Without the record of a trial, Demo-crats contended, Nixon would argue that he'd been railroaded from office. Wounded by Ronald Reagan's challenge in the Republican primaries, Ford collided with an anti-Nixon in the 1976 election—the temperate Jimmy Carter—and lost. "I will never lie to you," Carter promised Americans.

THE PARDON WAS a wise gesture, proof of Ford's decency and his wish to put the "long national nightmare" of Watergate behind him and his country. It was spurred, as well, by his concern for Nixon's health. Julie and Tricia conveyed the fear, in private and via the press, that their father had slid into a dangerous depression. He had lost the will to fight—maybe even to live. The phlebitis in Nixon's left leg had flared anew, and he had to be hospitalized. He could not disguise his fear. "If I go to the hospital, I'll never come out alive," he told Dr. John Lungren. The doctor saw "deep despair, anguish and mental torment" in Nixon. "It reminded me of the anxiety that often overwhelms patients who are suffering a fatal disease . . . reviewing their life, dwelling on last things, suffering great depression of mind and soul."

Cynics suggested that the illness was a hoax, to free Nixon from hav-ing to testify at the trials of his former aides. He seemed to recover, went home, but was back in the hospital for urgent surgery in early October. In the recovery room, he was bleeding internally. His blood pressure crashed. He slipped into shock. A nurse slapped his face, saying, "Richard! Richard!" Lungren was summoned. "Nixon was alabaster-white, incoherent and slip-ping into unconsciousness," he recalled. It was "an extremely close encoun-ter with death." The medical team pulled Nixon off Charon's ferry, and slowly he improved. But Lungren remained worried about his emotional health. Ford, hoping to boost Nixon's morale, visited the hospital while on a trip to California and was shocked by the former president's condition.

Others were not so charitable. "I don't think he should ever be for-given," Barry Goldwater would conclude. "He came as close to destroying America as any man in that office has ever done."

NIXON WAS RELIEVED when a panel of doctors appointed by Judge Sirica confirmed Lungren's diagnosis and freed him from the ordeal of traveling to Washington to testify. But along with relief, he felt guilt. John Mitchell, Bob Haldeman, John Ehrlichman, Charles Colson, and more than fifty other men and corporations would be convicted for Watergate-related crimes. They were not innocents. They had conspired to conduct and cover up political sabotage. But neither did they get a fair trial.

Prosecutors and judges have discretion; they are supposed to serve justice. But the ideal can give way as, incessantly confronted with man's wickedness, the officers of the court grow cynical. In a frenzy like Watergate, perspective was abandoned. "History may conclude that the way in which those guilty of crimes in the Watergate affair were brought to justice did more lasting damage to the highest purpose of American law than did the crimes themselves," wrote Richard Harris in *The New Yorker*. "The prosecutors—with an astonishing disregard for fairness—fell back on all the means that could reasonably be justified by the end, including the use of some of the same legal practices that had been so freely and perniciously employed by the Nixon Administration."

Mitchell, Haldeman, and the others were latecomers to the cause of civil liberties. They did not raise objections when they wielded power— when their demands for "law and order" and a "war on drugs" packed first-time offenders in prison cells, demonstrators were shot, and law enforcement agencies muzzled dissent. It was fair sport, perhaps, to see them hoist on their petard. But it is also true that the Watergate defendants were dispatched to prison by a process that denied them a called-for change of venue, bent the rules of evidence, and was tainted by ex parte collaborations between the judge and partisan prosecutors. Sirica's threat to impose "extraordinarily harsh sentences" to coerce defendants to testify, Harris argued, violated "the Fifth Amendment's prohibition against involuntary self-incrimination and the Constitutional right to due process of law." Immunizing witnesses, in exchange for testimony that convicts higher-ups, is a recognized prosecutorial tactic. But any process that let the more culpable John Dean escape the scourge of prison while other young men, like Donald Segretti and Dwight Chapin, were jailed was skewed.

"It was a lynching," the liberal columnist Nicholas von Hoffman wrote. At one end of town, the liberal elites screamed bloody murder over the wiretapping of journalists. At the other, wrote von Hoffman, "Sirica was conducting his kangaroo court" to their cheers. "The whole thing should make us queasy."

The lionization of Archibald Cox led to another overcorrection: Congress passed an independent counsel statute, giving prosecutors almost unlimited mandates and budgets, and huge staffs who ranged far and wide, looking for cases to justify their existence.

If the Pentagon Papers had ended "the implicit infallibility of presi-dents," as Haldeman put it, Watergate went further: it changed the default setting. For a generation, America's top leaders would be viewed as guilty, unless proven innocent. It was a mindlessly corrosive game, from which the nation suffered, until the lewd compositions of Kenneth Starr soiled the office beyond cleansing, and the statute was allowed to expire. Water-gate was its progenitor; another Nixon legacy.

SAIGON FELL IN the spring of 1975. The United States refused to intervene when the North Vietnamese launched the probing attack that, through Thieu's blundering, turned into a rout. It was time, the American people and their elected representatives concluded, for South Vietnam to stand alone. The U.S. commander in Vietnam, General Creighton Abrams, "feels strongly that the time has come for us to get out and that we simply have to cut the umbilical cord and have this baby walk by itself," Nixon had written in his diary back in 1972. "If they can't do it now, with all we have fed it in the way of arms and ammunition and training, etc., they will never be able to do it."

After the loss of Vietnam, Nixon and Kissinger would promote a fantasy that, had Congress approved the Ford administration's full aid requests in 1974 and 1975, the South would have prevailed. (Congress had appropriated $700 million of the $1.6 billion that Ford requested in 1975, and was on the verge of passing another $325 million in emergency aid when Thieu and his entourage fled Saigon.) Had he not so thoroughly bungled Watergate, Nixon told newsman David Frost, he could have given a national televised address and "the people, having supported the actions we had taken previously to get the peace, I think, would have supported what we had to do." The air attack on North Vietnam would have been "swift, it would have been massive and it would have been effective," he insisted.

In private, Nixon was more realistic. He always accepted that cutbacks of military aid were inevitable, and what the results would be. Once he got the POWs back, no waves of bombers would fly to save Thieu's regime, Nixon told Kissinger's aide, Brent Scowcroft, in the spring of 1973. "After the last American leaves . . . the whole feeling of Congress and the country would be, 'Now for Christ's sake, we're out of Vietnam. Let's don't go back in,'" Nixon said. "That's going to be the fact."

"Of course, we've told Thieu we'd do it and all that," Nixon said. "But we've also told the American people that we've gotten [South Vietnam] ready to defend themselves, and they've got an air force and all the rest, and [Americans will demand] 'Why the hell don't *they* do it?'"

Later that spring, Nixon and Kissinger had analyzed the South's chances. "I must tell you honestly," Kissinger told the president. He did not believe South Vietnam would survive "beyond 1974."

BLAMING CONGRESS FOR the loss of Vietnam was a sour, divisive, and selfish act, worthy of the pejorative adjective *Nixonian*. He would have been better off to argue that he had inherited a catastrophe, played a bad board well, lost knights and sacrificed rooks, and salvaged what he could. In the long view, if at an awful cost, Americans did succeed in "buying time" for other Asian nations "to avoid becoming dominos and to become tigers instead," Winston Lord, the former adviser to Kissinger and Nixon, averred.

Hundreds of thousands of Cambodians and South Vietnamese died in the terrors that followed the fall of Saigon and Phnom Penh. But the next thirty years gave freedom a victory. Marxism was a creature of the industrial age; it prospered in a world of factory lines and clanking tanks, five-year farm plans and sullen labor. Transistors and computer chips were pathogens. The next stage of economic progress put a premium on free thought, creativity, and nimbleness that captive state economies, run by sluggish bureaucracies, could not match.

George Kennan's design—Nixon's goal—was fulfilled in their lifetime: the Wall and the Iron Curtain fell, the Soviet Union collapsed, and Hanoi and Beijing, bending to a different wind, began to open their societies. By the early twenty-first century, Vietnam had become a trading partner and a tourist attraction to the generation of Americans who fought the war, and to their children. They found, in its mystique, its green beauty, and its proud people, a peace unimaginable to the warriors of old. Nixon would have been better to claim credit for his successes, and accept the responsibility for his mistakes, instead of blaming Congress for stabbing Thieu in the back.

If Nixon and Kissinger thought that the fate of the South Vietnamese people was an essential priority in their global strategy, they would have fought to win. They never did. As Nixon saw it, the American interests at stake in Southeast Asia were worth what he gave them—a face-saving retreat, with a chance that the South could survive. But he knew all along it was but a chance. "We didn't think a loss was inevitable" was his best

defense of his policy. Nixon did what leaders do—what he had seen Roosevelt and Churchill do in World War II. He inherited a war, with an army
of 500,000 men in the field. He analyzed America's national interest, and
chose a strategy. It was cold, excessive, brutal, and flawed. It could not save
the government in Saigon, and led to the Cambodian holocaust. These
were ghastly failures in a larger conflict in which America, at terrible cost,
nevertheless, finally prevailed.

NIXON'S MOST CONSISTENT claim of injury—that he was judged by a
double standard when it came to executive misconduct—was validated,
in spades, in that spring of 1975, as a Senate select committee chaired
by Senator Frank Church of Idaho began to hold hearings on the broad
range of abuses committed by the U.S. government during the Cold War.
There had been hints during the Watergate hearings, and charges made by
Nixon loyalists, about the iniquities of other presidents. The White House
taping systems, the political use of the IRS and the FBI, the black bag jobs
and wiretapping of reporters were just a few of the practices said to have
been used by Nixon's predecessors. Watergate took a lid off. In December
1974, Seymour Hersh and the *New York Times* revealed how the CIA had
violated its charter and spied on dissidents in America, and soon the country was treated to a series of revelations that vitiated what reverence still
existed for the presidency and other institutions of government.

Ford had named Nelson Rockefeller as his vice president and assigned
him to lead a presidential commission to investigate the Hersh disclosures,
but the material was politically scalding, and Rocky quickly yielded the
field to Church and his House and Senate colleagues. They unearthed
a cesspool. The CIA had built a computerized index of nearly 1.5 million suspect Americans. The FBI held more than half a million "domestic intelligence" files. Military intelligence agencies had collected 100,000
dossiers. The National Security Agency had intercepted millions of private telegrams and cables.

Those were the bold strokes. The FBI, the CIA, the IRS, the NSA, and
other agencies had also maintained "watch lists" targeting more than ten
thousand political activists and groups (the NAACP, Young Americans for
Freedom, the John Birch Society, the ACLU) for surveillance, disruption,
or discrediting. Included were civil rights leaders (Martin Luther King
Jr., Elijah Muhammad), feminist groups, entertainers and movie stars
(Joan Baez, Sammy Davis Jr.), writers (Norman Mailer, John Steinbeck),
businessmen, antiwar activists (Students for a Democratic Society, the

Vietnam Moratorium Committee), journalists (Jimmy Breslin, *Playboy* magazine), and political candidates (Hubert Humphrey, George Wallace, and Richard Nixon). Mail was opened. Political organizations were infiltrated by government agents. Telegrams and cables intercepted. Offices burglarized. Phones tapped. Microphones planted. The public got its first introduction to surveillance schemes and provocateur tactics like the CIA's Operation Chaos, the FBI's COINTELPRO program, the IRS "Special Services Staff," and the NSA's Shamrock and Minaret eavesdropping ops. The names of at least twenty-six thousand Americans, it turned out, were on a list for preventive detention—to be used by the FBI to round up and incarcerate U.S. citizens in the event of a "national emergency."

Some of the revelations were literally mind-blowing: the CIA had conducted drug experiments on random American citizens without their knowledge, in one case opening a string of brothels in San Francisco with two-way mirrors, where the courtesans administered LSD so the agency could observe its effects on unknowing patrons. The Kennedys had authorized the bugging of Martin Luther King Jr., and the FBI—as part of its relentless campaign to destroy the civil rights leader—had played the tapes of his extramarital liaisons to individuals around Washington.

Then there was Operation Mongoose—the CIA's assassination program. There were five major CIA plots, of which at least two—against Fidel Castro and Patrice Lumumba of the Congo—reached the operational stage. Three other foreign leaders—Rafael Trujillo in the Dominican Republic, Ngo Dinh Diem in South Vietnam, and General René Schneider in Chile—were killed in coups d'etat by American-supported forces. Both Kennedy and Eisenhower officials were involved in the plotting against Castro. Some of the details were resoundingly sordid. As the CIA was engaging the Mafia to help them kill Castro, John Kennedy was sharing a mistress with one of the Mob chieftains—Sam Giancana—who was then gunned down before he could testify to Congress. Before long, the reports of JFK's sexual license yanked the gauzy cloak from Camelot.

It put Watergate in a different context: it was part of a continuum, no sole breach of faith. "The sins of the fathers visiting upon their sons," Bryce Harlow said.

"The whole mess fell on Nixon," but "it had been endlessly building up until the White House was distorted and deformed. There had to be a reckoning," said Harlow. "The White House had proven too powerful, too irresponsible, too independent, too self-satisfied and arrogant. It felt too big; it acted too big. It was dangerous. It had to be restrained."

Nixon's predecessors earned the brunt of the vilification, but he did not escape unscathed. Tom Huston, the Nixon White House aide and author of the "Huston plan," was one of the first called to testify before the Church panel. Appearing contrite, he now analyzed the dangers of the path he had once suggested. "The risk," Huston said, was how the security agencies would invariably move "from the kid with a bomb to the kid with a picket sign, and from the kid with a picket sign to the kid with the bumper sticker." And thus was liberty eroded.

Nixon's innovation was that, frustrated by the aging J. Edgar Hoover's aversion to risk, he had brought the black bag boys in-house. There was no deniability: Liddy and Hunt left a trail to the West Wing, and the tapes revealed how the president had inspired their operations. Len Garment paraphrased Oscar Wilde: the problem with vice is not so much the sin, as the character of the people one meets to practice it. "Some president was going to get it: and it was Tricky Dicky," said Harlow. "And he did his part. He kicked the cannoneer when he had his head in the muzzle of the cannon."

THE CHURCH REPORT broke ground, as well, on the role that Nixon, Kissinger, and the CIA played in the overthrow of Salvador Allende in Chile. When Allende and his left-wing coalition won a plurality in the September 1970 election, Nixon ordered the CIA to intervene, and to foment a coup d'etat before the voting could be certified. "One in 10 chance perhaps, but save Chile! Worth spending. Not concerned risks involved," wrote CIA director Richard Helms in his notes of his meeting with the president.

To the CIA station in Chile went the order: "Parliamentary legerdemain has been discarded. Military solution is objective."

Years later, Helms recalled how "we were under pressure," from Kissinger and Nixon. "A hell of a lot of pressure."

In order to stop Allende, the agency's Chilean allies needed to overcome the opposition of the army commander, General Rene Schneider, who supported the constitution and the electoral process. The CIA furnished arms to its conspirators. But before the agency's men could "displace" him, Schneider was shot by other plotters. His murder backfired on his assassins, as it spurred the army to defend the constitution. To Nixon's dismay, Allende took office. When a claque of Chilean generals led by right-wing strongman Augusto Pinochet finally did overthrow Allende, in 1973, Nixon and Kissinger assured each other that—although hostile U.S. policies had targeted the Chilean economy—they had not played a direct role in the coup.

"Our hand doesn't show on this one," Nixon said.

"We didn't do it," Kissinger agreed.

BY THE SUMMER of 1975, Nixon was well enough to testify in several court cases that required his appearance. On June 23, the third anniversary of the smoking gun conversation, he welcomed a delegation of Watergate grand jurors and prosecutors who had traveled to California to question him. The transcript of that testimony, released in 2011, shows Nixon fully recovered, combative, and evasive—frustrating the prosecutors' efforts to ensnare him.

When the lead prosecutor, Henry Ruth, opened the questioning by reminding Nixon he could still be subject to prosecution for perjury, Nixon claimed to be wounded by the suggestion. He turned to the grand jurors and explained that the danger that "Mr. Ruth has so graciously pointed out" might require him to rely on the phrase "to the best of my recollection," which he otherwise abhorred. The government, Nixon noted, was still holding the records that could refresh his memory. The prosecutors had brought documents along, Ruth said. Well, that was "highly improper," Nixon shot back, "unless the purpose of this proceeding is to flash a document on the witness with the idea of entrapping him."

"Not at all," said Ruth, defensively.

"That is not your purpose?" Nixon taunted him.

THE INQUISITION WAS five minutes old, and Nixon had put Ruth on the defensive and lodged the suggestion in the jurors' minds that the prosecutor's use of documentary evidence was selective and unfair. The lawyers regrouped, and one of Ruth's assistants began to ask Nixon about the "sale" of ambassadorial posts. Was there not a political element in these appointments? Of course, said Nixon, "as has been the case in every presidency from the time this republic was founded." He happened to have statistics on hand which showed that his appointees were, percentage-wise, less political than those of previous presidents.

Again he turned to the jurors, with a winning intimacy. "Some of the things I will say will be with all of the bark off," Nixon confided. The problem with career diplomats is that they tend to be timid bureaucrats, afraid to take bold stands, he said: "Most of them are a bunch of eunuchs." That is one reason Nixon had searched for wealthy businessmen, or labor leaders—"the 'deese' and 'dose' guys," he called them—instead of elite Ivy League professionals.

"I point it out that—and this is in defense of not only my presidency, but of President Kennedy, President Johnson, President Eisenhower, President Truman, all of the others . . . that some of the very best ambassadors we have have been non-career ambassadors," Nixon said. Consider William Bullitt, who had served Franklin Roosevelt so ably in Russia and France: "He got his job because he had contributed a half million dollars to Mr. Roosevelt's campaign." And "Perle Mesta wasn't sent to Luxembourg [by Harry Truman] because she had big bosoms," Nixon winked. "Perle Mesta went to Luxembourg because she made a good contribution."

Why, to think any different would be un-American. "I don't want the record of this grand jury even to indicate that people of wealth, because they do make contributions, therefore should be banned from being ambassadors," he said. "The fact that an individual has proved himself on the American scene, has proved himself by legitimately building a great fortune, rather than being a disqualifier is a factor that can be considered."

At this point Ruth stepped in to save his overmatched assistant.

"Could I just say something here?" he asked.

"Sure," said Nixon. "In fact, you're in charge."

If his aides had broken the law, then surely Nixon would want to help the prosecutors pursue wrongdoing, Ruth said.

"I am quite aware of the fact that as far as anything I did . . . that because of the presidential pardon—which was terribly difficult for me to take, rather than stand there and fight it out—but I took it—that I can admit anything with impunity," Nixon said. But he would not be a rat, a snitch, an informer. "You are not going to use me to try to nail somebody else simply because I am not guilty of something," he said. "I am not going to . . . cooperate with you in a vendetta."

"I trust . . . that you are pursuing with the same tenacity . . . the over 150 charges of campaign violations that are in your files with regard to Democratic candidates," Nixon said.

"You gentlemen are making history, too," he told the prosecutor. "I have made mine; now you are making yours, and the question in the future will be: do you have a single standard, or did you have a double standard?"

"Think of your children. They are going to judge you in the pages of history," he told them.

—

RUTH QUESTIONED NIXON on a range of Watergate offenses: the eighteen-minute gap, the $100,000 gift from Howard Hughes, attempts to use the IRS to harass political opponents, the national security wiretaps, and more.

Eavesdropping was an old political trick, Nixon told the jurors. J. Edgar Hoover had told him, in 1968, how Lyndon Johnson ordered the FBI to bug Nixon's campaign plane during the Chennault affair. "There are differing versions as to whether they did or did not," Nixon said. "Mr. Hoover once told me that they did." As for the IRS, well, its agents had leaked information from his tax returns in 1952, 1962, and 1973. It didn't make up for what happened in Watergate, Nixon said, but it underscored his point about a double standard.

When he first heard about the eighteen-minute gap, Nixon said, he instantly saw how bad it looked. But he had not erased the tape, or covered up the act, or had aides like Rose Woods take a fall.

"Did I coach them? Did I tell them what to say? Did they ask me what to say? The answer is no," said Nixon. "I don't know how it happened."

"If you are interested in my view . . . it is very simple. It is that it was an accident," Nixon said. "I believe her totally," he said of Woods. "She would never lie to me."

That brought them to the Hughes donation and Nixon's assertion, during the "cancer on the presidency" talk with Dean, that "you could get a million dollars" to use as hush money. Just where, the prosecutor asked, would the money come from?

"I had a number of friends who are very wealthy, who if they believed it was a right kind of cause could have contributed a million dollars, and I think I could have gotten it within a matter of a week," Nixon told the jurors. "I felt . . . I had at least an obligation to see what kind of an option we had." In the end, he said, he had stood up to Hunt's blackmail: "We decided not to do it."

Nixon told the jurors how Bebe Rebozo had saved the $100,000 from Hughes for the 1974 congressional campaign, along with $100,000 from businessman Dwayne Andreas that Woods was holding for them in a White House safe. The $200,000 was eventually returned to the donors because "the heat was so great," Nixon said. It was not spent, as the Ervin committee suspected but he denied, on diamond earrings for Pat, or other Nixon family comforts. He had quizzed his brothers, Woods, and Rebozo personally, he said, and was satisfied that the committee's suspicion "was totally false."

The inquisitors brought up the IRS, and how Nixon had ordered Ehrlichman to have the agency investigate Larry O'Brien. In September 1971 the White House tapes had captured Nixon raging to Haldeman that all the Democrats' big donors—especially the "Jewish contributors . . . the cocksuckers"—should be audited.

"What I do recall is only a suggestion that the McGovern contributions might be checked," Nixon primly told the grand jury. He harped again about a double standard. "When nothing . . . developed out of the O'Brien investigation," he said, "instead of conducting two years of harassment against him, as they have against Mr. Rebozo . . . they [the IRS] simply dropped the matter."

Some of the tricks by Nixon's men were deplorable but—and he noted this proudly—George McGovern had never been shouted down by Nixon's agents. "It was not all that altruistic, to be quite honest," Nixon acknowledged. "My decision was based on the fact that I didn't think it would do any good. Why martyr the poor fellow? He was having enough trouble."

Yes, he had run the Plumbers from inside the White House, Nixon said. It was because Hoover "in his later years, became very sensitive about anything that happened in the press." He would have preferred to replace Hoover, but the old man knew too many of the capital's secrets, and might "pull down the temple with him, including me," Nixon told the jurors.

So Hunt and Liddy were hired.

SAN CLEMENTE WELCOMED Nixon back with equanimity. The surfers were happy to reclaim the beach, which had been shut by the Secret Service when he was president. Dog walkers and pot smokers sprawled on the sand below La Casa Pacifica at sunset, often with blankets and six-packs of beer. Dick joined the "Hole-in-One Club" at the local golf course.

Money was, momentarily, an issue. The transition funds allotted by Congress ran out in February 1975, and among those who had to depart was Ziegler, who had spent many hours in the previous six months as Nixon's senior aide and confidant. According to an accounting Nixon later gave British biographer Jonathan Aitken, the Nixons faced legal bills of over $750,000, tens of thousands of dollars in medical expenses, back taxes of $200,000, and what it cost to maintain a staff, offices, and the mansion at San Clemente. He was heavily mortgaged, could not practice law, and refused to accept the million-dollar honoraria that Ford, Reagan, Clinton, and other successors, breaking with long-standing tradition, would later collect from interest groups for making speeches. If he should die, Dick discovered, Pat would have to sell San Clemente.

Rebozo and Abplanalp helped by taking the Key Biscayne property off

Nixon's hands at a "generous" price, and he signed on as "adviser, a consultant or a provider of introductions" with various international tycoons, including Sir James Goldsmith of Great Britain, Ardeshir Zahedi of Iran, and Adnan Khashoggi of Saudi Arabia. But until these relationships bloomed, his $80,000 pension was what Nixon had to live on. At one point, in January 1975, he had just $500 in his bank account.

Yet by then Richard Milhous Nixon was one of the planet's most famous, recognizable figures. He had a story to sell, and as he regained his strength he began to dictate reminiscences. He hired a legendary talent agent—Irving "Swifty" Lazar—a goggle-glassed Angeleno known for a spectacular client list, which at times included Humphrey Bogart, Cary Grant, and Ernest Hemingway. A deal was concluded with Warner Books for a presidential memoir, and Lazar sold the rights to exclusive televised interviews as well. The winning bid came from David Frost, a British journalist and entertainer with a reputation as a bon vivant, for whom Nixon had neither enmity nor excessive regard. The contract with Frost was signed on August 9, 1975—the one-year anniversary of Nixon's resignation. He was to earn $600,000, plus a share of the profits.

Nixon slowly regained a sense of humor. When Lungren sent him a book proposal comparing his famous patient to the tortured King Lear, Nixon wrote back with a biblical reference that he thought was more apt: "The reference to Lear would be understood by only a few Shakespeare scholars. Job might be a better name."

THE FROST-NIXON INTERVIEWS, and publication of the memoirs, were delayed as the appeals filed by Nixon's former aides worked their way through the federal courts. The postponement turned out to be a boon for readers in that it allowed *The Final Days,* a blockbuster account of Nixon's last months in office by Bob Woodward and Carl Bernstein, to beat Nixon to print. Their book was a huge bestseller, stirring renewed interest in the ex-president, and requiring that he address such scenes as his late-night prayer session with Kissinger, which otherwise might have been left untold.

The Final Days was rough on Nixon and cruelly treated Pat, who, according to the authors' sources, had sought refuge in drink from a joyless marriage and the strain of Watergate. In July 1976, after reading the book, and while worrying about Dick's imminent disbarment, she suffered a stroke. "She suffered severe paralysis on her left side and considerable speech impairment as well. Coming as this did after having gone through the ordeal of the resignation and the merciless attacks by the media, no one would have been surprised if she had simply given up and become a permanent invalid," Nixon wrote a friend. "But she is not an ordinary person."

"I have nothing but utter contempt," he would say of Woodward and Bernstein. "I will never forgive them. Never."

Pat's recuperation required many arduous hours of therapy. Dick did what he could to help as he prepped for his encounter with Frost. Their twin confrontations with mortality, like other crises they had endured, seemed to bring the "two broken people," as Pat described them, together. "We've discovered in this time of crisis that we need each other," Dick said. They had reentered public life with a trip to China that winter. The voyage profoundly irritated Ford, who didn't need to have voters reminded of his association with the disgraced president on the eve of the New Hampshire primary. It was "the biggest 'Fuck You' I've ever seen in my life," said Ford's friend and White House photographer David Kennerly. "President Ford was not disagreeing with my assessment. . . . It was such a hideous thing to do." In China Nixon found further signs of time's passage: Zhou was dead, and Mao dying.

THE FROST-NIXON INTERVIEWS were conducted in a private home in swank, serene Monarch Bay, not far from Dana Point. Nixon was robust and confident, Frost recalled, though typically awkward in their personal exchanges. "Did you do any fornicating this weekend?" Nixon asked the interviewer. Frost opened with a question that was marginally unscrupulous, since both sides had agreed to save Watergate for a later show: "Why didn't you burn the tapes?"

Nixon parried with a tactic he would use throughout the interviews: he filibustered, with an exhaustive account of how Kennedy and Johnson had taped White House conversations before finally returning to his own decision to preserve the tapes. It would look bad if he burned the recordings, and he had mistakenly assumed they were privileged material. "I thought it would be an admission of guilt," said Nixon, and "I must admit in all candor that I didn't believe that they were going to come out."

It was an awful mistake, he realized now. "If the tapes had been destroyed," he told Frost, "I believe that it is likely that I would not have had to go through the agony of resignation. . . . It would have been well, looking at it from our standpoint, to destroy them all."

They went on to discuss the final days of his presidency and the Vietnam War. By the time the initial sessions were over, it was clear that Nixon was prevailing. Whenever Frost confronted him, Nixon would slide away with a self-promotional digression. James Reston Jr., one of the newsman's researchers, would come to call their quarry Proteus, after the shape-changing god of Greek mythology. It took until the seventh day, and a session on the national security state, for Nixon to let slip the first of the memorable comments for which the interviews would become famous. He defended the black bag burglaries, and the eavesdropping, and harassment of dissenters approved in the Huston plan with as strong and unadorned a statement of executive arrogance as any American president ever uttered.

"When the president does it, that means that it is not illegal," Nixon declared. Frost was near dumbstruck. "He had presented us with a stunning picture of his mind-set by advancing the proposition that the president has the inherent power to violate the law and, by doing so, to purge the entire transaction of its unlawful character," he would recall.

The pinnacle came on the eighth and ninth days of taping, when the two men turned to Watergate.

Nixon had agreed to do the interviews because he needed the money. But he also wanted to explain his behavior and make a case for the accomplishments of his presidency. He knew well that the public had no tolerance for further stonewalling. Yet he had not worked through, for Frost or his memoir, just how to phrase his admissions of misfeasance. He remained a proud, combative man. He believed he'd been a victim of a Democratic plot, a hateful press, and that irksome double standard. When Frost barked at Nixon like a district attorney, Nixon dug in and barked back. At that point Jack Brennan, Nixon's chief of staff, held up a sign, off camera, that caused Frost to call for a break in the proceedings.

"Let Him Talk," said Brennan's sign. During the time-out, he told Frost that Nixon was prepared to atone but would not do so in response to an interrogation. Changing tactics was a risk for Frost, who was finally scoring points after hours of being jerked around. But when the cameras rolled again, Frost tossed his clipboard to the floor and dramatically asked Nixon to clear his conscience. Admit that Watergate was "more than mistakes," Frost urged Nixon, or be "haunted for the rest of your life." What followed was magical television for the 40 million viewers who would watch it. For the next half hour, before reverting to his bitter, give-no-ground persona, Nixon was reflective and revealing.

He clung to a legal thread, insisting that, technically, he did not obstruct justice—but "these are legalisms," he admitted. He had lied, let down his countrymen, failed to prosecute the illegal behavior of his aides, joined in the cover-up, and "impeached myself" by resigning. "If they want me to get down and grovel on the floor, no. Never. Because I don't believe I should," he said. But "I brought myself down. I gave them a sword. And they stuck it in. And they twisted it with relish. And I guess if I'd been in their position, I'd have done the same thing."

NIXON'S ADMISSION WAS, in the jargon of his White House, a modified limited hang-out. Its power was less in what he said than in the image—*I gave them a sword*—he used to say it. It would take a redoubtable young woman by the name of Diane Sawyer to get him to enumerate his crimes. She had worked in the White House press office and followed him to San Clemente, and been given the task of helping Nixon frame the Watergate chapters for his memoirs. Sawyer armed herself with the evidence and spent long, intense hours in metaphysical combat with her boss—showing the skills that would later propel her to a standout career as a broadcast journalist. They would emerge from the sessions, which Nixon came to dread, both spent and exhausted. Shame was an element. "How can I face Mrs. Nixon if I have to admit this?" he would ask.

Sawyer and Frank Gannon, the lead researcher and co-creator of *RN: The Memoirs of Richard Nixon*, got Proteus to divulge. In his public statements, Nixon had always claimed that "the sole motive for calling in the CIA had been national security." But the June 23 tape proved, he now admitted, that "there was no doubt . . . that we had been talking about political implications that morning."

"Unless we could find some way to limit the investigation the trail would lead directly" to CREEP, Nixon wrote. "If the CIA would deflect the FBI from Hunt, they would thereby protect us. . . . I told Haldeman to say . . . that they should call the FBI in and say that for the sake of the country they should go no further into this case."

"I . . . talked to Colson about clemency," Nixon added. "I too had suspected Magruder was not telling the truth, but I had done nothing about my suspicions; I had been aware that support funds were going to the defendants; and on March 21 [in the cancer-on-the-presidency talk with John Dean] I had even contemplated paying blackmail."

"I had become deeply entangled in the complicated mesh of decisions, inactions, misunderstandings and conflicting motivations that comprised the Watergate cover-up," he wrote. "Instead of exerting presidential leadership aimed at uncovering the cover up, I embarked upon an increasingly desperate search for ways to limit the damage."

Or, as Nixon said in a 1978 speaking engagement at the Oxford Union: "*Mea culpa.*"

RN, for which Nixon received a $2.5 million advance, is one of the better presidential memoirs. It captured its writer's voice, and was reasonably candid (if anything, there is too much detail about Watergate), its tone consistent with its evocative, Dickensian opening line: "I was born in a house my father built." It rose, justifiably, up the bestseller lists in the summer of 1978.

"COURSE I'M RESPECTABLE, I'm old," said the dastardly power broker Noah Cross in Robert Towne's screenplay for *Chinatown,* one of several brilliant motion pictures with themes of corruption inspired by Watergate and its times. "Politicians, ugly buildings and whores all get respectable if they last long enough."

Nixon lasted for another twenty years after leaving the White House—long enough to get respectable.

The former president wrote nine books after leaving office, traveled widely, circulated his political insights among his loyal followers and friends, and took advantage of the conservative restoration led by Ronald Reagan to resume the role of a foreign affairs savant, peppering the White House with advice during several administrations.

Reagan was grateful, but not others whom Nixon counseled. "Bush, Clinton, Dole and Yeltsin had all been targets of Nixon's direct advice on Russia. None had taken significant action based upon it," his foreign policy aide, Monica Crowley, recalled. "That his suggestions had gone unheeded inspired rage, disappointment and frustration."

"He was *wrong,*" explained Reagan's secretary of state, George Shultz, recalling Nixon's excessive assessments—*Gorbachev . . . is the most powerful Soviet leader since Stalin. . . . The Soviet military is leaner, but stronger. . . . Beneath the velvet glove he always wears there is a steel fist*—of the Soviet threat in the months before the collapse of the Soviet Union.

Like many who served with Nixon, Shultz had conflicting feelings about the former president, recalling brave acts and small kindnesses as well as venal behavior until, at last, the ex-Marine declared, "He was like the little girl in the poem." Drawing himself up like a schoolboy, Shultz recited the lines from Longfellow:

There was a little girl,
And she had a little curl
Right in the middle of her forehead.
When she was good
She was very, very good
And when she was bad she was horrid.

The Nixons ended their California years in 1980, after buying a brownstone on the Upper East Side of Manhattan whose backyard abutted that of an old nemesis, Arthur Schlesinger Jr. On Halloween, the stone-faced Secret Service agents handed candy to the historian's son Robert, who went trick-or-treating in a Nixon mask. Their last dinner guests, before leaving California, were a gay former aide and the aide's gay partner. If the country could not move beyond the cultural division of the 1960s, Richard Nixon could.

In 1981 the Nixons moved to a sprawling home in Saddle River, New Jersey. They went out to restaurants and sporting events, hosted the neighborhood children at Halloween, and mixed with the crowds at Radio City and Rockefeller Center during the Christmas holidays. There were no ugly incidents, and the couple gave up their Secret Service protection. To Pat's dismay, Dick insisted on adopting a stray, ill-mannered mutt. He named it Brownie.

Before leaving San Clemente, Pat had posed for her official White House portrait. If for no other reason, Julie told her, it would deny their enemies another victory. "Why not?" Pat said matter-of-factly. "They won, didn't they?" Of Washington and Watergate, she told the artist, "It was completely terrible."

The move put the Nixons back on the East Coast with their daughters and grandchildren. It also figured into his plans for rehabilitation—a matter of significant interest to Nixon and his old antagonists in the media. He invited reporters and editors to his home for dinner parties, in which he'd treat them to his famous martinis or daiquiris, sit himself at the head of the table, and cap the evening with well-honed commentary on American and international politics.

"When Nixon was President and Leader of the Free World we had troubles of our own here in the United States. We, too, had so-called student riots, protests, anarchy in the streets of Washington," he told a delegation of Chinese leaders a few weeks after the regime had crushed demonstrators in Tiananmen Square. "When Nixon was President and

Leader of the Free World, he found that *firmness paid.* You tell them that."

Nixon was protective of the American relationship with China, and the right man for Bush to delegate to mend and maintain things after the Tiananmen crackdown. His trip to Beijing in the fall of 1989 was his last meaningful contribution to world affairs. Nixon told the Chinese that, while the rapprochement would survive, Americans had been shocked by the brutality they witnessed on their television sets. "Another tragedy would be the death of a relationship," he warned.

In 1993 Nixon made his final trip to China, accompanied by his friends Rebozo and Abplanalp. He lingered in the guesthouse, and the Great Hall of the People, where he had made history twenty-one years before. "If Mao could see China now—my God, he's probably rolling in his grave!" he said. His latest Lazarus act paid dividends, most memorably when he was featured on the cover of *Newsweek* with the headline HE'S BACK: THE REHABILITATION OF RICHARD NIXON. Inside, he was christened THE SAGE OF SADDLE RIVER.

So HE LABORED, grinding out books; sharing his insights on television talk shows; overcoming his distaste for flying to make four journeys to China and ten trips to Russia, keeping up with world leaders like Mikhail Gorbachev, Boris Yeltsin, Deng Xiaoping. "I do not consider myself to be a legitimate author as writing is such an ordeal for me," he wrote Julian Amery, an MP in London, with whom he shared his admiration ("I consider *War and Peace* to be the greatest novel ever written") for Tolstoy. "My books will pass muster only because of their substance and not because of their literary quality."

Seeing how Reagan suffered from the distressing effects of senescence, Nixon stepped up a regime of mental exercises, which he had added to his daily early-morning walk and disciplined hours as a wordsmith. He was convinced that his longtime foes in the academy would malign him and fought a determined legal battle to keep his White House tapes and papers out of their hands. He once put the cost of his legal bills, in his twenty-year exile, at $2 million. After winning one round in an appellate court, he sat down at the piano and banged out an exultant "Happy Days Are Here Again."

"History will treat you well," Kissinger had told him, in their last days at the White House. "It depends who writes the history," Nixon replied. But his reputation could only improve. Though they suffered from the lack of primary sources—most notably the tapes—balanced biographies by Tom Wicker, Stephen Ambrose, Herbert Parmet, and Aitken were all published during Nixon's lifetime.

Washington is a jaundiced town. Nixon was welcomed back to the Capitol for Hubert Humphrey's funeral in 1978, and to a state dinner honoring Deng at the Carter White House in 1979. He was visibly proud to join Ford and Carter in 1981 and represent the United States at the rites for the assassinated Anwar Sadat. The trinity inspired Senator Bob Dole's arch description, at a Gridiron dinner, of the three former presidents as: "See no evil. Hear no evil. And evil."

"As soon as we got into the plane, Nixon was his old self again, trying to manipulate everybody and everything, dropping poisonous remarks, doing his best to set people against each other," Kissinger recalled. Later, when he and Ford were alone, Ford said: "Sometimes I wish I had never pardoned that son of a bitch." Americans named airports after Nixon's Republican successors, but the best he got was a gym in Kentucky and a stretch of highway in Yorba Linda.

Pat, at least, had an elementary school named after her. As a gift, she gave it a wishing well.

ON FATHER'S DAY in 1983, Julie gave her dad a copy of Paul Johnson's history of the twentieth century, *Modern Times*, which, in framing the century's great struggles as a battle between Western democracies and "gangster statesmen" of both left and right, had many kind things to say about the Nixon presidency. It had taken less than a decade for a noted historian to apply such perspective. "I only wish some of our American intellectuals were as fair in their appraisals of conservative leaders," Nixon wrote his friend Jack Drown. In fact, conservatism was triumphing—without him. The Reagan presidency would mark an end to the Nixon and Watergate— even the Cold War—eras in American history. With his moderate views on abortion, gun control, and homosexuality, Nixon was too liberal for the new right, which now had a hero who was all that Nixon was not—a charming, charismatic true believer. And the left, confronted by this forceful adversary, forgot their old piñata. Reagan's success left Nixon worse off than despised; he was now irrelevant.

The last years of his life saw Nixon struggling, somewhat pitiably, for attention. The score-settling material about Watergate in his 1990 book, *In the Arena,* left it the worst of his three memoirs. Two years later, as

George Bush was conducting an arduous reelection campaign, Nixon undermined his old aide with an op-ed piece that branded the administration's foreign policy as "pathetically inadequate."

It was a crude message from Nixon that, one way or another, attention must be paid. "If Bush wants distance from me, I'll give it to him," he swore. "Let them lose!"

Bush retaliated in 2013, when he released a volume of letters, including one long, perceptive note to his sons, written in the Watergate summer of 1974, about the "abysmal amorality" of the Nixon presidency and Nixon's "enormous" insecurities and resentments. "I feel battered and disillusioned," Bush told his sons. "I feel betrayed . . . by those who did wrong and tracked corruption and institutional subversion into that beautiful White House."

In private, Nixon derided Carter as a hypocrite, Ford and Reagan as intellectual lightweights, and Bush as lacking strength. For the draft-dodging, pot-smoking McGovernite Bill Clinton and his wife, Hillary—who had served on the Judiciary Committee staff during the impeachment hearings—Nixon wished all kinds of ills. "I am a square," Nixon told Monica Crowley, drawing a square in the air with his forefingers. "My values are traditional: God, country, family. I am absolutely opposed to the destruction of those values that came about during the Vietnam era. Free love, drugs, tearing down your country, denying God, selfishness and indulgence—everything I despise took root when I was president and there was so little I could do to stop it. . . . I represented everything they were trying to overthrow."

NIXON NEVER LEARNED that Mark Felt, the number two official at the FBI during Watergate, was the mysterious source Deep Throat—but he always had suspected that Felt was one of those leaking damaging information. It did not stop him from testifying on Felt's behalf when the G-man was prosecuted for ordering break-ins during the FBI's campaign against the violent Weather Underground. And when Felt ultimately survived the ordeal (he was pardoned by Reagan) Nixon sent him a bottle of champagne. Nixon showed more care and kindness when Republican campaign operative Lee Atwater was stricken by a brain tumor; Nixon came to his sickroom and, seeing the younger man's torment and debility, kept up both ends of the conversation.

The fall of the Soviet Union and the opening of the old Soviet archives in Moscow led to hasty news stories, soon corrected, alleging that Alger Hiss was innocent. "The handling of the Hiss 'exoneration' story by the prestige media has been as shockingly biased as the coverage of the case was 45 years ago," Nixon wrote Sam Tanenhaus, the biographer of Whittaker Chambers. The networks gave "massive" coverage to the initial report, and none when it was retracted. The *New York Times* "printed the retraction back with the corset ads," Nixon grumbled.

JULIE'S AND TRICIA'S marriages proved sturdy. The sunset days were generous. Grandchildren delighted Pat, and Dick. "In the years ahead you will have many happy moments, but in life you must expect some disappointments and sadness. At such times you will always be sustained by the fact that so many people love you very much," Nixon wrote his granddaughter Jennie Eisenhower on the day of her birth in 1978. "We all look forward to the excitement of watching you grow up into a lovely young lady. Your Great Grandfather, President Eisenhower, had the great gift of being able to light up a room with his smile. My fondest wish, which I know will come true, is that you will have that same gift."

Through peripatetic activity, he staved off the dread of infirmity or death unless something—Reagan's illness, the suicide of Clinton White House aide Vince Foster, the demise of John Connally—left him shaken and morose. He weathered a painful bout of shingles and surgery for prostate and cardiac troubles. His heart fibrillation forced him to give up alcohol. ("God, get a second opinion," Rebozo told him.) The years of smoking caught up with Pat, who suffered from emphysema and arthritis. As a concession to advancing age and Pat's condition they moved to a more manageable three-story town house with an elevator, in nearby Park Ridge in 1990.

Pat was a trouper, and a fighter—insisting that she would get better despite the grim news that cancer had joined her list of maladies. The first months of 1993 were terribly painful for Dick, as the love and great strength of his life slipped away. "Nixon made no attempt to conceal his despair. Sadness crept into everything he did and every word he spoke," Crowley wrote. "The end of her life was upon him, and he found her quiet suffering and the prospect of going through the rest of his own life unbearable."

On June 21, Nixon received word at his office that Pat now faced her final hours. Terrified, he begged Crowley to drive him through the old Saddle River neighborhood, with its happier memories, as he tried to compose himself. "I can't go home," he said. "I can't go home. Not yet."

As Pat clung to life that night, she seemed to perk up when she heard his voice. So he kept talking, telling her how much she was loved by her family, her country, the world. She smiled. He kissed her on the forehead. She died.

He was devastated. The pain in his face, in the photographs from the funeral, is difficult to view. She was buried in the plot they had chosen: in the garden of Dick's boyhood home, on the grounds of his presidential library. Nixon was furious at the Clintons, who did not attend the rites.

CROWLEY CAUGHT NIXON in a contemplative mood that fall. "As I look back, although it has been a rough ride, it has been worthwhile," he told her. "I might not want to do it again, but I wouldn't have missed it. . . . I have lived for a purpose and for the most part achieved it."

One day in early 1994, Nixon paid a visit to his former aide Don Rumsfeld. It was a far-ranging conversation, and Nixon made several predictions about the approaching millennium, which Rumsfeld recorded in his notes.

The twenty-first century would be marked by technological advancement and great progress in the war on poverty and hunger, Nixon said. The threat of a superpower showdown, with a planet-killing nuclear exchange, had ebbed. But without American leadership, there could well be outbreaks of smaller conflicts, he told Rumsfeld. And unless the world acted to stop nuclear proliferation, one or more cities could suffer the fate of Hiroshima. It was a mixed bag of hope and realism. He left Rumsfeld with a little-known quote from Churchill's Iron Curtain speech.

"The earth is a generous mother," Nixon said. "She will provide in plentiful abundance food for all her children if they will but cultivate her soil in justice, and peace."

NIXON THOUGHT HE had another decade. He was brooding about history, and great men, and peace—and working on another book—when, on an April evening in 1994, sitting in the fading sun, he suffered a stroke. The symptoms—paralysis, blindness, muddled speech—were doubtless as terrifying as those suffered by Ike so many years before. There was hope he could recover, but he faltered and slipped into a coma. He died on a Friday night, April 22, 1994, at the age of eighty-one.

His daughters chose his epitaph, to be carved into his tombstone, there in the backyard of the little house that Frank had built, on the lemon farm in Yorba Linda. It is a line from his first inaugural address. "The greatest honor history can bestow is the title of peacemaker," it says. He had come so long a way, chasing the whistles of trains in the night, and never so far at all.

A biography of Richard Nixon has much to tell.

Nixon's life spanned the Depression, World War II, and the Cold War. His early campaign tactics broke trail for McCarthyism. He was on the Republican Party's national ticket five times between 1952 and 1972, and his 1968 comeback campaign is justly storied—in a year that also saw the Tet Offensive in Vietnam, the abdication of Lyndon Johnson, the candidacies of George Wallace and Eugene McCarthy, the assassinations of Robert Kennedy and Martin Luther King Jr., and the riots at the Democratic convention in Chicago.

The five and a half years of his presidency were dominated by war in Southeast Asia and the Middle East, racial strife, antiwar protests at home, and the Watergate scandal. Yet amid partisan wrangling, he joined with the Democratic Congress and the federal judiciary to integrate southern schools, safeguard the environment, and meet other noble ends. He signed strategic arms treaties with the Soviet Union. And, of course, he went to China.

Stephen Ambrose, writing during Nixon's lifetime, took three volumes to tell the story of the thirty-seventh president. And he did not have access to any but a few of the thirty-seven hundred hours of White House tape recordings, or the four hundred oral history interviews of Nixon's friends and family members conducted by Whittier College, or Nixon's grand jury testimony from the Alger Hiss and Watergate cases, or H. R. Haldeman's diaries, or the transcriptions of Henry Kissinger's White House telephone conversations—all of which have since been opened to scholars.

Nor could Ambrose tap such treasures of the Nixon presidential library as the 150 oral history interviews conducted in the past decade with the leading aides and figures of his presidency, or Pat Nixon's correspondence with her friend Helene Drown, or Herman Perry's accounts of the Nixon family finances and the 1946 congressional campaign, or Aylett Cotton's diary of the 1952 Republican convention. The "contested" and "returned" segments of the White House Special Files—which Nixon and his legal team battled for decades to keep private—were not made public until 2007, and have yielded illuminating details for this book, especially on the 1968 "southern strategy" and his actions in the "Chennault affair."

Next year brings the fiftieth anniversary of the tumultuous 1968 election, and Nixon's ascension to the presidency. The immense scope of the recent releases, the centrality of Nixon's career to postwar political history, and the passions he still engenders have led scholars like Melvin Small to call for a single-volume biography that integrates all the new material—and prompted others, like David Greenberg, to wonder if it is even possible. "Richard Nixon still remains one of the most elusive for biographers," professor Iwan Morgan wrote in 2011, in Small's atlas, *A Companion to Richard M. Nixon*. "The absence of anything approaching a definitive biography of Nixon stands in marked contrast to those gracing the lives of most of his significant predecessors." When my editors at Doubleday suggested, six years ago, that I pursue this leviathan, I worried, more than a little, that I might end up like the captain and crew of the *Pequod*. But I, only, do not tell this story. Many good hands helped.

I dedicated my last book to my children, Caitlin and John, and this one to my sister Marjorie and brother Craig. But they know, as I do, that only the love of Catharina, my wife, makes any of this possible.

Two young men helped me in my research. My son John took time from his studies to mine the libraries at Harvard. And Dr. Brian Robertson, a thoughtful scholar of the Vietnam War, served as my guide to the foreign policy files of the Nixon presidential library.

For their friendship and support, I thank the Anspach, Donadio, and Kupka clans, Steve Kurkjian, Peter Gosselin, and Caledonia Kearns.

Irwin Gellman, a dean of Nixon scholars, read the manuscript, and helped me enlist Jeffrey Kimball and David Nichols as readers. These learned, generous men offered expert advice on Vietnam, civil rights, and other issues. Mark Feeney, author of *Nixon at the Movies*, and journalist Jack Torry—two more experts on the life of Richard Nixon—helped shape my thinking and gave me thoughtful critiques of the early drafts. Geoff Shephard, a Nixon White House veteran, read (and contested) my take on Watergate. Frank Gannon served Nixon as a White House fellow and a member of his staff in exile, and joined in the writing of *RN*, the former president's memoir. Like the others, he read the manuscript and offered valuable corrections, arguments, and suggestions. I am grateful for all of this input. In the end, any errors that remain, of fact or reasoning, are mine alone.

Almost twenty-five years ago, agent David Black dared me to chase a dream. As my friend and literary representative, he has been with me each step of the way, and I thank him once again. For more than a decade, the good folks at Doubleday have been handing me checks and telling me to come back in a few years with a book. For taking that leap of faith, and entrusting me with their guidance, time, and resources, I am indebted to senior editor Kristine Puopolo and editor in chief Bill Thomas. On our voyage in search of Richard Nixon, Kris and I have been ably aided by associate editor Dan Meyer, senior production editor Nora Reichard, creative director John Fontana, and publicist Victoria Chow.

Thanks go, as well, to George Mitrovitch, Greg Moore, Sandy Johnson, Ron Fournier, Susan Glasser, Rob Schlesinger, Bob Cohn, David Maraniss, Mike Barnicle, Diane Rehm, Gerry O'Neill, Jon Sawyer, Charles Lewis, Curtis Wilkie, David Shribman, Jim Toedtman, William Crawley, the folks at C-SPAN, the Biographers International Organization, and James Kitfield and the Center for the Study of the Presidency & Congress for their rewarding assignments, and to the Hoover Institution at Stanford University for a research fellowship.

Edward Nixon, the president's brother, invited me to visit him at his home outside Seattle. No interview was more valuable. Among the old Nixon hands who honored my request to share their memories, I owe thanks to George Shultz, Mel Laird, Alan Greenspan, Dwight Chapin, Pat Buchanan, Fred Malek, Henry Cashen, Morton Halperin, Frank Gannon, Bob Bostock, Roger Stone, and Geoff Shephard. Before taking on this particular challenge, I spent hours in conversation with John Kerry and Gary Hart about the Nixon era, spoke with John McCain about Vietnam, interviewed Richard Goodwin about the sixties, and quizzed Richard Ben-Veniste about Watergate and Ron Liebman about Spiro Agnew. I shamelessly eavesdropped, at a forum on Watergate at which I was a panelist, on the lunchtime conversation between Alexander Butterfield and Daniel Ellsberg, and sat down over coffee with my neighbor, John Haynes, to discuss the Hiss case, Cold War espionage, and McCarthyism. Julie Nixon Eisenhower patiently answered several urgent e-mailed queries that I sent her, shared family photographs, and allowed me to quote from her correspondence with Jonathan Aitken. And I had the good fortune, before they died, of talking with Leonard Garment, Bob Healy, Edward Kennedy, Dick Donahue, Don Edwards, Stanley Kutler, Jack Anderson, Ben Bradlee, James Cannon, David Cohen, Chuck Colson, Mary McGrory, William Gibbons, Robert Drinan, Jerry Zeifman, Bill Sutton, Ted Sorensen, Jerome Grossman, Neil MacNeil, Jim Wright, Arthur Schlesinger Jr., Dave Powers, John Ehrlichman, Elliot Richardson, and Gerald Ford about events reported here.

Bob Woodward shared his expertise with me, as did authors and biographers Tim Naftali, Will Swift, Evan Thomas, Roger Morris, Larry Harnisch, Ken Hughes, James Reston Jr., Dan Moldea, and Chris Tudda. I owe a special thanks to Irwin Gellman, James Rosen, Len Colodny, Herbert Parmet, Ray Locker, Joseph Dmohowski, and Jonathan Aitken, who opened up their files for me. Robert Caro encouraged me and his work served as a paragon; I'll not forget an evening swapping stories about Lyndon Johnson and Richard Nixon at a Tex-Mex restaurant in Austin with Bob and his bride, Ina. Among the many journalists who covered Richard Nixon, and helped me to understand him, I owe special thanks to Martin Nolan, Jimmy Breslin, Adam Clymer, Jim Doyle, Jules Witcover, and Mark Shields. The transcripts of my interviews will be deposited with my papers at the University of Virginia.

Winston Lord directed me to the collection of thorough, candid oral histories on Nixon-era foreign affairs that he and his colleagues contributed to the Association for Diplomatic Studies and Training. I attended several Nixon Legacy Forums conducted by the Richard Nixon Foundation at the National Archives, and listened as Nixon administration veterans like Lord, Don Hughes, Bobbie Kilberg, Richard Allen, Robert McFarlane, John Lehman, Richard Solomon, John Negroponte, Richard Smyser, Fred Fielding, Jack Brennan, Tom Korologos, Lee Huebner, and Ken Khachigian reminisced. Many agreed to take a question or two afterward, as did Egil "Bud" Krogh, who talked with me about Elvis and ethics at a fortieth anniversary gathering of Watergate veterans at the Watergate office building, where I toured the former Democratic National Committee offices, looked across at the old Howard Johnson's building, and found I was standing beside Carl Bernstein.

A Nixon biographer has an unparalleled resource in the White House tape recordings, a few of which surfaced during Watergate and the trials that followed, but most of which were kept from the public until the late Stanley Kutler and Public Citizen went to court, and triumphed in 1996. The initial review, and periodic releasing, of the thirty-seven hundred hours of tapes was not completed until 2013, though several hundred hours of classified or personal material remains closed. Kutler's initial book of transcripts—*Abuse of Power: The New Nixon Tapes*—came out in 1997, and two excellent volumes by professors Luke Nichter and Douglas

Brinkley—*The Nixon Tapes* and *The Nixon Tapes, 1973*—were published in 2014 and 2015. The Nixon presidential library, Luke Nichter's website—www.nixontapes.org—and the Miller Center of Public Affairs at the University of Virginia offer the finest online collections of tapes and transcripts.

At the Nixon presidential library, in Yorba Linda, I profited from the expert guidance of Director Michael Ellzey, Pamla Eisenberg, Carla Braswell, Jon Fletcher, Meghan Lee-Parker, Ryan Pettigrew, Craig Ellefson, Jason Schultz, Gregory Cumming, Abigail Malangone, Olivia Anastasiadis, and Dorissa Martinez. Jonathan Movroydis was my patient and courteous contact at the Richard Nixon Foundation, and Joe Dmohowski was equally helpful at Whittier College. The Gerald Ford, Franklin Roosevelt, John F. Kennedy, Harry Truman, Lyndon Johnson, Herbert Hoover, and Dwight Eisenhower presidential libraries are national treasures—as, of course, is the Library of Congress—and I thank the archivists at all these institutions for their help on this project.

My research also took me to UCLA; Claremont College; California State Polytechnic University in Pomona; the University of California at Berkeley; Stanford University; the University of Southern California; the Hoover Institution; the California State Archives; Scripps College; the New York Public Library; Boston University; Boston College; Harvard University; the National Archives; Columbia University; Drew University; California State University, Fullerton; the University of Utah; Princeton University; the University of North Carolina; the University of Texas; the University of Virginia; Kent State University; Whittier College; Georgetown University; and Bowdoin College. I thank them all.

There are several helpful online collections for Nixon scholars. The U.S. State Department's Foreign Relations of the United States series was an invaluable aid. So was the American Presidency Project, with its online collection of the public papers of the presidents, at the University of California, Santa Barbara. The Central Intelligence Agency and the Federal Bureau of Investigation allow electronic access to many Nixon-era documents and reports. The National Security Archive has fought the good fight against mindless secrecy laws for many years. And the University of Georgia has kindly posted the Nixon-Gannon interviews. The private benefactors and institutional advocates who champion this constructive, worthy use of the Internet should know how I and other scholars appreciate them.

Notes

ABBREVIATIONS IN NOTES
AP: Associated Press Archives
ASP: Arthur Schlesinger Papers, New York Public Library
Berkeley: Bancroft Library, University of California, Berkeley
BKP: Bela Kornitzer Papers, Drew University
BU: Boston University
CIA: Central Intelligence Agency
CSA: California State Archives, Sacramento
CSUF: California State University, Fullerton
DDEL: Dwight D. Eisenhower Presidential Library
DDEP: *The Papers of Dwight David Eisenhower,* ed. Alfred D. Chandler Jr., Stephen E.
    Ambrose, Louis Galambos, Daun van Ee, Joseph P. Hobbs, Elizabeth S. Hughes, and
    others, Johns Hopkins University Press
FBI: Federal Bureau of Investigation archives
FD: Foreign Affairs Oral History Program, Association for Diplomatic Studies and
    Training (ADST)
FDR: Franklin D. Roosevelt Presidential Library and Museum
FMB: Fawn McKay Brodie papers, University of Utah
FRUS: *Foreign Relations of the United States,* Office of the Historian, U.S. Department of
    State
GFF: Gerald R. Ford Presidential Foundation
GFL: Gerald R. Ford Presidential Library and Museum
HI: Hoover Institution, Stanford University
HJC: House Judiciary Committee
Hofstra: "Richard Nixon: A Retrospective on His Presidency," November 19–21, 1987,
    Hofstra University
HRH diary: H. R. Haldeman Diaries, Richard Nixon Presidential Library and Museum
HST: Harry S. Truman Library and Museum
HUAC: House Un-American Activities Committee
JFK: John F. Kennedy Presidential Library and Museum
JNE, *Pat:* Julie Nixon Eisenhower, *Pat Nixon*
LAT: Los Angeles Times
LBJ: Lyndon Baines Johnson Library and Museum
LOC: Library of Congress
NARA: National Archives and Records Administration
Nixon-Gannon: Nixon-Gannon interviews, University of Georgia
NSA: National Security Archive, George Washington University
NYHT: New York Herald Tribune
NYT: The New York Times

OH: oral history
PPP: Public Papers of the President, American Presidency Project, University of California, Santa Barbara
RNL: Richard Nixon Presidential Library and Museum
SEP: Saturday Evening Post
SSC: Select Committee on Presidential Campaign Activities, U.S. Senate (Watergate Committee)
Strober: Deborah H. Strober and Gerald S. Strober, *The Nixon Presidency: An Oral History of the Era*
Thompson: *The Nixon Presidency,* ed. Kenneth W. Thompson, Miller Center, University of Virginia
Warren project: *Richard M. Nixon in the Warren Era,* Earl Warren Era Project, University of California, Berkeley
WB: The Woodward and Bernstein Watergate Papers, University of Texas
WDN: Whittier Daily News
Whittier: Whittier College
WHSF-R: White House Special Files, Nixon Presidential Returned Materials Collection, Richard Nixon Presidential Library and Museum
WHSF-RC: White House Special Files, Nixon Presidential Returned Materials Collection: Contested Materials, Richard Nixon Presidential Library and Museum
WP: The Washington Post
WSPF: Records of the Watergate Special Prosecution Force, National Archives

CHAPTER 1: THE DRAGON SLAYER

2   "Somebody might remember": John Renneburg OH, John Buckley OH, Whittier; John Renneburg OH, University of Baltimore; Nixon-Gannon; Baltimore *Sun*, Jan. 26, 2008; Nixon to Jim Stewart, Oct. 22, 1945, RNL; *Time*, July 30, Aug. 20, 1945; Ken Burns and Lynn Novick, *The War,* PBS, 2007.

2   Representative Jerry Voorhis: Jerry Voorhis papers and Voorhis OH, Claremont College.

3   Richard Nixon—Dick, to his friends: Hubert Perry, interview with author; Nixon-Gannon; Frederick Albrink OH, Margaretha Lohmann OH, Whittier.

3   "He looked so different": Pat to "Folks," undated 1942, RNL. After five weeks at officer training school in Rhode Island, Dick was given a weekend leave. Pat met him in New York City, where they dined at the Rainbow Room. Garry Wills, *Nixon Agonistes: The Crisis of the Self-Made Man* (Boston: Houghton Mifflin, 1969).

3   He wasn't easy to like: "I'm not a very lovable man," Nixon told David Frost. See Frost-Nixon transcripts, RNL.

3   "sour puss brother": Nixon to Laurene Mae Nixon, Aug. 4, 1943, RNL. The remembrances of those who knew him as a boy and a young man are filled with comments about Richard's "distance." See oral histories by Frances King, Marshall Clow, Anne Gillmore, George Irving, Alice Nixon Linton, Jo Marcelle, Rose Olive Marshburn, and Evlyn Dorn, Whittier; Herman and Angela Smith Brannon OH, CSUF. For Nixon's early life see Roger Morris, *Richard Milhous Nixon: The Rise of an American Politician* (New York: Holt, 1990), Richard Nixon, *RN: The Memoirs of Richard Nixon* (New York: Grosset & Dunlap, 1978), and Irwin Gellman, *The Contender* (New York: Free Press, 1999). Mark Feeney, in *Nixon at the Movies: A Book About Belief* (Chicago: University of Chicago Press, 2004), winningly uses Nixon's fondness for motion pictures as a means of exploring his "fundamental yearning and loneliness."

4   He was a striver: Donald Jackson, "Coming of Age in America," unpublished manuscript, Aug. 28, 1970; Duke University letter to Nixon, Apr. 3, 1934, Thomas Evans unpublished memoir, Aitken papers, RNL. Nixon's papers also include an application for a

scholarship to Harvard Law School, with notes indicating that Dick applied for financial help in the spring of 1934, claiming that his father was "totally disabled at present."

4 "not only fun, he was joyous": Ola Florence Jobe OH, Whittier; Joseph Hiatt OH, Whittier; Raymond Burbank OH, Martha Cato OH, Wilma Funk OH, CSUF.

5 bright, left-leaning Jewish attorneys: "Some Jews, but not too bad," Nixon reported to his law partner, Tom Bewley, immediately after arriving at OPA. Nixon to Bewley, "Sunday Morning," Jan. 1943, RNL. For Nixon and anti-Semitism, see the notes to chapter 22, page 654.

5 "crying his heart out": Harrison to Mendall, Dec. 5, 1942, RNL.

5 Dick should leave the fighting: Bill Ryan to Pat, undated, 1942, RNL. "His main ambition was to get out in the Pacific where the fighting was," said Dorris Gurley, his commanding office in Iowa. "That's what his main purpose in life at Ottumwa was." Dick to his parents, June 1941, RNL; oral histories by Charles Cooper, Benjamin Horack, Edith Holt, Alyce Koch, Ralph Burnight, and Dorris Gurley, Whittier; *Collier's*, July 9, 1954; William Butler Yeats, "When You Are Old."

5 In the South Pacific: *Life*, Nov. 6, 1970. Nixon to Pat, Jan. 28, 1944, and Nixon World War II military record, J. Paull Marshall interview by Kornitzer, RNL; Hollis Dole OH, James Stewart OH, Whittier.

6 *The most virtuous hearts:* The "hell's fire" quote appears in an issue of *Collier's* from 1943: "Christie raised her dark head. The flecks in her eyes were like fire flashing through the green of leaves. 'There's a poem of Tennyson's, Johnny—I've forgotten just the poem and the line but there's this in it. The most virtuous hearts have a touch of hell's own fire in them.'"

6 "He was struck by what he was learning": Oral histories by Albert Upton, Carl Fleps, Hollis Dole, J. Willard Dyer, and James Stewart, Whittier; Nixon-Gannon. See Nixon's letters home to Pat from the South Pacific, 1943–1944, RNL, and those included in Julie Nixon Eisenhower's biography of her mother, *Pat Nixon: The Untold Story* (New York: Simon & Schuster, 1986).

6 he proved a shark at cards: Dick told his family he won $8,000 playing poker—about $100,000, accounting for inflation, in 2016 (see Edward Nixon OH, RNL). But during the "Checkers" controversy in the fall of 1952, Dick estimated that he and Pat had saved $5,500 before the war and $4,500 from their combined incomes while he was in the service. That would reduce his winnings to a few thousand dollars, a more reasonable but still impressive amount. Nixon said later that he and Pat spent $4,000 of their $10,000 savings in living expenses during the 1946 campaign. In this period, Pat received $3,000 from her parents' estate, and Dick inherited $1,600 from his grandfather. Dick to Pat, May 14, 1944, RNL; Nixon financial history and accounting, Sept. 1952, and summary of tax returns, 1947–1951, RNL.

6 his tour was over: In his memoirs, Nixon said his plane from Guadalcanal to Hawaii stopped to refuel on Wake Island, where a military cemetery held "row after row" of graves. If this walk took place, it was not on Wake Island, which was held by the Japanese until the end of the war. Nixon to parents, Aug. 15, 1945, Nixon to Douglas Hayward, May 15, 1961, RNL; Gretchen King interview with Bela Kornitzer, Ed Nixon OH, RNL; Albert Upton OH, Adela Rogers St. Johns OH, Whittier.

7 he was still Dick from Whittier: Nixon-Gannon; Thelma Nixon Lucas OH, Harry Schuyler OH, Edith Nunes OH, Edward Nixon OH, Whittier; *SEP,* July 12, 1958; Wallace Black OH, Merton Wray OH, CSUF; "Richard M. Nixon: A Self Portrait," documentary script for the 1968 presidential campaign, RNL, and Jessamyn West, interview with Fawn Brodie, FMB; Jessamyn West to David Abrahamsen, Dec. 3, 1974, Abrahamsen papers, Columbia University; Richard Nixon, "Remarks on Arrival in New Orleans, Louisiana," Aug. 14, 1970, PPP.

8 What he had was Herman Perry: Perry to Nixon, Sept. 29, 1945, RNL; How-

ard Marshburn OH, Donald Fantz OH, Whittier; M. F. K. Fisher, *Among Friends* (Emeryville, CA: Shoemaker & Hoard, 1970); Fisher to Weare Holbrook, June 24, 1969, quoted in Joan Reardon, *Poet of the Appetites* (New York: Macmillan, 2005); Jorgensen OH, Warren project; Harry Schuyler OH, CSUF.

10   Lycan promised Perry: Hubert Perry OH, RNL; Perry handwritten memo, "The Beginning of Dick Nixon" and typewritten memos "Re: Senator Nixon" and "The Early Political Career of the Honorable Richard M. Nixon," RNL.

10   Voorhis, a graduate of Hotchkiss: McLaughlin to Perry, Oct. 21, 1945, RNL; Voorhis OH, Claremont. California farmers called their spreads "ranches," even if they had no cattle.

10   Perry knew a young man: Perry memos cited above, Hubert Perry OH, RNL; Harold Lutz OH, Whittier.

11   "a dragon slayer": Nixon interviews with Stewart Alsop, *SEP,* Sept. 6, 1952 and July 12, 1958; Murray Chotiner to Earl Warren, Jan. 21, 1949, report on the 1948 campaign in Southern California, SAC; Upton OH, Hubert Perry OH, Whittier; JNE, *Pat;* Nixon-Gannon; Eric Goldman, *The Crucial Decade* (New York: Vintage, 1956).

12   "tear Voorhis to pieces": Perry memo, "The Early Political Career of the Honorable Richard M. Nixon" and Nixon to Perry, Oct. 6, 1945, RNL; *WDN,* Oct. 11, 1945 and Dec. 21, 1945. The Patton candidacy was a newspaper pipe dream; the general rebuffed all suggestions he run for any office. See Carlo D'Este, *Patton: A Genius for War* (New York: HarperCollins, 1995).

12   The Republican establishment: Earl Adams OH, Bullock papers, UCLA.

12   "My first impression of Nixon": Kyle Palmer interview with Kornitzer, BKP.

13   "the Amateurs": Roy Day OH, Whittier; Day to Walter Dexter, Oct. 13, 1945, RNL.

13   "We younger men": Frank Jorgensen OH, Whittier; Jorgensen OH, Warren project; *Covina Argus-Citizen,* Aug. 24, 1945; *Pomona Progress-Bulletin,* Sept. 20, 1945.

14   Babbitts, not Vanderbilts: Kruse, the treasurer for the Nixon committee, is illustrative. After serving in World War I and graduating from the University of Iowa, he joined the great migration to California, where he became a member of the Lions, the Elks, the Masons, and the American Legion and chairman of the First Federal Savings & Loan Association. He attended church in San Marino, golfed at the San Gabriel Country Club, and served as director of the local Community Chest and United Fund, and as president of the Chamber of Commerce. He, like the others, was as Main Street as Main Street gets. Roster, Committee of 100, RNL; Day to Dexter, Oct. 13, 1945, RNL; Jorgensen OH, Warren project; Adams OH, Bullock papers, UCLA.

14   search for a Cinderella: Before he would quit his state job to campaign, Dexter wanted a guarantee of employment if he lost, which the Amateurs could not provide. Yet to Perry's irritation, Dexter temporized and would not close the door. "Having supported you financially and in every other way in all of your campaigns," Perry told Dexter, he wanted a decision. The arm-twisting worked, and Dexter announced he would not run. Jorgensen OH, Warren Project; Day OH, Whittier; Perry to Lance Smith, Oct. 3, 1945, Day to Perry, Oct. 12, 1945, RNL; Perry telegram to Dexter and Dexter telegram to Perry, Oct. 9, 1945, and Perry to Dexter, Oct. 10, 1945, RNL.

14   Dexter was out of the race: Dexter was stricken by a heart attack and died that fall. *WDN, Alhambra Post Advocate,* Oct. 17 and 22, 1945.

15   "That's saleable merchandise": *WDN,* Nov. 2 and 3, 1945, Jan. 18, 1969; Day OH, Whittier; Nixon to Perry, Oct. 19, 1945, Nixon to Jim Stewart, Oct. 22, 1945, RNL; Rockwood Nelson to Day, Oct. 26, 1945, Perry telegram to Nixon, Oct. 25, 1945, Perry to Nixon, Oct. 16, 1945, RNL; Day to "Fellow Republicans," Oct. 18, 1945, Nixon to Moscow, Aug. 21, 1961, RNL.

15   Nixon cleared the next hurdle: No guest list for the luncheon survives in Nixon's pub-

lic papers. The names and number of those who actually attended are subject to old men's memories. In a letter to Faries, Nixon recalled that there were six to nine of them there that day, but there may have been more. It seems likely that Faries, Garland, Jorgensen, Day, Bewley, and Kepple were there. Others who may have attended include "Amateurs" Boyd Gibbons, Rockwood Nelson, Roy Crocker, Earl Adams, and Willard Larson, and Republican club leaders Harrison McCall, Herbert Spencer, and Lance Smith. The *Los Angeles Times* may have been represented by someone other than, or in addition to, John Garland. See text of Nixon letter to Faries, published in Faries's memoir, *Rememb'ring* (Glendale, CA: Griffin Publishing, 1993). See also Day, Jorgensen, and Adams oral histories, Warren project; Jorgensen to Rose Mary Woods, Jan. 12, 1972, and Day to Rockwood Nelson, Oct. 27, 1945, RNL; Garland interview, BKP; *WDN,* Oct. 17, 22, 1945; Day OH, Bullock papers, UCLA.

15   fund-raising would not be a problem: Faries OH, Jorgensen OH, Warren project; Garland interview, BKP.

15   "practical" liberalism: Harold Lutz OH, Whittier; *WDN,* Nov. 3, 1945; *LAT,* Nov. 3, 1945; Nixon to Day, Nov. 7, 12, 1945, Bewley to Nixon, Nov. 7, 1945, RNL.

16   "He had sold his soul": Stout OH, CSUF.

16   "Dick, the nomination is yours!": *LAT,* Nov. 26, 29, 1945; Kepple to Nixon, Nov. 29, 1945, Bewley to Nixon, Nov. 7, 1945, Perry to Nixon, Nov. 30, 1945, Nixon to Day, Nov. 22, 1945, Perry to Nixon, Nov. 24, 1945, Day to Nixon, Dec. 9, 1945, Nixon to Bewley, "Friday" (probably Nov. 9, 1945), RNL; JNE, *Pat; WDN,* Nov. 29, 1945; Nixon-Gannon.

16   Nixon was exhilarated: Nixon to Perry, Nov. 15, 1945, Nixon to Perry, Dec. 2, 1945, Nixon to Perry, Dec. 17, 1945, RNL.

16   the "fellow travelers": Nixon to Perry, Dec. 2 and 17, 1945, Nixon to Kepple, Dec. 4, 1945, RNL.

17   *spies in V. camp:* Nixon foolscap notes, 1946 campaign, RNL. Nixon's craving for political intelligence was evident in his first campaign. In early September he wrote his campaign manager: "We should get better reports on Voorhis' activities than we are at the present time. If necessary one person should be assigned the duty of tailing him and reporting everything he says." See Nixon to McCall, Sept. 3, 1946, RNL.

CHAPTER 2: "I HAD TO WIN"

18   back to the nowhere: Day, Florence Sucksdorf, Judith Wingert Loubet, Evlyn Dorn OH, Whittier; Nixon to John Evans, Nov. 13, 1946, RNL; *SEP,* Sept. 6, 1952; Edith Milhous Timberlake OH, CSUF.

18   Nixon's uneasiness with women: Day OH, Whittier; Herbert Spencer to Nixon, Jan. 15, 1946, RNL.

19   Organizations like the Elks: *WDN,* Jan. 15, 16, 19, 29, Feb. 28, 1946; *Pomona Progress Bulletin,* Feb. 18, 21, Mar. 20, 26, 28, 1946; *Alhambra Post-Advocate,* Feb. 28, 1946.

19   Nixon titled his talks: *WDN,* Jan. 15, 19, Feb. 1, 1946; *Alhambra Post-Advocate,* Feb. 28, Apr. 19, May 24, 1946; *South Pasadena Review,* Mar. 8, 1946; *Pomona Progress Bulletin,* Mar. 20, 22, May 11, 1946; Powell to Nixon, Feb. 27, 1946, Day to Pitkin, Mar. 14, 1946, Nixon 1946 speech file, RNL.

20   Patricia "Tricia" Nixon: JNE, *Pat;* Nixon to Perry, Dec. 2, 1945, RNL; Bullock papers, UCLA.

20   hundreds of minks: Waymeth Garrett OH, Edith Holt OH, Whittier; JNE, *Pat.*

21   Their campaign headquarters was no palace: Ed Nixon, interview with author; Boardman to Nixon, Jan. 10, 1956, RNL.

21   his first partisan disquisition: Nixon 1946 speech file, RNL.

21   iron curtain speech: Nixon 1946 speech file, RNL.

22 "He is dangerous": W. Earl Emick to Voorhis, May 2, 1946, "Report on Mass Meeting held by Republican Nixon for Congress Committee at Huntington School, San Marino," May 3, 1946, Voorhis papers, Claremont College.

22 Veterans were treasured targets: Long to Voorhis, Apr. 1, 1946, Voorhis papers, Claremont.

23 "Richard Nixon is one of us": Bewley OH, Weegar OH, Tolbert Moorhead OII, Whittier; Nixon 1946 campaign brochure, RNL; *SEP,* Sept. 6, 1952.

23 daily and weekly newspapers: Long to Voorhis, Feb. 16, 1946, Voorhis papers, Claremont; Faries OH, Warren project. On buying news stories, see also W. E. Smith to Drew Pearson, Oct. 27, 1952, Drew Pearson Papers, LBJ, and Klein exit interview, RNL.

23 building a grassroots movement: Gibbons to RN, Dec. 11, 1945, Gibbons to Day, Jan. 25, 1946, RNL; Jorgensen OH, Warren project.

24 bookkeeping, by necessity, was creative: The shortage of funds kept Nixon from some early skullduggery. John Hoeppel, a disgraced former congressman (he had been caught selling appointments to West Point), was running as a prohibitionist, looking to shake down the major party candidates. "The Republicans will pay him several hundred dollars and then he will peddle all the dirt in the campaign so Nixon will not have to engage in any mud-slinging," Voorhis fretted. To keep Hoeppel off the ballot, Voorhis organized a write-in campaign to clinch the Prohibition Party's nomination himself and fueled the scheme by sponsoring a bill to divert grain from U.S. liquor companies. But he need not have gone to the trouble: Nixon didn't have the funds to meet Hoeppel's $400 price. Day OH, Whittier; Voorhis to Jack Long, Mar. 28, 1946, Long to Voorhis, May 10, 1946, Voorhis notes on "Hoepple," Voorhis papers, Claremont; Adams OH, Bullock papers, UCLA; Adams OH, Warren project.

24 no infusion of funds: Nixon long recalled how Donald Jackson, an ex-Marine running for Congress in a west side district of Los Angeles, invited Dick to join him in a fund-raising pitch at the Beverly Hills home of a constituent who, it was said, wanted to donate to promising young Republicans. They stumbled into a scene from a film noir movie: a gated mansion on a two-acre property, where a butler showed them into a hall that reeked, as Nixon recalled, with "that musty smell and feel of great wealth . . . fallen on bad days." The owner, wearing a handsome smoking jacket, met them in the library before a blazing fire and was expounding on his crackpot economic theories when the butler reentered, armed with a .45-caliber pistol. "Young fellows," the servant said, "don't have a thing to do with this son of a bitch. He's no good. He's murdered two wives already." As the butler waved the gun at his employer and described in detail the horrific crimes, the two candidates rose, backed out of the room, and fled. "I think we need a drink," said Jackson. Nixon agreed, mournfully regretting that they could not be seen in a bar in mid-election. Maybe not in the Twelfth District, said Jackson: "In the 16th District we campaign in bars." Nixon-Gannon; Beatrice Hawkins OH, Whittier; undated 1950 letter from Harrison McCall to Pat Nixon, Day 1946 "newsgrams," RNL; *SEP,* Sept. 6, 1952.

24 Even the staunch had doubts: Day OH, Harrison McCall OH, Whittier; Adams OH, Bullock papers, UCLA; Nixon to John Evans, Nov. 13, 1946, RNL.

24 opposition remained confident: Charles Voorhis to Jerry Voorhis, Feb. 8, 1946, Voorhis papers, Claremont.

25 "Many people were disappointed": Nixon to Day, June, 1946, RNL; *SEP,* Sept. 6, 1952.

25 Dick stayed in the hotel room: Curtis Counts OH, Virginia Counts OH, Whittier.

25 Perry would tap Oil: Nixon had many supporters from the oil industry in 1946, including Willard "Swede" Larson, an oil engineer who served on the Nixon campaign committee; Frank Blake, an oil developer; and John Reilly of Standard Oil, whose daughter, Patricia Reilly Hitt, would one day serve in President Nixon's administra-

tion. Herbert Hoover Jr., an oilman, raised funds for Nixon in 1946 after his father, the former president, visited with him in Pasadena and asked if there wasn't anyone in the district who could beat Voorhis. According to President Hoover's associate John D. Hamilton, the Hoovers then met with Nixon, and the younger Hoover promised to "personally underwrite the campaign and, furthermore, through his relationship with several large corporations . . . [to] assure Mr. Nixon . . . win or lose . . . that he got sufficient . . . corporate business [as a lawyer] to make it worth his while." See G. Keith Funston OH, and John D. Hamilton OH, Herbert Hoover Presidential Library and Museum; Jorgensen OH, Warren project; Bewley OH, Ray Henle OH, John Reilly OH, Homer Rosenberger OH, Whittier; Judith Wingert Loubet OH, CSUF; Bewley to Rose Mary Woods, Mar. 15, 1954, Nixon to Mosher, Jan. 2, 1959, Perry memos, RNL. On the tidelands controversy see *Fortnight,* Apr. 14, 1952, and "The Tidelands Oil Controversy," Ernest Bartley, *Western Political Quarterly,* Mar. 1949.

26 letter from J. Paull Marshall: Marshall to Nixon, Feb. 20, Apr. 23, Nov. 7, 1946, Nixon to Marshall, Mar. 29, Nov. 13, 1946, Nixon to Perry, Aug. 16, 1946, RNL.

27 Perry forwarded Nixon's list: Perry to Stanley Natcher, Floyd Bryant, Aug. 22, 1946, Perry to Stanley Natcher, Nov. 20, 1946, RNL. In a 1979 letter to biographer Fawn Brodie, William Ackerman, a financial officer for Gladding, McBean & Co., a leading manufacturing company, noted how he and several dozen other executives were told to kick back $100 for the Nixon campaign and hide it on their expense accounts. Atholl McBean, the firm's chairman, was a Standard Oil director. See William Ackerman to Brodie, Jan. 2, 1979, FMB.

27 "money from Standard": There are several stories of Nixon distancing himself from the actual collection of money. When a California railroad told Day that it wanted to give its $500 directly to the candidate, for example, Nixon refused and said it should be sent to the campaign treasurer. "I don't want to know where it came from," he told Day. The state's Democrats also raised money through cutouts and "bag men," and promised judicial appointments and other plums to donors. See Lucien Haas OH, CSA; Lutz OH, Day OH, Hubert Perry OH, Whittier; Hubert Perry OH, RNL. On Ickes, Pauley, and the tidelands, see Bartley, *Western Political Quarterly,* Mar. 1949.

28 The campaign needed "meat": Chotiner to Nixon, Apr. 11, 1946, RNL.

28 His name was Murray Chotiner: In their divorce proceedings in 1962, Chotiner's wife, Ruth, testified that "he expressed a preference for younger women and told her she looked 103 years old," *LAT,* Jan. 23, 1962; Day to fact-finding committee, Oct. 18, 1945, Day to Nixon, Dec. 9, 1945, Day to Chotiner, Dec. 9, 1945, RNL; Day OH, Whittier; oral histories by Earl Adams, Victor Hansen, Warren Olney, Arthur Sherry, and Merrell Small, Warren project; Ken Chotiner interview, FMB.

28 Murray was his butcher: Lou Cannon OH, RNL; Chotiner, "Fundamentals of Campaign Organization," remarks to GOP campaign school, 1955, RNL; Nixon to Gerald Kepple, Dec. 4, 1945, Nixon to Perry, Dec. 17, 1945, Chotiner to Nixon, Aug. 14, 1946, Chotiner to Lowell, Feb. 15, 1946, Chotiner to Nixon, Mar. 13, 1946, Nixon to Chotiner, Nov. 13, 1946, thanking him for "the report on the Voorhis record which proved to be of tremendous value," RNL; Day OH, Whittier; Day OH, Jorgensen OH, Small OH, Warren project; Ken Chotiner interview, FMB; *People's Daily World,* July 3, 1946.

30 Gypsy Pat: JNE, *Pat.*

30 "Had enough?": Voorhis to Charles Voorhis, May 9, 1946, and Voorhis to Charles Voorhis, Feb. 13, 1946, Voorhis papers, Claremont; James T. Patterson, *Grand Expectations: The United States, 1945–1974* (New York: Oxford University Press, 1996).

31 "From a purely political standpoint": Voorhis to Charles Voorhis, May 9, 1946, Voorhis papers, Claremont; Voorhis remarks on tidelands oil, Cong. Rec., July 27, 1946, 10314; Bronson OH, Bullock papers, UCLA.

31 "a do-gooder who stumbles": Voorhis's office sent government pamphlets about child

care to new parents, and one was dispatched to the Nixons when Tricia was born. That prompted Nixon to write back, recalling how he and Voorhis had once met before the war. Voorhis then responded with a personal note, in which he offered to debate. Nixon to Voorhis, Apr. 1, 1946, RNL; Voorhis to Nixon, Apr. 16, 1946, Voorhis to Long, May 11, 1946, Voorhis to Nixon, May 11, 1946, Long to Voorhis, June 11, 1946, Harold Ickes to Florence Sebastian, Nov. 30, 1943, Voorhis papers, Claremont; Day OH, McCall OH, Whittier; Voorhis OH, Bullock collection, UCLA. Nixon saw in himself, and in Voorhis, a bit of Jefferson Smith, the idealistic hero of the Frank Capra film *Mr. Smith Goes to Washington.* See Stewart Alsop, *Nixon and Rockefeller* (New York: Doubleday, 1960).

32   Communism was a factor: *Life,* July 1, 15 and Aug. 12, 1946; Richard Powers, *Not Without Honor: The History of American Anticommunism* (New Haven, CT: Yale University Press, 1998); John Sullivan to Francis Matthews, Jan. 21, 1946, HST, quoted in Robert Griffith and Athan Theoharis, *The Specter: Original Essays on the Cold War and the Origins of McCarthyism* (Littlehampton Book Services, 1974).

32   "There was a lot of fear": Jorgensen OH, Warren project.

32   "the PAC": Perry to Palmer, Oct. 31, 1946, RNL; Charles Voorhis to Voorhis, Dec. 6, 1945, Voorhis to Loren Grey, May 22, 1946, Charles Voorhis to Voorhis, Apr. 1, 1946, Voorhis to Long, Apr. 6, 1946, Voorhis to Charles Voorhis, Apr. 6, 1946, Voorhis papers, Claremont.

33   "Not sent": Angered by the congressman's support of Truman's hard-line approach to the Soviet Union, the national NC-PAC ultimately sent Voorhis "one of the most bitter letters I have ever received in my life," he recalled, and "I never received the endorsement." Voorhis to William Miller, Mar. 28, 1956, Voorhis papers, Claremont; Voorhis OH, Richards OH, Bullock collection, UCLA; Voorhis to Loren Grey, May 22, 1946; Voorhis to Chester Watson, June 14, 1946, Voorhis papers, Claremont.

33   "a gut issue": *LAT* and district newspapers, Apr. 24–25, 1946; John Balch, "Richard M. Nixon vs. H. Jerry Voorhis For Congress, 1946," Voorhis papers, Claremont; undated 1960 newspaper profile of Roy Day, *San Gabriel Tribune,* RNL; McIntyre Faries, *Rememb'ring* (Glendale, CA: Griffin Publishing, 1993).

34   "'stooge' of the CIO-PAC": Paul Bullock to Voorhis, Aug. 26, 1946, Charles Voorhis to Voorhis, Aug. 27, 1946, Voorhis papers, Claremont. *Alhambra Post Advocate,* Oct. 29, 1946.

34   trading their "political soul": *Pomona Progress-Bulletin,* Sept. 3, 1946; *Alhambra Post Advocate,* Aug. 28, Sept. 11, 1946; *Whittier Daily News,* Aug. 29, Sept. 11, 1946, and other district papers. The newspapers appear to have received the order for the Voorhis ad and offered the Nixon campaign a chance to respond in the same edition.

34   a meet-the-candidates forum: *LAT,* Sept. 18, 1946; *WDN,* Sept. 14, 16, 20, 1946; Bullock, "Rabbits and Radicals," Richard Nixon's 1946 Campaign Against Jerry Voorhis, *Southern California Quarterly* 55, no. 5 (Fall 1973); Jorgensen OH, Warren project; Lyle Otterman OH, CSUF; Chester Holifield OH, Berkeley.

36   "Money came in very slowly": The Southern California Republican finance committee began the fall campaign with a $525,000 budget, with some $75,000 pledged to its seven congressional candidates in the southland. See Edward Shattuck to Earl Warren, with attached "confidential" budget, Aug. 17, 1946, Earl Warren Papers, CSA. Financial, manufacturing, and railroad representatives were among those who came to donate as the prospects for a Republican year, and a Nixon victory, became apparent. Harbison to Nixon, Apr. 11, 1946, R. N. Gregory to associates, Sept. 18, 1946, and Nov. 14, 1946, RNL; Day OH, McCall OH, Whittier; Ackerman to Brodie, Jan. 2, 1979, FMB; Chandler interview, BKP; Crocker OH, Richards OH, McCall OH, Bullock papers, UCLA; Bullock, "Rabbits and Radicals," *LAT,* Oct. 20, 1946; *WDN* and *Alhambra Post-Advocate,* Sept. 17, 1946; *WDN,* Oct. 21, 1946.

37　"Under the law": Nixon to Perry, June 29, 1948, RNL. Nixon ally Carter Barrett, for example, had a secretary who was tasked to make phone calls for Nixon at the rate of $40 a month. Carter Barrett OH, Whittier.

37　Nixon campaign, in its official report: Day OH, addendum, Bullock papers, UCLA.

37　four more debates: Nixon, *RN; WDN,* Oct. 12, 24, 29, 1946. The *Whittier Daily News* estimated that Nixon and Voorhis appeared before more than 500 people in South Pasadena; some 200 veterans in Whittier; 1,800 in Pomona; 1,200 in Monrovia; and 2,000 in San Gabriel. Holifield OH, Berkeley; Stout OH, CSUF.

38　"more Socialistic and Communistic": *Covina Argus Citizen,* Oct. 18, 1946.

38　federal jurisdiction over rabbits: Day OH, Whittier; Voorhis OH, Bullock papers, UCLA.

38　PAC issue reared up again: Newspaper ad, undated, after San Gabriel debate, Voorhis papers; Voorhis OH, Claremont.

38　thrum of one Nixon ad: Voorhis interview, Bullock papers, UCLA; Day OH, Whittier; *WDN,* Oct. 18, 1946. In a January 1947 letter Nixon attributed his victory to "the national swing and to the tremendous interest which was engendered by the series of public debates." Nixon to Hause, Jan. 21, 1947, RNL. In a 1968 interview, he also acknowledged that he "repeatedly" raised the issue of Communist infiltration of the CIO-PAC. "My blunt questions to my opponent about the politics and affiliation of some of his supporters were taken by some of his partisans as offensive," he said. "They were not. I stuck to the facts." See *Chicago Sun Times,* Nov. 18, 1968.

39　a hatchet man: Thomas Erwin, the Republican state assemblyman who represented the Whittier district and served in the Nixon campaign, was another Nixon adviser who "felt awful bad" about the Red-baiting. He was friends with Charles and Jerry Voorhis and was heartbroken when, in a post-election visit to Erwin's home, Charles Voorhis broke down and wept. "I'd liked Jerry Voorhis. I thought he was a very fine congressman," Erwin recalled. "I was just caught between the devil and the deep sea." Erwin OH, CSA. John Reilly, another who helped lead the Nixon campaign, remembered that he and his wife both thought Nixon was "rather intolerant . . . he just drove hard." *WDN,* Jan. 18, 1969; Folger to Nixon, Dec. 26, 1946, Nixon to Folger, Jan. 11, 1947, RNL; Faries, *Rememb'ring.*

39　Voorhis campaign was a shambles: Voorhis OH, Zetterberg OH, Bullock papers, UCLA.

39　persuaded voters to answer their telephones: The tale of the phone calls surfaced in the 1950s (see Ernest Brashear, "Who Is Richard Nixon?" *New Republic,* Sept. 1, 1952, and Richard Donovan, "Birth of a Salesman," *Reporter,* Oct. 14, 1952) and, though Nixon and the Amateurs all denied any knowledge of or participation in such a campaign, soon became political gospel (see Theodore White, "The Gentlemen from California," *Collier's,* Feb. 3, 1956).

　　Chotiner argued, convincingly, that in an election where 100,000 votes were cast, a meaningful phone campaign would have had to employ a significant number of Republican phone banks, which would have been impossible to conceal. See Alsop, *Nixon and Rockefeller.*

　　Voorhis did not complain about the phone calls in his 1947 book *Confessions of a Congressman,* but he later told inquirers that he heard about such calls from his supporters, and that "many" times Nixon had made private remarks to voters implying "that I was, at the very least, subject to communist influence." Voorhis to Lindley, Apr. 22, 1960; see also Voorhis to Miller, Mar. 28, 1956 ("Too many of my friends told me of receiving such calls for me to doubt that they occurred"). Both letters are in Voorhis papers, Claremont.

　　Earl Adams, an Amateur and future law partner of Nixon, also recalled the phone calls but insisted the campaign was not involved. See Adams OH, Bullock papers, UCLA.

For examples of Democratic partisans who claimed to have firsthand knowledge of the anonymous phone calls, see Zita Remley (who said she confirmed it by sending her niece to infiltrate a Nixon boiler room in Alhambra) to Brodie, 1980, FMB; Zita Remley OH and Stanley Long OH, Bullock papers, UCLA, and Lucien Haas OH, CSA.

Remley, at least, is a troublesome source: a Nixon hater who fed at least one demonstrably false story about Nixon's taxes to the press and claimed (more than twenty years later) that Nixon slapped her outside a public function—an assault that, if verified, would have ended his career but that she didn't care to report to the police at the time. See Brodie papers, Utah.

"Probably there were a few people who were for Nixon who made some wrongful accusations," said longtime Nixon press aide Herb Klein (see Klein OH, Columbia University), echoing several of the Amateurs, in what may be the best assessment of the episode.

40   Election Day verdict: Nixon, *RN;* Waymeth Garrett OH, Whittier. The final results were Nixon 65,586, Voorhis 49,994, and Hoeppel, 1,476. As a goal, or in exultation on the occasion of his election, Nixon wrote "VICTORY!" in his datebook for Nov. 5, 1946. See RNL; Nixon private archives, quoted in Jonathan Aitken, *Nixon: A Life* (Washington, D.C.: Regnery, 1993).

40   Voorhis was destroyed: Voorhis to Nixon, Dec. 7, 1946, RNL. In a March 1947 letter to a supporter, Voorhis noted that "vested interests" had worked "quietly and behind the scenes" to defeat him, but he acknowledged the times as well. "You asked me to give you the reasons why I was defeated and one of them was that the big Bank of America and several other powerful organizations were determined that I should not go back to Congress. However, I believe there were several other factors in the situation, one of the most important of which was that the people, tired of the war and governmental restrictions and controls which come with it, were determined to have a change." Voorhis to Raven, Mar. 4, 1947, Voorhis papers; Bronson OH, Bullock papers, UCLA.

41   "I had to win": Long OH, Bullock papers, UCLA. A Whittier College classmate, Kenneth Ball, said, "I don't think that Dick felt in his heart that what he was doing was dirty politics. I don't think he meant it to be dirty politics. . . . He was very competitive." His uncle Oscar Marshburn agreed: "It was just rough, and he was in there to win." Oscar Marshburn OH, Kenneth Ball OH, CSUF.

CHAPTER 3: AS AMERICAN AS THANKSGIVING

42   "the boy who lived down the block": *Washington Times Herald,* Jan. 21, 1947. Nixon was "a husky ex-footballer, OPA lawyer and lieutenant commander in the Pacific," *Newsweek* reported, some of which was actually true. (He was not husky, and rose only to lieutenant during the war.) *Time* found Nixon "lank," as opposed to "husky," but otherwise shared *Newsweek*'s penchant for error. He had, the magazine reported, "politely avoided personal attacks on his opponent." There were seven women in the House of Representatives in the 80th Congress, and two black men. The cherry blossom photo appeared in the press in April 1947; see the *Philadelphia Inquirer,* Apr. 14, 1947, and George Tames OH, Senate Historical Office, U.S. Senate.

42   He was born: For Nixon's early years see Jonathan Aitken, *Nixon: A Life* (Washington, D.C.: Regnery, 1993); Stephen Ambrose, *Nixon,* Vol. 1, *The Education of a Politician* (New York: Simon & Schuster, 1987); Fawn Brodie, *Richard Nixon: The Shaping of His Character* (New York: Norton, 1981); and Roger Morris, *Richard Milhous Nixon: The Rise of an American Politician* (New York: Holt, 1990).

42   His father was exultant: Frank Nixon had his own ten acres, and a team of men and boys helped him tend the groves of absentee landowners. He hailed the hired hands:

"I've got another boy!" Joseph Dmohowski, "From a Common Ground," *California History,* Fall 1994; Homer Bemis OH, Hoyt Corbit OH, Whittier.

Except for Francis Donald Nixon, who was named after his father, Hannah named her boys—Harold, Richard, Arthur, and Edward—after English kings. In Dick's case it was not Richard II or Richard III, the two Shakespearean monarchs with whom he is sometimes compared, but Richard the Lionhearted.

42 Nixons were Scotch-Irish Protestants: U.S. Adjutant General's Office, Aug. 2, 1865, response to application for pension to survivors of George Nixon; Raymond Martin Bell, "From James to Richard: The Nixon Line," genealogical paper, Washington and Jefferson College, 1969; Nixon genealogy files, WHSF-R.

43 Their third child was Frank: Alice Nixon Linton OH, Whittier; E. L. Nixon to Kornitzer, Mar. 8, 1959, Mar. 26, 1959, BKP.

43 warmth and promise of Southern California: "I immediately stopped going with five other girls I was dating," Frank recalled. Richard Gardner, *Fighting Quaker,* unpublished manuscript, Whittier College; Edwin Hoyt, *The Nixons: An American Family* (New York: Random House, 1972); Edward Nixon, interview with author; Edward Nixon OH, Whittier.

43 "I loved at first sight": Frank Nixon, undated manuscript, circa 1931, Nixon Family Papers, RNL.

44 Milhous clan: Richard's cousins remember their grandfather standing at the bottom of the stairs after being disturbed in his reading by the ever-present passel of children, saying: "If thee doesn't stop that now, I'm coming up there to give thee a thrashing." See Edith Nunes OH, Whittier. According to family lore, there were Milhous families among the local abolitionists who helped runaway slaves. If so, Jessamyn West could not confirm it. See Charles W. Milhous OH and Jessamyn West OH, Whittier.

44 became more materialistic and self-satisfied: Jessamyn West, "On Words and Men," *Whittier College Bulletin,* May 1960. See also Oscar Marshburn OH, Whittier.

44 clan's transcontinental passage: Jessamyn West OH, Whittier.

45 It was an act of escape: "She felt that he really needed her," Richard said of Hannah and Frank. "I mean, my mother had such a heart . . . and I think . . . she realized that this boy hadn't had a mother and . . hated his stepmother . . . and he had never really had much of a chance in life." Nixon-Gannon; Hannah to Kornitzer, 1960, BKP; *Whittier News,* July 3, 1908; Elsie Haigler OH, Whittier. See also Jessamyn West to Brodie on Hannah's motives ("Maybe she felt, you know, time to say yes to someone"), FMB, and Edith Milhous Timberlake OH, CSUF ("Hannah thought that would be a leap out of the fire").

45 Frank felt the scorn: Alice Nixon Linton OH, Jessamyn West OH, Rose Olive Marshburn OH, Whittier. For more on Frank's relationship with his in-laws see oral histories by Jane Milhous Barr, Leonidas Dodson, Priscilla Timberlake MacLeod, Elizabeth Timberlake Padanius, and Jane Milhous Beeson, Whittier. "The Milhous family was a big family, with various in-laws and they talked freely about each other," said Dodson. "The least popular member of that large family group was Frank Nixon." Said Jane Milhous Beeson of Frank and Hannah's marriage: "We didn't quite accept it." Added Jessamyn West: "I don't know about the men . . . but the Milhous women thought that Hannah had married beneath her." In the Nixon-Gannon interviews, Nixon reports his father's alienation from the Milhous clan: "The old man didn't like to go to those reunions. . . . He was pretty cantankerous about it." See also Edith Milhous Timberlake OH, CSUF, and Ed Nixon OH, RNL.

45 ten-acre plot in Yorba Linda: Franklin Milhous letterhead, "Nursery Stock and Real Estate." Frank bought one-fourth interest in forty acres for $500. Nixon Family Papers, RNL.

45   Yorba Linda in 1912: Jessamyn West OH, Whittier; Jessamyn West, *Double Discovery* (New York: Harcourt, 1980); Hoyt Corbit OH, David Cromwell OH, Mrs. Cecil Pickering OH, CSUF.

46   His citrus stock was poor: For opinions on the Yorba Linda property and Frank's talent for farming see Hoyt Corbit, Joe Johnson, Helen Neushutz, Mary Skidmore, Russell Harrison Sr., Oscar Marshburn, and Austin Marshburn oral histories, Whittier, and Hoyt Corbit OH, CSUF. "I don't know whether Franklin Milhous examined it carefully or why he bought it or why they got it. I don't know the history of it. But it was a very poor piece of ground . . . [and] I don't think Frank was a very good horticulturalist," said Austin Marshburn. Frank "was a very stubborn man," said Mary Skidmore. "He found it difficult to follow advice." As Hannah told Bela Kornitzer, one of Richard's early biographers: "My husband was a stubborn man, and arguments stiffened him." See Bela Kornitzer, *The Real Nixon: An Intimate Biography* (New York: Rand, McNally, 1960).

46   "*miserably poor* all the while": Hannah Nixon to sister, July 8, 1913, Nixon Family Papers, RNL; *Good Housekeeping,* June 1960; *Orange County Register,* June 12, 2012; Russell Harrison OH, Whittier; Mary Elizabeth Guptill Rez OH, CSUF.

46   "horny old devil": Mary Rez and Jessamyn West OH, Whittier; Hannah Nixon to her mother, Feb. 1920, Nixon Family Papers, RNL; Thomas Bewley and Jessamyn West interviews, FMB.

47   *Only a dad neither rich or proud:* Nixon Family Papers, RNL.

47   hair-trigger temper: Mary Rez OH, Merle West OH, Jessamyn West OH, Austin Marshburn OH, Whittier. In the collections at the RNL is a draft obituary for Frank Nixon, prepared by Dick's family and staff, which notes: "He used the strap or rod on the boys when he felt they needed it. . . . He expected obeyance [*sic*] under all circumstances. He was impatient, he had a hot temper."

      It is difficult to overstate Frank's hotheaded disposition. See Whittier College oral histories by Jessamyn West ("Frank was a tempestuous man and was filled with anger. And when he was filled with anger he spoke up. And when he spoke up, the children on both sides of the ditch quailed") and others such as Homer Bemis ("Frank came up behind Dick one day and threw him in the ditch"), Jane Milhous Barr ("He had a wild temper"), Joe Johnson ("We were always afraid of him"), Edith Milhous Timberlake ("He gave them the stick"), and Edward Nixon ("I remember the old stick coming out every once in a while. Sure."). See also Brodie interviews with Jessamyn West, Tom Bewley ("He'd use the strap on him . . . Dick never used the word 'beat'"), and Dr. Arnold Hutschnecker ("Nixon's father was brutal and cruel"), FMB. The oral histories at Fullerton and Whittier are replete with descriptions of Frank that employ terms like *hotheaded, belligerent, argumentative, explosive, stubborn, hot tempered,* and *antagonistic.* In his interviews with David Frost, Nixon listed his father's good qualities but said "he could be belligerent" and had "a terrific temper."

47   dish it back: Jessamyn West interview, FMB; Merle West OH, CSUF.

47   Hannah was quite the opposite: "Richard M. Nixon: A Self Portrait," documentary script for the 1968 presidential campaign, RNL; Nixon, *RN;* Richard Nixon, *In the Arena* (New York: Random House, 1990); *Good Housekeeping,* June 1960; *WDN,* May 9, 1959; Jane Milhous Beeson OH, Lawrene Nixon Anfison OH, Whittier.

48   Alger hero: Stans, quoted in *The Nixon Presidency,* a collection of essays and interviews edited by Kenneth W. Thompson of the University of Virginia (Lanham, MD: University Press of America, 1987) (hereafter Thompson). See also H. R. Haldeman, *The Ends of Power* (New York: Times Books, 1978). "we see exaggerated narcissism": Harlow interview, Thompson; Harlow interview, *New Republic,* May 13, 1978. See also Henry Kissinger, *Years of Upheaval* (Boston: Little, Brown, 1982); Heinz Kohut, *The Restoration of Self* (Chicago: University of Chicago Press, 1977); Brodie, *Nixon.*

Heinz Kohut's description of a narcissistic personality is striking to anyone who has spent hours listening to the White House tapes, digesting the opinions of Dr. Hutschnecker, and studying the thousands of pages of oral histories recorded from Nixon's relatives and childhood friends by historian Richard Arena for Whittier College.

There are several "psychobiographies" of Nixon. As David Greenberg notes, those published in the clamorous era of Vietnam and Watergate tend to offer more pathological diagnoses. But a study made after Nixon's death presents a measured account.

"Nixon's maintenance and regulation of his self-esteem were handled according to psychological processes typical of a narcissistic personality," the team of scholars concluded. "His internal demands would lead him to irrational and/or self-defeating decisions and actions." Yet his narcissim, while "exaggerated," was "*not* malignant," they concluded. See Vamik Volkan, Norman Itzkowitz, and Andrew Dod, *Richard Nixon: A Psychobiography* (New York: Columbia University Press, 1997).

See also Bruce Mazlish, *In Search of Nixon* (New York: Basic Books, 1972); David Greenberg, *Nixon's Shadow* (New York: Norton, 2003); Arnold Hutschnecker, *The Drive for Power* (Lanham, MD: M. Evans, 1974); David Abrahamsen, *Nixon v. Nixon* (New York: Signet, 1978); James David Barber, "The Nixon Brush with Tyranny," *Political Science Quarterly,* Winter 1977–78. See also Abrahamsen notes, transcripts, and manuscript, Abrahamsen papers, Columbia.

49 competed for emotional nourishment: Nixon defended his mother's nature and praised her for not indulging in "nauseating" shows of affection with her children. "Only one of those rather pathetic Freudian psychiatrists would suggest that her love of privacy made her private even from her sons," he told Jonathan Aitken. Russell Harrison Sr. OH, Whittier; Lucille Parsons, Floyd Wildermuth OH, CSUF. See also Nixon-Gannon: "I don't object to the way people today slobber all over everybody else . . . [but] in our family we expressed our love through our deeds in a quiet way rather than feeling that we had to burp it out."

49 Harold was a classic eldest child: West quoted in Donald Jackson, "Coming of Age in America," unpublished manuscript, Aug. 28, 1970, and in West interview with Brodie, FMB; Olive Marshburn to Kornitzer, July 12, 1959, BKP.

49 first six months of life: Hannah to sister, July 8, 1913, Nixon Family Papers, RNL; Nixon-Gannon; Russell Harrison Sr. OH, Whittier. Frank was out and about that Sunday, and Austin Marshburn, a neighbor, wrapped a towel around Dick's head and drove Hannah to the hospital in Fullerton. "His brain is not hurt. It's just a scalp wound," he told Hannah. "No small baby could have a brain injury and flap his arms like he's doing and bleed like he's doing and yell." See also Austin Marshburn OH, Whittier with correspondence between Richard Nixon and Marshburn, 1971.

50 "My emotions are controlled": Richard to Hannah, Feb. 4, 1924, Nixon Family Papers, Frost-Nixon transcripts, RNL; Jane Milhous Beeson OH, Whittier; Sheldon Beeson OH, CSUF; Richard Nixon interview with Kornitzer, BKP.

50 when frustrated, he raged: Nixon-Gannon; Jessamyn West OH, Russell Harrison Sr. OH, Edith Nunes OH, Ed Nixon OH, Whittier; Mary Rez, Gerald Shaw OH, CSUF.

50 "plenty of character": West, *Double Discovery.* Oscar Marshburn OH, Jessamyn West OH, Whittier.

50 "tempted to run away": Nixon campaign script, 1968, RNL. He may have picked up his Polonius-like wriggling from Hannah. "Richard, for his part, calls me Mother— not Mom or any other diminutive—but the formal tone does not in any way represent our true relationship, for we have been very close," she would tell a reporter. "He has always confided in me and discussed things with me—even though he isn't the gushy

type and doesn't pour out his heart." And "I have never heard him express a desire to be a financial success. I don't mean to imply, though, that Richard doesn't have a good business head.... He knows how to make an extra penny." *Good Housekeeping,* June 1960.

51   "fear, not love": Mary Rez OH, Oscar Marshburn OH, Jessamyn West OH, Russell Harrison Sr. OH, Whittier; Nixon, *RN;* William Safire, *Before the Fall* (New York: Doubleday, 1975).

51   Yorba Linda had its glories: Oral histories by Ralph Shook, Ralph Howe, Wilbur Page, Joe Johnson, and Howard Bemis, Whittier; Virginia Shaw Critchfield OH, CSUF; Jessamyn West, *Hide and Seek* (New York: Harcourt, 1973).

51   steep-banked irrigation ditch: Wilbur Page and many other oral histories, Whittier.

51   town's little school: Mary George Skidmore OH, Ellen Cochran OH, Whittier; Mary G. Skidmore OH, CSUF. The Nixon Family Papers, RNL, contain several book reports and essays. "One of the things that I like to do better than anything else is to read a good book, magazine or a paper. I also like music pretty well," he wrote in his eighth-grade "Autobiography."

52   wail of a train whistle: Rose Olive Marshburn OH, Delphine Smith OH, Floyd and Ruby Wildermuth OH, Whittier; Ollie Burdg OH, William Barton OH, Floyd Wildermuth OH, CSUF; Nixon-Gannon; "Nixon: A Self Portrait."

As he got older, there were other visitants from the outside world. One uncle was an entomologist who lived in Hawaii (and brought his butterfly net to family picnics); another had served in the Red Cross in World War I and let the Nixon boys play with defused artillery shells. And when the Nixon family moved to Whittier, a famous Arctic explorer—Ernest de Koven Leffingwell—was a neighbor.

52   opened a gas station: Frank had helped out at his brother Hugh's gas station and foresaw the opportunities presented by the growing numbers of automobiles. In the process of leaving Yorba Linda, he looked at a tract in Santa Fe Springs where drillers would later strike oil but, without the capital with which to speculate, he apparently chose the Whittier gas station as the safer bet. The regional oil boom gave rise to several family myths. In the most common version—spread by Hannah and Richard for years—Frank was said to have sold the Yorba Linda farm before oil was found on the property, thus losing a chance to become a millionaire. In fact, oil was never discovered on the property, which was eventually purchased by the town for an elementary school. In another story, retold by Richard Gardner in *Fighting Quaker,* Frank claimed to have turned down an offer of $45,000 by an oil company for his farm. There is some evidence to support this: in bank records from the 1920s Frank for a time valued his property at $40,000. See Russell Harrison Sr. OH, Floyd Wildermuth OH, Charles Post OH, Anne Gilmore OH, Whittier.

52   "He had failed": Merle West interview, Abrahamsen papers, Columbia. Using bank records recently donated by Herman Perry's family, it is possible to track the financial fortunes of Nixon's family during Dick's early years and reconcile the varying reported descriptions of their status, which range from poor to middle class.

In 1917, when applying for a line of credit with the First National Bank of Whittier, Frank reported that he had $215 in the bank and owed $1,200, and that his farm was worth $8,500. In 1922, as he left Yorba Linda, Frank had $1,100 in savings, owed $1,900, and his farm was worth $11,700; he also owned a house and a lot in Whittier. By 1926 Frank was doing much better, with savings, securities, and the store giving him a net worth of $36,450—almost $500,000 today. The Depression, and medical bills, rocked the family—their net worth slipped to $17,000, and the Bank of America refused to loan Frank money when he tried to mortgage the store in 1932—but did not wreck them. The grocery store had gross sales of from $40,000 to $50,000 a year, and net profits of $3,000 to $5,000 in the mid-1930s. By 1939, as Frank and Hannah prepared to move into an upscale neighborhood in Whittier, he declared a net worth of $41,000 (about $700,000 today), with the store and several rental properties on Whittier Boulevard.

52 Whittier: M. F. K. Fisher to Georges Connes, Feb. 15, 1969, quoted by Joan Reardon, *Poet of the Appetites* (New York: Macmillan, 2005); Robert Blake OH, Tolbert Moorhead OH, Jessamyn West OH, Cecil Sperring OH, Whittier. Quakerism "was their religion, but six days of the week they were selling real estate and you better believe it," Torbert Moorhead recalled. "This was one of the hardest towns to get started in that you could almost believe," said Glenn Shay. "It was real hard to break into this town in a business way. . . . They cut the people out here that they didn't want," Shay OH, Whittier. John Reilly would become one of the town's leading citizens, but as a young oilman he and his family were turned away by landlords in Whittier. "We're not going to have your kind of people in this town," they told him. John Reilly OH, Judith Wingert Loubet OH ("There was a clique. . . . terribly petty"), Paul Smith OH, CSUF; Nixon-Gannon; "Richard Nixon: Man and President," A&E documentary, 1996.

53 Sundays and holidays: The church played a commanding role in the boys' early years. There was Sunday school and a morning service at the Quaker meetinghouse, a youth group meeting called Christian Endeavor, and evening services, Nixon recalled. As he grew older he sang in the choir, gave religious talks, and taught some Sunday school himself. See oral histories by Jane Milhous Barr, Carleton Milhous, Charles Eric Milhous, Franklin Milhous, Howard Marshburn, Russell Harrison Sr., and Edith Nunes, Whittier; *Whittier News*, Feb. 3, 1919.

53 added a small store: "It was mostly study and work. Not much play and Sundays were all taken with church activities," Nixon recalled. See "Nixon: A Self Portrait."
      Frank's brother Ernest defended him: "The test of his accomplishment was not how high he attained, but how far did he travel." Ernest Nixon to Kornitzer, Mar. 26, 1959, BKP. The oral histories at Fullerton and Whittier, however, are stocked with descriptions of the dreary lives of the family in those early days. See oral histories by Leonidas Dodson, Harry Schuyler, Forrest Easley, Dorothy Bishop, Roger and Mabel Schuyler, Russell Harrison Sr., and Alice Nixon, Whittier. "They were so hard working, I was appalled. [Hannah] went around exhausted. She looked like she was going to drop all the time. And Uncle Frank. I just couldn't believe it," said Alice. The name of the store was "F.A. Nixon's General Merchandise," his son Edward recalled, and "probably anything that could be sold, dad was willing to try." Edward Nixon, interview with author; Edward Nixon OH, RNL; Loubet OH, CSUF.

54 known to perform charitable acts: The earthquake caused considerable damage in Whittier. Dick remembered the thunderous roar that accompanied the tremor. See oral histories by Jane Milhous Barr, Richard Harrison, Russell Harrison, Sheldon Beeson, Stephen Schatz, and Charles Eric Milhous, Whittier.

54 loud, crotchety self: Merle West interview, Abrahamsen papers, Columbia. In his eighth-grade "Autobiography," Richard wrote of Frank: "He is a very talkative man, liking to talk about politics, current events, and happenings of the day. He is a very ready debater on any subject." Jane Milhous Barr OH, Roger and Mabel Schuyler OH, Anne Gillmore OH, Whittier.

54 his beliefs: Frank became a Republican after a boyhood encounter with William McKinley and voiced his disapproval when Hannah voted for Democrat Woodrow Wilson on the eve of World War I. Richard's precocious sermons to his teachers and chums on behalf of Republican Warren Harding during the 1920 election were surely inspired by his father. But in hard times Frank could swing left. A portrait of the great populist and pacifist William Jennings Bryan hung in their Yorba Linda home. After reading (and ranting) about the Teapot Dome scandal, Frank refused to sell

Standard Oil products at his gas station. In 1924 he left the GOP to vote for the Progressive Party's presidential candidate, Senator Robert "Fighting Bob" La Follette of
Wisconsin, a defender of the little guy. When Southern California became a hotbed of
crackpot economic schemes, Frank was an enthusiast. And during the Depression, he
at first backed Franklin Roosevelt. It was only later, after becoming disillusioned with
the New Deal's welfare policies, that Frank returned to the Republican fold. See oral
histories by Hurless Barton, George Irving, Russell Harrison, Charles Eric Milhous,
and Edward Nixon, Whittier; Hannah Nixon interview with Bela Kornitzer, BKP.

55   little brother whom he adored: Nixon-Gannon. In his autobiography, Dick wrote:
"The cause of his death is not known but it is generally conceded that it was caused by
tuberculosis of the brain," RNL.

There were persistent family stories, however, that Arthur's illness was brought on
by an incident in which he was struck by a rock in the schoolyard. Gardner uses the
story in *Fighting Quaker* and says Arthur died from a concussion. It is possible that the
Nixon family misled Gardner, because tuberculosis then carried a stigma. (In recounting the death of Frank's mother, Gardner declines to mention that she also died from
tuberculosis.) The cause of death on Arthur's death certificate is listed as tuberculosis
or encephalitis, and neither is brought on by injury.

Nixon's medical confidant, Dr. Arnold Hutschnecker, assured Fawn Brodie that it
was not Dick who threw the rock, closing that particular door on presidential psycho-
biographers. Frank saw God's wrath at work in Arthur's death, punishing the family
for keeping the store open on Sundays.

Anne Gillmore, Thelma Nixon Lucas, Joe Johnson, Mildred Gibbons Fink, Russell Harrison Jr., Ed Nixon OH, Whittier; Ed Nixon, interview with author; Arthur
Nixon death certificate, RNL. The "good dog" letter and the college essay on Arthur
are in the Nixon Family Papers, RNL, with other school assignments. Hannah Nixon,
"Richard Nixon: A Mother's Story," *Good Housekeeping,* June 1960.

56   Harold returned from a boarding school: Merle West interview, Abrahamsen papers,
Columbia; Cecil Sperring OH, Whittier; Ralph Palmer OH, CSUF. Before leaving
for New England, Harold worked for a fumigating outfit, applying cyanide gas in
the orange groves. "His father thought that it would be fine, that he needed the extra
money for school," Sperring recalled. "Had any of us known that he had the slightest
bit of lung trouble . . . we never would have had him on that kind of job. . . . It was very
dangerous work."

56   Dick's teenage years: Jonathan Aitken and Maurice Stans both argue that Nixon's
upbringing was not as gothic as some biographers, like Fawn Brodie, would have it
seem. Many young people in Nixon's generation were compelled to endure disease,
economic uncertainty, and war—and emerged with their psyche relatively intact.
Nixon appeared to think so too. In his copy of a favorite biography of Benjamin Disraeli, Nixon underlined the opening words: "His career was an extraordinary one but
there is no need to make it seem more extraordinary than it really was. His point of
departure . . . was neither as humble nor as alien as some people have believed." Nixon
"resented the mythology" of deprivation that painted his father as cruel and his mother
as cold, wrote Aitken. In the interviews with Frank Gannon, Nixon called all such
speculation "fatuous nonsense." See Aitken, *Nixon;* Stans interview, Thompson; Robert Blake, *Benjamin Disraeli* (New York: St. Martin's Press, 1967); Nixon-Gannon.

56   Prescott, Arizona: Nixon-Gannon. To mark Independence Day, Prescott staged Frontier Days events to raise funds for local charities. Cowboys competed in a rodeo, and
various games of chance were permitted at the "Slippery Gulch" carnival downtown.
Richard was a barker, most memorably for a wheel of fortune where his grandmother
won a ham. Brodie interview with Jessie Lynch Brandt, FMB; Henry Akard, Marshall
Clow, Verna Hough, Edith Milhous Timberlake OH, Whittier. (Nixon's correspon-

dence uses "Clow," as do the Whittier College oral histories. Fawn Brodie has the name as "Clough.")

56 Dick lost himself in work: Richard Nixon "Autobiography" school paper, 1925, East Whittier school graduation program, 1926, Longfellow verse from *Psalm of Life* with inscription, inventory, Nixon children's books, all RNL; Rose Mary Woods to Kornitzer, May 20, 1959, BKP; Josephine Harrison OH, Whittier. Hannah Nixon, "Richard Nixon: A Mother's Story," *Good Housekeeping*, June 1960.

57 He was an A student: "Our Privileges Under the Constitution," reprinted in Nixon's Whittier High School yearbook; Merle West interview, Abrahamsen papers, Columbia; Beatrice Hawkins OH, Helen Netzley OH, Whittier.

58 Fullerton High School: East Whittier graduates generally attended Whittier High School, but some families in the community, like the Nixons, chose the option of sending their child to Fullerton. James Grieves OH, Virginia Shaw Critchfield OH, Gerald Shaw OH, CSUF; oral histories by A. H. Brannon, Linniel Taylor, Edward Flutot, Rose Milhous Marshburn, Ralph Howe, Lyman Dietrick, and Charles Eric Milhous, Whittier; Merle West interview, Abrahamsen papers, Columbia.

59 "you have studied too hard": Almira to Richard, Mar. 11, 1930, Nixon Family Papers, RNL; oral histories by Anne Gillmore, Thelma Nixon Lucas, Harry Schuyler, Edith Nunes, and Edward Nixon, Whittier; *SEP,* July 12, 1958; Wallace Black OH, Merton Wray OH, Albert Haendiges OH, CSUF; "Nixon: A Self Portrait"; Jessamyn West, interview with Fawn Brodie, FMB; Jessamyn West to David Abrahamsen, Dec. 3, 1974, Abrahamsen papers, Columbia.

59 Girls were a new frontier: Jessamyn West OH, Ralph Palmer OH, Whittier; West, *Hide and Seek*. "He was an absolute straight arrow. . . . He told me he hadn't slept with anyone in his life except Pat," Navy lieutenant James Stewart told Jonathan Aitken.

60 "there was a warmth underneath": Alice Nixon Linton OH, Rose Olive Marshburn OH, Ed Nixon OH, Jo Marcelle OH, Whittier.

60 "I have to apologize": Excerpts of letters from Richard Nixon to Ola Florence Jobe, Aitken papers, RNL; Nixon-Gannon; Ola Florence Jobe interview, Aitken papers, RNL.

60–61 Whittier College: The glee club performed sacred music and standards like "Home on the Range" and "Short'nin' Bread." The Apr. 27, 1934 edition of the campus newspaper noted how the club capped its season with a portrayal of "Negro Heaven" called "De Glory Road." Joseph Cosand OH, Harley McClure OH, Robert Watson OH, Whittier; Manville Saxton OH, CSUF. "He was noted in debating for being able to tear the other side down and he carried that into politics," Lyle Otterman recalled. "If they wanted to get nasty, he could play with them." Otterman OH, CSUF; Albert Upton, interview with Kornitzer, BKP.

61 the grocer's boy: Hannah's notes to Dick offer a glimpse of the family's long workday. "Dick: Let's get up at a quarter to four, 3:45 to load the truck and make out lists," she reminded him. After he was away at Duke, she continued to update him: "Nearly daylight. Dad is up making a cake and I must get to fixing the vegetable and meat case." Nixon Family Papers, RNL; Joseph Cosand OH, Clint Harris OH, Whittier. "He went from one class to another with his hands full of books and his head down," Lyle Otterman OH, CSUF.

61 Orthogonians: Stewart Alsop, *Nixon and Rockefeller* (New York: Doubleday, 1960). As a founder of the Orthogonians, Nixon did not have to endure the club's initiation rites. When he joined the glee club, however, he was stripped and paddled. Nixon-Gannon; oral histories by John Arrambide, Thomas Bewley, Edward Breitkreutz, William Brock, Nathaniel George, and Clint Harris, Whittier; Hubert Perry, interview with author; Emmett Ingrum OH, Dean and Jewel Triggs OH, CSUF; Keith Wood to Kornitzer, Mar. 25, 1959, BKP. See also Helen Larson to Kornitzer, Mar. 15, 1959:

"The thing which I recall as most impressive about his personality was his intensity of purposiveness. This tended in youth toward an almost ruthless cocksureness which perhaps was the reason some students disliked him."

62   promoting his classmates' interests: Dick was proud of a three- or four-hole privy he and some pals hijacked to feed the campus bonfire. He also led a caravan of Whittier students to invade the offices of the *Los Angeles Times* to protest its coverage of the college's athletic teams, and joined in a football team tradition of crashing the local movie theater without buying tickets. Tolbert Moorhead OH, Edith Nunes OH, Whittier; Richard Spaulding OH, Robert Halliday OH, Kenneth Ball OH, Joe Gaudio OH, William Soeberg OH, CSUF; see also Keith Wood to Kornitzer, Mar. 25, 1959, BKP.

The 1934 Whittier yearbook sang Dick's praises. "After one of the most successful years the college has ever witnessed, we stopped to reminisce and came to the realization that much of the success was due to the efforts of this very gentleman. Always progressive and with a liberal attitude, he has led us through the year with flying colors. After a fairly quiet political season and a campaign in which mud-slinging was noticeably lacking, the student body chose its officers for this year. Although political dictators managed to cause as much trouble as possible, Dick Nixon came through the melee unscathed with the title of Student Body President. On a platform advocating a new deal for those who enjoy the social niceties, he stormed to his position. But contrary to precedent and traditions he lived up to his promises."

63   Ola helped: Jackson, "Coming of Age"; oral histories by Clint Harris, Marjorie Knighton, Margaretha Lohmann, Camilla Simmons, and William Simmons, Whittier; Triggs and Gibbs OH, CSUF; Ola Florence Jobe interviews, Aitken papers, RNL, and Brodie, FMB; Clint Harris interview, Abrahamsen papers, Columbia.

63   Dick focused on French: Nixon transcript in Nixon Family Papers, RNL; oral histories by Charles Cooper, Paul Smith, Albert Upton, Wallace Newman, and Hubert Perry, Whittier; oral histories by Dean and Jewel Triggs, Albert Haendiges, Charles Kendle, Byron Netzlery, Sheldon Beeson, and Setsuko Tani, CSUF; Paul Smith interview with Kornitzer, BKP. "In the first place there aren't many Quakers, and in the second place there aren't many Quakers with money, and in the third place the Quakers with money are tightwads," Upton recalled. "So Whittier College was gradually starving to death."

64   Harold died: *Whittier News,* Mar. 7, 1933; Nixon-Gannon; Harold Nixon death certificate and Brodie interview with Ola Florence Jobe, FMB; Merle West interview with Abrahamsen, Columbia; Nixon, "A Mother's Story"; Edith Milhous Timberlake would say: "Richard took over after Harold died." Edith Milhous Timberlake OH, CSUF.

CHAPTER 4: DEATH, GOD, LOVE, AND WAR

66   "A process of enlightenment": "What Can I Believe?" is the title for a series of essays written by Nixon in his senior-year course Philosophy of Christian Reconstruction, RNL.

66   Nixon entered law school: Nixon to parents, fall, 1934, Nixon to Ola Florence Welch Jobe, Jan. 14, 1935, Charles Rhyne interview, Aitken papers; Duke University correspondence, Dean Horrack to Nixon, June 15, 1935, June 12, 1936, RNL; "Record of Richard Nixon," transcript, May 31, 1937, RNL. See also results of FBI preemployment investigation, July 1939, available at FBI website.

66–67 Gloomy Gus: There were more than thirty members of Phi Beta Kappa in Nixon's first-year law school class, which started out at forty-four but shrank dramatically. William Adelson OH, Whittier. See also Lyman Brownfield, "Reminiscences About Nixon," BKP; Brownfield to Stewart Alsop, undated 1959 or 1960, RNL.

67   Whippoorwill Manor: Nixon, "Notes—Anaheim Homecoming," WHSF-R, RNL; Nixon to Ola Florence Welch Jobe, Jan. 5, 1936, Aitken papers, RNL; Brownfield,

"Reminiscences About Nixon," BKP; Lyman Brownfield to Stewart Alsop, undated 1959 or 1960, RNL.

67 Who knows why couples drift apart: Lael Morgan, "Whittier '34," *LAT,* May 10, 1970; Ola Florence Welch Jobe interview, Nixon to Ola Florence Welch Jobe, Jan. 15, Feb. 2, 1936, Aitken papers, RNL; Jonathan Aitken, *Nixon: A Life* (Washington, D.C.: Regnery, 1993).

68 "never really knew him": Donald Jackson, "Coming of Age in America," unpublished manuscript, Aug. 28, 1970, RNL.

68 Milky Ways for breakfast: Nixon to parents, undated, Nixon Family Papers, RNL; Nixon to Ola Florence Welch Jobe, undated, probably January 1936, Aitken papers, RNL; Nixon campaign press release on Duke University days, Aug. 16, 1960, RNL; Nixon, "Changing Rules of Liability in Automobile Accident Litigation," *Law and Contemporary Problems,* Duke University Law School quarterly, October 1936; oral histories by Dorothy Airheart, Frederick Albrink, Les Brown, Lyman Brownfield, and Richard Kiefer, Whittier.

68 "a kind word": Mollenkopf to Nixon, Mar. 27, 1959, and Nixon reply, June 29, 1959, RNL. "It was the first time I had been so far from home, and more than once I was tempted to head back to the West Coast!" Nixon wrote his former classmate.

69 law school escapade: Dick stayed in Durham for the summer between his second and third year of law school. The previous summer, of 1935, he spent in Whittier and had something of a social life. Marie Actis remembers dating him and recalls one memorable night when they took a water taxi out beyond the three-mile limit to where the gambling ships—floating forerunners of Las Vegas casinos—operated outside the reach of the law. Dick hit a jackpot on a one-armed bandit, and the $20 winnings paid for their date. See oral histories by Marie Actis, Frederick Albrink, Lyman Brownfield, Joseph Hiatt, and Farley Hunter, Whittier; Brownfield, "Reminiscences About Nixon"; Brownfield to Nixon, May 8, 1973, WHSF-R; Frost-Nixon transcripts, RNL.

69 Federal Bureau of Investigation: Nixon's FBI records, including the history of his application and the results of the preemployment investigation, are available on the bureau website. His interest in the FBI was inspired by an agent who gave a recruiting speech at Duke. Dean Horrack wrote to J. Edgar Hoover recommending Nixon, as did the special agent who interviewed him in Los Angeles that summer. See also Lon Fuller OH, Whittier.

70 prevailed upon Tom Bewley: Tom Bewley OH, Whittier; Lucille Parsons OH, CSUF; Evlyn Dorn interview with Brodie, FMB. In an interview with Bela Kornitzer, Bewley said that Nixon did get an offer from a New York firm.

70 bungled his first big case: The case was Los Angeles Municipal Court Action No. 457600, in which Marie Schee sued her uncle and aunt, Otto and Jenneive Steuer, over a $2,000 debt. Nixon's mistakes led to Action No. 436435, a complaint of negligence against Wingert & Bewley in Los Angeles Superior Court. Fawn Brodie compiled an extensive file on the case, which is available in her papers at the University of Utah.

Nixon started at $50 a month, finished the year at $100 a month, and then earned "a very modest percentage" of the firm's profits. He and Pat found the life dull. They didn't especially crave wealth but wanted "to live a life that was exciting, interesting and fulfilling." See Nixon reminiscences, Mar. 19, 1976, Irwin Gellman, private collection.

70 He was terrible at divorce cases: Bewley, Loubet OH, Whittier; Bewley interview with Kornitzer, BKP; Evlyn Dorn interview with Brodie, FMB; Allen file for *Time* cover story, Jan. 1954; Tom Evans, unpublished manuscript on Nixon law career, Aitken papers, RNL.

71 "Citri-Frost": With the help of Herman Perry and Tom Bewley, Dick was still paying back Citri-Frost investors during the war—even from the South Pacific in 1944.

Nixon to Bewley, Feb. 28, 1943, "Tuesday," 1943, Aug. 25, 1943, Perry to Nixon, June 13, 1944, Citri-Frost legal file, RNL. Bewley OH, Edith Holt OH, Evlyn Dorn OH, Whittier. Whittier College, for one, was not put off by Dick's professional troubles. In 1939 he was elected to the college board of trustees, the youngest member in its history. See Joseph Dmohowski, "From a Common Ground: The Quaker Heritage of Jessamyn West and Richard Nixon," *California History,* Fall 1994.

71   golden boy had soured: Wallace Black OH, Judith Wingert Loubet OH, Whittier; Dorn interview with Brodie, FMB. His partners were patient but clear-eyed. "I remember my father saying that Dick was a better politician than he was a lawyer," said Judith Wingert Loubet.

71   met at a local theater group: Elizabeth Cloes OH, Grant Garman OH, Whittier. For the Nixon marriage, see Will Swift, *Pat and Dick: The Nixons, an Intimate Portrait of a Marriage* (New York: Simon & Schuster, 2014).

72   Pat had fled: JNE, *Pat.* Her nickname at home was "Babe," and in school they called her "Buddy." She chose Patricia when her father died. A student poll at Whittier High, where she taught typing and business skills and was the faculty sponsor for the cheerleaders, found her "very purty" and "not crabby like the other teachers." Pat Ryan Nixon papers, Drown remarks, 1960, Dick to Pat, Mar. 17, 1944, Pat to Dick, Mar. 18, 1938, RNL; Virginia Counts OH, Betty Kenworthy OH, Frances King OH, Whittier; Helene Drown interview with Kornitzer, BKP.

72   "a world of make believe": "He is very interesting but quite unusual," Pat told her friend Edith Holt. Edith Holt OH, Beatrice Hawkins OH, Whittier; JNE, *Pat.*

72   "Irish gypsy who radiates": Pat to Dick, Sept. 19, 1938, Pat to Dick, undated, RNL. She improved him right away. At Pat's suggestion he had a gold-rimmed bridge in his front teeth (he had lost a tooth playing basketball in college) replaced with a more distinguished porcelain appliance. Harold Stone OH, Whittier; JNE, *Pat.*

74   She and Dick were prodigious strivers: Dick to Pat, undated, Dick to Pat, "Wednesday afternoon," 1940, RNL; Alyce Koch OH, Thomas Ryan OH, Whittier. "My Aunt Pat had done housework all her life. She wanted to make sure she didn't have to do it the rest of her life" was her niece Lawrene's analysis. Lawrene Nixon Anfinson OH, Whittier; JNE, *Pat;* Gloria Steinem, "In Your Heart You Know He's Nixon," *New York,* Oct. 28, 1968.

74   accepted his proposal of marriage: Dick to Pat, "11:35 p.m.," 1940, RNL; Judith Wingert Loubet OH, Edith Milhous Timberlake OH, CSUF; JNE, *Pat.*

74   wedding was a modest affair: JNE, *Pat;* Pat Nixon, "I Say He's a Wonderful Guy," *Saturday Evening Post,* Sept. 6, 1952; *Whittier News,* June 22, 1940; Alyce Koch OH, Whittier; Nixon to Bewley, "Tuesday," 1943, RNL.

       Ed Nixon said that the bride chose the modest wedding. "Pat was not one for ostentation in any form. She wanted it simple." Ed Nixon OH, RNL.

       The young couple had earning potential, but modest resources. Dick earned $1,170 in 1938, $1,689 in 1939, and $2,400 in 1940, according to the Nixon Family Papers, RNL. "He didn't leave a lucrative practice," said Whittier lawyer Wallace Black in his Whittier oral history.

       On Citri-Frost and Pat, see also Evlyn Dorn interview with Brodie, FMB: "He instructed that she not be told."

75   lesson of Munich: Nixon, *RN;* Paul Johnson, *Modern Times* (New York: HarperCollins, 1983).

75   likely to lead to politics: WDN, Nov. 29, 1940, Harold Stone OH, Whittier.

76   Whittier had not welcomed: David Ginsburg, General Counsel, OPA, to Nixon, Sept. 29, 1941, RNL; Milton Viorst, "Nixon of the OPA," *NYT,* Oct. 3, 1971; Judith Wingert Loubet OH, Virginia Counts OH, Whittier.

76　he felt an obligation: Nixon to Bewley, "Sunday Morning" (n.d.), Jan. 25, 1942, Feb. 8, 1942, David Ginsburg, General Counsel, OPA to Nixon, Sept. 29, 1941, Pat Nixon to Helene Drown, Jan. 10, 1942, RNL; Robert Blake OH, Tom Bewley OH, Whittier.

76　marked time in Iowa: Nixon to Bewley, May 25, 1942, Oct. 19, 1942, Jan. 3, 1943, Mar. 14, 1943, July 26, 1943, RNL; Nixon U.S. Navy records, RNL; Dorn OH, Whittier.

77　war in the South Pacific: Nixon arrived in the South Pacific in June 1943 and remained until July 1944. JFK arrived earlier and left sooner, but he and Nixon shared the same waters from June 1943 until January 1944, and, they later agreed, it is not inconceivable that they met.

77　"the smell of combat": Carl Fleps OH, Hollis Dole OH, James Stewart OH, J. Willard Dyer OH, Whittier. Both Dole and Dyer, who was one of Nixon's commanding officers, recalled coming under Japanese artillery fire with Dick on Bougainville. Stewart served on Green Island with Nixon and remembered the Japanese bombing raids. Dyer recalled how Dick, worn out from his exertions on Bougainville, had to be ordered to the rear for a week's rest and recuperation: "I could see that he needed a rest," said Dyer, and "he was visibly angry with me." In *RN*, Nixon said the crashed bomber was a B-29, a strategic bomber used against Japan. It was more likely a B-24, or perhaps a B-25, that carried out the raids on Rabaul.

78　"When I knew that I didn't have the cards": Nixon White House tapes, Apr. 19, 1972, RNL; Hollis Dole OH, James Stewart OH, J. Willard Dyer OH, Whittier.

78　"All of me loves": JNE, *Pat.*

78　prepared a handwritten will: Nixon will, Dick to Pat, Sept. 8, 9, 1943, Jan. 28, 1944, Apr. 29, 1944, RNL.

79　rediscovered her taste for freedom: JNE, *Pat.*

79　"satisfied my yen *to do* something": Dick to Pat, Apr. 15, 1944, RNL.

CHAPTER 5: A KIND OF MAN THE COUNTRY NEEDS

81　A fraught and chilly capital: JNE, *Pat;* Roy McLaughlin to Raymond Haight, Mar. 5, 1947, Haight to McLaughlin, Mar. 7, 1947, Nixon to Perry, Mar. 28, 1947, Nixon to Garland, Dec. 24, 1946, RNL.

82　The Cold War: "Killing Japanese didn't bother me very much at the time," said General Curtis LeMay, a choreographer of the attacks on Japan. "I suppose if I had lost the war, I would have been tried as a war criminal." See "Report on the Covert Activities of the Central Intelligence Agency," CIA, Sept. 1954; *Air Power and Warfare: The Proceedings of the 8th Military History Symposium, United States Air Force Academy,* ed. Alfred Hurley and Robert Ehrhart (Honolulu, HI: University Press of the Pacific, 2002); *Time,* Aug. 20, 1945.

　　For general Cold War history, see Richard Rhodes, *Dark Sun: The Making of the Hydrogen Bomb* (New York: Simon & Schuster, 1995) and *The Making of the Atomic Bomb* (New York: Touchstone, 1988); Joe Martin, *My First Fifty Years in Politics* (New York: McGraw-Hill, 1960); John Lewis Gaddis, *George F. Kennan: An American Life* (New York: Penguin, 2011), *Strategies of Containment* (New York: Oxford University Press, 2005), and *The Cold War: A New History* (New York: Penguin, 2005); Paul Johnson, *Modern Times* (New York: HarperCollins, 1983); Robert Donovan, *Conflict and Crisis* (New York: Norton, 1977); David McCullough, *Truman* (New York: Simon & Schuster, 1992); Stephen Ambrose, *Eisenhower,* Vol. 1 (New York: Simon & Schuster, 1983).

82　Whittier Narrows Dam: Nixon campaign press release, Oct. 26, 1946, Nixon to Perry, Apr. 2, 1947, RNL.

83　Plan B settlement: "Whether or not this [pressure] made any profound impression on him, I don't know," said Pauley, "except that I do know that the matter of the Whittier Narrows . . . was shortly resolved and Congressman Nixon won the Republican primary and then afterwards became the Senator." Edwin Pauley, J. Paull Marshall, interviews with Kornitzer, BKP; Perry to Nixon, Jan. 15, 1947. Nixon to Perry, Jan. 25, 1947. Nixon to Perry, Feb. 17, 1947, Nixon to Perry, Mar. 10, 1947, Nixon to Perry, May 3, 1947, Perry to Nixon, May 15, 1947, Perry to Nixon, Jan. 17, 1948, Nixon to Perry, Jan. 20, 1948, Perry to Nixon, Mar. 12, 1948, Nixon to Perry, Mar. 22, 1948, Nixon to Day, Feb. 27, 1948, Mar. 23, 1948, Apr. 21, 1948, RNL; H. E. Hedger to Los Angeles County Flood Control District, May 2, 1947, RNL.

83   pleased with his committee assignments: Pat Nixon to Frank and Hannah, undated, 1947, RNL. Nixon and Martin differ on the HUAC assignment. In his memoirs (*My First Fifty Years in Politics*) Martin recalled being urged by California interests to give Nixon a seat he craved on HUAC; in *RN*, Nixon says he accepted Martin's request "with considerable reluctance." Pat's letter seems to tip the scales toward Martin. So does aide Bill Arnold's memoir (*Back When It All Began*, Vantage, 1972), which says that "with characteristic prescience" Nixon sought appointment to HUAC, a "politically dangerous" choice because "the committee had earned itself a measure of disrepute as a witch hunting group."

84   Taft-Hartley legislation: It was during the Taft-Hartley debate that Nixon revealed an early preference for no-nonsense tough guys in the union movement, like Teamster leader Dave Beck. "Beck stopped in to see me," Nixon wrote Perry. "He was far more reasonable in his attitude than some of the CIO boys. He, at least, has no Communist leanings and is a believer in the free enterprise system." In the 1950s, Beck was convicted and imprisoned on corruption charges. Nixon to McCall, Apr. 23, 1947, Nixon to Perry, Mar. 4, 1947, RNL; Eric Goldman, "The 1947 Kennedy-Nixon 'Tube City' Debate," *Saturday Review*, Oct. 16, 1976; Judith Wingert Loubet OH, CSUF; Nixon, *RN*.

85   Nixon's staff was tiny: Harlow interview, Thompson; William Robinson to *Saturday Review*, Nov. 14, 1962, RNL; Arnold, *Back When It All Began;* Irwin Gellman, *The Contender* (New York: Free Press, 1999).

86   Truman decided to act: McCullough, *Truman.* McCullough suggests that Truman did not believe homegrown Reds posed a threat but instituted the loyalty program to defend his administration against charges that it was soft on Communism. If so, it was at some cost. More than three million government employees would be investigated, several thousand would resign, and 212 would be dismissed. The program did not stop, and may have fed, the rise of McCarthyism. Alonzo Hamby, in *Man of the People: A Life of Harry Truman* (Oxford University Press, 1995), puts the number of those dismissed between 400 and 1,200 and those who resigned between 1,000 and 6,000. Eric Goldman, *The Crucial Decade* (New York: Vintage, 1956); James T. Patterson, *Grand Expectations: The United States, 1945–1974* (New York: Oxford University Press, 1996).

86   "so called Marshall Plan": Letter to Nixon signed by Roy Crocker and five others, with supporting note from Frank Jorgensen, Aug. 12, 1947, Asa Call to Kyle Palmer, Aug. 10, 1948, Perry to Nixon, Apr. 23, 1948, RNL. The Marshall Plan and the Truman Doctrine had some support among the Amateurs. Whittier newspaper editor Rex Kennedy and John Garland, who was active in the Olympics movement, both wrote Nixon in support of an internationalist foreign policy. "If we are to hold a dominate [*sic*] leadership in helping to build a new civilization in the world, we can't falter when the first crisis hits us," said Kennedy. Kennedy to Nixon, Mar. 13, 1947, Nixon to Kennedy, Apr. 3, 1947, Nixon to Garland, Aug. 21, 1947, RNL.

87   a select bipartisan committee: Nixon to Charles Kersten, Aug. 1, 1947, Nixon to Perry, Mar. 4, 1947, Mar. 21, 1947, Nixon press releases, July 2, 1947, Aug. 5, 28, 1947, RNL; *NYT,* July 30, Aug. 3, 1947; Alsop column, "The Herter Experiment," *St. Petersburg Times,* Aug. 2, 1947; Nixon, *RN.*

88   "hectic pace continues": Phil Potter, J. Edward Murray interviews, Halberstam papers,

BU; Dick to Pat, Sept. 1, 13, 14, 22, 1947, Jenkins to Nixon, Dec. 10, 1947, RNL. It is not known if the delegation availed themselves of the company of three young ladies in Paris whose names Kennedy gave Nixon before Dick left. See Jonathan Aitken, *Nixon: A Life* (Washington, D.C.: Regnery, 1993).

89   Economic activity was indeed lagging: In a March 12, 1958, memo to Rose Mary Woods, who met Dick while working for the Herter committee and ultimately became his aide, secretary, and confidante, Nixon says that his diary of the trip contained both nightly notations he made in Europe and his immediate recollections after he arrived home, which were used in his speeches on behalf of the Marshall Plan. For further details of the visit to Greece, see Trip Report, American Embassy, Athens, Oct. 24, 1947, RNL; *NYT,* Sept. 18, 26, 1947; Ochs obituary, *WP,* Nov. 29, 2011 (Nixon mistakenly called him "Oaks"); Gellman, *The Contender.*

90   Rosetta Rubsamen: Rosetta to Dick, Oct. 1, Nov. 18, 1947, Mar. 22, 1948, RNL. Rubsamen is listed in the embassy records as "legal assistant." She was Italian born, according to census records, and had lived in Los Angeles before the war.

     A veteran of the Office of Strategic Services, Allen Dulles would go on to serve as CIA director under Presidents Eisenhower and Kennedy; he is listed on the committee travel records as accompanying the congressmen on the *Queen Mary.* Chip Bohlen addressed the members of the Herter mission before they departed; Lucius Clay—an intimate of Dwight Eisenhower—met with them in Berlin. All three would play important roles in the Cold War, and in Nixon's future.

91   he needed to sell George Marshall's plan: Congress passed a short-term foreign aid bill, then adopted the Marshall Plan in March. Nixon was opposed in the 1948 election by Stephen Zetterberg, an unknown, underfunded Democratic attorney. When polls showed that he could knock Zetterberg out in the primary, Nixon and the Amateurs went all in, winning the Democratic nomination by more than four thousand votes. Klein OH and exit interview, Nixon speech notes, RNL; for Nixon speaking schedule, see Nixon press releases, Oct. 14, 20, 23, 1947, RNL, and *Los Angeles Times,* Oct. 26, Nov. 3, 5, 12, 13, 1947; Robert Finch OH, Columbia University; Finch interview, BKP; William Bundy, *A Tangled Web* (New York: Macmillan, 1999).

CHAPTER 6: HUAC

93   McCarthyism: Nixon maiden address, Feb. 18, 1947, RNL; *Life,* Feb. 17, 1947. Though Eisler was a leading Communist Party organizer in the 1930s, he was not a "mastermind" of Soviet espionage. John Earl Haynes and Harvey Klehr, *Venona* (New Haven, CT: Yale University Press, 1999). See also John Earl Haynes, Harvey Klehr, and Alexander Vassiliev, *Spies* (New Haven, CT: Yale University Press, 2009); Harvey Klehr, John Earl Haynes, and Kyrill Anderson, *The Soviet World of American Communism* (New Haven, CT: Yale University Press, 1995); Dean Acheson, *Present at the Creation* (New York: Norton, 1969); John Ehrman, "A Half-Century of Controversy: the Alger Hiss Case," Center for the Study of Intelligence, 2007, Central Intelligence Agency, www.cia.gov/library/center-for-the-study-of-intelligence/kent-csi/vol44no5/html /v44i5a01p.htm; *Thirty Years of Treason: Excerpts from Hearings Before the House Committee on Un-American Activities, 1938–1968,* ed. Eric Bentley (New York: Viking, 1971).

96   "The Committee": During the Alger Hiss case, Nixon admitted to a federal grand jury that "some of our individual members of the committee had been from time to time accused of being anti-Semitic, with probably good cause." The *Washington Post* decried the "stump speeches, gavel beating, general indecorum, and contempt citations which intensified the carnival or Halloween atmosphere" of the committee's hearings. The Republican *Herald Tribune* of New York lambasted HUAC's "expedition with blunderbuss and klieg lights." The *New York Times* detailed the committee's flaws: it trampled the rights of witnesses, intimidated worthy social criticism, and chilled free speech.

Nixon Grand Jury testimony in the Hiss case, HST; Nixon to "Friend," May 10, 1947, RNL; Stripling quote from Weinstein Papers, HI. For Stripling's background see his grand jury testimony in the Hiss-Chambers case, HST. *Investigation of un-American Activities and Propaganda,* Report of the Special Committee on Un-American Activities, Jan. 1939; Cong. Rec., Feb. 18, 1947, May 19, 1948; *U.S. Congressional Serial Set,* Issue 13151; *Time,* Feb. 14, 1944; *NYT,* Oct. 23, 1947; *WP,* Oct. 31, 1947; *NYHT,* Oct. 29, 1947; George Reedy OH, LBJ.

99   Hollywood Ten: "Whenever the going got rough for Hollywood's befuddled and intimidated executives, Nixon could be counted on to ask a question or two that could be answered in a self serving fashion," Edward Dmytryk, a Hollywood Ten screenwriter, would recall in his memoir *Odd Man Out.* "It would be uncharitable, but not unjust, to suggest that he did so because they were, or could be, a source of support in his future campaigns." Stripling agreed, complaining to Alan Weinstein that Nixon had gone "limber tail" during the Hollywood hearings and "run out" to save himself politically. Neither Stripling nor Dmytryk credits Nixon for a third possibility: that he showed discernment by absenting himself from the spectacle.

Trumbo won Oscars for *Roman Holiday* and *The Brave One,* and shattered the blacklist when hired to write the screenplays for the blockbusters *Exodus* and *Spartacus,* for which he was given credit. While blacklisted, he used fronts and pen names like Felix Lutzkendorf and Sally Stubblefield.

On Nixon and HUAC and the Hollywood Ten: "Richard M. Nixon: Investigator of Communism," a memoir prepared for Bela Kornitzer by Rev. John F. Cronin, BKP. Congressional Record, Nov. 24, 1947. Nixon to Day, Apr. 21, 1948; Nixon to Perry, June 17, 1947, Nixon to McCall, Dec. 8, 1947, Perry to Nixon, Nov. 30, 1948, RNL. For film industry lobbying of Nixon see Paul McNutt to Nixon, Oct. 26, 1947, RNL.

For HUAC history and Hollywood Ten see Alistair Cooke, *A Generation on Trial* (New York: Knopf, 1950); Edward Dmytryk, *Odd Man Out* (Carbondale: Southern Illinois University Press, 1996); Stefan Kanfer, *Plague Years* (New York: Atheneum, 1973); Robert Carr, *The House Committee on Un-American Activities* (Ithaca, NY: Cornell University Press, 1952); Victor Navasky, *Naming Names* (New York: Viking, 1980); John Sbardellati, *J. Edgar Hoover Goes to the Movies* (Ithaca, NY: Cornell University Press, 2012); Athan Theoharis, *From the Secret File of J. Edgar Hoover* (Chicago: Ivan R. Dee, 1991); Bentley, *Thirty Years of Treason.*

For FBI cooperation with HUAC see the bureau's HUAC and Nixon files, including Nichols to Tolson, Mar. 18, 19, 25, 1947, and Hood to Director, May 12, 13, 14, 1947, with Hoover notation on May 13, 1947, letter from Nichols: "Expedite. I want Hood to extend every assistance to this committee." The record shows that on that day the FBI delivered a mass of material to Stripling. See also McNaughton to Tasker, Sept. 10, 1948, McNaughton Papers, HST.

100   Mundt-Nixon bill: The Mundt-Nixon bill outlawed any efforts to establish a totalitarian dictatorship controlled by a foreign government in the United States, and membership in organizations that attempted to do so. It required Communists to register with the government and regulated certain political liberties. Hays HUAC testimony, Feb. 10, 1948, in Bentley, *Thirty Years;* Hays to Nixon, Mar. 1, 1948, Rev. John Cronin to Nixon, May 11, 1948, with legal analyses, RNL; John Heselton to Nixon, May 19, 1948, Kenneth Parkinson to Nixon, Jan. 12, Feb. 13, 1948, Nixon to John Foster Dulles, Jan. 17, May 17, 1948, Dulles to Nixon, Feb. 3, 1948, Nixon "Dear Friend" letter to supporters, Apr. 28, 1948, Nixon to R. A. Robinson, Feb. 25, 1948, Nixon to McCall, Mar. 13, 1948, Mundt to Thomas, July 27, 1948, RNL; *NYT,* Dec. 7, 1947, Mar. 5, 6, May 2, 20, Aug. 15, 1948; *LAT,* May 18, 1948; Cong. Rec., May 14, 19, 1948; *Time,* May 31, 1948; Herblock cartoon, *WP,* May 15, 1948; McNaughton to Bermingham, Apr. 30, 1948, McNaughton Papers, HST; Bert and Peter Andrews, *A*

Tragedy of History: A Journalist's Confidential Role in the Hiss-Chambers Case (Washington, D.C.: Luce, 1962); Bill Arnold, *Back When It All Began* (New York: Vantage, 1972); Cooke, *Generation on Trial.*

101 leaking HUAC's confidential files: Stripling to Nixon, Apr. 1, 1948, with memo, Nixon to Perry, Apr. 19, 29, 1948, with reports, Nixon to Perry, June 12, 1951, with reports, RNL.

102 Edward Condon: Stripling grand jury testimony, HST; Condon to Nixon, July 17, 1947, Nixon notes on "Condon," undated, Nixon to Douglas Maggs, Mar. 16, 1948 (one of a dozen sent to various acquaintances), Nixon telegram to Harriman, Mar. 5, 1948, RNL; Earl Mazo OH, Columbia University.

CHAPTER 7: A TRAGEDY OF HISTORY

104 needed it to refresh their marriage: JNE, *Pat;* Frederick Albrink OH, Whittier; Representative Lindy Boggs, interview with author; Pat Nixon correspondence files, Nixon to Smith, July 6, 1948, RNL. Ed Nixon OH, RNL; Albrink quoted Pat as saying: "If I were a young lawyer, there is a little town out here on the edge of the desert; it doesn't amount to much, but it has a great future. If I were a young lawyer I think I'd settle out there and buy up some of the land around there that you can get for $5 an acre. . . . It's a little place called Palm Springs." Then, said Albrink, "Pat made the statement, not too strongly, but she sort of wished that they were going to be doing that . . . rather than going to Washington."

105 foreign minister Jan Masaryk: Jeremy Isaacs and Taylor Downing, *Cold War* (Boston: Little, Brown, 1998); Paul Johnson, *Modern Times* (New York: HarperCollins, 1983); Eric Goldman, *The Crucial Decade* (New York: Vintage, 1956); Stephen Ambrose, *Eisenhower,* Vol. 1 (New York: Simon & Schuster, 1983).

106 Bentley, a Vassar graduate: When asked by a grand juror about the committee's motivations, Stripling said, "Congress is made up of people in politics, sir." Stripling Grand Jury testimony in the Hiss case, HST; Thomas to Mundt, July 26, 1948, Mundt to J. D. Coon, Aug. 3, 1948, Weinstein papers, HI. The *New York World Telegram,* in its July 20, 1948, edition, under the headline RED RING BARED BY BLOND QUEEN, called Bentley a "svelte and striking blonde"; *Time,* Aug. 9, 1948.

106 "a forlorn shot in the dark": The grand jury testimony given in 1948 and 1949 by Chambers, Nixon, and other HUAC members and staff, describing how the Hiss case unfolded, was made public in 1999 and is available at the Truman presidential library.

Nixon, Stripling, and the others faced a grand jury of skeptics led by federal prosecutors who were infuriated by HUAC's charges of a cover-up. As in their various memoirs, the witnesses tended to stress their own role in the affair. Nevertheless, recounted when memories were fresh, bound by oath, and open to challenge, their grand jury testimony is likely the most reliable record of the origins of the case. In resolving differences in published accounts, and other mysteries, I found it most valuable.

The notes, tapes, and transcripts of interviews conducted by historian Allen Weinstein for his landmark work *Perjury* (Knopf, 1978) are in his papers at the Hoover Institution at Stanford University; the Stripling interviews and his tape-recorded recollections are especially rich in behind-the-scenes material. The helpful papers of Sam Tanenhaus, the author of *Whittaker Chambers* (Random House, 1997), and Nixon biographer Ralph de Toledano are also housed there.

In the decade after Hiss was found guilty, Nixon composed memos on his role for biographers de Toledano and Earl Mazo, which can be found at the Nixon library.

Father John Cronin gave an important written account of the origins of Nixon's Red-fighting days—"Richard M. Nixon: Investigator of Communism"—to biographer Bela Kornitzer. The memo can be found in the Kornitzer papers at Drew University. In it Cronin states, definitively, that he told Nixon about Alger Hiss in 1947.

Finally, the Nixon library has transcripts of Nixon's dictated memories of the events chronicled in the 1962 memoir *Six Crises,* including an account of the Hiss case.

107 on his list was Alger Hiss: Chambers took a long, twisty road to the witness table. In 1939 a friendly journalist—Isaac Don Levine—had brought him, via the White House staff, to the State Department's Adolf Berle. Berle was wary. He thought the distraught Chambers was suffering from "some deep emotional strain" and might be mentally disturbed. Neither Hiss nor the other officials whom Chambers named were then in powerful positions. So Berle kept notes, did some checking, but let the matter slide. It took three years for the FBI to catch up with Chambers, for the first of many interviews, in 1942.

Meanwhile, Hiss's star was rising in the government. Levine, Chambers, and other reformed ex-Communists, like HUAC aide Benjamin Mandel, feared a cover-up. Government security officials, most notably the FBI and the State Department's Ray Murphy, shared their frustration and leaked the Chambers allegations to reporters and investigators like Father Cronin, who spread them, over the years, among church and business officials, Red-hunting journalists, and members of Congress like Charles Kersten and Richard Nixon. The Hiss story "was generally scuttle-butted around Washington," Karl Mundt recalled—one of the worst-kept secrets in the capital. The HUAC files and closed-door hearings were chock-full of Hiss's name.

In 1945, the defector Igor Gouzenko warned Canadian and U.S. authorities that the Soviets had a high-ranking spy in the State Department. Hiss fit the description, and he was visited by the FBI in 1946 and 1947. He soon left the government, under a cloud, for the Carnegie Endowment. He was called before the grand jury investigating subversion in 1948 and denied he was a Communist.

In early 1948, looking for information that would tie Condon to the Communists, Stripling sent Mandel and another HUAC investigator to call on Chambers but found him reluctant to testify. "They gave me a brief memorandum in which Chambers related this underground operation," Stripling told the Grand Jury. "I believe the memorandum contains the name of Alger Hiss."

Bentley's renunciation of Communism took the saga public. It was a staggering loss to the Soviets. She handed the FBI leads that closed down several working spy rings and gave credence to the alarms of the anti-Communists. After listening to Bentley, and spurred on by Mundt and others, Stripling subpoenaed Chambers to corroborate her story.

When Chambers showed up to testify on August 3, Stripling professed surprise at the passion, the detail, and the names in the witness's prepared statement. *Time* had never been kind to HUAC, and Stripling was expecting a reluctant witness. "You want to testify to *this?*" he asked Chambers. They moved immediately into the closed-door HUAC session, and then to the public hearing.

Stripling, Mundt, Nixon, Chambers, Hiss grand jury testimony, HST; Cronin, "Richard M. Nixon: Investigator of Communism," BKP; Cronin, Stripling interviews, Weinstein papers, HI; unsigned "Memorandum of Conversation, Tuesday, Mar. 20, 1945, Westminster, Md.," and memos from Nichols to Tolson, Oct. 9, 10, 1947, FBI; Isaac Don Levine, *Eyewitness to History* (New York: Hawthorn, 1973).

107 Hiss and Chambers were alike: "That dying world, which, in the death throe of the First World War, had just destroyed eleven million lives, and was visibly preparing to destroy as many more in its next convulsion, that dying world, of which my family was a tiny image, and whose poisons had also killed my brother . . . stirred a grimness in me," Chambers would recall, describing his conversion to Communism in *Witness.*

Stripling, Berle grand jury testimony, HST; Marbury interview, Weinstein papers, HI; Roosevelt "devil" quote in John Lewis Gaddis, *Strategies of Containment* (New York: Oxford University Press, 2005), from Keith D. Eagles, "Ambassador Joseph E.

Davies and American-Soviet Relations, 1937–1941" (PhD dissertation, University of Washington, 1966); William F. Buckley Jr., "The End of Whittaker Chambers," *Esquire,* Sept. 1962; Arthur Schlesinger Jr., "Whittaker Chambers & His *Witness,*" *Saturday Review,* May 24, 1952; Robert Stripling and Bob Considine, *The Red Plot Against America* (Drexel Hill, PA: Bell, 1949); John A. Farrell, *Clarence Darrow: Attorney for the Damned* (New York: Doubleday, 2011). The Steffens quote is from an Apr. 3, 1919, letter to Marie Howe, published in *The Letters of Lincoln Steffens* (New York: Harcourt, Brace, 1938). For the liberal letter see the *New Republic,* Aug. 23, 1939. For the life stories of Chambers and Hiss see Chambers, *Witness* (New York: Random House, 1952), Sam Tanenhaus, *Whittaker Chambers: A Biography* (New York: Random House, 1997), and Allen Weinstein, *Perjury: The Hiss-Chambers Case* (New York: Knopf, 1978). Levine, *Eyewitness.*

109 cost of Hiss's treason: The Hiss case was a celebrated cause of both left and right, hotly debated—despite such persuasive accounts as Weinstein's *Perjury*—until the fall of the Soviet Union in 1991. For a few years afterward, some Western scholars, including Weinstein, got limited access to Soviet intelligence archives. At the same time, the U.S. government revealed the secrets of its Venona project, which broke the Soviet code in the 1940s. When combined with the evidence presented at Hiss's trials and collected elsewhere since 1948, the new evidence leaves little doubt of his work as a spy. John Earl Haynes, interview with author; see John Earl Haynes and Harvey Klehr, *Venona* (New Haven, CT: Yale University Press, 1999), John Earl Haynes, Harvey Klehr, and Alexander Vassiliev, *Spies* (New Haven, CT: Yale University Press, 2009), and Allen Weinstein and Alexander Vassiliev, *The Haunted Wood* (New York: Random House, 1999).

Grover, Hersey, Hughes interviews, Halberstam papers, BU; Prosecutor Thomas Murphy quoted in Cooke, *A Generation on Trial* (New York: Knopf, 1950).

Years later, as president, Nixon would dismiss the documents that Hiss smuggled to Chambers as "old and outdated and unimportant," according to aide H. R. Haldeman. See HRH diary, June 20, 1971.

109 the "unkempt, disorderly": Chambers: Nixon dictation, Aug. 26, 1961, Hiss Case, RNL; Nixon-Gannon; Nixon grand jury testimony, HST; HUAC transcript, Aug. 3, 1948; *NYT,* Aug. 4, 1948; *NYHT,* Aug. 4, 1948; *Evening Star* (Washington), Aug. 3, 1948. The press fudged the distinction between espionage and infiltration. RED "UNDERGROUND" IN FEDERAL POSTS ALLEGED BY EDITOR, the *Times* declared in a page-one headline the next day.

110 Hiss now faced a choice: HUAC transcript, Aug. 5, 1948; Nixon dictation, Aug. 26, 1961, RNL; Nixon-Gannon; *Evening Star,* Aug. 5, 1948; *NYT,* Aug. 6, 1948; Mundt, Stripling grand jury testimony, HST; Chambers, *Witness.*

112 Nixon's audacity: Nixon, Stripling, Berle, Mundt, grand jury testimony, HST; Nixon dictation, Aug. 26, 1961, "Memorandum on the Hiss-Chambers Case," Feb. 1, 1949, RNL; White House tape, Nixon and Timmons, July 2, 1971, RNL; *Time,* Aug. 25, 1952; Nixon-Gannon; HUAC transcript, Aug. 5, 1948; Chambers, *Witness.*

113 Father John Cronin had told him: John Cronin told several Nixon biographers that he informed Congressman Nixon that Hiss was a Communist in early 1947. See Cronin memo to Kornitzer, "Richard M. Nixon: Investigator of Communism," BKP; Earl Mazo, *Richard Nixon: A Political and Personal Portrait* (New York: Avon, 1960); Garry Wills, *Nixon Agonistes: The Crisis of the Self-Made Man* (Boston: Houghton Mifflin, 1969).

In his 1962 memoir *Six Crises* and ever after, however, Nixon insisted that the August 3, 1948, HUAC hearing was "the first time I had ever heard" of Alger Hiss. Nixon told biographer Herbert Parmet that either Kersten or John F. Kennedy introduced him to Cronin in early 1947 and that while he and the priest discussed the

Communist threat, "I do not recall any discussions with Father Cronin of the Hiss-Chambers case at that time." See Nixon to Parmet, Dec. 10, 1986, Nov. 17, 1988, RNL.

Weinstein and others alleged that Nixon, trying to dramatize his role, purposefully concealed his knowledge of Hiss and the head start it gave him in leading the chase. But it is also possible that, in his busy first weeks as a freshman congressman, Nixon paid no attention to the name, filed it away, or forgot it.

Gellman supports Nixon's version in *The Contender,* noting how Cronin, at the end of his life, qualified his story when telling Jonathan Aitken that he "might have" alerted Nixon. But Cronin's initial recollection, given to Kornitzer in the late 1950s, would surely be more accurate.

It's a teapot tempest. If Nixon did recall Hiss's name, the information would not have given him much of an advantage: Cronin and others had spread the allegation throughout the capital. At HUAC, Stripling, Mandel, Mundt, and others knew. The challenge was not in the knowing, but the proving. Nixon showed nerve, performed ably, exposed a spy, and was justly rewarded.

For an analysis of the dispute, see John T. Donovan's biography of Cronin, *Crusader in the Cold War* (New York: Peter Lang, 2005). See also Day to Nixon, Aug. 21, 1948, Cronin to Nixon, Dec. 3, 1952, RNL; Weinstein interview with Cronin, Weinstein papers, HI; Cronin, "The Problem of American Communism," Francis Matthews papers, HST; Tames OH, Senate Historical Office, U.S. Senate.

114   Nixon had a personal reason: The "Harvard . . . Whittier" exchange with Hiss may be apocryphal. But Stripling insisted to Weinstein that it took place. Even as a contrived memory, it is worth noting for how it captured, in Stripling's mind, the essence of Nixon's animosity toward Hiss. HUAC transcript, Aug. 5, 1948; Nixon dictation, Aug. 26, 1961, Nixon to Bert Andrews, "Memorandum on the Hiss-Chambers Case," RNL; Stripling interview, Weinstein papers, HI. Nixon was impressed, as well, by the fact that Chambers was willing to take a lie detector test, but Hiss was not. See Nixon to Jerry Morgan, Sept. 28, 1948, RNL.

115   Nixon led a HUAC delegation: Nixon grand jury testimony, HST; HUAC transcript, Aug. 7, 1948; Nixon dictation, Aug. 26, 1961, Nixon to Dulles, Sept. 7, 1948, Nixon to Bewley, Sept. 1, 1948, Kersten to Mazo, July 11, 1958, Dorothy Cox interview, Aitken papers, RNL; Dulles to Nixon, Feb. 10, 1950, Allen file for *Time* cover story, Jan. 1954, Nixon to Andrews, "Memorandum on the Hiss-Chambers Case," RNL; Allen Dulles and Nixon oral histories, Princeton University; William Rogers interview, Cronin, "Richard M. Nixon: Investigator of Communism," BKP; Levine, *Eyewitness;* JNE, *Pat;* Stripling, *Red Plot;* Andrews, *Tragedy;* Chambers, *Witness; NYHT,* June 2, 3, 4, 1952; Earl Chapman OH, Whittier; see also Mundt to Brownell, Aug. 13, 1948, Dulles to Brownell, Aug. 20, 1948, Weinstein papers, HI.

117   hearings that transformed the case: Nixon to Dulles, "Personal," Sept. 7, 1948, RNL; Chambers, *Witness; NYT,* Aug. 18, 19, 1948; *NYHT,* Aug. 18, 1948; HUAC transcript, Aug. 16, 17, 1948.

Hiss was right to accuse Nixon of leaking. "I leaked everything," Nixon told Henry Kissinger and Haldeman in a July 1, 1971, conversation captured by the White House taping system. "Convict the son of a bitch in the press. That's the way it's done," Nixon told Haldeman, Charles Colson, and John Ehrlichman in another conversation captured on tape that day. RNL.

118   final showdown took place: *Evening Star,* Aug. 25, 26, 1948; *NYT,* Aug. 26, 1948; *WP,* Aug. 26, 1948; *The Nation,* Sept. 4, 1948; *Time,* Sept. 6, 1948; HUAC transcript, Aug. 25, 1948; Levine, *Eyewitness.*

"I got to say for Hiss. He never ratted on anybody else. Never. He never ratted," Nixon told his aides, on July 2, 1971. As for Chambers: "They finished him. . . . The informer is not wanted in our society," Nixon told counsel John Dean on February 28,

1973. White House tapes, Nixon, Haldeman, and Colson, July 2, 1971, Nixon and Dean, Feb. 28, 1973, RNL.

121 bombshell in the slander case: When asked why he had lied about the espionage, Chambers later told the grand jury: "It was my desire not to inflict greater damage on these people than was necessary in the course of revealing Communist activities. That seemed to me to be the ultimate perfidy. . . . If the result is technically perjury, I can only say that my mind is at peace."

In *Six Crises,* Nixon hogs credit for the "bombshells" by omitting from his account the valuable tip given to HUAC by Vazzana, the suggestion by Bert Andrews that Nixon subpoena Chambers, and Stripling's role in persuading a reluctant Nixon to travel to Westminster on December 1. "Playing a long hunch," Nixon wrote, "I suggested to Stripling that we drive to Westminster at once."

The Chambers, Nixon, and Stripling memoirs differ on who said what at the Westminster meeting. I have relied, where possible, on their grand jury testimony.

Hugh Scott to Nixon, Aug. 24, 1948, William Arnold to Robert Finch, Aug. 30, 1948, Arnold to William Jenner, Sept. 9, 1948, Brownell to Nixon, Sept. 27, 1948, Nixon to Bewley, Sept. 1, 1948, Nixon to Gerald Kepple, Jan. 25, 1949, Nixon speaking calendars, RNL; Nichols to Tolson, Dec. 20, 1948, FBI; Stripling, Wheeler, Chambers grand jury testimony, HST; Frank McNaughton to Don Bermingham, Dec. 4, 1948, McNaughton papers, HST; Vazzana interview, Weinstein papers, HI.

122 carved-out pumpkin in his garden: FBI memo, Los Angeles office to Hoover, Mar. 30, 1949, FBI; Stripling, Appell, Chambers grand jury testimony, HST. The HUAC press release and telegrams from Arnold (Dec. 4, 1948), Andrews (Dec. 2, 4, 1948), and Stripling (Dec. 3, 5, 1948), and Nixon's replies (Dec. 4, 1948), are at the Nixon presidential library. Nixon, *Six Crises* (Garden City, NY: Doubleday, 1962); *Evening Star,* Dec. 3, 4, 5, 6, 1948; *NYT,* Dec. 4, 1948; *NYHT,* Dec. 3, 4, 1948.

123 gone off and bought poison: Nixon and Stripling grand jury testimony, HST; Weinstein interview of Stripling, HI; FBI memo, Los Angeles office to Hoover, Mar. 30, 1949; Chambers, *Witness;* Nixon, *Six Crises;* Stripling, *Red Plot; NYHT,* Apr. 9, 1952, Dec. 11, 1948; Ladd to Hoover, Dec. 7, 1948; Nichols to Tolson, Dec. 20, 1948, FBI.

124 "You can't indict your main witness": See Stripling, Nixon, and Mundt grand jury testimony, HST; Cronin interview, Weinstein papers, HI; Donovan, *Crusader;* Wills, *Nixon Agonistes; Evening Star,* Aug. 19, 1948; *NYT,* Dec. 14, 1948; Alexander Campbell to Mundt, Dec. 8, 1948, Nixon to McGohey, Dec. 11, 1948, Nixon to Parmet, Dec. 10, 1986, Nov. 17, 1988, RNL; FBI memo, Los Angeles office to Hoover, Mar. 30, 1949, Nichols to Tolson, Sept. 29, 1948, Ladd to Hoover, Dec. 8, 1948, Whitson to Fletcher, Dec. 9, 1948, Nichols to Tolson, Dec. 2, 1948, Ladd to Hoover, Dec. 9, 1948, Hoover to Clark, Dec. 9, 1948, Nichols to Tolson, Jan. 14, 1949, FBI. The Nixon diary entry is in the Hiss case files at the RNL. The "double weapon" quote is from a March 27, 1973, conversation between Nixon and William Rogers, captured on the Nixon White House taping system.

On December 22, 1971, the taping system caught Nixon telling John Mitchell and John Ehrlichman that he believed Chambers and Hiss were homosexuals. "They were both that way," Nixon said. "And relationships sometimes poison a lot of these things."

124 they will prosecute the poor bastards: Nixon's relationship with the FBI was complex. From his service on HUAC, and via Father Cronin, the congressman had a working relationship with assistant director Lou Nichols, who handled congressional and public affairs for the FBI, and with agent Ed Hummer, who worked on the Hiss case. Throughout the fall of 1948, Nixon and HUAC leaked information to the FBI, and it passed tips to the committee.

Citing these relationships, Hiss's defenders have tried to tie Nixon to J. Edgar Hoover and an alleged FBI conspiracy to frame Hiss. The record does not support the charge. Hoover was a bureaucratic infighter, mindful that Truman was his boss. The FBI director thought Cronin was indiscreet, and Nixon an unknown quantity, and initially did not want his agents helping them.

By December, however, Nixon and Stripling were in frequent contact with Nichols, and their first calls after the discovery of the pumpkin papers were to the FBI.

Nixon then launched an extensive, multiyear project of wooing Hoover—spending weekends with him in California, throwing him a surprise party for his birthday, and praising the director and the bureau in speeches. Hoover responded by leaking Nixon helpful information from FBI files and introducing him to wealthy conservatives like oilman Clint Murchison.

For Nixon's candid recollections on the Truman administration and the FBI ("We won the Hiss case in the papers. We did. I had to leak stuff all over the place. Because the Justice Department would not prosecute it. Hoover didn't even cooperate"), see White House tapes, Nixon, Kissinger, and Haldeman, July 1, 1971, and Nixon, Colson, Haldeman, and Ehrlichman, July 1, 1971, RNL; Hoover to Nixon, Jan. 31, 1950, Nixon to Hoover, Aug. 25, 1955, Hoover to Nixon, Sept. 7, 1955, Nixon to Murchison, Feb. 27, 1955, Hoover to Nixon, Jan. 2, 1958, Hoover to Nixon, Aug. 28, 1959, Hoover to Nixon, Apr. 5, July 21, 1960, Hoover to Pat Nixon, Dec. 12, 1960, RNL.

124   Nixon had amazed the capital: *Newsweek,* Aug. 30, 1948; *Guardian,* July 22, 1960.

125   pejorative impressions of Nixon: Nixon, Chambers, Stripling, and Andrews all wrote bestselling memoirs about the Hiss case. Stripling believed that Andrews and Chambers, with Nixon's approval, belittled Stripling's role. In 1949 or 1950, Stripling ran into Dick and Pat and shared an elevator with them. They apologized to Stripling and sought his approval to keep exaggerating Nixon's role for the boost it would give Dick in the Senate campaign. See Stripling interview, Weinstein papers, HI.

    Nixon was effusively grateful to Andrews throughout the Hiss case. See Nixon to Andrews, Sept. 7, 1948, W. E. O'Brien to Nixon, Jan. 22, 1950, RNL; Nichols to Tolson, Sept. 29, 1948, FBI.

126   Laurence Duggan: Duggan was a KGB asset, but the evidence that HUAC possessed was sketchy. Feeling the heat, Nixon's colleagues strove to disassociate themselves: Representatives John Rankin and F. Edward Hebert called the Mundt-Nixon press conference an "atrocious" blunder. *NYT,* Dec. 23, 1948; *NYHT,* Dec. 25, 1948; *Time,* Jan. 3, 1949; *New Republic,* Jan. 10, 1949; John Earl Haynes, Harvey Klehr, and Alexander Vassiliev, *Spies;* Sam Tanenhaus, *Whittaker Chambers: A Biography.*

126   left Nixon and Chambers marked men: Hiss to Thomas, Aug. 24, 1948, RNL; Chambers, *Witness;* Chambers to James Rorty, undated, cited in Allen Weinstein, *Perjury: The Hiss-Chambers Case;* Lionel Trilling, *The Middle of the Journey* (New York: Scribner, 1976); Arthur Schlesinger, "Whitaker Chambers and his 'Witness,'" *Saturday Review,* May 24, 1952.

127   "unprincipled and vicious smear campaign": Frank Gannon, interview with author. Nixon dictation, Nov. 13, 1961, *Six Crises* file, RNL; Levine, *Eyewitness.*

127   an "epitomizing drama": "The Hiss case . . . went far beyond the usual congressional investigation," Nixon would recall. It "was considered by Hiss's supporters and defenders as being an attack on the whole elite establishment, on the foreign service, on Roosevelt." Nixon-Gannon; Chambers, *Witness.*

CHAPTER 8: THE PINK LADY

129   Central Valley runs for five hundred miles: Immense wealth was at stake. Paul Taylor, a pioneering Western economist, found that in places like Tulare and Kern counties, where mammoth spreads were the rule, some twenty landowners with more than 360,000 acres each might qualify for subsidies worth more than $8 million annually

if the acreage limit was removed. The limit remained on the books but—with the compliance of the Bureau of Reclamation—was rendered almost toothless by loopholes. Clayton Koppes, "Public Water, Private Land: Origins of the Acreage Limitation Controversy, 1933–1953," *Pacific Historical Review,* Nov. 1978; Robert de Roos, *The Thirsty Land* (Beard Books, Washington, D.C., 2000 or Stanford University Press, 1948); Paul Taylor, "Central Valley Project: Water and Land," *Western Political Quarterly,* June 1949; *LAT,* June 19, 1949; *Fortnight,* Feb. 4, 1949.

130   "La Gahagan": See oral histories by Helen G. Douglas, Tilford Dudley, India Edwards, Frank Rogers, Arthur Goldschmidt, Chet Holifield, Evelyn Chavoor, and Alis De Sola, Berkeley; Ed Lybeck memo, "Present Situation in the 14th California District," Douglas autobiographical notes and biographical sketch, 1944, and Ed Lybeck to Evie, Sept. 9, 1949, Lybeck Papers, UCLA; Truman to Downey, Jan. 7, 1948, Sheridan Downey papers, Berkeley; Douglas to Truman, Oct. 26, 1949, HST; Douglas OH, LBJ; *LAT,* Oct. 6, 1949; *Fortnight,* Jan. 21, 1949.

The Helen Gahagan Douglas unit of the California Women Political Leaders Oral History Project, conducted by the regional oral history office at the University of California, Berkeley, is indispensable for information on her life and campaigns and on issues like the 160-acre limit.

The best biographical works on Douglas are *Center Stage* by Ingrid Winther Scobie (New York: Oxford University Press, 1992) and the congresswoman's autobiography, *A Full Life* (New York: Doubleday, 1982). The "prima-donna" quote is from *Center Stage.* Her romance with Lyndon Johnson is detailed in Robert Caro, *Master of the Senate* (Knopf, 2002).

Downey participated in several populist movements in Depression-era California, including the End Poverty In California (EPIC) campaign of 1934, the Townsend Plan, and the Ham and Eggs movement, which guaranteed the elderly a weekly or monthly government pension check. Frank Nixon is remembered, in oral histories, giving the trademark "Ham and Eggs!" salutation in his store. Carey McWilliams, *Southern California: An Island on the Land* (Salt Lake City, UT: Gibbs Smith, 1973).

132   "the Senator deal": Douglas to Nixon, with June 1949 clipping from the *Alhambra Legionnaire,* June 4, 1949, Jorgensen to Nixon, Jan. 31, 1949, Nixon to Brennan, Mar. 14, 1949, Nixon to Bewley, Jan. 2, 1949, Bewley to Nixon, Feb. 16, 1949, Perry to Nixon, June 17, 1949, Nixon to Bewley, June 21, 1949, Nixon to Perry, June 21, 1949, Brennan to Nixon, Mar. 15, 1950, RNL; William Hughes OH, William Emmons OH, Donald Fantz OH, Whittier; Baus OH, CSA; Nixon-Gannon. Nixon signaled his presidential ambitions to aide William Arnold as well. See Bill Arnold, *Back When It All Began* (New York: Vantage, 1972).

133   to woo Brennan: Palmer's unique role is outlined in a letter written by Perry to Nixon in June 1949 after Perry and Jorgensen dined with the kingmaker. The newsman informed them that the Chandlers' support had been secured and promised that Warren and Knowland would support Nixon as well. Palmer also pledged to help them raise the $100,000 to $125,000 of the "do-re-me" they would need to launch the campaign by vouching for Nixon with Southern California's network of business-minded moneymen. Nixon had wanted San Francisco oilman Albert Mattei to serve as finance chairman, but since Mattei and Warren were feuding, Palmer advised Nixon not to take a side. (See Perry to Nixon, June 17, 1949, RNL.) Nixon took the advice and enlisted insurance man Asa Call, Pasadena attorney Dana Smith, and other veteran Republican fund-raisers instead. In November, after Nixon declared his candidacy, Brennan wrote to thank Palmer, accepting the newsman's invitation to host Nixon at one of Kyle's "intimate and attractive evenings," at which they would further plan the campaign's strategy and fund-raising. (See Brennan to Palmer, Nov. 14, 1949, RNL.)

When the campaign was over, Perry wrote to Palmer, thanking him for "the marvelous cooperation received from you and the paper." (See Perry to Palmer, Dec. 11, 1950, RNL.)

Jorgensen to Nixon, Jan. 31, 1949, Perry to Nixon, Feb. 1, 1949, Nixon to Perry, Feb. 8, 1949, Jorgensen to Nixon, Feb. 16, 1949, Nixon to Day, Mar. 2, 1949, Nixon to Brennan, Mar. 14, 1949, Brennan to Nixon, Mar. 15, 1950, Norman Chandler to Tyler Woodward, July 19, 1949, Nixon to Jorgensen, July 28, 1949, RNL; *LAT,* Feb. 19, 1950; Robert Finch OH, Columbia University; Robert Finch interview, Halberstam papers, BU.

135   The *Times* had emerged: Robert Hartmann interview, Halberstam papers, BU; Jorgensen OH, Berkeley; Nixon to Brennan, Mar. 14, 1949, Nixon to Jorgensen, May 24, June 10, 1949, Nixon to Perry, June 21, 1949, Nixon to David Saunders, Aug. 26, 1949, RNL; John A. Farrell, *Clarence Darrow* (New York: Doubleday, 2011); William Kahrl, *Water and Power* (Berkeley: University of California Press, 1982).

135   Palmer, jolly cynic: Palmer was "a cocky little fellow, very bright, very conservative . . . the single most important person in the state," Pat Brown recalled. "He loved Nixon with a passion."

A Stanford University study of newspaper coverage of the 1950 election showed how the *Los Angeles Times* characterized the candidates. Sixty percent of the references to Douglas were unfavorable, and 23 percent were favorable. The paper was far more loving to Nixon, with 62 percent of the references favorable, and only 5 percent unfavorable. The study found a similar pattern in the *San Francisco Chronicle,* the Hearst press, and nine other California newspapers. Altogether, Douglas received 70 percent of the critical comments. Stanford University News, Jan. 1951, RNL.

"We could not get anything in the *Times* about Manchester Boddy," said William Ross, a Democratic campaign adviser. Boddy could have been "throwing coconuts at everybody at Seventh and Broadway, nothing would have been printed. Unless you had a story where Manchester Boddy was attacking Helen Gahagan Douglas: that got printed." See Ross OH, CSA.

It wasn't just the newspapers. In an FCC hearing in 1950, a newscaster for Los Angeles radio station KMPC—the popular "Station of the Stars"—testified how his conservative and anti-Semitic owner, George Richards, had ordered him to favor Republican candidates, link Democrats to Communism, slander Jews, and give Douglas and others "nothing but critical notices" when he broadcast the news. See *NYT,* Mar. 15, 1950.

Leone Baxter, Verne Scoggins, Paul Ziffren, Dorothy Chandler, Pat Brown interviews, Halberstam papers, BU; Warren OH, Brown OH, Jorgensen OH, Berkeley; Haldeman OH, CSA; Lou Cannon OH, RNL; Lybeck memo, "Present Situation," Ruth Lybeck Papers, UCLA. The Catledge-Palmer exchange is from David Halberstam, *The Powers That Be* (New York: Knopf, 1979). The description of the Malibu dinners is from Harrison McCall to Hope McCall, Aug. 5, 1947, RNL.

138   "admittedly a long shot": Day said he had a brisk argument over Nixon's future with Herman Perry, and painted it as a dramatic showdown. (See Day OH, Bullock papers, UCLA; Day OH, Berkeley; Day OH, Whittier.) Yet the only written account of such a disagreement between the two men places it much earlier, in January 1949, during the dinner at Jorgensen's home. (See Jorgensen to Nixon, Feb. 16, 1949.) In his correspondence with Nixon in the summer of 1949, Perry generally supports the idea of a Senate race, and so it is possible that Day—whose relationship with Perry ruptured over local politics that fall—conflated occasions to make Perry a goat and himself more of a hero.

Aylett Cotton interview, BKP; Herb Klein OH, Columbia; David Sounders to

Nixon, July 27, 1949, Nixon to Jorgensen, May 24, July 28, Aug. 11, Aug. 30, 1949, Jorgensen to Nixon, Feb. 16, June 6, July 21, Sept. 26, Oct. 5, Nov. 14, 1949, Day to Nixon, July 7, 1949, Nixon to Day, July 15, Aug. 27, Oct. 6, 1949, Nixon to Perry, Jan. 3, June 21, Oct. 7, 1949, Nixon to Brennan, Oct. 7, 1949, Norris Poulson to Carlson, Oct. 6, 1949, Nixon to McCall, July 11, 1949, Nixon to Bewley, Oct. 7, 10, 1949, Mildred Younger to Nixon, Dec. 7, 1949, Day to Perry, Dec. 31, 1949, Nixon campaign press release, Nov. 3, 1949, RNL; *LAT,* May 20, 1949, Nov. 4, 1949, Dec. 18, 1949.

139   Attack was Chotiner's metier: "Congressman Richard Nixon for United States Senator" press release, Nov. 17, 1949, Adela Rogers St. Johns to Nixon, "Friday," 1960, Chotiner to Nixon, Oct. 19, 1940, Brennan to Nixon, Mar. 15, 1950, Chotiner to Walter Forward, Dec. 29, 1949, Feb. 3, 1950, Brennan to Dana Smith, with "Tentative Monthly Budget Up to January 31, 1950," Nov. 7, 1949, Chotiner, "Fundamentals of Campaign Organization" talk 1955, list of volunteers, 1950 campaign, RNL; Lynn Bowers and Dorothy Blair, "How to Pick a Congressman," *SEP,* Mar. 19, 1949; "Digest of Confidential Reports Submitted by Murray Chotiner and Pat Hillings," Earl Warren Papers, CSA; Patricia Reilly Hitt OH, Jorgensen OH, Berkeley; Ken Chotiner interview, FMB.

   "While they like to see someone who's friendly with the philosophy of the . . . paper, still their main purpose is to make money . . . and they like to get political ads," Nixon fund-raiser Roy Crocker said, when asked about journalistic standards of the day. "They'll kind of lean your way." One publisher opened the bidding by telling Chotiner that a rival candidate had offered to buy one thousand subscriptions to the paper in return for its backing.

141   party of "No": Jorgensen OH, Warren project; Chotiner to Hillings, Nov. 8, 1949, Chotiner to Nixon, Nov. 30, 1949, Brennan "Confidential Memorandum" to campaign committee, undated, Nixon press release, Feb. 14, 1950, RNL; Chotiner to Warren, with campaign report, Jan. 21, 1949, EWP.

141   Kyle Palmer liked him: For Ziffren quote see Jan. 1954 *Newsweek* cover story files, RNL; Merrell Small OH, John W. Dinkelspiel OH, Roy Crocker OH, Warren project; Gladwyn Hill, Paul Ziffren, Nancy Chotiner interviews, Halberstam papers, BU; Herb Klein OH, Columbia; *LAT,* Jan. 29, 30, 1950; Patrick Hillings, *The Irrepressible Irishman* (Harold D. Dean, 1994).

142   his pursuit of Alger Hiss: Nixon speech, House of Representatives, Jan. 26, 1950, Chotiner to Nixon, Nov. 30, 1949, Nixon press release, Nov. 17, 1949, RNL; *LAT,* Jan. 22, 1950; Dinkelspiel OH, Warren project; Willard Edwards interview, Halberstam papers, BU; *NYHT,* Jan. 26, 27, 1950; Dean Acheson, *Present at the Creation* (New York: Norton, 1969).

143   "Tail Gunner Joe": Reporters reveled in the fray, giving every charge and countercharge a headline. "We used to talk in the gallery about the propriety of just automatically running Joe's charges," newsman Willard Edwards recalled. "There was an uneasiness about it, but everybody else was doing it and it was a story, and it got us on Page One." See Willard Edwards interview, Halberstam papers, BU.

144   aid package for French Indochina: FRUS, 1950, Vol. 1, National Security Affairs; William Conrad Gibbons, *The U.S. Government and the Vietnam War* (Washington, D.C.: US Senate, Committee on Foreign Relations, Congressional Research Service, 1984); *Reporter,* Aug. 19, 1952; *Time,* Oct. 22, 1951; Stanley Karnow, *Vietnam* (New York: Viking, 1983); Fredrik Logevall, *Embers of War* (New York: Random House, 2012); *The Pentagon Papers,* ed. Neil Sheehan (New York: Bantam, 1971); Thomas Reeves, *The Life and Times of Joe McCarthy* (Lanham, MD: Madison Books, 1997); David Oshinsky, *A Conspiracy So Immense: The World of Joe McCarthy* (New York: Oxford University Press, 2005); Richard Rovere, *Senator Joe McCarthy* (New York: Meridian

Books, 1970); Walter Isaacson, *Einstein* (New York: Simon & Schuster, 2007); Acheson, *Present at the Creation;* John Negroponte address, "The American Experience in Southeast Asia, 1946–1975," U.S. Department of State, Sept. 30, 2010.

145   Nixon defended Oppenheimer: Oppenheimer was a victim of guilt by association. His brother was a Communist, and Oppenheimer and his lovers and friends dabbled in Communism when he was at Berkeley before the war. See Kai Bird and Martin Sherwin, *American Prometheus* (New York: Vintage, 2005).

The physicist appeared before HUAC in 1949, so Nixon had listened to him testify and no doubt read his file. It's worth wondering if Robert King, a friend who later joined Nixon's staff, didn't also influence his view of the scientist. King was an FBI agent during the war, charged with tracking Communists in the Bay Area, including those at Berkeley. See Cong. Rec., A2195, Mar. 28, 1955.

In *Embattled Dreams* (New York: Oxford University Press, 2002), California historian Kevin Starr suggests another potential explanation for Nixon's defense of the physicist: Oppenheimer may have given HUAC names and affiliations of the Communists at Berkeley.

Nixon dictation Aug. 12, 1961 (platter #1, "Fund"), White House tape, Nixon and Mitchell, June 22, 1971, Nixon speech, House of Representatives, Jan. 26, 1950, "The Red Record of Senator Claude Pepper," pamphlet, Nixon to Brennan, Mar. 3, 1950, Chotiner, "Fundamentals of Campaign Organization" talk 1955, Nixon to Chotiner, Mar. 6, 1950, Nixon to Albert Mattei, Mar. 7, 1950, Mundt to Nixon, May 8, 1950, Brennan to Nixon, Mar. 15, 1950, Jeffery to Arnold, May 3, 1950, Chotiner to campaign committee, May 1950, Nixon campaign press release, Apr. 6, 1950, "A Chronology of Joe McCarthy," RNL; Dinkelspiel OH, Warren project; Drown OH, Champlin OH, Whittier; Roy Cohn interview, FMB; *NYT,* May 11, 1950; *LAT,* Apr. 6, May 11, 1950; Nixon, *RN;* Michael Bowen, *The Roots of Modern Conservatism* (Chapel Hill: University of North Carolina Press, 2011).

146   The Democratic primary was as tumultuous: Several years after the 1950 election, a prospective buyer of Boddy's paper told Douglas that it was being kept afloat by Hearst, and loans from oil interests. See Douglas OH, Crocker OH, Warren project; Douglas, *A Full Life.*

147   Dick and Pat set off: *Fortnight,* Mar. 17, 1950; *Daily News* (Los Angeles), Mar. 2, 29, 1950; *LAT,* Feb. 28, Mar. 5, 29, Apr. 2, 18, 29, 1950; wall map and "Itinerary for Congressman Richard Nixon" for 1950, Nixon campaign press release, Apr. 4, 1950, RNL; George Milias OH, BKP; Eugene Koch OH, S. Truman Reeves OH, Whittier; Berkeley letter quoted in Scobie, *Center Stage.*

148   beware of "Tricky Dick": *San Bernadino County Sun,* May 11, 1950; *Daily News,* June 5, 1950; *LAT,* May 16, 20, Sept. 10, 1950; Chotiner to Campaign Committee, undated, 1950, Perry to Natcher, May 2, 1950, Perry to Mario Giannini, May 2, 1950, Downey radio address, RNL; Douglas, *A Full Life;* Don Bradley OH, CSA.

148   "women can best be appealed to emotionally": Chotiner to Nixon, Nov. 30, 1949, RNL. Nixon, *RN.*

149   United States was again at war: Louis Fisher, "The Korean War: On What Legal Basis Did Truman Act?," *American Journal of International Law* 89, no. 21 (1995); Brennan to Perry, June 5, 1940, RNL.

151   The pink sheet: Pink Sheet, undated, 1950, Chotiner, "Fundamentals of Campaign Organization" talk, 1955, RNL; Perry to Natcher, July 25, 1950, Lonigan to Nixon, July 25, Sept. 3, 1950, Nixon to Lonigan, Aug. 17, 1950, Lonigan to Chotiner, Oct. 3, 1950, Nixon to Nelson Dilworth, Aug. 1, 1950, Nixon to Arnold, Sept. 2, 1950, Nixon to McCullah St. Johns, Aug. 30, 1950, Nixon to T. M. Hanrahan, Aug. 28, 1950, RNL; Douglas speech, Aug. 18, 1950, Long Beach, CA, memo, Nixon "smears" file, RNL; Douglas,

speech, Aug. 18, 1950, radio address, Sept. 6, 1950, Lybeck Papers, UCLA; Ingrid Winther Scobie, *Center Stage*.

"I know we were affected by Nixon's tactics but at the time I thought I was rising above them. Perhaps our approach should have been different. Perhaps I shouldn't have been so above-it-all, sticking to my record all the time with Gahagan stubbornness," Douglas wrote in her memoirs. "I don't mean I should have played his game—winning isn't everything—but that I should have defended myself better. Still, every time I heard myself explaining that I really was a good, loyal citizen, I felt ashamed and debased. . . . I failed to take his attacks seriously enough. The communist thing was so ludicrous, so preposterous. I wasn't nearly shocked enough when I saw the pink sheet."

151 Brennan kicked off the fall campaign: Brennan, undated campaign bulletin, 1950, Nixon campaign "Manual of Information," RNL.

152 why others believed she was a fool: Lybeck papers, UCLA; *NYT*, Nov. 1, 1950; *Evening Star*, Oct. 15, 1950. Edmund Brown OH, Douglas OH, Chavoor OH, Berkeley; J. Paull Marshall, Edwin Pauley interviews, BKP; Douglas, *A Full Life*.

152 Kennedy dropped by Nixon's office: In his autobiography, *RN*, Nixon says he personally accepted the envelope from JFK. In his own memoir, Bill Arnold claimed that he received the money on behalf of an absent Nixon. The correspondence in Nixon's files supports Arnold's version. Kennedy was a friend of Nixon, and Joe Kennedy was an admirer of Joe McCarthy. They had philosophical reasons to oppose the Pink Lady. But the Kennedys may also have wanted to do their bit in removing a charismatic liberal from the field of future rivals. There was already talk about Douglas as a vice-presidential candidate. Like many donations, the $1,000 was not reported at the time, nor does it appear in the available records. Arnold, *Back When It All Began*; Nixon, *RN*.

153 "slap her around a little bit": When the *Los Angeles Times* did feel compelled to print a story about Douglas, it was usually accompanied by a piece with the Nixon campaign's countercharges. *LAT*, Apr. 2, May 21, Aug. 30, Sept. 10, Sept. 24, 29, Oct. 1, Oct. 5, 6, 12, 13, 18, 22, 29, Nov. 1, 3, 7, 1950; Norman Chandler interview, BKP.

153 "The contest centers on . . . Communism": Loubet OH, CSUF; Juanita Barbee OH, Berkeley; Nixon campaign attacks, Aug. 30, Sept. 18, 25, Oct. 11, 15, 16, 24, 27, 29, Nov. 1, 2, 1950, RNL; *LAT*, Sept. 19, 29, Oct. 17, 24, 1950.

153 "Asian scholar Owen Lattimore": McCarthy labeled Lattimore as the "top Russian espionage agent" in the United States. When U.S. cryptologists in the Venona project broke a Soviet code, they identified dozens of Russian agents. Lattimore, a university professor, was not among them, nor has other evidence surfaced to prove he was a spy.

154 Douglas campaign: This is an incommensurable comparison, as the Douglas campaign figure comes from official reports and the Nixon estimate (about $7 million in 2014 dollars) is his personal recollection, given to Jonathan Aitken. Douglas, in her memoir, estimated that Nixon spent $1.75 million.

The campaign finance laws were chock-full of loopholes. Checks made out to Nixon, cash gifts, and in-kind donations—like corporate billboards, studio time, and the services given the campaign by a public relations firm paid by Taiwanese interests—were not reliably recorded, nor were all the local get-out-the-vote and advertising expenses.

The firm of Dick's friend J. Paull Marshall, the lawyer-lobbyist with ties to California oil interests, paid the salary of an employee who was detailed to "go and come at the beck and call" of the Nixon campaign, Herman Perry noted in a May 19, 1952, letter to Nixon. "A lot of water has gone under the bridge since I sent my son-in-law up to Bakersfield with $8–10,000 to help you out in the stormy days of your campaign against that communistic Helen Gahagan Douglas," aerospace executive C. C. Moseley recalled, in a September 7, 1960, letter to Nixon (both letters in RNL).

In 1971, Nixon told his aides that the Teamsters union had secretly supported him in the race against Douglas—the beginning of a long alliance. See White House tape, Nixon, Haldeman, and Colson, June 23, 1971, RNL.

With all these caveats, Nixon's estimate seems reasonable: it fits the universal conclusion that Douglas was significantly outspent. For a discussion, see Morris, *Nixon,* and Gellman, *Contender.*

John Phillips to Nixon, Nov. 15, 1950, Nixon campaign press release, Sept. 6, 1950, and Sept. 18, 1950, itinerary, Nixon campaign budget summary, Nov. 2, 1950, Perry to Nixon, Nov. 13, 1950, and May 19, 1952, Hancock to County Chairman, Oct. 4, 1950, RNL. Douglas Aug. 18, 1950, speech, Lybeck papers, UCLA; Roger Morris, *Richard Milhous Nixon: The Rise of an American Politician* (New York: Holt, 1990); Jonathan Aitken, *Nixon: A Life* (Washington, D.C.: Regnery, 1993); *Reporter,* Oct. 14, 1952.

156 "In the last few days": Nixon press release, Nov. 4, 1950, RNL. For how the news from Korea transformed the campaign, see the *New York Times,* which on Monday, October 30, confidently reported that "troops of the United Nations continued their advances on both sides of the peninsula yesterday," but then led the next day's paper with the stunning headline: CHINESE RED UNIT HELPS FOES DRIVE ALLIES BACK IN KOREA. The bad news continued all that last week. *NYT,* October 30–November 7, 1950; Chavoor OH, Alvin Meyers OH, Berkeley; Don Bradley OH, CSA; *Nation,* Nov. 4, 1950.

156 Nixon was anxious on Election Day: Dorothy "Buff" Chandler interview, Halberstam papers, BU; *SEP,* Sept. 6, 1952; Norman and Dorothy Chandler interview, BKP. Sometime in the 1970s, Mrs. Chandler told David Halberstam that the milk and whiskey incident took place on election night, 1946, and it has been thus reported in several Nixon profiles and biographies. But in the late 1950s, much closer to the event, the Chandlers told Kornitzer it occurred on the night that Dick was elected to the Senate. Aside from the fact that their memories were fresher when they spoke to Kornitzer, it is far more likely they had Nixon join them as a senator-elect than as an unknown congressman-elect from Whittier.

CHAPTER 9: THE GREAT TRAIN ROBBERY

158 "menace to liberalism": Bryce Harlow interview, Thompson; Dean and Jewel Triggs OH, Richard Harris OH, Oscar Marshburn OH, CSUF.

159 "helluva shoddy way to win": The "shoddy" anecdote was told by Jack Sinclair, the executive director of the California Young Republicans in 1950, to a *Time* reporter in 1954, after Sinclair had soured on Nixon and become a Democrat. He also told *Time* that unnamed "Nixon supporters" had run a "massive" anti-Semitic telephone campaign against Douglas. "I don't say that Nixon was responsible for everything that happened or that he even knew about some of it," Sinclair said. "But for sheer, unadulterated viciousness, I've never seen anything worse." See McCulloch file for *Time* cover, Jan. 1954, RNL; Helen Douglas OH, Berkeley; *Nation,* Nov. 4, 1950.

160 as storm-tossed as most: There are many reports of trouble in the Nixon marriage in the 1950s. Jim Bassett told Brodie that he once surprised Nixon and Rogers with female companions in a Washington restaurant and had to take the drunken vice president home. Leonard Hall alluded to such behavior when he told Brodie that "Pat at times hated Rogers." The Rose Mary Woods comment ("Not speaking? You should have seen the days when the door was locked") was related by Jessamyn West to Brodie, as was the story about Dick calling on Hannah to mediate. See FMB. In interviews with Allen Weinstein, HUAC investigator Robert Stripling also spoke of Rogers and Nixon chasing girls, and John Cronin reported that in the 1950s the Nixon marriage was "a marriage of convenience." See Weinstein papers, HI.

Dwight Eisenhower would note that while Nixon was "energetic—physically strong—politically astute—ambitious," the "weakness I can detect . . . is that he is very fond of nightlife in Washington. Sometimes has a bedraggled morning appearance." See Irwin Gellman, *The President and the Apprentice* (New Haven, CT: Yale University Press, 2015).

Later, in the mid-1960s, Nixon enjoyed a warm relationship with Marianna Liu, a hostess in the cocktail lounge of the Hong Kong Hilton. The FBI, worried that she may have been a spy for Red China, investigated reports of an alleged affair. The *New York Times* caught wind of the probe and, after chasing the story for months, reported that "the Bureau never found any evidence suggesting that Mrs. Liu was an intelligence agent, that Mr. Nixon maintained an intimate relationship with her or that their friendship represented a threat to national security." Liu told the *Times* that Nixon sent her flowers and perfume, and that she once visited him in his room, but that their relationship was not intimate. See *NYT,* June 22, 1976, Sept. 18, 1976.

160 Nixon was in motion: Nixon's travel shows he always had an eye on the main chance. He told Herman Perry, "A few friends in other states may prove to be of considerable value in the future." See Nixon to Perry, Feb. 15, 1951, list of speaking engagements, 1951, Nixon to Day, Jan. 19, 1952, Pat Nixon to Helene Drown, undated, Mar. 12, 1951, May 20, 1951, Sept. 4, 1951, Nov. 3, 1951, Jan. 8, 1952, May 23, 1952, summer of 1953, Aug. 31, 1953, RNL; *NYT,* Sept. 23, 1952; Donald Shannon interview, Halberstam papers, BU; Frank Gannon, interview with author; "Nixon Diary," Sept. 9, 1970, Safire papers, LOC; Alice Longworth, Aylett Cotton interviews, BKP; Jim Bassett unpublished diary, "Ugly Year, Lonely Man," James E. Bassett Jr. papers, Bowdoin College; Whittaker Chambers, *Witness* (New York: Random House, 1952).

161 "the turmoil becomes almost unbearable": Nixon to Jack Drown, Mar. 24, 29, 1952, Bewley to Nixon, Oct. 30, 1951, Pat Nixon to Helene Drown, Sept. 4, 1951, Nov. 3, 1951, Jan. 8, 1952, RNL; Aitken, "File Note Visit to RN," Mar. 8, 1989, Woods to Bewley, May 22, 1954, Hutschnecker to Woods, Nov. 30, 1959, Hutschnecker to Nixon, "Thanksgiving Day, 1957," June 12, 1961, Nixon to Hutschnecker, Dec. 14, 1957, July 24, 1958, Mar. 16, 1959, RNL.

162 "Bebe" Rebozo: Woods to Nixon, May 30, 1959, Nixon to Rebozo, Nov. 28, 1952, Jan. 15, 1955, Apr. 22, Nov. 15, 1957, Jan. 22, Dec. 12, 1958, Rebozo to Nixon, Jan. 5, 1952, Mar. 4, 1954, Apr. 13, 1956, Jan. 16, 30, Apr. 16, May 4, Nov. 5, 1957, July 3, 1962, RNL; Nixon to Danner, Jan. 9, 1952, Smathers to Nixon, Jan. 14, 1952, with attached newspaper clipping, Jan. 3, 1952, RNL; *Newsday,* Rebozo investigative series, Oct. 6–13, 1971; Lady Bird Johnson OH, "Memo for Drew," Nov. 22, 1952, memo from Anderson to Pearson, Sept. 27, 1968, Pearson files, LBJ; see also Danner testimony cited in SSC, Final Report, June 1974.

A Rebozo file compiled by the FBI showed J. Edgar Hoover's ongoing surveillance of Nixon. Agents had investigated the vice president's new pal by 1953 and reported to Hoover via his friend and deputy Clyde Tolson that Bebe "has a good reputation, is generally well-liked and reportedly is reliable and efficient."

Rebozo's friendship with Nixon remained a source of gossip over the years, and the FBI collected tips and rumors about Rebozo's activities but concluded in a report to acting director William Ruckelshaus in 1973 that "no derogatory information is known regarding Mr. Rebozo."

The Senate Watergate committee and the Watergate prosecutors conducted long, detailed investigations of Rebozo and found no substantial evidence of wrongdoing. After checking out one tip, the prosecutors concluded: "Like so many, it lacked critical details. And like so many, it proved utterly baseless." See Rebozo file, FBI and Michel to Ruth, closing memo for Hughes-Rebozo probe, Oct. 16, 1975; *Frontier,* Sept. 1952; Cotton interview, BKP; Smathers OH, Senate Historical Office, U.S. Senate; Nixon-Gannon; James Cannon, *Time and Chance* (New York: HarperCollins, 1994); Jonathan

Aitken, *Nixon: A Life* (Washington, D.C.: Regnery, 1993); Richard Nixon, *Six Crises* (New York: Doubleday, 1962); Gellman, *President and the Apprentice.*

163 Harriman, a friend of Helen Douglas: The wife of Stewart Alsop told the Harriman story to Brodie in a Mar. 1978 interview, and Brodie included it in her biography, *Richard Nixon: The Shaping of His Character* (Norton, 1981). For Pearson fight, see Washington *Evening Star,* Dec. 14, 1950, and other contemporary news accounts; Nixon, *RN;* Perry to Nixon, Dec. 14, 1950, Nixon to Creel, Dec. 18, 1950, RNL.

163 maiden speech in the Senate: Cong. Rec., Apr. 11, 1951.

164 laundered a $5,000 donation: Senator Owen Brewster, a Republican from Maine, was chairing the Republican Senate Campaign Committee in early 1950 when Nixon and another senator pressed him for funds. The committee rules forbade preprimary contributions, so Brewster laundered $5,000 for each senator through Henry Grunewald, a shady figure involved in the Truman administration scandals. Brewster assumed full responsibility. *NYT,* Mar. 21, 1952; Chotiner to Nixon, May 13, 1952 with draft and final "Statement Concerning Sen. Brewster Campaign Advance," memo, Jim Gleason to Chotiner, "Brewster-Grunewald Affair," July 25, 1952, Nixon to Dave Saunders, Mar. 6, 1950, McIntyre Faries to Carl Beehner, June 18, 1952, Pat Nixon to Helene Drown, May 20, 1951, RNL.

For Nixon and Truman administration scandals, see *NYHT,* Oct. 8, 1951, Mar. 9, 11, 13, 16, 1952; *NYT,* Oct. 8, 1951, Feb. 1, Mar. 12, 13, 1952.

164 Nixon liked Eisenhower's chances: Nixon Platter #1—Fund—8/12/61, RNL; Perry to Nixon, Mar. 26, 1952, Perry to Brennan, May 12, 1952, Nixon to Perry, May 9, 1951, Alfred Kohlberg to Nixon, May 1, 1951, Nixon to Creel, Aug. 30, 1951, Nixon to Kohlberg, May 30, 1951, Nixon to Brennan, June 9, 1952, RNL; Richard Norton Smith, *Thomas E. Dewey and His Times* (New York: Simon & Schuster, 1982); Thomas Dewey OH, Robert Finch OH, Columbia University; Harold Stassen OH, Berkeley; Eisenhower to John Stephens Wood, June 20, 1949, Eisenhower to Edward Meade Earle, Sept. 2, 1952, Eisenhower diary, June 14, 1951, PDDE; Ellis Slater diary, *The Ike I Knew* (Ellis Slater Trust), 1980.

165 Warren, who wanted to be president: Aylett Cotton to Nixon, June 17, 1952, Perry to Kyle Palmer, June 23, 1950, Perry to Nixon and Brennan, Nov. 6, 1950, Bewley to Nixon, June 4, 1952, Helyn Noid to Nixon, June 9, 1952, reminiscence of 1946 campaign dictated by Harrison McCall, Jan. 3, 1959, Pat Nixon to Helene Drown, May 23, 1952, RNL; Verne Scoggins to Governor Warren, Sept. 30, Oct. 15, 1946, Warren papers, CSA; Verne Scoggins interview, Halberstam papers, BU; Merrell Small to Warren, Aug. 25, 1972, with Warren memoir manuscript, Berkeley; Earl Adams OH, Bartley Cavanaugh OH, Walter Jones OH, Berkeley; William Rogers OH, Columbia; Merrell Small memoir, "The Country Editor and Earl Warren," Berkeley; Arnold, *Back When It All Began.*

In 1946, Warren had written to Voorhis in the middle of the campaign, hailing his "splendid cooperation" in getting disability insurance legislation through the House. The governor's letter ran against the Nixon campaign theme, that Voorhis was an ineffective radical. See Arnold to Warren, Oct. 10, 1946, with attached Voorhis pamphlet, RNL.

In 1950, Helen Douglas and Warren tried to stay out of each other's races, but Chotiner had Young Republicans dog her on the campaign trail, demanding to know whom she favored, until she at last blurted Democrat James Roosevelt's name. That put the governor on the spot, but he still could not summon full-throated support for Nixon. In full, his statement read: "I have no intention of being coy about this situation. As always, I have kept my campaign independent from other campaigns. The newspaper reports from San Diego that Mrs. Douglas has said she hopes and prays Mr. Roosevelt will be the next governor of California do not change my position. In view of her statement, however I might ask her how she expects I will vote when I mark my ballot for United States Senator next Tuesday." Warren papers, CSA.

167 becoming the general's running mate: In a recorded reminiscence a decade later, Nixon noted how the conversations he had with Eisenhower's aides were necessarily prospective. "Cynics have the impression that I knew it was all cut and dried long before I ever arrived in Chicago—that Dewey had decided that I should be the candidate, had so informed me and that from that point on I was simply putting on an act when I indicated surprise," Nixon said. That was "patent nonsense." But he had "been for Eisenhower from the beginning," he acknowledged. See Nixon Platter #1—Fund—8/12/61, RNL.

    Nixon to Perry, May 5, 1952, Nixon to Persons, Jan. 13, 1961, Aitken, "File Note Visit to RN," Mar. 8, 1989, RNL; Smith, *Dewey and His Times;* Herbert Brownell, *Advising Ike* (Lawrence: University Press of Kansas, 1993); *NYT,* May 9, 1952; *NYHT,* May 9, 1952; Lucius Clay OH, Columbia.

167 California's seventy delegates: Nixon Platter #1—Fund—8/12/61, RNL; Nixon to William Knowland, Dec. 23, 1951, Brennan to Perry, Mar. 18, 1952, Perry to Brennan, Apr. 21, May 12, 1952, Perry to Nixon, May 5, June 4, July 7, 1952, Nixon to Perry, June 2 (with statement on Werdel delegation), June 16, 1952, Nixon to "Dear Friend" polling letter, June 11, 1952, and results (3,902 for Taft and 3,784 for Eisenhower), Nixon to Drown, Dec. 13, 1951, Bewley to Nixon, Oct. 30, Nov. 7, 1951, May 28, 1952, Nixon to Brennan, June 9, 1952, RNL; Keith McCormac OH, John Dinkelspiel OH, Faries OH, Berkeley; William Rogers OH, William Knowland OH, Columbia; Robert W. Kenny, "The Crisis Nixon Forgot," *Frontier,* Apr. 1962; *LAT,* June 20, 1962.

    McCormac and other conservatives claimed that Taft and his supporters also felt double-crossed by Nixon. Taft was famously quoted as calling Nixon "a little man in a big hurry." The apparent source of the quotation is a 1959 statement by Joseph Polowsky, a peace activist who claimed that Taft made the remark in a private conversation they had at the 1952 convention. According to Polowsky, Taft said "that while Nixon was clever, he had a mean and vindictive streak in him which came close to the surface when he couldn't get his way," that "Nixon's personality tended to radiate tension and conflict," and that Taft hoped Nixon would never become president. These were common evaluations made by Nixon critics like Polowsky in 1959. Taft would have had to be prescient to reach them in 1952. See *Desert Sun,* Aug. 1, 1959.

168 South as the pivotal region: Brownell, *Advising Ike;* Michael Bowen, *The Roots of Modern Conservatism* (Chapel Hill, University of North Carolina Press, 2011); *Time,* July 14, 1952; *WP,* July 3, 1952; *NYT,* July 3, 1952; Brownell OH, Berkeley; Harold Stassen OH, Columbia; Eisenhower to H. J. Porter, May 17, 1952, PDDE; Brownell OH, DDEL.

169 "The convention train": Aylett Cotton, who had worked for Nixon during the 1950 campaign, wrote almost daily letters in diary form to his wife, Martha Jane, from the delegation train and the convention, beginning July 3 and ending July 15, 1952. They give an unmatched firsthand account of events in the Nixon camp by someone who shared time and meals with Pat and Dick that week. Listed here as Cotton diary, RNL.

    Pat Nixon to Drown, May 23, 1952, RNL; James Bassett interview, Halberstam papers, BU; Earl Warren memoir manuscript, Berkeley; oral histories by Dinkelspiel, Frank Jorgensen, Edmund Brown Sr., Victor Hansen, Thomas Mellon, Percy Heckendorf, Verne Scoggins, and Roy Crocker, Berkeley.

171 "We have a traitor in our delegation": The Taft forces dangled the vice-presidential nomination in front of Bill Knowland, who did what he could for Taft but, because of his family's deep ties to Warren, did not have the free hand that Nixon had to undermine the governor. See Faries OH, Emelyn Knowland Jewett OH, Berkeley.

    Taft died the following summer. Had he won the nomination and the election after choosing one of the Californians as his running mate, either Knowland, Nixon, or Warren would have become president six months into Taft's first term.

Nixon to Adams, Dec. 31, 1958, RNL; *LAT,* July 6, 7, 1952; *WP,* July 9, 1952; *NYT,* July 9, 1952; Richard Bergholz interview, Halberstam papers, BU; oral histories by Brownell, Scoggins, Faries, Dinkelspiel, Milton Polland, and James Hagerty, Berkeley; Warren memoir manuscript, Berkeley; Merrell Small memoir manuscript, Berkeley; Knowland OH, Columbia.

172 the penultimate showdown: Technically, the skirmish over the "Fair Play Amendment"—like similar debates in the 1912 Republican convention and the 1972 Democratic convention—was over the question of whether and when delegates involved in credential challenges could vote. Thanks to Brownell's foresightedness, and a bad feeling left among the delegates by the arrogant behavior of the Taft forces, Eisenhower prevailed on the issue, exposing Taft's weakness. The first vote on a challenge concerned Louisiana and Georgia, and the Eisenhower forces won, 607 to 531, with the Californians and other favorite-son delegates making the difference. Taft then caved on Texas.

The delegates stayed in the Loop, though the convention was out at the stockyards. In addition to the Knickerbocker suite, Nixon wanted a private room at the Ambassador Hotel, and Bill Arnold was assigned the task of securing the extra space, which he acquired through the efforts of Judge Julius Hoffman, a machine politician who would one day become famous presiding at the trial of the Chicago Eight. In the end, fearing his fellow Californians might think him uppity, Nixon didn't take the Ambassador quarters. He instead used a room at the Stockyard Inn, next to the convention hall, for rest and consultations. That's where he was, with Chotiner and Hillings, when Brownell phoned him with the news that he was Ike's choice as a running mate.

The press baron John Knight wrote the signed front-page story on July 9 naming Nixon as the likely running mate—apparently after being tipped off by Dorothy Chandler. Kyle Palmer seethed at missing the scoop.

Arnold letter, 1952 campaign file, Cotton diary, RNL; Brownell, *Advising Ike; LAT,* July 10, 11, 1952; *NYT,* July 10, 11, 1952; *NYHT,* July 10, 11, 1952; Milton Polland OH, Herb Brownell OH, James Hagerty OH, Warren OH, Berkeley; Small memoir manuscript, Berkeley; Knowland OH, Columbia; Brownell OH, DDEL.

173 final roll call began: Thus did two future chief justices—Earl Warren and Warren Burger—help the men who would appoint them (Eisenhower and Nixon) along the road to power; *LAT,* July 11, 1952; Asa Call interview, Halberstam papers, BU; Sherman Adams OH, Columbia; Hagerty OH, Berkeley.

173 importance of the vice presidency: The Founders tried giving the vice presidency to the runner-up in the presidential election, and so great men like John Adams and Thomas Jefferson served in the office. But amid the growing factionalism of the Federalist period, that proved unsatisfactory, leading to the Twelfth Amendment, which was adopted in 1804, making the veep a second banana.

174 responded with a list of names: Ike remembered writing out a list. Brownell gave varying descriptions of the process. According to Brownell's memoir, *Advising Ike,* the general had indeed produced a written list with Nixon's name. But in another version given by Brownell, Ike relied on Brownell's recommendation, made in the presence of Dewey and Clay. Ike "thought for a moment, said he had met Senator Nixon, and that he would be guided by our advice. Then he told us to clear Nixon's name with the other leaders of the party. And that was it," Brownell told Jean Edward Smith, in *Lucius D. Clay: An American Life* (New York: Henry Holt, 1990). There are minor differences on other matters as well—like who chaired the vice-presidential selection meeting or first suggested Nixon—in the recollections given years later in interviews, oral histories and memoirs, and contemporary accounts like a *St. Louis Post-Dispatch*

article of Sept. 28, 1952, written with Brownell's input. See Brownell OH, Columbia; Brownell OH, Berkeley; Eisenhower press conference, May 31, 1955, PPP.

Among the other men considered were Taft, Bill Knowland, and Senator Everett Dirksen of Illinois. But the hard feelings between the Taft and Eisenhower forces were still raw, and Dirksen had crossed a line when, amid the tumult of the fair-play fight, he chastised Dewey from the podium.

Nixon had one final factor in his favor: the party would not lose the Senate seat if he were picked, as Warren could select a fellow Republican to finish his term.

David, Moos, and Goldman, *Presidential Nominating Politics in 1952* (Baltimore: Johns Hopkins Press, 1954); Sherman Adams, *Firsthand Report* (New York: Harper, 1961); Brownell, *Advising Ike;* Smith, *Dewey and His Times; St. Louis Post-Dispatch,* Sept. 28, 1952; *Time,* June 13, 1955; Adams OH, Clay OH, Columbia; Eisenhower to Paul Hoy Helms, Aug. 2, 1952, PDDE; Brownell OH, DDEL.

174 how Nixon was caught napping: *WP,* July 12, 1952; *NYT,* July 12, 1952; *LAT,* July 12, 1952; *SEP,* Sept. 6, 1952; Nixon, *RN;* Earl Mazo, *Richard Nixon: A Political and Personal Portrait* (New York: Avon, 1960); Patrick Hillings, *The Irrepressible Irishman* (Harold D. Dean, 1994).

176 "Lightning has struck": Cotton diary, RNL; Nixon to Sherman Adams, Dec. 31, 1958, Adams to Chotiner, Jan. 5, 1959, RNL; Harlow interview, Thompson; *WP,* July 12, 1952; *NYT,* July 12, 1952; *LAT,* July 12, 1952; *NYHT,* July 12, 1952; *SEP,* Sept. 6, 1952; Nixon, *RN.*

CHAPTER 10: CHECKERS

177 The television cameras were there: Mazo places the incident of the train's premature departure in Pomona; in *Six Crises,* Nixon recalled it, and his clash with Drown, taking place the next day in Tulare. Earl Mazo, *Richard Nixon: A Political and Personal Portrait* (New York: Avon, 1960); Richard Nixon, *Six Crises* (New York: Doubleday, 1962); *NYT,* Sept. 18, 1952; program and schedule, Pomona ceremonies, Sept. 17, 1952, Nixon itinerary commencing Sept. 15, 1952, RNL; *SEP,* Sept. 6, 1952.

178 Democrats chose Adlai Stevenson: Decades later, Nixon was still sore about the press's affection for Stevenson. "The media loved him, because the media loves froth. They like fashion. They liked the titillating humor that he used," Nixon complained in the Nixon-Gannon interviews.

On the FBI reports on Stevenson's sexuality, see Athan Theoharis, *Chasing Spies* (Chicago: Ivan R. Dee, 2002). Nixon dictation, Aug. 12, 1961 (platter 1, "Fund"), "RN Fund tape #5," fund story "Chronology and Analysis," RNL; Nixon to Link, Aug. 20, 1952, Perry to Cox, Aug. 4, 1952, Rogers to Nixon, Sept. 11, 1952, Cronin to Nixon, Cronin to Cox, Sept. 5, 1952, Nixon to MacKinnon, Sept. 15, 1952, Gleason to Nixon, Sept. 13, 1952, RNL; *NYHT,* Sept. 3, 7, 1952; *SEP,* Sept. 6, 1952; *NYT,* Sept. 3, 1952; *Lewiston Evening Journal,* Sept. 6, 1952; *Baltimore Sun,* July 21, 1952; Irwin Gellman, *The President and the Apprentice* (New Haven, CT: Yale University Press, 2015).

179 Liberal journals: The *New Republic* was a small liberal journal, but like the *Nation* and the *Reporter,* it was widely read by writers and editors in New York and Washington, and served as a launchpad for anti-Nixon commentary that molded elite opinion. The Brashear articles, for example, introduced the fiction that a telephonic "whispering campaign" branding Jerry Voorhis as a Communist was a more important factor in Nixon's 1946 victory than the defeats he had handed Voorhis in debate. Though attributed only to "many observers," this was thereafter embraced as fact by journalists who should have been wary. In addition to working for the Democratic *Daily News,* Brashear was an unsuccessful Democratic candidate for a state assembly seat in 1950. See Irwin Gellman, *The Contender* (New York: Free Press, 1999).

179 "Some of the Warrenites": The Nixon-Warren feud would persist for many years. A year after the Checkers speech, Tom Bewley advised Dick that "the Warren following still resent your ability and popularity and a true Warrenite would still like to slip the knife into you." Bewley to Nixon, Sept. 9, 1953, RNL.

180 charge of anti-Semitism: Perry to Hillings, Sept. 3, 1952, Peter Edson to A. T. Richardson, July 27, 1952, RNL; *Intermountain Jewish News,* Aug. 14, 1952; *NYHT,* Aug. 19, 1952; *New Republic,* Sept. 1, 8, 1952; *Reporter,* Oct. 14, 1952; Milton Polland OH, Emelyn Knowland Jewett OH, Edmund "Pat" Brown OH, Berkeley.

180 "slush fund" was another matter: The subsequent legal and financial audits would find that there were actually *two* funds, with $18,235 (about $160,000 in today's dollars) collected before the Chicago convention—"the Richard M. Nixon Expense Fund"— and almost $11,000 (about $100,000 nowadays) raised afterwards in "the Dana C. Smith Trust account." The total at Nixon's disposal—the equivalent of a quarter of a million dollars today—was no small matter.

The accompanying list of disbursements supported Nixon's claim that the money was spent on legitimate political expenses; he was very fortunate that the two funds contained no record of Smith's "surprise" offer to hire household help. The use of the money to pay for a maid would have undermined the common-man themes of the Checkers speech, and probably ruined Nixon's candidacy.

Henry Clifford, a Republican businessman who had served in the South Pacific with Nixon, challenged his claim that the funds were public knowledge. "I seriously question that," Clifford said in a letter urging Nixon to step down from the ticket. "After checking with numerous friends in Pasadena and Los Angeles, I find that the only persons who had knowledge of it were those who had been approached by Dana Smith or his associates." Warren Olney, a Warren aide who later served with Nixon in the Eisenhower administration, also said the fund-raising was "done in secrecy." Olney OH, Adams OH, Berkeley; Clifford to Nixon, Sept. 22, 1952, RNL; Gibson, Dunn & Crutcher to Sherman Adams, Sept. 23, 1952, Price, Waterhouse & Co. to Sherman Adams, Sept. 23, 1952, "Dana C. Smith, Trust Account, First Trust and Savings Bank of Pasadena" record of contributions and disbursements, Nov. 1950–July 1952, "Chronology and Analysis" of the 1952 campaign and the Fund, Aug. 5, 1961, RNL; Kruse to Nixon, Dec. 17, 1946, Lutz to Nixon, July 29, 1948, Perry to Bryant, Oct. 19, 1948, Jorgensen to Perry, Oct. 22, 1948, Perry to Natcher, Dec. 3, 1948, Nixon to Chotiner, Feb. 22, 1950, Elwood Robinson to Smith, Feb. 2, 1951, Smith to Walter Forward et al., Aug. 21, 1951, RNL; Nixon to Smith, Aug. 30, 1951, Nixon to Smith, Sept. 10, 1951, Smith to Arthur Crites, Sept. 25, 1951, Smith to Lutz, Nov. 6, 1951, Nixon to Perry, Nov. 12, 1951, Perry to Nixon, Dec. 10, 1951, Nixon to Victor Ryland, Jan. 9, 1952, Smith to Herbert Hoover Jr., Feb. 26, 1952, Nixon to Smith, June 9, 1952, Smith to Nixon, June 11, 1952, Nixon to Smith, June 16, 1952, Smith to Dick and Pat Nixon, July 23, 1952, RNL; Irving Salomon OH, Columbia University.

181 "created a firestorm": Katcher later changed his story, but at the time he told the United Press that the tip came from "a Warren Republican . . . unhappy over Nixon's being chosen as the Republican vice-presidential nominee." As for Warren, he happily let Nixon dangle in the wind, telling the press that he wanted to wait "until all the evidence has been presented" before voicing his support for the embattled vice-presidential candidate. See Humphreys to Chotiner, Sept. 23, 1952; *NYT,* Sept. 23, 1952.

Nixon dictation, Aug. 12, 1961 (platter 1, "Fund"), Edson to Richardson, July 27, 1952, Edson to Nixon, with attached proof of story, Sept. 17, 1952, Nixon to Edson, June 10, 1953, Pat Nixon to Helene Drown, June or July 1953, Aug. 31, 1953, RNL; *Time,* Sept. 29, 1952; Nixon-Gannon; Edith Holt OH, Whittier; Virginia Knudsen interview, BKP.

182 Stevenson had his own: *Chicago Tribune,* Sept. 30, 1952. For details see John Bart-

low Martin, *Adlai Stevenson of Illinois* (New York: Doubleday, 1976), which offers an accounting of the $84,000 Stevenson fund, of a type "long customary in the use ... by Illinois governors," as the records maintained. Martin found that Stevenson had disbursed $18,000 to supplement aides' salaries, $52,000 in donations to other Democratic candidates, $2,300 to charity, and $1,266.35 for the Christmas hams and other "gifts for news men." Another set of worksheets indicated that when all donations to Democratic campaigns are included, the Stevenson funds from 1948 to 1952 may have reached $146,000.

182   His first reaction: Nixon and his aides gave various accounts of when they learned of the impending fund stories. In *Six Crises* Nixon placed it before the Pomona kickoff on Wednesday, September 17. In his dictated reminiscences (see platter 1, "Fund," Aug. 12, 1961, in RNL), he says it took place as the train moved up the valley the next morning. *NYHT,* Sept. 19, 1952; *NYT,* Sept. 19, 1952; AP, Sept. 19, 1952; Hillings, *Irishman;* Rogers OH, Columbia.

183   ensnared in speculation and rumor: Nixon dictation, Aug. 12, 1961 (platters 1 and 2, "Fund"), "Election Digest," Radio Reports, Inc., Sept. 19–21, 1952, Woods to Perry, Aug. 26, 1953, Pat Nixon to Helene Drown, summer, 1953, Aug. 31, 1953, RNL; Jack Anderson to Drew Pearson, Sept. 23, 1952, Pearson Papers, University of Texas; *NYHT,* Sept. 20, 1952; *NYT,* Sept. 20, 1952; *WP,* Sept. 23, 1952; *Look,* Feb. 24, 1953; AP, Sept. 19, 20, 1952; *Time,* Sept. 29, 1952; Earl Adams OH, Berkeley; Rogers OH, Milton Eisenhower OH, Sherman Adams OH, Columbia; Eisenhower to Nixon, Sept. 19, 1952, PDDE; Herbert Brownell, *Advising Ike* (Lawrence: University Press of Kansas, 1993); Robert Cutler, *No Time for Rest* (Boston: Little, Brown, 1966); Emmet J. Hughes, *The Ordeal of Power* (New York: Atheneum, 1963).

185   the strokes of a plan: Ted Rogers remembered that the notion of a television broadcast first arose in a conversation he had with Chotiner on Friday. After getting the go-ahead, Rogers called New York adman Carroll Newton early Monday and asked him to book time. "Tuesday night ... in those days was BERLE NIGHT on TV," Rogers recalled. "I told him to get us as close to Berle as he could." Others credit the RNC's Robert Humphreys with the idea of a televised speech. See Rogers, "Fund Telecast" memo, RNL; Rogers interview, Halberstam papers, BU.

         Conrad Black notes, sagaciously, that Nixon was fortunate to have Bill Rogers and Murray Chotiner along. "They were free of Nixon's mercurial moods and inner Shakespearean fears that a dark, unstoppable destiny was afoot that could only be combated (if at all) by fearful acts of desperate courage." Conrad Black, *A Life in Full: Richard M. Nixon* (New York: Public Affairs, 2007).

         Nixon, audiotapes, Aug. 14, 1961 (tape 2, "Fund"; tape 3, "Fund Tape"), MacKinnon memo to Nixon train, Sept. 21, 1952, RNL; Jack Anderson to Drew Pearson, Sept. 20, 1952, Pearson Papers, University of Texas; Sherman Adams, *Firsthand Report* (New York: Harper, 1961); *NYHT,* Sept. 21, 1952; AP, Sept. 20, 1952; *Look,* Feb. 24, 1953; Adams OH, Clay OH, Knowland OH, Columbia; Eisenhower to William E. Robinson, Sept. 20, 1952, PDDE; William Bragg Ewald, *Eisenhower the President* (Englewood Cliffs, NJ: Prentice-Hall, 1981); Humphreys to Adams, Feb. 7, 1959, reprinted in *Smoke-Filled Rooms, The Confidential Papers of Robert Humphreys,* ed. Harold Lavine (Englewood Cliffs, NJ: Prentice-Hall, 1970).

187   "shit or get off the pot": There are several versions of the talk between Ike and Dick. I have used a memorandum of the conversation found among his papers at the Nixon presidential library: "September 20, 1952, Memorandum, Conversation (telephone) between Senator Nixon and Eisenhower."

         Hannah may have sent her love, but Frank Nixon was furious at his son for getting himself into such a predicament. See Joseph Johnson OH, Whittier.

         Nixon got some better news from Bert Andrews on Monday. Andrews was on the Eisenhower train and reported to Nixon how, in an off-the-record conversation with reporters, Ike had spoken of how much he liked Nixon and revealed that the telegrams he received were running six to one in favor of keeping Dick on the ticket. Andrews advised Nixon "not to do anything drastic" and to "take about four sleeping pills tonight and get on that television tomorrow night rested." See memo, "Quotes from Bert Andrews—9/22/52," RNL.

Nixon, audiotape, Aug. 14, 1961 (tape 3, "Fund Tape"), Nixon and Tom Dewey, telephone conversation (memorandum), Sept. 20, 1952, Nixon, audiotape, Aug. 14, 1961 (tape 4, "RN Fund tape"), MacKinnon to Nixon, Sept. 20, 1952, MacKinnon to Chotiner, Sept. 19, 1952, "Report on New York Post—Telephone conversation with Alfred Kohlberg," Sept, 21, 1952, RNL; HUAC report on James Wechsler, unsigned staff reports on fund receipts and expenditures, Nixon assets and federal tax law, Stassen to Nixon, Sept. 21, 1952, Don Mozley, CBS radio script, Mozley collection, RNL; telegram, "Mother" to Nixon, Sept. 20, 1952, BKP; *NYHT,* Sept. 22, 1952; *NYT,* Sept. 22, 1952; Gannon-Nixon; Hillings, *Irishman;* Patricia Hitt OH, Berkeley.

188   a settled speechwriting routine: Nixon, audiotapes, Aug. 14, 1961 ("RN fund Tape #5," "RN fund tape #4"); Rogers and Kissinger, telephone conversation transcript, Dec. 1, 1969, RNL.

189   It was Tom Dewey: In *Six Crises,* Nixon said that while hanging up he barked at Dewey, "And tell them I know something about politics, too!"

Dewey had many fine attributes, but the personal touch was not among them. The sheer ham-handedness of this eleventh-hour phone call may help explain why he lost two presidential elections. Ike's role in Dewey's phone call has never been fully settled. It is known that the general and his aides discussed the formal process of naming Nixon's replacement that day, but it may have been contingency planning.

Ike adviser Paul Hoffman, the president of the Ford Foundation, arranged for the legal and accounting reports after Adams summoned him to duty from a hospital, where he was being treated after being struck by a golf ball. *Life,* Dec. 14, 1953; Richard Whalen, *Catch the Falling Flag* (Boston: Houghton Mifflin, 1972); Jean Edward Smith, *Eisenhower in War and Peace* (New York: Random House, 2012); Richard Norton Smith, *Thomas E. Dewey and His Times* (New York: Simon & Schuster, 1982); *NYHT,* Sept. 23, 1952; *NYT,* Sept 23, 1952; Brownell, *Advising Ike; Time,* Oct. 6, 1952; Charles Cooper OH, Whittier; Paul Smith and Albert Upton interview, BKP; Brownell OH, Rogers OH, Adams OH, Clay OH, Columbia. Nixon's handwritten notes for the speech were reproduced in *Look* magazine, Feb. 23, 1953; Brownell OH, DDEL; Harlow OH, Thompson.

193   Checkers speech: Rogers did get a half hour with Nixon—whom he remembered as working with his legal pads, clad in a red dressing gown—at the hotel on Tuesday afternoon. That's where he first learned that Dick wanted Pat on the set.

Rogers did not remember Pat and Dick retiring to a dressing room for a last private moment; he recalled them getting some light makeup onstage and going right into the broadcast. Nixon's memories were hazy; in *Six Crises* he said their private talk took place in a dressing room; in the Nixon-Gannon interviews, he placed his conversation in the control room, and in *RN* he described it as "a small room at the far side of the stage." See Rogers, "Fund Telecast" memo, RNL.

There is no doubt that Nixon knew what he was doing by bringing up the finances of the other candidates. His staff had warned Nixon that his challenge to Stevenson and Sparkman to reveal their finances would no doubt be applied to Ike as well. See 1952 campaign files, RNL.

Both Checkers and Fala were immortalized on a September 23—Fala in the campaign of 1944 and Checkers eight years later. The comparison ends there, however. Roosevelt portrayed his Scottie as a scrapper, irate at the Republican lie that a destroyer had been sent, at great cost to the taxpayer, to retrieve him from an Alaskan island. The Fala joke was biting, and funny, and made Roosevelt's foes seem silly. The Checkers imagery—of heartbroken little girls about to lose their puppy to a sinister "they"—was in keeping with the pathos that characterized Nixon's speech.

Nixon to Helene Drown, Sept. 24, 1952, RNL; *NYHT,* Sept. 24, 1952; *NYT,* Sept. 24, 1952; AP, Sept. 23, 24, 1952; Nixon-Gannon interviews; Eisenhower to Arthur Vandenberg, Oct. 11, 1952, PDDE; Hughes, *Ordeal of Power;* Nixon, *Six Crises, RN.*

197 "You're my boy": Ike was still intent on establishing primacy. In private, he grilled Pat and Dick on rumors that they had used the fund to decorate their new home. "Tape #6 Fund," "Fund Tape #6," "Fund tape #7," Mozley script, Sept. 24, 1952, and reminiscence, Rogers interview, Aitken papers, RNL; *Wall Street Journal,* Sept. 25, 1952; *NYHT,* Sept. 25, 1952; *NYT,* Sept. 25, 26, 1952; AP, Sept. 24, 25, 1952; *Time,* Oct. 6, 1952; Olney, Edmund "Pat" Brown OH, Berkeley; Rogers OH, Klein OH, Clay OH, Adams OH, Columbia; Rogers interview, Halberstam papers, BU; Harlow interview, Thompson; Eisenhower to Nixon, Sept. 23, 1952, Eisenhower to Edgar Eisenhower, Sept. 24, 1952, Eisenhower to Benjamin F. Caffey, Sept. 23, 1952, PDDE; Nixon, *RN;* Hillings, *Irishman;* Hughes, *Ordeal of Power.*

CHAPTER 11: A CANDIDATE FOR THE LITTLE MAN

198 who spoke for the little guy: Franklin Roosevelt, address announcing the second New Deal, Oct. 31, 1936, radio address, Oct. 12, 1937, Inaugural Address, Mar. 4, 1933, radio address, Apr. 7, 1932, FDR; Theodore Roosevelt had also clashed with the "malefactors of great wealth"—marching his progressives out of the GOP in 1912 and running as the leader of the Bull Moose party.

198 New Deal coalition was fraying: Nixon speech files, Oct. 1952, RNL; Eric Goldman, *The Crucial Decade* (New York: Vintage, 1956); Lee Huebner, "The Checkers Speech After 60 Years," *Atlantic,* Sept. 22, 2012; Robert Ruark, "Human Republican," *New York World-Telegram,* Sept. 25, 1952.

199 Chambers published *Witness:* Hiss to Thomas, Aug. 24, 1948, RNL; Whittaker Chambers, *Witness* (New York: Random House, 1952), Chambers to James Rorty, undated, cited in Allen Weinstein, *Perjury* (New York: Knopf, 1978).

201 "honest, common man": Polly Ryther to Pat Nixon, Sept. 23, 1952, Hauser to Finch, Haldeman, and Hall, Jan. 26, 1960, WHSF-R; *NYT,* Oct. 6, 1952; William White, "Nixon: What Kind of President?" *Harper's,* Jan. 1958; Murray Kempton, "TIME and Nixon," Nov. 13, 1962, reprinted in *America Comes of Middle Age* (Boston: Little, Brown, 1963).

202 "traitors to the high principles": David P. Smith to Nixon, Nov. 10, 1952, RNL; Richard Nixon, "Statement on the Death of General Eisenhower," Mar. 28, 1969, PPP; *NYHT,* Oct. 17, 1952, Sept. 4, 1956; AP, Oct. 27, 1952; *NYT,* October 6, 9, 10, 14, 17, 1952; Rogers interview, Halberstam papers, BU; Abraham Ribicoff OH, Columbia University; Bryce Harlow OH, George Reedy OH, LBJ; Merle Miller, *Plain Speaking* (New York: Berkley-Putnam's, 1974); Helen Gahagan Douglas, *A Full Life* (Garden City, NY: Doubleday, 1982); David Halberstam, *The Powers That Be* (New York: Knopf, 1979); D. B. Hardeman and Donald Bacon, *Rayburn* (Austin, TX: Texas Monthly Press, 1987); Richard Rovere, *The Eisenhower Years: Affairs of State* (New York: Farrar, Straus and Cudahy, 1956); Harlow interview, Thompson; Nixon, *RN.*

203 "Inquiring Photografer": *Washington Times-Herald,* Nov. 1952; Cotton interview, Kornitzer papers, BKP; Klein, Rogers OH, Columbia; McConaughy file for *Time* cover story, Jan. 1954, RNL.

JFK sent his own note of congratulations to Nixon: "I was always convinced that you would move ahead to the top—but I never thought it would come this quickly; You were an ideal selection." Nixon, *RN.*

203 attributed to the press: It is difficult to explain Nixon's conviction that the press sav-
     aged him in the Hiss case. He was angered when a panel of Washington reporters, led
     by the *New York Times* correspondent James Reston, grilled Chambers on *Meet the
     Press*. Nixon took no pleasure from the editorial page of the *Washington Post*, which
     likened HUAC's targets to innocent pedestrians "spattered with mud." And he was
     criticized, harshly, when Laurence Duggan died. Yet the *Post*'s news stories on the
     Hiss case, like those of most newspapers, were more than fair; often, the paper ran
     the stories of Nixon's ally and confidant Bert Andrews on its front page. And once the
     pumpkin papers were discovered, even the *Post* editorial page conceded that "it seems
     pretty clear [that HUAC] has got hold of something real this time."
        It is possible that, when citing the Hiss case as the cause of his troubles, Nixon was
     using it as shorthand for the era, which included HUAC, the Hiss case, the Senate
     campaign, the fund episode, his alliance with Joe McCarthy, and his nasty attacks on
     Adlai Stevenson. By the end of 1954, Nixon was truly a polarizing figure. Robinson to
     Nixon, Dec. 31, 1959, Robinson to *Saturday Review*, Nov. 14, 1962, "RN Fund Tape
     #3," "RN Fund Tape #7," Klein OH, RNL; James Bassett, Ted Rogers, Earl Mazo,
     James Keogh, and Robert Finch interviews, Halberstam papers, BU; Hal Bruno OH,
     GFF; Aylett Cotton, Bill Rogers interview, BKP; Brownfield OH, Whittier; JNE, *Pat;*
     Walter Trohan, *Political Animals* (New York: Doubleday, 1975).

206 Herblock was a constant vexation: Herblock cartoon, *WP*, Oct. 29, 1952; Herblock
     interview, Halberstam papers, BU; Nixon-Gannon.

206 Drew Pearson was another tormentor: Nixon, audiotape, Aug. 21, 1961, "Supplemen-
     tal Memo for Moscow on the Fund Chapter" (Tape #2), Nixon to Henry Knoop, Nov.
     28, 1952, Nixon to St. Johns, undated, fall, 1952 and Mar. 7, 1953, Nixon to Willard
     Beaulac, American Embassy, Havana, Cuba, undated, and Beaulac replies, Sept. 5, Oct.
     1, 1952, Consul General Paul Reveley to Smith, Sept. 29, 1952, Cuban Tourist Divi-
     sion to Smith, Nov. 6, 1952, Nixon to *St. Louis Post-Dispatch*, Nov. 2, 1952, and Nixon
     springtime 1952 calendar, Blasé Bonpane to Drew Pearson, Nov. 1, 1952, Nixon to
     Creel, Nov. 28, 1952, Nixon to "Dear Colleagues," Aug. 1, 1947, RNL.
        Handwritten notes of reply to India Edward statement on Pat Nixon legal name and
     birthdate, Nov. 3, 1952, Dorothy Christie to Nixon, Nov. 19, 1952, and Murray Chotiner
     to Christie, Dec. 5, 1952, RNL; transcript, Chotiner telephone conversation with *Post-
     Dispatch* editor, Oct. 13, 1952, De Toledano to Sen. Frank Barrett, Feb. 12, 1953, Barrett
     to Brownell, Feb. 5, 1953, Pearson column on Nixon family finances, undated, Radio
     Reports transcriptions of Pearson broadcasts, Sept. 21, 28, Oct. 5, 12, 26, Nov. 2, 1952,
     Bewley to William Arnold, Sept. 10, 1951, "Malaxa" chronology, Nixon and Knowland
     to Defense Production Administration, Sept. 14, 1951, Bewley to Nixon, Apr. 2, 23,
     1952, Apr. 15, 1953, Bewley to Rose Mary Woods, Dec. 16, 1955, Nixon to Bewley, Apr.
     18, 1953, Bewley to Woods, "Memorandum on Nicolae Malaxa," Dec. 16, 1955, Eleanor
     Harris interview, Mar. 5, 1960, RNL.
        Thomas Harrington to Pearson, Nov. 3, 1952, Pearson to Harry Hoyt, Nov. 4,
     1952, George Arnold to Pearson, Nov. 7, 1952, "Open Letter to Editors and Readers,"
     Drew Pearson papers, Lyndon B. Johnson Presidential Library; *St. Louis Post-Dispatch*,
     Oct. 30, 1952; *NYT*, Oct. 30, 1952, Dec. 18, 1957; Rogers, Reston interview, Hal-
     berstam papers, BU; Pat Brown OH, Berkeley; Hal Bruno OH, GFF; *Time*, Dec. 13,
     1948; Mark Feldstein, "Fighting Quakers," *Journalism History*, Summer 2004; Cong.
     Rec., Oct. 5, 1962. See also Jack Anderson and James Boyd, *Confessions of a Muckraker*
     (New York: Random House, 1979) and Anderson with Daryl Gibson, *Peace, War and
     Politics* (New York: Forge, 1999).

207 The effect was cumulative, and lingering: Nixon, audiotape, Aug. 21, 1961, "Sup-
     plemental Memo for Moscow on the Fund Chapter" (Tape #2), RNL; Mazo OH,
     Columbia. Mazo interview, Halberstam papers, BU. For more on how liberal myth

took on the cloak of fact over time, as noted by Mazo, see the *New Republic* 1952 series of stories by Ernest Brashear and its 1959 series by William Costello, as well as the Democratic Party magazine, *Democratic Digest,* Feb. 1960.

208 sufficient to sic the press: Bassett, Rogers, Finch, Phil Potter, Nancy Chotiner, Herb Block, James Reston, and William Price interviews, Halberstam papers, BU; Frank Gannon, interview with author; Nixon, audiotape, Aug. 21, 1961, "Supplemental Memo for Moscow on the Fund Chapter" (Tape #2), RNL; Bewley interview, FMB; Nixon-Gannon; Juanita T. Barbee OH, Berkeley; H. R. Haldeman, *The Ends of Power* (New York: Times Books, 1978); Reston memo, July 12, 1959, Katie Louchheim Papers, LC, cited in Robert Dallek, *An Unfinished Life: John F. Kennedy, 1917–1963* (Boston: Little, Brown, 2003); Christopher Matthews, *Kennedy & Nixon* (New York: Random House, 1996); Russell Baker, *The Good Times* (New York: Penguin, 1989).

CHAPTER 12: McCARTHY

210 transition of power: Ike snubbed Truman when invited to the White House during the campaign, and again that morning when he refused to make the customary courtesy call on the outgoing president at the mansion. Alonzo Hamby, *Man of the People* (New York: Oxford University Press, 1995); David McCullough, *Truman* (New York: Simon & Schuster, 1992); Bill Arnold, *Back When It All* (New York: Vantage, 1972).

210 relationship between the president and vice president: Nixon dictation, *Six Crises* file, RNL; James Bassett, unpublished diary, "Ugly Year, Lonely Man," Bassett papers, Bowdoin. Bassett kept a diary in 1954, and later annotated it with commentary. Nixon reminiscences, Mar. 15, 1976, Irwin Gellman, private collection; *NYT,* Mar. 28, 1954; Harlow interview, Thompson; Finch and Brownell interviews in Strober; Emmet J. Hughes, *The Ordeal of Power* (New York: Atheneum, 1963); Arthur Schlesinger Jr. diary, Apr. 8, 1962, ASP. For more see William White, "Nixon: What Kind of President?" *Harper's,* Jan. 1958; Leonard Hall interview with Brodie, FMB; William Bragg Ewald, *Eisenhower the President* (Englewood Cliffs, NJ: Prentice-Hall, 1981); Irwin Gellman, *The President and the Apprentice* (New Haven, CT: Yale University Press); Jeffrey Frank, *Ike and Dick* (New York: Simon & Schuster, 2013); John Malsberger, *The General and the Politician* (Lanham, MD: Rowman & Littlefield, 2014). Revealing views are also available in Ralph de Toledano, *One Man Alone: Richard Nixon* (New York: Funk & Wagnalls, 1969) and William Safire, *Before the Fall* (New York: Doubleday, 1975).

213 "a misuse of television": "Sure I put some corn in the Fund telecast," Nixon told Jim Bassett. "I did it deliberately. I believed Stevenson was the wrong man for the country and I was doing everything I knew how to beat him." See Bassett diary, Bassett papers, Bowdoin; *NYT,* July 26, Oct. 2, 1953. Hauser to Finch, Haldeman, and Hall, Jan. 26, 1960, WHSF-R; Eisenhower diary, June 1, 1953, and Eisenhower to Walter Bedell Smith, Aug. 14, 1952, PDDE; Whalen diary, Whalen papers, Mar. 17, 1970.

213 Joe McCarthy was now: Nixon platter dictation on early months as vice president, June 16, 1953, Nixon handwritten notes, meeting with Eisenhower, Mar. 24, 1953, "A Chronology of Joe McCarthy," RNL; David Oshinsky, *A Conspiracy So Immense* (New York: Oxford University Press, 2005); Thomas Reeves, *The Life and Times of Joe McCarthy* (New York: Stein and Day, 1982); de Toledano, *One Man Alone;* Sherman Adams, *Firsthand Report* (New York: Harper, 1961); *NYT,* May 26, July 26, 1953; *WP,* Mar. 23, May 26, June 2, June 21, 1953; Bassett diary, Bowdoin; Joseph McCarthy to Eisenhower, Feb. 3, 1953, Minnich memo, May 22, 1953, DDEL; Eisenhower to McCarthy, Apr. 1, 1953, PDDE; Roy Cohn interview, FMB; *Time,* Mar. 30, Apr. 6, 13, 20, July 27, 1953; Nixon-Gannon.

216 embraced a backstage role: Nixon notes of meeting with Eisenhower, Apr. 2, 1967, RNL; Eisenhower diary, June 1, 1953, PDDE; *NYT,* June 28, July 26, 1953; *WP,* June

21, July 16, 1953; *Time,* July 20, 1953, Jan. 18, 1954. Dwight D. Eisenhower, Address "The Chance for Peace" Delivered Before the American Society of Newspaper Editors, April 16, 1953, PPP.

216 set off on a two-month tour: Eisenhower to Nixon, July 1953, Eisenhower to Dulles, Oct. 23, 1953, Eisenhower to Syngman Rhee, Nov. 4, 1953, Mar. 20, 1954, Eisenhower to Nixon, Dec. 14, 1953, PDDE; briefing papers and Sept. 17, 1953, itinerary for Nixon trip, Pat Nixon diary and notes and Marje Acker translation of Pat's shorthand notes, Rose Mary Woods to Ralph de Toledano, Nov. 17, 1953, Pat Nixon to Helene Drown, June 9, 1953, and undated, from Taiwan, 1953, McConaughy file, Jan. 7, 1954, "Continuation of Tape One," dictated reminiscence, *Six Crises* file, Rogers to Nixon, Dec. 15, 1953, RNL; Julie Eisenhower remarks, "First Lady Pat Nixon: Ambassador of Goodwill," Apr. 5, 2012, Pat Nixon centennial forum, National Archives, Washington, D.C.; Adela Rogers St. Johns OH, Columbia University; Elizabeth Cloes OH, Whittier; Nixon-Gannon, *Time,* Dec. 7, 1953, Jan. 4, 1954; *NYHT,* Dec. 20, 1953; *NYT,* Oct. 11, Dec. 14, 1953; Jonathan Aitken, *Nixon: A Life* (Washington, D.C.: Regnery, 1993); Nixon, *RN.* In the NSC meetings, Nixon "showed a serious and professional approach to foreign policy," recalled William Bundy, a Democratic foreign policy and intelligence expert working in the Eisenhower White House. See William Bundy, *A Tangled Web: The Making of Foreign Policy in the Nixon Presidency* (New York: Hill and Wang, 1998).

219 planning to abandon politics: Pat Nixon to Helene Drown, Sept. 4, 1951, Nov. 3, 1951, Aug. 31, 1953, McConaughy file for *Time* cover story, Jan. 1954, RNL; Evlyn Dorn OH, Alyce Koch OH, Elizabeth Cloes OH, Whittier; Nixon reminiscences, Mar. 14, 1976, Gellman, private collection; Smith interview, FMB; Bassett diary, Bowdoin; JNE, *Pat.*

220 McCarthy had bolted the corral: Robert King to Nixon, Jan. 6, 1954, Nixon to King, Jan. 1954, Jackson to Nixon, Mar. 9, 1954, "A Chronology of Joe McCarthy," RNL; Eisenhower to Eugene and Helen Henley, Aug. 19, 1952, Eisenhower to Philip D. Reed, June 17, 1953, Eisenhower to Milton Eisenhower, Oct. 9, 1953, Eisenhower to Paul Helms, Mar. 9, 1954, Eisenhower to William Robinson, Mar. 12, 1954, Eisenhower to Aaron Berg, Apr. 7, 1954, PDDE; Bassett diary, Bassett to "My Darling Wife," Mar. 14, 1954, Bassett papers, Bowdoin; C. D. Jackson, daily notes, Nov. 27, 30, Dec. 2, 1953, Eisenhower to Swede Hazlett, July 21, 1953, Minnich memo, July 29, 1953, DDEL; *NYT,* July 9, 1953, Jan. 7, 1954; *WP,* July 13, 1953; *Time,* July 13, 20, 27, Dec. 14, 28, 1953; Milton Eisenhower OH, Bryce Harlow OH, Columbia.

221 he had deleted remarks: The paragraph defending Marshall was deleted from Ike's speech, but not before an advance text had been distributed to the press. See "Sixth Draft—Communism and Freedom," DDEL; Nixon handwritten notes, White House meetings on McCarthy, Feb. 9, 26, 1954, and undated, spring 1954, Bewley to Rose Mary Woods, Mar. 9, 1954, "Suggestions from Ralph de Toledano," Eisenhower to Nixon and the cabinet, Mar. 5, 1954, "A Chronology of Joe McCarthy," RNL; Eisenhower to Nixon, Oct. 1, 1952, and notes, Eisenhower to Harold Stassen, Oct. 5, 1952, and notes, Eisenhower to Walter Bedell Smith, May 27, 1953, Eisenhower to Brownell, Nov. 4, 1953, Eisenhower to cabinet members, Mar. 5, 1954, Eisenhower diary, Mar. 5, May 11, 1954, Eisenhower to Charles Wilson, May 13, 17, 1954, PDDE; Eisenhower to Harry Bullis, May 18, 1953, Hagerty diary, Feb. 25, Mar. 8, 10, 24, May 12, 14 1954, DDEL; Bassett diary, Bowdoin; Bryce Harlow OH, Thompson; William Lawrence OH, Columbia; Ike "still smiling" cited in Gellman, *President and the Apprentice;* Ewald OH, Goodpaster OH, Thompson; Hughes, *Ordeal of Power; WP,* Feb. 25, 26, Mar. 4, 1954; *NYT,* Feb. 25, 26, 28, 1954; *Time,* Mar. 1, 8, 15, 22, 1954; William Bragg Ewald, *Who Killed Joe McCarthy?* (New York: Simon & Schuster,

1984); Richard Rovere, *The Eisenhower Year: Affairs of State* (New York: Farrar, Straus and Cudahy, 1956); William S. White, "Nixon: What Kind of President?" *Harper's,* Jan. 1958. The Hagerty diary is available at the Eisenhower presidential library, and in printed form as Robert H. Ferrell, ed., *The Diary of James C. Hagerty: Eisenhower in Mid-Course, 1954–1955* (Bloomington: Indiana University Press, 1983).

223 "Army-McCarthy" hearings: Nixon diary, June 28, 1954, author's collection; Bewley to Nixon, Jan. 7, 21, 1954, Nixon to Bewley, Jan. 19, 1954, "A Chronology of Joe McCarthy," Brownell interview, Aitken papers, RNL; Bassett OH, Halberstam papers, BU; Bassett diary, Bassett papers, Bowdoin; Minnich memo, June 21, 1955, DDEL; *NYT,* Mar. 9, 10, 14, 1954; *Time,* Mar. 22, May 3, June 21, Oct. 4, Nov. 29, Dec. 13, 1954; Nixon-Gannon; Reeves, *Life and Times;* Oshinsky, *Conspiracy So Immense;* Herbert Brownell, *Advising Ike* (Lawrence: University Press of Kansas, 1993); de Toledano interview, Brodie, FMB.

226 The rough beast arrived: FRUS, 1952–1954, Vol. 13, Indochina, Part 1 and 2, Documents 632, 646, 705, 711, 756, 802, 814, 818, 819, and notes; William Conrad Gibbons, *The U.S. Government and the Vietnam War* (Washington, D.C.: U.S. Senate, Committee on Foreign Relations, Congressional Research Service, 1984); Stanley Karnow, *Vietnam* (New York: Viking, 1983); Eisenhower press conferences, Mar. 24, Apr. 7, 1954, PPP; Kennedy tape recording, Apr. 1954 dictated memo of conversation between Kennedy and Nixon, Ted Widmer and Caroline Kennedy, *Listening In* (New York: Hyperion, 2012).

227 light the way toward U.S. intervention: Nixon diary entry, Apr. 29, 1954, author's possession; Nixon reminiscences, Mar. 18, 1976, Gellman, private collection; FRUS, 1952–1954, Vol. 13, Indochina, Part 1 and 2; Dwight Eisenhower OH, William Knowland OH, Columbia. Nixon handwritten notes on Eisenhower meetings, 1954 and Apr. 2, 1967; Nixon handwritten notes on Dien Bien Phu, use of atomic weapons, and other White House debates on Indochina, undated, vice-presidential years, Frank Kuest to Nixon, Apr. 24, 1954, Nixon to de Toledano, Nov. 15, 1955, Cronin paper, "The Current Crisis," briefing notes, fall 1953 trip, "Some Notes on the Political Situation in Indochina," and "Political Situation in North Vietnam" and Nixon itinerary, RNL; Gibbons, *The U.S. Government and the Vietnam War;* Bassett diary, Bowdoin; *NYT,* Mar. 18, 1955; May 7, 1970; *Wall Street Journal,* Apr. 19, 20, 1954; *Time,* Apr. 26, 1954; Karnow, *Vietnam;* Adams, *Firsthand Report;* William Bragg Ewald, *Eisenhower the President* (Englewood Cliffs, NJ: Prentice-Hall, 1981); "Vietnam and the Paris Peace Accords," Nixon Legacy Forum, Dec. 5, 2014, NARA, Washington, D.C. (participants: Winston Lord, John Negroponte, and William Richard Smyser); David Halberstam, *The Best and the Brightest* (New York: Random House, 1972). Nixon insisted that his remarks on Vietnam were not an administration trial balloon—an assessment supported by Jim Bassett's contemporaneous account. See Bassett diary, Bowdoin.

228 Ike's final option: FRUS, 1952–1954, Vol. 13, Indochina, Part 1 and 2 (for the NSC debate of April 29, 1954, see document 818); "Eisenhower was a non-involvement man," Nixon recalled, criticizing his mentor two decades later: see White House tape, Nixon, Haig, and Rogers, June 14, 1971, RNL. Eisenhower's remarks about "the jungles of Indochina" are from a draft of his memoir, *Mandate for Change,* written with ghostwriter William Ewald, and published in Ewald's *Eisenhower the President.* They are consistent with what he told Nixon and the NSC in 1954, and with what Ike wrote in his diary before becoming president: "I'd favor heavy reinforcement to get the thing over at once, but I'm convinced that no military victory is possible in that kind of theater." Eisenhower diaries, Mar. 17, 1951.

229 the Nixon brand blighted: *Time,* Apr. 19, June 21, 1954, Mar. 12, 1956, Oct. 27, 1958;

NYT, Mar; 21, June 10, 1954; *WP,* May 2, 4, 1954; Cong. Rec., July 1, 1954; *Duke Chronicle,* Sept. 24, 2015.

230 Ike claimed to be fond: Monica Crowley, *Nixon Off the Record* (New York: Random House, 1996); de Toledano, *One Man Alone;* Nixon, *Six Crises;* Adams, *Firsthand Report;* Earl Mazo, *Richard Nixon: A Political and Personal Portrait* (New York: Avon, 1960); de Toledano interview, Maryland Center for Public Broadcasting, Oct. 1971; Eisenhower to Edward "Swede" Hazlett, Dec. 24, 1953, Dec. 8, 1954, Eisenhower to Edgar Eisenhower, Jan. 27, 1954, Eisenhower to Paul Helms, Dec. 29, 1954, PDDE.

Elliot Richardson recalled a cabinet meeting in which Nixon, by deftly posing a series of questions (Is there an ideological objection? Does it cost too much? Is there any doubt about the need?), persuaded Eisenhower to back federal aid for education, despite the objections of other advisers. See Richardson OH, RNL.

231 Nixon did the grubby work: Eisenhower to Nixon, June 28, 1954, and note, Eisenhower to Nixon, Sept. 29, 1954, and note, Eisenhower to John R. McCrary, Dec. 4, 1954, PDDE; *NYT,* June 28, 1954; *Time,* Nov. 1, 1954, Jan. 24, 1955; *Denver Post,* June 29, 1954, quoted in Mazo, *Richard Nixon;* Bassett diary, Bowdoin; Harlow interview, *New Republic,* May 13, 1978; Irving Salomon OH, Robert Finch OH, Columbia; Jack Drown OH, Whittier; White, *Harper's,* Jan. 1958; Nixon diary entry, 1956, *RN.*

232 "Ugly Year, Lonely Man": A few other samples:

24 February—At 7:30 p.m. he picked me up, his exceedingly excellent Negro chauffeur snaking the longest Cadillac I'd ever seen into the hotel's tiny curving driveway. Went to LaSalle de Bois, RN's favorite eating haunt. We ordered extra dry Gibsons (with RN darkly muttering it was a "great mistake.") Then a second round. Then, RN having relaxed enthusiastically, briskly demanded a third, all his darkling fears apparently gone. . . . We talked of the gruesome McCarthy affair ("It's probably time we dumped him," said RN.). . . . Both of us agreed McCarthy has now passed all bounds, and must be controlled.

27 February—RN phoned about noon to ask if I wanted to go around Burning Tree Golf Club. . . . At the adjoining table sat the President, grinning, laughing and joking, with his foursome. Lunch was hamburger. Nixon fired off the tee first: a wobbly shot into the woods. He hit six in all. Then the others; and by this time Ike and his party were breathing on our group's necks. So after some slight Alphonse & Gastoning, the Presidential group went through.

4 March—The man never rests, relaxes; but I guess he takes politics through his pores. . . . In RN's fabulous Cad, we tooled out to a place called Martin's in old Georgetown; a saloon-type café . . . where we feasted on corned beef, cabbage and great drafts of Michelob.

12 March—Yesterday I felt the old rapport with RN, as we were sharing a bourbon after kicking the speech around. . . . Since I knew RN in the '52 campaign he's become immensely assured, to the point of occasional arrogance, that suddenly is tempered by a flash of humbleness. . . . RN is the oldest young man in the world, bar none. . . . RN said wistfully at one point in our rambling chat that he'd love to slip a secret recording gadget in the President's office to capture some of those warm, offhand, greathearted things the Man says.

13 March—RN was in that "high" mood he always develops after a tough deal like this ("Hardest speech I ever gave," he said, maybe forgetting a certain September night of two years ago, maybe not.). . . . We had Scotches. RN took two of them fast, heavy and straight, thereby heightening his curious mood. I began to study him. And for the life of me, I cannot identify RN with the quietly tense young man who came into my Los Angeles newspaper office in 1948, as a freshman Congressman . . . Ted Rogers says he hasn't changed much since 1950 . . . except to retreat deeper into that almost mystic shell he wears. Then

we had to start calling people on the telephone at 1 a.m. . . . RN wanted to get Hildegarde, the singer, up to the suite for conversation . . . But Hildegarde was packing for New York City . . . So the weird day ended at 3 a.m.

2 July—I got Hagerty aside to tell him RN is lower than a snake's belly lately and that we've got to boost his morale. "Dick is our political spearhead—and as such he's going to catch a lot of Hell. . . . they're trying to drive a wedge between him and the President." Hagerty harrumphed: "They can't do it!" "Maybe so," I said, "but somebody damned well better tell RN that—and make him believe it. He has broad shoulders; but this is pretty lonely business, being the heat-taker while the Big Chief plays the high level game."

233 *I've Had It:* Bassett to his wife, Sept. 1954, Bassett diary entry, Sept. 7, 1954, Bowdoin.

234 "quit the game forever": Eisenhower to Nixon, Sept. 25, 29, Oct. 27, 1954, RNL; Bassett diary, Bassett to wife, Sept. 1954, Bowdoin; Minnich memo, June 21, 1955, DDEL; *WP,* Oct. 23, Nov. 15, 1954; *NYT,* Oct. 24, 1954; de Toledano, *One Man Alone;* Malsberger, *General and the Politician.* The date of Nixon's talk with Pat about quitting politics is difficult to pin down. His aides remember him talking about quitting before the 1954 campaign, but in his taped reminiscences for his memoir Nixon placed the conversation around Thanksgiving, at a time when Pat was "particularly depressed" after the 1954 election. They no doubt discussed it more than once. See Bassett papers and Nixon reminiscences, Mar. 16, 1976, Gellman, private collection.

CHAPTER 13: THE NEW NIXON

235 Eisenhower had suffered a heart attack: In those first moments after hearing the news, Nixon remembered how, when he was chosen as Ike's running mate, someone had quoted an old political saw: Vice presidents have two duties: to preside over the Senate, "and to check the morning's newspaper as to the President's health." It was "the morbid aura of the office," he would remember. "No one ever talks of it, least of all the President and his VP, still every political being knows."

Nixon's original draft of his conversation with Hagerty, in his *Six Crises* files, jibes with Hagerty's diary and is included here. A slightly modified version appeared in the book when it was published in 1962. Pat's contemporary accounts, like that given to *Redbook* magazine in May 1956, also differ in minor ways from *Six Crises.*

It is no slander to report that Nixon seemed in shock. In his diary, Hagerty recorded the reactions of other White House aides. He described himself as shaken, Jerry Persons as shocked, and Ann Whitman in tears.

"The Heart Attack" and "Notes," Nixon *Six Crises* file, Woods transcribed shorthand notes, Sept. 1955, Eleanor Harris interview, Mar. 5, 1960, RNL; Rogers interview, BKP; Clarence Lasby, *Eisenhower's Heart Attack* (Lawrence: University Press of Kansas, 1997); *Redbook,* May 1956; *NYHT,* Oct. 9, 1955; Hagerty diary, Sept. 24, 25, 1955; *Time,* Oct. 3, 10, 1955.

237 target being pinned to his back: Nixon was not the only one under scrutiny. Ike's brother Milton, a formidable figure in his own right, had to curtail his visits to the ailing president because they roused suspicion he was angling to replace him. See Eisenhower to Milton Eisenhower and note, Oct. 25, 1955, DDEP; "The Heart Attack" and "Notes," Nixon *Six Crises* file, Eisenhower to Nixon, Oct. 1, 1955, Woods transcribed shorthand notes, Sept. 1955, transcript of Nixon phone conversation with Mosher, Oct. 5, 1955, RNL; Jorgensen to Nixon, Nov. 17, 1954, Oct. 3, 1955, transcript, RN phone conversation with Mosher, Oct. 10, 1955, Cotton to Nixon, Nov. 23, 1955, Guylay to Woods, Sept. 25, 1955, Chotiner to Nixon, Sept. 27, 1955, Mosher to Nixon, Sept. 28, 1955, Jackson to Nixon, Sept. 28, 1955, Nixon to Jackson, Sept. 29, 1955, RNL; Cronin "Political Analysis," undated, Bassett to Nixon, Oct. 2, 1955, Hancock to Nixon, Oct. 2, 1955, Mosher to Nixon, Oct. 3, 1955, Palmer to Nixon, Oct. 3, 1955,

Chotiner to Nixon, Oct. 5, 1955, RNL; White House tape, Nixon and Haldeman, April 13, 1973, RNL; Safire, "Nixon Diary," Mar. 16, 1973, Safire papers, LOC; Clay OH, Brownell OH, Milton Eisenhower OH, Columbia University; *New Republic,* Oct. 17, 1955; *NYHT,* Oct. 9, 1955; *NYT,* Sept. 25, 26, 27, 1955; *NYHT,* Oct. 2, 4, 1955; *Time,* Oct. 10, 17, 1955; *New Yorker,* Richard Rovere, "Letter from Washington," Sept. 29, 1955; *Wall Street Journal,* Aug. 22, 1956; Anderson to Pearson, undated, Drew Pearson papers, LBJ; Lasby, *Eisenhower's Heart Attack;* Sherman Adams, *Firsthand Report* (New York: Harper, 1961); Herbert Parmet, *Eisenhower and the American Crusades* (New York: MacMillan, 1972); Jonathan Aitken, *Nixon: A Life* (Washington, D.C.: Regnery, 1993); Rogers interview, Aitken papers, RNL.

239   prepared to run for reelection: "The Heart Attack" and "Notes," Nixon *Six Crises* file, Nixon handwritten notes on Eisenhower heart attack, RNL; Eisenhower Diary, May 14, 1953, Eisenhower to Hazlett, Dec. 24, 1953, Eisenhower to Hazlett, Dec. 8, 1954, Eisenhower to Hazlett, Oct. 26, 1955, Eisenhower to Nixon, July 15, 1955, DDEP; Hagerty Diary, Dec. 1955 and Jan. 1956; Slater Diary, Sept. 25, 1955, Jan. 6, 7, 1956; Clare Booth Luce OH, Columbia; Dulles memos, Oct. 11, 1955, and Jan. 15 and Feb. 9, 1956, Dulles papers, Princeton University; Ann Whitman diary, Feb. 9, 1956, Mar. 13, 19, Apr. 9, 1956, cited in Stephen Ambrose, *Eisenhower,* Vol. 2 (New York: Simon & Schuster, 1984); Arthur Larson, *Eisenhower: The President Nobody Knew* (New York: Scribner, 1968); Emmet J. Hughes, *The Ordeal of Power* (New York: Atheneum, 1963); Adams, *Firsthand Report;* William Bragg Ewald, *Eisenhower the President* (Englewood Cliffs, NJ: Prentice-Hall, 1981).

241   He was taking Equinal: Historian Irwin Gellman was given access to some of Nixon's medical records during a window of time when they were open to researchers at the Nixon presidential library. They have now been closed by the private Richard Nixon Foundation, despite the author's appeals to the National Archives on grounds that records held in presidential libraries should not be shown selectively to favored researchers. The response by the Archives was to cite a technicality, and return the documents to the custody of the Foundation. Gellman, however, shared the information with the author, along with the notes of the Nixon-Woods-Hutschnecker vacation consultation, which is dated "1956?"

In his account of the Eisenhower presidency, *The President and the Apprentice,* pages 277–84, Gellman notes: "Nixon was taking three Equanil, a tranquilizer, during the day. . . . He also took Dexamyl, a stimulant that could elevate mood and lead to psychic dependence. . . . During the evening he had two or three drinks. . . . Before going to sleep he had half a Doriden, a potentially addictive drug for those who had trouble sleeping." His physicians also prescribed the barbiturate Seconal. In the 1950s and early 1960s, these and other medicines were often prescribed for depression, sleeplessness, and fatigue.

Nixon saw "at least ten different doctors in the first half of 1956," Gellman writes. "He also kept his flu, tension, insomnia, and other health problems secret, along with the drugs he was taking to relieve his symptoms. . . . The combination of Ike's well-known illnesses and Nixon's unreported ones means that at the height of the Cold War, both the president and the vice president could easily have been simultaneously incapacitated. . . . Those health conditions were never known at the time."

Ike's secretary, Ann Whitman, described how she and others on the White House staff also relied on Dexamyl. "We call them jolly pills . . . after about three in a day then you have to take a sleeping pill to get some rest." Ike did not take the uppers, but relied on scotch and Seconal. See Robert Donovan, *Confidential Secretary* (New York: E. P. Dutton, 1988) and Evan Thomas, *Ike's Bluff* (Boston: Little, Brown, 2012).

242   a "dump Nixon" campaign: Safire, "Nixon Diary," Mar. 16, 1973, Safire papers, LOC; Eisenhower OH, Hall OH, Shanley OH, Clay OH, Columbia; Hall interview, Hal-

berstam papers, BU; Nixon-Gannon; Dorn interview, FMB; Dr. I. N. Kraushaar OH, Whittier; transcript, Eisenhower press conferences, Feb. 29, 1956, Mar. 7, 1956, PPP; Eisenhower to Jackson, Mar. 11, 1956, Eisenhower to Whitney, Mar. 12, 1956, Eisenhower to Bermingham, Mar. 14, 1956, Eisenhower to Clay, Apr. 24, 1956, and notes, DDEP; Nixon handwritten notes, spring 1956, on consultation with Eisenhower and the vice-presidential nomination and his determination to withdraw from consideration; transcript, Nixon press conference, Apr. 26, 1956, Leonard Hall statement, Jan. 11, 1955, Cronin to Nixon, "Random Thoughts on the 1956 Campaign," undated and Cronin to Nixon, Mar. 15, 1956, RNL; Knoop to Nixon, Mar. 13, 1956, Garland to Nixon, Mar. 11, 1956, Garland to Eisenhower, Feb. 27, 1956, Cotton to Nixon, Mar. 7, 1956, Nixon to Cotton, Mar. 29, 1956, de Toledano to Nixon, Mar. 2, 1956, Waldron to Moscow ("Ileitis Attack"), *Six Crises* file, RNL; statement of Harold E. Stassen and Stassen press conference transcript, July 23, 1956, Stassen letter to Republicans, Aug. 9, 1956, Stassen to Nixon, July 23, 1956, Aug. 16, 1956, Hartmann notes on Stassen press conference, July 31, 1956, Jorgensen to Nixon, Nov. 7, 1956, anti-Nixon booklet, Americans for Democratic Action, 1956, RNL; *New Republic*, Oct. 22, 1956 and (Harlow interview) May 13, 1978; *Time*, Mar. 12, 19, 26, May 7, Aug. 6, Sept. 3, 1956; *NYT*, Jan. 16, Mar. 4, 1956; *NYHT*, Aug. 23, 1956; Guylay interview, Theodore White papers, Harvard University; Anderson to Pearson, undated 1956, Pearson papers, LBJ; Charles Thomson and Frances Shattuck, *The 1956 Presidential Campaign* (Washington, D.C.: Brookings, 1960); Ewald, *Eisenhower the President;* Nixon, *RN;* Schlesinger diary entry, July 19, 1959, ASP; Ellis Slater, *Ike I Knew* (Ellis Slater Trust, 1980).

243 Stevenson described "Nixonland": See John Kenneth Galbraith, *Name-Dropping* (Boston: Houghton Mifflin Harcourt, 2001); *NYT*, Nov. 6, 1956; *Time*, July 4, 1955.

245 the "new Nixon": Nixon began the fall hoping to demonstrate that, as Ike put it, he was "taking a new high level" when campaigning. But both Eisenhower and Nixon were conflicted, and ultimately they realized the futility of the act. "You ought to take notice of some of these attacks that have been made on the administration and me," Ike ordered "I want them to be called on it. I would like you to do so."

     Nixon tried the high road until, sleepless in Oregon one night, he decided it just wasn't him. Having reached that conclusion, "I felt as if a great weight had been lifted from me. I had not realized how frustrating it had been to suppress the normal partisan instincts and campaign with one arm tied behind my back," he recalled. He went over to the piano in his hotel suite and launched himself into a joyous version of Brahms's Rhapsody in G. The music brought Pat into the room. "What on earth are you doing?" she asked him. "You'll wake up the whole hotel." "Memorandum of Conversation at Lunch," May 22, 1956, "Reaction to Lincoln Day Talk," Nixon "memo to the file" on phone call from Eisenhower, Sept. 12, 1956, Cronin to Nixon, Jan. 5, 1957, Cronin "Suggestions for the Next Two Years," and "J.C. Comment on Miss Waldron's letter," RNL; Basset interview, FMB; Rogers, Bassett, Phil Potter interviews, Halberstam papers, BU; *NYT*, Nov. 6, 1956; *Time*, Nov. 5, 1956; *New Yorker*, Sept. 1, Oct. 13, 1956.

245 Nixon took the oath of office: Nixon to Marshburns, Feb. 27, 1957, RNL; Julie Eisenhower, note to author; *Time,* Jan. 28, Feb. 4, 1957.

CHAPTER 14: THE DESOLATE NIGHT OF MAN'S INHUMANITY

248 Ike didn't get there quickly: See Whitman diary, Aug. 14, 1956, and Eisenhower to McGill, Feb. 26, 1959, DDEL; "Report by the Attorney General on the Administration's Efforts in the Field of Racial Segregation and Discrimination," Jan. 26, 1955, "Racial Tension and Civil Rights," Hoover to Rabb, Mar. 9, 1956, Robinson to Eisenhower, May 13, 1958, Eisenhower to Robinson, June 4, 1958, Eisenhower to Billy Graham, Mar. 22, 30, 1956, Morrow to Adams, Dec. 16, 1955, June 4, July 12, 1957,

Eisenhower to Hazlett, July 22, 1957, Eisenhower to Brown and other Little Rock parents, Oct. 4, 1957, DDEL; Eisenhower to Martin Clement, Mar. 19, 1952, Eisenhower to James F. Byrnes, Aug. 14, 1953, Eisenhower to Nixon, Sept. 4, 1953, DDEP; Lawrence O'Brien OH, LBJ; Nixon dictation, Sept. 15, 1958, L. P. Gray to Mrs. Benjamin Pease, Oct. 27, 1960, RNL; Brownell interview transcript, *Eyes on the Prize*, PBS; *NYT*, Oct. 3, 1952; Michael S. Mayer, "Eisenhower and Racial Moderation," in *The Eisenhower Presidency and the 1950s* (Boston: Houghton Mifflin, 1998); David Nichols, *A Matter of Justice* (New York: Simon & Schuster, 2007); Herbert Brownell, *Advising Ike* (Lawrence: University Press of Kansas, 1993).

249 Nixon was a man of his times: Eisenhower to Thompson, Aug. 17, 1960, DDEP; Val Washington to Nixon, Mar. 3, 1958, Charles McWhorter to Nixon, Mar. 4, 1958, McWhorter to Susan Holt, July 29, 1960, Harrison McCall, dictated reminiscence regarding Jackie Robinson, Jan. 3, 1959, Cushman to Anna Bentley, Mar. 7, 1960, Chotiner to Faries, Brennan, and Hancock, Oct. 9, 1952, RNL; Nixon deed, July 5, 1951, Cronin to Nixon, Sept. 5, 1952, Bewley to Nixon, June 22, 1960, Nixon to Bewley, July 14 1960, David P. Smith to Nixon, May 15, 27, 1952, Nixon to Smith, May 19, 1952, Nixon to Mrs. W. B. Reynolds, May 31, 1952, Brock to Nixon, Aug. 1, 1952, Mar. 26, 1953, Nixon to Brock, Mar. 9, 1953, RN to Chris, Feb. 2, 1954, and "Notes for Telephone Call to Bill Brock," Mar. 29, 1954, RNL; King to Mazo, Sept. 2, 1958, *The Papers of Martin Luther King Jr.* (Berkeley: University of California Press, 2000); Finch OH, Columbia University; Lee Simmons OH, GFF; King interview, BKP; *U.S. News & World Report*, Aug. 29, 1952; *Time*, Aug. 24, 1953, Nov. 7, 1955.

251 political problems with civil rights: "Summary of RN-JFC Conversation of 10/6/56" and "Race Relations Outline," undated, 1956 or 1957, King to Nixon, Aug. 30, 1957, Andrade to Nixon, Sept. 9, 1958, Brownell interview with Aitken, Aitken papers, RNL; "Civil Rights" position paper, 1960 campaign, WHSF-R; Eisenhower to Cardinal Francis Spellman, Oct. 26, 1956, DDEP; J. William Barba to John Sengstacke, Sept. 2, 1955, Memorandum for the Record, Frederic Morrow, Nov. 22, 1955, Cabinet Paper, "The Civil Rights Program," with letter from Brownell to Nixon, Apr. 10, 1956, DDEL; Hall OH, Brownell OH, Columbia; Warren Olney OH, Berkeley; J. W. Anderson, *Eisenhower, Brownell and the Congress: The Tangled Origins of the Civil Rights Bill of 1956–1957* (University of Alabama Press, 1964); Stephen Bailey, "The Dynamics of the Centripetal System: A Decade of Civil Rights Legislation," in *The New Congress* (New York: St. Martin's Press, 1966); Denton Watson, *Lion in the Lobby* (New York: William Morrow, 1990); Robert Caro, *Master of the Senate* (New York: Knopf, 2002); Nichols, *Matter of Justice; Reporter*, Sept. 5, 1957.

253 1957 civil rights act: William White, *Citadel* (New York: Harper, 1957); Lawrence O'Brien OH, LBJ.

253 The Senate governed itself: King to Nixon, Aug. 30, 1957, RNL; *Time*, Jan. 14, 21, 1957; Cong. Rec., Jan. 3, 4, 1957; *NYT*, Jan. 6, 1957; Martin Gold and Dimple Gupta, "The Constitutional Option to Change Senate Rules and Procedures," *Harvard Journal of Law & Public Policy*, Winter 2005; Richard Beth, Congressional Research Service, "Entrenchment of Senate Procedure and the Nuclear Option for Change: Possible Proceedings and Their Implications," Mar. 28, 2005.

255 the most dangerous man in America: King to Mazo, Sept. 2, 1958, *The Papers of Martin Luther King*.

255 Despite rigorous opposition: C. Vann Woodward, "The Great Civil Rights Debate," *Commentary*, Oct. 1957; Watson, *Lion in the Lobby*.

255 wooing black voters: Caro, *Master of the Senate;* Irwin Gellman, *The President and the Apprentice* (New Haven, CT: Yale University Press, 2015); Howard Shuman OH, Senate Historical Office, U.S. Senate; Olney OH, Berkeley; Nichols, *Matter of Justice*.

256 With Eisenhower wavering: Mitchell telegram to Nixon, summer 1957, "Richard

Nixon's Public Record on Civil Rights Measures," 1962, King to Nixon, May 15, 1957, Nixon to King, May 23, Sept. 17, 1957, Nixon handwritten notes, MLK meeting, June 1957, Robinson to Nixon, Aug. 7, Dec. 24, 1957, Feb. 5, 1958, Nixon to Robinson, Aug. 8, 1957, Jan. 23, 1958, RNL; Rabb to Adams, June 24, 1957, Morrow to Adams, July 12, 1957, Eisenhower to Hazlett, July 22, 1957, Adam Clayton Powell Jr., press release, Aug. 30, 1957, Val Washington to Eisenhower, July 18, 1957, Val Washington to Lyndon Johnson, Aug. 6, 1957, DDEL; Nixon reminiscences, Mar. 22, 1976, Irwin Gellman, private collection; Nixon interview with Theodore White, Dec. 2, 1968, White papers, Harvard; Harry McPherson OH, George Reedy OH, Clarence Mitchell OH, LBJ; Floyd Riddick OH, Senate Historical Office, U.S. Senate; Kasey Pipes, *Ike's Final Battle* (Los Angeles: World Ahead Media, 2007); Caro, *Master of the Senate;* James McGrath Morris, *Eyes on the Struggle* (New York: Amistad/HarperCollins, 2015); Nichols, *Matter of Justice;* William White, "Nixon: What Kind of President?" *Harper's,* Jan. 1958; *Reporter,* Aug. 8, Sept. 5, 1957; *Time,* July 1, July 22, Aug. 5, Aug. 12, Sept. 9, 1957; *NYT,* Aug. 26, 1957; *Boston Globe,* Aug. 30, 1957.

258   Central High in Little Rock: Nixon statement, Sept. 24, 1957, Batcheler to McWhorter, fall 1957, McWhorter to Batcheler, Oct. 2, 1957, transcript of Nixon appearance, National Conference of Editorial Writers, Oct. 12, 1957, Eisenhower to Nixon, Oct. 2, 1957, RNL; Ann Whitman diary, "Notes dictated by the President on October 8, 1957 concerning visit of Governor Orval Faubus," Russell to Eisenhower, telegram, Sept. 26, 1957, Eisenhower to Russell, telegram, Sept. 27, 1957, Stennis to Eisenhower, Oct. 1, 1957, Eisenhower to Stennis, Oct. 7, 1957, Eisenhower to General Alfred Gruenther, Sept. 24, 1957, Oscar Eckford and other Little Rock parents to Eisenhower, telegram, Sept. 30, 1957, Little Rock Mayor Woodrow Wilson Mann to Eisenhower, telegram, Sept. 24, 1957, Eisenhower handwritten notes, draft, and Sept. 24, 1957, speech, DDEL; Eisenhower diary, Oct. 8, 1957, DDEP; Juan Williams, *Eyes on the Prize* (New York: Penguin, 1987); Brownell OH, Berkeley; Brownell OH, Columbia; Brownell interview, PBS, *Eyes on the Prize;* Brownell, *Advising Ike.*

CHAPTER 15: THE FIELD OF PENDING BATTLE

260   a silver Russian beach ball: NSC minutes, Oct. 10, 1957, DDEL; Paul Dickson, *Sputnik* (New York: Walker, 2001); Central Intelligence Agency, Center for the Study of Intelligence, Historical Collections, "The Missile Gap"; Central Intelligence Agency, Gregory Pedlow and Donald Welzenbach, "The Central Intelligence Agency and Overhead Reconnaissance," 1992; Fred Kaplan, *The Wizards of Armageddon* (Stanford, CA: Stanford University Press, 1991); Yanek Mieczkowski, *Eisenhower's Sputnik Moment: The Race for Space and World Prestige* (Ithaca, NY: Cornell University Press, 2013); "*Sputnik,* 1957," Office of the Historian, U.S. Department of State; a recording of the Sputnik signal, American and Soviet documents, and other records can be found on NASA's "50th Anniversary of the Space Age" web page.

260   a slough of somnolence: Lucius Clay OH, Columbia University; Nixon to Robinson, Apr. 1, 1958, St. Johns to Nixon, undated, 1960, Cronin to Nixon, Oct. 5, 1958, Nixon to Nofziger, May 11, 1982, Klein to Nixon, Dec. 12, 1957, RNL. *NYT,* Dec. 8, 1957, Oct. 26, 1958; *Time,* Dec. 2, 9, 1957; *New Yorker,* Dec. 7, 1957; John Eisenhower, *Strictly Personal* (New York: Doubleday, 1974); Sherman Adams, *Firsthand Report* (Harper, 1961); Jeffrey Frank, *Ike and Dick* (New York: Simon & Schuster, 2013). For the change in the zeitgeist, see Margaret Halsey, "Little Brown Jugular, I Love Thee," Nov. 10, 1958 (bowl of tapioca) and "Beware the Tender Trap," Jan. 13, 1958, *New Republic;* Richard Rovere, "Eisenhower Revisited," *NYT,* Feb. 7, 1971; Emmet J. Hughes, *The Ordeal of Power* (New York: Atheneum, 1963).

262   "Poor brave Jack": Nixon's vice-presidential office was across the hall from Kennedy's suite in the Senate Office Building, and they and their aides came to know each other

well. For Nixon's early relationship with Kennedy, see transcript of Nixon phone call to Herter, Sept. 22, 1958, Rose Mary Woods memo of Mar. 3, 1960, recounting Kennedy's $1,000 donation to Nixon's Senate campaign, Kennedy to Nixon congratulating him on the vice-presidential nomination, undated, and Nixon reply, Aug. 9, 1952, Rex Scouten interview, Aitken papers, RNL; Kennedy to Nixon thanking Dick for sponsoring his membership at the Burning Tree golf club, Feb. 4, 1954, RNL; Jacqueline Kennedy to Nixon thanking him for a parliamentary courtesy, Dec. 5, 1954 ("I don't think there is anyone in the world he thinks more highly of than he does you—and this is just another proof of how incredible you are"), Nixon offering Kennedy, who was recovering from surgery, the use of his office off the Senate floor, Feb. 5, 1955, and Kennedy transcript, *Face the Nation,* July 1, 1956, advising the Republicans to keep Nixon on the ticket, RNL.

262 Murray Chotiner was subpoenaed: Chotiner's finagling was known and tolerated by Nixon. "I have abided faithfully by the rules you set down through Chotiner that I was not to trade on my former association with you for the purpose of getting business for myself in Washington," former aide Bill Arnold told the vice president in 1953. "Now, as you know, Chotiner himself is doing that very thing here, in the case of North American Airlines." See Arnold to Nixon, Aug. 3, 1953, also Chotiner Senate hearing transcript, "Statement by Murray M. Chotiner, June 4, 1956," and de Toledano phone call to Woods, May 7, 1956, RNL; *Time,* May 14, 1956; *Frontier,* Aug. 1958.

Among Chotiner's clients, Robert Kennedy pointed out, was Marco Reginelli, a New Jersey mobster, whom Chotiner had represented in a deportation case. See "Textile Procurement in the Military Services," hearings before the U.S. Senate Committee on Government Operations, Permanent Subcommittee on Investigations, 1955, and Clark Mollenhoff, *Game Plan for Disaster* (New York: Norton, 1976).

Warren Olney said that William Rogers was furious upon hearing that Chotiner was boasting that he could "square cases" with the Justice Department. See Warren Olney OH, Berkeley.

For Nixon acknowledging Chotiner's behavior, see Ted Rogers to Nixon, May 1956, Nixon to Rogers, June 16, 1956, RNL.

Though reportedly banned from Nixon's good offices, Chotiner did offer advice from time to time and rejoined Nixon for the 1968 campaign, after which he was rewarded with a job at the White House. Nixon, however, warned Bob Haldeman about Chotiner's "weaknesses," including his facility to "lead . . . in the wrong direction." See Chotiner to Nixon, May 12, 1958, Chotiner to Nixon, Sept. 18, 1958, Nixon to Chotiner, Sept. 22, 1958, Woods to Chotiner, Jan. 22, 1958, Nixon to Haldeman, Dec. 21, 1970, RNL.

Throughout, Chotiner was a source of friction to many Nixon associates who thought he was trading, clumsily, on his ties to Nixon. See Lutz to Nixon, Aug. 12, 1954, Perry to Brennan, May 23, 1951, Perry to Woods, Sept. 3, 1953, Woods to Perry, Aug. 26, 1953, Elwood Robinson to Robert Finch, Jan. 29, 1960, Brennan to Nixon, Aug. 26, 1954, Bewley to Nixon, Aug. 12, 1954, RNL; for Chotiner profile see *National Journal,* May 30, 1970. On loyalty see Knudsen to Nixon, Apr. 22, 1960, RNL, and de Toledano correspondence with Chotiner, May 23, 1970, and with Chambers in de Toledano Papers, HI, published as *Notes from the Underground* (Regnery, 1997).

262 Kennedy had notable political impediments: On knowledge of Kennedy's womanizing see DeLoach to Tolson, June 10, 1959, FBI, also reprinted in Athan Theoharis, *From the Secret File of J. Edgar Hoover* (Chicago: Ivan R. Dee, 1991). For Kennedy and family see Richard Whalen, *The Founding Father* (Washington, D.C.: Regnery Gateway, 1993); Arthur Schlesinger Jr., *A Thousand Days* (Boston: Houghton Mifflin, 1965); Theodore Sorensen, *Kennedy* (New York: Harper & Row, 1965); Doris Kearns Goodwin, *The Fitzgeralds and the Kennedys* (New York: St. Martin's Press, 1987); Nigel

Hamilton, *JFK: Reckless Youth* (New York: Random House, 1993); David Nasaw, *The Patriarch* (New York: The Penguin Press, 2012).

263 Sputnik's beeps were manna: NSC minutes, Oct. 10, 1957, DDEL; Klein to Nixon, Jan. 31, 1958, Nixon to Klein, Feb. 5, 1958, transcript of Nixon-Cronin phone call, Aug. 21, 1958, Elliot Richardson OH, RNL; Charles Lichenstein interview, WB; Stewart Alsop, "The Mystery of Richard Nixon," *SEP,* July 12, 1958; Nixon interview, 1958, Joseph Alsop and Stewart Alsop Papers, LOC; Robert Norris and Stephen Schwartz, "Growth and Evolution of the U.S. Nuclear Stockpile," Brookings Institution, 1998.

264 a mob in Caracas, Venezuela: Transcripts, tapes 1 through 10, dictated recollections and memoranda, "Caracas section," *Six Crises* files, transcript of Nixon press conference, May 21, 1958, National Press Club, Bill Brammer to Lyndon Johnson, June 18, 1958, with account of *Time-Life* correspondent in Caracas, Don Hughes, interview, Aitken papers, manuscript, Sherwood profile, Rogers to Nixon, "Saturday," 1956, RNL; Robert Amerson OH, FD; Julie Eisenhower, Don Hughes, remarks, Pat Nixon centennial forum, Apr. 5, 2012, National Archives, Washington, D.C.; Nixon-Gannon; Horace Busby OH, LBJ; "U.S. Secret Service, Moments in History," Department of the Treasury newsletter, National Security Archive; *NYHT,* Apr. 29, 30, May 8, 9, 13, 14, 1958; *Time,* May 19, 26, 1958; Vernon Walters, *Silent Missions* (New York: Doubleday, 1978).

267 The 1958 election: Key to Drummond, June 25, 1958, Nixon to Luce, Feb. 13, 1959, St. Johns to Nixon, undated, fall, 1958, Nixon to Agnes, Aug. 10, 1961, "Tape Number Nine" and "New Page 77," and Nixon and Lichenstein, memo, "The Odds Against Us," Sept. 16, 1961, RNL; *Six Crises* file, Robert Finch, postmortem "Address to the Presidential Associates Dinner," Occidental College, Feb. 18, 1961, WHSF-R; Lutz to Hillings, forwarded to RN, July 9, 1958, Robinson to Nixon, Oct. 13, 1958, Garland to Nixon, Feb. 9, 1959, RNL; *Life,* May 26, 1958; Dwight Eisenhower, *The Eisenhower Diaries,* ed. Robert Ferrell (New York: Norton, 1976), Jan. 10, 1955; Richard Norton Smith, *On His Own Terms: A Life of Nelson Rockefeller* (New York: Random House, 2014); *Time,* May 6, Nov. 11, 1957, June 30, Oct. 27, Nov. 17, 1958; *New Yorker,* Mar. 1, 1958, Nov. 15, 1958.

267 known as the Big Switch: Knight seethed when Nixon seemed to snub him at public appearances. The governor fought Nixon over a period of many months for control of the California delegation at the 1956 convention, hoping to replace Dick on the ticket. Knowland initially sided with Knight but later joined the Nixon forces.

For the Big Switch, see Helen Knowland to Finch, Oct. 24, 1958, Nixon to Charles Brownson, Dec. 30, 1958, Finch to Nixon, Jan. 27, 1959, Nixon statement, Nov. 5, 1957, RNL; oral histories by Virginia Knight, Emelyn Knowland Jewett, Jorgensen, Brown, Adams, Call, and Polland, Berkeley; William Knowland OH, Finch OH, Columbia; Stu Spencer OH, GFL; Caspar Weinberger OH, Clem Whitaker OH, CSA; Smathers OH, U.S. Senate Historical Office; Eisenhower to Jones, Aug. 22, 1958, Eisenhower to Roberts, Sept. 4, 1958, Eisenhower to Stassen, Nov. 15, 1958, DDEP; Theodore White, "The Gentlemen From California," *Collier's,* Feb. 3, 1956; Patrick Hillings, *The Irrepressible Irishman* (Harold D. Dean, 1993); James Worthen, *The Young Nixon and His Rivals* (Jefferson, NC: McFarland, 2010).

There are ample samples of Knight-Knowland-Nixon intrigue. See the following, all in RNL: Woods and Nixon memos and letters, 1954 and 1955, Robinson to Nixon, Dec. 10, 1954, Mosher to Nixon, Apr. 27, 28, 1955, Mosher to Nixon, May 25, 1955, Barrett to Nixon, Oct. 10, 1955, Mosher to Nixon, Oct. 10, 1955, Nixon phone conversation with Mosher, transcript, Oct. 10, 1955, Arbuthnot to Nixon, Oct. 13, 1955, Jan. 21, 1955, Bassett to Nixon, Oct. 17, 1955, Palmer to Nixon, Oct. 18, 1955, Palmer to Nixon, Oct. 19, 1955, Mosher to Nixon, Oct. 28, 1955, Chotiner to Nixon, Nov. 2, 1955, Cotton to Nixon, Nov. 23, 1955, Johnson to Nixon, Jan. 13, 1956,

King to Nixon, Feb. 4, 1956, Chotiner memo on Palmer advice, Feb. 16, 1956, Palmer to Nixon, Feb. 16, 22, Mar. 5, Apr. 5, 1956, Hillings to Nixon, Apr. 1, 1957, Nixon to Jorgensen, Aug. 30, 1957, Finch to Nixon, June 23, 1958, Mosher to Nixon, Nov. 12, 1958, McWhorter to Nixon, Aug. 5, 1958, Nixon to Moley, Aug. 19, 1958, Klein to Nixon, July 22, 1958, and undated Nixon handwritten notes, "Knowland—Feb. 21." *Wall Street Journal,* Jan. 9, Sept. 17, 1957; *Time,* May 30, 1955.

270   the "kitchen debate": "Tape No. 1 of The Kitchen" and accompanying tapes 2 through 5 of Nixon reminiscences, Aug. 1961, *Six Crises* file, RNL; Nixon to Eisenhower, July 27, 1959, Milton Eisenhower to Dwight Eisenhower, reports on the effects of the Russian and Polish visits, Aug. 1959, Robert Cushman to Nixon, July 22, 1959, U.S. Department of State, Memorandum of Conversations, July 24–26, 1959 with "Passages Excised or Paraphrased From Khrushchev's Conversations with the Vice President," RNL; Thompson to Herter, Jan. 20, 1960, Herter to Nixon, Jan. 28, 1960 (containing the disregarded advice that Nixon burn the letter after reading it), Nixon to Mansfield and transcript of Mansfield remarks, Aug. 17, 1959, Rogers to Nixon, July 21, Aug. 14, 1959, Robinson to Nixon, June 17, Aug. 6, Sept. 17, Sept. 22, 1959, Klein to Kornitzer, Dec. 7, 1959, de Toledano, "Notes on the 'Kitchen Conference,'" Klein OH, Safire OH, RNL; "Nixon Trip" documents, with note on Kitchen Debate, FRUS, 1958–1960, Volume 10, Part 1, E. Europe Region, Soviet Union, Cyprus; Vladimir Toumanoff OH, FD; *NYT,* July 25, 1984; *Esquire,* Apr. 1960; Michael Beschloss, *Mayday* (New York: Harper & Row, 1986); William Safire, *Before the Fall* (New York: Doubleday, 1975).

When Khrushchev met with President John Kennedy in 1961, he boasted of how the Soviets, by waiting until after the election to release captured American pilots, had helped beat "that son-of-a-bitch Nixon." When Kennedy joked about the unattractively dour foreign minister Andrei Gromyko, Khruschchev replied, "People say Gromyko looks like your Richard Nixon." See Richard Reeves, *President Kennedy* (New York: Simon & Schuster, 1993).

271   to take too much vodka: Nixon's postspeech routine—grabbing a beverage and working the phones for feedback as he decompressed—is familiar to scholars of his presidency and listeners to the White House tapes. Milton Eisenhower, Safire, and Toumanoff all noted this episode of intemperance on the 1959 trip, though they differed on details.

272   Rockefeller wasn't happy: Nixon reminiscences, Mar. 31, 1976, Irwin Gellman, private collection; Hall interview, FMB; Herbert Hill report on Rockefeller, with McWhorter to Nixon, Aug. 24, 1959, Hutcheson to Wood, Apr. 1, 1960, Hutcheson to McWhorter, Apr. 5, 1960, Finch to Spindell, June 16, 1960, Nixon to Dunham, undated, RNL; Eisenhower to Ackers, July 1, 1959, Eisenhower to Nixon, Aug. 18, 1959, DDEP; Eisenhower press conference, Apr. 30, 1958, PPP; Finch OH, Columbia; transcript, Nixon press conference, July 23, 1960, Theodore White papers, JFK; Alsop papers, LOC; Nixon diary entry, Dec. 11, 1969, in Nixon, *RN; New Yorker,* Aug. 6, 1960; Dart interview, BKP; William Bragg Ewald, *Eisenhower the President* (Englewood Cliffs, NJ: Prentice-Hall).

273   the action was with the Democrats: Lady Bird Johnson OH, Harry McPherson OH, Harlow OH, LBJ; Brown OH, Berkeley; Lou Harris, "An Analysis of the 1960 Election for President," Nov. 16, 1960; Anderson to Pearson, July 25, 1960, Pearson Papers, LBJ; Dilworth interview with White, Reedy comments, White papers, Harvard; for FDR Jr. smearing Humphrey see Schlesinger diary entry, Feb. 12, 1975, ASP; Theodore Sorensen, *Kennedy* (New York: Harper & Row, 1965); Theodore White, *The Making of the President 1960* (New York: Atheneum, 1961); Robert Caro, *The Passage of Power* (New York: Knopf, 2012).

274   "Rockefeller's behavior is simply inexplicable": Finch to Spindell, June 16, 1960, RNL; Hall interview, FMB; Stewart Alsop, *Nixon and Rockefeller* (New York: Doubleday,

1960); Gregory D. Pedlow, Donald E. Welzenbach, and Chris Pocock, *The Central Intelligence Agency and Overhead Reconnaissance* (New York: Skyhorse, 2016); Beschloss, *Mayday;* Richard Norton Smith, *On His Own Terms* (New York: Random House, 2014).

275 "If you give me a week": Arnold Hutschnecker, *The Drive for Power* (New York: M. Evans, 1974); Eisenhower press conference, Aug. 24, 1960, PPP; Brownell OH, Strober.

CHAPTER 16: NIXON VS. KENNEDY

276 formidable assets, and major deficiencies: Bliss to Miller, Jan. 2, 1962, with report on 1960 election, WHSF-R. Nixon and Lichenstein, "The Odds Against Us," memorandum, Sept. 16, 1961, Nixon to Waldron and Lichenstein, Sept. 12, 1961, *Six Crises* file, Martin to Nixon, Oct. 14, 1958, Hillings to Nixon, Jan. 12, 1959, Cotton to Nixon, Nov. 8, 1956, Nixon to Hall, Dec. 17, 1956, Robinson to Nixon, Sept. 1, 1960, Robinson to Nixon, Hall, and Finch, Sept. 22, 1960, RNL; "Tactics for First Television Debate," Finch, Occidental College address, Nixon Lodge Campaign, Summary of Opinion in the News, Finch address to Eisenhower officials, May 9, 1960, "Nixon the Statesman," 1960, Rita Hauser, "Report on Trip to Virginia and North Carolina," Mar. 31–Apr. 4, 1960, "Assets—Debits," and "Public Relations Themes to be Developed," 1960 campaign files, WHSF-R; Dart interview, BKP; Kristin Burnett, "Congressional Apportionment," U.S. Census Bureau, 2011. The Khrushchev shoe incident took place on Oct. 12, 1960; see *NYT,* Oct. 13, 1960.

278 "in the lap of the Fates": Haldeman undated postmortem notes for speech to Bel Air Republican women's club, WHSF-R; Nixon to Waldron and Lichenstein, Sept. 12, 1961, memo, Hall telephone call on polling results, Feb. 26, 1960, Robinson to Nixon, Dec. 31, 1959, Burns to Nixon, July 8, 1960, Finch, Occidental College address, RNL; Nixon interview, Stewart Alsop, Joseph Alsop and Stewart Alsop Papers, LOC; Bassett to wife, Oct. 24, 1960, Bassett papers, Bowdoin; Finch OH, Salomon OH, Columbia University; Jorgensen OH, Berkeley; unpublished biography of Leonard Hall, ACW, Aug. 30, 1960, DDEL; Al Smith Jr. statement, Mahoney to Finch, Oct. 26, 1960, and Nixon campaign pamphlet, "Bigotry is a Two-Way Street," Safire papers, LOC; "Massachusetts is Democratic," DNC briefing paper, JFK; O'Brien OH, LBJ; Nathan Glazer and Daniel P. Moynihan, *Beyond the Melting Pot* (Cambridge: MIT Press, 1963); William V. Shannon, *The American Irish* (New York: Macmillan, 1963); James Beatty, *The Rascal King* (Reading, MA: Addison-Wesley, 1992); Maurice Stans OH, Strober.

278 issue of the candidates' religious beliefs: The Nixon campaign saw the early signs of Catholic solidarity. It polled Wisconsin when Kennedy beat Humphrey in that state's open primary and discovered that 52 percent of Republican Catholics had crossed over to support Kennedy.

   The Kennedys saw it too. To persuade the Democratic bosses that a Catholic would be a boost to the national ticket they circulated a memo in 1956 which reported that in the urban centers of the big Electoral College states, "the Catholic voters in each of these cities can usually determine the size of the Democratic margin in those cities; the size of the Democratic margin in those cities usually determines whether these states go Democratic, and whether these states go Democratic usually determines whether the Democrats win the election." See "Catholic Voters and the Democratic National Ticket," JFK, Julie Nixon Eisenhower to Aitken, Aitken papers, RNL; Finch address to Eisenhower officials, May 9, 1960, WHSF-R.

279 charged that the pastor: The Quaker pastor Charles Ball had posed for a nonpolitical pamphlet that was included in an anti-Kennedy mailing by anti-Catholic evangelicals. Nixon to Lichenstein and Waldron, Sept. 12, 1961, Finch address to Eisenhower

officials, May 9, 1960, "Senator Jackson Press Conference," Sept. 14, 1960, Unruh to Ball, Sept. 13, 1960, and Ball to Unruh, Sept. 14, 1960, Peale to Nixon, Jan. 29, 1961, Knoop to Nixon and Nixon reply, May 1960, Knoop to Nixon, Sept. 2, 1960, RNL; McWhorter to Nixon, Mar. 28, 1959, Graham to Nixon, June 21, Aug. 22, Sept. 1, Oct. 17, Nov. 2, 1960, Robinson to Nixon, Mar. 7, May 11, 1960, Feb. 8, Nov. 12, 1962, Nixon to Robinson, June 3, 1960, NAACP, "Monthly Report of the Washington Bureau," Sept. 9, 1960, with analysis of Nixon and Kennedy voting records, Nixon to Mitchell, Sept. 25, 1960, Robinson to Nixon, Sept. 5, 1958, Nixon to Robinson, Sept. 15, 1958, RNL; Finch OH, Columbia; Earl Mazo interview with Theodore White, White papers, Harvard.

280 "Religion has become an issue": The ultimate impact of religion is debatable and depends on which statistic is used. When the election was over, Robinson said that 26 percent of Catholic voters went Republican—far below Ike's totals in 1952 (44 percent) and 1956 (48 percent), yet exactly how Catholics voted in the off-year election of 1958. The Protestant vote for Nixon rose 10 percent, to 60 percent, over what the party's candidates got in 1958—but stayed below Ike's 1952 (63 percent) and 1956 (63 percent) totals. Four out of five Republican Catholics stuck with Nixon and four out of five Democratic Protestants stayed with Kennedy, Robinson said. The Gallup organization mirrored these results.

Kennedy pollster Lou Harris concluded that Kennedy brought Catholic Democrats and independent Catholics who leaned Democratic back to the party after their dalliance with Eisenhower, but he also noted how both Catholic and Protestant Republicans stuck by Nixon, and that even Irish Catholics split their votes fifty-fifty. "Kennedy got little more than a bare majority of the Irish vote in New York City," Moynihan noted in *Beyond the Melting Pot*. "The students at Fordham gave him as much, but it appears it was the Jewish students in the College of Pharmacy who saved that ancient Jesuit institution from going on record as opposed to the election of the first Catholic President of the United States." Kennedy himself remarked, after watching an audience of Catholic business leaders give Nixon the warmer welcome when the two spoke at the Al Smith dinner, that "It all goes to show that when the chips are down money counts more than faith." See Schlesinger diary entry, Oct. 20–Nov. 8, 1960, ASP.

"If Kennedy had been a Protestant," Robinson ultimately concluded, "his percentage might have been 51.1 instead of 50.1."

See Claude Robinson, "The Weight of Church Membership in 1960 Presidential Preferences," Sept. 1958, "Campaign Evaluation as of October 7, 1960 (Second Debate)," Oct. 13, 1960, "Campaign Evaluation as of October 22, 1960 (Fourth Debate)," Oct. 28, 1960, "The Religious Issue in the Campaign," Nov. 16, 1960, "Shift, 1956–60," Nov. 11, 1960, "The Influence of Religion in the 1960 Campaign," Nov. 30, 1960, RNL; Harris, "An Analysis of the 1960 Election for President," Nov. 16, 1960, Alsop papers, LOC; and RNC, "Building For Victory '62" citing Gallup results, Theodore White papers, JFK; Richard Scammon interview, "Meet the Press," Nov. 13, 1960; Theodore White, *The Making of the President 1960* (New York: Atheneum, 1961); Emmet J. Hughes, *The Ordeal of Power* (New York: Atheneum, 1963).

280 Nixon walled himself off: Bassett memorandum to Hall and Finch, Nov. 4, 1960, Theodore White papers, JFK; Finch address to Eisenhower administration officials, May 9, 1960, memo on Ev Hart phone conversation, Rose Mary Woods to Haldeman, Oct. 7, 1968, WHSF-R; Hughes to Nixon, Oct. 7, 1962, Hughes interview with Aitken, Aitken papers, Haldeman to Gaunt, May 1, 1956, Haldeman to Nixon, May 22, 1956, Haldeman to Gaunt, May 22, 1956, Gaunt to Arbuthnet, May 26, 1956, Nixon press release, Aug. 21, 1960, Haldeman OH, RNL; Bassett to wife, Oct. 3, 9, 1960, Bassett papers, Bowdoin; Sheply to White, White papers, Harvard; Finch OH,

Columbia; Jorgensen OH, Berkeley; H. R. Haldeman, *The Ends of Power* (New York: Times Books, 1978); Nunes OH, Whittier.

280   "He is his own campaign manager": Nixon to Finch, Apr. 14, 1960, May 27, 1960, WHSF-R; Nixon to Robinson, Apr. 9, 1960, RNL; Confidential Notes on Schedule Meeting, July 8, 1960, WHSF-R; Cornelius Cotter, Stanford University, "Technical Specialists and the 1960 Republican Campaign," paper prepared for delivery to the American Political Science Association, 1961, WHSF-R; Valley to Nixons, Apr. 22, 1960, Finch to Nixon, Oct. 12, 1960, Robinson to Nixon, Sept. 28, 1960, Elliott to Nixon, Sept. 27, 1960, RNL; Guyluy interview, Theodore White papers, Harvard; Finch, Hall OH, Columbia; Bassett to wife, May 27, 1960, Bassett papers, Bowdoin; John K. Galbraith, *A Life in Our Times* (New York: Ballantine, 1982).

284   "the most important telecast of his life": In his defense, Ted Rogers contended that he had been deceived by Haldeman and others about Nixon's physical condition and by CBS about the color of the set, and that Kennedy had a chemically enhanced tan. See Rogers to Hall and Finch, Oct. 25, 1960, WHSF-R. But Nixon's features and complexion were ill suited for the black-and-white television of the day, and continued to be a challenge. His friend, TV producer Paul Keyes, warned Haldeman during the 1962 campaign: "When a man shows with dark hair, shows a dark beard, and then if his eyes get dark too, it just makes him look mean. . . . if the Boss comes off looking mean we are all in trouble. I don't care how well he answers questions, he must be *liked as the man* and we must get the *warmth and the friendliness of a kind face* through to them." Keyes to Haldeman, Oct. 13, 1962, WHSF-R. Rogers Memorandum, "First Debate—1960" and Lichenstein to Nixon, "Memorandum on the Debates," Sept. 19, 1961, *Six Crises* file, RNL. White, *The Making of the President, 1960*.

284   "I felt like the wrath of God": Rogers Memorandum, "First Debate—1960" and Lichenstein to Nixon, "Memorandum on the Debates," Sept. 19, 1961, *Six Crises* file, RNL. Finch memo on Lodge reaction to the first debate, Sept. 27, 1960, St. Johns to Nixon, undated, fall, 1960, "Tuesday," and Aug. 2, 1960, Burns to Nixon, Sept. 28, 1960, Robinson to Nixon, Aug. 1, 1960, Robinson to Nixon, Hall, and Finch, Oct. 1, 1960, Kruse to Nixon, Nov. 10, 1960, Newton to Hall, "Studies of the Effects of Political Debate III," Oct. 19, 1960, Klein speech to broadcast executives, Mar. 9, 1961, Herb Klein OH, RNL; Hewitt to Stanton and Mickelson, Oct. 5, 1960, and Mazo interview with White, White papers, Harvard; Hewitt, Wilson interviews, Halberstam papers, BU; Bassett to wife, Bassett papers, Bowdoin; Edward Morgan broadcast transcript, Sept. 27, 1960, Theodore White papers, JFK; Marshall McLuhan, *Understanding Media* (New York: McGraw Hill, 1964); Sidney Kraus, *The Great Debates: Kennedy vs. Nixon, 1960* (Bloomington: Indiana University Press, 1977).

286   debates ended on October 21: When all four debates were finished, 42 percent of Gallup's respondents said Kennedy won the debates, 30 percent favored Nixon, and 23 percent called it even.
          "Essentially, Senator Kennedy had to blunt the Nixon argument that the Senator was too young and inexperienced for the job, and that the Senator could not deal as effectively in the field of foreign policy. The debates, won by Senator Kennedy . . . eliminated the inexperience argument," said Kennedy pollster Lou Harris. (See Harris, "An Analysis of the 1960 Election for President," Nov. 16, 1960, Alsop papers, LOC.) "This threw Nixon on the defensive, a stance he was able to get off of only in the final closing days."
          Nixon pollster Robinson agreed. "On the average, the four debates have been a draw. Kennedy, however, started the campaign as the less well-known candidate and with many of his adherents wondering about his maturity. He has done a good job of dissipating the immaturity label and has increased his standing on every issue test. Kennedy has succeeded in creating a victory psychology. . . . Nixon-Lodge can win,

but the margin is very small." See Robinson to Nixon, Hall, and Finch, Oct. 28, 1960, "Campaign Evaluation as of Oct. 22, 1960 (Fourth Debate)," and Robinson to Nixon, Hall, and Finch, "Campaign Evaluation as of September 26, 1960," Oct. 5, 1960, RNL; Knowland OH, Columbia.

Many years later, after leaving office, Nixon wrote to an aide, "There is no question but that Kennedy did better in the first debate than I did, but the others balanced it out." See Nixon to Khachigian, Oct. 2, 1984, Aitken papers, RNL.

287 Martin Luther King Jr. was arrested: Gallup showed the race with Nixon ahead, 50 to 44, after the Republican convention; tied at 47 to 47 at Labor Day; Kennedy ahead, 51 to 45 on November 4; and clinging to a one-point lead, 49 to 48, over Nixon on November 7.

Gallup estimated that Nixon took 32 percent of the nonwhite vote in 1960. If so, it was a significant accomplishment for a white Republican who was not, like Ike, a famous hero in his own right.

Both Nixon and Kennedy ran on progressive civil rights platforms, yet were mindful of feelings in Dixie. When Lodge predicted that Nixon would name a black man to his cabinet, Kennedy criticized the idea as reverse "racism," and Nixon hedged, declining to second Lodge's promise and alienating black voters. As the campaign progressed, Kennedy more explicitly sought the votes of African Americans—citing their plight, for example, in the first debate, and making the calls on behalf of Martin Luther King.

Years later, Nixon told Jonathan Aitken: "Herb Klein told reporters I had no comment. What I had told Herb was that Robert Kennedy as a lawyer had acted unethically. Despite my personal feelings that Dr. King was being treated shamefully, what I expected Herb to say was that I had no comment at that time, but there was a fatal communication gap. Kennedy's quick action was measured against my apparent indifference and of course the black community acted accordingly. . . . I still believe that Robert Kennedy did the wrong thing in calling the judge." See Nixon to Aitken, "RN Unpublished Comment on the Martin Luther King Incident," Aitken papers, RNL.

In an April 14, 1987, column in the *New York Times*, William Safire recalled how Jackie Robinson rushed to the Midwest to meet with Nixon after hearing of King's arrest, "to urge him to show concern in some tangible way." Robinson emerged from his meeting with Nixon with "tears of frustration in his eyes," Safire wrote. And Robinson told Safire: "Nixon doesn't deserve to win."

In a November 4, 1960, letter from Nixon to Robinson, Nixon explained his inaction. "It is easy for one who is not in the Administration to make what our good friend Joe Louis called a 'grandstand play' but you and I know that real progress in the civil rights field is best advanced by the day to day consistent application of the principles which we know are sound." Nixon to Robinson, Nov. 4, 1960, RNL.

Robinson was not persuaded and ended his allegiance to Nixon. In a March 1968 newspaper column, Robinson wrote, "I will never vote for Mr. Nixon." And in a letter to Nelson Rockefeller in 1968 Robinson decried "the all things to all men phoniness of Richard Nixon." See Arnold Rampersad, *Jackie Robinson: A Biography* (New York: Ballantine, 1998).

Kennedy was delighted, of course, to get the King family's support, but bemused by "Daddy" King's slur about Roman Catholics. "Imagine Martin Luther King having a bigot for a father," Kennedy said. "Well, we all have fathers, don't we?" See Arthur M. Schlesinger Jr., *A Thousand Days* (Boston: Houghton Mifflin, 1965).

Nixon and Lichenstein memorandum, "The Odds Against Us," Lichenstein, "Pre-Election News Coverage," Waldron to Moscow, "The Negro Vote and Martin Luther King," *Six Crises* file, RNL; "The Los Angeles Negro Community" (report), "Civil Rights and the South," from campaign booklet, *Become Better Acquainted with Richard Nixon*, WHSF-R; "Mr. Nixon and the Negro National Community," unsigned and undated report, WHSF-R. Safire report to Finch et al. on minority voting in 1960 election, Nov. 11, 1960, Robinson to Nixon, Hall, and Finch, "The Negro Vote," Dec. 1, 1960, Mitchell to Nixon, Oct. 26, 1960, Nixon to Robinson, Nov. 4, 1960, Safire OH, Klein OH, RNL; Nixon reminiscences, Mar. 23, 31, 1976, Irwin Gellman, private collection; Harris Wofford, "Memorandum to Senator Kennedy RE: Civil Rights," June 9, 1960, "Kennedy and the Negro Vote," and Kennedy campaign pamphlets, Theodore White papers, JFK; S. Ernest Vandiver OH, Georgia State University; Finch OH, Columbia; Harris, "An Analysis of the 1960 Election for President," Nov. 16, Alsop papers, LOC.

    The Papers of Martin Luther King Jr. (Berkeley: University of California Press, 2000); Clifford Kuhn, "'There's a Footnote to History!' Memory and the History of Martin Luther King's October, 1960 Arrest and Its Aftermath," *Journal of American History,* Sept. 1997; *New York Post,* Mar. 9, 1961; *NYT,* Mar. 10, 1961, Mar. 27, 1962, Apr. 14, 1987; *Ebony,* Apr. 1962; Taylor Branch, *Parting the Waters* (New York: Simon & Schuster, 1988); Harris Wofford, *Of Kennedys and Kings* (New York: Farrar, Straus, Giroux, 1980); Rampersad, *Jackie Robinson.*

289   his final regret involved Eisenhower: After visiting Nixon in the hospital, Eisenhower "mentioned again, as he has several times, that the VP has very few friends," Whitman noted in her diary. "Of course, the difference to me is obvious. . . . [Nixon] sometimes seems like a man who is acting like a nice man rather than being one." Julie Nixon Eisenhower to author, Aug. 21, 2015, correcting Safire, *Before the Fall* (New York: Doubleday, 1975); see also Dwight Eisenhower OH, Milton Eisenhower OH, Finch OH, Mazo OH, Columbia; Hall interview, Halberstam papers, BU; Bryce Harlow OH, Thompson; Harlow OH, LBJ; Steve Hess OH, RNL; Harlow interview, *New Republic,* May 13, 1978; Dwight Eisenhower interview, *Today* show, Oct. 27, 1965; Nixon-Gannon; Ellis D. Slater, Ernestine Durr, and Elsie Maki, *The Ike I Knew* (Ellis D. Slater Trust, 1980); Safire, *Before the Fall;* Clarence G. Lasby, *Eisenhower's Heart Attack* (Lawrence: University Press of Kansas, 1997); JNE, *Pat;* Harlow OH, Thompson; Nixon, *RN;* Edmund Kallina, *Kennedy v. Nixon* (Gainesville: University Press of Florida, 2010); Evan Thomas, *Ike's Bluff* (Boston; Little, Brown, 2012).

290   its share of chicanery. There was plenty of hardball in the 1960 election. The Nixon camp dispatched advance man John Ehrlichman to infiltrate the Rockefeller campaign, while the Democrats, via Adam Clayton Powell Jr., raised the old chestnut about the restrictive covenant on Nixon's home. There were also whispers that Nixon was anti-Semitic. See McWhorter, Memo to File, Sept. 30, 1960, Nixon to Lichenstein and Waldron, Sept. 12, 1961, Klein OH, RNL; Roosevelt press release, Nov. 3, 1960, Safire papers, LOC; John Ehrlichman, *Witness to Power* (New York: Simon & Schuster, 1982).

    Kennedy's philandering was common knowledge in political and journalistic circles, but protected by the gentleman's code of the day. His womanizing and the sins of his piratical father were known but not exploited by the Nixon high command. See Finch OH, Columbia, and Bozell and Jacobs to Finch, Nov. 1, 1960, Safire papers, LOC.

    Nixon also turned down a deal offered by Teamsters president Jimmy Hoffa, who hated the Kennedys and offered to attack the Democratic candidate in return for favorable treatment by the Department of Justice. See Hunter to Nixon, Dec. 21, 1959, Hunter to Hoffa, Dec. 8, 1960, Hunter to Hillings, Oct. 13, 1968, Hunter to Mollenhoff, Jan. 22, 1970, RNL.

    Years later, amid the Watergate scandal, Republican Party chairman George H. W. Bush produced affidavits alleging how the Democrats sought to eavesdrop on Nixon's hotel room before the second presidential debate. The evidence was inconclusive, but it would not have been terribly unusual. Throughout the 1950s and 1960s, electronic eavesdropping was viewed as a somewhat underhanded but trifling offense. CBS had bugged the closed-door sessions of the credentials committee at the 1952 Republican convention. Journalist Jack Anderson was caught bugging during the Sherman Adams case, and NBC newsmen admitted they bugged a private session of the Democratic platform committee at the 1968 convention. Harold Lipset, the chief investigator for the Watergate Committee, resigned from that role after someone remembered that he had been convicted for an illegal bugging in 1968. All these incidents were quickly forgotten.

Among those bugged by the U.S. government during the Kennedy-Johnson years were Martin Luther King Jr.; foreign embassies; journalists; the Mafia; civil rights groups at the 1964 Democratic convention; and Frank Capell, an anti-Communist who, among other things, authored a 1964 book about the Kennedys and Marilyn Monroe. See the *Chicago Tribune,* Sept. 7, 1968; *LAT,* Dec. 10, 1997; "Interview with Carmine Bellino," Aug. 14, 1973, and "Statement by Honorable George Bush" with affidavits, author's collection; Jack Anderson with Daryl Gibson, *Peace, War and Politics* (New York: Tom Doherty Associates, 1999).

Walter Cronkite, *A Reporter's Life* (New York: Ballantine, 1997); the Church Committee findings and "Project Mockingbird" in the CIA "family jewels" report.

290   Nixon's brother Donald: Klein OH, Hoover to Nixon, June 3, 1960, Hoover to Woods, Oct. 5, 1960, Hoover to Nixon, Ed Nixon OH, Nov. 2, 1960, Bewley to Woods, Oct. 17, 28, 1955, Nov. 13, 1956, and Woods to Bewley, Nov. 15, 1955, RNL; Haldeman to Nixon, Aug. 28, 1962, Nixon campaign release, Oct., 1962, WHSF-R; Statement by Hughes Tool Company, RNL; Drew Pearson, "Documents in the Nixon-Hughes Loan Case," undated ms; Pearson Oct. 1960 column, Pearson papers, LBJ; Ann Whitman diary, Nov. 5, 1960, quoted in Stephen Ambrose, *Nixon,* vol. 1, *The Education of a Politician* (New York: Simon & Schuster, 1989); *NYT,* Nov. 13, 1960, Jan. 24, 1972, May 3, Aug. 4, 1973; *WP,* May 3, 1973; Jan. 14, 2011; Peter Edson, "How Nixon Brother Failed," *New York World Telegram,* Oct. 27, 1960; *New York Post,* Nov. 2, 3, 1960; James Phelan, "The Nixon Family and the Hughes Loan," *Reporter,* Aug. 16, 1962, AP, Nov. 1, 1960; Kennedy campaign press release, July 4, 1960, Theodore White papers, JFK; Lasby, *Eisenhower's Heart Attack;* Drew Pearson diary entries, Oct. and Nov. 1960, Pearson and Peter Hannaford, *Washington Merry-Go-Round: The Drew Pearson Diaries, 1960–1969* (Washington, D.C.: Potomac Books, 2015); Jack Anderson with James Boyd, *Confessions of a Muckraker* (New York: Random House, 1979).

292   was predicting a Kennedy victory: Hughes memo, Jan. 28, 1961, Sherwood to Nixon, Nov. 8, 1961, "Bessie" memo to Nixon on Julie and Tricia, no date, Nixon election night notes and calculations and network and wire service election night chronologies, *Six Crises* file, "Remarks of the Vice President at 12:18 PST," RNL; O'Brien OH, LBJ; "See-Saw returns Made Election Watch Tense," *Times Talk,* Theodore White papers, JFK; *NYT,* Nov. 10, 1960; Benjamin Bradlee, *Conversations with Kennedy* (New York: Norton, 1975); *The New York Times: The Times of the Sixties,* ed. John Rockwell (New York: Black Dog & Leventhal, 2014); White, *Making of the President, 1960.*

No one can definitively calculate the 1960 popular vote—or even say who won it—because of the confusing situation in Alabama, where voters made their choice by voting for pledged and unpledged electors, not directly for the presidential candidates. Kennedy took twenty-two states and five pledged Alabama electors, for a total of 303 electoral votes. Nixon won twenty-six states and 219 electoral votes. But six unpledged Democratic electors in Alabama, one Oklahoman, and eight electors from Mississippi cast votes for segregationist senator Harry Byrd, a Democrat from Virginia. Because many Alabamans voted for the unpledged electors, the popular votes awarded Kennedy in the state are a judgment call. History usually grants Kennedy the number of votes cast for the leading Democratic elector, or for the leading Democratic elector who publicly declared for JFK. But by another formula—awarding the popular vote in proportion to the electoral vote—Nixon would win the popular vote in Alabama and the nation. See footnote, Arthur Schlesinger Jr., *Robert Kennedy and His Times* (Boston: Houghton Mifflin, 1978), p. 220.

CHAPTER 17: WILDERNESS

294   Texas was worth twenty-four electoral votes: Nixon to Peale, Jan. 18, 1961, Robinson to Nixon, Dec. 1, 1960, Hillings to Nixon, Dec. 21, 1960, Burns to Nixon, Nov. 14, 1960, Hutcheson to McWhorter, Dec. 7, 1960, Hutcheson to Nixon, Dec. 16, 1960, RNL; Finch, Occidental College address, WHSF-R; Drown OH, Whittier; Adams OH, Berkeley; Safire, "Nixon Diary," Sept. 9, 1970, Safire papers, LOC; Robert Caro, *The Passage of Power* (New York: Knopf, 2012); Robert Caro, *Means of Ascent* (New York: Knopf, 1990); *Look*, Feb. 14, 1961; *NYHT*, Nov. 11, Dec. 4, 5, 7, 1960.

295   election fraud was a work of art: Arends to Nixon, Nov. 16, 1960, Derwinski to Nixon, May 22, 1961, Rentschler to Nixon, Nov. 14, 1960, Adamowski to Nixon, Feb. 24, 1961, Robinson to Finch, Oct. 30, 1960, memorandum, "Voting Irregularities," GG to Finch, Dec. 22, 1960, memorandum, "1960 Presidential Election," Harriman to Taylor, July 16, 1999, RNL; *NYHT*, Nov. 11, Dec. 6, 7, 1960; John A. Farrell, *Clarence Darrow* (New York: Doubleday, 2011).

296   "the night of the gnomes": "Frauds Part"—Campaign Section 6, *Six Crises* file, Dec. 5, 1961, RNC "Fact Memo," Dec. 1960, Fay and Hutcheson to McWhorter, Dec. 12, 1960, Hutcheson to Republican State Executive Committee, Dec. 15, 1960, Pat Nixon to Drown, Dec. 1960, Nixon to Mazo, Mar. 19, 1963, "Chronology of Events Relating to the Meeting Between Vice President Nixon and President-Elect Kennedy, November 14, 1960," RNL; Lawrence O'Brien OH, LBJ; Finch OH, Mazo OH, Columbia University; Brownell OH, Klein OH, Strober; Hall interview, FMB; Nixon-Gannon; Edmund Kallina, *Courthouse over White House* (Orlando: University Presses of Florida, 1988); William Bragg Ewald, *Eisenhower the President* (Englewood Cliffs, NJ: Prentice-Hall, 1981); Earl Mazo, *Richard Nixon* (New York: Avon, 1960); Earl Mazo, "The Nixons: A Family's Comeback From Defeat," *Good Housekeeping*, Mar. 1962.

298   "*I'll be back*": Over the years, in telling his "I'll be back" story, Nixon seems to have compressed inauguration eve and inauguration night. He went to the Capitol on inauguration night, he told Gannon, but could not get into his office because he had already surrendered the key. He had gazed from his balcony at the Mall through the famous snowstorm the night before. See Nixon-Gannon; Hall interview, FMB; Mazo account in "The Nixons," *Good Housekeeping*, Mar. 1962; Robinson to Nixon, Hall, and Finch, Nov. 11, 16, 30, Dec. 1, 1960, Robinson to Nixon, "Observations for the Future," Nov. 15, 1960, Safire to Finch et al., Nov. 11, 1960, RNL; Bliss, "Report of the Committee on Big City Politics," WHSF-R; Klein OH, RNL.

298   Pat was stricken too: Julie Nixon Eisenhower to Aitken, RNL; Julie Nixon Eisenhower to author, Aug. 21, 2015; Nixon to Lichenstein and Waldron, Sept. 12, 1961, *Six Crises* file, RNL; Schlesinger diary entries, Aug. 6, Oct. 16, 1960, Mar. 31, 1962, ASP; Nixon-Gannon; Helen Thomas OH, GFF; Roger Johnson OH, Whittier; Ehrlichman OH, Strober; Hall interview, FMB; DDE diary, memo dated Dec. 28, 1960, quoted in David Nichols, *A Matter of Justice* (New York: Simon & Schuster, 2007); Ewald, *Eisenhower the President;* Henry Kissinger, *White House Years* (Boston: Little, Brown, 1979); Pierre Salinger, *With Kennedy* (New York: Doubleday, 1966). Jacqueline Kennedy Onassis gave a series of oral history interviews to Arthur Schlesinger Jr., published as *Jacqueline Kennedy: Historic Conversations on Life with John F. Kennedy*, ed. Michael Beschloss (New York: Hachette, 2011).

299   the campaign press corps: The nation's publishers, far from the campaign trail, main-

tained their pro-business and pro-Republican tilt: Nixon received four times as many endorsements as Kennedy. Editorials, of course, are properly slanted. News stories are supposed to be objective. See *Journalism Quarterly*, Spring 1974.

For biased reporters, see Nixon campaign press reports, WHSF-R; Klein to Woods, Sept. 2, 1959, Doris to Finch, Sept. 17, 1960, Willard Edwards to Nixon, Nov. 25, 1960, Hauser to Nixon, Mar. 15, 1960, Hauser to Finch, Haldeman, and Hall, Jan. 26, 1950, Ehrlichman to Nixon, Apr. 6, 1961, RNL; Paul Niven Analysis, July 8, 1961, Sulzberger to Patterson, Oct. 29, 1956, Robinson to editors, *Saturday Review*, Nov. 14, 1962, Lichenstein, "Memorandum On Theodore H. White's *The Making of the President 1960*," *Six Crises* file, RNL; see also Edwards, "Did Biased Reporters Cost Nixon the Election?" *Human Events*, Apr. 7, 1961; "New Disturbing Journalistic Era Opens," with analysis of wire service reporting, *Human Events*, Oct. 13, 1961; "Kennedy and the Press," *Time*, July 25, 1960; "Remarks of the Vice President of the United States, Rear Train Platform, Centralia, Illinois, Oct. 28, 1960," PPP; Harlow interview, Thompson; Klein OH, Strober; Hall, Bassett interview, FMB; Lawrence OH, Columbia; Simons, Friedrich, Mazo interviews, Halberstam papers, BU; Russell Baker, *The Good Times* (New York: Penguin, 1989). The Lincoln memento correspondence is in the Safire papers, LOC.

300 "when the land gives out": Robert Penn Warren, *All the King's Men* (New York: Harcourt, 1946), p. 270.

"Supplemental Memo for Moscow on the Fund Chapter" (Tape #2, Aug. 21, 1961), *Six Crises* file, Nixon to Milburn and Robinson, Aug. 15, 1961, Milburn and Robinson to Nixon, Aug. 13, 1961, Nixon to Woods, July 20, 1962, RNL; Haldeman to Moscow, Apr. 18, 1962, WHSF-R; Haldeman to Woods, Feb. 29, 1962, McCormick to Haldeman, Feb. 23, 1962, Haldeman to Lichenstein, Feb. 27, 1962, Lichenstein memo to Haldeman, Mar. 8, 1962, WHSF-R; Nixon to Stark, Dec. 12, 1961, Nixon to Cronin, Nov. 11, 1961, St. Johns to Nixon, Jan. 9, 1961, Apr. 1961, Nixon to St. Johns, Aug. 16, 1961, Nixon to Eisenhower, Feb. 20, 1962, RNL; Les Brown OH, Adela Rogers St. Johns OH, Whittier; Stephen Hess, interview with author; Mazo, "The Nixons," *Good Housekeeping*, Mar. 1962; Nixon introduction, *Six Crises*, 1990 edition; *LAT*, Nov. 5, 2006; *Esquire*, Feb. 1962; *Redbook*, July 1962; Adams OH, Berkeley; Los Angeles Fire Department Historical Society and Educational Institute, "Bel Air Fire"; Nixon, *RN*.

Nixon was offered the chairmanship of the Dreyfus Corporation and a chance to serve as commissioner of Major League Baseball. See Nixon-Gannon. He got a $60,000 advance for *Six Crises*, of which $20,000 was paid to researcher-writer Alvin Moscow, one of several aides who helped him. See royalty statement, WHSF-R.

302 nasty brawl over Cuba: Among the casualties of the 1960 election was Nixon's relationship with the CIA. He believed that the agency had allowed the "missile gap" controversy to help Kennedy. "The agency's standing with Nixon was never very good," former director Richard Helms said in a CIA oral history. "From the very first day he came to office, the Agency had an uphill battle with Richard Nixon." "Rough Draft of Summary of Conversation between the Vice President and Fidel Castro," and accompanying letter, Nixon to Mansfield, Apr. 25, 1959, NSA; FRUS, 1958–1960, Vol. 6, Cuba; Senate Select Committee to Study Governmental Operations with Respect to Intelligence Activities (Church Committee), "Final Report" and "Alleged Assassination Plots Involving Foreign Leaders"; Jack Pfeiffer, "Official History of the Bay of Pigs Operation," Vol. III, Dec. 1979, CIA.

See also Nixon handwritten notes, Allen Dulles conversation, undated, Bay of Pigs, AW to RN, memorandum, "Kennedy Briefings from CIA during the 1960 Campaign," Mar. 16, 1962, RNL; Nixon memo to Woods, Mar. 19, 1962, Nixon memo to file, Oct. 16, 1962, Statement Released by Allan Dulles, Mar. 20, 1962, "Salinger's

Statement," Mar. 20, 1962, reports of phone calls: Leonard Hall, Mar. 19, 1962, Ann Whitman, Mar. 20, 1962, and Robert Finch, Mar. 20, 1962, Robinson to Nixon, Apr. 25, 1961, Cushman 1959 memo, "Fidel Castro," with "Briefing Paper For Castro Visit," undated, Abplanalp interview, Aitken papers, RNL; Nixon-Gannon; Pfeiffer to Brodie, Mar. 1, 1978, Bissell to Brodie, Feb. 23, 1977, Cushman and Bissell interviews, FMB; *NYHT,* Mar. 21, 1962; Schlesinger diary, Mar. 31, 1962, ASP; Richard Bissell and Jonathan Lewis, *Reflections of a Cold Warrior* (New Haven, CT: Yale University Press, 1996); David Atlee Phillips, *The Night Watch* (New York: Ballantine, 1982); Peter Wyden, *Bay of Pigs* (New York: Touchstone, 1979); Richard Goodwin, *Remembering America* (Boston: Little, Brown, 1988).

304 challenge California governor Pat Brown: "He didn't want to be governor," Haldeman recalled. "He had little interest in the state of California.... He lost, and I think he should have lost." See Haldeman OH, CSA; notes, Sept. 28, 1961, campaign organizational meeting, notes, Oct. 6, 1961, campaign organizational meeting, WHSF-R; Nixon to Eisenhower, July 13, July 25, Sept. 6, 1961, Eisenhower to Nixon, Aug. 8, Sept. 11, 1961, St. Johns to Nixon, July 30, 1962, Chambers to Nixon, Feb. 2, 1961, Dinkelspiel to Nixon, Nov. 10, 1960, Burns to Nixon, Aug. 29, 1961, Phillips to Nixon, Oct. 2, 1961, Robinson to Nixon, July 24, 1961, RNL; Cronin to Nixon, Apr. 14, 1961, Nixon to Cronin, Aug. 26, 1961, Cronin to Nixon, Sept. 4, 1961, RNL; "Derogatory Questions Most Often Asked About Dick Nixon Among Democratic and Minority Groups.... August 1954—June, 1959," WHSF-R; Klein to RN, Aug. 7, Sept. 15, 1961, Lou Cannon OH, Stephen Hess OH, RNL; Harris poll and analysis, Aug. 1962, Theodore White papers, JFK; Nixon-Gannon; Day OH, Whittier; Finch OH, Columbia; Roger Kent OH, CSA; Adela Rogers St. Johns interview, FMB; Don Bradley OH, Weinberger OH, Adams OH, Berkeley; *LAT,* Apr. 30, 1961; *Esquire,* Feb. 1962.

305 team of young professionals: The "tailed and tapped" comment comes from notes taken at a Sept. 28, 1961, campaign meeting of Nixon, Haldeman, Woods, and other aides found in the White House Special Files. It appears that wiretapping was Nixon's suggestion, though the notes are not explicitly clear. See WHSF-R, Box 57.

Another memo casts revealing light on the campaign ethics of the time. In September 1962, a savings bank official sent by his firm to work for the Nixon campaign (though retained on the bank's payroll) sent a memo to Haldeman noting that the thrift's owner "is very conscious of the fact that RN, when sitting in Sacramento as Governor, will have a profound effect on the savings and loan industry," particularly when approving branch offices. In that light, the bank official promised Haldeman that "if handled properly, a request (to the owner) for a *very large* campaign contribution would probably be granted." See Madden to Haldeman, Sept. 24, 1962, WSHF-R.

See the following, all in WHSF-R: Haldeman correspondence files; "First General Memorandum on 1962 Campaign," Oct. 9, 1961; Chotiner to Nixon, Oct. 24, 1961; Nixon to Haldeman, May 10, 1962; Nixon to Haldeman, May 10, 1962; Nixon to Haldeman, July 25, 1962; Nixon to Haldeman, Aug. 1, 20, 1962; Nixon to Haldeman et al., Aug. 14, 1962; Haldeman to Chotiner, Aug. 21, 1962, and Oct. 5, 1962; Haldeman to Hess, Sept. 4, 1962; Nixon campaign remarks, May 26, 1962; Haldeman to Nixon, Aug. 20, 1962; Nixon to Finch, Haldeman et al., Oct. 14, 1961. See also Hall to Nixon, Nov. 20, 1961, Roper to Finch, Oct. 1, 1962, Klein OH, RNL; Champion OH, Brown OH, Berkeley; *LAT,* Sept. 13, 14, 1962; *San Francisco Examiner,* Sept. 14, Sept. 27, Oct. 23, 1962; *Frontier,* Oct. 1962; *New Republic,* June 9, 1973; Cong. Rec., May 7, 1973.

306 a nasty campaign on both sides: In the 1962 race, "we were wondering how everything was getting out, and we finally found a bug," Nixon told the Watergate grand jurors in

1975. See Nixon grand jury testimony, NARA. See also Brown OH, Berkeley; Lucien Haas OH, CSA; Rogan to Pearson, with Oct. 10, 1962, Mickey Cohen affidavit, Nov. 6, 1962, Drew Pearson papers, LBJ; Dwight Chapin, interview with author; "Text of Nixon-Brown Discussion at National Conference of UPI Editors and Publishers," Oct. 1, 1962; Brown campaign letter on Nixon restrictive covenant, Oct. 31, 1962, "Citizens Fact-Finding Committee on Governor Brown," undated pamphlet, news release, Committee to Re-elect Governor Brown, Oct. 22, 1962, Robinson to Finch, Apr. 25, 1960, Robinson to Nixon, Mar. 6, 1962, Roger Kent, "Complaint to the Fair Campaign Practices Committee of Northern California," Oct. 25, 1962, RNL; "Kent Questions and Answers," undated, WHSF-R; "Report on 1962 Gubernatorial Race Between Edmund Brown and Richard Nixon," unsigned and undated, WHSF-R. Nixon For Governor press release, May 3, 1962, Haldeman statement, Oct. 18, 1962, RNL.

308 desertions from the right: White House tape, Nixon, Finch, and Rumsfeld, Apr. 15, 1971, RNL. Goldwater to Farrington, Mar. 27, 1962, Farrington to Goldwater, Apr. 11, 1922, Joe Shell for Governor newsletter, Chotiner to Haldeman, Oct. 16, 1962, WHSF-R. Kalmbach to McClellan, undated, WHSF-R, "Statement of Richard Nixon to California Republican Assembly," Mar. 1, 1962, Knott to Nixon, June 11, 1962, Smith to Nixon, June 21, 1962, Nixon to Eisenhower, Mar. 5, 1962, Eisenhower to Nixon, Mar. 6, 1962, Garland to Nixon, Nov. 26, 1962, Hoover to Nixon via Woods, Nov. 8, 1961, RNL; Haldeman to Nixon, May 4, 1962, WHSF-R; Haldeman to Nixon, "Meetings with GOP Congressmen," Feb. 27, 1962, WHSF-R; Farrington to Haldeman with transcript of Nixon remarks on Jack Paar show, Feb. 15, 1962, WHSF-R; Woods memo, Nov. 27, 1961, WHSF-R; Haldeman to Moscow, May 10, 1962, WHSF-R; Polling memo, fall 1962, WHSF-R; St. Johns to Haldeman, no date, 1962, WHSF-R; Day to Nixon, June 1, 1962, WHSF-R; John Birch Society and Joe Shell files, WHSF-R; Hess OH, Cannon OH, Huston OH, RNL; Nixon column, "Draw the Line on Demagogues," *LAT*, Mar. 16, 1962; *LAT*, May 2, 1962; *NYT*, May 13, Oct. 9, 1962; Harris poll and analysis, Aug. 1962, Theodore White papers, JFK; Finch OH, Columbia; oral histories by Brown, Gerald O'Gara, Richard Kline, Hale Champion, Weinberger, Hitt, Bradley, Adams, and Knight, Berkeley; Kent OH, CSA; Patrick Hillings, *The Irrepressible Irishman* (Harold D. Dean, 1994); Kissinger, *White House Years;* Merrell Small unpublished memoir, Berkeley; *Newsweek*, Oct. 29, 1962; *New Yorker*, Aug. 30, 2004.

309 the media had undergone its own transformation: Dorothy Chandler, McCullough, Harris, Kossen, Bassett interviews, Halberstam papers, BU; Lucien Haas OH, CSA.

310 "You don't have Nixon": Recordings of Nixon's remarks are clear, but for one word. Some hear Nixon saying that the press "won't" have him to kick around; others, including the author, hear "don't."

The IRS launched an "exhaustive" audit of Nixon's tax returns a few months after the election, Nixon claimed in *RN:* "They had me down," he said of the Kennedy brothers. "They wanted to put a couple of nails in the coffin."

What affection Kennedy and Nixon had for each other ended in 1960. In a 1964 oral history for the Kennedy library, Jacqueline Kennedy Onassis said that her husband thought Nixon was "dangerous, you know, and that he was a little bit . . . sick." Ben Bradlee recorded similar comments. See Benjamin Bradlee, *Conversations with Kennedy* (New York: Norton, 1975). Kennedy and Brown, transcript of JFK dictabelt conversation, Nov. 7, 1962, Miller Center, University of Virginia; Hitt OH, Brown OH, Berkeley; Haldeman OH, Klein OH, 1962 postmortem files, WHSF-R; Klein exit interview, RNL; Ehrlichman OH, Thompson; Drown OH, West OH, Eisenhower OH, Whittier; *NYT*, Nov. 8, 9, 1962; Jules Witcover, *The Resurrection of Rich-*

ard Nixon (New York: Putnam, 1970); Arthur Schlesinger, *A Thousand Days* (Boston: Houghton Mifflin, 1965); Hillings, *Irrepressible Irishman;* Richard Reeves, *President Kennedy* (New York: Simon & Schuster, 1993).

CHAPTER 18: THE GREATEST COMEBACK

312 it would have been Richard: Oswald's wife, Marina, claimed that she once stopped the assassin from trying to shoot Nixon. See FBI report, Feb. 20, 1964, Warren Commission report; Woods to Manchester, Aug. 4, 1964, Kennedy to Nixon, no date, late 1963, RNL; Nixon-Gannon; Janet Goeske OH, CSUF.

313 Nixon had moved to New York: Garment, interview with author. Dwight Chapin, Garment OH, Donald Kendall interview, Aitken papers, RNL; Nixon datebooks, 1963 and 1964, and personal address book, WHSF-R; William Safire interview, WB; Safire, "Nixon Diary," Mar. 16, 1973, and Nixon, memo to Garment on the Hill case, Apr. 23, 1966, in Safire papers, LOC; Adams OH, Berkeley; Helen Thomas OH, GFF; Garment, "The Hill Case," *New Yorker,* Apr. 17, 1989; Leonard Garment, *Crazy Rhythm* (New York: Da Capo, 1997); Mazo and Hess, *Nixon;* JNE, *Pat;* Evans manuscript, Aitken papers, RNL.

The Nixons bought the co-op apartment at 810 Fifth Avenue for $100,000 on May 14, 1963, and made $66,000 in improvements before selling it for $312,500 in the summer of 1969. With the help of Robert Abplanalp and Bebe Rebozo, they purchased a twenty-seven-acre estate on the ocean in San Clemente that summer for $1.4 million, keeping six acres for themselves and selling the rest of the property to their two wealthy friends. The Nixons also owned two $100,000 homes in Key Biscayne, purchased in late 1968: one for use as a vacation residence and the other as an office. See "Examination of President Nixon's Tax Returns for 1969 through 1972," Joint Committee on Internal Revenue Taxation, U.S. Congress, Apr. 3, 1974. The apartment transaction file is in WHSF-R.

313 admiring corporate chiefs: Nixon's great corporate champions were Elmer Bobst, chairman of the Warner-Lambert Pharmaceutical Company, who matched him up with his new law firm, and Donald Kendall, the CEO of Pepsi-Cola. His comments on practicing law are from a presidential memo to John Ehrlichman, WHSF-R.

314 Kennedy had gone to war: Kennedy may have recognized the danger he was courting. A few weeks before he was killed, the president signed an order, and issued a press release, announcing the withdrawal of one thousand troops by the end of 1963, and stating the goal that all U.S. forces could return home by the end of 1965. "We need a way to get out of Vietnam. This is a way of doing it," said Defense Secretary McNamara in an Oval Office conversation captured on Kennedy's White House taping system. Yet Kennedy and other aides can be heard expressing their concerns that the planned withdrawal must not look like a retreat, leaving Kennedy's actions ambiguous and his future intentions unknowable. Kennedy White House tape recording, Kennedy and McNamara et al., Oct. 2, 1963, Tape114/A49, JFK; FRUS, 1961–1963, Vols. 1–4 (Vietnam); FRUS 1964–1969, Vol. 1, Vietnam; *NYT,* Feb. 18, 1962; Ball to Rusk et al., "Cutting Our Losses in Vietnam," June 28, 1965, White papers, Harvard; Flanigan interview, White papers, JFK.

Harold P. Ford, *CIA and the Vietnam Policymakers: Three Episodes 1962–1968* (Langley, VA: Center for the Study of Intelligence, 1998); Johnson speeches, Oct. 21, 1964, Dec. 18, 1964, Jan. 4, 1965, PPP; Alexander Haig OH, Nixon to Eisenhower, Aug. 16, 1963, Eisenhower to Nixon, Sept. 25, 1963, Nixon to Rusk, Mar. 6, 1964, RNL; Gibbons, *The US Government and the Vietnam War,* Part II, Committee on Foreign Relations, U.S. Senate; *United States—Vietnam Relations, 1949—1967* (The Pentagon Papers), NSA; Stanley Karnow, *Vietnam* (New York: Viking, 1983); Henry

Kissinger, *Ending the Vietnam War* (New York: Simon & Schuster, 2003); Robert McNamara, *In Retrospect* (New York: Times Books, 1995); Rick Perlstein, *Nixonland* (New York: Scribner, 2008); *CT,* Apr. 12, 1965; AP, Feb. 7, 20, 1968; *Life,* Dec. 26, 1969; Kenneth O'Donnell and David Powers, *Johnny, We Hardly Knew Ye: Memories of John Fitzgerald Kennedy* (Boston: Little, Brown, 1972).

317 "It was my life": Nixon would revisit the decision one final time, over the Christmas holidays in 1967, before securing and proceeding with his family's support. Nixon to Aitken, May 29, 1991, Robinson to Nixon, Nov. 12, 1962, Graham to Nixon, Nov. 11, 1962, Peale to Nixon, Nov. 29, 1962, Nixon to Peale, Apr. 9, 1963, Perry to Nixon, Nov. 15, 1962, H. L. Hunt to Nixon, Jan. 24, 1963, WHSF-R, Garment OH, Huston OH, RNL; Frank Sorg interview, Tom Wicker Papers, University of North Carolina; Roland Evans and Robert Novak, "The Unmaking of a President," *Esquire,* Nov. 1964; *Reporter,* Aug. 11, 1966; *New Republic,* June 20, 1964; *NYT,* Apr. 6, 1964; *Time* correspondent files, Miller to Parker, Nov. 14, 1963, White papers, Harvard; Robert Novak, *The Prince of Darkness* (New York: Three Rivers Press, 2008); Theodore White, *The Making of the President 1964* (New York: Atheneum, 1965); Rick Perlstein, *Before the Storm* (New York: Hill and Wang, 2001); Tom Wicker, *One of Us* (New York: Random House, 1991); Monica Crowley, *Nixon in Winter* (New York: Random House, 1998); Nixon, *RN.*

317 "it is a fine trait": Nixon to Hannah, no date, Nixon to Drown, Apr. 29, 1978, RNL; Nixon, *RN;* Chris Duran interview with Brodie, FMB.

318 a loud insistent voice for escalation: (For Nixon on Vietnam see *NYT,* Apr. 4, 10, 17, 19, July 27, Oct. 3, 11, 15, 1964, Jan. 27, Feb. 11, Aug. 10, 29, Sept. 5, 8, 13, 15, Nov. 22, 23, 1965, Jan. 31, Feb. 2, 6, Aug. 6, Oct. 15, Nov. 4, 5, 1966); White note, undated, JFK; Murray Kempton, "Mr. Nixon's Return," *Spectator,* May 11, 1967; Nixon, "The Choice in Vietnam," Mar. 15, 1965, Buchanan to Nixon, Oct. 17, 1966, Safire papers, LOC; Evans manuscript, Aitken papers, RNL; Ellsberg OH, Strober; Nixon, "Needed in Vietnam: The Will to Win," *Reader's Digest,* Aug. 1964; Andrew Johns, "A Voice from the Wilderness: Richard Nixon and the Vietnam War, 1964–1966," *Presidential Studies Quarterly,* June 1999; Daniel Ellsberg, *Secrets* (New York: Penguin, 2003).

318 Nixon again took to the road: Chapin, Buchanan interviews with author; Chapin OH, RNL; Johnson speech, Jan. 10. 1967, PPP; McPherson to Johnson, Mar. 18, 1968, author's possession; Patrick J. Buchanan, *The Greatest Comeback* (New York: Crown, 2014); Nixon, *RN.* Nixon bridled when GOP chairman Ray Bliss declined to use party funds to pay for his travels, or for an election-eve television show to let him respond to Johnson. Nixon aide John Whitaker proposed to send a telegram to Bliss: SCREW YOU. STRONG LETTER FOLLOWS. One of Nixon's first acts after being elected president was to fire Bliss. See Jules Witcover, *The Resurrection of Richard Nixon* (New York: Putnam, 1970).

320 an imminent enemy offensive: "It is essential to get out, get out right away, it is distorting all of American life, distorting our entire foreign policy," Nixon told Theodore White. See Nixon interview, Mar. 12, 1968, White papers, Harvard. Nixon radio address, Mar. 7, 1968, WHSF-R; Garment OH, RNL; Winston Lord OH, FD; FRUS, 1964–1968, Vols. 4–6, Vietnam; "Notes of the President's Meeting with the President-Elect Richard Nixon," Nov. 11, 1968, Intelligence report, Nov. 25, 1968, on conversation with Le Duc Tho, LBJ; Rostow to Johnson, Feb. 12, 1968, Wheeler to Director, CIA, "North Vietnam's Ability to Withstand Manpower Attrition," June 11, 1968, Peter Braestrup OH, LBJ; Whalen diary entry, Mar. 17, 29, 1968, Whalen papers, HI; CIA, CSI, *CIA and the Vietnam Policymakers: Three Episodes 1962–1968;* E. Allen Wendt, ADST, *"Viet Cong Invade American Embassy"—The 1968 Tet Offensive;* Don Oberdorfer, *Tet!* (New York: Doubleday, 1971); William T. Allison, *The Tet Offensive: A Brief History with Documents* (New York: Routledge, 2008); Lien-Hang T.

Nguyen, *Hanoi's War* (Chapel Hill: University of North Carolina Press, 2012); James Willbanks, "Tet 1968: The Turning Point," Foreign Policy Research Institute, 2012; *WP,* Mar. 13, 1968; *NYT,* Feb. 2, Mar. 13, 1968.

323   *like your whole world depended on it:* Chapin, interview with author. For Nixon on RFK, see Whalen diary entries, Mar. 17, Mar. 30, 1968, Whalen papers, HI; McPherson to Johnson, Mar. 18, 1968, author's possession; Nixon campaign commercial, 1968, Haldeman notes, July 3, 1968, WHSF-R; Chapin OH, RNL; *NYT,* Apr. 6, 1968; Nixon-Gannon; Schlesinger diary entry, May 5, 1968, ASP.

324   new Nixon: When Rockefeller met with the editors of the *Washington Post,* he brought an entourage. Nixon arrived alone and appeared so calm, knowledgeable, and persuasive that his old antagonists were shocked. Editorialist Meg Greenfield said she had to go home and lie down—to reconcile the image of the Nixon she disliked with the Nixon she just met. See Katharine Graham, *Personal History* (New York: Alfred Knopf, 1997).

Chapin, interview with author; Buchanan, interview with author; Ray Price, "Recommendations for General Strategy from now through Wisconsin," Nov. 28, 1967, WHSF-R; Nixon appointment book, 1963, WHSF-R; Haldeman notes, July 3, 1968, WHSF-R; Safire to Keogh, "Re: Nixon Image Abroad," Nov. 20, 1968, WHSF-R; Woodward OH, Sears interview with Aitken, RNL; Opinion Research Corp. poll, May 1967, Sears interview, Nov. 19, 1970, Whalen diary, July 14, 1968, Whalen papers, HI; Theodore White, "Travels of—and Reactions to Richard Nixon, 1966–1967," Nelson Rockefeller, George Hinman, Herb Brownell, Clifton White interviews, White papers, Harvard; Nixon interview, Nov. 21, 1967, Peter Flanigan interview, White papers, JFK; Safire, "Nixon Diary," Mar. 23, 24, Apr. 1968, Price notes on Johnson withdrawal, Safire papers, LOC; *WP,* Mar. 13, 1968; *NYT,* Mar. 13, 1968; Dick Schaap, "Will Richard Nixon Trip Over Himself Again on His Way to Victory?" *New York,* June 10, 1968; *Time,* Aug. 16, Oct. 11, 1968; Norman Mailer, *Miami and the Siege of Chicago* (New York: New American Library, 1968); Lewis Chester, Godfrey Hodgson, and Bruce Page, *An American Melodrama, The Presidential Campaign of 1968* (New York: Viking, 1969); Hunter Thompson, "Presenting: The Richard Nixon Doll (Overhauled 1968 Model)," *Pageant,* July 1968, reprinted in *The Great Shark Hunt* (New York: Summit Books, 1979); Buchanan, *Greatest Comeback; JNE, Pat.*

328   South was the key to the nomination: The southern strategy was not so crucial to Nixon's general election victory as it was to his primary campaign. The 1960 U.S. census determined the allocations of votes in the Electoral College in 1968, and the historic growth of the Sunbelt had barely begun to register. It was only as air-conditioning made the South and Southwest more habitable (fewer than one in five southern homes had air-conditioning in 1960; almost three in four enjoyed it in 1980) that those regions boomed and assumed more important roles in Congress and the Electoral College. Of the 301 electoral votes Nixon collected in 1968, 57 came from the South, and most of them were from states (Virginia, Tennessee, Florida) that Republicans had carried in 1952, 1956, and 1960. Humphrey won Texas, and deepest Dixie (Georgia, Mississippi, Alabama, Arkansas, and Louisiana) went to Wallace. For the Sunbelt, air-conditioning, and politics see James T. Patterson, *Restless Giant* (New York: Oxford University Press, 2005) and Nelson Polsby, *How Congress Evolves* (New York: Oxford University Press, 2003). Rockefeller campaign strategy paper, July 15, 1968, WHSF-R, RNL. John C. Whitaker, "Nixon's Domestic Policy: Both Liberal and Bold in Retrospect," *Presidential Studies Quarterly,* Winter 1996; Ellsworth interview, Aitken papers, Ellsworth OH, RNL; Democratic Party platform, July 12, 1948; *NYT,* May 7, 1966; Brock OH, Spencer OH, GFF; Nixon interview, Nov. 23, 1968, White papers, Harvard; Hall interview, Columbia University; Thurmond interview, WB; Richard Scammon and Ben Wattenberg, *The Real Majority* (New York: Capricorn, 1971); Thomas

Byrne Edsall and Mary D. Edsall, *Chain Reaction: The Impact of Race, Rights, and Taxes on American Politics* (New York: Norton, 1991); Harry Dent, *The Prodigal South Returns to Power* (New York: Wiley, 1978); Dan T. Carter, *The Politics of Rage: George Wallace, the Origins of the New Conservatism, and the Transformation of American Politics* (Baton Rouge: Louisiana State University Press, 1995).

329 compulsory busing: Chester et al., *American Melodrama;* Carter, *Politics of Rage;* Dent, *Prodigal South;* Michael Dukakis OH, Moakley project, Suffolk University; Patterson, *Restless.*

330 "Law and order": The FBI crime statistics for the 1960s show that the violent crime rate doubled, from 160.9 per 100,000 in 1960 to 328.7 in 1969, and that the absolute number of violent crimes rose from 288,460 in 1960 to 661,870 in 1969. See FBI, Uniform Crime Reporting Program, U.S. Department of Justice.

In *Breach of Faith,* the most critical of his books on Nixon, Theodore White absolved him of the charge of racism in the 1968 campaign. Nixon made a "hard decision," White wrote, "to win, if possible, in a way that would make him a conservative President who could nonetheless govern without having mobilized majority white prejudice against minority black Americans."

The WHSF-R files contain a wealth of strategic plans and memoranda from the 1968 Nixon campaign, with many pages of Haldeman notes, and many analyses of the "law and order" theme. See Phillips to Garment, undated, Oct. 1968, "Last Four Weeks' Strategy," WHSF-R; Sears to Nixon, July 19, 1968, WHSF-R; Safire to Keogh, "Re: Nixon Image Abroad," Nov. 20, 1968, WHSF-R; Haldeman notes, Aug. 3, 1968, WHSF-R; Colson, Hallett, and Porter, "Report on Middle America," Nov. 2, 1971, with lengthy Wallace analysis—"It is not felt that we should compete with Wallace for redneck support"—WHSF-RC.

Nixon's men were moved by what they saw around them. Former congressman Robert Ellsworth, serving as a campaign aide, urged Nixon to pursue a policy of "national unification, rather than continued drift to further division." He forwarded a paraphrased quotation from novelist Albert Camus's 1957 Nobel Prize acceptance speech. "Probably every generation sees itself as charged with remaking the world," Camus said. "Mine, however, knows that it will not remake the world. But its task is perhaps even greater, for it consists in keeping the world from destroying itself." Ellsworth to Chapin et al., June 24, 1968, WHSF-R.

See also Ellsworth to Nixon, Feb. 13, 1968, Robinson to Nixon, Jan. 23, 1957, Robinson, "What Ails the GOP," presentation to RNC, Jan. 22, 1959, Nixon to Eisenhower, Mar. 17, 1968, Buchanan to Nixon, July 13, 1968, Cannon OH, Colson OH, RNL; Whalen memo, Nov. 20, 1967, Sears interview, Nov. 19, 1970, Whalen papers, HI; Ehrlichman interview, "Cold War," NSA; *Newsweek,* May 19, 1968; Walter Lippmann syndicated column, Oct. 7, 1968; Richard Nixon, "What Has Happened to America?" *Reader's Digest,* Oct. 1967; Richard Nixon, "If Mob Rule Takes Hold in U.S.," *US News & World Report,* Aug. 15, 1966; Garry Wills, *Nixon Agonistes* (Boston: Houghton Mifflin, 1979).

For more on 1968 campaign themes see Scammon and Wattenberg, *Real Majority;* Dan Carter lecture, "George Wallace, Richard Nixon and the Transformation of American Politics," published by Baylor University Press, 1992; Richard Kleindienst, *Justice* (New York: Jameson Books, 1985); James Sundquist, *Dynamics of the Party System* (Washington, D.C.: Brookings, 1983); Buchanan, *Greatest Comeback;* Taylor Branch, *At Canaan's Edge* (New York: Simon & Schuster, 2007); and Pete Hamill, "The Revolt of the White Lawn Middle Class," *New York,* Apr. 14, 1969.

For Nixon speaking "with insight and decency" see Nixon radio speech, Mar. 7, 1968, WHSF-R; *NYT,* Sept. 22, 1968; Hugh Davis Graham, Introduction, "Civil

Rights During the Nixon Administration, 1969–1974," Microfilm Document Collection (Bethesda MD: University Publications of America, 1989).

332 Reagan was on the move: Haldeman notes, WHSF-R; Bruno OH, Brock OH, GFF; Chester et al., *American Melodrama. Time,* Aug. 16, 1968.

333 Maryland governor Spiro Agnew: Nixon invited a score of top Republicans to consider a list of running mates in a series of meetings in Miami Beach. But Haldeman's notes show that Nixon was leaning toward Agnew well before the convention, despite concerns that he was "not [a] hard worker." The others on Nixon's short list, according to Haldeman's notes, were Bob Finch, Ronald Reagan (who didn't want the honor, Haldeman wrote, and "hurts in North—doesn't add enuf in So."), and three moderates— Governor John Volpe of Massachusetts, Senator Mark Hatfield of Oregon, and New York City mayor John Lindsay. Nixon told Safire that Lindsay was a personal favorite, but that the mayor would cost them the border states and help only, perhaps, in Pennsylvania; see Haldeman notes, "VP," Aug. 1, 1968, WHSF-R; Derge to Nixon, July 31, 1968, WHSF-R, RNL. Nixon acceptance speech, Aug. 8, 1972, PPP; *WP,* Sept. 25, 1968; Safire, *Before the Fall;* Novak, *Prince of Darkness;* Graham, *Personal History.*

333 his "forgotten" Americans: Nixon liked, as one of his favorite poems, Carl Sandburg's book-length ode to popular wisdom and endurance, *The People, Yes.* See Nixon to Woods, Jan. 8, 1969, WHSF-R; Nixon to Aitken, undated, Colson to Haldeman, Nov. 10, 1972, Nixon handwritten notes, Anaheim homecoming, Jan. 1969, WHSF-R; Nixon to Haldeman and Mitchell, Sept. 10, 1968, WHSF-R; Buchanan to Ehrlichman, Haldeman, and Colson, Sept. 23, 1971, WHSF-RC; Whitaker to Haldeman, July 11, 1968, "RN '68 Campaign Schedule," WHSF-R; Nixon to Haldeman, May 15, 1968, WHSF-R; Haldeman to Flanigan, Sept. 5, 1968, WHSF-R; Woods to Sherwood, Aug. 27, 1968; WHSF-R; Dent to Allison, Nov. 4, 1969, WHSF-R; Buchanan to Nixon, July 13, 1968; Huston OH, Garment OH, Haldeman OH, RNL; Gary Wills, "Dunces," *New York Review of Books,* Apr. 6, 1978; Theodore White, *The Making of the President 1968* (New York: Atheneum, 1969); Wills, *Nixon Agonistes;* Richard Goodwin, *Remembering America* (Boston: Little, Brown, 1988).

339 "man in the arena": Keyes to Haldeman, Oct. 13, 1962, WHSF-R; Haldeman to Nixon, June 20, 1967, WHSF-R; Haldeman paper, June 9, 1968, WHSF-R; Price, "Recommendations for General Strategy from now through Wisconsin," Nov. 28, 1967, WHSF-R; Ailes to Garment and Shakespeare, Sept. 27, 1968, WHSF-R; Shakespeare to Haldeman, Sept. 24, 1968, Nixon to Garment, July 9, 1968, RNL; Ailes to Garment, July 6, 1968, Whalen papers, HI; Joe McGinniss, *The Selling of the President* (New York: Penguin, 1988).

339 Nixon started the fall campaign: See Hatfield in *Ripon Forum,* Oct. 1968. Nixon to Keogh and Haldeman, Sept. 17, 1968, WHSF-R; Phillips to Garment, no date, Oct. 1968, "Re: Wallace, HHH and the need for an RN Second Offensive," WHSF-R; Moley to Nixon, with Nixon notes, March 26, 1968, WHSF-R, RNL; Greenspan, "1968 Presidential Election Simulation based on Gallup Poll (September 20–22)," WHSF-R; Buchanan to Nixon, Aug. 15, 1968; Hallett to Haldeman, June 28, 1972, WHSF-RC; Sears to Nixon, June 26, 1972, WHSF-RC; Haldeman to Flanigan, Sept. 5, 1968, WHSF-R; Haldeman notes, July 3, 1968, WHSF-R; Nixon radio address, Mar. 7, 1968, WHSF-R; Teeter to Haldeman, "1960 and 1968 elections," June 29, 1972, WHSF-R; O'Brien OH, LBJ; Safire to Haldeman, "Campaign Assessment," undated, and "Nixon Diary," Aug. 8, 1968, Safire papers, LOC; Jeffrey Bell memo, July 13, 1968, Whalen papers, HI.

342 the Chennault affair: Years later, when asked about Chennault in his television interviews with David Frost, Nixon insisted that he "did nothing to undercut" the peace talks and "had no knowledge of any contact with the South Vietnamese," adding: "I

couldn't have done that in conscience." Nixon also denied "the Chennault canard" in a May 29, 1991, memo to Jonathan Aitken. See Frost-Nixon transcripts; Nixon to Aitken, May 29, 1991, RNL.

Haldeman's notes from the fall of 1968 show that Nixon was lying, WHSF-R. For Haldeman's notes and other documents on the Chennault Affair, see Boxes 1, 6, 32, 33, and 34.

On September 12, 1968, John Mitchell reported that Kissinger was "available" as a confidential source. Haldeman's notes from September 23 and September 27, 1968, reflect communications from Kissinger ("just back from Paris . . . thinks better than even J will have bombing halt mid Oct . . . ⅓ likelihood of movement before election . . . K's really concerned about moves J will take") and the resultant flurry of activity as Nixon and his campaign grappled with the threat.

The Haldeman notes from October 16 contain Nixon's analysis of a telephone conversation in which Johnson informed the three presidential candidates of the state of play, and how a bombing halt could hurt the Republicans. ("RN thinks attempt by LBJ to get pause before election . . . danger is attempt to build up idea war is at end.")

Three days later, Nixon told Haldeman what Mitchell was learning from his conduits with the South Vietnamese: ("LBJ and Bunker have been putting tremendous pressure on SVN to go along w/ bomb halt—w/o conditions—they propose to hold out long as poss. They'd like RN to ask what is quid pro quo.")

The most damning segment in Haldeman's notes is from his late-night conversation with Nixon on October 22. He reports the instruction from Nixon to Mitchell to "Keep Anna Chennault working on SVN." Further on, Haldeman reports Nixon asking, "Any other way to monkey wrench it? Anything RN can do" and Nixon's suggestion that Rose Mary Woods call their old friend Louis Kung, a nephew of Madame Chiang Kai-shek, and get him "going on the SVN—tell him hold firm." Nixon himself wrote Chiang, via Kung, with "a personal message of great importance," on October 29.

Nixon also told Haldeman to get in touch with Bebe Rebozo, who was to contact Senator George Smathers and "have Smathers threaten J" that "N is going to blast him . . . in major speech on VN" if he used the bombing halt to help Humphrey. Nixon also ordered Agnew to probe CIA director Richard Helms for information on the peace talks. "Tell him we want the truth—or he hasn't got the job" in the Nixon administration.

On November 2, according to Haldeman's notes, Johnson's tirade with Dirksen about Chennault made it back to the Nixon campaign in a report from Harlow to Haldeman: "LBJ called Dirksen—says he knows Repubs through D. Lady are keeping SVN in present position if this proves true—and persists—he will go to nation & blast Reps & RN. Dirksen very concerned." Nixon's advice to Haldeman was to rally congressional Republicans to turn on the Democrats and "kick them hard . . . [saying] this is a political gimmick" that could "risk Am lives w/o any return."

Further confirmation of Chennault's role comes in the internal correspondence among Nixon aides after the election, also contained in the WHSF-R files.

In December 1968 Chennault wrote a long letter to Nixon, asking the president-elect to make her his Asian affairs adviser. Rose Mary Woods passed it on with a note to Peter Flanigan, instructing him to keep Chennault at arm's length. Several months passed, and then Harlow reported Chennault's discontent in a note to Haldeman.

"Seems she is being cut up by press etc. for her alleged activities during the campaign involving South Vietnam. Certain aspects of this you and I know; she asserts that everything she did was with the full knowledge of John Mitchell" and other Nixon advisers, Harlow wrote. "She feels forsaken . . . as she is subjected to severe criticism for activities which she insists were undertaken at the direct request of the Nixon campaign group." See Harlow to Haldeman, Aug. 27, 1969, RNL.

In 1973, Chennault's friend and frequent escort, lawyer-lobbyist Thomas Corcoran, visited Nixon in the Oval Office. In the conversation, captured on the White House tapes, he solicited a favor for her, reminding the president how she "kept her mouth shut" on Nixon's behalf when the press dug into the Chennault affair. "Oh yeah," Nixon said and agreed to see her. See White House tape, Mar. 6, 1973, RNL.

The WHSF-R files also contain a series of memos from Nixon's and Mitchell's law partner and campaign aide Thomas Evans listing his extensive contacts with Chennault that fall. The Evans files show a lunchtime meeting took place on October 25, 1968, and telephone calls were exchanged on September 30 and October 3, 4, 10, 11, 17, and 31, 1968. Evans was an aide to Mitchell, in charge of handling wealthy donors.

Looking back, Rostow posited that the success of the Chennault affair gave Nixon and his aides a taste for illegal intrigue and a false sense of confidence, which led them to Watergate. "They got away with it," Rostow wrote, in a memo to his files. "As the same men faced the election of 1972 there was nothing in their previous experience with an operation of doubtful propriety (or, even, legality) to warn them off; and there were memories of how close an election could get and the possible utility of pressing to the limit—or beyond." See the X Envelope, "Memorandum for the Record," May 14, 1973, LBJ.

Bundy believed that the Chennault affair gave Thieu the leverage to blackmail Nixon, restricting the new president's freedom to take bold actions to end the war. See Bundy, *A Tangled Web* (New York: Macmillan, 1999).

Johnson White House tapes, Johnson and Russell, Oct. 30, 1968, Johnson and Dirksen, Oct. 31, 1968, Johnson and Dirksen, Nov. 2, 1968, Johnson and Smathers, Nov. 3, 1968, Johnson and Nixon, Nov. 3, 1968, LBJ; Thomas Allen OH, Miller Center, University of Virginia; "October 26–31, 1968: The Bombing Halt" and "November 1–12, 1968: South Vietnamese Abstention from the Expanded Peace Conference; the Anna Chennault Affair," FRUS, 1964–1968, Vol. 7, Vietnam, September 1968–January 1969.

Waldron to Buchanan, "Administration Actions to Influence the 1966 Election," Oct. 2, 1968, WHSF-R, Chennault to Nixon, no date, 1968, WHSF-R; Haldeman notes, Sept.–Nov. 1968, WHSF-R; Huston OH, Haldeman OH, Huston report to Haldeman, "Vietnam Bombing Halt—The Chennault Affair," Feb. 25, 1970, White House tape, Nixon and Thomas Corcoran, Mar. 6, 1973, RNL.

The "X Envelope" files, bombing halt files, and supporting documents at the LBJ presidential library offer revealing glimpses of Johnson administration thinking, especially George Elsey's notes of Defense Secretary Clark Clifford's morning staff conferences, May 1966–Jan. 1969; "Summary Notes of President's Meeting with the Joint Chiefs on Vietnam," Oct. 14, 1968; State Department cable, Bunker and Abrams to Rusk, Oct. 12, 1968; Rostow to Johnson, Oct. 28, 1968; Rostow to Johnson, "The Bombing Halt and U.S. Politics," Oct. 29, 1968, and "Notes on Tuesday Luncheon," Oct. 29, 1968; "Notes on Foreign Policy Meeting," Oct. 29, 1968, and Rostow to Johnson, "Literally Eyes Only," Oct. 29, 1968; Bunker to Rusk, Nov. 6, 1968; Bunker to Rusk, Nov. 12, 1968; "Key Chronology of Total Bombing Cessation" and "Bombing Cessation" narrative, Nov. 10, 1968, and Rostow, "Memorandum for the Record," May 14, 1973.

See also oral histories by James Rowe, Lawrence O'Brien, Arthur Krim, Dean Rusk, Cartha DeLoach, Clark Clifford, Benjamin Read, Cyrus Vance, and Harlow, LBJ; White interview with Haldeman, Nov. 22, 1968, and Nixon Nov. 23, 1968, White papers, Harvard; AP, Oct. 26, 1968; *Evening Star,* Aug. 21, 1968; UPI, Oct. 25, 1968; *WP,* Nov. 1, 1968, Feb. 15, 1981; *NYT,* May 23, June 13, 1991.

For early journalistic reports on the Chennault affair, see *Chicago Daily News,* Nov. 15, 1968; Drew Pearson column, Nov. 17, 1968; *St. Louis Post-Dispatch,* Jan. 6, 1969;

Theodore White, *Making of the President 1968; NYT,* July 23, 1969; transcript, "Phone Conversation, Tom Ottenad of the *St. Louis Post-Dispatch* and W. W. Rostow, Jan. 3, 1969," LBJ.

In their memoirs, Anna Chennault and Bui Diem acknowledge clandestinely meeting with Nixon and Mitchell early in the 1968 campaign. See Anna Chennault, *The Education of Anna* (New York: Times Books, 1980) and Bui Diem with David Chanoff, *In the Jaws of History* (Boston: Houghton Mifflin, 1987); Gregory Tien Hung Nguyen and Jerrold Schecter, *The Palace File* (New York: Harper and Row, 1986).

A reader who requires further evidence may turn to the correspondence between Haldeman and Tom Charles Huston, and a long report made by Huston to Haldeman in 1970, released by the Nixon library at the request of the author and other researchers.

After Nixon's election, Haldeman gave Huston the assignment of assessing Nixon's and Johnson's vulnerability on the matter. In a February 25, 1970, memo, attached to an eleven-page report, Huston warned: "The evidence in the case does not dispel the notion that we were somehow involved in the Chennault affair and while release of this information would be most embarrassing to President Johnson, it would not be helpful to us either."

The report and Huston's subsequent oral history with the Nixon presidential library convey his belief that there was high-level contact via Mitchell and Chennault with the Thieu government, and that Nixon directed it: "Clearly Mitchell was directly involved," Huston said in his oral history, and "it's inconceivable to me that John Mitchell would be running around, you know, passing messages to the South Vietnamese government, et cetera, on his own initiative." See Huston to Haldeman, Feb. 25, 1970, Huston, "Vietnam Bombing Halt—the Chennault Affair," Feb. 25, 1970, Huston, "The Negotiations for a Bombing Cessation," June 1, 1973, and Huston OH, RNL.

In his oral history for the LBJ library, Harlow reports that, though Nixon denied his involvement in the Chennault affair, "I'm not convinced that it was not true. It was too tempting a target." See Harlow OH, LBJ.

For accounts of the Chennault affair, see Bundy, *A Tangled Web;* Ken Hughes, *Chasing Shadows* (Charlottesville: University of Virginia Press, 2014); Catherine Forslund, *Anna Chennault* (Wilmington, SR Books, 2002); Jules Witcover, *The Year the Dream Died* (New York: Warner, 1997); James Rosen, *The Strong Man* (New York: Doubleday, 2008); Jack Torry, "Don't Blame Nixon for Scuttled Peace Overture," RealClearPolitics, Aug. 9, 2015.

345   separate suites at the Waldorf: Johnson White House tape, Johnson and Dirksen, Oct. 31, 1968, LBJ; Price OH, Strober; Nixon election night notes and Electoral College calculations, WHSF-R; Lasky manuscript, Box 17, WHSF-RC; Sears to Haldeman, Dec. 18, 1968, "Analysis of Election Results," WHSF-R; Phillips to Haldeman, undated, late 1968, "Trends of the Last Three Weeks of the Campaign—Their Causes and Effects," WHSF-R; Phillips to Garment et al., undated, Oct. 1968, "Last Four Weeks' Strategy," WHSF-R; Safire to Keogh, "Re: Nixon Image Abroad," Nov. 20, 1968, WHSF-R; Haldeman notes, Nov. 3, 1968; Haldeman to Flanigan, Nov. 1, 1968, WHSF-R, RNL; Glen Moore, "Richard Nixon: The Southern Strategy and the 1968 Presidential Election," Hofstra; Safire, "Nixon Diary," Nov. 20, 1968, Safire papers, LOC. JNE, *Pat;* Nixon-Gannon; Nixon, *RN;* Bundy, *A Tangled Web.*

CHAPTER 19: NIXON'S WAR

347   power of a million Hiroshimas: "Comprehensive Study on Nuclear Weapons," United Nations Centre for Disarmament, Department of Political and Security Council Affairs, 1981.

348 Nixon swore the oath of office: Nixon Inaugural Address, PPP. The author was a spectator at the 1969 inauguration and witnessed the scenes at the Capitol and on Pennsylvania Avenue. Theodore White papers, Harvard; HRH diary, Jan. 20, 22, Feb. 3, 1969; Harlow interview, Thompson; JNE, *Pat;* Henry Kissinger, *White House Years* (Boston: Little, Brown, 1979); Nixon, *RN; WP,* Dec. 23, 1968; *Star,* Dec. 19, 1968; Anatoly Dobrynin, *In Confidence* (New York: Times Books, 1995).

349 had been Woodrow Wilson's: The provenance of the desk serves as a cautionary tale for historians. The White House staff soon discovered that "the Wilson desk" was not used by Woodrow Wilson at all, but instead (or so they believed) named after Vice President Henry Wilson, who served with President Ulysses Grant in the early 1870s. Because Nixon referred to it as President Wilson's desk in many discussions and at least one famous (Silent Majority) speech, a correction was quietly slipped into the Public Papers of the President.

But even the correction was in error: according to Senate records the desk was not purchased for the Vice President's Room in the Capitol until the turn of the century by Vice President Garret Augustus Hobart, who was President William McKinley's first vice president. And so neither Henry nor Woodrow Wilson used it—though the room is associated with Vice President Wilson, who died there after suffering a stroke in 1875, and by doing so may have caused all the confusion. The desk in "the Wilson room" became "the Wilson desk."

See Nixon, "Remarks at a Reception of Campaign Workers," Jan. 21, 1969, PPP; Safire, *Before the Fall;* Mark Hatfield, Senate Historical Office, *Vice Presidents of the United States, 1789–1993* (Washington, D.C.: GPO, 1997); United States Senate, *The Vice President's Room,* Office of Senate Curator, S. Pub. 106–7.

350 Heinz Alfred Kissinger: Chapin, interview with author; Buchanan to Nixon, Oct. 18, 1968, Buchanan to Haldeman, Dec. 20, 1968, Garment OH, RNL; Niall Ferguson, *Kissinger* (New York: Penguin, 2015). For a glimpse of Kissinger's blarney, see telcon, Nixon and Alsop, Mar. 12, 1973, RNL. Lord OH, FD; Nixon interviews, Dec. 2, 1968, Jan. 23, 1969, White papers, Harvard; Moynihan to Glazer, May 25, 1973, quoted in Steven Weisman, "How to Govern a Divided Country," *New York,* Sept. 19, 2010; Leonard Garment, *In Search of Deep Throat* (New York: Basic Books, 2000).

351 "short term problem": "I was determined to avoid the trap Johnson had fallen into, of devoting virtually all my foreign policy time and energy to Vietnam, which was really a short term problem," Nixon wrote in *RN.* "Kissinger said he was delighted that I was thinking in such terms."

352 "if jobs in government for women": For Nixon on women appointees see Finch to Nixon with Nixon handwritten reply, Apr. 15, 1971, cited in Stephen Ambrose, *Nixon,* vol. 2, *The Triumph of a Politician* (New York: Simon & Schuster, 1989).

353 "an introvert in an extrovert profession": "I knew that I could absorb far more material by reading it than by talking about it, and I have invariably found that staff members will present problems more concisely and incisively in writing than they will in meetings," Nixon reported in his memoirs. Alexander Butterfield's testimony before the House Judiciary Committee during the impeachment hearings provides an inside glimpse of the day-to-day workings of the Nixon presidency. Gannon, Chapin interviews with author; Safire, "Nixon Diary," Apr. 4, 1969, Safire papers, LOC; Butterfield OH, Chapin OH, Nixon to Ehrlichman, Jan. 3, 1968, WHSF-R; Rose Mary Woods to Stans, Jan. 29, 1969, WHSF-R; Nixon to Haldeman, Dec. 1, 1969, in *From: The President, Richard Nixon's Secret Files,* ed. Bruce Oudes (New York: Harper & Row, 1989); Garry Wills, *Nixon Agonistes* (Boston: Houghton Mifflin, 1979); Nixon, *RN.*

354 The racehorse had his quirks: Nixon memorandum for Woods and Haldeman, Mar. 31, 1971, Haldeman OH, RNL. Buchanan, interview with author; oral histories by Halde-

man, Huston, Schlesinger, Butterfield, Colson, Garment, Price, Safire, RNL; White House tape, Nixon and NSC, Feb. 2, 1972 (Napoleon), Nixon and Kissinger, Apr. 4, 1972 (Churchill), RNL; Safire, "Nixon Diary," Dec. 29, 1969, Aug. 24, 1972, Safire papers, LOC; Alexander Butterfield testimony, House Judiciary Committee, impeachment hearings, July 2, 1974; Ehrlichman OH, Thompson; Henry Kissinger, *Years of Upheaval* (Boston: Little, Brown, 1982); Nixon's exhortations to himself are from his White House personal files at the RNL; the prologue to Reeves, *Nixon*, offers a fine selection.

356   Haldeman supplanted even Rose Woods: Sorg, Ehrlichman, and Bryce Harlow interviews, Wicker papers, UNC; Safire, "Nixon Diary," Sept. 14, 1970, Safire papers, LOC; Kehrli to Haldeman, Mar. 14, 1972, WHSF-RC; Haldeman OH, RNL.

356   "so enmeshed in details": On the night before announcing the invasion of Cambodia in the spring of 1970, Nixon phoned a dumbstruck Haldeman to discuss the location of the new White House pool table. Butterfield testimony, House Judiciary Committee; Haldeman notes and Nixon memos, WHSF-R; Haldeman to Chapin, Aug. 19, 1970, WHSF-R; Nixon to Haldeman, Jan. 26, 1970, RNL; HRH diary, Jan. 27, 29, Apr. 29, 1970; Butterfield OH, RNL; Nixon to Mrs. Nixon, Jan. 25, 1969, Nixon to Haldeman and Ehrlichman, Jan. 29, 1969, Nixon to Haldeman, Feb. 17, 1969, Nixon to RMW, Feb. 17, 1969, Nixon to Haldeman, June 16, 1969, Nixon to Scouten, July 9, 1969, Haldeman to Higby Aug. 11, 1969, Haldeman to Winchester, Aug. 19, 1969, Haldeman to Hughes, Sept. 1, 1970, Oudes, *From: The President;* Safire, "Nixon Diary," Sept. 24, 1970, Safire papers, LOC; Nixon-Gannon; Ehrlichman notes, "Bumper Stickers," July 5, 1972, HI; Haldeman, Hofstra.

358   menacing commands to his aides: Ehrlichman OH, RNL; Nixon to Haldeman, Jan. 4, 1969, WHSF-R; oral histories by Haldeman, Huston, Colson, Garment, Price, Safire, RNL; *Newsweek,* Dec. 2, 1996; Safire, "Nixon Diary," Aug. 18, 1969, Jan. 27, 1971, Mar. 16, 1973, Safire papers, LOC; Douglas Hallett, "A Low-Level Memoir of the Nixon White House," *NYT,* Oct. 20, 1974; Leonard Garment, *Crazy Rhythm* (New York: Times Books, 1997) and *In Search of Deep Throat.*

360   secret plan was to win: "I'm not going to end up like LBJ, holed up at the White House, afraid to show my face on the street," Nixon told Haldeman. "I'm going to stop that war. Fast." See H. R. Haldeman, *The Ends of Power* (New York: Times Books, 1978); see also Nixon news conferences, Mar. 4, June 19, Sept. 26, 1969, PPP; Pat Buchanan, Morton Halperin interviews with author; Ehrlichman interview, "Cold War," NSA; Lord OH, FD; handwritten memcon, Nixon and Eisenhower, Apr. 2, 1967, Nixon to Kissinger, July 7, 1958, Sept. 15, 1969, Buchanan to Nixon, July 28, 1968, with attachment, "Memo from Jeff Bell," Robert Ellsworth OH, RNL.

      O'Brien OH, LBJ; Moynihan interview, *Playboy,* Mar. 1977; memcon, Nixon, Kissinger, and Dobrynin, Oct. 20, 1969, Keogh memo, May 15, 1969, National Security Council minutes, Jan. 25 and Mar. 28, 1969, Kissinger to Nixon, Apr. 3, 1969, and Sept. 11, 1969, Kissinger telcon, Oct. 20, 1969, Nixon to Kissinger, Feb. 1, 1969, FRUS, 1969–1976, Vol. 6, Vietnam, January 1969–July 1970; meeting, LBJ and Nixon, July 26, 1968, FRUS, 1964–1968, Vol. 6, Vietnam, January–August 1968; White House tape transcript, Nixon and Kissinger, Apr. 19, 1972, FRUS, 1969–1976, Vol. 8, Vietnam, January–October 1972; essay, "Ending the Vietnam War, 1969–1973," Milestones in the History of U.S. Foreign Relations, Office of the Historian, U.S. State Department; Haldeman, Hofstra; "Vietnam and the Paris Peace Accords," Nixon Legacy Forum, Dec. 5, 2014, NARA, Washington, D.C. (participants: Winston Lord, John Negroponte, and William Richard Smyser); Kennan testimony, Feb. 10, 1966, U.S. Congress, Senate, Committee on Foreign Relations, *Supplemental Foreign Assistance, Fiscal Year 1966-Vietnam* (Washington, D.C.: 1966); Dobrynin memcon, May 14, 1969, in Edward Keefer, David Geyer, and Douglas Selvage, *Soviet American Relations:*

The Détente Years, 1969–1972 (Washington, D.C.: U.S. Department of State, 2007); *Miami Herald,* Aug. 7, 1968; memcon, Nixon, Thompson, and Kissinger, Oct. 17, 1969, in Jeffrey Kimball, *The Vietnam War Files* (Lawrence: University Press of Kansas, 2004); Goodpaster, "Memorandum of Meeting with the President 17 February 1965," LBJ, NSA; for Kennan on withdrawal see *NYT,* Nov. 10, 1969; Robert Dallek, *Nixon and Kissinger* (New York: HarperCollins, 2007); Dobrynin, *In Confidence.* Kimball's book *The Vietnam War Files* contains a rich collection of documents supporting the findings and analysis he makes in an authoritative earlier volume, *Nixon's Vietnam War* (Lawrence: University Press of Kansas, 1998).

362 "I call it the Madman Theory": Haldeman, *Ends of Power.* For the "madman" theory on the White House tapes, see Nixon and Kissinger, Apr. 23, 1971, Nixon and Kissinger, July 19, 1971, Nixon, Haldeman, and Kissinger, Sept. 21, 1971, RNL. See also telcon, Nixon and Kissinger, Oct. 20, 1969, RNL; Garment, *Crazy Rhythm;* William Burr and Jeffrey Kimball, *Nixon's Nuclear Specter* (Lawrence: University Press of Kansas, 2015).

363 bombing the Communist camps: The article of impeachment failed, in a 26-to-12 vote, largely because Nixon had informed Democratic senators Richard Russell of Georgia and John Stennis of Mississippi and a few other members of Congress about the bombing. Kissinger contended in his memoirs that the dual bookkeeping scheme was designed to deceive the press and public, not Congress. See *Impeachment of Richard M. Nixon, President of the United States, Report of the Committee on the Judiciary, House of Representatives, Aug. 20, 1974* with Kissinger affidavit, Nov. 26, 1973, from *Ellsberg v. Mitchell* and Kissinger telcon with Nixon and Stennis, Apr. 24, 1970, FRUS, 1969–1976, Vol. 6.

Nixon was preparing to strike at the North Vietnamese in Cambodia even before taking office. "In making your study of Vietnam I want a precise report on what the enemy has in Cambodia and what, if anything, we are doing to destroy the buildup there," he wrote Kissinger on January 8, 1969. "A very definite change of policy toward Cambodia probably should be one of the first orders of business when we get in." Nixon to Kissinger, Jan. 8, 1969, WHSF-R.

Bunker to Rogers, Feb. 12, 1969, Nixon, "Memorandum for the Record," Mar. 15, 1969, Kissinger to Nixon, Mar. 16, 1969, Kissinger telcons with Laird, Mar. 15 and 16, 1969, "Summary of Interagency Responses to NSSM 1," Mar. 22, 1969, FRUS, 1969–1976, Vol. 6; Jacob Van Staaveren, Office of Air Force History, "The Air Force in Southeast Asia, Toward a Bombing Halt, 1968," Sept. 1970; *The Final Report of the Select Committee on Presidential Campaign Activities,* U.S. Senate, June 1974 (hereafter SSC, final report).

"Statement of Information," Hearings Before the Committee on the Judiciary, House of Representatives, 93rd Congress; "Memorandum of the Record Relating to the Conduct of the Surveillance," *Halperin v. Kissinger,* Civil Action 1187-73, U.S. District Court for the District of Columbia, RNL; Nixon-Frost interview transcript (when pressed about civilian casualties, Nixon told Frost: "If we did it, mistakes were made, yes, but it was not policy") and White House tape, May 4, 1972, RNL; telcon, Kissinger and Safire, Aug. 3, 1973, NSC Vietnam subject files, Nixon deposition, Jan. 15, 1976, *Halperin v. Kissinger,* RNL; Kissinger interview with David Frost, Oct. 11, 1979, NBC.

In defense of the secret bombing of Cambodia, Nixon offered a World War II analogy to Halperin's lawyers. "I can think of no one who objected to the United States bombing the Nazi occupied portions of Western Europe, France and so forth," Nixon said. "We weren't bombing France, we were bombing the Nazis. In this case, we were not bombing the Cambodians, we were bombing the North Vietnamese."

Kissinger confessed to Congress in 1975 that "our guilt, responsibility, or whatever you may call it toward the Cambodians is that we conducted our operations in Cambodia primarily to serve our purposes related to Vietnam, and that they have now been left in a very difficult circumstance." For discussion, see Kimball, *Files;* Walter Isaacson, *Kissinger* (New York: Simon & Schuster, 1992); William Shawcross, *Sideshow* (New York: Simon & Schuster, 1979).

364 Nixon called in J. Edgar Hoover: As the Senate Watergate Committee and House Judiciary Committee would later note, in 1969 the law was in flux and there were as yet no statutes or Supreme Court rulings prohibiting warrantless electronic eavesdropping in matters of national security. The loophole had been exploited by most of the Cold War presidents, but they generally followed a procedure requiring written authorization by the attorney general. The Kraft bug did not meet even that safeguard and, though never tested in court, was widely judged illegal. Hedrick Smith, Morton Halperin interviews with the author; SSC, final report; "Statement of Information," Hearings Before the Committee on the Judiciary, House of Representatives, 93rd Congress.

 "Memorandum of the Record Relating to the Conduct of the Surveillance," *Halperin v. Kissinger,* Civil Action 1187-73, U.S. District Court for the District of Columbia; Nixon to Kissinger, Feb. 1, 1969, Kissinger to Nixon, Feb. 19, Hoover to Mitchell, Re: Colonel Alexander M. Haig Technical Surveillance Request, May 12, 13, 20, 1969, Miller to Rosen, Oct. 20, 1971, and Jacobson to Walters, May 12, 1973, "Sensitive Coverage Placed at Request of the White House," FBI; Kissinger testimony, Senate Foreign Relations Committee, Sept. 17, 1973; *NYT,* May 9, 1969; Nixon, *RN;* Kissinger, *White House Years.*

365 It came to be called Vietnamization: Laird to Nixon, Mar. 13, 1969, National Security Council minutes, Mar. 28, 1969, Kissinger to Nixon, Apr. 3, 15, Aug. 7, 1969, Kissinger notes, June 11, Sept. 27, 1969, meetings with Anatoly Dobrynin, Kissinger notes, Oct. 20, 1969, meeting with Nixon and Dobrynin, Kissinger telcon with Nixon, Sept. 27, 1969, FRUS, 1969–1976, Vol. 6; Dobrynin memcon, Oct. 20, 1969, Keefer, Geyer, and Selvage, *Soviet American Relations;* Nixon press conference, Sept. 26, 1969, PPP; memcon, Le Duck Tho and Kissinger, Feb. 21, 1970, Frost-Nixon transcripts and telcon, Nixon and Kissinger, Nov. 5, 1975, RNL; Lord OH, FD; "Vietnam and the Paris Peace Accords," Nixon Legacy Forum; George W. Ball, *The Past Has Another Pattern* (New York: Norton, 1982); Kimball, *Files;* Nixon, *RN.*

367 the morality of such a war: The sorties include supply, transport, and reconnaissance missions. Nixon-Gannon; White House tapes, Nixon, Haldeman, and Kissinger, June 2, 1971, Nixon and Colson, Jan. 20, 1973, RNL; Frost-Nixon transcripts, RNL; HRH diary, Apr. 22, 1973; Nixon press conference, June 1, 1971, PPP; *NYT,* Feb. 7, 1968; Edward Miguel and Gerard Roland, "The Long Run Impact of Bombing Vietnam," NBER, 2006; Micheal Clodfelter, *Vietnam in Military Statistics* (Jefferson, NC: McFarland, 1995); John Schlight, *A War Too Long: The USAF in Southeast Asia* (Washington, D.C.: Air Force History and Museums, 1996). Ball, *Pattern.*

369 "the great Silent Majority": White House tape, Nixon and Kissinger, Apr. 7, 1971, Nixon Silent Majority speech, Nov. 3, 1969, Haldeman notes, Sept. 26, 1969, Moynihan to Haldeman, Oct. 1, 1969, Buchanan memos on "our Americans" and speech, Oct. 8, 1969, RNL; HRH diary, Oct. 3, 8, 9, and 17, 1969; telcons, Laird and Kissinger, Oct. 21, Nov. 14, and Nov. 21, 1969, Moynihan to Nixon, Jan. 3, 1969, RNL; memcon, Kissinger et al., Paris, Aug. 4, 1969, Nixon to Kissinger, Aug. 6 and 30, Sept. 10 and Oct. 2, 1969, FRUS, 1969–1976, Vol. 6; *WP,* Oct. 7, 1969; *NYT,* Nov. 16, 1969; Stephen Hess, *The Professor and the President* (Washington, D.C.: Brookings Institution Press, 2015); Tom Wells, *The War Within* (Berkeley: University of California Press, 1994); Kimball, *Files.*

 Moynihan described what was happening, and the peril Nixon faced, in a private letter to Haldeman and Ehrlichman. "The administration took office and did brilliantly for six months. The initiative was all with us. Then, inevitably, a counterattack began. . . . Attacked, we attacked back. We began to raise our voices. Mistakes began to engender mistakes. All along there was one repeated phenomenon: we acted in such ways as to increase the moral authority of our opponents and to diminish our own. We tried to invoke the moral authority of the silent majority: the plain, good Americans who still Believe in God, and in America, and are proud to display the flag. *The problem with this strategy is that it positioned the President on the side of one group of Americans, against another,*" Moynihan wrote, while the "adversary culture" of the universities, the press, and other elites was "more in opposition now than perhaps at any time in history" (emphasis by Moynihan). Moynihan to Haldeman and Ehrlichman, "Personal & Confidential," July 24, 1970; Daniel Patrick Moynihan, *Daniel Patrick Moynihan: A Portrait in Letters of an American Visionary,* Steven R. Weisman, ed. (New York: PublicAffairs, 2010).

370 a hamlet called My Lai: Nixon press conference, Dec. 8, 1969, PPP. Haldeman's notes on the "dirty tricks" conversation are at the RNL and were published by CBS News on its website on March 23, 2014. Bob Woodward's book *The Last of the President's Men* (New York: Simon & Schuster, 2015) contains lengthy notations from Alexander Butterfield's notes from November 1969, in which Nixon wondered if army witness Ronald Ridenhour was a "lib Jew" and ordered that Ridenhour, Sy Hersh, and others be investigated. In 1971, when Army Lieutenant William Calley was convicted for murdering civilians at My Lai, Nixon bowed to public pressure, interceded, and had him moved from the stockade to house arrest.

CHAPTER 20: NOT FISH NOR FOWL

371 first twelve months: Safire, "Nixon Diary," Jan. 23, 1970, Safire papers, LOC; Nixon-Frost transcript, RNL; HRH diary, Jan. 25, 1969; Huston OH, Nixon to Haldeman, Nov. 22, 1970, RNL; Greenspan, interview with author; Greenspan OH, GFF; Moynihan interview, Tom Wicker Papers, University of North Carolina; Price interview, Dec. 18, 2008, American History TV, C-SPAN. The music box was given to Nixon, according to Haldeman, by PR executive Robert Gray.

372 Eisenhower's understudy: Ambrose, Hofstra; Schlesinger OH, RNL; HRH diary, Mar. 28, 1969; Nixon to Haldeman, Oct. 1, 1969, WHSF-RC; Strachan notes to file, Oct. 30, 1971, WHSF-RC; Haldeman to Butterfield, Pat Nixon, and Rose Woods, and Haldeman to Colson, "Church Services," Nov. 13, 1970, WHSF-RC; Nixon to Woods and Haldeman, Jan. 31, 1970, Nixon to Aitken, undated, RNL. On lapel pins and purposefully coopting the American flag see Ehrlichman notes, "Buttons," July 5, 1972, HI. Nixon to Haldeman, Apr. 13, 1970, Strachan to file, Oct. 30, 1971, RNL, and Nixon to Keogh, no citation, Reeves, *Nixon,* Nixon, *RN.*

374 White House staff: Price to Nixon, "Thoughts On Dealing With Youthful Unrest," Oct. 2, 1969, Moynihan to Nixon, Jan. 16, 1970, Nixon to Haldeman, Dec. 11, 1970, Moynihan to Ehrlichman and Finch, Nov. 18, 1970, Moynihan to Nixon, Jan. 3, 1969, and Nixon to Moynihan, Jan. 8, 1969, response, WHSF-R; Wilkinson to Haldeman, Dec. 6, 1968, WHSF-R; Haldeman to Keogh, Jan. 15, 1969, WHSF-R; Harlow OH, GFL, cited in Reeves.

375 president's pen stayed busy: White House tapes, Nixon and Haldeman, June 12, 1971, and June 15, 1971, Cole to Nixon, with May 31, 1974, memo from Weinberger, RNL; Brownell to Dent, Oct. 29, 1969, WHSF-RC; oral histories by Peter Flanigan, Robert Dole, Garment, and Huston, RNL; Ehrlichman to Haldeman, Nov. 6, 1971, WHSF-RC; Buchanan to Haldeman, Jan. 14, 1971, WHSF-RC; Hallett to Colson and Nixon, Jan. 3, 1972, WHSF-RC; Buchanan to Haldeman, July 28, 1971, WHSF-RC; Haldeman to Klein, "Minority Groups," WHSF-RC; Buchanan to Nixon, May 7, 1971,

WHSF-RC; Burns interview, WB; Ehrlichman notes, "Gun Control," May 16, 1972, HI; Alan Greenspan, Robert DuPont OH, GFF; Moynihan interview, Tom Wicker Papers, University of North Carolina; *Congressional Quarterly Almanac,* 1969; Nixon, Finch interviews, 1968, White papers, Harvard; Joan Hoff-Wilson, "Outflanking the Liberals on Welfare," Hofstra; "Nixon on the Home Front," *Prologue,* NARA.

376   Nixon's "self-determination" policy: "He feels very strongly," Haldeman said of Nixon, "that we need to show more heart, and that we care about people, and thinks the Indian problem is a good area for us to work in." Haldeman to Keogh, Jan. 13, 1969, WHSF-R; Haldeman to Klein, "Minority Groups," WHSF-RC.

      John A. Farrell and Jim Richardson, "The New Indian Wars," *Denver Post,* Nov. 1983; Nixon Legacy Forums, "Restoring Rights for Native Americans," May 23, 2012, and "Richard Nixon and the American Indian: The Movement to Self-Determination," Nov. 15, 2012; Leonard Garment, *Crazy Rhythm* (New York: Times Books, 1997).

376   federal health insurance: In an interview with the author, Kennedy said that spurning Nixon's health care plan was the biggest policy mistake of his career. Nixon's "Comprehensive Health Insurance Plan" was designed to address rising costs and the large number of Americans who lacked adequate health insurance. See Nixon message to Congress proposing his Comprehensive Health Insurance Plan, Feb. 6, 1974, PPP.

377   "On abortion—get the hell off it": See Nixon White House tape, Nixon and Colson, Jan. 23, 1973, RNL; Safire, "Nixon Diary," Sept. 9, 1970, Safire papers, LOC.

378   gay rights movement: The Archie Bunker remarks are from Nixon White House tape, Nixon, Haldeman, and Ehrlichman, May 13, 1971, RNL. The gay marriage prediction is from Safire, "Nixon Diary," Aug. 11, 1970, Safire papers, LOC.

378   "War on Drugs": As with affirmative action, which drove a wedge between the Democratic core groups of minorities and labor, a public health crusade against drugs had the added appeal of disrupting Nixon's political enemies, John Ehrlichman said. "By getting the public to associate the hippies with marijuana and blacks with heroin, and then criminalizing both heavily we could disrupt those communities. We could arrest their leaders, raid their homes, break up their meetings and vilify them night after night on the evening news," Ehrlichman told a writer in 1994. See Dan Baum, "Legalize It All," *Harper's Magazine,* Apr. 2016.

      Nixon, "Special Message to the Congress on Drug Abuse Prevention and Control," June 17, 1971, and "State of the Union Message to the Congress on Law Enforcement and Drug Abuse Prevention," Mar. 14, 1973, PPP; "Briefing: American Prisons," *Economist,* June 20, 2015; Ta-Nehisi Coates, "The Black Family in the Age of Mass Incarceration," *Atlantic,* October, 2015. Michael J. Graetz, Linda Greenhouse, *The Burger Court and the Rise of the Judicial Right* (New York: Simon & Schuster, 2016).

379   environment was emerging as a potent issue: Moynihan to Ehrlichman, Sept. 17, 1969, RNL; Garment to Nixon, Dec. 23, 1968, WHSF-R; Malek to Richardson, June 22, 1970, Malek to Haldeman, Oct. 6, 1970, Whitaker to Nixon through Ehrlichman, June 29, 1971, Whitaker to Nixon through Ehrlichman, Sept. 21, 1971, RNL; Moynihan to Lewis, June 10, 1991, Nixon to Haldeman, Jan. 20, 1971, Nixon-Frost interviews, Day 7, RNL; White House tapes, Nixon and Kissinger, June 2, 1971, Nixon and Goldwater, Nov. 10, 1971, RNL; HRH diary, Mar. 25, Oct. 8, 1969, July 13, 1970; Ruckelshaus OH, Huston OH, Haldeman OH, RNL; Teeter to Haldeman, Jan. 6, 1972, WHSF-RC; Ehrlichman interview, Wicker papers, UNC; Safire, "Nixon Diary," Jan. 20, 1970, Safire papers, LOC; Burns interview, WB; Moynihan interview, *Playboy,* Mar. 1977; Ehrlichman notes, "Reorg," Dec. 5, 1970, HI; James Farmer interview, Strober; Charles Warren and John Whitaker, discussants, the Nixon environmental record, Joan Hoff-Wilson discussant, "Outflanking the Liberals on Welfare," Hofstra; David Roberts, "The Greenest Presidents," *Corporate Knights,* Summer 2012; J.

Brooks Flippen, *Nixon and the Environment* (Albuquerque: University of New Mexico Press, 2000).

383 "nods and winks": Garment, interview with author; Shultz, interview with author; Ehrlichman to Haldeman, Apr. 15, 1970, Ehrlichman OH, RNL; Nixon press conference, Sept. 26, 1969, PPP. Nixon's handling of civil rights was debated at the 1987 conference at Hofstra University, attended by many of his former advisers. The scholarly papers and responses were printed in *Richard M. Nixon: Politician, President, Administrator,* ed. Leon Friedman and William Levantrosser (New York: Greenwood Press, 1991). For commentary see discussion by Michael Genovese, Alvy King, Hugh Graham, Robert Finch, Sallyanne Payton, and Roger Wilkins; Hugh Davis Graham, "Richard Nixon and Civil Rights: Explaining an Enigma," *Presidential Studies Quarterly* 26 (Winter 1996): 93–106; John Ehrlichman, *Witness to Power* (New York: Simon & Schuster, 1982); Garment, *Crazy Rhythm.*

384 "The laws have caught up with our conscience": Nixon Inaugural Address, PPP; Alexander to Harlow, "Report: Blacks," June 17, 1970, and memo on Haynsworth loss, undated, winter of 1969–70, Thurmond to Finch, no date, winter 1968–69, WHSF-R; Dent to Nixon, "Report on Meeting of Southerners and Other Conservatives with the President," Aug. 6, 1970, Garment OH, Panetta OH, RNL; Evans and Novak, *Cincinnati Enquirer,* Dec. 26, 1968; Taylor Branch, *Parting the Waters* (New York: Simon & Schuster, 1988); Dean Kotlowski, *Nixon's Civil Rights* (Cambridge: Harvard University Press, 2001); Dan Carter lecture, "George Wallace, Richard Nixon and the Transformation of American Politics," published by Baylor University Press, 1992; Bob Woodward and Scott Armstrong, *The Brethren* (New York: Simon & Schuster, 1979).

385 "I have the greatest affection for them": White House tape recordings: Nixon, Haldeman, and Ehrlichman, May 13, 1971, Nixon and Colson, Feb. 13, 1973, Nixon and Rumsfeld, July 22, 1971, RNL; Nixon to Ehrlichman and Haldeman, Jan. 28, 1972, Ehrlichman OH, RNL; Dent to Mitchell, Haldeman, and Morgan, Nov. 4, 1971, WHSF-RC; Ehrlichman notes, Feb. 12, 1970, "School deseg—Panetta," HI.

In his memoirs, Nixon attributed the racial polarization of the country to unforgiving black voters. "In 1960 I had received 32 percent of the black vote: in 1964 Goldwater received only 6 percent. I was able to increase the Republican share of the black vote to 12 percent in 1968, but the false impression that Goldwater was a racist was too prevalent for an easy relationship to exist between the black community and a Republican administration," he wrote in *RN.*

Jackie Robinson declined to support Nixon in the 1968 election. Their break was complete. The FBI kept a file on the ballplayer, which included a 1969 request by Nixon aide John Ehrlichman that the bureau investigate Robinson. See FBI file, Hoover to Ehrlichman, July 24, 1969.

386 Busing was a virulent issue: Nixon to Ehrlichman re busing, May 1972, WHSF-RC; Haldeman to Chotiner and Dent on Nixon and busing, Sept. 10, 1970, WHSF-RC; Colson to Nixon, re busing, May 1972, WHSF-RC; transcript of telcon, Colson and Lou Harris, Apr. 26, 1972, WHSF-RC; Colson to Mitchell, May 19, 1972; McWhorter to Flemming, July 26, 1971, WHSF-RC; Colson to Haldeman, May 17, 1972,WHSF-RC; HRH diary, Feb. 27, Nov. 7, 1970, Apr. 20, Aug. 2, 1971; Price OH, Colson OH, RNL.

386 presented a tantalizing opportunity: Colson to Nixon, May 19, 1972, WHSF-RC; Colson to Haldeman, Nov. 10, 1972, RNL; Richard Parker, "Those Blue-Collar Worker Blues," *New Republic,* Sept. 23, 1972; Thomas and Mary Edsall, *Chain Reaction* (New York: Norton, 1991); Stanley Greenberg, *Middle Class Dreams* (New York: Times Books, 1995); James T. Patterson, *Grand Expectations* (New York: Oxford University, 1996).

387   *The Real Majority:* Buchanan to Nixon, re *The Real Majority,* Aug. 24, 1970, WHSF-RC; Balzano to Nixon, "The Ethnic Vote in the 1972 Election," Dec. 31, 1971, with copies to Colson, Strachan, Haldeman, and others, WHSF-RC; Buchanan to Agnew and Harlow, Sept. 26, 1970, Buchanan to Nixon, Aug. 24, 1970, "Research" to Haldeman and Mitchell, "Dividing the Democrats," Oct. 5, 1971, Buchanan to Nixon, Apr. 3, 1972, RNL; Colson et al., "Report on Middle America," Nov. 2, 1971, WHSF-RC; Shultz, "Memorandum for the Working Group on the Blue Collar Worker," Mar. 16, 1970, RNL; Buchanan to Ehrlichman, Haldeman, and Colson, Sept. 23, 1971, WHSF-RC; Safire, "Nixon Diary," Sept. 9, 1970, Safire papers, LOC; Boyd "Nixon's Southern Strategy, 'It's All in the Charts,'" *NYT,* May 17, 1970; Phillips, "Post-Southern Strategy," *WP,* Sept. 25, 1970; Ehrlichman OH, Cold War series, NSA; Richard Scammon and Ben Wattenberg, *The Real Majority* (New York: Capricorn, 1971); Kevin Phillips, *The Emerging Republican Majority* (New Rochelle, NY: Arlington House, 1969).

389   retirements on the U.S. Supreme Court: Cong. Rec., Mar. 24, 1970; Dent to Haldeman, "Report on Meeting of Southerners and Other Conservatives with the President," Aug. 1970, Harlow to Staff Secretary, report on meeting among Nixon, Agnew, and Sen. Richard Russell, Feb. 19, 1970, RNL; Burger to Mitchell, Oct. 13, 1971, RNL; HRH diary, Sept. 25, Oct. 2, 15, 19, 20, 21, 1971; "Statement About Nominations to the Supreme Court," Apr. 9, 1970, PPP; Ehrlichman notes, "Haynesworth," 1969, and "Carswell," Mar. 26, 1970, "Supreme Court," Oct. 2, 1971, "Supreme Court," Oct. 25, 1971, HI; Buchanan OH, Thomas Kauper OH, GFF; Graetz and Greenhouse, *The Burger Court;* Henry J. Abraham, *Justices, Presidents and Senators* (Lanham, MD: Rowman & Littlefield, 2007); Woodward and Armstrong, *Brethren; New Yorker,* Apr. 18, 1970. Apr. 18, Dec. 5, 12, 1970; Fred Fielding, Wallace Johnson, Tom Korologos, Kevin McMahon, Nixon Legacy Forum, "Nixon to Reagan: Reshaping the Supreme Court," Nov. 13, 2012.

      John Mitchell was blamed for the Carswell fiasco, but Carswell had been recommended to Mitchell by Chief Justice Warren Burger. See Burger to Mitchell, Apr. 4, 1969, RNL.

390   striations in his character: King to Mazo, Sept. 2, 1958; *The Papers of Martin Luther King Jr.* (Berkeley: University of California Press, 2000); Garment OH, Huston OH, RNL; Nixon press conference, Dec. 8, 1969, PPP; Ehrlichman notes, Mar. 25, 1970, "Deseg Stmnt—game plan," HI.

391   local advisory committees: Shultz, interview with author; Nixon, "Statement About Desegregation of Elementary and Secondary Schools," Mar. 24, 1970, "Remarks Following a Meeting in New Orleans With Leaders of Seven State Advisory Committees on Public Education," Aug. 14, 1970, PPP; Shultz OH, Price OH, Garment OH, RNL; HRH diary, Feb. 20, Mar. 24, Aug. 4, 1970; Nofziger to Dent, Oct. 27, 1969, WHSF-RC; Dent to Nixon, Jan. 12, 1971, WHSF-RC; Higby to Haldeman, Dec. 6, 1971, WHSF-RC; Dent to Haldeman, June 16, 1972, WHSF-RC; Magruder to Mitchell, "The Black Vote in 1972," July 3, 1971, WHSF-RC; Sears to Haldeman, Dec. 9, 1970, WHSF-RC; Moynihan to Nixon, Jan. 16, 1970, RNL; Dent to Morton, Apr. 1, 1969, WHSF-RC; Finch to Nixon, Oct. 26, 1971, WHSF-RC; Ehrlichman interview, Wicker papers, UNC; Ehrlichman notes, "Southern Schools," Feb. 7, 1970, "Desegregation," Aug. 4, 1970, "Deseg-New Orleans," Aug. 12, 1970, HI. In his memoir, *Crazy Rhythm,* Garment says that the idea for the citizens' committees came to the White House from white and black leaders in Greenville, South Carolina, who had organized a group in their community.

393   "I wanted to bring the South": Nixon-Frost interviews, RNL; Panetta OH, Chapin to Haldeman, Aug. 10, 1970, WHSF-RC; Payton commentary, Hofstra; Kotlowski, *Nixon's Civil Rights;* William Safire, *Before the Fall* (New York: Doubleday, 1975); Law-

rence McAndrews, "The Politics of Principle: Richard Nixon and School Desegregation," *Journal of Negro History,* Summer 1998; Hugh Davis Graham, "Richard Nixon and Civil Rights: Explaining an Enigma," *Presidential Studies Quarterly* 26 (Winter 1996): 93–106; Mitchell quote: *Life,* July 25, 1969.

394 Nixon received little credit: Moynihan interview, *Playboy,* Mar. 1977; Dent to Nixon, Nov. 17, 1969, WHSF-RC; Dent to Nixon, Dec. 11, 1969, WHSF-RC; Khachigian to Buchanan, July 26, 1971 ("RN has brought some calm into a difficult situation. Sure, he followed the Supreme Court mandate on desegregation, but he didn't bully around the South and he didn't stomp the Black under his foot"), WHSF-RC.

395 should have tax-exempt status: Harlow to Haldeman, Mar. 16, 1970, WHSF-RC; Harlow to Haldeman, June 17, 1970, RNL; Ehrlichman notes, Jan. 1979, "Private Schools in South," HI.

395 first broad affirmative action plan: Shultz, interview with author; Safire, *Before the Fall;* Dean Kotlowski, "Richard Nixon and the Origins of Affirmative Action," *Historian,* Spring 1998; Ehrlichman interview, Wicker papers, UNC; Safire, "Nixon Diary," Dec. 22, 1969, Feb. 20, 1970, May 9, 1970, Safire papers, LOC.

396 1970 Gridiron Dinner: AP, Mar. 16, 1970; *WP,* Mar. 22, 1970; HRH diary, Mar. 14, 1970, RNL.

396 Duke Ellington's seventieth birthday: *NYT,* Aug. 25, 2002; Garment, *Crazy Rhythm;* HRH diary, Apr. 29, 1969, RNL; *New Yorker,* May 10, 1969.

CHAPTER 21: DRAWING THE SWORD

397 president's dark moods: HRH diary, Jan. 9, 1970, Chapin OH, White House tape, Nixon and Kissinger, Apr. 19, 1972, RNL; Nixon to Haldeman et al., Sept. 1968, WHSF-R.

397 "the day will be a disaster": Julie Nixon Eisenhower to Ehrlichman, Apr. 28, 1970, cited in Ehrlichman, *Witness to Power;* O'Neill to Higby and Brown, Aug. 15, 1969, *From: The President,* ed. Bruce Oudes (New York: Harper & Row, 1989); Nixon to Ehrlichman, Jan. 4, 1969, WHSF-R, RNL. John Prine, "Sam Stone."

398 snarl of incitements: Alan Greenspan, interview with author; James Wright diary, Wright papers, Texas Christian University; Ailes interview, Halberstam papers, BU; Elliot Richardson, Hugh Sidey interviews, Thompson; Henry Kissinger, *Years of Upheaval* (Boston: Little Brown, 1982); Monica Crowley, *Nixon in Winter* (New York: Random House, 1998); George H. W. Bush, *All the Best: My Life in Letters and Other Writings* (New York: Scribner, 2013).

399 Discipline was paramount: Dwight Chapin, interview with author; Chapin OH, RNL; *WP,* special section, "The Nixon Years," Aug. 9, 1974; Arthur Schlesinger Jr. diary entry, May 22, 1970, ASP; Earl Mazo, *Nixon* (New York: Avon, 1960); H. R. Haldeman, *The Ends of Power* (New York: Times Books, 1978); Nixon interview with Alsop, Joseph Alsop and Stewart Alsop Papers, LOC, published in Alsop, *Nixon and Rockefeller* (New York: Doubleday, 1960).

400 Pat Nixon: Pat was not forever solemn. She liked a cigarette and an occasional cocktail, and both she and her husband's guy pals—interestingly enough—played the same practical joke on Dick: sticking an inflatable sex doll in a bed where he would find it. Abplanalp interview, Aitken papers, RNL; Helen Thomas interview, GFF; Helen McCain Smith, "Ordeal!" *Good Housekeeping,* July 1976.

Chapin, interview with author; Gannon, interview with author; Hal Bruno, Richard Keiser, Helen Thomas interviews, GFF; Haldeman OH, Chapin OH, Butterfield OH, RNL; Leonard memo, "Mr. President . . . the Man," Mar. 29, 1971, WHSF-RC; Nixon handwritten comment on media analysis, Sept. 25, 1972, WHSF-RC; Price to Haldeman, July 21, 1972, WHSF-RC; Colson to Nixon, Jan. 19, 1972, WHSF-RC; Stuart to Haldeman, June 9, 1970, WHSF-RC; Stuart to Magruder, Mar. 12, 1970,

RNL; Dean interview, FMB; Ailes to Haldeman and Chapin, May 4, 1970, WHSF-RC; Colson to Higby with attached telcon, Aug. 20, 1971, WHSF-RC; Strachan to Haldeman, Sept. 30, 1971, WHSF-RC; Colson to Haldeman, Jan. 20, 1972, WHSF-RC; John Taylor, "The Episconixonian," July 1, 2013; Nixon-Gannon; Tom Wicker, *One of Us* (New York: Random House, 1991). For more on Dick's relationship with Pat, see telcon, Kissinger and Valenti, Oct. 28, 1975, RNL, and Helen Smith and Charles Lichenstein interviews, WB; Lord OH, FD; Ehrlichman, *Witness to Power*.

402   forceful action to save Cambodia: Brennan to Woods, May 4, 1970, RNL; HRH diary, Apr. 17, 1970; Hughes to Kissinger, Apr. 20, 1970, telcon, Nixon and Kissinger, Apr. 20, 1970, telcon Rogers and Kissinger, Apr. 21, 1970, Nixon to Kissinger, Apr. 22, 1970, memorandum of meeting, Nixon, Rogers, Laird, and Mitchell, Apr. 28, 1970; telcon, Nixon and Kissinger, May 4, 1970; telcon, Kissinger and Rogers, May 7, 1970, and editorial notes, FRUS, 1969–1976, Vol. 6, Vietnam, Jan. 1969–July 1970; Safire, "Nixon Diary," May 3, 1970, Safire papers, LOC; Henry Kissinger, *White House Years* (Boston: Little, Brown, 1979)*;* Jeffrey Kimball, *Nixon's Vietnam War* (Lawrence: University Press of Kansas, 1998).

404   Kent State: When the father of Kent State victim Allison Krause read Nixon's sorrowful account of the shooting in his memoirs, he measured it against the polarizing actions of the White House at the time. "Is there to be no end to your deceptions, omissions and outright distortions of historical fact?" Arthur Krause asked in an open letter to Nixon. Arthur Krause, "A Memo to Mr. Nixon," *NYT,* May 7, 1978.
      HRH diary, May 4–9, 1970; Nixon, "Address to the Nation on the Situation in Southeast Asia," Apr. 30, 1970; "Statement on the Deaths of Four Students at Kent State University, Kent, Ohio," May 4, 1970; "The President's News Conference," May 8, 1970, PPP; Ehrlichman diary entry, Apr. 30, 1970, and notes, "Scranton Comm'n," June 18, 1970, HI; *The Report of the President's Commission on Campus Unrest,* 1970; *NYT,* May 2, 1970; Garry Wills, "Richard Nixon's Seventh Crisis," *NYT,* July 8, 1973; *Newsweek,* May 18, 1970; "Vietnam and the Paris Peace Accords," Nixon Legacy Forum, Dec. 5, 2014, National Archives, Washington, D.C. (participants: Winston Lord, John Negroponte, and William Richard Smyser); Nixon-Gannon; John Ehrlichman, *Witness to Power* (New York: Simon & Schuster, 1982); Nixon, *RN;* Kissinger, *White House Years.*

405   "Searchlight is on the lawn!": Egil Krogh, interview with author; Nixon dictabelt recording of May 9 visit to the Lincoln Memorial, Robert Moustakas OH, Egil Krogh OH, RNL; HRH diary, May 9, 1970; Truman diary, HST; Ehrlichman interview, "Cold War," National Security Archive; Nixon press conference, May 8, 1970, and transcript of Ziegler briefing, May 9, 1970, PPP; "The Day Nixon Cracked," *Atlantic* website; Egil Krogh, *Integrity* (New York: PublicAffairs, 2007). A transcript of Nixon's dictation about his visit to the Lincoln Memorial is also in Oudes, *From: The President;* William Safire, *Before the Fall* (New York: Doubleday, 1975); Nixon, *RN.*

407   Nixon was not a mirthless man: Ed Nixon, Krogh interviews with author; Richard Keiser OH, Larry Buendorf OH, GFF; "When Nixon Met Elvis," NARA online exhibit; White House tapes, Julie and Richard Nixon, Dec. 9, 1972, Nixon and Lyndon Johnson, Jan. 2, 1973, Nixon to Woods and Haldeman, Mar. 31, 1971, RNL; Leonard memo, "Mr. President . . . the Man," Mar. 29, 1971, WHSF-RC; Butterfield to Haldeman, Jan. 26, 1970, WHSF-RC; HRH diary, June 26, 27, 1972; Chapin, Abplanalp interviews, Aitken papers, RNL; Steve Bull OH, Butterfield OH, Haldeman OH, RNL; Butterfield testimony, July 2, 1974, House Judiciary Committee; Smith, "Ordeal!" *Good Housekeeping,* July 1976; Brodie interview with Jessamyn West, FMB; Sears, *LAT,* Apr. 24, 1994; Mark Feeney, *Nixon at the Movies* (Chicago: University of Chicago Press, 2004).

409 Jacqueline Kennedy Onassis and her children: HRH diary, Sept. 9, 1971; oral histories by Haldeman, Butterfield, Bull, and Robert Dole, RNL; White House news summary, May 28, 1971, Jacqueline, Caroline, and John Kennedy to Nixon, Feb. 4, 1971, Nixon to John and Caroline Kennedy, Feb. 28, 1971, Woods to Nixon, Nov. 20, 1972, Woods to Nixon, undated with draft letter, Nixon to Jacqueline Kennedy Onassis, Aug. 30, 1971, RNL; Butterfield to Nixon, Jan. 16, 1970, Nixon to Haldeman, Dec. 4, 1970, RNL; Buchanan to Nixon, May 3, 1971, WHSF-RC; Hullin to Campbell, Sept. 12, 1972, WHSF-RC; Lee Simmons OH, GFF; Safire, "Nixon Diary," Feb. 27, 1969, Safire papers, LOC; Nixon to Haldeman, Jan. 9, 1970; Rose Kennedy to Nixon, Aug. 28, 1971, Oudes, *From: The President.* The letter to Terry Eagleton, Aug. 2, 1972, is reproduced in Nixon, *RN.*

411 acquaintance with alcohol: Chapin, Gannon, Adam Clymer interviews with author; HRH diary, Apr. 17, 1970, Feb. 27, 1972; telcon, Kissinger and Scowcroft, Oct. 11, 1973, RNL; oral histories by Colson, Garment, Haldeman, Chapin, Safire, Price, and Butterfield, RNL; Ehrlichman diary entry, Aug. 3, 1970, HI; Bassett interview, Halberstam papers, BU; Lord OH, FD; Hall OH, Columbia University; oral histories by Stu Spencer, Hal Bruno, Gerald Warren, and Tom DeFrank, GFF; Haig interview, WB; Chapin interview, Aitken papers, RNL; Price, Ehrlichman, and Sorg interviews, Tom Wicker Papers, University of North Carolina; George Reedy OH, LBJ; Ehrlichman OH, Thompson; Patrick Buchanan, *The Greatest Comeback* (New York: Crown, 2014); Leonard Garment, *Crazy Rhythm* (New York: Times Books, 1997) and *In Search of Deep Throat* (New York: Basic Books, 2000); JNE, *Pat;* David McCullough, *Truman* (New York: Simon & Schuster, 1992); Marshall Frady, *Billy Graham: A Parable of American Righteousness* (New York: Simon & Schuster, 2006); Robert Novak, *The Prince of Darkness* (New York: Three Rivers, 2008); Carl Bernstein and Bob Woodward, *The Final Days* (New York: Simon & Schuster, 1976).

412 Dilantin: See Nixon to Woods re Dreyfus and Hutschnecker, Mar. 3, 1973, WHSF-R, and Dreyfus interview, June 11, 1990, Aitken papers, RNL; see also *NYT,* Aug. 27, 30, and Oct. 24, 2000, and Jonathan Aitken, *Nixon: A Life* (Washington, D.C.: Regnery, 1993). In his interview with Aitken, Dreyfus noted that the side effects of mixing alcohol and Dilantin include slurred speech, "particularly in the evening just after it's been taken, when you're too high anyway and you use both alcohol and Dilantin to bring you down." Aitken suggests that Nixon's use of the two drugs created the impression of drunkenness, "a rather more credible theory than the crude suggestion that he was something of a drunkard."

414 "Huston plan": Huston had "a rather uncompromising, acerbic and at times paranoid reaction to positions less dogmatic than his own," Egil Krogh warned Haldeman. See Krogh to Haldeman, Jan. 26, 1970. For Huston zeal, see Huston to Haldeman, "Domestic Intelligence Review," June 16, 1970; "Domestic Intelligence," Aug. 5, 1970; Huston to Haldeman, "IRS & Ideological Organizations," Sept. 21, 1970, and Huston to Helms, "Domestic Intelligence," July 23, 1970. Haldeman's memo conveying Nixon's approval of the Houston plan is Haldeman to Huston, "Domestic Intelligence Review," July 14, 1970. Huston's plan was formally titled "Domestic Intelligence Gathering Plan: Analysis and Strategy" and was conveyed to Haldeman by Huston in July 1970. The illegal tactics are included in the accompanying section, "Operational Restrictions on Intelligence Collection." These documents can be found, along with Huston's testimony to the Church Committee, in the published transcript of hearings, Senate Select Committee to Study Governmental Operations with Respect to Intelligence Activities, Sept. 23, 1975. See also SSC, final report and Richard Helms OH, CIA.

415 Election Day results: Author interview, Richard Goodwin; oral histories by Dean,

Cannon, Huston, and Price, RNL; HRH diary, Oct. 29, 31, Nov. 2, 1970; Keogh to Nixon, Nov. 13, 1970, WHSF-RC; Buchanan to Nixon, May 21, 1970, RNL; Keyes to Haldeman, Nov. 4, 1970, WHSF-RC; Harlow to Nixon, Nov. 1970, WHSF-RC; Ehrlichman to Haldeman, Nov. 18, 1970, WHSF-RC; Price to Haldeman, May 28, 1970, with speechwriters' draft of letter on Smith College graduation, WHSF-RC; Buchanan to Haldeman, Nov. 18, 1970, WHSF-RC; Nixon via Buchanan to Agnew and Harlow, Sept. 26, 1970, WHSF-RC; Sears to Haldeman, Dec. 9, 1970, WHSF-RC; Harlow to Brown, June 2, 1970; Timmons to Chapin, July 6, 1970; Buchanan, relaying Nixon's instructions, to Harlow and Agnew, Sept. 26, 1970; Nixon to Haldeman, Nov. 22, 1970, Ehrlichman to Haldeman, Apr. 15, 1970, Magruder to Haldeman, Apr. 24, 1970, Odle to Amis et al., Oct. 30, 1970, with attached Keogh statement on San Jose incident, Moynihan to Nixon, Nov. 13, 1970, Nixon to Haldeman, Dec. 11, 1970, Timmons to Nixon, Apr. 1, 1971, Huston to Nixon, Nov. 13, 1970, RNL; White House tapes, Nixon, Kissinger, et al., June 23, 1971, Nixon and Haldeman, July 6, 1971, Nixon and Ehrlichman, Sept. 8, 1971, Nixon and Buchanan, Sept. 22, 1971, Nixon and Colson, June 13, 1972, RNL; Haldeman to Bull, Chapin, and Walker, 1970, WHSF-RC; Frost-Nixon transcripts, RNL; Safire, "Nixon Diary," Sept. 9, 1970, Safire papers, LOC; Nixon June 3, 1970, and Oct. 31, 1970, addresses, PPP; Ehrlichman notes, "Agnew: Nov. 1, 1970," HI; Andy Logan, Around City Hall, *New Yorker*, June 6, 1970; John A. Farrell, *Tip O'Neill and the Democratic Century* (New York: Little, Brown, 2001); *Time*, Sept. 21, 1970; Agnew "dividing" speech, *WP*, Oct 6, 1971, cited in James Sundquist, *Dynamics of the Party System* (Washington, D.C.: Brookings Institution, 1983).

CHAPTER 22: THE ROAD TO WATERGATE

416   Tricia's wedding: White House tape, Nixon telephone calls with Rose Mary Woods, June 12, 1971, and Ron Ziegler, June 13, 1971, RNL; *NYT*, June 13, 1971; Tricia Nixon diary entry in Nixon, *RN*. Among those looking on was Alice Roosevelt Longworth, eighty-seven, who had been married in the East Room in 1906. At one level Nixon was happy, at another he chafed at having to perform. "I get a lot of advice on PR and personality and how I've got to put on my nice-guy hat and dance at the White House, so I did it," Nixon told his cabinet on June 29. "But let me make it clear that's not my nature." HRH diary, June 29, 1971, RNL.

417   "Women all want to see the damn thing": White House tape, Nixon telephone call with Haldeman, June 14, 1971, RNL.

417   "run for the hills": White House tape recording, Nixon telephone call with George Shultz, June 14, 1971 RNL; Higby to Chapin, June 25, 1971, RNL; for White House worries, see Sears to Haldeman, Dec. 9, 1970, and Dec. 28, 1971, WHSF-RC; Nixon, *RN; NYT*, June 13, 14, 1971.

417   raged, sequentially, about his enemies: White House tape, Nixon and Haldeman, June 12, 1971, RNL. Nixon also analyzed his daughters as political performers. "Tricia's got the right theory, and it's quite different from Julie's, but each does damn well," he said. "Julie believes in being outgoing, kind and sweet to everybody.... She's a kind person.... Tricia, on the other hand, believes in mystery.... With me, frankly, I'm more on the Tricia side." *New Yorker*, Nov. 14, 1970, May 1, 1971.

418   three transformative initiatives: White House tape, Nixon and Kissinger, June 4, 1971, RNL; Kissinger, *White House Years*.

419   "devastating security breach": White House tape recording, Nixon and Haig, June 13, 1971, RNL.

419   summa cum laude graduate of Harvard: Ellsberg, oral history, RNL; Ellsberg conversation with author and remarks at symposium, "The Lessons of Watergate," Mar. 13, 2013; *NYT*, June 13, 14, 15, 1971.

421   worked himself into a frenzy: Garment interview with author; White House tapes, Nixon and Haig, June 13, 1971, Nixon and Kissinger, June 13, 1971, RNL; Colson to Haldeman, July 12, 1971, WHSF-RC; HRH diary, June 13, 1971. Haldeman was prescient; on Tuesday night he wrote in his diary of the danger that "we're going to be tied into it and get blamed for the same kind of deception that was practiced by the Johnson administration."

421   Nixon's foes were legion: Nixon acknowledged to aides that the arrest tactics were "not legal" but dismissed those arrested as "a bunch of dope addicts and the rest." See White House tape recordings, Nixon telephone calls with Kissinger and with Haldeman, June 1, 1971. The detainees would later win a class-action lawsuit against the government. See "The President's News Conference," June 1, 1971, PPP.

      Nixon, remembering the disastrous routing of the Bonus Army by Herbert Hoover in 1932, had the authorities treat the veterans gently. But behind the scenes, after identifying VVAW leader John Kerry's political promise, the White House launched a clandestine effort to discredit the young navy veteran. Kerry would go on to serve as a U.S. senator from Massachusetts, the 2004 Democratic presidential nominee, and secretary of state. Kerry, interview with author; *Boston Globe*, June 17, 2003; White House tape recordings, Nixon and Colson, Apr. 20, 1971, Nixon and Dean, Apr. 21, 1971, Nixon and Colson, Apr. 22, 1971, Nixon and Haldeman and Kissinger, Apr. 23, 1971, Nixon and Rainwater, Apr. 23, 1971, Nixon and Colson, Apr. 28, 1971, Nixon and Haldeman, June 2, 1971, Nixon and Colson, June 4, 1971, RNL.

      In his conversation with Haldeman about enlisting the Teamsters to smash noses, Nixon railed about Jews and singled out yippie leader Abbie Hoffman. Two days earlier, Hoffman had been beaten, and his nose broken, during the protests, by unknown assailants. No arrests were made. See *Chicago Tribune*, May 7, 1971; *NYT*, Sept. 24, 1981; FBI FOIA file, Abbott Hoffman.

      See White House tapes, Nixon, Haldeman, and Kissinger, Apr. 23, 1971, Nixon and Woods, Apr. 27, 1971, Nixon and Agnew, Apr. 27, 1971, Nixon and Haldeman, May 5, 1971, RNL; see also Buchanan to Haldeman, Apr. 21, 1971, and Colson to Shumway, June 15, 1971, in *From: The President*, ed. Bruce Oudes (New York: Harper & Row, 1989); Tom Wells, *The War Within* (Berkeley: University of California Press, 1994); *New Yorker*, Nov. 14, 1970, May 1, 1971.

422   "a little bit of the totalitarian": NSA, *American Cryptology during the Cold War*, National Security Archive, 2013; Bruce Ragsdale, "The Chicago Seven: 1960s Radicals in the Federal Courts," Federal Judicial Center, 2008; John Le Carré, *Smiley's People* (New York: Knopf, 1979); John Lewis Gaddis, *George F. Kennan* (New York: Penguin, 2011); Jon Wiener, *Gimme Some Truth* (Berkeley: University of California Press, 2000); PBS, *The American Experience*, "My Lai," 2010; Senate Select Committee to Study Governmental Operations with Respect to Intelligence Activities, 1975–76 (Church Committee hearings and report).

422   "We were obsessed with secrecy": Nixon grand jury testimony, June 24, 1975, NARA; White House tapes, Nixon and Kissinger, June 13, 1971, Nixon and Haldeman, June 14, 1971, Nixon and Colson, June 15, 1971, Nixon and Haldeman, June 16, 1971, Nixon and Kissinger, Ehrlichman and Haldeman, June 17, 1971, RNL. Haldeman had gotten the "gobbledygook" theory from Donald Rumsfeld on Monday morning, June 14, 1971. See also Colson affidavit, Apr. 29, 1974, *US v. Ehrlichman*. During that first week, Nixon and his aides were advised that a set of the Pentagon Papers had been delivered to the Soviets, but when the White House checked, the CIA scoffed at the report. See David Young Memorandum of Conversation, HJC, Book 4, July 21, 1971, and Ehrlichman diary, June 1971, Ehrlichman papers, HI; Lord OH, FD; Charles Colson address, Hofstra; Nixon-Gannon.

423   not limited to military history: White House tape, Nixon and Kissinger, June 15,

1971, RNL. Nixon also expressed his concern about exposure of the secret bombing in a conversation with Kissinger on June 13, and in one with Haldeman on Monday, June 14.

423 cellar of the presidential psyche: White House tapes, all in RNL: Nixon and Ehrlichman, June 14, 1971; Nixon, Mitchell, and Kissinger, June 14, 1971; Nixon, Rogers, and Haig, June 14, 1971; Nixon and Mitchell, June 15, 1971; Nixon and Colson, June 15, 1971 ("What the Times has done is placed itself above the law," said Nixon. "They say . . . 'We consider this an immoral law, it's our responsibility to print it.' Now, goddamn it, you can't have that . . . in a free country"); Nixon and Haldeman, June 15, 1971; Nixon and Colson, June 17, 1971.

424 "the wicket of suppression": HRH diary, June 24, 1971; White House tapes, Nixon and Haldeman, June 17, 1971, Nixon and Mitchell, Ehrlichman, Haldeman, and Ziegler, June 22, 1971, Colson OH, RNL; Colson to Haldeman, June 25, 1971, HJC, III. Nixon toyed with the idea of arguing the case before the Supreme Court himself. Perhaps he should have. The Supreme Court decision is *New York Times Co. v. United States,* 403 U.S. 713 (1971). See *The Day the Presses Stopped,* David Rudenstine (University of California, 1996) for analysis of the legal arguments and the ruling, and the websites of the Miller Center, at the University of Virginia, and the National Security Archive for analysis of the White House tapes that week. Also helpful are Ellsberg's oral history at the RNL; his memoir, *Secrets;* and *Inside the Pentagon Papers* by John Prados and Margaret Pratt Porter (University Press of Kansas, 2004).

425 A swarm beset him: Ehrlichman interview, Tom Wicker Papers, University of North Carolina; H. R. Haldeman, *The Ends of Power* (New York: Times Books, 1978); John Ehrlichman, *Witness to Power* (New York: Simon & Schuster, 1982); White House tapes, Nixon, Kissinger, Haldeman, and Ehrlichman, June 17, 1971, Nixon and Haldeman, June 18, 1971, RNL; Haldeman OH, RNL. Later in the June 17 conversation, Nixon qualified his charge that Kennedy "ordered the murder" of Diem. "He ordered the coup," Nixon said, "and he set in motion the train of events that any reasonable man knew would lead to murder." Kissinger, the courtier, agreed: "Without any doubt whatever."

425 "implemented on a thievery basis": White House tapes, Nixon and Ehrlichman, Haldeman and Kissinger, June 17, 1971, Nixon and Haldeman, June 24, 1971, RNL; see also Haldeman, *Ends of Power.*

425 start a fire at Brookings: SSC, final report and executive session, Mar. 23, 1974; Dean OH, Krogh OH, Colson OH, White House tapes, Nixon, Kissinger, and Haig, July 1, 1971, RNL. See also Ehrlichman, *Witness to Power* and John Dean, *Blind Ambition* (New York: Simon & Schuster, 1976).

426 Nixon's latent anti-Semitism: The Jews were "born spies," Nixon told Haldeman, but rarely were blacks involved in espionage. "There are damn few Negro spies," said Nixon. "Not smart enough," Haldeman suggested. "It may be," said Nixon. White House tapes, Nixon and Haldeman, July 3, 1971, Nixon and Haldeman and Ziegler, July 5, 1971, Nixon, Haldeman, and Ehrlichman, July 24, 1971, Nixon, Haldeman, Mitchell, Ehrlichman, and Ziegler, June 22, 1971, RNL.

In September, hearing from evangelist Billy Graham that he was being audited by the IRS, Nixon launched into another anti-Semitic rant. "Bob, please get me the names of the Jews, you know, the big Jewish contributors of the Democrats. . . . Could we please investigate some of the cocksuckers? . . . They've gone after Abplanalp. They've gone after Rebozo. They've gone after John Wayne. . . ." And, the next day: "IRS is full of Jews, Bob. . . . I think that's the reason they are after Graham, is the rich Jews." White House tapes, Nixon and Haldeman, Sept. 13, 1971, Nixon, Haldeman, and Colson, Sept. 14, 1971, RNL.

The tapes also reveal Nixon and Graham sharing their alarm about Jewish influence in America in deplorably ignorant private conversations. See White House tapes, Nixon and Graham, Feb. 1, 1972, Feb. 21, 1973, Miller Center transcript, UVA.

The Jews on Nixon's staff—Burns, Kissinger, and Garment, for example—did not hear these ugly rants or, when informed of them, gave balanced responses. "In my presence Nixon never made a derogatory comment on Jews. I don't think he is an anti-Semite. But there are vulgar strands of thought in his psyche," Burns told Bob Woodward after Nixon's resignation. "Nixon did not have much love for humanity. So why should he love Jews any more than Japanese or Italians or Catholics? He found epithets for large sections of mankind. He had great admiration for the Israelis. He admired their energy and enterprise and patriotism. On the other hand, if Jews or Israel stood in his way he'd be ready to destroy all of them."

At one meeting, when Nixon was told of political difficulties the White House was facing with the Jewish community, "his eyes glazed when he talked of the anti-Semitism that might descend on the Jews of this country if they persisted," Burns said. "He was clearly not an anti-Semite, but they might be destroyed because they were standing in his way. . . . The awful thought ran through my mind: Will he stop at anything?" Burns said that he and Kissinger often discussed this. "Kissinger never liked him," said Burns. "That's where Kissinger and I differed. He never liked him and he never trusted him." Halfway into Watergate, "Kissinger felt very strongly Nixon had to go." See Burns interview, WB.

The rumors of Nixon's anti-Semitism go back to his earliest campaigns. They persisted and were prevalent enough to disturb Dwight Eisenhower. "I have been repeatedly told by different people that Dick Nixon will be unable to obtain any significant portion of the Jewish vote," Eisenhower wrote Hollywood producer Sam Goldwyn in the spring of 1960. "Time and again I have asked for an explanation, and the only one I get is that they 'hate him.'" See Eisenhower to Goldwyn, Mar. 25, 1960, DDE.

For reports of anti-Semitism see Ehrlichman OH, Nixon to Chotiner, Dec. 12, 1949, Smith to Brennan, Chotiner, and Arnold, Oct. 26, 1950, Chotiner to Silberberg, July 25, 1952, Bewley to Chotiner, Aug. 1, 1952, Becker to Chotiner, Aug. 13, 1952, Nixon to Pacht, Aug. 20, 1952, Chotiner to Faries, Oct. 8, 1952, Black to Nixon, Nov. 10, 1952 ("There are rumors abroad in every level of Jewish society to the effect that you were anti-Semitic"), RNL; Nixon to Black, Dec. 8, 1952, Knoop to Nixon, May 24, 1956, Greenman to Nixon, July 19, 1956, Nixon to Greenman, July 20, 1956, Robinson to Finch, May 19, 1959, RNL; campaign statement from Rabbi Abba Hillel Silver, Oct. 27, 1960, defending Nixon, WHSF-R; Hauser to Finch, undated ("There is a presumption among many Jews that Nixon holds this feeling"), 1960 campaign, WHSF-R; *WP*, Dec. 11, 1996; *LAT*, Mar. 22, 1997; *NYT*, Dec. 10, 2010.

426   "couldn't get into our golf clubs": On June 21, 1971, the Supreme Court had declined to hear the case *MacDonald v. Shawnee Country Club*, in which the club's exclusion of Jews was at issue. That appears to be the case that Mitchell referred to.

426   "Leak it": White House tapes, Nixon and Haldeman, June 16, 1971, Nixon and Agnew, June 22, 1971, RNL. "I think they'll come up with Kennedy," said Agnew. "I think so too," said Nixon.

The president also suggested that Mitchell discredit Ellsberg by leaking testimony from a federal grand jury, a practice that could land the attorney general behind bars. See White House tape, Nixon, Haldeman, Mitchell, Ehrlichman, and Ziegler, June 22, 1971, RNL: "If I'm going to jail I want to go in a hurry," Mitchell joked, "so I might get a pardon."

Haldeman's diary of June 16, 1971, offers a cautionary lesson about the commercially published version, which omits his account of Nixon's intent to leak the Kennedy material. Wills, "Richard Nixon's Seventh Crisis," *NYT,* July 8, 1973; Nixon, *Six Crises.*

427   "They are using any means": White House tapes, Nixon and Haldeman, June 22, 1971, Nixon, Haldeman, and Kissinger, July 1, 1971, RNL; HRH diary, June 22, 1971; Ehrlichman to Nixon, Oct. 7, 1971, RNL.

427   retired CIA agent named Howard Hunt: The "fabrication was intended to alienate the Catholic vote" if Ted Kennedy ran in 1972 by framing John F. Kennedy with the murder of a Catholic chief of state, Hunt would testify. SSC, final report and hearing, Sept. 24, 1973.

427   "Convict the son of a bitch": White House tapes, Nixon, Haldeman, Colson, and Ehrlichman, July 1, 1971, Nixon and Mitchell, June 29, 1971, RNL; SSC, hearing, July 26, 1973; see also Ehrlichman, affidavit, Apr. 30, 1974, *US v. Ehrlichman.*

427   They called themselves the Plumbers: Nixon, May 22, 1973, televised address; Dean OH, Colson OH, RNL. See also Krogh affidavit, May 4, 1973, Krogh testimony, Jan. 11, 1973 to Senate Commerce Committee, Krogh and Young to Ehrlichman, July 30, 1971, HJC, and Ehrlichman diary, July 15, 1971, HI. Buchanan was offered the job of leading the Plumbers and wisely turned it down as "a waste of my time and my abilities."

427   "tough guys" like Hunt and Liddy: Ray Price, in his memoir *With Nixon* (Viking, 1977), wrote: "The President's 'dark side' came to be personified, to many of us, by . . . Colson." White House tapes, Nixon, Haldeman, Kissinger, and Ehrlichman, June 23, 1971, RNL. In his memoir *White House Years,* Kissinger wrote, "I was not aware of . . . steps later taken, the sordidness, puerility and ineffectuality of which eventually led to the downfall of the Nixon Administration." For "dead mouse," see Richard Ben-Veniste, "Watergate at 40," June 11, 2012. For the gardener's raise, see Strachan to Haldeman, "Political Matters," Feb. 16, 1972, HJC, and for the campaign song, slogan, lapel pins, and other minutiae, see campaign strategy memos, July 1972, WHSF-C.

428   a plan to discredit Ellsberg: A July 28 memo from Hunt to Colson includes the plan to collect "overt, covert and derogatory information" to "destroy his [Ellsberg's] public image and credibility." In an August 11 memo, Young and Krogh propose to Ehrlichman that the Plumbers launch "a covert operation . . . to examine all the medical files still held by Ellsberg's psychoanalyst." Ehrlichman initialed his approval "if done under your assurance it is not traceable." In an exchange of memos on August 26 and 27, Young, Ehrlichman, and Colson then discussed how best to use the fruits of "Hunt/Liddy Special Project #1" in "the damaging of Ellsberg's image and those associated with him." The doctor's files may have revealed the names of Ellsberg's confederates, as well as his foibles. The documents are available in the SSC record and cited in the SSC report. See also Helms OH, CIA.

429   wannabe James Bonds: Liddy deposition, *Dean v. St. Martin's Press,* Dec. 6, 1996. Among their many limitations, Hunt and Liddy failed to learn from mistakes. They presumed that the security at Dr. Fielding's office building would be lax and that they could slip in unnoticed. As would happen again at the Watergate, their clumsiness alerted a guard, who surprised them by locking the doors.

429   "We had one little operation": White House tape, Nixon and Ehrlichman, Sept. 8, 1971, RNL. The "impetus" for the burglary at Fielding's office came from the Oval Office, Krogh recalled. But at a meeting in San Clemente after Nixon's resignation, Krogh told Nixon that he did not believe the president specifically authorized the actual break-in. Nixon "was always a little unclear . . . which break-ins he did authorize," Krogh said. Nixon, no doubt worrying that some contrary evidence would surface to contradict him, always declined to give an unqualified denial that he had known of the Fielding operation in advance. If he did know, Nixon said in his memoirs, he

would have approved it because Ellsberg was a threat to national security. See Krogh OH, RNL. For Ehrlichman recounting of the episode, see his SSC testimony and the SSC report.

430 "that bunch of jackasses": White House tapes, Nixon and Ziegler, Apr. 27, 1973, Nixon and Ziegler, May 21, 1973, Dean OH, RNL.

431 "more use of wiretapping": White House tape, Nixon and Haldeman, May 28, 1971, RNL. See also Haldeman to Strachan, Apr. 22, 1971, RNL, in which Haldeman reports, after meeting with Mitchell, that "we need to do a better job of coordinating infiltration activities, polling, intelligence, etc. You and Magruder should get to work on this and perhaps there should be a meeting with Mitchell and me and the two of you and some others." On May 20, 1971—more than a year before the Watergate break-in, and just a few weeks after Haldeman's memo to Strachan—Magruder wrote to the attorney general, reporting how spies had been sent to every rival campaign headquarters, to map the layout of the offices, the security measures, and the locations of each telephone. See Magruder to Mitchell, May 20, 1971, WHSF-RC.

431 hip deep in sabotage and surveillance: SSC, final report. Nixon joined in the planning and was kept informed about many of the dirty campaign tricks. See, for example, White House tapes, Nixon and Colson, Dec. 23, 1971 (New Hampshire write-in campaign), Nixon and Colson, Nov. 3, 1971 (Hunt and the Cubans), Nixon and Haldeman, Sept. 18, 1971 (enemies and the IRS), Nixon and Haldeman, May 28, 1971 (Chapman's friend), Nixon and Haldeman, May 5, 1971 (Segretti's network), RNL; HRH diary, Dec. 5, 1970; White House tapes, Nixon, Haldeman, and Ziegler, Apr. 9, 1971, Chotiner to Dent and Ehrlichman, Aug. 22, 1969, Chotiner to Mitchell, May 17, 1971, and Nov. 8, 1971, Strachan to Haldeman, Nov. 10, 1971, Magruder to Howard, June 14, 1972, Strachan notes, May 17, June 3, 1971, RNL; Strachan to file, Nov. 5, 1971, WHSF-RC; Dean OH, Magruder OH, Butterfield OH, RNL; Strachan, "Political Matters Memoranda," HJC; Chotiner interview, FBI, June 1973, Watergate files, FBI.

432 "this rinky-dink crap": Nixon was furious when Chapin was nailed by the press for his role in Segretti's pranks. "They excused the Dick Tuck and other operations as being just good clean fun, but where we are doing it it is grim and vicious espionage and sabotage of the worst type," he wrote in his diary. See Nixon diary, Oct. 15, 1972, in Nixon, *RN*. Chapin oral history, RNL; White House tape, Nixon and Haldeman, May 5, 1971, RNL; Strachan "Political Matters Memoranda," HJC; SSC, final report.

432 Wallace: Dan T. Carter, *The Politics of Rage* (New York: Simon & Schuster, 1995); Shultz, interview with author; affidavits, Johnnie Walters; Haldeman talking points, HJC; Haldeman notes, June 23, 1971; telcon transcript, Aug. 29, 1972, Ehrlichman conversation with Shultz and Walters; White House tapes, Nixon, Haldeman, and Ehrlichman, May 13, 1971, Mollenhoff to Haldeman, Apr. 1, 1970, RNL; Dent to Haldeman, Feb. 24, 1970, WHSF-RC; Ehrlichman notes, Aug. 3, 1972, Dec. 7, 1972, HI. Nixon believed that the Kennedy brothers had used the IRS to harass him, and to have his taxes audited, in the early 1960s. As president, he repeatedly urged his aides to employ such tactics against Democratic Party chairman Lawrence O'Brien, scores of Democratic leaders, liberal donors, and celebrities, journalists, and other political "enemies." Despite the sometimes intense White House pressure, Treasury Secretary George Shultz and IRS Commissioner Johnnie Walters resisted.

433 project called "Gemstone": In a memo to Haldeman, Strachan complained that Dean was insufficiently enthusiastic about the dirty tricks assignments. "All political surveillance from the EMK tail to Sandwedge is just where it was two months ago—non-productive," Strachan wrote. "Dean should get mentally out of the clean 'in house counsel' job and into the knees and elbows part of the campaign. . . . He should han-

dle . . . the political surveillance with a vengeance, and the down and dirty tricks with dispatch." See Strachan to Haldeman, Sept. 30, 1971, WHSF-C.

In April 1973 Magruder and his lawyers met with Ehrlichman, and Magruder gave a full account of the events leading up to the Watergate break-in.

Gordon Liddy's memoir, *Will* (St. Martin's Press, 1976), contains details not found elsewhere, including his fondness for self-mutilation and Nazi nomenclature and an elaborate account of the January 27 meeting with Mitchell, Dean, and Magruder. At one point, Liddy says, he promised to recruit hit men to handle demonstrators at the Republican convention. "These men include professional killers who have accounted between them for 22 dead so far, including two hanged from a beam in a garage," Liddy told them. "And where did you find men like that?" Mitchell is said to have asked. Organized crime, Liddy told him, and they didn't come cheap. "Well, let's not contribute any more than we have to to the coffers of organized crime," Mitchell replied. It was the closest he came to a rebuke. To the Senate Watergate Committee, Mitchell later lamented: "I should have thrown him out of the window."

In his famous "cancer on the presidency" conversation with Nixon, Dean explained that Liddy rose because Caulfield failed to win Mitchell's confidence. "Uh, in retrospect, that might have been a bad call, cause [Caulfield] is an incredibly cautious person and, and wouldn't have put the situation where it is today," Dean told Nixon. White House tape, Nixon and Dean, Mar. 21, 1973, Dean, Magruder OH, RNL; Dean to Haldeman, Feb. 7, 1972, WHSF-RC; Strachan, "Political Matters Memoranda," HJC; Liddy deposition, *Dean v. St. Martin's Press.*

434 Nixon's wily old pal: "As he got older he began reading his press clippings," Nixon told David Frost about Hoover's sensitivity to public relations (see Frost-Nixon transcripts, RNL). Nixon also expressed his desire for more domestic wiretapping and complained about Hoover's reluctance at a June 5, 1971, meeting of the President's Foreign Intelligence Advisory Board, RNL.

"We wanted to make the president happy": "I do not believe that Nixon did order the break in. Nor that he even knew about it," Haldeman would conclude. "But I do believe he caused it." See Haldeman OH, RNL.

"The President always wants something done and we got into this mess because people reacted," Kissinger said (see telcon, Kissinger and Laird, June 28, 1973, RNL). "We knew the president wanted as much information as we could get. And the more information he got the happier he was. We wanted to make the president happy," said Magruder (see Magruder OH, RNL). Nixon "indicated certain wishes in broad general language," Leon Jaworksi said. "And the specifics were worked out by subordinates" (see Jaworski interview, WB).

See also oral histories by Haldeman, Huston, Krogh, Garment, and Magruder, RNL; Huston to Haldeman, "Domestic Intelligence Review," June 16, 1970, Liddy to Krogh, Oct. 22, 1971, "The Directorship of the FBI," RNL. For double standard see Moynihan to Nixon, Mar. 8, 1971, cited in Stephen Ambrose, *Nixon*, vol. 2, *The Triumph of a Politician* (New York: Simon & Schuster, 1989); Moynihan interview, *Playboy*, Mar. 1977; Garment, Stanley Kutler interviews with author; Tom Hayden, Bob Haldeman discussions, Hofstra University, reprinted in Leon Friedman and William Levantrosser, *Watergate and Afterward: The Legacy of Richard M. Nixon* (Westport, CT: Greenwood Press, 1992).

CHAPTER 23: THE WEEK THAT CHANGED THE WORLD

435 Nixon went to China: "Think of what could happen if anybody with a decent system of government got control of that mainland. Good God," Nixon told Walter McConaughy, the American ambassador to Taiwan. "You put 800 million Chinese to work under a decent system and they will be the leaders of the world." White House

tapes, Nixon and McConaughy, June 30, 1971, Nixon and Kissinger, Apr. 21, 1971, RNL.

Nixon to Aitken, May 29, 1991; White House tape recording, Nixon, Kissinger and Rush, June 14, 1971 ("Everything is linked"), RNL; William Kintner and Robert Pfaltzgraff, *SALT: Implications for Arms Control in the 1970s* (Pittsburgh: University of Pittsburgh, 1973); Nixon, "Remarks to Midwestern News Media Executives Attending a Briefing on Domestic Policy," July 6, 1971, PPP; Kissinger to Nixon, "My Talks with Chou En-Lai," July 14, 1971, University of Southern California.

436 diplomatic breakthrough: Roger Sullivan, a U.S. diplomat in Singapore, Singapore prime minister Lee Kuan Yew, Romanian president Nicolae Ceausescu, Chester Bowles, then the U.S. ambassador to India, and Pakistani leader Ayub Khan remembered similar conversations with Nixon when he toured Asia in 1965 and 1967. Nixon to Bishop, Jan. 28, 1964, and Bishop to Nixon, Feb. 6, 14, 1964, RNL; Marshall Green OH, Strober; Green interview, "Cold War," NSA; Green OH, FD; *Foreign Affairs*, Oct. 1967; Chris Tudda, *A Cold War Turning Point* (Baton Rouge: Louisiana State University Press, 2012); James Mann, *About Face* (New York: Knopf, 1999). Nixon offered a similarly insightful tour d'horizon to his staff on June 21, 1971—see Safire notes on "productivity" meeting, Safire papers, LOC.

438 "exploring rapprochement with the Chinese": Tudda interview with author; Nixon to Kissinger, Feb. 1, 1969, Frost-Nixon transcripts, NSC files, "Files for the President," China material, RNL; telcons, Sneider and Kissinger, Jan. 27, Feb. 4, 1969, Kissinger and Mansfield, July 18, 1969, Kissinger and Nixon, Dec. 11, 1969, RNL; *Time*, Oct. 5, 1970; FRUS, 1969–1976, Vol. 17, China, 1969–1972, Vol. 41, Western Europe, NATO, 1969–1972; Vol. E-13, Documents on China, 1969–1972; Nixon interview, Mar. 12, 1968, White papers, Harvard; Winston Lord OH, FD; Safire, "Nixon Diary," Aug. 18, 1969, Safire papers, LOC; Jing Zhicheng, Henry Kissinger interviews, *Nixon's China Game*, PBS; Winston Lord remarks, U.S. Department of State, Office of the Historian, *Transforming the Cold War: The United States and China, 1969–1980*; Tudda, *Turning Point*; Henry Kissinger, *White House Years* (Boston: Little, Brown, 1979); Nixon, *RN*; Alexander Haig, *Inner Circles* (New York: Warner, 1992); Patrick Tyler, *A Great Wall* (New York: PublicAffairs, 1999); Monica Crowley, *Nixon in Winter* (New York: Random House, 1998); Thomas Robinson, "The Sino-Soviet Border Dispute: Background, Development, and the Mar. 1969 Clashes," *American Political Science Review*, Dec. 1972; Chen Jian and David Wilson, "All Under the Heaven Is Great Chaos," *Cold War International History Project*, Bulletin 11, Winter 1998.

The National Security Archive, from 1999 to 2003, published a series of "briefing books" and articles on the Nixon administration rapprochement with China, putting many key documents on the Internet, including the Aug. 18, 1969, memcon from the State Department's William Stearman to his superiors, outlining the Soviet proposal that the United States join the Soviet Union in an attack on China's nuclear weapons facilities. (See "The Sino-Soviet Border Conflict, 1969: U.S. Reactions and Diplomatic Maneuvers," June 12, 2001, NSA.) The FRUS volumes are another rich online source, as are the articles, documents, and film clips at the University of Southern California's U.S.-China Institute.

The China initiative was Nixon's, but while he sometimes bridled at Kissinger's grandstanding, he was generous in sharing credit. "Many of those who are fascinated by the Nixon-Kissinger relationship miss the point when they try to choose one or the other as the prime innovator of our foreign policy initiatives," Nixon wrote to scholar Robert Litwak in 1984. "The truth is that we moved on parallel courses prior to the time I became President and found that our views were similar when major decisions had to be made. For example, I had already determined to embark on the China initiative before I had met Kissinger. . . . I am sure that he was thinking along the same lines, but did not dream that with my reputation I would be willing to embark on such a bold course. He could not have been more delighted when I did so." See Nixon to Litwak, Aitken papers, RNL.

440 the stuff of thrillers . . . a touch of farce: Winston Lord OH, John Holdridge OH, FD; Kissinger, *White House Years;* Lord remarks, *Transforming the Cold War;* Kissinger interview, *Nixon's China Game.* A startled Secret Service agent, confronted by a Red Chinese welcoming committee aboard the jet (which included Mao's niece), was ready to shoot it out, Lord recalled. In his diary, Haldeman recounts how he and Nixon lied to cushion the blow to Rogers, telling him that Kissinger's trip was an unplanned event. And in his July 14 report to Nixon, Kissinger delighted in telling how the Chinese, having admitted James Reston of the *New York Times* to China, stuck him on a slow train from Canton until the secret talks were over.

441 only Nixon could go to China: Kissinger to Nixon, "My Talks with Chou-En-Lai," July 14, 1971, Alexander Haig OH, Polo 1 memorandum, China material, NSC files, RNL; Safire to Haldeman, Apr. 20, 1971, Safire papers, LOC; Kissinger interview, "Cold War," NSA; Lord OH, FD; Lord remarks, *Transforming the Cold War;* Kissinger, *White House Years.* Kissinger waxed poetic when describing his talks with Zhou: "One of the rewards of my public life has been that in a moment, however brief in the pitiless measurement of history, I could work with a great man across the barriers of ideology in the endless struggle of statesmen to rescue some permanence from the tenuousness of human foresight."

442 agreement on a summit: Kissinger to Nixon, "My Talks with Chou En-Lai," July 14, 1971, USC; Lord to Kissinger, "Memcon of your conversations with Chou En-lai," July 29, 1971, USC; HRH diary, July 10, 1971; Margaret MacMillan, *Nixon and Mao* (New York: Random House, 2007).

442 Perino's Restaurant on Wilshire Boulevard: Kissinger to Nixon, "My Talks . . . ," July 14, 1971, USC; HRH diary, July 13, 1971; Kissinger, *White House Years; WP,* July 16, 1971; John Scali interview, WB. In *Witness to Power,* Ehrlichman says that when the bill arrived he dickered the cost of the wine from $600 down to $300. It had been selected with much foofaraw by Nixon and Kissinger. "I had the feeling neither one knew what he was talking about," Ehrlichman recalled.

443 Americans were stunned: Mansfield, the Senate's Democratic leader and foremost expert on Asian affairs, said he was "astounded, delighted and happy," AP, July 15, 1971. White House tapes, Nixon and Kissinger, May 27, 1971, Nixon and Kissinger, Apr. 14, 1971; Buchanan to Nixon, Jan. 7, 1971, quoted in Richard Reeves, *President Nixon: Alone in the White House* (New York: Touchstone, 2002); Rusher in Strober and Strober, *The Nixon Presidency* (Washington, D.C.: Brassey's, 2003).

444 Taiwan was collateral damage: Nixon and Kissinger, wisely as it turned out, preached patience to the Taiwanese. "Many things can happen. You are under no pressure to settle. Mao could disappear. Zhou could disappear," Kissinger told Taiwan's crestfallen ambassador after Nixon's trip to China. "It would be a mistake for you to panic, or do anything rash." White House tape, Nixon, Kissinger, and Ambassador James Shen, Mar. 6, 1972. For fist metaphor, see White House tape, Nixon and Brandt, June 15, 1971, RNL.

445 "We cooled off the economy": White House tape, Nixon, Agnew, et al., June 18, 1971; 'Report of the Cabinet Committee on Economic Policy," Apr. 10, 1969, quoted in Allen Matusow, *Nixon's Economy* (Lawrence: University Press of Kansas, 1998). Matusow contends that gradualism was working, but that Burns and others missed its impact because of faulty forecasts and forecasting tools. Ehrlichman notes, "Economists," Nov. 19, 1970, HI; Richard Smyser remarks, *Transforming the Cold War.*

445 "His features became twisted": Arthur Burns, *Inside the Nixon Administration: The*

Secret Diary of Arthur Burns (Lawrence: University Press of Kansas, 2010), Mar. 8, Aug. 12, 1971, Jan. 8, 1974.

446   stagflation: Safire, "Nixon Diary," Camp David events, Aug. 1971, Safire papers, LOC; Burns, *Inside the Nixon Administration,* Nov. 23, 1970; William Safire, *Before the Fall* (New York: Doubleday, 1975); White House tape, Nixon, McCracken, and Shultz, Nov. 16, 1971; Luke A. Nichter, "Richard Nixon and Europe: Confrontation and Cooperation, 1969–1974," PhD dissertation, Bowling Green State University, 2008.

446   "close the gold window": FRUS, 1969–1976, Vol. 3, Foreign Economic Policy; FRUS, 1969–1976, Vol. 3, International Monetary Policy, 1969–1972; White House tape, Nixon, Haldeman, Ehrlichman, and Weinberger, June 8, 1971; see Nichter, "Richard Nixon and Europe."

447   conclave at Camp David: It was a Nixon maxim to let the act speak for its import: "Where action is so powerful, the words should be very brief." White House tape, Connally, Nixon, and Shultz, Aug. 12, 1971, Ehrlichman OH, RNL; White House tape, Nixon, Connally, Shultz, Peterson, and McKracken, July 22, 1971, RNL; Nichter, "Richard Nixon and Europe." The Democratic Congress in 1970 had given the president the power to impose temporary wage and price controls, and dared him to use them. For an early discussion between Nixon and Burns about stagflation and the need for controls, see Ehrlichman notes, Sept. 11, 1969, cited in Matusow, *Nixon's Economy.* For the day-by-day details of the Camp David meetings, see Safire's memoir and diary and HRH diary, Aug. 2 and 12–15, 1971. Burns quote from Safire, *Before the Fall.*

449   wage and price freeze: Author interview with Alan Greenspan; Burns, *Inside the Nixon Administration;* Kissinger, *White House Years;* Nichter, "Richard Nixon and Europe"; Nixon, Aug. 15, 1971, address on the New Economic Policy, PP; *Variety* headline from *NYT,* Aug. 22, 1971, and Friedman in *Newsweek,* Aug. 30, 1971, quoted in Matusow, *Nixon's Economy;* Kissinger and Peterson memo to Nixon, Sept. 20, 1971, from FRUS, 1969–1976, Vol. 3. "The country needs a psychological lift," Nixon told Connally in early August. "We've got to shake this country and say, 'Look, you people have got to get off your ass and go to work. We've got to be more competitive.'" White House tapes, Nixon and Connally, Aug. 2, 1971, Nixon, Burns, and Connally, Sept. 11, 1971, Shultz OH, RNL; Richard Cheney OH, GFF.

449   Inflation: The Great Inflation ravaged the American economy for more than a decade. The inflation rate rose from 1.07 percent in January 1965 to 13.70 percent in March 1980 before President Reagan and Fed chairman Volcker resolutely paid the price— the 1982 recession—to end it. See Allan Meltzer, "Origins of the Great Inflation," *Federal Reserve Bank of St. Louis Review,* Mar./Apr. 2005, and Shultz OH, RNL.

    For an accounting of the Fed's loose money policy, see Burton Abrams, "How Richard Nixon Pressured Arthur Burns: Evidence from the Nixon Tapes," *Journal of Economic Perspectives,* Fall 2006. The M1 supply grew by 4.5 percent in 1970, 6.8 percent in 1971, and just more than 7.5 percent annually in the first half of 1972, Abrams reports. The M2 grew even faster, hitting double digits in 1971 and 1972. At the same time, the Fed pared interest rates. The discount rate, at 6 percent in the beginning of 1970, was lowered to 4.5 percent for 1971 and 1972. The federal funds rate dropped by 4 percentage points from 1970 through the first half of 1972.

    See also Ehrlichman interview, "Cold War," NSA; James T. Patterson, *Restless Giant* (New York: Oxford University Press, 2005). The "Santino" analogy, of delayed but inevitable consequences, is from the film *The Godfather* (1972).

450   Moscow summit: White House tapes, Nixon, Kissinger, and Haig, June 29, 1971, Nixon, Haldeman, and Kissinger, Aug. 11, 1971, RNL.

450   Jimmy Hoffa's prison sentence: On Hoffa and Hoover, see Ehrlichman notes, "Hoover,"

Sept. 20, 1971, HI, and Strachan notes of Haldeman-Mitchell conversation, Dec. 8, 1971, RNL.

Nixon conducted a career-long flirtation with the Teamsters union and its tainted leadership that culminated during his presidency, when he and Charles Colson plotted to make organized labor part of a Nixonian "New Majority." The president courted AFL-CIO and Teamsters officials and, to please Hoffa supporters, commuted Hoffa's prison sentence in late 1971.

Nixon and Hoffa shared a common enemy in the Kennedys, and pardoning Hoffa fulfilled a debt Nixon owed to conservative New Hampshire publisher William Loeb, a Hoffa ally whose newspaper had survived on Teamster loans. In late 1969 Loeb responded to a White House request to support the Haynsworth nomination by griping in a letter to Nixon aide Harry Dent that "if it were not in the interest of the United States to have Haynsworth on the Supreme Court, I would tell you guys to go to hell because you have not done a damn thing for me in connection with my request regarding Mr. Hoffa." In his letter, Loeb claimed the credit for keeping Ronald Reagan out of the 1968 presidential race and accused Nixon of ingratitude. "If it had not been for my persuading . . . to keep Reagan out of New Hampshire," Loeb wrote, "Nixon would not have received the backing he did in New Hampshire and Reagan might have come close to beating him, and you fellows would not be in the White House now. But you show all the gratitude of a passel of rattlesnakes." See Loeb to Dent, Oct. 29, 1969, RNL.

For details of the early Hoffa-Nixon relationship, see Allen O. Hunter to Nixon, Dec. 21, 1959, Jan. 5, 1960, Hunter to Hoffa, Dec. 8, 1960, Hunter to Hillings, Oct. 14, 1968, Hunter to Mollenhoff, Jan. 22, 1970, RNL.

451   SELECTIVE GENOCIDE: Consul general Archer Blood oral history, FD. More than three weeks before the massacres began, NSC aides Harold Saunders and Samuel Hoskinson warned of the coming crisis, and in a March 1, 1971, memo to Kissinger framed the policy question: "How active should the U.S. be in trying to avoid bloodshed?" When the army crackdown began, Blood, who was in Dacca, reported the systematic extermination of separatist sympathizers. Among other such tactics, the army was setting fire to college dormitories and other buildings and mowing down unarmed men and women as they fled the flames. See the following in FRUS, 1969–1976, Vol. 11, South Asia Crisis, 1971, and companion volume FRUS, Vol. E-7, Documents on South Asia, 1969–1972: Blood telegrams, Mar. 28–30, 1971; "Telegram from the Embassy in Pakistan to the Department of State," Mar. 31, 1971; "Memorandum Prepared in the Office of National Estimates," CIA, Sept. 22, 1971. On Hindu persecution, see "Telegram from the Embassy in Pakistan to the Department of State," May 14, 1971, and memcon, Kissinger and Keating, June 3, 1971. See also Keating to Rogers, Mar. 29, 1971, NSA.

451   "we have no control": Minutes of Senior Review Group Meeting, Mar. 6, 1971. The group favored a policy of "massive inaction," and Nixon was so advised by Kissinger in a March 13, 1971, memo. When it came, on March 25, the crackdown caught Washington by surprise. "Yesterday it looked as though an agreement was in sight," Kissinger said at the emergency WSAG (Washington Special Actions Group) meeting. The State, Defense, and CIA advisers all agreed with Kissinger: "There is nothing we can do except evacuate our citizens." The United States did not want to be blamed for encouraging "the split-up of Pakistan," they concluded. See Minutes of Washington Special Actions Group Meeting, Mar. 26, 1971. Nixon agreed. "The main thing to do is to keep cool and not do anything," he told Kissinger. "There's nothing in it for us anyway." Kissinger telcon, Kissinger and Nixon, Mar. 30, 1971. All from FRUS, 1969–1976, Vols. 11 and E-7.

452   "charge of moral insensitivity": Blood oral history, FD; Hoskinson to Kissinger, Mar.

28, 1971, Blood telegrams from Dacca, Mar. 28–30, 1971, Kissinger telcon, Kissinger and Nixon, Mar. 28, 1971, Minutes of Senior Review Group Meeting, Apr. 9, 1971, FRUS, 1969–1976, Vols. 11 and E-7; Kissinger, *White House Years.* Blood was recalled to Washington and given an administrative job, his career in tatters. See White House tape, Farland, Kissinger, and Nixon, July 28, 1971, RNL. To his face, Nixon derided Keating as "brainwashed" by the Indians and privately resolved to force the "soft sonofabitch" out: see White House tapes, Kissinger, Keating, and Nixon, June 15, 1971, Kissinger and Nixon, Dec. 6, 1971, and telcon, Nixon and Kissinger, July 27, 1971, FRUS, 1969–1976, Vols. E-7 and 11. An argument for the moral imperative of American intervention in East Pakistan, and other cases of genocidal violence, is made by Gary J. Bass in *The Blood Telegram: Nixon, Kissinger, and a Forgotten Genocide* (New York: Knopf, 2013). On the need and potential effects of a Nixon protest, see Telegram from the Embassy in Pakistan to the Department of State, Apr. 6, 1971, and Special National Intelligence Estimate 32-71, CIA, Apr. 12, 1971. For the "tilt," see Minutes of Senior Review Group Meeting, July 30, 1971, Minutes of Washington Special Actions Group, Dec. 3, 1971, and White House tape, Nixon, Rogers, and Kissinger, Nov. 24, 1971, FRUS, 1969–1976, Vols. 11 and E-7.

453   "one blip in the battle": Kissinger telcon, Kissinger and Nixon, Mar. 29, 1971, RNL.
454   "Don't squeeze Yahya": Christopher Van Hollen OH, Harold Saunders OH, FD. In FRUS 1969–1976, Vols. 11 and E-7, see memcon, Kissinger and Farland, May 7, 1971; memo from Kissinger to Nixon, Apr. 28, 1971; telcon, Kissinger and Nixon, May 23, 1971; White House tape, Nixon, Kissinger, and Keating, June 15, 1971; Minutes of Senior Review Group Meeting, July 23, 1971.

Kissinger and Nixon recognized that Yahya was a thin thread on which to hang their breakthrough initiative. "I will, when I'm talking to the Chinese, set up a separate channel so that we're not so vulnerable," said Kissinger. "It just may be that the poor sonofabitch can't survive," Nixon agreed.

454   Nehru dynasty: White House tapes, Kissinger and Nixon, May 26, 1971, Kissinger and Nixon, June 4, 1971, Nixon and Kissinger, Dec. 6, 1971, RNL; memcon, Kissinger and Keating, June 3, 1971, Nixon notes, 1954 trip, RNL.

Nixon acknowledged his anti-Indian "bias" to his advisers. The Indians were "a slippery, treacherous people," he said. See memcon, Nixon, Rogers, and officials, July 16, 1971, RNL.

For Helms see Minutes of Senior Review Group Meeting, July 23, 1971, FRUS, 1969–1976, Vols. 11 and E-7; Kissinger, *White House Years.*

455   curtain for aggression: *NYT,* June 22, 1971. In FRUS, 1969–1976, Vol. 11, see Minutes of Senior Review Group Meeting, July 23, 1971; White House tape, Kissinger and Nixon, June 4, 1971; memcon, Nixon, Rogers and officials, July 16, 1971; Memorandum Prepared in the Office of National Estimates, CIA, Sept. 22, 1971 (as of that day it estimated the number of dead at 200,000 and the number of refugees at eight million).

456   "stilettos": White House tape, Nixon, Kissinger, and Haldeman, Nov. 5, 1971, FRUS, 1969–1976, Vol. E-7.

457   "a high possibility of disaster": In FRUS, 1969–1976, Vols. 11 and E-7, see Nixon to Brezhnev, Dec. 10, 1971; telcon, Nixon and Kissinger, Dec. 4, 1971; White House tapes, Nixon and Kissinger, Dec. 6, 1971, Nixon, Kissinger, and Mitchell, Dec. 8, 1971, Nixon and Kissinger, Dec. 8, 1971, Nixon and Kissinger, Dec. 9, 1971; CIA Intelligence Information Cable, Dec. 7, 1971. Not for the last time, the attorney general of the United States sat silent as a crime was proposed in his presence.

457   "lobbing nuclear weapons": White House tape, Nixon, Kissinger, and Haig, Dec. 12, 1971, FRUS, 1969–1976, Vol. 11; Dobrynin, *In Confidence.*

458   "ranted and raved": Safire, "Nixon Diary," Jan. 18, 1972, Safire papers, LOC; Burns

diary entry July 8, 1971, *Inside the Nixon Administration*. See Ehrlichman, *Witness to Power:* "Nixon wondered aloud if Henry needed psychiatric care," and he urged Ehrlichman to suggest it to Kissinger. For Kissinger tirades, see HRH diary, Dec. 7, 1971, through Jan. 15, 1972.

459 "a heroic act": Intelligence Information Cable, CIA, December 12, 1971, White House tape, Kissinger and Nixon, Dec. 12, 1971, FRUS, 1969–1976, Vol. E-7; Lord OH, FD, Christopher Van Hollen, "The Tilt Policy Revisited," in Lloyd and Susanne Hoeber Rudolph, *The Regional Imperative* (Atlantic Highlands, NJ: Humanities Press, 1980). In *White House Years*, Kissinger defended "the decision to risk war," contending that "history's assessment of Nixon ... must not overlook his courage and patriotism in making such a decision, at risk to his immediate political interest, to preserve the world balance of power for the ultimate safety of all free peoples."

Van Hollen dissented. "Contrary to his [Kissinger's] claims, the United States did not need to remain mute to the Pakistan Army's repressions in East Pakistan to protect the White House opening to China ... it was both unnecessary and unwise to raise the Bangladesh regional crisis to the level of global geopolitics. ... Kissinger is wrong in concluding that Nixon's willingness to risk war with the Soviet Union ... saved West Pakistan."

See also Nixon grand jury testimony, June 24, 1975, NARA.

459 Charles Radford: The liaison office had long been used as a Pentagon listening post: Laird told Ehrlichman that the Chiefs bartered information with Republicans in Congress during the Kennedy and Johnson years. See Dec. 23, 1971, transcript of Ehrlichman-Laird telephone call, RNL.

Nixon wanted to know if Radford was Jewish, then if he was gay. But Laird warned Ehrlichman that if the news got out that the White House was smearing Radford and Anderson it would be highly damaging. Radford was transferred to Oregon, where a tap was kept on his telephone. Anderson never admitted that Radford was his source, but when the columnist won the Pulitzer Prize for his columns on the "tilt," Radford called to congratulate him, as the FBI listened in.

See also Ehrlichman diary, Dec. 1971, and Ehrlichman notes, Jan. 5, 1972, Ehrlichman papers, HI; Ehrlichman OH, RNL; White House tapes, Haldeman, Ehrlichman, Mitchell, and Nixon, Dec. 21, 1971, Nixon, Mitchell, and Ehrlichman, Dec. 22, 1971, Nixon, Mitchell, and Ehrlichman, Dec. 23, 1971, Nixon, Ehrlichman, and Kissinger, Dec. 24, 1971, RNL; David R. Young, "Record of Investigation into Disclosure of Classified Information in Jack Anderson Articles December 14 and 16, 1971," undated (1972), "Unauthorized Disclosure of Classified Defense Information Appearing in the Jack Anderson Columns in the Washington Post dated December 14 and December 16, 1971," DOD, Dec. 20, 1971, telcon, Kissinger and Stennis, Jan. 28, 1974, RNL; see also Nixon grand jury testimony, June 24, 1975, NARA; James Rosen, "Nixon and the Chiefs," *Atlantic*, Apr. 2002.

460 Mao would receive them: FRUS, 1969–1976, Vol. 17, China, 1969–1972; Tudda, *Turning Point;* MacMillan, *Nixon and Mao;* Nixon, *RN*.

462 the trip played out on cue: Toasts of the President and Premier Chou En-lai of the People's Republic of China at a Banquet Honoring the President in Peking, Feb. 21, 1972, PPP. FRUS, 1969–1976, Vol. 17, China, 1969–1972; Colson memo to file, July 28, 1971, WHSF-RC; Julie Eisenhower remarks, "First Lady Pat Nixon: Ambassador of Goodwill," Pat Nixon centennial forum, Apr. 5, 2012, National Archives, Washington, D.C.; Henry Kissinger, Brent Scowcroft, Stapleton Roy remarks, "The Week That Changed The World," U.S. Institute of Peace and Richard Nixon Foundation conference, Mar. 7, 2012; Remarks, Hillary Rodham Clinton, Secretary of State, U.S. Institute of Peace, March 7, 2012, U.S. Department of State; HRH diary, Feb. 21–27, 1972; Green interview, "Cold War," NSA; Green OH, Lord OH, FD; *Time*, Mar. 6,

1972; Walter Lippmann interview, *New Republic,* Nov 1, 1971; Lord, *Transforming the Cold War;* MacMillan, *Nixon and Mao;* Tudda, *Turning Point;* Mann, *About Face; Nixon, RN.*

Nixon did believe he had changed the world, but as with most matters, his dark and cynical side would denigrate even this, his greatest achievement. "The China thing was important from one standpoint only—hope. The American people are suckers," he told Kissinger. "Getting to know you—all that bullshit. . . . the gray, middle America—they're suckers." See White House tape, Nixon and Kissinger, May 4, 1972, RNL.

CHAPTER 24: A THIRD-RATE BURGLARY

465 "As far as I was concerned, anything went": Liddy, *Will* (New York: St. Martin's Press, 1976). It was that very conviction—that individuals could make their own moral judgment and act above and beyond the law—that Nixon found objectionable and condemned in Daniel Ellsberg and other intellectuals.

 Liddy's code name for the Plumbers was ODESSA—which he borrowed from a secret Nazi group thought to have helped war criminals flee from justice after World War II. Robert Odle OH, RNL; Lord OH, FD.

466 "a little bit carried away": For Helms on Hunt, see SSC, Book 8. For Hart, see Hart OH, FD.

466 "good healthy right-wing exuberants": See White House tape, Colson and Nixon, Jan. 8, 1973, RNL; H. R. Haldeman, *The Ends of Power* (New York: Times Books, 1978). "I left the campaign committee under the actual direction of a young man whom I would never have considered qualified for that level of responsibility," Haldeman wrote of the "smooth-talking but weak" Magruder. "Because I just didn't want to be burdened with the additional responsibility for the campaign, I conveniently overlooked the problem."

 Given the ties that McCord, Hunt, and the other burglars had to the CIA, there were those—Republicans on the Senate Watergate committee, White House aides, and Nixon himself—who suspected that the CIA played a role in his downfall. The evidence of CIA involvement was like "animals crashing around in the forest," Senator Howard Baker said. It could be sensed, if not seen.

 It is possible—maybe likely—that the CIA was vexed by the cloak of secrecy cast by Nixon and Kissinger over foreign affairs and had spies like Hunt reporting what they heard at the White House. Spying is what spies do. There is evidence that Hunt sent envelopes (he said they were pension forms) back to Langley via a CIA liaison office at the National Security Council.

 There is evidence, as well, of a CIA cover-up—and of a cover-up of its cover-up. After the burglars were arrested, agency officials sought to hide its embarrassing links to McCord and Hunt. Tapes were wiped. Records were burned. And when some CIA personnel objected, their protests were buried in the files.

 And as Nixon operatives Hunt and McCord made such hideous blunders, it raised the question: Had they tried to get caught? They left proof of their identities everywhere—on banquet reservations, hotel bills, security logs, and long-distance telephone records. Once they were arrested, the trail led straight to the White House. To Nixon, Haldeman, and others, it looked like the break-in was purposefully botched.

 Yet from all the many Watergate probes, the FBI investigation, the CIA's internal reviews, and the work of the Rockefeller commission and the Church committee—substantive inquiries that unearthed assassination plots and other sins far more reprehensible than Watergate—no proof emerged that Hunt, McCord, or the others were out to sabotage the Nixon presidency.

 Who was the alternative: George McGovern? The CIA's director, Richard Helms, may have been a sleek Ivy League operative, a trait sure to raise Nixon's hackles, but the two deputy directors involved in the Watergate saga—Vernon Walters and Robert Cushman—were retired military officers and longtime Nixon admirers.

Occam's razor applies. Hunt and McCord were CIA has-beens. In their deterioration in the months after their arrests, they each displayed signs of instability. And many of their goofs—like those of Gordon Liddy—can be consigned to carelessness, stupidity, or venality, not a CIA conspiracy. See Metropolitan Police Department, Supplementary Evidence Report, June 20, 1972, HJC.

Hunt to Lakewood Country Club, see Metropolitan Police report, HJC. For the FBI's analysis of CIA involvement see Watergate Summary, July 5, 1974, Watergate files, FBI. See also House Committee on Armed Services, "Inquiry into the Alleged Involvement of the Central Intelligence Agency in the Watergate and Ellsberg Matters," Oct. 23, 1973, and "Minority Report on CIA Involvement," submitted at the request of Senator Howard H. Baker Jr.; SSC and related testimony including "CIA Employee Statement, January 17, 1974" and "CIA Employee Affidavit, May 18, 1973," HJC. See also Liddy deposition, *Dean v. St. Martin's Press*. For the minority staff's theories and inquiries see Fred Thompson, *At That Point in Time* (New York: Quadrangle/New York Times Books, 1975).

467   "throw the Battle Override": Liddy, *Will*.

467   ITT scandal: White House tape, Nixon and Kleindienst, Apr. 19, 1971, Haldeman and Nixon, May 5, 1971, Colson OH, Chapin OH, RNL; SSC, Book 8 and final report; Richard Kleindienst, *Justice* (Ottawa, IL: Jameson Books, 1985).

467   added Gemstone to the agenda: Who ordered the Watergate break-in? Jeb Magruder did. He consistently told and testified how, feeling pressure from Colson and Haldeman, he launched the Gemstone operation after meeting with Mitchell in Key Biscayne and obtaining his approval on March 30, 1972. See Ehrlichman notes of Magruder meeting, Apr. 14, 1973, SSC and HJC, and transcript of Magruder telephone call with Higby, Apr. 13, 1973, HJC.

Mitchell swore he killed the plan and had nothing more to do with it. But Fred LaRue, who was the only witness at Key Biscayne, says Mitchell merely postponed the decision. And as Liddy's plan became operational, LaRue became convinced that his friend Mitchell knew what was going on.

Magruder certainly showed no signs of going behind Mitchell's back. He notified Stans, the finance chairman, who checked with Mitchell before handing the first $83,000 of the $250,000 budget to Liddy.

Magruder also informed Strachan, who sent news to Haldeman that Liddy's "sophisticated political intelligence gathering system" had been approved, and put it on the agenda for Haldeman's April 4 meeting with Mitchell.

According to Liddy's memoir, *Will*, it was Magruder who chose the DNC offices at the Watergate as a primary target near the end of April 1972, and Magruder who ordered the team back in on the night of June 16 after Strachan and Mitchell had complained about the meager results of the initial wiretaps.

On the White House tape recordings, Haldeman can be heard telling Nixon that "we all knew that there were some activities, and we were getting reports, or some input anyway." Nixon's guess was that Mitchell, wanting deniability, signaled Magruder: "Don't tell me about it, but you go ahead and do what you want."

Nixon likely had it right. "Frankly, it was a non-decision," Magruder told Ehrlichman, in their Apr. 14, 1973, meeting. Mitchell was well aware that the plan was hideously illegal and would not have wanted to leave his fingerprints. Magruder, feeling the breath of Haldeman and Colson on his neck, and with a shrug from Mitchell, would have concluded that he had the approval he needed.

See White House tapes: Nixon and Haldeman, June 20, 1972, Nixon and Haldeman, June 21, 1972, RNL; Colson to Dean, Aug. 29, 1972, with Colson "Memorandum for the File, Subject: Howard Hunt," Colson OH, Magruder OH, RNL. See also Magruder, Reisner, and LaRue grand jury testimony, HJC. For further testimony, see SSC, Books 2, 4, and 6 and final report; interviews conducted by Robert Mardian's defense team in his papers at the Hoover Institution; Mitchell and Haldeman grand jury testimony and Haldeman's notes in the Haldeman papers, RNL, and the trial record, *U.S. v. John N. Mitchell et al.*

Strachan's handwritten notes were opened by the Nixon presidential library in 2010. His "talking paper" for the April 4 meeting escaped the shredders and can be viewed on the library's website, along with his notes from his meetings with Haldeman on political intelligence and Liddy's operation. His interview with the FBI, and results of a lie detector test, are in the FBI Watergate files, also online.

The Cubans were told by Hunt that he was reporting to Colson and that the Watergate bugging was done "for Mitchell." See Henry Rothblatt interview, WB; sentencing studies and other material, "Unsealed Materials from *U.S. v. Liddy,*" NARA.

468   Muskie was leading: The Nixon campaign's dirty tricksters had an effect on Muskie's deterioration, though it is not possible to gauge the final impact. In a most celebrated incident, a bogus letter to the Manchester, New Hampshire, *Union Leader* (a rightwing newspaper that had been baiting Muskie and his wife) accused the senator of laughing along at an ethnic slur comparing those of French Canadian ancestry to blacks. Muskie went to confront the paper and, while standing in a wet snow on a flatbed truck outside the building, was overcome by emotion. The scene struck at the heart of Muskie's image as a strong, dependable leader, a blow inflated by the contemporaneous televised scenes of Nixon's visit to China. Muskie won the New Hampshire primary, but his 9-point margin over McGovern was judged a Pyrrhic victory by the press, triggering his slide. Months later, the *Washington Post* reported that Ken Clawson, a White House aide, had boasted to one of its reporters of writing the so-called "Canuck letter." Clawson denied it.

468   shift his sights from Muskie to McGovern: For the switch from Muskie to McGovern, see White House tape, Nixon and Haldeman, Apr. 5, 1972, RNL; Higby note to self, June 13, 1972: "Follow-up on checking on getting the McGovern tapes from Magruder," WHSF-RC; Dean and Strachan notes, undated, Haldeman notes, Apr. 5, 1972, RNL; see also SSC, Strachan testimony, Book 6 and final report, and Liddy, *Will.*

The May 15 attempt on Wallace's life offered another glimpse of Nixon's authorial role in dirty tricks. That evening, in a conversation with Colson, the president suggested it would be beneficial if the would-be assassin, Arthur Bremer, were identified as a crazed "left-winger." Colson called on Hunt and asked if he could break into Bremer's apartment. Colson also phoned the FBI, planting the suggestion that Bremer had ties to McGovern and Kennedy. See Fred Emery, *Watergate* (New York: Times Books, 1994); SSC, final report; White House tape, May 15, 1972, Nixon and Colson, Colson OH, RNL.

469   kickback scheme with Florida vendors: The alleged Democratic kickback scheme was no small matter in the eyes of the Nixon White House. Both Liddy and Caulfield were assigned the task of investigating the funding for the Democratic convention, the White House records show, under the watchful eye of Mitchell, Dean, and Haldeman. See SSC proceedings, Book 3. See also Higby to Colson, Apr. 3, 1972, RNL; Higby to file, Apr. 17, 1972, Higby to Dean, Apr. 3, 12, 1972, WHSF-RC; Henry Rothblatt interview, WB.

469   O'Brien, fifty-four: "One item that needs to be fully and carefully explored is the fact that Lawrence O'Brien was on retainer by Howard Hughes and probably still is," wrote Lawrence Higby, relaying Nixon's and Haldeman's desires to Colson in January 1972. "We should really try and stir this up since there was such a big stink made about the Nixon loan situation." See Higby to Colson, Jan. 24, 1972, WHSF-RC. See

also Higby to Haldeman, Oct. 16, 1970, on using the Justice Department to pressure Hughes for campaign donations, WHSF-RC.

Anthony Lukas, Jeb Magruder, Earl Silbert exchange, Bob Haldeman, David Simon remarks, Hofstra; HRH diary, Mar. 4, 1970; telcons, Rebozo and Kissinger, July 16, 1969, Nixon and Kissinger, July 16, 1969, Nixon to Haldeman, Nov. 22, 1970, RNL; Buchanan to Nixon, Sept. 13, 1968, WHSF-R; Dent to Morton, May 28, 1969, WHSF-RC; Chotiner to Haldeman, Mar. 10, 1970, WHSF-RC; Nofziger to Haldeman, Mar. 9, 1970, WHSF-RC; Colson to Dean, Mar. 2, 1971, Dean OH, Butterfield OH, RNL; O'Brien OH, LBJ; Ehrlichman notes of Apr. 14, 1973, meeting with Magruder, HJC and SSC; Michel to Ruth, Oct. 16, 1975, closing memo for Hughes-Rebozo, NARA; Whittaker to Kelley, July 23, 1973, Whittaker to file, June 18, July 19, 1973, Kelley to Alexander, Aug. 1, 1973, Walters to Shultz, Feb. 23, 1973, Rebozo file, FBI.

For Nixon's desire to hold O'Brien accountable, see Nixon to Haldeman, Jan. 14, 1971, *From: The President,* ed. Bruce Oudes (New York: Harper & Row, 1989). For his subsequent explanation of the Hughes money and the Hughes and O'Brien relationship, see Nixon grand jury testimony, June 23 and 24, 1975, NARA.

The White House got jittery whenever the name of Howard Hughes came up. One of the first assignments that Dean received after becoming the president's counsel was to rein in an unrelated tax case involving Hughes, for fear that it would stir memories about the Hughes loan. "As you probably remember there was a Hughes/Don Nixon loan controversy several years ago, and the prosecution of this case could re-open that entire issue which could be very damaging politically," Lawrence Higby told Dean. See Higby to Dean, Aug. 10, 1970, Oudes, *From: The President.*

For the Caulfield warnings about a "counter scandal," see Caulfield memos to Dean of Jan. 22, Jan. 25, and Feb. 1, 1971, Dean memo to Haldeman, Jan. 26, 1971, and Haldeman response to Dean, Jan. 28, 1971, in SSC, Book 21 and SSC executive session interview of Roger Barth, June 5, 1974, with Walters memo to Shultz, Feb. 23, 1973. See also Ehrlichman notes, Sept. 4, 1969, Jan. 24, 1972, Feb. 7, 1972, Ehrlichman diary, Feb. 9, 1972, HI; telcon, Kissinger and Ziegler, Jan. 23, 1974, RNL; Nixon press conference, Oct. 26, 1973, PPP; Jerry Jones OH, GFF; *NYT,* Jan. 4, 1976. Nixon's postwar friend and vice-presidential chief of staff Robert King was a partner of Maheu after leaving Nixon's office. See *NY Post,* Nov. 3, 1960.

The Anderson column on Don Nixon's renewed involvement with Hughes ran on February 16, 1972. Anderson broke the news of the $100,000 contribution on August 6, 1971, and January 24, 1972. It is likely that Maheu was also a source for Anderson's January 18 and 19, 1972, columns on the CIA assassination plots, in which Maheu had recruited John Rosselli, a Mafia figure in Las Vegas, to enlist Mob hit men to kill Fidel Castro.

471 some prurient conversations: Were the Watergate burglars looking for evidence that would tie the DNC to a call-girl ring? The trope endures, along with other theories about the break-in, because the legal and political focus in Washington shifted so quickly from "what" happened on June 17 to "who" ordered the break-in. The crime seemed solved. The bad guys had been caught red-handed. The "why," at the time, seemed unimportant.

But as word spread that Baldwin had been listening to intimate conversations on DNC official Spencer Oliver's line, rumors "gave rise to unconfirmed reports that the telephone was being used for some sort of call-girl service," J. Anthony Lukas reported in his book on Watergate—*Nightmare: The Underside of the Nixon Years*—in 1976. Politics and sex are known to intersect. It was not beyond the pale to think that employees of a political party maintained a list of party girls or prostitutes to serve visiting dignitaries.

Then, in 1984, author Jim Hougan published *Secret Agenda,* which proposed that the CIA was running a call-girl ring in a nearby apartment building, utilized by the Democrats, and that Hunt and McCord were assigned to sabotage the Watergate burglary to keep the operation secret. Hougan was the first to comb through the FBI files on Watergate, and he found puzzling gaps in the official version on when and where the bugs were installed, and what the burglars were searching for. *Secret Agenda* inspired even more elaborate conjectures, including the bestselling *Silent Coup,* in 1991, by Len Colodny and Robert Gettlin, suggesting that White House counsel John Dean ordered the break-in to suppress evidence of his girlfriend's connections to the call-girl ring.

Aside from the Everest of evidence that bolsters the official version, and the conspiracy theorists' proclivity to take one or two facts and spin webs of supposition, there are outstanding flaws in the alternate history.

The first challenge to the call-girl theories is Baldwin's testimony. He has consistently said that while he heard men and women discussing assignations over Oliver's phone, they were not the paying kind. There was no sign of a call-girl ring. "I can categorically state from the conversations that were obtained that no such operation was conducted," Baldwin said in his deposition in the case of *Dean v. St. Martin's Press.* These were young people, at the peak of the "sexual revolution," talking dirty on the phone or arranging trysts, said Baldwin. They were definitely not clients haggling with pimps.

Baldwin's later accounts jibe with what he told the FBI at the time, that the "only information obtained on tap was relative to marital problems of Spencer Oliver and Oliver's efforts to pull delegates away from Senator McGovern." (See FBI summary, July 11, 1972, and report on Baldwin interview with federal prosecutors, July 11, 1972, and other contemporary FBI reports, Watergate files, FBI.) None of the Watergate testimony and reports, memoirs by White House aides and Watergate prosecutors, or conversations captured on the White House tapes challenge Baldwin's account. Indeed, the tapes support his testimony: Ehrlichman can be heard griping that instead of useful political material—information that could actually help Nixon get reelected—the wiretaps showed only that Oliver had an active love life.

The other grave flaw in the call-girl theory is the extent to which it rests almost exclusively upon the testimony of a deranged procurer. In the 1970s, Phillip Bailley emerged from federal prison—where he had served time with the scandal superstars Liddy and Hunt—convinced that Watergate was all about him. Over the years, he told Hougan and others an ever-shifting tale, replete with salacious detail, about running a call-girl ring in cahoots with employees at the DNC.

When former DNC secretary Ida Wells sued Liddy in federal court for spreading Bailley's story, the court determined not only "that Bailley was the sole source for all of the variations of the prostitution ring theories of the June 17, 1972 break-in including *Silent Coup* and *Secret Agenda,*" notes a summary of the litigation by the U.S. Court of Appeals for the Fourth Circuit in 1999, but that "Bailley, who is a disbarred attorney and convicted felon with a long history of substance abuse and mental illness, had changed his story about the prostitution ring several times and was not a reliable source."

When the Wells case came to trial in Baltimore in 2001, "Bailley acknowledged that he was a mental patient who had taken a variety of medications for his illness and for a severe drinking problem. Alternately sobbing and insisting he had no memory about many of the Watergate details . . . [he] wove a disjointed narrative, saying he had no memory of Wells," one newspaper account noted. "Instead, Bailley told the jury that he once was forced to flee in the Seattle hills from a threatening group of people dressed as witches, and he admitted . . . that he once told Maryland police during an arrest that he was waiting on a lonely road for a spaceship to transport him to Alpha Centauri." See Stephen Braun, "It's Déjà vu as Watergate Flavors Liddy Trial," *LAT,* Jan. 30, 2001. See also *Wells v. Liddy,* 1 F. Supp.2d 532 (1998) and *Wells v. Liddy,* No. 98-1962, (CA-97-946-JFM) U.S. Court of Appeals for the Fourth Circuit (1999). See also Dean, Strachan, and Baldwin depositions, *Dean v. St. Martin's Press,* U.S. District Court, D.C.

Dean and Wells had mixed success suing the conspiracy theorists in the courts. Dean halted sales of *Silent Coup* by St. Martin's Press, but Wells failed to persuade a jury that Liddy had defamed her. Nixon experts who gave credence to the call-girl theory, in one iteration or another, included Jonathan Aitken (*Nixon: A Life*), Joan Hoff (*Nixon Reconsidered*), and James Rosen (*The Strong Man*).

471   "to keep the lid on": "We decided, you know, that, you know, that there was no price too high to pay to let this thing blow up in front of the election," Dean told Nixon on March 21, 1973. "Bob is involved in that. John is involved in that. I am involved in that. Mitchell is involved in that. And that's an obstruction of justice."

Liddy deposition, *Dean v. St. Martin's;* Liddy, *Will;* SSC, final report; Powell Moore, Jeb Magruder, Robert Mardian, Richard Kleindienst, Fred Vinson, Jake Stein interviews, Mardian papers, HI; Nixon-Gannon; White House tape, Nixon and Dean, Mar. 21, 1973, CREEP "Statement by Honorable John N. Mitchell," June 17, 1972, FBI Summary Reports, July 21, 1972, Watergate files, FBI, Dean OH, Magruder OH, Colson OH, RNL; Dean commentary, "Watergate at 40," June 11, 2012; *WP,* June 18, 19, 1972; Angelo Lano, "Watergate: Forty Years Later," *Grapevine,* Society of Former Special Agents of the FBI, June/July 2014.

The prominence of the victims ensured that the crime could not be "disappeared" by the administration. The Democrats were immediately notified of the break-in by police, and since the party shared Edward Bennett Williams's law firm with the *Washington Post*—and Williams was one of Ben Bradlee's best friends—editors were awakened and had reporters dogging the story within hours of the arrests.

473   Democratic convention in Miami: Daley paid a humiliating price for the actions of the Chicago police at the 1968 convention. Four years later, in Miami, the left had seized control. Daley and his delegates were ejected from the hall by a McGovern credentials challenge. Tom Wicker, "Nixon's First Year," *New Republic,* Jan. 24, 1970. See also Buchanan to Colson, July 23, 1972, with attachment from Krupnick & Assoc. and response from Colson, Buchanan to Nixon, Aug. 6, 1972, RNL; Sears to Nixon, June 26, 1972, WHSF-RC; Teeter to Haldeman, Aug. 1, 1972, "Second Wave Polling Results"; Khachigian to Buchanan, Nov. 7, 1972, WHSF-RC; Haldeman notes, July and Aug. 1972, WHSF-RC. The WHSF-RC collection, Box 14, has an array of campaign strategy memos.

474   payment of hush money: SSC, final report; Ehrlichman, "Watergate Report to the President," Apr. 1973 ("Thereafter began an effort to insure that the five burglars— 4 Cubans and McCord—and Hunt and Liddy did not implicate anyone else"), Ehrlichman papers, HI.

474   Nixon did not know beforehand: Nixon grand jury testimony, June 23, 1975, NARA; White House tapes, Nixon, Haldeman, and Colson, June 21, 1972, Nixon and Haldeman, May 28, 1971, Nixon and Ehrlichman, Sept. 8, 1971, Nixon and Petersen, Apr. 19, 1973, Chapin OH, RNL.

The White House tapes are not comprehensive. Nixon had many private, unrecorded conversations with Haldeman, Ehrlichman, and Mitchell while in, to, and from San Clemente, Key Biscayne, *Air Force One,* and Camp David, and on untapped lines in the White House. Of the conversations that were taped, hundreds of hours of "personal" or classified excerpts are still secret, as is Nixon's personal diary and private correspondence. But until conflicting evidence emerges, the tapes that we do have, checked against Haldeman's diary and handwritten notes, Ehrlichman's personal notes, and the testimony given under penalty of perjury by Nixon and his aides provide a degree of confidence in a judgment that Nixon did not know about the Watergate break-in before it occurred.

But if Nixon did not know about Liddy's plans, Haldeman almost certainly knew something. The White House Special Files show Haldeman and his minions consumed by the Nixon reelection campaign that summer, with the chief of staff reviewing and ruling on strategy, polling, advertising, scheduling, and such trivia as the campaign song and lapel pins. (Haldeman even kept track of the toilet paper reserve at Camp David; see Terry O'Donnell OH, GFF.) After examining those records—and the recently unearthed notes of Gordon Strachan, quoted in the text—it is impossible to accept Haldeman's claims that he was kept in the dark about Liddy's operation, though easy to see how it and its risks might be overlooked in a tide of other duties.

475 brought down Alger Hiss: White House tape, Nixon, Haldeman, and Colson, June 21, 1972.

476 "Us Against Them": Sherwood to Staff, Jan. 23, 1960, WHSF-R; Hallett to Haldeman, Aug. 7, 1972, WHSF-RC; Garment to Haldeman, Aug. 8, 1972, RNL.

476 "that's my public line": Nixon grand jury testimony, June 23, 1975, NARA; White House tape, Nixon and Haldeman, June 20, 1972, Robert Odle OH, Colson OH, president's daily diary, June 17, 1972, RNL; AP, June 19, 1972; Ehrlichman diary, June 18, 1972, Ehrlichman papers, HI. In *RN,* Nixon said he learned of the break-in from the Sunday edition of the *Miami Herald* after returning to Key Biscayne on Sunday. (Haldeman thought it was the *New York Times.*) If so, then Abplanalp and Rebozo told fanciful stories of Nixon laughing it off on the beach in the Bahamas on Saturday. It makes little difference, except that both versions reveal a desire to portray the president as uninvolved and unconcerned. Colson's contrary tale, of Nixon hurling an ashtray, comes from his testimony before the House Judiciary Committee.

476 Nixon brooded about Colson: Nixon was not alone in his initial reaction that Colson was to blame. Haldeman's first thought upon being informed of the Watergate arrests was "Good Lord—they've caught Chuck Colson." And Haldeman's reconstruction of an infamous eighteen-minute gap in a June 20, 1972, tape was included in his book *The Ends of Power.* He has Nixon saying: *"Colson can talk about the President, if he cracks. You know I was on Colson's tail for months to nail Larry O'Brien on the Hughes deal."*

Haldeman's account was thought far-fetched and self-serving—the act of a bitter man, at the gates of prison, sensationalizing to make money. He would later distance himself from his memoir. Then a White House tape was released, in 1996, of Nixon ordering his aides to stage a black bag job at the Brookings Institution (*I want it implemented on a thievery basis. Goddamn it, go in and get those files. Blow the safe!*) and another made public in 1997, capturing Nixon telling Haldeman to bug the Democratic candidates. Haldeman's reconstruction of the June 20 tape no longer seemed far-fetched.

Nixon surely worried that a zealous aide had carried out one of his off-the-cuff orders, and countenanced the cover-up.

477 "get one jump ahead of them": White House tape, Nixon, Haldeman, and Colson, June 21, 1972, RNL.

477 "It's got to be done": L. Patrick Gray, in his memoir *In Nixon's Web,* said that Ehrlichman phoned Henry Petersen, the head of the criminal division at the Justice Department, on Sunday, June 18, and told him: "That's it. You have the burglars. Close it out in the next 24 to 48 hours." According to Gray, Petersen told Ehrlichman: "Screw you. We're not going to."

According to the White House tapes, Ehrlichman was instructed to call FBI director Gray on Wednesday, June 21, with the express purpose of "turning off" the bureau's work. "It's got to be done by Ehrlichman," the president told Haldeman. White House tape, Nixon, Haldeman, and Colson, June 21, 1972, RNL.

478   bring the CIA into the cover-up: The Minority Report on CIA Involvement, submitted by Senator Baker and the Republican senators and staff of the Senate Watergate Committee, and attached to the SSC final report, is the starting point for all discussions of the agency's involvement in Watergate, its cover-up of that involvement, and its cover-up of that cover-up. See also Liddy deposition, *Dean v. St. Martin's Press.*

479   "the smoking gun": White House tapes, Nixon and Haldeman, June 23, 1972, RNL; Helms OH, CIA; Ehrlichman interview, Tom Wicker Papers, University of North Carolina; FBI summary report, July 21, 1972, Watergate file, FBI. The pressing concern was the money trail. The CREEP fund-raising team, to beat a deadline set by a new campaign finance law, had collected $10 million from corporations and individual donors who were promised anonymity. The corporate donations were illegal, and some of the individuals were Democrats, who didn't want their betrayals publicized. Liddy had joined in a scheme to wash some of the money via Mexico and the Miami bank account of one of his burglars—and then used the cash to help fund the break-in.

Nixon's references to the Bay of Pigs and "the Cuban thing" have spurred learned speculation that he was using code to warn—or threaten—the agency that the continued pursuit of Hunt would lead to disclosure of the CIA-Mafia plots against Castro. See James Cannon, *Time and Chance* (New York: HarperCollins, 1994).

479   Dean became the "desk officer": "Just so we keep it all in one hat here, it's Dean with you, or Dean with Bob, or both?" Nixon asked Ehrlichman on July 19.

"Both," Ehrlichman replied. "The two of us have been talking to him, more or less together right along."

White House tape, Nixon and Haldeman, July 20, 1972. See also Ehrlichman OH, Nixon and Haldeman, July 22, 1972, Nixon and Ehrlichman, July 19, 1972, Chapin to Haldeman, June 30, 1970, Dean OH, Chapin, OH, RNL; Dean grand jury testimony, HJC.

481   "They have to be paid": Nixon, *RN;* Gray phone call, SSC, Book 9 and final report; White House tapes, Nixon and Haldeman, July 22, 1972, Dean to Haldeman, Sept. 12, 1972, Dean OH, RNL; Ehrlichman notes, "Agnew and Press," July 7, 1972, Ehrlichman papers, HI; Gray grand jury testimony, HJC.

482   Felt was the one they called Deep Throat: Howard Simons interview, Woodward and Bernstein papers, University of Texas; William Ruckelshaus OH, Price OH, Haig OH, RNL; *LAT,* Oct. 5, 1972; Belz to Bates, Oct. 12, 1972, Watergate files, FBI; Bob Woodward, *The Secret Man* (New York: Simon & Schuster, 2005).

A lawyer for *Time* magazine tipped off the White House that Felt was leaking to the press. "Now why the hell would he do that?" Nixon asked, when Haldeman told him. "I think he wants to be in the top spot," Haldeman guessed, correctly. They wrongly concluded that Felt must be Jewish. But, as with Admiral Moorer and the Radford case, they decided that punishing Felt was too risky. White House tapes, Nixon and Haldeman, Oct. 19 and Oct. 20, 1972, RNL.

483   sleeping with Bradlee's sister-in-law: In his autobiography, Bradlee claimed that he did not know of Kennedy's philandering. He was surprised as anyone, he wrote, to discover that Kennedy had bedded his sister-in-law, Mary Pinchot Meyer. When she was murdered in 1964, on the towpath of the C&O Canal in Georgetown, and James Angleton, a CIA counterintelligence specialist, was discovered in her house searching for a diary that confirmed her White House love affair, Bradlee decided it wasn't a story. Bradlee, *A Good Life* (New York: Simon & Schuster, 1995); David Remnick, "Last of the Red Hots," *New Yorker,* Sept. 18, 1995.

483   more muscular means of persuasion: Benjamin Bradlee, *Conversations with Kennedy*

(New York: Norton, 1975); Bradlee oral history, Strober; "Eyes Only" memo, Colson to File, Jan. 15, 1973, Colson OH, RNL; Graham interview, Halberstam papers, BU; Katharine Graham, *Personal History* (New York: Knopf, 1997).

For White House pressure on broadcasters over Watergate, see Colson to Haldeman, Nov. 3, 1972, containing telcon transcript between a craven William Paley ("I just wanted to call up and say please have a little faith in me") and Colson ("Paley was pleading," Colson told Haldeman. "He sounded like a whipped dog and almost on the verge of tears"), WHSF-RC; Woodward OH, RNL; Woodward and Bernstein papers, University of Texas; Halberstam papers, BU; Carl Bernstein and Bob Woodward, *All the President's Men* (New York: Simon & Schuster, 1974).

484 "That's an exciting prospect": White House tapes, Nixon, Haldeman, and Dean, Sept. 15, 1972, RNL; Watergate documents collection, FBI reading room.

CHAPTER 25: A FAIRLY REASONABLE INTERVAL

486 "We want a decent interval": "If the agreement breaks down, then it is quite possible that the people in Vietnam will fight it out," Kissinger told Zhou. "If the government is as unpopular as you seem to think, then the quicker our forces are withdrawn, the quicker it will be overthrown. And if it's overthrown after we withdraw, we will not intervene. . . ."

"But you have a prerequisite with that," Zhou said, "that is, a ceasefire throughout Indochina."

"For some period of time," said Kissinger. "We can put on a time limit, says eighteen months or some period."

See memcons, Kissinger and Zhou Enlai, July 9, 10, 1971, NSA and RNL.

Further evidence of Nixon's strategy can be found in the handwritten notation that Kissinger made in a briefing book for that trip to China. "Let objective realities shape the political future. . . . If the Vietnamese people themselves decide to change the present government, we shall accept this," read the text. Beside it, Kissinger jotted: "We want a decent interval. You have our assurance." See reproduction in Jeffrey Kimball, *The Vietnam War Files* (Lawrence: University Press of Kansas, 2004).

Nixon and Kissinger first suggested that the North Vietnamese army could remain in South Vietnam in a 1970 "standstill cease-fire" offer. "That North Vietnamese forces would remain in the South was implicit in the standstill proposal," Kissinger wrote in his memoirs. "No negotiation would be able to remove them if we had not been able to expel them by force." The United States made the offer explicit in May 1971. See Henry Kissinger, *White House Years* (Boston: Little, Brown, 1979).

Kimball tracks the "decent interval" approach in *The Vietnam War Files* and *Nixon's Vietnam War,* and more recently, with Burr, in *Nixon's Nuclear Specter.* See also White House tapes, Nixon and Kissinger, Feb. 14, 1972, Nixon and Kissinger, Mar. 14, 1972, Nixon and Kissinger, Aug. 2, 1972, Nixon, Kissinger, and Kraemer, Oct. 24, 1972, Nixon and Kissinger, Jan. 3, 1973, Nixon and Haig, Oct. 23, 1972, Haig OH, RNL. See also Kissinger, "The Viet Nam Negotiations," *Foreign Affairs,* January 1969.

For the North Vietnamese thinking, see Kimball, *Vietnam War Files* and Lien-Hang T. Nguyen, *Hanoi's War* (Chapel Hill: University of North Carolina Press, 2012).

See also White House tapes, Nixon, Laird, et al., Mar. 26, 1971, Nixon and Kissinger, Connally and Haldeman, May 4, 1972, Nixon, Kissinger, and Connally, May 8, 1972, RNL; HRH diary, Dec. 15, 21, 1970, Mar. 23, 1971; Kissinger to Nixon, Sept. 18, 1971, Nixon to Kissinger, Mar. 11, 1972, memcon, Kissinger and Gromyko, May 27, 1972, RNL; John Barriere memo, Kissinger briefing to members of Congress, Jan. 26, 1973, Carl Albert Papers, University of Oklahoma; FRUS, Volume XIV, Soviet Union, October 1971–May 1972; Dobrynin memcon, May 14, 1969, in Edward Keefer, David Geyer, and Douglas Selvage, *Soviet American Relations: The Détente Years,*

1969–1972 (Washington, D.C.: U.S. Department of State, 2007); notes from Nixon meeting with congressional leaders, Feb. 9, 1971, Safire papers, LOC; Dobrynin, *In Confidence.* Ken Hughes, "Fatal Politics: Nixon's Political Timetable for Withdrawing from Vietnam," *Diplomatic History* 34, June 2010.

486 Nixon did not forfeit all hope: At a State Department forum in 2010, Kissinger defended the "decent interval" strategy. "We had to act . . . within what was possible," he said. "We knew it was a precarious agreement. We knew that the North Vietnamese had not fought for 50 years in order simply to become a North Vietnamese state. . . . We could not commit ourselves for all eternity to maintain a [South Vietnamese] government against all conceivable contingencies. So in that sense, the decent interval phase has a meaning." But it did not mean, said Kissinger, that he and Nixon believed that the South was irrevocably doomed. After watching the South Vietnamese performance during the Easter Offensive of 1972, "we thought . . . that they could sustain a significant shock and survive politically and even militarily," he said, with continued U.S. military assistance. See Kissinger remarks, U.S. Department of State, "The American Experience in Southeast Asia, 1946–1975," Sept. 29, 2010.

See White House tapes, Nixon and Kissinger, Mar. 11, 1971, Nixon and Kissinger, Mar. 19, 1971, Nixon and Kissinger, Aug. 3, 1972, telcon, Kissinger and Laird, Jan. 17, 1973, RNL; HRH diary, Dec. 15, 21, 1970; Nixon diary entry, 1972, Nixon, *RN;* Jeffrey Kimball, "Decent Interval or Not?" Society for Historians of American Foreign Relations (SHAFR) newsletter, Dec. 2003; Jusi Hanhimaki, "Some More 'Smoking Guns'? The Vietnam War and Kissinger's Summitry with Moscow and Beijing, 1971–73," SHAFR newsletter, Dec. 2001; "Vietnam and the Paris Peace Accords," Nixon Legacy Forum, Dec. 5, 2014, National Archives, Washington, D.C. (participants: Winston Lord, John Negroponte, and William Richard Smyser).

490 "two out of three": The cynical side of Nixon surfaced during the SALT negotiations, as it did after the China trip. "I know that this kind of agreement isn't worth a damn," he assured Kissinger. "We're having it for politics reasons. . . . Because the American people are so peace-loving, they think agreements solve everything." See White House tape, Nixon, Haldeman, and Kissinger, Apr. 17, 1971, RNL.

CIA, National Intelligence Estimate, Feb. 27, 1969, and Nixon administration memoranda in FRUS, 1969–1976, Vol. 12, Soviet Union, January 1969–October 1970. See also National Intelligence Estimate, June 1, 1973, in FRUS, 1969–1976, Vol. 15, Soviet Union, June 1972–August 1974; U.S. Department of State, Office of the Historian, conference transcript, "U.S.-Soviet Relations in the Era of Détente, 1969–1976"; U.S. embassy, Amman to Secretary of State, Sept. 21, 1970, White House tapes, Nixon and Kissinger, Mar. 12, 1971, Nixon, Haldeman, and Kissinger, Mar. 18, 1971, Nixon and Kissinger, Apr. 14, 1971, Nixon, Haldeman, and Kissinger, Apr. 17, 1971, Nixon and Kissinger, May 18, 1971, Nixon and Kissinger, July 19, 1971, Nixon to Kissinger, May 20, 1972, RNL; White House tapes, Nixon, Haldeman, and Kissinger, Aug. 11, 1971, Nixon and Ehrlichman, Jan. 24, 1972, memcon, Nixon and de Gaulle, Mar. 1, 1969, RNL; Dobrynin and Kissinger memcons, 1969–1971, in Keefer, Geyer, and Selvage, *Soviet American Relations;* Gerard Smith, *Doubletalk* (New York: Doubleday, 1980); *New Yorker,* John Newhouse, Annals of Diplomacy, May 5, 12, 19, 26, June 2, 1973, and Richard Rovere, "Letter from Washington," Mar. 22, 1969; Kissinger, *White House Years.*

490 Easter Offensive: White House tapes, Nixon and Haldeman, May 2, 1972, Nixon and Kissinger, May 3, 1972, Nixon and Connally, Moorer and Kissinger, May 4, 1972, Nixon and Kissinger, Jan. 20, 1972, National Security Council, Feb. 2, 1972, RNL; Lord OH, FD; "Vietnam and the Paris Peace Accords," Nixon Legacy Forum; Politboro Guidance Cable 119, Mar. 27, 1972, trans. Merle Pribbenow, from *Collected Party*

Documents, ed. Nguyen Thi Nhan (Hanoi, Vietnam: National Political Publishing House, 2004) cited in Stephen P. Randolph, *Powerful and Brutal Weapons* (Cambridge: Harvard University Press, 2007).

492 "Operation Linebacker": White House tapes, Nixon, Connally, Moorer, and Kissinger, May 4, 1972, Nixon, Moorer, and Kissinger, Apr. 3, 1972, Nixon and Kissinger, Apr. 4, 1972, Nixon and Kissinger, Mar. 30, 1972, RNL. Communication between Nixon and his commanders was difficult, Moorer told Haig, and the difficulty was compounded by Nixon's late-night "reinforcement" of alcohol. Telcon, Haig to Moorer, Apr. 5, 1972, RNL, cited in Randolph, *Brutal Weapons.*

492 "Slop over": White House tapes, Nixon, Connally, and Kissinger, May 8, 1972, Nixon and Kissinger, May 5, 1972, RNL.

493 "I'll destroy the goddamn country": White House tapes, Nixon and Kissinger, Apr. 15, 1972, Apr. 18, 1972, RNL; White House tape, Nixon and Kissinger, Apr. 19, 1972, FRUS, 1969–1976, Vol. 8, Vietnam, January–October 1972.

493 "Sitting in this chair": White House tapes, Nixon and Kissinger, Apr. 15, 1972, Nixon and Kissinger, Apr. 17, 1972, RNL.

494 "We shouldn't fool ourselves": Lehman OH, White House tape, Nixon and Haig, Apr. 20, 1972, RNL; "Vietnam and the Paris Peace Accords," Nixon Legacy Forum.

494 ABM and SALT treaties: Morton Halperin, Gerard Smith interviews, Tom Wicker Papers, University of North Carolina; "Vietnam and the Paris Peace Accords," Nixon Legacy Forum; John Lehman OH, Schlesinger OH, RNL. The SALT treaty's biggest weakness was its MIRV loophole, which both nations exploited to grow their arsenals.

496 The "morality" worried him: White House tape, Nixon and Kissinger, Oct. 6, 1972, Miller Center, University of Virginia; HRH diary, Oct. 12, 1972; "Vietnam and the Paris Peace Accords," Nixon Legacy Forum.

497 "Peace is at hand": White House tapes, Nixon and Haldeman, June 23, 1971, Nixon and Kissinger, Sept. 17, 1971, Nixon, Kissinger, and Haig, Sept. 29, 1972, Nixon and Kissinger, Oct. 6, 1972, Nixon, Kissinger, Haig, and Haldeman, Oct. 12, 1972, Nixon, Kissinger, and Haig, Dec. 14, 1972, RNL; memcon, Kissinger and Tho, Sept. 15, 1972, Haig to Kissinger, Oct. 22, 1972, Kissinger to Haig, Oct. 22, 23, 1972, Bunker to Haig, Oct. 22, 1972, Nixon to Kissinger, Nov. 24, 1972, RNL; memcon, Nixon, Kissinger, Haig, and Duc, Nov. 29, 1972, Kissinger to Haig, Dec. 14, 1972, Rush to Nixon, Dec. 7, 1972, RNL; John Scali interview, WB; Kimball, *Vietnam War Files;* Ehrlichman notes, "Vietnam negotiations," Dec. 6, 1972, HI.

497 the hour was strangely sour: Nixon, *RN.* Nixon to Haldeman, Nov. 29, 1972, White House tape, Nixon and Kissinger, Nov. 8, 1972, RNL. Kissinger, *White House Years.*

498 "exhausted volcanoes": Like Eisenhower, Nixon wanted to remake the American political system. Ike had wanted to move the Republican Party to the center, and jettison its right wing. Nixon, with Colson, schemed at creating a new majority, in which southerners, organized labor, Jewish and Catholic traditionalists, and others from the "forgotten" working class abandoned the New Deal coalition, giving the Republicans command of the political terrain. "I have more in common with them from a personal standpoint than does McGovern or the intellectuals generally," Nixon told his diary. He called it "revitalizing the Republican Party." The project went by several names— the Real Majority, the Silent Majority, and the New American Majority were the best known—and the tectonic political shifts that he recognized, and fortified, survived Watergate. Recast as "Reagan Democrats," these segments of his silent majority would join with the former Democrats of the Solid South and contribute to Republican landslides in 1980 and 1984, and to two-party parity in congressional elections. Chapin OH, HRH diary, Nov. 8, 1972, RNL; Evans-Novak Political Report, Nov. and Dec. 1972, White papers, JFK; Buchanan OH, Jerry Jones OH, GFF; Safire, "Nixon Diary,"

no date, Nov. 1972, Safire papers, LOC; Schultz OH, Strober and Strober; Nixon diary entry, Dec. 31, 1972, *RN*.

499   Watergate lingered like Banquo's ghost: Ehrlichman OH, White House tape, Nixon and Haldeman, Dec. 10, 1972, Ehrlichman to Haldeman, Jan. 25, 1973 (Too late, Ehrlichman warned Haldeman that Colson's "judgment is not just bad. In combination with Richard Nixon's proclivities it could be fatal"), RNL; John Ehrlichman, *Witness to Power* (New York: Simon & Schuster, 1982); Ehrlichman interview, Tom Wicker Papers, University of North Carolina.

499   before and after Christmas Day: White House tapes, Nixon, Kissinger, Haig, and Haldeman, Oct. 12, 1972, Nixon, Kissinger, and Haig, Dec. 14, 1972, Nixon and Kissinger, Dec. 17, 1972, Nixon, Kissinger, and Haldeman, Dec. 20, 1972, RNL.

   Long before the negotiations stalled, Nixon had looked forward to bombing North Vietnam as the United States departed—civilian casualties or not. "That's a hell of a good time to bomb," he told Kissinger. And "I wouldn't worry about a little slop over, and knock off a few villages and hamlets and the rest. . . . And then, everybody would say, 'Horrible, horrible, horrible.' That's all right. You agree?" Said Kissinger: "Absolutely!" See White House tape, Nixon and Kissinger, Nov. 20, 1971.

500   Paris Peace Accords put an end: telcon, Nixon and Kissinger, Apr. 21, 1973, RNL; oral histories by Alexander Haig, Scowcroft, Ehrlichman, and Schlesinger, RNL; telcon, Nixon and Kissinger, Dec. 17, 1972, FRUS, Volume IX, Vietnam, October 1972–January 1973; Lord OH, FD; Ehrlichman diary entry, Oct. 31, 1972, Ehrlichman papers, HI. *NYT*, Jan. 9, Apr. 24 and 25, May 1, 1975; *CQ Almanac*, 1975; Nixon, *RN*; Nixon letters to Thieu, Nov. 14, 1972, Jan. 5 and Jan. 17, 1973, from Gregory Tien Hung Nguyen and Jerrold Schecter, *The Palace File* (New York: Harper & Row, 1986); Elmo Zumwalt, *On Watch* (New York: Quadrangle/New York Times Books, 1976); John Negroponte, remarks, "Vietnam and the Paris Peace Accords," Nixon Legacy Forum; Kimball, *Vietnam War Files* and *Nixon's Vietnam War*; Kissinger, *Years of Upheaval* (Boston: Little, Brown, 1982); Randolph, *Brutal Weapons*; Ball, *Pattern*. After visiting Hanoi and conferring with former North Vietnamese officials, Jeffrey Kimball, a leading authority on the war in Indochina, reached the conclusion that a deal along the lines of that struck in 1973 might have been reached in 1969. See Kimball, "Why the US War in Vietnam Did Not End Sooner," unpublished conference paper, New York University, Apr. 30, 2015.

502   final American casualty: Frost-Nixon, RNL.

CHAPTER 26: CANCER ON THE PRESIDENCY

503   confronting their imminent incarceration: In his memoirs, Liddy claimed that Dean promised him $30,000 in living expenses for his family, a pardon within two years, a medium-security prison cell, and payment of his legal fees.

504   "Surely your cheapest commodity": Colson recorded the phone call and gave the tape to Dean, who says he played it for Haldeman and Ehrlichman, SSC, final report. According to testimony at the Watergate trials, $429,500 in hush money was distributed, with the Hunts receiving $210,000, see AP, Nov. 25, 1974.

504   he would expose the "seamy things": Sirica was "a tough, hard-boiled, law and order judge . . . a Republican . . . very decent guy, dedicated to you and to Eisenhower," Colson told Nixon on Feb. 3, 1973. "This case just got under his craw for some reason, and he is a hot-headed Italian and he blew." White House tapes, Nixon and Colson, Feb. 3, 1973, Nixon and Haldeman, Mar. 2, 1973, Nixon and Pappas, Mar. 7, 1973, RNL; Colson to Dean, Jan. 2, 1973, RNL; Colson memos to files, Jan. 5, Mar. 23, 1973, Hunt grand jury testimony, July 17, 1973, transcript of telephone call, Hunt and Colson, Nov. 1972, HJC; *Nomination of Earl J. Silbert to Be United States Attorney,*

Senate Judiciary Committee, 1975; McCord testimony, SSC, final report; Nixon diary entry, *RN*.

505 there was John Dean: Justice Department officials failed to recognize the significance of Hunt's photographs. In the pre-Google era, it was no easy thing to connect a photo of Liddy standing before a California office building with Daniel Ellsberg.

505 Pat Gray, in his confirmation hearings: Gray had developed a case of "confirmation-itis," Dean complained to Nixon. "He's panting after the Goddamn job and is sucking up," the angry president replied.

White House tapes, Nixon and Dean, Mar. 7, 1973, Mar. 17, 1973, Nixon, Ehrlichman, and Gray, Feb. 16, 1973, Dean OH, RNL.

506 "awful hard rap to prove": White House tapes, Nixon and Haldeman, Nov. 24, 1972, Nixon, Haldeman, and Ehrlichman, Dec. 11, 1972, Nixon and Colson, Feb. 3, 1973, Nixon and Dean, Feb. 28, 1973, Mar. 14, 1973, Nixon and Kissinger, Mar. 16, 1973, RNL.

506 "We have a cancer": White House tape, Nixon and Dean, Mar. 21, 1973, Dean OH, RNL; Ehrlichman, interview with author; Nixon grand jury testimony, June 23, 1975, NARA; Nixon, "Transcript of Dictabelt Recording," Mar. 21, 1973, HJC; McCord to Sirica, Mar. 19, 1973, GFL, original in *US v. Liddy* files, NARA, read by Sirica in court on Mar. 23, 1973.

Ehrlichman was an early and consistent proponent of full disclosure, as long as it didn't apply to him. From the summer of 1972, he urged Nixon to pin the blame for Watergate on John Mitchell and make a fresh start. He thought he and Nixon could cloak their role in the Fielding break-in as a matter of "national security."

Haldeman was constantly preaching about the need to get ahead of the scandal, and not letting it corrode the presidency, drip by drip. Though Haldeman was more willing to sacrifice himself than his colleagues were, he and Nixon always, ultimately, shrank from the pain they would suffer by making a clean breast of things.

Dean's early nobility vanished when he began to suspect that his new best friends Nixon, Haldeman, and Ehrlichman were setting him up as the fall guy.

507 The frenzy was on: LaRue, Kalmbach, Hunt, and Young were right behind Dean and Magruder in cooperating with the prosecutors. So was Robert Reisner, who was Magruder's administrative assistant at CREEP. The FBI had failed to interview Reisner, but the Senate committee put him on its witness list after hearing his name from McCord. Despite Magruder's frantic pleading ("If this gets out of hand they're going to impeach the president!"), Reisner, who knew the whole Gemstone saga, declined to commit perjury, dooming his former boss.

In an unsuccessful attempt to stop this parade of cooperative witnesses, Nixon issued a presidential directive (aimed primarily at Dean) that no White House aide trade immunity from prosecution for his testimony. Dean OH, RNL; Howard Simons, Fred Buzhardt interviews, WB; transcript, *Dick Cavett's Watergate*, PBS, Aug. 8, 2014; Monica Crowley, *Nixon in Winter* (New York: Random House, 1998); Magruder testimony, SSC, executive session, June 12, 1973; Max Friedersdorf OH, GFF. In HJC, see Dean memos to file on "Meeting with Fred LaRue," Apr. 13, 1973, and "Meeting with John Mitchell," Apr. 12, 1973; transcript, Magruder and Haldeman, Apr. 14, 1973; transcript, Magruder and Higby, Apr. 13, 1973 ("The game is over . . . I'm not going to lie anymore. I've committed perjury so many times . . . our lives are all ruined right now anyway . . . I'm going to jail. The question is for how long"). *LAT*, Mar. 26, 27, 1973; *WP*, Mar. 29, 1973.

508 toward a roaring finale: This time it was Ehrlichman who talked tough, assured Nixon he would carry the "message to Garcia," and then quailed when meeting Mitchell face-to-face. See transcript, Mitchell and Ehrlichman meeting, Apr. 14, 1973, HJC; Friedersdorf OH, GFF.

509   Petersen called Kleindienst: White House tapes, Nixon and Kleindienst, Petersen and Silbert, Nixon and Petersen, all Apr. 15, 1973, RNL; Nixon, *RN*.

509   Ellsberg was then on trial: At Nixon's bidding, Ehrlichman had offered Judge Matthew Byrne, who was presiding over the Ellsberg trial, the job of FBI director, to replace Pat Gray. When word of the Fielding break-in reached him, Byrne recognized how he had been compromised, announced the news of the burglary in open court, pressed the government for evidence of other impropriety, and ultimately dismissed the charges, freeing Ellsberg and his leading associate, Anthony Russo, from further prosecution. Ehrlichman, Krogh, and others were later convicted for their role in the Fielding break-in. White House tape, Nixon and Kleindienst, Apr. 25, 1973, RNL; Petersen grand jury testimony, HJC; John Ehrlichman, *Witness to Power* (New York: Simon & Schuster, 1982); Fred Emery, *Watergate* (New York: Times Books, 1994).

510   "separability," as he called it: In their struggle to hang on (and stay out of jail), Haldeman and Ehrlichman made crude threats, which Nixon swallowed without comment. "I cannot sit by quietly. If I take a leave, and I go out of here, I am going to very vigorously defend myself," Ehrlichman told him. "And I'll do it by fair means or foul." White House tapes, Nixon, Rogers, Haldeman, and Ehrlichman, Apr. 17, 1973, Nixon and Ehrlichman, Apr. 19, 1973, RNL.

510   the two aides were summoned: Nixon grand jury testimony, June 23, 1975, NARA. It was the first time, Haldeman recalled, Nixon ever shook his hand—see HRH diary, Apr. 29, 1973. H. R. Haldeman, *The Ends of Power* (New York: Times Books, 1978); Ehrlichman, *Witness to Power;* Nixon, *RN*.

510   Nixon's televised address: Later that night, Nixon spoke to his friend Hobart Lewis, the publisher of *Reader's Digest*. "Isn't it a shame," he told Lewis. "It's all about a crappy little thing that didn't work. . . . Nobody ever got a goddamn thing out of this damn bugging." "No goddamn thing . . . just a bunch of schoolboys." Lewis said. "Assholes," said Nixon. White House tapes, Nixon and Haldeman, Nixon and Lewis, Apr. 30, 1973, Chapin OH, RNL; Emery, *Watergate.*

511   Nixon walled out Pat: JNE, *Pat;* Tricia Nixon, diary entry, May 24, 1973, Nixon, *RN*.

511   the fissures spread: Kissinger would also speculate, in private, about the "weird" and "slightly homosexual" atmosphere of the Nixon White House. See Schlesinger diary, Jan. 27, 1975, ASP. Chapin OH, telcon, Kissinger and Alsop, Aug. 8, 1973, RNL; Moynihan diary entry, July 17, 1974, in *Moynihan: A Portrait in Letters;* Kissinger "normalcy" quote from *Dick Cavett's Watergate*, PBS, 2014; Nixon, *Six Crises;* Leonard Garment interview with author; Kissinger, *White House Years* (Boston: Little, Brown, 1979).

512   plenty to help Nixon into the tumbrel: Gerald Ford, Neil MacNeil interviews with the author. Ford interview, WB; William Timmons OH, GFF; Richard Helms OH, CIA; Wright to O'Neill, Jan. 19, 1973, Thomas P. O'Neill Jr., Congressional Papers, Boston College; Barriere to Albert, Feb. 14, 1973, Carl Albert Papers, University of Oklahoma; Nixon to Haldeman, Sept. 4, 1972, Buchanan to Haldeman, Dec. 12, 1972, RNL; Higby to Colson and Buchanan, Nov. 2, 1972, Higby to Timmons, Dec. 5, 1972, WHSF-RC; Magruder and Malek to Nixon, Nov. 29, 1972, WHSF-RC; Colson to Chapin, Feb. 8, 1972, WHSF-RC; Dent to Haldeman, July 10, 1972, WHSF-RC; Nixon to Mitchell, June 6, 1972, WHSF-RC; Nixon to Haldeman, May 18, 1972, FRUS, 1969–1976, Vol. 2, Organization and Management of U.S. Foreign Policy, 1969–1973; Failor to Magruder, Sept. 4, 1972, Magruder and Malek to Nixon, "Critique of the 1972 Campaign," Nov. 29, 1972, Magruder papers, HI; Henry Kissinger, *White House Years;* Stephen Ambrose, *Nixon*, vol. 3, *Ruin and Recovery* (New York: Simon & Schuster, 1991); Garment, "The Guns of Watergate," *Commentary,* Apr. 1987; John Farrell, *Tip O'Neill* (New York: Doubleday, 2011); Monica Crowley, *Nixon in Winter* (New York: Random House, 1998).

514 torch-and-pitchfork crew: Carmine Bellino, a longtime Kennedy family investigator and surveillance expert, moved from Ted Kennedy's Subcommittee on Administrative Practices to become the chief investigator for the Ervin Committee.

514 plucked Archibald Cox: With Cox's appointment, Henry Petersen and the original Watergate prosecutors—U.S. attorney Earl Silbert and his aides Seymour Glanzer and Donald Campbell—lost control of the case.

    The leading Kennedy hands on the Watergate Special Prosecution Force (WSPF) were Cox, Philip Heymann, James Vorenberg, Henry Ruth, Thomas McBride, James Neal, William Merrill, and Charles Ruff. Terry Lenzner was another veteran of the Kennedy Justice Department, and joined Carmine Bellino as a top investigator for the Ervin Committee. Charles Shaffer, who represented John Dean, and William Bittman, who represented Howard Hunt, had also worked for RFK. The House Judiciary Committee staff included a young Hillary Rodham Clinton. Its chief, John Doar, reached into Kennedy mythology when sending his staff a group photograph that quoted, as Robert Kennedy was fond of doing, the Tennyson line from the poem *Ulysses:* "To strive, to seek, to find and not to yield." See Banchero to Brodie, Dec. 20, 1975, FMB; Geoff Shepard, interview with the author; JNE, *Pat;* David Halberstam, *The Powers That Be* (New York: Knopf, 1979); Raymond Price, *With Nixon* (New York: Viking, 1977).

515 It was great public theater: Nixon got some imaginative advice. Barry Goldwater urged him to make a dramatic appearance at the Ervin hearings and "face the committee down." White House aide David Parker suggested that Nixon take advantage of his status as a former member of the House to stride into the chamber and take on all questioners. See Harlow to Haig, July 24, 1973, Parker to Haig, July 31, 1974, RNL.

    Harlow to Haig, Aug. 13, 1973, telcon, Kissinger and Nixon, Aug. 12, 1973, Kehrli to Haig, Sept. 20, 1973, with attached Opinion Research poll, Woodward OH, RNL; William B. Dickinson and Janice L. Goldstein, eds., *Watergate: Chronology of a Crisis* (Washington, D.C.: Congressional Quarterly, 1973); *Time,* Sept. 24, 1973; Moynihan to Glazer, May 25, 1973, in *Moynihan: A Portrait in Letters.*

CHAPTER 27: THE FINAL DAYS

517 White House tapes: Nixon recalled that Kissinger, Agnew, Connally, and others urged him to eradicate the tapes. So, by their own account, did Buchanan and Goldwater. Nixon did not consult Pat. She said later that she, too, would have told him to destroy the recordings. Leon Jaworski, who succeeded Cox, said Nixon could have "burned the tapes early in the game and gotten away with it" and that "it would have been very difficult" for the special prosecutors to succeed without them.

    Kennedy taped 325 meetings and 275 telephone conversations in some 260 hours of taping. Johnson taped 9,300 telephone conversations, totaling more than 400 hours, as well as 200 hours of cabinet meetings. Nixon had about 3,700 hours of tapes. See Edward C. Keefer, "Key Sources for Nixon's Foreign Policy," *Passport* 38 (Aug. 2007): 27–30.

    "They must be used with caution because Nixon had a tendency to exaggerate, vent, and posture," said Keefer, the former editor of the *Foreign Relations of the United States* series. "What Nixon says on one day in the heat of the moment is not in itself absolute proof of his intentions, just evidence of his state of mind at that particular time."

    Geoffrey Shephard, interview with author; Harlow to Nixon, Sept. 1969, Timmons to Nixon, Sept. 1, 1973, Haig OH, Garment OH, RNL; Butterfield testimony, SSC, Book 5, July 16, 1973; Gannon-Nixon; Leon Jaworski, William Safire interviews, WB; John Lungren, *Healing Richard Nixon* (Louisville: University Press of Kentucky, 2003); *McCall's,* May 19, 1975; Alexander Haig, *Inner Circles* (New York: Warner, 1992).

519 Agnew had taken bribes: Gerald Ford, James Cannon, Neil MacNeil, Ronald Lieb-

man interviews with author; Rodino and O'Neill, transcripts of interviews with James Cannon, author's collection; Beall to Richardson, "Status Report on the Investigation of Vice President Agnew and Others," Sept. 11, 1973, Ford interviews with Trevor Armbrister, GFL; Cannon OH, Pat Buchanan OH, Tom Korologos OH, GFF; Timmons to Haig, Oct. 24, 1973, Cole notes, Oct. 21, 1973, Blair to Butterfield, Apr. 2, 1970, Agnew to Mansfield, Oct. 10, 1973, Price to Nixon, Oct. 11, 1973, Buchanan to Nixon, Oct. 26, 1973, Conable to Timmons, Oct. 10, 1973, Harlow to Woods, Oct. 11, 1973, RNL; White House News Summary, Sept. 22, 26, 27, Oct. 11, 21, 22, 24, 26, 1973, Timmons to Haig, Oct. 26, 1973, RNL; Ehrlichman notes, Nov. 14, 1969, HI; Carl Albert OH, Abzug to Albert, Sept. 26, 1973, Albert lecture, OSU, Jan. 17, 1974, Carl Albert Papers, University of Oklahoma; Albert, O'Neill, Rodino statements, Oct. 23, 1973, O'Neill statement, Oct. 24, 1973, O'Neill papers, Boston College; *WP,* Oct. 11, 1973, Aug. 9, 1974, Nov. 28, 1982; *NYT,* Oct. 11, 1973; *CQ Almanac,* 1973; Edward Mezvinsky, *A Term to Remember* (New York: Coward, McCann & Geoghegan, 1977); Richard M. Cohen and Jules Witcover, *A Heartbeat Away* (New York: Viking, 1974).

520 Yom Kippur War: *WP,* Oct. 11, 1973; Henry Kissinger, *Years of Upheaval* (Boston: Little, Brown, 1982); Brent Scowcroft OH, RNL.

521 Saturday Night Massacre: Nixon was correct about the breadth of Cox's inquiries. A July 1973 memo from Cox to acting FBI director William Ruckelshaus listed forty-two different areas of inquiry regarding campaign contributions and election laws—all of which ranged far and wide from the original Watergate burglary. A memo from Ruckelshaus to incoming FBI director Clarence Kelley a week later, listing the various "areas of investigation," devoted two paragraphs to the Watergate case and then ran for an additional itemized nine pages. See Cox to Ruckelshaus, July 2, 1973, and Ruckelshaus to Kelley, July 9, 1973, Watergate files, FBI; Neil MacNeil, interview with author; Eisenhower interview with Blackman, AP, Nov. 5, 1973; MacNeil files to *Time* editors, January–August 1974, author's collection; Nixon to Haig, July 7, 1973, Clawson to colleagues Nov. 16, 1973, Timmons to Haig, Oct. 22, 1973, Ruckelshaus OH, RNL; Harvard Law School report on Special Prosecutor Archibald Cox, "Press Conference with Special Prosecutor Archibald Cox," Oct. 20, 1973, White papers, JFK; briefing paper, "The Saturday Night Massacre and the Impetus to Impeachment," undated, Ari to O'Neill, "The Legal Aspects of the Dismissal of Cox and Turnover of the Tapes," O'Neill papers, Boston College; Elliot Richardson interview, WB; Bork interview, FMB; Helen Thomas OH, GFF; Cong. Rec., Oct. 23, 1973; *Time,* Feb. 4, 1974.

523 moved to DEFCON III: Haig, the only aide to deal with Nixon on the night of the nuclear alert, insisted that the president was not drunk. See Haig OH, RNL.

To reports that Nixon was fortifying himself with liquor that fall, his daughter Julie said this: "The drinking rumors were the most persistent, perhaps because it seemed he *was* drinking a little more than he ever had before, but at dinnertime, when he was trying to unwind. He still adhered to his self-imposed code of no alcohol on nights he was attending receptions or dinners, nor did he drink during the day."

On alcohol, see telcon, Kissinger and Scowcroft, Oct. 11, 1973 (S: "The switchboard just got a call from 10 Downing Street to inquire whether the president would be available for a call within 30 minutes from the prime minister. The subject would be the Middle East." K: "Can we tell them no? When I talked to the president he was loaded"). See also telcon, Haig and Kissinger, Aug. 17, 1973 (Haig: "We're incommunicado at the moment . . . you know, we're relaxing . . . you understand?" Kissinger: "Oh, I understand very well"), both RNL. See also Doar interview, FMB. When asked if Nixon drank a lot in the final days, Doar replied: "It would be abnormal if he had not."

In his 1995 memoir, *In Confidence*, the former Soviet ambassador Anatoly Dobrynin accused Nixon and Kissinger of manufacturing a superpower crisis to boost Nixon's public approval, and to buy time for Israel to win back territory in the Sinai. "There was no threat of a direct military clash between us ... we took no measures to put our armed forces on high combat alert," Dobrynin wrote. The Soviet leaders believed Nixon and Kissinger acted in bad faith, and the episode "cooled the excitement about détente that had reigned in Moscow after the summits." In the weeks after the Yom Kippur War, both Nixon and Kissinger expressed regret for their actions to the Soviets, Dobrynin said.

Nixon press conference, Oct. 26, 1973, PPP; telcons, Nixon and Kissinger, Oct. 24, 25, 1973, telcon, Kissinger and Dinitz, Oct. 26, 1973, telcon, Kissinger and Haig, Oct. 24, 25, 26, 1973, telcon, Haig and Dobrynin, Oct. 26, 1973, telcon, Kissinger and Ziegler, Jan. 23, 1974, telcon, Nixon and Sidey, Aug. 9, 1974, RNL; "President Nixon and the Role of Intelligence in the 1973 Arab-Israeli War," symposium program, essays, and documents, RNL; Stein to Gergen, Nov. 28, 1973, Ash to Nixon, Jan. 3, 1974, Timmons to Garment, Oct. 29, 1973, Harlow to Haig, Oct. 31, 1973, Scowcroft OH, Schlesinger OH, RNL; telcon, Haig and Kissinger, Oct. 24, 1973, and Admiral Thomas Moorer, diary entry, Oct. 26, 1973, FRUS, 1969–1970, Vol. 25, Arab-Israeli Crisis and War, 1973; Alexander Haig, Arthur Burns interviews, WB; Lord OH, FD; "The 1973 Arab-Israeli War: Overview and Analysis of the Conflict: Intelligence Report. September 1975," CIA.

Office of the Historian, U.S. Department of State, Milestones: 1969–1976, "The 1973 Arab-Israeli War," "Oil Embargo, 1973–1974," "Shuttle Diplomacy and the Arab-Israeli Dispute, 1974–1975"; "Waging Peace: Richard Nixon and the Geopolitics of the Middle East," Apr. 23, 2012, Nixon Legacy Forum, National Archives, Washington, D.C.; Nixon Legacy Forum; May 12, 2014; Melvin Goodman, "Inside the Kremlin during the Yom Kippur War," *Middle East Journal*, Spring 1996; Henry Kissinger, *Crisis: The Anatomy of Two Major Foreign Policy Crises* (New York: Simon & Schuster, 2003); Kissinger, *Years of Upheaval*.

For the birth of the Arab oil embargo see Helms to Nixon, Feb. 22, 1973, Ash to Haig, Nov. 14, 1973, and Haig to Kissinger, Oct. 13, 1973, with attached "Memorandum to the President" from the chairmen of Mobil, Exxon, Texaco, and Standard Oil, Oct. 12, 1973, on the dire consequences of an embargo, RNL.

524 eighteen-and-a-half-minute gap: Nixon's own experts objected to the panel's certainty and left open the possibility that a faulty tape recorder contributed to the erasure. See "Review of a Report Submitted to the U.S. District Court for the District of Columbia Entitled 'The Tape of June 20, 1972,'" May 31, 1974, White papers, JFK. Nixon grand jury testimony, June 23, 1975, Ruth to files, July 7, 1975, Denny to Davis, June 6, 1975, "J. Fred Buzhardt Testimony, Grand Jury #3—Tapes" and "Testimony of Rose Mary Woods Before DCGJ 3 on Feb. 1, 1974," NARA. J. Anthony Lucas, *Nightmare: The Underside of the Nixon Years* (New York: Viking, 1976).

524 federal income-tax payments: "Examination of President Nixon's Tax Returns for 1969 through 1972," Joint Committee on Internal Revenue Taxation, Apr. 3, 1974; William Samson, "President Nixon's Troublesome Tax Returns," *Tax Analysts*, Apr. 11, 2005. *Baltimore Sun*, Sept. 11, 1973. Question-and-Answer Session at the Annual Convention of the Associated Press Managing Editors Association, Orlando, Florida, Nov. 17, 1973, PPP.

525 Nixon met the new year: Nixon diary notes, Jan. 5, 1974, and Tricia Nixon diary excerpt, undated, in Nixon, *RN*. Buchanan to Nixon, Nov. 5, 1973, RNL.

525 On the morning of: Nixon was in the residence of the White House that morning. One of his scheduled events that day was a meeting to thank the Secret Service for its handling of a previous incident—the February 17, 1974, landing by a disgruntled soldier

in a stolen army helicopter on the White House lawn. President's Daily Diary, Feb. 17, 22, 1974, RNL; Byck hijacking plot file, FBI; *NYT,* Feb. 23, 24, 27, 1974; *WP,* Feb. 23, 1974; *Baltimore Sun,* Nov. 13, 2005; *The 9/11 Commission Report* (New York: Norton, 2004); *The Plot to Kill Nixon,* The History Channel, 2005.

526 a final, futile attempt to turn things around: Garment, Sheppard interviews with author; Buchanan to Haig, May 10, 1974, Buchanan to Haig, May 23, 1974, Timmons to Nixon, May 10, 1973, Scott "dugout" remarks, May 7, 1974, Haig OH, Garment OH, RNL; Laird OH, Cannon OH, GFF; John Scali, Agnes Waldron, John Rhodes, Walter Tkach, Fred Buzhardt interviews, transcript, Hugh Scott dugout chatter, May 7, 1974, WB; *WP,* July 12, 1973; *Newsweek,* Jan. 28, May 13, 1974; Dobrynin, *In Confidence;* Address to the Nation Announcing Answer to the House Judiciary Committee Subpoena for Additional Presidential Tape Recordings, April 29, 1974, PPP. JNE, *Pat.* Stanley Kutler, *The Wars of Watergate* (New York: Norton, 1990).

527 impeachment hearings: Of the seventeen Republicans on the committee, ten voted against every article of impeachment. But after the release of the smoking gun tape and Nixon's resignation, the ten joined the other Republican members in reporting to the House of Representatives, "We know that it has been said, and perhaps some will continue to say, that Richard Nixon was 'hounded from office' by his political opponents and media critics. We feel constrained to point out, however, that it was Richard Nixon who impeded the FBI's investigation of the Watergate affair . . . it was Richard Nixon who created and preserved the evidence of that transgression and . . . concealed its terrible import, even from his own counsel, until he could do so no longer. And it was a unanimous Supreme Court of the United States, which in an opinion authored by the Chief Justice whom he appointed, ordered Richard Nixon to surrender that evidence to the special prosecutor to further the ends of justice. The tragedy that finally engulfed Richard Nixon had many facets. One was the very self-inflicted nature of the harm. It is striking that such an able, experienced and perceptive man whose ability to grasp the global implications of events little noticed by others may well have been unsurpassed by any of his predecessors, should fail to comprehend the damage that accrued daily to himself, his Administration and to the nation as day after day, month after month, he imprisoned the truth about his role in the Watergate cover-up so long and so tightly within the solitude of his Oval Office that it could not be unleashed without destroying his Presidency." HJC, final report.

Robert Drinan, Don Edwards, Francis O'Brien interviews with author; Bush to Armstrong et al., Nov. 12, 1973 w/ Sandman to Bush, Nov. 8, 1973, and Peckham to Bush, Nov. 9, 1973, Khachigian to Haig, July 16, 18, 1974, Timmons to Haig, Mar. 8, 1974, Timmons to Harlow, Mar. 9, 1974, "Congressional Commentary on Watergate," May 6, 9, 1974, RNL; Nixon diary entry, July 27, 1974, Nixon, *RN; Impeachment of Richard M. Nixon, President of the United States,* Report of the Committee on the Judiciary, House of Representatives, Aug. 20, 1974; Robert Drinan diary, Drinan papers, BC; Richard Keiser OH, GFF; John Rhodes interview, WB; Charles Wiggins address, Hofstra; *WP,* July 28, 30, 31, 1974; *Newsweek,* July 22, Aug. 5, 1974; *Time,* Aug. 5, 1974.

529 Haig had already begun to orchestrate: Charles Wardell, an aide to Haig, says the general decided, "We got to bring down the curtain on this charade" after the Supreme Court ruling on the tapes. When Nixon warned Haig and Buzhardt about the smoking gun tape, it was clear that the president had listened to it that spring and not disclosed the danger to his staff. Wardell interview, WB.

530 "Somebody leaves a pistol": Arthur Burns was one of several officials who feared that Nixon would commit suicide or, by not taking proper care of his phlebitis, fulfill a death wish. Haig told Woodward and Bernstein that he had the staff reduce the president's supply of sleeping pills. See Burns, Haig, Charles, Wardell interviews, WB; Haig OH, RNL.

531 He would certainly be impeached: Tom Korologos, the president's vote counter on Capitol Hill, said that after the transcript of the June 23 tape was released, the number of senators who would vote against impeachment had dwindled to less than ten. His colleague Friedersdorf, counting House and Senate, said the number of supporters in both houses of Congress had shrunk to less than forty. See Friedersdorf OH, Korologos OH, GFF.

Burch to Haig, July 5, 1974, Speakes to Haig, July 26, 27, 29, 30, 1974, Timmons to Haig, Aug. 1, 1974, reports on House Judiciary Committee deliberations, RNL; telcon, Kissinger and Burns, Aug. 10, 1974, Ellsworth OH, Schlesinger OH, Haig OH, Schlesinger interview, Aitken papers, RNL; Richard Nixon, "Statement by the President," Aug. 5, 1974; Richard Nixon, "Statement Announcing Availability of Additional Transcripts of Presidential Tape Recordings," Aug. 5, 1974, PPP; *US v. Nixon*, 418 U.S. 683, July 24, 1974; Minutes of Senate Republican Policy Luncheon, Aug. 6, 1974, Hugh Scott diary notes of White House visit, Aug. 7, 1974, Rhodes, Haig, Buzhardt, James Schlesinger, Barry Goldwater, William Simon interviews, WB; Alan Greenspan OH, Jerry Jones OH, Robert Bork OH, GFF; Bob Woodward and Carl Bernstein, *The Final Days* (New York: Simon & Schuster, 1976); Lou Cannon, "The Last 17 Days of the Nixon Reign," *WP*, July 25, 28, Aug. 6, 7, 8, Sept. 29, 1974; Howard Ball, *United States v. Nixon Reexamined*, Hofstra. Jim Newton, *Justice for All: Earl Warren and the Nation He Made* (New York: Riverhead, 2006). The Rehnquist papers at the Hoover Institution contain the correspondence among the justices as they considered the tapes case.

532 "you destroy yourself": Nixon had been playing with the theme of hatred and self-destruction all summer. In May he had told a sympathetic rabbi, "What really destroys an individual when he is under attack is if he allows the hate against him to become part of himself and then the fury that arises within him will destroy him." See Baruch Korff interview with Nixon, May 13, 1974, in *The Personal Nixon* (Washington, D.C.: Fairness, 1974). In his oral history with the Nixon library, Garment called it "the miraculous terminal insight."

The airplane took off from Andrews Air Force Base as *Air Force One*, and landed at El Toro as "SAM 27000." When Nixon climbed aboard, he told the pilot, Colonel Ralph Albertazzie, that he regretted he had never made him a general. "Sir, there's still time," the colonel said, gently joking. See Steve Bull OH, RNL.

Richard Nixon, "Address to the Nation Announcing Decision to Resign the Office of President of the United States," Aug. 8, 1974, and "Remarks on Departure from the White House," Aug. 9, 1974, PPP; telcons, Kissinger and Fulbright, Aug. 9, 1974, Kissinger and Burns, Aug. 10, 1974, Victor Lasky, "The Woodstein Ripoff," Frost-Nixon transcripts, RNL; oral histories by Bull, Garment, Price, and Odle, RNL; Helmut Sonnefeldt interview, FMB; Nixon-Gannon; Scott diary notes, Buzhardt, Glenn Davis interviews, WB; Lee Simmons, Max Friedersdorf OH, GFF; Ralph Albertazzie OH, Veterans History Project, LOC; Woodward and Bernstein, *Final Days; Star*, Aug. 11, 20, 1974; *NYT*, Aug. 12, 1974; Cannon, *WP*, Aug. 9, 10, 1974, Sept. 29, 1974; Bush, *All the Best.*

CHAPTER 28: EXILE

534 Richard Nixon's Elba: Ken Clawson, "Then: A Loyalist's Memoir," *WP*, Aug. 9, 1979; Finch interview, Abrahamson papers, Columbia University; telcon, Kissinger and Burns, Aug. 10, 1974, Acker interview, Aitken papers, Dole OH, Dean OH, Klein OH, RNL; Herbert Gold, "The Western White House Did Not Fall," *Esquire*, Apr. 1975; *Ladies' Home Journal*, Mar. 1978.

535 presidential pardon: After consulting with Nixon, Haig advised Ford more than a week before the resignation that the president expected to step down. At the same meeting,

Haig presented Ford with the option of pardoning Nixon. Ford seemed amenable. Haig then went back to Nixon and gave him a report on the conversation. Nixon subsequently resigned. But both Haig and Ford insist no explicit quid pro quo was struck. See Haig, Ford interviews, WB; Ford testimony, HJC.

Nixon clearly thought he had a deal. "We began to get the phone calls from San Clemente after Nixon was there and President Ford was in office about, 'Where in the hell's my pardon,'" aide Jerry Jones recalled. "A lot of phone calls, particularly to Haig. . . . The man [Nixon] was distressed and frantic." See Jones OH, GFF.

For cuff-link anecdote see Becker interview, WB, and Becker memo, "History and Background of Nixon Pardon," Sept. 9, 1974, GFL.

Oral histories by Benton Becker, Jack Marsh, Jerry Jones, Jim Cannon, and Hal Bruno, GFF; author interviews with Laird, Cannon, and Ford; telcons, Kissinger and Ziegler, Aug. 13, 1974, Kissinger and Childs, Sept. 9, 1974, RNL; O'Neill statement, BC; Haig, Becker, Marsh, Miller interviews, WB; Monica Crowley, *Nixon in Winter* (New York: Random House, 1998); John Farrell, *Tip O'Neill* (New York: Doubleday, 2011); JNE, *Pat*.

537 Cynics suggested that the illness: Nixon was in a newly built hospital ward with doors that could be bolted from the inside. His was accidentally locked when Ford arrived, and the president had to wait as workmen opened it with a hacksaw. See Cheney OH, GFF, and John Lungren, *Healing Richard Nixon* (Louisville: University Press of Kentucky, 2003).

John Lungren book proposal, Woods to Day, Mar. 11, 1975, Frost-Nixon transcripts, Aitken, "File Note Visit to RN," Mar. 8, 1989, *Today* show transcripts, NBC, Apr. 30–May 3, 1990, RNL; Barker to Kreindler, Oct. 15, 1974, memo to Davis and Dreindler from Ruth, "Re: Health Status of GJ Witness," May 1975, Watergate Special Prosecution Force, NARA; Becker interview, WB; Buchanan OH, GFF; affidavit of Herbert Miller, *US v. Mitchell*, U.S. District Court for the District of Columbia; John Sears interview, WB; *NYT*, Sept. 12, 1974; *Newsweek*, Nov. 11, 1974; *60 Minutes*, CBS, Mar. 9, 1980.

538 "It was a lynching": Dean OH, RNL; *US v. John D. Mitchell et al.*, trial transcripts and appellate files, Mardian papers, HI; Miller interview, WB; *New Republic*, June 23, 1982; Richard Harris, "Reflections: The Watergate Prosecutions," *New Yorker*, June 10, 1974; Leonard Garment, "The Guns of Watergate," *Commentary*, Apr. 1987; *Newsweek*, Jan. 13, 1975; SSC counsel David Dorsen speech, "The Lessons of Watergate," Sept. 23, 1974 ("I am far from convinced that such procedures are consistent with fairness," Dorsen said. "I also wonder whether there would have been more voices raised in protest if the defendants involved were Dr. Benjamin Spock or Daniel Ellsberg"), SSC; White papers, JFK; Geoff Shephard, *The Real Watergate Scandal* (Washington, D.C.: Regnery, 2015); George V. Higgins, *The Friends of Richard Nixon* (Boston: Little, Brown, 1975).

539 Saigon fell in the spring: White House tape, Nixon and Scowcroft, Mar. 20, 1973 (NB); telcon, Nixon and Kissinger, Aug. 9, 1973, RNL; Kissinger to Nixon, Dec. 7, 1972, FRUS, 1969–1976, Vol. 9, Vietnam, October 1972–January 1973. Niall Ferguson, *Kissinger* (New York: Penguin, 2015).

540 Americans did succeed in "buying time": Nixon blamed Congress for the fall of South Vietnam in the Frost-Nixon interviews, in his memoirs, and in his speech to the Oxford Union on November 30, 1978. In private, he was more objective. The great flaw in the Paris Peace Accords, he told Monica Crowley, was his surrender to Hanoi's demand that it maintain its army on the territory it held within South Vietnam. "We really tried with Vietnamization to make the South Vietnamese into a pretty effective fighting force. . . . We thought that since we had no choice but to withdraw, that we could substitute them for us," Nixon told Crowley, his foreign policy aide, in 1991. "Of

course, we knew that even with our equipment, they couldn't do the job we could, but since we had to get out, that was it." See Crowley, *Nixon in Winter.*

"Vietnam and the Paris Peace Accords," Nixon Legacy Forum, Dec. 5, 2014, National Archives, Washington, D.C. (participants: Winston Lord, John Negroponte, and William Richard Smyser); Kissinger-Frost interviews, NBC, Oct. 11, 1979; telcons, Nixon and Kissinger, Apr. 11, 1975, Kissinger and Reston, Apr. 16, 1975, Richardson OH, RNL; oral histories by Kissinger, Cheney, Cannon, Friedersdorf, Lee Hamilton, and Strobe Talbott, GFF; Lord OH, FD.

Kissinger could have resigned as Ford's secretary of state if he felt that Congress was betraying a viable ally, and Ford could have taken the case to the country. Nixon urged them to do so. Both knew it was useless. In two conversations with James Reston, on April 8 and April 16, 1975, Kissinger gave a reasoned explanation for South Vietnam's demise. The Soviets "kept their level of aid steady and ours declined for a variety of reasons including inflation and oil prices" and the showdown between Nixon and Congress, said Kissinger. "I think it is a casualty of Watergate."

On the secret agreements, see telcon, Kissinger and Reston, Apr. 8, 1975, RNL.

For Nixon's manipulation of the POW families ("Make a cosmetic offer on POWs.... I'm just looking for a gimmick"), see White House tape, Nixon, Haldeman, and Kissinger, Apr. 26, 1971.

541 select committee chaired by Senator Frank Church: See the following, all authored by the Select Committee to Study Governmental Operations with Respect to Intelligence Activities, U.S. Senate: *Alleged Assassination Plots Involving Foreign Leaders* (Washington, D.C.: GPO, 1975); *Intelligence Activities and the Rights of Americans,* Book 2 (Washington, D.C., Apr. 26, 1976); *Supplementary Detailed Staff Reports on Intelligence Activities and the Rights of Americans,* Book 3 and Richard Nixon interrogatories, Book 4 (Washington, D.C., Apr. 23, 1976). Richard Helms OH, William Colby OH, CIA; SAC NY to Director, FBI, "Highly Confidential and Anonymous Sources," Jan. 20, 1955, Brennan to Sullivan, "Electronic Surveillances," June 23, 1969, FBI; Smith to Sullivan, "Microphones—Policy Brief," July 12, 1966, Director, FBI to Attorney General, "Surreptitious Entries," June 1, 1976, Sullivan to DeLoach, "Black Bag Jobs," July 19, 1966, FBI; Tom Hayden address, Hofstra; Harlow interviews, Thompson, WB; Cartha DeLoach OH, LBJ; *NYT,* Dec. 22, 1974, June 5, Dec. 8, 1975; *Newsweek,* Jan. 13, 1975; Wicker, "Kennedy Without End, Amen," *Esquire,* June 1977; Garment, "The Guns of Watergate," *Commentary,* Apr. 1987; CIA Electronic Reading Room, "The Family Jewels," 1973 Report; *Report to the President by the Commission on CIA Activities Within the United States* (Rockefeller Commission), June 1975, GFL; Loch Johnson, *A Season of Inquiry* (Lexington: University Press of Kentucky, 1985); Kathryn Olmsted, *Challenging the Secret Government: The Post-Watergate Investigations of the CIA and FBI* (Chapel Hill: University of North Carolina Press, 1996).

543 overthrow of Salvador Allende: Richard Helms OH, CIA. Helms details how American business interests, especially ITT and Don Kendall, the Pepsi executive and long-time client and friend of Nixon, played a role in stirring fears about Allende's election; FRUS 1969–1976, Vol. 21, Chile, 1969–1973; telcons, Kissinger and Nixon, July 4, 1973, Sept. 16, 1973, and Aug. 6, 1975, Kissinger and Karamessines, Aug. 7, 1975, RNL; *Intelligence Activities,* Book 2; *Supplementary Detailed Staff Reports,* Book 3 and Richard Nixon interrogatories, 4; CIA white paper, *CIA Activities in Chile,* Sept. 18, 2000.

544 Watergate grand jurors: Nixon grand jury testimony, June 23, 24, 1975, and prosecutor files, NARA. After his sworn testimony, the prosecutors quizzed Nixon on other subjects, including his knowledge of the Watergate burglary team's assault on antiwar protesters during J. Edgar Hoover's funeral in early May 1972—an attack that Nixon and Haldeman discuss on the White House tape of April 25, 1973. Nixon's aides had

spoken several times about getting "a goon squad" or "thugs" to "beat the shit" out of anti-administration demonstrators. In the state of siege they were in, the president and his aides "probably did talk about some of the drastic things mentioned on the tapes," Nixon told the prosecutors, "but they never did anything, to his knowledge, that involved violence." See Ackerman to Ruth, May 15, 22, 27, 1975, Ruth to Miller, May 16, 1975, Davis to files, July 16, 1975, Ruth to files, July 7, 1975, NARA.

547   Money was, momentarily, an issue: When still in office, Nixon told Ehrlichman that writing a book was "agony," but that corporate law was "degrading," and the "idea of a former president accepting honorariums for speeches or for going on television is abhorrent to me." See Nixon to Ehrlichman, Feb. 1, 1972, WHSF-R.

The WHSF-R files contain several folders on Nixon's real estate and financial holdings at the time he left office. See, for example, Ehrlichman to Kalmbach, Dec. 27, 1971, with attached estate plan, WHSF-RNL. See also memo from John Taylor, Oct. 28, 1987, Aitken papers, Lungren to Nixon and reply, Dec. 21, 1975, telcon, Kissinger and Ziegler, Feb. 1, 1975, Dean OH, RNL; David Kennerly OH, Jim Cannon OH, Stu Spencer OH, GFF; *NYT*, Aug. 3, 1975; Paul Theroux, "Nixon's Neighborhood," *Sunrise with Seamonsters* (Boston: Houghton Mifflin Harcourt, 1986); *Esquire*, Apr. 1975; *Newsweek*, May 19, 1975, May 24, 1976; *Good Housekeeping*, July 1976; Woodward and Bernstein, *Final Days*; Jonathan Aitken, *Nixon: A Life* (Washington, D.C.: Regnery, 1993).

548   The Frost-Nixon interviews: Gannon, Reston, interviews with author; Frost-Nixon transcript, David Frost OH, RNL; Jonathan Aitken, "Nixon v. Frost," *The Mail Online*, Jan. 23, 2009; David Frost, *Frost/Nixon: Behind the Scenes of the Nixon Interviews* (New York: Harper Perennial, 2007); James Reston, Jr., *The Conviction of Richard Nixon* (New York: Harmony, 2007).

548   *The Final Days:* Nixon's "final days" were captured by Woodward, Bernstein, and a team of researchers who interviewed everyone from Fred Buzhardt and Al Haig to the White House barber and garage attendants. Nixon's friends fired back with op-ed pieces and a detailed thirty-four-page critique authored by Victor Lasky. The interview transcripts in the Woodward and Bernstein papers at the University of Texas, however, support the duo's reporting. Victor Lasky, "The Woodstein Ripoff," RNL; *Final Days* files, WB.

551   *RN: The Memoirs of Richard Nixon:* Gannon, interview with author. Gannon interview with Aitken, Frost-Nixon transcripts, RNL; Nixon, *RN.*

552   "Course I'm respectable": "In turning to [Gary] Hart," Nixon wrote in a typical political memo for his friends, "there is no question that he brought on his own demise. . . . Ironically, I think part of his problem may be due to the fact that throughout his political life he has always tried to pattern his conduct after Kennedy. He may have figured that since Kennedy got away with some extra-marital escapades he may be able to do so. But since so many reporters won Pulitzers and other prizes for their investigative reporting in Watergate, the media can't resist going after a public figure if they think they can strike pay dirt." See Nixon to Abplanalp et al., May 11, 1987, Aitken papers, RNL.

George Shultz, interview with author; Nixon to Aitken, with political tout sheet for friends, Sept. 11, 27, 1992, Nixon, "Political Memo #3," et al., 1984, RNL; Nixon to Nofziger, Dec. 6, 1989, Nixon to Amery, Apr. 3, June 26, 1987, Nixon to Abplanalp et al., Mar. 13, 1987, Amery to Thatcher, June 30, 1987, and Thatcher to Amery, July 2, 1987, Nixon to Aitken, Sept. 24, 1990, RNL; John Taylor, memo, Apr. 13, 1990, with undelivered Nixon speech, "The Real Gorbachev," Aitken papers, RNL; telcons, Nixon and Kissinger, Nov. 2, 1976, Dec. 17, 1976, Panetta OH, Cannon OH, Scowcroft OH, RNL; *NYT*, Mar. 10, 1994; Crowley, *Nixon in Winter*; Mark Feeney, *Nixon at the Movies* (Chicago: University of Chicago Press, 1994).

For Nixon letters to presidents, see the following, all in RNL: Nixon to Carter, Dec.

20, 1978; Nixon to Reagan, Nov. 17, 1980; Nixon to Clark, Jan. 14, 1982; Nixon to Clark, Nov. 21, 1982; Nixon to Reagan, Nov. 1, 1982; Nixon to Shultz, Jan. 27, 1983; Nixon to Reagan, Feb. 25, 1983; Nixon to Schultz, Mar. 4, 1983; Nixon to Shultz, Apr. 18, 1983; Nixon to Clark, Apr. 25, 1983; Nixon to Reagan, Oct. 17, 1984; Nixon to Baker, Sept. 25, 1984; Nixon to Regan, Jan. 28, 1985; Nixon to McFarland, Oct. 7, 1985; Nixon to McFarland, Oct. 21, 1985; Nixon to McFarland, Oct. 30, 1985; Nixon to Reagan, Nov. 14, 1985; Nixon to Regan, Mar. 17, 1986; Nixon to Reagan, July 25, 1986, Aitken Papers. Leon Panetta, who served Clinton as chief of staff, said Clinton found Nixon's advice quite helpful.

554 "Sage of Saddle River": Roger Stone, Robert Schlesinger interviews with author; Dole OH, RNL; Nixon to Drown, June 30, 1983, Taylor to Chiles, Oct. 23, 1987, John H. Taylor, memo, Jan. 17, 1990, Aitken papers, RNL; Price interview, Tom Wicker Papers, University of North Carolina; Michael Korda, "Nixon, Mine Host," *New Yorker,* May 9, 1994; *NYT,* Jan. 10, 2013; JNE, *Pat.*

554 "It depends who writes the history": All politicians lie, fib, shade, or dissemble. Nixon was adept at it, and conveniently flexible with history. After learning that chopsticks he had used in China had been lost, he told his aides that nobody would know the difference, so they could use any set for a museum display. In his interviews with Frank Gannon, Nixon added a crudity to a remark made by Lyndon Johnson, and confessed off camera to doing so because it made the story "better." He once told Len Garment that Garment would never be a good politician because he wasn't a good liar.

In his memoir *In the Arena* Nixon spun an egregious whopper, apparently seeking to secure himself a place among the Vietnam War veterans who professed to have been spit at when they returned home from war. He wrote of an incident—which he also mentioned in the Frost interviews, and in his appearance at the Oxford Union—in which a young girl supposedly broke through his Secret Service entourage in 1970 or 1971 (the year varied in the telling) on a trip to Williamsburg, Virginia, and covered Nixon's face with spit. It is an undocumented and highly unlikely story that— had a protester broken through the Secret Service cordon and assaulted him in that manner—would doubtlessly have been well publicized. There is no mention of the incident in the Haldeman diary, nor has one surfaced in the White House tapes. There is a line, however, in an April 20, 1971, memo from Pat Buchanan to the president's file, of Nixon telling congressional leaders how "a little teenager" had approached him in Williamsburg the previous day and asked him, "Mr. President, how does it feel to be a war criminal?" The teen was a boy, and if there was spitting involved, Nixon did not mention it. See Buchanan to Nixon, Apr. 20, 1971, Nixon to Amery, Aitken papers, Jan. 21, 1987, Nixon to Drown, June 30, 1983, RNL. Roger Stone interview with Aitken, RNL. Bush to "Lads," July 23, 1974, from Bush, *All the Best, George Bush* (New York: Scribner, 2013). *NYT,* Dec. 19, 2008; *LAT,* Dec. 19, 2008. Schlesinger diary entry, April 3, 1982, ASP; Crowley, *Nixon in Winter;* Monica Crowley, *Off the Record* (New York: Random House, 1996). Aitken, *Nixon.*

556 alleging that Alger Hiss was innocent: See Nixon to Tanenhaus, Jan. 8, 1993, Tanenhaus papers, HI.

558 "cultivate her soil in justice, and peace": Churchill had in turn cribbed the quotation from an Irish-American orator, William Bourke Cockran.

In the negotiations over the pardon, Nixon won control of his tapes and papers, and the right to destroy the tapes after all the Watergate trials and appeals were finished. But Congress passed a law seizing the material, which the Supreme Court upheld in 1977. For decades, as the tapes were processed by the National Archives, Nixon's lawyer fought to stall their release, and only a few transcripts from the Watergate trials became available before Nixon's death. Most, but not all, of the tapes are now available, with devastating results to his reputation.

After years of searching for a more majestic spot, Nixon chose the old Yorba Linda homestead for his privately funded museum and library, which was opened in 1990, with Presidents Ford, Reagan, and Bush attending. In 2007, as part of a settlement, it joined the presidential library system. Many, but not all, of Nixon's papers are now owned by the American people, and are slowly being opened to the public.

As president, Nixon told Haldeman that he wanted a simple funeral, with little pomp, no church service, and a grave next to his parents in the Whittier cemetery. He hoped that Billy Graham or Norman Vincent Peale would handle the prayers, and "doesn't want a Catholic or Jew to participate," Haldeman recorded. See Haldeman to Hughes, Apr. 20, 1970, WHSF-RC.

Aitken, "Notes on Meeting with RN," Mar. 14, 1992, Nixon to Abplanalp, Aug. 22, 1985, Amery to Thatcher, June 30, 1987, and Thatcher to Amery, July 2, 1987, Nixon to Nofziger, July 2, 1987, Aitken papers, Price OH, RNL; Nixon to Tanenhaus, Sept. 13, 1990, HI; Rumsfeld to files, Feb. 3, 1994, Rumsfeld Archives; see also Nixon to Price, Apr. 12, 1972, RNL; JNE, *Pat.*

Bibliography

Abraham, Henry J. *Justices, Presidents and Senators.* Lanham, MD: Rowman & Littlefield, 2007.

Abrahamsen, David. *Nixon v. Nixon: An Emotional Tragedy.* New York: Signet, 1978.

Acheson, Dean. *Present at the Creation.* New York: Norton, 1969.

Adams, Sherman. *Firsthand Report: The Story of the Eisenhower Administration.* New York: Harper, 1961.

Adler, Renata. *Canaries in the Mineshaft: Essays on Politics and Media.* New York: St. Martin's Press, 2001.

Agnew, Spiro. *Go Quietly . . . or Else.* New York: William Morrow, 1980.

Aitken, Jonathan. *Nixon: A Life.* Washington, D.C.: Regnery, 1993.

Allison, William T. *The Tet Offensive: A Brief History with Documents.* New York: Routledge, 2008.

Alsop, Stewart. *Nixon and Rockefeller.* New York: Doubleday, 1960.

Ambrose, Stephen. *Eisenhower: The President.* New York: Simon & Schuster, 1984.

———. *Eisenhower: Soldier, General of the Army, President-Elect 1890–1952.* New York: Simon & Schuster, 1983.

———. *Nixon: The Education of a Politician 1913–1962.* New York: Simon & Schuster, 1987.

———. *Nixon: Ruin and Recovery 1973–1990.* New York: Simon & Schuster, 1991.

———. *Nixon: The Triumph of a Politician 1962–1972.* New York: Simon & Schuster, 1989.

Anderson, J. W. *Eisenhower, Brownell and the Congress: The Tangled Origins of the Civil Rights Bill of 1956–1957.* Tuscaloosa: University of Alabama Press, 1964.

Anderson, Jack, and James Boyd. *Confessions of a Muckraker.* New York: Random House, 1979.

———, with Daryl Gibson. *Peace, War and Politics.* New York: Tom Doherty Associates, 1999.

Andrews, Bert, and Peter Andrews. *A Tragedy of History: A Journalist's Confidential Role in the Hiss–Chambers Case.* Washington, D.C.: Luce, 1962.

Anson, Robert Sam. *Exile: The Unquiet Oblivion of Richard M. Nixon.* New York: Simon & Schuster, 1984.

Arnold, William. *Back When It All Began.* New York: Vantage, 1975.

Bailey, Stephen. *The New Congress.* New York: St. Martin's Press, 1966.

Baker, Russell. *The Good Times.* New York: Penguin, 1989.

Ball, George. *The Past Has Another Pattern: Memoirs.* New York: Norton, 1982.

Bass, Gary. *The Blood Telegram: Nixon, Kissinger, and a Forgotten Genocide.* New York: Knopf, 2013.

Beatty, James. *The Rascal King: The Life and Times of James Michael Curley (1874–1958).* Reading, MA: Addison-Wesley, 1992.

Ben-Veniste, Richard, and George Frampton Jr. *Stonewall: The Real Story of the Watergate Prosecution.* New York: Simon & Schuster, 1977.

Bentley, Eric, ed. *Thirty Years of Treason: Excerpts from Hearings Before the House Committee on Un-American Activities, 1938–1968.* New York: Viking, 1971.

Berman, Larry. *No Peace, No Honor: Nixon, Kissinger, and Betrayal in Vietnam.* New York: Free Press, 2001.

Bernstein, Carl, and Bob Woodward. *All the President's Men.* New York: Simon & Schuster, 1974.

Beschloss, Michael. *The Crisis Years: Kennedy and Khrushchev, 1960–1963.* New York: HarperCollins, 1991.

———, ed. *Jacqueline Kennedy: Historic Conversations on Life with John F. Kennedy.* New York: Hyperion, 2011.

———. *Mayday: Eisenhower, Khrushchev and the U-2 Affair.* New York: Harper & Row, 1986.

———. *Reaching for Glory: Lyndon Johnson's Secret White House Tapes, 1964–1965.* New York: Simon & Schuster, 2001.

———. *Taking Charge: The Johnson White House Tapes, 1963–1964.* New York: Simon & Schuster, 1997.

Bird, Kai, and Martin Sherwin. *American Prometheus: The Triumph and Tragedy of J. Robert Oppenheimer.* New York: Vintage, 2005.

Bissell, Richard, and Jonathan Lewis. *Reflections of a Cold Warrior.* New Haven, CT: Yale University Press, 1996.

Black, Conrad. *A Life in Full: Richard M. Nixon.* New York: PublicAffairs, 2007.

Blake, Robert. *Benjamin Disraeli.* New York: St. Martin's Press, 1967.

Bowen, Michael. *The Roots of Modern Conservatism.* Chapel Hill: University of North Carolina Press, 2011.

Bradlee, Benjamin. *Conversations with Kennedy.* New York: Norton, 1975.

———. *A Good Life.* New York: Simon & Schuster, 1995.

Branch, Taylor. *At Canaan's Edge.* New York: Simon & Schuster, 2006.

———. *Parting the Waters.* New York: Simon & Schuster, 1988.

———. *Pillar of Fire.* New York: Simon & Schuster, 1998.

Breslin, Jimmy. *How the Good Guys Finally Won: Notes from an Impeachment Summer.* New York: Viking Press, 1975.

Brinkley, Douglas, and Luke Nichter. *The Nixon Tapes, 1971–1972.* Boston: Houghton Mifflin Harcourt, 2014.

———. *The Nixon Tapes, 1973.* Boston: Houghton Mifflin Harcourt, 2015.

Brodie, Fawn. *Richard Nixon: The Shaping of His Character.* New York: Norton, 1981.

Brownell, Herbert. *Advising Ike.* Lawrence: University Press of Kansas, 1993.

Buchanan, Patrick. *The Greatest Comeback.* New York: Crown, 2014.

Bullock, Paul. *Jerry Voorhis: The Idealist as Politician.* New York: Vantage, 1978.

Bundy, William. *A Tangled Web.* New York: Hill & Wang, 1998.

Burns, Arthur. *Inside the Nixon Administration: The Secret Diary of Arthur Burns.* Edited by Robert Ferrell. Lawrence: University Press of Kansas, 2010.

Burr, William, ed. *The Kissinger Transcripts: The Top Secret Talks with Beijing and Moscow.* New York: New Press, 1999.

———, and Jeffrey Kimball. *Nixon's Nuclear Specter.* Lawrence: University Press of Kansas, 2015.

Bush, George H. W. *All the Best, George Bush.* New York: Scribner, 2013.

Cannon, James. *Time and Chance.* New York: HarperCollins, 1994.

Cannon, Lou. *President Reagan: The Role of a Lifetime.* New York: Simon & Schuster, 1991.

———. *Reagan.* New York: Putnam, 1982.

Caro, Robert. *Master of the Senate: The Years of Lyndon Johnson.* New York: Knopf, 2002.

———. *Means of Ascent: The Years of Lyndon Johnson.* New York: Knopf, 1990.

———. *The Passage of Power: The Years of Lyndon Johnson.* New York: Knopf, 2012.

Carr, Robert. *The House Committee on Un-American Activities.* Ithaca, NY: Cornell University Press, 1952.

Carter, Dan T. *The Politics of Rage.* Baton Rouge: Louisiana State University Press, 1995.

Chambers, Whittaker. *Witness.* 50th anniversary edition. Washington, D.C.: Regnery, 2002.

Chennault, Anna. *The Education of Anna.* New York: Times Books, 1980.

Chester, Lewis, Godfrey Hodgson, and Bruce Page. *An American Melodrama, The Presidential Campaign of 1968.* New York: Viking, 1969.

Clifford, Clark, with Richard Holbrooke. *Counsel to the President.* New York: Random House, 1991.

Clodfelter, Micheal. *Vietnam in Military Statistics.* Jefferson, NC: McFarland, 1995.

Cohen, Richard, and Jules Witcover. *A Heartbeat Away: The Investigation and Resignation of Vice President Spiro T. Agnew.* New York: Viking, 1974.

Colodny, Len, and Robert Gettlin. *Silent Coup: The Removal of a President.* New York: St. Martin's Press, 1991.

Cooke, Alistair. *A Generation on Trial: U.S.A. v. Alger Hiss.* New York: Knopf, 1950.

Costello, William. *The Facts about Nixon: An Unauthorized Biography.* New York: Viking, 1960.

Cronkite, Walter. *A Reporter's Life.* New York: Ballantine, 1997.

Crowley, Monica. *Nixon in Winter.* New York: Random House, 1998.

———. *Nixon Off the Record.* New York: Random House, 1996.

Cutler, Robert. *No Time for Rest.* Boston: Little, Brown, 1966.

Dallek, Robert. *Nixon and Kissinger.* New York: HarperCollins, 2007.

———. *An Unfinished Life: John F. Kennedy, 1917–1963.* Boston: Little, Brown, 2003.

Dash, Sam. *Chief Counsel: Inside the Ervin Committee—The Untold Story of Watergate.* New York: Random House, 1976.

David, Lester. *Lonely Lady of San Clemente.* New York: Crowell Book, 1978.

David, Paul, Malcolm Moos, and Ralph Goldman, eds. *Presidential Nominating Politics in 1952.* Baltimore: Johns Hopkins Press, 1954.

Dean, John. *Blind Ambition.* New York: Simon & Schuster, 1976.

———. *Lost Honor.* Los Angeles: Stratford Press, 1982.

———. *The Nixon Defense.* New York: Viking, 2014.

Dean, Maureen. *"Mo": A Woman's View of Watergate.* New York: Simon & Schuster, 1975.

Dent, Harry. *The Prodigal South Returns to Power.* New York: Wiley, 1978.

de Roos, Robert. *Notes from the Underground: The Whittaker Chambers–Ralph de Toledano Letters: 1949–1960.* Washington, D.C.: Regnery, 1997.

———. *The Thirsty Land.* Washington, D.C.: Beard Books, 2000.

de Toledano, Ralph. *One Man Alone: Richard Nixon.* New York: Funk & Wagnalls, 1969.

———, and Victor Lasky. *Seeds of Treason: The True Story of the Chambers-Hiss Tragedy.* New York: Funk & Wagnalls, 1950.

Dickinson, William B., and Janice L. Goldstein. *Watergate: Chronology of a Crisis.* Washington, D.C.: Congressional Quarterly Press, 1975.

Dickson, Paul. *Sputnik: The Shock of the Century.* New York: Walker, 2001.

Diem, Bui, with David Chanoff. *In the Jaws of History.* Boston: Houghton Mifflin, 1987.

Dmytryk, Edward. *Odd Man Out: A Memoir of the Hollywood Ten.* Carbondale: Southern Illinois University Press, 1996.

Dobrynin, Anatoly. *In Confidence.* New York: Times Books, 1995.

Donaldson, Gary. *The First Modern Campaign: Kennedy, Nixon and the Election of 1960.* Lanham, MD: Rowman & Littlefield, 2007.

Donovan, John T. *Crusader in the Cold War: A Biography of Fr. John F. Cronin, S.S. (1908–1994).* New York: Peter Lang, 2005.

Donovan, Robert. *Conflict and Crisis: The Presidency of Harry S. Truman, 1945–1948.* New York: Norton, 1977.

————. *Confidential Secretary: Ann Whitman's 20 Years with Eisenhower and Rockefeller.* New York: Dutton, 1988.

Douglas, Helen Gahagan. *A Full Life.* Garden City, NY: Doubleday, 1982.

Doyle, James. *Not Above the Law: The Battles of Watergate Prosecutors Cox and Jaworski.* New York: William Morrow, 1977.

Drew, Elizabeth. *Richard Nixon.* New York: Times Books, 2007.

————. *Washington Journal: The Events of 1973–1974.* New York: Vintage, 1976.

Edsall, Thomas, and Mary Edsall. *Chain Reaction.* New York: Norton, 1991.

Ehrlichman, John. *Witness to Power.* New York: Simon & Schuster, 1982.

Eisenhower, Dwight. *The Eisenhower Diaries.* Edited by Robert Ferrell. New York: Norton, 1976.

————. *Mandate for Change.* Garden City, NY: Doubleday, 1963.

Eisenhower, John. *Strictly Personal.* Garden City, NY: Doubleday, 1974.

Eisenhower, Julie Nixon. *Pat Nixon: The Untold Story.* New York: Simon & Schuster, 1986.

Ellsberg, Daniel. *Secrets.* New York: Penguin, 2003.

Emery, Fred. *Watergate.* New York: Times Books, 1994.

Ervin, Sam. *The Whole Truth: The Watergate Conspiracy.* New York: Random House, 1980.

Evans, Rowland, and Robert D. Novak. *Nixon in the White House: The Frustration of Power.* New York: Random House, 1971.

Ewald, William Bragg. *Eisenhower the President.* Englewood Cliffs, NJ: Prentice-Hall, 1981.

————. *Who Killed Joe McCarthy?* New York: Simon & Schuster, 1984.

Faries, McIntyre. *Rememb'ring.* Glendale, CA: Griffin, 1993.

Farrell, John A. *Clarence Darrow: Attorney for the Damned.* New York: Doubleday, 2011.

————. *Tip O'Neill and the Democratic Century.* Boston: Little, Brown, 2001.

Feeney, Mark. *Nixon at the Movies.* Chicago: University of Chicago Press, 2004.

Feldstein, Mark. *Poisoning the Press: Richard Nixon, Jack Anderson, and the Rise of the Washington Scandal Culture.* New York: Farrar, Straus & Giroux, 2010.

Felt, Mark. *The FBI Pyramid.* New York: Putnam, 1979.

Ferguson, Niall. *Kissinger.* New York: Penguin, 2015.

Fields, Howard. *High Crimes and Misdemeanors.* New York: Norton, 1978.

Fisher, M. F. K. *Among Friends.* Washington, D.C.: Shoemaker & Hoard, 1970.

————. *M. F. K. Fisher: A Life in Letters: Correspondence 1929–1991.* Edited by Marsha Moran, Patrick Moran, and Norah Barr. Berkeley: Counterpoint, 1997.

Flippen, J. Brooks. *Nixon and the Environment.* Albuquerque: University of New Mexico Press, 2000.

Ford, Gerald. *A Time to Heal: The Autobiography of Gerald R. Ford.* New York: Harper & Row, 1979.

Forslund, Catherine. *Anna Chennault: Informal Diplomacy and Asian Relations.* Wilmington, DE: Scholarly Resources, 2002.

Frady, Marshall. *Billy Graham: A Parable of American Righteousness.* New York: Simon & Schuster, 2006.

Frank, Jeffrey. *Ike and Dick.* New York: Simon & Schuster, 2013.

Friedman, Leon, and William Levantrosser. *Richard M. Nixon: Politician, President, Administrator.* Westport, CT: Greenwood Press, 1991.

————. *Watergate and Afterward: The Legacy of Richard M. Nixon.* Westport, CT: Greenwood Press, 1992.

Frost, David. *Frost/Nixon: Behind the Scenes of the Nixon Interviews.* New York: Harper Perennial, 2007.

Gaddis, John Lewis. *The Cold War: A New History.* New York: Penguin, 2005.

————. *George F. Kennan: An American Life.* New York: Penguin, 2011.

————. *Strategies of Containment.* New York: Oxford University Press, 2005.

Gaiduk, Ilya. *The Soviet Union and the Vietnam War.* Chicago: Ivan R. Dee, 1996.

Galbraith, John Kenneth. *Name-Dropping.* Boston: Houghton Mifflin. 1999.

Garment, Leonard. *Crazy Rhythm.* Boston: Da Capo Press, 1997.

———. *In Search of Deep Throat.* New York: Basic Books, 2000.

Garrow, David. *Bearing the Cross: Martin Luther King, Jr. and the Southern Christian Leadership Conference.* New York: Morrow, 1986.

Gellman, Irwin. *The Contender.* New York: Free Press, 1999.

———. *The President and the Apprentice.* New Haven, CT: Yale University Press, 2015.

Gibbons, William Conrad. *The U.S. Government and the Vietnam War: The U.S. Government and the Vietnam War* (Vols. 1–4). Committee on Foreign Relations, U.S. Senate, 1984.

Gibbs, Nancy, and Michael Duffy. *The Presidents Club.* New York: Simon & Schuster, 2012.

Gitlin, Todd. *The Sixties: Years of Hope, Days of Rage.* New York: Bantam, 1987.

Glazer, Nathan, and Daniel P. Moynihan. *Beyond the Melting Pot.* Cambridge, MA: MIT Press, 1963.

Goldman, Eric. *The Crucial Decade.* New York: Vintage, 1956.

Goodman, Walter. *The Committee: The Extraordinary Career of the House Committee on Un-American Activities.* New York: Farrar, Straus & Giroux, 1968.

Goodwin, Doris Kearns. *The Fitzgeralds and the Kennedys.* New York: St. Martin's Press, 1991.

Gormley, Ken. *Archibald Cox: Conscience of a Nation.* Reading, MA: Addison-Wesley, 1997.

Gottlieb, Robert, and Irene Wolt. *Thinking Big: The Story of the Los Angeles Times, Its Publishers and Their Influence in Southern California.* New York: Putnam, 1977.

Graham, Katharine. *Personal History.* New York: Knopf, 1997.

Gray, L. Patrick. *In Nixon's Web.* New York: Henry Holt, 2008.

Greenberg, David. *Nixon's Shadow.* New York: Norton, 2003.

Greenberg, Stanley. *Middle Class Dreams.* New York: Times Books, 1995.

Greenstein, Fred. *The Hidden-Hand Presidency.* New York: Basic Books, 1982.

Griffiths, Robert, and Athan Theoharis. *The Specter: Original Essays on the Cold War and the Origins of McCarthyism.* New York: New Viewpoints, 1974.

Haig, Alexander. *Inner Circles.* New York: Warner, 1992.

Halberstam, David. *The Best and the Brightest.* New York: Random House, 1972.

———. *The Fifties.* New York: Villard, 1993.

———. *The Powers That Be.* New York: Knopf, 1979.

Haldeman, H. R., and Joseph DiMona. *The Ends of Power.* New York: Times Books, 1978.

———. *The Haldeman Diaries: Inside the Nixon White House.* New York: Putnam, 1994.

Hamby, Alonzo. *Man of the People.* New York: Oxford University Press, 1995.

Hamilton, Nigel. *JFK: Reckless Youth.* New York: Random House, 1993.

Hardeman, D. B., and Donald Bacon, *Rayburn.* Lanham, MD: Madison, 1989.

Hart, Gary. *Right from the Start: A Chronicle of the McGovern Campaign.* New York: Quadrangle, 1973.

Haynes, John Earl, and Kyrill Anderson. *The Soviet World of American Communism.* New Haven, CT: Yale University Press, 1995.

———, and Harvey Klehr. *Venona.* New Haven, CT: Yale University Press, 1999.

———, and Alexander Vassiliev. *Spies.* New Haven, CT: Yale University Press, 2009.

Hersh, Seymour. *The Price of Power: Kissinger in the White House.* New York: Simon & Schuster, 1983.

Hess, Stephen. *The Professor and the President.* Washington, D.C.: Brookings Institution Press, 2015.

Higgins, George V. *The Friends of Richard Nixon.* Boston: Little, Brown, 1975.

Hillings, Patrick, with Howard Seelye. *The Irrepressible Irishman.* Harold Dean, 1993.

Hoff, Joan. *Nixon Reconsidered.* New York: Basic Books, 1994.

Hougan, Jim. *Secret Agenda: Watergate, Deep Throat and the CIA.* New York: Random House, 1984.

Hoyt, Edwin. *The Nixons: An American Family.* New York: Random House, 1972.

Hughes, Emmet J. *The Ordeal of Power.* New York: Atheneum, 1963.

Hughes, Ken. *Chasing Shadows.* Charlottesville: University of Virginia Press, 2014.

———. *Fatal Politics.* Charlottesville: University of Virginia Press, 2015.

Hunt, E. Howard. *Undercover: Memoirs of an American Secret Agent.* New York: Berkley, 1974.

Hutschnecker, Arnold. *The Drive for Power.* Lanham, MD: M. Evans, 1974.

Isaacson, Walter. *Einstein.* New York: Simon & Schuster, 2007.

———. *Kissinger.* New York: Simon & Schuster, 1992.

Jacoby, Susan. *Alger Hiss and the Battle for History.* New Haven, CT: Yale University Press, 2009.

Jaworski, Leon. *The Right and the Power: The Prosecution of Watergate.* New York: Reader's Digest Press, 1976.

Johnson, Loch. *A Season of Inquiry, The Senate Intelligence Investigation.* Lexington: University Press of Kentucky, 1985.

Johnson, Paul. *Modern Times.* New York: HarperCollins, 1983.

Kahrl, William. *Water and Power.* Berkeley: University of California Press, 1982.

Kallina, Edmund. *Courthouse Over White House: Chicago and the Presidential Election of 1960.* Orlando: University Presses of Florida, 1988.

———. *Kennedy v. Nixon.* Gainesville: University Press of Florida, 2010.

Kanfer, Stefan. *A Journal of the Plague Years.* New York: Atheneum, 1973.

Kaplan, Fred. *The Wizards of Armageddon.* Stanford: Stanford University Press, 1991.

Karnow, Stanley. *Vietnam.* New York: Viking, 1983.

Katcher, Leo. *Earl Warren: A Political Biography.* New York: McGraw-Hill, 1967.

Kempton, Murray. *America Comes of Middle Age.* Boston: Little, Brown, 1963.

Keogh, James. *President Nixon and the Press.* New York: Funk & Wagnalls, 1972.

Kimball, Jeffrey. *Nixon's Vietnam War.* Lawrence: University Press of Kansas, 1998.

———. *The Vietnam War Files.* Lawrence: University Press of Kansas, 2004.

King, Martin Luther, Jr. *The Papers of Martin Luther King Jr.* Berkeley: University of California Press, 2000.

Kintner, William, and Robert Pfaltzgraff. *SALT: Implications for Arms Control in the 1970s.* Pittsburgh: University of Pittsburgh, 1973.

Kissinger, Henry. *Crisis: The Anatomy of Two Major Foreign Policy Crises.* New York: Simon & Schuster, 2003.

———. *Ending the Vietnam War.* New York: Simon & Schuster, 2003.

———. *White House Years.* Boston: Little, Brown, 1979.

———. *Years of Renewal.* New York: Simon & Schuster, 1999.

———. *Years of Upheaval.* Boston: Little, Brown, 1982.

Klein, Herbert. *Making It Perfectly Clear.* New York: Doubleday, 1980.

Kleindienst, Richard. *Justice.* Ottawa, IL: Jameson Books, 1985.

Kohut, Heinz. *The Restoration of Self.* Chicago: University of Chicago Press, 1977.

Korff, Baruch. *The Personal Nixon.* Washington, D.C.: Fairness Publishers, 1974.

Kornitzer, Bela. *The Real Nixon: An Intimate Biography.* New York: Rand McNally, 1960.

Kotlowski, Dean. *Nixon's Civil Rights.* Cambridge, MA: Harvard University Press, 2001.

Kraus, Sidney. *The Great Debates: Kennedy vs. Nixon, 1960.* Bloomington: Indiana University Press, 1977.

Krogh, Egil. *The Day Elvis Met Nixon.* Bellevue, WA: Pejama Press, 1994.

Kutler, Stanley, ed. *Abuse of Power: The New Nixon Tapes.* New York: Free Press, 1997.

———. *The Wars of Watergate: The Last Crisis of Richard Nixon.* New York: Norton, 1992.

Larson, Arthur. *Eisenhower: The President Nobody Knew.* New York: Scribner, 1968.

Lasby, Clarence. *Eisenhower's Heart Attack.* Lawrence: University Press of Kansas, 1997.

Lasky, Victor. *It Didn't Start with Watergate.* New York: Dial Press, 1977.

Lavine, Harold, ed. *Smoke-Filled Rooms, The Confidential Papers of Robert Humphreys.* Englewood Cliffs, NJ: Prentice-Hall, 1970.

Le Carré, John. *Smiley's People.* New York: Knopf, 1979.

Levine, Isaac Don. *Eyewitness to History.* New York: Hawthorn, 1973.

Liddy, G. Gordon. *Will: The Autobiography of G. Gordon Liddy.* New York: St. Martin's Press, 1980.

Logevall, Fredrik. *Embers of War.* New York: Random House, 2012.

———, and Andrew Preston. *Nixon in the World.* New York: Oxford University Press, 2008.

Lukas, J. Anthony. *Nightmare: The Underside of the Nixon Years.* New York: Viking, 1976.

Lungren, John. *Healing Richard Nixon.* Lexington: University Press of Kentucky, 2003.

Lyon, Peter. *Eisenhower: Portrait of the Hero.* Boston: Little, Brown, 1974.

MacMillan, Margaret. *Nixon and Mao.* New York: Random House, 2007.

Magruder, Jeb Stuart. *An American Life: One Man's Road to Watergate.* New York: Atheneum, 1974.

Mailer, Norman. *Miami and the Siege of Chicago.* New York: New American Library, 1968.

Mallon, Thomas. *Watergate: A Novel.* New York: Pantheon, 2012.

Malsberger, John. *The General and the Politician.* Lanham, MD: Rowman & Littlefield, 2014.

Mann, James. *About Face.* New York: Knopf, 1999.

Martin, Joe. *My First Fifty Years in Politics.* New York: McGraw-Hill, 1960.

Martin, John Bartlow. *Adlai Stevenson of Illinois.* New York: Doubleday, 1976.

Massing, Michael. *The Fix.* New York: Simon & Schuster, 1998.

Matson, Kevin. *Just Plain Dick: Richard Nixon's Checkers Speech and the "Rocking, Socking" Election of 1952.* New York: Bloomsbury, 2012.

Matthews, Christopher. *Kennedy & Nixon.* New York: Touchstone, 1996.

Matusow, Allen. *Nixon's Economy.* Lawrence: University Press of Kansas, 1998.

Mayer, Michael. *The Eisenhower Presidency and the 1950s.* Boston: Houghton Mifflin, 1998.

Mazlish, Bruce. *In Search of Nixon.* New York: Basic Books, 1972.

Mazo, Earl. *Richard Nixon: A Political and Personal Portrait.* New York: Avon, 1960.

———, and Stephen Hess. *Richard Nixon: A Political Portrait.* New York: Popular Library, 1968.

McCord, James. *A Piece of Tape: The Watergate Story: Fact and Fiction.* Rockville, MD: Washington Media Sources, 1974.

McCullough, David. *Truman.* New York: Simon & Schuster, 1992.

McGinniss, Joe. *The Selling of the President.* New York: Penguin, 1988.

McLuhan, Marshall. *Understanding Media: The Extensions of Man.* New York: McGraw-Hill, 1966.

McNamara, Robert. *In Retrospect.* New York: Times Books, 1995.

McWilliams, Carey. *Southern California: An Island on the Land.* Salt Lake City, UT: Gibbs Smith, 1973.

Mezvinsky, Edward. *A Term to Remember.* New York: Coward, McCann & Geoghegan, 1977.

Mieczkowski, Yanek. *Eisenhower's Sputnik Moment: The Race for Space and World Prestige.* Ithaca, NY: Cornell University Press, 2013.

Miller, Merle. *Plain Speaking.* New York: Berkley, 1980.

Mitchell, Greg. *Tricky Dick and the Pink Lady: Richard Nixon vs. Helen Gahagan Douglas—Sexual Politics and the Red Scare, 1950.* New York: Random House, 1998.

Mollenhoff, Clark. *Game Plan for Disaster: An Ombudsman's Report on the Nixon Years.* New York: Norton, 1976.

Montgomery, Gayle B., and James W. Johnson. *One Step from the White House: The Rise and Fall of Senator William F. Knowland.* Berkeley: University of California Press, 1998.

Morgan, Iwan. *Nixon.* London: Arnold, 2002.

Morris, James McGrath. *Eyes on the Struggle.* New York: Amistad, 2015.

Morris, Roger. *Richard Milhous Nixon: The Rise of an American Politician.* New York: Henry Holt, 1990.

Moynihan, Daniel Patrick. *Daniel Patrick Moynihan: A Portrait in Letters of an American Visionary.* Ed. Steven R. Weisman. New York: PublicAffairs, 2010.

Navasky, Victor. *Naming Names.* New York: Viking, 1980.

Newton, Jim. *Justice for All: Earl Warren and the Nation He Made.* New York: Riverhead Books, 2006.

Nguyen, Gregory Tien Hung, and Jerrold Schecter. *The Palace File.* New York: Harper & Row, 1986.

Nguyen, Lien-Hang T. *Hanoi's War.* Chapel Hill: University of North Carolina Press, 2012.

Nichols, David. *A Matter of Justice.* New York: Simon & Schuster, 2007.

Nichter, Luke. *Richard Nixon and Europe: The Reshaping of the Postwar Atlantic World.* Cambridge, UK: Cambridge University Press, 2015.

Nixon, Edward, and Karen Olson. *The Nixons: A Family Portrait.* Bothell, WA: Book Publishers Network, 2009.

Nixon, Richard. *In the Arena.* New York: Random House, 1990.

———. *Leaders.* New York: Warner Books, 1982.

———. *The Presidential Transcripts, with Commentary by the Staff of the* Washington Post. New York: Dell, 1974.

———. *RN: The Memoirs of Richard Nixon.* New York: Grosset & Dunlap, 1978.

———. *Six Crises.* Garden City, NY: Doubleday, 1962.

Novak, Robert. *The Prince of Darkness.* New York: Three Rivers Press, 2008.

O'Brien, Lawrence. *No Final Victories: A Life in Politics from John F. Kennedy to Watergate.* Garden City, NY: Doubleday, 1974.

Oberdorfer, Don. *Tet!* Garden City, NY: Doubleday, 1971.

O'Donnell, Kenneth, and David Powers. *Johnny, We Hardly Knew Ye: Memories of John Fitzgerald Kennedy.* Boston: Little, Brown, 1972.

Olmsted, Kathryn. *Challenging the Secret Government: The Post-Watergate Investigations of the CIA and FBI.* Chapel Hill: University of North Carolina Press, 1996.

Osborne, John. *The Fifth Year of the Nixon Watch.* New York: Liveright, 1974.

———. *The First Two Years of the Nixon Watch.* New York: Liveright, 1971.

———. *The Fourth Year of the Nixon Watch.* New York: Liveright, 1973.

———. *The Last Nixon Watch.* Washington, D.C.: New Republic Book Company, 1975.

———. *The Third Year of the Nixon Watch.* New York: Liveright, 1972.

Oshinsky, David. *A Conspiracy So Immense.* New York: Oxford University Press, 2005.

Oudes, Bruce. *From: The President: Richard Nixon's Secret Files.* New York: Harper & Row, 1989.

Parmet, Herbert S. *Eisenhower and the American Crusades.* New York: Macmillan, 1972.

———. *Richard Nixon and His America.* Boston: Little, Brown, 1990.

Patterson, James T. *Grand Expectations.* The Oxford History of the United States. New York: Oxford University Press, 1996.

———. *Restless Giant.* The Oxford History of the United States. New York: Oxford University Press, 2005.

Pearson, Drew. *Diaries, 1949–1959.* New York: Henry Holt, 1974.

———, and Peter Hannaford. *Washington Merry-Go-Round: The Drew Pearson Diaries, 1960–1969.* Lincoln, NE: Potomac Books, 2015.

Perlstein, Rick. *Before the Storm.* New York: Hill & Wang, 2001.

———. *Nixonland,* New York: Scribner, 2008.

Phillips, David Atlee. *The Night Watch.* New York: Ballantine, 1982.

Phillips, Kevin. *The Emerging Republican Majority.* New Rochelle, NY: Arlington House, 1969.

Pietrusza, David. *1960: LBJ vs. JFK vs. Nixon: The Epic Campaign That Forged Three Presidencies.* New York: Sterling, 2008.

Pipes, Kasey. *Ike's Final Battle: The Road to Little Rock and the Challenge of Equality.* Los Angeles: World Ahead Media, 2007.

Polsby, Nelson. *How Congress Evolves.* New York: Oxford University Press, 2003.

Powers, Richard. *Not Without Honor: The History of American Anticommunism.* New Haven, CT: Yale University Press, 1998.

Powers, Thomas. *The Man Who Kept the Secrets: Richard Helms and the CIA.* New York: Knopf, 1979.

Prados, John, and Margaret Pratt Porter. *Inside the Pentagon Papers.* Lawrence: University Press of Kansas, 2004.

Price, Raymond. *With Nixon.* New York: Viking, 1977.

Rampersad, Arnold. *Jackie Robinson: A Biography.* New York: Ballantine, 1998.

Randolph, Stephen. *Powerful and Brutal Weapons: Nixon, Kissinger and the Easter Offensive.* Cambridge, MA: Harvard University Press, 2007.

Reardon, Joan. *Poet of the Appetites.* New York: Macmillan, 2005.

Reedy, George E. *The Twilight of the Presidency.* New York: World Publishing, 1970.

Reeves, Richard. *President Kennedy: Profile of Power.* New York: Simon & Schuster, 1993.

———. *President Nixon: Alone in the White House.* New York: Touchstone, 2001.

Reeves, Thomas. *The Life and Times of Joe McCarthy.* Lanham, MD: Madison Books, 1997.

Reston, James. *The Conviction of Richard Nixon.* New York: Broadway Books, 2008.

Reuben, William A. *The Honorable Mr. Nixon and the Alger Hiss Case.* New York: Action Books, 1956.

Rhodes, Richard. *Dark Sun: The Making of the Hydrogen Bomb.* New York: Simon & Schuster, 1995.

———. *The Making of the Atomic Bomb.* New York: Touchstone, 1988.

Rockwell, John, ed. *The New York Times: The Times of the Sixties.* New York: Black Dog & Leventhal, 2014.

Rosen, James. *The Strong Man: John Mitchell and the Secrets of Watergate.* New York: Doubleday, 2008.

Rovere, Richard. *The Eisenhower Years: Affairs of State.* New York: Farrar, Straus & Cudahy, 1956.

———. *Senator Joe McCarthy.* Cleveland, OH: Meridian Books, 1960.

Rudenstine, David. *The Day the Presses Stopped.* Berkeley: University of California Press, 1996.

Rudolph, Lloyd, and Susanne Hoeber Rudolph. *The Regional Imperative.* Bloomington: Indiana University Press, 1980.

Safire, William. *Before the Fall.* Garden City, NY: Doubleday, 1975.

Salant, Richard. *Salant, CBS, and the Battle for the Soul of Broadcast Journalism: The Memoirs of Richard S. Salant.* Boulder, CO: Westview Press, 1999.

Sbardellati, John. *J. Edgar Hoover Goes to the Movies.* Ithaca, NY: Cornell University Press, 2012.

Scammon, Richard, and Ben Wattenberg, *The Real Majority.* New York: Capricorn, 1971.

Schell, Jonathan. *The Time of Illusion.* New York: Vintage, 1976.

Schlesinger, Arthur, Jr. *Journals, 1952–2000.* New York: Penguin, 2007.

———. *Kennedy or Nixon: Does It Make Any Difference?* New York: Macmillan, 1960.

———. *A Thousand Days: John F. Kennedy in the White House.* Boston: Houghton Mifflin, 1965.

Schlight, John. *A War Too Long: The USAF in Southeast Asia.* Washington, D.C.: Air Force History and Museums Program, 1996.

Schmitz, David. *Richard Nixon and the Vietnam War.* Lanham, MD: Rowman & Littlefield, 2014.

Schulte, Renee K. *The Young Nixon: An Oral Inquiry.* Fullerton: California State University, Fullerton, 1978.

Scobie, Ingrid Winther. *Center Stage.* New York: Oxford University Press, 1992.

Shannon, William V. *The American Irish.* New York: Macmillan, 1963.

Shawcross, William. *Sideshow.* New York: Simon & Schuster, 1979.

Sheehan, Neil, Hedrick Smith, E. W. Kenworthy, and Fox Butterfield. *The Pentagon Papers.* New York: Bantam, 1971.

Shephard, Geoff. *The Real Watergate Scandal.* Washington, D.C.: Regnery, 2015.

Shultz, George P. *Turmoil and Triumph: My Years as Secretary of State.* New York: Scribner's, 1993.

Sirica, John. *To Set the Record Straight: The Break-In, the Tapes, the Conspirators, the Pardon.* New York: Norton, 1979.

Slater, Ellis. *The Ike I Knew.* Ellis Slater Trust, 1980.

Small, Melvin, ed. *A Companion to Richard M. Nixon.* Malden, MA: Wiley-Blackwell, 2011.

———. *The Presidency of Richard Nixon.* Lawrence: University Press of Kansas, 1999.

Smith, Gerard. *Doubletalk.* New York: Doubleday, 1980.

Smith, Jean Edward. *Eisenhower in War and Peace.* New York: Random House, 2012.

———. *Lucius D. Clay: An American Life.* New York: Henry Holt, 1990.

Smith, Richard Norton. *On His Own Terms: A Life of Nelson Rockefeller.* New York: Random House, 2014.

———. *Thomas E. Dewey and His Times.* New York: Simon & Schuster, 1982.

Sorensen, Theodore. *Kennedy.* New York: Harper & Row, 1965.

Spalding, Henry D. *The Nixon Nobody Knows.* Middle Village, NY: J. David, 1972.

Starr, Kevin. *The Dream Endures: California Enters the 1940s.* New York: Oxford University Press, 1997.

———. *Embattled Dreams: Californians in War and Peace.* New York: Oxford University Press, 2002.

———. *Endangered Dreams: The Great Depression in California.* New York: Oxford University Press, 1996.

———. *Golden Dreams: California in an Age of Abundance, 1950–1963.* New York: Oxford University Press, 2009.

Steffens, Lincoln. *The Letters of Lincoln Steffens.* New York: Harcourt, Brace, 1938.

Stone, Oliver. *Nixon: An Oliver Stone Film* (annotated screenplay). Edited by Eric Hamburg. New York: Hyperion, 1995.

Stripling, Robert. *The Red Plot Against America.* Drexel Hill, PA: Bell, 1949.

Strober, Deborah Hart, and Gerald Strober. *The Nixon Presidency: An Oral History of the Era.* Washington, D.C.: Brassey's, 2003.

Sulzberger, Cyrus. *The World and Richard Nixon.* New York: Viking, 1978.

Summers, Anthony. *The Arrogance of Power.* New York: Viking, 2000.

Sundquist, James. *Dynamics of the Party System.* Washington, D.C.: Brookings Institution, 1983.

Sussman, Barry. *The Great Coverup: Nixon and the Scandal of Watergate.* New York: New American Library, 1974.

Swift, Will. *Pat and Dick: The Nixons, an Intimate Portrait of a Marriage.* New York: Simon & Schuster, 2014.

Tanenhaus, Sam. *Whittaker Chambers.* New York: Random House, 1997.

Theoharis, Athan. *Chasing Spies.* Chicago: Ivan R. Dee, 2002.

———. *From the Secret Files of J. Edgar Hoover.* Chicago: Ivan R. Dee, 1991.

Theroux, Paul. *Sunrise with Seamonsters.* Boston: Houghton Mifflin, 1986.

Thomas, Evan. *Being Nixon.* New York: Random House, 2015.

———. *Ike's Bluff.* Boston: Little, Brown, 2012.

———. *Robert Kennedy.* New York: Simon & Schuster, 2000.

Thompson, Fred. *At That Point in Time: The Inside Story of the Watergate Committee.* New York: Quadrangle, 1975.

Thompson, Hunter. *The Great Shark Hunt.* New York: Summit Books, 1979.

Thompson, Kenneth W., ed. *The Eisenhower Presidency.* Lanham, MD: University Press of America, 1984.

————. *The Nixon Presidency.* Lanham, MD: University Press of America, 1987.

Thomson, Charles, and Frances Shattuck. *The 1956 Presidential Campaign.* Washington, D.C.: Brookings Institution, 1960.

Trilling, Lionel. *The Middle of the Journey.* New York: Scribner, 1976.

Trohan, Walter. *Political Animals.* Garden City, NY: Doubleday, 1975.

Tudda, Chris. *A Cold War Turning Point.* Baton Rouge: Louisiana State University Press, 2012.

Tyler, Patrick. *A Great Wall.* New York: PublicAffairs, 1999.

Ulasewicz, Tony, and Stuart A. McKeever. *The President's Private Eye: The Journey of Detective Tony U. from N.Y.P.D. to the Nixon White House.* Westport, CT: MACSAM Publishing Company, 1990.

Vidal, Gore. *An Evening with Richard Nixon.* New York: Random House, 1972.

Volkan, Vamik, with Norman Itzkowitz and Andrew Dod. *Richard Nixon, A Psychobiography.* New York: Columbia University Press, 1997.

Voorhis, Jerry. *Confessions of a Congressman.* Garden City, NY: Doubleday, 1948.

————. *The Strange Case of Richard Milhous Nixon.* New York: P. S. Eriksson, 1972.

Walters, Vernon. *Silent Missions.* Garden City, NY: Doubleday, 1978.

Washington Post staff. *The Fall of a President.* New York: Delacorte Press, 1974.

Watson, Denton. *Lion in the Lobby.* New York: William Morrow, 1990.

Weiner, Tim. *One Man Against the World: The Tragedy of Richard Nixon.* New York: Henry Holt, 2015.

Weinstein, Allen. *Perjury.* New York: Knopf, 1978.

————, and Alexander Vassiliev. *The Haunted Wood.* New York: Random House, 1999.

Wells, Tom. *The War Within.* Berkeley: University of California Press, 1994.

West, Jessamyn. *Double Discovery.* New York: Harcourt Brace Jovanovich, 1980.

————. *Hide and Seek.* New York: Harcourt Brace Jovanovich, 1973.

Whalen, Richard. *Catch the Falling Flag.* Boston: Houghton Mifflin, 1972.

————. *The Founding Father.* Washington, D.C.: Regnery Gateway, 1993.

————. *Taking Sides: A Personal View of America from Kennedy to Nixon to Kennedy.* Boston: Houghton Mifflin, 1974.

White, Theodore H. *Breach of Faith: The Fall of Richard Nixon.* New York, Atheneum, 1975.

————. *The Making of the President 1960.* New York: Atheneum, 1961.

————. *The Making of the President 1964.* New York: Atheneum, 1965.

————. *The Making of the President 1968.* New York: Atheneum, 1969.

————. *The Making of the President 1972.* New York: Atheneum, 1973.

Wicker, Tom. *One of Us.* New York: Random House, 1991.

Wiener, Jon. *Gimme Some Truth.* Berkeley: University of California Press, 2000.

Williams, Juan. *Eyes on the Prize.* New York: Penguin, 1987.

Wills, Garry. *Nixon Agonistes: The Crisis of the Self-Made Man.* Boston: Houghton Mifflin, 1969.

Witcover, Jules. *The Resurrection of Richard Nixon.* New York: Putnam, 1970.

————. *The Year the Dream Died.* New York: Warner, 1997.

Wofford, Harris. *Of Kennedys and Kings.* Pittsburgh: University of Pittsburgh Press, 1980.

Woodward, Bob. *The Secret Man: The Story of Watergate's Deep Throat.* New York: Simon & Schuster, 2005.

————. *Shadow: Five Presidents and the Legacy of Watergate.* New York: Simon & Schuster, 1999.

————, and Scott Armstrong. *The Brethren.* New York: Simon & Schuster, 1979.

————, and Carl Bernstein. *The Final Days.* New York: Simon & Schuster, 1976.

Worthen, James. *The Young Nixon and His Rivals.* Jefferson, NC: McFarland, 2010.

Wyden, Peter. *Bay of Pigs.* New York: Touchstone, 1979.

Zumwalt, Elmo. *On Watch.* New York: Quadrangle, 1976.

Illustration Credits

INSERT A
Page 1 Courtesy of the Richard Nixon Presidential Library
Page 2 Top left: Courtesy of the Yorba Linda Public Library
Top right and bottom: Courtesy of the Richard Nixon Presidential Library
Page 3 Top and bottom: Courtesy of the Yorba Linda Public Library
Center: National Archives
Page 4 Top left and bottom: Courtesy of the Richard Nixon Presidential Library
Top right: Courtesy of the Richard Nixon Foundation
Page 5 Top right and left: Courtesy of the Richard Nixon Foundation
Bottom: Courtesy of the Richard Nixon Presidential Library
Page 6 All: Courtesy of the Richard Nixon Presidential Library
Page 7 Top: Courtesy of the Whittier College Special Collections & Archives, Wardman
      Library
Bottom left: Harris & Ewing Collection (Library of Congress)
Bottom right: Courtesy of the Richard Nixon Presidential Library
Page 8 Top and bottom: Courtesy of the Richard Nixon Presidential Library
Center: National Archives
Page 9 Top and bottom left: Courtesy of the Richard Nixon Presidential Library
Bottom right: Collection of the U.S. House of Representatives
Page 10 Top: National Archives
Bottom: Courtesy of the Richard Nixon Presidential Library
Page 11 Top left and right: Dwight D. Eisenhower Presidential Library
Bottom: National Archives
Page 12 Top: National Archives
Center: Courtesy of the Richard Nixon Foundation
Bottom: Courtesy of the Richard Nixon Presidential Library
Page 13 All: Courtesy of the Richard Nixon Presidential Library
Page 14 Courtesy of the Richard Nixon Presidential Library
Page 15 Top: LBJ Library photo by Yoichi Okamoto
Bottom left: National Archives
Bottom right: Courtesy of the Richard Nixon Presidential Library
Page 16 Courtesy of the Richard Nixon Presidential Library

INSERT B
Page 1 Top and bottom left: Courtesy of the Richard Nixon Presidential Library
Bottom center and right: National Archives
Page 2 Top left and right: Courtesy of the Richard Nixon Presidential Library
Bottom: Library of Congress Prints and Photographs Division
Page 3 All: Courtesy of the Richard Nixon Presidential Library

Page 4 All: Courtesy of the Richard Nixon Presidential Library
Page 5 Courtesy of the Richard Nixon Presidential Library
Page 6 Top: Courtesy of the Richard Nixon Presidential Library
Bottom: National Archives
Page 7 Top: National Archives
Bottom: Courtesy of the Richard Nixon Presidential Library
Page 8 All: Courtesy of the Richard Nixon Presidential Library
Page 9 All: Courtesy of the Richard Nixon Presidential Library
Page 10 Top left and bottom: National Archives
Top right: National Archives, courtesy of "The Smoking Gun"
Page 11 Top: National Archives
Center and bottom: Courtesy of the Richard Nixon Presidential Library
Page 12 Courtesy of the Richard Nixon Presidential Library
Page 13 All: Courtesy of the Richard Nixon Presidential Library
Page 14 Top left: Courtesy of the Richard Nixon Foundation
Top right: Courtesy of Julie Nixon Eisenhower
Bottom: Courtesy of the Richard Nixon Presidential Library
Page 15 All: Courtesy of the Richard Nixon Foundation
Page 16 Courtesy of the Richard Nixon Presidential Library

ABM treaty, 494
abortion, 377
Abplanalp, Robert, 353, 547
   RN's friendship with, 400, 408, 472, 554,
      633*n*
Abrams, Creighton, 343, 491, 494, 539
Abzug, Bella, 513, 520
Acheson, Dean, 94, 127, 143, 226, 230
Achilles, Theodore, 265
Acker, Marje, 535
Adamowski, Ben, 295, 296, 297
Adams, Earl, 12, 24, 166, 184, 300
Adams, Sherman, 172, 174, 186, 188, 212,
      230, 237, 238, 239, 241, 242, 257, 261,
      507–8
   resignation of, 267
affirmative action, 383, 395–96
Affordable Care Act, 376
Afghanistan, 217
Africa, 245
African Americans:
   Eisenhower's popularity with, 254
   in prisons, 379
   race riots and, 321–22
   Republican neglect of, 289
Agnew, Spiro, 384, 393, 397, 402–3, 514
   corruption charges against, 333, 519
   resignation of, 519
   as RN's 1968 running mate, 333, 637*n*
   RN's critics attacked by, 413
   as vice president, 370
Agricultural Adjustment Administration,
      109
Ailes, Roger, 339, 399, 401
Air Combat Intelligence, 5
Aitken, Jonathan, 162, 547, 555, 580*n*,
      592*n*, 638*n*, 651*n*
Alabama, University of, desegregation of,
      384

Alaska Pipeline, 381
Albert, Carl, 513, 520
Alexander, Lamar, 385
Algeria, French withdrawal from, 360
Ali, Muhammad, 335, 387, 422
Allende, Salvador, CIA-backed overthrow
      of, 543–44
Alsop, Joseph, 87, 163, 526
Alsop, Stewart, 87, 399, 511
Amateurs (Committee of 100), 13–16,
      23–24, 28, 29, 133
   Marshall Plan opposed by, 86, 87, 91
Ambrose, Stephen, 373, 555
American Civil Liberties Union (ACLU),
      101
Amery, Julian, 554
Anaheim Union Water Company, 51
Anderson, Jack, 207, 238, 459, 467, 470,
      471, 664*n*, 668*n*
Anderson, Robert, 240, 241, 272
Andreas, Dwayne, 546
Andrews, Bert, 85, 102, 116, 117, 119, 122,
      127, 184, 196–97
antiballistic missiles (ABMs), 488,
      489
anti-Communism, anti-Communists:
   McCarthy's discrediting of, 223,
      226
   Red threat exaggerated by, 94
   witch-hunting by, 95, 233
anti-Semitism, of RN, 417–18, 426, 653*n*,
      654*n*–55*n*
antiwar movement, 315, 350, 362, 397, 404,
      413, 417, 553–54
   construction workers' attack on, 414
   illegal surveillance of, 421–22
   mass arrests of, 421
   Mobilization and, 368, 370
   Moratorium and, 368

antiwar movement (*cont.*):
  RN's attacks on, 414–15
  RN's proposal for Teamsters assaults on, 421, 653*n*
Apollo 8, 348
Arbuthnot, Ray, 309
Arends, Leslie C., 295–96
Arkansas National Guard, Eisenhower's federalization of, 258
armed forces, U.S., desegregation of, 247, 248
arms race, 82, 83, 144, 215, 263, 347, 435, 487–88, 494–95
Armstrong, Anne, 352*n*
Army, U.S., McCarthy's attacks on, 220, 222
Army-McCarthy hearings, 223
  televising of, 224–25
Arnold, George, 206
Arnold, William, 85, 122, 210, 604*n*
ARPANET, 376*n*
Arrambide, John, 61
"Asia After Viet Nam" (Nixon), 437
Atkins, Oliver, 531
atomic weapons, 80–81, 94
  arms race in, 83, 144, 215
  Cold War tests of, 105
  Soviet acquisition of, 81, 94, 105, 144
Atwater, Lee, 556
Austria, German invasion of, 75
automobiles, postwar shortages of, 20, 39
Ayub Khan, Mohammad, 217

B-29 bombers, 105
B-52 Stratofortresses, 364, 494, 497
Bacall, Lauren, 98
Baker, Howard, 327, 330, 478, 480
Baldwin, Alfred, 468, 482, 483–84, 668*n*, 669*n*
Baldy, Mount, 51
Ball, George, 360, 368, 500
Balzano, Michael, 388
Bangladesh, 459
Bank of America, 8, 9, 14, 26
Bassett, James, 208–9, 232, 243, 244–45, 281, 291, 410*n*, 411
  on Eisenhower's relationship with RN, 232, 615*n*
  on McCarthy, 214, 215, 220–21, 224–25
  in RN's 1952 vice-presidential campaign, 182, 185, 194

RN's conversations with, 232–33, 614*n*
  on RN's increasing paranoia, 209
  "Ugly Year, Lonely Man" diary of, 232–33, 614*n*–15*n*
Baus, Herbert, 134
Bay of Pigs invasion, 303, 426
Beard, Dita, 467
Becker, Benton, 536
Bentley, Elizabeth, 106, 110, 116, 123, 590*n*
Bergholz, Richard "Dick," 171
Berle, Adolf, 108, 110, 113
Berlin, 93
  Allied bombing of, 367
  RN's postwar trip to, 89
Berlin crisis (1948), 105
Bernstein, Carl, 482, 483, 529, 536–37, 548, 549
Best Years of Our Lives (film), 97
Bewley, Kathryn, 23
Bewley, Thomas, 15, 16, 62, 70–71, 74, 77, 83, 167, 186, 207, 209, 250
Biafra, 451
Bilbo, Theodore, 29
Bill of Rights, 103
Black, Hugo, 424–25
"Black Day, The: To the Memory of Laurence Duggan" (MacLeish), 126
Blackmun, Harry, 377, 390, 395
Black Panthers, 335, 375, 387, 422
Blake, Robert, 53
Block, Herb, *see* Herblock
Boddy, Manchester, 149
  in 1950 Democratic primary, 146–47, 148, 153
Bogart, Humphrey, 96, 98
Boggs, Hale, 513
Bohlen, Charles "Chip," 90
  McCarthy's smearing of, 214–15
Book of the Month Club, 301–2
Bork, Robert, 521, 529
Bosnia, 451
Boston, Mass., school busing crisis in, 329
Boston Globe, 424
Bougainville, 77, 585*n*
Bowles, Chester, 299
Bradlee, Benjamin, 77, 476, 670*n*
  career of, 482–83
  Kennedy family and, 482–83
Bradley, Don, 155

Brandt, Willy, 444, 489
Brashear, Ernest, 179, 605*n*
Breach of Faith: The Fall of Richard Nixon
    (White), 296*n*, 636
Brecht, Bertolt, 98
Bremer, Arthur, 525, 667*n*
Brennan, Bernard, 167, 168
  in RN's 1950 Senate campaign, 133–34,
      138, 142, 145, 151–52, 155
Brennan, John "Jack," 403, 550
Brennan, William, 251, 528–29
Bretton Woods Agreement, 446
  RN's suspension of, 444, 448
Brezhnev, Leonid, 450, 457, 459, 494, 522,
    523
  RN's meetings with, 516, 527
Bridges, Styles, 242
Brock, William, 250, 327, 330, 332–33
Broder, David, 368
Bronson, Leisa, 31, 40
Brookings Institution, proposed burglary
    of, 425–26
Broun, Heywood, 130–31
Brown, Edmund "Pat," 136, 195, 204, 206,
    326
  in 1958 California gubernatorial race, 268
Brown, Edmund "Pat," 1962 gubernatorial
    campaign of, 304
  Cuban missile crisis and, 308
  dirty tricks used by, 306–7
  JFK and, 310–11
  Warren and, 309
Brownell, Herbert, Jr., 167, 169, 172, 174,
    188, 195, 202, 211, 221, 251, 252, 254,
    256, 258, 275
Brownfield, Lyman, 67, 68–69, 205
Brown v. Board of Education, 247–49, 251,
    254, 384, 385
Bryant, Floyd, 27
Buchanan, Patrick, 323, 326, 334, 340, 354,
    374, 388, 403, 414, 498, 525, 526, 535
  "Neither Fish Nor Fowl" memo of, 376–77
Buckley, William F., Jr., 108, 128
budget deficits, 445
Bui Diem, 342, 343
Bull, Steve, 408
Bullock, Paul, 34, 35
Bundy, William, 344
Bureau of Reclamation, 129
Burger, Warren, 173, 389*n*, 390, 529
Burke, Edmund, 87, 91–92, 315

Burma, 217
Burns, Arthur, 278, 375, 381, 444, 458, 512,
    524, 655*n*
  RN's confrontations with, 445
  RN's economic policies and, 448
Bush, George H. W., 327, 330, 398, 530,
    556, 627*n*–28*n*
Butterfield, Alexander, 353, 355, 408, 409,
    431, 518
Buzhardt, J. Fred, 518, 529
Byck, Samuel, in attempted assassination of
    RN, 525–26
Byrd, Harry, 395
Byrne, Matthew, 678*n*

Cady, Fred, 68
Cagney, James, 96
California:
  Central Valley Project in, *see* Central
      Valley Project
  Democratic voter advantage in, 304
  1962 gubernatorial race in, 304–11
  North-South divide in, 136, 140
  oil industry in, 25–27
  population explosion in, 137
  Southern, conservatism in, 22–23
California Republican Assembly, 142
Call, Asa, 173, 595*n*
Cambodia, 217, 361
  Khmer Rouge regime in, 364
  1970 coup in, 397
  North Vietnamese invasion of, 397, 402
  U.S. bombing of, 363–64, 367, 643*n*–44*n*
  U.S. invasion of, 360, 412–13, 439
Camp David, secret economic conference
    at, 447
Camus, Albert, 636*n*
Cardozo, Benjamin, 529
Carmichael, Stokely, 386–87
Carnegie Endowment for International
    Peace, 107, 116, 215
Caro, Robert, 295
Carr, Robert, 97
Carswell, G. Harrold, 389
Carter, Dan T., 433
Carter, Jimmy, 555, 556
  in 1976 election, 537
Castro, Fidel, CIA plots against, 302–3,
    470, 542, 668*n*
Catholicism, as issue in 1960 election,
    278–80, 623*n*, 624*n*

Catledge, Turner, 136
Caulfield, Jack, 431, 432, 433, 470, 504–5
  Senate testimony of, 515
Cavett, Dick, 418
CBS, 515
CBS radio, 186
Celler, Emanuel, 99, 103, 230
Central High School, Little Rock, 258
  desegregation of, 248
Central Intelligence Agency (CIA), 86, 215,
  265, 274, 302, 630n
  assassination plots of, 313–14, 433, 470,
    542, 668n
  Castro plots of, 302–3, 470, 542, 668n
  drug experiments by, 542
  foreign coups sponsored by, 302, 542,
    543–44
  illegal surveillance by, 433, 541–42
  RN's planned purge of, 512
  Watergate break-ins and, 665n–66n
  Watergate cover-up and, 477–79, 481,
    515–16, 536, 551
Central Valley Project:
  big agriculture and, 130
  160-acre water limit in, 129–30, 132, 147,
    155
Chamberlain, Neville, 75, 321
Chambers, Esther, 115, 124
Chambers, Whittaker, 96, 188, 204, 262
  anti-elitist attack on, 199
  background of, 107
  as Communist, 107, 108
  dropping of perjury charges against, 124
  grand jury testimony of, 123–24, 593n
  Hiss's slander suit against, 120
  homosexuality of, 107, 115, 124
  HUAC testimony of, 106–7, 109–10,
    590n
  liberal loathing of, 126–27
  mental instability of, 123, 590n
  poor dental hygiene of, 107–8
  on RN's decision to pursue Hiss case, 112
  RN's meetings with, 113, 115–16, 117,
    121
  as Soviet spy, 109, 122, 123
  in televised HUAC hearing, 119–20
Champlin, Malcolm, 145
Chancellor, John, 521
Chandler, Dorothy, 136, 157, 600n
Chandler, Harry, 135
Chandler, Norman, 135, 136–37, 157

Chandler, Otis, 309
Chandler family, 36, 204, 309, 311, 595n
Chapin, Dwight, 305, 323, 352, 353, 398,
  432, 538
  on RN's growing paranoia, 399–400
Chavoor, Evelyn, 155
Checkers (Nixon dog), 188, 193, 219, 301,
  608n–9n
Chennault, Anna, 342–43, 637n–39n, 640n
Chennault, Claire, 342
Chennault affair, 342–44, 425, 433, 546,
  637n–40n
Chessman, Caryl, 304
Chiang Kai-shek, 150, 217, 228, 439, 441
Chicago, Ill.:
  1968 Democratic Convention in,
    322–23
  voting fraud in, 295–96
Chicago *Daily News*, 173
Chicago Eight, 422
Chile, Allende coup in, 543–44
China, 218
  civil war in, 94, 441
  Cultural Revolution in, 347
  Japanese invasion of, 74
  Kissinger's secret trip to, 436, 440–42,
    453
  in Korean War, 156, 462
  "loss" of, 314
  nuclear weapons acquired by, 362
  purges and atrocities in, 436
  Quemoy and Matsu bombarded by, 228,
    235, 299
  RN in post-presidential trips to, 554
  RN's opening to, 418, 435–44, 450, 453,
    460–64, 465, 490
  and Soviet invasion of Czechoslovakia,
    438
  Soviet relations with, 438–39, 463
  Tiananmen Square protests in, 553–54
  U.S. table tennis team in visit to, 439–40,
    453
China Lobby, 436
Chinatown (film), 552
Chotiner, Murray, 35, 37n, 101, 166, 167,
  171, 174, 180, 234, 238, 282, 356, 386,
  431
  attack mentality of, 139
  influence-peddling charges against, 262,
    620n
  Kyle Palmer and, 141–42

national health plan promoted by, 141
in RN's 1946 campaign, 28–30, 573*n*
and RN's 1952 vice-presidential
  campaign, 175, 182, 184, 186, 194,
  196, 209
in RN's 1962 campaign, 305, 310
in RN's 1968 campaign, 345
in RN's Senate campaign, 138–42, 145,
  148–52, 602*n*
Christopher, George, 169
Church, Frank, 413, 541
Church committee, 541–43, 665*n*
Churchill, Winston, 30, 75, 85, 221, 227,
  491
  Iron Curtain speech of, 21, 558
  on McCarthyism, 225
CIO-PAC, 32–34, 573*n*
Citadel, The (White), 253
Citra-Frost, 71, 74
civil liberties, 538
Civil Rights Act of 1957, 328
  Brownell's draft of, 252–53
  Eisenhower and, 256
  House passage of, 255
  RN and, 253–57
  Senate attack on part III of, 255–56,
    258
Civil Rights Act of 1964, 257, 315, 327–28,
  329
Civil Rights Commission, U.S., 252, 257
Civil Rights Congress, 154
civil rights movement, 245–46, 321, 334
  Eisenhower and, 247–49, 254, 258–59
  growing militancy of, 386
  growth of, 251–52
  illegal surveillance of, 421–22, 628*n*
  JFK and, 329
  Johnson and, 257, 329, 384
  World War II in revitalizing of, 247
civil rights movement, RN and, 332
  affirmative action and, 395–96
  Brown decision disliked by, 385
  busing opposed by, 385–86
  and concern about loss of white votes,
    384–85, 395
  and deliberate encouragement of racial
    divisions, 388–89
  in 1960 campaign, 287, 626*n*
  1970 white paper of, 391
  as president, 384–96
  silent majority and, 388

threat of legal and budget reprisals as tool
  of, 393–94
as vice president, 245–46, 250–51,
  252–58, 259
vows to uphold law in, 391
Claar, John, 190–91
Clawson, Ken, 535
Clay, Lucius, 90, 167, 186, 195, 211, 241,
  261
Clean Air Act (1970), 380
Clean Water Act (1972), 381
Clifford, Clark, 321, 351
Clinton, Bill, 371, 378, 556, 558
Clinton, Hillary Rodham, 296*n*, 556,
  558
Coffin, William Sloane, 368
Cohen, Meyer "Mickey," 306
Cohn, Roy, 145, 215, 222–23, 224–25
Cold War, 93, 210, 226, 450, 541
  atomic bomb tests in, 105
  Berlin crisis in, 105
  emergence of, 81
  Hiss case and, 127–28
  McCarthyism and, 144
  "missile gap" myth in, 260, 274, 630*n*
  1971 India-Pakistan war in, 456–57
  nuclear arms race in, 82, 144, 215, 263,
    347, 435, 487–88, 494–95
  test ban agreement in, 313
  U.S. plans for war with Soviets in, 105
Colodny, Len, 669*n*
Colson, Charles, 306, 377, 386, 411–12,
  421, 423, 424, 431, 445, 466, 467, 476,
  514, 662*n*
  dirty tricks campaign and, 434, 671*n*
  hired as RN's political counselor, 359
  Plumbers and, 427, 428
  racial division encouraged by, 388
  on RN's relations with media, 402
  Watergate conviction of, 537–38
  Watergate cover-up and, 477, 503–4, 506,
    508, 551
Commager, Henry Steele, 200
Committee of 100, *see* Amateurs
Committee to Re-Elect the President
  (CREEP), 466, 476, 483–84, 513,
  551
  FBI investigation of, 474
  Liddy and, 467
  money-laundering scheme of, 478, 672*n*
  Plumbers and, 429–30

Communism, Communists, 14, 21, 29
   as global threat, 81, 93, 165, 314
   liberal infatuation with, 108
   popular fear of, *see* Red Scare
   in Southeast Asia, 314
   in Spanish Civil War, 74–75
Communist Party, U.S., 94, 101, 154
   federal indictments of, 106
Conant, James, 214
Condon, Edward, HUAC smear of, 102,
      105, 590*n*
Congress, U.S.:
   Democratic majority in, 372
   growing opposition to Vietnam War in,
      413, 415, 417, 423, 539, 540
   Southern Democrats' domination of, 247,
      253
   U.S. military operations in Vietnam
      ended by, 501
   War Powers Resolution passed by, 523–24
Congress of Industrial Organizations,
      radicalism of, 32–33
Connally, John, 519, 557
   as treasury secretary, 444, 447, 448–49
   Vietnam War and, 492–93
Conscience of a Conservative, The
      (Goldwater), 277
Contender, The (Gellman), 592*n*
Cooke, Alistair, 102, 125
Coolidge, Calvin, 174
Cooper, Gary, 98
Cooper, John Sherman, 413
Cooper, Lorraine, 211
Coral Sea, battle of, 76
Corcoran, Thomas, 638*n*–39*n*
Cotton, Aylett, 159, 161, 170, 172, 173,
      176, 203
Council on Environmental Quality, 379
Cox, Archibald, 538
   RN's firing of, 520–21, 680*n*
   as Watergate special prosecutor, 514,
      679*n*
   Watergate tapes and, 517, 518, 521
Cox, Dorothy, 178
Cox, Edward:
   Tricia's marriage to, 557
   wedding of Tricia and, 416–17
Cox, Edward Eugene, 89–90
Cox, Patricia Nixon "Tricia," 80, 101, 104,
      188, 193, 203, 217, 235, 245, 296, 301,
      310, 313, 324, 325

   birth of, 20, 31
   Edward's marriage to, 557
   and RN's long absences, 219
   RN's resignation and, 530, 531–32
   Watergate scandal and, 511, 525
   wedding of Edward and, 416–17
CREEP, *see* Committee to Re-Elect the
      President (CREEP)
crime rates, sixties and seventies rise in, 322,
      330
Crocker, Roy, 13, 36
Cronin, John, 32, 97, 116, 178, 233, 238,
      249, 252, 261, 263, 282
   anti-Communism of, 85, 113–14
   RN and, 113–14, 589*n*–90*n*, 591*n*–92*n*
Cronkite, Walter, 177, 482
Crowley, Monica, 399, 552, 556, 557,
      558
Crucial Decade, The (Goldman), 199
Cuba, 93
   Bay of Pigs invasion of, 303, 426
   Soviet Union and, 489
Cuban missile crisis, 308, 313
Cubans:
   Watergate break-ins and, 484
   Watergate cover-up and, 503, 506
Cushman, Robert, 302–3
Czechoslovakia, 347
   Nazi invasion of, 75
   Soviet invasion of, 438
   Soviet takeover of, 105

Dacca, 455, 456
Daily Worker, 150
Daley, Richard, 295, 296, 322, 473, 670*n*
Dart, Justin, 277
Davis, Paul, 171–72
Dawson, William, 249*n*, 288
Day, Roy, 13, 14, 15, 16, 18, 19, 21, 23, 24,
      25, 28, 29, 33, 34, 37, 83, 133, 138,
      142, 167, 596*n*
D-Day invasion, 201
Dean, John, 425–26, 432, 465, 466, 472,
      479, 670*n*
   enemies list and, 484
   federal testimony of, 509, 518
   Gemstone operation and, 433, 480, 507,
      657*n*–58*n*
   Hughes investigation of, 470
   in refusal to perjure himself, 508
   Senate testimony of, 516

in Watergate cover-up, 474, 479–80, 484, 503, 504, 505, 506, 507, 508, 515, 538, 551, 658*n*, 676*n*
as White House counsel, 479
Debs, Eugene, 108
DEFCON III alert, 523, 680*n*–81*n*
Defense Department, U.S., 86
de Gaulle, Charles, 349, 360, 439
Dellums, Ron, 513
Democratic National Committee, 155
Democratic National Convention, of 1968, 322–23, 422
Democratic Party, Democrats:
as champions of "forgotten man," 198
corruption in, 165, 183, 193
in 1948 election, 132
portrayed as elitists by RN, 200
postwar economy mismanaged by, 30
race issues and, 327–28
Deng Xiaoping, 554, 555
Dent, Harry, 384, 386, 391, 394
Denver Post, 223, 524
desegregation:
of armed forces, 247, 248
of public transit, 252
RN and, 383
of schools, *see* school desegregation
de Toledano, Ralph, 145, 215, 223, 224, 231, 262
Dewey, Thomas, 103, 150, 167, 168, 169, 173, 174, 183
in 1948 election, 103, 104, 116, 120, 133, 137, 141
RN urged to resign from 1952 campaign by, 189–90, 194, 608*n*
Dexter, Walter, 12, 14, 568*n*
Diem, Ngo Dinh, 314–15, 427, 542
Dien Bien Phu, battle of, 226, 229, 260, 314
Dies, Martin, 96, 97
Dilantin, 412
Dinkelspiel, John, 140, 145, 146, 180
Dirksen, Everett, 173, 342, 343, 605*n*, 638*n*
dirty tricks, political, 41, 306–7. 627*n*
in RN's 1972 reelection campaign, 429–34, 467–68, 472, 550, 657*n*, 665*n*
Dmytryk, Edward, 588*n*
Dobrynin, Anatoly, 94, 450, 681*n*
Kissinger in secret talks with, 362–63, 486, 488, 489
on RN's growing paranoia, 365

Dodson, Leonidas, 54
Doheny, Edward, 25–26
Dole, Hollis, 77, 78
Dole, Robert, 410, 555
Dominican Republic, 426
Dorn, Evlyn, 243
Douglas, Helen Gahagan, 99, 178, 206, 254
background of, 130–31
in Congress, 131
HUAC opposed by, 131, 146–47
LBJ's affair with, 131
liberal causes espoused by, 130, 131, 139, 146
in 1950 Democratic primary, 132, 138, 146–47, 148, 153
RN's view of, 138–39
small farmers championed by, 130, 131, 132
tidelands controversy and, 131, 132
Truman Doctrine opposed by, 131, 146
Douglas, Helen Gahagan, in 1950 Senate campaign, 148, 155, 602*n*
fund-raising problems and, 155, 599*n*–600*n*
ineptness of, 155, 159
portrayed as Communist dupe by RN camp, 150–52, 153–55, 158–59, 599*n*
Douglas, Melvyn, 99, 131
Douglas, William, 389*n*, 528–29
Downey, Sheridan, 114, 149, 159, 161, 595*n*
in 1950 Democratic primary, 132, 138
political career in, 130
RN's view of, 138–39
tidelands controversy and, 130
in withdrawal from Democratic primary, 146
Dresden, firebombing of, 82, 367
Dreyfus, Jack, 412, 651*n*
Drinan, Robert, 513
Drown, Helene, 72, 160, 163, 166, 169, 174, 205, 324, 514
Drown, Jack, 163, 169, 178, 205, 309, 310, 317–18, 324, 555
drug abuse, 378, 646*n*
Dudley, Tilford, 132
Duggan, Laurence, 126
Duke University, 230
Duke University Law School, RN at, 4, 66–70
Dulles, Allen, 90, 116–17, 263, 587*n*

Dulles, John Foster, 101, 116–17, 211, 215,
    235, 238, 240, 261, 460
Dust Bowl, 129

Eagleton, Thomas, 410, 473–74
Eastern Europe, Soviet control of, 81, 94
Eastland, James, 255
East Whittier, Calif., Nixon gas station
    in, 52
Ebony, 289
economy, global, rise of, 387
economy, U.S.:
    cost of Vietnam War and, 444–45
    decline in manufacturing segment of, 387
    inflation in, 445–46, 449, 661*n*
    1973–74 stock market crash in, 449–50
    recessions in, 445, 449
    RN's wage-price freeze in, 444, 446
    run on gold in, 447
    stagflation in, 446, 448
    trade deficit in, 449
    unemployment in, 449
    wage-price freeze in, 449
Edson, Peter, 182, 205
    RN slush fund reported by, 181
Edwards, India, 132
Egypt:
    Soviet Union and, 489
    in Suez war, 244
    in Yom Kippur War, 520, 522–23
Ehrlichman, John, 305, 323, 359, 375, 377,
    379, 385, 389, 393, 406, 411, 412, 424,
    425–26, 428, 460, 474, 546, 627*n*,
    646*n*
    domestic policy managed by, 381
    Plumbers and, 428, 429, 515
    on RN's decision-making process, 354
    RN's firing of, 510
    Senate testimony of, 516
    Watergate break-ins and, 473
    Watergate conviction of, 537–38
    in Watergate cover-up, 474, 479–81, 499,
        507, 508, 515, 677*n*
    as White House counsel, 352
Eighty-second Airborne, 523
Eisenhower, David, 245, 417
    marriage of Julie and, 348, 373, 557
Eisenhower, Dwight D., 79, 81, 149, 183
    common touch of, 201
    Communist threat viewed as overstated
        by, 221
    death of, 373

    gifts to, 182
    ileitis of, 212, 242
    incremental approach to civil rights issues
        favored by, 248–49, 256
    internationalism of, 164
    military career of, 211
    on morality of war, 366–67
    1953 inauguration of, 210
    professional politicians disliked by, 213
    RN's ambiguous relationship with, 263,
        274–75
    RN's early support for candidacy of,
        164–65
    RN TV appearance proposed by, 187
    strategic vision of, 231
    Truman and, 210
    in World War II, 201
Eisenhower, Dwight D., 1952 presidential
        campaign of:
    "Checkers" speech and, 195
    and delayed decision to keep RN on
        ticket, 196
    Democratic corruption as theme of, 183
    Dump Nixon Movement and, 183–84,
        185–86
    at Republican Convention, 168–76
    RN as choice for vice president, 174,
        604*n*–5*n*
    RN slush fund story and, 182–83
    RN's Paris meeting with, 165
    South and, 327
    whistle-stop tour in, 182–83
Eisenhower, Dwight D., as president:
    and CIA plots against Castro, 302–3
    civil rights movement and, 245–46,
        247–49, 254, 258–59, 383–84
    dropping of RN from reelection ticket
        denied by, 239–42
    farewell address of, 263
    heart attack of, 234, 235–40, 615*n*
    Indochina War intervention urged by,
        226–27, 613*n*
    Korean trip in, 211
    Korean War armistice announced by,
        215–16, 361
    McCarthy and, 214, 220–21, 222, 223
    1960 election and, 272, 278, 289–90
    1960 stimulus package rejected by, 278
    in plea for peace, 215
    in reelection campaign, 243–45
    RN's ambivalent relationship with,
        240–42, 289–90

RN's closer relationship with, 245
RN's uneasy relationship with, 210–11,
    230, 231–32
second inauguration of, 245
stroke of, 261
tape-recording system of, 517
unilateral U.S. intervention in Indochina
    opposed by, 228–29
use of nuclear weapons contemplated by,
    228
Eisenhower, Edgar, 197
Eisenhower, Jennie, 557
Eisenhower, Julie Nixon, 73, 74, 188, 204,
    217, 219, 245, 266, 292, 296, 298, 301,
    310, 313, 324, 325, 346, 350, 397, 411,
    417, 553, 555
    birth of, 91, 104
    marriage of David Eisenhower and, 348,
        373, 557
    RN's resignation and, 530, 531
    Watergate scandal and, 511, 522, 526
Eisenhower, Mamie, 239, 289–90
Eisenhower, Milton, 221, 269
Eisenhower administration:
    McCarthy's attacks on, 214, 220
    RN's uneasy relationship with, 211–12
Eisler, Gerhart, 95
elections, U.S.:
    of 1942, 12
    of 1944, 10, 12
    of 1948, 91, 103, 104, 116, 120, 132–33,
        137, 141
    of 1950, 114
    of 1950, *see* Douglas, Helen Gahagan,
        in 1950 Senate campaign; Nixon,
        Richard, in 1950 Senate campaign
    of 1954, 231, 233
    of 1956, 238, 242–45, 263, 617*n*
    of 1958, 267, 277
    of 1964, 316–17, 321, 327–28
    of 1966, 318
    of 1970, 412, 415
    of 1976, 537
elections, U.S., of 1946, 126, 149
    Republican sweep in, 39
    RN in, *see* Nixon, Richard, in 1946
        congressional campaign
elections, U.S., of 1952:
    California Republican primary in,
        167–68
    Eisenhower in, *see* Eisenhower, Dwight
        D., 1952 presidential campaign of

Eisenhower as possible candidate in,
    164–65
Eisenhower's victory in, 202–3
Republican Convention in, *see* Republican
    Convention of 1952
RN as Eisenhower's running mate in, *see*
    Nixon, Richard, 1952 vice-presidential
    campaign of
RN as possible vice-presidential candidate
    in, 165, 167
Stevenson in, 198, 202, 208
Taft and, 164, 166, 167, 168–73, 176
Warren and, 165–73, 176
elections, U.S., of 1960:
    African Americans and, 385
    dirty tricks in, 627*n*
    Eisenhower and, 272, 278, 289–90
    Electoral College in, 277–78, 287, 294,
        298
    JFK campaign in, *see* Kennedy, John F.,
        1960 presidential campaign of
    JFK's victory in, 292–93
    media in, 299
    popular vote in, 628*n*–29*n*
    recounts in, 297
    RN in, *see* Nixon, Richard, 1960
        presidential campaign of
    Rockefeller and, 272–74, 627*n*
    voter fraud in, 294–98
elections, U.S., of 1968:
    Humphrey in, 323, 324, 339–41, 343, 344,
        638*n*
    LBJ's decision not to run in, 321
    McCarthy in, 320
    Reagan and, 326–27
    RFK in, 320
    RN in, *see* Nixon, Richard, 1968
        presidential campaign of
    RN's victory in, 345–46
    Rockefeller and, 326–27, 333
    Romney and, 326
    Wallace in, 324, 329, 339–41, 344, 345*n*,
        468
elections, U.S., of 1972, 409
    Humphrey in, 431, 434
    McGovern in, 432, 468–70, 471, 473, 493,
        497–98, 547
    Muskie in, 431, 432, 434, 448, 468
    Nixon administration's dirty tricks
        campaign in, 429–34, 467–68, 472,
        550, 657*n*, 665*n*
    polls in, 431, 487

elections, U.S., of 1972 (*cont.*):
  RN in, 430–31, 468, 473–74, 487, 491,
    497–98, 550
  RN's economic speech and, 448
  RN's landslide in, 497–98, 513
  Ted Kennedy in, 431, 434, 468, 493
  Vietnam War and, 485, 486, 491, 493–94
  Wallace in, 431, 432–33, 473
Electoral College, 137, 255
  1960 election and, 277–78, 287, 294, 298
  in 1968 election, 345n, 635n
Elizabeth II, Queen of England, 349
Elk Hills, Calif., Navy oil reserves in, 26
Ellington, Edward Kennedy "Duke," 396
Elliott, John B., 152
Ellsberg, Daniel, 318, 419–20, 423, 425
  dismissal of charges against, 509, 678n
  Plumbers' burglary of psychiatric files of,
    429, 430, 468, 472, 476–77, 505, 509,
    515, 521, 656n–57n
El Monte, 82
Ely, Nev., 177
Emerging Republican Majority, The
  (Phillips), 387
Ending the Vietnam War (Kissinger), 342n
End Poverty in California (EPIC), 31
Eniwetok atoll, A-bomb tests at, 105
Enterprise, USS, 457
environmentalism, RN and, 379–81
Environmental Protection Agency (EPA),
  380
Ervin, Sam, 507, 514, 521
  see also Senate Select Committee on
    Presidential Campaign Activities
Esquire, 316–17
Europe:
  economic resurgence of, 446
  postwar devastation of, 85–86, 88–90,
    587n
Evans, Rowland, 385, 498
Evans, Tom, 323, 639n
Ewald, William, 224, 296
Executive Office Building, RN's hideaway
  at, 353, 403, 417, 428, 496
executive privilege, 514, 518, 529
Exodus (film), 99n

Fair Housing Act, 329
Fala (FDR's dog), 188, 608n–9n
Family Assistance Plan, 374, 382
Fantz, Donald, 9

Faries, McIntyre, 15, 33, 39
Farland, Joseph, 453, 454
Farmer, James, 374, 382
fascists, in Spanish Civil War, 74–75
Faubus, Orval, 258
Federal Bureau of Investigation (FBI), 69,
  95, 512, 546
  Hiss case and, 593n–94n
  illegal surveillance by, 433, 541–42, 628n
  Watergate cover-up and, 478–79, 483–84,
    515–16, 536, 551
  Watergate investigation of, 474
Federal Reserve Board, 10
  anti-inflation measures of, 445–46
Felt, Mark, 556
  Watergate cover-up and, 481–82, 483,
    672n
Fielding, Lewis, 429, 505
Field Poll, 156
Fifties, conflict between elites and common
  man in, 199–201
film industry, HUAC hearings on, 32, 96,
  97–100, 125
Final Days, The (Woodward and Bernstein),
  548, 549
Finch, Robert, 137, 204–5, 210, 268, 305,
  323, 356, 534–35
  as HEW secretary, 352, 382, 384
  in RN's 1960 campaign, 272–73, 274, 276,
    280, 281, 282–83, 286, 289
First Amendment, 425
Fisher, M. F. K., 9, 52
Flanders, Ralph, 223, 225
Flanigan, Peter, 323
Fleps, Carl, 77
Fletcher, Arthur, 395
Flippen, J. Brooks, 380
Folger, Herschel, 39
food, postwar shortages of, 20, 39
Ford, Betty, 161
Ford, Gerald, 389n, 404, 513, 555, 556
  in 1976 election, 537
  as president, 539, 541
  RN pardoned by, 535–36, 683n–84n
  on RN's moodiness, 161
  as vice president, 519–20, 527
Foreign Affairs, 437
Foreign Agents Registration Act (1938),
  100
Formosa, 150
Fortas, Abe, 389n

Fort Monmouth, 220
Foster, Vince, 557
Foster, William Z., 153
France, in Suez war, 244
Frankfurter, Felix, 114
Franklin, Benjamin, 65
Franklin Delano Roosevelt, USS, 523
Franklins (college society), 61–62
Friedersdorf, Max, 509
Friedman, Milton, 446, 449
Friendly Persuasion, The (West), 44
Frost, David, 364, 393
  RN's interviews with, 539, 548, 549–51,
    637*n*
Fuchs, Klaus, 144
Fulbright, J. William, 316, 420
Fuller, Lon, 69

Gabrielson, Guy, 164
Galbraith, John Kenneth, 243
Gallup Poll, 285, 286
Gandhi, Indira, 459
  RN's enmity toward, 454–55, 456
  in treaty with Soviet Union, 455–56
Gannon, Frank, 353, 551, 687*n*
Garland, John, 15, 24
Garment, Leonard, 323, 352, 356, 359, 374,
    383, 384, 390, 391, 404, 411–12, 434,
    512, 513, 518, 531, 543, 655*n*, 687*n*
  on strategic retreat, 421
Garrett, Waymeth, 20
Gavin, William, 339
gay rights, 377–78
Gellman, Irwin, 592*n*, 616*n*
Gemstone operation, 433, 466–69, 474, 476,
    478, 480, 507, 508, 657*n*–58*n*, 666*n*
  see also Watergate break-ins
Geneva, 269
Germany, Nazi, 60
  Allied bombing of, 367
  Austria invaded by, 75
  Czechoslovakia invaded by, 75
  persecution of Jews in, 75, 350–51
  in Soviet nonaggression pact, 75, 108
  surrender of, 80
Gettlin, Robert, 669*n*
Ghana, 245
Giancana, Sam, 542
Giap, Vo Nguyen, 226
Gibson, Dunn and Crutcher, 188–89,
    191–92

Gillmore, Anne, 58
Glenn L. Martin Company, Baltimore
    plant of, 1
Goldfine, Bernard, 267
Goldman, Eric, 11, 199
gold standard, RN's abandonment of, 444,
    446
Goldwater, Barry, 273, 274, 277, 303, 314,
    326, 330, 332, 333, 380, 531, 537
  1964 presidential campaign of, 316,
    327–28
Golos, Jacob, 106
Goodwin, Doris Kearns. *See* Kearns, Doris
Goodwin, Richard, 303, 335, 374
Gorbachev, Mikhail, 554
government, RN's distrust of, 69
Graetz, Michael J., 390
Graham, Billy, 280, 316, 318, 411, 412,
    654*n*, 655*n*
Graham, Hugh, 394
Graham, Katharine, 483
Grant, Ulysses S., 198
Grapes of Wrath, The (Steinbeck), 131
Gray, L. Patrick, 478, 482
  confirmation hearings of, 505, 514
  FBI Plumber files burned by, 474
  Watergate cover-up and, 479, 481–82,
    516
Great Britain:
  Soviet spies in, 94
  in Suez war, 244
Great Depression, 9, 54, 60–61
Great Society, 371
Greece, Communist threat in, 86
Green, Marshall, 436, 440, 462
Greenglass, David, 144
Greenhouse, Linda, 390
Green Island, 77–78
Greenspan, Alan, 339, 372, 398
Greenspun, Herman "Hank," 470, 471
Gregory, R. N., 36
Gregory, Thomas, 468
Gromyko, Andrei, 486
Guadalcanal, battle of, 77
Guatemala, CIA-backed coup in, 302
Gulf of Tonkin incident, 315
Guylay, Lou, 241, 280, 283

Haas, Lucien, 306, 309
Haendiges, Albert, 58
Hagerty, James, 222, 236, 242, 290

Haig, Alexander, 419, 420, 438, 494, 497,
    501, 517, 526, 528, 530, 536
  as RN's chief of staff, 521
Haight, Raymond, 36
Haiphong harbor, U.S. mining of, 492, 494
Halberstam, David, 213, 515
Haldeman, H. R. "Bob," 135, 302, 322, 323,
    330, 342, 343, 344, 347–48, 349, 350,
    362, 372, 385, 386, 396, 414, 417, 424,
    458, 640n
  access to Oval Office controlled by, 352
  as chief of staff, 352, 356–57, 358, 359,
    374, 381, 401, 427–28
  dirty tricks campaign and, 433, 434, 466,
    468, 665n
  Gemstone operation and, 467–68, 480,
    666n
  on Kissinger's mental state, 458
  Nixon family's resentment of, 356
  Pentagon Papers and, 420, 422–23
  Plumbers and, 429
  in RN's 1960 campaign, 281, 282
  as RN's 1962 campaign manager, 305–6,
    311
  in RN's 1968 campaign, 338
  RN's anti-Semitism fed by, 426
  RN's dark moods noted by, 397
  on RN's decision-making process,
    354
  RN's firing of, 510
  on RN's paranoia, 399
  RN's physical and mental stability as
    concern of, 407
  Senate testimony of, 516
  Watergate break-ins and, 473, 671n
  Watergate conviction of, 537–38
  Watergate cover-up and, 475, 476–78,
    479–81, 499, 503, 507, 508, 515, 516,
    677n
  as yes-man, 305–6, 431
Haldeman, Jo, 534
Hall, Leonard, 214, 237, 240, 242, 274, 278,
    281, 286, 290, 298, 300, 305–6, 327
Hallett, Douglas, 376, 476
Halperin, Morton, 374
Halsey, William "Bull," 77
Hamlin, Hannibal, 174
Hammett, Dashiell, 154
Hanoi, 218
  U.S. bombing of, 491–92, 497
Harlan, John Marshall, II, 251

Harlow, Bryce, 48, 85, 158, 176, 195, 202,
    211, 232, 241, 349, 385, 395, 413, 527,
    542, 543
Harper's, 325
Harriman, W. Averell, 163, 268, 428
Harris, Lou, 289
Harris, Richard (Whittier classmate), 158
Harris, Richard (writer), 538
Hart, Everett, 281
Hart, Samuel, 466
Hatfield, Mark, 332, 340, 413
Hauser, Rita, 200, 378
Hawaii, 297
Hayek, Friedrich, 22, 34
Haynes, John Earl, 95
Haynsworth, Clement, 389
Hays, Arthur Garfield, 101
Hazlett, Edward E. "Swede," 239
Health, Education, and Welfare
    Department, U.S., 384, 393
  civil rights and, 384
Hearst newspapers, 135
Helms, Richard, 454, 455, 465–66, 512,
    543, 630n, 638n, 665n–66n
  Watergate cover-up and, 478, 479, 481
Herblock, 102–3, 144, 159, 206
Hersh, Seymour, 370, 482, 541
Herter, Christian, 87, 90, 113, 116, 299
Herter, Christian, Jr., 262
Heselton, John, 103
Higby, Lawrence "Larry," 352
Hillings, Patrick, 142, 159, 174, 182, 277,
    323
Hillman, Sidney, 108
Hiroshima, atomic bombing of, 80–81
Hiss, Alger, 137, 158, 165, 178, 193, 204,
    206, 214, 311, 430, 556–57
  in Agricultural Administration, 109
  background of, 107
  Chambers sued for slander by, 120
  as Communist, 107, 108
  in decision to lie about Communist past,
    110–11
  guilty verdict of, 142–43
  HUAC appearances of, 111–12
  as member of East Coast elite, 200
  named as Communist by Chambers, 107,
    110
  perjury and trials of, 124, 142, 202, 475,
    506
  RN's dislike of, 114–15, 118, 592n

RN's pursuit of case against, 112–28, 132, 136, 137, 142, 145, 158, 165, 193, 200, 204–5, 589*n*–90*n*, 591*n*–92*n*, 610*n*
seen as victim of trumped-up charges, 204–5
as Soviet spy, 109, 122, 123, 590*n*, 591*n*
State Department career of, 107, 109
in televised HUAC appearance, 118–20
Hiss, Priscilla Hobson, 107, 123
"Hiss Case, The—A Lesson for the American People" (RN speech), 143
Hitler, Adolf, 81
Hitt, Patricia Reilly, 308–9, 310
Hobart, Garret, 174
Ho Chi Minh, 226, 369, 485
nationalism of, 314
Hoeppel, John, 570*n*
Hoffa, Jimmy, 450, 627*n*, 662*n*
Hoffman, Abbie, 653*n*
Hoffman, Julius, 604*n*
Hoffman, Paul, 195
Hofstadter, Richard, 200
Holifield, Chet, 35, 37
Hollywood Ten, 99–100, 125, 144, 588*n*
Holt, Edith, 20
Holton, Linwood, 395
Hoover, Herbert, 87, 149, 240, 297, 327*n*, 427
Hoover, J. Edgar, 101, 102, 125, 226, 301, 364, 414, 434, 450, 482, 543, 546, 547, 593*n*–94*n*, 658*n*
anti-Communist crusade of, 32, 94, 98
RN's 1960 campaign aided by, 290
Hougan, Jim, 669*n*
House Committee on Un-American Activities (HUAC), 29, 32, 83–84, 95, 226
Bentley's testimony to, 106, 107, 110, 590*n*
Chambers's testimony to, 106–7, 109–10, 119–20
Dies as chairman of, 96, 97
Helen Douglas's opposition to, 131, 146–47
Hiss's appearances before, 111–12, 114, 117–20
Hollywood hearings of, 32, 96, 97–100, 125
racist members of, 96–97
Reagan's testimony to, 98

reputation of, 96, 97, 112, 116
RN and, *see* Nixon, Richard, as HUAC member
Stripling as chief investigator for, *see* Stripling, Robert
Thomas as chairman of, 97–98
witch hunt of, 126
House Judiciary Committee, 514
impeachment proceedings begun by, 522, 526, 528, 682*n*
Watergate tapes and, 526, 527
House of Representatives, U.S., 255
Agriculture Committee of, 2
Democratic majorities in, 132
Education and Labor Committee of, 83–84
Houser, Fred, 142
housing, postwar shortages in, 19–20, 39
Hruska, Roman, 389
Hughes, Don, 263, 266, 281, 292
Hughes, Emmet, 183, 191, 212
Hughes, Howard, 291, 292, 306–7
donation to RN campaign by, 470, 546
Don Nixon's ties to, 306–7, 470, 668*n*
O'Brien and, 469–70, 471
RN's ties to, 470–71
Hughes, William, 134
Humphrey, George, 227
Humphrey, Hubert, 269, 436
funeral of, 555
1968 presidential campaign of, 323, 324, 339–41, 343, 344, 345, 638*n*
in 1972 election, 431, 434
Humphreys, Robert "Bob," 185–86
Hunt, Dorothy, 499, 504
Hunt, Howard, 427, 429, 432, 471, 543
CIA ties of, 466, 468, 478, 665*n*–66*n*
personality of, 465–66
trial of, 505
Watergate break-ins and, 471, 472, 476, 477, 484, 665*n*–66*n*, 667*n*
Watergate cover-up and, 481, 503–4, 506
Hunter, E. Farley, 69
Huston, Tom Charles, 334, 342, 358, 372, 377, 381, 391, 414, 425, 427, 543, 550, 640*n*, 651*n*
Hutcheson, Thad, 295
Hutschnecker, Arnold, 241–42, 275
as RN's personal physician, 161–62
hydrogen bomb, 144

Ickes, Harold, 28, 31
Illinois, voting fraud in, 296, 297
imports, taxes on, 444, 447
Inchon, MacArthur's landing at, 149
In Confidence (Dobrynin), 681*n*
Independent Review, 154
India, 217, 218
  in cease-fire with Pakistan, 459
  East Pakistani refugees in, 451, 454,
    459
  1947 partition of, 451
  in 1965 war with Pakistan, 452
  in 1971 war with Pakistan, 450, 454,
    456–59
  in treaty with Soviet Union, 455–56
Indochina War, 218
  Eisenhower's call for intervention in,
    226–27, 613*n*
  French withdrawal from, 360
  Geneva peace conference on, 229
  public opposition to U.S. intervention in,
    227–28
  U.S. aid to French in, 144, 226, 500
  use of nuclear weapons considered in,
    228
Indonesia, 217, 361
inflation, 445–46, 449, 661*n*
intercontinental ballistic missiles (ICBMs),
  260, 488
Internal Revenue Service (IRS):
  Hughes investigation of, 470
  Nixon administration pressure on,
    432
  O'Brien investigated by, 546
  political activists targeted by, 541
  RN tax returns leaked by, 546
international monetary system:
  exchange rates in, 446
  renegotiation of, 448–49
International Telephone and Telegraph,
  467, 469, 524
Internet, 376*n*
In the Arena (Nixon), 555, 687*n*
Iran, 218
  CIA-backed coup in, 302
Israel:
  in Suez war, 244
  in Yom Kippur War, 520, 522–23
Italy, prewar, 60

Jackson, Charles "C. D.," 238
Jackson, Donald, 570*n*

Jackson, Henry "Scoop," 279, 351, 374, 379
Japan, 217, 435
  China invaded by, 74
  economic resurgence of, 387, 421, 435,
    438, 446
  expansionism of, 74
  prewar, 60
  RN's opening to China and, 444
  surrender of, 80
Jaworski, Leon, 522, 527, 679*n*
Jefferson, Thomas, 65
Jenkins, Thomas, 88
Jenner, William, 428
Jesus Christ, 65
Jews:
  Nazi persecution of, 75, 350–51
  RN and, 417–18, 426, 653*n*, 654*n*–55*n*
Jiang Qing, 462
John Birch Society, 309
  RN's attack on, 308
John F. Kennedy, USS, 523
John F. Kennedy Center for the Performing
  Arts, 409
Johnson, Andrew, impeachment of, 518
Johnson, Edwin, 227
Johnson, Frank, 251
Johnson, Hiram, 12, 135, 136
Johnson, Lady Bird, 294, 416
Johnson, Lyndon B., 162, 256, 257, 260,
    289, 314, 366, 387, 408, 433, 436
  bombing halt ordered by, 341, 344, 638*n*
  bugging of RN's plane ordered by, 546
  civil rights and, 257, 329, 384
  in Glassboro summit, 488
  Helen Douglas's affair with, 131
  as JFK's 1960 running mate, 273, 294
  1948 Senate election stolen by, 295
  1957 Civil Rights Act opposed by, 254,
    255, 256
  in 1964 election, 328
  Paris peace negotiations and, 366
  public distrust of, 344
  southern strength of, 273
  tape-recording system of, 349, 517, 549
  Vietnam cease-fire proposed by, 318–19
Johnson, Lyndon B., as president:
  Chennault affair and, 342–43
  and decision not to seek reelection, 321
  escalation of Vietnam War by, 315, 319
  social programs of, 315
  Vietnam credibility gap and, 320
Johnson, Paul, 555

Johnson, U. Alexis, 451
Joint Chiefs of Staff, spying on Nixon
    administration by, 459–60
Joint Committee on Internal Revenue
    Taxation, 524
Jorgensen, Frank, 13, 14, 15, 24, 32, 40, 133,
    136, 138, 180, 238, 280–81
Just, Ward, 333
Justice Department, U.S.:
  Civil Rights Division of, 252, 257
  Communist Party investigation by, 106,
    107
  Watergate investigation of, 479, 481

Kallina, Edmund, 297
Kalmbach, Herbert, 305, 431, 432
  Watergate cover-up and, 474, 503
Karachi, 456
Kashmir, 456
Katcher, Leo, RN slush fund reported by,
    181–82
Kaufman, Samuel, 142
Kaye, Danny, 99
Kazan, Elia, 100
Kearns, Doris, 374
Keating, Kenneth "Ken," 451, 454
Kefauver, Estes, 177
Kelly, Walter "Walt," 229–30
Kempton, Murray, 200, 319, 325
Kennan, George, 226, 361, 421, 422, 540
  "long telegram" of, 81, 82
Kennedy, Caroline, 409, 410
Kennedy, Edward "Ted," 376, 415, 426, 455,
    476, 514, 646*n*
  Chappaquiddick accident of, 431
  in 1972 election, 431, 434, 468, 493
Kennedy, Ethel, 514
Kennedy, John F., 32, 77, 137, 162, 255,
    256, 260, 283, 303, 385
  Addison's disease of, 290
  assassination of, 257, 312, 315, 316
  background of, 261–62
  as Catholic, 262
  civil rights and, 329
  on Eisenhower's treatment of RN, 241
  Jacqueline Bouvier's wedding to, 84
  on media's smearing of RN, 208
  in meeting with RN on Indochina War,
    227
  political liabilities of, 262–63
  RN admired by, 92
  on RN's 1962 loss, 310–11

RN's relationship with, 84, 619*n*–20*n*,
    632*n*
  and RN's Senate campaign, 152, 599*n*
  unilateral invasion of Vietnam opposed
    by, 229*n*
  womanizing by, 542, 627*n*
Kennedy, John F., Jr., 409, 410
Kennedy, John F., 1960 presidential
    campaign of, 269, 276–93
  black voters and, 289
  Catholicism issue and, 278–80, 623*n*,
    624*n*
  health questions in, 290
  LBJ as running mate in, 273, 294
  MLK's jailing and, 288, 626*n*
  polls and, 285, 286, 289
  TV debates in, 283–86, 625*n*–26*n*
  voter registration advantage in, 277
  and voting fraud issues, 294–98
Kennedy, John F., as president:
  Bay of Pigs invasion and, 303, 426
  Cuban missile crisis and, 308, 313
  tape-recording system of, 517, 549
  test ban agreement and, 313
  Vietnam War and, 314, 341, 633*n*
Kennedy, Joseph, 262–63, 297
  in donations to RN's Senate campaign,
    152–53, 599*n*
Kennedy, Rex, 23
Kennedy, Robert F., 215, 262, 263, 288,
    330, 626*n*
  assassination of, 322, 323, 338
  1968 presidential campaign of, 320
  RN's dislike of, 323
Kennedy, Rose, 409
Kennedy family, RN's distrust of, 299, 303,
    308
Kent State massacre, 404, 413, 650*n*
Keogh, James, 203
Kepple, Gerald, 15
Kerry, John, 653*n*
Kersten, Charles, 113–14, 116, 132
Key Biscayne, Fla., Nixon houses in, 353,
    400, 467, 472, 476, 509, 524, 547–48,
    633*n*
Khachigian, Ken, 528
Khmer Rouge, 364, 397
Khrushchev, Nikita, 313, 622*n*
  mercurial personality of, 269–70, 274, 276
  RN's debates with, 270–71
King, Coretta, 287, 288, 289, 322
King, Gretchen, 7

King, Martin Luther, Jr.:
  assassination of, 322, 333
  Atlanta jailing of, 287–89, 626n
  FBI surveillance of, 433, 542, 628n
  on RN, 251, 254–55, 289
  RN's first meeting with, 245
  RN's relationship with, 254, 257–58, 287,
    385, 390
  Vietnam War opposed by, 321, 387
King, Martin Luther, Sr., 288
King, Robert, 221, 251
King Timahoe (Nixon dog), 349, 408
Kissinger, Henry, 341, 342n, 348, 359, 362,
    402, 418, 428, 435, 523, 554, 555,
    638n
  Allende coup and, 543–44
  in back-channel meetings with Dobrynin,
    488, 489
  background of, 350–51
  Cambodia bombing and, 364, 643n–44n
  East Pakistan crisis and, 452, 453–54
  India-Pakistan war and, 457
  as national security adviser, 350, 374
  on need for RN to resign, 524
  Nobel Peace Prize awarded to, 524
  Pentagon Papers and, 420, 425
  and RN's economic policies, 449
  on RN's insecurity, 398, 399
  and RN's opening to China, 436, 438,
    439, 440–44, 453, 460–61, 463, 464,
    659n–60n
  RN's relationship with, 351, 498, 655n
  in secret negotiations with Le Duc Tho,
    366
  in secret talks with Dobrynin, 362–63,
    486
  in secret trip to China, 436, 440–42,
    453
  state and defense departments reduced
    influence under, 350, 354
  tantrums of, 458
  unilateral Vietnam withdrawal and, 360,
    485–87, 495–96
  Vietnam cease-fire violations and,
    500–501
  on Watergate scandal, 511–12
Klehr, Harvey, 95
Klein, Herb, 23, 33, 151, 305, 309–10, 626
Kleindienst, Richard, 467, 472, 509
  resignation of, 510, 514
  Watergate break-ins and, 472
  Watergate cover-up and, 481

Knight, Goodwin "Goodie," 133, 135, 137,
    238
  in 1958 election, 267–68
Knight, Mrs., 268
Knoop, Henry, 207, 279
Knott, Walter, 308
Knowland, Helen, 267, 268
Knowland, William, 29, 35, 132, 133, 135,
    136, 168, 171, 179, 185, 197, 213, 228,
    238, 245, 255, 256, 603n, 605n
  in 1958 California gubernatorial race,
    267–68
  RN's 1950 Senate campaign supported by,
    137, 595n
Koch, Alyce, 219
Kohut, Heinz, 48–49, 577n
Korean War, 93, 155, 159, 165, 194, 201,
    462
  armistice in, 215–16, 361
  Chinese advances in, 156
  Inchon landing in, 149
  outbreak of, 149
Kosygin, Alexei, 341, 488
Kotlowski, Dean, 393
Kraft, Joseph, 365, 431, 644n
Krock, Arthur, 87
Krogh, Egil, 352, 405, 427, 428, 429, 466,
    656n–57n
  perjury indictment of, 521
Kruse, J. Arthur, 13, 568n
Ku Klux Klan, 29, 97
Kung, Louis, 343

labor unions, 108
  Communist infiltration of, 113
  HUAC investigation of, 96
  militancy of, 30, 32–33
Laguna Beach, Calif., 51
La Habra, Calif., 71
Laird, Melvin, 359, 527, 536
  as defense secretary, 351–52
Lake, Anthony, 374
Lansdale, Edward, 318, 419–20
Laos, 485
  South Vietnamese invasion of, 485, 486
  U.S. bombing of, 360
Lardner, Ring, Jr., 98–99
LaRue, Fred, 472, 509, 666n
  Watergate cover-up and, 503
Lasky, Victor, 142, 145
Lattimore, Owen, 153, 599n
Lausche, Frank, 240

"law and order":
  as euphemism for racism, 325, 330
  as response to urban violence and crime rates, 330–32
Lazar, Irving "Swifty," 548
le Carré, John, 422
Le Duc Tho, 366, 495, 524
Lee, George, 251
Leffingwell Ranch, 52, 367
LeMay, Curtis, 340–41
Lenin, V. I., 108
Lennon, John, 422
Levine, Isaac Don, 108, 116
Lewis, Fulton, 125
Lexington, USS, 76
liberals:
  Hiss case and, 126–28
  RN viewed as menace by, 158–59
Lichenstein, Charles, 263
Liddy, G. Gordon, 427, 429, 471, 543
  CREEP money-laundering scheme and, 478, 672*n*
  Gemstone operation and, 433, 466–69, 474, 477, 478, 480, 507, 658*n,* 666*n*
  personality of, 465
  Watergate break-ins and, 471, 472, 476–77, 484
  Watergate cover-up and, 480, 484, 676*n*
Life, 266, 427, 439
Lin Biao, 461
Lincoln, Abraham, 133, 193, 198, 249
  RN's admiration of, 6
Lindsay, John, 332
Linton, Alice Nixon, 43, 45, 59–60
Lippmann, Walter, 195, 325, 331
Little Rock, Ark., school desegregation in, 248, 383
Lodge, Henry Cabot, Jr., 167, 168, 174, 316
  as ambassador to South Vietnam, 314, 315
  as RN's 1960 running mate, 274, 282
Loeb, William, 662*n*
Long, Jack, 22
Long, Stanley, 31, 35
Longfellow, Henry Wadsworth, 57
Long March, 441
Longworth, Alice Roosevelt, 175
Lonigan, Edna, 150, 153, 154
Look, 183, 207
Lord, Winston, 351, 363, 374, 411, 460–61, 495, 500, 540

Los Angeles, Calif.:
  growth of, 8–9
  Owens Valley water scheme of, 135
  Watts riot in, 322
Los Angeles *Daily News,* 146, 148, 179
Los Angeles Times, 15, 36, 130, 309, 311, 482
  conservative politics of, 135
  RN's Senate campaign endorsed by, 136–37, 142, 596*n*
Loubet, Judith Wingert, 76, 84–85
Lucas, Scott, 156
Luce, Clare Boothe, 290
Lumumba, Patrice, 542
Lungren, John, 537
Lutz, Harold, 14, 15
Lybeck, Ed, 131
Lycan, Don, 10–11, 18, 26

MacArthur, Douglas, 149, 163
Machiavelli, Niccolò, 315
MacKinnon, George, 178, 186
MacLeish, Archibald, 126
Mafia, in CIA plot against Castro, 302, 470, 542
Magruder, Jeb, 465, 466
  dirty tricks campaign overseen by, 429–30, 431, 433, 471, 665*n*
  federal testimony of, 509
  Gemstone operation and, 433, 467, 474, 476, 507, 508
  perjury of, 505
  Plumbers and, 429–30
  Watergate break-ins and, 666*n*
  Watergate cover-up and, 472, 474, 480–81, 484, 551, 658*n*
Maheu, Robert, 470, 668*n*
Mailer, Norman, 325–26
Making of the President 1960, The (White), 296*n*
Malaxa, Nicolae, 207
Malaysia, 217, 361
Malcolm X, assassination of, 335
Malone, Dumas, 200
Malraux, André, 461
Manhattan Project, 81, 212
Mao Zedong, 228, 229, 347, 437, 438
  RN's meeting with, 460–62
  and RN's opening to China, 439–40
Marbury, William, 107
Marcantonio, Vito, 38, 146
  Helen Douglas linked to, 150–51

Marcelle, Jo, 59
March, Harry, 26–27
Mardian, Robert, 472
Marshall, George, 86, 95
  McCarthy's smearing of, 221
Marshall, J. Paull, 26–27, 83
Marshall Plan, 86–87, 93, 101
  RN's support for, 91–92, 124*n*, 587*n*
Marshburn, Austin, 47
Marshburn, Oscar, 158
Martin, Joe, 83
Marx, Karl, 108
Marx, Louis, 427
Masaryk, Jan, 105
Matsu, 228, 235, 299
Matthews, J. B., 220
Mazo, Earl, 177, 203, 207–8, 280, 290, 296,
  297–98, 410*n*
McCall, Harrison, 34, 36, 99
McCarthy, Eugene, 326, 330, 342
  1968 presidential campaign of, 320
McCarthy, Joseph, 77, 93, 95, 128, 149, 153,
  174, 202, 263, 314
  anti-Communist crusade of, 94, 143–44,
    145, 213, 233, 599*n*
  Army attacked by, 220
  in Army-McCarthy hearings, 224–25
  death of, 226
  Eisenhower administration attacked by,
    214, 220
  media's linking of RN with, 206
  RN and, 145, 163, 216
  RN's attempts to broker peace with, 214,
    215, 216, 222, 225
  Senate censure of, 225
  as Senate Government Operations
    Committee chairman, 213
  State Department attacked by, 215
  in Washington social life, 163
McCarthyism, 93, 144, 225–26
McCloskey, Pete, 432
McConaughy, Walter, 444
McCord, James, 466
  CIA ties of, 466, 478, 504, 665*n*–66*n*
  Gemstone operation and, 468, 507
  letter to Sirica from, 507
  Senate testimony of, 507, 515
  trial of, 505, 507, 508
  Watergate break-ins and, 471, 484
  Watergate cover-up and, 503, 504–5
McCormac, Keith, 168–69
McCormack, John, 131

McDowell, John, 117
McGill, Ralph, 249
McGovern, George, 413, 420, 473
  in 1972 election, 432, 468–70, 471, 473,
    493, 497–98, 547
McKay, Douglas "Doug," 185
McKeesport, Pa., 84
McKinley, William, assassination of, 175
McLaughlin, Roy, 10
McLuhan, Marshall, 285–86
McNamara, Robert, 314, 351*n*, 419, 633*n*
McNaughton, John T., 351*n*
McPherson, Harry, 322
McWhorter, Charlie, 232
McWilliams, Carey, 155, 159
Meany, George, 473
media:
  in calls for RN's resignation, 524
  Hiss case and, 204, 610*n*
  lies and distortions about RN spread by,
    207–8
  in 1960 election, 299
  RN linked to McCarthy by, 206
  RN's mutual enmity with, 203–8, 242–43,
    299, 305, 309–10, 397–98, 402, 416,
    418, 420, 421, 482, 499, 514–15, 610*n*
  Stevenson's rapport with, 208, 605*n*
  Vietnam War coverage by, 319, 320
  Watergate cover-up and, 482, 483–84,
    529
  Watergate scandal and, 514–15, 516
Medicaid, 315
Medicare, 315
Meet the Press (TV show), 181
Mencken, H. L., 334
Menjou, Adolphe, 98
Meredith, James, 391
Mesta, Perle, 545
Meyers, Alvin, 155
Miami Herald, 328
Middle East, 93, 397
  Soviet Union and, 488, 489, 520, 522, 523
Midway, battle of, 76
Milhous, Almira Burdg, 44–45, 53, 69
Milhous, Ezra, 53, 147
Milhous, Franklin (cousin), 53
Milhous, Franklin (grandfather), 45, 53, 61
  in move to Whittier, 44
Milhous, Joshua and Elizabeth, 44
Milhous, Olive, 45, 49
Milhous, Thomas and Sarah, 44
Milhous family, as Irish Quakers, 44

military, U.S., in plans for war with Soviets, 105
MIRVs (multiple, independently targetable warheads), 488–89, 495
"missile gap" myth, 260, 274, 630n
Mission Inn, Riverside, 74, 177
Mississippi, University of, desegregation of, 384, 391
Missoula, Mont., 196
Missouri, 297
Mitchell, Clarence, 257, 287–88
Mitchell, John, 77, 359, 392, 394, 414, 426, 433, 638n, 640n
  as attorney general, 351, 384
  dirty tricks campaign and, 472
  Gemstone operation and, 467–68, 480, 507, 658n, 666n
  Pentagon Papers and, 423–24
  as RN's 1968 campaign manager, 323, 332, 338
  Senate testimony of, 516
  Watergate break-ins and, 473, 667n
  Watergate conviction of, 537–38
  Watergate cover-up and, 471–72, 475, 477, 478, 479, 484, 504, 507–8
Mitchell, Martha, 467
Mitchell, Stephen, 183, 185
Mobilization (antiwar protest), 368, 370
Modern Times (Johnson), 555
Mohammad Reza Pahlavi, shah of Iran, RN's friendship with, 218
Mollenkopf, Oren, 68
Montgomery, Bernard, 201
Montgomery bus boycott, 252, 260
Moorer, Thomas, 459, 491, 492, 522
moral rearmament, RN's advocacy of, 6
Moratorium (antiwar protest), 368
Morrow, E. Frederic, 250, 287–88
Mosher, Samuel, 26
Moss, Annie Lee, 233
Moustakas, Robert "Bob," 406
Moynihan, Daniel Patrick, 352, 379, 391, 395, 414, 433, 512, 515, 644n–45n
  on inevitable defeat of U.S. in Vietnam, 368
  RN's relationship with, 374–75, 381
Mundt, Karl, 100, 101, 102, 103, 106, 112, 122, 125, 126, 146
Mundt-Nixon bill, 100–101, 103, 106, 124, 151, 588n
  see also Subversive Activities Control Act
Munich pact (1938), 75

Murphy, Thomas, 142–43
Murphy Ranch, 52
Murrow, Edward R., 223
Muskie, Edmund, 379, 415
  in 1972 election, 431, 432, 434, 448, 468, 667n
Mussolini, Benito, 60
My Lai massacre, 370, 526

NAACP, RN's membership in, 250, 258
Nagasaki, bombing of, 80–81
Natcher, Stanley, 27, 180
Nation, 94, 118, 155, 159, 605n
National Bureau of Standards, 102
National Citizens' Political Action Committee (NC-PAC), 32–33
  Voorhis endorsed by, 33, 35, 37–38
National Environmental Policy Act (1970), 379
National Oceanic and Atmospheric Administration (NOAA), 380
National Press Club, 205
National Security Act (1947), 86
National Security Agency (NSA), domestic surveillance by, 541–42
National Security Council (NSC), 86, 227, 228–29, 263, 304, 374
  RN's role in, 212, 218, 231, 238, 276
National University of San Marcos, 264
Native Americans, 376
Navy, U.S.:
  Aeronautics Bureau of, 1–2
  oil reserves of, 26
  RN's service in, 5–7
NBC, 319
Negroponte, John, 502
Nehru, Jawaharlal, 217, 454–55
Nelson, Jack, 482
Neushutz, Helen, 46
Nevins, Allan, 200
New Deal, 2, 10, 12, 15, 38, 84, 107, 130, 371
  postwar backlash against, 11, 19, 39, 333
  RN's skepticism about, 69, 76
New Deal coalition, fraying of, 2, 39, 198–99, 386
Newell, Frederick H., 129
Newman, Wallace, 63
New Republic, 94, 179, 605n
Newsweek, 330, 449, 483, 554
New York, 325
New Yorker, 242, 244, 268, 417, 482, 538

New York Herald Tribune, 184, 185, 297–98
New York Post, 186
  RN slush fund story in, 181–82
New York Times, 87, 101, 119, 136, 169, 216,
  217, 218–19, 232, 236, 260–61, 292,
  318, 320, 364, 416, 482, 524, 541,
  557
  Pentagon Papers published by, 419, 420,
    422, 423–24
  restraining order against, 424
  Watergate scandal and, 514, 515–16
New Zealand, 217
Ngo Dinh Diem, 314–15, 427, 542
Nguyen Van Thieu, 320, 341–43, 344, 365,
  369n, 485, 495–96, 497, 500, 539–40,
  639n, 640n
Nichols, Louis "Lou," 125, 593n–94n
Nietzsche, Friedrich, 315
Nixon, Arthur, 46, 48
  death of, 55–56, 64, 580n
Nixon, Donald, 46, 49, 157, 290–91, 292,
  306–7
  Hughes's ties to, 306–7, 470, 668n
  Nixon market and, 54
  outgoing personality of, 3, 49
Nixon, Edward, 18, 21, 46, 60, 64, 408
Nixon, Ernest, 43
Nixon, Frank, 8, 9, 15, 18, 21, 58–59, 71,
  105, 157, 177, 203, 219, 390
  birth and childhood of, 43
  charitable acts of, 54
  children beaten by, 47
  in conversion to Quakerism, 45
  courtship and marriage of, 43–44, 45
  credit given to struggling customers
    by, 54
  death of, 242
  farming abandoned by, 52
  gas station and market of, 52, 53–54,
    578n–79n
  grudges and resentments nurtured by,
    54–55
  ill health of, 46–47, 223
  as itinerant worker, 43
  Milhous family's scorn for, 45, 575n
  in move to East Whittier, 52
  in move to Southern California, 43
  Pennsylvania farm of, 85
  political beliefs of, 54–55, 579n–80n
  as taskmaster, 54
  temper of, 47, 49–50, 576n
  Yorba Linda farm of, 42, 45–46, 578n

Nixon, George, 43
Nixon, George, III, 43
Nixon, Hannah Milhous, 9, 15, 18, 54, 58,
  71, 105, 157, 160, 186, 219, 224, 243,
  245, 312, 390
  courtship and marriage of Frank and,
    43–44, 45
  death of, 317–18
  emotional coldness of, 47–48, 49, 50, 58,
    577n
  nervous breakdowns of, 47, 49
  Pennsylvania farm of, 85
  pregnancies of, 46, 49, 60, 64
  RN's idolization of, 68, 162, 318, 406. 532
  in Yorba Linda, 45–46
Nixon, Harold, 46, 47
  death of, 64
  outgoing personality of, 49, 58
  tuberculosis of, 56, 60, 64
Nixon, James, 42
Nixon, Mudge, Rose, Guthrie & Alexander,
  313
Nixon, Pat (Thelma Catherine) Ryan, 1, 2,
  197, 245
  background of, 4–5, 72
  Beverly Hills home of, 300–301
  "Checkers" speech and, 191
  childhood of, 73
  in China trip, 460, 462
  death of, 557–58
  difficult marital relations of, 160, 600n
  Eisenhower's heart attack and, 235, 236,
    237
  emotional reserve of, 74, 161
  financial worries of, 20–21
  first Whittier apartment of, 20–21
  grandchildren and, 557
  health problems of, 557
  "household expenses" fund for, 180–81,
    189
  isolation of, 219
  jobs held by, 72, 73
  in move to Saddle River, 553
  in 1940 move to Washington, 76
  in 1946 campaign, 20–21, 23, 24,
    29–30, 40
  and 1948 Caribbean vacation, 105,
    120–21, 122–23
  1952 vice-presidential campaign and, 169,
    201, 203, 205–6
  in 1953 tour of Asia and Middle East,
    216–18

in 1958 Latin American tour, 264–66
in 1959 trip to Russia, 272
in 1960 campaign, 290, 292, 296, 298
in 1963 move to New York, 313
in 1968 campaign, 324, 339, 345
in 1980 move to New York, 553
political life detested by, 175, 206, 219–20, 233, 305, 324, 553
post–White House years of, 553, 555
pregnancies of, 11, 18, 20
Price Administration job of, 78
RFK assassination and, 323
at RN's inauguration, 348
and RN's 1950 Senate campaign, 134, 157
and RN's 1952 vice-presidential campaign, 174–76
and RN's 1962 campaign, 304–5, 310
RN's courtship of, 4–5, 71–73, 74
and RN's first congressional term, 104
and RN's first House term, 80, 84
and RN's health problems, 162, 175
RN's political career supported by, 11, 75, 134
RN's political life as strain on, 104–5
and RN's promise to quit politics, 234, 238
RN's resignation and, 530, 531, 532–33
and RN's trip to postwar Europe, 87–88, 104
RN's wartime letters to, 78–79
on RN as target of liberals, 204
RN urged to fight back against Dump Nixon Movement by, 184
Saturday Evening Post article of, 178
self-reliance of, 72, 79
in station wagon campaign tour, 140–41, 147
stroke of, 548–49
teaching job of, 72
at USC, 72, 73
Washington house of, 160
in Washington social life, 163
Watergate scandal and, 511, 514, 526, 527, 528, 548, 553
wedding and honeymoon of, 5, 74
Nixon, Pat (Thelma Catherine) Ryan, as First Lady, 409
in humanitarian tour to Peru, 401–2
RN's remoteness from, 400–401
White House decor and social functions managed by, 356–57

Nixon, Richard:
abandonment of friends and allies by, 262
affection craved by, 49, 50, 62, 162
ambition of, 125
analytical mind of, 3
angry outbursts of, 59, 244, 281, 398
anti-Semitism of, 418, 426, 653n, 654n–55n
anxiety attacks of, 241
appearance of, 3
audacity and resourcefulness of, 41, 48
back taxes owed by, 524
Beverly Hills home of, 300–301
black and white view of, 209
brashness of, 211–12
civil liberties defended by, 145
civil rights and, 332
confrontation avoided by, 49–50
crisis and risk courted by, 399, 512, 520, 535, 683n
death of, 558
deep-seated insecurity of, 67, 69, 94, 162, 203–4, 211, 281, 337, 375, 398, 455, 463, 532
Democrats portrayal as elitist by, 200
drinking problem of, 411–12, 522–23, 651n, 680n
as driven to succeed, 74, 535
at Duke Law School, 4, 66–70
Eisenhower's ambiguous relationship with, 263, 274–75
Eisenhower's death and, 373–74
emotional reserve of, 19, 41, 48, 49, 50, 58, 62, 67, 69, 74, 78, 161, 162, 203–4, 353, 398, 399, 443
empathy of, 68, 374
expediency and dirty tricks of, 41
failed frozen orange juice business of, 71, 74
first Whittier apartment of, 20–21
fondness for nightlife of, 160, 600n–601n
Ford's pardon of, 535–36, 683n–84n
foreign policy as focus of, 371
Frost interviews of, 539, 548, 549–51, 637n
generosity of, 409–10
grandchildren and, 557
growing paranoia of, 209, 365–66, 373, 397, 399–400, 423
grudges and resentments nursed by, 58–59, 299–300, 303, 308, 398, 556
Hannah's death and, 317–18

Nixon, Richard (*cont.*):
  health problems of, 161–62, 175, 187, 219,
    241–42, 527, 537, 557
  idealism of, 7, 16
  inclination to intrigue of, 17, 164, 430–31,
    569*n*
  inhibitions of, 59, 70–71
  insomnia of, 412
  intellectuals' dislike of, 200, 204–5
  internationalism of, 164
  In the Arena memoir of, 555, 687*n*
  Kelly's caricature of, 230
  Kennedys mistrusted by, 299, 303, 308
  Key Biscayne houses of, 353, 400, 467,
    472, 476, 509, 524, 547–48, 633*n*
  lack of racial prejudice in, 249–51, 252,
    254
  lasting impact of Hiss case on, 126–27
  liberal enmity toward, 158–59
  liberalism of, 68–69, 85, 555
  loneliness of, 403, 430, 463, 499, 532
  Los Angeles law practice of, 300–301
  lying by, 687*n*
  McCarthy and, 145, 163, 216
  media's mutual enmity with, 203–8,
    242–43, 299, 305, 309–10, 397–98,
    402, 416, 418, 420, 421, 482, 499,
    514–15, 610*n*
  MLK assassination and, 322
  moodiness of, 161
  in move to Saddle River, 553
  as narcissist, 48, 577*n*
  at Navy Aeronautics Bureau, 1–2
  Navy service of, 1–2, 5–7, 11, 12, 19,
    76–79, 585*n*
  in 1948 election, 91
  1952 Republican Convention
    maneuvering by, 166–67, 169, 170–72,
    184
  in 1963 move to New York, 313, 633*n*
  1964 election and, 316–17
  1966 elections and, 318–19
  in 1980 move to New York, 553
  in Office of Price Administration, 5, 76
  as opportunist, 385, 390–91
  Pat and, *see* Nixon, Pat (Thelma
    Catherine) Ryan
  Pat's death and, 557–58
  phlebitis of, 527, 537
  poker playing by, 6, 78, 567*n*
  political instincts of, 171, 200, 212–13,
    271, 382, 390, 617*n*

post-presidential finances of, 547–48, 554,
    686*n*
  in post-presidential trips to China, 554
  in post-presidential trips to Russia, 554
  prescription drugs taken by, 162, 241–42,
    412, 616*n*, 651*n*
  presidential aspirations of, 133
  psychoanalysis scorned by, 48
  Quaker background of, 5, 6, 75, 249–50,
    279, 390
  racism of, 385–86
  resiliency of, 70
  RN memoir of, 551–52
  Rose Mary Woods as secretary of, 159–60
  San Clemente house of, 353, 425, 427,
    441, 442, 453, 497–98, 509, 516, 524,
    534–35, 547, 633*n*
  seen as opportunist, 113, 125, 200, 206,
    225
  self-discipline of, 399
  self-pity of, 196
  Senate career of, 159–60, 163–64
  Six Crises memoir of, 301–2, 303
  in South Pacific campaign, 77–79
  speechwriting routine of, 188
  "Tricky Dick" image of, 39, 148, 154, 158,
    159, 283, 304, 306
  as uneasy around women, 18–19
  vacations of, 162–63
  Vietnam War escalation supported by,
    314, 316, 318–19
  viewed as glory hound, 125
  Washington house of, 160
  Watergate grand jury testimony of,
    544–47, 685*n*–86*n*
  Whittier house of, 134
  Whittier law practice of, 2, 9, 14, 70–71,
    583*n*
  win-at-all-costs mentality of, 41, 63, 126,
    162, 445
  at Wingert & Bewley, 70–71, 74
  World War II as catalyst for, 7
Nixon, Richard, childhood and adolescence
    of, 8, 48, 49–60
  acting by, 60, 63
  Arthur's death and, 55–56
  birth of, 42, 46, 49
  on college football team, 61
  as driven to succeed, 56–57
  in extended stays with relatives, 55, 58
  girls and, 59–60, 62–63
  goals of, 57

and Harold's illness and death, 56, 64
illnesses in, 49, 59
jobs of, 52, 54, 56
Marshall Plan supported by, 91–92
musical ability of, 50, 51, 57, 61
as prize-winning orator, 57
scholastic achievements of, 50, 51, 55, 56–58
student acting experience of, 4
temper of, 59
tuberculosis and, 56
as voracious reader, 50, 51–52
at Whittier College, 4, 60–63, 582*n*
Nixon, Richard, in House of Representatives, 80–128
anti-Communist crusade of, 93–94
Education and Labor Committee seat of, 83–84
in Herter mission to Europe, 86–91, 104, 587*n*
Marshall Plan supported by, 101
national health insurance plan of, 141
in 1948 election, 132
Whittier Narrows Dam project and, 82–83
Nixon, Richard, as HUAC member, 83–84, 93, 95–96, 97–103
Chambers's meetings with, 113, 115–16, 117, 121
and Chambers's televised appearance, 119–20
Chambers's testimony and, 109–10
Chambers subpoenaed by, 122
Condon smear and, 102, 105
Hiss case pursued by, 112–28, 132, 136, 137, 142, 145, 158, 165, 193, 200, 204–5, 589*n*–90*n*, 591*n*–92*n*, 610*n*
Hollywood investigation avoided by, 98, 125, 588*n*
leaks by, 101–2, 124, 592*n*
liberal smear campaign against, 127
Mundt-Nixon bill and, 100–101
"Pumpkin Papers" and, 122–23
and Trumbo contempt citation, 99–100
Nixon, Richard, in 1946 congressional campaign, 2, 18–42, 136, 158
Amateurs in, 23–24, 28, 29
British Columbia vacation trip in, 25
cash shortage in, 24, 25, 27, 570*n*
Chotiner in, 28–30, 573*n*
Committee of 100 and, 14–16
fund-raising in, 27, 36–37, 570*n*

in grassroots movement, 23–24
oil money in, 25–28, 36, 38, 570*n*–71*n*
Perry and, 8, 10–12, 14, 16, 26, 27, 37, 568*n*
as political unknown, 7–8
primary in, 25, 27
Republican establishment and, 15
RN's landslide in, 40
and RN's uneasiness with women, 18–19
shortages as theme in, 21
Soviet containment as theme in, 21–22
speeches to service clubs in, 19, 22
veterans courted by, 22
Voorhis debates in, 34–36
Voorhis portrayed as Communist stooge by, 16, 28–29, 32–41, 126, 573*n*–74*n*
Nixon, Richard, in 1950 Senate campaign, 114, 120, 132–33
Brennan and, 133–34, 138, 142, 145, 151–52, 155
Chotiner and, 138–42, 145, 148–52, 602*n*
Douglas portrayed as Communist dupe by, 150–52, 153–55, 158–59, 599*n*
and Douglas's attack on RN's Korea bill vote, 149–50
Douglas's fund-raising problems and, 155
Downey and Douglas as viewed by, 138–39
fund-raising in, 135, 137, 599*n*–600*n*, 602*n*
ineptness of Douglas campaign and, 155, 159
Kennedy family support for, 152–53
Knowland's support for, 137, 595*n*
Korean War and, 149, 155, 156, 159
Los Angeles Times endorsement of, 136–37, 142, 596*n*
media attacks on Douglas in, 153
Palmer's support for, 136–37, 142, 153
Pat and, 134
Perry and, 134, 142, 596*n*
Red-baiting in, 145–46, 155
RN's landslide victory in, 156–57
spending by, 139, 154, 155
station wagon tour in, 140–41, 147–48
Warren and, 137, 166
Nixon, Richard, 1952 vice-presidential campaign of, 174–76, 177–97, 198–209
anti-Semitism allegations against, 180
as champion of common man, 198–201

Nixon, Richard, 1952 vice-presidential campaign of (*cont.*):
"Checkers" speech in, 187, 188–89, 190–95, 198–99, 201, 208, 212, 213, 334, 606*n*, 607*n*, 608*n*–9*n*
Dewey's urging of RN's resignation in, 189–90, 194
Dump Nixon Movement and, 183–84, 186–87
and Eisenhower's delayed decision to keep RN on ticket, 196–97
kick-off of, 177–78
Red-baiting in, 179, 202
in refusal to resign from ticket, 194
slush fund accusations in, 180–84, 205, 606*n*
whistle-stop tour in, 177–78, 182–83, 185
Nixon, Richard, 1960 presidential campaign of, 276–93
in agreement to TV debates, 278
Catholicism issue and, 278–80, 624*n*
changing image as preoccupation of, 283
civil rights issue in, 287, 626*n*
dirty tricks in, 627*n*
Eisenhower's help spurned by, 289–90
election results accepted by, 297–98
fifty-state pledge of, 280, 284, 287, 291
immediate aftermath of, 298–300
JFK's health as issue in, 290–91
Lodge as running mate in, 274, 282
MLK's jailing and, 287–89, 626*n*
polls and, 272–73, 276, 278, 285, 286, 291
RN's exhaustion in, 281
RN's obsessive micromanaging of, 280–82, 291
Rockefeller and, 272–74, 627*n*
staph infection of, 278, 284
TV debates in, 283–86, 625*n*–26*n*
unemployment rise and, 278
vice-presidential experience as both plus and minus in, 276–77
voter registration disadvantage of, 277
and voting fraud issues, 294–98
Nixon, Richard, 1962 gubernatorial campaign of:
Birch Society attacked by, 308
Brown portrayed as soft on Communism by, 306
counterintelligence operations in, 305
Cuban missile crisis and, 308
Haldeman as campaign manager of, 305–6, 311

Howard Hughes loan as issue in, 306–7
"last press conference" in, 310–11
Pat's concerns about, 304–5
RN's concerns about, 304
Nixon, Richard, 1968 presidential campaign of, 320, 323–24
Agnew as running mate in, 333, 637*n*
as champion of silent majority, 333–34
Chennault affair and, 342–44, 425, 433, 546, 637*n*–40*n*
Haldeman in, 338
innuendo and misstatements in, 344
"law and order" issue in, 330–32
"loser" label and, 324
mass media in, 338–39
in meeting with southern delegations, 328–29
mellower image of, 324–25
Mitchell as campaign manager in, 323, 332, 338
nomination acceptance speech in, 335–37
political IOUs redeemed in, 326, 332–33
polls and, 339–40
Reagan-Rockefeller alliance in, 326–27
right wing and, 327
RN's silence about Vietnam in, 340
southern strategy in, 329–30, 635*n*
staff of, 323
Nixon, Richard, as president:
abortion issue and, 377–78
Allende coup and, 543–44
ambassadorial appointments of, 544–45
angry outbursts of, 403
approval ratings of, 417
assassination attempt against, 525–26
"black ops" of, 431–34
Brezhnev's meetings with, 516, 527
Brookings Institution burglary proposed by, 425
cabinet decision-making sidelined by, 356
Chappaquiddick investigation by, 431
China trip of, 460–63, 465, 490
Congress's arms-length relationship with, 353
culture war and, 413–15
decision-making process of, 354
desegregation under, 383
and East Pakistan crisis, 451–54
economic policies of, 444–50
Eisenhower as role model for, 372–73
enemies lists of, 432, 484
environmentalism and, 379–81

Executive Office hideaway of, 353, 403, 417, 428, 496
expansion of government under, 372
farewell speech of, 532
first inauguration of, 347–48, 349–50
gay rights and, 377–78
health care plan of, 376, 646*n*
Hughes's campaign donation and, 470, 546
illegal surveillance by, 475, 657*n*
impeachment hearings and, 522, 526, 528, 682*n*
India-Pakistan war and, 450, 454, 456–59
interpersonal relationships avoided by, 353, 355, 373, 392
ITT scandal and, 467, 469, 524
and Jacqueline Onassis's visit to White House, 409–10
JFK as obsession of, 409
liberal domestic policy of, 372, 375–76
in Lincoln Memorial meeting with antiwar protesters, 405–6
Native Americans and, 376
in 1972 Moscow Summit, 450, 487–88, 489, 494–95
in 1974 tour of Europe and Middle East, 527
O'Brien targeted by, 469–70
as obsessed with minutiae, 356–58
in opening to China, 418, 435–44, 450, 453, 460–64, 465, 490, 659*n*–60*n*
Pentagon Papers and, 419–20, 422
Plumbers and, 427, 547
pragmatism of, 376–77
rants and tantrums of, 358–59, 377–78, 382, 417–18
reelection campaign of, 430–31, 468, 473–74, 487, 491, 497–98, 513, 550
resignation of, 530–33
rightward shift in, 382
SALT talks and, 418, 428, 489, 490, 491, 494–95
Saturday Night Massacre in, 520–21, 528, 680*n*
second inauguration of, 505
secrecy as obsession of, 422
secret tape-recording system of, 415, 429, 474, 476, 479, 517, 518
social welfare legislation under, 375–76
solitude preferred by, 408
southern strategy of, 389

state and defense departments reduced influence under, 350, 354
Supreme Court nominees of, 389–90
Taiwan and, 443–44
tax reform by, 375
"tilt" toward Pakistan of, 453, 459–60
Vietnam War and, *see* Vietnam War, under Nixon administration
"war on drugs" of, 378, 646*n*
Watergate and, *see* Watergate cover-up
Watergate tapes released by, 522, 524, 525, 526
Yom Kippur War and, 520, 522–23, 680*n*–81*n*
Nixon, Richard, as vice president:
anti-McCarthy speech of, 224
in attempts to broker peace with McCarthy, 214, 215, 216, 222, 225
in Caracas mob attack, 265–66
and CIA plots against Castro, 302–3
Civil Rights Act and, 253–57
civil rights movement and, 245–46, 250–51, 252–58, 259
Congress and, 213, 216
Eisenhower's heart attack and, 234, 235–40
Eisenhower's relationship with, 210–11, 230, 231–32, 240–42, 245, 289–90
filibuster rulings of, 253–54
Indochina War intervention urged by, 227
Khrushchev's debates with, 270–71
leaving politics contemplated by, 233, 234, 238
in 1953 tour of Asia and Middle East, 216–19
1954 election campaigning by, 231, 233
in 1956 reelection campaign, 243–45, 617*n*
1958 election campaigning by, 267–68
1959 Russia trip of, 269–72
NSC role of, 212, 218, 231, 238, 276
partisan rhetoric of, 230, 231
proposed dropping from 1956 ticket of, 239–42
in San Marcos University confrontation, 264–65
Nixon, Samuel, 43
Nixon, Sarah Wadsworth, 43
Nixon family, as Scotch-Irish Protestants, 42
"Nixon Sustaining Fund," 180
North, segregation in, 387

North Atlantic Treaty Organization
    (NATO), RN's support of, 165
North Korea, 217
  South Korea invaded by, 149
North Vietnam, 314, 485
  Soviet presence in, 341
  Soviet pressure on, 344
  U.S. underestimation of resolve of, 366
Novak, Robert, 316–17, 333, 385, 498
nuclear proliferation treaty (1968), 488
nuclear weapons, U.S. buildup of, 263
Nunes, Edith, 50, 62–63

Oakland Tribune, 135, 136
Obama, Barack, 376
O'Brien, Lawrence, 253, 340, 475–76
  background of, 469
  as DNC chairman, 469
  Hughes and, 469–70, 471
  IRS investigation of, 546–47
  Plumbers' bugging of office of, 471
O'Brien, W. E., 125
Occupational Safety and Health Act, 375
Ochs, William, 90
O'Donnell, Peter, 332
Office of Minority Business Enterprise,
    395
Office of Price Administration, 5
  RN's job at, 75–76
oil, price of, 449
oil industry:
  1946 election and, 25–28, 36, 38,
    570n–71n
  Teapot Dome scandal and, 25–26
  tidelands controversy and, 26–28
  Voorhis's attacks on, 26
oil money, 36
oil prices, Yom Kippur War and, 522–23
Oliver, Spencer, 668n, 669n
Olney, Warren, 28, 194–95, 256
Onassis, Jacqueline Bouvier Kennedy, 84,
    203n, 262, 298
  RN's correspondence with, 312
  in visit to Nixon White House, 409–10
101st Airborne Division, 248, 258, 383
O'Neill, Thomas P. "Tip," 314, 513–14, 520,
    522
Operation Mongoose (CIA assassination
    program), 542
Oppenheimer, J. Robert, 144, 221, 226
  RN's support for, 145, 221n, 598n
Orthogonians (college society), 61–62, 250

Ostrow, Ron, 482
Oswald, Lee, 312
Otis, Harrison Gray, 135
Ottumwa, Iowa, 5, 76–77, 79
Owens Valley, 135

Pakistan, 217, 218, 439, 440
  in cease-fire with India, 459
  massacre of East Pakistanis by, 451–54,
    459, 662n
  in 1965 war with India, 452
  in 1971 war with India, 450, 454, 456–59
  RN's illegal aid to, 457
  RN's personal relations with, 454
Palmer, Kyle, 12–13, 28, 36, 164, 168, 204,
    216–17, 238, 268, 309
  Chotiner and, 141–42
  Helen Douglas attacked by, 150
  as kingmaker, 135–36
  RN's Senate campaign supported by,
    136–37, 142, 153, 595n–96n
Panetta, Leon, 384
Pappas, Thomas "Tom," 504
Paris Peace Accords (1973), 500, 684n–85n
Paris peace talks, 319, 340, 341, 343, 366,
    495–97
Parks, Rosa, 251–52
Parmet, Herbert, 555
Parr, George, 295
Patton (film), 403, 491
Patton, George, 12, 14, 201
Pauley, Edwin, 27, 28, 83, 152
Payne, Ethel, 250, 256
Payton, Sallyanne, 383, 394
PBS, 515
Peale, Norman Vincent, 279–80, 294, 348
Pearl Harbor, Japanese attack on, 5, 76
Pearson, Drew, 163, 238, 291, 306, 397
  anti-Nixon vendetta of, 206–7
  distortions and errors of, 207
Penn, William, 44
Pennsylvania, 44
Pentagon Papers, 419–20, 422–25, 509, 514,
    526, 539
  Supreme Court ruling on, 424–25
Pepper, Claude, 145
Pepsi-Cola, 313
Peress, Irving, 220, 222
Perjury (Weinstein), 591n
Perry, Herman, 13, 14, 83, 98, 101–2, 133,
    166, 167, 178, 179, 180, 207
  banking career of, 8, 9

fading influence of, 134, 142
oil money solicited by, 25, 570n–71n
RN as surrogate son of, 9–10
and RN's 1946 congressional campaign, 8,
    10–12, 14, 16, 25, 26, 27, 37, 568n
as RN's political mentor, 80, 82–83
and RN's Senate campaign, 134, 142,
    596n
Perry, Hubert, 9–10, 27, 52
Persons, Wilton "Jerry," 237
Peru, 264
1970 earthquake in, 401–2
Petersen, Henry, 509, 519
Philadelphia Plan, 395
Phillips, John, 166
Phillips, Kevin, 330, 340, 387, 388
Phnom Penh, 218
Pinochet, Augusto, 543
Plessy v. Ferguson, 247
Plumbers (Special Investigative Unit), 427,
    434, 547
arrests of, 471, 476
in burglary of Ellsberg's psychiatrist,
    428–29, 430, 468, 472, 476–77, 505,
    509, 515, 521, 656n–57n
Cubans in, 429, 430, 468, 471
in Gemstone operation, 468, 477
Magruder given oversight by, 429–30
O'Brien's office bugged by, 471
trial of, 505, 507
in Watergate break-ins, *see* Watergate
    break-ins
Pogo (comic strip), 230
Poland, 272
division of, 75, 81
Political Obituary of Richard Nixon, The (TV
    special), 311
Pompidou, Georges, 458
Populists, 198
Porter, Herbert "Bart," 432
Potter, Philip "Phil," 89
Powell, Adam Clayton, Jr., 249n, 288,
    627n
Powell, Lewis, 390, 395–96
Prague Spring, 347
Presley, Elvis, 407
Price, Raymond, 323, 324, 339, 346, 359,
    374, 412, 413, 437, 515, 519, 535
Price Waterhouse, 188, 191–92
prisons:
African Americans in, 379
population of, 378–79

Project Apollo, 376
Protestants, 1960 election and, 279–80
"Pumpkin Papers," 122–23

Quakers, 9, 75, 390
materialist faction of, 9, 44
Milhous family as, 44
snobbishness of, 9, 52
Whittier founded by, 9, 44, 249–50
Quemoy, 228, 235, 299

Rabb, Maxwell "Max," 257
race riots, 321–22, 333
Radford, Charles, 459–60, 664n
Rahman, Mujibur, 452
Rand, Ayn, 98
Rankin, John, 96–97, 99–100, 131
racism of, 103
Rather, Dan, 417, 515
Rayburn, Sam, 94, 127, 131, 273
RN's smearing of, 202
Reader's Digest, 145
Reagan, Ronald, 328, 371, 378, 390, 472,
    537, 552, 556, 557
anti-Communist crusade of, 32, 98
HUAC testimony of, 98
in 1968 election, 326–27, 332–33
presidency of, 555
Real Majority, The (Scammon and
    Wattenberg), 387–88
Rebozo, Charles "Bebe," 241, 310, 353n,
    398, 470, 521, 546, 547, 557
RN's friendship with, 162–63, 400, 408,
    472, 554, 601n, 633n
Reconstruction, 327
recounts, procedures for, 297
Red Detachment of Women, The (ballet),
    462
Red peril, 21–22
Red Record of Senator Claude Pepper, The
    (pamphlet), 145–46
Red Scare, 32, 81–82, 95, 144, 226, 314
exaggerations of, 94
as theme of RN's Senate campaign,
    145–46
see also McCarthyism
Reece, Carroll, 32
Reed, Clarke, 333
Reed, John, 108
Reedy, George, 96
Rehnquist, William, 377, 390
Reilly, John, 186

religion, RN's rationalist approach to, 65–66

Remley, Zita, 40

Remnick, David, 482–83

Renneburg, John, 1–2, 11–12

Reporter, 179, 605*n*

Republican National Committee (RNC), 189, 194, 197, 280

Republican National Convention, of 1952, 168–76

  Eisenhower's first ballot victory at, 173

  "Fair Play" vote in, 171, 604*n*

  "great train robbery" and, 170–71

  RN's maneuvers on behalf of Eisenhower in, 166–67, 169, 170–72, 184

  seating of Southern Eisenhower delegates in, 172–73

  televising of, 173, 177

Republican National Convention, of 1968, 429–30

Republican Party, Republicans:

  black voters neglected by, 289

  corruption in, 267

  growing southern strength of, 327–28

  history and image of, 198

  in 1946 election, 39, 40

  in 1954 election, 233

  1958 election losses of, 267, 277

  "Old Guard" wing of, 86, 128, 149, 168, 171, 176, 273

  race issues and, 327–28

  right-wing vs. moderates of, 303–4

Reston, James, Jr., 550

Reston, James "Scotty," 119, 204, 208, 232, 260–61, 292, 311

Rez (hired girl), 47, 49

Rhee, Syngman, 217

Rhodes, James, 404

Rhodes, John, 527, 529, 531

Rhyne, Charles, 68

Richards, James, 90

Richardson, Elliot, 263, 374, 399, 510, 514, 519, 521

  resignation of, 521

Ridgway, Matthew, 222, 227

RN: The Memoirs of Richard Nixon, 551

Road to Serfdom, The (Hayek), 22

Robbins, Jerome, 100

Robeson, Paul, 154, 164

Robinson, Claude, 204, 276, 280, 283, 285–86, 291, 296

Robinson, Edward G., 99

Robinson, Elwood, 308

Robinson, Jackie, 248, 287-88, 289, 647*n*

  RN's friendship with, 250, 287, 288, 315–16, 331, 385, 626*n*

Robinson, William, 185, 204

Rockefeller, Nelson, 290, 303, 316, 317, 350, 351, 378, 436

  as New York governor, 304

  in 1958 New York election, 268

  in 1960 election, 272–74

  in 1968 election, 326–27, 333

  as vice president, 541

Rockefeller commission, 541, 665*n*

Roe v. Wade, 377

Rogers, Edward "Ted," 190–91, 194, 202, 208, 213, 244, 266–67, 269, 272, 284, 286, 607*n*

Rogers, Roy, 177

Rogers, William, 116, 160, 209, 214, 288, 313, 461*n*, 462, 510, 523

  Eisenhower's heart attack and, 235, 236, 237

  in 1952 presidential campaign, 169, 178, 182, 184, 189

  as secretary of state, 351–52, 354, 358, 402, 440

Rogers, Will, Jr., 29

Roman Holiday (film), 99*n*

Romania, 439

Rome, 90–91

Romney, George, in 1968 election, 326

Roosevelt, Eleanor, 131

Roosevelt, Franklin D., 2, 11, 14, 21, 109, 129, 131, 188, 198, 327*n*, 331–32, 426, 608*n*–9*n*

  death of, 79, 173

  Truman sidelined by, 212

Roosevelt, John, 290

Roosevelt, Theodore, 139, 174, 198

  RN's admiration of, 6

Rosenberg, Ethel, 144, 201–2

Rosenberg, Julius, 95, 144, 201–2

Rostow, Walt, 341, 343, 639*n*

Rovere, Richard, 242, 244, 268, 417

Ruark, Robert, 199

Rubsamen, Rosetta, 90–91

Ruckelshaus, William, 380, 521

Rumsfeld, Donald, 385, 558

Rush, Kenneth, 435

Rusher, William, 443

Russell, Richard, 254, 255–56, 257, 258–59, 390

Russia, RN's post-presidential trips to, 554
Russo, Anthony, 419, 678*n*
Rust Belt, 387
Ruth, Henry, 544–47
Rwanda, 451
Ryther, Polly, 201

Sacramento River, 129
Sadat, Anwar, 523, 527, 555
Saddle River, N.J., Nixon house in, 553
Safire, William, 270, 271*n*, 289, 313, 323,
    337–38, 355, 365, 393, 409, 412, 447
Saigon, 218
  fall of, 501–2, 539, 684*n*–85*n*
St. Johns, Adela Rogers, 7, 139, 261
Sanchez, Manolo, 346, 405, 408, 411–12
San Clemente, Calif., RN's house in, 353,
    425, 427, 441, 442, 453, 497–98, 509,
    516, 524, 534–35, 547, 633*n*
San Francisco Chronicle, 135, 596*n*
San Joaquin River, 129
Santa Ana Canyon, 51
Santa Ana winds, 46
Santa Barbara oil spill, 379
Sato, Eisaku, 444
Saturday Evening Post, 178, 199
Saturday Night Massacre, 520–21, 528,
    680*n*
Saturday Review, 200
Sawyer, Diane, RN and, 551
Scammon, Richard, 331, 335, 387–88
Schaap, Dick, 325
Schine, G. David, 215, 222–23, 224
Schlesinger, Arthur, Jr., 108, 126–27, 211,
    241, 322, 329*n*, 553
Schlesinger, James, 352–53, 372, 522,
    530
Schneider, René, 542, 543
school desegregation, 248–49, 383–84
  busing in, 329, 385–86
  RN's enforcement of Supreme Court
    decision on, 391–93
  white flight and, 329
Schroeder, Patricia, 513
Schuyler, Harry, 54
Scoggins, Verne, 136
Scott, Hugh, 140, 526, 531
Scottsboro boys, 108
Scowcroft, Brent, 539
Scranton, William, 375
Screen Actors Guild, 98
Scripps College, 19

Sears, John, 323, 365
Seaton, Fred, 183
Secret Agenda (Hougan), 669*n*
Seeds of Treason (Lasky and de Toledano),
    145, 165
segregation, RN's opposition to, 68
Segretti, Donald, 432, 467, 538
Senate, U.S.:
  Church committee hearings in, 541–43
  filibuster rule in, 253
  Government Operations Committee of,
    213
  Judiciary Committee of, 467, 476, 514
  part III of Civil Rights Act attacked by,
    255–56, 258
  Southern Democrats' domination of,
    253
Senate Select Committee on Presidential
    Campaign Activities, 514, 515
  Dean's testimony to, 516
  Ehrlichman's testimony to, 516
  Haldeman's testimony to, 516
  McCord's testimony to, 507
  Mitchell's testimony to, 516
  tape-recordings and, 516, 518
Sequoia (presidential yacht), 403, 445
service clubs, 19, 22
Sevareid, Eric, 183
Sheehan, Neil, 419
Shell, Joe, 308–9, 382
Sherwood, John "Jack," 264–66, 269, 475
Shriver, Sargent, 288
Shultz, George, 374, 392, 417, 446, 498,
    552–53
  school desegregation and, 391–93
Shuman, Howard, 256
Signal Oil & Gas, 10, 26
Sihanouk, Norodom, 217, 397
Silbert, Earl, 484, 509
Silent Coup (Colodny and Gettlin), 669*n*,
    670*n*
silent majority, 333–34, 369, 645*n*, 675*n*
Silvermaster, Nathan, 102
Simmons, Lee, 410
Simon, William, 529
Simons, Howard, 482, 507
Sinclair, Upton, 31, 130
Sirica, John, 505, 507, 518, 524, 537,
    538
Six Crises (Nixon), 301–2, 303, 506, 512
Skidmore, Mary, 51
Slater, Ellis, 165

Small, Merrell, 29, 142, 170, 171
Smathers, George, 145, 162, 298
Smith, Al, 279, 327n
Smith, Al, Jr., 279
Smith, Dana, 167, 180, 181, 188–89, 206, 595n, 606n
Smith, Gerald L. K., 29
Smith, Lamar, 251
Smith, Margaret Chase, 144, 163
Smith, Paul, 63, 219–20
Smith, Sandy, 482
Smith, Walter Bedell, 213, 214
Smith Act (1940), 100
Smyser, William, 404
Sobeloff, Simon, 251
Socialism, 108
Social Security, 375
  cost-of-living raises in, 449
Solomon Islands, 77
Sorensen, Ted, 274, 520
South:
  Eisenhower campaign in, 327
  growing Republican strength in, 327–28, 635n
  segregation of, 68
Southeast Asia, 93
  Communism in, 314
  RN's interest in, 313
Southern California, University of (USC), Pat Nixon at, 72, 73
South Korea, 217
  North Korea's invasion of, 149
South Pacific, World War II in, 77–79
South Pacific Air Transport Command, 77–78
South Vietnam, 315
  fall of, 501–2, 539, 684n–85n
  RN's "decent interval" strategy for, 486, 500–501, 673n–74n
  RN's goal of strengthening regime in, 360
  U.S. support for, 314
  Viet Cong demands for political role in, 341–42
Soviet Union:
  atomic bomb acquired by, 81, 94, 105, 144
  China relations with, 438–39, 463
  collapse of, 540, 556
  Cuba and, 489
  Czechoslovakia invaded by, 438
  economy of, 487
  in German nonaggression pact, 75, 108

India's treaty with, 455–56
Middle East and, 488, 489, 520, 522, 523
purges in, 108
SALT talks and, 418, 428, 489, 490, 491, 494–95
Sputnik launched by, 260, 263, 267
spying by, 93, 94
in test ban agreement with U.S., 313
in treaty with West Germany, 489
U-2 shot down by, 274, 276, 490
U.S. plans for war with, 105
U.S. relations with, 30, 269, 435, 444, 450, 463, 487–88, 494–95
Vietnam War and, 341, 344, 362–63, 464, 494
in World War II, 108–9, 221
Spanish Civil War, 74–75, 108
Sparkman, John, 182
Spartacus (film), 99n
Speck, Richard, 335
Spellman, Francis, 314
Spencer, Stu, 412
Sputnik, 260, 263, 267
stagflation, 446
Stagg, Tom, 333
Stalin, Joseph, 14, 21, 105
  death of, 215
  purges orchestrated by, 108
Standard Oil, 26, 27
Stans, Maurice, 48, 305, 323, 580n, 666n
Starr, Kenneth, 539
Stassen, Harold, 11, 77, 103, 137, 140, 165, 166, 183, 186, 228, 242
State Department, U.S.:
  coverup of Communist infiltration of, 110
  Hiss's career at, 107, 109
  McCarthy's crusade against, 143–44, 215
Steffens, Lincoln, 108
Steinbeck, John, 131
Steinem, Gloria, 73
Stennis, John, 229n, 259
Stettinius, Edward, Jr., 109
Stevens, Robert, 222
Stevenson, Adlai, 183, 218, 224, 233, 430
  alleged homosexuality of, 178–79
  as character witness for Hiss, 178, 202
  media's admiration of, 208, 605n
  in 1952 presidential campaign, 178, 198, 202, 208
  in 1956 presidential campaign, 243–45, 263
  "Nixonland" speech of, 243

RN's attacks on, 202
RN's enmity toward, 179
slush fund of, 182, 189
Stewart, James, 78
stock market, 1973–74 crash in, 449–50
Stoessel, Walter, 439
Stout, Osmyn, 16, 37
Strachan, Gordon, 352, 432, 433, 467–68, 476, 657*n*–58*n*, 666*n*, 667*n*
strategic arms limitations treaty (SALT), 418, 428, 489, 490, 494–95
Stripling, Robert, 85, 97, 112, 125, 301
Hiss case and, 106–7, 111, 113, 114–15, 117, 118, 121, 589*n*, 590*n*, 594*n*
Stryker, Lloyd, 142
Stuart, Constance, 400
Subversive Activities Control Act (1948), 151, 152
Helen Douglas's opposition to, 152
see also Mundt-Nixon bill
Sucksdorf, Florence, 18
Suez crisis, 244
Sukarno, Achmed, 217
Summerfield, Arthur, 185, 196, 197, 232
Sundquist, James, 330
Supreme Court, U.S., 252
affirmative action and, 395
Brown II decision of, 251
Brown v. Board of Education decision of, 247–49, 251, 254, 384, 385
busing decision of, 386
desegregation decisions of, 384
fights over Nixon nominees to, 389–90
Pentagon Papers ruling of, 424–25
Plessy decision of, 247
Warren appointed chief justice of, 216
Watergate tapes decision of, 527, 528–29, 682*n*
surveillance, illegal, 365, 421–22, 433, 475, 541–42, 628*n*, 644*n*, 657*n*, 658*n*
Symington, Stuart, 260
Syria, in Yom Kippur War, 520, 522–23

Taft, Robert, 86, 128, 150, 165, 605*n*
death of, 213, 216, 603*n*
1952 presidential campaign of, 164, 166, 167, 168–73, 176, 603*n*, 604*n*
Taft, William Howard, 240
Taft-Hartley Act, 83–84, 101, 124, 586*n*
Taiwan, 217, 439, 450, 461, 463
and RN's opening to China, 443–44
Tanenhaus, Sam, 557

taxes, on imports, 444, 447
Teamsters Union, 421, 586*n*, 600*n*, 627*n*, 653*n*, 662*n*
Teapot Dome scandal, 25–26
television:
Army-McCarthy hearings on, 224–25
"Checkers" speech on, 188–89, 190–95, 198–99, 201, 208, 212, 213, 334, 606*n*, 607*n*, 608*n*–9*n*
emerging power of, 177, 190, 195, 196, 208
HUAC hearings on, 118–20
1952 Republican Convention on, 173, 177
RN-JFK debates on, 283–86, 625*n*–26*n*
in RN's 1968 campaign, 338–39
Vietnam War coverage by, 319
Temple, Shirley, 96
Templer, Gerald, 218
Texas, voting fraud in, 294–95, 296, 297
Thailand, 361
theater, HUAC investigation of, 96
They Would Rule the Valley (Downey), 130
Thieu, Nguyen Van, 320, 341–43, 345, 365, 369*n*, 485, 495–96, 497, 500, 539–40, 639*n*, 640*n*
Tho, Le Duc, 366, 495, 524
Thomas, Helen, 401, 522
Thomas, J. Parnell, 102, 103, 116, 125
corruption conviction of, 97
as HUAC chairman, 97–98
Thompson, Hunter, 325
Thurmond, Strom, 332, 384, 391, 395
RN and, 328
tidelands, 26–28, 31, 130
Till, Emmett, 252, 256
Time, 80–81, 96, 97, 178, 194, 206, 219, 254, 258, 335, 439, 482, 524
Watergate scandal and, 514–15
Timmons, William, 415, 513
Title IX, 376
Tkach, Walter, 405, 527
Tokyo, firebombing of, 82
Tolstoy, Leo, 63, 554
Toumanoff, Vladimir, 271
Tower, John, 327
Train, Russell, 379, 380
Trieste, 90
Triggs, Dean, 158, 250
Triggs, Jewel, 62, 63, 158
Trilling, Lionel, 126, 127, 200

Trohan, Walter, 205
Trujillo, Rafael, 542
Truman, Harry, 21, 30, 79, 81–82, 86, 94,
102, 105, 126, 173, 174, 273
aid to French Indochina war approved by,
144, 226, 500
desegregation of armed forces ordered by,
247, 248
Eisenhower and, 210
FDR's sidelining of, 212
foreign policy blunders of, 30
and global Communist threat, 86
on HUAC witch hunt, 112
hydrogen bombs program announced
by, 144
loyalty probe launched by, 86, 586n
MacArthur fired by, 163
in 1948 election, 103, 120, 133
price controls maintained by, 20
RN's smearing of, 202
tidelands controversy and, 26, 27–28, 31
Truman Doctrine, 93, 131, 146
Trumbo, Dalton, 99–100, 588n
tuberculosis, 56
Tuck, Dick, 306, 432
Turkey, Communist threat in, 86
Tuttle, Elbert, 251
Twelfth Amendment, 604n
Twelfth Congressional District,
California, 2
Amateurs in, see Amateurs
eclectic nature of, 13–14, 23
redistricting in, 12
Republican establishment in, 12–13, 15
RN as political unknown in, 7–8
Twenty-fifth Amendment, 261n
Tydings, Millard, 156

U-2 spy planes, Soviet downing of, 274,
276, 490
Ulasewicz, Anthony, 431, 432, 503
Senate testimony of, 515
unemployment, 449
1960 election and, 278
United Auto Workers, 33
United Nations, 107, 131, 276, 452
Communist China as member of, 444
United States:
population growth in, 371
Soviet relations with, 30, 269
Soviet spies in, 93, 94

United States of America v. Richard Nixon,
528–29
United States, postwar era:
backlash against New Deal in, 11, 19
economic might of, 85
fraying of New Deal coalition in, 2, 39,
198–99
shortages in, 18, 19–20, 30, 39
University of California v. Bakke, 395–96
Upton, Albert, 6, 63
urban violence, 321–22, 330–32, 333
Uruguay, 264
U.S. Chamber of Commerce, 32, 95
Ut Nho, 320

Van Buren, Martin, 174, 240
Vandenberg, Arthur, 86
Van Doren, Mark, 200
Van Hollen, Christopher, 452
Vann, John Paul, 419–20, 472
Variety, 194, 448
Vazzana, Nicholas, 121, 123
Vella Lavella, 77
Venona project, 94–95, 591n, 599n
veterans, RN's 1946 courting of, 22
vice presidency, history of, 173–74, 604n
Vidal, Gore, 325
Vietnam, 217
French in, see Indochina War
partitioning of, 229
U.S. postwar relations with, 540
Vietnam Veterans Against the War, 421
Vietnam War, 93, 485
civilian death toll in, 500
Congress's growing opposition to, 413,
415, 417, 423, 539, 540
draft and, 319
fall of Saigon in, 501–2, 539, 684n–85n
Kissinger's view of, 351
LBJ's escalation of, 315, 319
LBJ's proposed cease-fire in, 318–19
lottery and, 370
media coverage of, 319, 320
MLK's opposition to, 321, 387
My Lai massacre in, 370
Paris peace talks in, 319, 340, 341, 343,
366, 495–97
secret negotiations between North
Vietnam and U.S. in, 366, 418
Soviet Union and, 341, 344, 362–63, 464,
494

Tet Offensive in, 320, 341, 369
U.S. bombing halt in, 341, 344, 638*n*
U.S. bombing in, 315, 367
U.S. casualties in, 500
U.S. self-esteem and international
    reputation damaged by, 368
U.S. troop strength in, 314, 315, 319
Vietnamization in, 365, 368
see also antiwar movement
Vietnam War, during Nixon administration:
appeal to silent majority in, 369
bombing of Cambodia in, 363–66, 367,
    643*n*–44*n*
bombing of Hanoi in, 491–92, 497
Cambodian invasion in, 360, 402–4, 439
cease-fire violations in, 500–501
"decent interval" strategy in, 486, 500–501,
    673*n*–74*n*
Dobrynin in secret talks on, 362–63, 486
escalation supported in, 314, 316, 318–19
Haiphong harbor mining in, 492, 494
Laos bombing in, 412
1972 Easter Offensive in, 490–91, 493–94
1972 U.S. elections and, 485, 486, 491,
    493–94
opening to China and, 442, 443–44,
    463–64
Paris Peace Accords and, 500, 684*n*–85*n*
return of U.S. POWs and, 485, 500, 501,
    511, 539
RN on morality of, 367
RN's desire for quick end to, 359–60, 420
RN's priorities in, 539–41
RN's self-imposed silence on, 340
RN's view of, 351
stepped-up bombing campaign in, 370,
    412, 420, 491–92, 497, 499–500, 676*n*
strengthening South Vietnam as goal of,
    360
threat to use nuclear weapons in, 362, 493
unilateral U.S. withdrawal in, 485–87,
    495–96, 500–501, 673*n*–74*n*, 685*n*
U.S. credibility as issue for, 361
U.S. troop withdrawals in, 363, 370
U.S. unilateral withdrawal rejected by, 360,
    362
Vietnamization policy in, 402, 403, 412,
    420, 485
Vo Nguyen Giap, 226
von Hoffman, Nicholas, 538
Voorhis, Charles, 24, 31, 32–33, 40

Voorhis, Jerry, 2, 8, 12, 14, 30–32, 82, 84,
    131, 150, 166, 178, 206
congressional career of, 10
in debates with RN, 34–36
leftist politics of, 10, 16, 28
NC-PAC endorsement of, 33, 35, 37–38
in 1944 election, 10
in 1946 campaign, 16, 22, 23, 24–25,
    28–29, 30, 136, 149, 158, 570*n*
oil industry attacked by, 26
political instincts lacking in, 31, 40
portrayed as Communist stooge by RN
    campaign, 16, 28–29, 32–41, 126,
    573*n*–74*n*
tidelands controversy and, 31
Voorhis Act (1940), 29, 100
Voting Rights Act (1965), 257, 315, 321, 329
RN's attempted dilution of, 384

Wagner Act, 84
Wallace, George, 384, 386, 387
attempted assassination of, 468, 525, 667*n*
1964 presidential campaign of, 321
in 1968 election, 324, 329, 330–31,
    339–41, 345, 346*n*
in 1972 election, 431, 432–33, 468, 473,
    667*n*
Wallace, Gerald, 432
Wallace, Henry, 30, 131
Wallace, Mike, 374
Walters, Vernon, 264
Watergate cover-up and, 478–79, 481,
    515
war on cancer, 375–76
Wardlaw, John, 288
War and Peace (Tolstoy), 554
Ware, Harold, 109
Warner, Jack, 98
war on drugs, 378, 646*n*
war on poverty, 315
War Powers Resolution (1973), 523–24
Warren, Earl, 12, 28, 133, 135, 136, 137,
    141, 186, 245, 251, 311, 389*n*, 528–29,
    595*n*, 602*n*
appointed chief justice, 216
Birch Society attacks on, 308, 309
Brown supported by, 309
mutual enmity of RN and, 166, 171–72,
    173
in 1952 presidential campaign, 165–73,
    176, 184

Warren, Earl, Jr., 309
Warren campaign song, 169–70
Washington, George, 43
Washington, Kenny, 250
Washington, Val, 250
Washington *Evening Star,* 112, 118
Washington Post, 102, 184, 206, 333, 348,
    416, 476, 481–82, 505, 670*n*
  Nixon administration's campaign against,
    483
  Pentagon Papers published by, 424
  Watergate scandal and, 514, 515, 529
Washington Times Herald, 42, 203
Watergate, DNC headquarters in, 469
Watergate break-ins, 471–72, 473, 476–77
  CIA and, 466, 478, 504, 665*n*–66*n*
  conspiracy theories about, 668*n*–70*n*
  Cubans and, 484
  Haldeman and, 473, 671*n*
  Hunt and, 471, 472, 476, 477, 484,
    665*n*–66*n*
  Liddy and, 471, 472, 476–77, 484
  McCord and, 471, 484, 665*n*–66*n*
  Magruder and, 666*n*
Watergate cover-up, 343*n*
  CIA and, 477–79, 481, 515–16, 536, 551
  Colson in, 477, 503–4, 506, 508, 551
  Cubans and, 503, 506
  Dean in, 474, 484, 503, 504, 505, 506,
    507, 508, 515, 538, 551, 658*n*, 676*n*
  Ehrlichman in, 474, 479–81, 499, 507,
    508, 515, 677*n*
  FBI and, 478–79, 484, 515–16, 536, 551
  Felt and, 481–82, 483, 672*n*
  Haldeman in, 475, 476–78, 499, 503, 507,
    508, 515, 516, 677*n*
  Hunt in, 481, 503–4, 506
  hush-money scheme in, 474, 481, 482,
    499, 503–4, 506, 551, 576*n*
  Kalmbach in, 474, 503
  Kleindienst and, 481
  LaRue in, 503
  Liddy in, 480, 484, 686*n*
  McCord in, 503, 504
  Magruder in, 472, 474, 480–81, 484, 551,
    658*n*
  media and, 482, 483–84, 514–15, 516,
    529
  Mitchell in, 471–72, 475, 477, 478, 479,
    484, 504, 507–8
  RN in, 475, 476–81, 499, 505–11, 515,
    529, 536, 543, 549, 551–52, 658*n*

  RN's Frost-interview admissions on,
    550–51
  Walters and, 478–79, 481, 515–16
  White House tapes in, 474, 476, 479,
    516, 517–18, 521, 522, 524, 525–27,
    528–30, 536, 543, 546, 549, 670*n*–71*n*,
    679*n*, 682*n*, 687*n*
  zealousness of prosecutors and, 537–38
Watergate Special Prosecution Force, 514,
    679*n*
Waterloo, battle of, 494
Watson, Denton, 255
Wattenberg, Ben, 331, 335, 387–88
Watts riot, 322
Weather Underground, 556
Wechsler, James, 186
Weegar, Hannah, 23
Weidenfeld, Sheila, 400
Weinberger, Caspar, 530
Weinstein, Allen, 591*n*, 592*n*
Welch, Joseph, 225
Welch, Ola Florence:
  RN's breakup with, 67–68
  RN's dating of, 60, 61, 63, 66
Wellington, Duke of, 494
Wells, Ida, 669*n*, 670*n*
Werdel, Thomas, 167–68
West, Eldo, 47
West, Jessamyn, 44, 49, 50, 51, 59, 310, 408
West, Merle, 47, 52, 54, 58
West Berlin, 105, 489, 490
West Germany, in treaty with Soviet Union,
    489
Whalen, Richard, 321, 331
Wheeling, W.Va., 197
Whitaker, John, 323, 379, 380
White, F. Clifton "Clif," 332
White, Harry Dexter, 106, 116
White, Theodore, 272, 283, 296, 319,
    324–25, 328, 349, 371, 437, 636*n*
White, William, 200–201, 230, 253
Whitman, Ann, 249, 517, 615, 616
Whitman, Charles, 335
Whittier, Calif., 398
  early history of, 8–9
  parochialism of, 7, 9
  Quakers as founders of, 9, 44, 249–50
Whittier College, 4, 60–63, 102, 250, 582*n*
Whittier Narrows Dam, 82–83
Whittier News, 45
Wicker, Tom, 317
  on "forgotten American," 473

Wilkins, Roger, 374
Will (Liddy), 465, 658*n*
Williams, Edward Bennett, 476, 670*n*
Willkie, Wendell, 75
Wills, Frank, 473
Wills, Garry, 331, 333–34, 335, 353
Will to Live, The (Hutschnecker), 161
Wilson, Charles, 227
Wilson, Harold, 349
Wilson, Woodrow, 179, 226
  RN's admiration of, 6, 66
  stroke of, 237
"Wilson desk," 349, 641*n*
Winchell, Walter, 206
Wingert & Bewley, 26, 71
  RN at, 70–71, 74
Wingert family, 70
Wisdom, John Minor, 251
Witness (Chambers), 188, 199
  RN's review of, 200
Wood, Keith, 62
Woods, Joe, 433
Woods, Rose Mary, 184, 196, 238, 241, 323,
    343, 356, 409, 416, 506, 524, 526,
    530
  as RN's trusted secretary, 159–60
  Watergate tapes and, 546
Woodward, Bob, 325, 482, 483, 516, 529,
    536–37, 548, 549
Woodward, C. Vann, 255

World War II:
  bombing campaigns of, 82
  civil rights movement revitalized by, 247
  Eisenhower in, 201
  Japanese surrender in, 7
  in South Pacific, 77–79
  Soviet Union in, 108–9, 221
  U.S. entry into, 5, 76, 108–9
Wright, Jim, 398, 514

Yahya Khan, 440, 451, 452–54, 456, 459
Yeltsin, Boris, 554
Yom Kippur War, 520, 522–23
Yorba Linda, Calif., 51, 398
  Nixon farm in, 42, 45–46, 578*n*
  Nixon museum and library in, 688*n*
Yorktown, USS, 76
Young, David, 427, 428, 429
Young, Whitney, 374
Yugoslavia, 90

Zetterberg, Stephen, 39
Zhou Enlai, 229, 436, 437, 439, 440, 457,
    460, 461, 462–63, 465, 486
  Kissinger's meetings with, 441, 453
Ziegler, Ron, 352, 358, 416–17, 534, 547
Ziffren, Paul, 137, 142
Zumwalt, Elmo, 354, 500
Zwicker, Ralph, McCarthy's defamation
  of, 222